Are you **AWARE** of how attitudes are about intimate relationships?

Discover your attitudes and knowledge about close relationships. By taking AWARE, you will also learn about how your ideas about relationships compare with marriage experts.

www.awareonline.net

©Oliver Hoffmann/Shutterstock

What is AWARE Online?

AWARE contains 15 categories that match the chapters in the *Marriages and Families* book. Your Personal Report provides a chapter by chapter summary of your knowledge and insight into relationships.

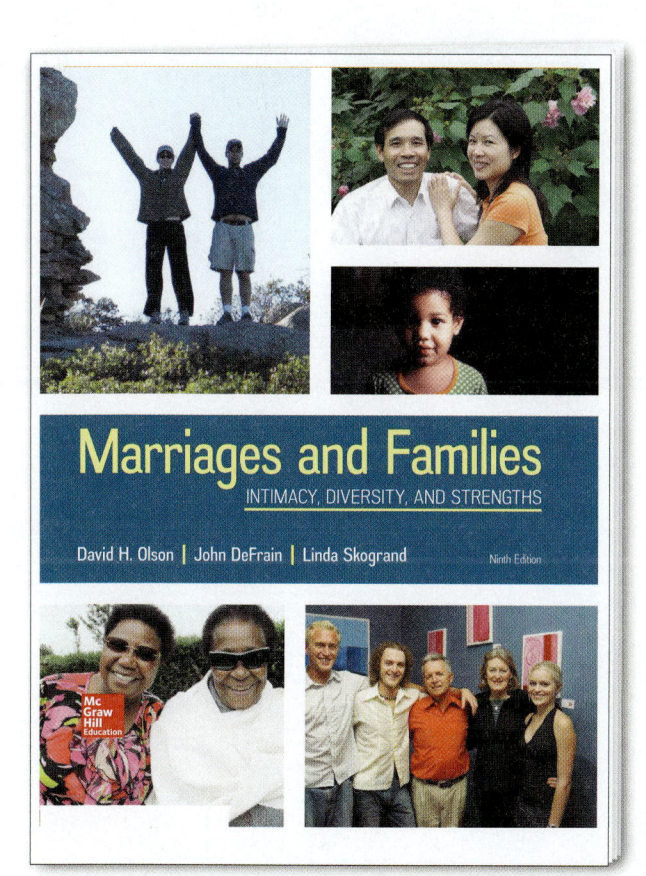

You receive an AWARE Personal Report
(20 pages)

After answering 150 questions about relationships, you will be able to view and print (in color or black/white) your AWARE Personal Report.

Advantages of AWARE to you:

- Helps to personalize the course by highlighting your attitudes and knowledge.
- Identifies your strengths and growth areas regarding relationships.
- Generates insight into your personal style and your past and current relationships.
- Stimulates your interest and curiosity about relationship issues.
- Helps you discover more about your family of origin and better understand your family dynamics.

www.awareonline.net

Marriages & Families

Intimacy, Diversity, and Strengths

Ninth Edition

David H. Olson
University of Minnesota

John DeFrain
University of Nebraska

Linda Skogrand
Utah State University

McGraw Hill Education

MARRIAGE AND FAMILIES

Published by McGraw-Hill Education, 2 Penn Plaza, New York, NY 10121. Copyright © 2019 by McGraw-Hill Education. All rights reserved. Printed in the United States of America. No part of this publication may be reproduced or distributed in any form or by any means, or stored in a database or retrieval system, without the prior written consent of McGraw-Hill Education, including, but not limited to, in any network or other electronic storage or transmission, or broadcast for distance learning.

Some ancillaries, including electronic and print components, may not be available to customers outside the United States.

This book is printed on acid-free paper.

1 2 3 4 5 6 7 8 9 LWI 21 20 19 18

ISBN 978-1-260-09159-5
MHID 1-260-09159-7

Cover Image: *Courtesy of John DeFrain*

All credits appearing on page or at the end of the book are considered to be an extension of the copyright page.

The Internet addresses listed in the text were accurate at the time of publication. The inclusion of a website does not indicate an endorsement by the authors or McGraw-Hill Education, and McGraw-Hill Education does not guarantee the accuracy of the information presented at these sites.

mheducation.com/highered

Dedication

This book about marriages and families is dedicated to our marriages and families.

Brief Contents

Preface xxiii

PART I — The Social Context of Intimate Relationships 1

Chapter 1	Perspectives on Intimate Relationships 1
Chapter 2	Cultural Diversity and Diversity in Family Structure: Family Strengths and Challenges 37
Chapter 3	Understanding Marriage and Family Dynamics 70

PART II — Dynamics of Intimate Relationships 106

Chapter 4	Communication and Intimacy 106
Chapter 5	Conflict and Conflict Resolution 129
Chapter 6	Sexual Intimacy 149
Chapter 7	Gender Roles and Power in the Family 185
Chapter 8	Managing Economic Resources 210

PART III — Stages of Intimate Relationships 234

Chapter 9	Friendship, Love, Intimacy, and Singlehood 234
Chapter 10	Dating, Mate Selection, and Living Together 264
Chapter 11	Marriage: Building a Strong Foundation 289
Chapter 12	Parenthood: Joys and Challenges 312
Chapter 13	Midlife and Older Couples 350

PART IV — Challenges and Opportunities 381

Chapter 14	Stress, Abuse, and Family Problems 381
Chapter 15	Divorce, Single-Parent Families, and Stepfamilies 433
Chapter 16	Strengthening Marriages and Families Worldwide 463

APPENDICES

Appendix A	Couple and Family Scales A-1
Appendix B	Family Science and Family Research Methods A-7
Appendix C	Contraception and Abortion Options (available online)
Appendix D	Pregnancy and Childbirth (available online)

Glossary G-1
References R-1
Name Index I-1
Subject Index I-11

Contents

Preface xxiii

PART I — The Social Context of Intimate Relationships 1

1 Perspectives on Intimate Relationships 1

Three Themes of Intimacy, Strengths, and Diversity 2

Defining Marriage and Family 3
- What Is Marriage? 3
- What Is a Family? 4

Trends in Marriage and the Family: Change and Continuity 6
- Trends in Marriage and Cohabitation 8
- Trends in Divorce and Remarriage 9
- Trends in Family Structure 11
- Continuity in Marriage and the Family 14

Focus on Marital and Family Strengths 14

BOX 1.1 Putting It Together: *Learning to Focus on Strengths* 15

Advantages of Marriage 15

Impact of the Social Environment on Relationships 18
- Stress, Change, and Materialism 19
- Lack of Time for Oneself and Significant Others 20
- Increasing Use of Child Care Outside the Family 21
- Instability of Couple and Family Relationships 22
- Violence, Criminal Victimization, and Fear 22
- Use of Alcohol, Tobacco, and Other Drugs 25
- The Internet and Human Relationships 27
- Changing Gender Roles and the Balance of Power 29
- Urban Migration and Overcrowding 30
- Financial Problems and the Global Economy 30
- Family and the Environment 31

Changing the Social Environment 33

Positive Responses to the Social Environment 34

Summary 35

Key Terms 35

Activities 35

Suggested Readings 35

2 Cultural Diversity and Diversity in Family Structure: Family Strengths and Challenges 37

Diversity and Strengths in Family Structure and Cultural Context 38

Why Culture Matters 38

Intimacy and Diversity 39

The Concepts of Race, Culture, and Ethnicity 39

BOX 2.1 Diversity in Families: *Race Has No Place* 40

U.S. Demographics and Future Trends 41

  The Hispanic Population 41
  The African American Population 42
  The Asian American Population 43
  The American Indian and Alaska Native Populations 43
  Immigration and Family Life 43
  What the Future Will Bring 44

Gay and Lesbian Couples and Families 45
  Same-Sex Couple Relationships and Marriages 45
  Gay and Lesbian Families 46
  The Challenges of Gay and Lesbian Couples and Families 47

Challenge to Researchers and Practitioners 49
  Research 49
  Practice 50

Cultural Competence 50
  Awareness 50
  Knowledge 51
  Skills 51

Kin Relationships Across Cultures 51

Family System and Sociocultural Characteristics 53
  Three Family System Characteristics 53
  Three Sociocultural Characteristics 54

Family Strengths and Challenges Across Ethnic Groups 55
  Strengths of European American Families 55

  BOX 2.2 Self-Assessment: *Rate the Strengths in Your Family* 56
  Strengths of African American Families 57
  Strengths of Latino Families 57
  Strengths of Asian American Families 59
  Strengths of American Indian Families 60

  BOX 2.3 At Issue: *Historical Trauma and American Indians* 62

Cross-Cultural Family Studies 63

Challenges for Ethnic Families 63
  Assimilation, Acculturation, and Segregation 63

  BOX 2.4 Diversity in Families: *The Tables Are Turned: Going from the Majority to the Minority* 64
  The Advantages of Being in the Majority 65
  Marriage Outside the Group 66
  Relationships Between Men and Women 66
  Relationships Between Parents and Children 67

Summary 68
Key Terms 68
Activities 68
Suggested Readings 68

3
Understanding Marriage and Family Dynamics 70

The History of Family Science 71
  Family Science in the Early Years 72
  Family Science Today 73

Conceptual Frameworks for Understanding Couples and Families 74
  Family Systems Theory 74

  BOX 3.1 Putting It Together: *Theories and Research* 76

  BOX 3.2 Putting It Together: *Reorganization of the Family System After a Car Accident* 79

  BOX 3.3 Diversity in Families: *Cultural Conflicts for a Female Chicana College Student* 81
  International Family Strengths Framework 82
  Family Development Framework 87
  Symbolic Interaction Framework 89
  Social Construction Framework 89
  Feminist Framework 90

Three Key Relationship Concepts 92
  Cohesion in Couples and Families 92
  Flexibility in Couples and Families 95
  Communication in Couples and Families 97

Couple and Family Map 97
  Balanced Versus Unbalanced Families 98
  Balanced Relationships Are Healthier 98
  Value of Couple and Family Map 100

Dynamics Change in Relationships over Time 101
Summary 102
Key Terms 103
Activities 103
Suggested Readings 103

PART II Dynamics of Intimate Relationships 106

4 Communication and Intimacy 106

Couple Strengths and Issues in Communication 107

Perspectives on Communication 108
Gender Differences in Communication 108

BOX 4.1 At Issue: *Communicating About Sex* 110

Cultural Differences in Communication 110
Communication with GLBT Individuals and Couples 111

BOX 4.2 Putting It Together: *All Together at Family Mealtimes* 112

Using Communication to Develop Intimacy 113
Communication as a Cooperative Endeavor 113
Content and Relationship Messages 114
Nonverbal Communication 114
Mixed Messages and Double Binds 115
Metacommunication: Clarifying Your Communication 116
Continuous Partial Attention 117

Using Communication to Maintain Intimacy 118
Speaking: The Art of Self-Disclosure 118
When Self-Disclosure May Not Be Healthy 121
Listening: A Difficult Skill 121
Assertive, Passive, and Aggressive Communication 123

BOX 4.3 Putting It Together: *Using Communication to Increase Intimacy* 124

Positive and Negative Communication Cycles 124
The Positive Influence of Assertiveness 125
The Negative Influence of Avoidance 125

Summary 126

Key Terms 127

Activities 127

Suggested Readings 127

5 Conflict and Conflict Resolution 129

Couple Strengths and Issues in Conflict Resolution 130

Conflict and Anger: An Overview 131
The Hierarchy of Conflict 131
Anger and Conflict Taboos 133
Myths, Theories, and Facts About Anger 134

BOX 5.1 Putting It Together: *Anger: Myths and Facts* 136

Intimacy and Conflict 136
Conflict Resolution for Couples 136
Love and Anger in Balance 137
The Dance of Anger 138
Conflict and Supportiveness in Heterosexual, Gay, and Lesbian Couples 140

BOX 5.2 At Issue: *Ways of Dealing with Conflict in Later Years* 141

Things to Consider in Resolving Conflict 141
Suggestions for Having a Healthy Conversation 141
Strategies for Communicating About Difficult Issues 142

BOX 5.3 At Issue: *Ending a Conflict and Learning to Forgive* 144

Conflict Between Parents and Children 146

Summary 147

Key Terms 147

Activities 148

Suggested Readings 148

6 Sexual Intimacy 149

Intimacy, Strengths, and Diversity 150

Couple Strengths and Sexual Issues 150

Sex and Society: An Overview 152
Sexuality, Sex, and Gender 152
Historical Perspectives on Sex and Society 152

Gay and Lesbian Couples 153
   Sexuality Across Cultures 155
   HIV/AIDS—The Epidemic Continues 158

American Sexual Health and Behavior 159
   National Survey of Sexual Health and Behavior 159
   The American Sex Survey by ABC News 160
   Sexuality in the Later Years 162
   Gay-Male and Lesbian Sexual Behavior 163

Sexual Behavior Among Adolescents and Young Adults 165
   Unintended Consequences: Teen Pregnancies and Sexually Transmitted Infections (STIs) 165
   Education for Sexuality 167
   Sexuality Education and Parents 168

   BOX 6.1 Putting It Together: *Father-Child Communication About Sex* 169
   Is Sex Education Effective? 170
   Sexual Behavior, Alcohol, and College 171

Marital and Extramarital Sexual Behavior 172
   Sex Within Marriage 172
   Marital Styles and Sexual Behavior 174
   Infidelity 174

Toward Sexual Health 176

   BOX 6.2 Diversity in Families: *What's Morally Acceptable? It Depends on Where You Live* 177
   Sexual Dysfunction 179
   Sex Therapy 181

Summary 182

Key Terms 183

Activities 183

Suggested Readings 183

7
Gender Roles and Power in the Family 185

Intimacy, Strengths, and Diversity 186

Facts About Women and Men in the United States 186

Gender Roles 186
   Gender Norms and Family Life 188
   Distribution of Family Work by Gender 190
   Emotion Work in Marriage and Family 191
   Spending Time with Children 191
   Maternal Gatekeeping 192

   Traditional versus Contemporary Views of Gender Roles 193
   The Move Toward More Egalitarian Roles 193

   BOX 7.1 At Issue: *The Work-Family Interface* 194
   An International Perspective 194

   BOX 7.2 Diversity in Families: *Ethnic Variations in Who Does Housework* 198

Gender Roles Across Ethnic Groups 198
   Latino/a Culture 198
   African American Culture 199
   American Indian Culture 199
   Asian American Culture 200
   Gender Issues for Immigrant Couples 200

Theories About Gender Roles 201
   Social Learning Theory 201
   Cognitive Development Theory 201
   Family Systems Theory 203
   Feminist Framework 203

   BOX 7.3 At Issue: *Gender Inequality as a Global Problem* 204

Power in Families 204
   Power in Couple Relationships 205
   Egalitarian Roles and Marital Satisfaction 206
   Suggestions for Minimizing Power Issues 207

Summary 208

Key Terms 209

Activities 209

Suggested Readings 209

8
Managing Economic Resources 210

Money and Happiness 211

Marriage and Money 213

   BOX 8.1 At Issue: *The Effects of Debt on Newlyweds* 215

Diversity and Financial Style 216

The Cost of Divorce 218

Why Do Finances Cause Problems? 218

   BOX 8.2 Putting It Together: *Steps to Financial Freedom* 219

Family Income and Expenses 220

Family Income 220

BOX 8.3 At Issue: *The Recession and Fertility Rates* 221
Does It Pay to Work Outside the Home? 224

Smart Money Management 225
Creating a Budget 225
Pooling Money: Pros and Cons 226

Credit: Uses and Abuses 227
Credit Cards—Dangerous Plastic 227

BOX 8.4 At Issue: *Debt in the United States* 228
Purchasing a Home 228
Avoiding Debt and Bankruptcy 231
Financial Counseling 231

Summary 232

Key Terms 233

Activities 233

Suggested Readings 233

PART III — Stages of Intimate Relationships 234

9 Friendship, Love, Intimacy, and Singlehood 234

Friends Versus Lovers 235
The Fabric of Friendship 235
The Tapestry of Love 237

BOX 9.1 Putting It Together: *Ten Traits of Love* 238
The Love Triangle 239
Jealousy: A Green-Eyed Monster or Real Love? 240

BOX 9.2 At Issue: *Love and Science* 241
Looking for Love on the Internet 242

Exploring Intimacy: From Experience to Relationship 244
Paths to Intimacy Differ in Males and Females 244
Intimacy and Communication 245
Intimate Experiences Versus an Intimate Relationship 246
The Paradox of Marriage and Intimacy 246

Developing Intimacy in Couple Relationships 247
Communication Skills 248
Couple Closeness 248
Couple Flexibility 248
Personality Compatibility 248
Conflict Resolution 249

Intimacy Games 249
Constructive Intimacy Games 251
Destructive Intimacy Games 251
Limiting Destructive Games 253

Attachment Theory and Intimacy 254

Being Single 255
A Historical Perspective on Being Single 257
Being Single Today 257

BOX 9.3 Diversity in Families: *Definitions of Singlehood* 258

Summary 262

Key Terms 262

Activities 262

Suggested Readings 263

10 Dating, Mate Selection, and Living Together 264

Courtship Patterns 265
Parent-Arranged Marriages 265
What Has Happened to Dating? 268
Trends in Searching for a Partner 270

BOX 10.1 Putting It Together: *Dating Do's and Don'ts* 272
Ongoing Relationships 272
Breaking Up Is Hard to Do 273
Dating Among Older People 273

Choosing a Mate 274
Those Who Are Like Us 275
Age and Finding a Mate 275
Birth Order 276
Similar Personalities or Different Personalities 276
Interracial and Interfaith Marriages 276
Finding a Good Mate 279

Patterns of Mate Selection 279

Conflict and Violence in Relationships 280

   BOX 10.2 At Issue: *Partner Violence Warning Signs* 282

Living Together 283
   Cohabitation's Dramatic Increase 283
   Reasons for Cohabiting 284

   BOX 10.3 Putting It Together: *Ten Ideas to Consider Before Cohabiting* 286
   Difficult Choices 286

Summary 287

Key Terms 287

Activities 287

Suggested Readings 287

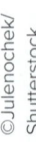

11 Marriage: Building a Strong Foundation 289

Intimacy, Strengths, and Diversity 290

Perspectives on Marriage Today 290
   The Benefits of Marriage 291
   Marriage and Black Americans 292
   Marriages over Time 292
   The Decline in Marriage 293

Components of a Successful Marriage 294

Marriage Education 296
   Premarital Education 297
   What Constitutes an Effective Premarital Program? 298

   BOX 11.1 Putting It Together: *The PREPARE Program for Premarital Counseling* 299

   BOX 11.2 At Issue: *Predicting Marital Success* 300
   Predicting a Successful Marriage 300

The Importance of Families of Origin in Marriage 301
   Kathy's Family of Origin 301
   Jim's Family of Origin 302
   Goals for the Marriage 302

Newlywed Years 303

Keeping Marriages Strong 305
   Five Types of Marriage 305
   Why Marriages Fall Apart 307
   Keeping Your Marriage a Top Priority 307
   The Role of Forgiveness in Marriage 307
   The Role of Sacrifice in Marriage 309
   Prayer in Marriage 309

Federal Healthy Marriage Initiative 310

Summary 311

Key Terms 311

Activities 311

Suggested Readings 311

12 Parenthood: Joys and Challenges 312

Roots and Wings 313

Children and Happiness 313
   Children and Individual Happiness 313
   Children and Couple Happiness 314

Couple Strengths and Issues in Parenting 314

The Challenge of Parenthood 315
   Myths and Realities of Parenthood 316
   The Transition to Parenthood 318
   Financial Issues and Children 320

Adoption 320

The Child-Free Alternative 322

Styles of Parenting 325
   Democratic Style 326
   Authoritarian Style 327
   Permissive Style 327
   Rejecting Style 327
   Uninvolved Style 327
   Democratic Parenting Works Best 328

Theories of Childrearing 328

Issues in Parenting 330
   The Need for Positive Discipline Today 331
   Corporal Punishment and Its Consequences 332

   BOX 12.1 Putting It Together: *The Mother's Book by Mrs. Child* 333
   Child Care 333

   BOX 12.2 Diversity in Families: *Child Care for the Growing Hispanic Population* 334

   BOX 12.3 At Issue: *Looking for a Very High Quality Child Care Program and Positive Caregiving* 336
   Coparenting 337
   Single Mothers 338
   Gay and Lesbian Parenting 339
   Fatherhood and Motherhood Today 339
   When a Child Dies 342
   Educational Programs and Resources for Parents 343

The Joy and Enduring Satisfaction of Parenthood 346

BOX 12.4 Putting It Together: *A Young Mother's Diary* 347

Summary 347

Key Terms 348

Activities 348

Suggested Readings 348

13

Midlife and Older Couples 350

Intimacy, Strengths, and Diversity 351

Family Life in the Middle Years 352
Defining Middle Age 352
Middle Age: A Crisis or An Opportunity? 353
The Middle-Aged Person and the Working World 354
Sexuality in Middle Age 354

BOX 13.1 Diversity in Families: *Childlessness: The Invisible Group* 355
The Middle-Aged Marriage 357
Divorce During the Middle and Later Years 358
Empty Nest, Spacious Nest, or Cluttered Nest? 358
Caught in the Middle: The Sandwich Generation 359
Grandparenthood 360
Grandparents Raising Grandchildren 362

BOX 13.2 Diversity in Families: *Grandparents and Grandfamilies* 364

Family Life in the Later Years 364
Defining Old Age 365
Conventional Wisdom About Old Age 366
Retirement 370

BOX 13.3 At Issue: *Alzheimer's* 371
Long-Term Marriages 372
Losing a Spouse 374
Couple Relationships in the Later Years 375

BOX 13.4 At Issue: *I Am Aware That I Am No Longer Anyone's "Most Important Person": The Desolation of Grief* 376
Changes in Family Dynamics in the Later Years 377

Summary 377

Key Terms 378

Activities 378

Suggested Readings 379

PART IV Challenges and Opportunities 381

14

Stress, Abuse, and Family Problems 381

Intimacy, Strengths, and Diversity 382

Cross-Cultural Perspectives on Couple and Family Stress 383

What We Know About Stress 383
Coping with Stress 384
Stress and Life Events 384

BOX 14.1 At Issue: *Ambiguous Loss: When We Are Uncertain If a Person Is In or Out of Our Family* 386
Top Five Stressors for Couples 388
Five Tips for Dealing with Stress in Your Relationship 388
The ABC-X Family Crisis Model 389
Life as a Roller Coaster 390
A Roller Coaster Course of Adjustment 391
Family Systems Changes Before and After the 9/11 Attacks 391

War and Its Effect on Families 393
Couples 394
Children 395

BOX 14.2 At Issue: *The Impact of War on Families Left Behind* 396
The Role of the Community in Supporting Military Families 398
Posttraumatic Stress Disorder and War 400

Family Coping Strategies 401
Theoretical Perspectives 401
Coping with 9/11 402

Contents xv

BOX 14.3 Putting It Together: *Strategies for Managing Stress* 404

Domestic Violence 404
Incidence of Domestic Violence 405
Diversity and Domestic Violence 407
National Survey of Domestic Violence 407
Relationship of Physical Abuse and Psychological Abuse 408
Factors Contributing to Domestic Violence 409
Patterns of Domestic Violence 412
Treatment and Prevention of Domestic Violence 412
Domestic Violence and Children 414

Child Abuse and Neglect 414
Incidence of Child Abuse and Neglect 415
Psychological Aggression and Spanking 415
Alternatives to Spanking 417
The Long-Term Consequences of Child Abuse and Neglect 417
Transcending Abuse 418
Families at Risk 419
Treatment and Prevention of Child Abuse 420

Sibling and Child-to-Parent Abuse 421
Sibling Abuse 421
Child-to-Parent Abuse 422

Alcohol Problems in Families 423
Alcohol and Family Violence 424
The Family's Reaction to Alcohol Abuse 424
Treatment and Prevention of Alcoholism 426
Acknowledging the Dangers of Legal Drugs 428

Summary 429
Key Terms 430
Activities 430
Suggested Readings 431

15
Divorce, Single-Parent Families, and Stepfamilies 433

Intimacy, Strengths, and Diversity 434

Divorce in Today's Society 434
Historical Trends 434

BOX 15.1 Diversity in Families: *The Globalization of Divorce* 436
Divorce Laws and Views on Divorce 437

Understanding Divorce 439
The Culture of Divorce 439
The Impact of Divorce on Adults 440

BOX 15.2 At Issue: *Fathers' Experiences with Marital Separation* 441
The Impact of Divorce on Children 442

Single-Parent Families 444
Fathers 446
Strengths of Single-Parent Families 448
Challenges of Being in Single-Parent Families 449
Benefits of Being in Single-Parent Families 451
What Resources Do Single-Parent Families Rely On? 452

Stepfamilies 453
Differences Between Nuclear Families and Stepfamilies 454
Children in Stepfamilies 455
Couples in Stepfamilies 456
Stepfamilies in Diverse Populations 458
Boundary Ambiguity in Stepfamilies 459
Stepfamilies in Later Life 459
Building Stepfamily Strengths 459

Summary 461
Key Terms 461
Activities 461
Suggested Readings 462

16
Strengthening Marriages and Families Worldwide 463

Global Perspectives on Family, Community, and Cultural Strengths 464
Family Strengths 465
Community Strengths 465
Cultural Strengths 465
Two Visual Models Integrating Family, Community, and Cultural Strengths 466

BOX 16.1 Diversity in Families: *The Perennial Philosophy* 468

Premarital and Marriage Programs 468
Premarital Programs for Marriage 469
Couple Education Programs 471

Marital and Family Therapy 471
Common Problems in Couple Relationships 471
Problems Related to Closeness and Flexibility 472
Common Questions About Marital and Family Therapy 473
Family Therapy Case Study 476

xvi   Contents

Strengthening Your Marriage and Family Relationships 479
  Building a Stronger Marriage 479

  BOX 16.2 Putting It Together: *Building a Stronger Marriage* 480
  Building a Stronger Family 480

  BOX 16.3 Putting It Together: *Building a Stronger Family* 481

The Future of Your Family 481
Summary 482
Activities 483
Suggested Readings 483

Appendices

Appendix A
Couple and Family Scales A-1

Appendix B
Family Science and Family Research Methods A-7

Glossary G-1
References R-1
Name Index I-1
Subject Index I-11

Note: Appendices C and D, added below, are available online. And, please visit the Web site: www.mhhe.com/olson9e **to access them.**

Appendix C
Contraception and Abortion Options

Appendix D
Pregnancy and Childbirth

Boxed Features

Box 1.1	**Putting It Together:**	*Learning to Focus on Strengths* 15
Box 2.1	**Diversity in Families:**	*Race Has No Place* 40
Box 2.2	**Self-Assessment:**	*Rate the Strengths in Your Family* 56
Box 2.3	**At Issue:**	*Historical Trauma and American Indians* 62
Box 2.4	**Diversity in Families:**	*The Tables Are Turned: Going from the Majority to the Minority* 64
Box 3.1	**Putting It Together:**	*Theories and Research* 76
Box 3.2	**Putting It Together:**	*Reorganization of the Family System After a Car Accident* 79
Box 3.3	**Diversity in Families:**	*Cultural Conflicts for a Female Chicana College Student* 81
Box 4.1	**At Issue:**	*Communicating About Sex* 110
Box 4.2	**Putting It Together:**	*All Together at Family Mealtimes* 112
Box 4.3	**Putting It Together:**	*Using Communication to Increase Intimacy* 124
Box 5.1	**Putting It Together:**	*Anger: Myths and Facts* 136
Box 5.2	**At Issue:**	*Ways of Dealing with Conflict in Later Years* 141
Box 5.3	**At Issue:**	*Ending a Conflict and Learning to Forgive* 144
Box 6.1	**Putting It Together:**	*Father–Child Communication About Sex* 169
Box 6.2	**Diversity in Families:**	*What's Morally Acceptable? It Depends on Where You Live* 177
Box 7.1	**At Issue:**	*The Work–Family Interface* 194
Box 7.2	**Diversity in Families:**	*Ethnic Variations in Who Does Housework* 198
Box 7.3	**At Issue:**	*Gender Inequality as a Global Problem* 204
Box 8.1	**At Issue:**	*The Effects of Debt on Newlyweds* 215
Box 8.2	**Putting It Together:**	*Steps to Financial Freedom* 219
Box 8.3	**At Issue:**	*The Recession and Fertility Rates* 221

Box 8.4   **At Issue:** *Debt in the United States* 228

Box 9.1   **Putting It Together:** *Ten Traits of Love* 238

Box 9.2   **At Issue:** *Love and Science* 241

Box 9.3   **Diversity in Families:** *Definitions of Singlehood* 258

Box 10.1   **Putting It Together:** *Dating Do's and Don'ts* 272

Box 10.2   **At Issue:** *Partner Violence Warning Signs* 282

Box 10.3   **Putting It Together:** *Ten Ideas to Consider Before Cohabiting* 286

Box 11.1   **Putting It Together:** *The PREPARE Program for Premarital Counseling* 299

Box 11.2   **At Issue:** *Predicting Marital Success* 300

Box 12.1   **Putting It Together:** *The Mother's Book by Mrs. Child* 333

Box 12.2   **Diversity in Families:** *Child Care for the Growing Hispanic Population* 334

Box 12.3   **At Issue:** *Looking for a Very High Quality Child Care Program and Positive Caregiving* 336

Box 12.4   **Putting It Together:** *A Young Mother's Diary* 347

Box 13.1   **Diversity in Families:** *Childlessness: The Invisible Group* 355

Box 13.2   **Diversity in Families:** *Grandparents and Grandfamilies* 364

Box 13.3   **At Issue:** *Alzheimer's* 371

Box 13.4   **At Issue:** *I Am Aware that I Am No Longer Anyone's "Most Important Person": The Desolation of Grief* 376

Box 14.1   **At Issue:** *Ambiguous Loss: When We Are Uncertain If a Person Is In or Out of Our Family* 386

Box 14.2   **At Issue:** *The Impact of War on Families Left Behind* 396

Box 14.3   **Putting It Together:** *Strategies for Managing Stress* 404

Box 15.1   **Diversity in Families:** *The Globalization of Divorce* 436

Box 15.2   **At Issue:** *Fathers' Experiences with Marital Separation* 441

Box 16.1   **Diversity in Families:** *The Perennial Philosophy* 468

Box 16.2   **Putting It Together:** *Building a Stronger Marriage* 480

Box 16.3   **Putting It Together:** *Building a Stronger Family* 481

About the Authors

David H. Olson, Ph.D.

David Olson is professor emeritus of family social science at the University of Minnesota. He is founder and president of Life Innovations. He is a past president of the National Council on Family Relations (NCFR) and a past president of the Upper Midwest Association for Marriage and Family Therapists (UMAMFT) and a fellow of the American Psychological Association (APA). Olson is also a member of the editorial boards of multiple family journals. He has received numerous awards, including the Distinguished Contribution to Family Therapy Research Award from both AAMFT and the American Family Therapy Association (AFTA).

Olson has written or edited more than 20 books, including *Couple Checkup; Remarriage Checkup; Empowering Couples; Building Relationships; Families: What Makes Them Work; Circumplex Model; Power in Families; Treating Relationships;* and 10 volumes of the *Inventory of Marriage and Family Literature.* He has published more than 100 articles with the theme of bridging family research, theory, and practice.

Olson and his colleagues at the University of Minnesota are well known for having developed the Circumplex Model of Marital and Family Systems and a variety of couple and family assessment tools, including PREPARE, ENRICH, FACES, PAIR, and AWARE.

Courtesy of David H. Olson

John DeFrain, Ph.D.

John DeFrain is a professor emeritus of family studies at the University of Nebraska-Lincoln. His professional focus has been the development of couple and family strengths nationally and internationally.

DeFrain's research on family strengths and challenges from a global perspective has been recognized around the world. He holds an Honorary Appointment as Conjoint Professor of Family Studies at the University of Newcastle, Callaghan, New South Wales, Australia; serves as a research scientist in the Center for Family Studies, Shanghai Academy of Social Sciences, People's Republic of China; received an Onassis Foundation Fellowship to work at Aristotle University of Thessaloniki, Greece; was a Fulbright Scholar at the University of the South Pacific in Suva, Fiji; has consulted with the Department of Family Development of the federal government of Mexico and other Mexican organizations; and has worked with the EMMA Foundation in Romania, helping to develop programs for families whose child has died. DeFrain was the 2014 recipient of the National Council on Family Relations Jan Trost Award for outstanding contributions to international family studies. He is currently working with the Doha International Family Institute in Qatar on a proposed study of the strengths and challenges of Arab families in 22 countries.

DeFrain co-founded the Global Consortium for International Family Studies. The organization links universities in the United States, Australia, India, and other countries, making it possible for students in many nations to learn about how to strengthen families from teachers in the global network.

Courtesy of John DeFrain

DeFrain's research has been published in 160 professional articles in books, journals, and Extension publications; and he has co-authored and co-edited 34 books, including: *Coping with Sudden Infant Death; Secrets of Strong Families; Stillborn: The Invisible Death; On Our Own: A Single Parent's Survival Guide; Parents in Contemporary America; Sudden Infant Death: Enduring the Loss; Building Relationships;* and *We Cry Out: Living with Developmental Disabilities.* His most recent books are: *Surviving and Transcending a Traumatic Childhood: The Dark Thread; Family Treasures: Creating Strong Families; Strong Families Around the World: Strengths-Based Research and Perspectives; The Strengths and Challenges of New Immigrant Families: Implications for Research, Education, Policy, and Service; Getting Connected, Staying Connected: Loving Each Other Day by Day; Family Violence from a Global Perspective: Strengths-Based Perspectives;* and *The World of Bereavement: Cultural Perspectives on Death in Families.*

John would like to thank his spouse Nikki DeFrain and his three daughters, three sons-in-law, and four grandchildren for teaching him so much of what he knows about marriage and family.

Linda Skogrand, Ph.D.

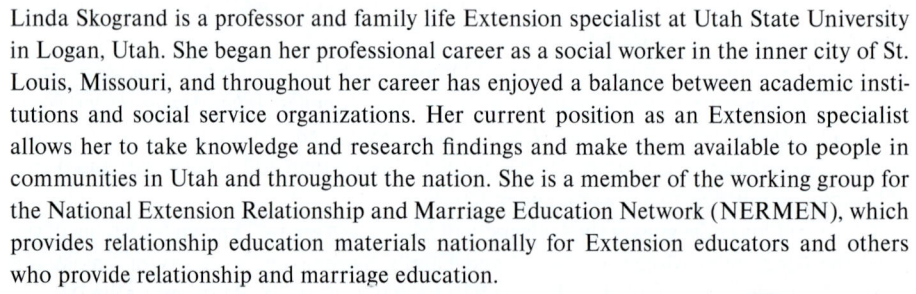

Linda Skogrand is a professor and family life Extension specialist at Utah State University in Logan, Utah. She began her professional career as a social worker in the inner city of St. Louis, Missouri, and throughout her career has enjoyed a balance between academic institutions and social service organizations. Her current position as an Extension specialist allows her to take knowledge and research findings and make them available to people in communities in Utah and throughout the nation. She is a member of the working group for the National Extension Relationship and Marriage Education Network (NERMEN), which provides relationship education materials nationally for Extension educators and others who provide relationship and marriage education.

Skogrand's social service experiences include providing HIV/AIDS education programs for street kids, people in prison, and gang members, and overseeing the design of an AIDS house for the Latino population. She also taught family courses at St. Olaf College in Northfield, Minnesota, for 17 years and was adjunct faculty at the University of Minnesota.

She has authored numerous journal articles focusing on topics such as transcending a traumatic childhood, diversity, strong Latino marriages, strong Navajo marriages, strong African American marriages, relationship and marriage education for low-income and diverse populations, and benefits of stepfamily education for Latino and low-income audiences. She is currently involved with a federal grant bringing fatherhood education to Utah fathers in communities as well as fathers in jails.

Skogrand is nationally known for her work with diversity—hearing the voices that are not typically heard in family research. With that focus in mind, she has conducted research with Latino couples and Navajo couples and created curricula for these populations based upon this research. These curricula include *Strong Latino Couple Relationships* for the Latino population and *Strong Marriages for Navajo Couples* for the Navajo people so members of these populations can strengthen their couple relationships in ways that are consistent with their cultural values. Currently, she is collaborating with the 4-H director in Alaska in conducting research in order to ultimately bring 4-H to youth in remote Native villages in culturally appropriate ways.

Courtesy of Linda Skogrand

Preface

Our colleague and friend, the late Dr. David R. Mace, once said, "Nothing in the world could make human life happier than to greatly increase the number of happy couples and strong families." Throughout nine editions, our goal in writing *Marriages and Families: Intimacy, Diversity, and Strengths* has been to provide students with information about marriage and family relationships that will help them move toward Mace's goal.

We have tried to make the concepts and ideas presented in this book useful and meaningful so students will be able to apply them to their own lives. We hope to help students integrate intellectual ideas and personal experiences, thereby enriching both. Although the text deals with some complex ideas and materials, it is written in a style that is accessible to students new to the field of family studies and to those wishing to learn more about intimate relationships.

Intimacy, Strengths, and Diversity

Three distinctive themes have guided our efforts in writing this book, and they are woven throughout the text. The first is *intimacy,* and our focus is on how to develop and maintain close relationships. Most people seek connectedness and want to be involved in intimate relationships, the most intimate being marriage and family. This book is full of ideas, principles, and suggestions for building and keeping intimate relationships in your life. As a result, we hope this will be a book that you will want to keep and refer to throughout your life.

The second key theme is *marital and family strengths.* The family strengths perspective is based on the premise that if you approach relationships from a "problem-oriented" perspective, you will find problems. If you look for strengths, you will find strengths. Growing numbers of family educators and family therapists are using this approach today, helping families recognize their own strengths and use them as a foundation for positive growth. In Chapter 1, we identify a number of strengths that have been found to be present in healthy marriages and families all over the world. Throughout the book, we show how these strengths help families provide healthy and nurturing settings that promote the growth and well-being of individual family members, better enabling them to face the challenges and solve the problems they encounter.

Although the theme of marital and family strengths is integrated throughout the book, three chapters focus especially on this theme: Chapter 2 highlights the couple and family strengths of diverse ethnic and cultural groups, including gay and lesbian couples and families; Chapter 14 examines how families can use their strengths to manage stress, abuse, and other family issues; and Chapter 16 looks at how families, communities, and cultures can work together to build a healthier world in the future.

The third key theme is *diversity,* and, wherever possible, we consider how concepts, research, and theories about the family apply to couples and families of diverse ethnic and cultural backgrounds. We also focus on the diversity in structure that characterizes families today, looking at the many different forms that *family* can take. Diversity in sexual orientation—gay and lesbian relationships and families in our society—is another type of diversity we explore. The theme of diversity is introduced in Chapter 1, discussed in detail in Chapter 2, and integrated into discussions throughout the book. One of the four categories of the boxes throughout the text is dedicated to exploring diversity in families.

Family Systems and Family Strengths

We present innumerable theories of family in this book, but we focus especially on family systems theory. Recognizing that the family unit is a system of interdependent parts, we look at how families maintain themselves, yet change; how family members can be separate, yet connected; and how communication facilitates the processes of change and growth. We focus on communication and conflict resolution skills as essential tools for creating healthy intimate relationships. We also look at how families can learn to function well within the larger systems of community and society.

The family strengths perspective was developed by Nick Stinnett, John DeFrain, and many of their colleagues across the country and around the world. We use this perspective throughout the text as a model for understanding and evaluating families. With it, we identify and focus on six key qualities of healthy families: commitment, appreciation and affection, positive communication, enjoyable time together, spiritual well-being, and the ability to manage stress and crisis effectively. The research driving this model has involved thousands of family members in the United States and other countries around the world.

In Chapter 3, we introduce the Couple and Family Map, an assessment tool that was developed by David Olson and his colleagues. The Couple and Family Map is based on concepts from family systems theory, and it focuses on the three dimensions of cohesion, flexibility, and communication. It has been used in hundreds of studies to help researchers understand and evaluate families. Throughout the text, we cite studies that have used the map as a theoretical base. An ongoing family case study, described in the Instructor's Manual, can be used to show students how the Couple and Family Map is applied. Appendix A contains the instructions and materials to apply the map to couple and family relationships.

Updates in the Ninth Edition

Like a healthy couple and family, a good textbook needs to identify major issues and change over time. We have tried to describe the current issues in marriage and families today and identify how these relationships are changing.

The field of relationships, especially marriages and families, is increasingly changing and becoming more diverse and complex. Marriage is being preceded and/or replaced by cohabitation, and two-parent families are becoming less common. Same-sex couples are increasing, as are single parents and people who are choosing not to marry. We will now highlight some of the changes we have made in each of the 16 chapters.

Overall, it is important for the reader to know that as we work on a new edition of the textbook, we check every citation to be sure that it is the most up-to-date source available. In addition, worldwide databases are tapped, organizations that collect the most recent data about marriages and family are searched, and the most reliable research and commentary are chosen to help keep the book current. This process takes 18 months.

To give the reader an idea of the magnitude of our task, this textbook has more than 1,500 references. For this ninth edition, we checked each of these references individually to make sure they represent the most current research and thinking on the subject; and we replaced those references which could be updated with new research and commentary. In total for this edition, nearly 850 new references were added and more than 700 old references were deleted. The task of revising this book took, literally, hundreds of hours. Was it worth the effort? You will have to be the judge.

Part I: The Social Context of Intimate Relationships

In **Chapter 1, Perspectives on Intimate Relationships,** we have completely updated national statistics on marriage and divorce in America. We have added some new definitions of *family* for the reader, and discussed the controversy between the so-called *exclusionists* and *inclusionists*. The latest developments in the struggle over same-sex marriage in the United States are discussed, followed by new statistics on cohabitation and remarriage. We present several propositions on how to look at couples and families from a strengths-based perspective, and go on to discuss why, from a statistical perspective, marital relationships look stronger than cohabiting relationships. New statistics are featured that show Americans are generally pessimistic about the prospects for the country's economy and for international peace in the near future, but the vast majority are optimistic about how they and their family will do in the coming year.

A number of major challenges Americans face in the broader social environment are described. This section includes the latest statistics on who's minding the kids, looking at the percentages of young children in the care of their parents, other relatives, child care centers, or nonrelatives in home-based arrangements. Violence and domestic abuse in this country are reviewed using very recent research. The latest data on the problems caused in families by tobacco use and excessive alcohol use are reviewed. New research is presented on how family socialization has dropped dramatically in recent years, attributed to increased internet use. And finally, we have added a section on Family and the Environment, which discusses the problem of overpopulation and environmental degradation, and how all of us in our families can help protect the earth. For the new Ninth Edition, Chapter 1 has been extensively revised and strengthened.

In **Chapter 2, Cultural Diversity and Diversity in Family Structure: Family Strengths and Challenges,** we have added information about the impact of the 2015 Supreme Court ruling to legalize same-sex marriages. There is new information about what the increase in diversity means for the projected U.S. population in the year 2060. Updated information about the ethnic population distribution in the United States is included.

Chapter 3, Understanding Marriage and Family Dynamics, features updated sections on the past, present, and future of the field of family studies or family science. The latest thinking on family systems theory, the international family strengths perspective, the family development, symbolic interaction, social construction, and feminist theoretical frameworks are presented. And the couple and family map show how family dynamics can change over time. All references in this chapter have been checked carefully and new material has been added in each section.

Part II: Dynamics of Intimate Relationships

In **Chapter 4, Communication and Intimacy,** there is new information about how communication differs between men and women and how this affects couple relationships. The chapter has a new Box about communicating about sex and how lack of communication affects sexual health. In addition, there is an added section about the challenges of gay and lesbian couples as they communicate with their friends and family.

In **Chapter 5, Conflict and Conflict Resolution,** there is a new section on guidelines for couples as they resolve conflict. A recent study about how couples deal with conflict in later years has been added in a new Box. Another new Box discusses how to end conflict and learn to forgive. There is also new information about conflict between parents and children.

Chapter 6, Sexual Intimacy, includes new data from a nationwide survey of married couples which focuses on the quality of their sexual relationship. The story of the international HIV/AIDS crisis is updated, more than three decades into the struggle to control the spread of the deadly disease. New insights from the National Survey of Sexual Health and Behavior are presented. And all the discussions on sexuality in the later years, gay-male and lesbian sexual behavior, sexual behavior and young adults, and marital and extramarital behavior are revised to include the latest thinking. Chapter 6 concludes with new developments in the understanding of sexual dysfunction and sex therapy.

Chapter 7, Gender Roles and Power in the Family, provides the most up-to-date information about gender roles, including facts about men and women such as poverty rates, educational achievement, labor force participation, use of health care, and being victims and perpetrators of crimes. There is also a new Box about ethnic variations about who does housework and why this occurs. There is a new section about power in couple relationships.

Chapter 8, Managing Economic Resources, has become an increasingly important topic as it relates to couple and family relationships. There is new information in this chapter about how spending money to help others increases one's sense of well-being. There is a new Box about how the Great Recession of 2007 affected fertility rates and also a new Box about debt for families in the United States.

Part III: Stages of Intimate Relationships

Chapter 9, Friendship, Love, Intimacy, and Singlehood, features updates of the research in all sections of the chapter, including the materials on friends compared to lovers, attachment theory and intimacy, and being single. Highlights focus on how researchers study love from a scientific perspective; looking for love on the internet; how straight couples met their partner; definitions of singlehood and statistics on singles; and new research explaining why marriage is still very popular in the United States, even while singlehood is on the rise.

In **Chapter 10, Dating, Mate Selection, and Living Together,** we added a new section about how dating has changed. There is also a new topic that focuses on recent trends in searching for a partner, including an extensive discussion about the use of the internet in finding a partner. There are also two new sections that discuss ongoing relationships and the challenges of breaking up.

In **Chapter 11, Marriage: Building a Strong Foundation,** the latest marriage statistics are reported. New information about how marriages fare over time is included. Prayer in marriage has become an increasingly important topic and research about this topic is presented.

In **Chapter 12, Parenthood: Joys and Challenges,** we have added updated information about the multiple costs of raising a child. New information about adoption has been included. Given that more and more same-sex couples are becoming parents, new information about gay and lesbian parenting is provided. A new Box presents the challenges faced by a young mother after childbirth.

Chapter 13, Midlife and Older Couples, has been thoroughly revised and updated, including the sections on family life in the middle years; middle age as a crisis or opportunity;

sexuality in the middle years; the empty nest, spacious nest, or cluttered nest; grandparenthood; family life in the later years; long-term marriage; and losing a spouse. Highlights of new material in the book include new insights from around the world on how long adult children should stay in the nest before they leave home; data from a new, nationally representative study of grandparenthood; and an Australian woman who lost her husband to cancer writes about the continuing story of her grief. In the eighth edition of this textbook she described grief from the perspective of a woman whose husband had died just five months to the day before she sat down write. In this ninth edition of the textbook she continues her story, telling us how her grief has evolved slowly over 4 years as she struggles to create a new life without her best friend.

Part IV: Challenges and Opportunities

In **Chapter 14, Stress, Abuse, and Family Problems**, new thinking has been added on war and how it affects the lives of service members and their families; dating violence and domestic violence statistics have been updated; statistics on the effects of alcohol abuse have been updated; the material on how the family adjusts to the crisis of alcoholism has been enhanced; the section on Alcoholics Anonymous and Al-Anon Family Groups has been revised extensively, including an update on the size and scope of these international organizations; the material on smoking has been extensively updated; and new statistics are presented on deaths each year caused by legal and illegal drugs in the United States.

Chapter 15, Divorce, Single-Parent Families, and Stepfamilies, has a new Box focusing on fathers' experiences with marital separation and other new sections describing the difficult and bumpy road of adjusting to divorce for all family members. There is also updated information about the increasing percentage of households headed by fathers.

Chapter 16, Strengthening Marriages and Families Worldwide, has new material in the discussion of the research on global perspectives of family, community, and cultural strengths; the section on couple education programs has been updated and strengthened; new data from a nationwide survey of the top 10 stumbling blocks for couples is presented; and many new *Suggested Readings* have been added.

Appendices

Appendix A, Couple and Family Scales, based on research over the past 35 years that continues today, remains helpful to students who want to learn how to describe and assess couples and families from a family systems perspective. Having students use these scales to evaluate their own family or another family is a very useful and insight-producing assignment. See the *Activities* section at the end of Chapter 3 for more details on the assignment.

Appendix B, Family Science and Family Research Methods, has been reviewed and all the references have been updated to include the most recent citations.

Appendix C, Contraception and Abortion Options, was thoroughly revised with new material added in the sections on methods of contraception; abortion laws; abortion procedures; and physical and emotional aspects of abortion. Several new *Suggested Readings* were also added. Appendix C is available online.

Appendix D, Pregnancy and Childbirth, saw complete updates of references, and a major revision of the section on alternative approaches to birth, including the latest new methods used around the country. The section on infant mortality was also extensively revised. Appendix D is available online.

How We Do Our Job

The field of family studies or family science continues to grow dramatically. Thanks to advances in computer technology and search engines scouring massive databases, we have been able to update this text to include the most current statistics and cutting-edge research studies. As noted earlier, nearly 850 new sources are cited in this volume, carefully gleaned from computer-driven searches, searching the top journals in the field of marriage and family, and keeping our eyes open literally every day of our lives for interesting new material for this textbook.

The tools listed below have proven to be especially useful as we do our job:

- *Google Scholar* is a web search engine owned by Google Inc., and is a widely used search engine on scholarly work on the internet. Google receives several hundred million queries each day through its various services. We have found Google Scholar especially useful when trying to track down the source of different ideas, quotations, or data that we have run across.
- *U.S. government web sites* of the federal government provide a wealth of information about families that proves useful for textbook writers. Some of our favorite web sites include Administration on Aging; Centers for Disease Control and Prevention; CIA *World Factbook;* Library of Congress; National Center for Health Statistics; National Council on Alcoholism and Drug Dependence; National Institutes of Health; U.S. Bureau of the Census; U.S. Department of Health and Human Services; National Youth Violence Prevention Resource Center; U.S. Office of Justice; and the Statistical Abstracts of the United States.
- *Professional organizations and other useful web sites* include the Alan Guttmacher Institute; Alliance for Children and Families; American Academy of Pediatricians; American Association for Marital and Family Therapy; American Psychological Association; Child Trends; Compassionate Friends; Mayo Clinic; M.I.S.S. Foundation; National Healthy Marriage Resource Center; National Council on Family Relations; National Marriage Project; Pew Research Center; Planned Parenthood; and WebMD.
- *The media* provide some of our favorite sources, including *The New York Times, The Washington Post, Associated Press, The Economist, The Nation, AARP Magazine, Time, Newsweek, The New Republic, The Atlantic Monthly, Business Week, Money Magazine, NPR,* and *PBS.*

Finally, but probably most importantly, to update this and every edition of *Marriages and Families: Intimacy, Diversity, and Strengths,* we literally go through every issue of the following 12 professional journals, searching for solid and interesting new research and thinking: *Journal of Marriage and Family, Family Relations, Marriage and Family Review, Journal of Family Issues, Journal of Marital and Family Therapy, National Council on Family Relations Report, Journal of Family Communication, Child Development, Journal of Family Psychology, Family Process, Families in Society,* and the *Journal of Family and Economic Issues.*

Online Resources

The Ninth Edition of *Marriages and Families: Intimacy, Diversity, and Strengths* is accompanied by a number of supplementary learning and teaching resources available on the Online Learning Center web site at www.mhhe.com/olson9e.

For the Student

AWARE Online. AWARE is a computerized assessment that contains 15 categories that match the chapters in the book. After completing the AWARE Online assessment, the student receives a 19-page *AWARE Personal Report* that identifies relationship areas and issues that are strengths for the student and problematic issues that need to be considered. AWARE helps personalize the course by showing students how their current relationship attitudes compare with those of professionals in the field. It also stimulates students' interest and involvement in the class by highlighting current relationship issues. To learn more about AWARE, go to the Online Learning Center web site at www.mhhe.com/olson9e.

Additional Student Resources. The Online Learning Center web site that accompanies this text offers a variety of resources for the student. Students will find interactive multiple choice and true/false chapter quizzes, and an annotated list of other online resources. Please visit the text OLC site at www.mhhe.com/olson9e.

For the Instructor

The ninth edition of *Marriages and Families* is now available online with Connect, McGraw-Hill Education's integrated assignment and assessment platform. Connect also offers SmartBook for the new edition, which is the first adaptive reading experience proven to improve grades and help students study more effectively. All of the title's web site and ancillary content is also available through Connect, including:

Instructor's Manual. For each chapter of the text, the Instructor's Manual provides a chapter outline, learning objectives, a chapter summary, a list of key terms, lecture notes, suggested activities, and suggested readings. The Instructor's Manual also can be downloaded from the Instructor's Online Learning Center.

AWARE Online. AWARE is an acronym for **AW**areness of **A**ttitudes and **R**elationship **E**xpectations. AWARE contains 15 categories that match the chapters in the textbook. After the students have completed the AWARE Online assessment, the instructor can view online and print a 20-page *AWARE Instructor Summary*. The summary provides an overview of the background areas, along with the strengths and issues for the class on 15 categories and the Couple and Family Map. There are several advantages for using AWARE with a class.

- First, the instructor can quickly and efficiently learn about the relevant relationship attitudes of the students in the class.
- Second, by knowing the strengths and growth areas for the class, the instructor can tailor the class to better serve the needs of that class.
- Third, AWARE provides background information about the students that an instructor could not easily ask in a class.
- Fourth, the instructor can provide the class with summary feedback about their relationship attitudes for each chapter in the book.
- Fifth, AWARE personalizes the class for the students and stimulates their interest and involvement in the class.
- Last, AWARE helps engage the students in the class and facilitates greater class interaction. For more information about AWARE, go to www.mhhe.com/olson9e.

Test Bank. The Test Bank offers multiple-choice, true/false, short-answer, and essay questions for each chapter in the text. The Test Bank can be downloaded as a Word file from the

McGraw-Hill connect®

McGraw-Hill Connect® is a highly reliable, easy-to-use homework and learning management solution that utilizes learning science and award-winning adaptive tools to improve student results.

Homework and Adaptive Learning

- Connect's assignments help students contextualize what they've learned through application, so they can better understand the material and think critically.
- Connect will create a personalized study path customized to individual student needs through SmartBook®.
- SmartBook helps students study more efficiently by delivering an interactive reading experience through adaptive highlighting and review.

Connect's Impact on Retention Rates, Pass Rates, and Average Exam Scores

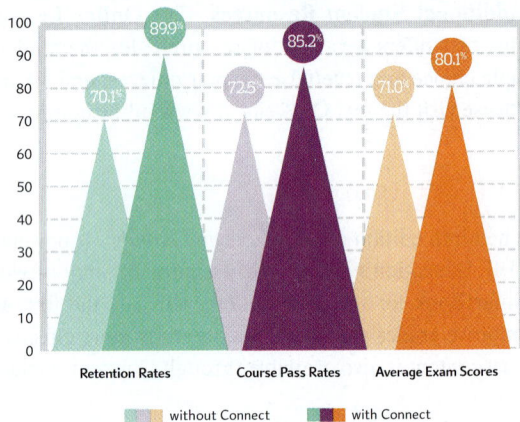

	Retention Rates	Course Pass Rates	Average Exam Scores
without Connect	70.1%	72.5%	71.0%
with Connect	89.9%	85.2%	80.1%

Over **7 billion questions** have been answered, making McGraw-Hill Education products more intelligent, reliable, and precise.

Using Connect improves retention rates by 19.8%, passing rates by 12.7%, and exam scores by 9.1%.

Quality Content and Learning Resources

- Connect content is authored by the world's best subject matter experts, and is available to your class through a simple and intuitive interface.
- The Connect eBook makes it easy for students to access their reading material on smartphones and tablets. They can study on the go and don't need internet access to use the eBook as a reference, with full functionality.
- Multimedia content such as videos, simulations, and games drive student engagement and critical thinking skills.

73% of instructors who use **Connect** require it; instructor satisfaction **increases** by 28% when **Connect** is required.

©McGraw-Hill Education

Robust Analytics and Reporting

- Connect Insight® generates easy-to-read reports on individual students, the class as a whole, and on specific assignments.
- The Connect Insight dashboard delivers data on performance, study behavior, and effort. Instructors can quickly identify students who struggle and focus on material that the class has yet to master.
- Connect automatically grades assignments and quizzes, providing easy-to-read reports on individual and class performance.

©Hero Images/Getty Images

Impact on Final Course Grade Distribution

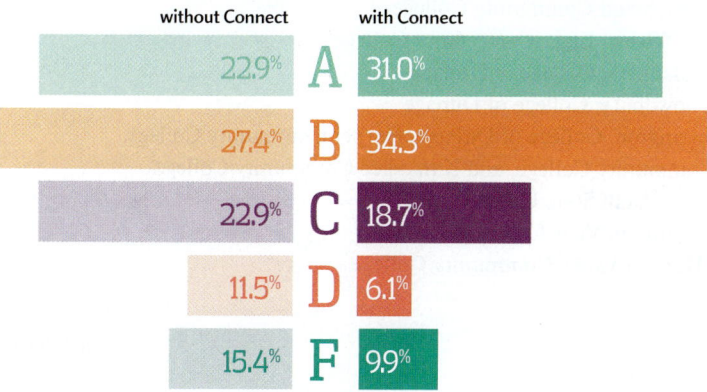

Grade	without Connect	with Connect
A	22.9%	31.0%
B	27.4%	34.3%
C	22.9%	18.7%
D	11.5%	6.1%
F	15.4%	9.9%

More students earn **As** and **Bs** when they use **Connect**.

Trusted Service and Support

- Connect integrates with your LMS to provide single sign-on and automatic syncing of grades. Integration with Blackboard®, D2L®, and Canvas also provides automatic syncing of the course calendar and assignment-level linking.
- Connect offers comprehensive service, support, and training throughout every phase of your implementation.
- If you're looking for some guidance on how to use Connect, or want to learn tips and tricks from super users, you can find tutorials as you work. Our Digital Faculty Consultants and Student Ambassadors offer insight into how to achieve the results you want with Connect.

www.mheducation.com/connect

Online Learning Center web site at www.mhhe.com/olson9e. A Computerized Test Bank is also available on the web site.

PowerPoint® Slides. A collection of tables and figures from the text, augmented by additional graphics, allows instructors to add visual content to their lectures. The PowerPoint® slides are also available on the web site.

Additional Online Resources. The Instructor's side of the OLC offers access to the student chapter quizzes, an annotated list of other online resources and internet exercises. The Instructor's Manual, PowerPoint® slides, and more can be accessed on this web site at www.mhhe.com/olson9e.

Acknowledgments

We are grateful to the following reviewers for providing us with their helpful comments and suggestions during the development of the ninth edition:

Rosie Miller, Coahoma Community College
Kristi Palmer, Richland Community College
Dr. Patricia H. O'Brien, Elgin Community College
Cari Beecham-Bautista, College of Dupage
Shaheen A. Chowdhury, College of Dupage
Norene A. Herrington, College of DuPage, Harper Community College, Waubonsee Community College, and Kankakee Community College
Bryan K. Spuhler, Utah State University
Ayre Harris, Mountain View College
Karen Nash, Hudson Valley Community College

David Olson
John DeFrain
Linda Skogrand

PART ONE
The Social Context of Intimate Relationships

1 Perspectives on Intimate Relationships

©Photodisc/Getty Images

Three Themes of Intimacy, Strengths, and Diversity

Defining Marriage and Family

Trends in Marriage and the Family: Change and Continuity

Focus on Marital and Family Strengths

Advantages of Marriage

Impact of the Social Environment on Relationships

Changing the Social Environment

Positive Responses to the Social Environment

Summary

Key Terms

Activities

Suggested Readings

Three Themes of Intimacy, Strengths, and Diversity

Most people need *intimate relationships* with other people. Intimacy is sharing intellectually, physically, and/or emotionally with another person. In this text we will focus on intimacy in marriage and family relationships and on how they are maintained and how they can become broken.

Intimacy usually occurs when individuals disclose information about themselves, allowing themselves to become vulnerable, and involves trusting that the other person will not use that information to cause harm. Sharing information that involves intimacy usually results in receiving support from the other person.

Intimacy will be discussed throughout this book in terms of dating, romance and courtship, sexual relationships, communication, dealing with conflict, and other aspects of marriage and couple relationships. Intimacy may look different at different times in the life cycle. In addition to having intimacy in couple relationships, intimacy occurs in parent–child relationships, relationships with extended family, and relationships with others who take the place of family. Most intimate relationships go through periods when that closeness is threatened or destroyed. Our goal is to provide you with ideas and exercises to help you improve your ability to develop and maintain intimate relationships throughout life.

Identifying and focusing on *strengths* and building on those strengths are essential for developing and maintaining successful marriage relationships. The focus of this textbook on couple and family strengths provides evidence from the United States and many other countries around the world on how families succeed in the face of life's inherent difficulties (DeFrain & Asay, 2007). By concentrating only on a family's problems and a family's failings, we ignore the fact that it takes a positive approach in life to succeed. The family strengths perspective is a worldview or orientation toward life and families that is positive and optimistic, grounded in research conducted among thousands of couples and families globally. It does not ignore family problems but restores them to their proper place in life: as vehicles for testing our capacities as families and reaffirming our vital human connections with each other. Not all families are strong, of course, but all families have strengths, and these strengths can be a foundation for continued growth. When one only looks for problems in marriages and families, that is all that one will find. By looking for a relationship's strengths, we create a more balanced and realistic picture of the couple and family situation. Finally, looking for what makes families strong helps us discover knowledge that is useful in helping other families. The strong families identified by researchers around the world become the experts for teaching other families how to create a happy and resilient family environment.

Focusing and building on strengths in relationships will be evident throughout this book in relation to couples, marriage relationships, single-parent families, gay and lesbian relationships and families, parenting practices, relationships in diverse cultures, and life in the middle and later years.

Today there is more *diversity* in family and couple relationships than ever before. There are a variety of family structures that are described in this book, including married couples, cohabiting couples, gay and lesbian couples, single-parent families, stepfamilies, and grandparents raising grandchildren. There is also greater cultural and ethnic diversity in the United States than ever before, with minority cultural groups becoming a greater proportion of the total population. These cultural groups bring a wide array of values, beliefs, and practices to our understanding of how marriages and families work. It is increasingly challenging to understand the diversity of couple and family relationships that exist today and will continue to increase in the future.

The three themes of intimacy, strengths, and diversity are critical in understanding couple and family relationships today. These themes and the research and literature surrounding these themes are essential for developing healthy and happy relationships. Knowledge about the latest research in each of these areas will help you develop healthy relationships and better understand and appreciate those around you.

Defining Marriage and Family

Not as many people today live in the so-called traditional family, with a dad at work and a mom at home with the kids—only about 20% of all families in the United States match this model (Tavernise, 2011, May 26). And a survey by the Pew Research Center (2015, January 16) makes it clear that the image of the American family popularized by television programs like "Leave It to Beaver," which aired from 1957 to 1963, does not reflect family life today. Using data from the American Community Survey and the U.S. Census Bureau, Pew researchers found that 46% of children under age 18 live in households headed by two heterosexual parents in their first marriage. Compare this to 1960, when 73% of children lived in this kind of household, and in 1980 when 61% of children lived with two heterosexual parents in their first marriage. The Pew Research team argued, "Rapid changes in American family structure have altered the image" of families. "While the old 'ideal' involved couples marrying young, then starting a family, and staying married till 'death do they part,' the family has become more complex and less 'traditional.'" In addition to the diverse types of family structure, families may vary in cultural or ethnic background, income, size, and longevity. There are many possible family structures rather than one "right" way for a family to be organized.

What Is Marriage?

Marriage is by nature a multifaceted institution. We define **marriage** as *the emotional and legal commitment of two people to share emotional and physical intimacy, various tasks, economic resources, and values.*

The following nine characteristics of marriage were identified by the late Carlfred Broderick (1992, 1993, 2016). A former president of the National Council on Family Relations, Broderick found these characteristics to be common across income levels, educational levels, and ethnic and cultural groups in the United States:

- *Marriage is a demographic event.* Each marriage creates a social unit in society.
- *Marriage is the joining of two families and social networks.* When individuals marry, they marry not only each other but their partner's family and friends. Their social network may comprise friends of both partners, but only those friends liked by both partners tend to remain friends of the couple.
- *Marriage is a legal contract between the couple and the state.* Each state specifies the rights and responsibilities of the partners.
- *Marriage is an economic union.* A married couple usually becomes a single financial unit for most purposes. As a group, married couples are probably society's most important financial decision makers—buying, selling, borrowing, and sharing resources as one.
- *Marriage is the most common living arrangement for adults.* Few people choose to live alone. Marriage is also the most popular living arrangement for adults.
- *Marriage is the context of most human sexual activity.* Most married couples rate sexual activity positively, especially in the early years.
- *Marriage is a reproductive unit.* Most married couples become parents and see parenting as an important goal and a valued purpose in their lives.

- *Marriage is a unit that socializes children* (although children can also be raised by single parents, extended families, grandparents, and other caregivers).
- *Marriage is an opportunity to develop an intimate, sharing relationship.* Although many marriages fail, many others provide a supportive context in which people develop and maintain intimacy.

Same-sex marriage. On June 26, 2015, the U.S. Supreme Court ruled in favor of the freedom to marry for same-sex couples nationwide. In a 5-4 decision in the case of *Obergefell v. Hodges,* the Court wrote:

> *No union is more profound than marriage, for it embodies the highest ideals of love, fidelity, devotion, sacrifice, and family. . . . [These men and women] ask for equal dignity in the eyes of the law. The Constitution grants them that right.*

The nation's highest court explained that the fundamental right to marry is guaranteed to same-sex couples by both the Due Process Clause and the Equal Protection Clause of the Fourteenth Amendment to the U.S. Constitution (Supreme Court of the United States, 2015; Freedom to Marry, 2016).

Gay rights advocates in the United States and around the world hailed the decision as a major victory in the struggle for equal protection under the law, while opponents decried the decision.

There are now 16 countries in the world that allow same-sex couples to marry. These countries are mostly in the Americas and Europe: Argentina, Belgium, Brazil, Canada, Colombia, France, Iceland, Ireland, Luxembourg, Norway, Portugal, South Africa, Spain, Sweden, the United States, and Uruguay. Also, certain subjurisdictions of five other countries (parts of Denmark, Mexico, the Netherlands, New Zealand, and the United Kingdom) allow same-sex couples to marry. A similar law in Finland is not yet in force. In addition, as of 2015, South Africa is the only African country where same-sex marriage is recognized, and no country in Asia allows same-sex marriage ceremonies. Israel accepts same-sex marriages performed overseas (Same-Sex Marriage, 2016).

There are 196 countries in the world today. Homosexuality is illegal in 76 countries (Erasing 76 Crimes, 2016, April 21). There are 10 countries where being gay may be punishable by death: Yemen, Iran, Iraq, Mauritania, Nigeria, Qatar, Saudi Arabia, Somalia, Sudan, and the United Arab Emirates (*Washington Post*, 2014, February 24).

What Is a Family?

Family can be defined in many ways. One dictionary offers the following definitions (*Merriam-Webster Dictionary,* 2016):

1. A group of people who are related to each other.
2. A person's children.
3. A group of related people including people who lived in the past.

There are innumerable other definitions of family, and following is a collection that represents a diversity of perspectives:

- A family consists of two or more people (one of whom is the householder) related by birth, marriage, or adoption residing in the same housing unit (U.S. Census Bureau, 2016).
- The term *family* is an inclusive term for people who "care, support and protect each other" (Australian Government, 2008).
- A family is a group of two or more people who are related by blood, marriage (registered or de facto), adoption, step or fostering, and who usually live together in the same household. This includes all families such as newlyweds without children, same-sex

Strong families are good for raising healthy and happy children. Extended families are a great source of support in raising children.
©Hill Street Studios/Blend Images LLC

partners, couples with dependent, single mothers or fathers with children, and siblings living together. At least one person in the family has to be 15 years or older. A household may contain more than one family (Australian Bureau of Statistics, 2013).

- A family is defined as two or more persons who share resources, share responsibility for decisions, share values and goals, and have a commitment to one another over time (American Association of Family and Consumer Sciences, 2015).
- The family is the most important unit of society and functions to fulfill its members' needs for both survival and well-being. "Families" come in many forms. A well-functioning family enhances its individual members' ability to function both within the family and in the larger community; such a family provides emotional, physical, and economic mutual aid to its members. Ideally, family is characterized by intimacy, intensity, continuity, and commitment among its members throughout the life cycle (Family Service Association, 2012).
- The definition of a family "should not rest on fictitious legal distinctions or genetic history" but instead should be based on the functional and psychological qualities of the relationship: the "exclusivity and longevity" of the relationship; the "level of emotional and financial commitment"; the "reliance placed upon one another for daily family services"; and how the couple (members) "conducted their everyday lives and held themselves out to society" (Braschi v. Stahl Assocs. Co., 1989).
- Definitions of the family vary along a continuum with biological conceptions on one end of the continuum and social conceptions on the other. Having a child through birth would be on the biological end, and adopting a child would be on the social end of the continuum. Both are legitimate definitions of family (Holtzman, 2005, 2011).
- Voluntary family or voluntary kin. People who care for us, support us, and feel like family to us, but are not related by blood or law (Braithwaite, 2008; Braithwaite et al., 2010).
- Call it a clan, call it a network, call it a tribe, call it a family. Whatever you call it, whoever you are, you need one (Howard, 2002).

How Americans define *family* is clearly evolving. A research team at Indiana University led by sociologist Brian Powell surveyed more than 2,300 people between 2003 and 2010

(Berman, 2010, September 15; Powell, Bolzendahl, Geist, & Carr Steelman, 2010). The researchers found that "people are moving away from a traditional definition of family towards a modern definition of family," Powell said. "That includes a greater array of living arrangements. They're including a much broader group of people, broader combination of people as families."

The Indiana research team identified three clusters of Americans, when it comes to defining family: *exclusionists* who hold onto a more narrow definition of family; *moderates* who are willing to count same-sex couples as family if children are involved; and *inclusionists* who have a very broad definition of family. In 2010, the researchers found that almost everyone—99.8%—agreed that a husband, wife, and kids count as a family. Ninety-two percent said that a husband and wife without the kids made a family. "Children provide this, quote, 'guarantee' that move you to family status," Powell said. "Having children signals something. It signals that there really is a commitment and sense of responsibility in a family."

The researchers also found that 83% of Americans say unmarried couples with children are a family. Only 39.6% said that an unmarried man and woman living together were a family, but adding kids jumped the number up to 83%. Thirty-three percent said a gay male couple was a family. Sixty-four percent said they became a family when they added children. This number rose from 54% to 64% between 2003 and 2010. "People right now are really reevaluating their views about same-sex couples," Powell said.

Sixty percent of Americans in 2010 said that if you considered yourself to be a family, then you were one.

We personally believe that any definition of family should be broad enough to encompass a range of family structures, dynamics, and functions. Our definition of family is *two or more people who are committed to each other and who share intimacy, resources, decision-making responsibilities, and values.* This definition is inclusive and allows for diversity in family structure, family values, and ethnic and cultural groups. At a Wimbledon tennis match, sisters Venus and Serena Williams were going to play each other and a sports writer asked, "Will this match hurt your relationship with your family?" The immediate answer was: "Tennis is just a game. Families are forever."

Trends in Marriage and the Family: Change and Continuity

What are marriage and the family like today? Current trends cited by the Pew Research Center (2016) include:

More breadwinner moms. A record 40% of all households with children under the age of 18 include mothers who are either the sole or primary source of income for the family, according to U.S. Census Bureau data. The share was just 11% in 1960.

Contemporary parenthood has changed dramatically in the past half century. Dads are doing more housework and child care; moms are doing more paid work outside the home. Neither dads nor moms have overtaken the other in their "traditional" realms, but their roles are converging.

The marriage rate has declined and the marriage age has risen. Barely half of U.S. adults are married, continuing a downward trend. In addition, the median age at first marriage for men and women has never been higher.

The American public is sharply divided in its judgments about sweeping changes in the structure of the American family. About a third generally accept the changes over the past half century; a third are tolerant but skeptical; and a third consider the changes bad for society.

More than 4 in 10 American adults have at least one step relative in their family—either a stepparent, a step or half sibling, or a stepchild.

There has been a decline in marriage and a rise of new families over the past half century. The preeminent family unit of the mid-20th century—mom, dad, and the kids—no longer has the stage to itself. A variety of new arrangements have emerged, giving rise to a broader and evolving definition of what constitutes a family.

The college marriage gap has reversed. In a reversal of a long-standing marital pattern, college-educated young adults are now more likely than young adults lacking a bachelor's degree to have married by the age of 30.

Statistics on divorce, domestic violence, and alcohol and other drug abuse, as well as stories of families in crisis, paint a rather negative picture of marriage and family life today. These snapshots of troubled families may be newsworthy, but the situations they describe are not new. For decades, many respected social scientists have predicted that the institutions of marriage and the family would not survive. For example, in 1927, psychologist John B. Watson predicted, "In 50 years, unless there is some change, the tribal custom of marriage will no longer exist." He believed marriage would disappear because family standards had broken down. In 1937, Pitirim Sorokin, a respected Harvard sociologist, wrote, "The family as a sacred union of husband and wife, of parents and children, will continue to disintegrate" (Bernard, 1970, p. 42). Ten years later, Carl Zimmerman, also a Harvard sociologist, noted, "There is little left now, within the family itself or the moral code, to hold the family together" (Bernard, 1972).

Although some professionals emphasize the decline of marriage and the family, others see them as being in a state of transition. As Ernest Burgess and his colleagues stated in 1954, "Certainly marriage and the family in the U.S. are in the process of rapid change. But is it change for the worse? Perhaps it may be for the better" (Bernard, 1972). In a similar vein, David and Vera Mace, pioneers in the marriage and family enrichment movement in Great Britain and the United States, argued that "marriage has not failed—it is simply in transition" (Mace & Mace, 1980, p. 260). Skolnick and Skolnick (1977), in their classic study *Family in Transition*, clearly illustrated the dramatic changes in family life over the centuries. In fact, one of the salient characteristics of the family is its ability to adapt to changing times and new challenges.

Today, pessimists and optimists disagree about how to interpret these trends and what to do about them. The pessimists see recent changes as an indication that marriage and family

Strong families enjoy leisure activities together.
©Ariel Skelley/Getty Images

Chapter 1 | Perspectives on Intimate Relationships | 7

are in serious trouble and are declining in their significance to society. They believe that we need to return to a more traditional value system to curtail these negative trends. The optimists, on the other hand, see recent changes as a reflection of the flexibility of marriage and family and the ability of these institutions to adapt to the increasing stresses of modern life. They believe marriage and the family will survive and thrive.

In fact, marriage and the family have survived over time despite all the predictions of their imminent collapse. Moreover, marriage remains the most popular voluntary institution in our society, with about 85% of the population marrying at least once (Popenoe & Whitehead, 2004).

Trends in Marriage and Cohabitation

There are several important trends in the United States that will be briefly described in this section: a decline in the percentage of those who are married, an increase in the number of those delaying marriage until they are older, an increase in the number of the never married, and an increase in the number of couples who choose to cohabit before—or instead of—marrying.

Marriage. Although marriage remains popular in the United States, it is not as popular as it once was. The percentage of people over the age of 18 who are married has steadily declined. In 1970, 68% of adults were married; in 1980, 66%; in 1990, 62%; and about 60% in 2000 (see Figure 1.1). In 2006, homes headed by married couples dipped to 49.7% (Roberts, 2006). This is the first time that married-couple households dipped below 50%, thus making married couples a minority in the United States. There are two reasons for this change: Many couples are choosing to stay single longer or are choosing to cohabit. There are also increased numbers of elderly people who have lost their spouse, which is adding to the number of single-family households. In addition, there are increasing numbers of same-sex couples who are not typically counted as being married.

More individuals are delaying marriage until their late 20s. Latest statistics indicate that the median age for first marriage is 28.4 years for men and 26.5 years for women, the oldest in U.S. history. Age at marriage has been on the increase for more than four decades. In 1960, the median age for a first marriage was 22.8 years for men and 20.3 years for women (U.S. Census Bureau, 2011a).

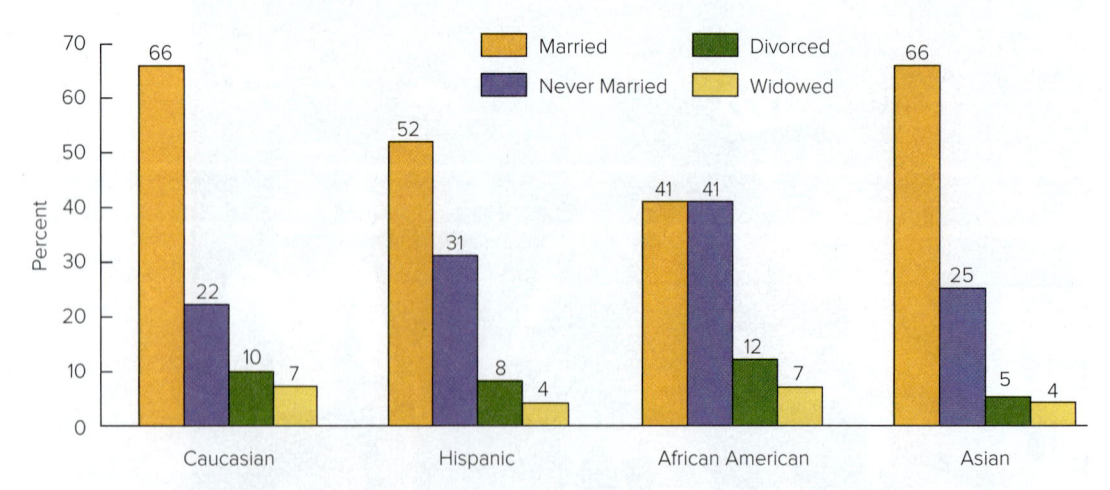

FIGURE 1.1
Marital Status of U.S. Population
Source: U.S. Census Bureau, *Statistical Abstract of the United States,* 2004/2005. Washington, DC: Government Printing Office, 2004/2005.

Cohabitation. Unmarried cohabitation, defined as the status of couples who are sexual partners, not married to each other, and sharing a household, is particularly common among young people. The rise of cohabitation has dramatically reshaped family life in the United States. Nearly nonexistent in 1960, the number of cohabiting couples increased 17-fold and reached 7.5 million by 2010. More than two-thirds of American adults cohabit before they marry, and about 40% of children live in a cohabiting family during childhood. Most young Americans are spending some time living together outside of marriage, and cohabitation commonly precedes marriage. An estimated 60% to 75% of first marriages are preceded by cohabitation, and up to 80% to 85% of remarriages (Kennedy & Bumpass, 2008; Kennedy & Fitch, 2012; Kreider, 2010).

Trends in Divorce and Remarriage

Although marriage is still popular, it is not necessarily lasting, with new estimates indicating that the lifetime probability of divorce or separation now falls between 40% and 50% (American Psychological Association, 2016; National Marriage Project, 2012, p. 67). However, the majority of those getting divorced will remarry.

Divorce. The majority of people who divorce eventually remarry. However, the increases in divorce rates in the United States and decline in remarriage rates have led to a steep increase in the percentage of adults in this country who are currently divorced. This percentage was

Cohabitation was once rare, but today a majority of young men and women of marriageable age live together without being married for some time, and about 40% of all children before reaching age 16 will spend some time in a cohabiting family.
©Don Hammond/Design Pics

only 1.8% for males and 2.6% for females in 1960, but quadrupled by the year 2000 and remains high today. The percentage of divorced persons is higher for females than for males, because divorced men are more likely to remarry than divorced women. Also, among those who remarry, men tend to remarry sooner than women (National Marriage Project, 2012, p. 69).

As we have seen, the chances of divorce for a first marriage entered into in recent years remains high—between 40% and 50%. But the likelihood of divorce varies considerably among different segments of the American population: the figures are higher for Blacks than for Whites, and higher in the South and West than in other parts of the country. These differences, however, are diminishing. The trend toward a greater similarity of divorce rates between Blacks and Whites has been largely attributed to the fact that fewer Blacks are marrying (National Marriage Project, 2012, p. 72).

There has been little change in such traditionally large divorce rate differences as between those who marry as teenagers and those who marry after the age of 21. Teenagers still have higher divorce rates than the rest of the population. And the divorce rate for the religiously committed remains lower than the divorce rate for the nonreligious (National Marriage Project, 2012, p. 72).

Why are there so many divorces and unhappy marriages in our society? Here are a few things to think about:

1. Many people enter marriage with unrealistic expectations.
2. Many marry the wrong person for the wrong reasons.
3. Marriage is a challenging type of relationship, even if one chooses a partner wisely.
4. Little time or effort is put into developing the relationship skills needed to create and maintain a strong marriage.

Remarriage. A remarriage occurs when a previously married person marries again. To understand the context of marriage in this country, we talk about whether and when Americans choose to marry, and we also talk about how many times they marry. Researchers at the U.S. Census Bureau report that the majority of recent marriages are first marriages for both partners. However, divorce rates are higher in the United States when compared with European nations, and remarried adults are more likely to divorce than those in their first marriage (Lewis, Kreider, & U.S. Census Bureau, 2015). Here are some of the highlights of the American Community Survey on Marital History:

- About half of all men (50%) and women (54%) aged 15 and over had married only once.
- The proportion of adults that had married only once has decreased since 1996, from 54% to 50% of men and 60% to 54% of women.
- Between 2008 and 2012, the share of those that had married twice or three or more times increased only for women aged 50 and older and men aged 60 and older.
- Non-Hispanic White men and women are most likely to have married three or more times, while Asian men and women in the United States are the least likely.
- Those with at least a bachelor's degree are more likely to have married only once (64%) than all adults (52%).
- The majority of recent marriages (58%) are first marriages for both spouses, although 21% of recent marriages involve both spouses marrying for at least the second time.
- States with a lower share of ever-married adults who had remarried are concentrated in the Northeast and Midwest, while Southern and Western states generally have a higher share.

The National Healthy Marriage Resource Center (2013) reports that though remarriages have always existed in the United States, until recently the majority of remarriages followed the death of a spouse rather than a divorce. From early colonial times until as late as the 1920s, remarriage was more likely to follow widowhood than divorce. But the trend changed and by 1987, only 9% of men and women remarried due to the death of a spouse. Remarriages also show higher divorce rates than first marriage. Researchers have found that 20% of first marriages end in divorce within 5 years, while 25% of second marriages end within this same time frame.

The presence of children is one factor associated with the failure of a second marriage. About 40% of remarriages involve children from a previous relationship, and women who had children before their second marriages were more likely to see that marriage fail within 10 years than women without children before the second marriage. Women who reported their children were *not wanted* were more likely to see the second marriage fail within 10 years than those who said their children *were wanted*. Also, failure of a remarriage is associated with remarriages in communities with higher poverty rates, low median family income, and a low proportion of college-educated residents (National Healthy Marriage Resource Center, 2013).

Table 1.1 provides some statistics on marriage and divorce trends. Divorce and remarriage will be discussed in greater detail in Chapter 15.

Trends in Family Structure

Family structure is becoming more complex through divorce and remarriage, which creates new kinship relationships. Contemporary families are more varied today than ever before. There are stepfamilies, same-sex parents and couples, child-free couples, grandparents raising grandchildren, surrogate parents, foster care families, families with disabled parents and children, and a variety of informal family arrangements.

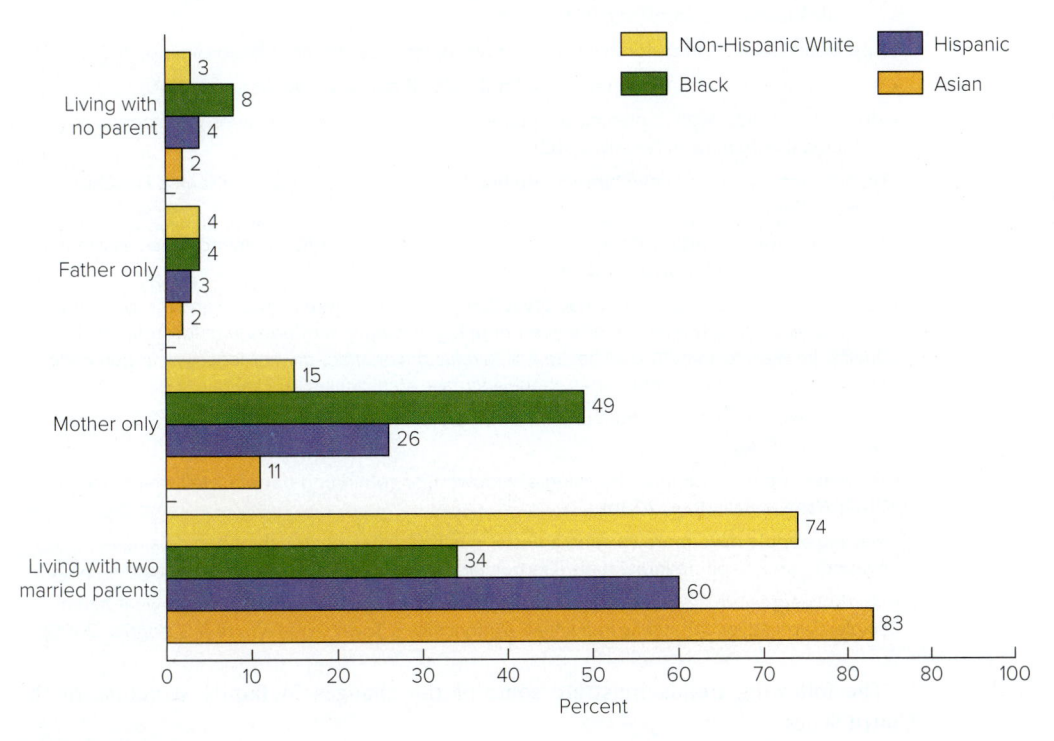

FIGURE 1.2
Living Arrangements of Children, by Race and Hispanic Origin: 2015
Source: Child Trends Calculations of U.S. Census Bureau, *Current Population Survey,* 2015. "America's Families and Living Arrangements: 2015." Table C-2. Available at: http://docplayer.net/21928353-Family-structure-updated-december-2015.html.

TABLE 1.1 Statistics on Marriage and Divorce

- 85% of the U.S. population will marry at least once (U.S. Census Bureau, 2008).
- Age at marriage has been on the increase for more than four decades. In 1960, the median age for a first marriage was 22.8 years for men and 20.3 for women. In 2009 the median age for first marriage was 28.4 years for men and 26.5 years for women (U.S. Census Bureau, 2011a).
- Over 75% of Americans report a belief that *being married* is an important value (Popenoe & Whitehead, 2010).
- Marriage among those with college degrees appears to be getting stronger, while marriage among those with a high school degree or less is becoming increasingly unstable and unhappy (Popenoe & Whitehead, 2010).
- In 2014 there were 2,140,272 marriages and 813,862 divorces and annulments (Centers for Disease Control and Prevention, 2015, November 23).
- 23.2 million Americans—about 9.1% of the U.S. population—are currently divorced (U.S. Census Bureau, 2009).
- People marrying today have a 40–50% chance of divorcing. Statistically, 40% of first marriages, 60% of second marriages, and 73% of third marriages end in divorce (American Psychological Association, 2016; Popenoe & Whitehead, 2010).
- About 75% of those who divorce will eventually remarry (U.S. Census Bureau, 2008).
- Of the marriages that do not end in divorce, the quality of some of those may be poor (Popenoe & Whitehead, 2010).
- After 10 years of marriage, it has been predicted that only 25% of couples will still be happily married (Popenoe & Whitehead, 2010).
- Most divorces involve children, and more than 1.5 million children are affected by divorce each year (*Scientific American*, 2013).
- Approximately 40% of children will experience divorce before adulthood (Amato, 2007).
- Women are more likely than men to file for divorce (Popenoe & Whitehead, 2010).
- Most adults adjust well to divorce over time. Thirty percent feel their lives were negatively impacted (Hetherington & Kelly, 2002).
- Divorce and unmarried child bearing are highly related to child poverty (Rank & Hirschl, 1999, 2015).
- A small number of studies have found positive individual benefits of divorce such as greater autonomy, personal growth, and happiness (Amato, 2000).
- With fewer barriers to divorce in society today, it becomes more common and more readily obtainable. As a consequence, the number of highly stable marriages with low relationship quality are likely to steadily decline. So-called *reluctant* or *make-do* marriages will lessen while the percentage of happy marriages should increase statistically (Xu, DeFrain, & Liu, 2017).
- Married people live longer than unmarried or divorced people (Liu & Reczek, 2012; Waite & Gallagher, 2000).
- Married people are happier than single, widowed, or cohabiting people (Helliwell & Grover, 2014; Waite & Gallagher, 2000).
- Married people have more sex and a better quality sexual relationship than do single, divorced, or cohabiting individuals (Herbenick, Reece, et al., 2010; Waite & Gallagher, 2000).
- Married people are more successful in their careers, earn more, and have more wealth than single, divorced, or cohabiting individuals (Antonovics & Town, 2004; Waite & Gallagher, 2000).

The following trends illustrate some of the changes in family structure in the United States:

- In 2015, 65% of all children lived in a nuclear family in which two parents were present. The percentage of two-parent families varies by ethnic/cultural group (Figure 1.2): 74% of Caucasian children live in two-parent homes; 60% of Hispanic children; 34% of African American children; and 83% of Asian American children (Child Trends, U.S. Census Bureau, 2015).

Single-parent families with children under the age of 18 have dramatically increased since 1970.
©Hill Street Studios/Stockbyte/Getty Images

- One of the largest shifts in family structure is the percentage of children who are living with an unmarried parent: 34% today compared to 19% in 1980 and 9% in 1960. In most cases, these unmarried parents are single. However, a small percentage of children—4%—are living with two cohabiting parents, according to U.S. Census Bureau data (Pew Research Center, 2014, December 22).
- About half (49%) of all African American families are headed by a single mother, while 26% of Hispanic families, 15% of Caucasian families, and 11% of Asian American families are headed by a single mother. A small but growing number of families in the United States (2% to 4% of families across ethnic/cultural groups) are headed by a single father (Child Trends, U.S. Census Bureau, 2015). Some social scientists have predicted that 60% of children in the United States will have lived in a single-parent household by the time they are 18 years old, if current divorce and remarriage rates hold.
- Families are typically having fewer children today, compared to earlier generations. A woman in the early 1900s in the United States could expect to give birth to about four children during her childbearing years, considered to be ages 15 to 44. A woman living during the Great Depression of the 1930s could expect to have only two children. After World War II, the number of births per woman climbed to 3.7 in 1957, but fell to 1.8 by the mid-1970s. Since then, the birth rate in the United States has hovered around two births per woman, with the most recent number at 1.9 in 2010. This is well below the replacement level of 2.1 births per woman. Similar declines in fertility rates have been reported in Ireland, Italy, Spain, Sweden, and several other European countries (Population Reference Bureau, 2012). See Figure 1.3.
- The share of mothers who do not work outside the home rose to 29% in 2012, up from a modern-era low of 23% in 1999, according to a Pew Research Center analysis of government data (2014, April 8). This rise over the past dozen years represented a reversal of a long-term decline in "stay-at-home" mothers that had persisted for the last three decades of the 20th century. The turnaround appears to be driven by a mix of demographic, economic, and societal factors, including rising immigration into the United States, as well as a downturn in women's labor force participation. And this is set against a backdrop of continued public ambivalence about the impact of working mothers on young children.

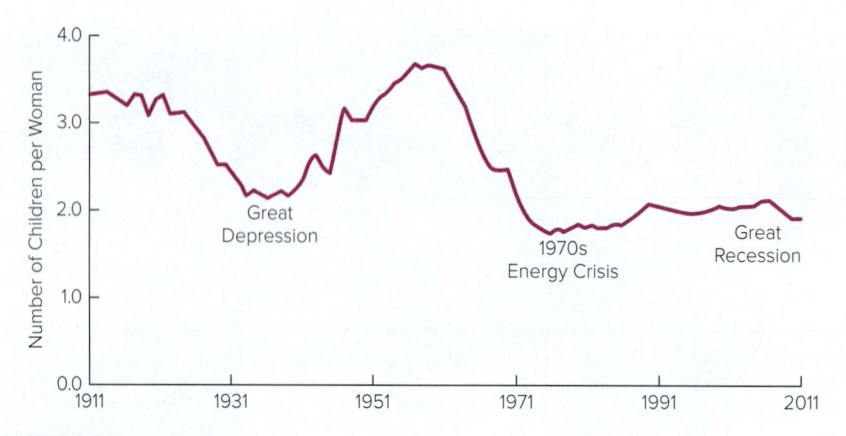

FIGURE 1.3
The U.S. Fertility Rate Has Fallen During Periods of Economic Decline
Source: Population Reference Bureau, *Fact Sheet: The Decline in U.S. Fertility,* 2012.

Continuity in Marriage and the Family

Although we tend to focus on how marriage and the family have changed, in many ways these institutions have remained the same over several decades and continue to provide stability in our lives. For example, most people in the United States want to marry, and most couples who do so see marriage as a lifelong commitment and do not plan to divorce. Many couples want to have an egalitarian marital relationship, but equality does not mean that they will share exactly the same roles around the house. Rather, equality means that they work together to accomplish the many tasks and responsibilities required by family life on a regular basis and divide these responsibilities fairly.

Most couples who marry want to have children. Parenthood is an important goal for many couples, a fact that becomes more evident when a couple is not able to have a child. Most parents want their children to have a good education and to be at least as successful as they, the parents, are in society. In fact, most parents would like their children to do better than they have in all aspects of life.

Most family members also have a commitment to each other, although they might not always get along. They have an emotional connection to their immediate and extended family network and feel it is appropriate to call on them in times of need. This family network is an important support system, although it is often taken for granted until a crisis arises. The family is an interdependent system of people who are emotionally connected to each other.

Most families also have a value system that encompasses spiritual and/or moral beliefs that provide the foundation for their attitudes and behaviors. These values become even more important to couples after they have children or in times of crisis. Also, there is an ongoing commitment and connection between parents and their children, even after divorce. This is particularly true if the parents are given joint custody of their children. Most people also feel that the family is the most effective and efficient way of socializing children.

In summary, marriage and family provide significant continuity in our society. Unfortunately, overemphasis on marriage and family problems can overshadow the stability and continuity that these intimate relationships offer us in our daily lives.

Focus on Marital and Family Strengths

A major theme of this book is strengths and the importance of focusing on strengths in a marriage and a family. This means paying attention to the good things your partner or children do and giving praise for the things you appreciate. Too often, married couples and family members tend to shift their focus from the positive to the things they do not like about each other.

BOX 1.1 Putting It Together
Learning to Focus on Strengths

Over the past 40 years, researchers looking at couples and families from a strengths perspective have developed the following propositions (DeFrain & Asay, 2007; DeFrain et al., 2012).

- *Families, in all their remarkable diversity, are the basic foundation of human cultures.* Strong families are critical to the development of strong communities, and strong communities promote and nurture strong families.
- *Not all families are strong, but all families have strengths.* If one looks only for problems in a family, one will see only problems. If one also looks for strengths, one will find strengths.
- *Function, not structure, is most important.* When talking about families, it is common to make the mistake of focusing on external family structure or the type of family rather than internal family functioning.
- *Strong marriages and intimate partners are the center of many strong families.* The couple relationship is an important source of strength in many families with children who are doing well. Parents need to find ways to nurture a positive couple relationship for the good of everyone in the family.
- *Strong families tend to produce great kids.*
- *If you grew up in a strong family as a child, it will probably be easier for you to create a strong family of your own as an adult.* But it's also quite possible to do so if you weren't so lucky and grew up in a seriously troubled family.
- *The relationship between money and family strengths is weak.* Once a family has adequate financial resources the relentless quest for more is not likely to increase the family's quality of life, happiness together, or the strength of their relationships with each other.
- *Strengths develop over time.* When couples start out in life together, they sometimes have considerable difficulty adjusting to each other, and these difficulties are quite predictable. Adjusting to each other is not an easy task. Many couples who are unstable at first end up creating a healthy, happy family.
- *Strengths are often developed in response to challenges.* A couple and family's strengths are tested by life's everyday stressors and also by the significant crises that all of us face sooner or later.
- *Strong families don't think much about their strengths, they just live them.* It is, however, useful to carefully examine a family's strengths from time to time and discuss precisely how family members use these strengths to great advantage.
- *Strong families, like people, are not perfect.* Even the strongest of families have difficulties and disagreements. A strong family is a work of art continually in progress, always in the process of growing and changing.
- *When seeking to unite groups of people, communities, and even nations, uniting around the cause of strengthening families can be a powerful strategy.*
- *Human beings have the right and responsibility to feel safe, comfortable, happy, and loved.*

Sources: DeFrain, J., & Asay, S.M. (Eds.), *Strong Families Around the World: Strengths-based Research and Perspectives.* London and New York: Haworth Press/Taylor & Francis, 2007; and DeFrain, J., & The University of Nebraska Extension Family Action Team, *Getting Connected, Staying Connected: Loving One Another Day by Day.* Indianapolis, IN: iUniverse, 2012.

Box 1.1 summarizes a number of important observations about relationship strengths. This includes the idea that all families have strengths, and you will observe them if you look for them rather than look only for problems. A strong marriage is the foundation for a strong family. This does not mean that single-parent families cannot be strong, but it is often harder for one parent to manage all the stressors and maintain the strengths. Strengths develop over time and are tested by struggles and ongoing issues that inevitably arise in marriage and parenting. Strengths also provide a framework for dealing with crises and for growing and changing over time.

Advantages of Marriage

Although people are delaying marriage and some are choosing not to marry, most people still value marriage. In one survey of adults, 93% rate having a happy marriage as one of the most important or very important objectives. For college freshmen, 94% said they personally hoped to get married, and they had a negative view of divorce. Over 70% agreed that children do better with both parents, and over 60% felt that children develop more emotional problems if their parents divorce (Waite, 2001, 2003; Waite & Gallagher, 2000; Waite & Lehrer, 2003; Waite, Luo, & Lewin, 2009).

But until recently, the positive impacts of marriage on the persons in the marriage have not been emphasized. Linda Waite and Maggie Gallagher (2000) made a major contribution in that regard in their book, *The Case for Marriage,* where they summarized over 200 studies that clearly demonstrated the major positive impacts of marriage.

First, Waite and Gallagher (2000) found that married people live longer than unmarried or divorced people. In fact, Waite and Gallagher stated, "Not being married can be hazardous to your health" (2000, p. 47). Nonmarried women have a 50% higher mortality rate than married women, and nonmarried men have a 250% higher rate than married men.

Married people live longer partially because they lead a healthier lifestyle. Single men typically engage in more risky behavior, including drinking, smoking, and drug use. Although single women typically have lower levels of risky behavior compared to men, being married also lowers the rate at which women participate in unhealthy behaviors. In addition, marriage improves a man's health as well as a woman's health. Married partners also tend to monitor each other's health more closely than cohabiting couples.

Married people are happier than single, widowed, or cohabiting people. About 40% of married people said they were very happy with their lives, whereas only 18% of divorced people, 15% of separated people, 22% of widowed, and 22% of cohabiting people were very happy.

On the basis of two national surveys, married couples have sex more frequently and find their sexual relationship more satisfying physically and emotionally than singles (Waite, 2001, 2003, 2016; Waite & Gallagher, 2000; Waite & Lehrer, 2003; Waite, Luo, & Lewin, 2009). In one study, 43% of the married men reported having sex at least twice a week, whereas only 26% of the single men who were not cohabiting had sex this often. The findings were similar for women; very few married women reported never having sex. Almost half (48%) of married men said sex is extremely satisfying emotionally compared to 37% of cohabiting men who found sex satisfying. There was less of a difference for married women compared to cohabiting women (42% for married versus 39% for cohabiting) who reported that sex was extremely satisfying.

Married sex is better sex because of four factors: *proximity, a long-term contract, exclusivity,* and *emotional bonding* (Waite & Gallagher, 2000). In terms of proximity, being married means your partner is more available, and partners are more comfortable with each other. Because they plan to remain married, married couples are often more willing to invest time, money, and energy in the relationship. By being more sexually exclusive, married couples are more willing to develop a mutually agreeable relationship. Emotionally, married couples feel more connected to each other than cohabiting couples.

Being married is also good for men in regard to their career and financial earnings (Waite, 2001, 2003, 2016; Waite & Gallagher, 2000; Waite & Lehrer, 2003; Waite, Luo, & Lewin, 2009). They argue that marriage is almost as important as education in predicting a man's success in a career. Their explanation of why this is so may raise the hackles of some readers, so let's discuss what they are saying in some depth. Why would marriage statistically predict a man's success in a career as much as his level of education? Waite and Gallagher propose that many married men are more successful because they can focus more on earning money and know that other tasks such as meals, laundry, and child care will be handled by their wives. Also, a wife often contributes ideas about her husband's job and generally supports the career of the husband.

The controversy ignites when wives don't feel equally supported in their careers, of course. And if an egalitarian relationship is not created—a genuinely 50/50 marriage—a couple runs the risk of ending up with two marriages, rather than one. Jessie Bernard, an eminent family sociologist, explained her two-marriages concept quite compellingly four decades ago in her classic book *The Future of Marriage* (1972). Bernard argued that marriage was simply better for men than for women because women take care of men, but men in a male-dominant society aren't as willing or capable or inclined to take care of women. She argued that in many cases there are two marriages: *his* marriage and *her* marriage, and his marriage is a much better deal because the wife attends to the husband's needs with more energy and interest than the husband attends to hers.

The argument looks like this behind closed doors, and it is still being fought today in some households:

She: "Well, I took your suits to the laundromat and got them cleaned and pressed. And I got a great present for your secretary's birthday. Oh, your mom called, and I told her you were too busy to go out to dinner this week, but I would take her to lunch Friday."

He [distracted as he looks through the mail]: "Oh, yeah, thanks...."

She [miffed as blood pressure rises]: "I could use a good wife!"

He [startled and angered by her sarcasm, responds in kind]: "You couldn't afford one!"

[And on and on.]

The concept of two marriages helps explain why women today are more likely to file for divorce than men: In essence, more women feel let down by marriage than men. The solution, of course, is not to bog down in *his* marriage and *her* marriage, but to work together to create *our* marriage. This, however, is no simple task.

Married couples accumulate more financial wealth, which is a total of their assets (home, car, investments, savings) after deducting their debts (mortgages, other loans, credit card debt). Married couples are able to combine their incomes, which is helpful inasmuch as more women work outside the home and increasingly are earning as much as or more than the husband. This pooling effect is worth 12% to 14% for couples at the age of 30 and it increases to 30% for retired couples compared to single individuals. Married couples are also more responsible in their spending because they have another person involved in the decision about spending. Conversely, if a person gets divorced the wealth is divided and each person starts over again (Waite, 2001, 2003, 2016; Waite & Gallagher, 2000; Waite & Lehrer, 2003; Waite, Luo, & Lewin, 2009).

Married people, especially women, are less likely to experience domestic abuse than cohabiting and separated women. The abuse rate for separated women is about 3 times higher than that for divorced women and 25 times higher than that for married women. Also, arguments between couples tend to lead to physical abuse in 4% of married couples compared to 13% for cohabiting couples.

Children generally fare better in families where their parents are married (Manning & Brown, 2006). Children from homes where the parents are married tend to be more academically successful, more emotionally stable, and more likely to assume leadership roles. This is, in part, because of the stability and guidance of two parents. Also, a married couple can model communication and collaborative behaviors, which helps childhood learning.

Marriage is much different from cohabitation (Waite & Gallagher, 2000). Cohabitation is seen by society and sometimes by the partners themselves as a temporary arrangement, whereas marriage is still seen as a lifelong commitment. Marriage is seen as a sexually exclusive relationship, and cohabitation is sometimes perceived as more sexually open to others. People who are cohabiting are typically less willing than married couples to be financially responsible for their partners. For married couples there are higher expectations to be seen and to operate as a couple socially than is true for cohabiting couples. Cohabiting couples have less-positive attitudes toward marriage and more-positive attitudes toward divorce than married couples.

In sum, marriage seems to have multiple benefits for both the husband and the wife. Married people live longer, are healthier and happier, and feel better emotionally. They also have more sex and a better sexual relationship. Married people are also more successful in their careers, earn more, and have more wealth. Married women experience less domestic abuse. Children raised by married parents tend to be more emotionally stable and academically successful. So, in many ways, married persons do experience numerous positive outcomes from being married that single and cohabiting couples do not receive.

This is not to say, of course, that if you are unhappy with the person you are living with and rush out and get married everything will work out fine. And this is not to say that if you are unhappy as a single person and rush out and get married you will suddenly be happy as a married person. All this is saying is that for many reasons marital relationships from a statistical perspective look stronger than cohabiting relationships, and married people tend to do better in life in many ways, compared to single people. This is not always the case when looking at individual situations, but on average it is true.

Impact of the Social Environment on Relationships

Human beings do not live and love in a vacuum. Just as we are connected to the special people in our lives—our friends and loved ones—so we are inextricably embedded in our social environment. The **social environment** comprises all the factors in society, both positive and negative, that impact on individuals and their relationships, such as the mass media, the internet, changing gender roles, and growing urban crowding. As individuals, we each have a modest influence on society, yet society clearly shapes our personal attitudes and behaviors and ultimately our couple and family relationships.

There is emerging interest about the interface between individual and family lives and community life. Basically, it has been found that the strengths of the community enhance life in the family (DeFrain & Asay, 2007; Asay, DeFrain, Metzger, & Moyer, 2014). A good example of this is a study showing that when neighborhood factors were controlled, African American students were less likely to drop out of school than White students (Van Dorn, Bowen, & Blau, 2006). Another way of saying this is that Black students are more likely to stay in school than White students when the Black students are living in a strong neighborhood. Bámaca, Umaña-Taylor, Shin, and Alfaro (2005) found that psychological outcomes for Latino adolescents were related to community assets, with more positive outcomes occurring in neighborhoods that had more assets. This occurred even when parenting influences stayed the same. Other researchers found that problem behaviors for African American children decreased when social assets in the neighborhood increased (Caughy, O'Campo, Nettles, & Lohrfink, 2006). It has also been found that the incidence of teen cohabitation and nonmarital births increased as ties with the community decreased (Houseknecht & Lewis, 2005). These studies make it apparent that there is an interface between families and the communities in which they live and that community strengths enhance family strengths.

We may be drawn to the Western ideal of rugged individualism—going boldly where no man or woman has gone before—but the reality of our lives is probably closer to the East Asian notion that each of us is but a drop of water in the ocean of life. Cultural norms and expectations have a powerful impact on us, especially if we try to behave against these norms. Visiting another culture is one way to experience the pervasive influence the social environment has on our lives, as the following personal account illustrates.

FIGURE 1.4

Elements of the Social Environment That Affect Couples and Relationships

Although families work and play together to create a haven in a sometimes bewildering and hazardous world, countless elements in the social environment can challenge a family's drive for balance and stability.

©Ingram Publishing/SuperStock

- Stress, change, and materialism
- Instability of couple and family relationships
- Urban migration and overcrowding
- Use of alcohol, tobacco, and other drugs
- Financial problems and the global economy
- The internet and human relationships
- Violence in our society
- Lack of time for self and significant others
- Changing gender roles and the balance of power in relationships
- Increasing use of child care outside the family
- Family and the environment

> *When my husband and I were living in China, everything was so different from what we were used to: the language, the food, the music, the dress, everything. Now this is a hard thing to explain to someone who has not already experienced it, but being out of my own culture, my own environment, I started to feel after a few months in China like my identity as a person was disappearing.*
>
> *It was like I was shrinking. Without my family and my friends at home, without our dog Jessie, without my music, without my food, without our crummy old car, I felt so disconnected, so insignificant. One day I would have given $50 for a genuine American cheeseburger. It sounds crazy talking about it now.*
>
> *We both finally did adjust pretty well to China. After about a year or so I kind of turned an emotional corner. And after 2 years I felt like an old hand at surviving culture shock. Today, I love China. But we also love home. And I learned something very important from all this: The social environment I'm used to is very, very important to me. I felt like a fish out of water for a while when taken away from what's familiar to me. I'm not the great individualist I thought I was."*

In general, the social environment shapes us much more than we can shape the social environment (see Figure 1.4). However, we are not puppets of the social environment. Growing up in an alcoholic family is not an excuse for being an alcoholic. Similarly, being abused as a child does not justify abusing one's own children. Countless people grow up in violent families but are able to rise above those life experiences. Individuals can make positive choices in their lives, regardless of their past lives.

Stress, Change, and Materialism

"Whatever you're doing," one anonymous observer noted, "it's not enough." The velocity of life in this country appears to many people to be increasing exponentially, and our inner demons press us to perform, to produce, to consume, to move. These voices accelerate as social change presses upon us. **Stress** is the body and mind's reaction to life. Stress is directly related to change, and the greater the change, the higher the level of stress. The continuous cascade of new developments in society today can be defined broadly as *progress* perhaps, but many of these developments add stress to our lives.

Chapter 1 | Perspectives on Intimate Relationships | 19

We now want and expect things to happen *fast*. We now have voice mail, email, and texting, and we even call regular mail snail mail. We used to have telephones in our homes and offices. Now we carry them in our pockets, purses, and packs and attach them to our belts. We also fool ourselves into thinking that we can multitask, trying to do several things at once: We drive cars while we talk on the phone, put on our makeup, sing along with the CD player, eat a cheeseburger, plan our day, and text, regardless if these activities while driving a vehicle are legal or not. Not only have these technological changes increased the volume of information we receive and must respond to, but the time in which we are expected to respond has been shortened—from a few days to return a letter to a few hours to return an email to seconds as we answer our ubiquitous cell phones and read our text messages.

As a society, we also have a great appetite for material possessions—for *stuff*. In fact, everything has to be new, if we are to believe media sales pitches: We need new cars, new houses, new clothes, perhaps a new nose. The business world is brimming with stories of corporate takeovers and downsizing. Companies come and go every day, and workers are cast off like old furniture. In this kind of consumer culture, it's not such a stretch to imagine that finding a new partner is the easiest option when there are problems with the old relationship. As the old male chauvinist joke goes, "I'm tired of my 40-year-old wife. I'm going to trade her in for two 20-year-olds."

When they are combined, technology and materialism increase our level of stress in all areas of life. We feel pressured to do more and to have more—and to run faster while grasping for all of it. The first casualty in such an environment is our individual sense of well-being. The second casualty is our bond of affection and closeness with each other.

You can counter these trends by being more proactive in your personal life. You can look for ways to be less materialistic and less caught up in the hectic pace of life. This is a personal choice that you can make, which will influence how much you let these factors affect you.

Lack of Time for Oneself and Significant Others

According to family researchers, one of the most difficult qualities to develop in many American families is the ability to spend enjoyable time together. Not only do we find ourselves challenged by a busy and competitive social environment outside the home, but once we return home, we often feel we need time to unwind from a hectic day before reconnecting with others.

For many in today's society, the boundaries between the home and work are being blurred. As sociologist Arlie Hochschild's (Hochschild, 1997, 2009, 2010; *Washington Post*, 2014, August 6) observed, work becomes more like home and home becomes more like work. Caught in the time bind, the more time we work, the more stressful home life becomes. The more stressful home life becomes, the more we want to escape back to work. Hochschild argues that we must challenge the economic and social system that invites or demands long hours at work, and focus our efforts on investing less time in the job and more time in couple and family relationships.

Families that have discretionary income can purchase labor such as child care and people who care for the household in order to free up time for families to eat out or engage in recreational or leisure activities. Low-income families may not have the option to purchase services and may experience greater challenges in finding time for themselves and other family members. Researchers have found that low-income families are less likely to spend time in activities outside the home but instead intentionally build relationship time into mealtime and other household activities (Tubbs, Roy, & Burton, 2005; Tubbs, 2016).

You can counter these trends by purposefully setting time aside for yourself and also time to be with your significant others. Some people have found their alone time is to have 15 minutes with coffee in the morning; others look for time alone at the end of the day, going for an hour-long walk or exercising at the recreation center. For couples, it is important that they purposefully find time to reconnect after a hectic day, even though on some days it might be for only 10 to 15 minutes together. Families also need time to be with each other, and although it is often hard to find time, more families are taking time to set up regular rituals, eating together as often as possible, and not allowing the world to steal their time together.

Increasing Use of Child Care Outside the Family

What do we do about our kids when both parents work outside the home? This is one of the most challenging questions our society faces today. In the United States today more than half of mothers with young children work outside the home, compared to about one in three in the 1970s. Working mothers are now the rule rather than the exception. Women have been moving into the workforce not only for career satisfaction but also because they and their families need the income. Many women who are married have husbands who make less than $30,000 a year (American Academy of Pediatrics, 2016).

While parents are working, who's minding the kids? The U.S. Census Bureau (2013, April) reported that in the spring of 2011 there were 20.4 million children in the United States under 5 years of age. In a typical week during that spring, 12.5 million of these children (61%) were in some type of regular child care arrangement. They spent an average of 33 hours a week in child care. Here are some highlights of the Census Bureau report: Families with children under 5 paid, on average, $179 per week, which sums to $9,300 per year for child care. Preschoolers (defined as children under 5 years old) were more likely to be cared for by a relative (42%) than by a nonrelative (33%), while 12% were regularly cared for by both. Twenty-four percent of young children were regularly cared for by a grandparent, and 18% were cared for by their father. More than one-third of the preschoolers (7.9 million) were not in a regular child care arrangement during the month preceding the Census Bureau survey.

Mothers and fathers struggle with questions about day care:

- Do I need to work outside the home? Is employment essential for our family's well-being? For my well-being? And how will it affect our child's well-being?
- Will I be able to develop a bond with my child if she spends so much time away from me?
- Will I spend more money on child care, extra clothes, lunches, and transportation than I make on the job?
- How will the stresses of the job affect me personally? Our family? Can all this be balanced effectively?
- How will our child adapt to outside care? Will he receive good care? Will it be as good as the care we can give him?
- Will our child enjoy being with other children? Will the child's social development be enhanced by these opportunities?

For parents, finding satisfactory answers to these and countless other child care–related questions is a considerable challenge.

Parents now are becoming more active in finding ways to balance time away from their children and quality child care. Parents are checking out day care centers more carefully and looking critically at how teachers relate to their children.

Instability of Couple and Family Relationships

Many observers have argued that our fast-moving and competitive social environment is directly responsible for the high rate of marital dissolution and the increase in single-parent families and stepfamilies. Although personality conflicts and troubles within a marriage clearly contribute to marital breakdown, societal factors and values also influence our intimate behavior.

Rather than come home from work and sit on the front porch to talk with family and neighbors, we often hide behind closed doors in a cocoonlike atmosphere, plopped down in front of the television or a computer. As a result, many of our personal impressions come from the media. We may know more about our favorite actor's marriage than we know about how the couple is doing next door. Perhaps we are choosing to live like this, of course, in the name of personal privacy. But married life on television and in the tabloids is far different from the average couple's life. It can be argued that the steady diet of extramarital affairs and marital conflict we receive from the media helps create a *culture of divorce* in this country.

However, we believe that more people are feeling the need to maintain their close personal relationships. People are seeking more stability in their relationships and are trying to stay more connected. Married couples are more interested in building a stronger marriage, and families are trying to find ways to spend more quality time together.

Violence, Criminal Victimization, and Fear

Violent and abusive behavior continues to be a major cause of death, injury, stress, and fear in our country. Here are some highlights from the most recent Federal Bureau of Investigation (2015) crime statistics:

- There were an estimated 1,165,383 violent crimes (murder and nonnegligent homicides, rapes, robberies, and aggravated assaults) reported by law enforcement.
- Aggravated assaults accounted for 63.6% of the violent crimes reported, while robberies accounted for 28.0%, rape 7.2%, and murders 1.2%.
- There were an estimated 8,277,829 property crimes (burglaries, larceny-thefts, and motor vehicle thefts) reported by law enforcement. Financial losses suffered by victims of these crimes were calculated at approximately $14.3 billion.
- Larceny-theft accounted for 70.8% of all property crimes reported, burglary for 20.9%, and motor vehicle theft for 8.3%.
- Police made an estimated 11,205,833 arrests during 2014—498,666 for violent crimes, and 1,553,980 for property crimes. More than 73% of those arrested during 2014 were male.

However, Gallup (2015, October 22) argues that Americans' perceptions of crime are not always on par with reality. Government data show that violent crime rates in the United States over the past two decades have declined, but majorities of Americans in Gallup's yearly survey still maintain that crime has increased nationally each year the survey is taken. U.S. Department of Justice statistics show that serious crime has decreased almost every year from 1994 through 2010. The overall violent crime rate for rape, sexual assault, robbery, aggravated assault, and simple assault fell from 80 victimizations out of every 1,000 persons in 1994 to 19 victimizations per 1,000 in 2010. Why do people tend to feel that crime is increasing rather than decreasing? Gallup argues that this unwarranted pessimism may stem from the imperfect views of crime that Americans receive from the news and other sources, as well as Americans' overall mood.

Sexual violence, stalking, and intimate partner violence are major public health problems in the United States and impact millions of people each year, according to the National Intimate Partner and Sexual Violence Survey conducted by the Centers for Disease Control and Prevention (2015, March 10). Consequences for survivors of these forms of violence can include mental health problems such as depression, anxiety, low self-esteem, and suicide attempts, and other health consequences including gastrointestinal disorders, substance abuse, sexually transmitted diseases, and gynecological or pregnancy complications. These can lead to hospitalization, disability, or death. Women are more likely to be affected by sexual violence, intimate partner violence, and stalking:

- Twenty people per minute are victims of physical violence by an intimate partner in the United States.
- Intimate partner violence affects both men and women. Nearly one in two women and one in five men experience sexual violence victimization other than rape at some point in their lives.
- Violence starts early: 79% of female victims of completed rape report being raped before age 25; and 28% of male victims report they were first raped before 10 years old or younger.
- More than half of female victims and nearly half of male victims of stalking report they were first stalked before age 25.
- Intimate partner violence impacts all ethnic groups: 4 in 10 women and 4 in 10 men among American Indians or Alaska Natives; 4 in 10 women and 3.5 in 10 men among non-Hispanic Blacks; 3.5 in 10 women and 2.5 in 10 men among non-Hispanic Whites; 4 in 10 women and 3 in 10 men among Hispanics; 5 in 10 women and 4 in 10 men among multiracial individuals; and 2 in 10 men and women among Asian or Pacific Islanders.
- Intimate partner violence varies by income. Women with a household income less than $50,000 have a significantly higher prevalence of intimate partner violence. For those making less than $25,000 per year, the intimate partner violence rate is 9.7%. For those making between $25,000 and $50,000, the rate is 5.9%. And for those making more than $75,000 a year, the intimate violence rate is 2.8%.
- Intimate partner violence impacts people of all sexual orientations: one in two bisexual women, one in six lesbian women, and one in eight heterosexual women have been raped during their lifetime.
- Among men, one in two bisexual men, two in five gay men, and one in five heterosexual men experienced sexual violence other than rape during their lifetime.

Nationwide, according to the latest available statistics in 2013, 679,000 children were victims of abuse and neglect. This is a rate of 9.1 victims per 1,000 children in the U.S. population (Child Welfare Information Gateway, 2015). Among the children confirmed as victims by Child Protective Services agencies during the year, children in the age group of birth to 1 year had the highest rate of victimization at 23.1 per 1,000 children. The youngest children are the most vulnerable to maltreatment. Slightly more than one-half of the child victims were girls (50.9%), and 48.7% were boys. Gender was unknown for less than 1% of victims. Three ethnic groups comprised more than 87% of victims: African American (21.2%), Hispanic (22.4%), and White (44.0%). African American children had the highest rates of victimization at 14.6 per 1,000 children in the population of the same race or ethnicity. Hispanic and White children had rates of victimization at 8.5 and 8.1 per 1,000 children, respectively.

As in prior years, neglect was overwhelmingly the most common form of child maltreatment, comprising 79.5% of victims. Eighteen percent suffered physical abuse; 9.0% sexual abuse; 8.7% psychological maltreatment; and 2.3% medical neglect. In addition, 10.0% suffered "other" maltreatment, such as threatened abuse or parents' substance abuse. Risk factors for maltreatment include poverty and socioeconomic status. Other possible risk factors: 14.4% of victims of child maltreatment and 8.8% of nonvictims had caregivers experiencing a financial problem; 29.9% of victims and 23.4% of nonvictims were receiving public assistance; 27.4% of victims and 8.1% of nonvictims were exposed to domestic violence. For the 43 states that reported on disabilities, 12.6% of victims were reported as having a disability (Child Welfare Information Gateway, 2015).

How many children died from abuse or neglect? This is the most tragic consequence of maltreatment. During 2013, the U.S. government estimates that 1,520 children died due to abuse and neglect. The overall rate of child fatalities was 2.04 deaths per 100,000 children; 71.4% of child fatalities were attributed to neglect only or a combination of neglect and another maltreatment type; and 46.8% died exclusively from physical abuse or from physical abuse in combination with another maltreatment type. Nearly three-quarters (73.9%) of the children who died due to child abuse and neglect were younger than 3 years old. Boys had a slightly higher child fatality rate than girls at 2.36 boys per 100,000 boys in the population compared to 1.77 girls per 100,000 girls in the population (Child Welfare Information Gateway, 2015).

Suicide is a major public health concern (National Institute of Mental Health, 2015, April). More than 41,000 people take their own lives each year in the United States. The rate of suicide hovers around 11 suicide deaths per 100,000 people each year. An estimated 11 suicide attempts occur for every person who actually ends her or his life. It is the tenth leading cause of death in this country. Suicide is tragic, and it is often preventable. Knowing the risk factors can help reduce the suicide rate. Suicide does not discriminate, as people of all genders, ages, and ethnicities can be at risk. The main risk factors are:

Depression, other mental disorders, or substance abuse disorder
A prior suicide attempt
Family history of a mental disorder or substance abuse
Family history of suicide
Family violence, including physical or sexual abuse
Having guns or other firearms in the home
Incarceration, being in prison or jail
Being exposed to others' suicidal behavior, such as that of family members, peers, or media figures.

Men are more likely to die by suicide than women, but women are more likely to attempt suicide. Men are more likely to use deadlier methods, such as firearms or suffocation. Women are more likely than men to attempt suicide by poisoning. Children and young people are at risk for suicide. It is the second leading cause of death for young people ages 15 to 34. Older adults are also at risk for suicide. Older adults have had the highest suicide rates for decades, but suicide rates for young adults and middle-aged adults (ages 24 to 62) have risen to comparable levels. Over age 65, White males account for 80% of all late-life suicides. Among America's various ethnic groups, American Indians and Alaska Natives tend to have the highest rate of suicides, followed by non-Hispanic Whites. Hispanics tend to have the lowest rate of suicides, while African Americans tend to have the second lowest rate.

Suicidal tendencies can be treated successfully, of course. Those in crisis, or those who have a loved one or friend in crisis, are encouraged to call the toll-free National Suicide Prevention Lifeline at 1-800-273-8255, which is open 24/7.

Gun violence in the United States is far greater than gun violence in any other of the G-8 countries that collect data. The Group of Eight includes the eight largest economies in the world (ABC News, 2012). There are an estimated 88.8 civilian guns per 100 people in the United States, according to the Small Arms Survey, a number unparalleled in the rest of the world and higher than the other G-8 countries for which there are data. The United States also has a much higher rate of homicides by gun—3.2 homicides by firearm per 100,000 people, according to the United Nations Office on Drugs and Crime Homicide Statistics. Italy, the G-8 country with the second highest rate of homicides by firearm, comes in far behind the United States. According to United Nations data, a person is 4.5 times more likely to die from gun violence in the United States than in Italy. In France, the homicide by firearm rate is 0.1 per 100,000. That is one in a million.

Use of Alcohol, Tobacco, and Other Drugs

Drinking and smoking are woven into the very fabric of American culture, and yet the use of legal substances—alcohol and tobacco—kills hundreds of thousands of Americans every year, far more deaths than can be attributed to illegal drugs.

Some statistics compiled by the Centers for Disease Control and Prevention (2016, February 29) give a good picture of the situation concerning alcohol:

> Excessive alcohol use led to approximately 88,000 deaths and 2.5 million years of potential life lost each year in the United States from 2006 to 2010, shortening the lives of those who died by an average of 30 years.
> In addition, excessive drinking was responsible for 1 in 10 deaths among working-age adults ages 20 to 64.
> The economic costs of excessive alcohol consumption in 2010 were estimated at $249 billion, or $2.05 per drink.

What, precisely, is a "drink"? In the United States, a standard drink contains 0.6 ounces (14.0 grams or 1.2 tablespoons) of pure alcohol. Generally, this amount of pure alcohol is found in 12 ounces of beer (5% alcohol content); 8 ounces of malt liquor (7% alcohol content); 5 ounces of wine (12% alcohol content); 1.5 ounces of 80-proof (40% alcohol content) distilled spirits or liquor (for example, gin, rum, vodka, whiskey).

Excessive drinking includes binge drinking, heavy drinking, and any drinking by pregnant women or people younger than age 21. Binge drinking, the most common form of excessive drinking, is defined as women consuming four or more drinks during a single occasion, and men consuming five or more drinks during a single occasion. Heavy drinking is defined as women consuming 8 or more drinks per week, and men consuming 15 or more drinks per week. Most people who drink excessively are not alcoholics or alcohol dependent. Moderate drinking is defined as up to one drink per day for women and up to two drinks per day for men.

Health researchers in the federal government recommend that nondrinkers should not start drinking. Some people are especially at risk if they drink: those who are younger than age 21; women who are pregnant or may be pregnant; those who are driving, planning to drive, or participating in other activities requiring skill, coordination, and alertness; those taking certain prescription or over-the-counter medications that can interact with alcohol; those suffering from certain medical conditions; and those recovering from alcoholism or those unable to control the amount they drink.

Short-term health risks related to excessive alcohol use are most often the result of binge drinking and include the following:

> Injuries, such as motor vehicle crashes, falls, drownings, and burns.
> Violence, including homicide, suicide, sexual assault, and intimate partner violence.

Alcohol poisoning, a medical emergency that results from high blood alcohol levels.
Risky sexual behaviors, including unprotected sex or sex with multiple partners. These behaviors can result in unintended pregnancy or sexually transmitted diseases, including HIV.
Miscarriage and stillbirth or fetal alcohol spectrum disorders (FASDs) among pregnant women.

Long-term health risks related to excessive alcohol use include the development of chronic diseases and other serious problems: high blood pressure, heart disease, stroke, liver disease, and digestive problems. Add to this list:

Cancer of the breast, mouth, throat, esophagus, liver, and colon
Learning and memory problems, including dementia and poor school performance
Mental health problems, including depression and anxiety
Social problems, including lost productivity, family problems, and unemployment
Alcohol dependence, or alcoholism

By not drinking too much, these short-term and long-term health risks can be reduced.

The research-based evidence on the negative effects of tobacco use is also overwhelming, regardless of what the advertisers say. Here are some statistics from the Centers for Disease Control and Prevention (2016, April 14):

- Smoking leads to disease and disability and harms nearly every organ of the body.
- More than 16 million Americans are living with a disease caused by smoking.
- For every person who dies because of smoking, at least 30 people live with a serious smoking-related illness.
- Smoking causes cancer, heart disease, stroke, lung diseases, diabetes, and chronic obstructive pulmonary disease (COPD), which includes emphysema and chronic bronchitis.
- Smoking also increases risk for tuberculosis, certain eye diseases, and problems of the immune system, including rheumatoid arthritis.
- Smoking is a known cause of erectile dysfunction in males.
- Smoking is the leading cause of preventable death.
- Worldwide, tobacco use causes nearly 6 million deaths per year, and current trends show that tobacco use will cause more than 8 million deaths annually by 2030.
- Cigarette smoking is responsible for more than 480,000 deaths per year in the United States, including nearly 42,000 deaths resulting from secondhand smoke exposure. This is about 1 in 5 deaths annually, or 1,300 deaths every day.
- On average, smokers die 10 years earlier than nonsmokers.
- If smoking continues at the current rate among U.S. youth, 5.6 million of today's Americans younger than 18 years of age are expected to die prematurely from a smoking-related illness. This represents about 1 in every 13 Americans aged 17 years or younger who are alive today.
- The tobacco industry spends billions of dollars each year on cigarette advertising and promotions. In 2012, $9.17 billion was spent on advertising and promotion of cigarettes—more than $25 million every day, or more than $1 million every hour.
- In the United States, 16.8% of all adults smoke (40 million people): 18.8% of males, 14.8% of females.
- Many adult cigarette smokers want to quit smoking. In 2011 nearly 7 in 10 (68.9%) adult cigarette smokers wanted to stop smoking. More than 4 in 10 (42.7%) adult cigarette smokers had made a quit attempt in the past year.

The number of deaths caused by alcohol is dwarfed by the number of deaths caused by tobacco, as we have seen: approximately 88,000 alcohol-related deaths in a recent year, compared to 480,000 tobacco-related deaths. These are legal drugs, killing 568,000 Americans each year.

Now, let's take a look at this problem from another angle: deaths caused each year by illegal drugs. The Centers for Disease Control and Prevention (2015, November 6; 2016, February 9) estimates that 17,465 died in 2015 from overdosing on illicit drugs such as heroin and cocaine. The number of deaths from marijuana last year remained steady from the year before, according to the CDC: once again, no one died from a marijuana overdose.

So, if we do the math, we divide 568,000 deaths from legal drugs (alcohol and tobacco) by 17,000 (the number of deaths from illegal drugs, such as heroin and cocaine), and we find that 33 times more people die from legal drug use each year, compared to illegal drug use.

An additional 25,760 people died in 2015 from overdosing on legal prescription drugs, including painkillers and tranquilizers like Valium, according to the CDC (2016, February 9).

You can counter these trends by limiting or eliminating altogether your use of tobacco and alcohol, which is easier if you choose friends who also have a similar lifestyle. By limiting your use, you can minimize the addicting quality of these drugs, which are very difficult to stop using once one is addicted. Because drugs negatively affect your body in the short and long run, adopting a lifestyle without them will bring you a healthier life.

The Internet and Human Relationships

In our continuous quest to market technological solutions to human problems, much has been made of the computer's potential for connecting human beings. In the fun movie *You've Got Mail,* Meg Ryan and Tom Hanks fall in love via email. It is a charming notion, but research tells a more complicated story.

According to Pew Research Center data, 84% of American adults use the internet. Since 2000, Pew researchers have conducted 97 national surveys of adults that document how the internet has become an integral part of everyday life across diverse parts of American society (Pew Research Center, 2015, June 26). For some groups, especially young adults, those with high levels of education, and those in more affluent households, internet penetration is at full saturation levels. In other words, most everyone in these groups use the internet. For other groups of Americans, such as older adults, those with less educational attainment, and those living in lower-income households, adoption of the internet has historically been lower but rising steadily, especially in recent years. But, a digital gap still persists:

Age differences: Older adults have lagged behind younger adults in their adoption, but now a clear majority (58%) of senior citizens uses the internet.

Class differences: Those with college educations are more likely than those who do not have high school diplomas to use the internet. Similarly, those who live in households earning more than $75,000 are more likely to be internet users than those living in households earning less than $30,000. Still, the class-related gaps have shrunk dramatically in 15 years as the most pronounced growth has come among those in lower-income households and those with lower levels of educational attainment.

Racial and ethnic differences: African Americans and Hispanics have been somewhat less likely than Whites or English-speaking Asian Americans to be internet users, but the gaps have narrowed. Today, 78% of Blacks and 81% of Hispanics use the internet, compared with 85% of Whites and 97% of English-speaking Asian Americans.

Community differences: Those who live in rural areas are less likely than those in the suburbs and urban areas to use the internet. Still, 78% of rural residents are online.

Too much time on the internet can create problems in relationships for many people.
©Peter Bernik/123

Parents and children use the internet for emailing, text messaging, listening to music, reading the newspaper, shopping online, and many other activities. Monitoring children's use of the internet is increasingly difficult as young people rely on it to do homework, which means they also have access to unsuitable web information.

Research at the University of Southern California indicates that more and more of America's internet-connected households report erosion of face-to-face family time, increased feelings of being ignored by family members using the web, and growing concerns that children are spending too much time online (USC Annenberg, 2009, 2016). The USC research team reported that the percentage of people who say they spend less time with household members since being connected to the internet nearly tripled during one 3-year period, from 11% to 28%. Total hours devoted to family socializing dropped by more than 30% over the same 3-year period, from about 26 hours per month to 17.9 hours per month.

According to another investigation, 1 in 7 youths have received unwanted sexual solicitations on the internet, 1 in 3 have experienced unwanted exposure to sexual material, and 1 in 11 have been subjected to threatening or other offensive behavior. The good news is that these numbers were lower than they were 5 years before, as a result of national internet safety programs (Wolak, Mitchell, & Finkelhor, 2006; see also Finkelhor, 2009).

Pedophiles often use the internet to lure children into participation in sexual behavior. Sexual exploitation of children on the internet is an increasing concern for parents, law enforcement agencies, and legislators (Wolak et al., 2006; Finkelhor, 2009). "It's an unfortunate fact of life that pedophiles are everywhere online," according to Special Agent Greg Wing, supervisor of a cyber squad in the FBI's Chicago Field Office (Federal Bureau of Investigation, 2011). Research indicates that parents have made efforts to monitor young people's use of internet sites, with one study indicating that 61% of parents regulated their teen's internet use (Wang, Bianchi, & Raley, 2005; see also Child Development Institute, 2015).

What about adult access to pornography on the internet? Is pornography additive? What effect does it have on marriage and family life? (American Psychological Association, 2014). It is estimated that 15% of individuals visiting internet porn sites develop sexual behaviors that interfere with their lives (Gustafson, 2005). On a very basic level, pornography is viewed in secret, which creates deception in marriage and contributes to divorce. In addition, Dr. Mary Anne Layden, a psychotherapist and expert on sexual addiction, concludes that involvement in pornography is the common theme in sexual violence. Layden says that pornography increases the likelihood of sexual addiction, and 40% of sex addicts will lose their spouse, 58% will have financial difficulties, and 27% will lose their jobs or be demoted (Gustafson, 2005).

Sex is big business, and some say it has become a national obsession. This trend has been fueled by an increase in internet sex reaching deep into our homes, causing problems for children and for marriage and family relationships.

Changing Gender Roles and the Balance of Power

Since the late-1960s there has been a dramatic increase in the number of mothers working outside the home. This development has helped fuel an ongoing discussion of the roles of women and men in America and how power should be allocated in society as a whole and between household partners in particular.

On a global scale, there are more than 175 current heads of state worldwide. How many of them are women? Eighteen—or just over 10% of those top posts. To this day, most presidents and prime ministers are men. Women are not even close, in spite of some progress (*Globalist,* 2016). Nevertheless, in the United States women are serving as associate justices on the Supreme Court, as senators and representatives of Congress, and in countless other positions of power and influence in both government and the business world. With the emergence of women in traditionally male roles, particularly in positions of power, **gender roles** (the traits and behaviors assigned to males and females in a culture) are being redefined.

Just as *supermoms* struggle to find a meaningful balance between work and family, so too men are challenged by their own changing world. Years ago, a man's home may have been *his* castle; today it's an *egalitarian haven*. Just how fairly power and work should be shared in American households is a topic of considerable discussion today. Some observers suggest that men still have a long way to go before true equality is reached in the home.

Many maintain that women have been the true pioneers of the gender revolution, arguing that wives have more quickly changed their roles *outside* the home than men have changed their roles *inside* the home. Still others question how equal we really want males and females to be in our society. They assert that females and males are biologically different and that wives should stay at home to better socialize our children. Regardless of one's position, it's impossible to deny that gender roles and relationship power balances are evolving in today's society.

Urban Migration and Overcrowding

"The history of American agriculture," according to Rex Campbell, a rural sociologist at the University of Missouri at Columbia, "is the history of technology in rural areas" (Campbell, cited in Graham, 1998, p. 9; also, Campbell, 2016). When farmers depended on animals for work and transportation, small towns dotted the rural landscape in the heartland about 6 miles apart. Eventually, trucks and tractors replaced horses and mules, farms got bigger, and the number of farmers and farm families declined steadily over the years. Small towns also shrank in size.

What do we lose when a small town vanishes? What do we lose when the kids grow up and leave the farm or ranch for the city? A realist, focusing solely on harsh economic forces, might say that the young person is leaving the farm to find work and a more stable life in an urban environment. An idealist might argue that we lose a little bit of the fabric of America, a small piece of the American dream. American rural societies tend to be caring environments in which many honest and hard-working individuals live and join together to help each other and their communities to succeed (Struthers & Bokemeier, 2000; Trussell & Shaw, 2009).

Another trend is that more people are moving away from the large cities to smaller communities within commuting distance. Although it may take a village to raise a child, a villagelike atmosphere can also be created in an urban neighborhood, in an apartment building, or among relatives and friends scattered about a city. The impersonal forces of urban living can be countered by the creation of villagelike social structures in the neighborhood, in the workplace, in religious institutions, and in community settings. Villages today are also being created in cyberspace. Many people enrich their already vibrant social lives by connecting to loved ones, friends, and colleagues globally via the internet. One's neighborhood may reach out through several continents.

Financial Problems and the Global Economy

Financial issues are the most common stressors couples and families face, regardless of how much money they make. Researchers have consistently found that economic distress and unemployment are detrimental to family relationships. More than one in five children in this country live in poverty (22%), and more than one in three poor people are children (36%) (National Poverty Center, 2016).

Food security in American households and communities is defined as access by all people at all times to enough food for an active, healthy life. The latest data indicate that 86% of U.S. households were food secure throughout 2014, while 14% were food insecure at least some time during that year (United States Department of Agriculture, Economic Research Service, 2015).

The National Coalition for the Homeless argues that it is very difficult to estimate how many people are without a home in the United States, but the best approximation comes from a study conducted by the Urban Institute, which found that 3.5 million people are likely to experience homelessness in a given year, and 1.35 million of these people are children. The most recent statistics available indicate that children under age 18 account for 39% of the homeless population; and that 42% of homeless children were under the age of 5. It is argued that two trends are largely responsible for the rise in homelessness in the past 20 to 25 years: a growing shortage in affordable rental housing and, at the same time, an increase in poverty (National Coalition for the Homeless, 2009, July).

Many Americans today are doing well financially, and yet many other Americans live close to the edge, lacking savings and chronically spending more than they earn. Easy credit lines have contributed to mounting debt and difficulty. Credit card debt, which carries extraordinarily high interest rates, plagues many Americans, and many are in over their heads from housing payments spurred, again, by easy credit. As we have seen, debt threatens not only individuals and families but also the well-being of the lenders and, eventually, the economy as a whole (Nasdaq, 2016).

Although economic survival is challenging for many people in the United States, residents of many countries around the world are in far worse straits. Nonetheless, their economic problems do not exist in isolation; as business commentators and politicians frequently point out, we are living in a global economy. The strength of the American economy is inextricably linked in complex ways to the economies of many other nations.

Thus the employment situation in Asia, Europe, or Latin America influences marriage and family relationships not only in those corners of the world but in this country as well. For example, if American farmers can't find markets for their produce in the United States or elsewhere, they aren't going to be able to buy American cars, Japanese televisions, or shirts crafted in Malaysia. Likewise, if the Japanese or Malaysians can't find markets for their products at home or abroad, income and employment will drop in those countries, and Malaysians won't be going to college in California and Japanese won't be vacationing in Hawaii.

Although individuals cannot directly influence the economic changes in the United States or internationally, they can control their own spending. The most positive approach is that people should have a saving and investment plan, which is only possible if a person stays out of debt by not getting hooked on credit card spending and other overspending.

Family and the Environment

Treat the Earth well . . .
It was not given to you by your parents . . .
It was lent you by your children.

— KENYAN PROVERB

The U.S. population is more than 323 million, while the world population is 7.3 billion. Both are growing relentlessly. By 2050 the United States is projected to grow to 438 million, while the world population is projected to grow to 9.7 billion (Pew Research Center, 2008; United Nations, 2015; U.S. Census Bureau, 2016, May 7). In the words of one environmental organization, "Human overpopulation is among the most pressing environmental issues, silently aggravating the forces behind global warming, environmental pollution, habitat loss, the sixth mass extinction, intensive farming practices and the consumption of finite natural resources, such as fresh water, arable land and fossil fuels" (Everythingconnects.org, 2013).

Five mass extinctions of life on earth can be distinguished from the fossil record (*Encyclopedia Britannica*, 2015). Ranked in descending order of severity, they are:

1. ***Permian extinction*** (about 266–252 million years ago), the most dramatic die-off, eliminating about half of all biological families, some 95% of marine species (nearly wiping out brachiopods and corals), and about 70% of land species (including plants, insects, and vertebrates).
2. ***Ordovician-Silurian extinction*** (about 444 million years ago), which included about 25% of marine families and 85% of marine species, with brachiopods, conodonts, bryozoans, and trilobites suffering greatly.
3. ***Cretaceous-Tertiary (K-T), or Cretaceous-Paleogene (K-Pg), extinction*** (about 66 million years ago), involving about 80% of all animal species, including the dinosaurs and many species of plants. Although many scientists contend that this event was caused by one or more large comets or asteroids striking the earth, others maintain that it was caused by climatic changes associated with the substantial volcanic activity of the time.
4. ***End-Triassic extinction*** (about 201 million years ago), possibly caused by rapid climate change or by an asteroid striking the earth. This mass extinction event caused about 20% of marine families and some 76% of all extant species to die out, possibly within a span of about 10,000 years, thus opening up numerous ecological niches into which the dinosaurs evolved.
5. ***Devonian extinctions*** (about 407–359 million years ago), which included 15% to 20% of marine families and 70% to 80% of all animal species. Roughly 86% of marine brachiopod species perished, along with many corals, conodonts, and trilobites.

In her book, *The Sixth Extinction: An Unnatural History*, Elizabeth Kolbert (2014) demonstrates that the earth is in the midst of a modern, human-made sixth extinction. Kolbert chronicles the five previous mass extinction events triggered by natural causes, and compares them to the accelerated, widespread extinctions during our present time. Kolbert received the Pulitzer Prize for her book.

The picture scientists paint today is one in which human imagination and determination to change is in a race with our other natural human tendency to greedily exploit and destroy our environment. Will we be on the list of species that die out in this sixth extinction? And, what does the earth's environment have to do with marriage and family relationships? Quite a bit, actually. As we have seen, the family is in the center of all these global changes, because "All the problems in the world either begin in the family or end up in the family" (Olson, Olson-Sigg, & Larson, 2008).

While the worldwide political struggle continues over the degradation of the earth and how governments can respond to mitigate the effects of human overpopulation, families will end up dealing with many of the problems governments do not have the will or the creative judgment to fix. But what can families do to share in the responsibility for treating the earth well, as the Kenyan proverb admonishes us to do?

Beginning with our children and grandchildren, we can teach them how to walk lightly on the earth. We can model this environmentally sensitive worldview through our own behavior. The list of things we can do all by ourselves to preserve the earth is a long one. The internet is alive with ideas. Here are a few we think make good sense (Metro.co.uk, 2015):

1. Throw less stuff away. Put recyclables in recycling; compost leftover food; reduce the amount you send to the landfill.
2. Turn things off when you're not using them.

3. Only boil the water you need.
4. Get a bike.
5. Buy second hand. Better yet, don't be so preoccupied with buying stuff at all. Think of the cost to the earth when you buy things.
6. Reuse plastic bags. Avoid accepting them at stores.
7. Don't leave chargers plugged in.
8. Think carefully about the various chemicals you wish to use. What are the long-term environmental consequences?
9. Reuse plastic bottles. Better yet, drink tap water. Find out if your tap water is clean, and if it is, use it rather than contributing to the heaps of plastic bottles flooding our world.
10. Eat less meat. The Union of Concerned Scientists argues that the second biggest environmental hazard facing the planet after fossil-fuel vehicles is meat-eating, and PETA argues that one hamburger uses enough fossil fuel to drive a small car 20 miles.

Every family is responsible for helping to make our world a better place, so it is important for all of us to be involved in the global conversation. Talk with loved ones and friends and make your own personal list. We can all be part of the solution, rather than part of the problem.

Changing the Social Environment

Recently, there have been a number of initiatives with the goal of improving the social environment in order to improve the lives of individuals and families in communities. An example of one of these initiatives is the Search Institute in Minneapolis, Minnesota, a nationally known organization that conducts research and creates programming around assets that promote healthy growth and development of young people (Search Institute, 2013). Twenty of the 40 assets that have been known to help youth have to do with positive experiences that young people receive from interactions in their communities. Several communities have enhanced community assets, such as schools, neighborhoods, and youth organizations, with the goal of ultimately improving the lives of young people.

William Doherty, a family scholar at the University of Minnesota, has developed the Families and Democracy Model, which provides strategies to engage citizens to make changes in their communities (Doherty, 2016). The model provides direction to family professionals and community citizens to come together to solve problems that affect individuals and families. After hearing from a family professional about the loss of family time in today's busy society, community members in one neighborhood decided to do something to change this societal trend. Using the Families and Democracy Model, the community developed and implemented the Putting Family First initiative, which encourages families and community institutions to make family time a high priority. One of the outcomes of this initiative was the cancelation one night a week of all community activities so that families could spend time together.

Many communities have schools, organizations, and religious institutions that provide positive experiences for the individuals and families who live in those communities. Even when those institutions are not present, community initiatives can create a social environment that will benefit the community's residents.

Positive Responses to the Social Environment

Because the social environment in which we live poses many problems for couples and families, it is important that couples and families be more proactive, beginning with their own relationships. There is growing evidence that people are happier, healthier, and wealthier if they are in a marriage (Waite & Gallagher, 2000). And a strong marriage brings even more positive benefits for the individuals, the couple, and their family.

Fortunately, there are countless ways to provide for oneself and one's close relationships and at the same time help make the world a better place. There are types of work and lifestyles that provide not only financial security but also emotional satisfaction and the comfort of knowing that one's life actually makes a difference. The following account illustrates the reciprocal value of giving to others. This is what Raedene, 20, an undergraduate student and volunteer in a Big Brothers Big Sisters program, had to report:

> *I felt it was my job as a college student as well as a citizen to give something that I had always received, a little love and attention. I signed up for training in the program and was contacted by one of the organizers. After attending many long hours of training, I wondered if I had gotten myself into something more than I had bargained for. They required me to spend at least 5 hours a week with my match. I didn't think that I possibly had time but decided to give it a shot.*
>
> *About 5 days after training, I received a phone call that I was going to be matched with a little 5-year-old girl. I met my supervisor at the home of Elizabeth, my new little friend. A little nervous, I walked into their home. It was really strange. The minute I sat down, Elizabeth jumped up on my lap like she had known me for years. "Could you read this book to me? ... Watch this! ... Come into my room!" She just couldn't stop talking.*
>
> *I did know from that minute on that this young child needed my love and attention more than 5 hours a week. I felt a sense of warmth come over me. To think that I was second-guessing 5 hours a week to give to a child who needed me. We played for a couple of hours until her mom felt comfortable with the match. I told Elizabeth that I would phone her Monday. Her response was, "Don't forget." When I left all I could do was smile. I knew I was in for some fun.*
>
> *Over the semester I have seen much growth in her, socially and intellectually. She's in kindergarten and is always telling me how much she likes it, and I always try to reinforce how much fun school is. I understand what she talks about, and I listen to what she has to say. I feel she has gained so much trust in me over the past 4 months.*
>
> *I am able to communicate openly with her mother. I offer suggestions to her on many topics. I am very honest with her mother, and her mother trusts me a lot, too. I have learned how difficult a time their family has dealing with finances, stepparents, and stepsiblings. I have seen much growth in their family over the past 4 months. I am very happy that I chose to volunteer my time. I wish everyone would volunteer because not only does the child benefit from the experience, but you do, too.*

The late Betty Friedan (1921–2006), a pioneer in the latest wave of the feminist movement, said, "People's priorities—men's and women's alike—should be affirming life, enhancing life, not greed." She argued for a basic restructuring of our economy and society, putting the lives and interests of people first. The restructuring cannot be accomplished in terms of women versus men, Blacks versus Whites, old versus young, conservative versus liberal. "It can't be done by separate, single-issue movements now, and it has to be political to protect and translate our new empowerment with a new vision of community, with new structures of community that open the doors again to real equality and opportunity" (Friedan, 1997; National Women's Hall of Fame, 2013).

Summary

- The family today is not in danger of extinction, but it is changing. The American family is more diverse today, in terms of family structure and ethnicity, than ever before.
- Somewhat under half the people marrying today will probably divorce at some time in their lives, often because they enter marriage with unrealistic expectations, marry the wrong person, marry for the wrong reasons, or have few skills to deal with the many challenges of marriage.
- Marriage is the emotional and legal commitment of two people to share emotional and physical intimacy, various tasks, economic resources, and values. A family is two or more people who are committed to each other and who share intimacy, resources, decision-making responsibilities, and values.
- Some of the major trends in family structure, marriage, divorce, and remarriage are the following: There are both more families headed by single women and more stepfamilies today than there were in the 1950s and 1960s; families are smaller today; women are more likely to work outside the home after marriage; both men and women are marrying at a later age; cohabitation before marriage has increased dramatically; the divorce rate increased but has now stabilized at somewhat under 50%; and about 75% of those who divorce later remarry.
- Though not all families are strong, all families have strengths, and strengths develop over time. Strengths help families cope with stress and problems and help families better manage change.
- Marriage has many advantages for individuals, including a longer life, better health and healthier lifestyle, more money and wealth, a better sexual relationship, less domestic abuse for women, and more successful children.
- Human beings do not live and love in a vacuum. Besides being connected to special people in our lives, we are inextricably embedded in our social environment. As individuals, couples, and families, we have little influence on society as a whole, but society has a great deal of influence on our personal attitudes and behaviors.
- There are many elements in our social environment that pose difficult challenges for couples and families. These include stress, change, and materialism; lack of time for oneself and significant others; the increasing use of child care outside the family; instability of couple and family relationships; violence; the use of alcohol, tobacco, and other drugs; the internet's effects on human relationships; changing gender roles and the balance of power in intergender relationships; urban migration and overcrowding; financial problems and the effects of the global economy and the environment on families.
- Community initiatives led by community members and family professionals have made some communities more supportive of youth development and building strong family relationships. These initiatives can be models for other communities.
- Surveys over the years indicate that the majority of Americans think their marriages and families are doing pretty well and that their lives are generally satisfying.

Key Terms

marriage
family
social environment
stress
gender roles

Activities

1. In small groups, write down your own definition of the family. Share your responses within the group and compare how your ideas are similar and/or different.
2. What is your definition of marriage? After writing your definition, compare it with the definition used in this book.
3. Interview a grandparent, great-grandparent, or another older person you would like to get to know better. Talk about family life in *the old days*—both positive and negative aspects. Some interesting areas to explore might be (1) growing up in a family, (2) *a woman's place* in the world 50 or more years ago, (3) gender roles, (4) the Great Depression of the 1930s, (5) World War II (1939–1945), (6) major family crises, (7) religion and/or spirituality, and (8) philosophies of child rearing.
4. What are the major stressors in your social environment? Make a list and discuss it with others. How did you deal effectively with these stressors?

Suggested Readings

Al-Anon Family Groups. (2016). Since 1951, "Al-Anon (which includes Alateen for younger members) has been offering strength and hope for friends and families of problem drinkers. It is estimated that each alcoholic affects the lives of at least four other people . . . alcoholism is truly a family disease. No matter what relationship you have with an alcoholic, whether they are still drinking or not, all who have been affected by someone else's drinking can find solutions that lead to serenity in the Al-Anon/Alateen fellowship." Web site: http://www.al-anon.alateen.-org/english.html.

Alcoholics Anonymous. (2016). In their own words, AA is "a fellowship of men and women who share their experience, strength and hope with each other that they may solve their common problem and help others to recover from alcoholism. The only requirement for membership is a desire to stop drinking." AA charges no dues or fees for membership and is self-supporting through member contributions. It is not allied with any sect, denomination, politics, organization, or institution. AA does not wish to engage in any controversy, and neither endorses nor opposes any causes. "Our primary purpose is to stay sober and help other alcoholics to achieve sobriety." Web site: http://www.aa.org/lang/en/subpage.cfm/page=1.

Asay, S. M., DeFrain, J., Metzger, M., & Moyer, B. (2014). *Family violence from a global perspective: A strengths-based approach*. Thousand Oaks, CA: Sage.

Bryant, J., & Bryant, J. A. (2001). *Television and the American family* (2nd ed.). Mahwah, NJ: Erlbaum.

Cherlin, A. (2009). *The marriage-go-round: The state of marriage and family in America today.* Clashing values have caused more partnering and repartnering in the United States than elsewhere in the world, Cherlin argues. The reason, in part, is that Americans value both marriage and individualism.

Cherlin, A. (2014). *Love's labor lost: The rise and fall of the working-class family in America.* New York: Russell Sage Foundation.

Dalla, R., DeFrain, J., Johnson, J., & Abbott, D. A. (2009). *Strengths and challenges of new immigrant families: Implications for research, education, policy, and service.* Lanham, MD: Lexington Books/Rowman & Littlefield. Explores the lives of East Indian, Sudanese, Somali, African, Asian Indian, Korean, Irish, Egyptian, Israeli, Chinese, Mexican, and other immigrants to the United States. "A wonderful introduction for those wanting to study or work with immigrant families."

Deal, R. L., & Olson, D. H. (2010). *The remarriage checkup: Tools to help your marriage last a lifetime.* Minneapolis, MN: Bethany House. Ways in which remarried couples can build on their strengths and overcome relationship problems.

DeFrain, J., & Asay, S. M. (Eds.). (2007). *Strong families around the world: Strengths-based research and perspectives.* London and New York: Haworth Press/Taylor & Francis.

Esteinou, R. (2009). *Construyendo relaciones y fortalezas familiars: Un panorama internacional.* Mexico, D.F.: Centro de Investigaciones y Estudios Superiores en Anthropologia Social. This book, published in Spanish in Mexico City, is the first book in Latin America to focus on family strengths. The book is the result of the Mexican Family Strengths Conference held in Cuernavaca, and includes articles from Mexico, Australia, Botswana, China, Italy, Korea, and the United States.

Freedom to Marry. (2016). Winning the freedom to marry nationwide. Web site: http://www.freedomtomarry.org/.

Kartemquin Films. (2008). *The new Americans.* Web site: kartemquin.com. Follows 4 years in the lives of a diverse group of contemporary immigrants and refugees as they start new lives in America. An Indian couple is viewed through the dot-com boom and bust in Silicon Valley. A Mexican meatpacker struggles to reunite his family in rural Kansas. Two families of Nigerian refugees escape government persecution. Two Los Angeles Dodgers prospects follow their big dreams of escaping the barrios of the Dominican Republic. And a Palestinian woman marries into a new life in Chicago, only to discover that in the wake of 9/11 she cannot leave behind the pain of the conflict in her homeland.

National Marriage Project. (2016). Mission. Web site: http://nationalmarriageproject.org/about/. The National Marriage Project (NMP) is a nonpartisan, nonsectarian, and interdisciplinary initiative located at the University of Virginia. The project's mission is to provide research and analysis on the health of marriage in America, to analyze the social and cultural forces shaping contemporary marriage, and to identify strategies to increase marital quality and stability. NMP publishes *The State of Our Unions,* which monitors the current health of marriage and family life in the United States.

National Stepfamilies Resource Center. (2016). Web site: http://stepfamilies.info.

Northern Territory Government. (2008). *Strong families: Sharing cultural parenting knowledge.* Darwin, N.T., Australia: Department of Health and Community Services. Focuses on four strong families in Australia: the Ahmed family from Somalia; the Albert family from Thailand and Australia; the Gray family from Papua New Guinea; and the Casimiro-Branco family from East Timor. The families share their personal stories, their family traditions, and how they have dealt successfully with the challenges of life they face in Australia today.

Olson, D. H., Olson-Sigg, A., & Larson, P. J. (2008). *The couple checkup.* Nashville, TN: Thomas Nelson. Based on a survey of 50,000 couples, the book is an effort to help couples find the strengths in their relationship and build on these strengths.

Straus, M., Gelles, R., & Steinmetz, S. (2006). *Behind closed doors: Violence in the American family.* New Brunswick, NJ: Translation Publishers.

U.S. Census Bureau. (2016, May 7). U.S. and world population clock. Web site: http://www.census.gov/popclock/. Visit this web site and watch the human population on the clock grow relentlessly.

Visit the text-specific Online Learning Center at **www.mhhe.com/olson9e** for practice tests, chapter summaries, and PowerPoint slides.

Design Element: © Alicia Grünkind/EyeEm/Getty Images

2 Cultural Diversity and Diversity in Family Structure: Family Strengths and Challenges

©Sean Gallup/Staff/Getty Images

Diversity and Strengths in Family Structure and Cultural Context

Why Culture Matters

Intimacy and Diversity

The Concepts of Race, Culture, and Ethnicity

U.S. Demographics and Future Trends

Gay and Lesbian Couples and Families

Challenge to Researchers and Practitioners

Cultural Competence

Kin Relationships Across Cultures

Family System and Sociocultural Characteristics

Family Strengths and Challenges Across Ethnic Groups

Cross-Cultural Family Studies

Challenges for Ethnic Families

Summary

Key Terms

Activities

Suggested Readings

The world in which you were born is just one model of reality. Other cultures are not failed attempts at being you: they are unique manifestations of the human spirit.

—WADE DAVIS

Diversity and Strengths in Family Structure and Cultural Context

Our goal in this chapter is to point out some of the major strengths of various **ethnic groups** in the United States. Although most of the information in this chapter is about ethnic diversity, we are also including information about an increasingly common diverse family structure, gay and lesbian couples and families. One of the reasons our country has prospered is that the various ethnic groups have different strengths. The strengths of each of these groups can be seen at the individual level, family level, and cultural level. Some ethnic groups place a high value on the importance of kin networks and are very group oriented; other cultures emphasize more individual achievement. Some ethnic groups value both individual achievement and group connection relatively equally.

Diversity and strengths are also interconnected. There are strengths in diversity, and diversity helps build further strengths. The different abilities, interests, attitudes, and values of each diverse group provide a broad range of options and ideas that can improve the ability to solve problems and create new ideas. These diverse strengths can help people at all levels of society from the personal level, to school, and at work.

When we see people from different ethnic groups, we typically do not focus on their strengths. When we see gay and lesbian couples and families, we typically do not focus on their strengths. The more common reaction is to notice how they are different from us. The next reaction can be that the difference is seen as interesting or it could be perceived as a potential problem. But after getting to know someone who is different from yourself, you will be able to see that some of the differences can be both personal strengths and things you value about your relationship with them.

So one way to increase our appreciation of diversity is to seek out opportunities to talk with people who have ethnic backgrounds different from our own. Sharing feelings about oneself with someone who is different can be a mutually rewarding experience, an opportunity to learn more about others and their uniqueness.

Why Culture Matters

Families are families, right? Does it really matter that families have cultural histories? Yes, it does. For example, strong marriages look different in Navajo (Skogrand et al., 2008), Latino (Skogrand, Hatch, & Singh, 2009), and African American (Skogrand & Chaney, 2010) cultures. The findings of a study of Latino couples who had strong marriages indicated that in order to have strong marriages, couples needed to have children (Skogrand et al., 2008). The African American couples indicated that prayer, God, and church were highly important to have a strong marriage (Skogrand & Chaney, 2010). Everything that happens in families happens within a cultural context. Family members learn, and pass on to their children, the definition of family, how intimacy is expressed, what it means to be male and female, and role expectations (Waldegrave, 2009).

Most often programs and policies focus on the values evident in mainstream society (Waldegrave, 2009). In the United States that is primarily white, middle-class individuals. White, middle-class individuals and families typically focus on individualism and self-determination, whereas, many members of diverse cultures think more collectively in that they value the group over oneself, and the group may be family or the community (Waldegrave, 2009). The result is that programs do not fit the values and needs of diverse populations. An example is that in the field of family finance, it is expected that you save money, plan for retirement, and take care of yourself. However, based upon one study of strong African American couples, it was sometimes more important to help others, such as family and friends, than have financial security for oneself (Anderson, 2010). Most financial education programs would not provide information that would be consistent with these collectivist values. The result is the African Americans know they are not going to get their needs met in programming, so they do not attend. Or if they do attend, they do not see the relevancy of the information to their lives. This lack of fit is also evident in family policy, therapy, and counseling.

To be effective and relevant in the lives of individuals and families from diverse cultures, we need to understand their values and experiences. This chapter provides information to begin the process of understanding members of diverse populations. It will become clear, however, that understanding cultural differences is a long process.

Intimacy and Diversity

While some people have relatively stable family lives evidenced by two-parent families, some do not. Poverty, prejudice, education level, and life experiences affect the ability to maintain intimate family relationships such as extended-family relationships, parent–child relationships, and couple relationships (Bent-Goodley, 2005; Perreira, Chapman, & Stein, 2006; Sarkisian, Gerena, & Gerstel, 2006).

Some people had historical experiences that have long-term effects on their ability to maintain intimate family lives today. For example, American Indians in the United States historically had land, language, and culture taken from them (Chilisa, 2012). In the mid-1900s, children were taken from their homes and put in boarding schools where they were to become "civilized" and adopt the ways of White Americans. These experiences created a legacy of trauma, which contributed to multiple psychiatric disorders such as alcoholism and violence (Chilisa, 2012). These issues affect intimacy in American Indian families.

How members of **cultural groups** entered the United States, when they entered the country, and how they were received may also impact their ability to develop intimacy among family members. Did they come as refugees with nothing but the clothes on their backs? If so, these refugees will need to focus on survival with little time or energy to develop intimate relationships. The following example is a real event that could impact close and intimate family relationships:

> Recently, there was a raid by immigration officials at a food processing plant in a small community that employed a large number of Latino immigrants. A significant number of Latino breadwinners were arrested for prosecution and deportation. Members of the Latino community were afraid to leave their homes, go to work, and send their children to school, and many had limited or no financial resources. In some cases both parents were arrested, and children were being cared for by friends or relatives.
>
> Financial, social, and emotional stress prevailed for these families. Survival and safety were foremost in the minds of these family members, which negatively impacted their intimate family relationships.

The Concepts of Race, Culture, and Ethnicity

Race refers to the common physical characteristics of a group and generally describes skin color and the texture of hair (Murry, Smith, & Hill, 2001). The concept of race originally arose as a way to explain the diversity of the human population worldwide but can be problematic, since it does not describe what happens to people regarding socialization and environment (Murry et al., 2001). These authors indicate that ethnicity, on the other hand, refers to nationality or ancestry. Further, culture is usually used to describe how people make sense of their environment and their experiences. It describes their values, beliefs, and practices. Toni Morrison, the Nobel Prize–winning author of such novels as *Song of*

BOX 2.1 Diversity in Families

Race Has No Place

The following are segments selected from a play called *VOICES*, created by Twin Cities Youth (in collaboration with Stacey Parshall) from Minneapolis and St. Paul for an exhibition on the concept of "race" at the Minnesota Science Museum in 2007. "The words you hear, the stories, the definitions, the statements and wishes, are those of some of your teenage youth across the Twin Cities. A sacred space was created for them to write these words. They were told their voices are absolutely necessary for all of us to move forward, beyond the pain and confusion that the subject of race conjures up. . . .

Will you tell me about race. R. A. C. E. What does that mean to you? What does that stand for?

Respect All Colors Everywhere
Respect All Cultures Equally
Radical Awesome Cultures Everywhere
Rare Assortment of Color and Ethnicity
Rights And Confusion Expressed
Race Always Changes Everything
Rage Amongst Conflicting Ethnic groups
Revolutionize All Concepts that Enslave
Real Answers Can (help shape) Equality
Race Absolutely Costs Everybody

Race is just another word.
Race is just a title.
Race is not necessary.

Black, White, yellow, tan and they're just colors.
Color is what you get when White light is broken up.

Color defines merely what is on the outside.
Skin color? In my mind means nothing.
There is a saying, "it's only skin deep."
I always try to look deeper.

People are different races and come from different places, but we all have faces. Treat all with respect, no matter their races, even in tough cases. We are one human race."

Source: Adapted from *VOICES*, a publication of the Science Museum of Minnesota, St. Paul, Minnesota, 2007. Adapted with permission.

Solomon, Beloved, and *Tar Baby,* puts it this way: "Race is the least reliable information you can have about someone. It's real information but it tells you next to nothing" (cited in Gray, 1998, p. 67). This view is still generally held by social scientists today. With the recent influx of Latinos into the United States, many people talk about cultural groups or use the term *ethnicity* because Latinos are not a race (Murry et al., 2001). Selections from a creative play about the problems with the concept of race are provided in Box 2.1.

Therefore, we will try to avoid using the term *race* in this book; rather, we will use the terms *culture* (or *cultural group*). Culture is thought of as the social context in which we live

Ethnic or cultural differences are not always evident. A mother may look like her child but may have adopted this child from a country where everything is different from the United States, including language, religious beliefs and traditions, and cultural values.
©Tetra Images/Getty Images

40 Part I The Social Context of Intimate Relationships

(McGoldrick & Ashton, 2012). These authors further describe culture as how we raise our children, what we eat, how we celebrate, and how we die. These ways of doing things are learned from those around us. Ethnicity refers to peoples' common ancestry, when values, beliefs, and customs have been passed down from previous generations (McGoldrick & Ashton, 2012). Because of the great diversity within groups, however, even calling them *ethnic* or *cultural* groups can be misleading. Jews, for example, are often classified as an ethnic group, but doing so stretches the imagination considerably, for a number of reasons: (1) Jews hold a wide variety of religious views, from very conservative to very liberal—some are Orthodox believers, and others are atheists; (2) Jews speak a variety of languages, and many Jews today cannot speak Hebrew, the language of tradition; (3) Jews are of many nationalities as a result of Judaism's expanding influence worldwide over the centuries; and (4) Jews exhibit a variety of physical characteristics, ranging from dark-skinned, black-haired African Jews to light-skinned, blue-eyed, blond European Jews. From a cultural viewpoint, a nomadic Jewish shepherd in Ethiopia has much more in common with other Africans than he does with a Jewish dentist in suburban Chicago.

Perhaps the key issue in determining membership in an ethnic or cultural group is whether the individual *believes* he or she is a member of that group and has a **cultural identity.** Clearly, human beings are diverse. Classifications cannot be based solely on religious views, language, ancestry, or physical characteristics.

U.S. Demographics and Future Trends

The United States is more ethnically diverse than ever before, with the Hispanic population making up the largest ethnic group, followed by African American, Asian American, and American Indian. The 2015 estimates by the U.S. Census (U.S. Census Bureau Quick Facts, n.d.) provided new information on the estimated population distribution in the United States. The estimates are as follows: White 77%, Hispanic or Latino 18%, African American or Black 13%, Asian 6%, and American Indian or Alaska Native 1% (U.S. Census Bureau Quick Facts, n.d.).

There are differences in minority population changes by regions in the United States (Humes et al., 2011). The fastest rate of increase of minority populations was in the West, with the next largest increase in the South. As of 2010, California has the largest *total minority* population of any state, followed by Texas and New York. States with the *largest percentage* of minority populations, which are all over 50% minority, are Hawaii (77%), California and New Mexico (60%), and Texas (55%). These states have what is called a "majority-minority" population (Humes et al., 2011). Our nation's capital, Washington, D.C., also has this majority-minority status with a 65% minority population.

See Figure 2.1 for some demographic characteristics of families from various ethnic groups.

The Hispanic Population

The Hispanic population, also referred to as "Latino," includes people from Spanish-speaking cultures. In 2005, the Hispanic population became the largest ethnic group, surpassing the African American population for the first time in U.S. history and this trend is continuing (U.S. Census Bureau, n.d.). The growth in the Hispanic population is primarily due to new births and immigration. It should be noted, however, that this growth has slowed in recent years, reaching a record low in 2014. There has been a decrease in births and a decrease in both legal and illegal immigration (Gomez, 2016, September 9–11).

The largest number of Hispanics in the United States immigrated from Mexico (64%) (Stepler & Brown, 2016, April 19), with the remainder coming from other Central American, South American, or other Hispanic countries (Ennis, Rios-Vargas, & Albert,

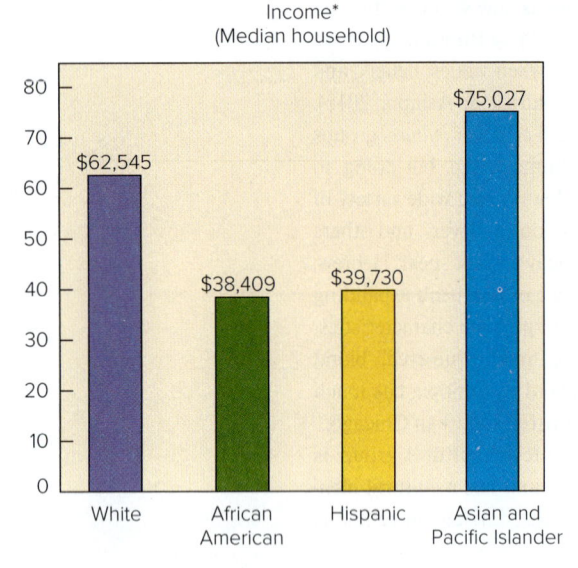

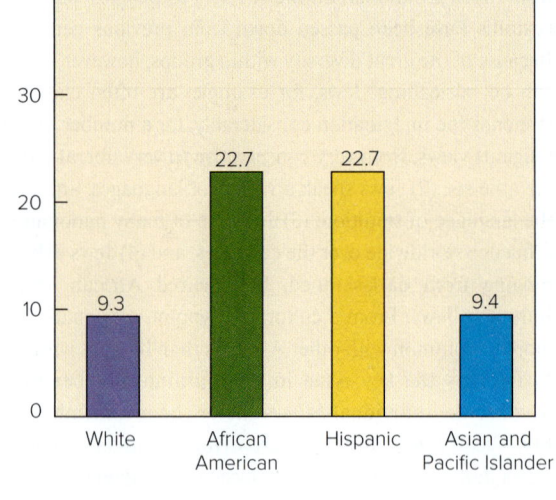

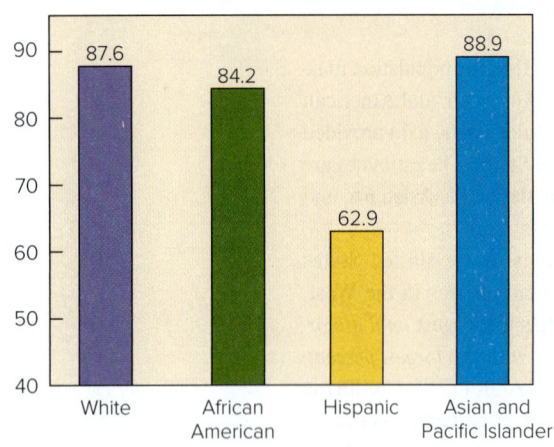

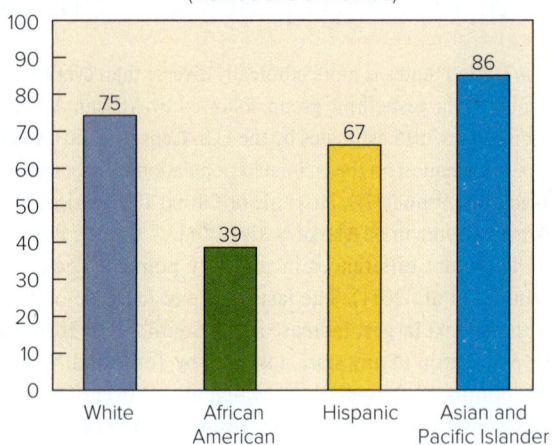

FIGURE 2.1

Characteristics of Families from Various Ethnic Groups

*U.S. Census Bureau, *The 2012 Statistical Abstract,* Tables 696, 715, 229, 69.

2011). The Hispanic population in this country is very young, with a median age of 28 years in 2014 (Stepler & Brown, 2016, April 19). Approximately 35% of the Hispanic population was foreign born in 2014 and the median household income was $42,200.

The African American Population

The African American population is the second-largest minority population in the United States with the 2015 estimate at 13% of the population (U.S. Census Bureau Quick Facts, n.d.). African Americans, or Blacks, refer to people having origins in any of the Black race groups of Africa. Although many African Americans came to the United States as slaves years ago, 9% are immigrants (Anderson, 2015, April 9). These new immigrants are very diverse and very different culturally from African Americans who have lived in the United

States for several generations. These refugees and immigrants have come from the Caribbean and from African countries such as Nigeria, Ghana, and Ethiopia and have very little in common with their native-born counterparts. Because of this increasing diversity in the Black population, we need to be more aware of the diversity of cultural values and beliefs in what we once thought of as a relatively homogeneous cultural group.

In 2013 the median age for African Americans was 37 years (Anderson, 2015, April 9). Blacks have a household income which is substantially lower than the national average (Noel, 2014, November).

The Asian American Population

Asian Americans refer to people having origins in the Far East, Southeast Asia, or the Indian subcontinent. The Asian American populations differ greatly in their culture, language, and length of residency in the United States. More recent immigrants and refugees include Hmong, Vietnamese, Laotians, and Cambodians, while people coming from China and Japan typically have been in the United States for several generations. In 2012 Asians became the nation's fastest growing ethnic group (U.S. Census Bureau, 2013, June 13).

The median age of Asian Americans is 36 years. Asian Americans have the highest income level of all the minority groups and higher than that of Whites. It is important to note, however, that there is a wide disparity in education and affluence among different groups who identify themselves as Asian American. For example, the Hmong are, on average, very poor with limited education, whereas Asian Indians are, on average, highly educated and affluent (Pew Research Center, 2013, April 4).

The American Indian and Alaska Native Populations

There are over 560 tribes that make up the American Indian and Alaska Native (AI/AN) population in the United States (Sue & Sue, 2016; U.S. Department of the Interior, 2014, January 16), with a wide range of tribal cultures. The largest tribe by population is the Navajo tribe in Arizona, New Mexico, and Utah (Norris, Vines, & Hoeffel, 2012, January).

One of the unique characteristics of the AI/AN population is that their communities are sovereign political entities with tribes having their own form of governance, culture, and history. Many AI/AN people live on tribal land or reservations, however most live off away from tribal lands in rural and urban communities throughout the country (Sue & Sue, 2016). The median age for American Indians and Alaska Natives is lower than other U.S. minority groups.

Immigration and Family Life

According to Grieco et al. (2012, May), immigration has continued to be at record highs in recent years. In 2010 those who were **foreign born,** or whose birth place is somewhere other than the United States, made up 13% of the U.S. population (Grieco et al., 2012, May). The ethnic composition of **immigrants,** or those who came to this country for a better life, is primarily Latino and Asian, with Mexicans making up the majority of Latinos coming into the United States (Camarota & Zeigler, 2014, September). Historically, men made up the majority of immigrants, but more recent data indicate that immigrants are about equally male and female. The increasing numbers of women who have come to the United States have left their own children behind in their country of origin to care for children and clean houses of the more wealthy in this country. These women are leaving their children behind in the care of extended family members and send money to their families back home (Cherlin, 2010).

Many immigrants come to the United States without documentation or have allowed documentation to expire. There are indications that one-third of children who have

FIGURE 2.2

Increasing Diversity in America from 2014 to 2060

Source: Colby, S. L., & Ortman, J. M. (2015). "Projections of the Size and Composition of the U.S. Population: 2014 to 2060," *Current Population Reports,* 25-01143. Washington, DC: U.S. Census Bureau.

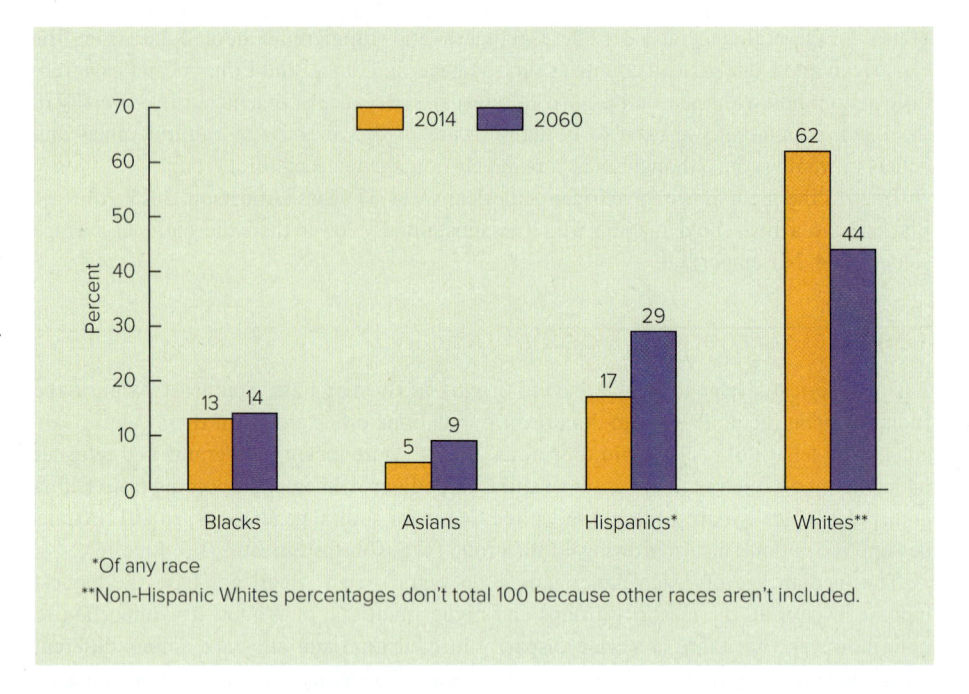

Group	2014	2060
Blacks	13	14
Asians	5	9
Hispanics*	17	29
Whites**	62	44

*Of any race
**Non-Hispanic Whites percentages don't total 100 because other races aren't included.

immigrant parents have at least one parent that is undocumented. These parents may not have access to services for themselves or their children and are very vulnerable because they risk deportation if they ask for help.

Refugees make up another group of folks who come to the United States. Refugees come to the United States because conditions in their country of origin are unsafe or they wanted to avoid persecution. They often come to this country as families and are able to access social and financial services, but often face other challenges. Refugees have often experienced trauma due to war or other kinds of oppression prior to their arrival in the United States. Many come having spent years in refugee camps that provided for their physical safety, but that in no way provided for optimal family life.

These families come to the United States with enormous issues and challenges as they begin their lives anew. They need to learn about the American culture, find ways to make a living, and help their children enter a world that is foreign to them. In addition to challenges for their families, there are also challenges for the communities where they reside. Social services are not always prepared to meet the extreme variety of needs presented by these new neighbors (Martinez-Brawley & Zorita, 2011).

What the Future Will Bring

Estimates have been made about what the White and ethnic populations might look like in the year 2060 (Figure 2.2). The minority populations will grow faster than the White population. The nation's Hispanic and Asian populations are predicted to double by 2060 and non-Hispanic Whites will decrease to less than half of the population (Colby & Ortman, 2015, March).

If the trend of multiracial marriages and relationships continues to increase as they have in recent history, there will be increasing numbers of multiracial children in the country. This combined with the increase in minority groups means it is possible that by the year 2050 cultural groups may cease to be an issue that will be written about in marriage and family textbooks.

Gay and Lesbian Couples and Families

Although most of this chapter is about ethnic diversity and families, we also want to include information about a family form that is increasing in this country—gay and lesbian couples and families. There has been increased contention about whether or not gay and lesbian people have a right to legally marry and raise children. People's views about these issues often have roots in religious beliefs. Religious groups are not all opposed to gay and lesbian marriages and families. Some religious groups have struggled internally with these issues, and splits within denominations have resulted.

In a landmark decision in June of 2015, the Supreme Court ruled to legalize same-sex marriages, which meant that individual states could not ban same-sex marriages, but rather needed to recognize these marriages. This ruling provided increased state and federal benefits for same-sex couples who choose to marry. This meant that, along with other benefits, same-sex married couples can file federal and state income taxes and can receive health insurance and retirement benefits in the same way heterosexual couples receive these benefits (Berman, 2015).

Although there are studies about same-sex couple relationships and families, most of this research is focused on samples that are European American and middle class (Goldberg, 2007). We know very little about ethnic minority same-sex couples and families. Gay and lesbian same-sex couples and families who are from ethnic minorities not only are dealing with discrimination related to their family structure, but also are dealing with issues around racism. Low-income couples and families have the added stress of financial insecurity to contend with.

Same-Sex Couple Relationships and Marriages

There is no way of knowing how many gay and lesbian people are in relationships. It is estimated, however, that 40% to 60% of gay men and 45% to 80% of lesbians are involved in romantic relationships (Kurdek, 2004). Because being public about being in a same-sex relationship can result in discrimination, it is likely these estimates are low.

Studies generally conclude that healthy gay and lesbian couple relationships are similar to healthy heterosexual couple relationships (Kurdek, 2004; Porche & Purvin, 2008). According to findings provided by Kurdek, same-sex couples functioned as well, relationshipwise, as heterosexual couples. On some relationship variables, same-sex couples functioned better than heterosexual couples. Kurdek did find, however, that gay and lesbian couples experienced less social support than heterosexual couples.

It is reasonable to assume that gay and lesbian couples could benefit from couple education in the same way heterosexual couples benefit. In fact, because of the lack of social support same-sex couples experience, these couples may need it even more. However, couple education for this population is typically not available. In a very small, nonrepresentative sample of therapists and researchers, researchers asked about existing relationship education and needed modifications (Whitton & Buzzela, 2011). Their research revealed three things. First, relationship skills used in couple education of heterosexual couples, such as communication skills, conflict resolution skills, developing and maintaining positive couple connections, and individual self-regulation, were found useful for same-sex couples. Second, the clinicians who have provided couple education for same-sex couples found they needed to modify the information presented. One example of such changes was the use of gender terms and another was the issue of commitment as symbolized through marriage. Third, clinicians found that there were unique issues experienced by same-sex couples that were not addressed in curricula developed for heterosexual couples. An example of one of these issues was how to deal with discrimination and stigma for themselves and their children. In addition, in one study of the benefits of stepfamily education developed with heterosexual couples in mind, two lesbian couples found the course very useful (Skogrand, Mendez, & Higginbotham, 2012). In fact, these two same-sex couples felt they shared many of the same issues as heterosexual couples and experienced a feeling of normalcy by attending the class. In this case no modifications were made to the course.

Because same-sex marriages are relatively new, we do not know what the effect of the Supreme Court's ruling will be. Historically, couples were not allowed to enter into a legally binding marriage relationship and, therefore, cohabited. Thus, it was difficult to make comparisons between stable gay and lesbian couples who were not married because they could not be married and heterosexual couples who were in marriage relationships (Patterson, 2009; Regnerus, 2012). We do not know what the impact of being legally married will have on these couple relationships.

Gay and Lesbian Families

The number of same-sex couples raising children has risen in the past 20 years with individuals feeling more comfortable coming out and being open about being in **gay and lesbian families**. Approximately one-fourth of gay and lesbian couples have children, and approximately 45% want to have children (Gates, 2008). The majority of the children of same-sex couples are a result of previous heterosexual relationships. Although we may think of gay and lesbian families as being primarily European American, African American and Latino men are three times more likely to be raising children in same-sex relationships than are European American men. More than half of the children being raised by same-sex couples are non-White.

Children being raised by same-sex couples have not been studied until recently. In the 1990s, researchers wanted to know if children raised by gay and lesbian couples would, in some way, be damaged by the experience of growing up in a gay family (Berkowitz, 2009). The answer was that there was no difference in developmental outcomes—there were no adverse effects (Patterson, 2009). In the 2000s, other researchers (Stacey & Biblarz, 2001; Todd, 2011) criticized the earlier work, suggesting that these researchers have been so concerned that "there was no difference" between children raised by same-sex parents and those raised by heterosexual parents that they missed differences that might be viewed as positive. One such finding by Gartrell and Bos (2010) found that adolescents raised by lesbian mothers since birth had healthy psychological adjustment. These authors concluded that, in fact, these youths were doing better than their age-matched counterparts.

Although there is no typical gay and lesbian family, Brenda and Lori provide one example of what family life might be like:

> *Lori and Brenda have lived together for 5 years. They met at work, dated for about a year, and then moved in together. Each had two children from prior heterosexual relationships, ranging in age from 7 to 15. Lori and Brenda also have a 2-year-old child together through assisted reproduction with an unknown donor.*
>
> *At one point Brenda was not allowed to have any contact with her children because her former husband obtained sole custody of the children, as a result of the claim that she was an unfit mother because she was lesbian. Later, however, she got visitation rights and now*

has the children for one month in the summer and two weekends out of each month. Lori has shared custody of her children, and they spend the majority of their time with Brenda and Lori.

Generally speaking, their family has been well received in their suburban neighborhood, schools, and the church they attend. Both Brenda and Lori teach Sunday School and attend other church events. They both attend their children's school conferences. There is one other lesbian couple in the neighborhood with whom they spend lots of time.

There have been challenges. Although Lori's extended family is supportive of their relationship, Brenda's extended family members blame Lori for Brenda's being gay. Their relationships with Brenda's extended family members are strained, and they spend little time with them. This has resulted in Brenda's children having limited time with their grandparents.

Because they are a stepfamily, their biggest challenge is parent/child relationships. It has been difficult having all the children together and disciplining effectively and treating them all fairly. Brenda and Lori feel their relationship is strong, but if things do not go well for the children, it could put stress on their couple relationship. There has been a problem with Brenda's ex-spouse who says derogatory things about her to the children. Brenda and Lori have decided to "take the high road" and not say negative things to Brenda's children about their father. They have both worked hard to put the children's needs first, and the children are generally doing well. One of the children has learning disabilities and struggles with school. This means both Brenda and Lori spend considerable time each evening helping him with schoolwork.

They try to do things together like any other family. They go on camping trips, generally around some theme. For example, one year they visited several historic homes of Laura Ingalls Wilder. Before the trip the family members read several of her books to learn about her life and her books.

One of the questions often asked is, "Don't children need both a mother and a father?" In other words, does the gender of parents matter? Biblarz and Stacey (2010) reviewed studies comparing same-sex families, opposite-sex families, and single-mother and single-father families. They found that the long-held conviction that children need both a mother and a father did not hold true. After looking at the studies that have been conducted, these researchers suggested that children who had two mothers did as well as children who had a mother and a father. There is not enough research to conclude the same is true for children who had two fathers. Single-parent families did less well. These authors concluded that two parents provide advantages over a single-parent trying to raise children. These findings, however, are looking at averages, and single-parent families also have strengths and children can do just fine in these families. These authors concluded that two parents can do well raising children and it is not dependent on gender or marital status. It appears that committed and compatible parents are most important in providing strong families. In some aspects of raising children, Biblarz and Stacey (2010) found that lesbian parents actually outperformed heterosexual couples. According to these authors, this may be due to women typically having better parenting skills than men.

The Challenges of Gay and Lesbian Couples and Families

It is obvious that same-sex relationships can be more difficult because of societal pressures. Researchers have addressed how the stigma of being in a same-sex relationship affects intimacy in the couple relationship because these relationships are not seen as equal to heterosexual relationships (Frost, 2011). When Frost interviewed

99 individuals about their gay and lesbian relationships, he found that individuals in couple relationships developed six different ways to allow intimacy and stigma to coexist in their lives:

- Many individuals in this study said stigma weighed heavily on their relationships. These individuals described stigma from society and family members as an ever-present negative force on their relationships. This weight was not only difficult to endure but contributed to couples' thoughts about ending the relationships because it was just too difficult to stay together.
- Other individuals did not describe negative stigma as ever-present but, rather, were generally able to maintain normal family relationships. They were able to have children, buy houses, and attend family events. There were times, however, when these experiences were "contaminated" by family members or individuals in society. Even though they could do typical couple things, people could dampen their happiness. For example, even though a couple had a commitment ceremony that was generally very positive, it could be dampened by parents' not attending because they did not approve.
- Another group of individuals said that stigma had, at one time, been a significant factor in their lives, but currently they did not allow it to affect their couple relationships. These individuals were most likely to live in accepting and liberal communities and neighborhoods.
- Some individuals said they almost never experienced discrimination, and then went on to describe a very difficult situation. It appears these individuals were reluctant to acknowledge that negative things happened. Therefore, it appears these couples distanced themselves from it and did not let stigma affect their couple relationships.
- Other individuals described experiencing discrimination and stigmatization in their relationships, but they did not view these experiences as negatively affecting their couple relationships. Rather, these individuals used these experiences to strengthen their couple relationships and solidify their commitment to each other. They also saw this societal discrimination as coming from the outside and did not let it affect their intimacy.
- Some individuals recognized the stereotypical heterosexual relationship models that existed. For themselves, however, they developed their own process for becoming a couple and a family even though it mirrored the heterosexual norm. These individuals redefined what was important in their relationships and created opportunities for commitment and public recognition of their relationships.
- Finally, some individuals described discrimination and intimacy but indicated no connection, either positive or negative, between the two in their couple relationships. Frost (2011) speculates that these individuals deliberately distanced themselves from the stigma and did not allow it to affect their couple relationships.

This study (Frost, 2011) makes it clear that society's stigma can positively or negatively affect intimate, same-sex couple relationships. It is important to note from this study that most couples are able to maintain a positive couple experience, even in the context of discrimination.

Gay and lesbian couples having children adds another layer of complexity to family life (Hare & Skinner, 2008). To give birth to a child in a lesbian relationship, there must be a sperm donor. This donor can be anonymous, which gives no rights to the father. However, many states do not give any rights to the lesbian partner and do not allow same-sex adoption. If the sperm donor is a person selected by the couple, the father's involvement in the child's life must be negotiated and in some cases legally defined. Because neither partner in a gay male relationship can give birth, gay men having children is even more complicated (Berkowitz & Marsiglio, 2007). One option is to employ a surrogate mother to carry and deliver the child. Again, multiple legal issues must be resolved, and same-sex adoptions may not be legal in the state in which they reside. It is clear that family policy and family law have not caught up with the increased number of gay and lesbian couples who want to have children.

Once a couple brings children into the relationship, solidifying their family identity in society becomes an issue (Suter, Daas, & Bergen, 2008). Sometimes the couple creates a common family last name, typically the hyphenated last names of both partners. They often create regular family activities (Suter et al., 2008). These regular events are recognized by others as ordinary family interactions. The events can include such things as taking regular walks as a family, attending school or church events as a family, or putting up family pictures in the workplace. Families often create their own family rituals around holidays or other celebrated events. These events help family members and members of society see their family as a cohesive group.

Challenge to Researchers and Practitioners

Most research that informs programs and services is based on White, middle-class families, and, yet, this research is typically used to provide programs and services for all ethnic groups (Skogrand et al., 2009). Most of these programs and services are not a good fit for families from other cultures, because the information is not culturally relevant. There is, therefore, a need for research to be conducted within a cultural context to inform programming for the members of diverse ethnic groups.

Research

Mohatt and Thomas (2006) indicate that we need to include members of diverse cultures in decision making about how we conduct research, analysis of findings, and interpretation of results. There are a variety of things we should be doing differently when conducting research with minority populations, which will take a shift in our thinking (Trimble & Fisher, 2006):

- We need to be respectful of the wishes of cultural groups regarding the research we do, how it should be used, and how those communities might benefit from the research findings.
- We need to collaborate with and develop partnerships with members and organizations in diverse cultures and accept the conditions imposed by the community when conducting research.
- We need to know about belief systems and show respect for these values in conducting research.
- Participants in research studies need to provide informed consent in a language and reading level that they understand.
- Interpretation of findings requires involving members of the population studied, because cultural meanings may not be understood by the researchers.

Practice

We might ask, Why is it important to address the issue of marriage and family from the perspective of one's culture? There are two responses to this question. First, if there is a cultural clash between the information and services provided and the values of a cultural group, people will usually not participate. If they do participate, they will not benefit from the information provided. Harm to members of the cultural group may result if individuals embrace programming ideas that destroy aspects of their cultural heritage (Fowers & Davidov, 2006; Skogrand et al., 2008).

Second, there is evidence that relying on one's cultural heritage, the way one's people deal with struggles, is the most effective way for people to be resilient and capable of handling difficulties (Skogrand et al., 2008). Several studies have shown that a positive **ethnic identity** has a positive influence on the lives of youth (Kiang, Gonzales-Backen, Yip, Witkow, & Fuligni, 2006; Perreira et al., 2006; Spencer, 2006). Consequently, it is important to draw on and reinforce the existing family values that are evident in minority cultural groups. In addition, there is evidence that maintaining one's cultural heritage and also learning about the dominant culture contribute to positive mental health (Chapman & Perreira, 2005; Kiang et al., 2006; Perreira et al., 2006).

Cultural Competence

With the increasing numbers of people of diverse cultures becoming part of society, it is critical that professionals develop culturally appropriate ways to provide effective family education and services. This ability has been described as **cultural competence**. Cultural competence has been defined in a variety of ways. A general definition is that one is effective in working with a variety of cultural groups. Cultural competence is often viewed as having three parts: awareness, knowledge, and skills. Fowers and Davidov (2006) discuss these three components and also emphasize the importance of having an *openness* to learning about oneself and others throughout the process.

Awareness

According to a classic article by Fowers and Davidov (2006), a person must begin with self-exploration, which leads to self-awareness. This is a process that starts with an understanding of one's own cultural heritage and belief system, which leads to the ability to recognize how one's own culture affects how one views those from other cultures. People who are African American have values and beliefs that come from a long history of racial and ethnic experiences, and a person who is African American sees others based on those cultural experiences.

People who are German or Norwegian also have cultural perspectives that affect how they view people from other cultures. Many who have a European ancestry see themselves as blending into the dominant culture in the United States and may not think of themselves as having a culture, but everyone has values and beliefs with which they grew up that affect how they view the world.

To better understand our own belief system, we might ask ourselves the following questions:

- What are my basic beliefs about family, children, and extended family?
- Do I think the individual or the collective group has the higher priority?
- How do religion and spirituality play into my belief system?
- What rituals do I carry out, and how and why have I developed these rituals?
- What foods do I eat and what kinds of clothes do I wear that make me feel like I am part of my family or community?

How we think about these questions may be influenced by a variety of things, but many of the answers might have resulted from our cultural experiences. Once we understand who we are and how our concept of self has been developed, we can think about how those views affect how we interact with those who are different from us.

Knowledge

The second component described by Fowers and Davidov (2006) is gaining the knowledge or factual information necessary to understand another person's culture. Knowledge may be general in nature and may include understanding discrimination, prejudice, and oppression and how these experiences affect a person or group of people. Specific knowledge about a cultural group might include the group's history, cultural beliefs and values, and family dynamics. The knowledge that one gains contributes to being more open to work with members of a culture because there is cross-cultural understanding. Not everyone within a cultural group is the same, but having knowledge about some cultural characteristics and features is necessary for one to become culturally competent. Once a person has knowledge about a culture as a whole, there can be additional learning about the subcultures within the larger group.

How does a person gain knowledge about a cultural group? Several strategies have been identified by Skogrand (2004) that are useful in learning about a cultural group. First, reading scholarly information that describes the history of the culture, beliefs and values, and family organization will provide much needed knowledge about a cultural group. A second strategy is to attend activities, markets, art galleries, or places of business that are frequented by members of the culture. For example, attending events such as pow-wows and Juneteenth Day celebrations would help one learn about history and spiritual practices. Visiting markets, art galleries, or places of business would provide information about food preferences, clothing worn, and other cultural beliefs. Learning about family life will also occur as we pay attention to who goes to the market, how mothers and fathers interact with their children, and the presence or absence of extended-family members. Respectfully attending these events can contribute to learning about family life, customs, and heritage.

Skills

Developing and practicing appropriate skills in effectively working with people who are culturally different from us is the third component of cultural competency (Fowers & Davidov, 2006). Being aware and having knowledge are of little use unless they are put into action.

Cultural competence skills can be demonstrated by the language used and by showing knowledge of history, beliefs and values, and cultural practices in implementing programs and providing services. Fowers and Davidov (2006) make it clear that it is not easy to teach skills in being culturally competent, but, rather, these skills are an outcome and are expressed naturally and in individual ways once one is self-aware and has knowledge about a cultural group.

Kin Relationships Across Cultures

Most of us learn about kinship early in our lives, with little or no theoretical explanations. We learn, for example, about brothers and sisters and about aunts, uncles, and cousins; but we identify with them as people rather than focus on specific kinship principles. We know who Uncle Jack and Aunt Libby are long before we understand the concepts of "mother's brother" or "father's sister."

All cultures recognize **kinship**, the relatedness of certain individuals within a group, and have norms and expectations that structure and govern kin behavior. The diversity of these norms is wide ranging. These kinship concepts describe kinds of kinship groups and the norms that govern marital forms, family structure and organization, inheritance, authority, and residence.

As people get divorced and remarried, forming new stepfamilies, family and kin relationships become more complex.
©Monkeybusinessimages/iStock/Getty Images

Kinship groups range from nuclear families to various forms of extended families and may even include symbolic relationships. The **nuclear family**—the smallest, most elementary kinship unit—usually consists of two parents and their dependent children. Even in societies in which the nuclear family is embedded within a larger group, it is recognized as a distinct entity. The nuclear family is a **conjugal family system**, one that emphasizes the relationships formed through marriage. Typically, a conjugal system comprises only two generations and is relatively transitory, dissolving when the parents die or the children grow up and leave. Because nuclear families are comparatively small and short lived, they are less likely to develop traditions that are handed down through the generations.

Many family functions are better performed by composite family groups, or **consanguineal family systems**, which emphasize blood ties more than marital ties. In consanguineal systems, married couples and their children are embedded in a larger kinship group of three or more generations related by blood. Consanguineal systems can include extended families or families resulting from plural marriages. An **extended family** consists of a nuclear family and those people related to its members by blood ties, such as aunts, uncles, cousins, and grandparents.

A **plural marriage**, or **polygamy**, is a marriage in which a man has more than one wife (**polygyny**) or, more rarely, a marriage in which a woman has more than one husband (**polyandry**). In **monogamy**, a man or woman has only one mate. Although people from monogamous societies often perceive potential hazards in plural marriages, family patterns appear to operate in a relatively smooth fashion in groups in which plural marriages are the norm.

A third kind of kinship group is a **pseudo-kin group**, in which relationships resembling kinship ties develop among unrelated individuals. Relationships within these groups range in intensity, from close friendships to godparent-godchild connections to individuals living together and caring for each other without any legal or blood relationship.

Cultural norms influence family structure, but they also influence concepts of **lineage** or lines of descent; of who holds authority in a family; and of where newly married couples should reside. Lineage is important in determining membership in a particular kinship group, patterns of inheritance, and kinship obligations or responsibilities. In some societies, descent is traced by gender: **matrilineal societies** trace descent through females, and

patrilineal societies trace descent through males. In a matrilineal society, for example, a man inherits group membership through his mother; lines of descent through his sister(s) are also important. Although a man may live with his wife or wives, he perceives the households of his mother and sisters as his true home. In a patrilineal society, a man's sister will be in his descent group but her children will not; they belong to their father's descent group.

Bilateral descent is common in many Western societies, with children tied equally to relatives of both the mother and the father. In this "family tree" approach to descent, in which ancestors and descendants multiply geometrically, true descent kinship groups are not formed unless limited by generation or to particular ancestors and descendants.

Norms for lines of descent may or may not be linked to lines of authority within a kinship group. If females exercise the authority, a kinship group is considered a **matriarchal group.** If males are dominant and exercise the authority, the kinship group is considered a **patriarchal group.** Note that these terms emphasize femaleness and maleness rather than motherhood and fatherhood. In a patriarchal group, for example, the grandfather is likely to wield more authority than the father of a nuclear family. But the criterion of gender always supersedes that of age in matriarchal and patriarchal kinship groups.

In **egalitarian groups**, such as those found in the United States, the ideals of democracy suggest that the rights and perspectives of both genders and all generations be respected. A given family's structure and interactions may lean toward the patriarchal or matriarchal, but the norms of the group would most likely be considered egalitarian.

Norms of residence for newly married couples can also be categorized by a society's emphasis on biological sex. In a **matrilocal society**, newly married couples normally live with or near the wife's kin, especially her mother's kinship group. Newly married couples in **patrilocal societies** are expected to live with or near the husband's kin, usually his father's kinship group. In a **neolocal society**, norms encourage newly married couples to establish a separate, autonomous residence, independent of either partner's kinship group.

Although a society may have norms regarding marital and family organization and interaction, diversity is generally also evident within that society's families and kinship groups. Understanding the concept of kin relationships, however, enables observers to compare and analyze the structure and dynamics of a broad range of kinship groups.

Family System and Sociocultural Characteristics

Family system framework is very useful for understanding and improving the quality of life for couples and families. These family system characteristics are cohesion, flexibility, and communication. Three sociocultural characteristics that also give us insight into families are the extended family, the social system, and the belief system. Figure 2.3 graphically illustrates how the family system characteristics and the sociocultural characteristics can be synthesized.

Three Family System Characteristics

There has been a great deal of research looking at the characteristics of strong families, focusing on their family system. The three dimensions (clusters of concepts) of family systems that have been found are cohesion, flexibility, and communication (Olson, 2011; Walsh, 2006). These three dimensions also relate directly to the six characteristics of strong families described by DeFrain in the international family strengths model (DeFrain & Asay, 2008).

FIGURE 2.3
Family System and Sociocultural Characteristics

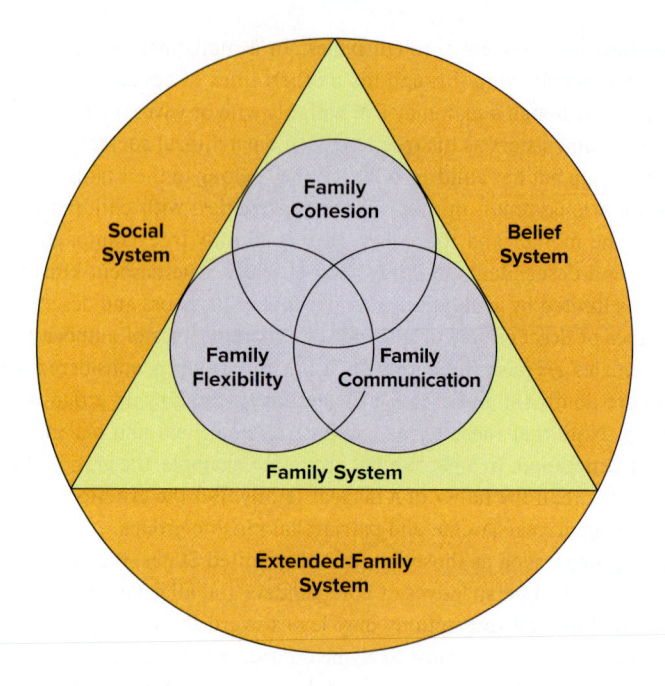

Family cohesion is *the emotional closeness a person feels to other family members*. Cohesion includes both commitment and spending enjoyable time together from the family strengths model. Commitment to the family includes trust, honesty, dependability, and faithfulness. Spending time together means committing a considerable amount of quality time to sharing activities, feelings, and ideas, and enjoying each other's company.

Family flexibility is *the ability to change and adapt when necessary*. Flexibility also relates to dealing effectively with stress and having helpful spiritual beliefs from the family strengths model. Coping abilities include using personal and family resources to help each other, accepting crises as challenges rather than denying them, and growing together by working through crises. Spiritual well-being includes happiness, optimism, hope, faith, and a set of shared ethical values that guide family members through life's challenges.

Family communication is *the sharing of information, ideas, and feelings with each other*. Communication is generally positive in strong families because angry outbursts and other negative interchanges simply don't work well. Appreciation and affection are regularly shared. Positive communication includes having open, straightforward discussions, being cooperative rather than competitive, and sharing feelings with one another. Appreciation and affection include kindness, mutual caring, respect for individuality, and a feeling of security.

Three Sociocultural Characteristics

In describing successful families, we have emphasized three important family system characteristics, but it is also important to consider the sociocultural context in which families live. The three sociocultural characteristics that are particularly useful in describing and understanding families from diverse ethnic groups are the *extended-family system*, the *social system*, and the *belief system* (Walsh, 2006).

The **extended-family system** encompasses *relatives, kin, and other family members connected to the family system*. These are very important resources for most families and are a particularly important resource for families of color.

The **social system** includes *the economic, educational, and other related resources available*. Families of color are often at a disadvantage in the social system because they are more likely to be of middle or lower socioeconomic status. Because of their relative lack of both education and economic resources, the social system is often more a liability than an asset to families of color.

The **belief system** refers to *a family's spiritual beliefs and values*. All families have a value system, and families of color often have a spiritual belief system that helps them maintain a strong and successful family.

Family Strengths and Challenges Across Ethnic Groups

This section describes some of the most salient family strengths and family challenges of the major ethnic groups in the United States. The summary lists that follow were created from reviewing several hundred publications related to the various ethnic groups. We tried to rely on studies done by *insiders* rather than *outsiders*—studies done by researchers who were members of the particular ethnic group under study, rather than studies done by researchers on the outside looking in. Although the characteristics in each list are commonly found in a particular ethnic group, it does not mean that every family has these particular characteristics. Each family in the world is a culture all to itself. It is unique and different from all the other families in the world, even though it is quite likely to share many similarities with other families in its own ethnic group and similarities with families outside its ethnic group.

So that you may identify the strengths in your own family, we have put together a short quiz you can take. Box 2.2 lists 10 characteristics that you can use to rate your own family. We hope you find it a useful way to think about the good things in your family.

Strengths of European American Families

Understanding of the strengths of European American or White families has been highly influenced by the research of John DeFrain and Nick Stinnett. Their work began in the mid-1970s and very early they developed a model of six major traits that make a family strong (Stinnett & DeFrain, 1985; Stinnett, Sanders, & DeFrain, 1981; Stinnett & Sauer, 1977). Their ongoing later research continues to confirm that these six qualities of strong families apply to many ethnic groups around the world (DeFrain & Asay, 2008):

- *Commitment to family*. Strong White families are very committed to one another and are able to give all family members the freedom and support they need to achieve their individual goals.
- *Enjoyable time together*. White families that remain strong throughout the family life cycle find ways to spend time together and enjoy each other.
- *Ability to manage stress and crisis effectively*. Although all families encounter marital and family stress, strong families see stress as a challenge and deal directly with issues as they occur.
- *Spiritual well-being*. Strong White families have spiritual beliefs and values, often including religious beliefs, that help them deal with ongoing life issues.

BOX 2.2 Self-Assessment

Rate the Strengths in Your Family

This Family Strengths Inventory was developed by researchers who have studied strengths as perceived by more than 30,000 family members in 39 countries. Put an "S" for *strength* beside the qualities you feel your family has achieved, and a "G" beside those qualities that are an area of potential *growth*. If the particular characteristic does not apply to your family or is not a characteristic that is important to you, put an "NA" for *not applicable*.

_____ 1. We enjoy expressing appreciation and affection for each other.

_____ 2. We are committed to our well-being as a family and the well-being of each individual.

_____ 3. Communication is usually positive, straightforward, and honest.

_____ 4. We share an adequate amount of enjoyable time together.

_____ 5. We share beliefs and values that give us meaning and a sense of belonging in the world.

_____ 6. We see challenges in life as opportunities for growing closer together.

_____ 7. We love one another.

_____ 8. Life in our family is satisfying to us.

_____ 9. We are happy as a family.

_____ 10. All things considered, we are a strong family.

How Can a Family Use This Inventory?

Partners or family members can fill out a copy of this Family Strengths Inventory separately and then share their answers with each other. If discussed in a positive manner, they will be able to identify those areas they would like to work on together to improve, and those areas of strength that will serve as the foundation for their growth and positive change together.

Source: From John DeFrain, *Family Treasures: Creating Strong Families.* Lincoln, NE: University of Nebraska, iUniverse, 2007. Reprinted by permission.

- *Positive communication.* One of the most important characteristics of healthy Caucasian families is that they feel good about their communication with one another.
- *Appreciation and affection.* Sharing the positive feelings they have about one another helps keep relationships positive in strong White families.

Enjoyable time together is critically important for families in American society. In a fast-paced environment, loved ones need to s-l-o-w d-o-w-n and relearn why they care for each other so much.
©Ingram Publishing/SuperStock

Strengths of African American Families

Throughout the past four decades researchers have been interested in strengths of African American families (Billingsley, 1992; Hill, 1971). In recent years there has also been increased interest in strengths of African American marriages (Chaney & Skogrand, 2009; Marks et al., 2008; Sue & Sue, 2016). Both areas of research help us identify and better understand the strengths of this population:

- *Strong kinship bonds.* The extended family is very important to many African American families, and African Americans tend to take relatives into their households (Hine, 2007; Marks, Nesteruk, Hopkins-Williams, Swanson, & Davis, 2006; Sarkisian, 2007).
- *Flexibility in family roles.* Role flexibility serves as an effective coping mechanism in healthy African American families. Because it has been necessary for many mothers to work outside the home, Black mothers tend to have considerable power in the family. The typical strong African American family is not matriarchal or patriarchal but is egalitarian in style. African American families have a longer tradition of egalitarian marriages than White families (Sue & Sue, 2016).
- *Strong motivation to achieve.* African American parents believe education is important, and many would like to see their children go to college (Sue & Sue, 2016).
- *Strong religious orientation.* Recent research has found that African American couples who have strong marriages actually incorporate their religious beliefs into all aspects of their lives. For example, they sought out a religious person to marry, incorporated God into important issues they encountered in their marriages, and passed those beliefs on to their children (Chaney, Shirisia, & Skogrand, 2016; Chaney & Skogrand, 2009; Marks et al., 2008).

Strengths of Latino Families

Because Latinos have recently become the largest U.S. minority group (U.S. Census Bureau, 2006a), there has been increased literature about the cultural characteristics of

In 2011 the Martin Luther King, Jr., Memorial was dedicated. Dr. King's leadership in the civil rights movement of the 1960s brought hope to many Black Americans that freedom and liberty could be a reality for all people. Martin Luther King has become a symbol of civil rights for people around the world.
Source: NPS Photo

this population. Although family strengths can vary depending upon country of origin and migration experience, there are several strengths that most Latinos have in common, and several of these characteristics are also common in families from other cultures:

- *Familism*. The family is highly valued in Latino culture and is viewed as sacred. There is cohesion among family members, and family members usually include the extended family or friends that might be viewed as family (Skogrand, Barrios-Bell, & Higginbotham, 2009; Sue & Sue, 2016).
- *Children are highly valued.* Children are sometimes viewed as more important than the marriage relationship (Skogrand et al., 2009). Children are typically not left with child care providers, and if children need to be cared for by someone other than parents, it is often an extended family member (Olsen & Skogrand, 2009).
- *Religion.* Members of the Latino culture are highly likely to self-identify as having a religious affiliation, with the majority identifying as Catholic (Skogrand et al., 2009). Religion influences decisions about marriage, having children, and divorce (Sue & Sue, 2016).

Family members provide support to each other. The Latino culture is collectivistic, which means that the group, or the family, is more important than the individual. Therefore, family members provide social and financial support for those in need, sometimes at the expense of their own well-being (Halgunseth, Ispa, & Rudy, 2006; Sue & Sue, 2016).

Linda Skogrand and colleagues interviewed 25 Latino couples who had strong marriages to find out what made their marriages strong (Skogrand et al., 2009). The study was conducted using open-ended interview questions with the questions being developed within a cultural context. These couples indicated three things that were essential in making their marriages strong: children, communication, and religion.

Children were important to these Latino couples because they were the reason for getting married and they were the "glue" that kept the marriages together. These couples saw there marriages subsumed within and a part of their family lives—marriage relationships

Latinos in the United States have managed to preserve a strong family system in spite of the difficult challenges they face. As in other ethnic and cultural groups, Latino families are changing as mothers become more involved in the workforce and fathers become more involved in family responsibilities at home.
©Monkeybusinessimages/ iStock/Getty Images

were not separate, but a part of their family. Participants in the study also said communication was essential for a strong marriage. Finally, religion was important in making a marriage strong. Religion provided a strong base for the relationship with support from other congregational members. Religious beliefs were also the context for their strong sense of commitment in the marriage. Making a commitment before God and the church helped the couples stay in the marriage even through difficult times (Skogrand et al., 2008).

The Latino marriage study supported extensive literature identifying family and religion as important values in the Latino culture. These values provide resources and strength to Latino families.

Strengths of Asian American Families

Families of Asian descent are another very resilient group in this country. Although Asian Americans have faced prejudice and discrimination throughout their history in the United States, they have fared better than other ethnic minorities economically and have managed to preserve their family ties, traditions, and values. Asian Americans come from many diverse national origins and also represent diverse economic backgrounds (Pew, 2013, April 4; Zhou & Lee, 2008). Asian Americans who come here to get additional education and seek high-paying jobs do very well economically in this country. Others, however, have come as refugees with minimal skills and have settled in poor inner cities.

A period of disruption occurred in the 1940s, which affected many early Asian American immigrants. Following the bombing of Pearl Harbor, fear of further attacks by Japan led the U.S. government to resettle Japanese Americans—even those born in this country—in what were essentially prison camps until the war ended. Four decades later, the federal government agreed to modestly recompense surviving family members for the ill treatment they had suffered.

Many Asian Americans share a cultural heritage that values discipline, family commitment, hard work, and education (Pew, 2013, April 4). Young people reared in such an environment become challenging competitors in a society such as ours, which values

Many Asian Americans share a cultural heritage that values discipline, family commitment, hard work, and education.
©Dann Tardif/LWA/Getty Images

competition and individual initiative. Asian American families are very diverse, but they commonly share many of the strengths of other cultural groups. Following are six major strengths of Asian American families:

- *Strong family orientation*. Both the nuclear and the extended family are very important historically and today.
- *Filial piety*. The great respect Asian American families have for their elders is noteworthy. It helps explain the high level of mutual support each generation receives from the other generations.
- *High value on education*. Asian American families emphasize the importance of education, from nursery school through college.
- *Well-disciplined children*. Traditionally, children are expected to be quiet, well behaved, and somewhat passive.
- *Extended-family support*. Financial and emotional support is provided by the extended family when the nuclear family needs it.
- *Family loyalty*. Family members support each other and protect each other's privacy.

Strengths of American Indian Families

American Indians and Alaska Natives (AI/ANs) are people having origins in any of the original peoples of North and South America (including Central America) and who maintain tribal affiliation or community attachment (U.S. Census Bureau, 2000c). The greatest concentrations of American Indians and Alaska Natives are in the West, Southwest, and Midwest, especially in Alaska, Arizona, Montana, New Mexico, Oklahoma, and South Dakota. American Indian families in the United States are members of 566 federally recognized tribes, plus an unknown number of tribes that are not federally recognized (U.S. Department of the Interior, 2014, January 16).

American Indians and Alaska Natives are classified together in the U.S. Census. Native Hawaiians and other Pacific Islanders are included in a separate group. In this section on the strengths of American Indian families, we are looking only at the groups living in North America.

There is great diversity within the American Indian population based upon tribal affiliation and whether they live on reservations or in metropolitan communities. Several strengths of American Indians have been identified by researchers and others who write about the cultural characteristic of this population (Sue & Sue, 2016; Trimble & Gonzalez, 2008).

- *Extended-family system*. The extended family is very strong in American Indian families.
- *Spiritual beliefs*. The belief system of American Indian tribes focuses on harmony with nature and the value of contentment. There is a connection among the spirit, mind, and body.
- *High family cohesion*. The connectedness of the family is important. The family is broadly defined to include the nuclear family, the extended family, friends, and the tribal community.
- *Respect for elders*. Elders are the most respected individuals in traditional American Indian tribes, and the family reinforces this attitude.
- *Bilingual language skills*. Most American Indians work hard to maintain their native languages, but this objective is becoming more difficult because the children attend school off the reservations and are increasingly exposed to television and other mass media.
- *Tribal support system*. Many American Indians rely on their tribal support system for all types of problems. Only when that is inadequate do they turn to outside support.

There are a variety of ways people conceive of the coming together of cultures. This is the *Monument of Three Cultures* on the grounds of El Santuario De Chimayo in Chimayo, New Mexico. The three cultures are American Indian, Protestant, and Catholic. This monument may only have meaning in this particular part of the country where differing religious/spiritual beliefs learned to coexist.
©Russell Contreras/AP Images

Spirituality is probably one of the most pervasive themes in the American Indian culture (Limb & Hodge, 2008). Health and wellness are based upon the ability to create balance and harmony among the mental, physical, and spiritual aspects of one's life, and thus spirituality is an integral component of most aspects of one's life. One of the authors of this textbook was conducting research with one of the tribes and after several attempts could get no answer about how to ask about spirituality. This author concluded that spirituality is so much a part of individual and collective lives in this tribe that it is not talked about as a separate concept—it is part of all that is. Historically, efforts have been made to destroy the spiritual expressions and practices of American Indians, but these beliefs remain for many. Spiritual practices have been a source of strength by reminding American Indians where they came from, giving them strength from their ancestors, and also contributing to the maintenance of a cohesive bond between the individual, the community, and the Creator. There is an increase in research about historical trauma (see Box 2.3), and the impact of this trauma as well as the importance of reconnecting with culture to address this trauma.

Although American Indian families are characterized by diversity, some investigators have asserted that the family remains the basic unit of the American Indian community and that the American Indian family can be characterized as having traditional beliefs, practices, and languages and a unique history and lifestyle. American Indian families derive support from both individual family members and the clan or tribal group to which they belong.

The extended family is still a source of strength for many American Indians, but this is changing as more family members leave the reservation to seek opportunities elsewhere. American Indian youths may have a wider array of people to whom they are attached than do non-Indians. In fact, children may live in multiple households during their growing up years (Sue & Sue, 2016). In times of crisis, support from both the extended family and the tribal community helps people survive. Nuclear families are important, but the tribal community also acts as a safety net, assuming a great deal of responsibility for the welfare of its individual members. Many fathers actively care for their own children along with the mothers and serve as father substitutes for children whose fathers have died or deserted the family.

How an individual behaves, in both positive and negative ways, reflects upon the individual's family and tribe. Therefore, cooperation is important (Sue & Sue, 2016). The group is in part collectively liable for the transgressions of its individual members, so the group provides a collective conscience and consciousness that emphasize individual responsibility. Respect for elders is common among American Indian tribes, and grandparents often

BOX 2.3 At Issue

Historical Trauma and American Indians

In recent years several researchers have written about the trauma American Indians have experienced through history with the loss of land, language, and culture (Brown-Rice, 2013; Evans-Campbell, 2008). This trauma has at times been referred to as **historical trauma**, historical consciousness, intergenerational trauma, or unresolved grief. These terms generally refer to the result of what has been taken from them by European Americans over several generations. Land—often sacred land—was taken when American Indians were placed on reservations. Language was taken from them when children were put in boarding schools and were not allowed to speak their native language or practice their traditional ways. They experienced genocide when large numbers of people died due to exposure to illnesses for which they had no immunity. Promises were made and were broken. These multiple losses have gone on for several generations, and the trauma that resulted has affected individual and family lives.

Brown-Rice (2013) describes three phases which are part of a conceptual framework of historical trauma. The first phase involves the dominant culture causing devastation on a population which involves losses for individuals, families, and the culture. The second phase involves the original generation showing symptoms of those losses, which may be psychological, societal, and biological.

These losses, sometimes referred to as "soul wounds" (Trimble & Gonzalez, 2008), have resulted in social and individual problems such as alcoholism, suicide, homicide, abuse, and domestic violence. In essence, part of their selves has been taken, resulting in tremendous loss. The third phase is when these these symptoms get passed on to future generations. Many believe that to recover, and to address the social problems such as alcoholism, they must reclaim their culture—reestablish rituals and traditional practices, sometimes called "cultural recovery" (Gone, 2009; Heart, Chase, Elkins, & Altschul, 2011; Trimble & Gonzalez, 2008).

Many tribes are making efforts to heal themselves. Some are teaching children their almost lost tribal language, because culture is embedded in language. Many are becoming gatekeepers of research, which can be done on the reservation, such as the Navajo Nation, in order to control what is said about them in research findings. Some tribes have their own schools and colleges so that what young people learn is taught within a cultural context. In essence, many American Indians are "taking back their culture" as a way to address social issues and become healthy. Here is the true story of one man:

A 50-year-old Lakota man was adopted as a child into a European American family. He took on the ways of White society from living in a White home, attending White schools, learning White history, and attending White churches. Even though he had dark skin, he did everything he could to fit in as a White person.

As an adult he drank heavily and became an alcoholic. He went through alcohol treatment several times with little success. Finally a case worker said that he needed to find out who he was as an American Indian man before he could become healthy. The process was long because he had to create an entire new identity. He had to get over his internal shame about being Indian and learn Lakota ways. For a period of time he cut off contact with his White family and friends and became immersed in his Lakota culture. It was very difficult to be proud of being Indian. Through a long, painful process he developed his American Indian identity—he knew who he was. Only then could he remain sober.

Although most researchers focus on historical trauma as it relates to the lives of American Indians, one might wonder if historical trauma might also be evident in the lives of members of other minority groups. For example, African Americans experienced multiple and painful losses when children, spouses, parents, and other family members were separated during slavery. It took years before Blacks were allowed to own land or participate in the social life of White communities. The civil rights movement brought hangings and other trauma to many who fought for their rights. Did the Hmong and other refugees who came to this country after the Vietnam War experience similar losses as they left family members behind and sailed on boats that had little hope of bringing them to safety? Future research may address such questions, and others may better understand how historical trauma may have impacted their lives.

---

hold a unique position, passing on cultural values and beliefs to their grandchildren and educating the young about the physical, social, and spiritual world. Social shame (that is, embarrassment) is a common tool for disciplining children. In general, physical punishment is not encouraged or condoned. Parents usually praise their children only for special accomplishments. The young are not socialized to expect praise, and it is not given lightly.

A number of tribes stress marriages based not only on an attraction between two people but on the consensus of their relatives and the tribal community. This approach to marriage recognizes the fact that an individual marries not only another individual but also that person's family and cultural community. Research suggests that these officially sanctioned marriages are more stable than those not recognized by the couple's family members or the tribe.

Cross-Cultural Family Studies

Cross-cultural family studies tend to focus on two interrelated questions. First, how are families in the United States different from those in other parts of the world? Second, how are they similar? At first glance, people are often struck by the obvious differences between family cultures. Clothing styles, food preferences, religious beliefs, housing, music, education—all these aspects of culture vary from one society to another. When visiting a new culture, people often look for the differences between it and their own culture. Eventually, they also begin to see the similarities. When learning about another culture, then, the key is to look for both similarities and differences.

Cross-cultural family studies focus on how particular cultural contexts influence a wide variety of issues: family values and behaviors, courtship patterns and weddings, marital and parent–child communication, power and gender roles, work and the family, ethical and religious values, childrearing patterns, sexuality, the role of grandparents and the extended family, and the role people outside the immediate family play in helping families in crisis.

We are all ethnocentric to some extent; we see others through unique lenses that are shaped by our own culture. **Ethnocentrism** is the assumption that one's own culture is the standard by which other cultures should be judged. Our ethnocentricity influences the extent to which we judge other people, families, and cultures as similar to or different from us. Tolerance of the traditions and values of other cultural and ethnic groups is the first step in transcending our overconcern with human differences. Understanding other ways of looking at life and the world around us can lead to genuine, mutual appreciation among people of different backgrounds (see Box 2.4).

Related to the issue of ethnocentrism is what anthropologists have called *perspective*. When one looks at a society from the outside, or from an **etic perspective**, one sees its characteristics in isolation rather than as they relate to the structure of the society as a whole. On the other hand, when one looks at a society from the inside, or from an **emic perspective**, one analyzes behaviors in terms of the internal structural elements of the society. The etic perspective tends to focus on and exaggerate differences, whereas the emic perspective makes it easier to see similarities between cultures.

Family researchers attempt to combine these two perspectives, recognizing the differences between cultures but also trying to identify similarities. Researchers from one culture can never completely discard their personal lenses. They can, however, try to become more open to new ideas and behaviors by submerging themselves in another culture, even learning that culture's language and living within that culture.

Challenges for Ethnic Families

Ethnic families in the United States face many challenges. Among them are intercultural marriage, the issue of assimilation, and relationships between men and women and between parents and children. Ethnic families do not experience the "advantages of being in the majority" that White Americans in the predominant culture do.

Assimilation, Acculturation, and Segregation

Newcomers to any society face a difficult set of choices: Should they swiftly reject their former life and the culture from which they came? Should they downplay their ethnic origins in an effort to fit the mainstream view? Or should they build their own ethnic enclave and

BOX 2.4 Diversity in Families

The Tables Are Turned: Going from the Majority to the Minority

In the following story, a father tells what it felt like when his family moved from being members of the dominant White majority in the United States to being members of the tiny White minority in the small country of Fiji in the South Pacific.

Living as a minority in another country was one of the most vivid experiences our family has ever had. It gave us all a great deal of insight into what it feels like to be an "outsider." We went from a city in which we were part of the 89% White majority and we were "insiders," to a village in which we were part of the 2% Caucasian minority.

We were used to being accepted, to being "normal," to "fitting in." When we arrived, everything was different to us, and it was clear that we just did not fit in. Instead of seeing the middle-class midwestern suburban neighborhood with well-kept homes, manicured yards, and new cars, we moved into an indigenous settlement. The settlement was set in a river valley ringed by low mountains that were covered with tropical rain forest. It rained 200 inches a year. The settlement was a 10-minute walk from a tropical lagoon where tiger sharks swam and women hunted for eels and shellfish to feed their large families.

The first evening we moved into our house we heard drums begin to beat a few hours after we had fallen into bed, exhausted; faint chanting was coming from the settlement. Lying underneath the mosquito netting in bed, we laughed about how the drums sounded like some kind of celebration. The islanders had given up cannibalism more than a century before: "Perhaps they're reviving the old ways to introduce us to the culture," we joked to each other, falling into cultural stereotypes that made us feel guilty for dredging them up. The next day we found out the drums were traditional instruments carved from large logs. They were being used to call members of the local church choir to Wednesday evening practice. We felt even stupider then.

The people of color who dominated the country had a different language than we did. They ate different foods, sang different songs, danced different dances, wore different clothes, held different religious beliefs, made different rules for their families and their communities and their government. And the color of their skin was different from ours. Frankly, everything was different to us.

At first these differences seemed exotic and interesting. After a while, we were worn down by being different, and a kind of chronic fatigue set in upon us, sprinkled with occasional outbursts of anger that we felt we should not express. You could see the stress on the faces of other Whites who were either visiting the small island or had decided to live there. Being different meant that they didn't quite understand all the cultural rules—all the patterns of behavior and thought and speech, all the do's and don'ts.

Being a member of the 2% White minority in our little South Pacific country turned the tables on us. When we visited with other Whites on the island, the conversation often focused on how difficult it was to live in a culture dominated by people of color. "You can't trust them. They're always trying to take advantage of you. They run the government. They make the rules. There's no way we can get ahead in this country," and so forth. The minority Whites often seemed sick and tired and miserable, though they put on brave, smiling faces when around the majority.

Fortunately, my family and I met people of color there who took us into their homes and their hearts, and served as our cultural guides, helping us understand their world and the wonderful things about life the islanders knew that we didn't know. Without these cultural guides, our life on the island would have been much more difficult. Instead, it turned into an unforgettable experience in seeing the world from the perspective of an ethnic minority.

---

try to create a safe microworld that reflects their cultural heritage? These questions are extremely difficult to answer, and minority-group members often disagree on how to proceed. Some families are torn apart by controversies of this nature.

There are three important processes that help explain what happens when a cultural group from another country encounters the dominant culture of the new country. **Assimilation** is *the process in which old cultural traits and values are relinquished and replaced by those of the dominant culture.* **Acculturation** is *the process whereby cultural traits and values from one ethnic group become blended with those of the dominant culture.* **Segregation** is *the process in which an ethnic group isolates itself or is forced into isolation within the dominant culture.* All three of these processes can occur in an interactive way as a family adapts to living in another culture.

Members of the majority culture whose families have been in the United States for two, three, or more generations sometimes do not understand why immigrants are hesitant about assimilation—adopting the values of the dominant culture. But it is clear that immigrants are in a difficult psychological position. They see and are attracted by the strengths of American culture, especially its abundance of economic resources. But they also see the weaknesses of American culture—materialism, competitiveness, wasteful exploitation of the natural world, a fast-paced and often impersonal existence. Immigrants are in some ways in a better position to see America's strengths and weaknesses than are Americans, for they have another culture with which they can compare this one.

Unfortunately, most of what people know about ethnic and cultural groups other than their own is based on **stereotypes**—standardized, oversimplified, and mean-spirited views. When a person from one group describes people from another, the description is often a stereotype. **Prejudice**, which literally means prejudging, is also closely linked with stereotyping; both attitudes reinforce each other. As a society, we need to move beyond stereotypes and focus on each group's strengths and challenges. Recognizing others' strengths helps reduce prejudice.

Racism is closely related to ethnocentrism and may even be a by-product of it. All the various "isms" tend to distance human beings from each other by accentuating differences and ignoring fundamental similarities, which, in turn, leads to tension and conflict. **Racism** develops when the most powerful group in a society creates an elaborate mythology (a set of beliefs that grossly distort reality) about a minority group. These prejudices often endure because of the need of the dominant group to feel superior to others. These prejudices can be significant stressors for members of the minority group, having serious psychological, social, and physiological effects.

The Advantages of Being in the Majority

If you're a member of the predominant culture in any society, there are innumerable benefits that accrue to you. You receive these benefits every day of your life, regardless of whether you worked for them—and, thus, "deserve" them—or didn't do anything at all to gain them. They are a birthright, like being born into a wealthy family. If you're a member of the majority culture, you take these benefits for granted. In fact, you hardly ever think about them.

We're not just targeting American culture here; we believe this is a cross-cultural phenomenon. Many countries throughout the world have a dominant culture. The dominant culture does not necessarily have to comprise the largest population, but it does hold most of the power.

What, in essence, are we talking about here? If you're a member of the majority culture:

- People speak the same language you speak.
- The educational system is patterned after your ways of thinking and honors your history, your beliefs, and your values.
- The job market is more open to you because you are the "right" color, gender, religion, sexual orientation, political affiliation, or social class, and you don't have a disability that makes the majority culture uncomfortable.
- People will not discriminate in renting an apartment to you or selling you a house in their neighborhood.
- The laws, the police, and the courts are sensitive to your cultural values and tend to deal with you in a relatively open-minded fashion.
- Religious and spiritual values of the culture are ideals that you can agree on and live with.
- Music, literature, movies, and art reflect your tastes and values.

The list of advantages accruing to those in the majority culture is almost endless. What advantages can you add to this list?

Marriage Outside the Group

In many countries throughout the world, marriage is seen primarily as an agreement between two families. An alliance through marriage between two successful families can enhance the power, prestige, and well-being of all the members of both families. In this sense, one marries not just an individual but also that person's family.

Because American culture stresses individuality, the importance of a good "fit" between families is often overlooked, and individuals who wish to marry often purposely ignore advice from family members. Sometimes that advice is based on ignorance of the proposed partner's personal strengths and/or on prejudice toward the cultural group from which the proposed partner comes. The greater the differences between the two families, the more likely the chance for conflict.

Our society has become more diverse and marriages with someone from a different race or ethnic group has increased dramatically. In 2010 15% of new marriages were multiracial (Frey, 2014, November 28). Only 17% of Whites were in **multiracial marriages;** however, almost half of Asians and Hispanics were in multiracial marriages (Frey, 2014, November 28). This is likely due to the increase of Asian and Hispanic immigrants coming to this country. African Americans are least likely to be in multiracial marriages. It must be noted that until 1967 it was illegal for Blacks to marry outside of their race (Frey, 2014, November 28). Most intermarrying is happening in the West and Southwest United States (Passel, Wang, & Taylor, 2010, June 4). Recent studies indicate that there are increasing numbers of interracial marriages between Whites and Blacks, and slower increases in interracial marriages between Whites and Latinos (Qian & Lichter, 2011). There has also been a decline in the number of White and Asian interracial marriages. The number of marriages between foreign born and U.S. born has also increased because Latinos born in the United States are now likely to marry new immigrants. This is also the reason why there is such a low percentage of Whites in interracial marriages. They have a large pool of potential marriage partners from which to choose from within their own culture.

The number of multicultural couples cohabiting has increased and is approximately twice as high as the number of multiracial marriages (Batson et al., 2006). Some couples choose to live together to avoid disapproval from extended family. The number of multiracial marriages is increasing, and the trend is expected to continue as public attitudes become more accepting of such unions.

Relationships Between Men and Women

Regardless of nationality or cultural background, friction occurs between men and women in intimate relationships. Although couples strive for mutual love and caring, different socialization processes and biological inheritances produce misunderstanding and conflict. Women in developed countries, because of greater education and more employment opportunities outside the home, tend to have more options. If they are dissatisfied with their marriages and can support themselves, they are not as likely to stay in these marriages. Women in rural areas and in developing countries have fewer options, even though they may be just as unhappy as their divorcing counterparts in developed countries. As a result, divorce rates tend to be higher in industrialized, urban-oriented societies around the world and lower in less-developed, agrarian societies. But the lower divorce rates in the more rural societies do not necessarily indicate happier marriages.

Ethnic identity is a social construction rather than a biological fact. The children in this family are of mixed European American and Asian heritage; their ethnic identity depends not on their physical characteristics but on the tradition within which they are being raised. Many young parents such as these work to rear their children in a bicultural environment, respectful of both family traditions.
©Rubberball/Getty Images

Relationships Between Parents and Children

Children often develop into adults much like their own parents. In the process of growing up, however, children and parents often experience much conflict. The younger generation strives to create a relatively independent life, and the older generation tries to maintain control of the children. These struggles are played out in countless cultures around the world. Family power structures in various cultures seem to change gradually over time, as societies move from agriculturally oriented economies to industrialized economies. In an agriculturally oriented family, the father, who is responsible for making sure the farm runs smoothly, has more control over his children. In the city, the father's influence lessens, and the influence of others (peers, school, the workplace) increases. Rural societies generally emphasize respect for the authority of the dominant males. In more modern societies, the rights of the individual, whether female or male, receive more weight because the family is more likely to succeed if all its members become well educated and find good jobs.

When a family moves from one culture to another, parent–child relationships can be especially strained, because the youngsters struggle to fit into the new culture and inevitably lose touch with past traditions. Kim, a 35-year-old woman who married an American and emigrated to the United States from Korea, explains why it is important for their children, born in Korea but being raised in the United States, to be able to speak not only English but her native language as well. It will be a delicate balancing act for the family to maintain connections to both Korean and American cultures, but the benefits of such an accomplishment can far outweigh the difficulties.

> *"Of course, they need to know English. They're going to end up being Americans. That's obvious. We aren't going back to Korea to live, only to visit.*
>
> *It's hard for them. They speak English in school and in the neighborhood, but in the home we speak Korean. They get confused sometimes and mix languages. Sometimes the neighbor kids tease them about it. It's especially difficult for Jared, our son, but Emily is doing great. I think they'll both catch on and see why it's important in the long run.*
>
> *I want them to appreciate their roots, to remember the wonderful civilization they come from. And, most important, I want them to know me, their mother. I live in the United States but probably always will be Korean deep down, because that's where I grew up. I can't help it. That's home. The language of emotion, the language of love is your native language. How can I show my true emotions, my true love for my children if they cannot understand my Korean? How can they really know me?"*

Summary

- When viewing people from different ethnic groups, it is important to look beyond their physical qualities and get to know their personal and family strengths.
- In families we learn what it means to be a family, how intimacy is expressed, what it means to be male and female, and gender roles. Families, however, exist within a cultural context—therefore culture matters.
- Cultural identity evolves from shared beliefs, values, and attitudes.
- Ethnic identity refers to the geographic origin of a particular group.
- Race is based on the physical characteristics of a group of people and is a concept that is losing value.
- The Hispanic, or Latino, population recently became the largest minority population in the United States, followed by African American, Asian American, and American Indian and Alaska Native populations.
- Historically, research has been primarily conducted with White, middle-class populations. Not only is there a need to include minority population in research studies, but there is also a need to include members of these populations in all aspects of research, including planning, analyzing data, and interpreting results.
- Professionals need to become culturally competent in order to more effectively provide family education and services.
- Strong families share the three family system traits of cohesion, flexibility, and communication. Three sociocultural characteristics are also useful for understanding families: the extended-family system, the social system, and the belief system.
- The strengths of White families in the United States include commitment to the family, enjoyable time spent together, the ability to manage stress and crisis effectively, spiritual well-being, positive communication, and appreciation and affection for each other.
- The strengths of African American families include strong kinship bonds, flexibility in family roles, strong motivation to achieve, and a strong religious orientation.
- The strengths of Latino families include familism, a supportive kin network system.
- The strengths of Asian American families include strong family orientation, filial piety, a high value on education, well-disciplined children, extended-family support, and family loyalty.
- The strengths of American Indian families include an extended-family system, spiritual beliefs, high family cohesion, respect for elders, bilingual language skills, and a tribal support system.
- There is evidence that children who have parents of the same sex will do as well as children in opposite-sex relationships.
- Multiracial marriages are increasing with the increase in diversity in this country.
- Male–female relationships and parent–child struggles are common issues in families from a variety of ethnic groups.
- The issues of assimilation, acculturation, and segregation must be faced by any new ethnic or cultural group.

Key Terms

ethnic group
cultural group
race
cultural identity
foreign born
immigrant
refugee
gay and lesbian family
ethnic identity
cultural competence
kinship
nuclear family
conjugal family system
consanguineal family system
extended family
plural marriage
polygamy
polygyny
polyandry
monogamy
pseudo-kin group
lineage
matrilineal society
patrilineal society
bilateral descent

matriarchal group
patriarchal group
egalitarian group
matrilocal society
patrilocal society
neolocal society
family cohesion
family flexibility
family communication
extended-family system
social system
belief system
historical trauma
cross-cultural family study
ethnocentrism
etic perspective
emic perspective
assimilation
acculturation
segregation
stereotype
prejudice
racism
multiracial marriage

Activities

1. Make a list of your family's strengths. How do they compare with the strengths identified by family researchers?
2. There will be multiple changes in population demographics in the United States over the next 40 years. With a group of classmates, discuss how life in this country will be different from the way it is today.
3. Find people in your class or on campus who have ethnic backgrounds different from yours. Talk with them about what positive and negative things they have experienced because of their membership in this ethnic group.
4. Try to learn more about the challenges and strengths of living in a gay or lesbian family. You might find a family through a gay and lesbian group on your campus who might be willing to talk with you about their family life. Pay particular attention to examples of family members being stigmatized and how they deal with it.

Suggested Readings

Chung, A. Y. (2016). *Saving face: The emotional costs of the Asian immigrant family myth.* Chapel Hill, NC: Rutgers University Press.

Coles, R. L., & Green, C. (2010). *The myth of the missing Black father.* New York, NY: Columbia University Press.

Coontz, S. (Ed.). (2008). *American families: A multicultural reader.* New York, NY: Routledge.

Dalla, R., DeFrain, J., Johnson, J., & Abbott, D. A. (Eds.). (2009). *Strengths and challenges of new immigrant families: Implications for research, education, policy, and service.* Lanham, MD: Lexington Press.

Dreby, J. (2010). *Divided by borders: Mexican migrants and their children.* Berkeley, CA: University of California Press.

Haynes, C., Merolla, J., & Ramakrishnan, S. K. (2016). *Framing immigrants.* New York, NY: Russell Sage Foundation.

Mohatt, G., & Thomas, L. (2006). "I wonder, why would you do it that way?" In J. E. Trimble & C. B. Fisher (Eds.), *The handbook of ethical research with ethnocultural populations and communities.* Thousand Oaks, CA: Sage.

Owings, A. (2011). *Indian voices: Listening to Native Americans.* New Brunswick, NJ: Rutgers University Press.

Putman, R. D. (2015). *Our kids.* New York, NY: Simon & Schuster.

Russell, S. T., & Horn, S. S. (2016). *Sexual orientation, gender identity, and schooling.* New York, NY: Oxford University Press.

Skogrand, L., Hatch, D., & Singh, A. (2009). Strong marriages in Latino culture. In R. Dalla, J. DeFrain, J. Johnson, & D. Abbott (Eds.), *Strengths and challenges of new immigrant families: Implications for research, policy, education, and service.* Lexington, MA: Lexington Books.

Skogrand, L., Mueller, M. L., Arrington, R., LeBlanc, H., Spotted Elk, D., Dayzie, I., & Rosenband, R. (2008). Strong Navajo marriages. *American Indian and Alaska Native Mental Health Research: The Journal of the National Center, 15,* 25–41. Web site: http://www.ucdenver.edu/academics/colleges/PublicHealth/research/centers/CAIANH/journal/Documents/Volume%2015/15(2)_Skogrand_Strong_Navajo_Marriages_25-41.pdf.

Tudge, J. (2008). *The everyday lives of young children: Culture, class, and child rearing in diverse societies.* New York, NY: Cambridge University Press.

Visit the text-specific Online Learning Center at **www.mhhe.com/olson9e** for practice tests, chapter summaries, and PowerPoint slides.

Design Element: © Alicia Grünkind/EyeEm/Getty Images

3 Understanding Marriage and Family Dynamics

- The History of Family Science
- Conceptual Frameworks for Understanding Couples and Families
- Three Key Relationship Concepts
- Couple and Family Map
- Dynamics Change in Relationships over Time
- Summary
- Key Terms
- Activities
- Suggested Readings

There are a variety of perspectives or ways of describing marriage and family dynamics. These perspectives are like different lenses through which we can observe the various aspects of close relationships. Each perspective, or framework, is built on different assumptions and has specific concepts that help define the relevant elements of each framework.

In this chapter we will present six major conceptual frameworks for describing marriage and family dynamics: *the family systems theory, the international family strengths framework, the family development framework, the symbolic interaction framework, the social construction framework*, and *the feminist framework*. We will also take a look at three major dimensions of couple and family dynamics that integrate many of the concepts from the six frameworks; these three central dimensions are cohesion, flexibility, and communication. To conclude, we will discuss the Couple and Family Map, which helps integrate and apply these more abstract frameworks and concepts to specific couple and family relationships.

Before we begin exploring the conceptual frameworks, we will define some of the relevant concepts related to conceptual and theory development. A **conceptual framework** is a set of interconnected ideas, concepts, and assumptions that helps organize thinking from a particular perspective. A **theory** consists of general principles that are composed of interrelated concepts, and **hypotheses** are presumed and testable relationships between variables. A **research study** can be designed to test one or more specific hypotheses.

Most family professionals maintain that there are many ways of looking at families. They use ideas and principles from several different conceptual frameworks to help them understand marriage and family life. This open-minded approach to learning and to life is often termed an *eclectic* approach, and most family researchers, family life educators, and family therapists subscribe to it. However, professionals with an eclectic approach can sometimes be too open and accepting of contradictory ideas.

There are two contrasting approaches to understanding how individuals and families operate: the idiographic approach and the nomothetic approach. Some family scientists maintain that human beings are unique and that it is difficult to construct a broad conceptual framework or theory that applies to all couples and to all families. This view has been labeled the **idiographic approach**, which focuses on the unique aspects of individuals or families. Professionals who use this approach are more interested in individual case studies and tend to have a clinical focus; they spend much of their professional life working directly with families.

On the other end of the theory spectrum is the **nomothetic approach**, which focuses on ideas that apply to the majority of individuals or families. Researchers using this approach try to develop a broader understanding of couples and families and to work toward a general theory. Both of these approaches have value and usefulness, because every marriage and every family *is* unique and yet has much in common with others. This textbook looks at families from both an idiographic perspective and a nomothetic perspective.

The History of Family Science

The field of family science (also called family studies) began many years ago, focusing on family relationships. Currently it is a multidisciplinary field integrating research from multiple areas. There have been changes in focus and content over the years, but many of the issues remain the same.

Family Science in the Early Years

Family science is a multidisciplinary field that originated almost 80 years ago. The National Council on Family Relations (NCFR), one of the major professional organizations in the field, was founded in 1938 and focuses on family research, practice, and education (ncfr.org). The first journal published by NCFR was called *Living,* and has evolved to a journal called *Journal of Marriage and Family.* In 1952, NCFR added a second journal that focused less on research and more on the application of research to family life. The earliest version of the journal was called *The Coordinator;* this evolved into a journal that is currently known as *Family Relations.* In 2009, NCFR added a third journal entitled *Journal of Family Theory & Review,* which focuses on all aspects of family theory.

The American Association for Marital and Family Therapy (AAMFT), which was founded in 1942, is made up of marriage and family therapists who focus on increasing understanding, research, and education and on helping individuals, couples, and families who have problems (aamft.org). Although most of their work involves therapy with individuals and families, marriage and family therapists also provided education for couples and families. They began publishing a journal entitled *Journal of Marital and Family Therapy* in 1975.

There are several journals in addition to those published by NCFR and AAMFT that are well known in the family science field and are widely read by family social scientists. Some of those journals include *Marriage and Family Review, Journal of Family Issues,* and *Family Process.* Others come from psychology and include the *Journal of Family Psychology.* Because family science is an interdisciplinary field, there are also journals in social work, education, communication studies, anthropology, and many other fields that have relevance for family science.

Family life education has also evolved as a part of family science. Early work included sex education for youth, with later educational programs focusing on parent education and marriage enrichment. In recent years there has been an increased focus on couple and relationship education (Administration for Children and Families, 2016), with federal funding supporting marriage education.

A study of the first three volumes of *Living* (Volume 1, 1939; Volume 2, 1940; Volume 3, 1941), which evolved into what is currently the *Journal of Marriage and Family,* places family science in its historical context (Osborn, 1939). Many of the issues in these first three volumes are similar to the issues that we still highlight in current family science literature. For example, there were concerns about the impacts of poverty and inadequate housing on family life. There were concerns about instability, focusing on the high divorce rate of that time, about 18%. Compare this to about 40% to 50% today (American Psychological Association, 2016). There were discussions about the need for casework and family counseling to help all families, but particularly poor families. There were also articles about what it takes to have a good marriage and the importance of healthy relationships to avoid divorce. Having healthy parent–child relationships also received attention in family science in the early years.

There were also topics that are no longer focused on in current family science literature. For example, there were several articles about **eugenics**, which refers to breeding to improve inherited characteristics. There was concern that contraception be available to limit births in cases where genetic defects would likely be inherited (Osborn, 1939). These articles used terms such as "superior heredity capacity," "physical, mental and social inadequacy," and "hereditary defectives, borderline cases, and persons with marked ability" (p. 34). There were also several articles describing marriage courses that had been successfully implemented at colleges and universities and explaining why these courses were successful. Authors indicated concerns about youths and the problems they were encountering. Mention is made of the Civilian Conservation Corps (CCC), which provided work, structure, and a small amount of money each month for young men, and at the same time provided service to the country and money for the young men's low-income families.

Although the concerns about the demise of the family were similar to what we experience today, the cause of those concerns might have been different. An article by Goldstein (1940, p. 9) describes the reasons for the "disorganization of the family":

> That the family is in danger today there can be no doubt in the minds of those who know the facts. Growing tensions and discords and disruptions in family relationships; the deepening rebellion of children; the widening revolt of women; the increasing restlessness of men; the almost incredible multiplication of estrangements, separations and divorces—and these are the symptoms of a serious disorganization in family life.

One author, in an article entitled *Seven Pillars of Family Strength,* identified the seven things that made families strong in the early years of family science (Faris, 1940). The seven pillars were (1) laws of the land about marriage and family life, (2) church, (3) schools, (4) neighborhoods, (5) communities, (6) welfare organizations, and (7) what they were learning through research about the problems of human nature, personality, and family life. It is interesting to note that six out of seven of these pillars are social structures and institutions outside of the family itself. And, because research about marriage and family was just beginning and was very limited, it was viewed as only a small part of what helps families.

Some of the articles in the early days of the field of family science provided very limited research evidence. The research that was conducted was both qualitative and quantitative. And many articles were simply the thoughts of the authors, making arguments for a stand they were taking on a particular issue. All things considered, these early writings show clearly where we began as a field nearly 80 years ago, and they provide a foundation that we continue to build upon today.

Family Science Today

The growing impact of the family profession is indicated by how many other professional groups now focus on family-oriented topics. Table 3.1 illustrates the topics and issues that

TABLE 3.1 Disciplines Contributing to Family Science

Discipline	Topics in Family Science
Anthropology	Cross-cultural studies; kinship; diversity in families
Biology	Conception and reproduction; growth, development, and aging
Child development	Development of infant and child; parenting
Communication studies	Family communication
Economics	Family finances; consumer behavior
Education	Family life education; marriage education
English	Marriages and families in literature (present and past)
History	Historical perspectives on the family throughout time
Human ecology	Ecosystem perspectives on family, nutrition, housing, and clothing
Law	Marriage and divorce laws; child custody laws
Medicine	Families and health; family practice
Psychiatry	Family therapy
Psychology	Family psychology; assessment of couples and families
Social work	Treating problem families; family policy
Sociology	Marriage and divorce statistics; sociological theories about families

the traditional disciplines are now studying and are making significant contributions. Increasingly, professionals from these other disciplines are now specializing in marriage and family. For example, there are lawyers who now specialize in family law. Even in the medical profession, there is a specialty that focuses on the family called *family practice*.

There is a growing awareness of the importance of close relationships in a person's life. Studies of personal happiness have consistently revealed that close relationships are the most important aspects of life and are essential to emotional well-being and good physical health (Berscheid, 2006, 2010). Conversely, many studies have documented that a troubled relationship, especially a distressed marriage and family, is the most common presenting problem of those seeking therapy.

While psychologists have traditionally focused on understanding individuals, family science is focused on *relationships*. The growing interest in relationship science was identified by Ellen Berscheid, a well-known social psychologist, who emphasizes the importance of studying interactions and interconnections between people (Berscheid, 2006, 2010). Relationship science assumes that a relationship is dynamic and resides between people and not within a person.

Relationships are the essence of life. "We are born into relationships, we live our lives in relationships with others, and when we die, the effects of our relationships survive in the lives of the living" (Berscheid, 2006). It is for this reason that there is increasing interest in family science, which focuses on studying, understanding, and helping to strengthen all types of close relationships.

Conceptual Frameworks for Understanding Couples and Families

This chapter will describe a variety of models or ways of understanding couples and families, which are called *conceptual frameworks*. (See Box 3.1 for a discussion of these theories and research.) The most popular of the conceptual frameworks is the *family systems theory*, which focuses on the family as an ongoing system of interconnected members. (Because it is a broad and comprehensive set of principles, this perspective is referred to more often as a theory than as a conceptual framework.) The *international family strengths framework* is becoming more accepted because it highlights from a global perspective the positive aspects of couples and families rather than only looking at their problems. The *family development framework* looks at how couples and families change over time. The *symbolic interaction framework* has historically been valuable to family professionals because it examines how family members learn roles and rules in our society. The *social construction framework*, which is growing in popularity, maintains that our views as partners and family members are shaped by our social world and that each of us has a different life experience and therefore a unique view of our own close relationships. The *feminist framework* is increasingly important to the family field because it emphasizes the value of women's perspectives on marriage and family life and on society.

Family Systems Theory

Everything that happens to you, happens to me.

—Nikki DeFrain

According to **family systems theory**, everything that happens to any family member has an impact on everyone else in the family (Goldenberg, Stanton, & Goldenberg, 2016). Because family members are interconnected and operate as a group, the group is called a

family system. This approach to describing the family as a system has become very popular in both theory and practice, particularly with family therapists who work with couples and families having relationship problems.

A pioneer family therapist Carl Whitaker was fond of saying that in a metaphorical sense "there are no individuals in the world—only fragments of families." In other words, individual human beings are inextricably tied to their family. How people think and behave is deeply influenced by their family background, and people are best understood by understanding their family. From a family therapist's standpoint, an individual can most effectively change if his or her family also changes. If a family is in trouble, both parents and children need to become involved in family therapy (Edwards, 2014; Whitaker, 2016).

When an individual has a problem, not only the family but also the whole community is often involved in finding a solution, an idea echoed in the popular statement "It takes a whole village to raise a child." A family simply cannot do it all alone. Troubled families often live in troubled communities, and if individuals are to be well, the community must find a way to create health for all its members.

Family systems theory grew out of the general systems theory, a conceptual framework developed in the 1960s by Ludwig von Bertalanffy (1968), and family therapists applied these ideas to marriage and family as a system. The **general systems theory**, a broad-based model used in a variety of fields, is a set of principles and concepts that can be applied to all types of systems, living and nonliving. The dictionary defines a **system** as (1) a set or arrangement of things so related or connected as to form a unity or organic whole and (2) a whole made of interacting parts.

Family systems theory was created by family therapists because family therapists working with troubled individuals over the years discovered that working with an individual alone did not produce long-term change in a child's behavior. A problem child might make some improvements in her or his functioning by working alone with the therapist, but the child often reverted back to problem behaviors unless the family changed. This is because the family system has such a powerful impact on a child's behavior.

Another important finding by family therapists was that when a child has problems, often there are problems in the family system. For example, family therapists have found that if there is a disturbed child in a two-parent family, there is often a troubled marriage or couple relationship which contributes to the child's difficulties.

A Hierarchy of Connected Systems. Proponents of the family systems theory have expanded on ideas and terminology developed by general systems theorists, and family therapists use these ideas in their practice. Several concepts of the general systems theory are particularly relevant to family systems. The idea of **multiple system levels** is that systems are embedded within other systems. Whenever attention is focused on a given system, a **suprasystem** (a larger system) and a **subsystem** (a smaller system) are usually also involved. If you are focusing on the couple as the system, the suprasystem is the family and the subsystem consists of the two individuals. If you are focusing on the nuclear family as the system, the suprasystem is the extended family and the subsystem is the couple or any other dyadic (two-person) unit, such as parent and child.

Systems are both connected to and separated from other systems by **boundaries**. The notion of a boundary also implies a hierarchy of interconnected systems, each system being separated by invisible boundaries from other smaller or larger systems (Goldenberg et al., 2016). Considering the family, there is a boundary between the family and the larger kin system and a boundary between parents and the children.

BOX 3.1 Putting It Together
Theories and Research

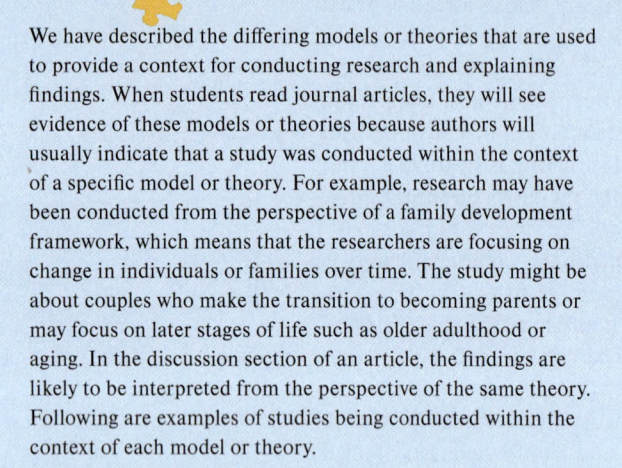

We have described the differing models or theories that are used to provide a context for conducting research and explaining findings. When students read journal articles, they will see evidence of these models or theories because authors will usually indicate that a study was conducted within the context of a specific model or theory. For example, research may have been conducted from the perspective of a family development framework, which means that the researchers are focusing on change in individuals or families over time. The study might be about couples who make the transition to becoming parents or may focus on later stages of life such as older adulthood or aging. In the discussion section of an article, the findings are likely to be interpreted from the perspective of the same theory. Following are examples of studies being conducted within the context of each model or theory.

Family Systems Theory

Research by Dolbin-MacNab and Keiley focused on relationships of adolescents who were raised solely by their grandparents (Dolbin-MacNab, 2016; Dolbin-MacNab & Keiley, 2009). The specific relationships that were analyzed were those between the child and the parents who did not raise the child and the child and the grandparents who did raise the child. The study used the ecological approach of systems theory to create the context of multiple environmental systems that influenced the child. Adolescents who were raised by grandparents became the most important people within the inner circle of the family system. The parents may be in one of the outer circles, depending upon their involvement with the adolescent.

In the discussion, these authors described the importance of community services and organizations in the outer circles that could be of help to these adolescents as they experience several sources of stress.

International Family Strengths Framework

A study conducted by Skogrand, Mueller, Arrington et al. (2008) focused on the components of strong marriages in the Navajo (Dineh) culture. This study used research about positive cultural characteristics of American Indians to develop the interview questions for the study, and the questions focused on what was going well in these marriages within their cultural context, rather than what was not going well. Navajo couples were interviewed so they could tell their stories about their marriages, and five components of strong marriages were identified: maintaining communication, nurturing the relationship, learning about marriage, being prepared for marriage, and having a strong foundation. The findings of this study were used to create a couple activity book (Skogrand, Mueller, Crook, et al., 2007) that other Navajo couples could use to strengthen their marriages.

Family Development Framework

The transition to parenthood has been identified as a key transition in the life cycle of families. This transition has been found to be stressful because of the reorganization that must occur in the family. The need to care for the child can also decrease marital happiness. Claxton and Perry-Jenkins (2008)

Human systems have many different system levels that can be characterized as a set of concentric circles (Figure 3.1). For example, the smallest circle at the center would be the individual; encircling this in graduated rings would be the couple (a dyad, or two-person human system), the family, the local neighborhood (including businesses, schools, etc.), the town, the nation, the continent, the world, and so on. Families do not function in a vacuum because they are a part of larger systems.

Thinking about human systems is considered an ecological approach; **ecology** is the study of how all the organisms in a system are related to each other. As Figure 3.1 illustrates, all the concentric circles are connected to one another and the people in each of the circles influence the people in the other circles—creating a **human ecosystem**. To really understand a specific family system, you also need to consider the various system levels it influences and that influence it. For these reasons, helping a middle-class, suburban family through a crisis would be a very different process from helping a family living in poverty in the inner city.

Another concept from general systems theory is **wholeness**, the concept that the whole is more than the sum of its parts. From a family systems perspective, the whole family is more

examined the effects of becoming parents on leisure patterns for dual-earner, working-class couples. They found that both husbands and wives experienced a decline in independent and shared leisure immediately after the birth of the child. Couples began to increase their leisure activities when the wife returned to work, but couples never fully returned to their previous level of leisure before the baby was born. These authors also found that a decrease in shared leisure during the transition to parenthood was associated with more positive marital outcomes.

Symbolic Interaction Framework

The role of trust in intimate unions of low-income mothers was the focus of a study conducted by Burton, Cherlin, Winn, Estacion, and Holder-Taylor (2009). This study was guided by the symbolic interaction framework and examined trust in developing intimate relationships. They found that although these women generally did not trust men, they developed differing types of intimate relationships depending upon the role and function men played in their lives. These researchers found that four forms of interpersonal trust emerged in the women: suspended, compartmentalized, misplaced, and integrated. This study was conducted within the context of shared meanings and definitions of the situations and the roles men played in their lives.

Social Construction Framework

One study examined how lesbian mothers perceived their young children's parental preferences when one mother was the biological parent and the other mother was not (Goldberg, Downing, & Sauck, 2008). The findings of the study indicated that as infants these children preferred the birth mother, due to factors such as breast-feeding which resulted in differing amounts of time spent with the birth mother compared to the nonbiological mother. As children grew older, however, they typically did not have a preference. In this case the social processes of the children changed when time spent with their mothers was not based upon biology. The children's social world changed, and so did the relationships with their mothers.

Feminist Framework

Hill, Freedman, and Enright (2007) have written a journal article about feminist theory and forgiveness. They describe a forgiveness therapy model that includes the uncovering phase, the decision phase, the work phase, and the deepening phase. It has been suggested that the use of this model with clients in therapy has yielded positive results. Feminist critics have said this model should not be used with some women clients who have been exploited by men, because it perpetuates traditional gender roles—that is it advocates change for women victims by having them forgive rather than having male offenders make changes. The authors provide an in-depth description of how the forgiveness therapy model could be modified to include and address the issues identified by feminist critics. For example, the therapist should make sure that there is no pressure, but rather free choice, for a woman to forgive a male offender, since women have historically been expected to forgive men.

than the total of all its individual members. This means that you cannot know the family simply by knowing each person as an individual because each individual will behave differently outside the family (Goldenberg et al., 2016).

For example, Carla, a student living in an apartment, has a certain identity related to her life at college and another identity back home with her family. If you observe Carla very carefully in her college environment, you get a good understanding of what she is like at college. But when Carla goes home to visit her family for a holiday break, she becomes a different person in many ways. She is transformed into a daughter, a granddaughter, a big sister, a little sister. At home she may return to some of the ways she previously behaved at home, even though she does not continue that pattern at school. This is partly because, although she might have changed in college, the family did not change, and when the family is all together again she fills the role she played in the family to create the wholeness of the family.

A good cook takes individual herbs, spices, and vegetables and combines them to create a wonderful and zesty sauce that has flavors of the individual ingredients but is more than and different from the separate ingredients. The whole family system is also more than the sum of its parts, and the family's behavior cannot be predicted from knowing only the individual persons. Conversely, it is difficult to predict the behavior of the individuals by knowing about the family as a whole.

FIGURE 3.1
An Ecological Approach to Human Systems

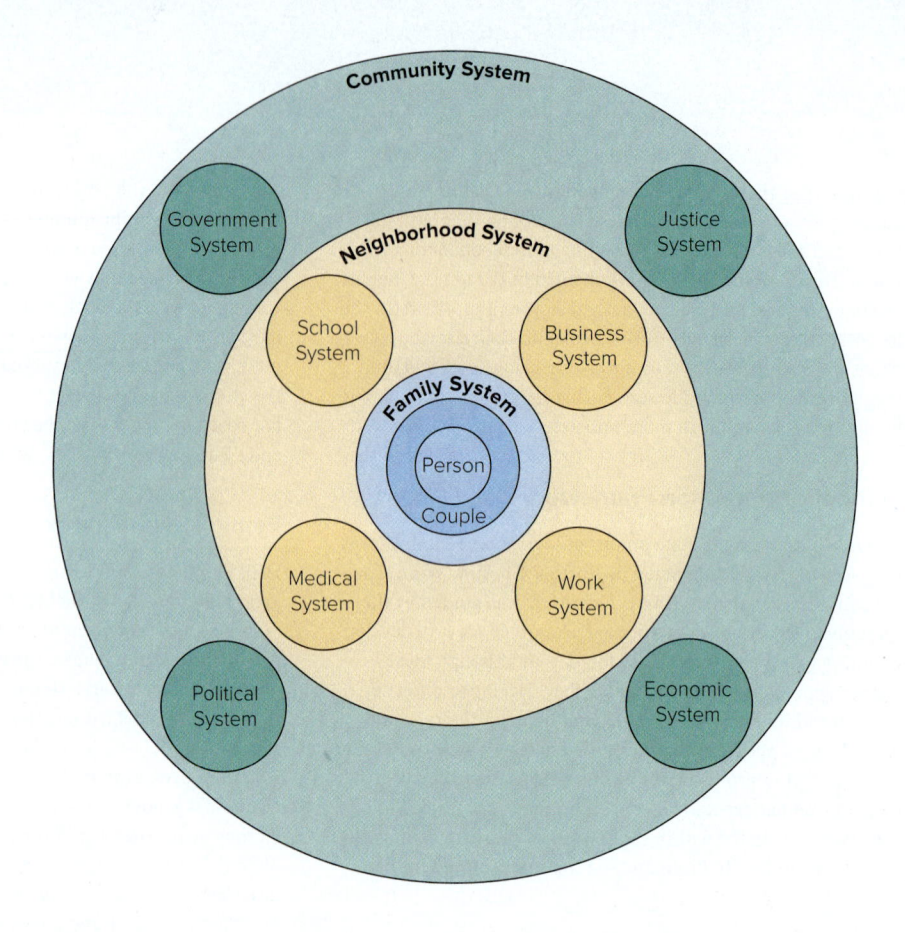

Another concept of the general systems theory is the **interdependence of parts**: The parts or elements of a system are interconnected in such a way that if one part is changed, other parts are also affected (Goldenberg et al., 2016). Visualize for a moment a mobile, an artistic creation suspended in midair, made up of many carefully balanced elements. Each element in the mobile is weighted and placed in such a way as to create not only an aesthetic effect but also a delicate system that can be easily set in motion by a slight ripple of wind or a soft touch. Anything stronger might knock it out of balance.

Healthy families, in a sense, are like a mobile: Each member fits into the whole in a unique way and adds to the beauty of the whole. If one individual changes—for better or worse—the total creation is affected. Consider how one event changed the family in the story presented in Box 3.2.

Flexibility: Balancing Stability and Change. Flexibility is the ability of a system to balance both stability and change. A flexible couple or family is like a flower in the wind because it is able to bend with the wind. General systems theorists use the term **open system**, or **morphogenic system**, when referring to a system that is open to growth and change. A **closed system**, or **morphostatic system**, is one that has the capacity to maintain the status quo, thus avoiding change (Goldenberg et al., 2016).

Family therapists have discovered that many couples and families are highly resistant to change, even though they need to adapt to solve the problems they face. They are likely to want to maintain the status quo out of habit, lack of insight, or fear of something new. A common observation is when one family member changes, there is also change in the other family members.

Part I | The Social Context of Intimate Relationships

> **BOX 3.2 Putting It Together**
>
> ## Reorganization of the Family System After a Car Accident
>
> Like other families affected by sudden changes, Julia's family will probably never return to the way things were before an accident occurred. But as Julia's case shows, the nuclear family, with the help of extended-family members, is capable of establishing a more connected family system.
>
> Julia was a single parent living with her two young children, Camille and Katy. Their life together was a hectic but satisfying round of school, work, family visits, and activities with friends. A year ago, Julia was involved in an auto accident and was seriously injured. She could neither work nor care for her children. Her family's delicate balance was upset until her mother, Eloise, her brother Tim, her sister Allison, and her best friend at work, Sheryl, all stepped in to help create a new sense of family balance.
>
> These four adults spent countless hours at the hospital, reassuring Julia and listening to her express her uncertainty and pain. They also worked out some new arrangements to make up for her absence. Camille and Katy temporarily moved in with Eloise. She took care of them, prepared their meals, made sure they had clean clothes for school, and took over many details of their lives. Tim, who lived nearby, drove Camille and Katy to and from school and took care of them afterward. Allison, who still lived at home, got them to bed at night and took them on outings on the weekends. Camille and Katy took on some new responsibilities themselves, like walking the dog and doing their homework without prompting. Sheryl kept things going at the office by taking on several of Julia's responsibilities herself.
>
> After an initial period of confusion and difficulty, all these individuals became familiar with their new roles and proud of their new skills. Julia was hospitalized for several weeks and had physical therapy for several months, but eventually she regained her strength and her courage. When she returned home, the whole family celebrated. In the months that followed, she established a new balance with her children, assimilating the experiences they had all had since the accident. She also had a stronger network of friends and family than she had before the accident.

As an example of a morphostatic system, consider the following story. By failing to deal openly and effectively with their relationship problems, Katherine and Ken are beginning a free fall into despair. They are an example of a morphostatic family system, unable or unwilling to change. A morphogenic system, one open to growth and change, might have been able to prevent such a scenario.

> *Ken and Katherine have been married for 15 years. Ken is an alcoholic, though he manages to hold on to his job as a floor supervisor at a printing plant. Ken has been having an extramarital affair with Winona a coworker at the plant, for 6 months. When Katherine discovers the affair, she tells Ken she is leaving him. He responds by begging for forgiveness and promising to give up the relationship with Winona.*
>
> *He wants to avoid divorce for a number of reasons: embarrassment at work, shame in his extended family, and severe financial consequences. Besides, although the thrill is gone from the marriage, he and Katherine have a long history together, and she is a good mother to their three children. Katherine is skeptical of Ken's promises. She tells him that she wants him to give up drinking as well. He says he can control his drinking and just drink "socially." He doesn't really need to go "cold turkey," he argues.*
>
> *Katherine remains skeptical; she has heard such arguments many times before. In spite of her skepticism, however, Katherine decides to forgive Ken, as she has before, and to stay. She genuinely loves him, even though she hates his drinking and, now, his seeing another woman. And he provides a good income for her and the children. Katherine also fears being on her own, both socially and financially. She dreads the thought of going back into the workplace after so many years at home. Whatever she has now, she feels, is better than what she would have as a divorced mother of three.*

The family systems framework assumes that systems operate on a continuum from extreme morphostasis to extreme morphogenesis. In a healthy system, there is a balance between these extremes. The couple or family needs to be open to change, but not to the point of being rootless or chaotic. Conversely, it needs to be centered and stable, but not to the point of being rigid.

Cohesion: Balance of Separateness and Connectedness. Couples and families need to find a balance between their separateness as individuals and their connectedness as a system. The dynamics that help systems maintain this separateness–connectedness balance are the opposing forces of centrifugal and centripetal interactions. **Centrifugal interactions** tend to push family members apart, thereby increasing separateness. **Centripetal interactions** pull family members together and increase family closeness (Goldenberg et al., 2016).

Family therapists have found that a family crisis can push families to an extreme of either centripetal or centrifugal interactions. Faced with a death of a family member, one family may pull together and come out stronger as a result of the loss, whereas another family may find itself torn apart by the events. The first family resolves to hold onto each other, communicate about feelings, and help each other. These centripetal interactions strengthen the bonds of love and concern. The members of the second family are afraid, cannot talk with one another, and attempt to deal with the death as individuals. They separate from the family and look for comfort outside it, or they bury themselves in personal despair.

An important aspect of understanding cohesion is whether a family system permits family members to develop their own independence from the family. In the personal account of a young Chicana woman recounted in Box 3.3, you will see that in her close Chicano family, most of the family system is opposed to a female (Julie) getting too much education. However, her mother and her husband are very supportive and enabled Julie to continue graduate school and develop her own independence within a very close family system.

Family therapists agree that a healthy balance of separateness and connectedness works best for families in crisis. In the face of death, family members can draw on each other's strengths and skills for comfort and at the same time seek out positive people in the community who can be growth enhancing for the family as a whole. If family members choose to go their separate ways as a result of the crisis, the likelihood of a positive outcome for the family as a whole lessens considerably.

Families that spend time together and enjoy fun activities build stronger relationships.
©Tanya Constantine/Blend Images/Getty Images

80   Part I   The Social Context of Intimate Relationships

BOX 3.3 Diversity in Families
Cultural Conflicts for a Female Chicana College Student

I am a Chicana graduate student who wants to complete a Ph.D. in family studies so I can teach at the college level and help the family field be more inclusive and up-to-date regarding Chicano families. Fortunately, the choices I've made are not in conflict with my family of procreation.

It was very difficult for my family of origin initially to understand why I wanted or needed to go to school for so long. Since my grandparents and parents struggled just to provide for adequate housing, food, and clothing, they find it difficult to see why education is so important. They were also somewhat threatened by the fact that I wanted to study families because I might learn too much.

Another conflict was regarding my interest in my own development versus their emphasis on the whole family. They felt I was focusing too much on myself and not giving back enough to the family. Also, they felt this was making me more competitive and less cooperative, which is a quality valued highly. Another issue is the use of the Spanish language and whether I would use both Spanish and English in my home. Since we decided to raise our children using English only, some family members viewed that choice as rejecting our heritage. Also, as my years of college education increased, my relatives tended to distance themselves more from me.

Fortunately, my husband, who is also Chicano, is totally supportive and is a house husband for our two small children. He takes care of the children, and I am the primary wage earner. This is not the traditional family model for most Chicanos, and so it does challenge some of our other family members and kin.

While I was not initially aware of the importance of my mother's support, I have lately become even more appreciative of her encouraging words. I have finally been giving her more credit for her support. She also served as a positive role model since she began working full-time when I was young. She also has strongly encouraged me to work outside the home and even to try to seek a career.

In general, I have made it because I am determined to have a professional career and have the strong support of my husband and my mother. My other relatives are less understanding and supportive since they question my goals and values. In spite of it all, education is necessary for me to help advance myself and my family.

Source: Julie Palacio, former graduate student in Family Social Science, University of Minnesota, St. Paul, MN.

Feedback Within the System (Communication). Another basic principle of the general systems theory is that communication in the system is essential. No matter how hard one might try, one simply cannot *not* communicate (Becvar & Becvar, 2013). Even if we completely withdraw from our family, we are communicating an important message: the family is not a safe, healthy, or happy place to live.

Family systems function better when important information is regularly exchanged among the members, which is the essence of communication. General systems theorists talk about information feedback loops, which can be either positive or negative (Goldenberg et al., 2016). **Positive feedback** in families is intended to create change, whereas **negative feedback** is designed to minimize change and keep things the same. Feedback can come either from family members or from people outside the family.

The words *positive* and *negative* do not connote value judgments or indicate whether a change is good or bad but rather whether change occurs in the system or not. For example, Sandy suggests that the members of her family exchange jobs around the house to add variety and give everyone a better understanding of what the various jobs entail. If Sandy's family members accept this idea and change their routine, then Sandy's feedback to the system is considered positive. However, if they resist her idea of change, the system feedback is negative.

In sum, openness to change is a key concept in the family systems framework. A common reaction of some couples and families under stress is to look inward and try to prevent new information or people from coming into the system. This would be an example of negative feedback because they are resisting change. When under stress, families would be helped if they were more open to change, which is an example of positive feedback.

International Family Strengths Framework

The **international family strengths framework** focuses on how couples and families succeed rather than on why they fail, from a global perspective (DeFrain & Asay, 2007; DeFrain et al., 2012). This perspective arose from the notion that strong families can serve as models for other families wanting to succeed. One advantage of the international family strengths framework is that it tends to change the nature of what one finds in families. Simply stated, if one studies only problems, one finds only couple and family problems. Similarly, if researchers and therapists are interested in couple and family strengths, they have to look for them. When these strengths are identified, they can be the foundation for continued growth and change.

Family therapists and other counselors are finding the international family strengths framework helpful in treating family problems (DeFrain, Cook, & Gonzalez-Kruger, 2005; Marsh, 2003). Many professionals have found that just solving problems is not enough. They need a model of healthy family development as a goal for troubled families to work toward. Identifying a family's strengths also boosts morale among family members.

The most extensive series of studies of family strengths hs been conducted by Nick Stinnett, John DeFrain, and colleagues around the world (DeFrain & Asay, 2007). In more than 40 years of work, the researchers have collected data from more than 29,000 family members in the United States and 39 countries, representing every major geocultural area of the world. Stinnett and DeFrain propose that six major qualities are commonly present in strong families (Table 3.2). These qualities are appreciation and affection, commitment, positive communication, enjoyable time together, spiritual well-being and shared values, and the ability to manage stress and crisis effectively.

All these family strengths are interrelated, overlap to some degree, and interact. Appreciation and affection for one another make family members more likely to spend

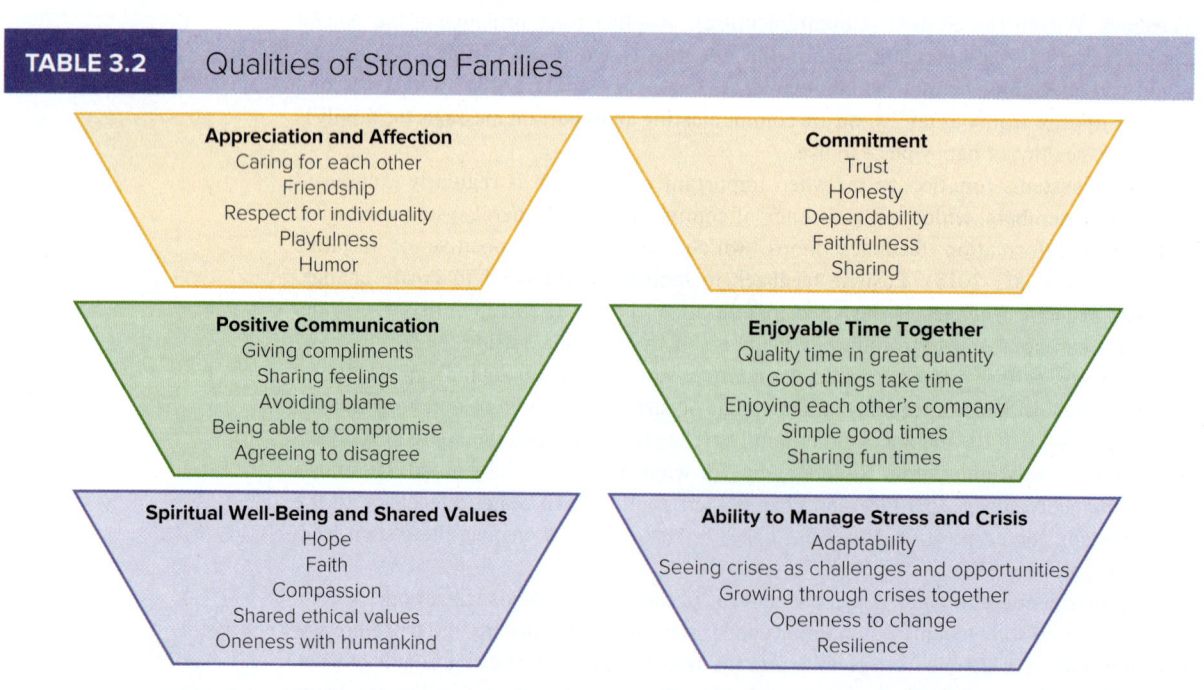

TABLE 3.2 Qualities of Strong Families

Appreciation and Affection
Caring for each other
Friendship
Respect for individuality
Playfulness
Humor

Commitment
Trust
Honesty
Dependability
Faithfulness
Sharing

Positive Communication
Giving compliments
Sharing feelings
Avoiding blame
Being able to compromise
Agreeing to disagree

Enjoyable Time Together
Quality time in great quantity
Good things take time
Enjoying each other's company
Simple good times
Sharing fun times

Spiritual Well-Being and Shared Values
Hope
Faith
Compassion
Shared ethical values
Oneness with humankind

Ability to Manage Stress and Crisis
Adaptability
Seeing crises as challenges and opportunities
Growing through crises together
Openness to change
Resilience

Source: DeFrain, J. & Asay, S. M., *Strong Families Around the World: Strengths-Based Research and Perspectives*. The Haworth Press, Taylor & Francis, 2007.

time together, and time together is enhanced by positive communication. Communication enhances commitment, and commitment leads to spending more time together. A feeling of spiritual well-being gives people the confidence to weather a crisis, and the ability to manage crises makes family members appreciate each other more. Family strengths are thus interconnected like a large, complex puzzle. Let's look at each strength in more detail.

Appreciation and Affection. People in strong families care deeply for one another, and they let each other know this regularly. Many people, however, don't express **appreciation and affection** in their families. Consider the response of one spouse: "She cooked dinner every evening, but it never occurred to me to thank her for it. She doesn't thank me for going to work every day." Such an attitude is unfortunate, because expressing affection and giving and receiving sincere thanks foster a positive atmosphere and help people get along better. A pat on the back, a smile, or a hug builds a bond of caring. One member of a strong family explained it this way: "He makes me feel good about me and about us as a couple. Very few days go by without him saying something positive."

People in dysfunctional families more often focus on the negative. These people gain energy by feeding off the self-esteem and good feelings of others. They believe that by putting other people down they can build themselves up. This approach usually backfires, however, often producing only countercriticism.

Researchers have found that sexual behavior in strong marriages is often a form of expressing appreciation for each other. "Foreplay does not begin at 10:30 P.M. on Saturday night," one husband explained. "It begins when I take out the garbage on Wednesday morning, when I cook dinner on Friday night, and when I help Jeannie solve a problem at her work on Saturday afternoon." Sex is a natural way to express warm feelings for the partner. Another person reported, "The times when sex was best have been times when we've felt especially close and in tune with each other, when we'd solved a problem or when we were working on a project together."

The international family strengths framework focuses on the positive qualities of families. Apparent in this family are such strengths as warmth, caring, appreciation, affection, trust, commitment, and enjoyment of each other's company.
©Kali9/E+/Getty Images

Chapter 3 | Understanding Marriage and Family Dynamics 83

Commitment. Members of strong families generally show a strong **commitment** to one another, investing time and energy in family activities and not letting their work or other priorities take too much time away from family interaction. "My wife and kids are the most important part of my life," one father said in describing commitment. Another noted that "what we have as a family is a treasure." Commitment does not mean, however, that family members stifle each other. "We give each other the freedom and encouragement to pursue individual goals," one wife noted. "Yet either of us would cut out activities or goals that threatened our time together."

Commitment includes sexual fidelity. Some of the people interviewed by the researchers admitted to having engaged in an extramarital affair earlier in the marriage. Some believed the affair precipitated a crisis that in the final analysis led to a stronger marriage. But marriages can change for the better without a crisis of such major proportions. "Being faithful to each other sexually is just a part of being honest with each other," one young woman noted. Honesty, indeed, is the best policy.

Positive Communication. When people are asked to list the qualities they consider essential to a strong family, most list **positive communication**. Yet many families don't spend much time talking to one another. Although successful families are often task oriented, identifying problems and discussing how to solve them, family members also spend time talking with and listening to one another just to stay connected. Some of the most important talk occurs when no one is working at communication. Open-ended, rambling conversations can reveal important information. How does your teenager feel about sex? Her grades? Her future? When parents and children get comfortable with each other, important issues arise.

Communication does not always produce agreement in strong families. Family members have differences and conflicts, but they speak directly and honestly about them without blaming each other. They try to resolve their differences but may agree to disagree. Dysfunctional families, on the other hand, are either overly critical and hostile in their communication with each other or deny problems and avoid verbal conflict. Although verbal hostilities are not productive, neither is avoidance of problems.

Studies reveal that communication in healthy families has several important aspects. Members of strong families are good at listening. "I'd much rather listen to other people talk," one father explained. "I learn a lot more when I'm listening to my loved ones than I do when I'm talking *at* them." Family members are also adept at asking questions, and they do not try to read one another's minds. Members of strong families also understand that people's views of the world change, and this can be a good thing.

Humor is another important aspect of healthy family communication. Strong families like to laugh. A study of 304 mothers, fathers, and teenagers revealed that humor is a valuable source of family strength. Wuerffel, DeFrain, and Stinnett (1990) reviewed the scientific literature on humor and found that humor can be used in many different positive and negative ways. Humor can reduce daily tension, facilitate conversations, express feelings of warmth and affection, lessen anxiety, point out mistakes made by others, and entertain. It can also help put others at ease and help maintain a positive outlook on life.

The study found positive correlations between the use of humor and how strong the families were based on their responses to a family strengths inventory. The stronger the family, the more likely the family members were to use humor to maintain a positive outlook on life, to entertain each other, to reduce tension, to express warmth, to put others at ease, to facilitate conversations, to lessen anxiety, and to help cope with difficult situations. The stronger families in the study reported negative effects, however, when humor was used to put down other family members. Put-downs and sarcasm were used less often by the stronger families.

The study concluded that families benefit from humor that points out the incongruous aspects of life—the inconsistent, bizarre, silly, illogical things that happen to people every day. Families, however, do not benefit from humor that places someone in a superior position or from sarcasm aimed at demeaning a family member. Sarcasm is often an attempt to mask anger; it is rarely used out of love.

Enjoyable Time Together. "What do you think makes a happy family?" a researcher asked 1,500 schoolchildren. Few replied that money or cars or fancy homes or television sets made a happy family. The most frequent response? A happy family is one that does things together and spends **enjoyable time together**. Although the response seems simple enough, family therapists see many couples and families who haven't figured this out. "I don't have a lot of time with my family," many people like to say, "but I try to make it quality time."

Happy memories result from quality time spent together in considerable quantity: "I remember stories Mom and Dad told me when they tucked me into bed." "Going with Dad to work on the farm. I felt so important." "Singing together—we had an old piano, and I

Spending fun time together and expressing love and affection are key components of strong families.
©Thinkstock Images/Stockbyte/Getty Images

Chapter 3 | Understanding Marriage and Family Dynamics

learned to play, and we would all sing corny old songs." "Vacation. We would go 50 miles to the lake and rent a cabin, and Dad would swim with us."

These happy memories share common threads. First, happiness often centers on activities that are shared as a family. Second, pleasurable time together often centers on simple activities that don't cost a lot of money. Strong families identified these popular family activities: meals together, house and yard chores, and outdoor recreation, including camping, playing catch and other yard games, canoeing, hiking, and picnicking.

Meaningful family rituals are one of the ways family members are brought together. Family rituals have been linked with positive outcomes for families, including greater marital and family satisfaction and better adjustment in children (Leon & Jacobvitz, 2003). Family rituals range from daily and weekly events like family dinners and weekend routines to family traditions like celebrating birthdays and holidays. These rituals contribute to a greater feeling of connection and stability in the family.

Spiritual Well-Being and Shared Values. Perhaps the most controversial finding of the family strengths researchers is the importance of religion or spirituality in strong families. Some families call this **spiritual well-being**. Others talk about faith in God, hope, or optimism about life. Some say they feel a oneness with the world. Others talk about their families in almost religious terms, describing the love they feel for one another as sacred. Others express these kinds of feelings in terms of ethical values and commitment to important causes.

Spiritual well-being can be the caring center within each individual that promotes sharing, love, and compassion. Spiritual well-being is the feeling or force that helps people transcend themselves. "I feel my family is a part of all the families of the world," said one respondent. An important aspect of membership in a religious or spiritual group is the caring, supportive community it provides. When illness strikes, a baby is born, or an accident occurs, friends in the group are often quick to help each other.

It is important to distinguish between *spiritual* and *religious* when talking about spiritual well-being. Spiritual beliefs can be seen as very personal, private beliefs individuals hold. Religious beliefs, in contrast, can be seen as being linked to a particular religious denomination or faith. Thus, some people would think of themselves as being spiritual but not religious, indicating that they have a strong personal belief system but are not connected to a religious institution. And other people would think of themselves as being *both* spiritual and religious, having a very personal belief system while being active in a religious institution. While spiritual beliefs focus on private and more universal beliefs, religious beliefs emphasize the public and external system linked more with denominations than with family dynamics. Families that are grounded spiritually have often integrated these beliefs into their family behavior and traditions.

Agreement by a married couple on spiritual beliefs has been found to be strongly linked to a more successful marriage (Larson & Olson, 2004). In a national study with 24,671 married couples who took the ENRICH couple inventory, couples with high agreement on spiritual beliefs not only were more happily married, but also had many other strengths in their marriages, including better communication, greater ability to resolve conflict, and feeling more couple closeness; they also had higher levels of couple flexibility.

Ability to Manage Stress and Crisis Effectively. Strong families are not immune to trouble, but they are not as crisis prone as dysfunctional families tend to be. Rather, they possess the **ability to manage stress and crisis effectively**. Strong families are often successful at preventing troubles before they occur, but some stressors in life are inevitable. The best a family can do is meet the challenge as efficiently as possible, minimizing its damage and looking for opportunities for growth together in the process.

Among the strategies strong families use to weather crises is pulling together rather than pulling apart. Each person, even a very young child, has a part to play in easing the burdens of the others. Additionally, strong families seek help if they cannot solve the problem themselves. Although this may surprise some people, members of strong families do get counseling in an attempt to learn better ways of coping with a crisis. In contrast, truly troubled families often do not have the strength to admit that they have troubles and need to seek advice.

Family Development Framework

Family development as a conceptual framework was originally designed to describe and explain the process of change in couples and families. Researchers and clinicians working from a **family development framework** are primarily interested in how partners and family members deal with various roles and developmental tasks within the marriage and family as they move through various stages of the life cycle. The family development framework assumes that the more efficient a family is at completing these tasks, the more successful the development of the various family members will be.

Many cultures embrace a form of family and community life that reflects what theorists think of as extended family systems. Among many American Indian tribes, for example, significant life events are marked with community-wide ceremonies. Individual problems are considered problems that can be solved only within the context of the group.
©Chris Cheadle/Alamy Stock Photo

Chapter 3 | Understanding Marriage and Family Dynamics   87

Evelyn Duvall, a major creator (with Reuben Hill) of the family development approach, has described some of the advantages of this framework (Duvall, 2001). For one thing, it focuses on development and change in individuals and the family over time. It also encourages attention to process. It approaches the family not as a static and unchanging group but as a dynamic system.

Some controversy surrounds the exact number of stages involved in the family life cycle. Duvall originally identified eight stages: Stage 1, The Married Couple; Stage 2, Childbearing; Stage 3, Preschool-aged Children; Stage 4, School-Aged Children; Stage 5, Teenage Children; Stage 6, Launching the Children; Stage 7, Middle-Aged Parents; and Stage 8, Aging Family Members. Her traditional family development framework in the early years assumed that a couple would marry and have children, raise the children until they are launched, retire, and become grandparents. The complexities of life as we witness them today were not really addressed in Duvall's early work: divorce, single parenthood, remarriage, voluntary childlessness, and so forth. Other family science professionals following in Duvall's footsteps have identified 4 to 24 stages in the family life cycle. The sequence of stages is clearest and easiest to apply when there is only one child in the family. The number of stages and the complexity of overlapping stages increase when there is more than one child or when the couple gets divorced and one or both partners remarry.

Researchers have identified what they believe to be a new stage of development, **emerging adulthood**, between childhood and adulthood, which is the age from 18 to 25 (Arnett, 2007, 2015; Nelson & Barry, 2005). This is a prolonged period of role exploration focusing on identity, and time is spent trying out career and relationship possibilities (Arnett, 2007). This is also a period of risk taking with substance abuse and alcohol. Sexual activity is also common during these years. Two studies focusing on emerging adulthood and sexuality found that most emerging adults engaged in sexual activity, although they typically used condoms or other forms of birth control, and marriage was not a high priority (Willoughby & Dworkin, 2009; Willoughby & Carroll, 2010). It will be interesting to see if emerging adulthood will develop as a well-recognized stage of development in future family science literature.

The family development framework is a useful framework for thinking about stages of the family life. However, it does not address the complexity of families today, which do not follow a traditional pattern of marrying, having a child or children, raising the children until they are launched, and retiring and becoming grandparents. Today's families often begin without marriage, and even those that begin with marriage often end in divorce. There is often remarriage that may include stepchildren from one or both parents, who might then have their own children.

There is a renewed interest in the family development framework (Hunt, 2005), likely because our longer life span affects many areas of social life. People born in the 1900s would have expected to live to about 65 years of age, while those born in the mid-1900s are living into their late 70s. In the future, life expectancy might be 110 years—medical advances and the ability to eliminate infectious diseases increase life expectancy.

Life cycle and *life stages* are terms we are familiar with in social science literature. These terms usually refer to specific age categories such as childhood or adolescence. However, according to Hunt (2005), **life course** is a more accurate term to describe the transitions one makes through life. *Life course* is more fluid, reflecting the unpredictable changes such as divorce, remarriage, or early retirement that are not tied to traditional age stages. That the family development framework has evolved and adapted to the changing roles, family structures, and life expectancy is evident in today's society.

Using Duvall's traditional family life cycle stages as a starting point, how would you adapt her model to fit the family life cycle stages that your parents and you are moving through? How traditional is your family, in this regard? And how nontraditional or more contemporary is your family?

Symbolic Interaction Framework

As the name indicates, the **symbolic interaction framework** focuses on symbols, which are based on shared meanings, and interactions, which are based on verbal and nonverbal communication (White, Klein, & Martin, 2015). This framework helps explain how we learn through communicating with each other about various roles in our society. The family is seen as a unit of interacting personalities, which according to Ernest Burgess (Burgess & Wallin, 1943) explains the importance of family interaction in creating an ongoing group.

A **role** is the expected behavior of a person or group in a given social category, such as husband, wife, supervisor, or teacher. Every family member plays a variety of roles at different times. For example, a man can be a parent, spouse, manager at work, and coach of a baseball team. A woman can be a parent, spouse, manager at work, and chairperson of a fund-raising committee. A young girl can be a daughter, student, and musician.

Roles are learned in society by **role taking**, the process whereby people learn how to play roles correctly by practicing and getting feedback from others. **Role making** involves creating new roles or revising existing roles. For example, as a couple's relationship changes from husband led to a more egalitarian relationship, the partners need to change the way they interact with each other.

One assumption is that meaning arises in the process of interaction between people. Shared meaning helps people understand each other and learn how to play various roles. Another important concept is **definition of the situation**, developed by William Thomas: Each person subjectively interprets a given situation, and different people will interpret an interaction or situation in different ways. This helps explain why there are often different perceptions of a marriage; there can be "his" marriage and "her" marriage, as initially described by Jessie Bernard (1970).

Another assumption is that people learn about themselves and develop a self-concept based on their interaction with others. An early theorist, Charles Cooley (1864–1929), developed the concept of the **looking-glass self**, the idea that you learn about yourself based on the feedback you receive from others who are reacting to your behavior. In other words, your feelings about yourself are derived from how others react to you. Another important theorist was George Mead (1863–1931), who described how the self-concept emerges in childhood. Mead explained that the child learns how to play out a certain role, and this helps her or him to take on the role of the *generalized other*. In essence, we learn to try to look at the world through others' eyes. In our behavior and social interaction with others, we learn how to react to the expectations of others, orienting ourselves to the norms and values of our community or group. This ability can be valuable in any situation because it enables a person to understand another's feelings.

Social Construction Framework

According to the **social construction framework**, human beings are profoundly immersed in the social world; our understanding of this world and beliefs about this world are social products. Similar to the earlier thinking of the symbolic interactionists, social construction theorists argue that because the self is a product of social processes, individuality is most difficult to develop because we live in a social environment: We are born into and live within social settings, as members of particular social groups. Our identities are shaped over time through our life experiences.

Social construction theories, which are compatible with the postmodernist and multicultural intellectual movements, are gaining attention today. **Postmodernism** thinking emphasizes the notion that we live in a complex world and that multiple perspectives or "truths" are in constant interaction and conflict with each other (Weinberg, 2008). In a postmodern era, then, there is no objective, universal truth that can be seen, once and for all, and readily agreed upon; rather, there is a collection of subjective truths shaped by the particular subcultures in which we live. These multiple subjective truths are constantly competing for our attention and allegiance.

When we look at the world, we are looking through a lens colored by our own beliefs and values, which we have developed in our own particular social worlds. In other words, we do not see the world the way *it is*, we see the world the way *we are*. Any "truth statement" is a statement about the observer as well as about what is being observed. The various perspectives on life that we encounter are called *knowledge-positions*. When one knowledge-position gains more power than the others in a particular culture, it becomes dominant and its adherents sometimes refer to it as the truth with a capital *T*. Traveling around the world, however, we find that there are innumerable truths from country to country; even within a particular country or particular family there are many different brands of truth.

From a postmodernist perspective, a dominant truth in a particular cultural group is simply the most popular and widely accepted story or narrative explanation about the way life is or should be. This story serves two purposes: to reinforce and maintain the power and cohesiveness of the particular group and to eliminate or minimize the stories and explanations of competing groups. But because this story or truth or knowledge-position is socially constructed, as society changes over time and countless new influences emerge, the story continuously evolves.

From an individual family's perspective, the truth about who the family is and what the family does can change as time passes. A troubled family can learn how to create a new, more positive story about who they are and where their family is going. Narrative therapy, which developed out of social constructionist and postmodern thinking, seeks to develop a new story for the individual and the family that works better than the old approach (Cook & DeFrain, 2005; White, 2016; White & Morgan, 2006). The family, as storyteller, relates the current perspective on reality that the family holds. In addition, the family therapist, in concert with the family members, helps develop a new narrative, or story, that helps the family meet its goals in a more effective manner.

Finally, from a social constructionist and postmodernist point of view, this textbook represents not necessarily *the truth* about marriage and family today but rather the perspective of three family scholars who see the world through particular conceptual lenses and whose worldviews are shaped by the unique sociocultural context in which they live. The articles and books we choose to quote in this textbook and the personal comments we make all reflect the social environment that has heavily influenced us.

Feminist Framework

> *I myself have never been able to find out precisely what feminism is: I only know that people call me a feminist whenever I express sentiments that differentiate me from a doormat, or a prostitute.*
>
> —REBECCA WEST, 1913

The feminist framework has grown in importance and has had a significant impact on theorizing about marriage and the family in recent decades (Switala, 2016). Central to the

feminist framework is the notion that women are exploited, devalued, and oppressed and that society should commit to empowering women and changing their oppressed condition (Tong, 2014).

While feminist thought can be traced back to ancient Greece, historians argue that the story of feminism in the United States can be described in three waves (Dorey-Stein, 2015). The first wave between the 1830s and early 1900s focused on women's fight for equal contract and property rights. Early feminists argued that women were often taken for granted, and that they must gain political power, including the right to vote, if they were to change their status in America. The political agenda expanded to issues concerning sexual, reproductive, and economic matters. The seed was planted that women had the potential to contribute just as much to this country as men, if not even more. The second wave of feminism in this country arrived in the 1960s to the 1980s. With millions of men gone from home to serve in the U.S. military in World War II, women were active on the home front in countless ways and worked in paying jobs formerly held by men. After the war ended in 1945, the men returned home and many women were forced back into their traditional role as homemakers. The second wave of feminism, then, focused on the workplace, sexuality, family, and reproductive rights. The second wave was stimulated by women like Betty Friedan, who wrote *The Feminine Mystique* in 1963. She argued that women needed a more active voice in decisions that affected them. She also pointed out that women are burdened by the guilt that they often feel because they are unable to balance motherhood and working outside the home. The second wave included a diverse group of people, both women and men, who were part of the Black civil rights movement, the anti-Vietnam movement, Chicano rights movement, Asian-American civil rights movement, Gay and Lesbian rights movement, and other groups pushing for equality. The third wave of feminism began in the 1990s and continues to the present. Issues faced today include disparities in male and female pay, the reproductive rights of women, violence against women, and working toward women's equality on a global level. Feminism has a wide variety of advocates arguing from diverse perspectives. In some ways it is a controversial and difficult concept to wrap one's mind around, but the dictionary does fine: "The theory of the political, economic and social equality of the sexes" (Dorey-Stein, 2015).

Feminist theories have a common interest in understanding the subordination of women with the goal of changing it (Fox & Murry, 2000). Feminists assume that women's experiences are central, not less important than those of men, and that gender must be explicitly used as a central focus. **Gender** is defined as the learned behaviors and characteristics associated with being male or female in a particular culture. Feminist theories examine gender differences and how gender-based distinctions legitimize power differences between men and women.

Feminists have also challenged the definition of family that is based on traditional roles. They see the family as a dynamic, changing, and open system that does not restrict roles and opportunities. They have criticized the structural/functional framework, which prescribed the roles of males and females. Parsons and Bales (1955) assumed that the family was most functional if the male played the **instrumental role**, being in charge of tasks, and the wife played the **expressive role**, being nurturing. Feminists maintain that both men and women can play both roles. This perspective provides couples with more flexibility because both members can play roles based on their unique skills and interests.

Even though some men today are offended and threatened by feminist thinking, feminism has considerable benefits for both men and women in family relationships. Some suggest that to be healthy, all human beings need to exhibit a full range of what were in the past thought of as traditionally masculine and traditionally feminine qualities (Tong, 2014). It encourages men to express their feelings, to share wage-earning responsibilities, and to focus less on their careers and more on their children. For men, the pressure of being the only wage earner is reduced when both partners are working outside the home. At the same time, working outside the home helps women enjoy an identity separate from their role within the family. It also provides them with independent economic security. Sharing the responsibility for child rearing allows men to participate in their children's development and women to pursue professional and personal interests. When work and power are shared, both partners have more opportunity to develop their full potential.

Feminism has affected thinking and research about family science in many ways (Tong, 2014). For some, feminist theory is about oppression and domination in many aspects of society, such as classism, racism, or ageism—not just sexism. Also, multicultural feminism focuses on how prosperity for women in developed nations might be achieved at the expense of women in developing nations. **Ecofeminism** is about the domination of nature or the nonhuman world. This has taken the form of environmentalism with concerns about global warming, waste disposal, and animal farming. Therefore, feminism can be about the voices not heard in a world of domination and oppression.

Three Key Relationship Concepts

[Authors' Note: In order for you to more easily understand the three dimensions of family cohesion, family flexibility, and family communication, it would be useful to assess your own family of origin before reading the following section. Complete Activity 2 at the end of the chapter and then read the following section.

Also read about the Couple and Family Scales in Appendix A at the back of the book.]

There is considerable agreement among theorists who have studied couples and families that the dimensions of cohesion, flexibility, and communication are central to understanding relationship dynamics. Although the descriptive terms vary from theorist to theorist, the majority of concepts relate to the three dimensions of relationships that we will now describe in more detail.

Cohesion in Couples and Families

Cohesion is a feeling of emotional closeness with another person (Olson & Gorall, 2003). Four levels of cohesion can be described in couple and family relationships: disengaged, connected, cohesive, and enmeshed (Figure 3.2). The extreme low level of cohesion is called

FIGURE 3.2
Four Levels of Family Cohesion: Balancing Separateness and Togetherness

Disengaged System	Connected System	Cohesive System	Enmeshed System
Separateness vs. Togetherness	Separateness vs. Togetherness	Separateness vs. Togetherness	Separateness vs. Togetherness
Too Much Separateness	More Separateness than Togetherness	More Togetherness than Separateness	Too Much Togetherness
Unbalanced	Balanced	Balanced	Unbalanced

disengaged, and the extreme high level, *enmeshed*. Although being disengaged or enmeshed is appropriate at times, relationships become problematic when they are stuck at one of these extremes. The two middle levels of cohesion—*connected* and *cohesive*—seem to be the most functional across the life cycle, in part because they balance separateness and togetherness. Both connected and cohesive relationships are classified as balanced family systems.

Balancing Between Separateness and Togetherness. Balance between separateness and togetherness is the essence of family cohesion. Family members need to balance between being intimate with and feeling close to other family members and being independent from the family so that they can develop as individuals. The concept of balance entails both autonomy and intimacy—and the ability to move back and forth between the two. Establishing a dynamic balance between the two requires shifting back and forth on a weekly, daily, or even hourly basis.

Table 3.3 illustrates the four levels of couple and family cohesion, from low to high. There is a balance between separateness and togetherness at both the connected and the cohesive levels of cohesion. *Connected relationships* place more emphasis on the individual than on the relationship. Levels of closeness are often low to moderate in a connected family system, with lower levels of loyalty; there is often more independence than dependence and more separateness than togetherness. *Cohesive relationships* place more emphasis on togetherness and less on separateness. There is some loyalty to the relationship, and there is often more dependence than independence.

Disengaged relationships (those with a low level of cohesion) emphasize the individual. There is often very little closeness, a lack of loyalty, high independence, and high separateness. *Enmeshed relationships* emphasize togetherness: very high levels of closeness, loyalty, and dependence on one another. Enmeshed relationships are often typical of couples in love. When this level of intimacy occurs between a parent and a child (for example, an enmeshed father–daughter relationship or an enmeshed mother–son relationship), the relationship often becomes problematic.

The relationship Gibran describes is an ideal. In the real world of loving relationships, few find this perfect balance with their partners. It is a useful goal but one that is difficult to maintain for long. It is also important to note that in intimate relationships, people can experience and even enjoy, at least for a short time, both extremes on the

TABLE 3.3   Levels of Couple and Family Cohesion

Characteristic	Disengaged (Unbalanced)	Connected (Balanced)	Cohesive (Balanced)	Enmeshed (Unbalanced)
Separateness–togetherness	High separateness	More separateness than togetherness	More togetherness than separateness	Very high togetherness
I–we balance	Primarily I	More I than we	More we than I	Primarily we
Closeness	Little closeness	Low-to-moderate closeness	Moderate-to-high closeness	Very high closeness
Loyalty	Lack of loyalty	Some loyalty	Considerable loyalty	High loyalty
Activities	Mainly separate	More separate than shared	More shared than separate	Mainly shared
Dependence–independence	High independence	More independence than dependence	More dependence than independence	High dependence

togetherness–separateness continuum. Couples can remain in love with each other while also enjoying being apart for periods of time.

Extreme Togetherness and Extreme Separateness. Too much togetherness can lead to relationship fusion, or enmeshment. People "in love" often feel they need each other. Although this feels good for a while, soon the enmeshment begins to prickle. After too much togetherness, lovers can get on each other's nerves.

Especially in the early stages of a relationship, couples enjoy being totally together. When two people are "falling in love," being away from each other for very long literally hurts. Each one aches and pines and feels pent-up emotion in the expectation of seeing the other again. Couples in this type of situation are enmeshed; being together so totally can be very exciting for a time. To expect to be totally sheltered from the storms of life by a loved one is a nice fantasy—but it *is* a fantasy.

Two of the most common reasons an enmeshed relationship becomes troublesome are jealousy and personification. People feel jealous when they fear they might lose their partner to another person. Tied closely to jealousy is **personification**, the notion that everything one's partner does is a personal reflection on oneself. A person who personifies his or her partner's actions will try to control the other's behavior. This may work in the short run, but it can destroy intimacy in the long run.

Enmeshment is problematic both for the people in the relationship and for the relationship itself because it romanticizes the relationship and puts impossible expectations upon

Within every family, each member must find a balance between autonomy and intimacy. If their family is like other families, these five people will experience periods of greater and lesser separateness and togetherness over the course of their lives.
©Blend Images/Getty Images

94　Part I　│　The Social Context of Intimate Relationships

the partners. It also tends to stifle individual development. One way to improve an enmeshed relationship is for each person to develop individual interests and abilities.

In the 1970s, one cultural theme in American society was "doing your own thing." Young people were dubbed "the me generation." This overfocus on self was problematic for relationships. "Doing your own thing" can lead to a disengaged relationship, in which there is very little emotional closeness.

A disengaged couple or family typically has very little emotional closeness. There is so much separateness that each person is mainly focused on himself or herself and not on each other. As a result, they have difficulty developing and maintaining intimacy with others. Most couples with marital problems have low levels of emotional connection as do families with problem children. Emotional closeness is the glue that helps couples and families stay connected even during difficult times. When emotional closeness is missing, individuals care more about themselves and there is little commitment and few resources to help the couple or family thrive.

A young former prostitute described the family she grew up in as very chaotic, saying, "It was like a sieve. Anybody could come into it, and anybody could leave, and anybody could fall through the gaps. The family wasn't safe or reliable for anybody at all." Her downfall at the hands of her family came at age 13 when she was raped by her mother's boyfriend, and then thrown out because her mother said it was all her fault.

Successful couples tend to be those who have figured out how to balance effectively between "I" and "we." Partners maintain both their own individuality and their intimacy as a couple.

Flexibility in Couples and Families

Flexibility is the amount of change that occurs in leadership, role relationships, and relationship rules (Olson & Gorall, 2003). Like cohesion, flexibility can be described as having four levels, ranging from low to high. These levels are rigid, structured, flexible, and chaotic (Figure 3.3). The extreme types of family systems—the *rigid* and the *chaotic*—can work well

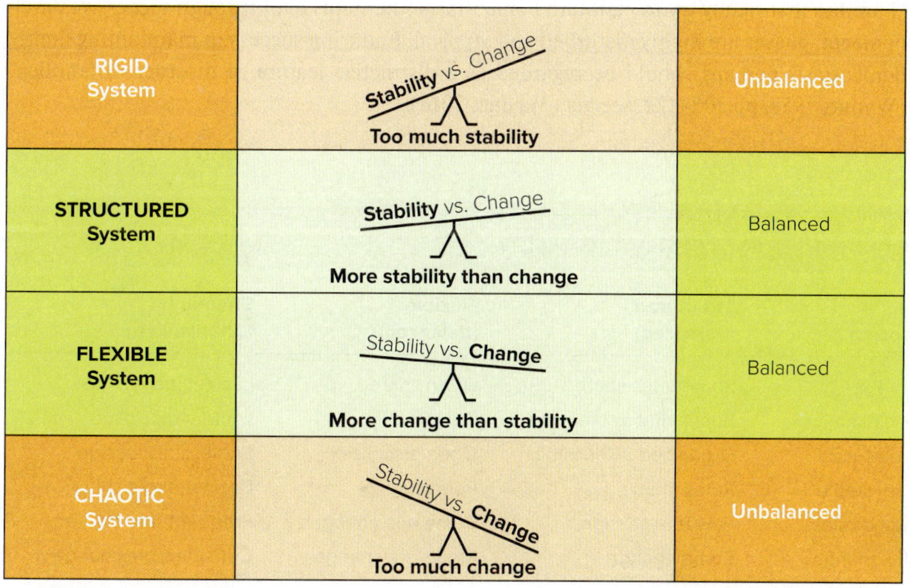

RIGID System	Stability vs. Change — Too much stability	Unbalanced
STRUCTURED System	Stability vs. Change — More stability than change	Balanced
FLEXIBLE System	Stability vs. Change — More change than stability	Balanced
CHAOTIC System	Stability vs. Change — Too much change	Unbalanced

FIGURE 3.3

Four Levels of Family Flexibility: Balancing Stability and Change

in the short run, but they have difficulty adapting over time. Conversely, the balanced types—the *structured* and the *flexible*—are more able to adapt to change over the family life cycle.

Balance Between Stability and Change. The essence of family flexibility is balancing stability and change. Families need a basic foundation that gives them stability, but they also need to be open to change when necessary. Change is particularly important when families are under stress and need to adapt in a crisis.

The two balanced levels of change are called *structured* and *flexible*. Of the two, structured relationships have more moderate levels of change, with leadership that is sometimes shared. Discipline is often democratic, and the roles are stable. In flexible relationships, there is more change. Often both the relationship between the couple and the relationships among family members are more democratic, and there is also more role sharing between the partners, as shown in Table 3.4.

The two extremes of change are described as *rigid*, indicating a very low degree of change, and *chaotic*, indicating an extremely high degree of change. Both extremes are unbalanced and problematic because families are often stuck at these extreme positions. In rigid relationships, the leadership is often authoritarian. As a result, the discipline is strict, and the roles are very stable. In chaotic relationships, there is too much change, often because there is a lack of leadership. Discipline is erratic and inconsistent, partly due to dramatic shifts in family roles.

Extreme Stability and Extreme Change. Families by nature tend to resist change; they are basically rigid. Most families function primarily to maintain the status quo: "When an organism indicates a change in relation to another, the other will act upon the first so as to diminish and modify the change" (Haley, 1959, p. 361; see also Haley, 2016).

In short, when one partner tries to make changes in a relationship, the other partner's first reaction is often to defend against the change or at least to slow it down until he or she can better understand what is happening. People often fear that the change will bring more harm than good. The family, which is maintenance oriented and conservative in its approach to change, often creates even more problems for itself. As Lyman Wynne sees it, "Families that rigidly try to maintain homeostasis [the status quo] through successive developmental phases are highly disturbed and atypical. Enduring success in maintaining family homeostasis perhaps should be regarded as a distinctive feature of disorder in families" (Wynne, 1958, pp.205-222; see also Wynne, 2016).

TABLE 3.4 Levels of Couple and Family Flexibility

Characteristic	Rigid (Unbalanced)	Structured (Balanced)	Flexible (Balanced)	Chaotic (Unbalanced)
Leadership	Authoritarian	Sometimes shared	Often shared	Lack of leadership
Discipline	Strict discipline	Somewhat democratic	Democratic	Lenient discipline
Negotiation	Limited discussion	Organized discussion	Open discussion	Endless discussion
Roles	Roles very stable	Roles stable	Role sharing	Dramatic role shifts
Rules	Unchanging rules	Few rule changes	Some rule changes	Frequent rule changes
Change	Very little change	Some change	Moderate change	Considerable change

TABLE 3.5 — Levels of Couple and Family Communication

Characteristic	Poor	Good	Very Good
Listening skills	Poor listening skills	Appear to listen, but feedback is limited	Give feedback, indicating good listening skills
Speaking skills	Often speak for others	Speak for self more than for others	Speak mainly for self rather than for others
Self-disclosure	Low sharing of feelings	Moderate sharing of feelings	High sharing of feelings
Clarity	Inconsistent messages	Clear messages	Very clear messages
Staying on topic	Seldom stay on topic	Often stay on topic	Mainly stay on topic
Respect and regard	Low to moderate	Moderate to high	High

Extreme stability is seen in rigid families, those in which there is little room for change. The family rules are always the same, even though the game of life outside the family continuously changes. This rigidity manifests itself in such relatively trivial matters as scheduling family meals. Family members do not permit one another to make even the slightest changes, even if the changes help one or more members. The rigidity may also be evidenced by resistance to changes in family roles. For example, a mother wants to find work outside the home but the father opposes it, or a son wants to become a musician but his parents are not supportive.

On the other extreme of change are chaotic families. These families are almost completely without structure, rules, and roles. No one knows what to expect. For example, a chaotic family operates on the premise that nothing is constant in life but change. It is difficult to go through life without some change—and individuals and relationships often do better if they are open to some change over time. However, constant change is problematic for most people.

Communication in Couples and Families

Communication is the grease that smoothes frictions between partners and family members. Family communication is linear: The better the communication skills, the stronger the couple and family relationship (Olson, Olson-Sigg, & Larson, 2009).

The following six dimensions are considered in the assessment of family communication: listening skills, speaking skills, self-disclosure, clarity, staying on topic, and respect and regard (Table 3.5). Positive *listening skills* involve empathy and giving feedback. *Speaking skills* include speaking for oneself and using "I" statements rather than speaking for others. *Self-disclosure* entails sharing personal feelings and ideas openly. *Clarity* involves the exchange of clear messages. *Staying on topic* is another important aspect of interpersonal exchanges. Last, *respect and regard* reflect the good intentions of family members and keep communication positive.

Couple and Family Map

The **Couple and Family Map** is built on the three major dimensions of cohesion, flexibility, and communication. Four levels of cohesion and four levels of flexibility are integrated to create a model that is useful for describing and understanding couple and family dynamics.

The Couple and Family Map (otherwise known in the field of family research as the *Circumplex Model of Marital and Family Systems*) was developed by David Olson and his colleagues at the University of Minnesota, especially Douglas Sprenkle and Candyce Russell, who worked on the original model. The model offers a way of mapping and understanding couple and family relationships. It can also be applied by therapists, counselors, and family members interested in understanding and changing the dynamics within a couple or family experiencing difficulties.

The Couple and Family Map is built primarily on principles and concepts from family systems theory, but it also has features in common with other frameworks. As a graphic model, it clearly represents the dimensions of cohesion and flexibility; the third dimension, communication, serves as a facilitating function. That is to say, good communication smooths the way as family members move through life together.

It is through communication that family members identify and work out their concerns about cohesion—issues of spending time together versus having enough separateness to retain a sense of oneself—and flexibility—issues of adapting to the demands of change versus minimizing such demands if they threaten the stability of the relationship. Communication thus helps families move between the extremes of cohesion and flexibility to find a balance that works for them. If couples or families have good communication skills, they are more likely to be able to maintain their cohesive structure, adapt to change, and work out whatever problems confront them (Olson et al., 2009).

Balanced Versus Unbalanced Families

The Couple and Family Map identifies 16 types of couple and family relationships (Figure 3.4). The logic of the map is quite simple: The dimensions of cohesion and flexibility are broken down into four levels each, and 4 × 4 = 16. A marriage or family relationship can be classified according to 1 of these 16 types depending on how a given family or couple relationship operates.

The 16 types of family relationships can be clustered into three general types of family systems: balanced families, midrange families, and unbalanced families. **Balanced families** are those that fit into the four central categories (yellow section) on the relationship map in Figure 3.4. Balanced families are labeled flexibly connected, flexibly cohesive, structurally connected, and structurally cohesive. **Midrange families** (light orange section) are extreme on one dimension (for example, cohesion) but balanced on the other (for example, flexibility). **Unbalanced families** (dark orange section) are those that score at extreme levels on both dimensions. In the Activities section at the end of this chapter, you will have the opportunity to classify your own family using the Couple and Family Scales.

Balanced Relationships Are Healthier

The Couple and Family Map is a valuable model because it is scientifically verifiable; in other words, researchers can validate (or invalidate) the Couple and Family Map by testing hypotheses derived from it. A few of the most important hypotheses that have been developed and tested in numerous studies are discussed next.

One hypothesis is: *Balanced couple and family systems* (those that fall under two central levels of cohesion and flexibility) *generally function more adequately across the family life cycle than unbalanced types* (two extremes on cohesion and flexibility). Families balanced on

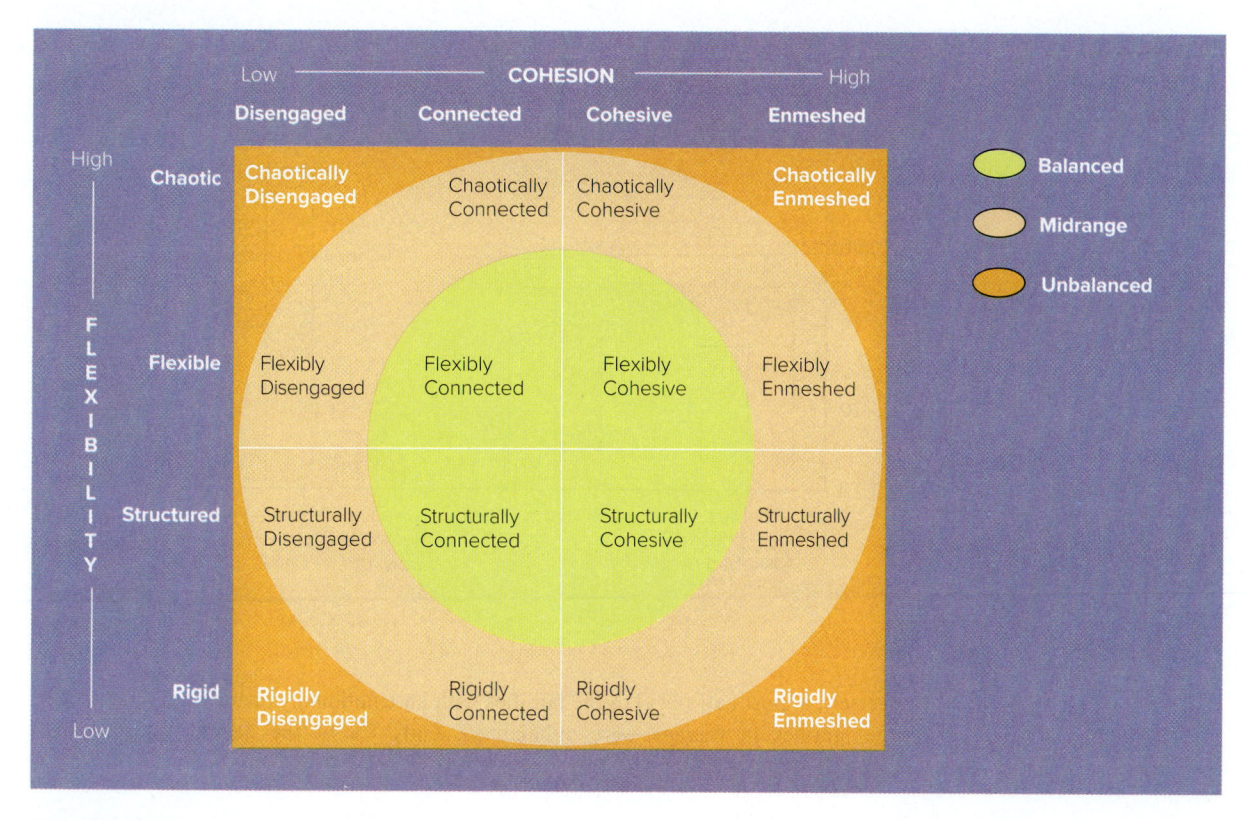

FIGURE 3.4
Couple and Family Map

cohesion allow their members to be both independent from and connected to the family. Families balanced on flexibility maintain some stability but are also open to change. Although balanced family types are located in the central area of the model, they can experience the extremes of the dimensions when necessary to deal with a situation, but they do not typically function at those extremes for long.

Conversely, couples and families with problems are more typically found at the extremes of the dimensions; they are unbalanced types. Problem families often experience too much separateness (disengaged type) or too much togetherness (enmeshed type) or cohesion. On flexibility, problem families tend to have too much stability (rigid type) or too much change (chaotic type).

There is considerable support for the main hypothesis derived from the Couple and Family Map: *Balanced family types are healthier and more functional than unbalanced family types*. One systematic study that found strong support for this hypothesis was by Volker Thomas and David Olson (1993). They tested four groups of families with an adolescent, videotaping each family while they discussed some family topics. The four samples included 35 families with an emotionally disturbed child, 25 families in family therapy for a variety of problems, 62 healthy families with a Down syndrome child, and 60 healthy families.

The findings strongly supported the hypothesis (Figure 3.5). As hypothesized, only 16% of the families with an emotionally disturbed child and 12% of the families in therapy were balanced types, whereas about 78% to 80% of the healthy families were balanced types.

Chapter 3 | Understanding Marriage and Family Dynamics

FIGURE 3.5

Degree of Balance in Problem and Healthy Families

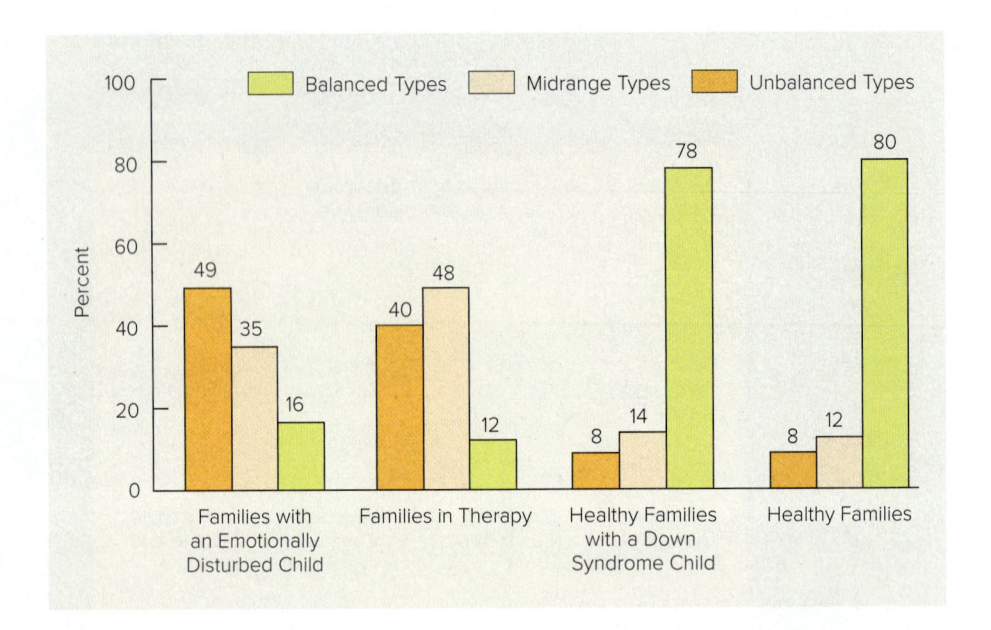

Bar chart showing percentages of Balanced Types, Midrange Types, and Unbalanced Types across four family groups:

- Families with an Emotionally Disturbed Child: Unbalanced 49, Midrange 35, Balanced 16
- Families in Therapy: Unbalanced 40, Midrange 48, Balanced 12
- Healthy Families with a Down Syndrome Child: Unbalanced 8, Midrange 14, Balanced 78
- Healthy Families: Unbalanced 8, Midrange 12, Balanced 80

Conversely, almost half (49%) of the families with an emotionally disturbed child and 40% of the families in therapy were unbalanced. Only 8% of the healthy families were unbalanced.

Value of Couple and Family Map

There are several advantages to using the Couple and Family Map to understand marital and family life. First, *the model provides a common descriptive language for talking about real couples and real families—a language the expert and the layperson can use to talk with each other.*

Second, the Couple and Family Map *draws on concepts and ideas from three of the major frameworks we have discussed—family systems, family strengths, and family development.* It offers a means of bringing together and applying all three frameworks to the examination of real families and their interactions. It grounds theory in examples of relationships based on intimacy and commitment.

Third, the Couple and Family Map *can help describe how a couple relationship or a family changes as time passes or as stresses and challenges appear.* The relationship map provides information about the present dynamics of a couple or family's relationship and what actions are necessary to bring about change. It provides a means to visualize where one is and where one might wish to be.

Finally, the Couple and Family Map *turns concepts into working themes so one can observe and measure couple and family dynamics.* Just where is a given family on the relationship map? Is this relationship a rigid, inflexible, suffocating environment? Is it an unpredictable, unsafe, chaotic place to be? Or is it flexible and nurturing? Can family members communicate what their problems are and express what kind of family they would like to become? What changes must they make to move toward that ideal or maintain the aspects they wish not to lose as they change others?

Dynamics Change in Relationships over Time

Another important characteristic of relationships is that they change over time. The Couple and Family Map is a useful tool that can help describe the changes in relationships, and they can be plotted onto the map. Figure 3.6 illustrates how a couple's relationship changed from the time they began dating, to marriage and as newlyweds, to the time when the couple became pregnant and had a baby.

As one views Figure 3.6 it is easy to see the dramatic changes in the type of couple relationship over a few years. This level of change in a couple's relationship is typical as relationships deal with changes, particularly related to major events like parenthood. Malik and Kayla began dating in college as seniors and had a "flexibly cohesive" relationship that was open to change and growing closer. Two years later they got married and as newlyweds were "structurally enmeshed." They were very structured because they both were very organized and wanted to be like their families. Being enmeshed is a common characteristic of many newly married couples. During the first 2 years of marriage, they each got busy with their own careers and had less time with each other. Emotionally, they moved apart more and changed from being enmeshed to being cohesive and then to connected levels of cohesion.

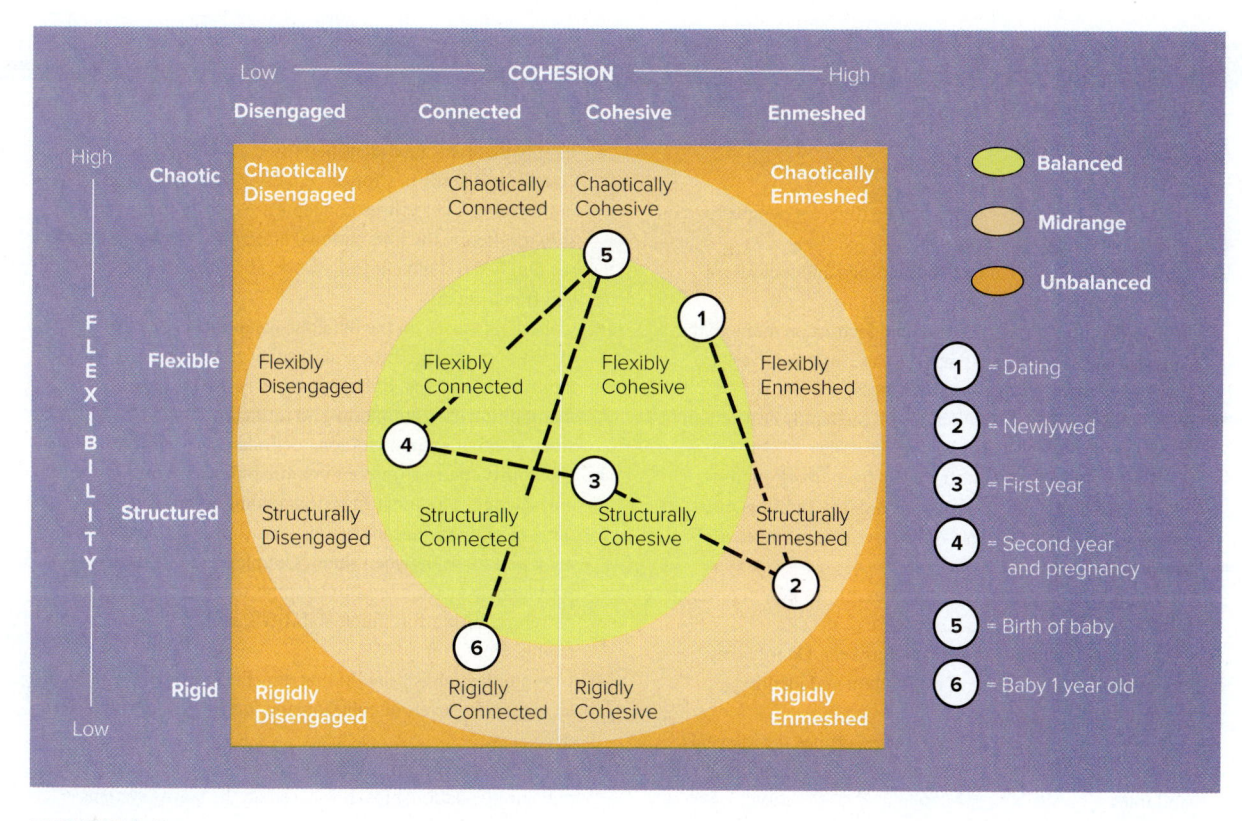

FIGURE 3.6
Couple and Family Map: Change over Time

Kayla became pregnant and the couple then had a "structurally connected" relationship. Once the baby was born, the couple moved to become a "chaotically cohesive" family. The birth of their first child brought them closer emotionally as a couple and new family. But the infant also added chaos to their typically stable life because life needed to revolve around the infant, which meant less sleep for both of them. As the child reached 1 year old, the couple was now "rigidly connected." The rigidity came from the need to establish a clear schedule for the child, and the child responded in a positive way to this structure by sleeping and eating at predictable times. But the couple became less close and moved from being cohesive to connected because Kayla felt stuck with mainly child care, while Malik continued to work and get more involved in his professional development.

In summary, this example illustrates how the Couple and Family Map can help a couple understand how their relationship changes over time. In terms of changes in the type of relationship over time, most couples and families simply experience the changes without knowing or thinking about them. But the model can also be used by couples and families in a more proactive way. Couples can jointly decide what type of relationship they want and they can work together to move the relationship toward that goal.

Summary

- Conceptual frameworks help describe different perspectives on couple and family dynamics.
- Family science began almost 80 years ago and focuses on family relationships.
- Early work in the family science field focuses on many of the same issues that receive attention today, such as poverty, housing, divorce, and marital happiness.
- The family systems theory focuses on the family as a system of interdependent parts.
- The international family strengths framework focuses on the positive characteristics of healthy families and couples, and how they use their strengths to meet life's challenges.
- The family development framework examines how couples and families change across the life cycle.
- Emerging adulthood (18-25 years) has been identified by researchers as a new stage of exploration and identity development.
- The symbolic interaction framework examines the internal perceptions of family members and how they learn social rules and roles.
- The social construction framework emphasizes the importance of multiple perspectives on reality and their use in helping families meet their goals more effectively.
- The feminist framework, which focuses on the world as women perceive it, aims to empower women in all aspects of their lives.
- Family theorists have identified three basic qualities that make couples and families stronger: cohesion, flexibility, and communication. These three concepts are central to the family systems theory, the international family strengths framework, the family development framework, as well as other theories and frameworks.
- Cohesion focuses on the dynamic balance between the extremes of separateness and togetherness in both couple and family relationships. Balancing these two extremes entails maintaining both autonomy and intimacy but not remaining stuck at either extreme for long periods.
- Flexibility focuses on the dynamic balance between stability and change. The most functional couples and family systems have both characteristics, and they are able to move back and forth between them. Couples and families with problems over time tend to become stuck at one of the extremes, either too much stability (rigid) or too much change (chaotic).
- Communication is a facilitating dimension that can help create change in the levels of cohesion and flexibility when change is necessary.
- The Couple and Family Map is a tool for understanding couple and family relationships. It is based on the family systems theory and is structured on the three dimensions of cohesion, flexibility, and communication.
- The Couple and Family Map describes three general types of family systems—balanced, midrange, and unbalanced—and can illustrate how systems change over time.

Key Terms

- conceptual framework
- theory
- hypothesis
- research study
- idiographic approach
- nomothetic approach
- eugenics
- family systems theory
- family system
- general systems theory
- system
- multiple system levels
- suprasystem
- subsystem
- boundaries
- ecology
- human ecosystem
- wholeness
- interdependence of parts
- open system
- morphogenic system
- closed system
- morphostatic system
- centrifugal interaction
- centripetal interaction
- positive feedback
- negative feedback
- international family strengths framework
- appreciation and affection
- commitment
- positive communication
- enjoyable time together
- spiritual well-being
- ability to manage stress and crisis effectively
- family development framework
- emerging adulthood
- life course
- symbolic interaction framework
- role
- role taking
- role making
- definition of the situation
- looking-glass self
- social construction framework
- postmodernism
- feminist framework
- gender
- instrumental role
- expressive role
- ecofeminism
- cohesion
- personification
- flexibility
- Couple and Family Map
- balanced families
- midrange families
- unbalanced families

Activities

1. Using Duvall's traditional family life cycle stages as a starting point, how would you adapt her model to fit the family life cycle stages that your parents and you are moving through? How traditional is your family in this regard? And how nontraditional or more contemporary is your family?
2. Use the Couple and Family Scales (Table 3.6) to describe your family of origin. Select a time period when you were all together (e.g., when you were in high school). Make a list of the people you are including in your family. Then do the following:
   a. Review the six categories shown in the scales (Table 3.6) for assessing cohesion, flexibility, and communication.
   b. On a separate piece of paper, rate your family on a scale of 1 to 8 for each of the categories in the three dimensions.
   c. To determine a total score for each dimension, review the scores and select a number that represents the best average score. Record the score below, and indicate the level for each dimension (e.g., for cohesion, enter *disengaged*, *connected*, *cohesive*, or *enmeshed*).

   Cohesion   Flexibility   Communication
   Score:_____   Score:_____   Score:_____
   Level:_____   Level:_____   Level:_____

   d. Now, plot the scores for cohesion and flexibility onto the Couple and Family Map (page 101) and identify the type of family system in which you grew up.
   e. After plotting your scores onto the model, consider the following questions:
   - What is/was it like to live in your type of family (e.g., flexibly connected, rigidly enmeshed, etc.)?
   - In what ways related to cohesion and flexibility is/was your family satisfying and in what ways is/was it frustrating?
   - How did your family change on cohesion and flexibility as you were growing up?
   - In what ways did communication affect your family's dynamics?
3. Plot on the Couple and Family Map (page 101) how your family changed over the years. Select at least three to five points in time and then plot them on the map. Then link those times and reflect on the changes. Also, were you and your family more happy at certain locations on the map than at others?
4. If you are dating someone, are engaged, or are married, both you and your partner should answer the questions on the Couple and Family Scales twice: first, in terms of your families of origin (as in Activity 1) and second, in terms of your couple relationship. Compare your partner's description of your couple relationship with yours and discuss the similarities and differences. Then compare the descriptions of each of your families of origin with those of your couple relationship.

(For more details on using the Couple and Family Scales, see Appendix A at the back of the book.)

Suggested Readings

Arnett, J. J. (2015). *Emerging adulthood: The winding road from the late teens through the twenties* (2nd ed.). New York, NY: Oxford University Press.

Boss, P., et al. (2009). *Sourcebook of family theories and methods: A contextual approach.* St. Paul, MN: Springer. An outstanding collection of family theories and family research methods.

Goldenberg, I., Stanton, M., & Goldenberg, H. (2016). *Family therapy: An overview* (9th ed.). San Francisco, CA: Cengage Learning.

Holstein, J. A., & Gubrium, J. F. (Eds.). (2008). *Handbook of constructionist research.* New York, NY: Guilford Press.

Hunt, S. (2005). *The life course: A sociological introduction.* New York, NY: Palgrave MacMillan.

TABLE 3.6 Couple and Family Scales

COHESION

Characteristic	Disengaged (Unbalanced)	Connected (Balanced)	Cohesive (Balanced)	Enmeshed (Unbalanced)
Score	1　　　2	3　　　4	5　　　6	7　　　8
Separateness–togetherness	High separateness	More separateness than togetherness	More togetherness than separateness	Very high togetherness
I–we balance	Primarily I	More I than we	More we than I	Primarily we
Closeness	Little closeness	Low-to-moderate closeness	Moderate-to-high closeness	Very high closeness
Loyalty	Lack of loyalty	Some loyalty	Considerable loyalty	High loyalty
Activities	Mainly separate	More separate than shared	More shared than separate	Mainly shared
Dependence–independence	High independence	More independence than dependence	More dependence than independence	High dependence

FLEXIBILITY

Characteristic	Rigid (Unbalanced)	Structured (Balanced)	Flexible (Balanced)	Chaotic (Unbalanced)
Score	1　　　2	3　　　4	5　　　6	7　　　8
Leadership	Authoritarian	Sometimes shared	Often shared	Lack of leadership
Discipline	Strict discipline	Somewhat democratic	Democratic	Lenient discipline
Negotiation	Limited discussion	Organized discussion	Open discussion	Endless discussion
Roles	Roles very stable	Roles stable	Role sharing	Dramatic role shifts
Rules	Unchanging rules	Few rule changes	Some rule changes	Frequent rule changes
Change	Very little change	Some change	Moderate change	Considerable change

COMMUNICATION

Characteristic	Poor	Good	Very Good
Score	1　　　2	3　　　4	5　　　6
Listening skills	Poor listening skills	Appear to listen, but feedback is limited	Give feedback, indicating good listening skills
Speaking skills	Often speak for others	Speak for self more than for others	Speak mainly for self rather than for others
Self-disclosure	Low sharing of feelings	Moderate sharing of feelings	High sharing of feelings
Clarity	Inconsistent messages	Clear messages	Very clear messages
Staying on topic	Seldom stay on topic	Often stay on topic	Mainly stay on topic
Respect and regard	Low to moderate	Moderate to high	High

Mahoney, A. (2010). Religion in families, 1999–2009: A relational spirituality framework. *Journal of Marriage and Family, 72* (August), 805–827. The role of religion "for better and worse," in marital and parent-child relationships.

Owens, T. J., & Suitor, J. J. (Eds.). (2007). *Advances in life course research: Vol. 12. Interpersonal relations across the life course.* Amsterdam: Elsevier.

Smith, S. R., & Hamon, R. R. (2012). *Exploring family theories* (3rd ed.). New York, NY: Oxford University Press.

Switala, K. (2016). *The feminist theory website.* Web site: http://www.cddc.vt.edu/feminism/enin.html. Research materials and information for students, activists, and scholars interested in women's conditions and struggles around the world.

Tong, R. (2014). *Feminist thought: A more comprehensive introduction* (4th ed.). Boulder, CO: Westview Press.

Walsh, F. (Ed.). (2015). *Normal family processes: Growing diversity and complexity* (4th ed.). New York, NY: Guilford.

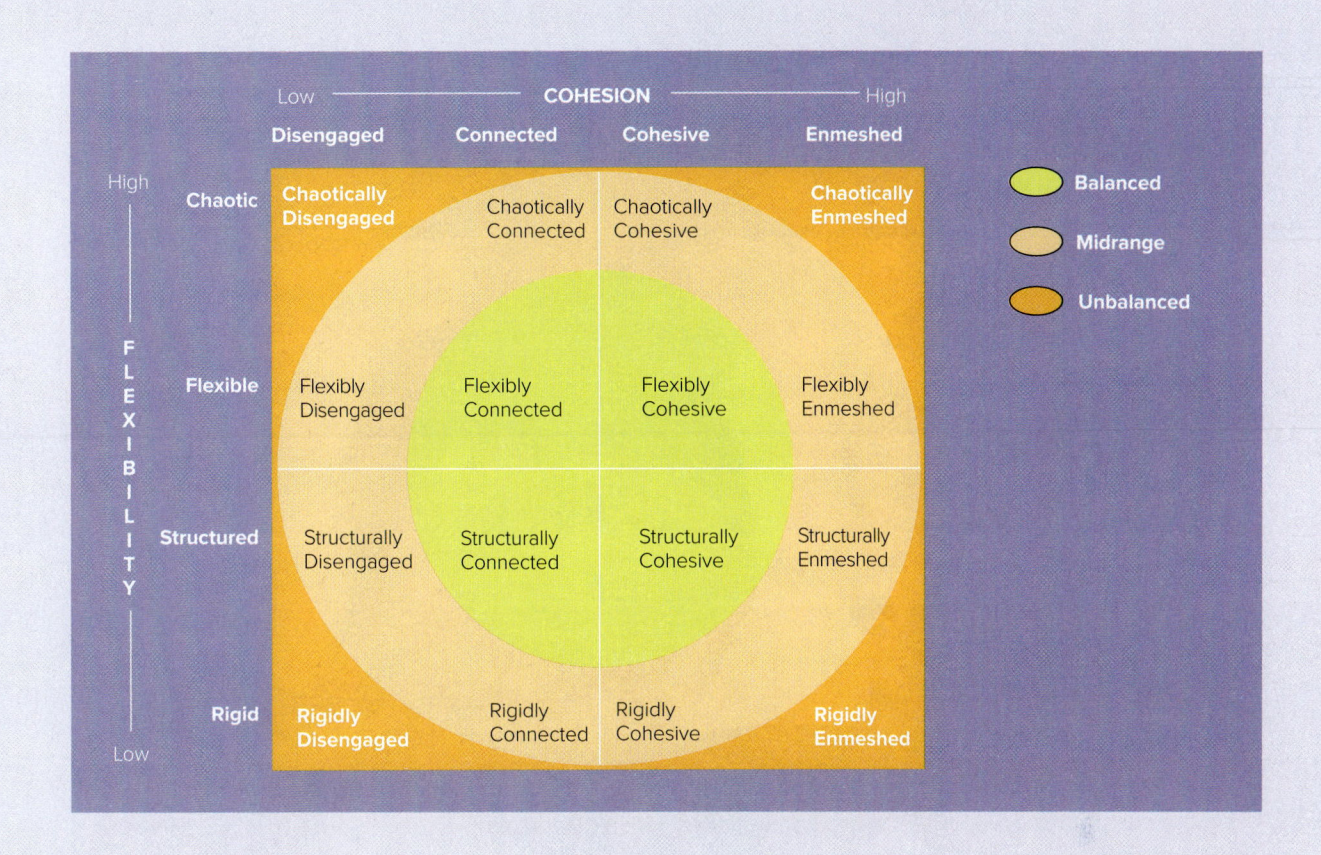

Visit the text-specific Online Learning Center at www.mhhe.com/olson9e for practice tests, chapter summaries, and PowerPoint slides.

	COHESION			
Low → High	Disengaged	Connected	Cohesive	Enmeshed
FLEXIBILITY High — Chaotic	Chaotically Disengaged	Chaotically Connected	Chaotically Cohesive	Chaotically Enmeshed
Flexible	Flexibly Disengaged	Flexibly Connected	Flexibly Cohesive	Flexibly Enmeshed
Structured	Structurally Disengaged	Structurally Connected	Structurally Cohesive	Structurally Enmeshed
Low — Rigid	Rigidly Disengaged	Rigidly Connected	Rigidly Cohesive	Rigidly Enmeshed

Legend: Balanced, Midrange, Unbalanced

Design Element: © Alicia Grünkind/EyeEm/Getty Images

PART TWO
Dynamics of Intimate Relationships

4 Communication and Intimacy

©Peopleimages/E+/Getty Images

Couple Strengths and Issues in Communication

Perspectives on Communication

Using Communication to Develop Intimacy

Using Communication to Maintain Intimacy

Positive and Negative Communication Cycles

Summary

Key Terms

Activities

Suggested Readings

Communication is at the heart of intimate human relationships—it is literally the foundation on which all else is built. **Communication** is the way humans create and share meaning, both verbally and nonverbally. As John Stewart said, "If humans really are social beings, then communication is where humanness happens" (2009, p. 7). He goes on to say that it is more than words; it defines who we are because in addition to conveying facts, it includes communicating in a close, supportive, and interpersonal way. The ability to communicate is one of a handful of essential skills individuals must master if they are to enjoy close relationships. In fact, the ability and the willingness to communicate have been found to be among the most important factors in maintaining a satisfying relationship.

In this chapter we will look at the art of interpersonal communication, focusing on several important principles of communication, as well as gender and cultural differences in communication styles. We will examine ways for people to become more aware of their communication patterns and styles. Finally, we will explore various approaches and techniques people can use to improve communication in their relationships, thereby increasing the level of intimacy they enjoy with friends, partners, and family members.

Because positive communication is critical to a successful couple relationship, we will open this chapter with some findings from a national survey (Olson, Olson-Sigg, & Larson, 2008). To identify the differences between happy and unhappy couples, the researchers conducted a study involving more than 50,000 married couples. Based on their scores on a marital satisfaction scale, the couples were classified as either *happily married* or *unhappily married*. There were 20,675 classified as happily married and 20,590 couples classified as unhappily married. A middle group of about 10,000 couples were not included in either group because their marital satisfaction scales were moderate or because one partner was high and one was low.

This national survey identified couple strengths in communication by comparing the happy couples and unhappy couples. Responses from the entire sample of 41,265 couples were used to identify specific issues for married couples in terms of their sexual relationship. The quality and quantity of a couple's communication are the key to the quality of other aspects of their relationship.

Couple Strengths and Issues in Communication

In a national study (Olson et al., 2008) comparing the major communication strengths of happy couples with those of unhappy couples, researchers found that happy couples were six times more likely (90%) than unhappy couples (15%) to agree that they are very satisfied with how they talk to each other (Table 4.1). Most happy couples (79%) feel that their partner understands them, but this is true for only 13% of unhappy couples. Almost all happy couples (96%) feel that they can express their true feelings, whereas this is true for only 30% of unhappy couples. Happy couples are good listeners (83%) compared to unhappy couples (18%). Most happy couples (79%) do not make comments that put each other down, but few (20%) unhappy couples could say the same thing.

In terms of problematic issues for all married couples, the survey focused on 41,265 couples regardless of whether they were happy or unhappy. As shown in Table 4.2, the vast majority of couples (76%) wished that their partner was more willing to share feelings. Sixty-nine percent of all couples had difficulty asking the partner "for what I want." Sixty-five percent did not feel understood, and 64% felt that their partner refused to discuss issues or problems. Also, 62% felt the partner made comments that put them down. Clearly, these are very common issues for the vast majority of married couples; the difference is that happy couples are more able to resolve these problems than unhappy couples.

TABLE 4.1 Communication Strengths of Happy Couples Versus Unhappy Couples

Percentage in Agreement Communication Issue	Happy Couples	Unhappy Couples
1. I am very satisfied with how we talk to each other.	95%	15%
2. My partner understands how I feel.	79	13
3. I find it easy to express my true feelings to my partner.	96	30
4. My partner is a very good listener.	83	18
5. My partner does not make comments that put me down.	79	20

Source: Olson, D., Olson-Sigg, A., & Larson, P. *The Couple Checkup.* Nashville, TN: Thomas Nelson, 2008.

TABLE 4.2 Top Five Communication Problems for Couples

Communication Issue	Percentage of Couples Having Problem*
1. I wish my partner were more willing to share his/her feelings.	76%
2. I sometimes have difficulty asking my partner for what I want.	69
3. My partner often does not understand how I feel.	65
4. My partner often refuses to discuss issues or problems.	64
5. My partner makes comments that put me down.	62

*One or both partners indicated this was an issue for them.

Source: Olson, D., Olson-Sigg, A., & Larson, P. *The Couple Checkup.* Nashville, TN: Thomas Nelson, 2008.

Perspectives on Communication

Communication difficulties often arise when partners have divergent communication styles. This section sheds light on three significant sources of communication-style differences: gender, culture, and sexual orientation.

Gender Differences in Communication

It needs to be understood that the differences between how men and women communicate is not true for everyone, but some of the differences may may sound familiar. These differences may be reflected in both verbal and nonverbal communication, and extend to sexual relationships as indicated in Box 4.1.

In general, according to Wood (2009), women typically see communication as the way relationships with others are sustained. For women talking is worthwhile in its own right, because it builds and sustains relationships. Of course, sharing emotions is a big part of this communication.

According to Wood (2009), men view communication as needed to settle a problem, achieve objectives, or to develop a plan. Communication is necessary to accomplish something and focuses on content. Men want closeness, but friendships can develop when doing projects together. Men may show they care about their wife or partner by doing something for them such as washing the car, making breakfast, or cleaning the garage.

The following example of one couple entering retirement makes these differences clear:

Richard has been retired for several years and has been doing woodworking as a hobby. He has built bookshelves, a desk, and has plans for many other projects. When people come to the house, he loves to show men his workshop, what he has made, and the plans for what he is going to make. The discussion usually moves quickly to the types of tools he has and what they accomplish. Men seem to love to talk about these things. He takes care of many tasks in the house such as changing filters, fixing things, and cooking. He is often heard saying, "I want to be useful."

Margaret, on the other hand, is looking forward to having more time to be with friends. She often is heard saying, "I think the next phase of life is going to be about relationships." She has not had time for such things while she was working. She has begun this process as she is phasing into retirement by meeting weekly with two different groups of women for coffee. They just talk. They talk about grandkids, activities they're involved with, and their husbands. These women have become good friends.

As one can imagine, these differences create problems between men and women. They are really from different places when it comes to communication. For example, if a woman has an issue in her life she wants to talk about, she might expect a man to acknowledge her feelings and empathize with her. He, on the other hand, wants to solve the problem and tells her how to fix the situation. She sees this as cold and uncaring; he sees it as fixing what needs to be fixed. Additionally, men want to do things together and women want to talk about feelings and relationships.

Wood (2009) concludes that these differences result from differing socialization for males and females. However, one might speculate that some of these differences are evident at birth. Watching young children play may give us clues.

Gender differences in conversational style can lead to misunderstandings if people are not aware of them. Women tend to view conversation as an opportunity to connect with another person; These young women are probably able to communicate with each other more easily than with a member of the other sex.
©Fancy/Alamy Stock Photo

BOX 4.1 At Issue
Communicating About Sex

Research indicates that communicating about sex is one of the most difficult things to do. Although this is true for any age group, it is especially true for adolescents (Widman, Choukas-Bradley, Helms, Golin, & Prinstein, 2014). In a sample of more than 600 youths, ages 12 to 15, more than half of the youths had not discussed any sexual topics with their dating partners. In addition, only about one-fourth of the students had talked to their parents or best friends about these topics. Communication was more likely if the youth was sexually active and/or female. Increased communication was also associated with more frequent use of condoms.

In a study with young adults ages 18 to 24 who were in a committed heterosexual relationship, most communication was initiated by men; 91% of the communication was nonverbal and 65% was verbal (Vannier & O'Sullivan, 2011). The responses by the partner typically matched the initiator's way of communicating. In other words, if the man initiated the communication verbally, the women responded verbally.

Earlier research supports some of these findings in that communication about sex was more likely to result in condom use (Noar, Carlyle, & Cole, 2006). They also found that conversations about one's sexual history may result in talking about condom use with their current partner. Men and women also differed in the extent of communication in that women were more likely to communicate about safer sex behaviors than men.

It seems that sexual relationships could be enhanced and responsible sexual behavior would improve if individuals communicated verbally about sex. In fact, Kristin Jozkowski (University of Arkansas News, 2013, July 2) concluded in her study of college students that when people rely on nonverbal cues, miscommunication can occur and result in unwanted sex.

Cultural Differences in Communication

The uses and interpretations of both verbal and nonverbal communication vary widely from culture to culture. In England, for example, nonverbal gestures are considered brash and undesirable. But in Italy, France, and the Polynesian islands of the southwest Pacific, among other places, nonverbal gestures are common.

Different cultures exhibit varying amounts of talking when it comes to communication. For example, in American Indian culture people do not have a need for lots of talking. Rather, they are likely to briefly state what they want to say and stop. It is not uncomfortable to have silence. Messages are also sometimes conveyed by way of stories. One such example is an American Indian man who would come into the office of one of the authors of this textbook and just sit for a period of time. Eventually, he would start telling a story about something that appeared to be totally unrelated to the topic at hand. The story would be told, and he would make a connection from the story to the issue that he wanted to talk about. Eventually the reason for having the conversation would become apparent.

Clearly, actions may be interpreted quite differently in different cultures. The nature and scope of our nonverbal communication are largely determined by our cultural heritage, as well. For example, studies have documented the different ways in which men react to beautiful women around the world: the American male lifts his eyebrows, the Italian presses his forefinger into his cheek and rotates it, the Greek strokes his cheek, the Brazilian puts an imaginary telescope to his eye, the Frenchman kisses his fingertips, and the Egyptian grasps his beard.

Westerners consider direct eye contact important, but many cultures see it as a personal affront, conveying a lack of respect. In Japan, for example, when shaking hands, bowing, and especially when talking, it is important to glance only occasionally into the other person's face. One's gaze should instead focus on fingertips, desk tops, and carpets. In the words of one American electronics representative, "Always keep your shoes shined in Tokyo. You can bet a lot of Japanese you meet will have their eyes on them" (Axtell, 2007).

Culture influences many aspects of communication, including such nonverbal elements as eye contact, facial expression, physical proximity, and touching. In addition, some cultures require few words or tell stories to communicate such as these two American Indian women.
©Szefei wong/Alamy Stock Photo

In most Latin countries, from Venezuela to Italy, the *abrazo* (hug) is as common as a handshake. Men hug men; women hug women; men hug women. In Slavic countries, this greeting is better described as a bear hug. In France, the double cheek-to-cheek greeting is common among both men and women. A traditional bow from the waist is the standard greeting for the Japanese, who are averse to casual touching. Many Americans, however, feel uncomfortable with bowing, but to the Japanese, it means "I respect your experience and wisdom."

Communication with GLBT Individuals and Couples

Communication for gay and lesbian couples is complex, given the discrimination and secrecy which often accompanies these relationships. One study about communication and resources to construct a sexual identity was conducted by Bond, Hefner, and Drogos (2009) and looked at how young people explore their gay, lesbian, and bisexual identities. These researchers found that the internet was the most common way for these participants to explore their sexual identity and the internet was the most helpful resource in the coming-out process. These findings differ from those of heterosexual individuals who are more likely to rely on face-to-face interaction with their peers and family to understand and explore their sexual identity.

The research conducted by Bond et al. (2009) also found that gay, lesbian, and bisexual participants relied so much on the internet relationships for understanding and support that they were less likely to communicate with family members. The virtual relationships found online were viewed as safe places to make connections, whereas family members were often viewed as unsafe sources of support. The researchers conclude that using the internet as a resource affects the family dynamics in a way that is different from young people who identify as heterosexual.

Another study explored how same-sex married and engaged couples communicated to their families about their marriage or upcoming marriage (Lannutti, 2013). Again, the issues they experienced in this communication were different from those experienced by couples in heterosexual relationships. This study found that for some couples announcing

Box 4.2 Putting It Together
All Together at Family Mealtimes

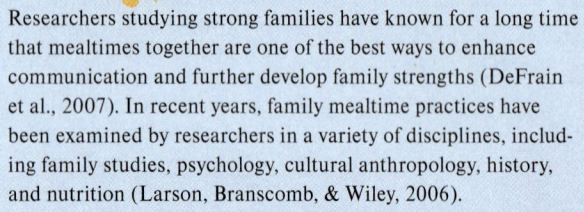

Researchers studying strong families have known for a long time that mealtimes together are one of the best ways to enhance communication and further develop family strengths (DeFrain et al., 2007). In recent years, family mealtime practices have been examined by researchers in a variety of disciplines, including family studies, psychology, cultural anthropology, history, and nutrition (Larson, Branscomb, & Wiley, 2006).

These researchers have been answering questions such as: What is the history of mealtime practices? Historically, how was mealtime different in differing socioeconomic classes? How does mealtime enhance the language skills of children? What role does mealtime play in the lives of those sitting around the dinner table?

For Linda Skogrand, mealtime on the farm in Minnesota in the 1950s and 1960s meant that work would stop and everyone could eat a large meal of meat, potatoes and gravy, vegetables, dessert, and coffee. The meal would have been prepared by the women in the family, including young girls, while the men and boys did the heavier farm labor outside. The conversation would be about the quality of the crop, whether rain would fall to interrupt the harvest, and how Grandma was doing with her recovery from the flu. There were two major mealtimes, dinner (the noon meal) and supper (the evening meal). Of course, there were lunches between these major meals.

During this same time period of the 1950s and 1960s, immigrant families might be having a different mealtime experience. The newcomers to this country might have been domestic servants providing meals to more affluent families in urban communities (Cinotto, 2006). The family mealtime was a time to serve others, and the domestic help would eat in the kitchen after everyone else had been fed. Those eating at the kitchen table were the hired help, which could include the immigrant workers' own family members.

So, what is family mealtime like today, and what purpose does it serve for family members? We might expect that family mealtime has decreased with all the competition for valuable time. Although the frequency of family mealtimes together has declined somewhat since the 1950s, in more recent years it has remained constant. Putman (2015) concludes that this may be true for middle-income families, however it may have diminished for low-income families because of the multiple responsibilities they have in order to survive. Family mealtimes today may be informal and may reflect the diversity of contemporary families today. A family member may have stopped at a restaurant on the way home from work, or families may go out to eat at a restaurant. Family mealtime may involve all members of the family participating in preparation of the meal to accommodate very busy schedules. Or an adult who has the major responsibility for homemaking may prepare the meal.

Mealtime activity can accomplish the goal of enhancing family well-being because family members can connect and share important happenings of the day. It provides opportunities for children to develop as they participate in conversations with other children and adults, solve problems, tell stories, and plan events (DeFrain & Asay, 2007; Larson et al., 2006). Putman (2015) in his book, *Our Kids*, discusses the importance of mealtimes together in having "serve-and-return" (p. 123) opportunities, referring to the give and take that goes on during family meals. Putman concludes that these mealtime opportunities have positive cognitive results for children. It is the place where communication skills are learned and cultural values are transmitted from one generation to the next (Ochs & Shohet, 2006). Although family mealtimes have changed over the years, this important time together is highly valued by most families today.

---

marriage plans or being married meant that family members treated them in a positive way, and in other cases they treated them in a negative way. For example, some family members talked about the same-sex couple in the same way other couples in the family were described, such as listing all members of the family coming to an event. Others, however, did include their adult child, but did not include the new same-sex in-law in discussions about the family. Some participants indicated family members only wanted to know about the lives of the straight members of the family. One participant in the study said that when planning a wedding the parents kept suggesting they keep the wedding small. The parent was uncomfortable "coming out" (Lannutti, 2013, p. 68) to those beyond the immediate family as having a gay or lesbian child. Participants in the study also indicated family members had varying kinds of support when it came to the couple having children.

Communicating with extended family members can be complicated when same-sex couples move into a more permanent relationship. Sometimes communication results in positive reaction and sometimes not. It is important to know that the experience is likely to be different for same-sex couples than it is for heterosexual couples.

Using Communication to Develop Intimacy

> *People forget what you say,*
> *They forget what you do,*
> *But they don't forget*
> *How you make them feel!*
>
> —Author Unknown

Good, positive communication is a hallmark of successful close relationships (Markman, Stanley, Jenkins, & Blumberg, 2004). A man might say, "We're best friends. We talk about everything. I don't know what I'd do if she weren't around to listen to my problems. She lets me know, very clearly, when she's upset about something. But I don't feel attacked. We both just sit down and work out a solution." Poor communication, on the other hand, often minimizes the possibility of establishing a close relationship. People may say, "We don't communicate." "He never talks." "She always nags." "He doesn't understand me."

Communication is important in every stage of a close relationship. The seeds of marital failure are often sown early in a relationship—sometimes even before marriage. Poor communication before marriage is likely to continue after marriage. In fact, one study showed that premarital communication was related to the likelihood of divorce 5 years after marriage (Markman, Rhoades, Stanley, & Ragan, 2010). They found that participants' self-reports of negative communication before marriage were associated with later divorce. Not surprisingly, negative communication was also related to lower levels of marital adjustment over the 5 years of their marriage. It is important, therefore, for couples to start out on the right foot when it comes to communicating, even before marriage.

Couples relationship education has been one way couples have shown to improve their communication skills. Prevention and Relationship Education Program or PREP has been one such program which has been used widely to improve couple relationships (Owen, Manthos, & Quirk, 2013). This program involved teaching couples the Speaker-Listener technique, which is when one partner communicates a concern and the other partner reflects back what the other partner was trying to convey. This study compared those who learned this technique and those who did not, and 6 months later the technique had helped these couples improve their communication skills.

Communication is a complex process, but understanding certain principles can help individuals improve their interactions with others. For example, it is useful to know that people send subtle verbal and nonverbal messages to each other no matter what they say or do, even when they aren't consciously trying to say or do anything. Therefore, one important principle of communication is that "you cannot *not* communicate." Noncommunication is also a form of communication.

Communication as a Cooperative Endeavor

When disagreement and conflicts arise, there is a natural tendency to blame the other person and deny or minimize personal responsibility for creating and maintaining the conflict. For example, a couple has an argument over the husband's refusal to discuss issues in the relationship that are important to the wife. The more she pushes him, the more the husband withdraws. He says to her, in effect, "I wouldn't withdraw so much if you stopped nagging me." To which the wife retorts, "I wouldn't nag you if you would discuss these important things with me." The discussion finally ends with the husband's withdrawing even more, which only reinforces the wife's negative feelings. This potential dialogue ends in two monologues: Each blames the other for what has happened and neither accepts responsibility for the outcome.

One model of interpersonal communication assumes a linear cause and effect. In the battle just described, the husband blames the wife because she nags and the wife blames the husband because he withdraws. This is an example of the **linear causality model**, which states that there is a direct, or linear, relationship between cause and effect. Interpersonal communication that reflects this linear model is usually destructive rather than productive. Both people end up saying, in effect, "If it weren't for you, I wouldn't act this way."

A family systems model better explains both what has happened and how to escape this type of situation. According to the **circular causality model**, both people deny responsibility for what has happened and for changing it and preventing it from happening again. In the circular causality model, one person sends out a message, which causes a change in and a response from the other person. That response causes a new response in the first person, and so on. The communication cycle usually escalates into conflict. The husband's and wife's responses to each other's comments trap them in a vicious circle of causality: He says, "I withdraw because you nag," and she says, "I nag because you withdraw." Each spouse sees her or his behavior only as a reaction to the other's behavior, not as a determining factor in the other's response. In essence, they are both escalating the conflict.

It is best to avoid the *blame game* and to focus on working together to find solutions that are acceptable to everyone involved. Whereas blaming is a competitive endeavor in which one side tries to beat the other, genuine communication is a cooperative endeavor in which the participants focus on agreement. (See Chapter 5 for a detailed discussion of various approaches to conflict resolution.)

Content and Relationship Messages

When people communicate with each other, they send out two kinds of information. The most obvious component of communication is content—that is, the facts, opinions, and experiences people relate to one another. This is also called the *report* component of communication. The report component is usually relatively straightforward and for the most part is given verbally. The other component of communication is the message—that is, what the individual conveys about the relationship at hand—for example, whether it is a friendly relationship. This is called the *relationship*, or *command*, component of communication. More subtle than the report component, the relationship component is often conveyed nonverbally. Although the content of the message being communicated may be straightforward, it is always interpreted in light of the accompanying message about the relationship between the people involved in the communication.

Nonverbal Communication

Verbal communication includes both spoken and written words. Spoken communication has various nonverbal aspects to it: tone of voice, volume, pitch, speed of speech, and rhythm of speech. Written communication also has nonverbal aspects: the style of writing (handwritten, printed, typed, sloppy, neat) and the medium (personal stationery, a card, a napkin).

Nonverbal communication takes a wide variety of forms (Knapp, Hall, & Horgan, 2014). It includes facial expressions, eye contact, gestures and other body movements, spatial behavior (for example, how far apart two people stand or sit from each other), body contact, nonverbal vocalizations (for example, sighs, grunts), and posture. Nonverbal communication is just as difficult to interpret as verbal communication. Is that yawn boredom, or is it a reflexive action?

People send some their most powerful messages nonverbally. This mother has her hand out with a frown on her face talking to her daughter. The daughter has her back to her mother, paying attention to the pile of clothes, rather than looking at her mother. Anyone looking at this picture can assume that their relationship is strained at this point.
©Andrew Olney/Stockbyte/Getty Images

The relationship component of communication has a central influence on the accurate transmission and interpretation of nonverbal messages. For example, if you saw two people hugging at the airport, you would assume that they have a close relationship. In other words, people make guesses about a relationship on the basis of nonverbal behavior and the context in which they observe the behavior.

Mixed Messages and Double Binds

People often send **mixed messages**—messages in which there is a discrepancy between the verbal and the nonverbal components. The receiver hears one thing but simultaneously feels something else. When the verbal and the nonverbal messages conflict, people tend to rely more on the nonverbal information. For example, a person collapses into her or his favorite chair to watch a favorite television show and says to another person, "Is there anything you want me to help you with now?" Although the verbal message conveys a willingness to help, the nonverbal actions express just the opposite. The person sending the message is hoping that the listener notices the discrepancy and responds to the nonverbal cues, enabling the speaker to watch the program while at the same time giving the impression of being willing to help out.

We all send mixed messages for a variety of reasons every day, but they often stem from an unwillingness to be direct and honest in our communication. Mixed messages can

Chapter 4 | Communication and Intimacy | 115

become a barrier to real understanding. Directness in communication minimizes misunderstanding and confusion.

Whereas a mixed message is a conflict between the verbal and the nonverbal components of a communication, a **double bind** occurs when the verbal and nonverbal messages (*interaction* component) relay information that causes some question or conflict about the relationship between the speaker and the receiver (the *relationship* component). The receiver is in a double bind when the speaker creates a situation—legitimate or not—that calls into question the type of relationship the receiver has with the speaker.

An example of a double bind is when one person tells a friend a secret and later learns from other people that the friend told them the secret. Because the supposed friend told a secret that was not to be shared, the speaker questions not only the trustworthiness of the friend but also the existence of the friendship. When one questions the relationship, one is caught in a double-bind situation.

Although a double bind can occur in any relationship, the probability of its occurring is greater if the relationship component is unclear. When the relationship between the two parties is established and clearly defined, the relationship component plays a less significant part in the interpretation of the message, and, consequently, the content can be more accurately understood. For example, if you say to someone, "You really are feebleminded," that message could be interpreted in a variety of ways, depending on the relationship you have with that person. If the person is a close friend, she or he would probably realize that you were just joking and might respond in a similar fashion. If, however, the other person was someone you just met, he or she might not only *not* know how to interpret what you said but might also question whether he or she would want a relationship with you at all.

Furthermore, the potential for a double-bind message hinges on the quality and mood of a relationship. If a husband brings his wife flowers, for example, the way she interprets this behavior will depend on the mood of their current relationship. If she is feeling good about the relationship, she will likely interpret the flowers as a sign of affection. Depending on recent events, however, she might also see them as a bribe, an apology, or a preparation for something to come. She might worry about what this act means, an indication that she is unsure or distrustful of her husband's behavior. Again, the interpretation depends on the quality and current mood of their relationship and on past experiences related to this event.

In summary, when the relationship between the two parties is established and clearly defined, the relationship component plays a less significant part in the interpretation of the message, and, consequently, the content is more accurately understood.

Metacommunication: Clarifying Your Communication

The original description of double-bind communications by Gregory Bateson (Bateson, Jackson, Haley, & Weakland, 1956) described a situation in which a mother visited her schizophrenic son in the hospital. When the man tried to embrace his mother, she stiffened, pulled away from him, and asked, "Don't you love me anymore?" On the verbal level, she was implying love, but nonverbally she was rejecting him. Because of his dependent relationship with her, he was unable to respond verbally to the double-bind situation she had created.

The primary way of preventing or unbinding a double bind is known as **metacommunication**—simply, communicating about communicating. It is sometimes easier for children to pick up and respond to conflicting messages than it is for adults, as illustrated in this exchange: A man was talking with an 11-year-old boy he liked very much. The boy was describing how much he disliked girls. The man commented that he really liked girls but disliked boys. After a moment of perplexity, the boy responded, "You're teasing!"—

When a couple wants to really connect with each other, they have to use all their communication skills—speaking honestly, listening attentively, requesting clarification, giving constructive feedback. Such efforts pay off in high-quality moments like the one this couple is enjoying.
©IKO/123RF

and they both laughed. In spite of the conflicting message about their relationship, the child was able to understand and to point out the incongruence. Because the man acknowledged the discrepancy, they were both able to see the humor in the situation. It did not turn into a double bind.

It is often more difficult to respond to a double-bind message that occurs within a close and dependent relationship. Because of the significance of the relationship, the possibility exists that metacommunicating might create more problems. Paradoxically, the more dependent the relationship in which the double-bind messages occur, the greater the resistance to clarifying these messages. The dilemma is this: In order to improve a relationship, one must be willing to risk losing it. Consequently, the more one has invested in a relationship, the less willing one is to discuss or change it, even though change is often necessary if the relationship is to remain vital or to grow. Because many individuals are not willing to take this *existential risk*, their relationships become increasingly predictable and routine.

Although double binds are usually seen as detrimental to a relationship, they can also prove beneficial. They can, first of all, create a situation in which one person feels the need for a clearer definition of the relationship. This can be accomplished by discussing the nature of the relationship directly, to clarify and possibly to renegotiate its nature.

Continuous Partial Attention

There can be no doubt that new technologies have improved our lives in countless ways, connecting us with each other in our communities and helping to develop human relationships around the world. These new technologies demand our attention and in many ways have speeded up our lives. Thus, they have become a double-edged sword: in some ways they help to increase human intimacy, and in other ways they diminish human intimacy.

To keep up with the relentless flow of information, ideas, and exchanges, we often find ourselves in a state of **continuous partial attention**. As we attend to our email, smartphone, computer, television, laptop, iPod, iPad, and so forth, we also are often trying to hold a genuine conversation with a friend. This form of multitasking, when it comes to developing and maintaining intimate relationships, simply does not work.

Facebook (FB) is used by many people these days, and one study found that 80% of undergraduate students used FB daily (Thompson & Lougheed, 2012, March). Today that number might be higher and would likely include many other social media venues.

Chapter 4 | Communication and Intimacy | **117**

Thompson and Lougheed found that women use FB more than men (62% versus 44%). Women also were on FB for longer periods of time than men, were more likely than men to feel stress and anxiety from their FB experience, and were more likely than men to feel they were addicted to FB. In addition to distracting people from having more intimate, one-on-one relationships, FB may also be creating negative feelings for many users.

Being employed often means being available 24/7. According to Korman (2016, December 9), the majority of employees feel they need to be available at all times and, therefore, their employers also need to be available. People often check for messages and emails before they get out of bed or shortly thereafter. Given these expectations, it is very difficult to separate work for home life. Although it adds flexibility, it also adds stress for many who feel their workday never ends. All of the increase in the use of technology can add to productivity and can help us connect to people everywhere, but it has its downside in diminishing intimacy with those who are physically in our presence.

Using Communication to Maintain Intimacy

Developing and maintaining communication skills are lifelong processes (Gottman, Schwartz Gottman, & DeClaire, 2006). Being good at communicating takes time, practice, and attention to detail. In this section we will focus on specific speaking and listening skills.

Speaking: The Art of Self-Disclosure

It is very important that as a speaker you speak for yourself, not for others. Communication problems often occur when a person tries to speak for another person, especially in a close relationship. A good way to avoid unnecessary friction is to stay away from *you should's* and *we's*. Again, the issue is one of power and control.

Self-disclosure occurs when an individual reveals to one or more people some personal information or feelings that they could not otherwise learn. We acquire information about an individual in many ways—from mutual acquaintances, from the person's behavior, and even from the clothes he or she wears. Self-disclosure differs from these other ways in that the individual willingly and with some forethought discloses the information. (Self-disclosure does sometimes also occur inadvertently.)

Self-disclosure requires both an awareness of information (reactions, goals, feelings, etc.) about oneself and a predisposition to disclose that information. For example, an adolescent may want to discuss her vocational goals with her parents, goals that do not include college. Her parents, however, are set on her going to a particular college. The daughter complies with her parents' wishes to avoid conflict and never discloses her true feelings about going to college. Thus, although she is aware of her feelings, her predisposition to disclose does not overcome her desire to avoid conflict.

Females receive more disclosures from other people than men do. Females also disclose more than men. However, these differences in disclosure can be small and are moderated by the situation and the sex of the other person. Dindia (2000) completed a comprehensive review of studies on gender and disclosure and found the following:

- Females receive more disclosures than do males.
- Females disclose more to females than males do to males.
- Females disclose more to males than males do to females.

- Females disclose more to females than males do to females.
- Females that are attractive receive more disclosure from males.

In general, there is a strong relationship between the amount of disclosure and liking a person. People disclose more to people they like, and the more they disclose, the more the other person discloses in return. More disclosure between people leads to greater feelings of closeness. So self-disclosure helps to build closeness and intimacy between people.

Self-Disclosure and Intimacy. Patterns of self-disclosure vary with each type of relationship, but relationship type is not the sole determinant of self-disclosure. High and low levels of disclosure occur among strangers, friends, and intimates. But factors such as motivation for and frequency of disclosure are likely to be related to relationship type. Let's look at three different relationships—between strangers, between friends, and between intimates—and compare the patterns of self-disclosure among them.

If you were to ask your average city bus rider why he or she never reveals personal information to the bus driver, the answer you'd probably get is "that wouldn't seem right." What this means is that disclosure does not seem appropriate between people who don't really know each other. Personal disclosure to strangers seems inappropriate because there is no relationship history to serve as a foundation for the disclosure. There are, of course, exceptions to the general rule. When one stranger discloses to another, it may be because the discloser knows that he or she will never see the other person again and therefore feels there is little risk.

"I was on a plane trip from Texas to Chicago," related Lydia, a young art student. "I found myself seated next to a young man who, like myself, was a student. We talked casually for a few minutes, mentioning where we had spent our vacations. However, by the time the plane had reached cruising altitude, he began asking me questions about my relationship with my boyfriend, future plans for marriage, motivations for marrying, and a host of other pointed and personal questions.

"I was rather surprised to be asked to reveal such personal information, but I was even more surprised to find myself answering his questions. At first I was wriggling with discomfort at disclosing to a complete stranger. But although the questions were startling, his manner was not at all offensive. In fact, he seemed rather likable. Because he also revealed some information about himself, I revealed more personal information and feelings to him. I guess I felt I had nothing to lose because I would never see him again."

Strangers also engage in self-disclosure in structured support groups such as Weight Watchers, Alcoholics Anonymous, grief groups, or group psychotherapy. Here, self-disclosure is encouraged so that the group may help the person work through feelings related to a specific goal or task. Because the group's purpose is to help the group member deal with problems that he or she might feel uncomfortable expressing in another situation, there is less concern about the appropriateness of self-disclosure.

Self-Disclosure in Friendships and Intimate Relationships. Although self-disclosure is not expected between strangers, it is expected and desired between good friends. The discloser is usually aware of how the receiver will react to a disclosure on the basis of what has gone on previously in the relationship. Although self-disclosure between friends may be quite selective, it may also become quite intimate and personal as the friends increase their mutual trust and exclusivity. In a relationship between friends, self-disclosure increases the listener's obligations because the listener also feels compelled to self-disclose.

Some couples, even though they are physically together, are more focused on their cell phones, work, newspaper, etc., and less focused on each other.
©Mediaphotos/iStock/ Getty Images

Mutual disclosure helps the friendship develop more equally on both sides. Their close relationship and previous knowledge about each other allow friends to move quickly from impersonal to personal communication: One moment they may be talking about a mutual friend's wedding and the next about their personal feelings about their own marriages.

Figure 4.1 summarizes some research on self-disclosure, positive comments, and negative comments in various types of relationships. (The positive and negative comments were about the partner and sometimes about the relationship.) Interactions with strangers tend to involve low-to-moderate self-disclosure and many more positive than negative comments. The greatest degree of self-disclosure and a high level of positive comments are seen in

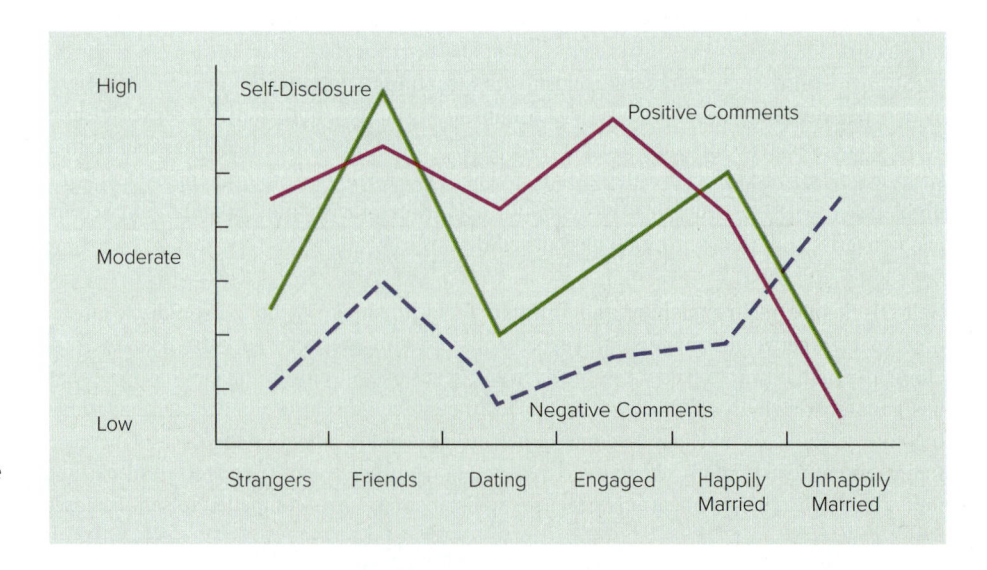

FIGURE 4.1
Self-Disclosure and Positive and Negative Comments by Relationship Type

120   Part II   Dynamics of Intimate Relationships

close friendships, which are also characterized by a moderate amount of negative comments. Dating relationships tend to have a higher level of expression of positive feelings and lower levels of both self-disclosure and negative comments. As couples move toward engagement, positive comments are at their highest, and both self-disclosure and negative comments increase. Happily married couples tend to be moderate to high on both positive and negative comments, as well as on self-disclosure. In contrast, unhappily married couples are very low on positive comments, very low on self-disclosure, and very high on negative comments.

When Self-Disclosure May Not Be Healthy

There are times and situations, however, where self-disclosure is not helpful even in intimate relationships. For example, individuals may not complete self-disclosure because they want to keep their own stress from affecting others in negative ways. One such example is when a spouse is in the military and the spouse who is not deployed hides concerns which can interfere with the health and safety of the person deployed (Joseph & Afifi, 2010). There are going to be times when a person feels they must protect their deployed spouse from stressful information so the person can stay focused on the task at hand. These authors suggest that other military spouses who have had experience with disclosure be a resource as to when to disclose information and when to buffer their deployed spouses.

There are other times when sharing all thoughts may not be helpful (Caughlin & Basinger, 2015). One example is when a person is in a potentially abusive situation with her or his spouse. A wife, for example, may not say what she wants to say because the words may put her at risk for further abuse. Divorced parents might not want to be totally open with children about their feelings toward their ex-spouse (Caughlin & Basinger, 2015). This would not be helpful for children and would only create conflict in the shared parenting responsibilities.

Caughlin and Basinger (2015) conclude that even happy couples and families are not completely open and honest all the time. These researchers suggest that there needs to be moderation when it comes to openness in couples and families. Individuals need to balance openness with discretion, politeness, and other values.

Listening: A Difficult Skill

We hear only half of what is said to us, understand only half of that, believe only half of that, and remember only half of that.

—MIGNON MCLAUGHLIN, JOURNALIST

People have a tendency to judge one another, listening to what others say and then deciding whether they are "right" or "wrong." "Being right" usually means that we agree with the other person, and "being wrong," that we disagree with the other person. Good listening skills require suspending judgment and spending more energy trying to understand other people. An important listening skill is to restate the speaker's ideas and feelings for verification. Although this approach slows down communication, it minimizes misunderstanding and conflict. When the goal of communication is to control other people, listening skills are of little importance. If the goal is to connect with other people and to develop genuine emotional intimacy, however, listening is essential.

Sherod Miller and his colleagues consider listening to be the process of developing a full understanding of another person's *story* (situation, concern, point of view). Effective listeners are aware of and make choices about how much they will attempt to direct or influence the speaker's telling of the story. Miller and his colleagues note that the listener's motives are paramount and identify three basic motives, or goals, among listeners: (1) to lead by persuading, (2) to clarify by directing, and (3) to discover by attending (Miller & Miller, 2012).

The distinguishing factor of each of these three listening motives is the degree of control, or power, the listener desires over the situation. Does the listener follow the leader, allowing the speaker to relate the story in her or his own way? Or does the listener become the leader—getting the speaker to tell the story in the way the listener wants to hear it? Either approach affects the quality and integrity of the information that is exchanged.

Persuasive listening is hardly listening at all; the "listener" is really looking for an opening to jump in and control the direction of the conversation. Sometimes the persuader resembles a television reporter trying hard to get that 10- to 15-second sound bite for the evening news.

Directive listening involves less control than persuasive listening, but it does attempt to channel, or direct, the conversation. Studies indicate that excellent salespeople (those most likely to make the sale) ask four times as many questions as the average salesperson (Miller & Miller, 2012). The questions control the direction of the conversation, steering it where the directive listener wants it to go. Directive listening has certain advantages. It quickly focuses a conversation, and if the speaker cooperates, it allows the directive questioner to take charge of the dialogue. The major disadvantage of directive listening, however, is that in the interest of efficiency, crucial elements of the story may be lost. Directive listeners who use the approach in a very curt manner often fail to really understand what they are being told. By controlling the direction of the conversation, the directive listener may also lead the speaker down a blind alley into a trap.

Attentive listening is a mode in which the listener simply lets the speaker tell the story spontaneously and without interruption, encouraging rather than directing the teller. Busy people sometimes feel that attentive listening is too time consuming. In fact, it is more efficient than the other approaches because it lets the speaker get to the *real* point, avoiding misunderstanding and confusion. It is clearly the most effective listening mode for building

Attentive listening is a rare skill worth cultivating. It not only builds trust and intimacy in a relationship but also most efficiently allows the speaker to get a point across—without interruption or distraction.
©Image Source

rapport and trust. People who practice this skill, usually described as *good listeners*, find this a positive trait to have in both their professional and personal lives. Here's how one attentive listener, a retired newspaper editor, described the benefits of learning how to listen well:

> *"I hope I don't sound immodest, but I think the main reason people have always liked me over the years is because I'm a good listener. I really enjoy hearing what other people have to say. I don't have any desire to sit in judgment of them, or to feel superior, or to give out a lot of advice. I simply like to listen and try to understand how their world works. It's always very interesting."*
>
> *"People take this as a supreme compliment. They smile when they see me coming, and they're always coming up to me to tell me the latest story about their lives because they know I'll appreciate it if it's funny or sympathize with them if it's sad. It's really kind of fun. I always know what's happening, more than anyone else I know. My ability to listen served me well all those years in the newspaper business, too."*

Assertive, Passive, and Aggressive Communication

Be careful of your thoughts: They may become words at any moment.
—Proverbs 16:23

Researchers have identified three styles of responses in interpersonal communication: passive, aggressive, and assertive (Olson et al., 2008). Each response style has effects on both the respondent and the partner. Assertive statements were consistently found to be the most accurate, expressive, self-enhancing, and productive in terms of achieving a goal.

Assertive communication involves the expression of thoughts, feelings, and desires as one's right as an individual. Because it is self-expressive, assertive communication frequently uses the personal pronouns *I* and *me*. Assertiveness is associated with feelings of self-esteem, self-confidence, and determination to express opinions or feelings. Assertiveness, in sum, is giving yourself the right to be who you are without infringing on the rights of your partner to be who he or she is. Assertiveness enables people to feel good about themselves and increases the likelihood of achieving personal goals. Because assertiveness encourages expressiveness rather than defensiveness, it facilitates intimacy between partners.

Passive communication is characterized by an unwillingness to say what one thinks, feels, or wants. Passive behavior is frequently associated with feelings of anxiety about others' opinions, overconcern about the feelings of others ("I just didn't want to hurt her"), and fears about saying or doing anything that can be criticized ("I was afraid of saying the 'wrong' thing"). Passive responses reinforce feelings of low self-esteem, limit expressiveness, leave a well of hurt and anxious feelings, and make achievement of personal goals unlikely. Receivers of passive responses often feel anger at and lack of respect for the sender, realizing that their goals have been achieved at the sender's expense. Passive behavior does little to enhance either person's feelings about oneself or the other and creates distance rather than intimacy.

Aggressive communication aims to hurt or put down another person and to protect the self-esteem of the aggressor. Aggressive statements are characterized by blame and accusation ("You always? . . . ," "You never . . ."). Aggressive behavior is associated with intense, angry feelings and thoughts of getting even. When people act in an aggressive manner with their partners, it reinforces the notion that the partner is to blame for the aggressor's frustration, that it is the partner's responsibility to make things "right." Aggressiveness is expressive behavior, but it is all too often self-enhancing at the other's expense. Goals may be

> **Box 4.3 Putting It Together**
>
> *Using Communication to Increase Intimacy*
>
> Using simple communication techniques like those listed below can help you increase and improve intimacy.
>
> - Look for the good in your partner and give compliments.
> - Praise your partner as much as possible.
> - Take time to listen, listen, listen.
> - Listen to understand, not to judge.
> - After listening carefully, summarize your partner's comments before you share your reactions or feelings.
> - Be assertive. Share your feelings by using "I" statements (i.e., "I feel," "I think," or "I would like").
> - Share personal feelings.
> - When issues arise, avoid blaming each other, and talk directly about how to deal with the issue differently.
> - If issues persist, focus on creating as many new solutions as you can and then try them one at a time.
> - If problems still persist, seek counseling early, when it's easier to find solutions.
> - Give your relationship the priority and attention you did when you were dating.

achieved, but only by hurting and humiliating the other. The partner may also retaliate in kind. Because aggressive behavior focuses on the negative aspects of people rather than the negative aspects of the *situation*, it generally escalates in negative spirals, leaving both partners feeling hurt and frustrated and creating distance in the relationship.

Assertiveness, passiveness, and aggressiveness are not personality traits; they are types of responses or behaviors. In most cases, it is inappropriate to label oneself or another an assertive, passive, or aggressive person. Some people use certain types of behaviors in specific situations or with certain people. For example, some women report that they have difficulty expressing their feelings or desires assertively in sexual relationships.

(Box 4.3 offers some excellent suggestions for improving intimacy through communication.)

Positive and Negative Communication Cycles

A study of over 50,000 married couples revealed that a positive communication cycle involves assertiveness and self-confidence and that a negative communication cycle is characterized by avoidance and partner dominance (Olson et al., 2008). The definitions of assertiveness, self-confidence, avoidance, and partner dominance are as follows:

Assertiveness is a person's ability to express her or his feelings and desires to a partner.
Self-confidence is a measure of how a person feels about herself or himself and the ability to control things in her or his life.
Avoidance is a person's tendency to minimize issues and a reluctance to deal with issues directly.
Partner dominance is the degree to which a person feels her or his partner tries to be controlling and dominant in their relationship.

In a positive communication cycle, as people become more assertive with their partner, they also tend to become more self-confident. This occurs, in part, because assertiveness often enables people to get more of what they want from others. Getting more of what they want tends to make them feel more self-confident. And as they gain more self-confidence,

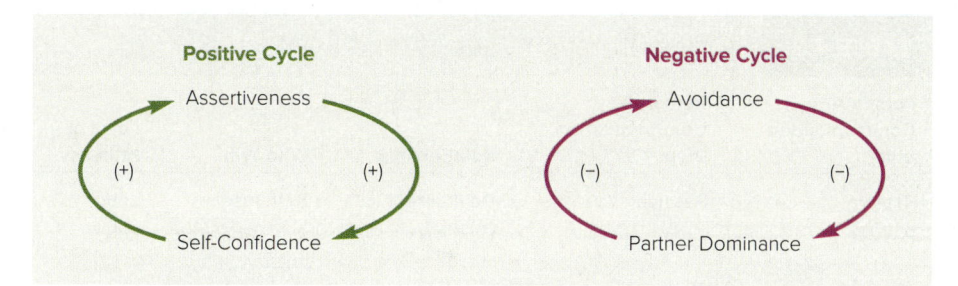

FIGURE 4.2
Positive and Negative Communication Cycles

they tend to be more willing to be assertive. This positive cycle illustrates how communication skills can help people develop more positive feelings about each other (Figure 4.2).

In a negative communication cycle, as one person avoids making decisions, the other partner will take over and become more dominant, and as one partner becomes more dominant, the other partner may further withdraw (that is, become avoidant). The combination of avoidance and partner dominance creates the negative communication cycle.

Research has found that couples in which both partners are assertive and self-confident tend to have very happy marriages. Conversely, couples in which one partner is dominant and the other is avoidant tend to have unhappy marriages.

The Positive Influence of Assertiveness

Assertive communication involves the expression of thoughts, feelings, and desires as one's right. It is self-focused and, therefore, favors "I" statements rather than "you" statements. An assertive person is able to ask for what she or he wants without demanding it or infringing on the rights of others. Assertive people tend to feel better about themselves because they are able to express themselves.

One goal in helping a couple improve their relationship is to try to help both people become more assertive with each other. Increasing assertiveness tends to increase each person's self-confidence and decrease avoidance and perceived partner dominance. Assertiveness generally has a positive impact on the person and on a couple's relationship (Olson et al., 2008).

In general, assertive individuals feel better about their partners and their relationships than nonassertive individuals. When both persons are assertive with each other, the level of intimacy increases because both partners are able to ask for what they want and, therefore, increase the probability that they will get what they want.

The Negative Influence of Avoidance

Avoidance, or a person's unwillingness or inability to deal with problematic issues, tends to be highest in people who are passive or nonassertive. Conversely, people who are very assertive tend to be low in avoidance.

Increasing evidence suggests that avoidance creates problems in close relationships. John Gottman and his colleagues (Gottman et al., 2006) describe the *avoidant style* quite well. Avoidant couples often minimize conflict by *agreeing to disagree*. Another common technique that avoidant couples use is *stonewalling*—shutting out the other person and not responding to her or him.

In a couple skills program called PREP (Prevention and Relationship Enhancement Program), developed by Howard Markman and Scott Stanley, counselors discovered that avoidance was very problematic for couples. In their book *12 Hours to a Great Marriage*

TABLE 4.3 Communication Patterns and Intimacy

Person A Communication Style	Person B Communication Style	Relationship	Who Wins	Level of Intimacy
Passive	Passive	Devitalized	Both lose	Low
Passive	Aggressive	Dominating	One wins, one loses	Low
Aggressive	Aggressive	Conflicted	Both lose	Low
Assertive	Passive	Frustrated	Both lose	Low
Assertive	Aggressive	Confrontational	Both lose	Low
Assertive	Assertive	Vitalized	Both win	High

(2004), Markman and colleagues describe the process of avoidance. They define avoidance as the reluctance to have any discussion that would raise problematic issues. When couples regularly avoid talking about risky issues, this is a sign that avoidance is becoming a more common style that will lead to problems in the long run.

The communication style a couple develops influences how intimate and close they will feel toward each other. Table 4.3 lists communication styles and their associated relationship styles, outcomes, and intimacy levels. For example, passive couples typically do not ask for what they want, and so partners usually will not get what they want. The result is a devitalized relationship with a low level of intimacy. When one partner is aggressive and the other passive, the aggressive partner tends to dominate the relationship, and this also results in a low level of intimacy. And when both partners use an aggressive style, the relationship is likely to be conflicted and low in intimacy (Olson et al., 2008).

In summary, it is clear that assertiveness (not aggressiveness) has a very positive impact on a couple's relationship, whereas avoidance has a negative influence. Learning assertiveness tends to help people overcome the more negative style of avoidance, so the more both people in a relationship can help each other become assertive with each other, the greater chance they will have in building each other's self-confidence and decreasing their feeling of being dominated by the partner. Couples in which both partners are high in assertiveness and self-confidence will feel better about their communication, how they resolve conflict, and, ultimately, how happy they are with their relationship.

Summary

- Communication, the process of sharing messages, is an integral part of intimacy.
- In a national survey of couple communication strengths, happy couples agreed more often than unhappy couples that they were satisfied with how they talked to each other as partners, had no trouble believing each other, felt their partners did not make comments that put them down, were not afraid to ask their partners for what they wanted, and felt free to express their true feelings to their partners.
- The top five communication issues identified by couples in a national survey were the following: They wished their partners would share their feelings; they had difficulty asking their partners for what they wanted; their partners did not understand how they felt; their partners often refused to discuss issues/problems; and their partners made comments that put them down.
- Men and women tend to have different priorities when it comes to communication. Men are more likely to be concerned with doing things and women are more concerned with developing and maintaining relationships.

- To keep up with the relentless flow of information, ideas, and exchanges, we often find ourselves in a state of continuous partial attention. As we attend to our email, smartphone, computer, television, laptop, iPod, iPad, and so forth, we also are often trying to hold a genuine conversation with a friend. This form of multitasking, when it comes to developing and maintaining intimate relationships, simply does not work.
- Facebook is used by many individuals and can actually create stress because of what they see and read. Women spend more time on Facebook and are more likely to be stressed as a result.
- Self-disclosure—individual revelations of personal information or feelings—is a key to the development of intimacy.
- Listening is the process of developing a full understanding of another person's *story* (situation, concern, point of view).
- Persuasive listeners and directive listeners try to control the conversation. Attentive listeners aim at fully understanding the other person's point of view, an approach that encourages the development of genuine intimacy.
- Assertive communication assumes that expressing thoughts, feelings, and desires is the right of the individual. Passive communication is characterized by an unwillingness to say what one thinks, feels, or wants. Aggressive communication aims at hurting or putting down the other person.
- Assertiveness and self-confidence are key elements of a positive communication cycle. A negative communication cycle is characterized by avoidance and partner dominance.
- The more assertive, and less avoidant partners are, the more satisfying their relationship will be.

Key Terms

communication
linear causality model
circular causality model
nonverbal communication
mixed message
double bind
metacommunication
continuous partial attention
self-disclosure
persuasive listening
directive listening
attentive listening
assertive communication
passive communication
aggressive communication
assertiveness
self-confidence
avoidance
partner dominance

Activities

1. As adults, men are more likely to communicate about content or projects, whereas women are more likely to communicate about relationships and feelings. Observe young children and see if there is evidence of these differences at an early age.
2. Because males and females are socialized differently, adult male culture differs somewhat from adult female culture. What can parents do for their children in the early years to minimize confusion and misunderstanding between the sexes later on?
3. Use the Couple and Family Scales in Appendix A to rate the communication in your family of origin now or at some time in the past. Identify the most positive and most negative aspects of that communication.
4. Use the Couple and Family Scales in Appendix A to rate the communication at various stages of a current relationship (friendship, dating, cohabiting, marriage). How has the communication changed over time on each aspect of the scale?
5. Focus on assertive, passive, and aggressive behavior in this exercise. Form groups of four. Two people will role-play the following styles for 2 to 3 minutes while the other two people observe. After each segment, discuss what it felt like to play the assigned role or to observe the role playing. When your group has role-played all three styles, compare and contrast the various styles.
   a. Passive and aggressive (one person acts passively; one acts aggressively)
   b. Assertive and passive (one acts assertively; one acts passively)
   c. Assertive and assertive (both people are assertive)

Suggested Readings

Axtell, R. E. (2007). *Essential do's and taboos: The complete guide to international business and leisure travel.* Hoboken, NJ: Wiley. A fun and funny book.

Gottman, J. M. (2011). *The science of trust: Emotional attunement for couples.* New York, NY: W. W. Norton.

Gottman, J. M., Schwartz Gottman, J., & DeClaire, J. (2006). *Ten lessons to transform your marriage: America's love lab experts share their strategies for strengthening your relationships.* New York, NY: Crown. The latest book from the University of Washington research team.

Journal of Family Communication. Philadelphia, PA: Routledge. JFC publishes original empirical and theoretical papers that advance the understanding of the communication processes within or about families. JFC is also committed to publishing manuscripts that address issues related to the intersection between families, communication, and social systems, such as mass media, education, health care, and law and policy. Web site: http://www.tandf.co.uk/journals/hjfc

Knapp, M. L., Hall, J. A., Horgan, T. G. (2014). *Nonverbal communication in human interaction* (8th ed.). Boston, MA: Wadsworth.

Markman, H. J., Stanley, S. M., Jenkins, N. H., & Blumberg, S. L. (2004). *12 hours to a great marriage: A step-by-step guide for making love last.* San Francisco, CA: Jossey-Bass. Most recent popular book from Markman, the marriage communication authority, and his colleagues.

Monaghan, L., Goodman, J. E., & Robinson, J. M. (Eds.). (2012). *A cultural approach to interpersonal communication.* Malden, MA: Wiley-Blackwell.

Olson, D. H., Olson-Sigg, A., & Larson, P. J. (2008). *The couple checkup: Finding your relationship strengths.* Nashville, TN: Thomas Nelson. Based on a national survey of 50,000 marriages.

Seiler, W. J., & Beall, M. L. (2011). *Communication: Making connections* (8th ed.). Boston, MA: Pearson/Allyn and Bacon.

Visit the text-specific Online Learning Center at **www.mhhe.com/olson9e** for practice tests, chapter summaries, and PowerPoint slides.

5 Conflict and Conflict Resolution

©Stuart Jenner/Getty Images

Couple Strengths and Issues in Conflict Resolution

Conflict and Anger: An Overview

Intimacy and Conflict

Things to Consider in Resolving Conflict

Conflict Between Parents and Children

Summary

Key Terms

Activities

Suggested Readings

Because people view the world from a wide variety of perspectives and have different goals, conflict is an inevitable part of intimate human relationships. In fact, the more intimate our relationships, the more chances there are for interpersonal conflict. Although conflict may be *normal* in a statistical sense, it does not have to escalate into verbal and physical violence. There are many constructive approaches to settling disagreements. **Conflict** is defined as one person opposing another person's position (Canary & Canary, 2013). It can occur between adults, between adults and children, and between children.

In this chapter we will begin with the results of a national survey (Olson, Olson-Sigg, & Larson, 2008) that identified the strengths of happily married couples versus unhappily married couples in how they resolve conflict. We will also review the five major conflict resolution issues reported by couples in this survey. These data set the stage for the rest of the chapter, in which we will discuss conflict and anger and the relationship between intimacy and conflict. We will also explore 16 rules for fair fighting and some basic approaches for constructive versus destructive conflict resolution.

Couple Strengths and Issues in Conflict Resolution

A national survey of more than 50,000 married couples focused on happy and unhappy couples in the group and revealed the most common strengths for happy couples regarding conflict resolution (Olson et al., 2008). The researchers found that happy couples (78%) are much more likely than unhappy couples (20%) to say that during a discussion of problems their partner understands their opinions and ideas. The survey also found that happy couples (78%) are much more likely than unhappy couples (25%) to say that they can share feelings and ideas with their partner during a disagreement. Happy couples were nearly five times (58%) as likely as unhappy couples (12%) to feel that they are able to resolve their differences. Nearly three-fourths (72%) of happy couples, compared to 28% of unhappy couples, have similar ideas about how to settle a disagreement. Finally, happy couples were nearly four times as likely (54%) as unhappy couples (14%) to feel that their partner takes their disagreements seriously (Table 5.1).

TABLE 5.1 Strengths of Happy Couples Versus Unhappy Couples Regarding Conflict Resolution

RELATIONSHIP ISSUE	PERCENTAGE IN AGREEMENT	
	Happy Couples	Unhappy Couples
1. When we discuss problems, my partner understands my opinions and ideas.	78%	20%
2. I can share feelings and ideas with my partner during disagreements.	78	25
3. We are able to resolve our differences.	58	12
4. We have similar ideas about how to settle disagreements.	72	28
5. My partner takes our disagreements seriously.	54	14

Source: Olson, D., Olson-Sigg, A., & Larson, P. *The Couple Checkup.* Nashville, TN: Thomas Nelson, 2008.

TABLE 5.2 Top Five Conflict Problems for Couples

Conflict Issue	Percentage of Couples Having Problem*
1. One person ends up feeling responsible for the problem.	80%
2. I go out of my way to avoid conflict with my partner.	78
3. We have different ideas about the best way to solve disagreements.	77
4. Some of our differences never seem to get resolved.	77
5. We sometimes have serious disputes over unimportant issues.	76

*One or both partners indicated this was an issue for them.

Source: Olson, D., Olson-Sigg, A., & Larson, P. *The Couple Checkup.* Nashville, TN: Thomas Nelson, 2008.

In terms of the most common conflict resolution problems for couples, the national sample of married couples revealed that among the vast majority (80%), the partners agreed that during a conflict one person ends up feeling responsible for the problem rather than both. Seventy-eight percent of the couples reported that they go out of their way to avoid conflict with their partner. Most couples (77%) feel that they have different ideas about the best way to solve disagreements, and most couples (77%) report that some of their differences never seem to get resolved. Finally, most couples (76%) said they sometimes have serious disputes over unimportant issues (see Table 5.2).

Conflict and Anger: An Overview

> *For one human being to love another: that is perhaps the most difficult of all our tasks, the ultimate, the last test and proof, the work for which all other work is but preparation.*
>
> —Rainer Maria Rilke (1904)

If conflict is not resolved, it continues to grow. In this section we will focus on the hierarchical process of conflict and discuss the value of early decision making in preventing problems and crises. We will explore some myths and taboos that limit our ability to express anger in a constructive manner and prevent us from establishing intimate relationships.

The Hierarchy of Conflict

The hierarchy of conflict, illustrated in Figure 5.1, can be thought of as a continuum, ranging from discussions of daily events to crises. The lowest three levels in the conflict hierarchy represent common reasons for individuals to get together to have a discussion: to chat about daily events, to discuss ideas, and to express feelings. These discussions generally operate at a low level of tension and usually entail little or no pressure for making decisions. The next four levels in the hierarchy involve increasing tension and the need for a decision. An awareness of the need for a decision precedes decision making. If a decision that should be made is not made, this could lead to the development of a problem, which would then need to be solved. If the problem is not solved, it could lead to a crisis, which is more difficult to resolve.

FIGURE 5.1
The Hierarchy of Conflict

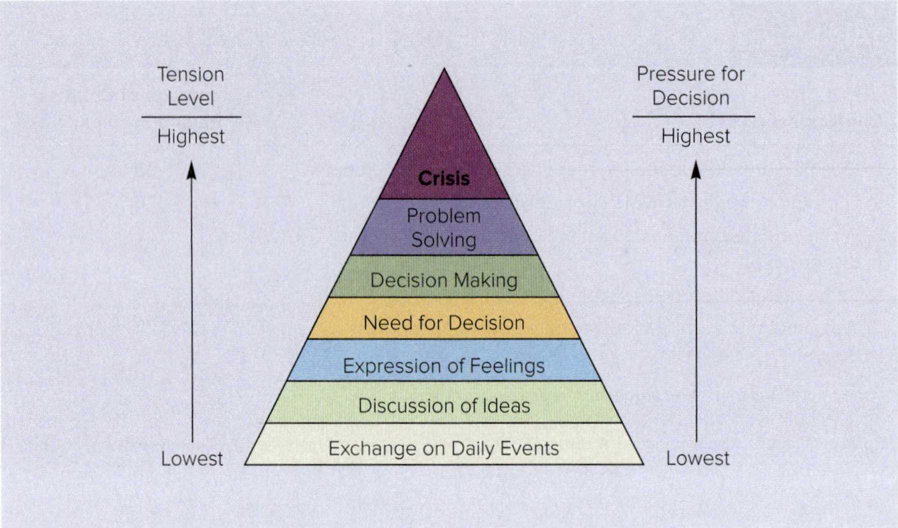

Tension Level
Highest
Lowest
Crisis
Problem Solving
Decision Making
Need for Decision
Expression of Feelings
Discussion of Ideas
Exchange on Daily Events
Pressure for Decision
Highest
Lowest

As an example of the hierarchical process of conflict, let's consider a couple, Joanne and Gary, who need to make a decision about birth control. The process involves three phases: the decision-making phase, the problem-solving phase, and the crisis-resolution phase.

Decision-Making Phase. If Joanne and Gary are aware that they need birth control, then they need to make a decision about the type of method(s) to use. If they are not aware, then they won't make a decision; this could lead to pregnancy (a potential problem), and an unwanted pregnancy could become a crisis. Even if they are aware of the need for a decision, however, they may not be willing or able to make a decision, which could also lead to crisis. In other words, deciding not to decide *is,* in fact, a decision, but it is one that often produces undesirable consequences. Even if they do make a decision, it may be either effective or ineffective. An effective decision might be to use the birth control pill, which would greatly minimize the chance of an unwanted pregnancy. An ineffective decision would be to choose, say, withdrawal as their sole form of birth control.

Problem-Solving Phase. Problems can arise for Joanne and Gary if they made no decision or if the decision they made was ineffective. If Joanne becomes pregnant and neither Gary nor Joanne wants to have a baby, they have reached the problem level. In the problem-solving phase, Joanne could consider whether to have an abortion. If she does not want an abortion or fails to decide within three months, the problem becomes more serious.

Crisis-Resolution Phase. Not dealing with the unwanted pregnancy could lead Joanne and Gary into a crisis. A crisis has the highest level of tension and creates the most pressure for a decision. Both tension and pressure increase the difficulty of making an adequate decision. The failure to make a decision earlier (to decide, for example, on a type of birth control) or the failure to make an effective decision (deciding, for example, to use a lower-risk, but relatively less reliable, method of birth control) forces Joanne and Gary to make a more difficult decision (whether to have the child or an abortion, whether to get married, whether to relinquish the child for adoption).

One would expect Joanne and Gary to be aware of potential problems and to therefore make an early effective decision to prevent problems and avert crisis. However, many

If this couple is in a situation that requires a decision, they should deal with it as early as possible. When decisions are avoided, problems arise; when problems are ignored, crises develop.
©Digital Vision/Getty Images

individuals, couples, and families put off making easier, less complex preventive decisions. As a result, they are later faced with problems or crisis situations. This hierarchy of conflict model illustrates the sequential flow toward crisis and points up the importance of awareness and early decision making in preventing problems and crises.

Anger and Conflict Taboos

Most couples are afraid of negative emotions—anger, resentment, jealousy, bitterness, hurt, disgust, and hatred—and have a difficult time learning how to deal with them. A common tactic is to suppress negative emotions, hoping they will disappear with time. There are two predominant reasons for suppressing negative emotions. One is sociological in nature; the other is psychological.

Our culture and many others have a taboo against the expression of anger. This message, transmitted verbally and nonverbally from generation to generation, says that nice and competent people do not show anger, that anger is wrong, and that anger indicates that something is terribly wrong in a relationship. This message requires individuals to deny their genuine feelings and keeps them from being in touch with their true emotions. Repressed anger can lead to high levels of stress for individuals and their relationships, as Doris, a young woman married for five years, describes:

> *I don't know what to do or think anymore. I know he loves me . . . I guess. He's just got so many rules he lives by, and so many rules I'm supposed to live by and the kids are supposed to live by. Maybe it's easier for him to live by these rules. Maybe he doesn't really think about them. I don't know. I just can't live by them anymore. The tension in me is volcanic. I find myself crying uncontrollably sometimes. I never have been able to express my feelings. My body expresses them. And now my feelings have built up so I can't seem to keep from exploding.*

The psychological reason for suppressing negative emotions has to do with human insecurity. Individuals think, "If I let other people know what I am really thinking and who I

Chapter 5 | Conflict and Conflict Resolution | 133

really am, they won't love me and I will be abandoned." In intimate relationships, partners struggle to find a delicate balance between dependence on each other and independence from each other. Some observers call that balance *interdependence*. In families, too, children and adolescents struggle to differentiate themselves from their parents and their siblings, to stake out territory and beliefs that are their own. People search for individuality while at the same time trying to maintain close relationships.

Some have been socialized to believe that all disagreements in a relationship are wrong, falsely assuming that the essence of marriage is harmony at any price. Such beliefs can be devastating to a relationship in the long run. Drew, a 30-year-old man, describes his relationship with his wife, Estelle:

> *When I was growing up, my parents gave me the impression that fighting was wrong in a happy family and that kids should be shielded from it. When they wanted to have a good argument, they would wait until we kids were out of the house or asleep. I grew up believing that my mom and dad never fought.*

Fortunately, Drew and Estelle were both intelligent, creative, and committed to the marriage. They stuck with each other long enough to find out how to face and deal with conflict in a positive and productive way.

> *Estelle, my wife, is from an alcoholic family. Her father would get drunk and pull the telephone cord out of the wall, push her mom around, and hit the kids. The meeting of these two approaches to conflict in one marriage was quite perilous for a number of years. My wife sometimes pushed and pushed until I blew up. She expected violence from men and pushed so she could get it over with and ease the tension. I would try to hold in my anger, but eventually I couldn't stand it any longer. One evening I got so mad I picked up a hamper full of clothes and was going to throw it at her.*

People tend to have negative attitudes toward conflict because of the popular assumption that love is the opposite of hate. Both love and hate are intense feelings. Rather than being opposites, however, they are more like two sides of the same coin. The line between the two is a fine one, with feelings of love often preceding those of hate. Nevertheless, when negative feelings are stifled, positive feelings also die. People often say, "I don't feel anything toward my spouse anymore. Not love or hate. I'm just indifferent." Indifference—lack of feeling—is the opposite of anger and love and hate. In the words of one loving father about his children, "If I didn't give a damn, I wouldn't get mad." Anger and love are connected; we often are angriest with the ones we love.

Rollo May (1969) described the dynamic connection between love and hate when he said:

> A curious thing which never fails to surprise persons in therapy is that after admitting their anger, animosity, and even hatred for a spouse and berating him or her during the hour, they end up with feelings of love toward this partner. A patient may have come in smoldering with negative feelings but resolved, partly unconsciously, to keep these as a good gentleman does, to himself; but he finds that he represses the love for the partner at the same time as he suppresses his aggression. . . . The positive cannot come out until the negative does also. . . . Hate and love are not polar opposites; they go together.

Myths, Theories, and Facts About Anger

In all matters of opinion, our adversaries are insane.

—MARK TWAIN (1907)

Bill Borcherdt (1996, 2000) offered an insightful perspective in his discussion of anger: "Of all the human emotions, anger has created the most harm and caused the greatest destruction within individuals, couples, families, and between social groups and nations" (1996, p. 53). This perspective seems to be as true today as it was when he wrote about it several years ago. Anger is a double-edged sword; just as it is directed at others, so it becomes internalized by the angry individual. As Borcherdt put it: "It is impossible to hate, despise, or resent somebody without suffering oneself." Although anger can sometimes make people feel good, it can also make them feel guilty and less positive about themselves.

Anger can also produce a feeling of strength and power. It deludes people into thinking that they are doing something constructive about the problems they face, when actually they are only making things worse. Anger lets people substitute feelings of superiority for those of hurt and rejection. It also allows them to think anything they want about another person without fear of retaliation.

Four common but false beliefs about anger are that it is externally caused, that it is best to express anger openly and directly, that it can be a helpful and beneficial emotion, and that it will prevent other people from taking advantage of you (Borcherdt, 1996, 2000). Let's take a closer look at these beliefs.

- *Anger is caused by others.* Many people believe that "somebody or something outside of you magically gets into your gut and makes you angry or gets you upset" (Borcherdt, 1996, p. 54). One's happiness or unhappiness, however, is not externally caused, Borcherdt points out. Anger, like any other human emotion, is self-created, usually when someone else does something we don't like.
- *The best way to deal with anger is to let it all out.* Although venting anger may make people feel better for the moment, it won't help them get any better. Letting it all out does not resolve the underlying issues. In fact, it tends to bring out those same feelings in others, increasing both people's anger.
- *Anger is a beneficial emotion.* This is simply not true. Individuals may find in the short run that they get their way by getting angry, but in the long run they will push others away from them or provoke them to get even.
- *You're a wimp if you don't get angry.* Some people believe that if they don't get angry, others will take advantage of them or consider them weak and inferior. Borcherdt urges people to decide how they want to feel, rather than how someone else is going to make them feel. Firm and assertive statements, such as "I disagree" or "I don't like that," let us take more control of situations. We do not *have to* get angry; we *choose* to get angry—and we can therefore choose a different approach.

Common myths and facts about anger are presented in Box 5.1.

Researchers have found that how well an individual controls anger has a powerful impact on a person's health. Investigators at Ohio State University gave 98 study participants blisters on an arm and monitored how quickly the wound healed. The participants, ages 24 to 72, also completed questionnaires that measured how they expressed and managed anger. Those who managed anger well healed faster, within four days. Those who reported that they did not control anger well were four times more likely to take more than four days to heal from the blister. These participants also produced higher levels of cortisol, a stress hormone linked to delayed healing. The consequences of slow healing include an increased risk of infection of the wound, which makes recovery take even longer. The researchers concluded that people who do not deal with anger well end up with a compromised immune system. And, for example, this could affect how quickly an individual heals after surgery (Gouin, Kiecolt-Glaser, Malarkey, & Glaser, 2008).

BOX 5.1 Putting It Together

Anger: Myths and Facts

When it comes to anger, the ability to distinguish fact from myth helps to provide the insight needed to manage anger, promoting both emotional health and a positive and nurturing couple relationship. Below are some common facts and myths about anger to keep in mind:

Facts

- Anger is a feeling, with psychological components.
- Anger is universal among human beings.
- The nonexpression of anger leads to an increased risk of coronary disease.
- The venting of anger—*catharsis*—is of value only when it sets the stage for resolution.
- Aggression leads to further aggression, not resolution.
- Most anger is directed toward those close to us, not toward strangers.
- Depression, shyness, and suicide are expressions of anger at oneself.

Myths

- Venting (by yelling or pounding pillows) *releases* anger and therefore *deals* with it.
- Women get less angry than men.
- Some people never get angry.
- Anger always results from frustration.
- Aggressive behavior is a sure sign of an *angry person*.
- TV violence, active sports, and/or competitive work release anger.

Source: Adapted from Alberti, R. E. and Emmons, M., *Your Perfect Right: Assertiveness and Equality in Your Life and Relationships,* Ninth Edition. Impact Publishers, 2008.

Intimacy and Conflict

Someone once joked, "The major cause of divorce is marriage." Living together as a couple can be one of the most difficult challenges people face in life. Although conflict for couples is an important aspect of marriages, it is also important to recognize that conflict also occurs between parents and children.

Conflict Resolution for Couples

Hennigan and Ladd (2015) explored existing research about how couples successfully deal with conflict. They emphasize that these techniques may be useful for many kinds of couples, including gay and lesbian couples as well as cohabiting couples. According to these authors, couples need to communicate by clarifying relevant issues, sharing their thoughts, and talking about solutions. Couples may use a variety of ways to communicate. They might write their thoughts down for the other person, or they may decide to have a conversation at a particular time and place. Many couples know that trying to solve a problem in the heat of the argument is not always productive. Talking when they are relaxed and sharing a meal together might set a positive tone for talking about an issue which is causing conflict. Men and women both need to have a shared understanding about the issues and perspectives.

Couples also seem to do better when they use positive communication, stay calm, and initiate topics softly. According to Hennigan and Ladd (2015), research suggests that humor, being open and honest, and being respectful helps couples resolve conflict. A positive and approachable manner on the part of both individuals helps put the relationship above the issues which created the conflict. These ways of interacting are also likely to keep the conversation focused and are less likely to result in anger and an escalation of the conflict. If individuals get upset and angry, they may need to stop and take a break and take up the conversation later when tempers have calmed. Even taking a break should be done in a way that is respectful, according to Hennigan and Ladd (2015), so that both individuals' time line in coming to a resolution is respected.

These ways of dealing with conflict may sound easy, but they are not. If there are issues that have festered over time and have never gotten resolved, there are lots of emotions which go along with such a discussion. Couples need to stay at it and not give up if conflict is not resolved on an initial try. This is hard work.

These strategies are also useful in communicating before a conflict develops. For example, if couples always have challenges getting along on vacations, they might talk about the areas where they seem to have difficulties before they go on a trip. Do conflicts develop over meals and eating or do they develop over the kinds of things to do each day? Having a shared understanding about where conflicts arise and how they might be addressed in advance may be a way to avoid them altogether. This entire process also means that accommodating each other's wishes needs to occur. There is often a need for compromise, and each individual will not get her or his way in every situation.

Love and Anger in Balance

In marriage counseling, couples commonly bring up the issue of balancing separateness and togetherness (the cohesion dimension on the Couple and Family Map). The challenge—or *growing edge*, as family therapists call it—is for couples to learn how to find a way to preserve a workable balance between giving each partner the freedom to grow and change and be a full and capable individual, while at the same time maintaining their deep commitment to each other, and to share life with each other, together. Somehow finding a way to balance *I* and *We*. With too much togetherness, marriage becomes a form of bondage. With too much separateness, the relationship dies from lack of attention. Finding the balancing point is difficult for each and every couple, and the partners are likely to differ in their individual needs and expectations. The balancing point between togetherness and separateness is likely to be quite different from individual to individual, and couple to couple, and that is why togetherness issues are difficult to resolve, but resolution remains crucial.

Similarly, love and anger must be kept in balance. In every marriage it can be argued that these two dynamic forces serve to draw partners together and also drive them apart. Anger, thus, can be a healthy emotion if it helps a couple create a balanced relationship. This is a relationship in which the partners are not too independent of each other, not too dependent upon each other, but a relationship in which they are somewhere in between—*interdependent*.

Anger becomes an ally of the partners when they use it to attend to those areas in the relationship that need work. If the partners do not find a constructive way to use anger, however, they may gradually drift apart. Thus, the most common divorce scenario, many family therapists would argue, is not one of fireworks but one of a gradual loss of closeness. In short, fear of anger and hostilities can lead to disengagement, and disengagement can lead to emotional divorce, which often leads to legal divorce.

In a mature marriage, anger is seen not as an enemy but as a friend. Nevertheless, partners must use it carefully and at appropriate times. Experts suggest that couples make a contract never to attack each other when angry. Feelings of anger signal that something is not right with the relationship. Rather than act on these feelings as they arise, partners should wait until they have calmed down and cooled off, so that they can calmly and rationally work things out. In other words, if they use anger as a barometer that is signaling an impending storm, partners can work together to prevent major damage to the relationship.

People send some of their most powerful messages nonverbally. We don't know the content of this couple's conversation, but we can guess something about their relationship.
©Robert Koene/Photodisc/ Getty Images

The Dance of Anger

It is our job to state our thoughts and feelings clearly and to make responsible decisions that are congruent with our values and beliefs. It is not our job to make another person think and feel the way we do or the way we want them to.

—HARRIET GOLDHOR LERNER (2014)

In her groundbreaking book *The Dance of Anger*, Harriet Goldhor Lerner urges people to closely observe how they manage anger. She graphically describes her own style of managing anger when she is under stress: "When stress mounts, I tend to underfunction with my family of origin (I forget birthdays, become incompetent, and end up with a headache, diarrhea, a cold, or all of the above); I overfunction at work (I have advice for everyone and I am convinced that my way is best); I distance from my husband (both emotionally and physically); and I assume an angry, blaming position with my kids."

Lerner developed a guide to various styles of anger management and labeled these styles pursuer, distancer, overfunctioner, underfunctioner, and blamer. Lerner's styles can be categorized in terms of the Couple and Family Map on the basis of the types of intimate relationships they tend to lead to.

In terms of the Couple and Family Map, **pursuers** tend to want to create connected or enmeshed types of intimate relationships that are very high in cohesion. Lerner describes pursuers as people who react to their anxiety by seeking greater togetherness in a relationship. Pursuers place a high value on talking and expressing feelings, believe other people should do the same, and tend to criticize a partner who can't tolerate feelings of closeness. When the partner wants more emotional space, the pursuer feels rejected and pursues the partner more vigorously before coldly withdrawing.

Distancers tend to create disengaged or separated types of intimate relationships that are low in cohesion. Distancers want emotional space when stress is high. They are private, self-reliant people rather than help-seekers. They have difficulty showing neediness, vulnerability, and dependency. Partners tend to describe them as being emotionally unavailable, withholding, and unable to deal with feelings. Distancers often manage anxiety by

Although most people have an impulse to blame others when things go wrong, some people habitually avoid responsibility for their part in problems. "Blamers" such as this man tend to expend a great deal of energy trying to get others to change.
©Katarzyna Bialasiewicz/Getty Images

retreating into their work and may terminate a relationship entirely when things become too intense. Distancers tend to open up the most when they are not pushed or pursued.

The **dance of anger** is Lerner's metaphor to describe how human beings relate to each other. Think about the dance of a pursuer and a distancer. As the pursuer moves closer, the distancer retreats. Then, as the pursuer unhappily backs off, the distancer's comfort level increases and the distancer moves toward the pursuer. The pursuer warms up again and moves in on the distancer, who again begins to retreat. Back and forth, ebb and flow. Just as people have different tastes in food, clothing, and cars, so they have different needs and feelings about closeness. In terms of the Couple and Family Map, pursuers and distancers have difficulty finding a comfortable balance between separateness and togetherness. Left to their own devices, family relationships would move back and forth between the extremes of being enmeshed or being disengaged.

Lerner describes **underfunctioners** as people who in many areas of life just can't seem to get organized. These people are too high in flexibility (chaotic). Underfunctioners tend to become less competent under stress, letting others take over or fill in. These people are described at work and in the family as "the fragile one," "the sick one," "the problem," "the irresponsible one." Underfunctioners have difficulty showing their strong and competent side to intimates.

Overfunctioners, on the other hand, know what is best not only for themselves but for everybody else as well. These people are low in flexibility (rigid or structured). In difficult times, overfunctioners move in quickly to advise, rescue, and take charge. They can't seem to stay out of the way and let other people solve their own problems. In this way they avoid thinking about their own problems. Overfunctioners are commonly characterized as "always reliable" and "always together" people. They have difficulty showing their vulnerable, underfunctioning side, especially to people who are having troubles.

In terms of Lerner's dance metaphor, how would a couple composed of an overfunctioner and an underfunctioner dance? The overfunctioner would hide feelings of inferiority and incompetence by swooping in to "save" the underfunctioner, making the underfunctioner's task more difficult in the long run by depriving her or him of the opportunity to develop personal strengths.

Some may think that a couple made up of an overfunctioner and an underfunctioner would be a complementary couple, each helping to meet the needs of the other person. However, this type of relationship is actually quite tenuous. The overfunctioner eventually tires of saving the underfunctioner, or the underfunctioner tires of looking and feeling so incompetent. In both cases, the end result can be the breakdown of the partnership. For the relationship to endure and become strong, the partners need to find relative equality in terms of competence and functionality, both contributing a reasonable share to the common good.

Lerner's fifth style, the **blamer,** is a person who has a short fuse and responds in times of stress with emotionally intense feelings. Blamers often fall in the rigidly enmeshed category, an unbalanced type of family system. Blamers spend a lot of energy trying to change other people. They involve themselves in repetitive cycles of fighting, which may relieve tension but which also perpetuate old patterns. Blamers hold others responsible for their feelings and see others, rather than themselves, as the problem.

Lerner notes that women in our society are encouraged to overfunction in the areas of housework, child care, and *feelings work*. In all other areas of endeavor, however, women are socialized to be pursuers and underfunctioners. Men, on the other hand, are socialized to be distancers and overfunctioners. Both sexes are good at blaming other people, but Lerner believes that women today do it more conspicuously than men because most women still feel they have less power in our society and resent their subordinate status.

All five ways of managing anger can be useful at times, but problems occur when one style dominates. It is important to find a balance between pursuing and distancing, underfunctioning and overfunctioning, blaming and taking the blame. In Lerner's (2014) words, "You will have a problem . . . if you are in an extreme position in any one of these categories or if you are unable to observe and change your pattern when it is keeping you angry and stuck." While many people do get stuck in their habitual styles of dealing with anger, Curt, a perceptive husband and writer, describes his experience with the dance of anger, noting that it *is* possible to change old patterns:

> *I think dance of anger is a good metaphor for how we operated in the early years of our marriage. It almost seemed choreographed, it was so predictable. Eileen would do her part of the dance, and then I would respond with my part of the dance, back and forth, back and forth, and then all hell would break loose. It could get really ugly. I was so mad at her once, I thought I could kill her.*
>
> *I think a big part of the problem was we were simply replaying old videotapes of the families we grew up in. Her family in Puyallup was a soap opera par excellence. They loved to fight and did it well all their lives. My dad was an attorney in Bellingham, and he could really pour on the B.S. as well. He'd filibuster over the dinner table in his melodramatic way for ages, and my mother would finally crack and become a bitch on wheels. It was pretty predictable. It made me sick to my stomach. I left home when I was 17.*
>
> *Fortunately, Eileen and I could see the pattern in our own marriage. We read some books and articles about more positive approaches to settling our differences. We experimented and finally found better ways to get along. Luck probably played a part in it all—as did the fact that we mellowed a bit with age and just simply didn't enjoy a good brawl anymore. For whatever reason, we don't dance and brawl as much. Nobody's thrown anything for a long time. We don't fall into the old habits. We simply sit down and work things out. Thank God.*

Conflict and Supportiveness in Heterosexual, Gay, and Lesbian Couples

Very few studies have compared couples with different sexual orientations (heterosexual, gay, and lesbian) in terms of their positive and negative communication. A recent study compared these three groups as the couples were videotaped while completing tasks designed to generate couple conflict and encourage supportive behavior (Julien, Chartrand, Simard, Bouthillier, & Begin, 2003).

> **BOX 5.2   At Issue**
>
> *Ways of Dealing with Conflict in Later Years*
>
> One would expect that the way couples deal with conflict would remain somewhat consistent as they age. Not true. Holley, Haase, and Levenson (2013) studied 127 middle- and later-age couples and observed how they dealt with conflict over a 13-year time period. The middle-aged couples were at least 40 years old when the study started, and by the time it ended they were at least in their 50s. The researchers specifically looked at demand-withdrawal communication patterns. Demand-withdrawal, according to Holley et al. (2013), is when one partner tries to talk about a problem, blames the other person for the problem, and then wants the other person to change so the problem can go away. The other partner, however, tries to avoid the discussion and withdraws from any talking about the problem.
>
> Demand-withdrawal communication is not healthy in a relationship and is usually associated with marital dissatisfaction. According to Holley et al. (2013), this behavior is often gender specific in that it is typically the woman who is demanding and wants the problem solved, and the man is the one who withdraws.
>
> The researchers found that middle-age and older couples are more likely to use avoidance or withdrawal behavior more than is typical for younger couples, and this finding was true for both husbands and wives. Older couples were more likely to avoid the conflict and, instead of dealing with it, they moved on to talking about something positive. In other words, couples would agree to disagree. When comparing the middle-age group to the later-age group in their study, the researchers found that the middle-age couples were slightly more likely to push for a solution. These researchers speculate that as couples grow older, there are less ramifications of not solving conflicts; whereas, the middle-age group were still dealing with conflicts that really needed to be solved before these problems would drastically interfere with their lives.
>
> It appears that as couples grow old together, having had years of working on conflicts, they are willing to "live and let live." As Holley et al. (2013) speculate, older couples engage in less demand-withdrawal activity, or at least do not insist on a solution to conflicts. This might not be a maladaptive solution, but actually an adaptive solution.

The study found that there was no difference in the level of conflict or supportive behaviors between the heterosexual, gay, or lesbian couples. This was based on their observed communication patterns, and it is consistent with past studies in the field. A surprising finding was that for all the couples, positive communication during conflict was particularly important. Couples who had more positive communication during conflict resolved more issues and had higher couple satisfaction. So, for example, if a partner received positive comments when he or she was talking about a current problem, this helped them resolve the issue and maintain a happy relationship.

Box 5.2 summarizes ways of dealing with conflict in later years.

Things to Consider in Resolving Conflict

We have been resolving conflicts, and we all know how to do it, right? In reality it takes a lot of work and involves skills and strategies that may not come naturally. Here are some ways to help resolve conflict.

Suggestions for Having a Healthy Conversation

According to Foote, Wilkens, and Kosanke (2014), there are several things to keep in mind before communicating about a conflict even begins. They suggest you begin by practicing the conversation in advance by talking to a mirror, rehearsing with a good friend, or talking to yourself during a drive home. The important thing is that you have thought through what you are going to say in advance. Keep in mind the 16 strategies discussed in the next section as you do this. Foote et al. (2014) suggest you consider carefully when to bring up a topic. We usually want to talk about the issues that are bothering us on our own time line, and usually that time line is as soon as possible. There is an urgency we all feel when there is a problem. Instead, think about when the other person might be relaxed and ready to talk. It is likely to be a time when the other person does not feel stressed.

Strategies for Communicating About Difficult Issues

Marital and family therapists offer many tips for resolving disagreements between individuals in a couple relationship. These strategies, however, would be valuable to use between multiple family relationships. Here are 16 of our favorites (DeFrain & The University of Nebraska Extension Family Action and Research and Writing Team, 2012):

- *Focus on the positive aspects of the other person.* Don't get so terribly wound up about a handful of negative things when the vast majority of things the other person does are commendable. Being habitually negative and dwelling on the other person's faults doesn't work. It leads to an endless cycle of hurt and anger. Being habitually positive does work.
- *Call a time-out.* Parents often use time-outs today when children are getting too wound up. Adults sometimes need a time-out, also. Simply agree that the situation is getting out of hand and that you will get back together in a half hour or a day or two when adrenalin has stopped pumping and you can be reasonable.
- *Listen very carefully to the other person. Check out what he or she is saying:* "Let me see if I understand your point here: are you saying that....?" And then repeat back to your partner what you think she is saying. Many arguments go on needlessly because the other person has no idea what the other is really trying to say.
- *Get to the point. Say what you mean—what you really mean.* Besides listening carefully to the other person, make sure that when you speak you are speaking clearly and to the point. Often times, individuals are afraid to say what they are really feeling, so they mask these feelings by attacking the other person on another front. For example, a husband might disagree with how his wife disciplines the children but he does not know how to talk with her about this, so, instead, he becomes very harsh with the kids when they act up. She then becomes puzzled: "Why is he so angry with little children? What's wrong with him?"
- *Don't expect the other person to be able to read your mind.* You may think that *they should just know,* but this is not realistic.
- *Don't humiliate the other person in front of others.* Shame and embarrassment don't work. The hostilities will simply continue when you're alone together, and the level of anger may be even higher.
- *The dance of nagging-and-avoidance doesn't work.* Family members often get into the trap of nagging and avoiding that can easily escalate. For example, instead of a wife and husband acting like adults, she acts like his mother, nagging him endlessly to do his jobs around the house, and he acts like her son, ignoring her, avoiding her, running away from her. This type of game usually escalates: she nags even more as he refuses to comply. Finally, he is likely to have a temper tantrum, throw things, hit, and run away. To get out of this trap, the husband and wife must sit down together and admit to each other that this is just a childish game each person is playing. Then they will find an adult solution to the problem calmly and rationally. She's not his mother and he's not her son, so it's silly to act like it.
- *Avoid giving ultimatums.* Don't get into the game of saying things like, "If you do that again I will *never ever . . .*" or "You had better do this *or else!*" This is one of the most heavily confrontational ways people have for arguing with each other and such a strategy does not cool things down, it tends to heat things up. When someone gives an ultimatum they are trying to put themselves in an adult position, looking down on the other person, who is supposed to feel like a child. However, the response usually is anger and defiance and the battle escalates.

Couples need to observe certain conventions when arguing with each other; they will feel safer voicing disagreement if they know that it will not get out of hand. The goal is not winning the argument. The goal is to strengthen the relationship.
©Tetra Images/Getty Images

In some cases the situation can get so out of hand that the couple is setting themselves up for one person to walk out or even divorce. Don't give ultimatums because you may find yourself doing something you really don't want to do. Ultimatums are the stuff of silly TV shows but in real-life they don't work.

- *Grow up. Calm down. Act like an adult.* Do we sound like your mother here? We're just trying to get your attention. The trouble is, a sad thing often happens when couples and family members get into a conflict situation. Individuals quickly become reduced to behaving like small children, yelling and throwing tantrums. This is precisely how they look to outsiders. This childish behavior may work when we're little kids but as adults we just look foolish to others.
- *Don't fight dirty. Avoid attacking the other person.* Conflicts in a relationship are not resolved by attacking each other. Things only become worse. Avoid the temptation to fight dirty, to win by damaging the other person. What good can possibly come from making our loved one feel bad?
- *Hate begets hate. Love begets love.* When we are kind to the other person, they will be likely to respond with kindness. Similarly, when we are nasty to the other person, we are likely to get nastiness in return.
- *The silent treatment is fighting dirty.* When family members get into the game of "What's-wrong?"—"Nothing . . ." the likelihood of successfully resolving the conflict goes down dramatically. The silent treatment does not end a conflict. To end a conflict, people have to sit down and listen to each other and talk with each other in a respectful and kind manner.
- *Use "I" statements rather than "you" statements. "I" statements are more gentle and work better.* Blaming each other doesn't work to resolve conflicts effectively and efficiently. It only makes people angry. "You" statements commonly are blame statements: "You shouldn't do that!" or "You always make me so mad!" or "You always sound so stupid when you talk with her!" On the other hand, "I" statements aim toward minimizing blame and working, instead, toward understanding and joint problem-solving.
- *Discuss one thing at a time until it is resolved.* When conflicts get out of hand in relationships, the combatants commonly start throwing everything from the past into the

Box 5.3 At Issue
Ending a Conflict and Learning to Forgive

As we have seen, conflicts within loving relationships are inevitable. Because each of us is a unique and different human being—and often on a different trajectory in life—we view the world differently, and we are puzzled and often frustrated and angered by the differing views our partner has and the strange or thoughtless or hurtful things our partner sometimes does. It needs to be mentioned, of course, that there are different levels of disagreement, different levels of conflict. As partners we forgive and forget mistakes and differences on an almost daily basis. We have to do this to maintain order and civility in the household. Frankly, the vast majority of things that irritate or anger us are simply not that important, not worth mentioning, not worth arguing about. Pick your quarrels carefully, or your life will be one endless battle.

There are, however, genuinely devastating mistakes loved ones make, and hurtful things they do. Forgiveness is much more difficult in these situations. The list includes: infidelities, major lies, drastic unilateral financial decisions, and other similar humiliations and betrayals (Cano, Christian-Herman, O'Leary, & Avery-Leaf, 2002). If partners cannot learn how to forgive each other and effectively resolve the conflict, these betrayals can leave lasting emotional scars on marital functioning, particularly in terms of psychological closeness (Gordon & Baucom, 2003).

What exactly is forgiveness? Professionals who study intimate relationships commonly discuss three elements that comprise forgiveness: (1) regaining a more balanced and compassionate view of the offender and the event; (2) decreasing negative feelings regarding the offender and the event; and (3) giving up the right to seek revenge or lash out toward the offender (Coop Gordon, Hughes, Tomcik, Dixon, & Litzinger, 2009).

Some researchers talk about two dimensions of forgiveness (Fincham & Beach, 2002; Worthington, 2005): (1) a negative dimension which involves the degree to which a person holds a grudge, withdraws from the relationship, and desires revenge or punishment for the betrayal; and (2) a positive dimension, which involves the degree to which a person experiences a readiness to forgive, an increase in empathy, and a release from anger.

A serious betrayal affects not only the couple relationship but parent-child relationships and the lives of children in the family. For these reasons, the help of professionals in dealing with the wounds should be seriously considered. Some conflicts caused by marital betrayal will not be resolved and the partnership will end in divorce. But even in these cases, parents may need to keep a reasonable working relationship going for the sake of the children. The marriage may not be a good one, but both parents may still be reasonably good parents and children in these cases benefit from positive contact with both parents (American Association for Marital and Family Therapy, 2012a and b; Coop et al., 2009).

To illustrate the challenges individuals endure when faced with serious betrayal and humiliation in life, we talked at length with two friends who we felt would have some good ideas in regard to forgiveness. Our first friend said that when her husband took off with another woman for several weeks that she was overwhelmed by a feeling of deep hurt: "Why would he do this to me? What have I done?" She hurt and felt somehow she might have contributed to his errant behavior. A few weeks later, however, she concluded that she "was getting high on feeling low." At this point her feelings turned from hurt to anger: "Damn him!" From this point on, she stood up for herself and her sense of honor and what is right, and let her husband know she could live quite happily without him.

When this errant husband did come home a few weeks later, with his tail between his legs, she eventually forgave him, but with qualifications. She would take him back. She would forgive,

argument. Rather than calmly talking about an issue until it is resolved, they bring up one sore point after another until the chance of anything good happening is almost zero. Instead of falling into this trap, pick the most important issue to talk about and save your discussion of other issues until you have resolved the most important issue.

- *Win-Win is much better than Win-Lose.* Loving relationships are not athletic contests nor are they wars between ethnic groups or nations. Loving relationships work well when couples in conflict clearly see that they need to join together and work as a team to find a solution to the issue at hand that is good for everyone involved. Loving relationships fall apart when the people get into Win-Lose types of conflicts, when each is trying to dominate the other.

This approach implies that someone in the household is supposed to be the boss and someone is supposed to be the employee. The problem is that people usually

but she would never forget. And the two reconciled with the agreement that both of them would carefully guard the sanctity of their partnership by not getting too close to others outside of their marriage. They both agreed to be watchful so that neither would be led into temptation again. The promise held water, and the couple are still together today, many years later.

The second friend we talked with at length had gained several valuable insights from her experience, also. She told her story in the context of her upbringing, which was in a very conservative and religious rural community. Being sheltered and shy, she was knocked a bit off her feet when she left home for the bright lights and big city, and met her husband-to-be, who was significantly older and significantly more experienced in life. She fell for him in a way she would not have fallen if she had been older and wiser.

The marriage was not a good one from early on. Her husband tried to dominate her verbally, physically, and emotionally. She was overwhelmed raising baby after baby pretty much by herself, and he was verbally and physically abusive to her and the children.

Why didn't she leave him? "Where would a mother with many little kids go in those days?" The marriage dragged on year after year, until things finally unraveled when he admitted to a series of affairs over many years. He assumed she would accept the humiliation and his infidelities. But she most certainly did not accept this, and she filed for divorce.

Her main feeling at that point was relief at no longer having to try to make him happy and make the marriage a success.

Now, 14 years later, she has created a happy single life for herself, with support from her children, many friends, and her church family. "Have I forgiven him? In my faith tradition, you have to ask forgiveness from God. My husband never asked to be forgiven by God, or by me. Never. In his view, I was the one who was wrong. I should simply accept who he is."

She feels today she is reasonably healed from the experience, and said that "You have to forgive yourself, also."

Why would that be? "You keep asking yourself, 'Why was I so stupid putting up with all this?' and I don't know why. I guess I was from another generation of women. When I met him he was exciting, showed me a world I hadn't seen." But all of his running around with multiple sexual partners turned out to be part and parcel of the excitement he embodied. In the beginning she was naïve, she never dreamed this would happen. And when it did happen, she did not have the emotional resources to deal with an errant husband. She raised child after child with little help, only discovering his infidelity after the children were gone.

She agrees with the adage that you need to forgive, but not forget. "If you forget, you're setting yourself up to make the same mistake over and over." But you need to forgive for your own good. Otherwise, your soul is destroyed by anger and hatred: "Anger is poisonous to you, personally."

Looking back over the years, she believes that in the final analysis, "You never get over it. You learn to live with it." She believes a person should let go of the anger and heal. And what does healing mean to her? "You're not angry. You learn to accept what happened. You understand the way the other person looks at the world, but you don't have to agree with that reality. You don't have to join that craziness. You learn to be assertive. You see the truth."

She went on to explain that when she was growing up a long time ago, she was groomed by the community and culture in which she lived to be meek and mild. To be subservient to men. To follow all the rules, even though men don't seem to follow all the rules. But not anymore: "I learned how to be my own person. To stand up on my own two feet. God has really helped me through all this. God doesn't want me to be a doormat."

---

don't love their bosses. They might respect or fear their boss, but they are not particularly likely to love their boss. There is usually an emotional distance between the boss and the employee. And who wants to live in a home that feels more like the workplace?

The reality is, if one person wins and one person loses, both are losing. They are losing because a loving relationship between equal partners has broken down. They are acting like they are not playing on the same team but on opposing teams.

- **Solve the conflict, make things better, create a peaceful and harmonious relationship.** Long-term loving relationships are much more important than endless bickering. Find a way to love each other and agree on the vast majority of issues. Life is too short to be spent trying to change each other. See Box 5.3 for more about ending conflicts and learning to forgive.

Conflict Between Parents and Children

Much of this chapter has been about conflict between adults and especially about adults in couple relationships. Many of us who are parents might reflect on parent/child conflict and speculate that it takes more time and energy than conflict between the adult parents. One also might expect that once a child reaches adulthood all conflict stops and all family members get along wonderfully, but many of us only have to look back to a recent holiday to realize parents and children often have conflict into adulthood. For some it never ends.

Canary and Canary (2013) describe the parent/child conflicts that occur throughout childhood beginning at about 2 years. This is the time when children begin to communicate verbally and have cognitive skills to challenge their parents. According to these authors, a summary of studies that show the number of conflicts that occur between parents and toddlers range from around 4 to 55 conflicts per hour! For someone who has not been around children, this upper range may seem exceedingly high. For those of you who are parents or are around toddlers, you may think these higher numbers reflect some children that you have known. There are other children who are very easy going and rarely protest an action.

When there is conflict between adults and toddlers or preschoolers, it is often about correcting or reprimanding or about a rule that is not being followed. According to Canary and Canary (2013), common issues for young children are behaviors that are destructive or harmful to other children such as hitting or throwing things. Although the actions of the child are not necessarily a problem long term, the way the adult responds to the conflict is important. It is suggested that distracting, negotiating, or reasoning is best for healthy child development, whereas, criticism and threatening are not helpful for children (Canary & Canary, 2013).

According to Canary and Canary (2013), there is little research about adult/child conflict in elementary school. One might speculate that these years are less conflict-ridden and, therefore, less research is done. I remember one parent who said, "When my children turn 12,

Conflicts occur among and between all family members. A common time for a parent and a child to have conflict is during adolescence. The parent is often hanging on and the youth is pulling away.
©Digital skillet/Getty Images

I am going to send them to live with their grandparents." This statement implies that the elementary years are, indeed, easy compared to what is coming next. The elementary school years are when children have the cognitive ability to reason and, yet, are somewhat dependent on their parents for most social interactions.

Many parents would agree that conflict is at its peak when children become adolescents. Child development theorists such as Erikson (1963) make it clear that the task of adolescents is to move toward adulthood. This means that they will spend less time with their parents and establish their own identities, which typically results in conflict. As Canary and Canary (2013) state, "One side pulls at how things used to be; the other side pulls at how things will be" (p. 90). Adolescents want to try new things—piercings, staying out late, stretching all rules, dressing in new ways. This is normal adolescent development. Conflicts center on their appearance, chores, schoolwork, and relationships.

Generally, reasoning and searching for compromise were most effective in solving conflicts between parents and adolescents (Canary & Canary, 2013). Younger adolescents had more trouble doing that, however, and withdrawing and aggression were more likely to occur. As these authors summarized their review of literature, it was clear that conflicts between parents and adolescents also affect the parents' couple relationships and can spill over into the relationships with other siblings. These relationship issues can carry over into the adulthood. As stated previously, some parent/child conflict never ends.

Summary

- According to a national survey of married couples, happy couples are more able than unhappy couples to understand each other's opinions and ideas when they discuss problems; can share feelings and ideas with their partner during disagreements; are able to resolve differences; have similar ideas about how to settle disagreements; and take disagreements seriously.
- According to the same national survey, the major conflict resolution problems that married couples experience are the following: one person ends up feeling responsible for the problem; they go out of their way to avoid conflict with their partner; they have different ideas about the best way to solve disagreements; some of their differences never seem to get resolved; and they sometimes have serious disputes over unimportant issues.
- Conflict is inevitable in any intimate relationship. It can be thought of as a process that moves from decision making to problem solving to crisis resolution; making decisions when they are called for helps prevent crises.
- Most couples are afraid of negative emotions and have a difficult time learning how to deal with them. A common tendency is to suppress anger for fear of damaging the relationship. Because love and hate are so closely tied, however, the suppression of anger can lead to loss of affection in a relationship.
- Popular myths about anger include the belief that anger is caused by others, that the best way to deal with anger is to let it all out, that anger is a beneficial emotion, and that you're a wimp if you don't get angry.
- Intimacy and conflict are inextricably tied together. Anger keeps people from developing unhealthy dependencies on each other. Interdependence, a balance between dependency and independence, seems to work best.
- People manage stress and anger in a number of ways: Pursuers seek greater togetherness in a relationship; distancers want emotional space when stress is high; underfunctioners become less competent under stress; overfunctioners tend to take charge in tough times; and blamers believe everyone else is responsible for their problems.

Key Terms

conflict
pursuer
distancer
dance of anger
underfunctioner
overfunctioner
blamer

Activities

1. Using Harriet Lerner's ideas about the various styles of managing anger, focus on someone with whom you have an important relationship. Does one of you tend to be a pursuer or a distancer? An overfunctioner or an underfunctioner? A blamer or a blame taker? Rate each of you on a scale from 1 (low) to 10 (high) on each of the dimensions. Are you performing any dance based on these style differences? If so, how might you create a healthier dance?
2. It is often hard to express negative emotions. In a group, reflect on past experiences in expressing negative emotions. Talk about why it is hard. Also talk about how it has worked well and how it has not been successful in dealing with conflict.
3. Observe young children playing together. How often is there conflict? What is the conflict typically about?

Suggested Readings

Alberti, R., & Emmons, M. (2008). *Your perfect right: Assertiveness and equality in your life and relationships* (9th ed.). Atascadero, CA: Impact.

American Association for Marital and Family Therapy (2012a). Infidelity. Web site: http://aamft.org/imis15/content/Consumer_Updates/Infidelity.aspx.

American Association for Marital and Family Therapy. (2012b). Online infidelity. Web site: http://www.aamft.org/imis15/Content/Consumer_Updates/Online_Infidelity.aspx.

Borcherdt, B. (2000). *You can control your anger! 21 ways to do it.* Sarasota, FL: Professional Resource Press. A practical guide for people who would like to change.

Canary, H. E., & Canary, D. J. (2013). *Family conflict.* Cambridge, UK: Polity Press.

Coop Gordon, K., Hughes, F. M., Tomcik, N. D., Dixon, L. J., & Litzinger, S. C. (2009). Widening spheres of impact: The role of forgiveness in marital and family functioning. *Journal of Family Psychology, 23*(1), 1–13.

DeFrain, J., & The University of Nebraska Extension Family Action Research and Writing Team. (2012). *Getting connected, staying connected: Loving each other day by day.* Bloomington, IN: iUniverse. A practical guide for couples and families built around the research-based six key couple and family strengths.

Emery, R. E. (2012). *Renegotiating family relationships* (2nd ed.). New York, NY: Guilford Press.

Gottman, J. M., Schwartz Gottman, J., & DeClaire, J. (2006). *Ten lessons to transform your marriage: America's love lab experts share their strategies for strengthening your relationships.* New York, NY: Crown.

Lerner, H. G. (2012). *Marriage rules: A manual for the married and the coupled up.* New York, NY: Gotham Books. Good advice from the much-admired couple and family therapist.

Lerner, H. G. (2014). *The dance of anger.* New York, NY: HarperCollins.

Olson, D. H., Olson-Sigg, A., & Larson, P. J. (2008). *The couple checkup: Find your relationship strengths.* Nashville, TN: Thomas Nelson.

Robinson, J. (2012). *Communication miracles for couples. Easy and effective tools to create more love and less conflict.* San Francisco, CA: Red Wheel.

Visit the text-specific Online Learning Center at **www.mhhe.com/olson9e** for practice tests, chapter summaries, and PowerPoint slides.

6 *S*exual Intimacy

©John Lund/Drew Kelly/Sam Diephuis/Blend Images/Brand X Pictures/Getty Images

Intimacy, Strengths, and Diversity

Couple Strengths and Sexual Issues

Sex and Society: An Overview

American Sexual Health and Behavior

Sexual Behavior Among Adolescents and Young Adults

Marital and Extramarital Sexual Behavior

Toward Sexual Health

Summary

Key Terms

Activities

Suggested Readings

Intimacy, Strengths, and Diversity

> It seems a matter of elementary logic: love leads to sex, which leads to greater love, which in turn leads to better sex—and so it goes.
> — WILLIAM H. MASTERS AND VIRGINIA JOHNSON (MAIER, 2009, P. 262)

Intimacy in relationships can be expressed in a variety of ways, and the sexual relationship we have with another person can be a key element of intimacy. Men and women differ in the importance they place on the sexual relationship, compared to emotional closeness. They also often view sex and love differently: women are more likely to view sex and love as highly connected, and men are more likely to separate love and sex (Blow & Hartnett, 2005; Hyde & DeLamater, 2014; Insel & Roth, 2014; Kelly, 2011; Yarber & Sayad, 2013).

Sexual intimacy is an integral part of healthy marriage relationships. Studies show that marital satisfaction and the satisfaction couples have with their sexual relationship are related (Blow & Hartnett, 2005). The quality of the sexual relationship in a marriage relationship can strengthen a marriage, and the quality of the marriage relationship increases the couple's sexual satisfaction (Olson, Olson-Sigg, & Larson, 2008).

Although much of the discussion in this chapter focuses on sexual attitudes and behaviors in the United States, there is evidence that attitudes and behaviors differ in other countries, and these differences will be discussed. There are also differences based on gender and the type of couple relationship (Blow & Hartnett, 2005; Scheinkman, 2005).

Nationwide research is described in this chapter about the sexual practices of women and men (Herbenick et al., 2010). This research indicates that couples experience a variety of sexual practices, but vaginal intercourse is the most common for men and women.

One of the changes that has occurred over the years is that Americans are increasingly more open in their discussions of sex. References to sex are pervasive in the media—we hear about medications that address sexual dysfunction on prime-time television—and discussions of sex and sexuality are common in our daily lives. Many schools are teaching young people about sex, as well as HIV/AIDS and other sexually transmitted diseases. Couples talk about how to improve their sexual satisfaction. We go to doctors to talk about what is not working and get information and treatment about how to make it work. This increasingly open communication about sex means young people and adults know more about sex than ever before in history.

Couple Strengths and Sexual Issues

A major strength for a happily married couple is the quality of their sexual relationship. In a nationwide survey of married couples, researchers revealed distinct differences between happy couples and unhappy couples in terms of their sexual relationships (Olson et al., 2008). Happy couples agreed much more (68%) than unhappy couples (17%) that they were completely satisfied with the affection they received from their partner (Table 6.1). Most of the happy couples (76%) reported that their sexual relationship was satisfying and fulfilling, while only 28% of the unhappy couples reported being satisfied. Happy couples were more likely (82%) than unhappy couples (36%) to agree that their partner does not use or refuse sex unfairly. More than twice as many happy couples (84%) as unhappy couples (40%) did not have concerns that their partner might not be interested in them sexually. Similarly, most happy couples (86%) were not worried that their partner might consider having an

TABLE 6.1 Strengths of Happy Couples Versus Unhappy Couples Regarding Sexuality

SEXUALITY ISSUE	PERCENTAGE IN AGREEMENT	
	Happy Couples	Unhappy Couples
1. I am completely satisfied with the affection I receive from my partner.	68%	17%
2. Our sexual relationship is satisfying and fulfilling.	76	28
3. My partner does not use or refuse sex in an unfair way.	82	36
4. I have no concerns that my partner may not be interested in me sexually.	84	40
5. I do not worry that my partner may consider an affair.	86	45

Source: Olson, D., Olson-Sigg, A., & Larson, P. *The Couple Checkup.* Nashville, TN: Thomas Nelson, 2008.

TABLE 6.2 Top Five Sexual Problems for Couples

Sexual Issue	Percentage of Couples Having Problems*
1. I am dissatisfied with the amount of affection I receive from my partner.	68%
2. Our levels of sexual interest are different.	66
3. Our sexual relationship has become less interesting and enjoyable.	62
4. Our sexual relationship is not satisfying or fulfilling.	58
5. I am dissatisfied with the level of openness in discussing sexual topics.	52

*One or both partners indicated this was an issue for them.

Source: Olson, D., Olson-Sigg, A., & Larson, P. *The Couple Checkup.* Nashville, TN: Thomas Nelson, 2008.

affair, as compared to 45% of unhappy couples. Looking at these research findings, it is clear that many couples could benefit by learning how to communicate openly, honestly, and positively about sex.

In this same study the researchers looked at the total sample of more than 50,000 couples and identified common sexual problems (see Table 6.2). A majority of couples (68%) were dissatisfied with the amount of affection they received from their partner. About two-thirds of the couples (66%) said the level of sexual interest differed from their partner. More than 6 in 10 couples (62%) said their sexual relationship had become less interesting and enjoyable; 58% said their sexual relationship was not satisfying or fulfilling; and 52% of the couples said they were dissatisfied with the level of openness in discussing sexual topics. Looking at these research findings, it is clear that many couples could benefit by learning how to communicate openly, honestly, and positively about sex.

Sex and Society: An Overview

A person's sexual identity is an important part of who she or he is. A number of factors, including biology and culture, influence sexual identity. In this section we will discuss these factors, look at historical and cultural perspectives on sexuality, and explore the ways in which Americans receive information about sexuality.

Sexuality, Sex, and Gender

The formation of a person's sexuality is a complex process, involving continuous interaction among a wide variety of biological influences, family and cultural influences, and each individual's relatively unique set of personality characteristics. **Sexuality** is a broad term that encompasses the set of beliefs, values, and behaviors that defines each of us as a sexual being. One aspect of an individual's sexuality is whether a person identifies himself or herself as **heterosexual, homosexual, bisexual**, or **transgender**. This identity is otherwise known as one's **sexual orientation**.

Heterosexual means that one's sexual orientation is toward members of the other sex. Homosexual means that one's sexual orientation is toward members of the same sex. Bisexual indicates that one is sexually oriented toward both sexes. Transgender refers to people who believe they were assigned a gender at birth based on their genitals, but who feel that is a false or incomplete description of themselves. A majority of transgender persons are biological males who identify themselves as females, usually early in their childhood.

You will notice in these definitions that we did not use the term "opposite sex" because that term is imprecise. This is because males and females are much more similar than different, not only biologically but also in other ways. In fact, in the early phases of an infant's development, there is little visible difference in the genital development of the male and female.

Other aspects of sexuality include a person's interest in having a variety of sexual partners or only one and a person's preference for specific types of sexual acts. There are countless beliefs, values, and behaviors associated with sexuality. Therefore, individuals vary widely in how they define themselves as sexual beings.

In our society, the term **sex** can refer either to being biologically female or male or to sexual activity. The term **gender** refers to the learned characteristics and behaviors associated with being male or female in a particular culture.

Historical Perspectives on Sex and Society

Throughout history, human sexual behavior and thinking about sex have been guided by religious teachings and cultural beliefs. Many religions, including some Christian groups, have attempted to regulate sex outside marriage by condemning it as sinful. Some religions, such as Islam, although also condemning sex outside of marriage, allow men to take more than one wife. Other ideas about sex evolve out of, and are part of, general cultural beliefs. For example, Western male-dominated culture has held the idea that women have little interest in sex. Other cultures—for example, that of the Inuit—consider female sexual activity to be on a par with that of males.

Advances in science as early as the 17th century led to a more technical approach to sex. Little was known about the biological aspects of sexuality until Dutch microscopist Anton van Leeuwenhoek (1632–1723) and his student John Ham discovered sperm swimming in human semen. Oscar Hertwig was the first to observe fertilization of the egg by the sperm in sea urchins in 1875, yet the human ovum was not directly observed until the 20th century.

Today, we have a great deal of scientific knowledge about sex—about conception, contraception, and sexual functioning, as well as about how to treat infertility and sexual

In our society, most information about sexual behavior and intimate relationships comes from the media. Not surprisingly, many people have misconceptions and distorted ideas about both the physical and the emotional dimensions of sexuality.
©McGraw-Hill Education/ Christopher Kerrigan, photographer

dysfunction. We talk openly about sex and are complacent about the ubiquity of sexual images in our society. Yet religion still plays a role in many people's sexual attitudes and behavior, and there is still conflict between those who espouse an open, objective, scientific, informational approach to sex and those who wish to regulate people's sexual behavior and their access to information on moral grounds.

Gay and Lesbian Couples

There are more than 8 million adults in the United States who are lesbian, gay, or bisexual. This is approximately 3.5% of the adult population. In total, research suggests that there are about 9 million Americans—roughly the population of New Jersey—who identify themselves as lesbian, gay, bisexual, or transgender.

Among adults who identify as lesbian, gay, or bisexual, bisexuals comprise a slight majority (1.8% compared to 1.7% who identify as lesbian or gay). Women are much more likely than men to identify as bisexual. There are also nearly 700,000 transgender individuals in the United States (Gates, 2011, April).

Estimates of those who report having engaged in any same-sex sexual behavior during their lifetime and any same-sex sexual attraction during their lifetime are substantially higher than estimates of those who identify as lesbian, gay, or bisexual. An estimated 19 million Americans (8.2%) report that they have engaged in same-sex sexual behavior and nearly 25.6 million Americans (11%) acknowledge at least some same-sex sexual attraction (Gates, 2011, April).

On June 26, 2015, the U.S. Supreme Court ruled 5-4 to legalize same-sex marriage. The Court ruled that states cannot ban same-sex marriage. This was seen by advocates of gay rights as their greatest victory yet (CNN, 2015, June 27). According to Gallup, when the Supreme Court was adjudicating the issue, there were about 390,000 married same-sex couples in the United States, and there were also 1.2 million adults living in a same-sex domestic partnership. All told, about 4 in 10 of all same-sex couples in the United States were married before the Supreme Court's ruling. With the Court's ruling in favor of same-sex marriage, it was predicted that the dramatic rise in same-sex marriages in recent years would continue (*Washington Post*, 2015, April 28).

Over recent decades there has been a slow but steady change in societal attitudes toward **GLBT** (gay, lesbian, bisexual, transgender) individuals. During this time, gays and lesbians have increasingly moved in the direction of developing and maintaining ongoing relationships with one person (Gotta et al., 2011; Kurdek, 2008). Increasingly, both gays and lesbians have had to struggle with coming out and have often experienced considerable rejection by their parents and other relatives. This struggle has helped some of them develop a variety of strengths that are valuable in relationships (Kurdek, 2008).

Historically, most of the focus on gays and lesbians has been on their sexual orientation. Looking at this from a strengths-based perspective, the following are some of the characteristics that have been found to be strengths of gay and lesbian couples:

- *High emotional connection with partner and others.* A common strength for many gays and lesbians is their ability to connect in an emotional way with people of both the same sex and the other sex.
- *High role flexibility.* In their same-sex relationships, they often have a flexible role relationship that gives them the ability to adapt to each other (Green, 2012).
- *Egalitarian decision making.* The ability to negotiate and make decisions in a sharing manner enables them to establish and maintain an egalitarian relationship (Gotta et al., 2011; Green, 2012). Same-sex couples are more egalitarian than heterosexual couples.
- *Positive parent–child relationships.* Gay and lesbian couples are on par with heterosexual couples when it comes to raising healthy, well-adjusted children (Green, 2012).
- *Psychologically perceptive.* Whether it is because they have had to struggle to come out or because of their lifestyle, they often tend to be very perceptive in terms of psychological dynamics.
- *Effective communication skills.* A common characteristic of many of the same-sex relationships is that they have been able to achieve very good communication skills and more equality in communication within their couple relationship (Gotta et al., 2011).

A 12-year study of gay and lesbian couples by John Gottman, Julie Schwartz Gottman, and their colleagues (2016) focused on what makes same-sex relationships succeed or fail. The research demonstrated that all couple types—straight or gay—have many of the same problems and the same approaches to couple satisfaction. The researchers outlined some qualities of strength that are especially critical for same-sex partnerships:

- *Gay and lesbian couples are more upbeat in the face of conflict than heterosexual couples.* Gay and lesbian couples in the Gottman study used more affection and humor when they were engaged in a disagreement.
- *Gay and lesbian couples use fewer controlling, hostile, and emotional tactics than heterosexual couples when communicating with each other.* Fairness and power sharing between partners is more important and more common among gay and lesbian couples, Gottman found.
- *In a fight, gay and lesbian couples take it less personally.* Compared to straight couples, gay and lesbian partners have a tendency to accept some degree of negativity without getting hurt feelings.
- *Unhappy gay and lesbian couples tend to demonstrate low levels of physiological arousal.* This is measured by elevated heart rate, sweaty palms, and jitteriness. Straight couples tend to get more aroused during a disagreement than gay and lesbian couples.

It is difficult to study gay and lesbian couples for several reasons. First, many couples are not willing to be open about their sexual orientation and are less willing to be part of a research project. Second, laws and policies are still in place, along with prejudice and oppression, that impact the lives of gay and lesbian couples and families. Even though the U.S. Supreme Court has made same-sex marriage a nationwide right, discrimination against LGBT people still remains in most states. This discrimination occurs in the areas of employment, housing, and public accommodation. For example, in many states a person could marry someone of the same gender and then be fired at work for being gay (Brown, 2015; LGBT Rights in the U.S., 2016; Reid, 2015).

Even though there may be an expectation that gay couples function like heterosexual couples, this may be an unrealistic expectation. These differences regarding laws, rights, and the degree of acceptance make it difficult to compare gay and lesbian couples and families with heterosexual couples and families (Pawelski et al., 2006). Many gay and lesbian individuals have been in heterosexual relationships and have had children in those relationships. Their extended families may have disowned them, or, at best, they have strained relationships. These past and current life circumstances greatly affect one's family and other network relationships.

Third, we compare gay and lesbian couple relationships to heterosexual relationships with the assumption that heterosexual relationships provide the gold standard for how couple relationships should be—and this may not be a fair way to assess these relationships. Even though these issues are often identified in the literature, the majority of studies continue to compare gay and lesbian relationships to heterosexual relationships.

Kurdek (2006), in a large national study, compared gay couples, lesbian couples, and heterosexual cohabiting couples to heterosexual couples with children regarding their relationship adjustment. The findings of this study showed that these couples did not differ markedly from each other in terms of relationship adjustment. Some relatively insignificant differences were reported. For example, Kurdek found that gay couples were more likely to rely on friends for support, and heterosexual sexual couples were more likely to rely on family for support. Kurdek also found that gay and lesbian couples and unmarried heterosexual couples were more prone to separation than married couples with children. What we know from current research is that children from same-sex couples typically fare about the same as children from other family structures (Chamberlin, 2005; Herek, 2006; Pawelski et al., 2006).

While the lesbian, gay, bisexual, and transgender community is increasingly visible in U.S. culture, same-sex relationships are often hidden and forbidden in many other cultures. The International Lesbian, Gay, Bisexual, Transgender and Intersex Association (ILGA) (2016), a worldwide federation of 1,100 member organizations in 110 countries, reports that being lesbian, gay, bisexual, or transgender is illegal in almost 80 countries, and in at least 5 countries it is still punishable by death. A total of 2.7 billion people in the world live in countries where being gay is a crime.

Sexuality Across Cultures

Attitudes toward sexuality and sexual behaviors vary markedly from one culture to another, and ethnocentrism encourages people to believe that their culture's thinking and practices are the only "right" or "natural" way to live. An important generalization cross-cultural researchers make about sexuality is that all societies regulate sexual behavior in some way, although the regulations vary greatly from culture to culture (Hyde & DeLamater, 2014). Sex is a powerful force, and societies around the world have found it necessary to develop some rules regarding sexual behavior. For example, **incest taboos**, which prohibit intercourse between parents and children and between siblings, are nearly universal; most societies also condemn forced sexual relations, such as rape (Hyde & DeLamater, 2014).

Standards of Attractiveness. Cultural standards of sexual attractiveness vary widely. In many non-Western cultures, a plump woman is considered more attractive than a thin woman. But in the United States, the ideal woman has a slim body, well-developed breasts, and long, shapely legs; the ideal man is tall and moderately muscular, with broad shoulders and narrow hips. Physical attributes are often more important for women in Western societies because women tend to be judged by their appearance, whereas men are judged by their accomplishments and power.

In some cultures, the shape and color of the eyes are most important; other cultures value good-looking ears. The Nawa of Africa value elongated labia majora (the pads of fatty tissue on either side of the vagina), and Nawa women reportedly tug on them to enhance their length. Although the specifics vary, most cultures identify certain physical traits as attractive and valuable (Hyde & DeLamater, 2014).

Sexual Behavior. Gender roles in sexual behavior differ considerably across cultures. In a few societies, including the Maori and the Kwoma of the South Pacific, females generally initiate love affairs. Although rape in American society is primarily committed by men, the anthropologist Bronislaw Malinowski (1929) reported groups of Trobriand Island women in the South Pacific who regularly raped and sexually humiliated male strangers who were unfortunate enough to wander through the area near their village.

Sexual techniques also vary considerably from culture to culture (Hyde & DeLamater, 2014). Kissing is common in most societies; however, when the Thonga of Africa first saw Europeans kissing, they were amused and could not believe the Europeans were sharing saliva. In some societies, one partner inflicts pain on the other partner during lovemaking. Apinayean women of South America have been known to bite off bits of their partner's eyebrows; Trukese women in the South Pacific poke fingers in the man's ear when sexually excited; and partners in some societies draw blood and leave scars as a result of sexual passion.

In many cultures around the world, the breast is not a sexual object, according to Marilyn Yalom, author of *A History of the Breast* and *A History of the Wife*. Yalom argues that

Standards for physical attractiveness, which we take for granted, are actually culturally determined. Although these two women are very different from each other in appearance, each is considered beautiful in her culture.
(a) ©Wasif Hassan/Getty Images
(b) ©Ingram Publishing

the breast is over-eroticized in the Western world. In African cultures, breasts are for babies and not for men. In African sexual tradition, the erotic focus is on the buttocks. The Chinese make a sexual fetish of the foot, while the Japanese concentrate on the nape of the neck ("Breasts Shaped by Evolution for Babies, Not Men," 2010; Yalom, 2016).

The frequency of sexual intercourse varies from society to society. American society today is about average when compared with other cultures. The range of frequency of intercourse for married couples runs from a low of about once a month among the Keraki of the South Pacific to a high of a few times a night for young couples among the Aranda of Australia and the Mangaians of the South Pacific (Hyde & DeLamater, 2014).

Sexual Attitudes. Attitudes toward **masturbation**, the self-stimulation of the genitals, vary widely from culture to culture. It is tolerated among children and adolescents in some societies but condemned at any age by other societies (Bhugra, Popelyuk, & McMullen, 2010). Most societies tend to disapprove of adult masturbation; if it is discovered, the consequences range from mild ridicule to punishment.

Similarly, attitudes toward same-sex behavior vary widely from culture to culture. Although some cultures tolerate same-sex sexual activity among children, they disapprove when adults engage in it. Other societies force such behavior on all their male members, most often during puberty rites (Bhugra et al., 2010). Often sexual attitudes are influenced by religious practices and beliefs.

Female Circumcision in Africa. The story of female circumcision is graphically told by the supermodel Waris Dirie in her book *Desert Flower* (1998; see also French, 2014; U.S. Department of Health and Human Services, 2016; World Health Organization, 2016). She was circumcised at age 5 in Africa as a member of a Somalian tribe and had an arranged marriage to an older tribal member when she was 13. In her teens, she served as a maid in London, England, to an ambassador family and then became a model. After a successful career, she became a special ambassador for the United Nations (UN) to promote cultural change away from female genital mutilation (FGM).

Most African cultures have practiced female circumcision for centuries. The UN estimates that it has been performed on more than 130 million women. This still happens to at least 2 million girls a year and over 6,000 women a day. The practice varies by geographic location, cultural group, and tribe. At a minimum, the hood of the clitoris is destroyed. But in over 80% of women in Somalia, the most severe form is infibulation, in which the labia minora and labia majora are also removed, leaving only a small opening to urinate.

The practice of female genital mutilation has been promoted by men and maintained in the culture by women. Men demand a circumcised woman because they feel the woman is otherwise dirty and oversexed. The mothers support it because otherwise their daughters would not be selected by men for marriage.

Female circumcision is dangerous because many women get infected and die from the surgery. They often suffer from immediate health problems from the surgery, including infections and shock. They also suffer long-term problems like chronic urinary infection and depression. In addition, the surgery eliminates the possibility of achieving any sexual satisfaction. Waris Dirie continues to work to eliminate FGM.

Cultural Change. Cultural beliefs and attitudes regarding sexuality change, often dramatically, over time. In China, economic and social reforms over the past three decades have been the catalyst for remarkable changes in Chinese family dynamics (Xu, DeFrain, & Liu, 2017). For example, a research team in suburban Shanghai reported that an increasing number of Chinese adolescents are engaging in premarital sexual activity. This has led to a marked increase in unplanned pregnancies and sexually transmitted infections (STIs).

The Shanghai research team developed a comprehensive sex education program for young people, including information on abstinence, contraception, and healthy sexual behaviors. The program provided information and services for unmarried 15- to 24-year-olds over a 20-month period. Results were compared with a control group in a comparable town who did not receive a similar intervention. The researchers found that the intervention program was not associated with delayed sexual initiation, but it was associated with reduced odds that youth coerced a partner into having sex, and with increased odds of contraceptive use and condom use during the intervention program. The researchers also found that pregnancy involvement was significantly lower in the intervention group (19%) when compared to the control group (26%). The research team concluded that comprehensive, community-based interventions may be effective in reaching large numbers of Chinese young people, and in the promotion of sexual negotiation, contraceptive use, and pregnancy and STI/HIV prevention (Wang, Hertog, et al., 2005).

HIV/AIDS—The Epidemic Continues

Human immunodeficiency virus (HIV) can lead to acquired immunodeficiency syndrome, or AIDS. Unlike some other viruses, the human body can't fight off or rid itself of HIV. Once infected with HIV, a person has it for life (Centers for Disease Control and Prevention, 2016e).

No safe and effective cure currently exists, but scientists around the world continue to search for one and remain hopeful. Meanwhile, with proper medical care, HIV can be controlled. Treatment for HIV is often called antiretroviral therapy or ART. This treatment can dramatically prolong the lives of many people infected with HIV and lower their chance of infecting others. Before the widespread use of ART in the mid-1990s, people with HIV could progress to AIDS in just a few years. Today, however, someone diagnosed with HIV and treated before the disease is far advanced can have a nearly normal life expectancy (Centers for Disease Control and Prevention, 2016e).

The HIV virus is spread through certain body fluids and attacks the immune system, specifically the CD4 cells, often called T-cells. These special cells help the immune system fight off infections. Untreated, HIV reduces the number of CD4 cells (T-cells) in the body. This damage to the immune system makes it increasingly difficult for the body to fight off infections and some other diseases. Opportunistic infections or cancers take advantage of a very weak immune system and signal that the person has AIDS (Centers for Disease Control and Prevention, 2016e).

By the end of 2012, an estimated 1.2 million persons aged 13 and older were living with HIV infection in the United States, including 156,300 persons (12.8%) whose infections had not been diagnosed. Around the world, HIV disease continues to be a serious health issue. Worldwide, there were about 2 million new cases of HIV in 2014. About 36.9 million people are living with HIV around the world, and as of March 2015, around 15 million people living with HIV were receiving antiretroviral therapy (ART). An estimated 1.2 million people died from AIDS-related illnesses in 2014. About 39 million people worldwide have died of AIDS-related causes since the epidemic began more than three decades ago. Seventy percent of all people living with HIV in 2014 were living in Sub-Saharan Africa, which bears the heaviest burden of HIV/AIDS worldwide. Other regions significantly affected by HIV/AIDS include Asia and the Pacific, Latin America and the Caribbean, and Eastern Europe and Central Asia (Centers for Disease Control and Prevention, 2016e).

Today, someone diagnosed with HIV and treated before the disease is far advanced can live nearly as long as someone who does not have HIV. And, more tools than ever are available to prevent HIV. To be as safe as possible: limit your number of sexual partners, never share needles, and use condoms the right way every time you have sex. You also may be able to take advantage of newer medicines such as pre-exposure prophylaxis (PrEP) and post-exposure prophylaxis (PEP). PrEP (pre-exposure prophylaxis) is used when people are at very high risk for HIV. They can take HIV medicines daily to lower their chances of getting infected. PEP (post-exposure prophylaxis) means that an individual can take antiretroviral medicines (ART) after being potentially exposed to HIV to prevent becoming infected. PEP should be used only in emergency situations, and the procedure must be started within 72 hours after a recent possible exposure to HIV. If you think you've recently been exposed to HIV during sex or through sharing needles and other injection-preparation related activities, or if you've been sexually assaulted, talk to your health care provider or an emergency room doctor about PEP right away (Centers for Disease Control and Prevention, 2016e).

American Sexual Health and Behavior

Married couples have sex 58 times a year. However, this average number comes from interviews with newlyweds, young couples, couples in the middle years, and elderly couples. Broken down by age group, couples in their 20s have sex 109 times a year on average, and the frequency drops off steadily over time, about 20% per decade, as couples get older. Put in simpler terms, young couples have sex slightly more than twice a week and the frequency declines steadily as the years pass. Couples 70 and older have sex about 17 times a year (General Social Survey, 2016; Smith, 2006). There have been a handful of large-scale sex surveys in the United States since Alfred Kinsey's landmark study in the early 1950s. These studies include the General Social Survey conducted by the University of Chicago; the National Survey of Sexual Health and Behavior conducted by Indiana University Bloomington; the American Sex Survey conducted by ABC News; and the American Association of Retired Persons study of Sex, Romance, and Relationships: AARP Survey of Midlife and Older Adults. These surveys reveal, among other things, information regarding the frequency with which Americans engage in sexual activity and the kinds of sexual activities they engage in.

The first study we will discuss in some depth is the National Survey of Sexual Health and Behavior conducted in 2009 and first reported on in 2010 (Herbenick et al., 2010; Indiana University Bloomington, 2016). We believe that this research deserves considerable discussion in this chapter because it is the most recent large-scale study of sexuality in the United States. We will also report the findings of a sex survey conducted by ABC News in 2004. Finally, we will summarize the study commissioned by AARP,* focusing on sexuality in the later years (Fisher et al., 2010). These three studies are the most prominent large-scale studies of sexuality in the United States that we have found in our research literature investigations. Major studies of sexual behavior, as the reader can readily imagine, are not easy to conduct. These investigations are expensive, time consuming, and politically charged because they focus on sensitive and very personal aspects of people's lives. For these reasons, large-scale studies of sexual behavior are not conducted very often.

National Survey of Sexual Health and Behavior

Researchers in this national study surveyed 5,865 randomly selected adults and teens 14 to 94 years of age to understand sexual behavior in the United States. This study included information about masturbation, vaginal intercourse, noncoital sex (that is, mutual masturbation), anal intercourse, and same-sex behavior (Herbenick et al., 2010; Indiana University Bloomington, 2016).

---

*The American Association of Retired Persons officially changed its name to AARP in 1999.

Men's Sexual Behaviors. Most men (from 28% to 69%) reported masturbating during the past year, with the exception of younger teens and older men (701 years), and most masturbation was done alone (Herbenick et al., 2010; Indiana University Bloomington, 2016). This research also found that although most men from 18 to 19 years of age had the experience of vaginal intercourse, it was not common. Eighty-five percent of men in their 20s and 30s experienced vaginal intercourse at least once in the previous year, with the percentages dropping to 74% among men in their 40s, and 58% of men in their 50s. Men in the 25 to 49 year age categories experienced vaginal intercourse more often than other sexual behaviors.

Some, but not many, men experienced partnered noncoital behaviors such as partnered masturbation or oral sex, across all age categories (Herbenick et al., 2010; Indiana University Bloomington, 2016). The highest rate of these behaviors happened with men who were between 25 and 49 years of age. Anal intercourse was less common, but not rare, by men across all ages. However, anal sex was most common in men ages 25 to 49 years of age. Almost half of the men between 25 and 59 years reported participating in anal sex during their lifetime.

Same-sex behavior was not very common, but approximately 6% of men from 18 to 59 years had engaged in same-sex behavior, such as oral or anal sex, with another man in the past year (Herbenick et al., 2010; Indiana University Bloomington, 2016). However, approximately 14% reported such behavior over their lifetime.

Women's Sexual Behaviors. Approximately 40% of women across all age groups reported having masturbated during the past year, except for women over 70 years of age (Herbenick et al., 2010; Indiana University Bloomington, 2016). As was true of men, approximately 43% of women reported vaginal intercourse being the most common sexual behavior with which they engaged. The percentages of women engaging in vaginal intercourse began decreasing in their 30s and continued to decrease through old age. Approximately 80% of women over 70 years had no vaginal intercourse in the previous year.

Masturbating with a partner, or noncoital sex, was reported most often in women between 25 and 49 years of age (Herbenick et al., 2010; Indiana University Bloomington, 2016). Oral sex was more common with women, with more than half of women from 18 to 49 years of age having had oral sex from a male partner in the past year. Anal sex was a behavior approximately 40% of women engaged in during their lifetime, which is similar to the rate of anal sex for men.

Same-sex behavior was reported by less than 5% of women during the past year, again being very similar to men (Herbenick et al., 2010; Indiana University Bloomington, 2016). Oral sex with another woman was the most prevalent same-sex behavior.

Common Findings for both Men and Women. In general, both men and women begin partnered sexual relations at age 14, with sexual activity increasing sharply for 18 to 24 year olds (Herbenick et al., 2010; Indiana University Bloomington, 2016). Findings show these sexual activities continue during the 20s and through the 40s, with a decline beginning in the 50s and continuing into older age. These changes in sexual activity as one ages is considered to be attributed to health issues and the loss of a partner.

The American Sex Survey by ABC News

We would also like to discuss the results of the American Sex Survey conducted by ABC News. The ABC survey confirms much of what the earlier research found, concluding, "the vast majority of Americans are monogamous and happy about it, expressing satisfaction with their sex lives and a broad preference for emotional commitment in sexual relationships. Most by far prefer marriage to the single life" (Langer, Arnedt, & Sussman, 2004, p. 1).

Young people become sexually active at an earlier age than in previous generations of Americans, and they also tend to have more sexual partners over a lifetime. But there seems to be a trend toward more conservative sexual behavior, perhaps because of the threat of sexually transmitted diseases.
©Olegdudko/123RF

ABC conducted a telephone poll of 1,501 randomly sampled American adults. Differences between men and women were illuminating:

- Forty-three percent of the men in the survey said they thought about sex several times a day; only 13% of the women thought about sex that much.
- Eighty-three percent of the men said they enjoyed sex "a great deal"; 59% of the women said they enjoyed sex "a great deal"; women, however, were equally likely to say they were satisfied with their sex lives.
- Women, on average, reported that they had 6 sex partners in their lifetime; men reported 20. A better measure of sexual activity, however, was the median for both. (The median is the midpoint where half the participants scored higher, and half of the participants scored lower.) Women reported a median of three sex partners, and men a median of eight. ABC explained that the averages are higher than the medians because a small number of individuals, especially men, reported a very high number of sex partners. Five percent of the men in the ABC sample said they had 99 or more sex partners, including four men who reported 200, three who reported 300, and one who reported 400. For the women, 1% reported more than 99 sex partners, and the high was 100 (reported by two women).
- Forty-two percent of the men reported having had sex on a first date, while only 17% of the women reported this.
- Women were more conservative than men on other sexual attitudes and behaviors as well: 84% said there was too much sex on TV, while 62% of the men agreed; 54% of the women condoned sex before marriage, compared to 68% of the men; 31% of the men said they slept in the nude, while only 14% of the women said they did; 51% of the women preferred sex with the lights off, while only 27% of the men liked it this way; 54% of the men thought participating in a sex chat room was cheating on the partner, while 72% of the women thought it was cheating; 15% of all men had paid for sex, and 30% of single men had paid for sex. None of the women reported this.
- About half the women said they had faked an orgasm.

Chapter 6 | Sexual Intimacy | **161**

Sexuality in the Later Years

The American Association of Retired Persons (AARP) commissioned a survey of sexual attitudes and practices among Americans 45 and older in 2009, similar to surveys in 1999 and 2004. The research team argued that the sexual revolution continued in the older population as baby boomers continued to age. The researchers found that opposition to sex among those who are not married was down by half over the previous 10 years, and the belief that there was too much emphasis on sex in our culture was also down since 2004 (Fisher et al., 2010).

However, data for the latest AARP study were collected from 1,670 adults in August, 2009, during the Great Recession, when unemployment in the United States was peaking and the economic environment was adding stress and financial anxiety. Thus, the research team was not surprised to find that the frequency of sexual intercourse and overall sexual satisfaction were down since 2004, while the frequency of self-stimulation and sexual thoughts and fantasies had not changed.

The researchers found that men continue to think about sex more often than women, see sex as more important to their quality of life, engage in sexual activities more often, are less satisfied if they are without a partner, and are twice as likely as women (21% to 11%) to admit to sexual activity outside their relationships.

Those individuals who were the most satisfied with their sexual relationship tended to have the following:
— A sexual partner (but not necessarily a spouse, because dating singles are more sexually satisfied)
— Frequent sexual intercourse (more than once a week, but not necessarily daily)
— Good health (self and partner)
— Low levels of stress
— Absence of financial worries

Sexual frequency and sexual satisfaction were both higher among unmarried and dating or engaged individuals than among those who were married. Forty-eight percent of those who were single and dating said they had intercourse at least once a week, compared to 36% of those who were married. And 60% of dating singles were satisfied with their sex lives, compared to 52% of those who were married.

The research team found that sexuality remains an essential element in the lives of many adults ages 45 and older. Although 2 out of 3 older Americans in the study believed that there was too much emphasis placed on sex in today's culture, nearly 6 out of 10 continued to agree that sexual activity is critical to a good relationship, and less than 1 in 20 felt sex was only for younger people.

For those respondents who had a current or recent sexual partner, 41% had sexual intercourse once a week or more often on average in the last 6 months, and 60% had intercourse at least once a month. These numbers, collected during the Great Recession, were about 10 points lower than in 2004 when the economy was functioning better. Those individuals who were partnered but unmarried had higher rates of both sexual intercourse and sexual satisfaction than those who were married.

More than one in five (22%) engaged in self-stimulation at least once a week, virtually identical to 2004 figures. Whether the individual had a sexual partner or not did not matter, as 25% of those with sexual partners reported they engaged in self-stimulation at least once a week also.

Forty-three percent of the respondents said they were satisfied with their sex lives, down from 51% in 2004 during better economic times. Younger participants in the research were more likely than older participants to be satisfied with their sex lives, and men were more satisfied, overall, than women. For the majority of individuals, the presence of a sexual partner appeared to be a prerequisite to sexual satisfaction, though not a guarantee. Among all of the participants with a sexual partner, 57% were satisfied with their sex lives.

Four in 10 considered themselves to be in excellent or very good health, and 36% said their health was good. One in five (21%) said their health condition was either poor or fair. The health of the partners in the relationship had an important effect on sexual satisfaction, with health problems identified as the most significant factor affecting sexual satisfaction. Medical conditions and medication were often cited as the reason for sexual dissatisfaction. Some of the health conditions that had a negative effect on sex were high blood pressure, high cholesterol, arthritis or rheumatism, back problems, diabetes, and depression.

Overall, midlife and older adults had a positive outlook on life, on average, though less so than 2004 in better economic times. But, nevertheless, they were optimistic about what life would bring in the coming 5 years.

It is clear from the AARP study that the majority of individuals age 45 and older seek a healthy and satisfying sex life. They talk about improving their sex life with their partner, they seek out medical care for sexual dysfunction, and they take medications to enhance sexual functioning. Sexuality plays an important part in couple relationships.

Gay-Male and Lesbian Sexual Behavior

Gays and lesbians are people who are attracted to members of the same sex. When speaking of a person's *sexual orientation,* this means that an individual has an enduring pattern or disposition to experience sexual, affectional, or romantic attractions primarily with people of the same sex. Sexual orientation also refers to the individual's feelings of personal and social identification as a gay or lesbian, based on these attractions, behaviors expressing them, and membership in a community of other people who share these attractions (American Psychological Association, 2016; GLAAD, 2016).

Heterosexual refers to people who are attracted to the different sex. *Bisexuals* are those attracted to both sexes. The term *gay* can be used to include both gay males and female lesbians. Gays, then, comprise one of the three main categories of sexual orientation, along with heterosexuality and bisexuality. These three together make up what can be seen as a sexual orientation continuum. Basically, human sexuality is commonly seen by many professionals as not an either/or type of issue, but on a continuum. In essence, researchers have consistently found that some people throughout life have always been heterosexual, some people throughout life have always been oriented toward the same sex, and other people have had a mix of feelings toward and experience with both men and women. The most common terms used today are gay for males and lesbian for females, though some people prefer other terms or none at all. Sometimes gays and lesbians, when talked about as a group, are called gays (American Psychological Association, 2016; GLAAD, 2016; Kinsey Institute, 2016).

We have chosen not to use the term "homosexual" in this textbook because of the clinical history of the word. It has been aggressively used by anti-gay extremists to suggest that gay people are somehow diseased or psychologically/emotionally disordered, and this type of thinking has been discredited by both the American Psychological Association and the American Psychiatric Association since the mid-1970s (GLAAD, 2016).

The number of people who identify as gay or lesbian, and the percentage who have had same-sex sexual experiences, have always been difficult for researchers to reliably determine (American Psychological Association, 2016). This is because individuals are often quite guarded about issues surrounding their sexuality, especially in the case of gays and lesbians. One study found that 20% of the participants anonymously reported some homosexual feelings, though relatively few of the participants identified themselves as homosexual (McConaghy, Hadzi-Pavlovic, Stevens, & Manicavasagar, 2006).

According to a study conducted by Gotta et al. (2011), both heterosexual couples and same-sex couples reported having less non-monogamous sex in 2000 compared with 1975. Gay men reported the greatest decrease during that time. Agreements about monogamy are likely to be a result of the HIV/AIDS disease and fears about contacting other sexually transmitted diseases (Gotta et al., 2011).

In many ways, gay male and lesbian relationships are like heterosexual relationships. In the past, gay male couples have been less likely to maintain monogamous relationships (Green, 2012). However, men in general are less likely to have monogamous relationships than women. Over the past 30 years gay men and lesbians have increasingly moved toward developing and maintaining ongoing relationships with one person.

Perhaps the greatest difference between gays and straights in American culture has to do with the stigmatization that same-sex relationships face in this culture. Gay people are frequently the targets of prejudice, have to endure malicious jokes and bullying, and sometimes experience violence against them. They experience discrimination in the employment and housing markets, and in most communities they hold little political power. Gangs of teenagers and young adults have terrorized gays, and stories of brutality against gays by police and military personnel are not uncommon. As we reported earlier in this chapter, on June 26, 2015, the U.S. Supreme Court ruled 5–4 to legalize same-sex marriage. The Court ruled that states cannot ban same-sex marriage. The GLBT community and its supporters saw this as a recognition of their rights as gay and lesbian couples in the same way that rights of heterosexual couples are honored through marriage.

Looking back, the first gay couple to apply for a marriage license in the United States were two University of Minnesota students. The couple applied for the license on May 18, 1970, and were turned down by the district court clerk because they were both men. The issue went to the Minnesota Supreme Court, and in 1971 the court ruled that "the institution of marriage as a union of man and woman uniquely involving the procreating and rearing of children within the family is as old as the book of Genesis." As we now understand, the struggle continued and was not legally resolved until the decision of the U.S. Supreme Court in 2015 more than 45 years later (ProCon.org, 2016).

Meanwhile, the arguments in our society and in our families continue. Looking back over past decades, attitudes in America have changed significantly. In 1985 researchers asked Americans, "If you had a child who told you he or she was gay or lesbian, what would your reaction be?" Nine percent of the respondents said they would not be upset; and 89% said they would be upset. This question was asked five times over 30 years. By 2015, the responses had shifted dramatically: 57% of respondents said they would not be upset; and 39% said they would be upset (Pew Research Center, 2015, June 29). See Figure 6-1.

FIGURE 6.1
Changing Reactions to a Gay Child: 1985–2015.
Source: Pew Research Center, "Most Americans Now Say Learning Their Child is Gay Wouldn't Upset Them," June 29, 2015.

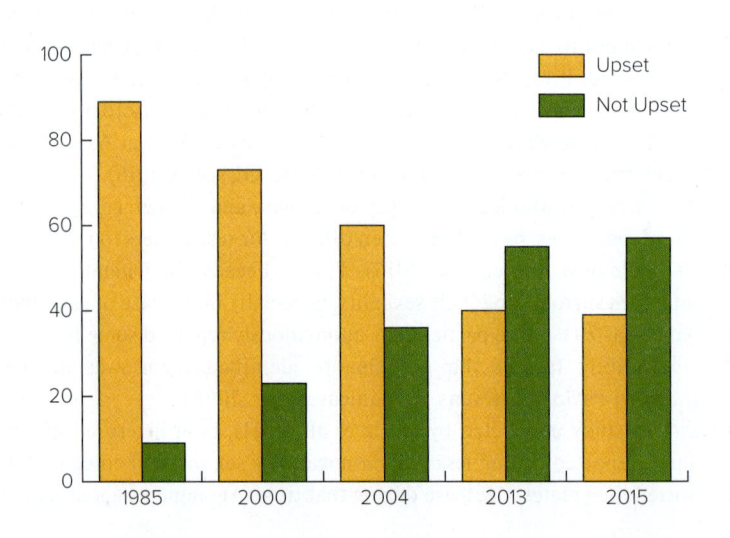

Sexual Behavior Among Adolescents and Young Adults

Research indicates that by the time adults in this country reach age 44, generally seen as the end of the childbearing years, 99% of Americans have had sex; 95% have had sex before being married; and 74% have had sex before age 20. Even among young people who abstain from sex until age 20 or later, 81% eventually had sex before marriage. (The average age for marriage, as we have seen, is 25 for women and 27 for men.) And, contrary to the widespread public perception that premarital sex is much more common today than in the past, even among women born in the 1940s, nearly 9 in 10 had sex before they were married. In other words, premarital sex is almost universal and has been so for decades (Finer, 2007). See Figure 6.2.

Clearly, sex before marriage is statistically normal. Sex among young people is also common. By the time young women in this country reach their 18th birthday, 6 in 10 of them will have had sexual intercourse. By the time young men reach their 18th birthday, more than 5 in 10 of them will have had sexual intercourse (Abma et al., 2004; Abma, Martinez, & Copen, 2010).

Unintended Consequences: Teen Pregnancies and Sexually Transmitted Infections (STIs)

Approximately 750,000 teen pregnancies occur each year, and 82% of these are unintended. More than one-fourth of teen pregnancies end in abortion (Finer & Zolna, 2011). However, rates of teen pregnancy, birth, and abortion have declined dramatically in this country since their peak in the early 1990s. In 2010, some 614,000 pregnancies occurred among teenage women aged 15 to 19, at a rate of 57.4 pregnancies per 1,000 women in that age group. This is a 51% decline from the 1990 peak. Similarly, the teen birthrate declined 44% from the peak in 1991 (from 61.8 births per 1,000 to 34.4 per 1,000); and the teen abortion rate

FIGURE 6.2

Premarital Sex in America.

Source: From Boonstra, H. D., "The case for a new approach to sex education mounts: Will policymakers heed the message?", *Guttmacher Policy Review*, 2007, 10(2):2–7.

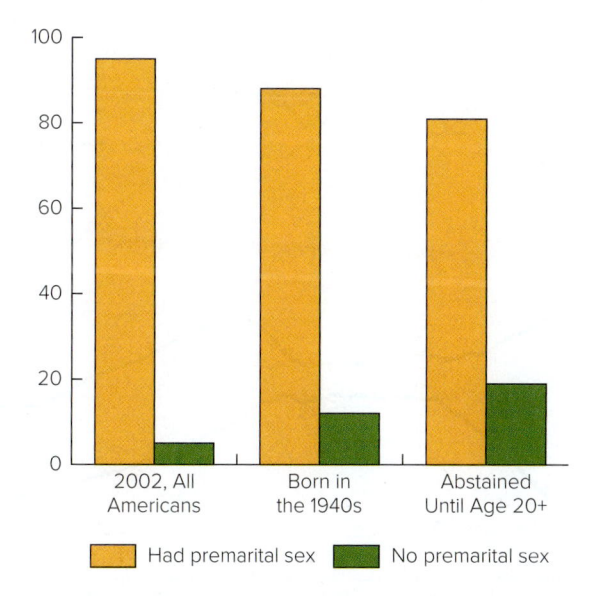

Note: Percentages are of Americans who had premarital sex by age 44.

declined 66% between its 1988 peak and 2010 (from 43.5 abortions per 1,000 to 14.7 per 1,000) (Guttmacher Institute, 2014, May 5). See Figure 6.3. Even though teen pregnancy rates have declined considerably over the past few decades in this country and in most of the other 20 countries with complete statistics, the teen pregnancy rate is still highest in the United States (57.4 per 1,000 for 15- to 19-year-olds), followed by New Zealand (51) and England and Wales (47). The lowest rate was in Switzerland (8 per 1,000), followed by the Netherlands (14), Slovenia (14), and Singapore (14). Teen pregnancy rates were higher than the highest rates (of those just mentioned in the previous text) in some former Soviet countries with incomplete statistics and in developing countries in Sub-Saharan Africa and Latin America for which estimates could be made (https://www.guttmacher.org/news-release/2015/teen-pregnancy-rates-declined-many-countries-between-mid-1990s-and-2011).

So, what is the long-term impact of teen pregnancy? In a recent study, over 500 participants who had a child before the age of 20 were followed until the age of 53 (Taylor, 2009). These participants were compared to delayed child bearers, who had children at an average age for that time. The researcher in this study found that early child bearers were more likely to have less education and less prestigious careers, and were less physically healthy. They also had less stable marriages. These participants who were pregnant as teens were as likely as later child bearers, however, to have satisfying marriages and to feel good about their jobs, and they experienced a high degree of social and psychological support. The author of this research concludes that there are areas where adolescent pregnancies create vulnerabilities, but there are also areas where individuals adapt and rise to the challenges they experienced with a teenage pregnancy.

Another unintended consequence of sexual activity among adolescents and young adults is a high rate of sexually transmitted infections (STIs) in this country. It has been estimated that young people aged 15 to 24 years acquire half of all new STIs, and that one in four sexually active adolescent females have an STI, such as chlamydia or human papillomavirus (HPV). Compared with older adults, sexually active adolescents aged 15 to 19 years and young adults aged 20 to 24 years are at higher risk of acquiring STIs. There are a number of reasons for this: For some STIs, such as chlamydia, adolescent females may have increased susceptibility to infection because of increased cervical ectopy. The higher prevalence of

FIGURE 6.3

U.S. Teen Pregnancy, Birth, and Abortion Rates: 1970–2010.

Source: Kost,Kathryn and Henshaw, Stanley.,"U.S.Tennage Pregnancies,Births and Abortions, 2010: National and State Trends by Age, Race and Ethnicty".
https://www.guttmacher.org/news-release/2014/us-teen-pregnancy-birth-and-abortion-rates-reach-historic-lows

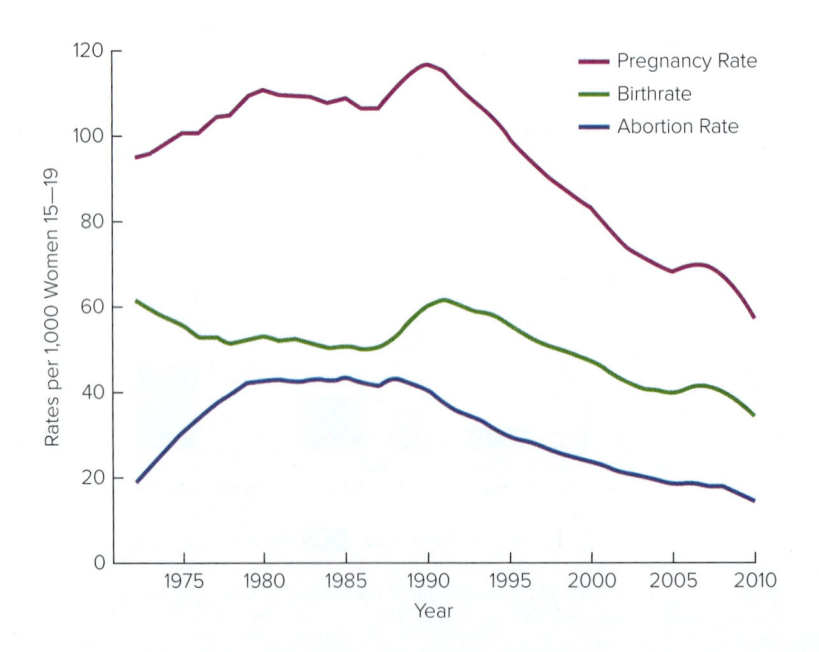

STIs among adolescents also may reflect multiple barriers to accessing quality STI prevention services, including lack of health insurance or ability to pay, lack of transportation, discomfort with facilities and services designed for adults, and concerns about confidentiality (Centers for Disease Control and Prevention, 2015, November).

Education for Sexuality

As we have seen, rates of teen pregnancy, birth, and abortion have declined dramatically in this country since their peak in the early 1990s (Guttmacher Institute, 2014, May 5). Two competing approaches to sex education in America have emerged in recent decades: the comprehensive approach to sex education, which stresses abstinence and responsible decision making, but also includes information on contraception and avoiding sexually transmitted infections; and the abstinence-only-until-marriage approach, which argues that nonmarital sex is immoral behavior and people should "just say no."

Both sides are convinced that much of the decline in teen pregnancy can be attributed to their efforts. The abstinence-only proponents have received approximately $1.5 billion since 1996 from the federal government for just-say-no programs in schools (Advocates for Youth, 2010a). The comprehensive sex education proponents report that their research indicates that improved contraceptive use and the use of more effective birth control methods among teenagers explain 86% of the recent declines in teen pregnancy, not teens simply abstaining from sex. They also argue that abstinence-only is unrealistic, because research indicates that 9 out of 10 Americans have sex before marriage and this has been true for decades; and that two decades of research have failed to find evidence that abstinence-only programs delay sexual activity or reduce teen pregnancy.

A study by National Public Radio (NPR), the Kaiser Family Foundation, and the Kennedy School of Government at Harvard University found that only 7% of Americans believed that sex education should not be taught in schools. "The debate over whether to have sex education in American schools is over," NPR declared. "Moreover, in most places there is even little debate about what *kind* of sex education should be taught, although there

Because parents tend to be poor at providing their children with clear, useful information about sex, the responsibility for sex education in our society has fallen largely to schools and communities. Sex education is more effective when combined with access to a health clinic where contraceptives are available.
©Radius Images/Getty Images

TABLE 6.3   Ten Ridiculous Ideas That Will Make You a Father

- You can count on your partner to use birth control.
- Men have stronger sex drives than women do.
- Men need to have sex with different women to learn to be better lovers.
- If a woman uses birth control, then she has probably been sleeping around.
- A woman would do anything to keep from getting pregnant.
- It is easy for a woman to get on the pill.
- If a man hasn't gone all the way by the time he's 16, then something is wrong with him.
- I don't like condoms.
- When a woman says no, she really just wants to be talked into it.
- I could never talk to my partner about birth control.

Source: Adapted the brochure "Ten Ridiculous Ideas That Will Make a Father Out of You", Planned Parenthood of Central Oklahoma, 2000.

---

are still pockets of controversy" (NPR, 2004.) A national poll by the Pew Research Center found that 78% of American adults favored allowing public schools to provide students with birth control information, while 18% opposed such instruction. Seventy-six percent of adults said they believed that schools should teach teenagers to abstain from sex until marriage. Solid majorities in every major religious group said schools should be allowed to provide students with information on birth control, but a sizeable minority of white evangelical Protestants (30%) opposed this. White evangelicals are also among the most supportive groups believing that schools should teach teenagers to abstain from sex until marriage. Secular respondents to the Pew survey expressed the greatest number of reservations about schools promoting abstinence: 62% support that approach, while about one-third (34%) were opposed (Pew Research Center, 2007, September 14).

The most recent study we could find concurred. A random-digit-dial survey of 1,284 California parents found that overall 89% of the parents reported a preference for comprehensive sex education and 11% favored abstinence-only education (Constantine, Jerman, & Huang, 2007).

Planned Parenthood, a national private nonprofit organization, has developed a wide variety of presentations and materials to benefit young people. (See their web site: https://www.plannedparenthood.org/.) A sample of the organization's materials, displayed in Table 6.3, lists some common misconceptions young people have about sex—"ridiculous ideas" that can lead to trouble.

Sexuality Education and Parents

Although people disagree about sexuality, there is agreement on one issue—that education about sexuality should begin in the home. The reason that schools, religious institutions, and agencies such as Planned Parenthood have become involved in sex education is that most parents feel incapable of or uncomfortable about talking seriously with their offspring about sexual matters. A subtle conspiracy of silence exists between parent and child. Parents tell themselves that they are willing to answer any questions their children might have about sex, but children sense that their parents really do not want to talk about these sensitive issues. Because both feel uncomfortable talking about sexuality, they avoid the subject (Advocates for Youth, 2016; Kaufman, 2011).

Joyce, a 45-year-old single mother of three, describes growing up in a home in which her parents avoided any mention of sex, her early self-consciousness about her own sexuality,

> **Box 6.1 Putting It Together**
>
> ## *Father-Child Communication About Sex*
>
> Looking at 49 studies about communication between fathers and children about sex, Paul J. Wright found that fathers play an important role in their children's sexual development. Here are some of the findings of studies from 1980 through 2009, with most of the studies conducted in the 2000s:
>
> - In order of the extent to which fathers communicate with their children about sex, Black and Latino fathers communicated the most, then White fathers, and finally Asian fathers. We can conclude that culture impacts father-child communication about sex.
> - Generally, fathers who are more educated communicate with their children about sex more often.
> - Fathers talk more to their sons than they talk to their daughters about sex.
> - Fathers whose parents talked with them about sex are more likely to talk to their children about sex. This positive communication about sex from one generation to the next is worth noting.
> - Fathers with permissive attitudes about sex are more likely to talk with their children about safe sex, and more conservative fathers are likely to talk to their children about values.
> - The frequency and quality of discussions about sex are related to the extent to which fathers communicate with their children about other issues. If they talk often about nonsexual issues, they are more likely to talk about sexual issues.
> - There are no conclusive findings that children's sexual behavior is related to the extent to which they talk with their fathers about sex. Therefore, positive communication about sex does not necessarily affect children's sexual behavior.
>
> *Source:* Wright, P.J., "Father-Child Sexual Communication in the United States: A Review and Synthesis," *Journal of Family Communication,* 9, 2009, 233–250.

and her unease in talking to her own children about sex. Through sexuality education, she overcame her anxieties and can now talk freely about sexual matters.

> "My parents were intelligent, sensitive individuals, and yet they treated the subject of sex like it was the plague. All I knew for sure was this must really be something if it was such a big secret! What happened with my brothers and sister (and me) was there were a lot of misconceptions and a lot of guilt.
>
> As a parent, what kind of message did I give my children? In my head I knew what I wanted to give them, but in my gut I was still at war with my own sexuality. So I, too, gave mixed messages to my children about sex. It wasn't until I went back to college full-time after my divorce and got into a human sexuality class that the shift really came for me internally. I began to stop feeling self-conscious and began to relax—to enjoy being human. I still have one child living at home, and I'm able to talk openly and honestly with him about any subject regarding sex."

Few children receive direct instruction from their parents in the areas of sexuality, sexual intercourse, or birth control (Advocates for Youth, 2010a; Miller, 2002; Miller, Benson, & Galbraith, 2001; Miller, Sage, & Winward, 2006). See more about father-child communication in Box 6.1. This is sad because good parental communication about sex might forestall or postpone a child's sexual activity. Among those daughters who are sexually active, parental communication appears to help promote more effective contraceptive practices on the part of the adolescent. In one study describing how African American mothers talk to their children about sex, it was found that mothers talk more to their daughters about sex than they talk to their sons (Kapungu et al., 2010). This finding is consistent with research with other populations. Reasons for this might be that mothers do not know how to talk to sons, talking about menstruation to daughters may be a way to start the discussion, and they experience real concern about their daughters getting pregnant.

There is less pregnancy risk if adolescents have intercourse less often or with fewer partners, as well as by using contraception at first or most recent intercourse and by using contraception consistently over time. Elevated risk of adolescent pregnancy is associated with living with a single parent and living in a lower socioeconomic status family. There is also more risk if a woman has older sexually active siblings, has been a victim of sexual abuse, or is residing in a disorganized/dangerous neighborhood (Miller et al., 2006).

A nationally representative survey of 15- to 17-year-old youth in the United States complements Gordon's findings (Advocates for Youth, 2010b). *Seventeen* magazine and the Henry J. Kaiser Family Foundation studied sexual health communication between teens and their parents. The researchers found:

- 51% of teens (61% of females, 42% of males) had discussed with their parents "how to know when you are ready for sex."
- 43% of teens (53% of females, 33% of males) had discussed with their parents how to talk to a boyfriend or girlfriend about sexual health issues, such as pregnancy, birth control, and STIs.
- Among male teens, 50% had discussed condoms, but only 35% had discussed other forms of birth control, with parents. Overall, 52% of teens had discussed condoms, and 49% had discussed other forms of contraception.
- 56% of teens (64% of females, 48% of males) had discussed HIV/AIDS with their parents.
- 50% of teens (56% of females, 44% of males) had discussed STIs with their parents.

Why can't parents and teens talk about sex? The study found that:

- 83% of the teens worried about their parents' reaction.
- 88% worried that parents would think they have had sex or are going to have sex.
- 78% cited embarrassment as a big reason.
- 78% of teens (83% of females, 71% of males) said they didn't know how to bring the subject up with parents.

Brent Miller and his colleagues studied how strictness of parenting was related to adolescents' sexual attitudes and behaviors (Miller et al., 2001). These researchers hypothesized and found a curvilinear relationship between flexibility in parenting and sexual behavior. Sexual promiscuity and the experience of intercourse were highest among teenagers who saw their parents as not being strict or as not having any rules (chaotic on the Couple and Family Map; see Chapter 3), lowest among those teens who reported that their parents were moderately strict (flexible on the Couple and Family Map), and intermediate among teenagers who saw their parents as being very strict and having many rules (rigid on the Couple and Family Map). The results of this study suggest that if parents are concerned about adolescent sexual behavior, they can err in two directions: by being either too lenient (chaotic) or too strict (rigid). The more balanced levels (being structured or flexible on the Couple and Family Map) are related to more responsible sexual behavior on the part of adolescents.

Is Sex Education Effective?

In a review of research findings, Advocates for Youth (2010b) concludes that comprehensive sex education helps delay the onset of sexual activity, reduce the frequency of sexual activity, reduce the number of sexual partners, and increase condom and contraceptive use. The organization also says the evidence shows that youth receiving comprehensive sex education are not more likely to become sexually active, increase sexual activity, or experience negative sexual health outcomes. Effective programs have been implemented for young people from a variety of racial, cultural, and socioeconomic backgrounds.

Advocates for Youth began in 1980 as the Center for Population Options and concluded that it could best serve young people by advocating for a more positive and realistic approach to adolescent sexual health. The organization reviewed research on abstinence-only programs and found "little if any evidence" that the programs are effective. Advocates for Youth concluded, "No abstinence-only program has yet been proven through rigorous evaluation to help youth delay sex for a significant period of time, help youth decrease the number of sex partners, or reduce STI or pregnancy rates among teens" (Advocates for Youth, 2010b, p. 2).

The nationwide controversy is not likely to end soon. Because the best sex education of all begins in the home, parents are encouraged to learn how to talk calmly, openly, and honestly with their children from a young age when the questions start coming. Sex education should not be left up to the television set, the movies, the Internet, the pornography industry, or a child's friends on the street. Because schools and religious institutions face so many political obstacles in providing comprehensive sex education, including the discussion of GLBT issues, it is essential that parents begin to prepare themselves to be sex educators for their children.

Sexual Behavior, Alcohol, and College

Less than 2% of adolescents have had sex by the time they reach their 12th birthday. However, adolescence is a time of rapid change, and by age 15, 16% of teenagers have had sex. By age 16, one in three have had sex. By 17, 48%; by 18, 61%; and by 19, 71%. There is little difference by gender in the age of first having sex (Guttmacher Institute, 2014, May). During this developmental period in life, the sexual experience tends to be sporadic, furtive, and poorly managed. Even sexually experienced students entering college therefore have much to learn in the sexual arena (Centers for Disease Control and Prevention, 2016f).

In a culture that glorifies sex and drinking, it is of no surprise that the college campus is probably little different from anywhere else. Alcohol use and risky sexual behavior among college students are strongly linked, including sexual assault. A *Washington Post*/Kaiser Family Foundation poll of 1,053 current and recent college students found that heavy drinking is one of the most significant predictors of sexual assault in college, and women who say they *sometimes* or *often* drink more than they should are twice as likely to be victims of

It has been estimated that 400,000 college students between age 18 and 24 have had unprotected sex after drinking in a given year, and an estimated 100,000 had sex when they were so intoxicated they were unable to consent.
©William87/iStock/Getty Images

TABLE 6.4 — Risky Sexual Behavior

Percentage of sexually active young people who say . . .

	Teens 15 to 17	Young Adults 18 to 24
Alcohol or drugs influenced their decision to do something sexual.	29%	37%
They did more sexually than planned because they had been drinking or using drugs.	24	31
They worried about STDs or pregnancy because of something they did sexually while drinking or using drugs.	26	28
They used alcohol or drugs to help them feel more comfortable with a sexual partner.	13	16
They had unprotected sex because they were drinking or using drugs.	12	25

Source: The Henry J. Kaiser Family Foundation and the National Center on Addiction and Substance Abuse at Columbia University, *Substance Abuse and Risky Behavior: Attitudes and Practices among Adolescents and Young Adults: Survey Snapshot,* February 6, 2002.

completed, attempted, or suspected sexual assault. Several male victims also noted alcohol's role in their assault. Alcohol, in essence is *the* date-rape drug (Brown, Hendrix, & Svriuga, 2015, June 14).

Estimates indicate that 400,000 college students between the ages of 18 and 24 had unprotected sex after drinking in a given year, and an estimated 100,000 had sex when they were so intoxicated they were unable to consent (Hingson & Howland, 2002). (See Table 6.4.) Another investigator looked at the connection between drinking and teen childbearing and found that teenage girls who binge drink are up to 63% more likely to become teen mothers (Dee, 2001).

Marital and Extramarital Sexual Behavior

Premarital sex is nearly universal among Americans, and has been for decades. The most recent research available indicates that 95% of individuals have had sex before marriage, with 93% indicating they did so by age 30 (Finer, 2007). In fact, this study indicates that this high percentage of people having premarital sex has been evident for a long time, with nearly 9 out of 10 women born in the 1940s indicating they had sex before marriage. The fact that couples are waiting to get married until their late 20s means that individuals have more years available to have sexual relationships before they enter into marriage (Finer, 2007). After marriage, the sexual relationship gradually changes. Some people have jokingly asked, "Is there sex after marriage?" Research indicates there is.

Sex Within Marriage

Years ago when newspaper columnist Ann Landers asked her readers, "Has your sex life gone downhill since you got married?" 82% of the 141,210 people who responded said yes, sex after marriage was less exciting (Landers, 1989). However, intimacy—feelings of warmth and closeness between two people who love each other—does not appear to diminish with time. Within the intimate environment of a happy marriage, sexual experiences can become more satisfying and meaningful—and retain their excitement—over time.

Premarital relationships are often highly sexual, and most young people have intercourse before marriage. After marriage, the sexual relationship becomes more meaningful as the strength of the partnership increases. Friendship may deepen as the partners grow together through both good times and bad times. And even though sex drive may slowly diminish over time, the bond remains strong.

A hectic life often gets in the way of an active sex life. Long hours on the job, caring for children, continual interruptions, and countless other stresses tend to tire people out and decrease their sexual activity. For those couples with two jobs, the phenomenon has been called the **DINS** (double income, no sex) **dilemma**. Therapists have labeled it *inhibited*, or *hypoactive, sexual desire*. In addition to sheer fatigue, boredom is also a factor for some individuals. Most of the time, couples can resuscitate the sexual relationship with some tender care and concern, such as having dinner out together, seeing a movie, or going to bed early. Consulting a marriage and family therapist or a sex therapist may be useful for persistent sexual problems. The preeminent sex researchers and therapists William Masters and Virginia Johnson, along with Robert Kolodny (*Encyclopedia Britannica*, 2015; Masters, Johnson, & Kolodny, 1998), argued that half of all American couples are troubled at some time by some type of sexual distress, ranging from disinterest to genuine sexual dysfunction.

For many people, sex is not the most important thing in life. A landmark nationwide survey of 815 men found that the most important thing in a man's life is not sex, career, fame, or fortune, but marriage, according to 75% of the married men in the sample. About 90% of these husbands called their wives their best friends. Friendship, based on trust and sharing of responsibilities, becomes more important as life's challenges mount and sexual energy decreases (Hellmich, 1990).

Although sex is clearly not everything, it is important to an intimate relationship. Barry McCarthy (American University, 2016; McCarthy, 2001, 2003, 2009) explained that when sex goes well, it is 15% to 20% of a relationship; but if there are sexual problems, then it has a much more powerful role of 50% to 75%, and it robs the marriage of intimacy and vitality. Sex is more than a simple physical need; it also impacts the quality of the marriage.

Different people have different needs for sexual intimacy, and those needs affect how they perceive their sexual behavior. For this reason, couples must communicate clearly about sex if they are to maintain a satisfying relationship. The classic movie *Annie Hall* depicts two lovers with different perceptions of their sexual relationship. When friends ask them (separately) how often they have sex, the character played by Woody Allen answers, "Hardly ever, maybe three times a week"; the character played by Diane Keaton replies, "Constantly, three times a week."

Overall, it appears that in many marriages sex is very important for long-term happiness. It has powerful symbolic value in a successful marriage, reaffirming the bond between the individuals. It is an indication that everything is still okay despite wrinkles, sags, and love handles. To keep the spark in their lovemaking, married couples need to keep the relationship alive through communication and sharing. It is very difficult to have a successful sexual relationship if each partner does not feel good about herself or himself or about other aspects of the relationship. Serena, a middle-aged woman in St. Louis, describes the "sexy relationship" she has with her husband, a relationship founded not just on physical attraction but on a number of elements that make her marriage strong and healthy.

> *"Our sexual relationship is great today. It's a lot better than it was early in our marriage. I don't know why exactly, but I think we're more used to each other, more comfortable with each other. Perhaps we really love each other more. As the years pass, you look back and see a long-term tradition of commitment and kindness, and recognize that you have really created a wonderful marriage together.*
>
> *That's very special, and it makes you feel so very close to each other. It's hard to explain, but we do have a very sexy relationship with each other. Perhaps not as often as before, but it sure can be full of fire and tenderness."*

Marital Styles and Sexual Behavior

Four types of marital dynamics have been identified by Barry McCarthy (American University, 2016; McCarthy, 2001, 2003, 2009, 2014). He found that each style had sexual strengths and problems. The four styles were complementary couples, conflict-minimizing couples, best-friend couples, and emotionally expressive couples. These are not "pure" styles, and couples can sometimes change their styles over time.

Complementary Couples. This was the most common marital style (also called validating or supportive), and each partner has power in certain domains and moderate levels of intimacy. They validate each other's worth and value the marital bond. Sex for them becomes a low priority and often becomes routine, like watching the evening news. Usually the male is in charge of sexuality, and he overemphasizes intercourse at the expense of affection and intimacy. As the couple ages, sexuality drops considerably.

Conflict-Minimizing Couples. These couples are the most stable couple style (also called traditional) and usually have traditional roles. Strong emotional expression is discouraged. The male initiates sex and decides on the sexual style. Sex is very predictable and is rarely discussed.

Best-Friend Couples. This style values intimacy the most and considers friendship to be a strong foundation of their marriage. When the relationship works well, sex is an integral part of the marriage. Sex energizes the relationship and the marital bond is strong. The major pitfall is that it is a difficult style to maintain and it has a high rate of divorce. High expectations and disillusion rob the marriage of its excitement and pleasure.

Emotionally Expressive Couples. This style is full of feelings and can range from intense feelings of love and anger (also called volatile or explosive). Sex is often passionate, exciting, fun, and playful. A healthy pattern can be that sex occurs as a way of making up from conflict or a fight. The problem is that the conflict can often drive the couple apart and it could end in a "divorce from hell."

In summary, each marital style has both positive and negative consequences on the sexual relationship. Most couples develop a style that works for them and find it hard to change it over time, even when they are dissatisfied.

Infidelity

Extramarital friendships are common in American society. As one husband put it, "It doesn't make a whole lot of sense to deny friendships across-the-board to half the human race. If I enjoy talking with a person at work, it doesn't make sense to lose this friendship just because she's a female." Ideally, couples should allow each other the freedom to develop relationships outside the marriage. But if they are not properly handled, friendships with members of the other sex can harm a marriage. These friendships can sometimes develop into extramarital sexual relationships, which are commonly cited as one of a number of reasons for divorce. Opinion is divided on whether men and women can be friends—loving, affectionate, accepting, and so on—without becoming sexually involved.

Blow and Hartnett (2005) reviewed the research conducted on infidelity from 1980 through 2005. They summarized the research from the perspectives of attitude toward infidelity, prevalence, type of infidelity, infidelity by gender, and several other demographic characteristics. Based on this review, they drew the following conclusions:

- Attitudes about infidelity are related to actions, and those with more positive attitudes about infidelity are more likely to engage in infidelity.
- Attitudes about infidelity differ based on culture, gender, type of couple relationship (e.g., heterosexual, gay/lesbian, dating, marriage), behaviors that make up the infidelity (e.g., kiss, intercourse, emotional connection), and prior experience with infidelity.
- Internationally, differences in attitudes and behaviors vary by country and culture.
- Men are more likely to see a distinction between love and sex than women, with men more likely to view infidelity as only sexual and not emotional.
- Men are more likely to engage in sexual infidelity than women.
- Over the course of married heterosexual relationships in the United States, extramarital sex occurs in less than 25% of committed relationships.
- Dissatisfaction with the marital relationship is related to increased incidence of infidelity.
- There appear to be at least three types of infidelity: emotional-only, sexual-only, and combined sexual and emotional infidelity. Most research is about sexual infidelity.
- Some studies show that gay men are less concerned about infidelity than heterosexual couples. Lesbian couples are less likely to experience infidelity than gay male couples.

Emily Brown, a social worker, offers a different perspective on affairs. She identifies six stages in the process of infidelity (Brown, 1999, 2000, 2016). The first stage occurs when a climate develops in which infidelity can germinate, such as a couple's allowing hurt, dissatisfaction, and differences to go unresolved. Betrayal occurs in the second stage. The more dissatisfied spouse "slides" into the infidelity. The unfaithful spouse denies it is happening, and the other spouse may collude by ignoring obvious signs. The infidelity is revealed in the third stage. At this stage, both partners realize they will never be able to picture themselves or their marriage again in the same way. According to Brown, this stage requires a lot of time for partners to process; both need to experience the shock and fury of what happened, why it happened, what it means, and what the underlying issues might be. The impact can be as severe as the revelation of sexual abuse. The fourth stage involves admission of a crisis in the marriage. Brown believes that too often the infidelity itself is seen as the crisis rather than the problem she believes underlies the infidelity. In the fifth stage, the partners make a decision either to address all of the issues involved or to bury them and get on with rebuilding the marriage. The sixth and final stage involves forgiveness. Brown believes this can take place only if the preceding five stages have been successfully addressed and resolved.

There is an assumption that couples typically have equal power in a relationship and intervention strategies are carried out with that assumption. However, for some couples and in some cultures, power may not be equal and because of this unequal power, infidelity can be viewed very differently (Williams, 2011). For example, many cultures are male-dominated and there may be an acceptance of infidelity on the part of men, but no acceptance on the part of women. Researchers in China found that attitudes and behaviors regarding infidelity were very different between men and women. Men had a more permissive attitude and were more likely than women to engage in sex outside of marriage (Zhang, 2010; Zhang, Parish, Huang, & Pan, 2012). Therefore, the cultural context of the couple is an important component in understanding how a couple will respond to acts of infidelity and how the issue is resolved, if it is resolved.

The American Association for Marriage and Family Therapy (AAMFT, 2016) argues that the disclosure of infidelity can be devastating to a relationship. Intense emotions and recurrent crises are the norm. But AAMFT also notes that the majority of marriages not only survive an affair but can become stronger and more intimate. Couple therapy can be a useful tool for helping this growth begin. Approximately 50% of couples who seek couple therapy do so because an extramarital involvement has occurred.

Family therapists counsel couples dealing with the crisis of infidelity and try to help them work through the situation in a cautious and rational manner. It is clearly challenging, on the part of family therapists, how to deal with infidelity when the offending partner wants to keep the infidelity a secret (AAMFT, 2016; Butler, Harper, & Seedall, 2009). The challenge is whether to honor the confidentiality of the person who wants to keep it a secret, or to honor the rights of the partner for equality and justice in the couple relationship. A professional therapist can be very helpful by encouraging spouses to be calm and honest in disclosing their motives. Infidelity can signal the end of a relationship, or it can be a catalyst for dramatic and positive growth in a marriage. (See Box 6.2.)

A research team described the benefits of marriage education for couples in which there has been a history of infidelity in their marriage (Allen, Rhoades, Stanley, Lowe, & Markman, 2012). The researchers found that couples who had experienced infidelity and who participated in a marriage education program showed a significant increase in marital satisfaction and in communication skills, as compared to a control group. However, these couples did not experience an increase in marital satisfaction that was as high as couples in the marriage enrichment program who had not experienced infidelity in their marriage. But, the increase in marital satisfaction they experienced was still statistically significant. The findings of this research suggest that couples who have experienced infidelity can improve their marriage by attending marriage education classes.

Toward Sexual Health

Sex is an important part of human life, health, and happiness. It's a crucial ingredient in individual well-being and in intimate relationships, especially marriage. Problems in sexual functioning therefore need to be addressed if people are to have successful relationships.

A landmark study of sexuality in America by the University of Chicago identified the most frequent sexual problems of women and men (Laumann, Gagnon, Michael, & Michaels, 1994). About one-third (33.4%) of women reported a lack of interest in sex, as compared to only 15.8% of men. The second most frequent issue for nearly one-quarter of the women surveyed was an inability to reach orgasm (24.1%) and to find sex pleasurable (21.2%). In contrast, roughly one-quarter of the men reported that they reached climax too early (25.5%) or had anxiety about their sexual performance (17%). These symptoms are very similar to the common complaints heard from married couples in which the male feels the female is not interested in him sexually—often because he climaxes too early and does not satisfy her needs. (See also Gagnon, 2004, 2016; Laumann, 2016; Laumann & Michael, 2000; Laumann et al., 2004.)

BOX 6.2 Diversity in Families

What's Morally Acceptable? It Depends on Where You Live

Couple therapists view extramarital affairs as one of the most damaging relationship events a couple can face, and one of the most difficult problems to treat in couple therapy. A review of ethnographic accounts of marital dissolution in 160 societies found that infidelity was the single most common cause of the breakup (Whisman, Coop, Gordman, & Chatav, 2007).

The Pew Research Center has focused on global morality and asked people in 40 countries about what is morally unacceptable, morally acceptable, or not a moral issue. The list had a lot to do with sex, and focused on the following eight issues: married people having an affair, gambling, "homosexuality" (gays and lesbians), having an abortion, sex between unmarried adults, drinking alcohol, getting a divorce, and using contraceptives.

In the Pew Research Center study, a median of 78% of the respondents across 40 nations said married people having an affair was morally unacceptable, with only 7% saying it was morally acceptable, and 1 in 10 saying it was not a moral issue. Clearly, extramarital affairs are a hot button issue around the world.

Take a look below at feelings around the world regarding all eight moral issues:

Morality of Extramarital Affairs Around the World

Of all eight moral issues in the international survey of 40 countries, people seemed most comfortable with the use of contraceptives. Only a median of 14% said using contraceptives was morally unacceptable, while 54% believed contraceptive use was morally acceptable, and 21% said this was not a moral issue. Only in Pakistan, Nigeria, and Ghana did a majority of respondents say contraceptives were morally unacceptable.

Regarding the morality of premarital sex and alcohol usage, people in the 40 countries were more divided. Though a median of 46% saw sex between unmarried adults as immoral, an almost equal number believed it was morally acceptable (24%) or not a moral issue at all (16%). Similarly, in regard to alcohol usage, 42% said it was morally unacceptable, while 22% said it was acceptable and 24% said drinking was not a moral issue. Country by country there was a wide range of views. For example, in Pakistan 94% said premarital sex and alcohol usage were morally wrong. While in Japan, 21% said sex between unmarried adults was morally unacceptable and 66% said drinking was morally acceptable.

In regard to moral views in the United States, the Pew Research Center team found that an overwhelming majority of Americans (84%) believed that extramarital affairs were morally unacceptable. Fewer Americans said that abortion was morally unacceptable (49%), while 17% said abortion was morally acceptable and 23% said it was not a moral issue. Meanwhile, 37% said "homosexuality" (gay and lesbian behavior) was morally unacceptable; premarital sex (30% morally unacceptable); gambling (24% morally unacceptable); divorce (22% morally unacceptable); and alcohol usage (16% morally unacceptable). For these issues, the majority of Americans said they were either morally acceptable or were not moral issues. And in regard to contraception, only 7% said this was morally unacceptable. See the details on American morality in Figure 6.6:

From a global standpoint, it seems clear that extramarital affairs cause the greatest amount of moral indignation.

FIGURE 6.4
Global Morality
Source: Pew Research Center, "What's Morally Acceptable? It Depends on Where in the World You Live," April 15, 2014.

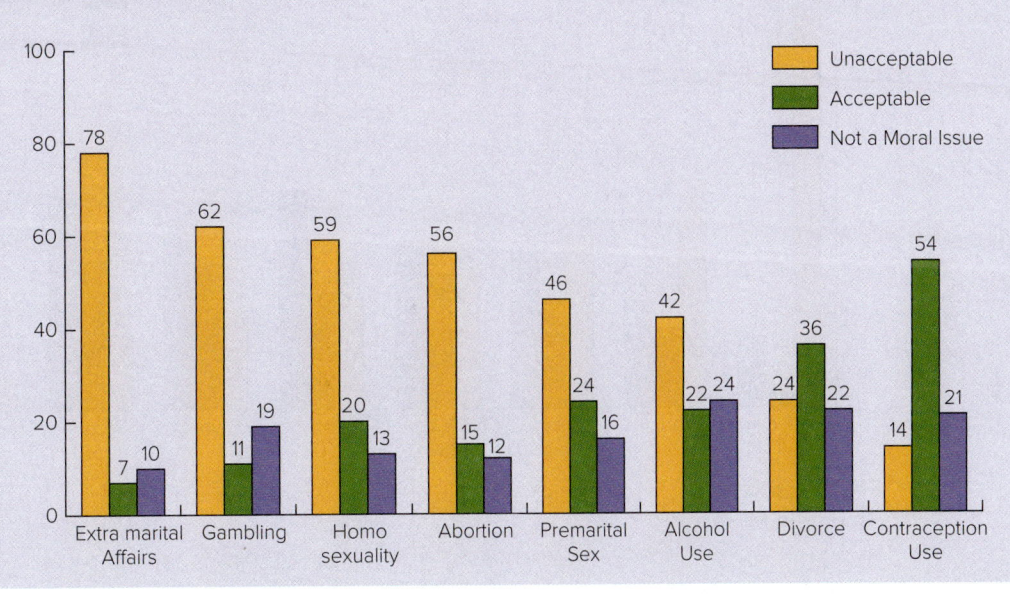

Issue	Unacceptable	Acceptable	Not a Moral Issue
Extra marital Affairs	78	7	10
Gambling	62	11	19
Homosexuality	59	20	13
Abortion	56	15	12
Premarital Sex	46	24	16
Alcohol Use	42	22	24
Divorce	24	36	22
Contraception Use	14	54	21

Chapter 6 | Sexual Intimacy

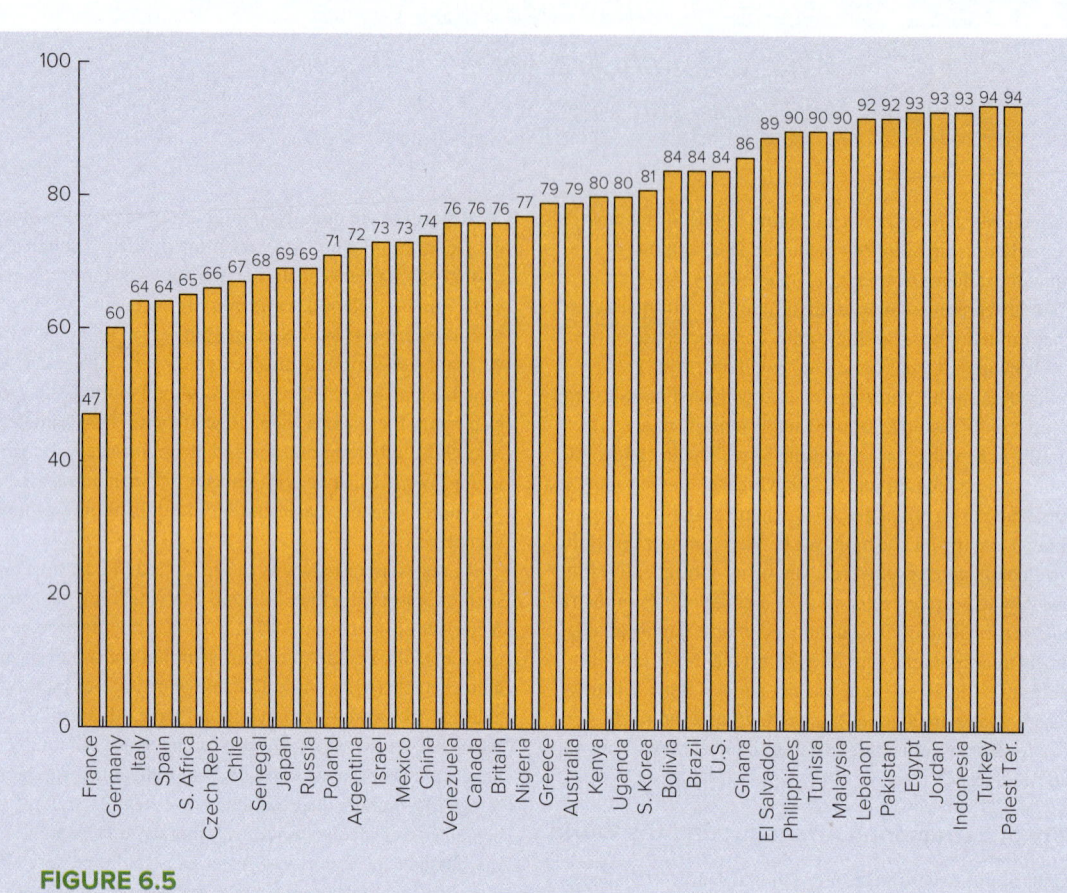

FIGURE 6.5
The Morality of Extramarital Affairs Around the World
Source: Pew Research Center, "French More Accepting of Infidelity Than People in Other Countries," January 14, 2014.

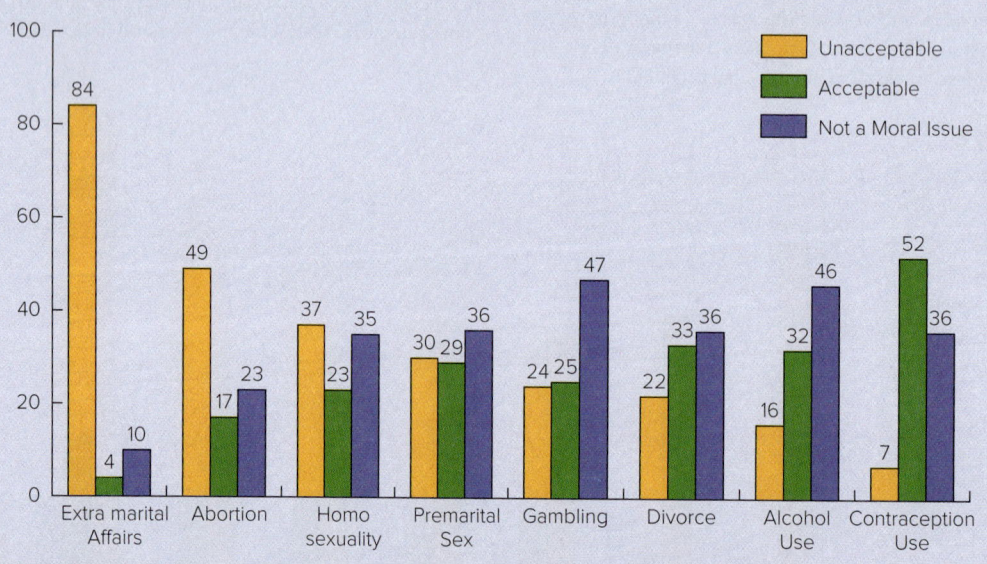

FIGURE 6.6
American Morality
Source: Pew Research Center, "What's Morally Acceptable? It Depends on Where in the World You Live," April 15, 2014.

178 Part II | Dynamics of Intimate Relationships

Sexual Dysfunction

Sexual dysfunction has been defined as a state in which sexual behavior or the lack of it causes anxiety, anguish, and frustration, which can lead to unhappiness and distress in a couple's relationship (Binik & Hall, 2014). A review of research about sexual dysfunction is provided by Simons and Carey (2008), where they summarized the findings of 52 studies. These authors suggest that sexual dysfunction may be among the more prevalent disorders, from a psychological perspective. The use of medications such as Viagra and Cialis for men and estrogen therapy for women indicate this may be true (Mayo Clinic, 2016a, 2016b).

Researchers believe that it may not be possible to identify the precise cause of a particular form of dysfunction, and that some dysfunctions may have multiple causes. Psychological factors that can result in sexual dysfunction are numerous. Developmental factors include troubled parent–child relationships, negative family attitudes toward sex and sexuality, traumatic childhood or adolescent sexual experiences, and conflict over one's gender identity (one's sense of being male or female). Personal factors include a variety of fears: of poor sexual performance, of pregnancy, of venereal disease, of rejection, of pain, of becoming close to someone, of losing control, or even of success. Interpersonal factors that can be related to sexual problems include poor communication and frequent power struggles between partners; hostility, distrust, and deceit; lack of mutual physical attraction; and gender-role conflicts.

Female Sexual Dysfunction. Many women report that their sex life has lost some of its spark because their body feels unresponsive or they are just not interested. This can happen at any age, but is most common when hormones are in flux—just after having a baby or during the transition into menopause. Sexual concerns also may occur during a major illness, such as cancer (Hyde & DeLamater, 2014; Kelly, 2011).

Symptoms include the following: the woman's desire to have sex is low or absent **(low sexual desire);** the woman cannot maintain arousal during sexual activity, or cannot become aroused even when she wishes to have sex **(sexual arousal disorder);** she cannot experience an orgasm **(orgasmic disorder);** she experiences pain during sexual contact **(sexual pain disorder)** (Hyde & DeLamater, 2014; Kelly, 2011).

Findings vary widely in terms of the prevalence of these disorders for women because so many different criteria are used in the various studies. However, Simons and Carey (2008) found that from 6% to 19% of women experienced sexual arousal disorder, depending upon the study. They also found that from 4% to 9% experienced orgasmic disorder, and approximately 12% experienced sexual pain disorder.

Causes of female sexual dysfunction often are a complex interaction of emotions, past experiences, physiology, beliefs, and lifestyles:

- *Physical conditions* that may contribute to sexual problems include arthritis, urinary or bowel difficulties, pelvic surgery, fatigue, headaches, other pain problems, and neurological disorders such as multiple sclerosis.
- *Hormonal conditions* include lower estrogen levels during menopause, leading to changes in genital tissues and sexual responsiveness. The folds of the skin covering the genital region (labia) become thinner during the menopausal transition and expose more of the clitoris. This sometimes reduces the sensitivity of the clitoris or causes unpleasant tingling or a prickling sensation. The vaginal lining also thins and becomes less elastic, especially if the woman is not sexually active. The vagina requires more stimulation to relax and lubricate before having intercourse, and this can lead to painful intercourse (dyspareunia). Achieving orgasm may also take longer.

- *Psychological and social causes* include untreated anxiety or depression, and long-term stress. The worries of pregnancy and demands of being a new mother can have similar effects. Long-term conflicts with one's partner—conflicts about sex or any other aspects of the relationship—can lead to lack of interest and diminished sexual response. Cultural and religious issues can also contribute, as well as body image problems the woman might have (Clay, 2009; Mayo Clinic, 2016a, 2016b).

Male Sexual Dysfunction. This is expressed in a variety of ways. **Erectile dysfunction** (formerly called impotence) is the inability to achieve or maintain an erection that is firm enough for intercourse. (Isolated episodes of the inability to achieve or maintain an erection are nearly universal among men.) **Premature ejaculation,** or rapid ejaculation, is difficult to define precisely, although it is a common sexual dysfunction. It causes problems in a sexual relationship when the woman is dissatisfied because the man reaches orgasm much more quickly than she does. **Orgasmic dysfunction,** the opposite of premature ejaculation, is a dysfunction in which prolonged and strenuous effort is needed to reach orgasm. **Painful intercourse,** often believed to be a problem only for women, can also affect men. Pain can be felt in the penis and/or testicles or internally; the pain is often related to a problem with the seminal vesicles or the prostate gland (Insel & Roth, 2014; Mayo Clinic, 2016a, 2016b).

According to Simons and Carey (2008), erectile dysfunction is identified as an issue with approximately 25% of men. Erectile dysfunction is more common for people with health issues or who take medicines that can effect the ability to have an erection. These same authors indicated that orgasmic dysfunction ranges from 9% to 25% of men, depending on the particular study. Premature ejaculation is reported by approximately 25% of individuals and orgasmic dysfunction is evident for approximately 15% of men. Finally, painful intercourse for men is relatively low, with pain reported 8% of the time. Again, these numbers are our conclusions after reading the decade review of 52 studies that used a variety of ways and criteria to gather their data.

Sexual interactions can be a source of frustration and disappointment, but they can also be a source of happiness and great joy. A satisfying sexual relationship is an important ingredient in a healthy intimate relationship.
©Goran Bogicevic/Shutterstcok

Sexual dysfunctions are generally something people are uncomfortable admitting to themselves and discussing with others. We can laugh and leer about sex in our society, but we have a difficult time talking honestly and openly about sex.

Sex Therapy

Many people with sexual difficulties go without help for a long time. This is unfortunate, because most **sex therapy** is simply a process of education. Sex therapists instruct clients (people who seek sex therapy are not called patients) in the gentle art of lovemaking.

Reputable professional sex therapists are trained in the subjects of sex and sexuality and have experience working with many different people regarding sexual needs and dysfunctions. A national organization, the American Association of Sexuality Educators, Counselors, and Therapists (AASECT), has established criteria for certifying sex therapists who have met its training standards. AASECT has also developed ethical principles for the practice of sex therapy. Certified counselors and sex therapists can be found on their web site (www.aasect.org/).

Sex educators typically work with relatively large groups of people and teach general information and principles that are useful to a variety of individuals. **Sex therapists** typically work with individuals, couples, or small groups of individuals and couples and focus more on individual concerns and problems. On the basis of content alone, a sex therapy session can be difficult to discern from a sex education session. The two approaches overlap considerably, so much so that some professionals do not distinguish between sex education and sex therapy.

Solving Sexual Problems. Sex therapy can involve a number of different components, including the following:

- Learning more about basic anatomy.
- Learning what one's true feelings are about the body.
- Learning what one's basic attitudes toward sex and sexuality are.
- Learning to relax with a partner and to get in a sexually responsive mood.
- Learning to sense one's own body and how the setting affects the body's responses.
- Learning sexual techniques.
- Exploring one's own and one's partner's body.
- Developing new sexual attitudes and techniques and maintaining them over time.

Sex therapists are quick to point out that couples with sexual problems should not rush into intercourse but should take time to enjoy each other's company and to touch each other in a variety of loving ways.

Two of the most common self-help techniques for overcoming sexual problems are body exploration and masturbation. Clinicians have found that masturbation exercises are helpful for treating orgasmic dysfunction in women and lack of ejaculatory control in men. Once a woman learns how to reach orgasm through self-stimulation, she can teach her partner the best ways to bring her to orgasm through intercourse. Self-help techniques that help men slow down during masturbation often help them delay ejaculation while making love with a partner (Kelly, 2011).

Susan Iasenza (2010, 2014) has written an interesting article about sex as a queer experience. She suggests that therapists need to expand their way of thinking about sex as they work with clients. She indicates that many sex acts are considered either in the gay or straight category and that individuals often feel guilty if they enjoy or get aroused by what is considered in the domain of same-sex couples, if they are heterosexual. She suggests that sexual behavior does not need to be viewed as gay or straight, but that therapists need to create a safe place for couples to enjoy and express their sexual desires in a variety of ways without guilt.

Behavioral exercises may also be prescribed to help couples enrich and expand their sexual awareness and enjoyment (Hyde & DeLamater, 2014; Kelly, 2011). These exercises include sensate focus, the stop-and-go technique, and the squeeze technique.

- *Sensate focus.* This technique teaches couples how to give each partner pleasure without expecting anything in return. The goal is not sexual arousal or intercourse but education. Each partner directs the other, showing her or him what kinds of touches are the most enjoyable and where the sensitive places are. The exercise helps people learn to communicate better sexually.
- *The stop-and-go technique.* This technique teaches men how to control ejaculation and orgasm. The man's partner manually or orally stimulates his penis until he is just about to ejaculate. Then, the partner stops the stimulation, resuming it only when the man is in control. Stimulation and rest may be alternated several times in a session before orgasm and ejaculation are triggered. Repeated sessions over weeks or months help men control rapid or premature ejaculation.
- *The squeeze technique.* In this variation on the stop-and-go technique, when the partner stops stimulating the man's penis, the partner immediately applies pressure to the penis, squeezing it with the thumb and two fingers until there is a tolerable degree of pain. This pattern is repeated seven or eight times until the man learns to tolerate intense stimulation while delaying ejaculation. The squeeze technique further shortens the time it takes to resolve the problem of premature ejaculation.

Summary

- According to a national survey, happily married couples compared to unhappily married couples reported: they were more satisfied with the affection they receive from their partners; they did not have as many concerns about their partner's level of interest in sex; they were less likely to be concerned that their partner was interested in having an affair; they were less likely to feel the partner used sex unfairly; and they had a more satisfying and fulfilling sexual relationship.
- The most commonly reported problems for married couples in terms of their sexual relationship were differing levels of interest in sex between husband and wife, dissatisfaction with the amount of affection received from one's partner, sexual disinterest between partners, difficulty talking about sexual issues, and an inability to keep the sexual relationship interesting and enjoyable.
- Attitudes toward sexuality, including sexual attractiveness and sexual behaviors, vary markedly from one culture to another.
- Sex surveys—such as the General Social Survey, the National Survey of Sexual Health and Behavior, the ABC News Survey, and the AARP study of midlife and older adults—reveal useful information about the sexual behaviors of Americans.
- Nearly four decades after AIDS was first identified, there is still no cure; however, new drug treatments have helped people live longer. Those infected with HIV can spread the virus to others because they may not know for years that they are infected.
- The most effective sex education programs are those that encourage abstinence but at the same time offer an alternative of effective contraceptives to those who choose to remain sexually active or become sexually active.
- Father-child communication is an important component of the sexual development of children.
- Although sexual activity often decreases after marriage, this decline is not inevitable. Key elements in keeping the sexual relationship vital include communication, commitment, and investing time to enjoy each other.

- The majority of individuals, even as they age, seek healthy and satisfying sex lives. Health issues and medication are often reasons for a decrease in sexual behavior as people age.
- Types of male sexual dysfunctions include erectile dysfunction, orgasmic dysfunction, premature ejaculation, and painful intercourse. Female sexual dysfunctions include vaginismus, anorgasmia, rapid orgasm, and painful intercourse.
- Sex therapy involves a number of different components, including learning more about basic anatomy, learning what one's true feelings are about the body, and discovering one's basic attitudes toward sex and sexuality.

Key Terms

sexuality
heterosexual
homosexual
bisexual
transgender
sexual orientation
sex
gender
GLBT
incest taboo
masturbation
human immunodeficiency virus (HIV)
DINS dilemma
sexual dysfunction
low sexual desire
sexual arousal disorder
orgasmic disorder
sexual pain disorder
erectile dysfunction
premature ejaculation
orgasmic dysfunction
painful intercourse
sex therapy
sex educator
sex therapist

Activities

1. Is sex truly everywhere in our society? For a day, keep a log, noting what, when, and where you see or hear something with a sexual theme. Several people in the class can work together and report their findings to the larger group.
2. In small groups, discuss the following situation: You are the parent of a 15-year-old son. He is interested in your views on premarital sex. What would you tell him?
3. What are your personal beliefs about premarital sexual behavior? Write a brief essay articulating and supporting your views.
4. Ask someone whose children are grown how they talked to their children about sex.

Suggested Readings

American Association of Retired Persons. (2016). AARP: Real possibilities. Web site: http://www.aarp.org/. An excellent resource for older persons and those interested in the process of aging.

Advocates for Youth. (2016). Rights. Respect. Responsibility. "Established in 1980 as the Center for Population Options, Advocates for Youth champions efforts that help young people make informed and responsible decisions about their reproductive and sexual health. Advocates believes it can best serve the field by boldly advocating for a more positive and realistic approach to adolescent sexual health." The work focuses on 14- to 25-year-olds in the United States and internationally. Web site: http://www.advocatesforyouth.org.

American Association of Sexuality Educators, Counselors and Therapists (AASECT). (2016). A not-for-profit, interdisciplinary professional organization promoting the understanding of human sexuality and healthy sexual behavior. "AASECT members include sexuality educators, sexuality counselors and sex therapists, physicians, nurses, social workers, psychologists, allied health professionals, clergy members, lawyers, sociologists, marriage and family counselors and therapists, family planning specialists and researchers, as well as students in relevant professional disciplines. Web site: http://www.aasect.org/.

American Association for Marriage and Family Therapy. (2016). AAMFT is the key national organization for advancing the professional interests of marriage and family therapists, and it has excellent educational resources for professionals and laypersons on its web site: http://www.aamft.org.

Berzon, B. (2004; see also 2016). Permanent partners: Building gay and lesbian relationships that last (Rev. ed.). New York, NY: Penguin. Suggestions by a psychotherapist specializing in same-sex relationships for resolving conflicts over power and control, jealousy, differences in sexual desire, money, and family demands.

Blow, A. J., & Hartnett, K. (2005). Infidelity in committed relationships II: A substantive review. *Journal of Marital and Family Therapy, 31,* 217–233.

Boston Women's Health Book Collective. (2011). *Our bodies, ourselves.* New York, NY: Touchstone. The classic book for women.

Centers for Disease Control and Prevention. (2016e). HIV/AIDS. Web site: http://www.cdc.gov/hiv/.

Clay, R. A. (2009). The debate over low libidos: Psychologists differ on how to treat a lack of desire among some women. *APA Online Monitor on Psychology, 40*(4), 32. Web site: http://www.apa.org/monitor/2009/04/libidos.html. Is it a medical problem or a relationship problem? An excellent discussion of the issues.

Consumer Reports. (2005). CR's guide to contraception. *Consumer Reports* (February), 34–38. Sections on condoms for extra protection; birth control, more and safer choices; a comparative guide to contraceptives; and abortion options.

Fisher, L. L., et al. (2010). Sex, romance, and relationships: AARP survey of midlife and older adults. American

Association for Retired Persons. Web site: http://assets.aarp.org/rgcenter/general/srr_09.pdf.

Giles, J. (2008; see also 2016). *The nature of sexual desire.* Lanham, MD: University Press of America.

Guttmacher Institute. (2016). "Now in its fifth decade, the Guttmacher Institute continues to advance sexual and reproductive health and rights through an interrelated program of research, policy analysis and public education designed to generate new ideas, encourage enlightened public debate and promote sound policy and program development. The Institute's overarching goal is to ensure the highest standard of sexual and reproductive health for all people worldwide." Web site: https://www.guttmacher.org.

Harvey, J. H. (Ed.). (2004). *The handbook of sexuality in close relationships.* Mahwah, NJ: Erlbaum. Enhances the dialogue about the centrality of sexual issues in close relationships.

Hyde, J. S., & DeLamater, J. D. (2014). Understanding human sexuality (12th ed.). New York, NY: McGraw-Hill. An excellent comprehensive textbook.

Insel, P. M., & Roth, W. T. (2014). *Core concepts in health* (13th ed.). New York, NY: McGraw-Hill. A very useful health education textbook with important sections on sex and sexuality.

Kelly, G. F. (2011). *Sexuality today* (10th ed.). New York, NY: McGraw-Hill. A fine source for a better understanding of human sexuality.

Kinsey Institute for Research in Sex, Gender, and Reproduction. (2016). The Kinsey Institute at Indiana University promotes interdisciplinary research and scholarship in the fields of human sexuality, gender, and reproduction. Web site: http://www.kinseyinstitute.org/.

Levin, D. E., & Kilbourne, J. (2008). *So sexy so soon: The new sexualized childhood and what parents can do to protect their kids.* New York, NY: Ballantine Books. Sex is everywhere in American commercial culture. How to help children live in such an environment.

Maier, T. (2009). *Masters of sex: The life and times of William Masters and Virginia Johnson, the couple who taught America how to love.* New York, NY: Basic Books. Tells the story of the research team whose pioneering studies helped couples around the world learn to talk openly and honestly about sex and sexuality.

Mayo Clinic. (2016). Excellent resources on extramarital sex, male and female sexual dysfunction. Web site: http://www.mayoclinic.com.

McCarthy, B., & McCarthy, E. (2014). Rekindling desire (2nd ed.). London: Routledge/Taylor & Francis Group. Web site: https://www.routledge.com/products/9780415823524?utm_source=web&utm_medium=cms&utm_campaign=SBU2_JKG_2PR_8cm_4PSY_00000_Self%20Improvement%20Month.

McCarthy, B. W. (2007). *Men's sexual health: Fitness for satisfying sex.* London: Routledge Mental Health, Taylor & Francis Group.

National Right to Life. (2016). Protecting life in America since 1968. "National Right to Life is the nation's oldest and largest pro-life organization. National Right to Life is the federation of 50 state right-to-life affiliates and more than 3,000 local chapters. Through education and legislation, National Right to Life is working to restore legal protection to the most defenseless members of our society who are threatened by abortion, infanticide, assisted suicide, and euthanasia. Web site: http://www.nrlc.org/.

Peluso, P. (Ed.). (2007). *Infidelity: A practitioner's guide to working with couples in crisis.* London: Routledge Mental Health, Taylor & Francis Group. When one partner in a relationship is unfaithful to the other, salvaging the relationship takes a lot of work by both parties.

Planned Parenthood. (2016). Care. No matter what. "Planned Parenthood is one of the nation's leading providers of high-quality, affordable health care for women, men, and young people, and the nation's largest provider of sex education. Planned Parenthood also works with partner organizations worldwide to improve the sexual health and well-being of individuals and families everywhere. Planned Parenthood has 59 independent local affiliates that operate over 650 health centers throughout the United States, providing high-quality services to women, men, and teens." Web site: https://www.plannedparenthood.org/.

Sexuality Information and Education Council of the United States (SIECUS). (2016). Founded by Dr. Mary S. Calderone in 1964, who was concerned about the lack of information about sexuality for both young people and adults. So, at the age of 60, "with determination to live in a world in which sexuality was viewed as a natural and healthy part of life," she founded SIECUS, which publishes books, journals, and resources for professionals, parents, and the public. Web site: http://www.siecus.org/.

Wincze, J. P. (2009). *Enhancing sexuality: A problem-solving approach to treating dysfunction: Therapist guide* (2nd ed.). New York, NY: Oxford University Press. An excellent overview of sex therapy today.

Yarber, W. L., & Sayad, B. W. (2013). Human sexuality: Diversity in contemporary America (8th ed.). New York, NY: McGraw-Hill. Filled with good information.

Visit the text-specific Online Learning Center at **www.mhhe.com/olson9e** for practice tests, chapter summaries, and PowerPoint slides.

Design Element: © Alicia Grünkind/EyeEm/Getty Images

7 Gender Roles and Power in the Family

©Asiseeit/E+/Getty Images

Intimacy, Strengths, and Diversity

Facts About Women and Men in the United States

Gender Roles

Gender Roles Across Ethnic Groups

Theories About Gender Roles

Power in Families

Summary

Key Terms

Activities

Suggested Readings

Intimacy, Strengths, and Diversity

All animals are equal, but some animals are more equal than others.
—GEORGE ORWELL (1951)

Contemporary models of intimacy stress gender equality in marriage and other types of partnerships. Egalitarianism is the trend among many couples making a serious commitment to each other. But if women continue to make less money for the work they do outside the home and if men continue to avoid child care and household labor, the fabric of intimate relationships is threatened. The fragile bonds of intimacy can easily be damaged when one spouse is subordinate to the other, has more power than the other, or receives less respect and dignity in society.

Individual and couple strengths result when there is equality and a balance of power in family relationships. This chapter provides a description of some of the gender differences between men and women, along with a discussion about the respective influences of nature and nurture to explain these differences. There are clearly cultural differences when it comes to gender roles. Does that mean strengths cannot exist when relationships are not equal? Or does it mean that there can be gender-role differences, but equal power? We will explore the complexity of gender roles and the quality of relationships in the United States and other cultures.

Facts About Women and Men in the United States

A lengthy report prepared by the U.S. Department of Commerce (2011) provides valuable information about men and women in the United States. The report covers comparisons between men and women in regard to such topics as health, crime and violence, education, and employment.

Here are some of the major findings:

- Women are more likely to be living in poverty than men. Poverty rates are especially high for single women with children.
- Women are more likely than men to get both graduate and undergraduate degrees.
- Labor force participation for women has steadily increased and for men has decreased. Men are more likely these days to opt for staying home and caring for children than in the past.
- Women's wages have increased over time, but women still earn only 80% of what men earn.
- Women are more likely than men to use health care for both health conditions as well as preventative care.
- Women are increasingly the victims of crime and are also increasingly the perpetrators of crime, resulting in an increase in incarceration rates for women.

There are societal changes and these changes have impacts on men and women. Although men and women increasingly are having equal opportunities, men and women still have differing life experiences.

Gender Roles

The different ways in which men and women behave are linked to, but not necessarily determined by, their biological sex. Individuals are identified as male or female on the basis of physical structures, which are determined by chromosomes, gonads, and hormones. This

Gender-role behaviors are less distinct today than they were in the past. One example is the degree to which girls play on sport teams that were historically restricted to males.
©Cathy Yeulet/123RF

labeling occurs at birth and is the first step in the process of developing **gender identity**—a sense of being male or female and what that means in one's society.

Although nature determines an individual's sex, culture determines the attitudes and behaviors appropriate for an individual on the basis of her or his sex. In each culture, individuals learn to adapt to these expectations as they shape their personal and professional lives. **Gender roles** are expectations about people's attitudes and behaviors in life based on whether they are male or female. When a child is born, **gender-role stereotypes** come into play. People comment, for example, that he is "a strong, healthy boy" or she is "a darling, adorable girl."

Labeling affects a child's psychological development in a variety of ways. The child begins to adopt personality traits, attitudes, preferences, and behaviors considered appropriate to her or his sex, and these affect how he or she walks, talks, eats, exercises, thinks, and later makes love. The gender-role patterns assigned to males and females influence all our roles in life.

Masculinity is the gender-linked constellation of traits that have been traditionally associated with men; **femininity**, the traits associated with women. In our society, the qualities stereotypically associated with masculinity include aggressiveness, independence, dominance, competence, and a predisposition for math and science. Qualities stereotypically associated with femininity include passivity, dependency, sensitivity, emotionality, and a predisposition for art and literature. These stereotypes are destructive because they imply that all males, and only males, have the so-called masculine qualities and that all females, and only females, possess the so-called feminine qualities. Obviously, any human being can have any of these qualities. Socially imposed gender-role stereotypes create inequality by prescribing—based on whether a person is male or female—certain qualities, behaviors, and opportunities and prohibiting or discouraging others.

Language is one of the most powerful tools people use both deliberately and inadvertently to establish and maintain rigid gender roles. The subtle ways we talk about people of the other sex reinforce stereotypes and segregate people by sex. We talk about men and women as being members of the "opposite" sex, reinforcing the notion that men and women are opposites and accentuating the differences rather than affirming the similarities.

Gender-biased language reinforces the misguided notion that men are more competent and rational than women. Terms used for men are often more positive and affirming, whereas equivalent terms for women are often more negative and degrading. These differences in terminology have an impact on how we perceive and feel about each gender.

Gender Norms and Family Life

Whether we like it or not, families are organized around expectations about gender roles. According to Knudson-Martin (2012), at times gender roles and expectations are so pervasive and ingrained into who we are that they are taken for granted. For example, Colette, age 60, describes how she views gender roles and how they have played out in her life:

> *"I have been a liberated woman all my life, and have fought for equal rights for women. I have been upset when men opened doors for me because I was perfectly able to do it myself.*
>
> *"I watched my mother do housework, care for us children, and focus on the family issues, while my father went to work and provided the paycheck. That wasn't all bad, but I wanted things in my life to be different—and they are. I have worked outside the home most all of my life. My husband and I both brought home paychecks. We shared in the raising of children, even though I probably did more than my share of the work in the home. Things weren't always equal, but we both worked hard to make it as equal as possible.*
>
> *"So, now I am ending my work life, my children are grown, and I like to bake cookies and take care of our house. I like sewing quilts while my husband shovels the drive after a snowstorm. What is the deal? Am I hardwired to enjoy certain things such as quilting, while my husband enjoys shoveling snow? After a lifetime of trying to make gender roles less stereotypical, I can't imagine my husband wanting to quilt, and me wanting to shovel the driveway."*

It is a complex question, with complex answers. People who study neuroscience say that boy and girl babies are different, but only slightly different, when it comes to the brain (Knudson-Martin, 2012). Environment most certainly has an impact on gender behavior, especially as behavior relates to language. Environment can be the family environment and the broader social environment. Therefore, parents can insist on a certain behavior in their families, but interaction in one's schools and communities also affects how children respond to gender issues. Therefore, Knudson-Martin (2012) concludes that biology, family, and the environment all interact to determine how one develops views and behaviors regarding gender.

According to a nationwide survey of more than 50,000 married couples, the happy couples agreed more often (82%) than unhappy couples (46%) that both partners are equally willing to make adjustments in their marriage (Olson, Olson-Sigg, & Larson, 2008). As indicated in Table 7.1, happy couples agreed more often (87%) than unhappy couples (54%) that both partners work hard to have an equal relationship. More happy couples (76%) than unhappy couples (42%) believed that both persons are satisfied with the division of

TABLE 7.1 How Happy Couples Versus Unhappy Couples View Their Roles

	PERCENTAGE IN AGREEMENT	
Role Issues	Happy Couples	Unhappy Couples
1. Both are equally willing to make adjustments in their marriage.	82%	46%
2. Both work hard to have an equal relationship.	76	42
3. Both are satisfied with the division of housework.	87	54
4. The partners make most decisions jointly.	87	59
5. Household tasks are divided on the basis of preferences, not tradition.	67	55

Source: Olson, D., Olson-Sigg, A., & Larson, P. *The Couple Checkup.* Nashville, TN: Thomas Nelson, 2008.

housework in their marriage. Happy couples also agreed more often (87%) than unhappy couples (59%) that they make most decisions jointly. Finally, this survey found that household tasks were divided on the basis of preferences rather than tradition more often in happy couples (67%) than among unhappy couples (55%).

Based on the national sample of more than 50,000 married couples, the major role relationship problem that couples faced (49%) was concern about the unfair division of the housework (Table 7.2). Less than half of the couples (44%) disagreed on the issue of whether housework was based on traditional roles versus their interests. Another common problem (44%) was that the husband was not willing to adjust as much as the wife. The couples also disagreed (43%) about whether or not the wife should work outside the home when children are young. And more than a third (36%) disagreed over the issue of whether both work to maintain an egalitarian relationship.

There is an interesting story about the role relationship of Bob and Elizabeth Dole, both former presidential candidates (Fadiman & Bernard, 2000). When Elizabeth Dole was appointed secretary of transportation in 1985, the press was curious about their role

TABLE 7.2 Top Five Role Problems for Couples

Role Issues	Percentage of Couples Having Problem*
1. Concern about unfair division of housework.	49%
2. Housework is based on traditional roles rather than interests.	44
3. The husband is not willing to adjust as much as the wife.	44
4. Disagree whether or not the wife should work outside the home when children are young.	43
5. Partners disagree that both work to maintain an egalitarian relationship.	36

*One or both partners indicated this was an issue for them.

Source: Olson, D., Olson-Sigg, A., & Larson, P. *The Couple Checkup.* Nashville, TN: Thomas Nelson, 2008.

relationship because Bob Dole was a senator and she would have a higher political position than he would. A photo was taken of them making the bed together, and a man wrote to Bob complaining, "You've got to stop doing the work around the house. You're causing problems for men across the country." Bob responded, "You don't know the half of it. The only reason she was helping was because they were taking pictures." Perhaps his willingness to do more housework contributed to their still being a married couple in spite of all the stress and public scrutiny they are under as a couple.

Distribution of Family Work by Gender

Extensive research has been carried out in the past several years about gender and the division of labor in the household. A summary of current findings (Meier, McNaughton-Cassill, & Lynch, 2006) include the following:

- Husbands and wives have both decreased the total number of hours spent on housework.
- Wives still do almost two-thirds of the work compared to husbands.
- Having children makes the imbalance even greater.
- Mothers spend twice as much time caring for their children as fathers.
- Even though fathers spend more time with children today than in the past, they still are often seen as "helpers" in providing care for their children.
- Perceptions of fairness regarding the division of household responsibilities are a more likely predictor of marital discord than actual behavior.

Husbands and wives disagree about how much housework each spouse does (Lee & Waite, 2005). These researchers found that wives typically make accurate estimates of husbands' time spent on housework, and husbands overestimate the time they spend. In addition, wives think they spend 13 hours more on housework each week, and husbands see the gap as only half as large. They also found that wives overestimated the numbers of hours worked in the home. These researchers concluded that what happens with housework depends on who you ask, and this gap in perception can lead to marital conflict. They also concluded that wives, in fact, do 9.4 hours more housework per week than their husbands, and the husbands perform about 40% of the work in the home.

So why is it that women still do most of the housework? There are several possible explanations. Poortman and van der Lippe (2009) discuss several factors, based upon past research. According to these authors, research might indicate that the partner that has the least amount of financial resources, such as money from paid employment, will have the least amount of power and, therefore, will be relegated to doing household chores—and in most cases that is the woman in the household. Other observers indicate that as a society we have beliefs about certain behaviors being gender specific, and activities such as cleaning and laundry are women's tasks, whereas household maintenance is relegated to men (Poortman & van der Lippe, 2009). These researchers, therefore, conducted a study to determine whether men and women have differing attitudes regarding household chores. They looked at individuals' enjoyment of household tasks and the standards for how well the chores should be completed.

Poortman and van der Lippe (2009) found that women did, indeed, have more positive attitudes about child care, cleaning, and cooking than men did. Women not only enjoyed these tasks, they felt they had more responsibility for these tasks than men had, and they also had higher standards for how well the tasks should be done. These researchers concluded that, along with power and resources brought into the home, attitudes contributed to the fact that women continue to do more household chores. The findings of the study indicated that attitudes toward the work that needs to be done in the home were more important for men and women, than their attitudes about child care, which tended to be similar. In other words, attitudes about caring for children were less likely to be different for men and women than attitudes about other household chores. The most preferred task for men was caring for children and the least preferred task was cleaning.

It is clear that the issue of who does what in terms of housework and child care is complicated. The studies that are described provide clues about why the inequities continue to occur, but do not provide conclusive answers for the phenomenon.

Emotion Work in Marriage and Family

Although most research on marriages relating to gender has focused on housework and care of children, recent research has conceptualized *emotion work* in families (Erickson, 2005). Emotion work, according to this author, includes such things as listening closely to a spouse's thoughts and feelings, recognizing feelings, offering encouragement, and showing appreciation. Women are deliberate about paying attention to the emotional well-being of other family members. This author concluded that emotion work is a gender issue and looks different to men and women, in that women see emotion work as part of their family work role and they recognize that they are held accountable for performing this work in their families.

Other researchers talk about mental work that happens in families, and this work is also divided unequally, with women performing more *mental work* than men (Meier et al., 2006). Mental work includes worrying about children and household tasks, planning and monitoring children's activities, seeking solutions to child care problems, and managing the division of labor and the delegation of tasks (Meier et al., 2006). This mental work is invisible and is very difficult to measure, but it is estimated that women are doing most of the mental work in families. Meier and colleagues also indicate that the unequal division of mental work affects women's marital satisfaction but not men's marital satisfaction.

Spending Time with Children

According to Lyn Craig (2015), the time parents spend with children has actually increased over recent years, even with more dual-earner households. This author speculates that the increase is due to the increase in expectations about what it means to be a good parent. If possible, parents are involved in every aspect of their children's lives, including friendships and education. Craig (2015) indicates that this intensive parenting most often falls on the mother since she spends more time with children. Fathers' time with children has increased as well, with children benefiting from an increase in overall time they receive from both parents.

The time spent by each parent does differ, however. Fathers typically spend time reading, talking, and participating in leisure activities. Mothers are more likely to do the routine care that needs to be done on a regular basis and is typically more constraining than the time spent by fathers. Fathers often work along side mothers rather than doing these tasks alone. In addition, Craig (2015) indicates that the more education parents have the more time is spent with children.

It needs to be noted that parents with less education may not be spending as much time with children because of other responsibilities necessary to meet the basic needs of the family. There may be more time available for children when parents have more education and are less likely to work multiple jobs. Putman (2015) indicates that both education and income affect the time parents spend with children, with low-income parents putting energy into making a living with little time for intensive parenting.

Maternal Gatekeeping

Maternal gatekeeping refers to behaviors that affect how women and men collaborate in the work of the family. This was defined by Allen and Hawkins (1999), and has continued to be addressed in literature (Schoppe-Sullivan, 2010). As we have seen, mothers continue to do significantly more child care than fathers, even though both parents realize the importance of father involvement and work at sharing equally in child care. As Schoppe-Sullivan (2010) reviews the recent literature, she talks about **maternal gatekeeping**. This is when mothers may be ambivalent about giving up their role as the parent with most knowledge about child care. They, in fact, might not want to share the role of being the major caregiver for their children, or they may not feel that the father is doing the caregiving well enough. Mothers may not even realize they send messages to fathers about the fathers' lack of expertise in caring for children.

Examples of maternal gatekeeping can be when a mother rushes in to fix what the father has done such as not putting on a child's hat correctly, or not wiping a child's mouth often enough while feeding. Mothers can roll their eyes in disapproval without even realizing they are doing it. How often does it happen in the media and how often does it happen in the lives of young children? Clearly, this mother-father dynamic is reciprocal. For example, if a father ignores the eye rolling and forges ahead, equality in caregiving can be achieved, and the family system has truly changed.

Schoppe-Sullivan (2010) also proposes that if women can close the gate, they can also open it. Fathers can be complimented as often as they are discouraged by a mother. In her research she found that these positive behaviors can, in fact, make a difference and that fathers are more involved in child care when mothers are encouraging. She indicates that it is only one of many factors that impact father involvement, but maternal gatekeeping should not be underestimated. She concludes that when both parents are invested in providing child care, the child benefits. Equality in child care can happen when:

- Fathers take the initiative some of the time, and do not wait to be invited to provide care.
- Fathers do not give up, even if there are signs of disapproval.
- Mothers think before action is taken or a response is given.
- Mothers give compliments. Society does not always view men as great child care providers, but mothers can change that.

A person's sex is biologically determined, but the abilities, behaviors, activities, social roles, and other characteristics that are considered appropriate for males and females are determined by one's culture.
©Bill Aron/PhotoEdit

Traditional Versus Contemporary Views of Gender Roles

In the traditional view of gender roles in our society, males are assumed to be superior to females and to have characteristics that are more desirable. A more contemporary view holds that neither males nor females are superior; both have desirable—and undesirable—traits not based specifically on sex.

To counter the traditional view of men and women in our society, humorist Garrison Keillor ends his radio show, *A Prairie Home Companion*, with the statement that in Lake Wobegon: "All the women are strong, all the men are good looking, and all the children are above average" (Keillor, 2009).

A Traditional View. The traditional view of gender roles in our society grew out of our male-oriented culture, but specific theories have been put forth in its support. One of the best known is that of sociologist Talcott Parsons (1955, 1965), whose theory of the family assumed that highly contrasting gender roles were essential for families and society. Parsons believed that, in this modern family, society required that men be instrumental and women be expressive. The man's instrumental role was to be the breadwinner, the manager, and the leader of the family. The woman's expressive role was to take care of the emotional well-being of the family through nurturing and comforting. Parsons saw these two roles as separate, one to be performed by the husband and the other by the wife.

The Parsons theory, which has been attacked by innumerable critics, is no longer considered valid. They charged that it was a mistake to assume that the traditional family structure was both a universal and necessary social institution—that only this traditional family structure could fulfill the needs of the individuals within the family and of the greater society. They further argued that the Parsons theory focused on the positive aspects of this traditional family structure but deemphasized potential problems. The traditional model emphasized stability rather than change, focused on harmony rather than conflict, and identified function but ignored dysfunction. The Parsons theory also tended to stereotype masculine and feminine traits, reinforcing differences and denigrating women.

A More Contemporary View. Today, it is more commonly assumed that both sexes are capable and can be successful in a variety of roles at home and at work. Women can be independent, strong, logical, and task oriented; men can be nurturing, sensitive, cooperative, and detail oriented. However, men and women can benefit by learning from each other: Men can learn the value of being more sensitive and caring from women; women can learn the value of independence from men; and both can learn to work together and become interdependent.

Women may be at an advantage in this more cooperative approach to living. Traditional culture has encouraged them to be good listeners and to be empathic, understanding, helpful, and supportive. These caring values fit well with the more cooperative approaches to group decision making that are gaining strength at home and at work.

See Box 7.1 for a closer look at the work–family interface.

The Move Toward More Egalitarian Roles

American society in many ways is moving away from male dominance and toward **egalitarian roles** (also called *equalitarian roles*)—social equality between the sexes. The process of change has been long and fraught with controversy. The struggle not only occurs in society

BOX 7.1 At Issue
The Work-Family Interface

Much of the current gender research is centered on dual career couples as they balance their family and work lives. It is appropriate, then, that we explain what the work-family interface looks like.

Managing the responsibilities of work and family life began to be an issue for researchers in the 1970s, as women increasingly entered the workforce. At that time, approximately one-third of women with children under the age of 6 worked outside the home (Halpern, 2005; Raley, Mattingly, & Bianchi, 2006). The issues of work and family in the 1970s focused primarily on how to manage work and child care responsibilities (Halpern, 2005). Researchers found that women became employed but also continued to be the major caretakers of children and other domestic responsibilities.

The number of women with children in the workforce has increased dramatically. Currently 70% of women with children under age 18 are currently in the workforce (U.S. Department of Labor, n.d.). Sixty-four percent of all part-time workers are women and 43% of all full-time workers are women.

Research has been consistent over time, indicating that mothers who work part time, versus not being employed or being employed full time, have improved mother and family well-being (Buehler & O'Brien, 2011). Mothers seem to like the balance of having both work and family in their lives.

Work-to-Family Influence

When we think about balancing work and family issues, we usually think about the effects of one's work life on one's family life. Work and family researchers often think about the multiple issues work places on family time and include such things as time-based demands and strain-based demands. Time-based demands focus on the idea that time at work means there is less time for family (Voydanoff, 2008). Therefore, when a person works extra hours, does shift work, or travels extensively, there is likely to be less time with the family. In addition, there are often strain-based demands that affect family life. Strain-based demands include such things as job insecurity, workload pressures, time pressures, or dealing with a demanding supervisor. Both time-based demands and strain-based demands have significant effects on family life.

Certainly there are times when both time-based demands and strain-based demands enter into one's work life. For example, when companies go through cycles of downsizing, which has happened in the past several years, employers will decrease the workforce with added responsibilities and longer hours for the workers who remain. In addition, there is the fear of additional downsizing, which also adds stress to the work environment. These stresses together can cause psychological spillover to the family (Voydanoff, 2008).

---

but is also played out each day in close relationships. Table 7.3 highlights some differences between traditional dating and marriage patterns and more contemporary practices. Looking back through the generations of one's own family illustrates how dramatically times have changed.

One of the most telling indexes of change is the decline of the double standard, the social convention allowing men more sexual and social freedom than women. Women are claiming more freedom for themselves, although some don't realize or acknowledge they are doing so. A number of social scientists have commented that today many women shy away from calling themselves nontraditional or feminist but are clearly living very different lives than their mothers or grandmothers. What is apparently happening is that as women's roles change, the definition of *traditional* also changes.

An International Perspective

Perhaps the classic description of how gender roles are rooted in culture comes from anthropologist Margaret Mead. In *Sex and Temperament in Three Primitive Societies,* Mead (1935) looked at "maleness" and "femaleness" in three New Guinea tribes: the Arapesh, the Mundugumor, and the Tchambuli. In American society, two traditional attributes of females are gentleness and unaggressiveness. Among the Arapesh, Mead found both the women *and* the men to be unaggressive. Not far away, among the Mundugumor tribe, Mead found that both males and females displayed an aggressiveness that Americans would characterize as

Family-to-Work Influence

Family-to-work influence refers to how family demands affect work performance (Voydanoff, 2005). The family demands drain one of time and energy to do well at work and affect one's ability to take advantage of opportunities to advance or take on more responsibilities. The behaviors that might be evident at work because of family demands include such things as absenteeism and lack of ability to concentrate on work tasks.

When family stresses occur at home such as marital issues or divorce, child behavior problems, financial difficulties, or a death, there is less energy for one's work life. For example, a couple may be having marital difficulties. This couple may be fighting more often and constantly feeling stressed over what might happen to the marriage and family life. There is little rest, relaxation, and sleep. Because of the stress the couple is experiencing, there is less quality time for children, and the children feel the stress about what might happen to their family. As a result, the children's behavior deteriorates, and now there is even more stress in the family. As one can imagine, the adults in the family have very little energy for their work. According to Voydanoff (2008), there is a reciprocal and positive relationship between work and family life. It is likely that when things go well at work, it positively affects family life, and when family life is positive, a person is more productive at work.

Current Issues That Affect Work and Family Life

Today, people are living longer, and, in addition to caring for their own children, they are also likely to be caring for aging parents (Halpern, 2005). For example, approximately 50% of working adults plan to assume significant caregiving responsibilities for aging relatives during the next 5 years, and many more are already doing so. Although women are most likely to provide such care, approximately 25% of care is provided by men.

Currently, there are also more family forms than in previous years. For example, there are stepfamilies, single-parent families, same-sex couples, cohabiting couples with children, and grandparents raising grandchildren. These family forms make the work and family relationship even more complex. A single parent balancing work and family will experience different stresses than a two-parent couple. In addition, there are cultural values with new and growing diverse populations that might view the work and family relationship very differently than is described by previous research (Halpern, 2005). For example, members of diverse cultures may be more likely to use extended-family members as a source of child care, which would affect the stress experienced by a dual-earner couple.

TABLE 7.3 Contemporary Versus Traditional Dating and Marriage Patterns

Contemporary	Traditional
Both women and men initiate dates.	The man initiates dates.
The woman keeps her maiden name after marriage.	The woman takes the man's last name.
The partners cohabit before marriage or may never marry at all.	The partners live apart before marriage.
Premarital sex is expected.	Premarital sex is not an option.
Both partners continue their education.	The wife supports the husband through school.
The birth of a child might precede marriage.	Children are conceived after marriage.
Both partners work, and both may have careers.	The husband's work is the priority.
Roles are flexible.	Roles are rigid.
Both partners share child care.	The mother is responsible for child care and housework.
Both partners initiate sex.	The husband initiates sex.
Both partners select the couple's friends.	The husband's friends become the couple's friends.

Source: The Henry J. Kaiser Family Foundation and the National Center on Addiction and Substance Abuse at Columbia University, *Substance Abuse and Risky Behavior: Attitudes and Practices among Adolescents and Young Adults: Survey Snapshot,* February 6, 2002.

Working parents are under increasing stress as they try to balance time for their career and family. Too often, the marriage is what suffers.
©Purestock/SuperStock

traditionally masculine. In both the Arapesh and the Mundugumor tribes, Mead found little contrast in temperament between the sexes.

The third New Guinea tribe Mead studied provided further evidence of cross-cultural differences. Among the Tchambuli, both men and women behaved in ways that are opposite to traditional behavior in Western societies. Tchambuli women were independent and aggressive, acting like traditional Western men; Tchambuli men were gentle and sensitive, like traditional Western women. Mead's conclusion was that the varieties in temperament she observed among these three "primitive" societies were not dictated by biology but were largely the creations of the societies.

Mead's work sparked a discussion in America and worldwide that has not ended yet, nor is it likely to ever reach a conclusion, because the discussion and the controversy are too much fun for everyone. One study by psychologist David Buss is a good example of another important perspective in the discussion of maleness and femaleness. Buss and his colleagues created a questionnaire to be used around the world, asking people to describe their ideal mate. Five categories were included: earning capacity, industriousness, youth, physical attractiveness, and chastity. Buss collected data from 37 groups of men and women in 33 different societies.

The researchers found that even though the participants in the study came from many different geographical and cultural areas, consistent patterns emerged. Females placed more value on wealth and ambition, and males were more interested in signs of youth and

Gender-role stereotypes limit people's choices by dictating what they are believed to be able to do. Today, however, it is more commonly assumed in the United States that both sexes are capable and can be successful in a variety of roles at home and at work.
©Iakov Filimonov/Shutterstock

fertility. A mate who was a "good financial prospect" was more important to females in 36 of 37 groups, and "good looks" were more important to males than to females in all 37 groups in the study (Buss, Shackelford, Kirkpatrick, & Larsen, 2001).

Treas (2011), who has focused her work on how couples internationally distribute the division of housework, concludes that cultural values also contribute to how couples divide up household tasks and that household routines are influenced by the examples that couples see around them. These values may also determine how much time, in total, is spent on housework. For example, she indicates that in countries where hygiene is important, the total time spent on housecleaning may be higher than in other countries where hygiene is less important.

Barstad (2014) conducted a study in Norway, which is one of the most gender-equal societies in the world. In Norway the employment rate for men and women is nearly equal, and men are encouraged to be involved with their children. According to Barstad (2014), household tasks are often in two categories, routine and intermittent. Women typically take care of routine tasks such as cooking, cleaning, and laundry. Men, on the other hand, take care of intermittent tasks such as household repairs and yard work. It has been found in past research that when men do their share of routine household tasks women have higher marital quality, but men who do no housework at all seem to be the happiest. Barstad (2014) found in the study of individuals in Norway that women who had partners who did little or no routine tasks around the house often had relationship problems and lower marital satisfaction. In addition, women who never had to do the intermittent work had the best relationship quality. Men who did more than their share of routine jobs around the house had more problems in their relationship. The author of this study concluded that when routine jobs were shared equally, both men and women had equally good relationships. One might speculate that because Norway is a gender-equal country, it has an impact on both men and women being happy when responsibilities are shared on an equal basis.

Judith Treas (2015) adds to this discussion about the international view of household work. She concludes that when women work long hours outside the home, they need their spouse to share in household work, and when they only work part time, they are more likely to continue

BOX 7.2 · Diversity in Families

Ethnic Variations in Who Does Housework

A large national study examined how men and women differed in time spent on housework, depending upon their racial or ethnic background (Wight, Bianchi, & Hunt, 2012). The study compared Hispanics, Asians, Whites, and Blacks.

Wight et al. (2012) found that women spent more time on housework than men for all ethnic groups. The gap was between men's and women's time on housework was largest for Asian and Hispanic couples. In other words, Asian and Hispanic women spent two and one half times as much time on housework than men. In general, these two ethnic groups are more traditional in their family roles. In this study White men spent the most time on housework compared to the other groups.

These researchers found that the number of hours worked outside the home was related to the amount of work women, and thus men, did in the home. If women worked outside the home, she was likely to do less housework. The same was true for men in that the number of hours they worked outside the home was related to the amount of housework they did. Time available to do housework determined how much time men and women spent on doing those tasks.

Treas (2015) adds to this discussion about household work done across cultures by raising the issue of differences in hygienic standards, which are often linked to income levels. She makes the point that some families would not think of making the bed without ironing the sheets. Others need to use their sheets for long periods of time. Some families do not have their own washers and dryers, and their sheets may be less clean over time because laundry needs to be done in a laundromat. In addition, they may not have the financial resources to pay for a laundromat.

---

to do the majority of the routine work in the home. Therefore, countries that support part-time employment are more likely to have women continuing to do more household work since they can manage it with their limited employment. Women in countries that do not have many part-time options, such as Southern Europe and formerly socialist countries, are more likely to work full time and will require more sharing of household tasks. Therefore, each country's policies regarding work affects the division of household labor between men and women.

Gender Roles Across Ethnic Groups

It is commonly believed that gender roles do not spring from innate characteristics individuals possess. Rather, they are learned behaviors, rooted in the social context of the particular culture in which people live. The gender roles women and men play vary widely from culture to culture and within each culture. This section examines some examples of cultural gender-role differences in the United States.

Latino/a Culture

Latino males, historically speaking, have often been stereotyped as being *macho*. Male exhibitions of aggressiveness—*machismo*—include bossing women around, being abusive to them, and having numerous extramarital affairs. But this macho attitude is not supported in the research literature (Falicov, 2010). Even though some Latinos act macho, this is not the predominant pattern for this group and it does not display the historical role of Latino men.

After reviewing historical and recent literature, Falicov (2010) concludes that Latino men have multiple ways to be masculine. However, when machismo is thought about within the context of history and the family, the term has positive attributes such as bravery, altruism, and being responsible for and providing for one's family (Falicov, 2010; Skogrand, Barrios-Bell, & Higginbotham, 2009). Being macho often means one does not show emotions. Latino men, however, often show affection, cry, or hug both men and women (Falicov, 2010).

There is also evidence that Latinos are often egalitarian and share equally in decision making, especially around child-rearing or household decisions (Falicov, 2010). This seems to be especially true when Latinos have immigrated to the United States, where the view of women may be different from in their country of origin. Also, many women join the workforce when they enter the United States, and they have more power since they contribute money to the household.

In addition to the unique ways Latino men may show their masculinity, Latinos can come from a variety of countries and these countries can have differing views about gender issues.

African American Culture

The majority of African American families are headed by women and, therefore, extended family members often help out when it comes to caring for children (Sue & Sue, 2016). In addition, the rearing of children can be done by older children, or even close friends. Therefore, the roles of African Americans within the family are flexible and adaptable, and men and women are used to adopting multiple roles.

One of the complexities in gender roles for African American families is that many African American men have been marginalized in their roles as a provider and as a marital partner (Boyd-Franklin, 2003; Franklin, 2006; Sue & Sue, 2016). African American males have often grown up in single-parent homes where they do not have a male model to learn from. African American marriages were most often egalitarian where the couple shared responsibilities and worked together to provide for their family.

Many African American women see feminism from a different perspective than do White women. African American women have rarely served only in the housewife role because economic circumstances have dictated that they work outside the home. African American women are also acutely aware of the disadvantages African American men have faced over the years, making it difficult for them to adopt a wholeheartedly feminist agenda. The dilemma: Am I more oppressed as a woman or as an African American? Because these two factors converge for African American women, life can be especially difficult for them.

American Indian Culture

Native American women confront many of the same problems that African American women face in American society in that there are more female-headed households than in the dominant culture (Sutton & Broken Nose, 2005). Because there are many single-parent families, the extended family members often help in raising children. Native American cultures in the United States vary widely, but some are identified by a matrilineal tradition such as is true in the Navajo, whereas in other tribes men hold the power (Sue & Sue, 2016).

Many Native American families also face racism, unemployment, poverty, and the abuse of alcohol and other drugs (Sutton & Broken Nose, 2005). Native American women play an important role in keeping the family and the tribe together. Some tribal traditions make it difficult for Native American women to attain leadership roles, and some tribes have religious beliefs against both contraception and abortion. But it has also been argued that tribal traditions are a source of strength for American Indian women.

The value orientation of Native Americans has considerable impact on why role relationships in their culture are more complex and less clearly defined (Sue & Sue, 2016). Native Americans emphasize communal living rather than a nuclear family and communal sharing rather than focusing on individual possessions. As one tribal member commented, "When I was little, I learned very early that what's yours is mine and what's mine is everybody's" (Sutton & Broken Nose, 1996, p. 40). Native Americans also have a tribal identity that puts

Wilma Mankiller, former chief of the Cherokee Nation, was the first woman ever elected to that position. Her election reflected the growing power of women in some Native American tribes.
©Jerry Willis/Muskogee Daily Phoenix/AP Images

a high value on the group. Time is also seen differently by Native Americans in that it is cyclical rather than linear, so minutes and hours are less important than seasonal rhythms. In summary, these cultural values greatly influence their lifestyle and how they function as a group.

Asian American Culture

Asian American families as a group have been very successful in the U.S. culture. They value education highly, and they have the highest family income of any ethnic group. They value tradition and respect their elders (called filial piety), and their children are well disciplined. Asian Americans have a family and group orientation, with the family being more important than the individual (Sue & Sue, 2016). The goal of parents is to train their children to be respectful, to work hard, and to be successful.

Traditionally, sex roles have been segregated so that the woman is very connected to the children, and the husband is most highly connected to his work. As a result, there is a strong mother–child bond and a weaker husband–wife bond (Asai, 2004). Traditional Asian American families are often hierarchical and patriarchal, with men and older individuals having more power (Sue & Sue, 2016). While marriage is important in Asian families, it is usually not as strong as the family system.

Gender Issues for Immigrant Couples

New immigrants often face challenges as they come to a new country. They may have had one set of rules regarding gender in their country of origin, and in the United States they not only need to learn the rules, but also must make decisions about adapting gender roles based on new norms. Many women come to the United States with relatively traditional roles, where men make many decisions, and they enter a culture where women often have power equal or nearly equal to men (Sue & Sue, 2016). According to Maciel, Van Putten, and Knudson-Martin (2009), who studied a group of new immigrant couples, such couples usually allow changes to evolve and do this through having lots of couple conversations, interpreting new experiences, and generally interacting with their new world. The end result is that gender roles and power evolve and are often a hybrid of the new and the old.

Often new immigrant women, who have experienced traditional roles in their country of origin, need to work after coming to the United States. This has an impact on power in marriage relationships because they are bringing money into the family. In addition, women see other women in places like the workforce having more power and they challenge past gender roles (Maciel et al., 2009). Men often face the loss of status that their prior job provided (Sue & Sue, 2016). The researchers found that women gained power in their couple relationships when they had opportunity, access to resources, and legal protection. How much men would let go of traditional gender roles varied greatly, however.

Theories About Gender Roles

Theorists interested in gender roles have focused on how children acquire gender-role identity during the early years of life and how changes in gender-role identity occur. Some observers believe that changes in gender-role identity are possible after early childhood, but it is generally assumed that once gender-role identity is formed, it remains stable and continues throughout adulthood. Four theories about gender-role development and change are described here: social learning theory, cognitive development theory, family systems theory, and the feminist framework.

Social Learning Theory

The **social learning theory** is concerned with how individuals learn the behavior patterns considered appropriate for their sex. Social learning researchers have particularly focused on direct observation of behavior and how people reinforce each other's behavior. Early in life, reinforcement of sex-related behavior by others is of primary importance. As individuals grow and develop, they assess personal situations and develop standards and rules by which to live. In the case of gender roles, individuals begin as very young children to internalize the standards and rules for being a boy or a girl in our society.

Social learning theorist Jerome Kagan (1964) argued that children at a young age dichotomize the world as female versus male and have a strong desire to match their own personal characteristics with the gender-role standards they learn from parents and society in general. Kagan believed that children want to develop a gender-typed identity and that they see variations from the gender-traditional ideal as failures. He noted that certain aspects of gender-role standards cause unnecessary anxiety and restrictions for individuals, and he proposed that perhaps these standards should be changed.

Cognitive Development Theory

The **cognitive development theory** links gender-role development (the progressive acquisition of gender typing) to the more general maturation of the child's thinking processes. Lawrence Kohlberg (1966), the developer of this theory, argued that children themselves actively create gender identity, gender-role stereotypes, and values in their minds in their efforts to understand the world around them (for example, "I can't do that! Only boys do that!"). He argued that the stereotypes do not necessarily become more rigid over time but follow a curvilinear pattern. In early childhood, the stereotypes develop quickly and are quite rigid. When the child realizes that not all gender-typed characteristics (hair, clothes,

Among earlier generations of American women, relatively few had the opportunity to learn skills traditionally assigned to men. Today, people are not limited as much by gender-role stereotypes, though barriers still remain for those who cross traditional gender lines.
©Stocktrek Images/Getty Images

sports, etc.) are crucial to maintaining gender identity, the child's thinking becomes less rigid. With increasing maturity, the child learns that variations are possible and becomes more flexible in her or his thinking.

Paul Mussen (1969) synthesized social learning and cognitive processes in looking at gender-role development. Mussen noted that labeling occurs early in the child's life and that the child must see the label as positive, rewarding, lovingly applied, and accepted by the labeler. This linkage between the label and love and acceptance helps motivate the child to perform gender-typed behaviors.

Both the social learning and cognitive development theories have been attacked in recent years. First, critics argue that these early theories erred by assuming that children of the same sex develop very similar gender-role identities (masculine for boys and feminine for girls). In fact, many boys engage in traditionally feminine behaviors, and many girls engage in traditionally masculine behaviors.

Second, the early theories were criticized for characterizing the traditional gender-role identities as desirable and a divergence from the norm as deviant. Today, many children enjoy the freedom to engage in a broad range of activities, despite the dictates of tradition.

Third, the theories were criticized for assuming that early childhood is a critical period in gender-role development and that an adult's gender-role characteristics spring directly from early-childhood experiences. Dramatic changes in gender-role behavior can take place later in life such as a female homemaker going back to school to become a lawyer and a male engineer retiring early to take care of the home and garden while his spouse begins a new career outside the home. Subsequent theorists have explored human development after childhood and suggest that individuals retain the capacity for growth and change in their gender-role identity.

Family Systems Theory

Family systems theory suggests that the family functions as an interconnected system. A change in one family member necessitates compensatory changes in other family members if the family is to achieve a new balance.

According to family systems theory, change is a difficult process for both individuals and families. If the individual is successful in growing in new directions, sometimes other family members will attempt to bring the individual back "into the fold."

Consider, for example, a young woman who desires more independence in a family wanting to maintain traditional family roles. The daughter feels stifled by the family's long list of rules and beliefs and finds support in feminist writings and rhetoric, but when she expresses her views, her parents react emotionally. "Are you telling me my life has been worthless?" her more traditional mother asks. "Those damned feminists!" her father sputters. Her mother becomes defensive because she has made a career of her children and her marriage. Her father becomes defensive because he feels he has done the right thing by supporting his wife and children.

Family systems that are balanced (on the Couple and Family Map; see Chapter 3) tend to be more open to change and are more supportive of independence in family members. In contrast, some types of unbalanced family systems, particularly rigidly enmeshed types, are resistant to change and restrict independence in family members.

Feminist Framework

Traditional gender-role patterns—stressing the differences between men and women, masculinity and femininity—have been criticized by many feminists, especially since the 1960s. The gender-role constraints under which men and women traditionally have lived have been revised considerably. Many women are doing things their mothers would not have deemed possible. Many men are also gaining the freedom to function outside the traditional boundaries of masculinity. Making these profound changes in life is a struggle, but it would be difficult—if not impossible—for many people to go back to the traditional patterns.

Feminist scholars have focused on the contributions that women have made to society. Feminists point out that, although women have made countless contributions to culture and to human life, the omission of these achievements from the historical record reflects the low status in which women have been held in society. Feminists point out that women have been exploited, devalued, and oppressed. In addition, as a result of their own experiences, feminists tend to be sensitive to other oppressed people.

Another focus of feminists is a commitment to change the conditions of women. Feminists strive to empower women by documenting oppression so that people recognize it when they see and experience it. Feminists take an affirming stance toward women, challenging the status quo of devaluation (see Box 7.3, which describes gender inequality from a global perspective). This affirmation of women does not imply a rejection of men or all things masculine. Instead, both men and women are accorded equal respect and value.

According to feminists, the boxes males and females are put in are too simple and too idealistic. In practice, many individuals—both men and women—feel stifled by the roles they have been assigned and have sought a way to transform the traditional family.

BOX 7.3 At Issue

Gender Inequality as a Global Problem

Thanks in large part to the work of feminists and activists around the world, gender roles have broadened, and many constraints about what is possible and/or appropriate for men and women to do have been lifted in many places. However, even in contemporary American society, the reality is that gender inequality continues.

In 1963, the U.S. Congress passed the Equal Pay Act to "prohibit discrimination on account of sex in the payment of wages by employers engaged in commerce or in the production of goods for commerce."

The act was intended to level the playing field for men and women in the workplace. However, the AFL-CIO and the Institute for Women's Policy Research (1999) found that working families in the United States lose more than $200 billion each year because of the wage gap between men and women, which amounts to an average of $4,000 per year per family.

According to USA Today (Dugas, 2012, October 24), women earned 82% of what men earned in this country. The gap was even larger for Latina and African American women.

This kind of gender inequality is by no means exclusive to the United States. In Scotland, for example, the Scottish Trade Union Congress found that as of November 2004, women earned, on average, 19% less than men, and in one city—Aberdeen—the discrepancy was closer to 30% in favor of men in the same job (BBC News, 2004).

The United Nations International Labour Office (2004b), in a report titled "Global Employment Trends for Women 2004," estimated that in 2003 there were 2.8 billion workers around the world, of whom 1.1 billion—or 40%—were women. This represented an increase of nearly 200 million over the past decade. The United Nations International Labour Office (2004a) concluded that women's share of managerial positions in more than 60 countries ranges between 20% and 40%—a figure that has remained the same since 2001.

In almost every country in the world, women are responsible for most of the unpaid, "nonmarket" work. In most societies, women care for the children, the elderly, and the ailing. Women do most of the household chores, which in developing countries can mean walking many miles to fetch water and firewood.

Of course, gender inequality—which exists in every part of the world—isn't limited to gaps in earnings. In an essay published in *Frontline* (India's national magazine), Nobel laureate Amarta Sen (2001) delineated seven kinds of disparity between men and women:

1. *Mortality inequality.* In some areas of the world (e.g., North Africa and Asia), women suffer unusually high mortality rates due to gender bias in health care and nutrition.
2. *Natality inequality.* Where boys are considered more desirable than girls, modern technology can determine the gender of the fetus, and the pregnancy can be terminated if it is a girl. Sex-selective abortion has become a common practice in China, South Korea, Singapore, Taiwan, and several other areas of the world.
3. *Basic institutional inequality.* In many countries women are denied access to education and other social and cultural institutions.
4. *Special opportunity inequality.* In some countries where women do have access to *basic* education, they are denied access to higher education and/or professional training.
5. *Professional inequality.* Even in countries where special opportunities exist, women often encounter great difficulties trying to gain and advance in managerial positions.
6. *Ownership inequality.* In many societies it is very difficult, if not impossible, for women to own land or homes, thus making it much harder for them to become economically independent.
7. *Household inequality.* Family arrangements in most cultures place the burden of unpaid work squarely on women's shoulders and take for granted that, whether they work outside the home or not, they will perform such duties as child care and housework.

One positive note is that many countries exhibiting a high degree of gender inequality are initiating government-led programs to try to reduce the gender gap. However, because gender bias has such a long cultural history and appears on so many fronts, the process ahead to overcome it will no doubt take many more years to accomplish.

Power in Families

The fundamental concept in social science is Power, in the same sense in which Energy is the fundamental concept in physics.

—Bertrand Russell

The words *family* and *power* are inextricably linked. Power, control, and authority are continuously exercised in families, and struggles for personal power in families are exceedingly common. Tradition has dictated that considerable power goes to the males in the family, but women often have more power than they or anyone else admit.

Power can be defined as the ability (potential or actual) of an individual to change the behavior of other members in a social system. By extending this definition to families, we can define **family power** as the ability of one family member to change the behavior of the other family members.

Many of the characteristics of power in close relationships were summarized by Kathleen M. Galvin and Bernard J. Brommel (2000). Power is a system property—a feature of a family system—rather than a personal characteristic of any one family member. Power is an interactive process involving one family member who desires something from one or more other family members; these members may affect all other members in the system. Power is also a dynamic process, not a static one. It creates reciprocal causation (that is, family members react to power attempts) in which one move leads to another, which leads to another, and so forth. Power also changes over time, particularly when the family is under stress. Power has both perceptual and behavioral aspects: The same power issue may be perceived differently by each family member.

Power in Couple Relationships

Although there may be a goal of being equal in power when it comes to couple relationships, according to Carmen Knudson-Martin (2012) that is typically not the case. Knudson-Martin (2012), a therapist, begins this discussion by stating that most couples operate under the assumption of invisible male power, indicating that women listen to and accommodate their partners more than men. There are multiple reason for this, most of which are societal stereotypes and patriarchy. Historical gender norms are alive and well in that women take care of relationships and are supposed to be available to care for others. Men, on the other hand, are supposed to have answers and are not supposed to be vulnerable. In addition, according to Knudson-Martin, men's needs and desires are often not questioned. These inequities are so common in society, they are not questioned by couples.

Women are more likely than men to have college degrees. However, those degrees have not translated into equal pay for women.
©Comstock/Stockbyte/Getty Images

Chapter 7 | Gender Roles and Power in the Family   **205**

TABLE 7.4 Role Relationships in Happy Couples Versus Unhappy Couples

Perception of Relationship	PERCENTAGE IN AGREEMENT	
	Happy Couples	Unhappy Couples
Both perceive as egalitarian.	81%	19%
Husband perceives as traditional; wife perceives as egalitarian.	50	50
Wife perceives as traditional; husband perceives as egalitarian.	37	63
Both perceive as traditional.	18	82

Source: Olson, D., Olson-Sigg, A., & Larson, P. *The Couple Checkup.* Nashville, TN: Thomas Nelson, 2008.

According to Knudson-Martin (2012), equal power or equal support is when individuals notice and respond to each other, are open to influence, and tune in to the emotions of each other. Couples who experience equal power also validate each other—they listen and respond, letting the other person know she or he has worth. Equality also promotes honest and direct communication rather than trying to manipulate the situation to get a certain outcome. These strategies not only equalize power but create intimacy and marital satisfaction because they allow each person to be vulnerable in communicating. This vulnerability results when individuals trust each other. Although power in a relationship is often held by men, power can change depending on what is happening with the couple. For example, power may move to a person who had indicated a need to leave the relationship, and power is not necessarily dependent on gender.

Knudson-Martin (2012) concludes that it is very difficult for a couple to assess the degree to which they have an equal relationship when it comes to power. They may need a therapist to help them understand power in their relationship and help them equalize it.

Egalitarian Roles and Marital Satisfaction

When it comes to the importance of an equal relationship versus a traditional relationship to marital satisfaction, the national survey by Olson et al., (2008) clearly demonstrated that more equal relationships are highly related to marital satisfaction (see Table 7.4). If both partners perceive their relationship as egalitarian, 81% of the couples describe their marriage as happy and only 19% are unhappy. Conversely, if both partners perceive their marriage as traditional, only 18% feel their marriage is happy and 82% are unhappy. These findings are rather dramatic and demonstrate the importance of an equal relationship for marital happiness.

Two interesting patterns emerged when the partners perceived their relationship differently with one person saying it is equal and the other saying it is traditional. When the husband says the relationship is traditional and the wife says it is equal, half the marriages are happy and half are unhappy. However, when the wife says the relationship is traditional and the husband says it is equal, only about one-third (37%) are happy and two-thirds (63%) are unhappy. It is the wife's perception of equality that is most predictive of couple satisfaction.

The quest for power, money, and material success in which so many men are immersed is accompanied by higher levels of stress, higher rates of heart disease, and shorter life spans. Some observers believe that over time as women continue to rise in the working world there will also be a concomitant increase in the stress-related health problems that women experience. The current life expectancy at birth in the United States for men is 76.4 and for women is 81.2 years (Copeland, 2014, October 9).
©Anton Vengo/Purestock/SuperStock

Suggestions for Minimizing Power Issues

Remember that power is a characteristic of relationships, not of people. Power is always relative, changing, and useful only to the extent that it is legitimate. Many of the conflicts that cause relationship stress are struggles over the power process (the way decisions are made) rather than disagreements about a specific issue. The person holding the authority to make each decision must have the responsibility for following through on the decision.

Decision making should be balanced by the value of the areas each partner controls, not by the number of areas each has. It is more efficient and more realistic to assign each partner primary responsibility for making decisions in certain areas, whether or not the other has veto authority, than to make all decisions a matter of mutual agreement.

Men may think they have a lot to lose by giving up some of their power over women and children, but, in fact, they have a great deal to gain. Men tend to die younger than women, often from a variety of illnesses related to stress and poor lifestyle choices. A macho, "win-at-all-costs" attitude is commonly thought to contribute to men's health problems. Rigid gender roles may have afforded men more power in our culture, but it is lonely at the top. The path toward intimacy is best walked side by side.

Summary

- Men and women have different life experiences and, as a result, men and women are not equal in the United States. For example, more women than men live in poverty, especially women who are single parents.
- According to a national survey, happily married couples agree more often than unhappily married couples that both partners are equally willing to make adjustments in roles, that they are satisfied with the division of housework, that it takes hard work to have an equal relationship, and that they make most decisions jointly and household tasks are divided on the basis of preferences rather than tradition.
- The most commonly reported issues for married couples in their role relationship were the following: concern about unfair division of housework, housework based on traditional roles, husband not willing to adjust, wife too involved in housework, and lack of working to maintain an equal relationship.
- Gender roles—the expectations every society has about people's attitudes and behaviors based on whether they are male or female—are rooted in biology but heavily influenced by culture.
- Women often open or close the gate to men's involvement with their children. Women often feel they can do a better job than men and, therefore, do not let men be involved with their children.
- Sociologist Talcott Parsons espoused a traditional view of gender roles. His theory of family roles assumed that men should be "instrumental" and women "expressive." Parsons's theory has been vigorously challenged and is no longer well received.
- Persistent gender-role patterns in marriage mean that women do much more of the housework in the family than men do, which often leads to relationship conflict.
- Internationally, couples may have equal responsibility in the home based upon such things as income level, the availability of part-time work, and family policy.
- New immigrants often have to adapt to new gender role dynamics as they enter the United States. Gender roles often become a hybrid of the new and the old.
- Historically prominent theories of gender-role development include the social learning theory, which is concerned with how individuals learn the behavior patterns considered appropriate for their sex; the cognitive development theory, which links the progressive acquisition of gender typing to the general maturation of the child's thinking processes; the family systems theory, which holds that the entire family must change when an individual member changes; and the feminist framework, which argues that women are exploited, devalued, and oppressed and affirms their equality with men.
- Family power is the ability of one family member to change the behavior of other family members. Power is an interactive process involving one family member who desires something from one or more other family members; these members may affect all other members in the system.
- Although most couples want to have equal power in their relationship, it is often difficult to do. Society's expectations about men's and women's roles in society have subtle, but powerful, impacts on how we interact as a couple. This lack of equality can affect couple satisfaction.

Key Terms

- gender identity
- gender role
- gender-role stereotype
- masculinity
- femininity
- maternal gatekeeping
- egalitarian roles
- social learning theory
- cognitive development theory
- power
- family power

Activities

1. In small groups, identify places in society where equal gender roles exist. Are they in certain kinds of families? Are they in certain kinds of workplaces? Where are they least likely to exist?
2. Study Table 7.3, Contemporary Versus Traditional Dating and Marriage Patterns. If you are in an intimate relationship, decide which aspects from the "contemporary" list and which from the "traditional" list apply to your relationship. Have your partner do the same exercise and compare your answers.
3. In small groups, discuss family power. How was power distributed in your family of origin? How do you know? (Give examples.) How do you want power to be distributed in the family you hope to create in the future?

Suggested Readings

Bass, B. L., Butler, A. B., Grzywacz, J. G., & Linney, K. D. (2009). Do job demands undermine parenting? A daily analysis of spillover and crossover effects. *Family Relations, 58,* 201–215.

Coontz, S. (2011). *A strange stirring.* New York, NY: Basic Books.

Davis, D. J., & Chaney, C. (2013). *Black women in leadership: Their historical and contemporary contributions.* New York, NY: Peter Lang Publishing.

Drago, R. W. (2007). *Work, family, life.* Boston, MA: Dollars & Sense Publishers.

Gerson, K. (2010). *The unfinished revolution: How a new generation is reshaping family, work, and gender in American.* New York, NY: Oxford University Press.

Gilbert, N. (2008). *A mother's work: How feminism, the market, and policy shape family life.* New Haven, CT: Yale University Press.

Halpern, D. F., & Cheung, F. M. (2008). *Women at the top: Powerful leaders tell us how to combine work and family.* West Sussex, UK: Wiley-Blackwell.

Kahn, J., Garcia-Manglano, J., & Bianchi, S. (2014). The motherhood penalty at midlife: Long-term effects of children on woman's careers. *Journal of Marriage and Family, 76,* 56–72.

Meier, J. A., McNaughton-Cassill, M., & Lynch, M. (2006). The management of household and childcare tasks and relationship satisfaction in parenting couples. *Marriage and Family Review, 40,* 61–88.

Rosenblum, K., & Travis, T. (2016). *The meaning of difference* (7th ed.). New York, NY: McGraw-Hill.

Treas, J., & Drobnic, S. (Eds.). (2010). *Dividing the domestic: Men, women, and household work in cross-national perspective.* Stanford, CA: Stanford University Press

U.S. Department of Commerce (2011). *Women in America.* Washington, DC: White House Council on Women and Girls. Web site: http://www.esa.doc.gov/sites/default/files/womeninamerica.pdf.

Wight, V. R., Bianchi, S. M., & Hunt, B. R. (2012). Explaining racial/ethnic variation in partnered women's and men's housework: Does one size fit all? *Journal of Family Issues, 34,* 394–427.

Visit the text-specific Online Learning Center at **www.mhhe.com/olson9e** for practice tests, chapter summaries, and PowerPoint slides.

8 Managing Economic Resources

Money and Happiness

Marriage and Money

Diversity and Financial Style

The Cost of Divorce

Why Do Finances Cause Problems?

Family Income and Expenses

Smart Money Management

Credit: Uses and Abuses

Summary

Key Terms

Activities

Suggested Readings

In this chapter we will focus on financial issues, particularly as they relate to intimate relationships and to families across the life cycle. The interest and research regarding the interface between couples and families and economic issues has grown substantially in the past 20 years (Dew, 2008b). This interest is expected to continue to grow as baby boomers move into retirement. Some of the topics that have received attention are financial management, women's labor force participation, balancing work and family, and economic issues and their impact on family relationships. The field of study of economic issues and families has, by nature, been interdisciplinary, including such areas as consumer economics, family studies, psychology, political science, nutrition, and sociology. In addition, much research has been done and many resulting journal articles have been written by authors from multiple disciplines. This allows for multiple perspectives to come together to address the issues around families and finances.

The economic recession that began in 2007 is also adding interest to the dynamics between money and families. Although the recession lasted only a couple of years, it affected everyone, and the majority of people expect the effects of the recession to last for several years. Even those who were relatively well off financially felt the strain and experienced feelings of vulnerability (Zvonkovic, Lee, Brooks-Hurst, & Lee, 2014). Researchers have found that even if the recession did not result in job loss, economic strain was experienced by many in terms of worry and uncertainty about the future, and this strain affected their children (Leininger & Kalil, 2014). Money problems are often related to an inability to develop an open and well-organized couple or family system. These financial problems then lead to more stress and conflict in the marriage or family. We will explore the field of financial resource management, whose aim is to achieve economic **goals** and harmony in intimate relationships.

Money and Happiness

Do money and happiness go together? It has been generally felt that when rich and very poor people are compared, the rich are happier. However, it has been thought that once people are out of poverty, the differences in happiness are relatively weak. As we shall see, the findings are mixed.

Some recent reports indicate that there is a strong relationship between money and happiness (*The Economist,* 2007, July 14). In an international study asking people how satisfied they are with their life on a scale of 1 to 10, in general people in wealthier nations (America, Europe, Japan, Saudi Arabia) reported being more happy than those from poor countries (primarily African countries). These findings were also true when it came to looking at those who were wealthy and those who were poor within countries—the wealthy people were happier. Another study, conducted by the Pew Research Center (Stokes, 2007, July 24), indicates that globally, countries that have had rising economic growth have also had rising happiness levels. This report also showed that once people reach a certain level of income, happiness levels off. Other investigators have argued that after families reach a household income of $50,000, the relationship between money and happiness is no longer strong (*Time*, 2009, April 27).

Another study, which was done in the United States, also showed that money and happiness go together (Pew Research Center, 2006, February 13). In this study, one-third of participants said they were very happy, with another 50% indicating they were pretty happy (see Figure 8.1). According to this study, these numbers have been stable over the past 35 years. Pew also found that annual family income correlated with peoples' happiness responses. For example, only 24% of those with annual family incomes of less than $30,000 said they were very happy, whereas 49% of families making $100,000 or more said they were very happy (see Figure 8.2). However, just because money and happiness go together does not mean one causes the other. Maybe money leads to happiness, or happiness leads to money. This study also showed that those who were healthiest were more likely to be very happy and those who

FIGURE 8.1

About One-Third of Americans Are Very Happy

Source: The Henry J. Kaiser Family Foundation and the National Center on Addiction and Substance Abuse at Columbia University, *Substance Abuse and Risky Behavior: Attitudes and Practices Among Adolescents and Young Adults: Survey Snapshot,* February 6, 2002.

How happy are you these days in your life?

- Pretty happy 50%
- Very happy 34%
- Not too happy 15%
- Don't know 1%

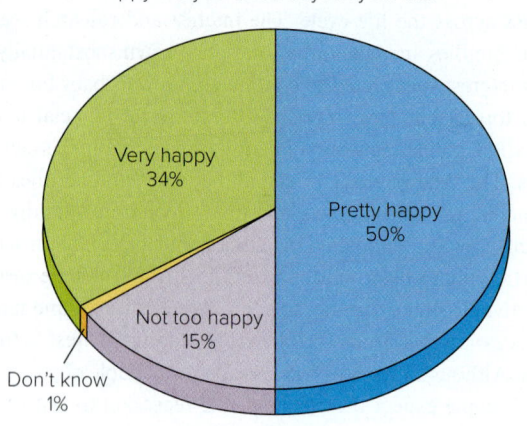

had poor health were least happy. It may be that those with poor health made less money, and it was health that made the difference, not money. One might ask: Is it the money that makes the difference or is it things that go along with having money that make the difference, such as home ownership, less stress, or having more choices. All we know from these studies is that wealth and happiness seem to go together. With that said, there are many people who would say that when it comes to happiness, there are many things more important than money. In fact, two of the wealthiest men in the United States, Warren Buffett and Bill Gates, have weighed in on this issue. Buffet has said, "The true measure of success is the number of people who genuinely care about and respect you when you near the end of your life" (Hoskins, 2005, winter, p. 33). Bill Gates said, "My goal for success outside of work is definitely raising a family. So far I haven't caused any damage; they seem to be doing OK" (Hoskins, 2005, p. 33).

There is also evidence that income is related to social problems. One study indicated that lower income was related to increased environmental and family risk (Jones-Sanpei, Homes, & Day, 2009). In other words, more things can cause problems in the lives of family members who were poor. In another study, poor, rural women who lived in trailer parks told

FIGURE 8.2

Does Money Buy Happiness?

Source: The Henry J. Kaiser Family Foundation and the National Center on Addiction and Substance Abuse at Columbia University, *Substance Abuse and Risky Behavior: Attitudes and Practices Among Adolescents and Young Adults: Survey Snapshot,* February 6, 2002.

Percentage Very Happy by Family Income:
- Under $30K: 24
- $30K to under $75K: 33
- $75K to under $100K: 38
- $100K and over: 49

Part II | Dynamics of Intimate Relationships

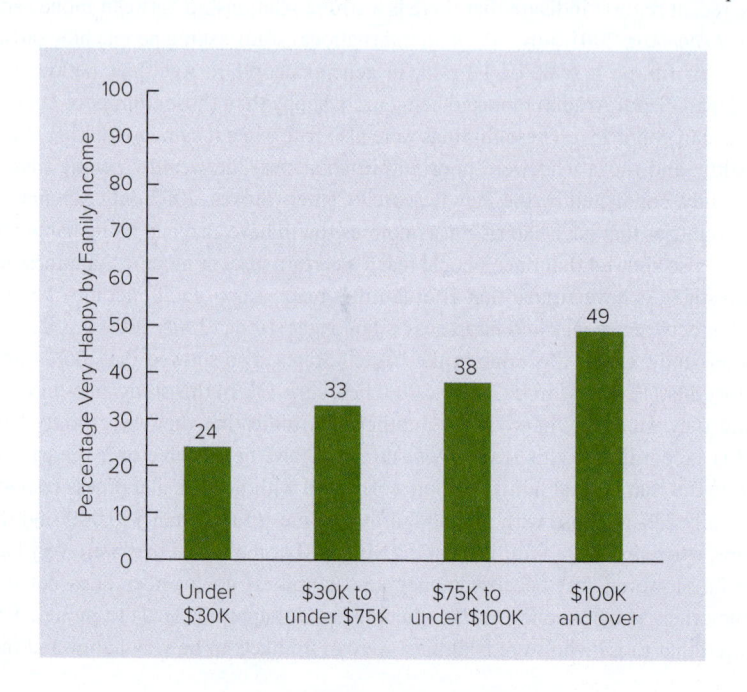

their stories about how they made their way across the life span (Notter, MacTavish, & Shamah, 2008). These women had multiple barriers to overcome, but they managed to be resilient. These women, however, also had persistent economic struggles and experienced social isolation. So poor people can overcome many barriers but still continue to struggle.

What might we conclude from this information? Being poor has multiple stresses, and it is likely that those in this country trying to raise a family on less than $50,000 per year experience many stresses that make them unhappy. They may be living in substandard housing, experiencing crime in their neighborhoods, and sending their children to schools that are unsafe and are not places where children can learn. Once families have earnings beyond a level that provides for basic needs, however, other things factor into happiness. These things may be marital happiness, having a supportive extended family, and doing things that one enjoys.

How people spend their money is also important in terms of contributing to happiness. Research findings indicate that spending their money to help others, or **prosocial spending**, provides positive emotional benefits for individuals. Dunn, Aknin, and Norton (2014) talk about this positive feeling as "the warm glow of giving" (p. 42). These researchers gave students on a university campus either $5 or $20 to spend by the day's end. They asked half of the individuals to spend the money on someone else and the other half of the individuals to spend the money on themselves. The result was that those who spent money on others were happier at the end of the day than those who spent it on themselves. Also, it did not matter whether the amount was $5 or $20; the results were the same. The conclusion one might draw is that the amount of resources shared with others is not important, but giving to others is personally beneficial.

Aknin et al. (2013) conducted a very large, international study in multiple countries throughout the world and had similar findings as Dunn et al. (2014). They found that prosocial giving, giving to others, rather than spending money on themselves, resulted in greater happiness for the individuals. This finding was supported in both rich and poor countries. They also found that this warm, fuzzy feeling was evident even if the giver did not know the person, and they would never meet the person, who received the money. This positive feeling was also evident even if no one knew the money had been given, so this feeling was not based on praise from others. These authors conclude that human beings around the world experience a sense of well-being and emotional rewards from using their finances to benefit others.

If people do not spend money on themselves, where do they donate their financial resources? According to Giving USA (2015, June 29), religious organizations were by far the largest recipients of charitable giving. Other destinations for gifts included education, human services, health, and arts. Individuals provided the majority of the donations (72%) as compared to corporations, foundations, and bequests (28%). Donations have increased since the recession of 2007 to an all-time high of $358 billion in 2014. One might wonder if people recognize the personal benefit they receive from giving.

Marriage and Money

A significant amount of research indicates there is a strong relationship between marital happiness and finances. One large study of over 50,000 couples shows that happy couples have different ways of viewing and managing money than unhappy couples (Olson, Olson-Sigg, & Larson, 2008). This study found that the financial management item that most distinguishes happy couples from unhappy couples is how much they agree on how to spend money (Table 8.1). Other issues that distinguish happy from unhappy couples include concerns about saving, concerns about debt, control of finances, and the use of credit cards. Couples can improve their couple relationship by discussing these issues and come to an agreement about these financial matters.

A national study asked 64 couples who had great marriages to tell, by way of a 31-page questionnaire, what made their marriages great (Skogrand, Johnson, Horrocks, & DeFrain,

TABLE 8.1 Strengths of Happy Versus Unhappy Couples Regarding Finances

Financial Issue	Happy Couples	Unhappy Couples
1. We agree on how to spend money.	85	43
2. I am satisfied with our decision to save.	67	29
3. Major debts are not a problem for us.	69	35
4. My partner does not try to control our finances.	74	43
5. Credit cards are not a problem for us.	69	42

PERCENTAGE IN AGREEMENT

Source: The Henry J. Kaiser Family Foundation and the National Center on Addiction and Substance Abuse at Columbia University, *Substance Abuse and Risky Behavior: Attitudes and Practices Among Adolescents and Young Adults: Survey Snapshot,* February 6, 2002.

2011). They answered questions about many aspects of their couple relationships, including how they managed their finances. Three themes regarding marriage and money emerged from the data. First, for most couples, one of the partners handled the day-to-day finances. The decision was based upon who had the expertise, who had the time, or who enjoyed doing it. When one person managed the money, however, it required trust and communication. Second, these couples with great marriages had little or no debt or had a goal of paying off debt. It was a shared goal to pay with cash or, if credit was used, to pay off the bill as quickly as possible. Third, couples lived within their means, and many considered themselves frugal. There was no trend toward having either joint or separate accounts. Either way seemed to work as long as they were in agreement. Although many of these couples with great marriages had experienced financial challenges during their married life, they had worked them out together. Therefore, one could conclude that managing finances well contributes to a great marriage. The authors of this study provide an alternative explanation, however, and suggest that having a strong marriage, which typically included having good communication and conflict resolution skills, helped couples more effectively manage their money. These strong marriages may have also helped them get through difficult financial times. They also suggest that teaching money management skills alone will not necessarily enable couples to strengthen their marriages. If couples do not know how to solve problems or deal with conflict in the marriages, they are unlikely to be able deal with the conflict that can result with money. It might be that helping couples strengthen their marriage will help them address financial issues. Only further research will address this question. It might be useful, however, for financial counselors and family life educators to work hand-in-hand in helping couples have healthy couple relationships, which would develop skills that will enhance their handling of financial issues—and developing skills in managing finances could enhance their marriage relationships. (See Box 8.1 for a discussion of the effects of debt on newlyweds.)

A significant amount of data shows a relationship between marital satisfaction and the emotional stress that goes along with finances. In one large sample of nearly 5,000 married couples it was found that couple financial strain contributed to both husbands' and wives' emotional distress (Gudmunson et al., 2007). This stress was related to marital instability. This study also found that there was a direct path from financial strain to disagreements in marriage, and disagreements provide a context for relationship decay. These authors also suggest that couples today have little time to spend together, and if this limited time together is spent arguing about money, it is likely to add to marital instability.

BOX 8.1 At Issue

The Effects of Debt on Newlyweds

Is it finances in general, or specifically debt, that causes problems for couples? Much has been written about the stress of finances and money in causing problems for couples in their marriages. One study, however, found that it was debt that caused the most problems in newlywed marriages, rather than finances in general.

In a study by Skogrand, Schramm, Marshall, and Lee (2005) of approximately 1,000 randomly selected newlywed couples who had been married from 3 to 9 months, debt brought into marriage was identified as the second-most-cited problem in their marriage by both husbands and wives. In this study, debt brought into marriage was separate from financial decision making, which was much farther down the list of 30 possible problematic areas for couples.

Couples in this study were asked to indicate their level of debt in areas of debt such as medical bills, credit card debt, auto loans, and school loans. Home mortgage debt was not included as a possible problem area in this study, because most newlywed couples do not own a home. Important findings of the study include the following:

- Seventy percent of husbands and wives brought debt into the marriage. Thirty-five percent of husbands and wives had more than $5,000 in debt when they married.
- Fifty-five percent of husbands and wives had automobile debt, 48% had credit card debt, 23% had school debt, and 12% had medical debt when they entered the marriage.
- Of the four kinds of debt, credit card and automobile loan debt had the highest correlation with lower marital satisfaction and adjustment scores for both husbands and wives.
- Higher levels of education were related to lower amounts of debt brought into marriage.
- Medical bills and school loans may have been viewed as necessary debt, because they did not have a high correlation with low levels of marital satisfaction and adjustment.
- The higher the debt brought into the marriage, the lower the marital satisfaction and adjustment scores of participants. Those who brought no debt into the marriage had the highest marital satisfaction and adjustment scores.

According to this study, debt is an important factor in marital satisfaction and adjustment. Why is this true? We suggest that debt and financial difficulties create stress, which takes away from developing and maintaining the marital relationship.

In a large national study, Dew, Britt, and Huston (2012) explored the direct relationship between financial issues and divorce. They found that financial disagreements were higher predictors for both men and women than other disagreements such as spending time together and household tasks. In fact, for husbands, disagreement about finances was the only type of disagreement that predicted divorce. For wives, disagreements about finances predicted divorce, along with disagreements about sex.

Debt and its relationship to marital happiness has been studied extensively in recent years. Dew's study of newly married couples showed that a change in consumer debt (for goods and services) predicted a change in marital satisfaction (2008a). If couples paid off their debt, their marital satisfaction increased. Dew suggests that having debt affects quality time together, which affects marital satisfaction. Lack of quality time together may be because of need to work more or being unable to spend time together without arguing about finances. Interestingly, changes in mortgage and school debt were not related to changes in marital satisfaction. It may be that mortgage and school debt are viewed as investments.

Along with debt, assets have also been studied in terms of their relationship to marital satisfaction. In another study Dew (2007) compared the impact of debt and assets on marital satisfaction. It was again found that debt was directly related to marital satisfaction—increased debt resulted in decreased marital satisfaction. In addition, however, it was found that assets reduced economic pressure and economic worries, but were not directly related to marital satisfaction. Based upon these findings, Dew suggests that paying down debt has a more direct impact on marital satisfaction than does the accumulation of assets.

Finally, Dew (2009) looked at assets as they related to divorce. The findings of this study showed that for women, assets were related to marital satisfaction, which kept them from wanting a divorce. This relationship was not true for men. It was suggested that assets may enhance wives' marital satisfaction so women do not want to divorce, and these women feel that divorce is not an option. It is possible that wives expect marriage to provide them with economic benefits and these assets, therefore, predict marital satisfaction. It is also important to note that Dew (2015) summarizes recent research by saying that issues such as consumer debt, assets, conflicts over money, and financial behavior are all associated with relationship quality. Income, however, is not associated with marital happiness. What people do with their money is a more important factor than the amount of income itself.

We can conclude from these findings that marital happiness and finances are related. Debt is negatively related to marital satisfaction, and couples who have little or no debt are happier than those with debt. Couples who are happy in their marriages trust each other and communicate about finances. It is expected that future studies will continue to enhance our understanding of this relationship between money and marital happiness.

Diversity and Financial Style

Little has been written about how finances are handled by low-income families and families from diverse populations. A major difference between low-income and middle- and higher-income spending practices relates to the difference between a **collective worldview** and an **individualistic worldview** (Skogrand, Hatch, & Singh, 2009). Low-income families and families living in poverty usually view things from a collective worldview. This means a family often gets through life because someone—a family member, friend, or neighbor—helped them when they really needed it. It follows, then, that when this family has a little extra money, it will be shared with the same people who helped them. People with an individualistic worldview typically use resources to better themselves such as buying a bigger house, furthering their education, or investing their money in the stock market.

Diverse cultural groups are also likely to have a collective worldview rather than an individualistic worldview and see helping family and friends as a high priority. This would be true of many Latino families. Family is the highest priority, and family needs would come before personal needs (Skogrand et al., 2008). Family is also viewed as the primary source of financial support. This perspective may be viewed by European American, middle-class folks as being irresponsible when, in fact, it is a cultural strength.

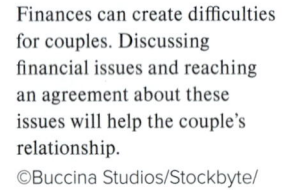

Finances can create difficulties for couples. Discussing financial issues and reaching an agreement about these issues will help the couple's relationship.
©Buccina Studios/Stockbyte/Getty Images

Low-income families may have had financial stresses in their lives to the point that they do not have a bank account because of bad credit. Other reasons for not having a checking account include not trusting banks, not trusting technology, or unavailability of banking services in some poorer neighborhoods. Because low-income families often do not have checking accounts, they often pay a fee for using money orders to pay bills or pay a fee for cashing checks. Because they do not have good credit, they may have to borrow money from payday loans (loans you pay back when you get a paycheck), which can have interest rates up to 1,000%. These costs add to an already stretched budget.

Because low-income families live from paycheck to paycheck, any unexpected expense has a domino effect. A bounced check of $20 can mean multiple overdraft charges that, according to one researcher, could run as high as 4,000% of the original bounced check. These overdraft charges can mean a car payment cannot be made, and a loss of a car can mean a loss of a job. There is often no opportunity to recover from an unexpected expense because there is no wiggle room in the budget for emergencies.

African American couples who had strong marriages talked about their experiences with economic issues and how those issues affected their marriages (Dew, Anderson, Skogrand, & Chaney, 2016). One of the findings of this qualitative study of 37 couples with strong and satisfying marriages was that they had financial struggles which put a strain on their marriages. These couples also talked about how they coped with those struggles, which included working together as a couple, using religious resources, and hanging in there until things got better. Some said that these struggles brought them closer as a couple. They also talked about how they worked together as a unit to overcome financial challenges. Individuals talked about how love, rather than materialism, is what helped them through hard times. In other words, they transcended the difficulties and rose above difficult financial issues. These results could be impacted by the collective worldview that is experienced by many African Americans. These ways of dealing with financial stress may be unique to African American couples.

Earlier experiences also affect how one manages finances. For example, new Latino immigrants often do not use banks because they were not always trusted in the country from which they emigrated (Holzner et al., 2006). Instead, money may be kept at home—literally under the mattress or in the cupboard, because those are more trusted places than a bank. Having a savings account, investing in a retirement account, or using credit, which involves banks, may not be something Latino families would do. Only a small percentage of Latinos have investment accounts (Holzner et al., 2006). In addition, substantial amounts of money are often sent to family members in their country of origin, rather than being used for improving quality of life for the family that is in the United States.

Somali immigrants have religious views about finances that are in contrast to the majority U.S. population (Solheim, 2008). According to Islamic law, unfair interest cannot be charged on loans, which stems from a belief that there should be economic justice between those who have and those who do not have financial resources. Low-interest loans, however, are acceptable, and paying off credit cards before they accumulate interest is acceptable under Islamic law. Earning interest on savings accounts is also problematic. This issue can be addressed by donating the interest to charity.

The issues that immigrants face in this country are significant, because 1 in 10 people in America were born in another country, with the number expected to increase (Solheim, 2008). Family finance professionals need to be aware of these cultural differences as they try to help new immigrant families manage money in their new country.

Couples and families use a wide range of strategies that are dependent on social class, family structure, life experiences, and culture. Stepfamilies have to negotiate ways to manage finances that account for each spouse having individual financial responsibilities involving their own children. They may have to manage several pots of money that include yours, mine, and ours to accommodate a complex family system. Child support and other types of financial commitments must be met that were made before the stepfamily relationship developed. Couples who have divorced and remarried later in life may not have young children to financially care for, but may have adult children who do not want their inheritance to go to a new spouse or that spouse's children.

The Cost of Divorce

We have always known that there is a tremendous emotional cost to families who experience a divorce. One researcher recently identified the potential economic cost of divorce. Divorce is necessary and in the best interest of the couple and the family in many cases, and to stay in the relationship would be financially costly as well in terms of physical, emotional, and mental well-being (Schramm, 2006). This study was conducted in a western state to determine the cost of divorce to the family and to the state and federal governments, with implications for social policy that would contribute to strengthening marriages.

The personal costs of divorce in the study were calculated based on legal and filing fees for the divorce, divorce education classes that were required in the state where the study was conducted, housing costs with required moves, and lost productivity due to distress (Schramm, 2006). Legal fees for a divorce vary, of course, but a conservative estimate of the costs was $7,000 per divorce for a couple with children, and a filing fee of $95 to start the divorce process. Some states have divorce education classes, especially for couples with children. Although this cost is somewhat minimal, in this western state it was $70 per couple.

Housing may be a substantial cost for divorcing couples. Schramm (2006) indicates that minimally there would be one geographic move in each divorce, and approximately one-third of the couples would have two geographic moves. It is estimated that the average housing cost for a family not going through a divorce would be $15,500, and the equivalent expenses for a divorcing family is estimated to be almost $20,000. Based on estimates of other studies regarding lost productivity related to stress, it is estimated that approximately $3,000 per year per couple is the cost of lost productivity. These costs total approximately $14,000 for the year of the divorce (Schramm, 2006).

Although a personal cost of $14,000 is considerable for any family, this amount would be especially burdensome for low-income families, where the divorce rates are the highest. Many couples may see only the anticipated added benefit of getting out of a marriage without being aware of the added financial costs.

In addition to the personal costs of divorce, Schramm (2006) calculates the cost to communities and local and federal governments and concludes that each divorce has a total average estimated cost of $30,000. Schramm suggests that resources might be invested in education to strengthen marriages, which would result in less money spent than the potential costs of divorce. Couples may also consider the personal investment in marriage therapy and education as being less costly than a divorce.

Why Do Finances Cause Problems?

There are several reasons finances cause problems for families:

- Money is a taboo topic in many families.
- Many couples do not create and stick to a budget.
- Some families overspend and rely too heavily on credit.
- Partners have different styles of spending and saving.

BOX 8.2 Putting It Together
Steps to Financial Freedom

There are some general principles that can help people control their financial resources. These steps can be utilized by individuals, couples, or families. If you are in a couple or family, it would be wise to take time as a couple or have a family meeting and make decisions about implementing these strategies.

Step 1: **Create a budget and stick to it.** Consider the money you have coming in, and identify the expenses that have to be paid. Expenses should include rent or house payments, utilities, loan repayments, groceries, car expenses, and any other regular costs. If you have insurance payments that are only made yearly or quarterly, find a way to put that money away on a monthly basis so that the payments can be made when they come due. It is also wise to put money into savings each month in case of a layoff or other emergency.

Step 2: **Identify your goals.** Think about the goals you have for the next 5 years. These goals will help you identify ways to spend your money in ways that are consistent with your goals. For example, if you want to buy a house, you may need to establish a savings account in order to have a down payment.

Step 3. **Cut up your credit cards.** Credit card debt can get out of hand and result in considerable interest being paid when a balance is maintained. Start paying off the credit cards that have the highest interest rates. When one credit card is paid off, use the money you would normally pay on that credit card to pay on the card with the next highest interest. It is a good idea to have one credit card for emergencies.

Step 4: **Make savings automatic.** If you do not put money aside for savings before other bills are paid, it usually does not happen. Taking a regular percentage out for savings, such as 15%, by way of automatic deposit or some other automatic system, makes it happen.

Step 5: **Protect your credit by making payments on time.** Regular, on-time payments help build good credit. Pay back aggressively if your budget allows for it. Late payments usually result in late fees and may eventually be reported to credit bureaus.

Step 6: **Have a savings account first, then worry about a retirement fund.** The first priority should be making sure you have money set aside for emergencies. Once that is in place, consider putting money away for retirement. It is especially important to contribute to a retirement fund if your employer is matching your contributions. It is free money.

Source: Adapted from Cynkar, A., "Early-career insights: Seven steps to stomp out debt," *Monitor on Psychology* 38 (5).

- One partner uses money as a tool to gain power and control over the other partner.
- Partners have different ideas about the meaning of money.

In the dating phase, couples are more likely to talk about any topic other than their financial situations; it's not very romantic to talk about potential income, the use of credit cards, and views on savings. In contrast, among married couples, money matters are the most common sources of arguments. Money can symbolize different things to different people, and if couples don't recognize these differences, they are often unprepared for the resulting friction. That's the situation described by Marcia, a 42-year-old computer technician, in the following account:

> "I thought we talked about everything before marriage. But we never seemed to get around to money—what it means to each of us and how it should be spent. Because I saw money as a symbol of security, I wanted to scrimp and save. I wanted to build a house, a nest, and feel safe inside. Because he saw money as a tool to achieve freedom and independence, he wanted to use it for adventure. We were doomed from the beginning to fight over money."

It isn't just married couples, however, who lack communication skills when it comes to finances. The discussion of money between parents and children is often nonexistent. Nonetheless, many financial advisers and counselors argue that it is essential to break the family pattern of financial silence. (See Box 8.2 for advice on steps to financial freedom.)

Money is not just the paper, coin, or plastic used to buy things. It can also be a perceived source of status, security, enjoyment, or control. If partners have incompatible attitudes about money and its uses, extravagant purchases are likely to cause conflicts between them over deeply held beliefs and values.
©VCG/Corbis/Getty Images

Family Income and Expenses

In this section we will focus on the average income of U.S. families and on income variations among different ethnic and cultural groups and between men and women. We will also explore typical family expenses and differences in family net worth. In Box 8.3 we will discuss the impact of the 2007 recession on fertility rates. Finally, we will examine the financial feasibility for both spouses to work outside the home, especially if they have children.

What does *living in poverty* mean? It means that people might not have adequate food or a decent place to sleep. (In the case of the homeless, it could mean living in a refrigerator box in an alley or under a bridge.) It means people cannot afford to see a physician when they are ill or to purchase medicine when they need it. Being poor may mean having no telephone, no radio, no television, no means of transportation. It often means that children attend substandard schools or that their parents move so often looking for work that the children do not attend school at all. Poverty is a very stressful state of affairs.

Lower-middle-income families, although not officially "poor" by government standards, also find it quite difficult to make ends meet. In both two-parent and single-parent lower-middle-income families, about three-quarters of all family expenditures can go for housing, food, and transportation. This leaves little money for anything else.

In 2015, the poverty rate was 13.5% (Proctor, Semega, & Kollar, 2016, September). The rate had decreased from 2014. The poverty rates are highest for children under 18 years of age and lowest for those 65 years and older. The poverty rate for Whites was 9%, for Blacks and Hispanics was 24%, and for Asians was 11%.

Family Income

As one can see from Figure 8.3, since the recession of 2007, the incomes for all racial and ethnic groups have increased. The highest household income level is for Asian Americans, followed in order by White, Hispanic, and Black Americans (Proctor et al., 2016, September).

BOX 8.3 At Issue
The Recession and Fertility Rates

There were many lessons learned from studying families during the Great Recession of 2007. It was a time of jobs loss, home foreclosures, and financial uncertainty (Schneider, 2015). One of the impacts on families was a reduction in fertility rates. Schneider (2015) found that states that had the highest levels of foreclosures and unemployment also had a reduction in the number of people having children. It was also evident in Schneider's research that, even in places where there were not high levels of foreclosure and unemployment, uncertainty about one's financial future also affected fertility rates.

During the recession, there was extensive media coverage about economic issues in the country. Foreclosure rates were in the news regularly. The downward trend of the stock market was reported in general news outlets and was often the focus of conversation over the dinner table or at social gatherings. Because people had such ready access to news about these economic issues, Schneider (2015) concludes that this also affected decisions to have children—even if the financial lows were not happening to a perspective parent directly.

It was assumed that this decrease in fertility resulted from use of contraception and an increased use of abortion to terminate a pregnancy. Schneider (2015) also speculates that there may have been an increase in stress-induced miscarriages. Although we know that stress can increase miscarriages, there has been no research done to show that miscarriages increased because of the recession.

Rates of fertility is one example of how economic issues can affect all aspects of individual and family life. Other issues that affected families during that time were an increase in partner violence (Schneider, Harknett, & McLanahan, 2016) and a decrease in the divorce rate (Cohen, 2014).

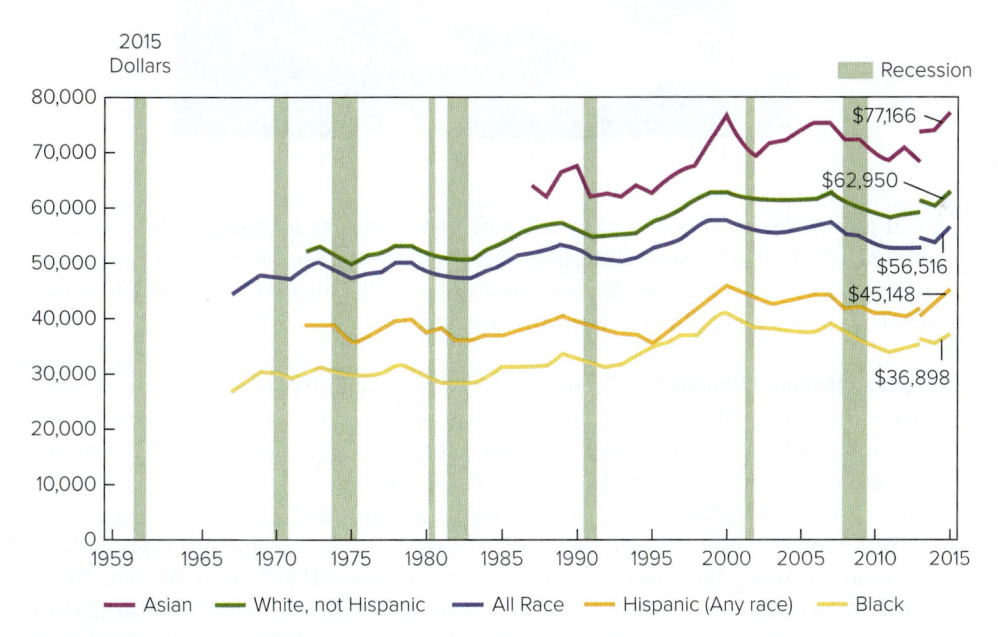

FIGURE 8.3
Household Income by Race and Hispanic Origin

Note: The data for 2013 and beyond reflect the implementation of the redesigned income questions. The data points are placed at the midpoints of the respective years. Median household income data are not available prior to 1967. For more information on recessions, see Appendix A. For more information on confidentiality protection, sampling error, nonsampling error, and definitions, see www2.census.gov/programs-surveys/cps/techdocs/cpsmar16.pdf

Source: Proctor, B. D., Semega, J. L., & Kollar, M., "Income and Poverty in the United States: 2015," U.S. Census Bureau, Current Population Reports, September 2016.

Although there is less gender segregation in the workplace than ever before, income differences between men and women still exist.
©Stuart Jenner/Shutterstock

It is important to note that the median household income increased by 5.2% between 2014 and 2015 (Proctor et al., 2016, September). During the same time period the poverty rate decreased by 1.2%. These changes indicate that families of all racial and ethnic groups are doing better financially after the 2007 recession.

Gender Income Differences. There is a large difference in the average income of males and females at all educational levels, with men making more than women at each level. According to Proctor et al. (2016, September) men, on average, earn $51,712 per year and women earn $40,742 per year. Therefore, women earn 80% of what men earn. The gap between men and women has not changed very much since 2007.

Education pays off financially as shown in Figure 8.4. As education increases for both males and females, their income progressively increases (U.S. Census Bureau, 2012). Individuals completing 9 years of schooling or less averaged $23,00, those with 9 to 12 years of schooling averaged $28,000, high school graduates averaged $38,000, and college graduates averaged $77,000. Individuals with professional degrees beyond college make even a larger increase in salary, some almost double those of a college graduate.

Education is also truly a great investment when you look at the total income individuals achieve in a lifetime of working full time. Individuals with a high school education earn about $1.2 million in a lifetime, while those with a college degree earn almost twice that amount, $2.1 million. Those with a master's degree earn about $2.5 million, with a doctorate (Ph.D. or Ed.D.) about $3.4 million, and with a professional degree (such as an M.D.), the total annual income is about $4.4 million over a lifetime.

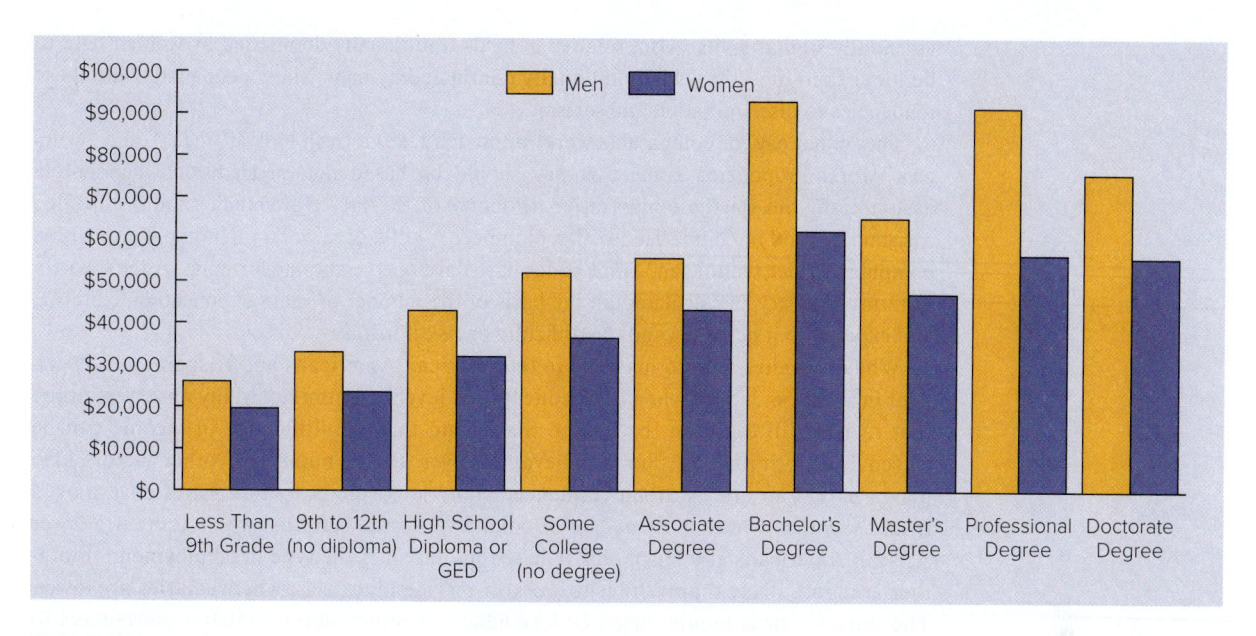

FIGURE 8.4
Median Earnings of Men and Women Age 18 and Older Who Work Full Time, Year Round by Educational Attainment
Source: U.S. Census Bureau, 2012.

Economists and other social observers cite a number of reasons for these income differences. Women often drop out of the labor force to have children and then stay at home to care for them for a few years. Meanwhile, men gain seniority in the labor force and get more job-related experience. Although it is illegal to pay women less for doing the same job, women have little legal recourse when they are paid lower wages for jobs that may require

As more women have joined the workforce and more families need two incomes to meet their expenses, debates have increased about the differences in salaries paid to men and women for similar kinds of work. If a female office assistant and a male computer technician, for example, have the same amount of education, experience, and job responsibility, why is the office assistant apt to be paid less?
©Eric Audras/Getty Images

essentially similar skills. Also, salaries in fields traditionally dominated by women tend to be lower than those in fields traditionally dominated by men. Many people attribute these tendencies to discrimination and sexism.

The "equal pay for comparable work" approach takes a fresh look at "men's" and "women's" work. Proponents argue that pay should be based not on traditional gender-role assumptions but on the comparative difficulty of the job. How much should an office assistant be paid in comparison with a plumber? A child care worker in comparison with a computer service technician? Some states have developed elaborate formulas. A job's worth, in terms of salary, is calculated on the basis of the number of years of education, training, and experience it demands and the difficulty or risk it involves.

Why do Whites tend to make more than African Americans and Hispanics, as is evident in Figure 8.3, even when their educational levels are similar? Many observers argue that racism still exists in the United States and that the difference in income can be traced to discrimination. Some believe, however, that a number of other factors also play a part. The first is urban residence. Many jobs sought by minorities have moved from the cities, where most people of color live, to the suburbs, where there are fewer African Americans and Hispanics. The second factor is the type of employment; minorities are more likely than Whites to work in service industries, where salaries are lower. The third factor is tenure; many college-educated minorities are relative newcomers to the labor market and have had less time than Whites to earn promotions and higher pay.

The controversy over the income gap between White males, females, and minorities in our country is not likely to end soon. The disparity in income between the haves and the have-nots is a problematic issue in a society where millions of people are living at or near the poverty level.

Does It Pay to Work Outside the Home?

One of the sobering facts of life for two-income families is that the second income often seems to disappear when the expenses associated with earning it are paid. A hypothetical example: Assume the second income in the family is a reasonably good one—$28,000 a year, or $2,333 a month. Each month, federal, state, and Social Security taxes could conceivably take about $942. Child care for two children under school age could easily take another $550 a month. Working

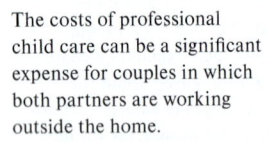

The costs of professional child care can be a significant expense for couples in which both partners are working outside the home.
©Image Source/Getty Images

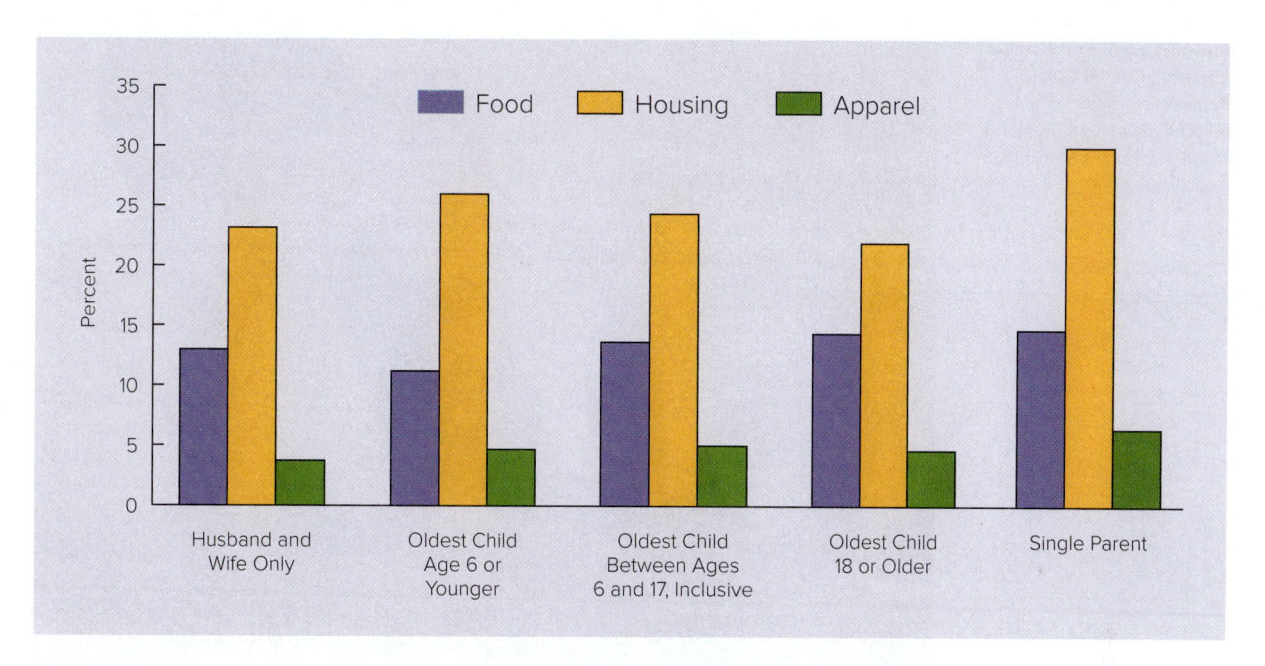

FIGURE 8.5
Annual Expenditures for Necessities
Source: U.S. Census Bureau, 2008.

outside the home also entails increases in clothing expenditures, say, $110 extra a month; personal-care and dry-cleaning bills may also go up an extra $45 a month. Lunch costs may rise about $110 monthly, and transportation to work could add at least $55 a month. After all is said and done, the $2,333 monthly salary is reduced to $521—about $3.25 an hour—in real income.

One woman who quit her $7-an-hour job in a family decision to rely solely on the husband's income said, "I had the feeling that all my money was going for clothes, lunch, and day care for my daughter." It is important to emphasize, however, that there are many reasons beyond financial ones for working outside the home, including personal and professional development, networking with others, and getting a break from child care at home. See Figure 8.5 for more information about expenses for necessities.

Smart Money Management

Managing money requires knowledge of how to budget, which is really how one manages expenses considering income, and to do this taking into account personal, couple, and family values. It also requires consideration of how two-income couples manage the different pots of money that they bring into the relationship. Smart money management also involves a plan for saving money for future needs, including unexpected crises.

Creating a Budget

Budgeting is the regular, systematic balancing of income and expenses. It is a personal system for making sure there is enough money to cover the essentials and, one hopes, a few extras.

To construct a workable budget, individuals need to examine their personal values about saving and spending; they must also have a good idea of what things really cost. To begin

Finances are one of the most stressful areas for couples because they reflect couples' power dynamics and values.
©Buccina Studios/Stockbyte/Getty Images

with, couples need to establish how much income they can count on. They should then outline their expenses by category: shelter, transportation, food, clothing, and so forth. After developing categories that reflect their particular circumstances, they must estimate how much money they will need to pay for each category.

Most people don't take the time to create a budget. An accurate budget requires that a couple or family record their expenses on a regular basis (for example, monthly) so they know how much they are spending in each category. At the end of the month, the couple can look at the recorded expenditures and develop a budget for the next month. Individuals usually find budgeting easier than families do because they don't need to negotiate decisions and work out priorities that are appropriate for the entire family.

Budgeting is a continuous process of assessment and adjustment. A good budget is simple, realistic, and clear. A good budget builds in some personal control for each family member. It also distinguishes between wants and needs, with needs given priority but a few wants satisfied if possible. A good budget treats credit as debt, not income. Charging something or deciding to pay for it "on time" creates a fixed expense that adds to a family's debt.

Pooling Money: Pros and Cons

Should two-income couples pool their money? This is a difficult question that partners have to answer together, and one they should discuss before marriage. Many newly married couples feel obligated to pool their money, believing that a refusal to do so might be interpreted as a lack of commitment. Married couples tend to favor pooling more than cohabiting couples, but those who remarry after divorce are more likely to maintain separate funds, perhaps because they worry about the permanence of the new relationship.

Pooling is simpler because there are fewer accounts to balance. But because each spouse must keep the other informed about financial transactions, pooling entails some loss of independence. If one partner forgets to record a check written on the joint account and causes an overdraft, a conflict is inevitable.

Another approach is to pool some of the money from each person to cover joint expenses and for each person to also keep a smaller but separate checking account and credit card. The problem with each individual having more freedom is when the total from the joint expenses and the two separate expenses cannot be paid.

In one study of 64 couples who had great marriages it was found that there was not a trend toward either joint or separate accounts (Skogrand et al., 2011). Although some couples had strong feelings about doing things one way or the other, it seemed most couples needed to work it out in a way that worked for them. This choice can depend upon many factors. For example, if couples marry late in life or are in a remarriage, they may want to continue to manage their own money rather than pooling their finances. If there is only one breadwinner in the family, it may make sense to pool their financial resources.

Credit: Uses and Abuses

There are both advantages and disadvantages to using credit. Buying on credit is easy, but it is important not to overdo it. Excessive debt can result in bankruptcy. Financial counseling can help those who have gotten into problems with credit.

Credit Cards—Dangerous Plastic

Having a credit card, actually several cards, has become the norm for most adults and with it has come credit card debt. The average credit card balance for the typical American household is $6,885, with average household credit card interest totaling more than $1,200 per year (El Issa, 2016). The amount of credit card debt actually decreased in recent years as people experienced the recession; however, it is now near the amount before the 2007 recession. It may be that people are being careful about incurring debt with the economy being so uncertain. About two-thirds of families carry a monthly balance and the interest rate ranges from 15% to over 20%. It would seem that if one has higher income they would have lower credit card debt, but this is not true. According to El Issa (2016), as income rises so does credit card spending. However, the percentage of credit card debt for lower income families is a higher percentage of total income than it is for higher income families. These plastic cards are creating a society where having a savings account is rare compared to having credit card debt.

College students are now offered "interest-free" credit cards with unspecified spending limits and these cards are very easy to obtain. College campuses are flooded with a large variety of credit cards that students can sign up to use. Unfortunately, it is too easy to spend money and abuse these cards, and most students find themselves having credit card debt. A common sign of financial problems is when people sign up for additional credit cards, which they use to pay off past credit card debt. (See Box 8.4.) A credit card bill enacted in 2009 did limit approval of credit cards for those under 21 years of age without a cosigner or proof of income to pay the bills (Gonzalez & Holmes, n.d.).

BOX 8.4 At Issue

Debt in the United States

Debt for families in the United States has increased in recent years. Even with the recession of 2007, which served as a warning to reduce debt because we do not know about future job loss or income reduction, we continue to go into debt. According to Dean, Joo, Gudmunson, Fischer, and Lambert (2013), we have become a culture where debt is seen as something we are entitled to, and avoiding debt is not a priority. Debt can escalate to the point of no return. Having accounts past due or spending over the credit card limit are often followed by becoming delinquent on other bills or filing for bankruptcy.

According to Dean et al. (2013), there are trends when it comes to those who get themselves into serious debt. They are more likely to be poor, have less education, and have higher risk tolerance. These authors indicate that financial problems are usually not because of money problems but, instead, are about how individuals view money. For example, money problems may result from trying to keep up with others around them, or they spend money to feel good about themselves.

Dean et al. (2013) conducted a study to find out if credit card debt was related to other forms of consumer debt. They found that negative credit card behavior was, in fact, an indication that these folks would also have difficulties with automobile debt, installment debt, and personal loan debt such as educational debt. Those who had no credit card debt were likely to have no other forms of debt. The person's gender or race did not predict the extent of individual debt. As these authors indicate, "debt begets debt" (p. 72). Additionally, not carrying a credit card balance was associated with financial well-being. It is also important to note that the level of income in this study was not associated with the extent of debt individuals had.

According to one study by Hancock, Jorgensen, and Swanson (2013), college students were more likely to have $500 or more in credit card debt if they had two or more credit cards and had parents who argued about finances. It is important to note that there are many factors that can enter into the accumulation of debt, including the behaviors of parents.

It is important to know that having a credit card is not problematic if balances are paid off each month. Some tips

---

Just paying the minimum amount on a credit card can be very costly. Let us assume that the interest rate is about 17%, which is about the average rate on most credit cards. If you had a monthly balance of only $1,000, it would cost you $2,590 and 17 years to pay off the balance. If you had a monthly balance of $2,500, your total cost would be $7,734, and with a monthly balance of $5,000, the total cost you would pay over 40 years would be $16,305. So the goal should be to pay off your credit card balance every month; otherwise, you will be in a difficult financial position very quickly, which will be hard to resolve. In a recent study by Lucia Dunn (*Chicago Tribune*, 2013), it was found that debt increases at younger ages, peaks when people are in their middle years of life, and tapers off at old age. Younger people not only have more debt, they also pay off their credit cards more slowly than older adults. These differences make sense in that older adults are likely to be living on a fixed income and they cannot assume they can pay off high credit card debt in the future.

Purchasing a Home

The family dwelling has psychological significance in virtually all cultures. It provides the family's space and binds them together as a unit. It can be a haven, a place of rest and enjoyment, somewhere to kick off one's shoes and escape the pretenses of polite society.

A home is usually the most expensive item Americans buy. Careful deliberation should go into its purchase. One rule of thumb is that, whether renting or buying, a family should spend no more than 1 week's take-home pay per month for housing expenses. Housing expenses are either rent or the total of all housepayment expenses (mortgage payment, insurance, and real estate taxes). One expense that many people do not consider in owning a home is maintenance (Moore, 2015). Families who can find adequate shelter for 20% to 25%

which can be helpful in applying for and using a credit card are listed below.

- Make sure you're ready to handle your own finances. Track spending and learn how money is being spent. A credit card may be the next step and a convenient way to manage monthly expenses.
- Get a secured card or a debit card. A secured card requires a security deposit of a certain dollar amount, and that is your credit limit (which can be as low as $200 to $500). A debit card is linked to your checking account balance, so you can't overspend easily.
- Compare rates and fees before you sign up for any card. You can go to web sites like www.bankrate.com to make comparisons.
- When comparing rates, look for details like annual fees, late fees, and charges for cash advances.
- Be sure to read the fine print of any credit card offer. Some cards offer a "teaser rate," which is an initial low interest rate that increases sharply after only a few months.
- Negotiate lower rates. Call the credit card company and ask for a lower rate. Companies are competitive, and if you have a good credit history, the company may give it to you.
- Pay your bills on time. Finance charges and late fees quickly add up to much more than the cost of the original product or service.
- Visit the Federal Trade Commission web site at either www.ftc.gov or www.consumer.gov for free information on dozens of topics relating to credit cards.

It is important to remember that being in debt at a young age can impact what happens as one gets older (Dean et al., 2013). If a family is constantly paying high interest rates on consumer debt, they are less likely to be able to invest money in things that are long lasting, such as a home or retirement. Financial counseling can be a valuable resource for those who feel they are constantly trying to catch up with bills.

Buying a home is an important aspect of family life. A home can be a great unifying benefit for families and can also be a major cost.
©Ryan McVay/Getty Images

of their take-home pay are likely to be in relatively good financial health. Unfortunately, many families find themselves paying 50% of their income or more for housing.

Renting versus Buying. Generally speaking, it is wiser to buy a home than to rent. Rent money is gone forever, whereas each mortgage payment gradually increases one's equity in the home and inflation increases the net worth of the dwelling. There are, however, many exceptions to this generalization, and families must carefully analyze their unique financial situation to decide if buying a home is the right choice for them. The recent housing crises have taught us that we can sometimes buy a house at a high dollar figure, only to have the home drop in value. The values of homes have stayed low in many areas of the country as a result of the housing crises, which causes problems for people who want to relocate. They find their home is not worth as much as they owe. To sell the house they would need to pay the lender an additional amount when they sell. We call this "being under water." Therefore, owning a home has not been as appealing as it once was, since we are not sure if housing values will continue to decline or if they are on their way up.

There are numerous advantages to both renting and buying. The advantages of renting include mobility, perhaps some amenities (pool, tennis courts, party rooms, laundry facilities), and a lifestyle that involves fewer responsibilities. No large down payment is needed (only a security deposit), and the relatively fixed housing expenditure (rent) makes budgeting easier.

The advantages of buying include pride of ownership, a better credit rating, and a monthly payment that remains constant for many years (that is, with a fixed-rate mortgage). The federal income tax deductions for mortgage interest and real estate property taxes are a major advantage, as is the potential for the home to increase in value over time. Owning a house forces one to save; each payment represents an asset that is growing in value. A homeowner can also borrow against equity as the value of the home increases. Furthermore, owners can make home improvements and alterations, which can increase the value of the home and/or add to the enjoyment of the dwelling.

The disadvantages of renting are that it offers no tax deductions and no potential gain from the rising value of the property. Furthermore, rents rise with inflation, and many rental units have restrictions on noise level, pet ownership, and children. One disadvantage of buying is the substantial down payment that is needed; this can reduce available funds for other things. Also, the cost of maintenance and repairs can be high. A home is a big commitment in time, emotion, and money.

The Cost of Home Loans. The average interest rate in 2016 for a 30-year home mortgage was only about 4.0%, a drop from about 10% to 11% in 2000. This drop has greatly increased the number of people purchasing homes. The savings on a loan with 4.5% interest versus 10% is substantial over the life of the loan, which is typically 15 to 30 years. Even 1% interest difference makes a difference in the interest for the lifetime of the loan. For example, a $200,000 mortgage over 30 years at 4.5% interest will result in a monthly payment of $1,013, not including taxes and insurance. If, instead, the interest rate is 6.5%, the monthly payment is $1,264. Over the lifetime of a 30-year loan, this is a substantial amount of money. At 4.5%, the total cost of the home including mortgage amount plus interest is $365,000. At 6.5%, the total cost of the mortgage amount plus interest is $455,000. Therefore, the interest rate is an important component to consider in purchasing a home. Therefore, it is clear that the low interest rates currently should mean people would be buying homes, and they are. The mortgage crises, however, have made qualifying for home loans more difficult. Buyers need more money down and higher credit scores to qualify for a loan than was true in the past.

Avoiding Debt and Bankruptcy

Bankruptcy is a legal term indicating that a person is financially insolvent and unable to pay her or his debts. In 2011, more than 1.3 million people declared personal bankruptcy in the United States, and about 35,000 businesses filed for bankruptcy (United States Courts, n.d.). That number has decreased somewhat in 2015 to less than one million people declaring bankruptcy. Although bankruptcy offers some protection from creditors, it is not a solution to financial problems because bankruptcy blemishes one's financial record for many years, making many financial matters more difficult. In our society bankruptcy signifies an individual's inability to handle money wisely, and society exacts various punishments on those who declare bankruptcy.

To stay out of debt and avoid bankruptcy, it is helpful to know why some people assume too much debt. It is interesting that level of income is not clearly related to debt. Debt-free families and debt-ridden families alike come from all socioeconomic levels.

Excessive debt may be due to any or all of the following reasons: credit spending, crisis spending, careless or impulsive spending, and compulsive spending. Unwise *credit spending* can lead to overextension. *Crisis spending*—resulting from unexpected events in life such as unemployment, uninsured illness, and business income decline or failure—can throw personal finances into turmoil. *Careless or impulsive spending* includes overpaying for items that could be purchased for less, purchasing inferior merchandise that does not last, and buying things one does not really need. *Compulsive spending* occurs because some people simply can't say no to salespeople or because they have an uncontrollable impulse to acquire material things.

Fortunately, there are a number of time-tested strategies for families who have become overextended. Although these solutions are not easy, they are far better than the alternative of bankruptcy:

- Develop and stick to a balanced budget.
- Avoid making any new financial commitments. Do not incur any new debt.
- Destroy all credit cards or lock them up so that they can't be used.
- Develop a plan for repaying all debts. If the budget cannot handle the repayment schedule, try to negotiate lower payments and lower payback periods.
- Pay off debts with the highest interest rates first.
- Work to reduce the total number of debts.
- Make a plan to pay at least a small amount on each debt each month.
- Avoid debt consolidation loans. These can set the stage for new borrowing, especially on credit cards.

Not only does moving toward and experiencing bankruptcy affect one's financial record, it also creates enormous stress for individuals, couples, and families. One study (Thorne, 2010) indicated that as couples moved toward bankruptcy, being in charge of finances meant not only paying the bills, but also increased work on the part of the bill payer. The work involved micromanaging of all debt and spending, dealing with bill collectors, and filing for bankruptcy. In the Thorne study, this work was typically done by wives rather than husbands. Thorne speculates, based upon other research, that marriage relationships are strained and power struggles about spending ensue. Whenever there is financial strain, time spent on finances can take away from other positive interactions in the couple and family relationships.

Financial Counseling

If individuals are overextended and they have made no progress in dealing with their debt in 3 to 6 months, they should seek financial counseling. Many large employers have budget counselors available through the human resources department or an employee assistance program. When financial difficulties are a symptom of a deeper marital or personal problem (alcohol or other drug abuse, depression, violence), a therapist may be the best way to approach the crisis.

For example, a single parent continues to support her 25-year-old son, even though his cocaine addiction is dragging her down financially. The son deals cocaine to come up with some of the $3,000 or $4,000 a month he needs to support his drug habit. He regularly borrows money from his mother and even steals and pawns her possessions. Consumed by guilt, she covers up for him, pays the bills, and lends him money, denying his drug habit. This mother needs not only a competent financial adviser to help her deal with the mountain of debts she has accumulated but also a personal therapist to help her come to grips with her son's drug problem, for which he must take responsibility.

People seeking financial counseling should avoid "credit clinics," which charge fees of $250 to $2,000 or more for their services. Some of these businesses advertise that they will negotiate new repayment schedules with creditors, but people in financial trouble can work directly with their creditors or can find help from nonprofit personal counseling organizations. Another possible resource is the network of more than 1,000 Consumer Credit Counseling Service (CCCS) agencies across the United States. Each year about a million people seek credit and budget counseling advice from CCCS.

Summary

- Studies about economic issues and family are relatively new. These studies often draw on different disciplines and involve researchers from different disciplines.
- There are studies that show that happiness and money often go together. However, we do not know if one causes the other. It may be that things that go along with having money make the difference, such as health, less stress, or having more choices.
- Giving financial resources to others increases happiness and well-being. These findings were true internationally in a study that included both rich and poor countries.
- According to a national survey of married couples, happy couples—as compared to unhappy couples—agree on how to spend money, have no concerns about how the partner spends money, are satisfied with decisions about savings, major debts are not a problem, and financial decisions are not difficult.
- Numerous recent studies indicate that marital happiness and money are related. One national study showed that couples with great marriages had little or no debt and lived within their means.
- It has been suggested that financial counselors and family life educators work together to help couples address both marriage issues and financial issues.
- It is not only money in general that causes difficulties for couples but debt in particular that causes stress. Research shows that as debt goes down, marital satisfaction increases. It is suggested that debt affects both the amount of quality time a couple has and also how they spend that time.
- People manage their economic resources in different ways, depending on their worldviews, life experiences, and family structures.
- Although couples often think that things will get better after a divorce, divorce is financially costly, and couples need to be aware of those potential costs as they contemplate this important life decision.
- White families in the United States make more money, on average, than Hispanic and African American families. Asian families have the highest median income. Males make more money than females, and there is a clear relationship between educational level and income.
- Budgeting is the regular, systematic balancing of income and expenses. To budget successfully, individuals need to examine their personal values about saving and spending and to monitor their plan monthly.
- Couples who pool their money are neither more nor less satisfied with money management issues in the relationship than couples who have separate accounts.
- Credit cards are not bad if bills are paid off each month. It is important to pay attention to all aspects of a credit card, including annual fees, monthly payments, late fees, and interest rates.

Key Terms

- goals
- prosocial spending
- collective worldview
- individualistic worldview
- budgeting
- bankruptcy

Activities

1. Write a few paragraphs describing how money was handled in your family of origin and how you handle money today. Then form groups of five or six for discussion. After having read the essays out loud, identify similarities and differences that emerge.
2. Think about a time that you spent money on others rather than yourself. How did it feel? Ask a family member or a friend how they felt when they gave to others rather than spending money on themselves. Were these answers surprising?
3. Think about the relationship between money and happiness in your life. Are there times when you have been very happy and you believe it was because of money? Are there times when you have been very happy and you feel money had nothing to do with it? Based upon what you have learned in this chapter and what you know about life, what advice would you give to your child about money and happiness?
4. Did the economic recession of 2007 affect you or your family? What happened? If you were too young to remember when it happened, ask someone older what her or his experience was like. Was there job loss? How did economic uncertainty affect yourself or someone else?
5. Keep track of your spending for 1 month. Write down everything you spend, including for small items such as snacks, newspapers, or bus fare. At the end of the month, evaluate your spending. Are you spending money in a way that reflects your values and what's important to you? If not, how would you change your spending?
6. Pair off into "couples" and discuss the following questions as if you were planning to marry. Then report your discussions to the class.
   a. Do you expect to share equally in financial decisions? If not, how do you plan to make financial decisions?
   b. Do you plan to use a budget? Why or why not?
   c. How do you feel about each partner's having a personal allowance for which he or she is not accountable to the other?
   d. How do you feel about buying small items on credit? Large items?
   e. Who will be the treasurer? The check writer? The bookkeeper? The investor?

Suggested Readings

Bailey, M. J., & Danziger, S. (2013). *Legacies of the war on poverty*. New York, NY: Russell Sage Foundation.

Desmond, M. (2016). *Evicted*. New York, NY: Crown Publishers.

Dew, J., Britt, S., & Huston, S. (2012). Examining the relationship between financial issues and divorce. *Family Relations*, *61*, 615–628.

Giving USA. (2015, June 29). Giving USA: *Americans donated an estimated $358.38 billion to charity in 2014: Highest total in report's 60-year history*. Web site: https://givingusa.org/giving-usa-2015-press-release-giving-usa-americans-donated-an-estimated-358-38-billion-to-charity-in-2014-highest-total-in-reports-60-year-history/.

Gonzalez, J., & Holmes, T. (n.d.). *Credit card debt statistics*. CreditCards.com. Web site: http://www.creditcards.com/credit-card-news/credit-card-debt-statistics-1276.php.

Healey, J. F., & O'Brien, E. (2015). *Race, ethnicity, gender, and class* (7th ed.). Thousand Oaks, CA: Sage Publications.

Proctor, B. D., Semega, J. L., & Kollar, M. (2016, September). *Income and poverty in the United States: 2015*. U.S. Census Bureau, Current Population Reports. Web site: https://www.census.gov/content/dam/Census/library/publications/2016/demo/p60-256.pdf.

Schramm, D. G. (2006). Individual and social costs of divorce in Utah. *Journal of Family and Economic Issues*, *27*, 133–151.

Skogrand, L., Schramm, D. G., Marshall, J. P., & Lee, T. (2005). The effects of debt on newlyweds and implications for education. *Journal of Extension*, *43*. Web site: http://www.joe.org/joe/2005june/rb7.shtml.

Xiao, J. J. (Ed.). (2008). *Handbook of consumer finance research*. New York, NY: Springer.

Visit the text-specific Online Learning Center at **www.mhhe.com/olson9e** for practice tests, chapter summaries, and PowerPoint slides.

Design Element: © Alicia Grünkind/EyeEm/Getty Images

PART THREE
Stages of Intimate Relationships

9 Friendship, Love, Intimacy, and Singlehood

©Carlos Enrique Santa Maria/123RF

Friends Versus Lovers

Exploring Intimacy: From Experience to Relationship

Developing Intimacy in Couple Relationships

Intimacy Games

Attachment Theory and Intimacy

Being Single

Summary

Key Terms

Activities

Suggested Readings

What is love? How do we develop genuinely intimate relationships? In this chapter we will explore various ways of defining love and the related concept of intimacy. We will also identify a number of constructive and destructive games people play in their intimate relationships. The goal of this chapter is to help you understand love and intimacy and learn how to enhance your own intimate experiences and relationships.

Love and friendship bind society together, providing both emotional support and a buffer against stress and thereby preserving our physical and psychological health. Love is clearly much more than friendship, and thus we treat love relationships more seriously. However, the strongest love relationships have roots in friendship. Satisfying and stable love relationships come from shared interests and values. When friends fall in love, they are adding passion to the emotional intimacy we call friendship.

Love means different things to different people. Definitions of love are almost endless (Table 9.1). No other topic demands so much attention and generates so much confusion in our society. We cannot go online, turn on the radio or TV, pick up a magazine or book, or converse with a friend for long without being confronted with words about love, thoughts of love, acts of love, or images of love. Despite the ubiquitous nature of love, it remains a mystery to many. Many regard it as a strange force that can overpower us and at times take control over our lives: People speak of being "under love's spell" or being "swept away" with passion. New scientific research has identified where love is located in the brain. These findings help us understand new love, sex drive, and couple attachment.

Finding a partner in some ways works differently today than in the past. People are using the internet more than ever before in their quest to find partners and develop intimate relationships. The internet can be a useful and efficient way to identify people who have similar interests and goals in life, though it comes with some risks. And, as we will see later in this chapter, research indicates that only a very small percentage of people who are married or in a committed relationship actually met online. And, even though most people still want to marry sometime, singlehood is more prevalent today than in the past. Some are very content to be single and take advantage of the multiple opportunities for education and career opportunities.

This chapter reminds us that many aspects of friendship, intimacy, and singlehood have not changed over the years. There are also many ways in which they look very different today, and these are likely to continue to emerge and develop as aspects of society change.

Friends Versus Lovers

Friendship and love are alike in many ways. In fact, if we regularly treated our marriage partners like our best friends, we might have better relationships. There are, however, crucial differences between lovers and friends.

Love, in short, runs deeper and stronger than friendship. And because the stakes are so high with love, the possibility of interpersonal difficulties increases, and we jealously guard this important relationship.

The Fabric of Friendship

When it comes to friendship, we can assume that two individuals participate in a reciprocal relationship as equals (Davis, 2004, 2014). The fabric of friendship includes eight important elements:

- *Enjoyment.* Friends enjoy each other's company most of the time, although disagreements and friction occasionally occur.
- *Acceptance.* Friends accept each other for who they are and don't try to change each other.

TABLE 9.1 On Love

Seize the moments of happiness, love and be loved! That is the only reality in the world, all else is folly.
—LEO TOLSTOY, *Writer and Philosopher*

In love the paradox occurs that two beings become one yet remain two.
—ERICH FROMM, *Psychiatrist*

Love doesn't just sit there, like a stone, it has to be made, like bread; remade all the time, made new.
—URSULA K. LE GUIN, *Writer*

Being in love isn't ever really loving, it's just wanting. And it isn't any good. It's all aching and misery.
—JAMES LEO HERLIHY, *Writer*

Love is the history of a woman's life; it is an episode in man's.
—MADAME DE STAËL, *Writer*

He who knows nothing, loves nothing . . . But he who understands also loves, notices, sees . . . The more knowledge is inherent in a thing, the greater the love.
—PARACELSUS, *Philosopher*

The trouble with some women is that they get all excited about nothing—and then marry him.
—CHER, *Actor*

When the satisfaction or the security of another person becomes as significant to one as is one's own security, then the state of love exists.
—HARRY STACK SULLIVAN, *Psychiatrist*

Chains do not hold a marriage together. It is threads, hundreds of tiny threads which sew people together through the years. This is what makes a marriage last—more than passion or even sex!
—SIMONE SIGNORET, *Actor*

Love is a state of perpetual anesthesia.
—H.L. MENCKEN, *Journalist*

There is only one happiness in life, to love and be loved.
—GEORGE SAND, *Writer*

To act intentionally, in sympathetic response to others (including God) to promote overall well-being.
—THOMAS J. OORD, *Scholar*

For one human being to love another is perhaps the most difficult task of all, the epitome, the ultimate cost. It is that striving for which all other striving is merely preparation.
—RAINIER MARIA RILKE, *Poet*

Happiness is love.
—GEORGE VAILLANT, *Psychiatrist*

- *Trust.* Friends assume that they will act in each other's best interest. "Even when he's hassling me, I know it's for my own good." "She would never intentionally hurt me, except in a fit of extreme anger."
- *Respect.* Friends respect each other; they assume the other has good judgment in making choices in life.
- *Mutual assistance.* Friends help and support each other; they can count on each other in times of need.
- *Confiding.* Friends share life experiences and feelings with each other.
- *Understanding.* Friends know each other's values and understand what is important to each other. "I know what makes her tick."
- *Spontaneity.* Friends feel free to be "real" around each other. They don't feel they have to play a role or hold back their true feelings.

According to Goodwin (2009), modern-day friendships have changed somewhat. Because of increased geographical and social mobility, friendships may emerge as people move to new situations, rather than being long lasting. There has also been a change from the acceptability of friendships being same sex to friends being from the different sex. The internet, texting, and other modern forms of communication have also affected how we communicate as well as our ability to maintain friendships around the world, if we choose to. Goodwin indicates that the result is that friendships can be somewhat superficial because we do not always maintain intimate relationships with friends.

Goodwin (2009) notes that culture affects how we develop and maintain friendships. For example, in ethnic groups in the United States and around the world, collectivist cultures typically value the group more than the individual. Therefore, friendships may be more important than and look different in individualist cultures. Also, where family is highly valued, friendships may be focused on family members rather than people outside the family. In individualistic cultures, friendships may be less important in general, and individuals may spend more time alone.

Immigrants may also have unique friendship patterns (Goodwin, 2009). For example, friendships for immigrants initially could focus on those who meet certain needs as people transition to a new country. We know that immigrants often relocate in geographical centers with others who came from the same country. Therefore, friendships may develop with people who have the same ethnic values and can provide social support. (See also Goodwin, 2016.)

The Tapestry of Love

Love is magical, changing, fragile, complex, and paradoxical. Amy and David Olson (2001) describe 10 traits of love that are common in our culture (Box 9.1). There are so many ways to think about love, and this has changed over time and has cultural impacts.

It is assumed that romantic love exists in all cultures (Goodwin, 2009). However, historically, love was not as important in romantic relationships and marriages, and relationships

William Adolphe Bouguereau, *Return of Spring* (*Le Printemps*), 1886. As artists have known for countless generations, love is magical, changing, fragile, complex, and paradoxical.
©The J. Paul Getty Museum/ Digital image courtesy of the Getty's Open Content Program

BOX 9.1 Putting It Together
Ten Traits of Love

These 10 characteristics of love are common in our culture, and knowing about them can help you become more realistic about the complexity of love.

1. **Love is often confused by chemistry.** People often claim to be in "love" when they experience a physical attraction to someone. There are many theories as to why people experience attraction in the first place. Attraction may be biologically/evolutionarily driven where we instinctively choose mates who will ensure survival of the species. Under this theory, men with overt alpha male characteristics and women whose vitality and health indicate she will bear children will be attractive. The social exchange theory says we choose mates whom we see as our equals, not only in terms of physical traits but things such as social status, intelligence, creativity, and so forth. The persona theory is such that a mate is determined by the degree to which he or she raises our self-esteem, including any pride or embarrassment we may attach to how we believe others perceive us in relation to our partner. To further complicate love, attraction releases chemicals from the human brain and these chemicals create a rush of euphoria lasting from between 6 months to 3 years, which can lead to the next trait.

2. **"Love" is often blind.** Studies show that the early stage of love (the attraction stage) changes the way we think. We can't help this as the brain is triggered to release chemicals and these chemicals make us feel energized (physically and emotionally), causing, among other things, an increased experience of joy and sociability and a decrease in appetite. The feeling of "floating on air" and excitement this brings also causes new couples to idealize their partners, seeing only their positive traits and not their flaws. This can make for a fun experience but not a very realistic and lasting one. It turns out that the human brain plays a vital role in the saying, "love is blind." This is one of the reasons why it is important for people to consider the input from family and from close friends about a potential date as they are often better able to "see" the other person with more objectivity.

3. **"Love" changes over time.** The beginning stages of romantic relationships are typically not very realistic due largely, perhaps, to brain chemistry. Some people find it difficult to sustain a long-term relationship because they become almost addicted to the rush of chemicals associated with the infatuation stage of a relationship. They become serial daters, moving from one partner to another once these chemicals subside (every 6 months to 3 years) in order to maintain this feeling of excitement. But over time if couples remain together upon finding their circumstances, personalities, and many other variables to be compatible, they move to "attachment," which is associated with a different set of brain chemicals. Attachment has been linked to chemicals known as endorphins that produce feelings of comfort and tranquility.

---

were often arranged or based upon economic considerations. For example, an 86-year-old woman describes her decision to get married some 68 years ago:

> "Paul and I grew up two miles apart in a rural, farming community in central Minnesota. We both grew up on farms, and farming was all we knew as a profession. We had known each other all our lives through church and school. Dating in those days was a challenge because everyone was related to everyone else. We had to find someone to date that was not a relative.
>
> "We were dating, but had not talked about marriage. Then a cash-crop farm became available for rent. Renting a farm in those days meant you gave half the income from the farm to the person who owned the land. It was really a 'share cropper'-type of arrangement, but we didn't call it that. Since those farms did not become available often, we thought we better get married and rent the farm. It was within a mile of each of our families, so we would have support from them. We eventually bought our own farm.
>
> "It wasn't that we weren't in love, because we probably were when we got married. However, love wasn't the deciding factor in our decision to marry, it was the availability of a farm to rent. In those days, coming out of the recession, we had to make practical decisions. We had to have a means of livelihood. We were married 56 years until Paul died, we raised four children, and had 13 grandchildren. I would definitely say love developed and we had a good life together."

In most countries around the world, arranged marriages are no longer the norm; however, there are many cultures that still seek family consent in marriage decisions (Goodwin, 2009). Therefore, love and romance are becoming more important in couple and marriage relationships.

238   Part III   Stages of Intimate Relationships

4. **Love-based marriages are more fragile than arranged marriages.** Because "love" is often confused with the chemicals of attraction, and arranged-marriages emphasize family and stability, divorce rates are very low (less than 4%) among arranged marriages. Other possible factors affecting the low divorce rates of arranged marriages may be that they occur in traditional cultures with a more practical view of marriage compared to the romanticized views of marriage in the United States.
5. **Love is not a feeling.** Love is often referred to as a feeling, but feelings are transient and ever changing. Joy and good feelings are one of the by-products of love, not love itself. Love needs no specific object to receive it, although love is often talked about in the context of an object, such as "I love my dog."
6. **Real love grows over time while superficial love will fade.** With real love, the positive feelings grow with time. With superficial love, the best feelings are usually at the beginning of the relationship. Over time, these feelings fade and the relationship dissolves as well. Real love realizes that love does not just "happen" but takes time, effort, and commitment to build.
7. **Our language for love is inadequate.** We are limited by the language we have to describe love. Love is much more complex than what we often express. Can we possibly be expressing the same idea when we say, "I love pizza," "I love football," and "I love you"? Similarly, while Eskimos have many different words to describe what we simply call "snow," we basically have one word to describe love. This vocabulary restraint gives limit to something infinite and beyond definition.
8. **Love is often "misdiagnosed."** Along the same lines as the language barrier in describing love is a common misdiagnosis of love. People often make the mistake of using the word "love" when what they are really describing is passion, excitement, enjoyment, or need. Or people profess to love a person but only when that person is doing what the individual wants. Real love is caring for the happiness of another person without any thought of what we might get in return.
9. **Love is paradoxical.** The "love" we throw around in our language system is paradoxical. We are told that love can conquer everything, yet it often does not. We are told that love is eternal, yet couples who claim to be in love later claim they have "fallen out of love." In a relationship, love may help get it started but it is not enough to make the relationship last.
10. **Giving love is receiving love.** You must give love to receive love. In fact, love is unique in that the more you give, the more you will have to give and the more you will receive.

Source: Olson, A., & Olson, D. H. (2001). "Ten Traits of Love." Levine, J. R. & Markman, H. J. (Eds.), *Why Do Fools Fall in Love? Experiencing the Magic, Mystery, and Meaning of Successful Relationships.* San Francisco, CA: Jossey-Bass, 2001.

The Love Triangle

Although the phrase *love triangle* usually brings to mind a relationship in which one person has two lovers, another sort of love triangle was developed by Sternberg and his colleagues (Sternberg, 2006, 2013a, 2013b; Sternberg & Weis, 2008). The three dimensions of the triangle are decision and commitment (the cognitive component), intimacy (the emotional component), and passion (the motivational component).

A relationship can start off with intimacy (friendship) and develop into love. A relationship can also start off with only passion and later develop the other two components. A relationship (such as an arranged marriage) can also begin simply with a commitment

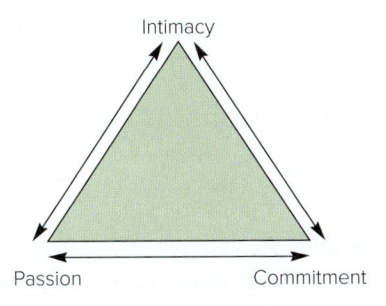

There are three dimensions to the love triangle.
R. J. Sternberg (2006). A duplex theory of love. In R. J. Sternberg & K. Weis (Eds.), *The new psychology of love* (pp. 184–199). New Haven, CT: Yale University Press. Reprinted with permission.

Chapter 9 | Friendship, Love, Intimacy, and Singlehood

between partners for economic reasons or for reasons dictated by the couple's families; even this type of relationship can later develop intimacy and passion and bloom into love.

Commitment is a cognitive attachment to another person. It develops over time, beginning slowly and increasing at a faster rate if the relationship is positive. If the relationship fails, commitment disappears. People express commitment when they move their relationship to a more advanced stage (from dating to engagement, from engagement to marriage), when they are faithful, or when they stay in the relationship during difficult times.

Intimacy involves sharing feelings and providing emotional support. It usually entails high levels of self-disclosure, the sharing of personal information not ordinarily revealed because of the risk involved. Intimacy gradually increases as closeness grows and deepens as a relationship matures. Few couples are likely to share everything with each other. People need some private space, a bit of their world that is closed to everyone else. But in a mature intimate relationship, most areas are open for discussion and sharing. By opening up, by earning each other's trust and becoming vulnerable to each other, people can build a strong emotional bond of intimacy. The paradox is that by expressing feelings of weakness and vulnerability, individuals can gain support and strength from trusted loved ones.

Passion is usually expressed by touching, kissing, and being affectionate, which are linked to physiological arousal; it is also expressed through sexual interactions. Because of its intensity, passion develops quickly but can also fade quickly. Passion is like an addiction; when it ends, a person can experience withdrawal symptoms such as irritability and depression.

Combining the three dimensions of love in various ways, Sternberg identified eight types of love relationships: non-love, liking, infatuation, empty love, romantic love, fatuous love, companionate love, and consummate love. **Non-love** occurs when there is no commitment, intimacy, or passion. **Liking** begins when there is just intimacy, but no passion or commitment. **Infatuation** involves passion only. In **empty love** there is commitment but no passion or intimacy. **Romantic love** has both intimacy and passion, but it is lacking in commitment. **Fatuous love** occurs when a couple is committed on the basis of passion but has not had the time to develop true intimacy. (For example, two people fall in love and, after seeing each other only on weekends for 2 months, get married.) **Companionate love** is more characteristic of couples who have been married for years. These couples have both commitment and intimacy, but they lack the passion they had when they were first married. Finally, **consummate love** is complete love, containing all three dimensions. It is the goal of most couples.

Most people have experienced several of these types of love and can recognize that each of them feels rather different. Even within one relationship, it is possible to experience two or more types of love over time. A couple, for example, may start out as close friends (liking) and then 2 years later become sexually involved (romantic love); a year later they may decide to live together (consummate love). However, 3 months later he has an affair; she finds out about it and moves out, ending the relationship (non-love).

A further description about what happens to one's brain chemistry is provided in Box 9.2. Science provides another description of how we physically respond in a new relationship.

Jealousy: A Green-Eyed Monster or Real Love?

He that is not jealous is not in love.

—Saint Augustine

Love, jealousy, and abuse are all interconnected (McGinley & Sabbadini, 2006; Puente & Cohen, 2003; Seidman, 2014). **Jealousy** is defined as an emotional response to a real or

BOX 9.2   At Issue
Love and Science

What, precisely, is this thing called love? Helen E. Fisher has been studying the phenomenon for much of her career (Fisher, 2010, 2016). Working with a team of researchers, Fisher has provided a description of the chemical changes that happen when people fall in love, and the chemical changes that follow when couples settle into the more mundane life when passion ends. We all go through it, and when it happens we ask ourselves, "What happened?" (Fisher, Aron, & Brown, 2006; Fisher, Brown, Aron, Strong, & Mashek, 2010).

In one groundbreaking study using MRI technology, the research team looked at the brains of 17 people who were intensely "in love" as these subjects looked at pictures of their loved one. Fisher's research team found that a part of the brain activates dopamine receptors. Dopamine creates intense energy, focused attention, obsessive following, and exhilaration. It allows one to focus attention and creates a motivation to get rewarded. The researchers explained that this process is a brain mechanism for courtship and is true of all humans; and it is comparable to what we see in mate selection for animals (Fisher et al., 2006).

It is also interesting to note that the serotonin levels in the blood of subjects who are in love are at levels similar to those in people who have an obsessive-compulsive disorder (Slater, 2006). Therefore, one can conclude that love and obsessive-compulsive disorder have similar chemical characteristics and that love and mental illness may be very similar. This author suggests that the use of some mental health medicines, such as those used for obsessive-compulsive behavior, may be useful for treating mental health but may also be jeopardizing a person's ability to fall in love. The medicine does not allow the dopamine receptors to respond and, thus, keeps romantic love from sweeping one away.

Fisher et al., (2006) also indicate that the brain response in new love relationships is different and longer lasting than sex drive. Sex drive is related to increased levels of testosterone, but is not related to romantic love. Sex drive and romantic love are related to two distinctly different aspects of the nervous system but work together to focus on potential mating partners and are also able to focus courtship attention on one individual. A person can sustain attraction and sexual arousal in a way that maintains a romantic relationship for a period of time and can set the stage for a long-term relationship. The sex drive, on the other hand, can be focused on several individuals—even someone on television or in the media—with a specific goal of a sexual union with a partner. It is also possible, then, for people to be sexually aroused and have sexual relationships with partners without having any interest in a romantic relationship. Romantic love, however, is focused on having an emotional union with the other person and does not go away by having sex.

These authors also consider a third neurological component that comes into play in couple relationships (Fisher et al., 2006). As described elsewhere in this chapter, partner attachment has a role in relationship intimacy. Attachment adds sustainability to sex drive and courtship attraction. Although attachment begins in childhood between child and parent, attachment remains active throughout one's lifetime and provides a foundation for the long-term attachment of couples, which ultimately provides a way to provide long-term care for the raising of children. The brain indicates a third neurological response, increased levels of oxytocin, which is related to attachment. Oxytocin is a hormone that promotes the ability to connect and bond with others. Therefore, sex drive, romantic love, and partner attachment occur in different parts of the brain, acting in ways that work together in helping couples form relationships, have children, and raise families.

One of the implications of these scientific findings related to love is that we now have a physiological explanation for why the intense passion evident at the beginning of a relationship moves to a much less intense attachment as time goes on. These findings also make the case for taking one's time when looking for a long-term relationship. Wait until the period of intense emotional feelings transition to partner attachment to see how that feels before getting married or making a commitment.

---

perceived threat to a valued relationship. When a person is in love with another person, there is always the possibility that he or she will feel some jealousy. In fact, some maintain that if there is no jealousy, there is no real love.

Certainly, some level of jealousy is functional in a relationship, but it can become problematic if it intensifies. It can be functional if it encourages a person to think about an intimate relationship and look for positive ways to develop a stronger relationship. But jealousy can be hurtful and can destroy a relationship as it creates more suspicion about the relationship. In the extreme, jealousy can lead to the greater probability of abuse and violence in an intimate relationship.

Both men and women become jealous when their partners become emotionally or sexually involved with other persons; there are no gender differences in the frequency, duration, or intensity of jealous feelings (Levy, Kelly, & Jack, 2006). However, there is often a sex difference as it relates to causes of jealousy. Men are more likely to feel jealous if the partner becomes sexually involved with a new partner, whereas women are more likely to be upset if the partner is emotionally connected with another person (Levy et al., 2006; Pines, 2005).

Jealousy is seen by therapists as a self-defeating emotion, and jealous people are often their own worst enemies. Jealousy leads to feelings of possessiveness, envy, and suspicion. The more jealousy takes over as a factor in an intimate relationship, the more it creates a vicious cycle of greater and greater jealousy. The jealous partner, who is often insecure about the relationship anyway, fears losing the relationship. When the partner tries to control the relationship and seeks greater closeness, the person they most fear losing is often driven away. Thus jealousy often leads to more problematic behavior, including various types of abuse (verbal, physical, sexual), and tends to push many couples apart.

Jealousy can be triggered by both external causes and internal causes. The external causes relate to behavior by a person that demonstrates the partner is (or appears to be) more interested in another person emotionally and/or sexually than in you. While you cannot control your partner's behavior, you can control how you perceive this external behavior. You can perceive it as a threat to your relationship, which will trigger jealousy, or as a sign that your partner is friendly and this person is not a threat to you. The greater your insecurity about the relationship, the greater the chances you will feel jealousy (Marelich, Gaines, & Banzet, 2003; Seidman, 2014).

Jealousy is often related to internal factors that are under your control and relate to such factors as your level of self-esteem, how dependent you are in the relationship, your level of insecurity about the relationship, your past experience about trusting others, and your perceived alternatives for another relationship (Levy et al., 2006). Findings from a variety of research studies have demonstrated that the lower a person's self-esteem, the more easily that person will become jealous. The more dependent you are on your partner or the more involved in the relationship, the more you will tend to become jealous. If you have been emotionally hurt in past relationships, trust in your partner is often not strong, which can lead to feelings of jealousy.

If you are feeling jealousy in an intimate relationship, it is very important to confront jealousy directly and to talk about it with your partner. Jealousy is a warning sign that things are not going well, and it should not be ignored. The person feeling jealousy should find a time and place to fully discuss the topic, and each person should openly share what he or she is feeling about the relationship. One significant issue to discuss is how much each person is committed to the relationship and wants to maintain it over time. If there is agreement on commitment to the relationship, then the couple should talk about ways that they can both work together to build a closer and more intimate relationship. In other words, jealousy can be a signal that you need to talk about your relationship and explore ways to make it grow.

Looking for Love on the Internet

Digital technology, and smartphones in particular, continues to transform our society, and this includes how people develop romantic relationships. The Pew Research Center began surveying online dating experiences in 2005 and found that few Americans had used technology in this way. Ten years later, the Pew research team found that 15% of U.S. adults reported using online dating sites and mobile dating apps (Pew Research Center, 2016, February 29).

Following are five interesting facts about online dating:

1. Online dating has lost much of its stigma, and a majority of Americans now say online dating is a good way to meet people (see Figure 9.1).
2. Online dating has jumped among adults under age 25, as well as those in their late 50s and early 60s (see Figure 9.2).

FIGURE 9.1

Attitudes Toward Online Dating Grow More Positive

Source: Pew Research Center, "Attitudes Toward Online Dating Grow More Positive," February 29, 2016. Website: http://www.pewresearch.org/fact-tank/2016/02/29/5-facts-about-online-dating/ft_16-02-29_onlinedating_attitudes/

Percent of U.S. adults who agree with the following statements

3. One-third of people who have used online dating have never actually gone on a date with someone they met on these sites.

4. One-in-five online daters have asked someone else to help them with their profiles. Many online daters, especially women, ask friends to help them craft the perfect profile (30% of women have done this, compared to 16% of men).

5. Five percent of Americans who are in a marriage or committed relationship say they met their significant other online. Even though 1 in 10 Americans are now using one of the many online dating platforms, the vast majority of relationships still begin offline. Even among those Americans who have been with their spouse for 5 years or less, 88% say they met their partner offline, without the help of a dating site.

Percent in each age group who have ever used an online dating site and/or mobile dating app

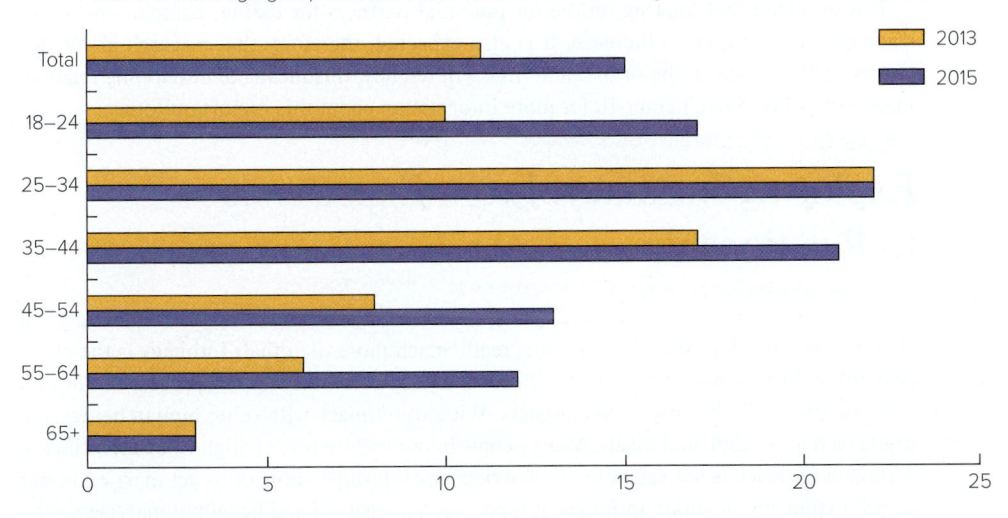

FIGURE 9.2

Online Dating Sites and Mobile Apps Usage: 2013–2015

Source: Pew Research Center, "15% of American Adults Have Used Online Dating Sites or Mobile Dating Apps," February 11, 2016. Web site: http://www.pewinternet.org/2016/02/11/15-percent-of-american-adults-have-used-online-dating-sites-or-mobile-dating-apps/

Chapter 9 | Friendship, Love, Intimacy, and Singlehood

People are looking for dating opportunities, companionship, or potential marriage partners. People might be seeking either long-term or short-term relationships. Here is one scenario about that experience:

> Nancy is a 48-year-old single woman with a 9-year-old daughter. She has been single for 7 years and has decided she wants to have a relationship with a man—mainly for companionship. She is looking for someone who is reasonably attractive and would have a lifestyle that is consistent with hers, which is someone from a small rural community, attends church, does not drink or party excessively, has wholesome values, and is committed to family. Nancy has supported herself most of her adult life and is financially independent, though not wealthy. She wants to be able to go out to dinner, or a movie, and have someone to spend time with. She is open to a relationship becoming permanent, but that is not her goal. She has been married twice before and does not want the legal entanglements of marriage. Currently, her primary goal in life is to raise her daughter in a healthy environment.
>
> She uses a free online dating service. Pictures and personal descriptions of other participants are available. The service allows her to connect with potential dates with a secure email. Multiple men contact her—many with offers for one-night stands, which is not what she is looking for. Others, however, offer what, in her mind, are very respectful invitations to talk or meet over coffee to get to know each other better. After several emails, she agrees to have a telephone conversation with one man. After several phone conversations, they agree to meet for coffee. They have agreed to go to a movie together. Where will the relationship go? Time will tell.

What people are looking for in a partner has evolved over time. In the late 1980s and early 1990s, mutual attraction and love were considered important qualities for both men and women (Najman, Dunne, Purdie, Boyle, & Coxeter, 2006). Current literature shows that women are more likely to want a partner with the ability or potential ability to earn money or have a high social status (deVries, Swenson, & Walsh, 2007; Mehta, 2013; Najman et al., 2006). Education has also been viewed as important by women because it indicates potential earning power. Men are more concerned about physical attractiveness. Other studies show that the attractiveness ratings of photographs determined success in attracting dates, with the most attractive people being selected most often. Attractiveness is usually determined by facial features. The self-descriptions, which included such things as resources (financial and nonfinancial), physical health, and social qualities, did not predict dating success (deVries et al., 2007).

It is expected that looking online for potential partners for dating, companionship, or marriage will continue to increase. It is also expected, therefore, that research about this process will increase in the future, and time will tell how this means of developing relationships will evolve. See Chapter 10 for more information about this important topic.

Exploring Intimacy: From Experience to Relationship

Like love, intimacy is also an elusive concept. The word generally brings to mind images of physical closeness and sexuality. But it is really much more than that. Intimacy is the closeness and feelings of warmth we have with certain people. It is an ongoing process of life with other people, and it has many components. Without intimacy with other human beings, life would be boring, cold, and lonely. Many people in our culture place a high value on intimacy. Although intimacy is not restricted to marriage relationships, most of us get married in our search to find and maintain intimacy. It is considered a reward and benefit of marriage.

Paths to Intimacy Differ in Males and Females

Although both males and females agree that the path to greater intimacy is one of greater personal self-disclosure, a variety of studies have found that females are more likely to follow that path (Fehr, 2004). In studying same-sex friendships, women consistently increase their intimacy with higher levels of self-disclosure about themselves. Males feel greater intimacy through doing activities together. So for many men, intimacy with other males is formed through attending sports events or doing activities together.

When seeking intimacy with those of the other sex, both women and men are often disappointed because they falsely assume that they will create intimacy the same way with the other sex that they do with their same-sex friends. So women often assume that they will achieve greater intimacy with a man by mutual self-disclosure, but many men are not very good at self-disclosure. Similarly, men often assume that it is by simply doing activities together that they will increase intimacy with a woman.

A more realistic goal for creating a more intimate relationship with the other gender is that there need to be both higher levels of self-disclosure on the part of the male and greater participation in activities by the female. By participating in activities with the male, females will find that doing things together opens the male up for more self-disclosure. A male will also appreciate the participation of the female in joint activities because this creates a feeling of greater bonding and intimacy to a male. And if men can learn to be more open and share personal beliefs and feelings, say, over lunch with their female partner, they will also benefit from this newfound emotional intimacy.

Intimacy and Communication

Honest communication is essential to true intimacy. We cannot feel close to another person if we are hiding or withholding important thoughts or feelings about that person, or even about ourselves. This doesn't mean, however, that we should lay bare our every thought or

The temptation is to let oneself be swept away by romance, but individuals falling in love should use some uncommon sense: Let things develop slowly, be honest with the other person and oneself, keep an open mind and a sense of humor. It's easier to fall in love than to stay in love.
©Blueskyimage/123RF

emotion. High self-disclosure can be detrimental to the development of intimacy at the beginning of a relationship, and it can damage a more established relationship if the "brutal truth" is too brutal. In the former case, when a relationship is just beginning, opening oneself up may threaten a partner who doesn't have the same commitment to the relationship and who therefore would not share in return. In the latter case, when a relationship is established, "honesty" may be a thin disguise for hostility or anger against the partner or spouse.

Nevertheless, open communication in appropriate doses, at appropriate times, and with good intentions can enhance a relationship and lead to greater intimacy. A couple who tries to maintain peace and stability by glossing over disputes or ignoring problems is headed for trouble. Finding a productive way of resolving differences, by meeting them head on and negotiating a workable compromise, is key.

Intimate Experiences Versus an Intimate Relationship

One can feel close to another person in a variety of ways and in different areas of one's life. Some of these ways include emotional intimacy, intellectual intimacy, social intimacy, recreational intimacy, and sexual intimacy.

An **intimate experience** is one in which we feel close or share ourselves with another person. For example, you may have 357 "friends" on Facebook, but a deep philosophic discussion can be a very intellectually intimate experience. Working together successfully on a project can also lead to an emotionally intimate feeling. The most commonly perceived type of intimacy is sexual intimacy. Nevertheless, people perceive experiences differently, and what one person perceives as an intimate experience may not seem so intimate to another. Think about it. . . .

An **intimate relationship** is one in which we share intimate experiences in several areas over time, with expectations that this sharing will continue. It is difficult to have and to maintain intimate relationships with more than a few people at once because intimacy is time consuming. For example, how many really good friends, intimate friends, do you have? Probably very few.

Also, it is quite clear from research with couples that no relationship can provide intimate experiences in all areas all the time. With apologies to Abraham Lincoln, "You can please some of the people some of the time, but you can't please all of the people all of the time." This is certainly the case with love relationships. Intimate partners may be able to satisfy each other in a number of ways—emotionally, intellectually, sexually—but both partners will most likely satisfy other intimacy needs outside the relationship. We do not suggest sexual intimacy as one of these areas, because an extramarital affair can destroy intimacy in all other areas of the relationship. But both partners can have friends of either gender at work or in other areas of their lives, friends who are very special and who provide something that the mate does not or cannot provide. These friendships can add to each partner's happiness and thus be a positive force in the couple or marriage relationship as long as the partners can minimize feelings of insecurity and jealousy, and avoid sexual entanglements.

The Paradox of Marriage and Intimacy

Most people in our culture seek marriage in their quest for intimacy. Marriage is an important source of intimacy, but, paradoxically, intimacy too often declines, and sometimes is completely destroyed, after marriage. For many, marriage increases intimacy; for others, however, it becomes an intimacy trap and smothers the very thing the two people desperately seek to enjoy. On the one hand, marriage is extolled as the path to happiness; on the other hand, it can be a source of conflict.

The basic question remains: Does marriage provide intimacy on a permanent basis? The answer is a qualified yes. Marriage can provide intimacy, but the partners must be very creative in making intimacy happen. Marriage in our society has become the classic great escape. People escape into marriage to avoid loneliness and to find intimacy. Later, when the marriage feels stifling or empty, some people escape from it to maintain their sanity and independence. Single people can feel lonely. So can married people (Rokach, 2005, 2006). In the next section, we'll look more closely at how couples can develop and maintain intimacy.

Developing Intimacy in Couple Relationships

With an extremely large sample, researchers have identified five areas in couple relationships that contribute to couple satisfaction (Olson, Olson-Sigg, & Larson, 2008). Although these findings are based on a study of married couples, they also provide information that is useful for dating couples, cohabiting couples, and premarital couples. These researchers found that there were distinct differences in the scores of five relationship characteristics between happily married couples ($n = 20,675$) and unhappily married couples ($n = 20,590$). These five areas, in order of importance, are communication, couple closeness, couple flexibility, personality compatibility, and conflict resolution. Olson and colleagues refer to these five areas as the five keys to intimacy, in that it is possible to predict with over 90% accuracy whether a couple will be happy or unhappy based on their scores in these five areas. These data were taken from the **ENRICH** Inventory (PREPARE-ENRICH, 2016), which has been used by over 50,000 couples who want to improve their couple relationships. These findings are depicted in Figure 9.3, and a more detailed description of each area is provided below.

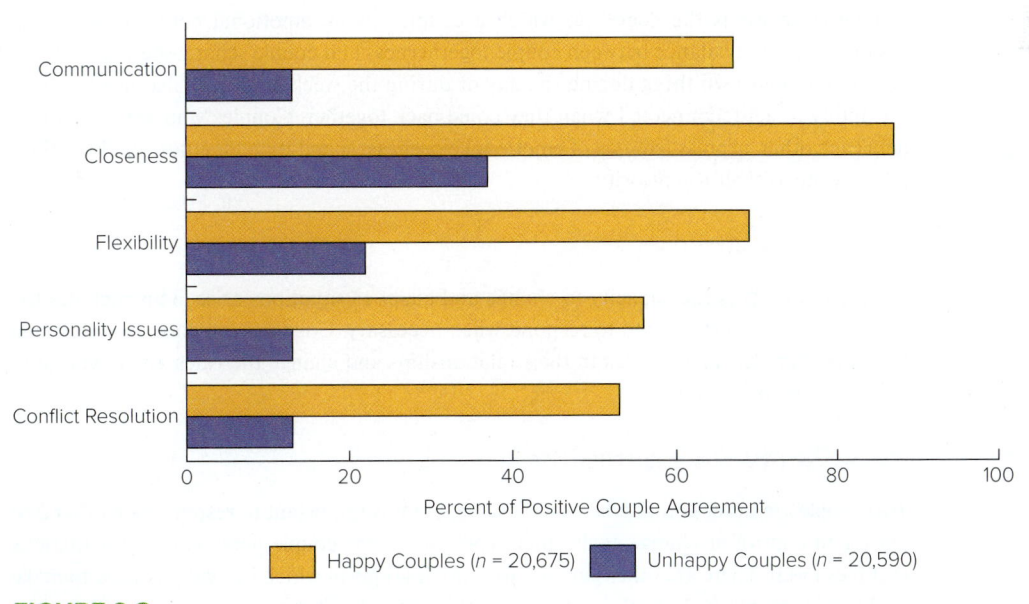

FIGURE 9.3

Happily Versus Unhappily Married Couples

Source: Olson, D., Olson-Sigg, A., & Larson, P. *The Couple Checkup.* Nashville, TN: Thomas Nelson, 2008.

Open communication is an essential component of a successful relationship, but talking about feelings—especially feelings about the relationship—can be a difficult experience for some individuals and couples. Fortunately, communication skills can be learned.
©Sigrid Olsson/PhotoAlto/Getty Images

Communication Skills

It is not surprising that communication is the area that most strongly distinguishes happy couples from unhappy couples. There is considerable agreement that good communication is essential for having an intimate relationship. Some people are more comfortable talking about their feelings than others. What appears to be critical for couples is that they are able to share important emotions and beliefs, they are able to both listen and speak, and they are able to communicate openly with their partner.

Couple Closeness

Couple closeness is the degree to which a couple has an emotional connection. It also assumes there is a balance between couple togetherness and couple separateness. People get busy doing their own thing during the day or during the week, and they also need to have the ability to get reconnected when they come back together. Couples who are close often help each other, express feelings of emotional closeness, spend time together, and have their relationship as their top priority.

Couple Flexibility

Couple flexibility is the capacity to change and adapt as situations arise. This includes the ability to deal with stress and to respond when necessary. Couples who do well in this area typically share leadership roles in their relationships and change the rules about who does what as situations change.

Personality Compatibility

Two people are never going to be exactly same, but it is important to respect each other and not try to control or change each other. There are some couple personality combinations that mesh well. There are other personality combinations in which individuals need to make slight adjustments in how they interact with each other because their personalities are extreme or out of balance. Sometimes the couple needs to develop an understanding and appreciation for personality differences.

Sharing leisure activities is one way couples can build and maintain the intimacy of their relationship. This couple has chosen an activity that allows for companionship and exercise.
©Purestock/Getty Images

Conflict Resolution

Couples who are happy resolve conflict by talking openly with each other and trying to understand each other's opinions and feelings. These couples generally deal with conflict openly and in a straightforward manner rather than avoiding issues that are difficult to talk about.

Intimacy Games

Two important aspects of any intimate relationship are honesty and straightforwardness. When one partner asks for or tells the other what he or she wants, the other partner is free to comply or not comply. But many people play **destructive intimacy games** with their partner, concealing what they really want and attempting instead to manipulate the partner into doing or giving them what they want. (As we will see later in this section, there are also constructive intimacy games.) Because destructive intimacy games tend to be effective in the short run—people often get what they want using these techniques—they can be rewarding. But in the long run, they undermine relationships. Closeness and sharing suffer, resentment grows, and the relationship may ultimately be destroyed.

Along these lines is what family therapists refer to as the **zero-sum game.** In this type of game, there is a winner and a loser. Unlike more cooperative games in which both people win by working together, the competitive zero-sum game results in one person winning what the other person loses; hence the score of the game comes to zero. For example, if I win by six points and you lose by six points, it all adds up to nothing. In human relationships, zero-sum games usually lead to problems, especially if the rules are constructed so that the same person wins most of the time. One partner might say, for example, that he or she will make the final decisions about how the couple's money is spent because he or she works outside the home and the other spouse doesn't.

Why do people play destructive intimacy games? Sometimes people don't really know what they want from a relationship. Sometimes they're embarrassed or afraid to ask for what they want, or they assume they'll be turned down. Sometimes they perceive a situation to be so difficult that the only way they can see to handle it is by playing a game. Then, because playing games often works in the short run, people tend to play them again and again.

Destructive intimacy games share many elements of such games as chess, bridge, and football: goals, players, rules, and strategies. But in football, for example, everyone knows what the goal is, who the players are, what the rules are, what the rewards and penalties are, when the game is over, and what the outcome is. In a destructive intimacy game, many of these elements are hidden or unclear. Intimacy games can be identified and defined by asking the kinds of questions listed in Table 9.2.

TABLE 9.2 Dimensions of Intimacy Games

Characteristic	Relevant Questions
Name of game	What name describes the game?
Players	Who were the players/opponents?
	Who were the spectators?
	Who were the referees?
Playing field	Where was the game played?
	When was the game played?
Objectives	What were the short-term objectives?
	What were the long-term objectives?
Rules	What were the rules?
	Were they implicit or explicit?
Strategies	How was the game played?
	What strategies did the offense use?
	What were the long-term objectives?
	What counterstrategies did the defense use?
Communication style	Did the participants express themselves verbally, nonverbally, or both?
Rewards and penalties	What were the rewards?
	What were the penalties?
Outcomes	How effective was the game in the short term? In the long term?
	How enjoyable was the game?
	Was there a winner and a loser?

Constructive Intimacy Games

Although most intimacy games are destructive, **constructive intimacy games** can enhance a relationship. Too often intimates focus on what they do *not* get from each other rather than on how often they benefit from the other person. This sets up a negative cycle: As one person becomes more negative and less willing to give, the other person reciprocates. Soon neither person in the relationship is giving to the other in a positive way.

One way to reverse this type of negative interaction is to focus on the positive, on what you can do for the other person and what the other person can do for you. Giving to another person in a positive way encourages the other person to do the same. Also, telling the other person what you want increases your chances of receiving it.

Marital therapists often find that when one partner does something positive for the other, the other will respond positively in return relatively soon. Over a period of 2 weeks, if one spouse did ten positive things for the other, the spouse would be likely to receive about the same number of positive gestures in return. In contrast, when individuals are negative, they receive negative responses, and the negative pattern repeats itself. Marital therapists often ask partners to double the number of compliments they give to their spouses each day for a week. Although both spouses commonly feel it would be strange to exchange so many compliments, they find that the recipient not only accepts the compliments but returns about the same number over the next few days. This approach develops a positive complementary cycle. Years ago, the Beatles put it more poetically when they sang, "In the end, the love you take/Is equal to the love you make."

Unlike destructive intimacy games, constructive games help develop positive cycles. In addition, constructive games have objectives that are specific, rules that are explicit, strategies that are cooperative rather than competitive, and outcomes that are mutually rewarding. Couples who would like instruction in constructive intimacy games can enroll in a couples communication workshop. Constructive games can be especially enjoyable in intimate relationships, which allow for a greater variety of ways in which partners can reward each other and develop more positive feelings toward each other.

Destructive Intimacy Games

As mentioned, many intimacy games are destructive. Identifying and analyzing a few can illuminate their pitfalls and provide the basis for developing more constructive and positive ways of relating. Two destructive intimacy games are "I Don't Care. You Decide" and "The Ties That Bind."

"I Don't Care. You Decide." Many times, when couples are involved in decision making, one partner genuinely wants the other partner to make the decision. However, when one partner knows what he or she wants but is afraid to tell the other person, or when the partner wants to make the decision but have it appear as if the other person has made it, the decision-making process can become a game.

The initiator often begins playing this game when he or she is relatively sure the other person will make the decision the initiator prefers. The initiator often opens the game with a loaded question, such as, "Do you want to stop here for dinner?" This really means, "I want to stop here, and I hope you will know that and make that decision." When the other player says yes, however, she or he can then be held responsible if the food is bad, the service is poor, or the bill is too high.

The following dialogue illustrates another common way this game begins. Lindy and Cooper have received an invitation in the mail from a couple they haven't seen in some time. The party-givers are primarily Cooper's friends, whom he has known for years. Lindy doesn't enjoy them because they argue so much.

Human relationships are too precious to risk by playing destructive games. Constructive interactions, positive feedback, and honest communication are the keys to successful, long-lasting relationships.
©Feverpitched/123RF

Cooper: What do you want to do about this party? Should we go?

Lindy: I don't care . . . [even though she does].

Cooper: Wouldn't you like to see them again?

Lindy: Well . . . don't you have other things you'd rather do this Saturday?

Cooper: No, I'd rather go. Okay?

Lindy: Okay, but . . .

Cooper: Are you sure you want to go?

Lindy: Yes, I guess so.

When Lindy and Cooper go to the party, Lindy will go reluctantly and will probably be frustrated by the experience. Lindy had hoped Cooper would realize she didn't want to go to the party and would decide they shouldn't go. But by not expressing her true feelings and not actively involving herself in the decision-making process, Lindy failed to achieve what she intended. This is one of the negative consequences of playing games.

Another negative consequence might be that when she gets home from the party, Lindy will feel so miserable or annoyed that when Cooper wants to make love, she will say quite honestly, "I don't feel like it tonight." Cooper suspecting Lindy's playing a game, might speculate, "She didn't want to go to their house all along, and now she's punishing me by withholding sex!" The merry-go-round continues, and both people feel frustrated.

"The Ties That Bind." The parent–child relationship is also fertile ground for destructive intimacy games, especially when the children become adults. Although supposedly played in the best interests of all concerned, these games are often disguised, and the players often do not enjoy playing them. Nevertheless, game playing between parents and their adult children is likely to exist. Giving up the role of parent is difficult.

The degree and type of involvement parents have with their married children causes difficulty in many families. The prevalence of in-law jokes attests to the significance of this issue in marital and family relationships. Some mutually agreed-upon degree of balance is important. But it can be difficult to successfully balance the dimension of separateness as individuals with that of connectedness to our families of origin. Some parents have difficulty accepting the fact that their children are grown up and desire a more independent lifestyle, one that is free from past traditions. Parents who are frustrated by their dwindling contact with their adult children often play games, such as the destructive intimacy game called "The Ties That Bind."

Limiting Destructive Games

Over the years, researchers and family therapists have devised a number of useful techniques for limiting gamesmanship in families and maximizing true intimacy. The four central techniques are (1) naming the game, (2) making implicit rules explicit, (3) identifying strategies and counterstrategies, and (4) discussing the disguised objectives and making them clear and specific. Each of these components is described in more detail below.

Naming the Game. Catching yourself and others playing intimacy games can be fun, as well as a way to increase intimacy in your relationships—as long as it is done in a playful and good-natured manner. A destructive intimacy game is a ploy someone uses to get something without directly asking for it. When you catch yourself or a loved one doing this, try very hard to describe what you see honestly. Encourage the loved one to be honest, too. Avoid blame or sarcasm. A matter-of-fact, caring approach is much more effective than a heavy-handed one.

Once the game playing is identified, try to give the game a catchy title. For example, everybody who has been in love is guilty at one time or another of playing the "If You Really Love Me, You'll Know What I Want" game. In this game we assume that the other person can read our mind at all times; if the loved one can't, then he or she must not care about us. Identifying and naming a game and focusing on the problem in a rational and calm manner are major steps in eliminating game playing.

Making Implicit Rules Explicit. Implicit (secret) rules are difficult to reveal, and they add confusion to the destructive intimacy game. Nevertheless, exposing implicit rules is an effective technique for ending the destructive intimacy game. The most common implicit rule is "Don't directly ask for what you want." This rule assumes that if you do ask directly, you will be refused. But playing by this rule puts you in a difficult situation. You don't ask directly because you think you'll be refused, but because you don't ask directly, people have to guess what you want. If they don't guess correctly, you won't get what you want.

By being direct, you give the other person a chance to choose how and when he or she might give you what you want. This places the responsibility for action on the other person and frees that person to give to you. And giving others what they want—making them feel good—makes the giver feel good also.

Identifying Strategies and Counterstrategies. Withdrawing quietly and sullenly from an argument is a common strategy in destructive intimacy games. Its intent is to keep the other player in the argument from continuing on the offensive. The "opponent" may then respond with a counterstrategy by saying, for example, "What's wrong, Dear?" And the obvious counterstrategy to this ploy is for the quiet and sullen "Dear" to respond, "[Sigh] Oh, nothing."

Unveiling game strategies like this isn't easy because, as in cards or tennis, players often try to confuse their opponents. Your intimate opponent may set you up by unveiling one game strategy, only to substitute another. Nevertheless, unveiling strategies can be an important step in building intimacy in a relationship.

Discussing the Disguised Objectives. Rather than directly asking for what they want, some people disguise their objectives. The loaded question is a common technique for disguising what one really wants and for making the partner think that he or she is making the decision. For example, suppose your partner asks, "Wouldn't you like to go to this movie?" To identify the hidden objective, you can ask your partner what movie she or he wants to see.

Attachment Theory and Intimacy

Attachment theory focuses on how children develop attachment to their caregivers, usually their parents, in infancy. The most important tenet of this theory is that a young child needs to develop a relationship with at least one primary caregiver, for social and emotional development to occur normally. Although this theory is a child development theory that can be traced back to the work of John Bowlby in the late 1950s and 1960s, since the late 1980s it has been applied to adult attachment, including the development of intimate and love relationships (Holmes & Fairfield, 2014). There is evidence that attachment follows a developmental trajectory throughout a person's life, beginning with parents, followed by peers, close friends, romantic partners, and a spouse. Romantic love and marriage (including sex), therefore, have recently been viewed as part of the attachment process.

Schachner, Shaver, and Gillath (2008) also found that long-term singles were most likely to view their siblings or a close friend as attachment figures. Some studies indicate that the extreme negative emotion adults experience around romantic breakups, divorce, or death parallels what happens with children. When the attachment figure is unavailable, adults express intense anxiety, sorrow, loneliness, and despair (Holmes & Fairfield, 2014). This intense emotion is comparable to the negative emotion experienced by a child who is separated from a parent.

Substantial research supports the notion that there are several attachment figures during adulthood in addition to romantic partners. For example, it was found that married adults viewed their spouse as their principal attachment figure, and as they got older they also mentioned their children as attachment figures (Schachner et al., 2008). Parents also continue to be a focus of attachment and serve as a secure base for adults to return to (Holmes & Fairfield, 2014). For example, when relationships do not work out, some people might go to their parents for comfort and security. During adulthood, siblings and friends are also important attachment figures.

Researchers Cindy Hazan and Phillip Shaver identified three types of attachment responses for adults to characterize their feelings and behaviors in romantic relationships (Mikulincer & Shaver, 2007). These responses parallel attachment theory for children. First, secure romantic attachment involves being comfortable with closeness and interdependence with one's partner and not being fearful of being abandoned by that partner. Second, avoidant attachment is feeling uncomfortable with closeness and interdependence. Finally, anxious attachment involves anxiety over abandonment and frustration over lack of closeness.

Sex is also part of attachment in adulthood, in that romantic love also involves sex (Mikulincer & Shaver, 2007). It is suggested that those who were securely attached as children are more likely to feel comfortable and relaxed and will be more likely to have enjoyable sexual experiences, being able to balance their own and their partner's needs. Insecure adults are likely to have more challenges and more conflict regarding sex in relationships. Avoidant individuals may abstain from sex or may have sexual relationships without intimacy and interdependence.

According to Mikulincer and Shaver (2007), when romantic couple relationships transition from flirtation and dating to a more permanent, long-term relationship, expressions of attachment also change. Mutual support and emotional intimacy become important. There is more disclosure, sharing of personal history, and a focus on long-term goals. The couple is providing a foundation for what they hope will be a committed, lasting, and mutually satisfying couple relationship. They are beginning the process of seeing themselves in a long-term, committed relationship and see their partner as an attachment figure who will be a sensitive and reliable source of comfort and support.

Another study examined the relationship between the family of origin's ritual patterns and the attachment of young adults (Homer, Freeman, Zabriskie, & Eggett, 2007). A family ritual can be thought of as a family celebration, a family tradition, and other patterned and predictable family interactions. With a sample of over 200 couples the research team found that the more meaningful the family of origin rituals, the more secure and less anxious the adult children were in their romantic relationships. The study also supports the idea that meaningful family rituals are associated with a higher sense of self-worth and greater self-confidence, which contribute to longer-lasting relationships.

Attachment theory provides a context for romantic relationships and marriage, and may provide explanations for happy and unhappy relationships and loss of a partner. Because this area of study is relatively new, it is likely that a deeper understanding about the relationship between attachment and intimacy will continue to evolve.

Being Single

Marriage is still very popular in the United States, with the vast majority of people marrying at some time in their lives. However, after decades of declining marriage rates and changes in family structure, the percentage of American adults who have never married has reached an historic high point. According to a Pew Research Center team analyzing U.S. Census Bureau data, by 2012, one in five adults ages 25 and older (about 42 million people) had never been married (Pew Research Center, 2014, September 24).

In 1960, only about 1 in 10 adults (9%) had never been married by age 25. Men are more likely than women to never have been married by this age (23% compared to 17% in 2012). This gender gap has widened since 1960, when 10% of men 25 and older and 8% of women of the same age had never married (Pew Research Center, 2014, September 24).

Why? Adults today are marrying later in life, and the percentage of adults cohabiting and raising children outside of marriage has increased significantly. For women, the median age at first marriage has reached 27; for men, 29. These ages are up from 20 for women and 23 for men in 1960. Also, 24% of never-married young adults ages 25 to 34 are living with a partner, according to the Pew Research analysis of the *Current Population Survey* data from the U.S. Census Bureau (Pew Research Center, 2014, September 24).

Other reasons for the decline in marriage and the rise in singlehood include shifting public attitudes, hard economic times, and changing demographic patterns. The Pew Research team found that the trend cuts across all major racial and ethnic groups. Among African Americans, 36% ages 25 and older had never married by 2012, up from 9% in 1960.

Once considered a sad fate to be avoided at almost any cost, singlehood is today recognized as a legitimate, happy, and healthy alternative to marriage. This single man in his 30s demonstrates some of the benefits of being single, including self-sufficiency and the time and space to cater to one's own tastes.
©Klaus Tiedge/Blend Images/Getty Images

Among European Americans, the percentage of never-married adults doubled over the same period of time. In 2012, 16% of whites had never been married, compared with 8% in 1960 (Pew Research Center, 2014, September 24).

Is society better off if people make marriage and having children a priority, or is society just as well off if people have priorities other than marriage and children? Pew researchers found that 46% of American adults chose the first statement, and 50% chose the second. Opinions were sharply divided by age. Younger adults were much more likely to say that society is just as well off if people have priorities other than marriage (67% of those ages 18 to 29, and 53% of those ages 30 to 49). While among those ages 50 and older, 55% said society is better off if people make it a priority to get married and have children (Pew Research Center, 2014, September 24).

Most Americans in the Pew survey (68%) said they continue to believe that it is important for couples to marry if they plan to spend the rest of their lives together (47% said this is very important; and 21% more considered it somewhat important). Even though Blacks are more likely than Whites to have never been married and less likely to be currently married, a much greater percentage of Blacks (58%) than Whites (44%) say that it is very important for a couple to marry if they plan to spend their lives together (Pew Research Center, 2014, September 24).

Following are some other interesting thoughts and statistics on singles from the U.S. Census Bureau (2015, September 15):

- Many unmarried Americans do not identify with the word "single" because they are parents, have partners, or are widowed.
- In 2014, 107 million Americans (45% of all U.S. residents age 18 and older) were not married.

- Fifty-three percent of unmarried Americans were women and 47% were men.
- Sixty-three percent of unmarried Americans had never been married; 24% were divorced; and 13% were widowed.
- Eighteen million unmarried Americans were 65 or older in the 2014 study. Seniors made up 17% of all unmarried people 18 and older.
- There are 88 unmarried men for every 100 unmarried women.
- Thirty-six percent of women aged 15 to 50 who gave birth in the last 12 months were either widowed, divorced, or never married.
- Thirty-nine percent of voters in the 2012 presidential election were unmarried, compared with 25% of voters in the 1972 presidential election.

See Box 9.3 for some definitions of singlehood.

A Historical Perspective on Being Single

An increasing number of people in the United States see singlehood as a legitimate alternative to marriage. This outlook represents a major shift in our society's attitude toward marriage. Throughout most of American history, the failure to marry (note how even the terminology is loaded) was considered undesirable. Of course, not everyone married in 18th- and 19th-century America, and many married in their late 20s or their 30s. But social circumstances or pure economics probably contributed to not marrying more than personal desires did, for marriage was highly valued. *Old maid* and *spinster* were certainly not flattering descriptions for unmarried women.

In colonial times in America (the 17th and 18th centuries), virtually all unmarried individuals lived in a family environment of some type—either in their parents' home or as servants in another's home. Unmarried people of all ages usually stayed dependent on the families with whom they lived until they married. Only then did they become fully independent members of society.

In the 19th century, the position of unmarried people began to change. They increasingly became involved in wage labor outside the family and often lived in boardinghouses. During the Industrial Revolution, many young people went to work in factories, often at some distance from the farms they grew up on. The boardinghouses exercised family-type controls but were still quite different from a traditional family environment. Although attitudes toward singlehood may have improved over the 19th and early 20th centuries, social custom held that marriage was by far the preferable state, and those who remained single were stigmatized.

Being Single Today

Being single can mean many things. It includes those who have never married, those who have been married and divorced or widowed, or those who are cohabiting. In 2015, 45% of Americans 18 years and older were single—63% of the unmarried had never been married; 24% were divorced; and 13% were widowed (U.S. Census Bureau, 2015, September 15). With the age of marriage increasing, currently at 27 years for women and 29 years for men, young people who eventually marry spend more years as singles (U.S. Census Bureau, 2015). With the divorce rate at approximately 40% to 50%, many people are single for periods of time after a divorce. The increase in cohabitation also affects the marriage rate, with many people living with a partner but officially single. As marriage rates have dropped, nonmarital cohabitation has increased, with over 50% of women ages 19 to 44 having cohabited for a portion of their lives (Popenoe, 2008; Popenoe & Whitehead, 2010).

Although many wish to be married some day, there are also substantial numbers of people who are enjoying being single and taking advantage of the opportunities available when

BOX 9.3 Diversity in Families

Definitions of Singlehood

Being unmarried in the United States, as well as in most other industrialized countries, is not what it used to be—especially for women. It has not been a long time since the words "spinster" and "old maid" have gone out of fashion. In the 1950s and early 1960s, for instance, if a young woman wasn't married by the age of 25, she was considered an oddity and was likely to be pitied. And an old joke in some rural areas had it that a girl out of high school better get married quick, before her opportunities dry up. Most young people married soon after they graduated from high school or college. But it's a different story today. According to the U.S. Census Bureau (2015, September 15), the median age for getting married is now 29 years old for men and 27 years old for women. Compare these figures to 1960 when it was 23 years for men and 20 years for women. And the most recent data indicate that 107 million people in this country age 18 and older are not married. This figure is fully 45% of all U.S. residents 18 and over.

For U.S. women, singlehood has its upsides and its downsides. On a positive note, increases in education and income have made single women the second largest category of buyers of condos, co-ops, townhouses, and single-family homes. One study reported that 21% of home buyers were single women, while only 11% were single men (Lisle, 2004).

However, the news for single women is not all good. Single women are often caught in the middle of two worlds. Like the four women on the TV show *Sex and the City*, they enjoy the freedom and sense of adventure that comes with being unattached, yet they spend much of their time searching for the perfect relationship. In an article in the *Journal of Mental Health Counseling*, Phyllis A. Gordon (2003) states that society does not prepare women for singlehood and that "from an early age, most young girls are prompted to think of an adult life that encompasses marriage and motherhood." She also says that although it is fairly acceptable for a man to remain single, women who do so are usually seen as less loving and nurturing, less sexually attractive, and more selfish. They often see themselves as being "less than," as lacking something fundamental, and they frequently experience low self-esteem. Many women feel great societal pressure to be part of a couple.

Traditionally, people married to fulfill parental expectations, for social and economic security, and for religious reasons. Contemporary reasons for getting—or not getting—married are often more personal and include the rise of feminism and the sexual revolution, the fact that many young people are staying in school longer to earn graduate degrees, and the cultural changes that affect the way people search for mates. Many people are no longer so concerned about meeting society's expectations.

That is not to say that intimacy is not still an important issue. Many young adults are postponing marriage until they find that one individual who is just right for them. According to Whitehead and Popenoe (2001) in a report for the National Marriage Project at Rutgers University, young adults are "searching for a deep emotional and spiritual connection with one person for life." The authors went on to say that 94% of never-married men and women ages 20 to 29 are searching for their soul mates "first and foremost."

In a global context, waiting for Mr. Right is a particularly Western notion. In other places around the world, marriage is often seen as an alliance between families for social, political, or there are no responsibilities to a spouse or family (Jayson, 2010). For example, Nancy, a middle-aged divorced woman in Alabama, is content with being single:

> "I don't know, perhaps I'll never get married again. At first, after the divorce, I was very panicky, like, 'Oh, I've got to be married, I've got to be married!' And then after several months of looking for the ideal mate, I discovered that I like myself quite a bit and actually was quite content having my own private space in the world. I'm a busy professional. Sure it gets lonely sometimes, but I've got lots of friends, male and female. I get on the phone and call someone, and we get together and talk and laugh, and I think, 'Hmmm, it could be a lot worse. I could still be dealing with Jerome's drinking.'"

Historically, people did not buy a house or have a child until they were married. In fact, many did not feel they could get on with their real life until they had someone to share it with. Today, singles buy homes, have babies, and make major career decisions without a spouse. Many singles choose to devote time to careers, with multiple job changes and multiple moves. Some of these lifestyles might be difficult if married.

economic reasons. The following are views of singlehood in several Asian countries:

- Phyllis A. Gordon (2003) reported in an article in *The Journal of Mental Health Counseling* entitled "The Decision to Remain Single: Implications for Women Across Cultures" that in Korea, choosing not to marry may reflect badly on the family, because it is perceived that the parents have been neglecting their duty to find a suitable mate for their child.
- In China, single women may face numerous problems, according to Philip A. Pan (2000) in a *Washington Post* article entitled "Thoroughly Modern Women Disconcert Many in China." Chinese men who are economically secure may choose to pursue extramarital affairs, but their wives usually choose to stay married to them, because divorced women in China are seen as tarnished. Single women in China are forbidden by law to bear children. And successful single Chinese women often find it difficult to find a mate. According to Pan, successful Chinese women want to marry men at least as successful as they are; however, Chinese men believe wives should be subservient, and ". . . less educated and less successful than their husbands, [and] university professors often advise their female students to get married before they pursue graduate studies, lest they end up 'overqualified' for marriage."
- In Japan, Anthony Faiola (2004) reports in an article in the *Washington Post* entitled "Japanese Women Live, and Like It, on Their Own" that Japanese women are entering the workforce in record numbers (with the percentage of women in the workforce hitting 40.8 in 2003). They are also becoming more financially independent, and many are choosing to remain single. In 2003, according to Faiola, 54% of Japanese women in their late 20s were single—a higher percentage than that found in any other country, including the United States. For many years, their icon was Princess Sayako, daughter of Emperor Akihito, who chose to remain single until she recently announced her engagement at age 35 (although every year on her birthday she was asked by the press about her marriage plans). However, single Japanese women are often criticized strongly for not taking their traditional roles of wife and mother seriously. Faiola quotes former Prime Minister Yoshio Mori as saying, "Welfare is supposed to take care of and reward those women who have lots of children. It is truly strange to say that we have to use tax money to take care of women who don't even give birth once, who grow old living their lives selfishly and singing the praises of freedom."
- In Thailand, a young woman named Saovapa Devahastin, 38, won a beauty contest and became the first woman ever to hold the title of "Miss Spinster." In an article in *The New York Times*, Seth Mydans (2004) reported that Miss Saovapa and ". . . a growing number of successful professional women like her are challenging not only the traditional imperative of marriage and family but also what they see as the delicate egos of Thai men." Not all traditions have changed, however. Before entering the contest, Miss Saovapa asked her father for his approval.

Throughout the world, marriage remains the norm. However, singlehood is increasing, and it is changing the makeup of many of the world's cultures.

A relatively new phenomenon is the increasing number of women between the ages of 25 and 60 years of age who are not married but are raising children alone (Marquardt, Blankenhorn, Lerman, Malone-Colon, & Wilcox, 2012). These women typically have not been married. This group of individuals is also likely to be less well-educated than those who are married with children. For example, more than half of births among women under age 30 now occur outside of marriage. The average woman who has a child and is not married has a high school diploma and is White. Thus, there is a decline in marriage for approximately 60% of Americans who have high school degrees, but do not have college degrees. These authors have concerns about this trend because we know that children, on average, do less well in single-parent homes than in two-parent homes.

These individuals do not necessarily want to be married or are unable to find the right person, but they do want children. Marquardt et al. (2012) conclude that these homes, with female heads of households with limited education, can quickly fall from being middle-income to low-income. These families, then, are less able to provide for their children and are less able to contribute to their communities. This increase in low-income families results in increased costs to our federal and state governments, which is adding to our financial debt. Therefore, this is not only a family issue, but is also becoming a public policy issue.

It is clear that being single today can mean several things. It can mean, "I am having the time of my life with a great career and few obligations," or it can mean, "I am struggling as I raise a child and am barely getting by."

The movie *Up in the Air*, starring George Clooney, is about a man with a job that has him traveling around the country firing people. A major focus of his life is his loyalty-program memberships and his frequent flyer miles. He loves his job because it leaves him with only a handful of days each year where he is not traveling—it leaves him no time for extended family or friends. When he is not traveling for work, he spends time in a very tiny apartment that is simple and plain, with no evidence of any life beyond his job. Ultimately, he falls in love and begins to have a glimpse of what he might have been missing in terms of relationships. The story ends when he finds out that the person with whom he has fallen in love is married and has no interest in a long-term relationship. One of the messages of this movie might be that this is a wake-up call for singles with a fast-paced career and no time for intimate relationships. Reviews of the movie were mixed, which may reflect the variety of ways singles view this issue. Some say it is, indeed, a wake-up call—if one is not careful, one could miss the most important things in life, having intimate relationships. Others say the man was happy and that he did not need relationships to complicate his life.

A recent study by Sharp and Ganong (2011) provided research findings of interviews conducted with 10 single women in their late 20s and early 30s about their experiences with being single. Even though being single is becoming very common, these women indicated that challenges still exist with family and friends considering them "losers."

These women had feelings of the eligible pool of men decreasing as they got older and were not married. The men who were available might be considered leftovers who could not find a partner earlier, or they had been married and divorced and many had children to bring into the relationship. Family and friends also reminded them regularly that they were on a different trajectory than others when they were not married and did not have children. On the other hand, the things they were accomplishing in their lives such as success in their careers were somewhat invisible to those around them. Although there were times when people acknowledged how lucky they were to be single, these comments were somewhat rare.

The book *Loneliness: Human Nature and the Need for Social Connection* by Cacioppo and Patrick (2008) presents pioneering research by Cacioppo on the physiological and psychological importance of human connections. He indicates that people today are living longer, having fewer children later in life, and are increasingly mobile, which can result in loneliness. Cacioppo's findings show that prolonged loneliness can have damaging effects and can be as harmful to one's health as smoking or obesity. For example, loneliness is related to greater resistance to blood flow through the cardiovascular system, higher levels of stress hormones, higher blood pressure, and increased levels of depression. The authors of this book suggest that mainstream society's focus on competition and individualism, rather than on family and community, is damaging to the health and well-being of individuals.

Many singles are enjoying lives without partners and are living healthy and happy lives. There are others, however, who would like to be in a couple relationship but for one reason or another are not, and these folks may feel lonely. Some advice for those seeking to cope effectively with loneliness:

- *Appraise your strengths.* What are the good things about yourself? If you have difficulty listing your attributes, ask some people who know you.
- *Develop a friendship network.* Spend time developing and connecting with a few close friends who can provide you with a caring network.

Women who remain single are likely to be high achievers of above-average intelligence. This can make it difficult for them to find an unattached man of equal status, because men sometimes prefer to marry "down."
©George Doyle/Stockbyte/Punchstock

- *Take a chance.* Reach out and take risks. You must tell people how you really feel and what you need. Say, "I'm really lonely today. I wish I just had somebody to talk to." Until you do this, people can't help you.
- *Don't expect too much.* When you go out socially, go out just to have fun. Many lonely people go out with a different motive: to find the perfect person, a lifelong friend. Convince yourself, instead, that you can enjoy relationships without long-term commitment.
- *Depend on yourself.* Looking for someone else to make you feel all right is seldom effective. You have to depend on yourself and participate in activities you enjoy.

Single people have the same basic desire for sexual intimacy that married people have, but they must take different approaches to fulfilling that need. For some, clubs such as this one offer the right mix of sociability and opportunity. Other singles seek partners in more tranquil settings.
©Rayes/Getty Images

Chapter 9 | Friendship, Love, Intimacy, and Singlehood 261

- *Rejoin your family.* Your family can be a great support. Regardless of how you treat your family or how they treat you, you still belong to that family.
- *Find an outside interest.* Try to find something that really interests or excites you and then work at it. If you join an organization, for example, don't just sit in the corner. Take some responsibility. Volunteer for things; really get involved.

In summary, these useful suggestions are not only for singles but also for anyone who wants to maintain healthy relationships with others. These time-tested ideas provide practical ways to live a happy and more connected life.

Summary

- Love and friendship are different. In addition, the dynamics of both have changed recently. Love and friendship can also look different depending on the culture.
- The love triangle, developed by Robert Sternberg, has three dimensions: decision and commitment, intimacy, and passion.
- Science shows that chemical changes occur in the brain when we fall in love and develop long-term relationships. This information may be useful in understanding why we respond as we do in courtship and marriage.
- Men and women are using the internet to find potential partners more than ever before. In the end, however, only 5% of people who are married or are in committed relationships found their partner using the internet.
- Jealousy is very connected with love and intimacy. The traditional approaches to meeting a partner—at school, at work, at a social gathering, through relatives or friends—still remain dominant in the quest for intimacy. Although jealousy can be both functional and dysfunctional in a relationship, it is more often seen as problematic. While both men and women get jealous, men are more likely to feel jealous if the partner becomes sexually involved with a new partner, while women are more likely to be upset if the partner is emotionally connected with another person.
- Men and women are in agreement that self-disclosure is related to greater intimacy. However, women tend to be better at self-disclosure. Men are likely to seek intimacy by participating in activities with others, while women are likely to use self-disclosure to create intimacy with others.
- Intimacy involves feeling close to and sharing oneself with another. Although marriage is an important source of intimacy, intimacy often declines after marriage and sometimes disappears completely. Intimacy takes a great deal of time, effort, and hard work to develop and maintain.
- The five keys to intimacy are communication, couple closeness, couple flexibility, personality compatibility, and conflict resolution. These keys are important for dating couples, cohabiting couples, premarital couples, and married couples.
- Attachment theory was developed by John Bowlby in the late 1950s and 1960s, when he focused on how infants and young children learn to bond with parents. Attachment theory today has been expanded to show how childhood attachment affects how we interact in our adult relationships.
- Intimacy games can be either destructive or constructive. To minimize destructive games, it's important to identify them, make their rules explicit, determine the hidden strategies, and make the disguised objectives clear and specific.
- An increasing number of people in today's society see singlehood as a viable alternative to marriage. This represents a major shift in behavior in the last decade.

Key Terms

commitment	consummate love
intimacy	jealousy
passion	intimate experience
non-love	intimate relationship
liking	ENRICH
infatuation	destructive intimacy game
empty love	zero-sum game
romantic love	constructive intimacy game
fatuous love	attachment theory
companionate love	

Activities

1. In a small group, discuss your friendships and how they are similar to and different from love relationships.
2. What does love mean to you? In a small group, share a description of an especially romantic time in your life. What are the similarities and differences among the descriptions group members provide?
3. Consider Box 9.2, "Love and Science." Think about times you have felt you were in love. Did you react in a way that seemed obsessive—like you could not think about anything else but the person you were in love with? Did you

experience intense energy around this person? In your experience, is this scientific description about what happens in our brains correct?
4. Take a class survey—using anonymous written responses—to find out how many times each student has been in love. What is the average number? What is the range (lowest to highest)?
5. Interview a divorced or remarried person. Ask how the individual's definition of love changed as she or he went through the following phases: dating, engagement, marriage, marital dissolution and divorce, singlehood, and remarriage. To do this exercise well, spend 45 to 60 minutes with the person to get a good understanding of what happened to the marriage and why.
6. What intimacy games have you personally played? Pick an intimacy game you have played and respond to the questions in Table 9.2. Then discuss your experiences with other members of a small group.

Suggested Readings

Baumbusch, J. L. (2004). Unclaimed treasures: Older women's reflections on lifelong singlehood. *Journal of Women and Aging, 16*(1/2), 105–121. Lifelong single women strongly emphasize their independence and "ability to be alone" as significant benefits, while discussing drawbacks, including loneliness and the absence of a social support network, which became more important as they experienced increasing age and frailty.

Buono, A. J., & Weisenbach, S. (Eds.). (2004). *We met online! Stories of married Catholics who met their spouses on the Internet*. Philadelphia, PA: Xlibris.

Cacioppo, J. T., & Patrick, W. (2008). *Loneliness: Human nature and the need for social connection*. New York, NY: W. W. Norton.

Chiriboga, D., Zettle, L., Connidis, I., Koropeckyj-Cox, T., Bluck, S., Luecking, G., Rook, K., Dykstra, P., DePaulo, B., Morris, W., & Hertel, J. (2004). The never-marrieds in later life: Potentials, problems, and paradoxes. *The Gerontologist, 44*(1), 145. A cross-national perspective on conceptual models and research findings, including discussions of social supports available to never-married men and women, advantages and disadvantages of never being married, how society views individuals representing this role status, and the variety of types of never-marrieds.

DePaulo, B. M. (2006). *Singled out: How singles are stereotyped, stigmatized, and ignored and still live happily ever after*. New York, NY: St. Martin's.

Ferguson, S. J. (2000). Challenging traditional marriage: Never married Chinese American and Japanese American women. *Gender and Society, 14*(1), 136–159. Why do some heterosexual Chinese American and Japanese American women never marry? The four most significant reasons are the effect of their parents' marriages, their status as eldest daughter, their pursuit of education, and the lack of eligible suitors. Parents' traditional marriages and duties as eldest daughter caused many to have negative views of marriage and childbearing. The number of suitors was limited for 46 of 62 respondents because their parents placed strict restrictions on them concerning the types of men they are allowed to marry.

Fisher, H. E. (2016). *Anatomy of love: A natural history of mating, marriage, and why we stray*. New York, NY: W. W. Norton.

Goodwin, R. (2009). *Changing relations*. New York, NY: Cambridge University Press.

Holmes, P., & Fairfield, S. (2014). *The Routledge handbook of attachment: Theory*. New York, NY: Routledge.

Mashek, D. J., & Aron, A. (Eds.). (2004). *Handbook of closeness and intimacy*. Mahwah, NJ: Erlbaum. Written by scholars in the field, this book provides the most comprehensive summary of a wealth of ideas about closeness and intimacy.

Mikulincer, M., & Shaver, P. R. (2007). *Attachment in adulthood*. New York, NY: Guilford Press.

Oord, T. J. (Ed.). (2008). *The altruism reader: Selections from writings on love, religion, and science*. West Conshohocken, PA: Templeton Foundation Press.

Pew Research Center. (2014, September 24). Record share of Americans have never married as values, economics and gender patterns change. Pew Research Center. Web site: http://www.pewsocialtrends.org/2014/09/24/record-share-of-americans-have-never-married/.

Puente, S., & Cohen, D. (2003). Jealousy and the meaning of violence. *Personality and Social Psychological Bulletin, 29*(4), 449–460.

Sternberg, R. J. (2013a). Measuring love. *The Psychologist, 26*(2), 101.

Sternberg, R. J. (2013b). Searching for love. *The Psychologist, 26*(2), 98–101.

Sternberg, R., & Weis, K. (Eds.). (2008). The new psychology of love. New Haven, CT: Yale University Press.

Straus, J. (2006). *Unhooked generation: The truth about why we're still single*. New York, NY: Hyperion.

Visit the text-specific Online Learning Center at www.mhhe.com/olson9e for practice tests, chapter summaries, and PowerPoint slides.

Design Element: © Alicia Grünkind/EyeEm/Getty Images

10 Dating, Mate Selection, and Living Together

- **Courtship Patterns**
- **Choosing a Mate**
- **Patterns of Mate Selection**
- **Conflict and Violence in Relationships**
- **Living Together**
- **Summary**
- **Key Terms**
- **Activities**
- **Suggested Readings**

Regardless of how intense a love relationship is, there are both good and bad reasons for getting married. Similarly, there are both good and bad reasons for remaining single. Today, marriage is a personal choice, not a social dictate. In this chapter we will examine theories that attempt to explain mate selection and the functions and stages of dating. We will focus on mate selection from a cross-cultural point of view, looking at arranged marriages around the world and comparing them with the customary couple-arranged *love matches* of more-developed societies.

We tend to find mates who are like us in some way, people from our group—ethnic, religious, or socioeconomic. But many of these rules are changing as a result of our increasingly multicultural population. So-called mixed or intercultural marriages are a growing phenomenon, causing many families to examine their attitudes and behaviors toward people outside their particular cultural group.

Later in this chapter we will take a close look at some serious problems in our society today: conflict and violence in relationships and the connection between premarital violence and violence after marriage. Finally, we will conclude with a discussion of the growing trend of couples living together—an arrangement that is becoming a new courtship stage but one with legal and relationship consequences.

Courtship Patterns

One of the chief reasons so many marriages fail is that the functions of a date and a mate differ radically—that of a date is to be charming; that of a mate to be responsible; and, unfortunately, the most charming individuals are not necessarily the most responsible, while the most responsible are just as often deficient in charm.

—SYDNEY HARRIS, JOURNALIST

All societies have created some system for matching individuals for marriage and parenthood. These systems range from the practice of bride purchase, to the selection of a mate by the village shaman according to astrological signs, to contractual systems in which a mate may serve as an indentured servant to the bride's parents, to individual choice based on personal attraction and love. In some cultures, couples are matched while they are still infants; in others, the bride and groom must prove their fertility by producing children before they are eligible for marriage. Although the customs of mate selection vary widely, all perform the necessary function of matching a couple for marriage and eventual parenthood.

Parent-Arranged Marriages

Throughout much of world history, courtships were generally brief. In most cultures, the parents of the bride and groom selected the future spouse and made most of the arrangements for the marriage ceremony. If the prospective couple were granted any freedom of choice, they were expected to complete their arrangements in a few days. The pattern common in modern industrialized nations, in which a couple spends months or even years dating and choosing a mate, developed largely over the past century. Parent-arranged marriages, however, still occur throughout much of the nonindustrialized world (Bhopal, 2008). Although young adults in the United States today might view the practice as archaic and uncivilized, many people worldwide prefer parent-arranged marriages.

Myers, Madathil, and Tingle (2005) compared arranged marriages in India with marriages of choice in the United States. Their study indicated differences in what couples from these two countries thought were important precursors to marriage. For example, couples from the United States felt that love was an important requirement before marriage and couples in India felt love was less important. The important finding from this study, however, was that in the end marital satisfaction between the two groups did not differ significantly. Couples from the United States felt that love was an important component to have before the marriage, whereas, couples from India felt that love could grow. Couples in the arranged marriages also saw the importance of accepting and adjusting to their partner after marriage.

Parent-arranged marriages are based on the principle that the elders in a community have the wisdom to select the appropriate spouse. Parents or elders are more likely to base their decision on economic, political, and social status considerations—to enhance the family's status and position through their choice. Considerations of lineage and family status are generally more important than love or affection in such decisions, although the parents may take the couple's preferences into account to some extent. Arranged marriages thus serve to extend existing family units rather than to create new units. They reinforce ties with other families in the community, strengthening the order and organization of the community (Bhopal, 2008).

Advantages of Arranged Marriages. Parent-arranged marriages are usually very stable, because it is the duty of the whole family to help the new couple get established in life. Divorce is almost unheard of—except for the reason of infertility—because of the potential disapproval a couple would receive from the parents and members of the community who were responsible for the selection. Although love between the couple before marriage is relatively unimportant, affection and respect usually grow through the years; arranged marriages are often quite harmonious. Because there is not really a courtship period, premarital intimacy is minimal or nonexistent.

In parent-arranged marriage systems, couples avoid many of the problems of *American-style* dating. There is virtually no risk of being rejected or of losing one's true love, and one does not have to determine whether one's partner is committed to the relationship. Although many people might not view these factors as advantages, they effectively ensure a

Parent-arranged marriages are usually very stable, because it is the duty of the whole family to help the new couple get established in life. Divorce is almost unheard of—except for the reason of infertility—because of the potential disapproval a couple would receive from the parents and members of the community who were responsible for the selection.
©Erica Simone Leeds

stable marriage. Remnants of arranged courtship and marriage systems are still found in our culture today; for example, a limited number of professional marriage brokers still operate among urban ethnic groups. Further, as most single people know, relatives and friends are often only too eager to help find that "perfect" partner.

Patterns of Change. The world, in general, appears to be moving toward freedom of choice in marriage. This approach is sometimes referred to as the *love match*, though love is not always the goal of marriage in Western industrial societies. Perhaps a better term would be **couple-arranged marriage.** Cross-culturally, the absence of economic means for women to gain financial independence leads to early marriage and little individual freedom. The ability of women to work leads to the decline of arranged marriages, enhances the possibility of love matches, and may slightly diminish the marriage rate. In general, the world is also moving toward monogamous marriage, although the rate of advance varies from country to country.

The movement away from arranged marriage appears to be related to industrialization. As countries shift from more rural to urban industrial societies, love marriages become more common. Data from Africa, India, Israel, and Malaysia indicate that love marriages are more likely among people who marry at a later age, have a higher level of education, have a higher socioeconomic status (or the promise of a higher status), and live in an urban setting. A woman who can support herself financially is more likely to want to decide for herself whom she will marry.

Cultural Variations. The ways people find marriage partners vary from culture to culture. In developing countries that are moving away from arranged marriages, the influence of cultural tradition may be combined with modern sensibilities. In India, for example, it is commonly believed that there is one predestined mate who will share life with the spouse through reincarnation. Therefore parents believe they should supervise their children's marriage choices to avoid mistakes. But many young people are unhappy with this approach, and a compromise is often reached. Semiarranged marriages, in which parental approval is obtained before the marriage, are becoming more common. The case of Dipendra, an Indian sociology lecturer at a university in the South Pacific, provides an example:

> *"I suppose you could call our marriage a 'semiarranged' marriage. My parents had a girl in mind for me, but there was this other beautiful girl in my classes at the uni. I hadn't talked with her much, but she seemed good for me. So, I had my brother talk with her and then he talked with my parents, and the families got together and worked it out. She came from a good family, so my parents were quite pleased. Officially, it was an arranged marriage in the traditional Indian fashion, but I had a lot to say about it!"*

In China, there has been a dramatic change in mate selection from parent-arranged marriage to love-based marriage, as in the United States (Pan, 2002; Xu et al., 2007). Love-based mate selection happens more often in the larger cities than in the small towns and rural areas where parent-arranged marriage continues to occur. A common problem is that many of the young people in China do not know how to date or how to select a mate, and so dating is a challenging adventure for Chinese couples. But China, like many places in the world, is changing rapidly.

Japan, one of the current industrial giants of the Pacific, has generally moved from arranged marriages to love-based marriages. The traditional *nakode*, or matchmaker, is still used in some rural areas of Japan, but the matchmaker's role has become increasingly ceremonial. As more women have entered the labor force and gained financial independence, they have moved away from marriages arranged by their parents. Japanese young people can find dating very awkward and uncomfortable, however, because they often do not have much social contact with members of the other sex.

The Scandinavian countries are perhaps the most liberal in the world in regard to marriage customs. Parent-arranged marriages disappeared decades ago in Scandinavia, and cohabitation has become the most common type of relationship until after the birth of a child. Research in Sweden indicates a steep drop in the marriage rate. Associated with this decline are an increase in cohabitation and an increase in state and parental support for children born outside of matrimony (Cherlin, 2009).

What Has Happened to Dating?

If one were to search the literature for the topic of **dating,** one would find that the most recent articles are in the mid-2000s. What has happened? Bogle (2007) provides an historical explanation of trends from 1960 to recent times. Bogle summarizes the research, which indicates that dating culture began to change in the 1960s with the sexual revolution. According to Murstein (1980), the traditional date, where a male picks up a female at her home and the male pays for the expenses of the date, was rapidly dying in the 1970s. Instead, couples began to be more comfortable congregating in groups and getting into couple relationships at these gatherings. Dating was still occurring at that time outside of the college campuses where it was more difficult to arrange for groups of people to gather.

On college campuses, young people were "partying" instead of dating (Murstein, 1980). Bogle (2007) indicates that college students were rejecting the formality of dating and found partners, sexual or otherwise, at these gatherings. Although research continued under the topic of dating into the 2000s, Bogle (2007) suggests that this was not dating in the traditional sense, but rather **hooking up.** Hooking up can be a sexual encounter that may include anything from kissing to intercourse. Bogle explains that traditional dating only occurred after a couple was in an exclusive relationship. Although couples may hook up, most do not result in an exclusive relationship. Most studies were conducted with college students, because they are an easy to reach population, but they likely do not represent the larger population that is more likely to date in a more traditional sense. However, even a more traditional date is likely to result in sharing the expenses of the date.

Couples may spend time together doing a variety of activities with others, or they may spend time together as couples.
©Radius Images/Alamy Stock Photo

Hooking Up: Sex, Dating and Relationships on Campus, written by Kathleen Bogle (2008a), studied hooking up at two unnamed universities—a large East Coast public university and a smaller Roman Catholic school in the Northeast. She found that hooking up involves a wide range of behavior, from those who do not participate at all to those who participate to a moderate degree to those aspects of hookup culture that might be "cause for alarm (or at least concern)."

Comparing a religious institution to a state university, Bogle found that most students she interviewed in the faith-based university did not believe that the religious affiliation affected hooking up in any way. College, by its very nature, is very conducive to hooking up. Bogle describes campuses as homogeneous populations of young men and women living close together with no strictly enforced rules or careful monitoring of their behavior. Students socialize among themselves, and this fosters feelings of safety and comfort. A *let loose and party* attitude pervades campuses, and this makes for an environment in which hookup culture thrives.

In many campus fraternities, freshman males are not allowed to attend a party unless they are a fraternity member, while freshman females are admitted to the party for free. Bogle argues that this practice fosters a *conquest mentality* toward sex among many fraternity members. She also believes that hookup culture more negatively impacts females than males. For one reason, women are far more likely to get a bad reputation for their conduct, including a bad reputation for how often they hook up, whom they hook up with, how far they go sexually during a hookup, and how they dress when they go out at night to a place where hooking up may occur. Men who are active in the hookup game are called *players,* while women are called *sluts.* A second reason hookup culture is harder on women than men is, Bogle believes, that women are not getting what they want out of the hookup system. Women often are seeking a stable, ongoing relationship rather than simply a sexual experience, and are dissatisfied with how often hooking up leads to nothing. Bogle concedes that there are certainly many cases in which a woman is not seeking a serious relationship, "but on average women are far more interested in a hookup turning into 'something more' than men are."

All this puts women in a difficult position. If they don't hook up at all, they are left out of the dominant cultural game on campus and may find it difficult to find opportunities to form sexual and romantic relationships with men. If they do hook up, though, they find themselves walking a fine line as they try to be part of the campus mainstream without being negatively labeled. Bogle observed that campus hookup culture was a 24/7 sexual arena in which students were constantly watching each other, gossiping about each other, and judging each other. When students leave college, Bogle says, there is a discernible shift away from hookup culture to more formal dating and, eventually, marriage, for many. Some college graduates in her study found the more formal dating system a big adjustment.

Several students described to Bogle what they called the *walk of shame.* This refers to a college student, usually female, walking home in the morning after a hookup in the same outfit she was wearing the night before. Because students dress differently when they go out at night, it is obvious to everyone she passes on campus where she has been. Bogle believes that this terminology alone underscores the point that many students on campus are struggling with the hookup system and want more (Bogle, 2008b).

Who hooks up, and with whom do they hook up? In a study of a large number of college students, Lewis, Granato, Blayney, Lostutter, and Kilmer (2012) found that most people hooked up with someone they knew. This could be a friend or ex-partner. Hooking up with an ex-partner was associated with an increased likelihood of using a condom, possibly because they felt more comfortable negotiating condom use. Additionally, alcohol use was associated with most of the hook ups. Having oral sex was seen more positively and vaginal sex was viewed more negatively by the participants in this study. These authors suggest that there are concerns about sexual safety based on the findings of this study. Over half of the

In the past, the pool of eligible partners was often limited by the difficulty of traveling long distances. Today, the internet allows people from across the country to chat online, making the pool of potential partners less restricted by physical proximity.
©Javier Pierini/Stockbyte/Getty Images

participants had sex during their last hook up, and only 47% used a condom. Less than 1% of the sexual encounters resulted in pregnancy or a sexually transmitted disease.

Owen and Fincham (2011) studied emotional reactions of college students after hooking up. They found that men had more positive feelings than women, but both men and women indicated the experience was more positive than negative. Women were more likely than men to hope that the hook up would lead to a committed relationship.

Hooking up is also a common practice for teens as well as college students (Manning, Giordano, & Longmore, 2006). Findings of hooking up in teen years have some of the same characteristics as those that occur while attending college in that people usually hook up with someone they know, such as friends or ex-partners. These authors found that one-third of the individuals hooking up hoped that a relationship will develop.

Trends in Searching for a Partner

The process of finding a heterosexual partner today is much different than it was several years ago, and it has even changed in recent history (Rosenfeld & Thomas, 2012). As Figure 10.1 shows, the internet and friends have become the most often cited connection sources of finding a mate. Historically, from the 1940s through about the 1990s, people typically met their partners in primary or secondary school or through their family. These sources were in close proximity to where people grew up and provided a likely place to meet people. These were safe ways to begin dating, because people often knew each other well and may have even been acquainted with each other's family background. Meeting someone with a similar background in terms of income level, race, and religion was very likely. In addition, meeting through family, coworkers, or friends provided a third party who could vouch for a potential partner.

According to Rosenfeld and Thomas (2012), meeting on the internet did not result in less stable relationships. These researchers found that those who had face-to-face relationships that had started online, were of the same quality and no more fragile than relationships that

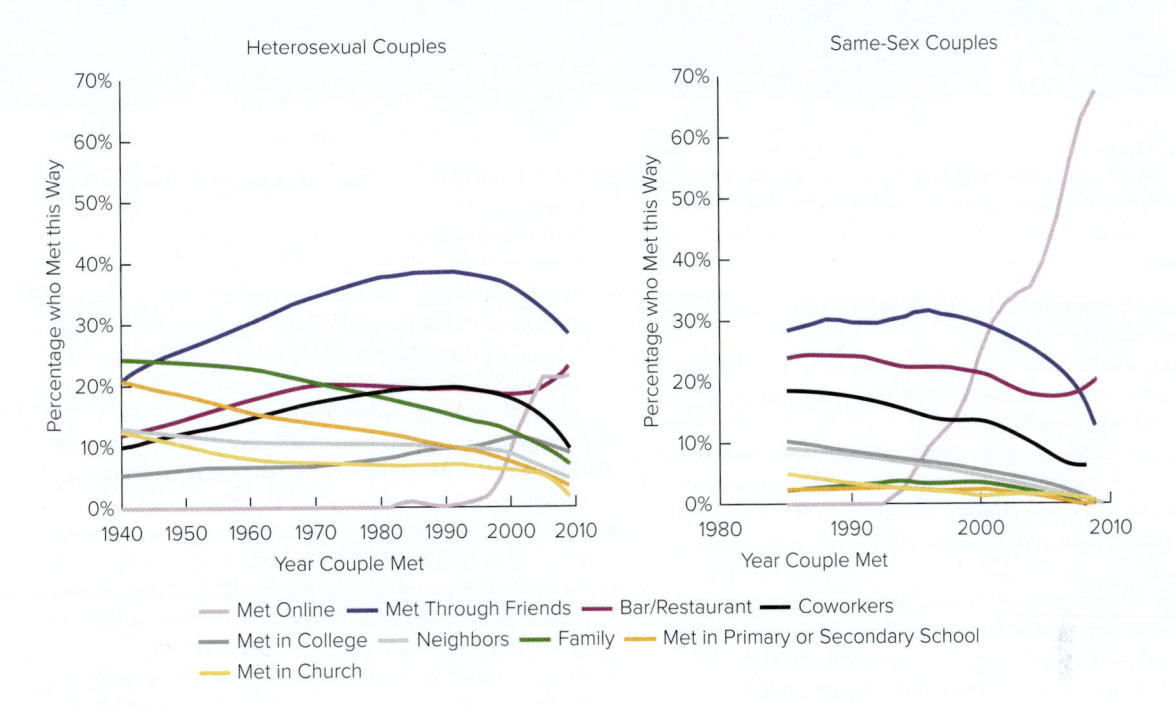

FIGURE 10.1
How Couples Meet
Source: Rosenfeld, M. J., & Thomas, R. J.," Searching for a Mate: The Rise of the Internet as a Social Intermediary," *American Sociological Review*, 77, 2012, 523–547.

did not begin on the internet. According to these authors, even people who meet someone on the internet rely on friends and family to help determine whether their partner is a good match. Rappleyea, Taylor, and Fang (2014) also found in their study of 18- to 25-year-olds, that although men and women used technology to connect with a potential dating partner, they preferred personal contact such as "hanging out" to truly develop the relationship.

As the second graph in Figure 10.1 shows, gay and lesbian couples are even more likely to search for a partner on the internet. According to Rosenfeld and Thomas (2012), the internet may be an especially important resource when there is a scarce dating market. Other resources such as friends and family are less likely to know about potential partners for this same-sex population. As data in the graph indicate, for same-sex couples the use of the internet increased, while the use of friends, coworkers, and meeting people in bars declined significantly.

So what do statistics around internet dating look like? According to Smith (2016, February 11), 15% of adults in America have used online dating sites. Since 2013, usage by emerging adults (18 to 24 years of age) has increased threefold. For the older population (55 to 64 years of age) it has doubled. In 2015 study conducted by Pew Research Center and cited by Smith, 12% of adults have used an online dating site. The growth has been greatest by emerging adults and those 50 years and older. It is important to note, however, that one-third of those who have used online dating never went on a date with someone (Smith, 2016, February 29). Smith (2016, February 11) also indicates that the more affluent are more likely than the less affluent to use online resources. Most (80%) of those who have used this means to find dating partners agree that it is a good and generally efficient way to meet people. According to Smith (2016, February 29), meeting someone online has lost the stigma it once had and the majority of Americans feel it is a good way to meet people.

BOX 10.1 Putting It Together

Dating Do's and Don'ts

As we have learned, currently dating is typically happening for those who are in a relationship and may have some level of commitment to each other. Here are some things to think about when dating:

- There are two main reasons for dating, for pleasure and to find a mate.
- Dating should be for fun and for mutual enjoyment. It gives two people a chance to get to know each other and enjoy each other's company.
- Take it slow. Don't jump into things. Gradually reveal more and more about yourself, rather than overwhelming the other person.
- Don't feel the need to become involved physically too soon because it is better for the relationship if you first become friends.
- Friendship is a better foundation to base a relationship on than sex. Sexual attraction and energy often confuse you and prevent you from getting to know each other in other ways.
- It's important to get to know a number of people before getting serious with one.
- Friends and relatives can give you good feedback about someone you are dating. They often can be more objective about what is happening than someone who thinks he or she is falling in love.
- Get to know the friends and family members of someone you are getting serious about. You often can learn a great deal about a person by visiting with those who have known him or her intimately over a long period of time.
- How do your prospective mate's parents get along? This can give you some clues about how you will get along after marriage.
- Whatever you see that you dislike while dating someone is likely to become magnified after marriage. Small problems before the wedding can become large ones later.
- Be especially cautious about how the prospective mate deals with angry feelings. If the person takes anger out on others, it is only likely to get worse after marriage.
- Notice how your date treats other people. Look for someone who is respectful and kind to everyone.
- Be realistic. Don't look at your prospective mate through rose-colored glasses, seeing only the positives. Sometimes there are serious negatives that have to be considered carefully.
- Be sure to talk with each other about what you like and what bothers you. Being positive is easy, of course, but you need to be honest and express those thoughts that are more difficult to bring up.
- Falling in love is easy. Staying in love takes intelligence, creativity, commitment, and a good heart.
- Trust your feelings and use your brain.

Ongoing Relationships

No matter how one begins the process of dating, some general guidelines about the do's and don'ts of dating are listed in Box 10.1. Basically, dating is a time to learn more about yourself and what you like and don't like in other people. These guidelines are suggestions that can help you make dating a more rewarding and useful experience.

So, how do romantic relationships develop? Weiser and Niehuis (2014) summarized and discussed earlier research which identifies multiple steps people go through in developing intimate relationships. Initially, a conversation between two people begins. Today this may begin with a face-to-face conversation or with an online dating experience. Next, the conversation may extend to learning about each other and may include basic information to get to know details about the other person's life. This gradual revelation may be happening over time through multiple dates and may take several months. Finally, the individuals in the couple learn to trust each other and develop some level of commitment. They may move forward to a committed long-term relationship or marriage. Many couples, of course, end the relationship before they get to a trusting and committed relationship. They may find out that the other person does not share basic core values, or that they do not like how the person treats them.

One of the trends seen in relationships is the "on-again/off-again" relationship (Lindstrom, Monk, & Vennum, 2014, p. F5). According to these authors, 60% of couples have experienced breaking up and reconciliation with a partner. Does it work better the second time? Couples who reconnect after breaking up often do so because they still have feelings for the person or they miss having the shared history with someone. These boomerang relationships usually do not work well. Lindstrom et al. (2014) found that the second time around there is poor communication, increased uncertainty about the relationship, and less stability. They may have slid back into something that felt comfortable rather than deliberately evaluating what was wrong the first time around. One might speculate that these couples get back together because they are not finding healthier, more satisfying relationships and decide to settle.

Breaking Up Is Hard to Do

Most individuals have experienced a breakup with someone they perceived as a potential long-term partner. In fact, most of us have had this experience multiple times. The effect of these breakups can be devastating. Depression is a common response to a breakup and may result in thoughts similar to those experienced when someone close to them dies (Graham, Keneski, & Loving, 2014). There may be insomnia, increased use of alcohol or medications, and increased susceptibility to disease. The person may feel increased distress and lower self-esteem as a result of the loss. Field (2011) has actually coined the feeling as "broken heart syndrome" (p. 382), which is pain in one's chest similar to a heart attack. Field indicates these symptoms are experienced across cultures.

It needs to be noted that not all breakups result in heartbreak (Graham et al., 2014). Some individuals are relieved to be ending a relationship. Because it is often difficult to end a relationship, it may have gone on too long. Staying together may cause stress and other symptoms identified in the previous text as well. The ability to get out from under that stress of staying in a relationship might result in a newly found freedom.

Dating Among Older People

The term *dating* has a decidedly youthful ring, but single people over 65 also date and are sexually active. Interest in dating, especially for older women, is typically the result of divorce; whereas, dating for older men is typically because they have never married (Sassler, 2010). Dating offers the single older person romance, the most exciting form of intimacy for human beings, no matter what age. When it goes well, dating can boost an older person's self-confidence and offer the potential for happiness and companionship at an age in life when future prospects are uncertain. When it goes poorly, dating can destroy self-confidence. In sum, dating in the later years can be thrilling, nerve-wracking, and complicated, just as it was in the younger years of life.

The proportion of older individuals in the American population has increased dramatically since 1900. About 15% of Americans are over 65 (Federal Interagency Forum on Aging-Related Statistics, 2016, August). Because women live longer than men, the ratio of women to men increases as they age. This affects the ability of women to find men with which to develop relationships. As life spans lengthen, the percentage of older individuals is expected to increase, to about 20% by the year 2030 (U.S. Administration on Aging, 2009; U.S. Census Bureau, 2009a). We also know that divorced or widowed men are more likely to remarry than women (Sassler, 2010). This is likely to be because of the lack of availability of men in relation to women.

Older people date, fall in love, and behave romantically in ways similar to the young. It is very common these days to see proms and dances at retirement facilities. There are also *kings* and *queens* crowned at these events—makeup and formal dress all around. These events are very successful and are well attended. What older people do on dates is similar to what younger individuals do but is often "far more varied and creative." In addition to pizza, movies, and dances, older couples went camping, enjoyed the opera together, and flew off to

Although we usually think of dating couples as being young, today more older couples are dating, cohabiting, and marrying.
©Ronnie Kaufman/Blend Images/Getty Images

Hawaii for the weekend. Also, the pace of dating is greatly accelerated. Older people realize they simply do not have much time to play the field. Therefore, they are very direct and forthcoming in their approach in building relationships. Sexual relationships may develop and older people may feel they need sexual intimacy more as they get older than they did earlier in their lives. Sex can reaffirm the fact that one is alive and important to at least one other person in the world.

Like younger individuals, older people face a number of dilemmas and difficulties in dating. Fear of disapproval leads many to be secretive about their dating activities. At this point in their lives, they may have adult children or grandchildren who disapprove of their romantic relationships. Adult children may worry about their aging parents having bad judgment about relationships, or they may feel that their parents are moving into relationships too quickly.

Marriage is another dilemma for older people. They may initially seek a marital partner, but many decide as time goes on that they are not willing to give up their independence. Women, especially, often like the new freedom divorce or widowhood offers (Sassler, 2010). Both men and women sometimes do not want to marry because they will lose their Social Security or do not want to have their assets merged through marriage. Some do not want the hassle of merging two households. Therefore, older adults are often entering into long-term companionship arrangements, but choose not to live together or get married. Older adults often view cohabitation as an alternative to marriage rather than a precursor to marriage (Sassler, 2010). Finally, many fear the burden of caring for someone in deteriorating health or being a burden themselves to someone else.

Choosing a Mate

Americans tend to choose partners who are similar to them in a variety of ways—in ethnic and cultural background, age, educational and religious background, and socioeconomic status. This section discusses the criteria that influence mate selection in the United States.

Appearance makes a difference in a person's life in several ways: Attractive individuals do better in school, believe they have a more promising future, and feel better about themselves than less-attractive individuals. Appearance is one of several features important in mate selection.
©Purestock/SuperStock

Those Who Are Like Us

Being similar in a variety of ways is one of the most powerful determinants in choosing a lifelong partner (Shpancer, 2014, December 2). We often live, go to school, or work in places where there are people like us. We often share common values, culture, income, and religion and, therefore, these are the people we often end up choosing to marry or to whom we make commitments. For example, if one marries someone who has a college degree, it is likely they will share views about the importance of education and also a similar income level.

According to Hutson (2015, January/February), it is true that people marry others who are similar in income levels and education, with education mattering more. Hutson also indicates that people with similar mental and emotional disorders such as depression and chemical dependency issues seem to end up together. According to Shpancer, we often even marry someone who is similar in attractiveness. It is just easier to relate to and understand someone who is like us.

Age and Finding a Mate

It has been estimated that in six out of every seven marriages in the United States, the man is as old as or older than the woman. Why is this the case? Physiologically, males mature more slowly than females and do not live as long. Furthermore, in the United States there are more males than females in their early 20s. Finally, there is the phenomenon social scientists have labeled the **mating gradient,** the tendency of women to marry men who are better educated or more successful than they are. Because men tend to "marry down" in terms of age and status, it can be difficult for successful older women to find an acceptable mate.

Although married men tend to be as old as or older than their spouses, the age difference between partners marrying today isn't very pronounced, especially among younger people. In the United States in the 1960s, the median age for males marrying for the first time was about 23, and the median age for females was about 20, about a 3-year difference in ages. By 2012, the estimated U.S. median ages at first marriage had risen, to 28.3 years for men and 25.8 years for women, about a 2.5 year difference in ages (Copen, Daniels, Vespa, & Mosher, 2012, March).

The term **sex ratio** indicates the relationship between the number of men and the number of women of a given age. Because of differences in birth and infant mortality rates, men have historically outnumbered—and continue to outnumber—women in the U.S. population. Most recent U.S. Census Bureau (Howden & Meyer, 2011, May) figures indicate there are

105 men for every 100 women. If every single man in this country wanted to marry, there wouldn't be enough women to go around. This problem is true for men across all age groups, except those 85 and older when women tend to start exceeding men, since women have a longer life span.

An increasing dilemma for women who want to pursue a career is that it is challenging to develop a career while also trying to find Mr. Right. An insightful discussion of the many issues confronting women today is provided by Barbara Whitehead (2003) in a book entitled *Why There Are No Good Men Left*. As women reach their 30s, there are fewer men available who are personally acceptable and can also match the income and achievements of the women. As a result, many career women are frustrated in their efforts to find and develop a relationship that will lead to marriage and a family.

Birth Order

One might wonder if birth order affects marital satisfaction. Should we be looking for a partner who has similar birth order, or differing birth order from ourselves? Historically, studies have had mixed findings. The assumption is that birth order affects personality and personality affects how we form friendships and select a mate and, thus, there would be a relationship between birth orders of friends and spouses (Hartshorne, Salem-Hartshorne, & Hartshorne, 2009). These authors completed two studies with sample sizes of 1,000 and 2,500 participants and found in both studies that people are more likely to be in long-term relationships, either friendships or romantic, if they share a birth order than if they do not.

In a recent study of a large random sample of 10,000 married couples, a researcher compared couple satisfaction and intimacy for couples who had a spouse with the same birth order with those who had a spouse with a different birth order (Raetz, 2011). This researcher found that there was no significant effect on marriage intimacy and satisfaction.

The answer to the question: Does birth order matter in mate section? We don't know yet.

Similar Personalities or Different Personalities

Are people attracted to personality types that are like themselves or different from themselves? Are relationships likely to work better if a couple is like *two peas in a pod*, or *the odd couple*? Kaufman (2011) conducted a study with 10,000 couples with five different couple types concerning their degree of relationship satisfaction. The first finding was that couples did not, in fact, marry someone like themselves. Two-thirds of the couples had personality scores that did not match up. Second, this researcher found that happily married couples were not significantly different or significantly similar to each other. The findings of this study indicated that whether individuals have similar personalities or different personalities, it does not impact marital satisfaction.

Interracial and Interfaith Marriages

Two other factors that influence mate selection are endogamy and exogamy. **Endogamy** is the culturally prescribed practice or tradition of choosing a mate from within one's own group. These groups might include ethnic, religious, socioeconomic, or general age groups. The principle of endogamy supposes, say, that middle-class Whites will marry middle-class Whites, Catholics will marry Catholics, and young people will marry young people. **Exogamy**—the practice or tradition of choosing a mate from outside one's own group—is typically discouraged in our society. There are no laws against marrying someone of a different socioeconomic status, religion, or ethnic group; however, outside groups tend to be off limits or less desirable as a source of marital partners.

The growing ethnic diversity in the United States and the increasing rate of marriage across ethnic groups are changing the *unwritten rules* regarding exogamy. This change reflects a common belief that in the United States all ethnic and cultural groups can live and work together. This belief is true to a certain degree—we have developed a relatively stable society and share certain democratic values—but the United States is by no means a blended and homogeneous society. Although the ethnic and cultural mix often works rather well, the elements that make it up remain distinct. Ethnic values and identifications endure for generations. When people marry out of their ethnic group, problems can arise; the difficulties inherent in intercultural marriage often intensify if the partners do not anticipate them. We confuse the idea that we are all created equal with the belief that we are all the same.

The marriage rate between members of different ethnic groups is difficult to assess accurately because the concept of race is elusive, and many people cannot be easily classified into ethnic groups. According to Wendy Wang (2012, February 16) from the Pew Research Center, in 2010 about 15% of new marriages were between people from different races or ethnic groups. This is more than double the number in 1980. No matter when they married, in 2010 existing intermarriages reached an all time high of 8.4%. Hispanics and Asians are the most likely to marry outside of their ethnic group.

Parents are often hesitant to bless an intercultural marriage. They may be aware of the problems their children will face, both within the relationship and in our society. They may also think the young partners are naive, idealistic, or blinded by love and need the guidance of their more experienced elders.

Some of these concerns are legitimate. When people marry, they are often idealistic in their beliefs. One common—and unrealistic—belief is that love conquers all. Another is that true love means that the couple either has few differences or that one partner can change the other after marriage. In the words of one family therapist, "Spouses tend to perceive their cultural differences as failings—either badness or madness. With insight, people are able to get some distance from their hurt feelings and stop taking inevitable differences personally." Although differences can be a source of strength in a marriage, they can also cause problems.

One study investigated the experiences of 10 White/Asian Indian mixed race marriages (Inman, Altman, Kaduvettoor-Davidson, Carr, & Walker, 2011). The findings of this study indicated that couples received support from outside the family, but not from families of origin. The most common concern on the part of families of origin was protecting future generations. This concern focused on diluting ethnic pride, not passing on cultural values, and the effect on religious values. For these couples there was often a difference in social class, specifically education and income, which also became a concern for families of origin. These couples also experienced power and cultural differences in their interracial relationships, which required extensive negotiation to resolve and address. The more they learned about each other's culture, however, the more it strengthened their marriages.

Ethnically mixed couples are more likely to divorce and to have a variety of marital and family problems (Wang, 2012, February 16). Children of intercultural marriages have more personal and relationship problems than children from ethnically homogeneous families. The greater the ethnic differences between individuals, the less likely they are to marry. After marriage, the greater the differences, the greater the difficulty the couple will have adjusting to each other. McGoldrick, Giordano, and Preto (2005, 2008) identify eight factors that they believe most influence the degree of adjustment:

- *Values.* The greater the discrepancy in values between the cultural groups, the more difficulty the couple will have. For example, a Puerto Rican–Italian couple will probably have less difficulty because of disparity of values than will an Irish–Italian couple.
- *Acculturation.* The greater the difference in the levels of acculturation of each partner, the greater the probability of conflict. For example, a couple is likely to have

more difficulty if one is a recent immigrant and the other a fourth-generation American.

- *Religion.* Adding religious differences to cultural differences can compound adjustment difficulties. An Irish–Italian couple will probably have an easier time adjusting to marriage than an Irish–Jewish couple because the Irish and Italian partners are likely to share a common Catholic heritage. This is one less area for misunderstandings.
- *Race.* Interracial couples are the most vulnerable of all couples, sometimes feeling isolated from both groups. The children of an interracial union are also sometimes subject to discrimination from both groups. As interracial children become more commonplace, however, this discrimination may decline. Former President Obama, the son of a white mother and black father, may be helping our thinking on all this to evolve.
- *Sex and sex roles.* Because women are generally reared to talk more about their feelings, an Irish wife, for example, will probably have an easier time adjusting to a Jewish husband than a Jewish wife would have adjusting to an Irish husband. Why? Because Jews are traditionally more verbal, and McGoldrick and colleagues presume that matching a verbal Irish wife and a verbal Jewish husband would work out better than matching a verbal Jewish wife and a relatively less verbal Irish husband.
- *Socioeconomic differences.* Partners from different socioeconomic circumstances have added difficulties adjusting to each other. The financial issues with which couples must contend can become even more problematic if the partners have different life experiences and expectations regarding them.

Marriages between individuals of different ethnic backgrounds involve special challenges. Partners must acknowledge and appreciate differences and make them a strength of the relationship rather than a source of conflict.
©Ryan McVay/Valueline/Getty Images

- *Cultural familiarity.* Partners who have some experience with each other's culture before marriage are more likely to understand and adjust to each other. Couples who live in a multiethnic neighborhood after marriage are also less likely to experience pressure and negative reactions from others.
- *Extended-family agreement.* If kin of both partners are supportive, the couple has a greater chance of success. If a couple feels forced to elope or if one partner's family refuses to attend the wedding, this can indicate future difficulties.

Every ethnic group has its own unique heritage, values, and behaviors that make it special. It is important for those who marry someone from a different group to be aware of these differences and to work toward making them an asset rather than a liability.

In the final analysis, it can be argued that couples who engage in a relationship as intimate and enduring as marriage are likely to have transcended the boundary between them to some degree. From this positive perspective, increasing intermarriage can be celebrated as evidence that ethnic and cultural boundaries are weakening. Intermarriage can also be seen as an engine of social change, because children of interracial and interethnic couples are not as likely to identify with a single group, and these children challenge group boundaries by their very existence (Fu, 2008).

Finding a Good Mate

People often meet and date someone, may eventually marry, and ultimately realize the person is not a good partner. In fact, they may realize he or she is really a jerk. A curriculum used around the country helps someone looking for a partner to discern what to look for when seeking a partner. The program is referred to as *How to Avoid Falling for a Jerk (ette)* (Pick Program, n.d.). It was developed by Dr. John Van Epp, a therapist, and the curriculum is research based. This is a 6-hour premarital curriculum for anyone who wants to learn what a couple needs in order to have a healthy relationship. Not only does one learn how to avoid falling for a jerk (ette), but one can also learn to identify how they might, at times, act like a jerk (ette).

Utah State University Extension faculty have used this curriculum in providing classes throughout the State of Utah. The goal of the project was to provide classes for 18- to 30-year-olds, primarily college-age individuals. As the program progressed, however, it became clear the need for such a course went well beyond college-age individuals, and participants have instead ranged from 18 to 80 years of age. Not only do those who want a healthy first marriage take the course, but those who are widowed and divorced one or more times also enroll. High school age youth also benefit from the course as they look forward to having healthy relationships.

Preliminary data with 300 participants indicated that there was a statistically significant positive change after taking the course in knowing how to have a healthy relationship, communicate well with a partner, and have effective conflict management skills (Morrill, Bradford, Higginbotham, & Skogrand, 2013). Also, after taking the course, 68% felt they needed to change how *they* were in relationships. They realized everyone can act like a jerk at times.

Patterns of Mate Selection

Research regarding mate selection is currently more complex than it was years ago. If we are to truly understand mate selection today, we need to be knowledgeable about internet dating, hooking up, marriage after child birth, cohabitation, and serial partnering, as well as the traditional research that focused primarily on how couples transitioned into marriage. However, the common denominator in selecting a mate is a great desire for sexual and emotional intimacy that is sought after with each of the kinds of romantic relationships listed above. In addition, how this partnering happens also changes throughout the life cycle (Sassler, 2010).

Earlier editions of this textbook have included three theories about mate selection. Today, that does not begin to cover all the theories that are used in explaining how we find intimacy. One of the popular theories used today is attachment theory, which assumes that the same kind of emotional bonds between parents and children are evident in adult intimate relationships (Cassidy & Shaver, 2008). A second theory that is often used is exchange theory, which focuses on how relationships are developed based upon rewards received between partners (Qian & Lichter, 2007; Sprecher, 2001). Equity theory, which focuses on what is fair and unfair in relationships, is also used to explain and describe mate selection behaviors (Sprecher, 2001). Life course theories are also used to describe how individuals and couples transition throughout different stages in life (Waller & Peters, 2008). Feminist theory, which focuses on gender, is also increasingly being used (Smiler, 2008). Additionally, sociobiological theory emphasizes how evolutionary factors affect romantic and sexual preferences (Shoemake, 2007). Certainly this is not an exhaustive list of theories used to understand and explain mate selection; however, it provides an understanding of how varied the use of theory is regarding this topic. In recent years, because there are so many issues around mate selection, many family theories are used. It is beyond the scope of this book to describe them all in detail.

One of the new areas of research is to include the population of emerging adults, that is, those whose ages range from 18 through their mid-20s. This stage of life has received attention because young people are spending more time transiting into adulthood (Willoughby & Dworkin, 2009). Therefore, the adolescent years of mate selection have been expanded to include those into their mid-20s (Sassler, 2010). A summary of the literature in recent years draws the following conclusions about mate selection with teens through young adulthood (Sassler, 2010):

- By mid-teens approximately half of these adolescents have had a romantic relationship.
- By the time they graduate from high school, almost three-quarters of teens have had such a relationship.
- As teens move into emerging adulthood, they move from spending time in friendship groups to developing more committed relationships.
- Those who are in romantic relationships during high school are more likely to marry or enter cohabiting relationships in their 20s.
- Most teens and emerging adults enter into romantic relationships with others who are like them. However, there are a significant number who date across racial lines.
- Teenagers typically date before engaging in sexual intimacy; however, for a minority sexual partnering occurs without a relationship.
- Although hookups are defined as having a sexual encounter, the majority of hookups do not result in intercourse.
- The overwhelming majority of people in this age group plan to marry.

Several other sections in this chapter provide additional research findings about the components of mate selection, such as cohabitation, dating among older people, hooking up, and internet dating. These topics indicate how complex mate selection is in the 21st century.

Conflict and Violence in Relationships

Intimate partner violence is verbal, emotional, physical, or sexual abuse directed at a romantic partner (Cui, Ueno, Gordon, & Fincham, 2013; Ouytsel, Ponnet, & Walrave, 2017). Because of the wide range of behaviors within this definition across age groups, it is difficult to know the prevalence of intimate partner violence.

Conflict is an inevitable part of every relationship, but areas of conflict change as partners become more committed to each other. In the early stages of a relationship, jealousy and other personality issues are the greatest sources of conflict; later, conflict arises from such issues as differences in background, the balance of power in the relationship, and parent relationships.
©Wavebreak Media ltd/Alamy Stock Photo

According to Ouytsel et al. (2017), teenage relationship violence is associated with substance use such as smoking and alcohol and marijuana use. It is also related to risky sexual behaviors such as not using condoms. And, it is linked to behavior problems such as fighting with peers as well as depression and suicidal behaviors. It is not clear whether the violence causes these behaviors or vice versa. For example, are those who are using substances going to be more vulnerable to intimate partner violence, or are those who have experienced violence more likely to use substances to alleviate the painful experiences?

There is a belief that behaviors are learned and reinforced, and that adolescents who have experienced violence in previous relationships may feel that violence is acceptable and allow these behaviors in subsequent relationships (Cui et al., 2013). This acceptance may be on the part of either the perpetrator or the victim. This behavior may continue throughout adolescence and into adulthood. Because this behavior might have been witnessed in childhood, it can also become intergenerational. In a very large national sample following middle- and high-school youth into adulthood, Cui et al. (2013) found that a person who experienced violence as an adolescent was likely to also become a victim in young adulthood. These researchers also found that those who had been a victim during adolescence were more likely to be a perpetrator in future relationships. Again, this initial victimization might have been at the hand of parents, other adults, or an intimate partner. In fact, this study and other studies show that parent/child violence is a strong predictor of later intimate partner violence.

Cui et al. (2013) also found that couples living together were more likely to experience intimate partner violence than couples who were dating but not living together. These researchers speculate that living together requires more effort to terminate the relationship than for couples who are dating but not living together. In other words, for those living together it is more difficult to get out of a violent relationship.

It is clear that intervention should begin in the home with parents who may be violent and also with teens who may be perpetrators or victims of violence. These behaviors might be stopped before they become adults and pass violence on to the next generation.

BOX 10.2 At Issue

Partner Violence Warning Signs

Young people generally do not tell others when they are involved in a violent relationship, so it is important to be alert for signs that an individual may be involved in a relationship that is, or has the potential to become, abusive. Some of the following signs are just part of being a young person. But when these changes happen suddenly, or without explanation, there may be cause for concern.

- Does the boyfriend or girlfriend lash out, criticize, or insult the individual?
- Do you see signs that the individual is afraid of his/her boyfriend or girlfriend?
- Does the boyfriend or girlfriend seem to try to control the individual's behavior, making all of the decisions, checking up on his/her behavior, demanding to know who the individual has been with, acting jealous and possessive?
- Does the individual have unexplained bruises, scratches, or injuries?
- Does the individual apologize to you and others for the boyfriend or girlfriend's behavior?
- Has the individual casually mentioned the boyfriend or girlfriend's temper or violent behavior, but then laughed it off as a joke?
- Have you seen the boyfriend or girlfriend be abusive toward other people or things?
- Does the individual seem to have lost interest or to be giving up on things that were once important? Has he/she lost interest in school or other activities?
- Has the individual's appearance or behavior suddenly changed?
- Has the individual stopped spending time with friends and family?
- Have you seen sudden changes in the individual's mood or personality? Is the individual becoming anxious or depressed, acting out, or being secretive? Is the individual avoiding eye contact, having "crying jags" or becoming "hysterical"?
- Has the individual recently started using alcohol or drugs?

Source: Adapted from *Dating Violence Warning Signs*. National Youth Violence Prevention Resource Center 2009.

It is not unusual for individuals in a couple relationship to hope that violence will end when they get married or when they have children, but this is not likely. In fact, unless there is an intervention and an effort is made to change behaviors, the violence will escalate as time goes on. One young woman from Chicago recounts her experience before and after her wedding:

> *"I thought it would get better after the wedding. We had planned so long and carefully for it, and I knew the wedding would be wonderful. But even on the day of the wedding, Marty slapped me in the face. I don't know. He was frustrated about something my brother said or something. I don't know.*
>
> *"After we got married, it really got bad. He would stay out with his friends till all hours and when he came home, if I said even one word about it, he would hit me. Hard. I stayed with him 2 years, but when he pushed me down when I was 7 months pregnant, I couldn't stand it anymore and I left for the domestic violence program shelter. He would have hurt the baby, and I would never have forgiven myself. I ended up leaving town, moving to my sister's in Indianapolis. I didn't have hardly anything . . . Alexis's baby clothes and her toys, my clothes, a small stereo system.*
>
> *"I didn't have anything, really, but I was free and that was what counted."*

It is clear that if an individual is violent early in a relationship, it is most likely this behavior will continue after marriage. In general, a violent date is a poor marriage risk. Violence breeds violence and quickly destroys an intimate relationship. It is important, especially for women, to watch for warning signals that a partner might become more abusive as the relationship becomes more serious. See Box 10.2, which lists several very useful warning signals.

It is important for people to trust their own feelings regarding abuse from a partner and not to confuse abuse with love. Following are four relevant questions to seriously consider before committing oneself to a relationship:

Does your love "turn you on" or "turn you off"?
Does your love "tune you in" or "tune you out"?
Does your love "make you sing" or "make you shout"?
Does your love "light your fire" or "put it out"?

Living Together

For many people, marriage is no longer considered a prerequisite for living with a romantic partner. **Cohabitation** is defined by the federal government as two unrelated adults of the opposite sex sharing the same living quarters. A broader definition would include both heterosexual and same-sex unmarried couples who have an emotional and sexual relationship.

Cohabitation's Dramatic Increase

Between 1960 and 2009, the number of unmarried couples living together increased by more than 15-fold (Wilcox, 2010). Cohabitation is more popular than ever as a way for many Americans to move from being single to becoming married. Though it remains a controversial issue for many people, from a statistical standpoint it has become the norm to cohabit before marriage. The majority of all marriages are preceded by cohabitation, with the rate being 68% for first marriages (Copen et al., 2012). Historically most couples cohabited as a step toward marriage to that person (Vespa, 2014). More recently, however, serial cohabitation is more common than intentions to get married. So, for many, cohabiting is not connected to marriage. The more often a person has cohabited, the more likely the relationship will not end in marriage. In addition, Willoughby and Belt (2015) found that cohabiting couples who were moving toward marriage were happier than those who were not.

Teens are increasingly seeing cohabitation as a testing ground for marriage (Anderson, 2016). In Anderson's study of high school seniors, more than 70% felt that cohabiting was a way to know if one should marry the person. More Hispanics and Blacks felt this to be true than Whites.

A later study concluded that most young adults are not replacing marriage with cohabitation but instead are cohabiting and then marry. The researchers argued that "adolescents are including cohabitation as part of their future life trajectory but rarely envision cohabitation as substituting for marriage" (Manning, Longmore, & Giordano, 2007).

More and more people over 50 years of age are choosing to live with their partner instead of choosing marriage (Brown, Bulanda, & Lee, 2012). The numbers of those cohabiting more than doubled between 2000 and 2010, with about 8% of persons over 50 cohabiting. Because people are living longer and because cohabiting has become more acceptable, people are making different choices regarding coupling than they did 30 or 40 years ago. Brown et al. (2012) found in her study of almost 400 older cohabitors over an 8-year time period that the majority of couples who were cohabiting in the beginning of the study were still in the same relationship 8 years later. Only 18% of the unions ended within or at the end of the 8 years. Only 12% of the couples ended up getting married. For most couples cohabiting was not about finances. For this older age group, cohabiting was not typically a pathway to marriage, but rather an end in itself.

Cohabitation is likely to spark spirited discussion in your family among the different generations, and it certainly generates controversy and study after study after study among researchers. Some investigators argue that their findings indicate that cohabitation is not a good way to prepare for marriage and that couples who cohabit before marriage have a higher risk of divorce (Popenoe & Whitehead, 2004). Later research indicates that if the cohabiting occurs after a couple has planned to marry or are engaged, there is no difference in marital success than with couples who did not cohabit (Copen et al., 2012).

The rate of living together is also related to religious orientation, with those who are more religious less likely to cohabit (Wilcox, 2010). In addition, those who have been divorced are more likely to enter into a cohabiting relationship, as are those whose parents have been divorced. Finally, those who grew up with marital discord or those who grew up without a father are more likely to cohabit.

Given the predominant rates of cohabitation, it is difficult to believe that in the recent past living together for unmarried heterosexual couples was both illegal and considered immoral by many people. This revolutionary change can be attributed to several factors. First of all, first marriages are occurring at a later age than ever before (median age for females, 25.8; for males, 28.3) (Copen et al., 2012). In addition, puberty and sexual activity begin earlier, resulting in an extended singlehood before first marriage. The social stigma that was attached to cohabitation in the past has significantly declined, in part because of the sexual revolution. The saturation of sexuality within the entertainment industry and the media has greatly contributed to this change. Another important reason for cohabitation's growth is the decline in the number of individuals who choose to marry. Though the current divorce rate has declined significantly to 17.5 per 1,000 married women from 22.6 in 1980, the marriage rate has also been on a steady decline: a 50% drop since 1970 from 76.5 per 1,000 unmarried women to 39.2 (National Marriage Project, 2009). Concern over the continuing high rate of divorce may lead couples to choose to live together as either an alternative to marriage or a precursor to marriage.

People cohabit for many reasons and have various types of cohabitation arrangements. Following are some common reasons that couples give for cohabitating:

- Living together enables us to spend more time together.
- Living together allows us to share sexual and emotional intimacy without the commitment of marriage.
- Economic advantage—"We can save money by sharing living expenses."
- We can better learn the habits and character of each other, and if the relationship does not work out, there is no messy divorce.
- We can "test" our compatibility for a potential future marriage—see how we operate on a day-to-day basis.
- Engagement—"We are planning to marry."

A new area of research focuses on a new practice where couples in a relationship are "staying over" with their partner (Willoughby, Madsen, Carroll, & Busby, 2015). This is being practiced by those who are not choosing marriage or cohabiting, but rather spend nights together while retaining their separate homes. These couples are in the category of living apart together, which is when two people are in a committed relationship but do not live together. Some of these couples will eventually cohabit or marry, or may not do either. The folks who are likely to stay over are those who are in older age groups.

Reasons for Cohabiting

In a recent study of working-class and middle-class individuals between 18 and 36, information about the reasons for **cohabiting** became apparent (Sassler & Miller, 2011). In addition, the reasons were different depending upon whether they were working class or

Men have as much to gain from egalitarian relationships as women do. The quest for power, money, and material success in which so many men are immersed is accompanied by higher levels of stress, higher rates of heart disease, and shorter life spans.
©BananaStock/Alamy Stock Photo

middle class. These researchers found that working-class participants moved in with their romantic partners more quickly than did middle-class participants. The reason for this move was primarily financial in that it was cheaper to live together rather than separately. The cohabiting relationships were felt to be *pushed* and were often not a good match. These couples often ended up having an unplanned pregnancy. Middle-class couples often had more resources in order to live independently and often had work requirements that made them slow down their move toward cohabitation. This was less likely to be true for working-class couples.

These researchers also found that middle-class participants were more likely to move in together as a step toward marriage, and that was less likely for working-class couples (Sassler & Miller, 2011). Middle-class couples were also more likely to have plans made for marriage when they moved in together. This was less likely to be true for working-class couples. In fact, some working-class couples eventually concluded that living together could be an acceptable alternative to marriage.

It is clear that cohabiting has differing risks for the two groups of couples. Middle-class couples were often moving toward marriage, whereas, working-class couples were often moving in together as a better financial alternative than living separately. The trajectory toward a healthy marriage is clearly affected depending on the reasons for cohabiting.

Another related study by Dew (2011), with approximately 500 cohabiting individuals, indicated that over time, 40% of participants married their partner, 35% broke up, and 25% remained in a cohabiting relationship. Financial disagreements and perceived unfairness with finances were the only types of disagreements associated with breaking up. Although couples had other disagreements, such as housework, sex, parents, and spending time together, these differences did not predict a breakup.

There are few studies that address cohabiting among minority populations. In one study conducted by Chaney (2014), however, it was found that among low-income African Americans, cohabiting couples choose their partner because they wanted to build a future with someone who would support them where they were financially. They wanted someone

BOX 10.3 Putting It Together

Ten Ideas to Consider Before Cohabiting

1. Make the decision to live with another person with great care—remember it is much easier to move in together than to move out.
2. Before you move in together, clearly define what your expectations are for the relationship. Are you both interested in marriage or is this arrangement just because it feels right?
3. Keep your expectations reasonable. Do not live together to change the other person.
4. Define the amount of time you are planning to cohabit. Is it 1 month, 6 months, 1 year, or whatever?
5. Draw up and sign a "living-together agreement" that clarifies how you plan to handle finances and property.
6. Use birth control and be clear about your interest in having children. Remember that an unplanned pregnancy is a common outcome of living together.
7. Take a couples education class together so that you can get to know each other and see if you can develop and maintain a healthy relationship together.
8. Ask your friends and family to honestly tell you what they think about your relationship and trust their opinion.
9. Remember that love "blinds you" and that love and your relationship will not always be like they are today.
10. Before you decide to marry, seek premarital counseling to build a stronger couple relationship.

Source: Adapted and revised from Solot & Miller, 2009.

---

who would not drain their finances, but it was not necessarily important that they had a partner that would increase their financial well-being. It is clear that much more research needs to be done with non-White populations.

It seems, therefore, that when finances are the reason for cohabiting, they also might become the reason for breaking up. These issues are complicated, but important to think about as individuals consider cohabiting. Box 10.3 provides additional things to think about when considering cohabiting.

Difficult Choices

The growing rate of cohabitation among couples adds a new step in the mate selection and courtship process. Many counselors have severely criticized traditional courtship because it emphasizes recreation and avoids conflictual issues. Also the strong erotic needs of premarital couples tend to decrease their interest or ability to deal with problematic issues in their relationship. As one husband said in counseling, "When you're in love, you're willing to compromise on anything." Many believe that traditional courtship provides partners with idealized views of each other, making early marriage a period of more severe and difficult adjustments for most couples. In a cohabiting relationship, however, couples are able to experience the realities of life together before they decide to tie the knot.

Just as cohabitation has its supporters, so it has its detractors. Some argue against cohabitation on moral, religious, and philosophical grounds. Others question whether cohabitation is an effective predictor of marital success; because it is not truly a marriage, they contend, it cannot serve as a test of marriage. In the opinion of many observers, it is only "playing house"; to test marriage, they say, you need to actually get married.

Nonetheless, living together won't keep partners from experiencing pain and misery if the relationship breaks up. For many couples who have cohabited, dealing with the hurt of a broken relationship can be as difficult as it would have been if they had been legally married.

This is a difficult decision to make. What do you think?

Summary

- Parent-arranged marriages remain common—and are effective—in many nonindustrialized cultures today, but in the United States, individual-choice courtship is the norm.
- Dating has changed since the 1960s to include partying and hooking up.
- Online dating has increased substantially in recent years, especially for those with scarce potential partners.
- Research on dating reveals that older individuals experience the same emotions as young people. They may be more direct and move more quickly into a relationship, because they have less time left in their life to develop meaningful relationships.
- Many older adults choose to enter into a cohabiting relationship rather than marriage because of financial and other considerations.
- We are most likely to find a partner who is like ourselves, since we frequent places where we meet like-minded people.
- Factors that influence mate selection are physical attractiveness, personality, age, life success, and the principles of exogamy and endogamy. The rise in ethnic diversity in the United States is changing the unwritten rules regarding mixed or intercultural marriages.
- Multiple theories are used today to explain and predict the various ways couples enter into relationships. In addition, there has been increased attention to how people choose a mate in different life stages.
- The percentage of people entering into marriages with people from other cultures is approximately 15% and has increased substantially in recent years.
- Intimate partner violence is likely to be learned and, therefore, can be intergenerational.
- Cohabitation is more popular than ever as a way for many Americans to move from being single to becoming married. Though it remains a controversial issue for many people, from a statistical standpoint it has become the norm to cohabit before marriage. The majority of all marriages are preceded by cohabitation, with the rate being 68%.
- Cohabitation is likely to spark spirited discussion in your family among the different generations, and it certainly generates controversy and study after study after study among researchers. Some investigators argue that their findings indicate that cohabitation is not a good way to prepare for marriage and that couples who cohabit before marriage have a higher risk of divorce. Other researchers argue that it depends: they have found that if the cohabiting occurs after a couple has planned to marry or are engaged, there is no difference in marital success than with couples who did not cohabit.

Key Terms

parent-arranged marriage
couple-arranged marriage
dating
hooking up
mating gradient
sex ratio
endogamy
exogamy
intimate partner violence
cohabitation
cohabiting

Activities

1. Share your thoughts on these questions in a small group: What forces are pushing you toward marriage? What forces are pulling you toward marriage? What attracts you to singlehood?
2. What initially attracts you to another person? Rank the following traits from 1 to 5 (1 being the highest and 5 the lowest): physical attractiveness, popularity, social status, personality, and financial security. Discuss your rankings in a small group.
3. Think about friends who are connecting with potential partners. How are they doing it? Are most going online? Are they finding partners socially? What are other ways your friends are connecting to potential partners? Think about which ways seem to work best.
4. Discuss intimate partner violence as a small group. Be sure to address these questions, among others: How frequently have you experienced abuse? What was your reaction to it? What can be done to reduce courtship violence?
5. What are the pros and cons of living together? Make a list of five advantages and five disadvantages.
6. Interview someone who lived with a partner as they moved toward marriage and also interview someone who chose not to live with a partner before marriage. Ask them why they made the decision they did and what were the ultimate pros and cons of their decisions.

Suggested Readings

Best, J., & Bogle, K. A. (2014). *Kids gone wild*. New York, NY: New York University Press.

Bogle, K. A. (2008a). *Hooking up: Sex, dating and relationships on campus*. New York, NY: New York University Press.

Bogle, K. A. (2008b). The sociology of "hooking up." An interview with Kathleen Bogle. *Inside Higher Education*. Web site: http://www.insidehighered.com/news/2008/01/29/hookups.

Cherlin, A. J. (2009). *The marriage-go-round: The state of marriage and family in America today*. New York, NY: Random House.

Cui, M., Ueno, K., Gordon, M., & Fincham, F. D. (2013). The continuation of intimate partner violence from adolescence to young adulthood. *Journal of Marriage and Family, 75*, 300–313.

Hamon, R. R., & Ingoldsby, B. B. (Eds.). (2003). *Mate selection across cultures*. Thousand Oaks, CA: Sage. The meaningful processes, traditions, and practices related to couple formation around the world, including chapters from North America, the Caribbean and South America, Africa, the Middle East, Europe, and Asia.

Karis, T. A., & Killian, K. D. (2008). *Intercultural couples*. London: Routledge, Taylor & Francis Group.

Marquardt, E., Blankenhorn, D., Lerman, R., Malone-Colon, L., & Wilcox, B. (2012). *The state of our unions 2012: The president's marriage agenda for the forgotten sixty percent*. University of Virginia, The National Marriage Project. Web site: http://www.stateofourunions.org/.

National Center for Family and Marriage Research. (n.d.). Bowling Green State University. Web site: http://www.bgsu.edu/ncfmr.html.

National Marriage Project. (n.d.). Research and analysis on the health of marriage and family in America. Web site: http://nationalmarriageproject.org/about/.

Schwartz, P. (2015). *Better sex: AARP's guide to sex after 50*. AARP. Web site: http://www.aarp.org/entertainment/books/bookstore/home-family-caregiving/info-2016/better-sex-after-50.html.

Tatkin, S. (2016). *Wired for dating*. Oakland, CA: New Harbinger Publications.

Van Epp, J. (2008). *How to avoid falling in love with a jerk*. New York, NY: McGraw-Hill.

Visit the text-specific Online Learning Center at **www.mhhe.com/olson9e** for practice tests, chapter summaries, and PowerPoint slides.

Design Element: © Alicia Grünkind/EyeEm/Getty Images

11 Marriage: Building a Strong Foundation

- Intimacy, Strengths, and Diversity
- Perspectives on Marriage Today
- Components of a Successful Marriage
- Marriage Education
- The Importance of Families of Origin in Marriage
- Newlywed Years
- Keeping Marriages Strong
- Federal Healthy Marriage Initiative
- Summary
- Key Terms
- Activities
- Suggested Readings

Intimacy, Strengths, and Diversity

For those who marry, marriage is generally the most intimate relationship people have. It involves emotional and physical intimacy, which has the potential to make us feel happy and fulfilled. Intimacy involves good communication, which requires couples sharing feelings and experiences, and good communication helps couples solve problems and make decisions. Physical intimacy is also an important part of the closeness spouses feel toward one another. The degree of intimacy in a marriage is an important barometer of the health of the couple relationship.

Every marriage relationship has strengths, and it has been determined that focusing on strengths, rather than problems, can be helpful for couples trying to make their marriages better. Marriage education inventories, such as **PREPARE,** help couples identify their strengths and also spend time addressing areas where they want to grow. Recently, there has been an increased interest in promoting healthy marriages through marriage education throughout the country.

Most research and marriage education is focused on White, middle-class couples. We know very little about the effectiveness of existing marriage education programs for low-income couples and couples from diverse populations. Because of the current interest in, and ongoing federal funding for, marriage education for such couples, we are seeing an increase in culturally appropriate programming for diverse audiences.

As you read this chapter, you will see that we talk about marriage. Given that many people choose not to marry or marry later in life, know that principles presented in this chapter will also help committed couples have healthy relationships. We think every couple deserves to have a healthy relationship, whether they have chosen marriage or not.

Perspectives on Marriage Today

Next to parenthood, marriage is the most important, challenging and rewarding relationship we ever undertake. But what happens in this most private of all relationships can have powerful effects on others, and on society as a whole.

—THEODORA OOMS (1998, P. 6)

Based upon a report provided by Lewis and Kreider (2015, March), approximately 50% of all people 15 years and older had been married only once. This number has decreased from 54% in 1996. Approximately 18% of women and 11% of men ages 20 to 24 had married.

More than half of currently married couples (55%) had been married for at least 15 years, and 35% had reached their 25th wedding anniversary. Six percent had passed their 50th wedding anniversary, the golden anniversary. These percentages are about one to two percentage points higher than they were in 1996, reflecting the leveling of divorce rates in recent years and increases in life expectancy, the Census Bureau reported (The U.S. Bureau of Census, 2011).

For most couples (72%) both partners were in their first marriage. Six percent of the people married included a wife in her second marriage and a husband in his first marriage; 8% included a husband in his second marriage and a wife in her first; and 8% of the marriages in which both spouses were in their second marriage. One percent of currently married couples included both a husband and a wife who had both been married three or more times.

The median ages at first marriages have been steadily increasing since 1970 (Elliott & Simmons, 2011, August). Currently the median age for men to marry is 28.4 years and for women is 26.5 years. This is about six years older than in 1970. The percentage of women marrying in their teens has also decreased considerably. Still, a greater number of women marry in their teens than men, since women typically marry men who are older.

According to Elliot and Simmons (2011, August), women who have been divorced recently are more likely to be living with their own children, living in poverty, and have less household income than recently divorced men. In addition, 1.5% of children are living with a parent who was divorced in the past year.

The Benefits of Marriage

Society has a large stake in strengthening marriages. Children should be our central concern and, in general, they are better when raised by two parents. Marriage also typically improves the health and economic well-being of adults, stabilizes community life and benefits civic society.

—Theodora Ooms (1998, p. 4)

Because the media so often focus on the negative aspects of marriage (marital violence, divorce), many people often fail to see the positive effects of marriage, which are numerous. In a very well-known publication, Waite and Gallagher (2000) reviewed multiple studies which examined the positive effects of marriage for individuals. By and large, these studies included White middle-class couples. The benefits for those who are married included

It is clear that all African American family members can benefit from stable marriages, however, the couple relationships can be complex.
©Tetra Images/Getty Images

leading a healthier lifestyle, having a more satisfying sexual relationship, and having more wealth and economic assets.

Marriage and Black Americans

Researchers have reviewed the studies conducted with Black American couples to determine if they benefited from marriage to the same degree as White Americans (Blackman, Clayton, Glenn, Malone-Colon, & Roberts, 2005). Here is what they found:

- Marriage for Black Americans was related to more income and less poverty, and couples were more likely to be happy and have better family relationship functioning.
- Physical health did not appear to improve for Black couples who were married.
- Black men benefited more from marriage than Black women in terms of family life and physical health.
- Children in Black families, especially male children, experienced great benefits from parents who were married.
- Black women who were married actually reported *poorer* health than unmarried Black women.
- Black women experienced no benefit in terms of quality of family life when they were married.

Why is it that Black men seem to benefit more in terms of health and quality of family life than Black women? The researchers speculate that Black marriages experience more conflict than White marriages, and women, in general, are more likely to experience stress from this conflict. Therefore, this conflict negatively affects the quality of family life and health for Black women (Blackman et al., 2005).

There are other things we know about Black marriages, according to Vaterlaus, Skogrand, Chaney, and Gahagan (2016). In general, these authors summarize the literature about Black marriages by saying they marry later in life, are married less time during their lives, and have lower marital quality than marriages of other groups. In addition, we know they have the highest rate of children born outside of marriage and the lowest marriage rate (Chambers & Kravitz, 2011).

A recent study of marital expectations of strong African American marriages gave new insights into what they expect when they do marry (Vaterlaus et al., 2016). In this study of 39 couples who had strong marriages, they found that couples generally feel they had unrealistic expectations at the beginning of marriage and they became more realistic over time. Core expectations, however, included open communication, similar values, and positive treatment of their spouse. They also realized that they needed to have autonomy in their marriage relationship and sometimes had to do things by and for themselves.

Marriages over Time

We are beginning to know more about marital quality for low-income and ethnically diverse populations over time. A study led by Spencer James (2014) interviewed more than 12,000 women between 1992 and 2008 on marital quality and duration. One of the findings was that those who cohabited before they married were no different from those who did not in terms of marital quality. James also found that communication declined for both those who divorced and those who remained married. For those who remained married, communication seemed to stabilize and they experienced higher levels of communication over time.

Although Whites were usually happier, communicated better, and had less conflict than Hispanics or Blacks when they got married, James (2014) found that this did not continue throughout the marriage. He found that Blacks had an increase in marital happiness over time that was not experienced by Whites. He also found that, for those who remained together, marital quality generally declined during the first 10 years and flattened during the second 10 years. Those who divorced showed a rapid decline in marital happiness.

The Decline in Marriage

There is no sign in any nation that cohabitation is in decline; quite the opposite, it is increasing everywhere.

—DAVID POPENOE

Marriage trends in recent decades indicate that Americans are less likely to marry, and the marriage rate in the United States continues to decline. For those who do marry, there has been a moderate drop since the 1970s in the percentage of couples who report their marriages to be "very happy," but in the past two decades this trend flattened out (Wilcox & Marquardt, 2011).

Americans have become less likely to marry, reflected by a decline of more than 50% from 1970 to 2010 in the annual number of marriages per 1,000 unmarried adult women. In real numbers, the total of marriages fell from 2.45 million in 1990 to 2.08 million in 2010. Much of the decline—though researchers cannot say just how much—can be attributed to delaying of first marriages until older ages. The median age of first marriage went from 20 for females and 23 for males in 1960, to about 26 and 28, respectively, in 2010. Researchers argue that the decline in marriage is also affected by the growth of unmarried cohabitation, and a small decrease in the tendency for divorced persons to remarry. The U.S. Census Bureau also reported that the decline in marriage has accelerated in the wake of the Great Recession since 2008 (Wilcox & Marquardt, 2011).

The number of unmarried couples increased dramatically over the past five decades. Most younger Americans now spend some time living together outside of marriage, and unmarried cohabitation is common before marriage. Between 1960 and 2010, the number of unmarried couples increased more than 17-fold. About one-fourth of unmarried women age 25 to 39 are currently living with a partner, and another quarter lived with a partner at some time in the past. More than 60% of first marriages are now preceded by living together, though cohabitation was rare 50 years ago (Wilcox & Marquardt, 2011). Reasons people chose cohabitation over marriage are that people now are socially permitted to have sex outside of marriage, and there is greater equality between men and women, so women are choosing careers, education, or other opportunities over marriage.

As these statistics suggest, the popularity of marriage is decreasing. Although most individuals choose to marry at least once, it appears that fewer are choosing to remarry and instead either stay single or choose cohabitation over marriage. Marriage has been on the decline for the last two decades, and it appears that increasingly fewer people will choose to get married or to remarry in future years. See Table 11.1 for more details.

TABLE 11.1	Facts About Marriage

According to a Pew Research Center analysis of U.S. Census Bureau data:

- Barely half of all adults in the United States—a record low—are currently married.
- The median age at first marriage has never been higher for brides (26.5 years) and grooms (28.4).
- In 1960, 72% of all adults ages 18 and older were married; today just 51% are. The share of adults who are currently married will drop to below half within a few years.
- Other adult living arrangements—including cohabitation, single-person households, and single parenthood—have all grown more prevalent in recent decades.
- The United States is not the only nation where marriage has been declining for the past century. The same trend holds true in most other advanced post-industrial societies, and this long-term decline does not appear to be related to the business cycle's ups and downs. The declines have persisted during good and bad economic times.
- The declines in marriage have occurred among all age groups, but are the most dramatic among young adults. Only 20% of adults ages 18 to 29 are married, compared to 59% in 1960. Over the past 50 years, the median age at first marriage has risen by about 6 years for both men and women.
- It is not yet known whether young adults today are abandoning marriage or merely delaying marriage. Even though only 51% of the total adult population is currently married, a much higher percentage, 72% of all adults, has been married at least once.
- However, this "ever married" percentage is down to 72% today from 85% in 1960.
- Public attitudes about the institution of marriage are mixed in the United States. Nearly 4 out of 10 Americans say marriage is becoming obsolete. Yet, the same survey in 2010 found that most people who have never married (61%) would like to marry someday.
- Why has marriage declined? The decline is far less among adults with college educations than among the less educated. And some of the increase in the median age at first marriage over the long term can be explained by the rising percentage of young adults enrolling in college, who tend to marry later in life. Divorce is also a factor in the diminishing percentage of adults who are currently married compared to 50 years ago.
- The decline of marriage is occurring in other developed nations, especially in Europe, and in some cases in less developed nations. The United Nations argues that the decline is due, in part, "to an increasing acceptance of consensual [cohabiting] unions as a replacement for marital unions."

Source: Cohn, D., Passel, J., Wang, W., and Livingston, G., "Barely Half of U.S. Adults are Married—A Record Low." Pew Research Center, December 14, 2011. Web site: http://www.pewsocialtrends.org/2011/12/14/barely-half-of-u-s-adults-are-married-a-record-low/.

Components of a Successful Marriage

Happy wife—happy life.

—A Chinese Proverb

A loving relationship can bring two people enormous benefits; it can help them grow as friends and lovers, and it can even heal wounds. Most counselors agree that the chances of marital success are greater if both partners enter marriage as friends; but the chances of achieving a successful intimate relationship are slim for a couple in which one plays the role of therapist and the other the role of patient. A careful review of research and clinical experience reported by many professionals indicates that a marriage has a better chance for success if potential partners meet the following conditions:

- *Both individuals are independent and mature.* The more mature and independent two people are, the easier it is for them to develop an interdependent relationship that

Independent and mature individuals are likely to have acquired the self-knowledge and self-confidence necessary for an intimate relationship and a successful marriage. Because they can express their needs honestly and assertively and respond unselfishly to each other's needs, such couples are more likely to be friends as well as lovers.
©Henry Rose/Photodisc/Getty Images

can facilitate intimacy. Independence and maturity often increase with age, a good reason for waiting to marry. In fact, the single best predictor of a successful marriage is the age of the couple. This is partly because older people are typically more stable and know what they want in marriage.

- *Both individuals love not only each other but also themselves.* Self-esteem is very important in an intimate relationship. It is difficult to truly love another person without also loving oneself. People need to feel secure and self-confident before they can be truly giving and loving to another.
- *Both individuals enjoy being alone as well as together.* To balance the separateness and togetherness that an intimate relationship requires, partners need to enjoy separate activities and time apart. Time apart reminds partners of the value of the relationship and increases the importance and value of time together. Too much togetherness can lead to such negative behaviors as attempting to control one's partner and failing to appreciate the partner.
- *Both individuals are established in their work or occupation.* A stable and satisfying occupation or job fosters both financial and emotional security. When people's jobs are going well, they are able to devote more time and energy to their relationships. Conversely, the greater the stress at work, the less positive energy there is for a relationship.
- *Both individuals know themselves.* An intimate relationship requires openness and honesty between partners. They must be able to evaluate their personal strengths and failings objectively and not blame their problems on other people. They must also know what they want from and can give to the partner.
- *Both individuals can express themselves assertively.* One key to developing intimacy is assertiveness—expressing oneself in a direct and generally positive manner. People who are not assertive in their communication often adopt a passive–aggressive approach. The more clearly partners can ask for what they want from each other, the better the chances for compliance. (See Chapter 4 for a detailed discussion on assertive communication.)
- *Both individuals are friends as well as lovers.* When people focus on their lover's needs, they find that the loved one tends to focus on their needs. This has been called the *law of enlightened self-interest.* Developed by social exchange theorists to describe

successful relationships, the principle holds that being less selfish is in a person's best interest because it helps build cooperative and intimate relationships that benefit everyone. Nonpossessive caring encourages the partner to grow and to reach her or his potential. Both partners generally benefit.

Marriage Education

Marriage education has had an interesting and sporadic history in the United States. In the 1970s, there were a significant number of marriage education programs. Such programs began with the work of David and Vera Mace, who founded the Association for Couples in Marriage Enrichment in 1973 (Doherty & Anderson, 2004). Marriage Encounter emerged during this time, which was used primarily by Catholics but by other denominations as well. Marriage Encounter became the largest national marriage education program during that time (Doherty & Anderson, 2004). Marriage Encounter was led by clergy along with laypeople, and marriage education was taught within the context of spiritual beliefs.

During the 1980s and 1990s, marriage education was less popular (Doherty & Anderson, 2004). Marriage was seen as promoting patriarchal norms and not allowing for the emerging gay and lesbian relationships that were becoming more and more publicly prevalent. In addition, cohabitation was becoming an acceptable partnership model. One program that continued to attract large numbers of premarital couples was PREPARE. During this time, however, new marriage programs began to emerge, such as the Prevention and Relationship Enhancement Program (PREP), Relationship Enhancement, and Couples Communication (Doherty & Anderson, 2004).

In the 1990s, research emerged about the negative effects of divorce and resulted in what we know today as the *marriage movement* (Doherty & Anderson, 2004). Healthy marriages were viewed as a necessary component of society for the benefit of the couples and their children. By 2002 there was the hope of federal funding to support marriage education nationally. This funding materialized in 2006. Today there are several well-known programs throughout the country that are being used to help couples develop marriage skills.

The Healthy Marriage Initiative (Administration for Children and Families, n.d.), which was funded at the federal level in 2006, has resulted in marriage and relationship education programs and evaluations of those programs around the country. For example, one study looked at the impact of relationship education for a sample of 340 adolescents from a range of socioeconomic backgrounds who were primarily African American (Adler-Baeder, Kerpelman, Schramm, Higginbotham, & Paulk, 2007). The results of the study indicated that participants had increased knowledge about relationships and decreased destructive verbal and physical conflict strategies, as well as increases in reasoning strategies and positive changes in relationship beliefs that support healthy relationships. These researchers concluded that, in fact, adolescents from a wide range of backgrounds can benefit from relationship education, which can ultimately improve future couple relationships.

A wide variety of relationship education programs have shown that relationship education programs resulting from the Healthy Marriage Initiative help couples in their marriages (Hawkins, Blanchard, Baldwin, & Fawcett, 2008). Hawkins and colleagues found that across programs relationship quality and communication skills often increased for couples. They also found that a higher dosage of education, 9 to 20 hours, was more beneficial than fewer hours.

Other studies showing benefits of stepfamily education also showed positive results. A stepfamily education program focusing on low-income European American and Latino stepfamilies was implemented throughout the state of Utah using a model that included both children and adults (Higginbotham, Skogrand, & Torres, 2010). Because a major challenge for stepfamilies is to effectively address the needs of stepchildren, this model is recommended so that the entire family can benefit from the educational intervention. In this case children and parents were in separate rooms learning parallel information during most of a class session, and then came together during the last half hour for a family-strengthening activity. A qualitative evaluation study indicated the children in these stepfamilies benefited from their parents' participation in the stepfamily course, because parents became more empathetic about their children's situations, they spent more time with their children, and they were able to communicate more effectively with their children. The children also benefited by learning to express feelings and worries appropriately, being more empathic with their parents' and stepparents' situations, and learning skills that improved their family relationships. By attending the course with other stepfamilies, they also learned they were not alone and that other children shared their experiences.

Although historically much of what we know about marriage education has been based on research with European American, middle-class populations, the two examples above indicate that this is changing. In addition, recent articles have described what marriage education for low-income and diverse populations should look like (Olsen & Skogrand, 2009; Skogrand, Barrios-Bell, & Higginbotham, 2009). For example, Skogrand et al. discuss what stepfamily education should look like for Latino stepfamilies. Religious and family values affect how Latinos view stepfamilies, and stepfamily education needs to be adapted to address those values. For example, divorce and remarriage are often viewed negatively in Latino culture, and advertising for and presenting information to stepfamilies may need to look different than it would for European American families. In fact, many Latinos view the term *stepfamily* negatively, and other terms may need to be introduced.

Because divorce rates are highest in low-income and diverse populations, it is increasingly important that we provide culturally appropriate marriage and couple education for these populations (Skogrand, Hatch, & Singh, 2008). It appears that the federal funding is helping make that happen. For example, Latina women experienced an increase in positive couple and family relationships after taking a stepfamily course (Skogrand, Mendez, & Higginbotham, 2014). In addition, there is some evidence that stepfamily education can benefit gay and lesbian couples (Skogrand, Mendez, & Higginbotham, 2013). Two lesbian couples who attended the same stepfamily course also realized improved couple and family relationships.

Premarital Education

Failing to prepare is like preparing to fail.

—Anonymous

Before the wedding, couples spend hours talking about the wedding flowers, the size of the diamond and the design of its mounting, the color of the groomsmen's ties, and so on, but they rarely discuss such topics as finances, in-laws, and role relationships. Without instruction and preparation, people are no more expert at developing intimate relationships than they are at parenting. Writing about his own family-building experiences, Norbert Wiener, one of the original developers of the modern computer, said, "One has only one life to live and there is not time enough in which to master the art of being a parent" (Wiener, 1956, p. 224).

If it weren't for concerned clergy who insist that couples meet with them at least once before marriage, many couples would have no premarital preparation. About 40% of couples getting married for the first time in a place of worship (church, synagogue, or mosque) receive some type of premarital services or programs. Many of these couples meet only once or twice with their clergy to discuss marriage issues. Some premarital couples attend small-group couples' workshops or retreats where they discuss marriage. Another group of couples complete a premarital inventory and receive some feedback in two or three sessions. However, very few premarital couples receive a comprehensive premarital program that includes all the components mentioned in the following section.

A growing number of couples are now seeking premarital preparation. This is, in part, because they see the large number of divorced people around them, including their parents, relatives, and even friends who had only been married a few years.
©Maica/E+/Getty Images

What Constitutes an Effective Premarital Program?

It is evident from the research that there are at least five essential components to an effective premarital program:

- *The couple should take some type of premarital inventory and should receive feedback on the results*. A premarital inventory increases the couple's awareness of the strengths and potential problem areas in their relationship. It also helps them discuss their relationship. In addition, the process establishes a relationship with a clergy member, a counselor, or a married couple with whom the couple can consult should they need intensive counseling for serious problems. Finally, it prepares them for later marriage enrichment.
- *The couple should receive training in communication and problem-solving skills*. These skills help the couple deal with various relationship issues by teaching them empathy as well as techniques for self-disclosure, resolving conflict, and problem solving.
- *The couple should participate in a small discussion group in which couples share their feelings and experiences*. This increases a couple's ability and willingness to share with other couples, lets the couple see how other couples relate and deal with issues, and may foster friendships with other couples.
- *A good premarital program should start 12 months before marriage and last 6 to 8 weeks*. Unfortunately, most premarital couples do not begin marriage preparation until 2 or 3 months before their wedding. When a couple cannot complete a comprehensive program before marriage, they should enroll in some sort of program after marriage.
- *A good premarital program should motivate the couple to want to continue marital enrichment after marriage*. Marriage is a process and one that takes continual effort to make it grow and deal with the stress and changes over time. Couples should ideally seek out couple enrichment programs after marriage to continue to sustain their relationship.

There are a variety of couple programs that contain most of the characteristics that are helpful to couples, both premarital and married couples. Many curriculum resources are available. These can be downloaded from a marriage resource web site (National Healthy

BOX 11.1 Putting It Together
The PREPARE Program for Premarital Counseling

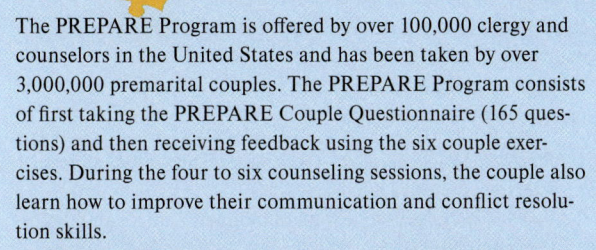

The PREPARE Program is offered by over 100,000 clergy and counselors in the United States and has been taken by over 3,000,000 premarital couples. The PREPARE Program consists of first taking the PREPARE Couple Questionnaire (165 questions) and then receiving feedback using the six couple exercises. During the four to six counseling sessions, the couple also learn how to improve their communication and conflict resolution skills.

The PREPARE Program has been demonstrated to be very effective in improving a couple's communication and ability to resolve conflict and has led to greater couple agreement (Knutson & Olson, 2003). By improving their relationship skills, they get their marriage off to a better start.

Six Couple Exercises

1. To help the couple explore their relationship strengths and growth areas.
2. To help the couple increase their communication skills (assertiveness and active listening).
3. To help the couple learn how to resolve couple conflict using the Ten Step Model.
4. To help the couple discuss their families of origin and what they want to bring, or not bring, from their families into their couple relationship.
5. To help the couple develop a workable budget and financial plan.
6. To help the couple develop their personal, couple, and family goals.

Over 25 Significant Relationship Areas in PREPARE/ENRICH Program

Interpersonal Area
Communication
Conflict Resolution
Role Relationship
Sexual Relationship
Financial Management
Family & Friends

Intrapersonal Areas
Realistic Expectations
Personality Issues
Spiritual Beliefs
Marital Satisfaction

SCOPE Personality Scales
Social
Change
Organization
Pleasing
Emotionally Stable

Relationship Dynamics
Self-Confidence
Assertiveness
Avoidance
Partner Dominance

Couple & Family System
Couple Closeness
Couple Flexibility
Family Closeness
Family Flexibility

To Locate a Professional Offering the PREPARE Program (www.prepare-enrich.com)

To locate a professional trained to offer the PREPARE Program in your area, go to the web site at www.prepare-enrich.com. You can insert your zip code and find professionals in your area. You can also take a Couple Quiz online, individually or as a couple, and learn more about your couple relationship.

Marriage Resource Center, n.d.). The resources include information for Hispanic couples, empty nesters, singles, and much more. Many of these resources have been developed with funds from the federally funded Healthy Marriage Initiative (Administration for Children and Families, n.d.). The 2015-2016 Strategic Plan developed by Administration for Children & Families promotes the safety and well-being of children, youth, and families and federal funds support this endeavor. This plan has resulted the development of federal grants for healthy marriage and healthy fatherhood programs. Helping couples have healthy relationships contributes to the safety and well-being of children. The most highly recommended programs are Couple Communication, PAIRS Program, PREP Program, PREPARE/ENRICH programs, and the Relationship Enhancement Program. See Box 11.1 for more detailed information about the PREPARE Program.

BOX 11.2 At Issue
Predicting Marital Success

We are taught, through fairy tales, TV movies of the week, romance novels, and our own fantasy lives, that love conquers all. And it does—in fairy tales, TV movies, novels, and fantasies. In real life, relationships (especially marriages) require continual care.

Couples often marry with unrealistic expectations of a life where both partners will always be happy, they will never fight, and conflicts will magically resolve themselves. They don't realize that fighting is an integral part of a relationship. Work conducted at the Gottman Institute (online at Gottman.com) indicates that marriages tend to settle into one of three styles of conflict resolution (Driver, Tabares, Shapiro, & Gottman, 2012):

1. *Validating*—couples argue, but they let each other know that they respect the other's points of view and emotions, even if they don't agree with them.
2. *Volatile*—passionate couples have intense fights and then intense make-up sessions; these couples see themselves as equal sparring partners.
3. *Conflict-avoiding*—couples often make light of their differences and learn to live with them.

Driver et al. concluded that no matter what the conflict resolution styles, the predictor of marital success is the ratio of positive-to-negative feelings and actions toward each other. "As long as there is five times as much positive feeling and interaction between husband and wife as there is negative," note the authors, "the marriage [is] likely to be stable over time."

The following are the specific signs they used to identify couples who would later divorce.

1. *Emotional disengagement*—those who display little interest, affection, concern, and humor.
2. *The four horsemen*—four ways of interacting that can sabotage communication:
   - *Criticism*—negative words that are global about the partner, attacking the partner's personality or character rather than a specific behavior.
   - *Contempt*—being overly critical and using such means of expression as insults, sarcasm, name calling, hostile humor, and mockery.
   - *Defensiveness*—denying one's own role in a problem or issue, thus blaming the partner.
   - *Stonewalling*—failing to respond, or tuning the partner out.
3. *Flooding*—feeling overwhelmed by the partner's negativity leaves the person shell-shocked.
4. *Bad memories*—when a marriage isn't going well, the couple rewrites the past in a more negative way.

The goal would be to identify those areas where couples are having difficulties and develop tailored interventions for couples, to help them avoid divorce.

Predicting a Successful Marriage

Love is not enough to make a successful marriage. The truth of this can be seen in divorce statistics. Most people who marry are in love, but roughly half of those who marry eventually divorce. If love at the time of marriage is a poor predictor of marital happiness, what characteristics do predict a happy marriage? Studies demonstrate that the type of relationship a couple has before marriage is very predictive of whether they will have a successful and happy marriage.

Two different approaches to predicting a successful marriage were conducted by two different research teams. Both teams could predict marital outcome (happiness versus divorce). One team directed by John Gottman (Driver et al., 2012) at the University of Washington focused on videotaping couples talking and resolving conflict based on microanalysis of the videotapes. The findings are summarized in Box 11.2.

The second team was directed by David Olson and colleagues (Olson, Olson-Sigg, & Larson, 2008) at the University of Minnesota, and they used couple questionnaires rather than videotaping couple interaction. The questionnaires are called PREPARE (for premarital couples) and ENRICH (for married couples). Both studies found that 90% of the time it was possible to predict, on the basis of their PREPARE inventory scores *before* marriage, whether a couple would later be happily married or divorced.

The Importance of Families of Origin in Marriage

When a couple gets married, each partner is also joining the other partner's family. As such, the Couple and Family Map can be useful for helping partners discuss and compare their **families of origin**—the families in which they were raised during childhood—before they marry. The case study that follows involves Kathy and Jim, a couple whose family backgrounds are quite different. They explored these differences in premarital counseling.

Kathy's Family of Origin

Kathy grew up in a *structurally enmeshed* family (Figure 11.1). She is the third oldest of six children, who at the time of counseling ranged in age from 18 to 27. Kathy's parents have been married for 28 years. All of the children except Kathy live and work in the town in which they grew up. Kathy's family is structured on the flexibility dimension of the Couple and Family Map for the following reasons: While growing up, the children knew what was expected of them. The parents were firm yet fair with discipline and enforcement of family rules. The mother was strong and a thorough organizer, and the father was equally strong and even stubborn at times. The father acted as the head of the household but respected his wife's education, contributions, and ability. The mother was comfortable playing a somewhat traditional role and worked hard at keeping the family organized.

FIGURE 11.1

Family of Origin and Ideal Type of Marriage

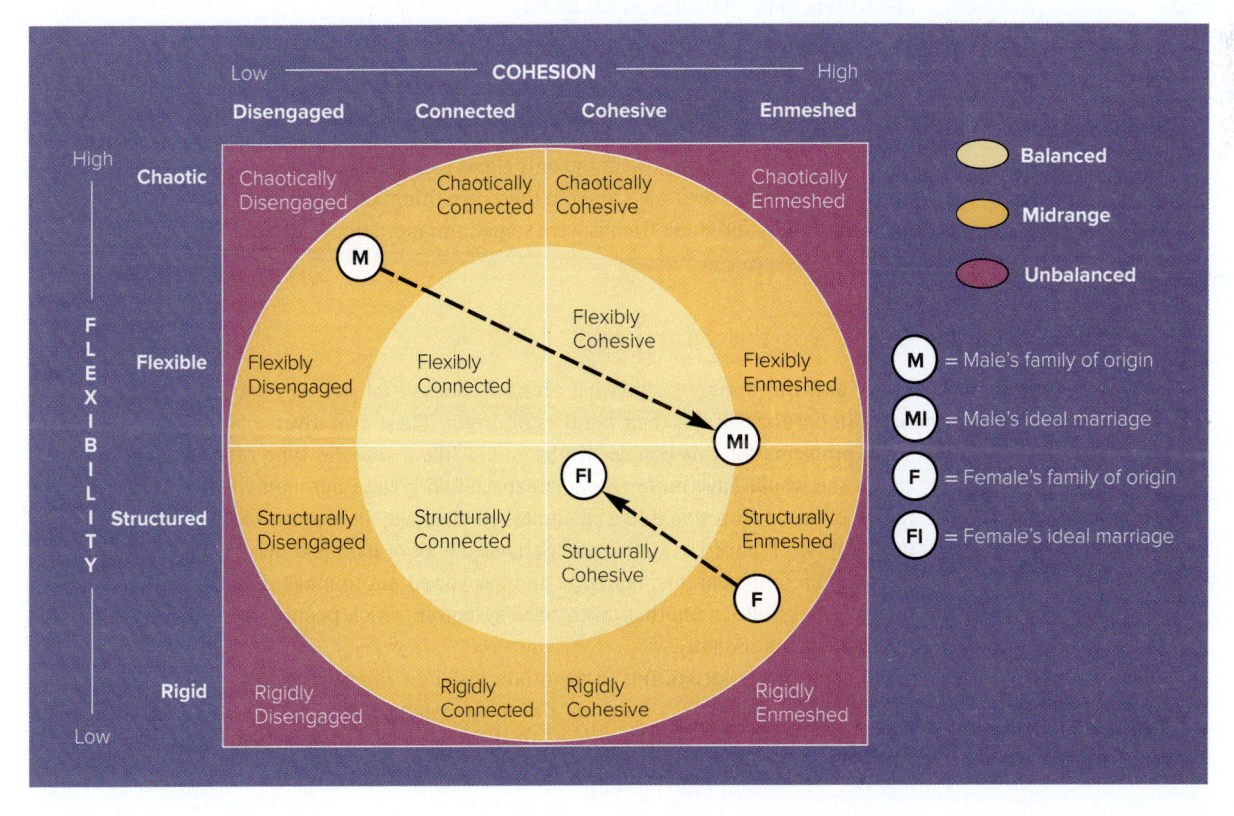

Chapter 11 | Marriage: Building a Strong Foundation   301

Kathy's family is enmeshed on the cohesion dimension. They are a close-knit Catholic family from a small town. Except for 18-year-old John, all of the children have left home, and all except Kathy have settled in the local community. The children drop by the family home several times a week. On weeknights, they play cards or just sit around and talk. The whole family gets together at least every other Sunday for dinner. The mother is heavily involved in each of her children's lives. She feels excited when they are excited and guilty when they are down, and she is always trying to help them. The father is less involved in the lives of his children but expects them to visit often, especially on weekends.

Jim's Family of Origin

Jim grew up in a *flexibly disengaged* family (see Figure 11.1). He is the older of two children; his brother is 4 years younger. His parents have been married for 27 years but are now separated. After several years of frustration, the mother decided that she had had enough and asked her husband for a separation; he moved out several months ago. He has been asking for a reconciliation, claiming he's changed, but she is suspicious of these "instant" changes and has decided to "wait and see" if they are permanent.

Jim's family is currently flexible in terms of how it functions, but over the past several years, it has undergone certain changes. For many years, it was closer to a structured family: The mother and father had traditional male and female roles; the father handed down the rules, and the mother backed him up. After 15 years as a homemaker, however, Jim's mother went back to school and got a 2-year certificate in bookkeeping. Her self-esteem improved, and she became more confident and assertive in her relationship with her husband. The family system became more flexible. Jim's father began helping out around the house. He became more lenient with the boys when he saw that they were fairly responsible and willing to pitch in around the house.

In terms of cohesion, the family is currently disengaged. When they were young, the boys were very involved in school activities, and the parents each had separate interests. The father hunted and fished, and the mother had her church activities. The father took the boys hunting and fishing when they got old enough, and they went on several canoe trips together. But these outings were the only times they were together. Most of the time, family members went their own ways and did their own thing. Each person in the family had her or his own friends, and these friends were sometimes more important to each person than family members were.

Goals for the Marriage

Kathy and Jim disagree somewhat on how cohesive (close) they want to be in their marriage, in part because of their families of origin. These two diverse family systems present some problems for this couple. Kathy would like a *cohesive* type of marriage but one in which she would have more emotional space and greater autonomy than in her *enmeshed* family of origin. Jim would like an enmeshed marriage, in reaction to his disengaged family of origin (see Figure 11.1). He has experienced a lot of pain and disappointment because of the breakup of his parents' marriage and has vowed not to make the mistakes they did. He doesn't want to be in another disengaged system in which people go their own way and do not connect emotionally.

This couple is struggling to negotiate just how much closeness they want from the relationship. Because it's hard for Jim to say what he is really feeling and to share his need for closeness in a direct way with Kathy, she sometimes interprets his desire for closeness as an attempt to control her. But Kathy wants to avoid the overcontrolling atmosphere of enmeshment that existed in her family. So she sometimes backs away from Jim when he is needy and wants closeness. Jim isn't always aware of how he tries to control Kathy or even why he wants to. He is more aware of the outcome of his efforts—her withdrawal.

What both Jim and Kathy have in common is the desire for a *structured* type of marriage. Although Jim sympathizes with his mother, he emotionally leans toward his father's value of a more structured type of system, with more stable male-female roles and predictable family rules and patterns. This is the level of flexibility with which he is most comfortable. Kathy would also like a structured marriage with fairly stable roles but with a distribution of responsibilities. She likes the predictability of a structured system but does not want it to become rigid like her family of origin. The desire for a structured system is a goal they both share and one they can work together to achieve.

Newlywed Years

The first years of marriage can be stressful, with spouses adjusting to the new relationship and with these marriages being especially vulnerable to dissolution. The newlywed years are also especially important for setting the tone that results in high marital satisfaction years down the road. In previous research, some of the difficulties that are related to later divorce include difficulty with finances, emotional dependence, immaturity, difficulties with families of origin, infidelity, jealousy, and substance abuse—to name a few (Schramm, Marshall, Harris, & Lee, 2005). This study focused on the negative things that can happen in couple relationships. A recent study of newlyweds looked at positive and negative emotions over the first 15 months of marriage and their impact on the relationship (Graber, Laurenceau, Miga, Chango, & Coan, 2011). They found that the positive emotions couples express are more predictive of marital success for newlyweds than negative emotions. This has important implications for therapists and educators who might want to focus on

Whether a wedding is simple or extravagant, it is a milestone in the lives of two families and public testimony of a couple's love for each other. Decisions about the date, the place, the kind of ceremony, the size of the wedding party, the guest list, and the reception often require negotiation among the couple and their relatives so that everyone will feel that their preferences have been considered. Preparation for the wedding sometimes becomes the couple's first major challenge together in life.
©Buccina Studios/Photodisc/Getty Images

He likes to make a quick circuit of the store, picking up whatever appeals to him. She likes to make a list of what they'll need for the week and shop for bargains. Newlyweds discover differences in their habits and preferences and must find ways to accommodate these differences if their marriage is to succeed.
©Milton Montenegro/Photodisc/Getty Images

positive feelings people have toward each other rather than responding to negative emotions. Table 11.2 provides further information about fantasies and realities of marriage.

The Schramm et al. (2005) study also found that marriage education was an important variable in marital satisfaction and marital adjustment. Having formal marriage education in college resulted in higher marital satisfaction and adjustment. This study indicates how important it is to develop knowledge about issues that cause problems in marriage before the wedding day. Because many couples get married shortly after leaving high school, information about the findings of this study should be introduced in high school.

TABLE 11.2 — Premarital Fantasies and Marital Realities

- She married him because he was such an assertive male;
  She divorced him because he was such a domineering husband.
- He married her because she was so gentle and petite;
  He divorced her because she was so weak and helpless.
- She married him because he could provide a good income;
  She divorced him because all he did was work.
- He married her because she was so attractive all the time;
  He divorced her because she spent too much time in front of the mirror.
- She married him because he was so romantic and sociable;
  She divorced him because he was a fun-loving playboy.
- He married her because she was so quiet and dependent;
  He divorced her because she was so boring and clinging.
- She married him because he was the life of the party;
  She divorced him because he was such a dud at home.
- He married her because she was so sociable and talkative;
  He divorced her because she could only discuss trivia.
- She married him because he was such a good athlete;
  She divorced him because he was always playing or watching sports.
- He married her because she was so neat and organized;
  He divorced her because she was too compulsive and controlling.

Happy couples learn to weather the stresses of life. They are, above all, best friends and enjoy spending time together. In fact, they are likely to find each other more interesting as the years go by.
©Purestock/Getty Images

Keeping Marriages Strong

Five Types of Marriage

Using a national sample of over 50,000 married couples, Olson et al., (2008) described five significantly different types of married couples: *vitalized, harmonious, conventional, conflicted,* and *devitalized.* These five types of marriage are described in more detail, and the impact of the type on other aspects of their relationship is described elsewhere. These five types were created with largely White couples (Figure 11.2).

Vitalized Couples. These couples composed 18% of the couples in the national survey. They had strengths in communication, conflict resolution, their sexual relationship, and finances. Only a small percentage of these couples had ever considered a divorce.

Harmonious Couples. Twenty-four percent of the couples fit into the harmonious category and had fewer strengths than vitalized couples. They were particularly satisfied with their ability to resolve conflicts and their role relationship.

Conventional Couples. Conventional couples made up 17% of the total sample. Although these couples were generally happy, they did not do as well as vitalized and harmonious couples when it came to personality compatibility, communication, and conflict resolution. They had strengths in spiritual beliefs, having traditional roles, and a network of supportive family and friends.

Conflicted Couples. These couples made up 22% of the couples. They were unhappy, with few strengths and multiple areas where they needed growth. Seventy-three percent of these couples had considered divorce. They had low scores in communication and conflict resolution.

FIGURE 11.2

Five Types of Married Couples

Source: Olson, D., Olson-Sigg, A., & Larson, P. *The Couple Checkup.* Nashville, TN: Thomas Nelson, 2008.

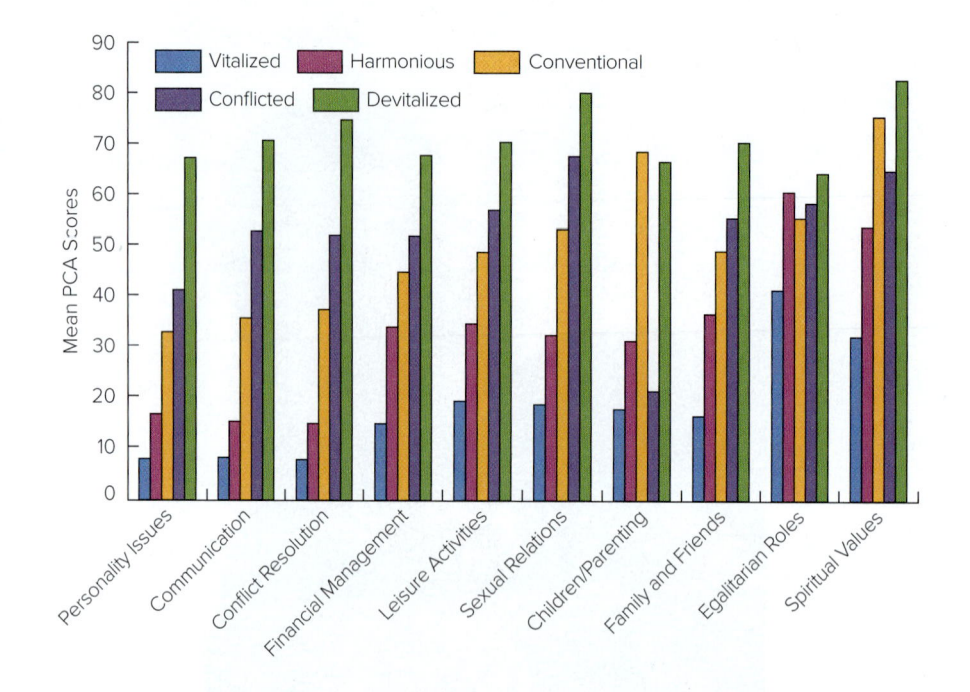

Devitalized Couples. These couples were very unhappy and made up 19% of the couples. Almost all had considered divorce. Many of these couples had sought marital therapy or marriage enrichment.

Some couples can maintain a healthy marriage with the advent of children, while others become less loving and more conflicted.
©Wavebreak Media Ltd/123RF

306   Part III   Stages of Intimate Relationships

Why Marriages Fall Apart

There are a number of reasons why couples drift apart over the course of the marriage. A major issue is that we begin to take marriage for granted and focus on other priorities in our life. William Doherty in his book *Take Back Your Marriage* (2001) identifies a variety of forces that negatively impact marriage: We are too busy for marriage; we get used to our mate; television and other media come between us; we stop dating, especially after having children; we don't know other couples' strategies for maintaining vibrant marriages; and the difference between spouses in their "work orientation" toward marriage gets resolved in the direction of less work.

This drifting apart is not usually done on purpose but gradually happens as a result of neglecting the marriage. William Doherty uses an interesting analogy in describing this process:

> Ever since I moved to Minnesota, I have thought that getting married is like launching a canoe into the Mississippi at St. Paul. If you don't paddle, you go south. No matter how much you love each other, no matter how full of hope and promise and good intentions, if you stay on the Mississippi without a good deal of paddling—occasional paddling is not enough—you end up in New Orleans. Which is a problem if you wanted to stay north. (Doherty, 2001, p. 11)

Keeping Your Marriage a Top Priority

One of the major things a couple can do to keep their marriage alive and growing is to make it a top priority—preferably number ONE. A good exercise for couples is to sit down and list the various important aspects of life and then rank them in terms of ideal priorities. Then rank them in terms of their actual priority in your life, which will probably be different from your ideal. The more you can keep your marriage the number one priority, the better your chances of success in the future.

There are a variety of specific things that you can do to keep your marriage or committed couple relationship a top priority in your life. Here are some suggestions:

- Remind yourself that the stability of your couple relationship will benefit the children in your family.
- Given that your children's needs are important, you also need to have time as a couple. Make sure you get that time. Your relationship depends on it.
- Make time for dates. Even if you do not have children, work and other obligations can distract you from your relationship.
- If your marriage is floundering, get professional help. Do not wait until you are so far down the road that it is difficult or impossible to get back on track.

The Role of Forgiveness in Marriage

Everyone says forgiveness is a lovely idea, until they have something to forgive.
—C. S. Lewis

The importance of forgiveness in marriage has become recognized as an important part of couple relationships, and it contributes to marital happiness and stability (Fincham, Hall, & Beach, 2006). In fact, forgiveness is important in our overall well-being and general health in that it helps us deal with everyday hurts (Gordon, Baucom, & Snyder, 2005; Harris & Thoresen, 2005). This has become such an important topic today that a scholarly book entitled *Handbook of Forgiveness* has been published to describe the benefits of forgiveness in all aspects of life (Worthington, 2005).

Forgiveness does not mean you have to be religious or that you forget about or accept the transgressions of your partner (Fincham et al., 2006). A person forgives in spite of the wrongful nature of the transgression and even if the transgressor does not deserve forgiveness (Fincham et al., 2006). An important component of forgiveness can be reconciliation, which may be helpful in allowing a couple to move on to a more positive place in their relationship. Forgiveness is about decreasing the negativity and increasing positive feelings and goodwill toward one's partner.

Forgiveness contributes to marital satisfaction when it becomes a part of conflict resolution (Fincham et al., 2006). Forgiveness helps couples move on from a conflict without having resentments that spill over into future conflicts, resulting in escalation of conflict over time. Forgiveness on the part of the victim involves understanding the impact of the offense, finding meaning for what happened, and moving forward—which may mean a change in the relationship. Here is an example of what the process of forgiving looked like for one couple:

> *Mary and Louis had been having difficulties in their marriage because each had a stressful work schedule, and they had been unable to spend much time together. Mary was working long hours and spending a considerable amount of time with a coworker. They ended up having an affair that lasted several months. Louis suspected the affair and confronted Mary. Mary had already ended the extramarital relationship, but admitted that it was true.*
>
> *Mary said she was sorry and declared her commitment to the marriage. Louis also wanted to stay married, but he was so angry. He both loved and was angry with Mary for betraying his trust. He wanted to forgive Mary, but he wasn't sure he could ever trust her again and have a healthy marriage relationship. He wanted to hurt her as much as she hurt him.*
>
> *After working with a therapist for almost a year, the relationship began to get back on track. Louis was able to forgive Mary and eventually, with the help of the therapist, was able to have positive feelings toward her. He shared with her how it had deeply wounded him since he had always been vulnerable when it came to being rejected. What happened would always cause him some pain.*
>
> *Mary and Louis also began cutting back on the hours spent on work and created a relationship that was very different from the one they had had before the affair. They would always set aside time to talk if either of them felt that things were not going well in their relationship. They fixed the problem rather than letting things go. Even though it took a long time, both Mary and Louis ultimately felt their marriage was better than before the affair. Forgiveness was definitely a necessary component of getting their marriage back on track in making their marriage healthy and stable.*

McNulty (2008) added to this research by conducting a longitudinal study with 72 couples over the first 2 years of their marriages. He found that if their partner did not act negatively very often, there was less to forgive, and there were positive marital outcomes. However, when there were more frequent times that needed forgiving, even if there was forgiveness, there was not an increase in marital satisfaction. The severity of the offense, even if it was forgiven, also affected marital happiness. This author concluded that forgiveness is, in fact, a good thing in marriage. However, if there are severe or regular problems that need forgiving, it does not result in a happier marriage.

More recent research expands on this idea of forgiving the other to also including self-forgiveness (Pelucchi, Paleari, Regalia, & Fincham, 2013). Self-forgiveness is the ability to show compassion to oneself when a wrong has been committed. In other words, providing love to oneself. This study found that both husbands and wives were more satisfied with their couple relationship when the offending partner had more positive feelings for themselves. These authors make it clear that the offender had to be truly sorry for the offense for the couple to have that satisfying relationship.

The Role of Sacrifice in Marriage

Sacrificing for the other person in a marriage and how it affects relationship functioning has become an area of research in recent years (Stanley, Whitton, Sadberry, Clements, & Markman, 2006). There are two components of sacrifice. First, an individual can make sacrifices for his or her partner, which means that a person puts the partner's needs before his or her own needs. A second component of sacrifice is that the partner puts the relationship above selfish interests, which means a person places the couple or marriage relationship above personal needs (Morrill, 2006).

Stanley and colleagues conducted a longitudinal study of those who were newly married in 1980 and studied the effects of sacrifice on the long-term relationship. They were interested in following newlyweds through the first several years of marriage, because that is the time when many couples experience difficulties in their relationship. These researchers found that sacrifice predicted marital success when those behaviors began early in the marriage. Morrill (2006) also contributed to our understanding of the role of sacrifice in marriage relationships in her qualitative study of couples who had great marriages. She found that couples who thought their marriages were great regularly made sacrifices for their spouse. They gave up personal wants and desires for each other and for the good of the marriage relationship. Here is how one husband from Morrill's study described sacrifice for his wife and his marriage:

> The promise is to always be there, willing to do whatever is needed to help the partnership, and to provide continuous support for, and encouragement to, your mate. . . . You are not the most important, they are. (p. 49)

There is also evidence that sacrificial behaviors appear to be symbols of overall commitment to the marriage and result in mutual trust (Stanley et al., 2006). Sacrificial behavior, then, can be instrumental in affecting several aspects of the marriage relationship in that it can be a tangible way that partners can show commitment on a daily basis.

Prayer in Marriage

We've all heard the saying, "The family that prays together, stays together." Recent research suggests that this is true for couples as well (Fincham & Beach, 2013). These researchers found that in both committed couple relationships as well as married couples, praying for each other enhance relationship satisfaction. Praying for each other increased commitment and, thus, enhanced relationship outcomes.

Other researchers have looked at adding prayer to relationship enhancement programs. Does adding prayer to marriage education increase the benefits of the program? Beach et al. (2011) found that there were better outcomes for the educational program if prayer was part of it. David and Stafford (2015) found in a study of over 300 married couples that one's individual relationship with God, the couple's communication about religion, and forgiveness predicted increased marital satisfaction. These authors concluded that one's own relationship with God was the cornerstone that led to communication about religion, which improved marital quality. In other words, one's relationship with God was a key component in enhancing the couple's relationship, and other things fell into place.

For so many years social scientists did not talk about spirituality and religion, and studies were not conducted to address benefits (Fincham, 2013). In recent years, however, we have learned that one's spiritual life is very much a part of marriage and family relationships. We expect there will be more research in this area in the future.

Federal Healthy Marriage Initiative

In 2006, the federal government passed legislation to fund the Healthy Marriage Initiative, which provided grant money of $100 million per year for 5 years to provide programs to promote healthy marriages around the country. These grants have continued, and in 2015 there were 91 organizations who received $150 million in funding to promote healthy marriage and provide relationship education, responsible fatherhood education, and reentry services for incarcerated fathers. According to the Administration for Children and Families (ACF), which is part of the U.S. Department of Health and Human Services, healthy marriages and healthy relationships promote the interest of children.

Funding was granted to 126 organizations to provide programs for couples, especially those in low-income and minority populations who have high rates of single parents and divorces. The programs were to teach relationship skills and knowledge to couples with the goal of forming and sustaining healthy marriages. There is a focus on low-income and ethnically diverse populations, because these couples are less stable.

This initiative has been controversial. At a policy level, some question whether the federal government should be involved in something as personal as marriage. Some feel that the initiative is a way to promote marriage rather than promoting *healthy* marriages, and that promoting marriage could result in couples staying married when the marriage is harmful to the partners. Because this initiative is supported by conservative religious organizations, some feel this initiative has a religious agenda. Given that there has been controversy about these grants, there is significant research which supports this initiative. We know, for example that children do better in stable, two-parent families that function well (Brown, 2010; Choi & Marks, 2013). Economic hardship often follows single parents, which adds another layer of stress for children and adults. Because the funding has now been in place for several years, there is some evidence to show that the initiative has worked. Programs that teach individual and couple relationship skills are making a difference in terms of couple stability and relationship satisfaction (Hawkins et al., 2008; Hawkins et al., 2013, February-March). There are studies that show that lower income and minority populations are benefiting from these programs. In fact, there seems to be more benefit to participants who have lower education. Studies show that these couples have lower rates of divorce, children's behavior improves, and parent–child relationships improve.

According to Hawkins et al. (2013a, February-March), these programs are reaching the most hard to reach audiences, which are those having the most unstable relationships. The grants, themselves require that barriers to attendance be addressed. Most programs do not charge and, in fact, provide incentives for attending. These incentives may be cash, meals, or gas cards to help make it more likely that they will be able to attend. In addition, facilitators are typically well versed in the cultural backgrounds of those attending, so that information may be provided in a culturally appropriate way. These authors conclude that even small effects may result in taxpayer savings by improving couple relationships.

Hawkins, Amato, and Kinghorn (2013b) conducted an ambitious study trying to determine if this funding stream has impacted states. They compared the amount of funding states received from these grants to the percentages of people living in single-parent families from 2000 to 2010. They found that federal funding did, in fact, cause a decrease in the percentage of children living with single parents. These authors clearly state that much more research needs to be done to substantiate these findings. However one feels about this initiative, it is an extensive policy change that can benefit many couples who want to have healthier relationships.

Summary

- Marriage offers a number of benefits. As compared to single or divorced individuals, married couples lead a healthier lifestyle, live longer, have a more satisfying sexual relationship, have more wealth and economic assets, and generally do a better job raising children.
- Three trends point to the changing role of marriage in the United States today. First, a decline in the popularity of marriage is indicated by a decrease in the number of marriages to an all-time low. Second, fewer couples who get divorced choose to remarry. And third, the number of couples living together has increased from 500,000 couples in 1970 to more than 5.5 million couples at present.
- Couples have a better chance for a happy marriage when both individuals are mature, love each other and themselves, enjoy being alone and together, are established in their work, are assertive with each other, and are friends as well as lovers.
- A very low percentage of couples in the United States enroll in a comprehensive marriage preparation program. The most useful programs include (1) a premarital inventory to assess strengths and areas of potential growth and a discussion of the assessment results with a trained counselor, (2) a small discussion group in which couples share feelings and concerns with each other, and (3) training in communication and problem-solving skills, which should start 12 months before marriage and last 6 to 8 weeks.
- Researchers have developed an inventory that couples can take before marriage to assess the strengths in their relationship. The inventory can predict a couple's chances of marital success or failure with 90% accuracy.
- A national survey identified five types of marriages: From most to least happy, they are *vitalized, harmonious, conventional, conflicted,* and *devitalized*. Studies suggest that these types exist across ethnic groups.
- The federal government has provided funding since 2006 to help couples have better relationships. The goal of programs resulting from this funding is to help children live in more stable two-parent families.

Key Terms

PREPARE
family of origin
vitalized couple
harmonious couple
conventional couple
conflicted couple
devitalized couple

Activities

1. List what you consider positive and negative reasons for getting married. Share the list with a partner or with others in a small discussion group.
2. How do you know if you are ready for marriage? Discuss this issue with a small group and formulate some guidelines to help people decide whether they are ready to marry.
3. For *dating or engaged couples:* Both partners should write down five things they like about the partner and five things that sometimes bother them. Then both partners should discuss the items on the lists very carefully and listen to each other so that the exchange is positive and constructive.
4. For those dating or engaged couples interested in taking the PREPARE Program, first contact a counselor or a member of the clergy in your area. If you cannot locate someone trained in PREPARE, go to the web site to locate one: www.prepare-enrich.com.

Suggested Readings

Administration for Children and Families (n.d.). *2015-2016 ACF Strategic Plan.* Web site: https://www.acf.hhs.gov/sites/default/files/assets/acf_2015_2016_strategic_plan.pdf.

Apter, T. (2009). *What do you want from me? Learning to get along with in-laws.* New York, NY: Norton.

Cherlin, A. J. (2009). *The marriage-go-around: The state of marriage and the family in America today.* New York, NY: Vintage Books.

David, P., & Stafford, L. (2015). A relational approach to religion and spirituality in marriage: The role of couples' religious communication in marital satisfaction. *Journal of Family Issues, 36,* 232–249.

Driver, J., Tabares, A., Shapiro, A. F., & Gottman, J. M. (2012). Couple interaction in happy and unhappy marriages. In F. Walsh (Ed.), *Normal family processes* (4th ed., pp. 57-77). New York, NY: Guilford Press.

Gottman, J. M. (2011). *The science of trust: Emotional attunement for couples.* New York, NY: W. W. Norton.

Knutson, L., & Olson, D. H. (2003). Effectiveness of PREPARE Program with premarital couples in a community setting. *Marriage and Family, 6*(4), 529–546.

Lerner, H. G. (2012). *Marriage rules: A manual for the married and the coupled up.* New York, NY: Gotham Books.

National Center for Family & Marriage Research. (n.d.). Bowling Green State University. Web site: http://www.bgsu.edu/ncfmr.html.

Olson, D. H., Olson-Sigg, A., & Larson, P. (2008). *The couple checkup.* Nashville, TN: Thomas Nelson.

Stanley, S. M., Whitton, S. W., Sadberry, S. L., Clements, M. L., & Markman, H. J. (2006). Sacrifice as a predictor of marital outcomes. *Family Process, 45,* 289–303.

Worthington, E. L. (Ed.). (2005). *Handbook of forgiveness.* New York, NY: Routledge.

Visit the text-specific Online Learning Center at www.mhhe.com/olson9e for practice tests, chapter summaries, and PowerPoint slides.

Design Element: © Alicia Grünkind/EyeEm/Getty Images

12 Parenthood: Joys and Challenges

©Jan Mika/123RF

Roots and Wings
Children and Happiness
Couple Strengths and Issues in Parenting
The Challenge of Parenthood
Adoption
The Child-Free Alternative
Styles of Parenting

Theories of Childrearing
Issues in Parenting
The Joy and Enduring Satisfaction of Parenthood
Summary
Key Terms
Activities
Suggested Readings

Roots and Wings

A parent's job is to give a child both *roots* and *wings,* which is no easy task. Rearing children may indeed be life's greatest mixed blessing. It is full of good times and bad times, frustrating challenges and genuine feelings of success. A baby's first stumbling steps and first words, a teenager's first love, a grown child's first baby—all are important transitions that parents remember. At the same time, children bring heavy responsibilities and drain parents of energy, finances, and time.

When we did a search on "parenting" using the Amazon.com web site, we found over 40,000 books listed in their database. Even so, we are quite confident that there is no book on rearing children that answers all the questions and no clear path to family happiness. The road is difficult, and there are no guarantees.

We begin this chapter with the results of a recent study about how children affect individual and couple happiness (Wilcox, 2011). We will examine the challenge of parenthood and take a look at some of the conventional wisdom that surrounds it. Among the challenges are the effects of parenthood on marriage, the decision whether to have children, and the financial burdens of raising children. We will discuss various parenting styles and how they relate to the family styles of the Couple and Family Map. This will be followed by an exploration of issues in parenting and some practical approaches to raising children, including coparenting. Then, we will touch on the benefits of parent education and family therapy and conclude with a summary of the many satisfactions of parenting.

We will report on the national survey that examined couple strengths and issues for married couples (Olson, Olson-Sigg, & Larson, 2008). We will begin with the results of the survey regarding the parenting strengths of happy couples versus unhappy couples. Next, we will review the five most common parenting issues as reported by more than 50,000 couples.

Children and Happiness

There is conflicting information about the effects of children on individual and couple happiness. A recent study by Bradford Wilcox (2011), using large data sets, looked at these issues, and the findings provide new insights into these issues.

Children and Individual Happiness

Most people want to have children, and yet, children can often create personal stress. Wilcox (2011) found that married men and women were equally happy regardless of their parental status. Parents who are cohabiting are next in terms of happiness, and single parents are least happy. This author concludes that those with a partner, whether that partner is a spouse or a person in a cohabiting relationship, have a higher degree of personal happiness raising children than do single parents.

When it came to being depressed, Wilcox (2011) found that married parents and cohabiting parents had an equal likelihood of being depressed, and single parents had a higher likelihood of being depressed. The similarity in general happiness between married parents and cohabiting parents is an important finding, given that 40% of those who cohabitate will have children (Wilcox, 2010). One might speculate that sharing the work, responsibility, financial costs, and stress of raising children is made easier when one has someone with which to share it.

Children and Couple Happiness

According to Wilcox (2011), although marital happiness does decline over time for all couples, it decreases more suddenly for parents versus nonparents. Childless couples have a more gradual decline in marital happiness, whereas for couples with children there is a significant decline that coincides with the birth of their first child. However, it should be noted that children do not create a higher degree of marital conflict or divorce proneness for married couples compared to those without children.

Are there benefits to having children? Both married men and women, according to Wilcox (2011), are more likely to indicate that their life has an important purpose than married couples who do not have children, and this was especially true for women. One might speculate that although marital happiness may decline with the addition of children, a sense of purpose may replace the marital satisfaction.

Wilcox (2011) looked more closely at the minority of couples who had higher levels of marital happiness after children arrived. What makes them have even better marriages than before children? This author identified eight factors that contributed to these couples having high marital quality even with children:

- Higher educational levels
- Higher level of financial resources
- Sharing of work and family responsibilities
- Support from family and friends
- Faith in a higher being
- Shared beliefs about marriage and parenthood
- High levels of sexual satisfaction
- Being generous to each other

Wilcox (2011) also explored differences in the number of children and marital happiness.

He found that couples who had no children and couples who had four or more children were happiest. How could this be, given the added financial and emotional stress of four or more children? This author speculates that several factors were evident with these couples that could have contributed to these findings. Wilcox (2011) found these couples were more likely to attend a place of worship, felt a sense of purpose in their lives, and experienced increased social support, which may have become an integral part of their marriage and family lives.

Couple Strengths and Issues in Parenting

In a national survey of married couples, Olson et al., (2008) identified a number of parenting strengths. As Table 12.1 shows, happy couples were more than twice as likely (61%) as unhappy couples (30%) to agree on how to share the responsibilities of raising their children. Happy couples were almost twice as likely (59%) as unhappy couples (31%) to be satisfied with the amount of attention they focus on their marriage versus the amount of attention they focus on their children. Almost twice as many happy couples (59%) reported agreeing on how to discipline their children as did unhappy couples (33%). Happy couples were much more likely (53%) than unhappy couples (33%) to feel that they had grown closer since having children. And 35% of the happy couples reported that they were more satisfied in their marriage since having children, compared to 19% for the unhappy couples.

TABLE 12.1 Strengths of Happy Couples Versus Unhappy Couples Regarding Parenting

	PERCENTAGE IN AGREEMENT	
Parenting Issue	**Happy Couples**	**Unhappy Couples**
1. I am satisfied with how childrearing is shared.	61%	30%
2. My partner focuses as much on the marriage as on the children.	59	31
3. We agree on discipline.	59	33
4. We feel closer since having children.	53	33
5. I am more satisfied in my marriage since having children.	35	19

Source: Olson, D., Olson-Sigg, A., & Larson, P. *The Couple Checkup.* Nashville, TN: Thomas Nelson, 2008.

TABLE 12.2 Top Five Parenting Issues for Couples

Parenting Issue	Percentage of Couples Having Problems*
1. Having children has reduced marital satisfaction.	82%
2. The father is not involved enough with our children.	65
3. My partner focuses more on the children than on the marriage.	64
4. I am dissatisfied with how childrearing is shared.	64
5. We disagree on discipline.	63

*One or both partners indicated this was an issue for them.

Table 12.2 identifies the top five parenting issues from this national sample of more than 50,000 couples. The biggest issue for parents (82%) is that children had a negative impact on their marital satisfaction, and they reported feeling more dissatisfied in their marriage since having children. The second most frequently reported parenting issue (65%) was that the father did not spend enough time with the children. Rounding out the top five parenting issues, 64% of the parents were dissatisfied with how childrearing responsibilities were shared; 63% disagreed on how to discipline their children; and 64% felt their partner focused more on their children than on the marriage.

The Challenge of Parenthood

Many authorities have noted that parenthood is the last bastion of amateurism in our society. Plumbers, bookkeepers, computer analysts—all need some kind of formal training, certificate, or license. About the only job that doesn't require some special kind of education is nurturing the young to adulthood.

Our society tends to shy away from "intruding" into family matters, and rearing children is certainly a family matter. But some have gone so far as to argue that education and even something like an internship should be mandatory before people can become parents—that is, that a license should be required for parenthood—although such a proposal has little chance of becoming law. Nevertheless, its proponents underscore the importance of parenting: Society benefits from parents' successes but also suffers from their mistakes.

Adults with problems often had problems as children, and many times they pass their problems on to the next generation. For example, one therapist described a counseling session with an abused woman who had fled from her husband after repeated beatings; the woman's 18-month-old son accompanied her. During the session, the toddler became angered over some minor issue and ran at his mother. In his frustration, he put his hands around her neck and tried to strangle her. He was imitating almost precisely what he had seen his father do a few days earlier. With counseling, this pattern could be changed so that the boy would not repeat his father's behavior.

Myths and Realities of Parenthood

All societies have folk beliefs or myths that are widely accepted and rarely examined. The myths about parenthood in our society often sugarcoat the subject, romanticizing a task that is too important for people to undertake with rose-colored glasses. What follows is a list of commonly held folk beliefs or myths in our society, along with some comments that offer a more balanced and realistic view.

Myth #1: *Children will turn out well if they have "good" parents.*
Reality: Parents are an important factor in a child's development, but they are only one influence among many, including siblings, schools, the mass media, and the child's peer group. The goal of parenting must be to instill values and model positive behaviors that children will internalize and use in their lives. But there are no guarantees. Some good parents work hard at parenting only to see their children get into great difficulty in life.

Myth #2: *Children are sweet and cute.*
Reality: Although children can be adorable, they can also be selfish and destructive, as well as extremely active. In fact, children possess the full range of human qualities—positive and negative—that adults must deal with in each other. Parents who have no break from watching over children can easily become exhausted.

Myth #3: *Good parents can manage any child, no matter what the child's nature.*
Reality: This myth is based on the notion that a human being is born a *tabula rasa,* a blank slate upon which the environment writes its script. But research on infants indicates that to some degree temperament is present at birth. Some babies are calm and content; others are cranky. Although the family environment that parents construct for their young is tremendously important, it is not the only influence or the sole determinant of a child's developmental outcome. It is important to note that children also strongly shape their parents' behavior. Parents, in sum, raise children. And children in many ways raise parents.

Myth #4: *Today's parents are not as good as yesterday's parents.*
Reality: Standards for raising children have gotten higher, making the challenge for today's parents even greater. Society now expects parents to be more democratic in their approach, to take the child's feelings into account when decisions are made, and to involve older children in the decision-making process.

Myth #5: *One child is too few.*
Reality: Although many believe that an only child is spoiled and selfish, countless studies worldwide have demonstrated that this belief is an unsubstantiated stereotype. The fact is, there are both advantages and disadvantages to having only

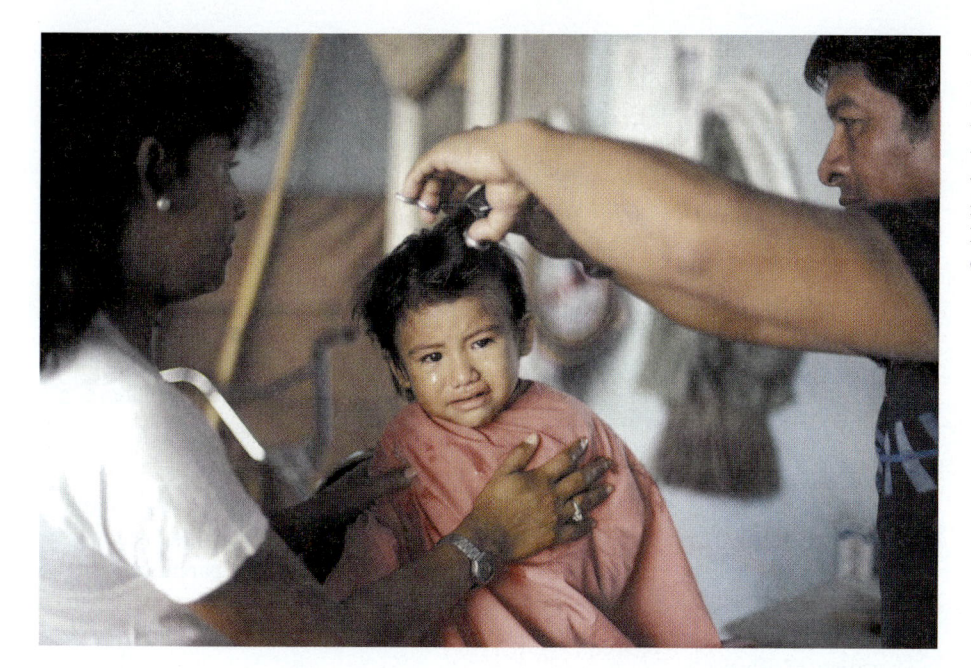

A first haircut is one of the many milestones that mark a child's growing up. Although this toddler may not remember the experience, his mother will likely remember this event in his transition from baby to little boy.
©Bonnie Kamin/PhotoEdit

one child. One child is less expensive to raise, is less demanding on the parents, places fewer limits on the parents' freedom, and receives more parental attention. On the downside, parents of only children sometimes focus too much attention on or overprotect the child, thus limiting the child's exposure to peer companions and possibly even causing the child to feel lonely. Also, having brothers and sisters can be a great source of support and joy throughout life: not only someone to fight with when you are young, but someone to cherish as a dear friend when you are grown up.

Myth #6: *All parents are adults.*
Reality: As reflected in our nation's teenage pregnancy rates, many adolescents unfortunately become parents. Government statistics indicate that 9% of all birth mothers are women age 15 to 19 years (U.S. National Center for Health Statistics, 2017, January 6). This is an historic low. Childrearing is difficult for adults, but it can be particularly challenging for teenage parents.

Myth #7: *Parenthood receives top priority in our society.*
Reality: Making money—not parenthood—receives top priority in our society. Parents are pressured to put their jobs first if they seek promotions—and sometimes even if they simply want to hold on to their jobs.

Myth #8: *Love is enough to guarantee good parental performance.*
Reality: Love certainly helps parents put up with the many difficulties of childrearing, but success at parenting also requires hard work and good parenting skills.

Myth #9: *Single-parent families are problematic.*
Reality: Single-parent families are often stigmatized in American society today, and the discussion of single-parent families' efforts to create a happy life together too often focuses on the negative. There is little question that many single-parent families face considerable challenges. Money and stress are very prominent on the list. The fact is, however, that there are countless strong single-parent families in which children are

Chapter 12 | Parenthood: Joys and Challenges

growing up happy and healthy. Simply knowing the structure of a family does not tell you how well a family is functioning.

Myth #10: *Parenting gets easier as children get older.*
Reality: Although most parents hope that parenting will get easier as their children mature, they typically find that their parenting issues change and become more difficult. Adolescence is the most challenging stage for many parents, because adolescents are seeking greater autonomy and freedom from parental control.

Myth #11: *Parenting ends when the children leave home.*
Reality: For most parents, parenting does not end when a child leaves home. Adult children often return home to live after a divorce, a job loss, or some other life crisis. Furthermore, parents are often called on to help with the care of their children's children; grandparenting brings joy, but it can also be exhausting.

Myth #12: *The empty-nest syndrome leaves many parents lonely and depressed.*
Reality: One observer noted, "After the kids leave home, some parents suffer from the empty-nest syndrome; others change the locks." Many parents enjoy the freedom that comes with not having adolescents at home. The middle-aged parent may get a job or change jobs, travel, or take up a new avocation. After they leave home, adult children are often surprised to watch their parents blossom and enjoy life in a variety of new ways.

The Transition to Parenthood

A 2011 Gallup survey showed that 49% of men said that if they could only have one child, they would want it to be a boy. Only 22% would want a girl and the remainder did not care. However, in another survey, once a man has a daughter, he is more concerned about gender equality. Little girls have power!

—REAL SIMPLE, JUNE 2012, P. 8.

Parenthood isn't something that happens gradually; the 9 months of a normal pregnancy should give prospective parents time to think about parenthood and to plan for the arrival of the baby. But many parents are unprepared for the challenges that will confront them when the infant arrives. They may take classes to prepare for childbirth, but few prepare for the responsibilities of parenting itself.

When the baby is born, parenting begins in earnest. For some it is a crisis. E. E. LeMasters gained prominence in the 1950s with his report in the *New York Times* of a study entitled "Parenthood as Crisis." LeMasters argued that because of romantic notions about parenthood, people go through a process of disenchantment when they have children. LeMasters was flooded with letters from parents, most of whom agreed with his findings. In his research, LeMasters interviewed 46 couples and found that 83% defined the coming of a child as a "crisis" for their marriage (LeMasters, 1957). Other researchers have debated these findings ever since, and the definition of the term *crisis* remains controversial (Lawrence et al., 2008).

One dictionary defines *crisis* simply as a *turning point,* which parenthood certainly is in the life of mothers and fathers. Ask new parents a few months or years into the process if they can remember what life was like before having a baby, and the responses tend to run like these:

> "I'm so tired, I can't remember what life was like yesterday, let alone what it was like before Lindy was born. We're just trying to figure out the everyday demands of parenting and do the best we can."

or

> "No, I don't remember at all. I know everything changed, but all in all, it's been a good change."

or

> "NO, I cannot imagine how life was like before he came. Everybody told me how your perspective and priorities change with a child, and I did not know the extent of it till now. It is the first time I am completely happy and do not feel guilty that I am not working. I used to work, even during vacations. Today, I am more than happy to just enjoy my son."

Another dictionary defines *crisis* as a time of great danger or trouble. New parents are not likely to use these terms, because they may seem melodramatic or overblown. However, most new parents will agree that life has changed, dramatically. Thus, in this section we will talk about the *transition to parenthood,* even though that may sound a bit dry and academic, not quite capturing the emotion and drama that surround the advent of a child into a new parent's life.

There are several changes that new parents can expect (Cowan & Cowan, 2011). First, as each person takes on the parent role, their identity as a spouse, lover, and successful employee takes second stage. A parent may be too tired to give time to her or his spouse, or may not be able to give 100% at work if the person spent all night taking care of a fussy baby. Second, the relationships with family of origin change. Some new parents want to parent just like their parents did and others want to avoid doing things their parents did in raising them. This may mean these new parents pull away from their parents, whereas others want to draw closer. Third, each new parent develops a new relationship with this child as part of the transition to parenthood. The parent tries to figure out why the child cries and how to satisfy every need. Fourth, there are new stressors as well as new sources of emotional support. Trying to go to work while worrying about a baby in someone else's care can be difficult for both mothers and fathers. Stressors can also come from changes in partners' roles. For example, a couple might have shared most responsibilities equally before the baby was born, and they want to continue this after the birth of the child. However, that typically does not happen and gender roles become quite traditionally stereotypical with a new baby. This change in the family system creates stress for both parents. Finally, the quality of the couple relationship changes, which has been supported by many studies. The couple relationship satisfaction declines after the birth of the first child and continues to decline for several years.

Chong and Mickelson (2016) conducted a study with mothers 9 months after the birth of a baby. These researchers looked at both household labor and child care as separate issues and found that perceived fairness when it came to both were equally important in terms of the mothers' relationship satisfaction with the father. In other words, when the mother felt there was fairness in how child care and household tasks were divided up, there was less conflict with her partner and, thus, resulted in greater relationship satisfaction.

According to Cowan and Cowan (2011), couples who attended family education classes addressing issues around the transition to parenthood were more likely to maintain high couple satisfaction with the birth of the first child, and these results were maintained long term. These authors also have the following suggestions for couples who cannot attend such classes:

- Communicate about issues that are creating stress for each parent.
- Develop a division of labor that is realistic and can work for both parents.
- Take time to keep the couple relationship strong. Take time for each other by building it into each day.

FIGURE 12.1

Cost of Raising a Child from Birth Through Age 17

Source: U.S. Dept. of Agriculture, Center for Nutrition Policy and Promotion.

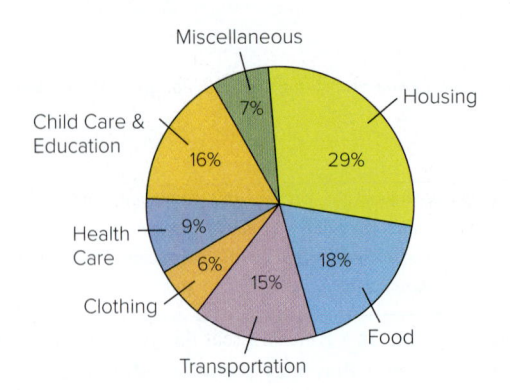

- Housing: 29%
- Food: 18%
- Transportation: 15%
- Clothing: 6%
- Health Care: 9%
- Child Care & Education: 16%
- Miscellaneous: 7%

Financial Issues and Children

One of the surprises for most parents is how much children cost, in terms of not just time and energy but also money. Raising children is a very expensive venture, no matter what a family's income. An analysis of the expense of raising a child, based on data from the U.S. Department of Agriculture, was summarized by Lino, Kuczynski, Rodriguez, and Schap (2017, January). The data were broken down into six major categories: housing, food, transportation, clothing, health care, and education.

It was found that a married, middle-income couple will spend approximately $233,610 to raise a child. The cost for lower-income families is estimated to be approximately $175,000 and for higher-income families approximately $372,000 (Lino et al., 2017, January). These costs are for a child born in 2015 and include the time from birth through age 17. These costs for middle-income families break down to approximately $13,000 per year. Housing is the largest expense at about 29% of total costs. This cost comes primarily from needing an extra bedroom for a child. Food averages 18%, transportation 15%, health care 9%, and clothing 6%. Child care and education take about 16% of the total cost. Although child care decreases as the child gets older, other educational expenses rise. (See Figure 12.1 for details.)

An important aspect of socializing children is helping them learn to understand and manage finances. One careful study of 182 parents by Sharon Danes asked when it was appropriate to introduce children to a variety of financial activities. About 70% of these parents felt that children 8 years or younger were mature enough to receive an allowance, and 64% felt that they could open their own savings account. Almost half of the parents surveyed felt that 12- to 14-year-olds could be responsible for their own clothing budgets, and 29% believed that they were mature enough to be told about the family's income. About half the parents felt that 15- to 17-year-olds should know about car insurance and have their own checking accounts. More than half the parents believed that by age 18 to 20, adult children should have and be responsible for their own credit cards and be able to apply for and make the payments on a loan (Danes & Haberman, 2007; see also CYFERnet, 2010).

Adoption

Adoption was once a secretive experience, with some children not knowing they are adopted until parents shared the information when the child became an adult. In fact, there were often efforts to match couples with children who looked like them so they would appear to be a biological child. According to Walkner and Rueter (2014), this has changed in the past 30 years. Adoption has become much less secretive and more normalized. Adoption across racial lines or adopting children in their teens has become more open and acceptable in today's society. In addition, there was a time when the identity of the birth parents were kept secret so that there would be no opportunity for the birth parents and the adoptive parents to interact. Today there are open adoptions where the biological parents and adoptive parents stay in contact over the years. There are also less children being adopted as infants today for several reasons. Those reasons include the acceptability of raising a child as a single parent and the availability of birth control and abortions. Therefore, the number of children adopted as infants has decreased and, instead, we see children adopted later in life.

Gay and lesbian couples are also adopting children with greater frequency, since gay and lesbian relationships and marriages are more common today. It needs to be noted, however, that although attitudes about civil rights of gay and lesbian relationships have become more positive, adopting children is still seen somewhat negatively (Rye & Meaney, 2010). As Meany reviews the literature, we know that men are more likely to have negative feelings toward gays and lesbians adopting than women are. Much of these negative feelings on the part of both men and women seems to come from peoples' fear that the couple may influence a child's sexual orientation.

It is estimated that approximately 2% to 3% of the population is adopted. However, adoption has affected many families in that the majority of individuals know someone who is adopted or they have an adopted person in their extended family. The research is mixed on how families do when there is an adopted family member (Walkner & Rueter, 2014). This often has to do with child factors. The research is pretty consistent that the older the child, the greater the stress for parents (Goldberg & Smith, 2014). An older child is likely to have been in multiple family situations, including foster care and/or challenging birth family environments. The extent of the emotional and behavior problems also affects the family's ability to welcome an adopted child into the family (Goldberg & Smith, 2014). These problems are often related to the age of the child. Some children, however, have been given up for adoption because of mental or emotional problems early on, and the birth parents did not feel they could care for the child. Or a child may have come from another country where she or he was in an orphanage or other family situation and, as a result, has cognitive or developmental problems. The relationships within the adoptive family are also important factors in adoption. If the family did not function well before the adoption, they are not likely to do well with the added stress of adoption. Goldberg and Smith (2014) also found in their study that no matter what issues the family encountered, support from family and friends was important in reducing stress for adoptive parents.

Six factors have been identified that contribute to the success of parents adopting a child:

1. Healthy adoptive parents explore their motivations and expectations for adoption in an open and healthy manner and are in agreement.
2. Healthy adoptive parents demonstrate stability and quality in their interpersonal relationships.
3. Healthy adoptive parents demonstrate flexibility and openness in the family system. They can accept and deal with change, they value differences among family members, they readily seek support and resources when help is needed.
4. Healthy adoptive parents know the importance of creating a family environment that openly acknowledges and communicates about adoption.
5. Healthy adoptive parents understand the core issues of adoption that may affect their child and the triggers that may create a crisis. These core issues include the child's grief and mourning over loss of her birth parents; and the child's feelings of loss and control, rejection and fear of abandonment, shame and guilt, loss of personal identity, and feeling different from other children.
6. Healthy adoptive parents understand that adoption is a lifetime commitment and maintain that commitment through difficult times (Schooler & Atwood, 2008).

The Child-Free Alternative

Attitudes in the United States regarding the importance of children to a successful marriage have shifted in recent decades. A Pew Research Survey on marriage and parenting found that children had fallen to eighth place on a list of nine factors that people associate with successful marriages, well behind *sharing household chores, good housing, adequate income, a happy sexual relationship,* and *faithfulness.* In a 1990 World Values Survey, children ranked third in importance among the same eight items, with 65% saying children were very important to a good marriage. Just 41% said so in the most recent study (Pew Research Center, 2007). (See Figure 12.2, which compares the percentages from 1990 and 2007.)

Various terms are applied to the choice not to have children, including *nonparenthood, voluntary childlessness,* and the **child-free alternative.** Acceptance of childlessness has increased since the 1970s, and researchers have found that women are more accepting of childlessness than men are. More than 86% of adults agreed or were neutral on whether childless adults could have fulfilling lives (Koropeckyj-Cox & Pendell, 2007, 2009). According to Agrillo and Nelini (2008), this trend toward childlessness has become more common in developed countries around the world.

The percentage of childless, middle-aged women aged 40 to 44—those at the end of their childbearing years—has increased from 10% in 1976 to about 18% (Wilcox, 2011). Rates of childlessness in the United States, including both women who choose not to have children and women who cannot have children, have varied substantially over the years. For example, for White women born in the mid-1880s, slightly over 15% remained childless. For White women born in 1910 and who reached childbearing age during the Great Depression of the 1930s, the childless rate was more than 25%. For White women born in 1935 who reached childbearing age during the baby boom of 1946 to 1964, the childless rate dropped dramatically to 10% (Morgan & Chen, 1992). The current recession has also had its effect on reproductive decisions. It has been found that 64% of women said that with the current economy, they could not afford to have a baby (Sandler, 2010, July 19).

FIGURE 12.2
Factors Americans Associate with Successful Marriage

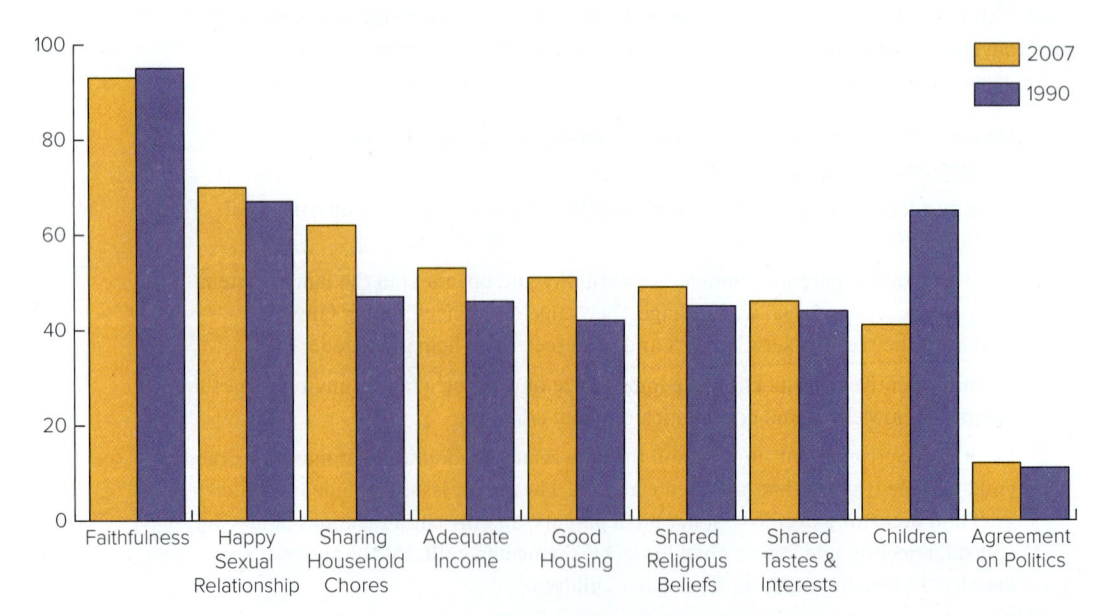

Source: Pew Research Center, "Modern Marriage," July 18, 2007. Website: http://www.pewsocialtrends.org/2007/07/18/modern-marriage/.

It was also found that 44% said they planned to reduce the number of children they plan to have because of the economy. Other reasons people choose not to have children include breaking the family violence cycle and not finding the right person with which to parent (Allen & Wiles, 2013).

These fluctuations indicate that even when modern, relatively efficient contraception is not available, parents have responded over the years to changing economic and social conditions. According to Gray (2015, April 9), the number of women giving birth between ages 15 and 44 in the United States is at an all-time low. According to Gray, the reasons may include the cost of raising a child, the gender wage gap, and the double duty of profession and domestic responsibilities. There are some estimates that 25% of women who are currently in child-bearing years may end up not having children. In addition, in Western countries, many women are choosing to have fewer children (Agrillo & Nelini, 2008; Wagner, Wrzus, Neyer, & Lang, 2015). Here are some findings regarding childlessness:

- *What long-term effects does voluntary childlessness have?* Although adult children are often very important to their parents in old age, older people without children also do quite well. Aging parents may even find themselves rejected or neglected by their adult children. Childless people in later years lead interesting and meaningful lives by creating intergenerational connections with others who have children (Allen & Wiles, 2013). These connections may be with family members or friends. In fact, those without children seem to have more freedom to become involved in experiences not available to those with children.

- *Is there something wrong with people who don't wish to have children?* The majority of studies on this topic concluded that nonparents exhibit no more psychopathology or deviance than a control group of randomly sampled parents. Culture affects one's attitude about whether or not to have children. For example, it has been argued that African Americans, American Indians, and Mexican Americans tend to be more family oriented than Whites and consider children an important part of marital life (Skogrand, Hatch, & Singh, 2009).

Parenthood is not for everyone. Couples who have decided not to have children can find happiness and fulfillment in life with each other, with their careers and avocational interests, and with friends and family.
©Andersen Ross/Blend Images LLC

Chapter 12 | Parenthood: Joys and Challenges   323

- *Do people without children do better in their careers?* Apparently, many people without children do very well. Voluntary childlessness leaves people with time and energy that can be focused on career goals. A disproportionate number of high-ranking businesswomen and professionals are childless.
- *Is the quality of a child-free marriage as good as that of a marriage with children?* Studies have found more vital and happy relationships among child-free couples than among those with children. This is, in part, because child-free couples can devote more time to their marriages and because they are more likely to divorce if they do not have a good relationship than would a couple with children.

How do couples decide to remain childless? What is the process they go through to decide not to have children even though there is no known reason why they could not have children? Durham and Braithwaite (2009) conducted a qualitative study, interviewing 32 individuals who were part of couples who were voluntarily childless. They found four trajectories that described the differing ways couples communicated about remaining childless.

The authors identified the first category of individuals who remained childless as being in the accelerated-consensus trajectory (Durham & Braithwaite, 2009). These individuals are deliberate about choosing a partner who wants to remain childless. These individuals often had political or other personal reasons for not wanting children. These couples discussed the issue of not having children early on in their relationship, and the issue typically did not come up with any regularity after that.

The second category of individuals who were childless was identified by the authors as being on the mutual-negotiation trajectory (Durham & Braithwaite, 2009). These individuals came into their relationships without prior discussion about having or not having children. Like those in the accelerated-consensus trajectory, these persons were on the same page as their partner, but in this case they had not made a decision about having children. They described their communication as going on over time about the pros and cons of having or not having children. They experienced times of being undecided or ambivalent about their reproductive preferences. Even though individuals described their relationships as being equal in terms of power, because each individual had uncertainty over the issue, many of the people on this trajectory experienced stress in their communication process. Even after they were beyond childbearing years, they wondered if they had made the right decision.

The third category of individuals in this study was identified as being on a unilateral-persuasion trajectory (Durham & Braithwaite, 2009). These individuals were part of couples where one spouse was committed to being child-free and that person convinced the undecided partner that being child-free was the best option for their marriage. Different from individuals in the mutual-negotiation trajectory who had equal power, one individual in the unilateral-persuasion trajectory had more power and influence in their communications about reproduction. All the individuals in this study in this trajectory resulted in the man being the undecided person and the woman being clear in wanting to remain childless. In many cases the man felt his spouse would eventually change her mind and they would have children. Individuals in this trajectory, as one would imagine, experienced lots of conflict and stress regarding the reproductive issue, and this conflict and stress spilled over into other aspects of their relationships.

Finally, the fourth category of individuals was identified as being on the bilateral-persuasion trajectory (Durham & Braithwaite, 2009). These individuals were in relationships in which they disagreed completely in their family planning perspectives. One spouse wanted to be child-free and the other wanted children. All the individuals who wanted children thought, incorrectly, that they would ultimately persuade their spouse to change their mind and they would have children. Individuals in these relationships described their communication as often being emotionally heated and negatively charged, resulting in lots of emotional turmoil. Often unilateral decisions were made on the part of one partner that resulted in hurt and anger on the part of the spouse. The impact on the marriage relationship was extensive.

Even though voluntary childlessness has increased, the joint decision to remain childless is not always easy. This decision, like all couple decisions, can support the marriage relationship or distract from the relationship. In general, remaining childless does not have a short-term or long-term negative effect on individuals or couples (Umberson, Pudrovska, & Reczek, 2010). Although the previous study included married couples, the decision to have children or remain childless also impacts the increased number of cohabiting couples who are also making reproductive decisions.

Styles of Parenting

There are two key aspects of parenting: parental support (family closeness on the Couple and Family Map) and parental control (family flexibility on the Couple and Family Map) (Figure 12.3). **Parental support** is defined as the amount of caring, closeness, and affection that a parent exhibits or gives to a child. **Parental control** is defined as the amount of flexibility that a parent uses in enforcing rules and disciplining a child.

There is considerable evidence that higher levels of parental support are related to positive outcomes in children, including better academic performance, higher self-esteem, more social competence, and better psychological adjustment (Bean, Barber, & Crane, 2006).

FIGURE 12.3
Parenting Styles and the Couple and Family Map

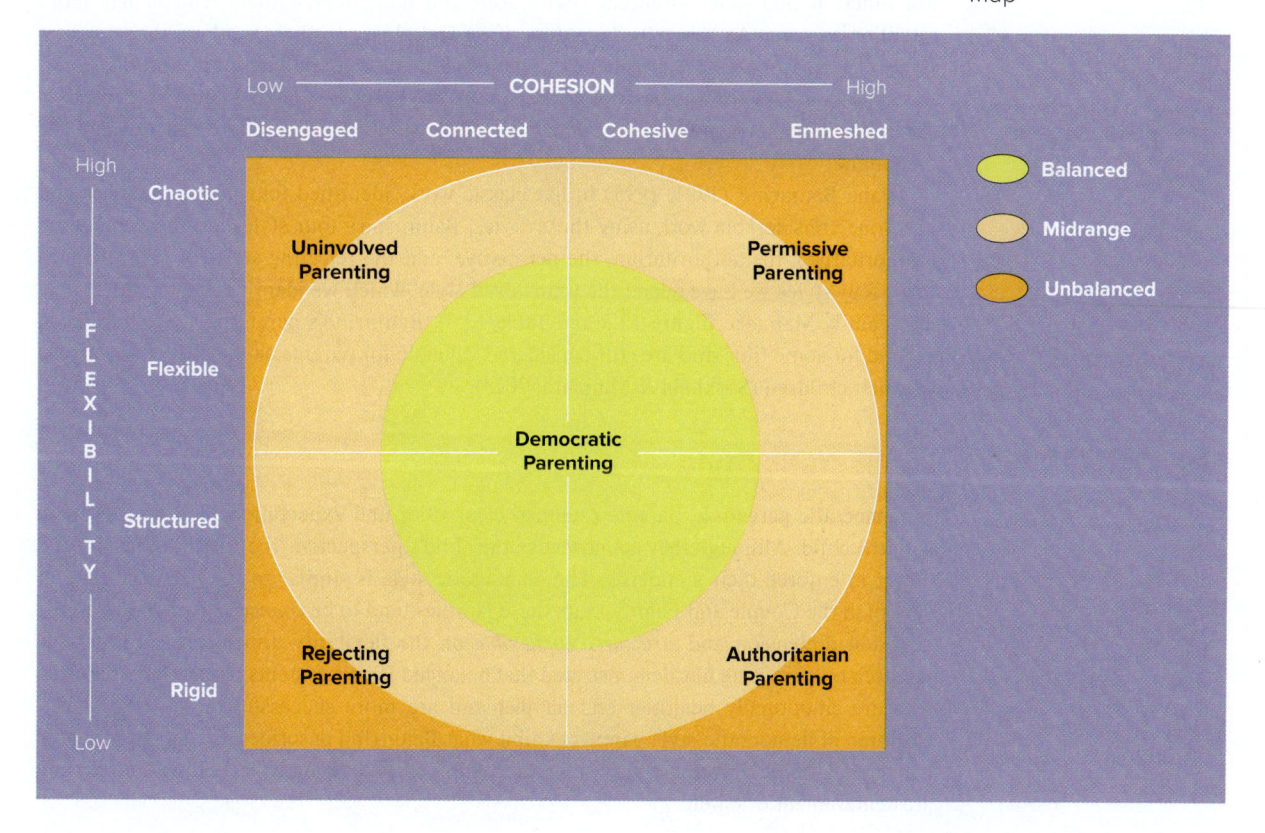

TABLE 12.3	Parenting Style and Children's Behavior
Parenting Style	**Children's Behavior**
Democratic style	Self-reliant, cheerful, achievement oriented
Authoritarian style	Conflicted, irritable, unhappy, unstable
Permissive style	Impulsive, rebellious, underachieving
Rejecting style	Immature, psychologically challenged
Uninvolved style	Solitary, withdrawn, underachieving

However, when you look at the extremes of family closeness using the Couple and Family Map, where there is very low closeness (disengaged) or very high closeness (enmeshed), children from these extremes tend to have more problems emotionally, socially, and academically (Manzi, Vignoles, Regalia, & Scabini, 2006).

Regarding parental control (family flexibility on the Couple and Family Map), there is considerable evidence that parenting that is too lenient (chaotic on the Couple and Family Map) and too strict (rigid on the Couple and Family Map) results in children with more psychological and academic problems. Conversely, parents who have a more balanced style of parenting (central level of the Couple and Family Map where parents are "structured" or "flexible" in parenting) have more positive outcomes with their children (Bean et al., 2006).

Sons and daughters often have different experiences growing up in the same family because they are treated differently by each parent. Although it appears that mothers do not function that much differently with sons and daughters, fathers tend to pay more attention to sons. As a result, daughters often feel closer to their mothers than to their fathers. Both parents have a tendency to punish sons more than daughters, and many still tend to assign tasks on the basis of gender—more boys mow the lawn, and more girls clean the house. In general, parenting style has about the same impact on both the sons and the daughters.

Diana Baumrind (1991, 1995) in her classic work, identified four parenting styles and has done considerable work using those styles. Baumrind's four styles are the democratic (authoritative), the authoritarian, the permissive, and the rejecting styles of parenting. To these four styles we have added the uninvolved style, which we identified using the Couple and Family Map (see Figure 12.3 and Table 12.3). Baumrind's parenting styles have been around for some time and are still considered valuable for parents as they think about raising their children (Sorkhabi & Mandara, 2013).

Democratic Style

In **democratic parenting,** parents establish clear rules and expectations and discuss them with the child. Although they acknowledge the child's perspective, they use both reason and power to enforce their standards. The democratic style is similar to the balanced type of system in the Couple and Family Map; these families tend to be *connected* to *cohesive* on the cohesion dimension and *structured* to *flexible* on the flexibility dimension. Considerable research on parenting has demonstrated that balanced family systems tend to have children who are emotionally healthier and happier and are more successful in school and life. Children of democratic-style parents exhibit what Baumrind describes as energetic-friendly behavior. These children are very self-reliant and cheerful. They cope well with stress and are achievement oriented.

Authoritarian Style

In **authoritarian parenting,** parents establish rigid rules and expectations and strictly enforce them. These parents expect and demand obedience from a child. The authoritarian style is located in the lower-right quadrant of the Couple and Family Map; these families tend to be *structured* to *rigid* on the flexibility dimension and *cohesive* to *enmeshed* on the cohesion dimension. As the authoritarian style becomes more intense, the family moves toward the *rigidly enmeshed* style. This type of family system is particularly difficult for adolescents, who tend to rebel against authoritarian parenting. In Baumrind's observations, children of authoritarian-style parents are often conflicted and irritable in behavior: moody, unhappy, vulnerable to stress, and unfriendly. A study of authoritarian parenting (Rudy & Grusec, 2006) in several European countries and the United States found that children from these families have more serious problems in a variety of areas (lower self-esteem, more behavior problems, less academic achievement).

Permissive Style

In **permissive parenting**, parents let the child's preferences take priority over their ideals and rarely force the child to conform to their standards. The permissive style is located in the upper-right quadrant of the Couple and Family Map; these families tend to be *flexible* to *chaotic* on the flexibility dimension and *cohesive* to *enmeshed* on the cohesion dimension. As the permissive style becomes more extreme, the family moves toward the *chaotically enmeshed* style, a style characterized by constant change and forced togetherness, which is not healthy for children. Baumrind observed that children of permissive-style parents generally exhibit impulsive–aggressive behavior. These children are often rebellious, domineering, and underachieving.

Rejecting Style

In **rejecting parenting**, parents do not pay much attention to the child's needs and seldom have expectations regarding how the child should behave. The rejecting style is located in the lower-left quadrant of the Couple and Family Map; these families tend to be *structured* to *rigid* on the flexibility dimension and *connected* to *disengaged* on the cohesion dimension. As the rejecting style becomes more extreme, the family moves toward the *rigidly disengaged* style, which leaves children feeling uncared for even though they are expected to behave and have many rules to follow. As a result, children from these homes are often immature and have psychological problems.

Uninvolved Style

In **uninvolved parenting**, parents often ignore the child, letting the child's preferences prevail as long as those preferences do not interfere with the parents' activities. The uninvolved style of parenting is located in the upper-left quadrant of the Couple and Family Map; these families tend to be *connected* to *disengaged* on the cohesion dimension and *flexible* to *chaotic* on the flexibility dimension. As the uninvolved style becomes more extreme, it moves toward the *chaotically disengaged* pattern, in which children are left on their own without emotional support and a lack of consistent rules and expectations. The uninvolved style of parenting is not often discussed in published research, but it is in many instances combined with the rejecting style. Children of uninvolved parents are often solitary, withdrawn, and underachieving.

Democratic parents are actively involved with their children. They set standards and discuss them with the child. Children of these parents tend to be self-reliant and achievement oriented, and they cope well with stress.
©ERproductions Ltd/Blend Images/Getty Images

Democratic Parenting Works Best

Diana Baumrind completed several studies that linked the four parenting styles and outcomes with children. She has done considerable work using these styles. Baumrind described three styles of behavior in preschool children—energetic–friendly, conflicted–irritable, and impulsive–aggressive—and correlated those behaviors with her parenting styles (Table 12.3). In general, the democratic style resulted in children who were self-reliant, cheerful, and achievement oriented. Children raised with other styles, which are more extreme on cohesion and flexibility, had more problematic behaviors and less academic success.

In contrast to the positive outcomes of democratic parenting, authoritarian parenting was related to greater psychological distress, lower self-esteem, a lower grade-point average, and—interestingly—lower substance abuse. Permissive parenting, considered the opposite of authoritarian parenting, was related to higher self-esteem, lower psychological distress, and lower substance abuse but also a lower grade-point average and some delinquency. Neglectful parenting was the most problematic parenting style. It was related to greater adolescent distress, lower self-esteem, a lower grade-point average, and greater drug use and delinquency compared to the other styles.

Research has been conducted to determine whether Baumrind's model applies to a variety of cultural groups. Sorkhabi and Mandara (2013) in summarizing the literature in this area, conclude that these styles and outcomes of these styles apply to a diversity of cultures. It is expected that these parenting styles will continue to be useful for parents for a long time.

Theories of Childrearing

Parenting is a complex process that raises many questions: How shall we raise the children? How strict should we be, and how will we discipline our children? How soon should we begin toilet training? Will day care meet all our children's needs if both of us work outside the home? How can we share household and parenting responsibilities so that neither one of us feels overburdened or resentful? Before we tackle the issues surrounding these and other questions, let's take a look at some interrelated and complementary theoretical approaches to parenting.

The family systems perspective is increasingly being used by those studying the parent-child relationship. Earlier work focused on the influence of the parent on the child and some focus of the child on the parent. In the 1980s, a strong consensus developed by child development researchers about the need to study **bidirectional effects**—both the effects of the child on the parent and those of the parent on the child—in order to understand parent-child dynamics. The idea was not new to proponents of family systems theory, but it was a breakthrough for traditional child development researchers. The book by Richard Bell, who described the research in *Child Effects on Adults* (1977), helped stimulate interest in bidirectional research. The family systems perspective takes this one step further, viewing the parent-child relationship as an interactive cycle, a circular process of mutual influence.

Several theories of child development have had an impact on approaches to raising children. Freud and his followers focused on the importance of childhood, when the foundation for later life is laid down. Freudians and other proponents of the **psychodynamic theory** emphasized the importance of providing a positive emotional environment for the child, who needs to believe that the world is a safe and good place and that parents can be trusted to be kind and consistent. Although individuals who have suffered enormously in childhood can make dramatic, positive changes later in life, it is best if we can help children succeed from the very beginning.

Jean Piaget and proponents of **organismic theory** were interested in cognitive development, the development of the mind. Piaget held that the mind develops through various stages over the course of childhood and adolescence. He observed that children think very differently than adults do. Child-thought is primitive and mystical; young children have only the beginnings of logical reasoning. Thought processes develop slowly toward higher forms into adulthood. This theory encourages parents to select toys and activities that are developmentally appropriate for their children and not to expect more than their children are capable of at any given stage.

Teaching a child appropriate behavior does not necessarily mean punishment for bad behavior. A more effective technique is reinforcing good behavior with praise and a hug.
©Big Cheese Photo/Getty Images

The **behaviorists**, operating from **learning theories**, have developed some practical, positive approaches for dealing with children's behavior. Rather than focusing on punishment, behaviorists encourage "accentuating the positive," known as **reinforcement**. When a child does something positive, reward the child. Picking the appropriate reinforcer is not easy; "different strokes for different folks" often applies. Most children respond quite well to money, but praise and a hug are usually equally or even more effective. (Adults, too, appreciate praise from a boss for giving that extra effort.) A parent's job is to be creative in developing new reinforcers.

Perhaps the greatest positive reinforcement is simply enjoying each other's company. For example, when invited to speak about our research on strong families at a conference, John DeFrain often goes on a "journey of happy memories" with the audience. He asks people to recall the "best time" they can remember as a child: "Close your eyes. Think back to when you were a kid. Picture the best time you can remember with your family. Go right back to the scene as if you were there once again. What are you doing with your family? What's happening? Who's there? Get into it. Feel it. . . ." Then, we ask them to open their eyes, and we call for volunteers to describe what they just saw in their mind's eye.

Some people recall holidays:

> *"I'm in the living room. It's Thanksgiving. The whole family is gathered together, standing and sitting around the piano. We're all singing songs. Us kids are giggling and squirreling around, too. It's wonderful."*

Some remember family nights together:

> *"I remember how we'd play games every Friday night. Just lie on the floor in the living room and play simple board games and laugh together."*

Some tell about working together:

> *"When I was 12, my job was to scrub the kitchen floor with Mom every Saturday morning. We'd be on our hands and knees—just the two of us—scrubbing and laughing and flicking water at each other. It was great!"*

Some remember times together outdoors in nature:

> *"We're on vacation. We're at the lake 2 hours north of our hometown. We're camping out. We're telling stories around the campfire."*

We have gone on this journey of happy memories with literally thousands of people over the past 25 years, and the most remarkable thing we have found is that adults rarely recall something that cost a lot of money. On only a handful of occasions has anyone recalled an expensive event: a costly vacation to a theme park, a big meal in a fancy hotel. The vast majority of our happiest memories from childhood come from experiences that cost almost nothing. The key element is this: People who love one another are together, enjoying each other's company, being kind to one another.

It's very clear: Simple things can be tremendously reinforcing to a good relationship. These good times not only enhance the bond between parents and children, they also foster cooperation in children.

Issues in Parenting

In this section of this chapter, we will focus on nine important issues that are regularly in the news today: the need for positive discipline; corporal punishment and its consequences; the need for high-quality child care; coparenting; single mothers; gay and lesbian parenting; the relationship between fatherhood and motherhood today; how families endure the death of a child; and educational programs and resources for parents.

The Need for Positive Discipline Today

Are parents today too lenient with their children and letting the children take over more? *Time* magazine featured this question with the theme "Who's In Charge Here?" (Gibbs, 2001). A Time/CNN poll indicated that 80% of parents felt that children are more spoiled today than 10 to 15 years earlier. Seventy-five percent of the parents felt their children did fewer chores. Over two-thirds (68%) of the parents felt that children today are somewhat to very spoiled. Last, 71% of the parents felt that children are exposed to too much advertising, which increases their desires for more things.

In reaction to this trend, a variety of authors have identified the problem and offer some solutions. Bill Doherty (2000) in his book *Take Back Your Kids* describes how parents are almost afraid to discipline their children. He describes how parents are willing to sacrifice time so their children can have endless opportunities for community and school activities. He identifies ways parents can stand up to their children and take more control of their lives. He believes it is important to balance family time together and the needs of the individual children to achieve their personal goals.

Dan Kindlon (2001) sounds a similar theme of parents giving in too much in his book *Too Much of a Good Thing: Raising Children of Character in an Indulgent Age*. After surveying 1,700 teens and parents, he concluded that parents today want to indulge their children emotionally and with things. He even felt that he was too lax with his children and did not expect enough of them. He compared children where the parents were not indulgent with parents who were indulgent. The study found that the nonindulgent parents used the TLC approach. Time: They spent more time with their children at supper, after school, and at bedtime. Limits: They set firmer limits and expected more of the child in a variety of areas. Caring: They took an interest in all aspects of the child's life. Nonindulgent families also shared four traits:

- Families frequently ate dinner together.
- Parents were not divorced or separated.
- Children were required to keep their rooms clean.
- Children did community service.

In summary, today's parents may be more indulgent and lenient with their children, and this trend can be problematic when carried to extremes. It is interesting that parenting styles may change over time on a scale from parent-dominant to child-centered. Harsh discipline and the old saying that "children should be seen and not heard" are indicators of a parent-dominant approach to childrearing. Letting children do whatever they wish in life would be an indicator of an extreme child-centered approach. We will always be arguing for a more balanced approach, of course. *Positive discipline,* as it is called today, focuses on teaching a child how to behave responsibly in life, while at the same time honoring and loving this child for the unique and beautiful person he or she already is.

Discipline as it is discussed today is often punitive. But why, in our efforts to make children do good in life, do we insist on making them feel bad? Positive discipline, on the other hand, seeks a win-win approach to childrearing: helping a child learn to do good and at the same time feel good about herself or himself for doing good.

Judith Rich Harris (2009) makes an interesting comparison between marriage and parenthood:

> *The relationship between a parent and a child is an important one, but it's important in the same way as the relationship between married partners. A good relationship is one in which each party cares about the other and derives happiness from making the other happy. A good relationship is not one in which one party's central goal is to modify the other's personality.*

Corporal Punishment and Its Consequences

Corporal punishment is the use of physical force, which causes the child to have bodily pain, with the goal to correct or change a child's behavior (Gershoff & Bitensky, 2007). Other countries, in addition to the United States, struggle with this issue, and many Western countries are banning corporal punishment. Even though evidence indicates that it does not have an overall positive effect in correcting a child's behavior, the majority of parents use it.

Research shows that, in the short term, corporal punishment may change behavior (Gershoff & Bitensky, 2007). In the long term, however, it is generally not effective. Parents expect children to develop acceptable behaviors while they are in their care as well as when they are out on their own. In other words, parents want children to internalize doing the right thing. There is little evidence that corporal punishment accomplishes this goal. We also know that children who start off with behavior problems often elicit more corporal punishment from parents. A child who has few behavior problems is less likely to be spanked or hit. In addition to corporal punishment not having the desired effect in changing behavior, we also know it is more likely to create additional behavior problems including poor mental health such as anxiety, depression, and general maladjustment (Gershoff & Bitensky, 2007). It also affects the child's relationship with her or his parents. Research indicates these findings have been true internationally.

The harm caused by spanking or hitting children also becomes part of their adult lives (Gershoff & Bitensky, 2007). Adults who have experienced corporal punishment are more likely to use physical means in efforts to change behavior in dating and marriage relationships. These individuals have learned that this is what you do to solve problems and use it in their own families as adults.

It needs to be noted, that parental stress can be a factor in physical punishment. Cumulative or **cascading circumstances** can build up to the point that parents use harsh discipline with their children such as hitting, spanking, or yelling (Arditti, Burton, & Neeves-Botelho, 2010). The circumstances that cause the stress can be a parent getting sick, which adds to losing a job, which results in getting evicted from an apartment. This is not uncommon when people are living at or near the poverty line, and one incident can result in a cascade of problems—with no resources with which to stop it. The stress pileup causes frustration and anger, and sometimes children ultimately experience the brunt of it. Stress does not excuse the parental behavior, but it might explain it. As these authors conclude, harsh disciplinary practices should not be condoned; however, suggesting alternative ways of disciplining may not make sense to those living in the context of poverty and extensive stress. Other sources of support in terms of resources might be more useful.

Although research is clear about the harm corporal punishment can cause children, many parents do not think spanking is wrong. According to the findings of a large national study (Ellison & Bradshaw, 2009), 73% of parents agree that a spanking is sometimes necessary. Beliefs about spanking can be associated with income levels, political, and religious beliefs. For example, Ellison and Bradshaw (2009) found that conservative Protestant beliefs are predictive of the use of spanking. These authors also found that parents who are politically conservative are more likely to approve of corporal punishment than those who are liberal or moderate politically.

In addition, internationally the use and results of differing forms of discipline have different results for children. One study drew a sample of almost 300 mothers and children from China, India, Italy, Kenya, Philippines, and Thailand (Gershoff et al., 2010). These parents and children within each country were considered middle class by the standards within those countries, and the sample focused on children from 8 to 12 years of age. The study focused on the relationship between mothers' disciplinary techniques and children's behavior. The study found that using corporal punishment (for example, spanking, slapping, hitting), expressing disappointment, and yelling or scolding were positively related to children's aggression. The study also found that the use of time-outs, corporal punishment,

BOX 12.1 Putting It Together

The Mother's Book BY MRS. CHILD

The roots of the word *discipline* go back through the millennia to the time of Jesus. The early followers were called disciples—*learners*—and Jesus was their teacher. Thus, the word *discipline* has always had an educational connotation. Similarly, parents, in essence, are teachers of children, and positive discipline techniques as they are defined today focus on ways to help children learn how to live successfully in a complex world. Positive discipline techniques demand that parents search for a reasonable balance between love, kindness, and thoughtful instruction, on the one hand, and firm insistence, on the other. This is not a new dilemma for parents, of course. *The Mother's Book* by Mrs. Child was a popular book on parenting, published in Boston in 1831. Mrs. Child was also the author of *The Frugal Housewife, The Girl's Own Book,* and *Evenings in New England* and the editor of *The Juvenile Miscellany*. As you read what Mrs. Child has to say on discipline, you may readily surmise that many of the challenges parents face today were challenges parents struggled with down through the centuries:

> *I have said much in praise of gentleness. I cannot say too much. Its effects are beyond calculation, both on the affections and the understanding. The victims of oppression and abuse are generally stupid, as well as selfish and hard-hearted. How can we wonder at it? They are all the time excited to evil passions, and nobody encourages what is good in them. We might as well expect flowers to grow amid the cold and storms of winter.*
>
> *But gentleness, important as it is, not all that is required in education. There should be united with it firmness—great firmness. Commands should be reasonable, and given in perfect kindness; but once given, it should be known that they must be obeyed.*

Source: Mrs. Child, *The Mother's Book.* Boston, MA: Carter & Hendee, 1831.

---

shaming, and expressing disappointment were positively associated with children's anxiety. It was also interesting to note that expressing disappointment on the part of mothers was more strongly associated with aggression in children in China, Italy, Philippines, and Thailand. So, although the authors do not speculate about the reasons for this, one might conclude that differing cultural views about disciplinary practices might have differing impacts on children. These researchers also found that the effects of certain forms of discipline did not have as strong a relationship with aggression and anxiety if it was considered normative by the child. For example, if children thought other children were experiencing corporal punishment, then they were not likely to be as anxious or aggressive.

So what can we conclude about corporal punishment and other forms of discipline? In the United States and in other Western countries, it is clear that corporal punishment has negative effects, yet it is still used by the majority of parents. It is likely to take years for parents to change these behaviors (Gershoff & Bitensky, 2007).

Child Care

Child care providers come in all shapes and sizes (Laughlin, 2013, April). They can be relatives, which can include nuclear family members or extended family members. Family day care providers also care for children from one, two, or more families, and the providers care for them in their own home. Organized child care facilities can be day care centers, preschools, nursery schools, and Head Start programs. These typically serve preschool children. School-age children may receive child care in after school programs or go to day care providers or other child care facilities before and after school.

Working mothers and fathers are increasingly needing child care for their children. In 2011, 61% of children under five were in some type of child care (Laughlin, 2013, April). Most preschoolers receiving care were cared for by a relative, with the majority being cared for by grandparents. On average, children spent 33 hours per week in child care (Laughlin, 2013, April). African American and Hispanic children were more likely to be cared for by relatives than were White children. More specific information about child care for one ethnic group is provided in Box 12.2.

BOX 12.2 Diversity in Families

Child Care for the Growing Hispanic Population

With so many mothers in the United States working outside the home, the issue of child care is a pressing concern. It is an issue that cuts across social and ethnic lines, as most families struggle to balance the need for work and the needs of their families.

Current statistics about Hispanic families provide a picture of the rising need for child care among Hispanic families:

- **45.5 million people.** This is the estimated Hispanic population of the United States as of July 1, 2007 (U.S. Census Bureau, 2008, May 1).
- **15.1%.** Hispanics accounted for about 1 in 6 Americans (U.S. Census Bureau, 2008, May 1).
- **16.** The Hispanic population exceeded 500,000 people in 16 states (U.S. Census Bureau, 2008, May 1).
- **One-half.** Hispanics accounted for about 50% of the nation's population growth between 2000 and 2006 (U.S. Census Bureau, 2009, September 21).
- **24.3%.** The Hispanic population growth rate was more than three times the growth rate of the total population (6.1%) (U.S. Census Bureau, 2009, September 21).
- **24.4%.** The Census Bureau estimates that by 2050, Hispanics will increase from just under 1 in 7 Americans to nearly 1 in 4 Americans (U.S. Census Bureau, 2009, September 21).
- **27.7.** This is the median age for Hispanics in the United States (27.0 for Hispanic males and 27.6 for Hispanic females). The median age for the total U.S. population is 36.8 (35.2 for males and 37.8 for females) (U.S. Census Bureau, 2008, July 1). These numbers indicate that the Hispanic population in America is closer to prime childbearing years than the general population.
- **11%.** Hispanics are the most likely ethnic group in America to be preschoolers (under age 5), with 11% in this age group (U.S. Census Bureau, 2005).
- **25%.** It is projected that by the year 2030 Hispanics will make up 1 in 4 of the total U.S. school-age population (National Child Care Information Center, 2004b).
- **Minorities will be in the majority.** By the year 2050, Hispanics and Blacks under the age of 5 will outnumber non-Hispanic Whites in the United States (National Child Care Information and Technology Assistance Center, 2004a, 2008, June).
- **Lower-quality child care, a lower supply of child care.** Although the Hispanic population is among the fastest growing and youngest segment of American society, families confront lower quality and lower supply of available child care in relation to the general public (National Child Care Information and Technology Assistance Center, 2004b, 2008, June).
- **About 15.5%** of Hispanic children of employed mothers were in organized care (child care centers, nurseries or preschools, Head Start programs, or other schools) (National Child Care Information and Technology Assistance Center, 2004b, 2008, June).

Some parents turn to relatives for child care, not only to save money but also because they prefer care from members of their extended family. Some parents value the developmental education approaches found in selected child care programs. Parents for whom hours, location, and cost of care are important issues often choose care in a home. And parents who think it is important that the child know the caregiver are more likely to choose family care. One research team found that in their sample of parents surveyed on the importance of various characteristics of child care, the top three factors were warmth of the caregivers, educational level of the caregivers, and utilization of a play-based curriculum (Kensinger-Rose & Elicker, 2008).

The cost of such child care is often more than parents can handle and high-quality child care is hard to find. The cost of child care in child care centers depends upon the age of the child, with younger children costing more. Another factor is the location, with centers in larger cities being more expensive than in smaller towns. The average cost of center day care in the United States is about $1,000 per month (Babycenter, 2011).

There are also employers, both public and private, who sponsor child care centers for their employees. These centers are either on site or near the place of employment, or companies pay to reserve space for employees' children at public and private care centers. There are a variety of ways employers subsidize the cost, such as providing the building or actually paying part of the cost of the care provided. These types of arrangements can actually benefit the employer by reducing turnover rates and absenteeism (American Planning Association, 2011).

The critical question for the parents of these children—and for our society as a whole—is how day care affects children, both positively and negatively. The National Institute of Child Health and Human Development Study of Early Child Care and Youth Development (NICHD) is by far the most ambitious study of the effects of nonmaternal child care, and about families who use child care as well as those who do not. Researchers tracked more than 1,300 children in various child care arrangements, including staying at home with a parent, being cared for by a nanny or a relative, or attending a large day care center. After the children reached school, the study used teacher ratings of each child, which assessed behaviors such as interrupting class, teasing, and bullying. This government-funded $200 million study began in 1991 (Eunice Kennedy Shriver National Institute of Child Health and Human Development, NIH, DHHS, 2006). Because of the importance of this ongoing research, we will examine it in some depth here.

The major goal of the study is to examine how differences in child care experiences relate to children's social, emotional, intellectual, and language development, and how these differences also relate to children's physical growth and health. Child care, for the purpose of the study, was defined as any care provided on a regular basis by someone other than the child's mother. This did not include occasional babysitting or any type of care for less than 10 hours per week (Eunice Kennedy Shriver National Institute of Child Health and Human Development, 2006).

Researchers, based at universities, collected data at 10 sites around the country. The study population was composed of children who were born healthy from a variety of socioeconomic backgrounds. The features studied were (1) cognitive and language development, (2) social behavior, (3) emotional development and relationships with parents, and (4) health and physical growth.

What were the major findings of the NICHD child care study?

1. *Higher-quality care was associated with better outcomes.* During the first 4½ years of their life, children in higher-*quality* child care had somewhat better language and cognitive development than those in lower-quality care. These children were somewhat more cooperative than those who experienced lower-quality care during the first 3 years of their life.

2. *Amount of time in care mattered to some degree.* Children who spent a higher *quantity* of time in child care (total combined number of hours) showed somewhat more behavior problems while in child care and in kindergarten classrooms than those who spent fewer hours in child care.

3. *The impact of child care type or setting was different for children of different ages.* Center-based child care has both positive and negative effects. This type of care is associated with better cognitive development through age 4½ and with more positive social behaviors through age 3. However, children attending child care centers also showed somewhat more behavior problems just before and just after entry into school than children who experienced other nonmaternal child care arrangements.

4. *Parent and family characteristics were more strongly linked to child development than any aspect of child care.* The researchers looked at the quality of the family environment, parental attitudes, maternal psychological adjustment, and mother's sensitivity. The following characteristics predicted children's cognitive/language and social development: parents' education, family income, and two-parent family compared to one-parent family; mothers' psychological adjustment and sensitivity; and the social and cognitive quality of the home environment.

BOX 12.3 At Issue

Looking for a Very High Quality Child Care Program and Positive Caregiving

Researchers in the pioneering National Institute of Child Health and Human Development Study of Early Child Care found that fewer than 10% of the child care arrangements they studied around the United States provided *very high quality child care,* which promotes the developmental well-being of children. What should parents look for when visiting child care programs? And what constitutes positive caregiving?

Professional Standards for Child Care Recommended by the American Academy of Pediatrics and the American Public Health Association

Adult-to-Child Ratios	Group Sizes	Training and Education of Staff
Children age 6 months to 1½ years—3 children to 1 staff person	Children age 6 months to 1½ years—maximum of 6 children in the group	Formal post–high school training, including certification or college degree in child development, early childhood education, or a related field
Children age 1½ years to 2 years—4 children to 1 staff person	Children age 1½ years to 2 years—maximum of 8 children in the group	
Children age 2 years to 3 years—7 children to 1 staff person	Children age 2 years to 3 years—maximum of 14 children in the group	

Percentage of Child Care Center Classes Observed in the NICHD Study Meeting Recommended Guidelines at Age 6 Months to 3 Years

Standard	6 Months	1½ Years	2 Years	3 Years
Adult-to-Child Ratio	36%	20%	26%	56%
Observed Group Size	35	25	28	63
Caregiver Training	56	60	65	75
Caregiving Education	65	69	77	80

Source: DeFrain, J., *Family Treasures: Creating Strong Families.* Lincoln, NE: University of Nebraska-Lincoln Extension, 2006.

In the NICHD study, only a small percentage of children received a lot of positive caregiving, and that percentage decreased as children got older, moving from 18% to 13% to 6% during the first 3 years of life. Poor-quality care, in which children received hardly any positive caregiving, also occurred for only a small percentage of children, changing from 6% to 8% to 4% during the first 3 years of life. The data suggest that most child care settings in the United States provide care that is "fair" (between "poor" and "good"). Fewer than 10% of child care arrangements were rated as providing very high-quality child care. At the other extreme, fewer than 10% of child care arrangements were estimated to provide children with very low-quality experiences (Eunice Kennedy Shriver National Institute of Child Health and Human Development, NIH, DHHS, 2006, p. 11). (Box 12.3.)

A follow-up study was conducted including a sample of these same children at age 15 (Vandell et al., 2010). This research was able to determine the longer-term effects of child care on children into their teens. High-quality care predicted increased cognitive and academic achievement for these 15-year-olds, and this was true for all income ranges. The higher quality of care also was predictive of less behavior problems for these adolescents. In addition, consistent with findings with children who were studied when they were 4½ years

What Is Positive Caregiving?

The NICHD researchers found that the more positive the caregiving, the higher the quality of care. When caregivers cared for a smaller number of children, they showed more positive caregiving, which in turn was associated with better outcomes in the children's lives. The same was true for caregiver education level. Caregivers with higher education levels were more positive in their caregiving and the children benefited. Positive caregiving was a primary indicator of child care quality. Positive caregiving behaviors include:

- **Showing a positive attitude**—Is the caregiver generally in good spirits and encouraging when interacting with the child? Is he or she helpful? Does the caregiver smile often at the child?
- **Having positive physical contact**—Does the caregiver hug the child, pat the child on the back, or hold the child's hand? Does the caregiver comfort the child?
- **Responding to vocalizations**—Does the caregiver repeat the child's words, comment on what the child says or tries to say, and answer the child's questions?
- **Asking questions**—Does the caregiver encourage the child to talk/communicate by asking questions that the child can answer easily, such as "yes" or "no" questions, or asking about a family member or toy?
- **Talking in other ways**—such as:
  - **Praising or encouraging**—Does the caregiver respond to the child's positive actions with positive words, such as "You did it!" or "Well done!"?
  - **Teaching**—Does the caregiver encourage the child to learn or have the child repeat learning phrases or items, such as saying the alphabet out loud, counting to 10, and naming shapes or objects? For older children, does the caregiver explain what words or names mean?
- **Telling and signing**—Does the caregiver tell stories, describe objects or events, or sing songs?
- **Encouraging development**—Does the caregiver help the child stand up and walk? For infants, does the caregiver encourage "tummy time"—activities the child does when placed on his or her stomach while awake—to help neck and shoulder muscles get stronger and to encourage crawling? For older children, does the caregiver help finish puzzles, stock blocks, or zip zippers?
- **Advancing behavior**—Does the caregiver encourage the child to smile, laugh, and play with other children? Does the caregiver support sharing between the child and other children? Does the caregiver give examples of good behaviors?
- **Reading**—Does the caregiver read books and stories to the child? Does the caregiver let the child touch the book and turn the pages? For older children, does the caregiver point to pictures and words on the page?
- **Eliminating negative interactions**—Does the caregiver make sure to be positive, not negative, in the interactions with the child? Does the caregiver take a positive approach to interacting with the child, even in times of trouble? Does the caregiver make it a point to interact with the child and not ignore him or her?

Source: DeFrain, J., *Family Treasures: Creating Strong Families*. Lincoln, NE: University of Nebraska-Lincoln Extension, 2006.

---

of age, these 15-year-olds experienced increased behavior problems the longer they were in child care. Those who had been in care longer hours were more likely to take risks and be impulsive. We can conclude, based upon this large national study, that high-quality child care can have positive effects on children more than 10 years later.

Although the interest and need for day care continue to rise, the United States is one of the few countries that does not have national day care policies or standards. Day care workers, who typically earn only minimum wage, often have little direct training. It is a sad commentary on our society that we fail to train and reward the people who are responsible for caring for, teaching, and nurturing so many of our children.

Coparenting

A growing number of parents have adopted a cooperative approach to parenting, known as **coparenting**. Traditional family roles—in which dad was the provider and mom the nurturer; dad was "tough" and mom was "tender"—are changing. More mothers are working outside the home, and more men are sharing in parenting tasks. An increasing number of mothers are providing income for their families and enjoying their connection to the world outside the home. At the same time, an increasing number of fathers are experiencing the joy of watching their children grow and learn.

Coparenting has been defined as the process by which mothers and fathers coordinate and support one another's parenting efforts (Kolak & Volling, 2007). Some couples share the responsibilities equally: Mother and father each do half the child care, half the housework, and half the work outside the home. But most couples do not divide up the tasks exactly equally. One young father explained, "I'm a better cook, so I tend to do more of that. She likes to see a neat, clean house, so she concentrates on that. We both like taking care of the girls, but I do baths and bedtimes because she's so tired at the end of a day of nursing." Flexibility is the key.

Researchers have found a number of advantages to the coparenting model. Parents report greater satisfaction with their marriage and family life than they had before they adopted the coparenting approach. They also report improved relationships with their children. Some partners even considered divorce before they changed their attitudes about childrearing. Coparenting frees men to spend more time relating to, caring for, and relaxing with their children and frees women to pursue outside interests. Both parents have much to gain from active involvement in their children's growth. Parenthood is much too important and much too time consuming to be left to one person (Smith, 2009).

Another important benefit of coparenting is that it brings fathers into the family on an emotional level. Some fathers enjoy being nurtured at home but don't want to nurture others in the home or don't have the capacity to do so. The experience of coparenting can help men learn how to attend to the emotional needs of others. This is a skill that has often been neglected because in our culture we tend to socialize men for competition, not cooperation.

A problem with coparenting is that sometimes the marriage gets lost in the shuffle. The mother is working outside the home, caring for the children, doing housework; the father is doing the same. Two outside full-time jobs and the job of maintaining a family and household add up to at least three full-time jobs for only two people. Often the marriage is neglected while the spouses concentrate on their employment responsibilities and their family and household tasks. The couple might be doing great at the office and great with the kids but still end up getting divorced because they forgot to focus on their relationship with each other. They need to remember that the foundation for the whole operation is a strong marriage.

Single Mothers

There is a growing number of single-parent mothers, primarily because women are having children while not being married to the father, and secondly because of divorce from the father (Dye, 2008). The percentage of children born into single-parent families is 40% of all births (Hamilton, Martin, Osterman, Curtin, & Mathews, 2015, December 23). African American mothers have the highest rate of nonmarital births at 71% (Hamilton et al., 2015, December 23). The rate of nonmarital births drops among Hispanic women (36%), is lower in Asians (27%), and is lowest in Whites (25%). Younger women have by far the highest rates of nonmarital births. About 90% of births to teenagers (15 to 19 years old) are nonmarital births, while the rate drops to 50% for women in their twenties and to 12% for women 30 years old and over (Martin et al., 2009). These single mothers typically experience a great deal of stress and are often low-income.

There are many women who choose not to marry or choose not to marry until later in life. These women may have careers and lead professional lives and also want to have children. There are options for women to have children without being married, and some women are choosing them.

This is the first generation in the United States where gay and lesbian couples have openly raised children who are now reaching adolescence and young adulthood.
©Creatas/Getty Images

Gay and Lesbian Parenting

Same-sex couples are increasingly becoming parents, with estimates of up to 45% of gay and lesbian couples raising children (Perrin & Siegel, 2013; Tasker & Patterson, 2007). The majority of same-sex couples with children are White. Couples become parents by having children from a previous heterosexual relationship, being foster parents, adoption, or donor insemination or surrogacy (Tasker & Patterson, 2007). In a review of existing literature, Tasker and Patterson (2007) conclude that children do well in same-sex families. Perrin and Siegel (2013) conclude from existing research literature that there are all kinds of things such as poverty, domestic violence, and parental substance abuse, which contribute to healthy and unhealthy development of children. However, research is clear that being raised by a same-sex couple is not a factor which contributes negatively to development. The strengths of the family relationships are crucial for healthy development in all families. There seems to be a fear that children raised in same-sex families will become gay or lesbian themselves. Research does not bear this out, with most children ultimately identifying as heterosexual (Tasker & Patterson, 2007).

In general, it appears that gay and lesbian couples are increasing their interest in raising children, and these families appear to be doing well. In addition to the normal challenges of raising adolescents, lesbian and gay couples and adolescents have to deal with the issue of social acceptance from others.

Fatherhood and Motherhood Today

Coparenting may be gaining popularity as an ideal, but the reality in many cases is quite different. Although the images of father as breadwinner and mother as nurturer are slowly breaking down, new images—especially for fathers—have not yet taken hold. More than half of American mothers with children under 18 are now in the workforce, but many fathers have not become proportionately involved in nurturing tasks. The value of fatherhood has not increased dramatically.

Margaret Mead once wrote that "motherhood is a biological necessity, but fatherhood is a social invention." James Garbarino explains that parenthood for women is clear, because it is tied to their essential biological role in the process of bringing children into the world. But the role of the father is ambiguous and relies on cultural prescriptions (Garbarino, 2000, p. 11).

Some scholars have gone so far as to ask, Is the father even a part of the family? David Blankenhorn (2004, 2007) has found that nearly 40% of children live in homes where the biological father is not present. Wade Horn (2010) estimates that 6 out of 10 children born in the 1990s will be "fatherless" before reaching adulthood. What forces are responsible for these trends? And what can be done about them?

The Absent Father. Two major threats to a father's presence in a child's life are divorce and nonmarital childbearing, both of which are increasing. Marriages are continuing to fail at a high rate, and a growing number of families are starting out without a father. Approximately 40% of births are to single women (Child Trends, 2017, January 4). Virtually all children born outside of marriage live with their mothers, and in two-thirds of these cases, the father never establishes paternity.

Many fathers, no longer living with their children, struggle to stay involved with them. But research has shown a pattern of gradual withdrawal by nonresidential fathers and growing alienation between fathers and children. Conflict between the former spouses also affects the quality of the father–child relationship by creating strains on the child that may offset any advantages of having the father actively involved.

When fathers remain in frequent contact and when conflict between the parents is low, fathers are more likely to make regular child support payments. There is a strong association between a divorced father's economic support and the well-being of his children. So frequent contact, low parental conflict, and economic support have a positive effect on the child's well-being. Nevertheless, many fathers would like to have the opportunity to contribute to their children's lives in deeper and more meaningful ways.

When a child is born, a father is born.

—Frederick Buechner

The Father as Nurturer. Research in child development has shown that fathers are just as capable as mothers in performing nurturing tasks (assuming the fathers are living with their children). Children can establish attachment relationships with fathers as they do with mothers. Fathers respond to the needs of their infants, picking up on their cues, just as mothers do. When mothers are present, however, fathers tend to back off and defer to them.

Fathers are more likely to be involved in the care of children if the parents are dual earners, but especially when the mother works different hours than the father. When parents work the same hours, mothers tend to come home to a "second shift" of family work.

Some studies report that women want men to be nurturing in their families, whereas other studies have shown that many mothers do not want increased father involvement (Gaunt, 2008; Goldberg, Downing, & Sauck, 2008). The home is said to be a place of power and control for women, whereas the workplace is where men have traditionally dominated. Some women do not want to share their power or their role as the "more important parent." Men's involvement as fathers can be shaped, positively or negatively, by the mothers' expectations and support.

Many fathers are fully capable of nurturing and caring for their children.
©Purestock/Getty Images

Schoppe-Sullivan (2010) discussed the gatekeeping of mothers and how mothers can have dramatic effects on how fathers father. This author makes the argument that fathers' behavior affects mothers' behaviors and vice versa. For example, if fathers are hesitant in responding to their children's needs, mothers are likely to step in and address those needs. On the other hand as gatekeepers, mothers can let fathers know that they are not doing things right, or can belittle their efforts. Schoppe-Sullivan suggests that both mothers and fathers should be aware of these possible family dynamics and take initiative to do what they need to do and want to do as parents.

In sum, countless fathers are fully capable of nurturing and caring for their children, but other factors—social, cultural, and interpersonal—tend to discourage them from doing so wholeheartedly. This is particularly unfortunate in light of the belief, put forth by some feminist scholars, that as more men become involved in nurturing tasks, inequalities in the workplace and the family will be reduced (Silverstein, 2010).

Responsible Fatherhood. What is the appropriate role for a father? It must first be acknowledged that every society constructs and defines roles for men and women; the role of father is no exception. In our society today, there is no single definition or description of this role. If a father is living at home with his children, he may be married and coparenting or single and parenting alone. Living apart from his children, he may be young and unwed, with or without paternity established. If divorced, he may have joint physical or legal custody or just visitation rights (Doherty, Erickson, & LaRossa, 2006; Lee & Doherty, 2007).

Although single fathers and divorced fathers with custody have nurturing roles thrust upon them, it appears that many other fathers in our society are given quite a wide latitude in how involved they want to be in the family. Unlike mothering, fathering appears to be a choice that men make in the face of contextual pressures. They can be very involved—or they can walk away.

To develop new roles, fathers need the support of mothers. They also need the support of society in general—in the workplace, in the courts, and in the social service agencies that serve families. This support may be forthcoming. Recognizing the holistic nature of family health, family service programs now attempt to involve fathers when they work with families. Additionally, new community-based programs have emerged to support fathers in their efforts to be responsibly involved in their families.

The best gift a father can give his children
Is to love their mother.

—ANONYMOUS

Good Fathering Makes a Real Difference in Children. Kristin A. Moore (2010) of Child Trends, a private organization that monitors research and policies related to children and parenting, conducted a major review of research on fathering. She found that fathers can have a very positive impact on their children's development—whether or not the father lives with the children or is a noncustodial partner. The specific conclusions from this review are as follows:

- The more fathers are involved in the routine activities of their children, the more likely the children will have fewer behavior problems, be more sociable, and do better in school.
- Fathers often promote children's development more through physical play, whereas mothers do it through talking and teaching.
- Across different ethnic groups, fathers tend to assume the important role of economic provider, protector, and caregiver.
- Fathers who provide economically for their children also stay more involved with their children, even if they live apart.
- Fathers who pay child support tend to have children who behave better and do better in school.

When a Child Dies

The loss of a child creates a unique crisis in a family. No individual experiences the crisis in the same way another does, and each family is different. Though common themes of grief and bereavement occur time and time again, each family experiences the crisis in its own desperate way.

We do not use the word *desperate* lightly here, because every parent we have talked with in our work as counselors and researchers over the past 30 years has been plunged into dreadful unhappiness in the aftermath of the child's death. Many parents consider suicide because of the death. Living becomes almost unbearable for most. Mothers and fathers have told us of slitting their wrists, trying to kill themselves in an automobile crash, trying to overdose on drugs, turning on the engine of the car in a closed garage.

The vast majority of parents who have experienced the loss of a child see the death as the most devastating crisis they have experienced in their lives. The child's death is clearly a catastrophe for families—mothers, fathers, brothers, sisters, grandmothers, grandfathers, and other close relatives and friends—and the responsibility falls to each of us in society to help these stricken people in any way we can. They are clearly crushed in a life-threatening and spiritually numbing situation.

And yet, parents do survive the loss of their child. They turn to each other for comfort, to their relatives and friends, and to professionals in their community. Many individuals suffering from the loss of a child say that their belief in God was helpful and that being able to tell themselves that their child was with God was one of the few comforts they received. But others caution that they sometimes couldn't sit back and wait for God to help, "You've got to get out of your rut yourself."

Commitment, togetherness, and the ability of partners and other family members to take turns being strong for each other are also seen as positive ways of enduring the loss of a child. A final common denominator seems to be a person's simple ability to survive—to get up in the morning and get through the day, to force concentration on tasks that may seem irrelevant to the situation. One woman found herself thinking, "How can I scrub this floor? My child is dead." But she knew she had to keep busy and involved, if even on such a basic level.

As the months and years after the death of the child pass, many parents and grandparents express surprise that they have survived the tragedy. Once the realization sinks in that they will live though their child did not, they find strength in themselves they never thought they had. Most of them grimly acknowledge the truth of one mother's words: "Now I can survive anything." (Visit the web sites of Compassionate Friends and the M.I.S.S. Foundation for excellent resources.)

Educational Programs and Resources for Parents

In meeting the challenges of raising children, parents often turn to professionals for guidance, either for education or for therapy. **Parent education** usually involves a presentation of information in a group setting followed by a group discussion of generic parenting problems, such as communication, discipline, imparting values to children, sibling rivalry, and choosing adequate child care. The focus is on common issues that parents face and general principles that are useful for thinking about and dealing with these challenges.

In **family therapy**, a therapist typically works with a single family with one or more specific problems, including sexual abuse, spouse abuse, child abuse or neglect, a runaway child, a child's attempted suicide, a child's coming out as a gay or lesbian, or the abuse of alcohol or other drugs. Though the dividing line between education and therapy tends to be somewhat blurry, educational programs tend to involve more participants and representatives of many families, while therapy tends to involve a single family and fewer people. Education for parents tends to aim at preventing problems before they begin, while family therapy tends to deal with more severe problems after they have occurred. The American Association for Marriage and Family Therapy (AAMFT) is the leading professional organization in the United States specializing in couple and family therapy. The National Council on Family Relations is the leading professional organization focusing on educational programs for parents and families in the United States. Founded in 1938, the NCFR awards Certified Family Life Educator (CFLE) to qualified professionals. This is the only international program that certifies family life educators.

Parent education has a long history in America, and has been traced back to 1700 (Bjorklund, 1977). Over the past 300 years, parent educators have developed a remarkable and evolving collection of educational programs for parents, meeting every imaginable need. Following is a sampling of the diverse programs currently available.

Abusive and Neglectful Parents. The explosion of child abuse and neglect reports that began in the 1970s, and the media attention that followed, prompted a nationwide response. Countless programs for parents under stress and in need of parenting advice and support were created and continue to thrive today.

Adoptive Parents. Adoptive parent associations and adoption agencies are teaming up to form support groups for adoptive parents, including support for parents involved in transracial and international adoption.

Alcohol and Other Drugs. AA, Al-Anon, Alateen, and countless other organizations have been created to help individuals and families deal with alcohol and other drug problems. Parent-child issues are common sources of discussion in these groups, of course. Special programs for adolescents who are chemically dependent abound, as do programs for the adult children of alcoholics.

Blue-Collar Parents and Parents with Lower Incomes. These parents have been unfairly criticized for lack of interest in parenting programs, but there is good evidence to indicate that if professionals design programs for the specific needs of these parents, the interest is there.

Bereaved Parents. Many local and national organizations have formed across the country to provide support and education for parents who have lost a child.

Business Community Programs for Parents. Increasing numbers of executives have begun to realize that worker productivity is intimately associated with how well the worker's family is doing. Employee assistance programs have sprung up in businesses and government to deal with the stresses of managing home and work, and wellness programs to focus on social and behavioral health issues, including parenting, are common.

Childbirth Education. Historically speaking, this has been one of the easiest types of parent education programs to get people involved in. Professionals complain all the time that it is difficult to fill a meeting room with parents. But childbirth educators are enjoying tremendous positive response. Perhaps it is the fear of childbirth that motivates many couples to attend prepared childbirth meetings. Whatever their reasons for attending, the classes can be very beneficial.

Couple and Family Enrichment Programs. Professionals are aware that parenting does not occur in a vacuum. The quality of a couple's relationship critically affects how well the partners are doing as parents. Many parent education programs target couple issues, for the couple is the foundation of a two-parent family.

Crisis Nurseries and Respite Care Facilities. Many social agencies around the country run crisis nurseries and other short-term care facilities for children and parents. The goals of the organizations vary, but the general idea is that the parent is helped in tough times, and the professionals get a chance to teach the parent new skills and enhance self-esteem so crises are not as common in the family.

Farm and Ranch Families. Programs for economically vulnerable and distressed farm and ranch families have been created by community-based mental-health teams, church groups, and the USDA's Extension Service. Economic problems of the family often have negative consequences for marriage and family relationships.

Foster Parents. Many communities have developed approaches to helping foster parents, including kin, understand and meet the challenges of this unique type of parenting.

Grandparents. The dramatic increase in past decades in the numbers of grandparents raising grandchildren has motivated the development of educational programs for grandparents.

The Mass Media. We have been rather hard on the media in this textbook, for much of what is seen on television, in the movies, on the internet, in magazines and newspapers, and on the radio are destructive to positive couple and family relationships. Fortunately, there are some wonderful parent education programs available via the mass media.

Military Families. Millions of families in the United States are relatively rootless, moving from base to base and assignment to assignment for the military. The stresses of picking up stakes regularly, and the enormous stress for families when a father or mother is serving in a war zone, affect parent–child relationships in many ways. Family support programs sponsored by the U.S. Department of Defense and many other governmental and private organizations bring needed resources to these parents under stress.

Minority-Group Parents. Support groups for parents of the various minority groups in our country are relatively common and are affiliated with religious institutions, counseling centers, and associations of various ethnic and cultural groups. These groups unite to reaffirm the beauty and importance of their cultural heritage, to gain strength through numbers in the quest for fair treatment, and to help each other deal with the problems parents of minority children face in America.

Parenthood Decision Making. To be a parent or not to be a parent? That is not an easy decision to make, and there are scattered reports in the professional literature of programs for people on the horns of this dilemma.

Parents of Children with Developmental Disabilities. The unique aspects of raising a child with a physical or mental handicap have created a demand for programs focusing on these issues. Parent support groups satisfy a number of needs: to vent frustrations among people in the same boat; to band together to gain political clout in the struggle to improve programs for special needs children in the schools and society; and to educate members as to the most successful ways of interacting with a special child and enhancing the child's growth and development.

Parents of Sexual Minorities. Over the years countless programs and support groups have been created that help parents of sexual minority children: gays, lesbians, bisexuals, transgender, transsexual, and two-spirited identities. Many parents find it difficult to understand their children, and seek ways to support them in a world that can be hostile to them.

Preparation for Parenting Classes. Colleges and universities offer classes for people who wish to become parents some day and for students who are already parents.

Sexuality Education. Sex education programs for young people are often presented in schools, and the communication about sexuality is between the school teacher and the students. Another model that can be very exciting is an education for sexuality model that links parents and their children. Typically, parents and their teens meet together to discuss the issues in a classroom setting with a professional teacher. Then, on the way home from the session and in the following days, the parents and their teens are more open to communicating about sexual issues. In this particular model of education, the goal is not only information about sex and sexuality, but improved communication between parents and their children. Ideally, parents and their teenage children will feel more comfortable talking about issues that often cause embarrassment and discomfort. This way, education for sexuality is family-centered, rather than driven by the internet, television, the movies, and other sources that generally have in mind, not the child's best interest, but money.

Single Parents. Parents Without Partners (2010) and many other social support and education groups have been created to help single mothers and fathers through local chapters, programs, and services. Joining the group expands the parent's network of supportive and understanding people to call upon in times of need.

Stepfamilies. Local organizations have developed programs for stepparents and stepchildren, and national stepfamily groups provide educational materials and conferences.

Teen Parent Programs. A good deal of energy has been focused on solving the problems teen parents face, and programs for them abound. The professionals and volunteers working with teen parents focus on enhancing the self-esteem of the young parent, helping to keep the parent in school, providing child care for the parent so she can further her education and have a brief respite from the pressures of parenting, and enhancing her skills in the day-to-day responsibilities of caring for a child.

Welcome Baby Programs and the First Three Years of Life. Motivated by consistent research findings in past decades on the importance of the early years of life, countless programs have been created to take over after the childbirth educators are finished with their work. These so-called Welcome Baby programs help the young family get off to a good start and stay with them until they are well established.

It scarcely needs to be said that some parents will need therapy even though they have attended parent education programs. Such parents should not feel guilty or incompetent—their problems are simply more complex than those that most parents have to face. For the majority of parents, however, it is hoped that educational materials found in the library, on the internet, and at parent support meetings will suffice to provide the information and emotional encouragement needed to be successful as a parent.

The Joy and Enduring Satisfaction of Parenthood

An enduring challenge for parents is how to translate philosophy into action. One important goal is to provide children with a basic foundation upon which they can build. Each day, parents are confronted with difficult questions that have complex answers. To find these answers, parents must learn to relate their personal philosophy to what is actually occurring with their children:

- "I don't believe in spanking, but this kid is driving me crazy!"
- "I love to watch my children grow, but I also need a life of my own. How do I balance the two?"
- "One child has a soccer game, but we had all planned to go to a children's play."
- "He flunked his math test again. I told him I would help him study for it, but he didn't want to study. Should I let him suffer the consequences of failing?"
- "We have not gone out as a couple to the movies or for dinner for almost a year, but our kids always want more of us."

"What was life like before you had children?" Box 12.4 provides a glimpse into what the first few months of parenting is like. Many parents respond, "I cannot imagine what it was like anymore. It has been such an emotional and overwhelming journey since the kids came along." Children take control of a parent's life and a parent's heart. They bring a considerable amount of stress to the parent's life; there is no question about that. But we cannot

BOX 12.4 Putting It Together
A Young Mother's Diary

We need to hear how some of the information in this chapter plays itself out in the lives of parents. What is it like to be a parent? What is life day to day like? Here is what life was like for one new mother over the first 18 months of her baby's life:

Breastfeeding: After 18 months, baby Lindy was weaned. This did not come easily, however. During those 18 months, she breastfed an average of 7 times every 24 hours. This comes out to 18 months × 30 days per month (on average) = 540 days × 7 breast feedings = 3,780 feedings in 18 months.

Diapers: There were approximately 12 diapers per day needed when Lindy was a little baby. This gradually declined to 6 per day at 18 months. Therefore, this averaged 9 diapers per day over the 18 months. This is 9 diapers per day × 30 days in a month × 18 months = 4,860 diapers.

Lost Sleep for Mom: In the beginning, Lindy was fed 4 times per night with each feeding lasting about 1 hour. At 18 months she was only fed once per night. Therefore, the average over 18 months was 2.5 hours per night × 30 nights in a month = 1,350 hours of lost sleep.

The experience of raising Lindy provides a context for the real challenges as people transition into being first time parents. The cost of diapers is only one of the many expenses that new parents encounter. One might get tired just thinking about getting up multiple times per night to feed a hungry baby.

---

afford to discount the engagement and fascination and joy they spark in our lives. Each day is a new day for a child, and watching the story unfold can be a delight to loving parents. What will the next chapter of the story bring? What will the children do next? What will they become in life? As one father put it so well, "I suppose I could have concentrated on my career more if I hadn't had children, but love has always counted far more to me than money. You can't hold a $100 bill in your lap and read a story to it."

Summary

- New research indicates that children add to individual happiness when people are in cohabiting or marriage relationships. Most couples experience a decline in marital satisfaction after the birth of their first child, but a minority of couples experienced increased marital satisfaction.
- A national survey of 50,000 married couples identified five key parenting strengths. Happy couples were more than twice as likely as unhappy couples to agree on how to share the responsibilities of raising their children. Happy couples were almost twice as likely as unhappy couples to be satisfied with the amount of attention they focus on their marriage versus the amount of attention they focus on their children. Almost twice as many happy couples reported agreeing on how to discipline their children as did unhappy couples. Happy couples were much more likely than unhappy couples to feel that they had grown closer since having children. And happy couples reported that they were more satisfied in their marriage since having children, compared to unhappy couples.
- Raising a child for the average parents cost over $200,000, with the largest percentage going toward housing.
- Conventional wisdom and folk mythology on the subject of parenthood in our society abounds. Although many people might believe the conventional "truths," research on parenthood indicates that the picture is more complex.
- Researchers have found that voluntarily childless individuals and couples can have just as satisfying a life as those who have children.
- Parenting styles differ, and some are more effective than others. The democratic style is favored today because it appears to produce self-reliant children who cope well with stress. Other parenting styles that are authoritarian, permissive, rejecting, and uninvolved tend to produce children with more behavioral and academic problems.
- How to discipline children is a major issue for many parents, as well as a source of some debate in our society.
- Corporal punishment is widely used in the United States. Stress can sometimes cause parents to use physical punishment as a result of cascading circumstances.

- Quality of day care can be a key component in determining whether child care is beneficial. These findings are also evident in following children long term.
- Numerous studies demonstrate the important role a father plays in a child's development—whether he lives with the child or is a noncustodial parent. Mothers' and fathers' behavior can affect how involved the other parent is in the lives of children.
- In the United States, many parent education programs have been developed as a response to the challenges of raising children and the diversity of American families. Many trained professionals provide both information and one-on-one therapy.

Key Terms

child-free alternative
parental support
parental control
democratic parenting
authoritarian parenting
permissive parenting
rejecting parenting
uninvolved parenting
bidirectional effects
psychodynamic theory
organismic theory
behaviorist
learning theories
reinforcement
cascading circumstances
coparenting
parent education
family therapy

Activities

1. Read Kahlil Gibran's poem *On Children* carefully and write a brief essay analyzing his philosophy of parenthood. On what points do you agree and disagree?
2. Set a time and place to interview a couple you know well about their beliefs on rearing children and the challenges and joys they have experienced over the years as parents. A good interview takes careful planning: Write down 15 to 20 questions you want to be sure to ask. Make sure to ask about how children affected their relationship. Then write up your interview in a short paper and share it with the class or a small group. You might like to audio-record or video-record the interview. (These might even become family treasures and make great gifts.)
3. Parenthood can be a challenging task; children are often too busy and too overwhelmed by their own problems and concerns to think about their parents' feelings. Write a letter to your parents, thanking them for all the things they have done for you and for their unique human qualities.
4. If you do not have children of your own, spend an afternoon with some children you know—your nieces and nephews, a neighbor's children, or a friend's kids. Reflect on your reactions to this brief "parenting" experience.

Suggested Readings

Bellous, J. E. (2010). *Children, spirituality, loss and recovery.* New York, NY: Routledge.

Belsky, J. (2006). Early child care and early child development: Major findings of the NICHD study of early child care. *European Journal of Developmental Psychology, 3,* 95–110.

Bloch, E. (2007). The daddy difference. *Parenting, 21*(5), 81–84. The author argues that fathers let kids take risks while mothers are too protective because of their attachment to the child, which developed during pregnancy. And fathers trust themselves more than experts, while mothers are more sensitive to getting it right; they tend to compare notes with other parents more than dads do.

Chong, A., & Mickelson, K. D. (2016). Perceived fairness and relationship satisfaction during the transition to parenthood: The mediating role of spousal support. *Journal of Family Issues, 37,* 3–28.

Clark, R. A., Richard-Davis, G., Hayes, J., Murphy, M., & Pucheu Theall, K. (2009). *Planning parenthood: Strategies for success in fertility assistance, adoption, and surrogacy.* Baltimore, MD: Johns Hopkins University Press.

Compassionate Friends. (2016). Supporting family after a child dies. Web site: http://www.compassionatefriends.org/home.aspx.

Diamond, M. (2007). *My father before me: How fathers and sons influence each other throughout their lives.* New York, NY: W. W. Norton.

Doherty, W. J., Jacob, J., & Cutting, B. (2009). Community engaged parent education: Strengthening civic engagement among parents and parent educators. *Family Relations, 58,* 303–315.

Douglas, S. J., & Michaels, M. W. (2004). *The mommy myth: The idealization of motherhood and how it has undermined women.* New York, NY: Free Press.

Eunice Kennedy Shriver National Institute of Child Health and Human Development, NIH, DHHS. (2006). *The NICHD study of early child care and youth development (SECCYD): Findings for children up to age 4½ years (05-4318).* Washington, DC: U.S. Government Printing Office. Web site: http://www.nichd.nih.gov/publications/.

Family Action Centre, University of Newcastle, Australia. (2010). Useful information and resources on parenthood. Web site: https://www.newcastle.edu.au/research-and-innovation/centre/fac/about-us.

Gottman, J. M. (2007). *And baby makes three: The six-step plan for preserving marital intimacy and rekindling romance after baby arrives.* New York, NY: Crown.

Hayes, A., & Higgins, D. (Eds.). (2014). *Families, policy and the law: Selected essays on contemporary issues for Australia.*

Melbourne: Australian Institute of Family Studies. Web site: https://aifs.gov.au/publications/families-policy-and-law.

M.I.S.S. Foundation. (2016). The MISS Foundation is a 501 (c) 3, volunteer-based organization committed to providing crisis support and long-term aid to families after the death of a child from any cause. Web site: http://www.missfoundation.org/.

National Center for Health Statistics. (n.d.). Centers for Disease Control and Prevention. Web site: https://www.cdc.gov/nchs/.

Schooler, J. E., & Atwood, T. C. (2008). *The whole life adoption book: Realistic advice for building a healthy adoptive family.* Colorado Springs, CO: NavPress.

Sheldon, A. (2009). *Big brother now: A story about me and our new baby* and *Big sister now: A story about me and our new baby.* Magination Press. Web site: http://www.apa.org/pubs/magination/.

Skogrand, L., Hatch, D., & Singh, A. (2009). Strong marriages in Latino culture. In R. Dalla, J. DeFrain, J. Johnson, & D. Abbott (Eds.), *Strengths and challenges of new immigrant families: Implications for research, policy, education, and service* (pp. 117–134). Lexington, MA: Lexington Press.

Smith, J. A. (2009). *The daddy shift: How stay-at-home dads, breadwinning moms, and shared parenting are transforming the American family.* Boston, MA: Beacon Press.

Sorkhabi, N., & Mandara, J. (2013). Are the effects of Baumrind's parenting styles culturally specific or culturally equivalent? In R. E. Larzelere, A. S. Morris, & A. W. Harrist (Eds.), *Authoritative parenting: Synthesizing nurturance and discipline for optimal child development* (pp. 113–135). Washington, DC: American Psychological Association.

Wilcox, B. (2010). *The state of our unions: When marriage disappears.* Retrieved from http://www.stateofourunions.org/2010/index.php.

Wilcox, B. (2011). *The state of our unions: When baby makes three.* Retrieved from http://www.stateofourunions.org/2011/SOOU2011.pdf.

Visit the text-specific Online Learning Center at **www.mhhe.com/olson9e** for practice tests, chapter summaries, and PowerPoint slides.

Design Element: © Alicia Grünkind/EyeEm/Getty Images

13 Midlife and Older Couples

Intimacy, Strengths, and Diversity

Family Life in the Middle Years

Family Life in the Later Years

Summary

Key Terms

Activities

Suggested Readings

Intimacy, Strengths, and Diversity

Intimacy in the middle and later years of life looks very different from intimacy in the earlier stages of the family life cycle. Freedom from raising children for couples in the middle years of life may pave the way for new sexual and emotional intimacy. For those in later years, sexual intimacy in marriage or couple relationships may change with added health problems. Emotional intimacy in couple relationships, however, may be very solid as couples grow old together. By the time they have reached their middle and later years, many couples have developed a considerable array of strengths and learned valuable lessons in life that can be passed on to younger generations.

Intimate emotional relationships among the older generation and their adult children may increase in quality as these adult children have children of their own. Now the older parents and the younger parents share the life-changing experience of having children. And the relationships among grandparents and grandchildren can flower, as grandparents learn the joy of watching a new generation in the family grow and develop.

Couples are likely to find themselves in the sandwich generation, which means they are caring for their aging parents and also have responsibilities for adult children who may have moved back into the home. This may create stress, but it also may create new opportunities to tap into family strengths and unexpected intergenerational family relationships (Skogrand, Henderson, & Higginbotham, 2006). The following text is a true story about such a family:

> *Sandra and Martin were in their mid-50s and for a couple of years they had been in an empty nest. Their children were off to college, and the major responsibilities of raising children were done. It was great. They could go out when they wanted, take trips on the spur of the moment, or sleep late, with no major responsibilities except their jobs to tie them down. The spark was back in their relationship with limited stress in their lives and more opportunity to spend time together.*
>
> *Several months later, however, their son, Adam, dropped out of school and moved home to make a decision about career goals and decide where he wanted to continue his education. It was to be temporary, but there was much ambiguity about future plans. He quickly got a low-paying job and lived with Sandra and Martin. He was really not much bother. He took care of his own meals, picked up after himself, and got himself to work. Sandra and Martin were looking forward to spending time with their son who was now an adult.*
>
> *About the same time Adam moved home, the decision was made that Sandra's elderly mother who lived 800 miles away would move to a nursing home in their town. Both Sandra and Martin viewed the move positively. For the first time in her adult life Sandra would be able to have quality time with her aging mother.*
>
> *Soon after the move, however, Sandra's mother's health began to decline. She needed daily visits and frequent medical appointments and conferences. Work for Sandra involved long days, ending with several hours spent at the nursing home in the evening. There were many 14- and 15-hour days for Sandra, who would drop into bed exhausted, only to do it again the next day. Martin's days also became longer as he picked up most of the household responsibilities in addition to his job.*
>
> *Although Adam generally took care of himself, he still counted on his parents' help in buying a new car and applying and making arrangements to enroll in school. He had anticipated that he would have his parents available to help him plan his future, but they were rarely available.*

This sandwich generation family was experiencing stress and responsibility at a time when the middle-aged couple expected a less stressful time. As you read this story, you may be feeling yourself tense up as you think about all the responsibilities in their lives. The couple reflected on this time a year after Sandra's mother died and their son had gone back to college. They said it had been stressful and they did not want to do it again. They also said, however, that there were many positive things that happened in their family relationships during this time. Adam got to know his grandmother as he sat by her bed in the last weeks of her life. Adam's grandmother had talked about how she loved getting to know her grandson as an adult—something that she had not anticipated before she died. Sandra developed the intimate relationship with her mother that she had hoped for. In fact, she says this special time was short and at times difficult, but was also one of the best times of her life. Martin and Sandra developed a closer couple relationship because they agreed that both generations needed them during this time.

The middle and later years of life are filled with surprises, some difficult and stressful, and also some positive things that are never anticipated. Individuals and couples in the middle and later years of life usually have developed skills to weather the storm and appreciate wonderful surprises.

In the middle and later years of life, there is a good deal of diversity in terms of couple and family relationships. Many couples who have been married 30 or 50 or more years are quite accepting and loving toward their children, grandchildren, and great-grandchildren who are all growing up in a very different world. These progeny may be living together with a partner outside of marriage, or may have been married and divorced. They may be living in stepfamilies or gay or lesbian relationships. But many in the older generation have adapted to changing times. In some families, however, members of the older generation have problems with the diverse family structures evolving in the United States, and even express outrage toward younger family members. While in other families, grandparents and even great-grandparents embrace this new diversity and show unconditional love for younger family members.

Family Life in the Middle Years

After the kids leave home, some parents suffer from the empty nest syndrome; others change the locks!

—ANONYMOUS

What images does the term *middle age* conjure up? For most young college students, their mom and dad are the first to come to mind. Middle age can be a relaxing time, a time of thankfulness that the challenges and fears of youth have been overcome. But middle age can bring new pressures, new challenges.

"Life begins at 40," an old saying goes. The kids may leave the nest. Family income may reach a peak. But *middlescence* can set in. In the middle years, some people mourn lost opportunities, the road not taken, and wonder what their lives would have been like if only they had been bolder, smarter, or luckier. Middlescents also often yearn for a taut young body and freedom from the grind.

In Erik Erikson's classic schema, middle age can be a time for generativity or stagnation (1950). The question in middle age becomes, "Can we remain productive despite boredom and malaise?" In essence, can an old dog learn new tricks? Millions of people transform their lives in the middle years by starting new careers or falling in love. Those who are flexible, who can adapt to new circumstances and "roll with the punches," will be much more likely to succeed. The inflexible ones may survive but will probably not excel—and they will be less likely to enjoy the process of living than those who are flexible.

Defining Middle Age

A popular societal definition of **middle age** is the period of life between ages 35 and 65. Scanning the research literature, we find the middle years defined as encompassing 40 to 59 years of age. If we don't think in numbers, middle age can be defined as the period of life beyond young adulthood but before the onset of old age (Feldman, 2015). But that, of course, can mean different things to different people. Indeed, there have been many attempts to define middle age, and the definition can vary among cultures and historic time periods. The eminent gerontologist Bernice Neugarten noted philosophically that the middle years are the time when people begin to think about how many years they have left rather than how many they've already lived (1968). One middle-aged man described life as a rainbow: At the beginning are infancy, early childhood, adolescence, and young adulthood; around the very highest point of the rainbow are the middle years; and nearing the end of the rainbow are the later years of life. When one reaches the crest of the rainbow, the middle years, one can clearly see the remainder of life for the first time. "When I reached middle age," the man explained, "I saw the rest of my life clearly. It looked like more of the same old stuff I had grown tired of over the past 10 years. Some people might call it a middle-aged crisis," he continued. "I thought of it as a middle-aged opportunity, and I've been changing steadily ever since."

The post–World War II baby boom period ran from 1946 to 1964. Now this group of Americans is well into middle age, and the oldest **Baby Boomers** are in their early 70s and many are collecting Social Security and receiving Medicare benefits. This group of aging adults will have a decisive impact on society. For example, the percentage of Americans who are 65 years and older is expected to double in the next 25 years, when one in five Americans will be 65 years or older. Currently the age group 85 years and older is the fastest-growing segment of society (U.S. Census Bureau, 2017).

The growing numbers of Baby Boomers will put increasing pressure on society to focus more on retirement, health care, and empty-nest issues. Their buying power will impact consumer goods and health care systems. While our society is often portrayed as a youth-oriented culture, Baby Boomers will have a growing impact on shifting more attention to their group.

Middle Age: A Crisis or An Opportunity?

For some, **midlife crisis** is an apt term. During their 40s and 50s, many people will experience the death of a parent or family member, career changes, physical changes in appearance and health, and noticeable changes in relationships with a spouse and children. The realization that one's life is half over and that many goals have not been attained or that there is nothing new to look forward to can cause emotional upheaval.

One of the biggest changes of middle age is the children's departure from home for college or a job. Parents who are flexible usually enjoy the freedom from daily responsibility for their children and are likely to develop new interests or even start new careers.
©Jules Frazier/UpperCut Images/Getty Images

Despite this common perception—and even the popularity of the term *midlife crisis*—evidence does not support the existence of a generalized midlife crisis. Although people do experience crisis and stress at important transition points in life, including midlife, data show that midlife is not any more stressful than other life stages. In fact, midlife is often a time of stability, freedom, and control, as well as a time to redefine life and relationships (Aldwin & Levenson, 2001; Lachman, 2004; Rosato, 2012).

Statistically, midlife does not bring about an increase in divorce, depression, suicide, or alcoholism. In fact, a survey found that people in their 40s find life more exciting than younger or older adults (National Opinion Research Center, 1996). With age comes greater work satisfaction and satisfaction with one's finances, a reduction in depression, and a rise in one's general happiness. Additionally, older people are less likely to divorce than younger people, and suicide rates drop during middle age (National Opinion Research Center, 1996). In fact, *early life* is more a time of crisis than midlife. The struggles of the young and less experienced, generally, are greater than the struggles of those in the middle years.

The Middle-Aged Person and the Working World

Middle age, especially for those in their 40s and 50s, can be a time when both men and women decide they can make a change in their work lives. Children might be leaving home, and financial obligations may seem less daunting. There are new opportunities for the major breadwinner to make a career change or for the caretaker of the children to go back to work or school. Some have even been able to retire early, in their late 40s and 50s, to explore new hobbies, start a business, or embark on a new career. Most recent data indicate that among men and women 55 and older, only about 40% were participating in the labor force (about 46% for men and about 35% for women) (Rix, 2014).

The economic downturn, called the Great Recession, hit many developed economies around the world in the wake of the financial crisis of 2007–2008. This widespread economic crisis made it difficult for many Americans to retire early. Many saw their retirement funds diminish dramatically when the stock market fell. In one study conducted in the middle of the economic crisis, 27% of those approaching retirement (ages 55 to 64) reported that they were postponing plans to retire. It was also found that 30% of those in the 45 to 54 age group felt it was somewhat likely that their job would be eliminated within the next year. Many who lost their jobs had considerable difficulty finding new employment in their field, and many of those who did find new jobs took a dramatic cut in pay. For these people in middle age, the opportunity to try out a new career in midlife was not an option.

During the collapse, unemployment in the United States soared. Since then the unemployment rate has gone down significantly, but the financial crisis affected the hopes and dreams, the plans and opportunities for many in their middle years, and many others in all age groups.

Sexuality in Middle Age

As noted in Chapter 6, sexual activity often declines steadily over the years of a marriage. Fortunately, among couples who are creative and committed, sex can remain a source of intense pleasure throughout the middle years. Two issues of concern during this time are menopause and male menopause (also referred to as androgen decline).

Menopause. The most dramatic age-related change in female reproductive functioning, after puberty, is **menopause**, the end of monthly menstrual periods. It has been referred to as the "silent passage" because it is so rarely discussed openly. Menopause occurs, on average, around the age of 50 but can begin as early as a woman's mid-30s or as late as her early 60s. Because of various hormonal changes, menopause signals the cessation of a woman's ability

BOX 13.1 Diversity in Families

Childlessness: The Invisible Group

Much of our discussion in this chapter implies that children are part of the lives of those in middle and later years of life. Parenthood is often central to how we think about psychological growth and the life cycle (Dykstra & Hagestad, 2007). What about those who remained childless? What is the pathway to childlessness? What are the lives of those without children like?

The Context

Even though one in five people older than 65 years of age will be without children, this group of people is often invisible and is left out of the family studies literature (Dykstra & Hagestad, 2007). We might feel sympathy for those who involuntarily are childless, and some of us might assume that there is something deviant about those who deliberately made that choice. This stigma was even more evident several decades ago—when those who are now in the later years of life were at childbearing age.

Over the years we have changed how we talk about having children or not having children. In the 1970s, we began using the term *childfree,* implying that for some not having children was a conscious decision (Dykstra & Hagestad, 2007). The women's movement has also contributed to the idea that women have a choice and have control in childbearing. In recent years we have also seen less connection between marriage and having children, with the increase of single parenthood and cohabitation.

Pathways to Childlessness

In addition to consciously choosing to not have children, there are several factors that came into play that affected the ability and decision to have children for men and women who are now in their middle or later years of life. Timing was important, especially for women (Hagestad & Call, 2007). For most who are currently in the middle and later years of life, societal expectations were that marriage came before childbearing. Caring for aging family members, economic conditions, war, and social policy were just a few of the factors that might have affected marriage and, thus, childbearing. For example, one couple who are now in their 80s chose to get married because a farm was available for rent and farms did not often become available in the community. The man had a means of making a living, thus marriage was possible. Another man in this same community enlisted in the military during World War II. After being away for several years, he came back to a community with a limited number of available women to marry. He never married and remained childless.

In addition to infertility or choosing to be childless, some life patterns were more likely to correspond with childlessness than others. For example, those who delayed leaving home were more likely to remain childless (Hagestad & Call, 2007; Koropeckyj-Cox & Call, 2007). Those who were slower to make life transitions, such as leaving home, getting an education, or getting a job, were also more likely to be childless.

The Lives of Those Who Are Childless

What are the lives of childless middle-aged and aging adults like today? Childless couples and individuals have typically been very involved in the lives of children of other family members, including nieces and nephews, siblings, and cousins. In some cultures, such as American Indian and African American cultures, there has been a tendency to share children, especially among the female family members (Dykstra & Hegestad, 2007). With the increasing number of stepfamilies today, some have become stepparents. Others were deeply involved in the lives of children by being foster parents, teachers, or involved with other professions that involve working with children. Therefore, we cannot assume that childless individuals have not had interactions with children.

Research indicates there are some differences between adults who remained childless and those who had children. Women who are childless, and less likely to be married, are more likely to have higher levels of education and occupational status. Childless men, on the other hand, are likely to have lower socioeconomic status (Koropeckyj-Cox & Call, 2007). It has also been found that behaviors that have a negative effect on health, such as smoking and alcohol consumption, are more prevalent for those who did not have children, and this is especially true for men (Kendig, Dykstra, Gaalen, & Melkas, 2007). We might speculate that those with children had developed positive role model behaviors.

We might also expect that childless individuals are less involved in their community than parents, because children might be the impetus for such involvement. However, it has been found that there are no real differences in community participation between those who have children and those who do not (Wenger, Dykstra, Melkas, & Knipscheer, 2007). In terms of relationships with extended family members, these researchers found that childless adults had more contact with siblings, nieces, and nephews than parents, whereas parents had most of their contact with their adult children. It was also found that adults without children were more at risk for loneliness and isolation than parents. In the end stages of life, parents were more likely to depend on a spouse or adult children, and childless adults, who do not have those resources, were more likely to rely on formal institutional services. In general, childless older adults were more likely to live alone or in institutions, and it was more likely that women would fit this pattern than men (Koropeckyj-Cox & Call, 2007)—perhaps because women live longer and are more likely to be widowed, thus not having a spouse to live with.

People between the ages of 43 and 50 usually come to terms with life, and are able to more realistically assess their strengths and weaknesses.
©Sirtravelalot/Shutterstock

to have children. Reproductive organs shrink, and the amount of fatty tissue in the breasts and other parts of the body decreases. The vulva becomes thinner, losing its capacity to engorge with blood, and the vagina shrinks and loses some elasticity. Vaginal secretions that provide lubrication during intercourse diminish (Boston Women's Health Book Collective, 2006, 2011; Mayo Clinic, 2015, January 7).

Many women experience distress—including irritability, insomnia, "hot flashes," headaches, and depression—during menopause. Historically, hormones to replace those no longer produced by the body have been prescribed to alleviate some of these effects. In 2002, however, a large clinical trial called the Women's Health Initiative reported that hormone treatment presented more health risks than benefits. Hormone therapy can increase the risk of heart disease, breast cancer, stroke, and blood clots. The benefits of hormone therapy include decreased risk of osteoporosis or colorectal cancer. Women need to talk to their doctor to determine whether hormone therapy is the best treatment for them. For some, such as women at high risk for osteoporosis, the benefits of hormone therapy outweigh the risks (Mayo Clinic, 2015, April 14).

In general, most women perceive menopause as a transition period rather than a problem. Even though physical responses change, a woman's perception of pleasure and satisfaction during intercourse may remain the same or may decrease or even become painful due to lack of lubrication and thinner vaginal tissues. There may also be a drop in libido with shifting hormones.

Male Menopause. Sexual changes related to age also occur in men. Production of the male hormone **androgen** declines slowly and steadily in most men until about age 60, when it levels off. For most men, this decline in hormone production does not cause the emotional and

Successful middle-aged couples tend to be those who have shared feelings and activities throughout their marriage, in spite of the competing demands of jobs and children. They continue to express love and concern both verbally and physically.
Source: U.S. Census Bureau, Public Information Office (PIO)

physical changes that some women experience during menopause. In other men, the symptoms are so similar to those experienced by menopausal women that physicians label the condition **male menopause**, a term that generates some controversy in the medical community.

As men get older, the amount of fluid ejaculated with orgasm tends to diminish, as does the strength of the ejaculation. The testicles become smaller and less firm; erections become less frequent and also less rigid. By age 50, the average male may require 8 to 24 hours after orgasm before he is capable of having another erection. Most men also require more time to reach orgasm, but this can be viewed as a benefit, as a lengthening of the period of pleasure for both the man and his partner (Hyde & DeLamater, 2014; Mayo Clinic, 2014, August 7; WebMD, 2014, August 17).

The Middle-Aged Marriage

Many marriages are happier before children arrive and after they leave home. For many couples in the middle years, marital satisfaction may reach a low point when the kids are teenagers and then increase as the adolescents leave home.

Strengthening Marriage in the Middle Years. A great deal can be learned about marriage from divorced people. Based on interviews with those who have experienced marital dissolution, here are some suggestions for strengthening marriage in the middle years:

- Establish priorities early in marriage, with the spouse at the top of the list. Do not allow parenthood to overshadow the marriage.
- Be alert for warning signs of marital problems, which include nagging, sarcasm, possessiveness, criticism, and personal discontent.
- Strive toward equality in all aspects of the marriage. Each partner should feel important and powerful.
- Seek a balance between togetherness and personal growth; either extreme can be harmful to a marriage.
- Good sex in a relationship in the middle years does not come naturally; it is a result of a positive daily life together.

- Develop a network of friendships with other couples who are concerned about maintaining a quality marriage.
- Evaluate the marriage from time to time and attend a marriage enrichment workshop.
- Avoid boring or frustrating work situations; a midlife career change may be beneficial.
- Consider a lifestyle change rather than a partner change in middle age to add pizzazz to the marriage.
- A happy marriage is the key to a content spouse. The best way to deal with infidelity is to prevent it from occurring.

Divorce During the Middle and Later Years

An AARP study of couples who got divorced later in life found the participants emerged from the difficulties of divorce far happier and emotionally healthier than most of them would have dared to hope at the beginning of their journey. The researchers surveyed 1,147 men and women who divorced in their 40s, 50s, and 60s. The researchers found that 66% of the women said they had asked for the divorce, while 41% of the men said they asked for the divorce. More men were caught off guard by the coming divorce than women (26% to 14%). Men were likely to remarry sooner (Montenegro, 2004; see also AARP, 2016b).

The AARP study found the causes of divorce at midlife and beyond are:

- Verbal, physical, or emotional abuse (34%)
- Different values, lifestyles (29%)
- Cheating (27%)
- Simply fell out of love/no obvious problems (24%)
- Alcohol or drug abuse (21%)
- Being a control freak (16%)
- Money problems (14%)
- Not carrying their weight in the marriage (14%)
- Fell in love with someone else (10%)
- Abandonment (10%)

Less than 5% to 8% of the respondents in the study checked *always being away*, *sexual problems*, *stepchildren*, and *in-laws* as reasons for the divorce. Not having children, religious differences, cultural differences, age differences, declining physical health, and homosexuality were named by less than 5% (Montenegro, 2004; see also AARP, 2016b).

The number of people ending long-term marriages after age 50 has increased dramatically. While the overall divorce rate in the United States has declined since 1990 somewhat, the divorce rate for those over age 50 has doubled. The surge spawned the term *gray divorce*. Jay Lebow, a psychologist at the Family Institute at Northwestern University, said, "If late-life divorce were a disease, it would be an epidemic" (Abrahms, 2012, p. 26).

What has caused the increase of divorces in the middle and later years? Sociologist Andrew Cherlin argues that as people's prospects for a long life have increased over the past decades, many are leaving unhappy marriages in quest of many more happy years ahead (Enright, 2004). One woman explained the reason for her divorce in midlife by saying, "If I hadn't been expected to live so long, I would have stayed with him. But I just couldn't see another 30 years in the marriage." (See also Brown & Lin, 2015.)

Empty Nest, Spacious Nest, or Cluttered Nest?

The term **empty-nest syndrome** describes the feelings of malaise, emptiness, and lack of purpose that parents sometimes experience when their children leave home. Some parents do suffer from these feelings, and most go through a period of adjustment when their children leave the nest. But the empty nest is a boon for most parents, giving them more time and energy to invest in their marriage. To emphasize the positive aspects of this time, we prefer the term **spacious nest**. There is more room in the home for the parents' things—and more money and time in the marriage for each other. Of course we need to keep in mind that not all couples choose to have children (Box 13.1), and may not experience this aspect of their midlife years.

The opposite of the spacious nest is the parental nest refilled with **boomerang kids**—adult children who return home for economic reasons, because they are going through a divorce, the need to find a safety net, extended education, drug/alcohol problems, or during a temporary transition period. The stereotypic image of this situation is of a self-centered young adult returning home to place an unfair economic burden on parents who resent the invasion of their new-found privacy. While this image may represent the experience of some, boomerang children are for the most part well tolerated by parents as long as the return home is temporary and does not happen too many times (Dickler, 2012; Nance-Nash, 2012; New York Life, 2012; Wang & Morin, 2009).

Societies around the world, even in the Western world, have been relatively hospitable to children staying or returning home. In Southern European countries, which have traditionally emphasized the extended family, many children do not move out of home until they marry. And since the Great Recession began in 2007, increasing numbers of adult children have either remained at home or boomeranged back. However, a variety of names for adult children living in the family home expresses ambivalence or negativity. In Italy they are called big babies (*bamboocioni*) or mama's boys (*mammoni*). In the United Kingdom they are called KIPPERS (Kids in Parents' Pockets Eroding Retirement Savings). In Japan, they are called parasite singles (*parasalto shingury*). And in the United States and Canada, where children might leave home earlier than they did in the mid-20th century, the cycles of leaving and returning sometimes are described as *accordion families* (Otters & Hollander, 2015).

Today, middle-aged parents of young adults are less likely to find themselves with empty nests than were their counterparts 40 years ago. More young adults are postponing marriage or are marrying and divorcing. A phenomenon called the **cluttered nest** occurs when adult children return to the parental nest to live after college graduation while they get established professionally and financially and save enough money to move into their own apartments or homes.

As one middle-aged mother in suburban Washington, D.C., asked rhetorically when recalling the time her daughter had returned home with two preschool-aged children after her divorce:

> *"What was I supposed to do? Slam the door in her face? She had no money. Her husband's lawyer was threatening to take the kids away, and she was so depressed I thought she might overdose on pills. I had to help. I love my daughter and I love my grandchildren.*
>
> *"I knew they wouldn't be with us forever. I knew she would be getting back on her feet soon enough. I knew I could help. What are families for?"*

Caught in the Middle: The Sandwich Generation

Besides struggling with adolescents, empty or cluttered nests, and boomerang kids, people in their middle years are also apt to have growing responsibilities for their aging parents. For this reason, middle-aged parents have been described as the **sandwich generation**. Data from the Pew Research Center (2013, January 30) indicate that almost half (48%) of adults ages 40 to 59 have provided some financial support to at least one grown child in the past year, while 27% were providing primary support. And, one in five adults ages 40 to 59 (21%) have provided some financial support to a parent age 65 or older in the past year.

Researchers agree that daughters are more likely to assume the caregiving role than sons, and somewhere between half and two-thirds of adult women will assume this role at some time in their lives (Cicirelli, 2001, 2003).

Caring for an elderly family member can be a burden for the caregiver, but it can also increase intimacy between a parent and an adult child. One study of 133 pairs of adult caregiving daughters and their elderly mothers reported that about half the mothers and daughters saw their relationship as having been positively affected by the caregiving situation, whereas most of the rest reported no change in the quality of their relationships (McGraw & Walker, 2004; Walker & McGraw, 1999).

For some middle-aged parents, though, the stress of caring for their children—whether adolescents or young adults—and for frail aging parents can be too great. Exhaustion and anger can reach a boiling point and can create intergenerational conflicts. These can also produce neglect or abuse of the elderly, which unfortunately is relatively common in the United States (National Center on Elder Abuse, 2016).

Caring for children and aging parents can cause stress for the marriage relationship (Skogrand et al., 2006). A married couple may be looking forward to freedom from caregiving responsibilities and to renewing that spark in their relationship. The opposite happens—instead there is added stress. There is evidence that having a healthy marriage going into the sandwich generation phase of life provides much needed support for the spouse who has the major responsibility for caring for two generations (Skogrand et al., 2006). It is, therefore, important to maintain a strong marriage relationship through the childrearing years, in preparation for what is sometimes a stressful time in life.

Grandparenthood

If I had known grandchildren would be this fun, I would have had them first.
—BUMPER STICKER

There are many ways to describe the experience of being a grandparent. Many grandparents talk about how they can spoil these children in a way they could not spoil their own children. Others describe the unconditional love they can provide to children whom they see only as delightful. Years ago, world-renowned cultural anthropologist Margaret Mead shared her thoughts on being a grandparent: "Grandparents and grandchildren get along so well because they have a common enemy," Mead chuckled. Then, getting serious, she added, "[Being a grandparent is] the extraordinary sense of having been transformed not by an act of one's own but by the act of one's child" (Mead, 1995, pp. 275, 277).
She went on to explain that grandparents do not have the anxiety and guilt experienced by parents.

As our life expectancy continues to increase, more and more Americans are living long enough to become grandparents. Data from the U.S. Census Bureau and from a nationally representative study by the Pew Research Center (2015, September 13) indicate the following:

- Most Americans (83%) ages 65 and older say they have grandchildren. Of these grandparents, two-thirds (67%) report they have at least four grandchildren, according to the Pew Research Center.
- More grandparents are living with a grandchild. About 7 million grandparents lived with a grandchild in 2013, compared to 5.8 million grandparents doing so in 2000, the U.S. Census Bureau reported. Among all these grandparents, 37% were serving as their grandchildren's primary caregiver.
- For most American grandparents, child care is only an occasional responsibility. In the Pew survey, among grandparents who had helped with child care in the past

12 months, nearly three out of four (72%) said they did so only occasionally. About one in five (22%) said they provided child care regularly.
- Grandparents living with their grandchildren are more racially and ethnically diverse than the U.S. population as a whole. Less than half (48%) of grandparents with grandchildren at home are White, while 75% of Americans 50 and older are White. Meanwhile, Hispanics, Blacks, and Asians make up a larger share of grandparents with grandchildren at home than they do of the age-50+ population as a whole.
- Older Americans say that having more time to spend with their family is by far the best part about growing old. When asked about the benefits of aging, the two most common answers were the benefits of spending more time with family (28%) and spending time with grandchildren (25%). The next-most popular answer was financial security, noted by 14% of the respondents in the Pew study.

For most people, grandparent–grandchild interaction is very enjoyable. Three-fourths of all grandparents have contact with their grandchildren weekly. Although most grandparents are not directly responsible for the well-being of their grandchildren, they do have a vested interest in their development. Research has shown that the resulting emotional closeness continues into adulthood if grandparents have provided support for grandchildren as they go through difficult times, especially when these life events occur before 12 years of age (Wood & Liossis, 2007). Grandparents were typically available to the grandchildren to provide child care, teach life skills, and provide recreational activities for the children, and they were seen as providing a stabilizing source of support and a buffer against stress.

Research has also found that the relationship between grandparents and grandchildren is related to the strength of the relationship between a parent and his or her own parent (Monserud, 2008). In addition, mothers, rather than fathers, are often the gatekeepers when it comes to the strength of the grandchild/grandparent relationship. For example, if a mother is close to her in-laws, it is more likely that the grandchild/grandparent relationship will be strong.

In a summary of the current research about grandparents, several dimensions of the grandparent role have been identified by Thiele and Whelan (2006, 2008). These aspects or dimensions include grandparents' attitudes and expectations, grandparent behaviors, the symbolic meaning of grandparenthood, and the affective outcome or feeling of satisfaction of grandparents.

- *Grandparents' attitudes and expectations.* The role is ambiguous, and grandparents have little control over how it plays out. There may be an expectation that there will be frequent contact with their grandchildren and that may or may not happen.
- *Grandparent behavior.* There is no single way for grandparents to behave. In some cultures where the elderly are viewed as authority figures, the relationship with grandchildren may be very formal. In other cultures, the expectation is that grandparents are fun loving and warm.
- *Symbolic meaning of grandparenthood.* Some grandparents view their role as a source of status. Others view their role as emotional self-fulfillment. Still others see the grandparent role as their opportunity to be a teacher to the next generation.
- *Grandparent satisfaction.* How enjoyable or how happy grandparents are in their role varies. The vast majority are very satisfied and happy with their role, but a small minority are not. The greatest satisfaction seems to come when involvement is moderate, not detached, but not providing custodial care.

The role of grandparents may differ greatly in different cultural groups. As Thiele and Whelan (2006, 2008) noted, some cultures view the elderly in ways that affect their relationship with grandchildren. For example, in a study conducted with American Indian grandparents, researchers found that these grandparents did many of the typical things all grandparents do such as engaging in a variety of activities with their grandchildren and providing unconditional love (Robbins, Scherman, Holman, & Wilson, 2005). In addition, however, these grandparents also engaged in activities where they had the opportunity to pass on American Indian traditions and knowledge. Almost all of the participants in this study were concerned that tribal culture would be lost if their grandchildren did not learn about it and pass these traditions on to future generations.

Thinking about one's relationship with one's own grandparents might help clarify the dimensions described by Thiele and Whelan (2006, 2008). What was your relationship with your grandparents like? What kind of a grandparent do you want to be?

By and large, the grandparent role is mutually enjoyable for grandparents and grandchildren, and it gives the parents a welcome break. Although grandparenting can sometimes overwhelm and tire out grandparents, the role is generally pleasurable: "I can enjoy these kids so much now . . . so much more than I really could my own kids. I don't have to worry about them. Their mom and dad can do the worrying."

Grandparents Raising Grandchildren

One child in 10 in the United States lives with a grandparent, and about 4 in 10 (41%) of those children are also being raised primarily by that grandparent (U.S. Census Bureau, 2014, October 22). The phenomenon of grandparents serving as primary caregivers is more common among African Americans and Hispanics than among Whites, but during the Great Recession of 2007–2009, the sharpest rise was among Whites. About 2.9 million children live with a grandparent, and almost half (49%) of children being raised by grandparents also live with a single parent; 8% have both parents in the household, in addition to the caregiver grandparent (Livingston & Parker, 2010). Grandparents are typically raising their grandchildren because of problems that exist with the parents of the grandchildren such as substance abuse, HIV/AIDS, mental illness, neglect or abuse, incarceration, or divorce (Dolbin-McNab, 2006; Inskeep & Ludden, 2014). For many adults in the grandparenting

Because they do not have to bother with the daily chores of childrearing, most grandparents are free to develop a more creative relationship with their grandchildren, sharing activities and interests with them. For most grandparents, one of the greatest satisfactions of grandparenthood is seeing a continuation of their family through another generation.
©Inmagine/Alamy Stock Photo

role, it means that they can care for their grandchildren, spoil them, and then give them back to the parents. For other grandparents, however, grandparenting means caring for their grandchildren in the same way they cared for their own children—taking care of their physical and emotional needs 24/7 (Dolbin-McNab, 2006; Inskeep & Ludden, 2014). In some cases, grandparents are providing care for several grandchildren, who may come from several different families, and they also may be caring for their own children (Bachman & Chase-Lansdale, 2005).

The amount of stress experienced by grandparents raising grandchildren is extensive with concerns about finances, parenting issues, and their own health (Bachman & Chase-Lansdale, 2005; Goodman & Silverstein, 2006; Ross & Aday, 2006). The majority of grandparents raising grandchildren do so without any formal custody of the grandchild and with resulting anguish about the long-term relationship (Cox, 2007). In addition, many grandparents experience grief if they are dealing with the loss of their own child to antisocial behavior. The emotional stress they are feeling about the family relationships that have gone wrong, or could go wrong, are also adding to the pain experienced by the grandparents raising grandchildren. There is a need for financial and emotional support for grandparents as they are highly committed, but highly stressed as they care for their grandchildren.

African American children are more likely to be raised by their grandparents than children of other cultural groups, including Whites (Gibson, 2005; Goodman & Silverstein, 2006). Statistics show that 5% of White grandchildren are being raised by grandparents, 15% of African American children, and 9% of Latino children (Ross & Aday, 2006). One researcher suggests that custodial grandparenting is more prevalent in the African American community because, historically, members of this cultural group have cared for their own rather than have children placed in the social service system (Gibson, 2005). Black women are most likely to care for their grandchildren because of parental drug use and incarceration (Gibson, 2005).

Goodman and Silverstein (2006) studied the differences among African American, Latina, and White custodial grandmothers. They found that African American and Latina grandmothers raised their grandchildren more often because of financial reasons, and White grandmothers were more likely to raise their grandchildren because of some other dire parental circumstances such as parental substance abuse, child neglect, and parental mental health issues. These researchers also found that Latina and African American custodial grandparents were less likely to experience extreme stress than White grandmothers in raising their grandchildren. These authors suggest that White grandmothers are more likely to expect their adult children to be independent, and, therefore, when they must intervene and become caregivers of their grandchildren, it creates a sense of disappointment in their child, which adds to the stress.

In a qualitative study of 55 American Indian and White grandparents raising grandchildren, it was found the American Indian grandparents had higher levels of depression than their White counterparts (Letiecq, Bailey, & Kurtz, 2008). Although American Indians have a rich history of providing care for their grandchildren and teaching them about their culture, these grandparents were providing care for their grandchildren because of a crisis with their own children. The authors of this study speculate that these high levels of depression may have resulted, in part, from the sadness they felt about unemployment, alcohol or drug addiction, or their children's inability to parent. These grandparents were trying to keep their grandchildren out of the foster care system and were overwhelmed with the full-time caregiving responsibility. These researchers also found that White and American Indian grandparents who had more financial resources were less depressed than those who had fewer resources. For more on grandparents and *grandfamilies,* see Box 13.2.

BOX 13.2 Diversity in Families

Grandparents and Grandfamilies

Grandparents have always been central to families. They have provided essential and often simultaneous assistance to two generations, their children and their grandchildren. Grandparents often take the role of the family historian, responsible for passing customs and the family lineage on to the next generations. Increasingly, grandparents are being asked to provide both emotional and instrumental support to their adult children as these children attempt to balance long work hours, distant military service, or other commitments with parenting responsibilities. Some modern grandparents act as coparents to their grandchildren by assisting their adult children with the daily responsibilities and care for their grandchildren.

Grandparenthood is a mutually reciprocal relationship for all generations interconnected. The grandparents benefit from seeing their family grow and the continuation of their legacy. The younger generations benefit from the past experiences and knowledge shared by the older generation.

Some grandparents have the responsibility of *parenting again* if they parent their grandchildren full-time. Grandparents provide child kinship care for their grandchildren if their adult children are absent, unwilling, or unable to parent (Gibson, 2002). While some grandparents have always cared for their grandchildren, *grandfamilies* are increasing in numbers with an estimated 5 million children residing with custodial grandparents (U.S. Census Bureau, 2010a). Grandfamilies are defined as households where the parents are absent or the grandparent is the head of the household (Saluter, 1996). These custodial grandparents often benefit from an increased sense of purpose in caring for their grandchild.

This is an excerpt from a story written by a custodial grandmother with the pseudonym of Dee:

Becoming a parent and raising your kids is an experience with many rewards, blessings, and disappointments. I had three daughters and desperately wanted a son but did not have one. You know the saying, "Be careful what you wish for because wishes do come true." Little did I know that after my girls were grown that I would literally become a full-time Grandma raising two of my grandsons.

These days there are many grandparents being-full-time caregivers for their children's children. My two grandsons are ages 8 and 6 and believe you me raising boys is a helluva lot harder than raising girls. I thought girls were difficult to bring up dealing with their attitudes and such, but I've discovered that little boys are totally different. They are very loud, extremely active (flying over furniture, very risk-taking requiring many trips to the emergency room) and just plain messy (hiding food, dirty clothes, and the like in places you would not believe).

My grandsons have special needs as they have been diagnosed with Attention Deficit Hyperactivity Disorder (ADHD). Their hyperactivity means their energy level knows no boundaries. They are always on the go like the energizer rabbit! I only wish I could tap into some of their energy, so that I could keep up with them.

I'm often asked, "How do you do it raising two very active grandsons with their special needs?" By the grace of God I've been blessed with a wonderful support system. Even when I have days when I'm not feeling my best, I still find a way to provide the care and guidance for my boys. They sing in the church youth choir, receive honors at school, and yes they can be quite the handful at times, and there are times when I wonder just what have I gotten myself into. But, after the crisis is over, whether it's mine or theirs, we are still a loving family with lots of hugs, kisses, and smiles. I predict the future for them will be very bright, full of rainbows and sunshine after we weather a few storms along the way.

Source: Dr. Toni L. Hill, Department of Family Studies, University of Nebraska at Kearney. Email: hilltl@unk.edu. Reprinted by permission.

Family Life in the Later Years

American society is going through a demographic revolution as the life span of the population increases. In 1900, the average life expectancy at birth was 47 years. The most recent data available projects a life span of 78.8 years. A baby boy at birth is projected to live to age 76.4, while a baby girl is projected to live to 81.2 years of age, women outliving men by an average of 4.8 years (Centers for Disease Control and Prevention, 2016, February 25).

Because of increased life expectancy, American society is growing older. Trends indicate that the population of older persons is increasingly rapidly. Most recent data indicate that people over age 65 in the United States make up 14.1% of the total population, about one in every seven Americans. By 2060 there are projected to be about 98 million older persons, more than double their number in 2013. In 2040 it is estimated that older people will represent 21.7% of the total population (Administration for Community Living, 2016, March 17).

The later years of life can be bittersweet. For those who were successful in raising a family and planning for retirement, the later years are easier than for those who have family or financial problems. Some older adults experience loneliness and isolation. Many must make do on limited funds. And elder abuse by younger family members occurs in some families.

Although many studies of older people have focused on the negative aspects of aging, a recent study demonstrated that many people become happier as they age. Mroczek and Spiro (2003) found that older men, especially those who are married, are happier than are younger men. Older men seem to regulate their emotions more effectively and are more able to maximize the positive and minimize the negative. In a sample of 2,727 men from ages 25 to 74, the older men reported having fewer negative emotions and, in general, were happier than the younger men. Younger people reported feeling sad, nervous, hopeless, or worthless more often than did older participants. Thus, aging seems to have some positive aspects when it comes to emotions.

A subsequent study by the same research team found that life satisfaction generally peaks around age 65 in men (Mroczek & Spiro, 2005). On average life satisfaction dropped in late life after peaking around 65, so that men around age 85 were about as happy as they were in their mid-40s. "But people vary significantly from that overall growth curve," Daniel Mroczek said. "Some people may keep going up, some people may never peak and some just keep going down. Finding a pattern doesn't mean everyone abides by it." The researchers also found that men with high levels of extroversion correlated with high levels of life satisfaction and relative stability in life satisfaction over the years; men with lower levels of extroversion had an overall lower level of life satisfaction and less stability in life satisfaction as the years passed. "So, people with high extroversion are happier throughout life, but importantly, they're also more stable," Mroczek concluded (Kersting, 2005).

More recent research by Gallup (Stone, Schwartz, Broderick, & Deaton, 2010) complements earlier findings. In a telephone survey of 340,000 people nationwide, ages 18 to 85, researchers found among many other things that by almost any measure people get happier as they get older. The researchers developed a global measure of well-being, including enjoyment in life, happiness, stress, worry, anger, and sadness. On this global measure people start out at age 18 feeling pretty good about themselves, on average, and then, apparently, life starts to make life more difficult. People tend to feel worse and worse on average until they reach age 50. At this point, there is a sharp reversal, and they keep getting happier and happier as they age. By the time they are 85, they are even more satisfied with their lives than they were at 18.

Defining Old Age

Old age is often said to begin at 65, which in our society is the typical age of retirement. But any exact chronological starting point for old age is bound to be arbitrary. In some parts of the world where life expectancy is lower, a person might be old at a much earlier age. Even in our own society, we see enormous variation among older adults. We all know active 75-year-olds and tired 50-year-olds.

Older adults are often divided into distinct groups: the young-old, the middle-old, and the old-old. There is not complete consensus on the ages of each of these groups, however, because human beings are so diverse. One approach puts the young-old between 65 and 74. These people tend to be retired and in good health and have abundant time to follow their interests. The middle-old, between 75 and 84, tend to be showing their age as health problems increase. The old-old, over age 85, as a group tend to have the most members who are frail, lonely, and poor. But some observers note that many of those over age 85 are in good shape in terms of health, income, and social relationships. So, a fourth group has been added to the discussion, the frail old. Even though the old-old tend to have the most health problems as a group, there are frail old people represented among the young-old and middle-old groups as well. By adding this fourth category, the fact is clearly being signified that human beings, for a variety of reasons, grow old at different rates.

Aging is in part a *psychological phenomenon*. How an older person feels depends to some degree on her or his mental attitude toward both the accomplishments of the past and the possibilities for the future. For most purposes, a person who feels "young at heart" is still young. Of course, aging is also a *biological reality*, and some variations among older adults are a result of their different genetic heritages. Aging is also a *social phenomenon*. If society forces people into retirement at 65, it is in effect declaring them to be old. Similarly, there are compelling data to argue that one's social standing or social class directly affects one's health and life expectancy. Similar to chickens, people have a pecking order, and the higher level of status one holds in the human pecking order, the longer, happier, and healthier one's life is likely to be (Marmot, 2004). Finally, aging is part of the family process, one that occurs in the context of ongoing interpersonal relationships with spouses, parents, children, and other family members whose attitudes help us define and redefine ourselves as we grow older.

Despite the challenges of aging—the lower energy levels, the failing eyesight or poor hearing, the serious health problems—many people adapt to these changes and continue to live fruitful lives. How we as individuals, and as members of families and communities, define the later years powerfully influences our well-being during this time.

Conventional Wisdom About Old Age

Grow old along with me! The best is yet to be, The last of life, for which the first was made.
—ROBERT BROWNING (1864)

Many people in our society accept the conventional wisdom about old age, most of which is negative. It is important, though, that we set the record straight about these myths or false beliefs, which foster a form of prejudice known as **ageism**, prejudging an older person negatively solely on the basis of age. In the following discussion, we hope to deconstruct some of the most common myths about old age.

Older couples often have more time to enjoy leisure activities together and see renewed happiness in their marriage. They may also return to hobbies or activities they previously did not have time to enjoy while working.
©Monkeybusinessimages/iStock/Getty Images

TABLE 13.1 Median Net Worth by Age of Householder, 1984 and 2009 (in 2010 dollars)

	1984	2009	Change
All	$ 65,293	$ 71,635	10%
Younger than 35	11,521	3,662	−68%
35–44	71,118	39,601	−44%
45–54	113,511	101,651	−10%
55–64	147,236	162,065	10%
65 and older	120,457	170,494	42%

Source: Pew Research Center tabulations of Survey of Income and Program Participation data and U.S. Census Bureau P–70, No. 7; *Household Wealth and Asset Ownership: 1984: Data from the Survey of Income and Program Participation,* Table E.

Myth #1: *At 65, You're "Over the Hill."*

Reality: Attitude has a good deal to do with how "old" one is. People whose attitudes toward life remain positive generally lead happier and more fulfilling lives in their later years. Many symptoms popularly associated with old age—cognitive impairment, falling, dizziness, loss of bladder control, and loss of appetite—are symptoms of disease, not of normal aging.

Myth #2: *Most Older Adults Are Poor.*

Reality: Actually, the financial situation for most people 50 and above is quite good. The Pew Research Center found that households headed by older adults have made dramatic gains compared to younger adults in terms of economic well-being over the past quarter century. Most recent data show that the typical oldest age household had 47 times as much net wealth as the typical household headed by someone in the youngest age group. (Net wealth can be defined as any asset owned minus any debt owed.) Households headed by persons 65 and older had an average net wealth of $170,494, while households headed by persons younger than 35 had an average net worth of $3,662 (Fry, Cohn, Livingston, & Taylor, 2011). Table 13.1 shows clearly how the accumulation of wealth has actually fallen off for young people in recent years, while wealth for 65 and older people has dramatically increased.

It is clear that, on average, older families are doing better than younger families from an economic perspective. However, other researchers have found that nearly half of all elderly Americans will encounter at least 1 year of poverty or near poverty between the ages of 60 and 90. Also, 58% of those between 60 and 84 will at some time fail to have enough liquid assets to make it possible for them to weather an unanticipated expense or downturn in income (Rank & Williams, 2010).

Myth #3: *Older Adults Are Not Interested in Sex.*

Reality: A major study by Lindau et al. (2007) focused on sexual behaviors of over 3,000 adults from ages 57 to 85 years of age. Men and women were approximately equally represented in the sample. The purpose of the study was to learn about the prevalence of behaviors, sexual activity, and problems in the older population and to learn about the relationship between sexuality and health conditions.

The findings of the Lindau et al. (2007) study indicated that sexual activity, including vaginal intercourse, oral sex, and masturbation, declined with age, and men were more sexually active than women. Women were less likely than men to be in a marriage or other intimate relationship, or more likely to have lost their sexual partner through death, which affected their level of sexual activity. Participants 75 to 85 years of age were involved in sexual activity less than those who were younger, but even at this age 54% were having sex at least two to three times per month, and 23% had sex once per week or more.

Both men and women in this study masturbated, with masturbation declining as age increased, with men masturbating more frequently than women. Approximately half of men and 25% of women in the 75- to 85-year-old age group had masturbated in the previous 12 months. This was true for adults who were in a relationship or marriage and those who were not. Although approximately half of the participants in the study, both men and women, reported sexual problems often related to health, one in seven men reported taking medication to improve sexual functioning.

Based upon the findings from this study, it is clear that older adults are, indeed, sexually active. Medications taken in middle and later years can, however, affect the ability to have and enjoy sex. For example, research shows that medications such as statins, which lower cholesterol, also lower sexual pleasure (WebMD, 2010, April 16). Men indicated that their sexual pleasure was reduced by one-half. Women's sexual pleasure was also decreased, but not as dramatically. Many who experienced sexual problems sought solutions through the use of medication.

Myth #4: *Older Adults Are Usually Sick.*
Reality: Actually, older adults are generally in good health. Even in the advanced stages of old age an overwhelming majority have little functional disability, and the proportion of the disabled is going down not up (Alliance for Aging Research, 2016). People over 65 have about half as many acute illnesses as those between 17 and 44. It is true, of course, that chronic conditions tend to accumulate over time, and older adults commonly suffer from sensory losses—hearing, vision, and taste. But as AARP regularly points out, these problems do not keep most older adults from enjoying an active, healthy life. People who have adapted to change throughout life will likely find ways to cope with most of the changes that aging brings (AARP, 2016a).

Myth #5: *Older Adults Become Senile.*
Reality: The term *senility* is not often used by gerontologists today, because it has little specific meaning. Although brain damage can be caused by a series of small strokes, most progressive organic brain impairment is caused by disease, such as **Alzheimer's disease** (Box 13.3). Assuming that memory loss or change in behavior in older adults is a function of age can cause one to overlook a disease that might be successfully treated. All too often, people attribute an older person's anger or depression to old age, when, in fact, it may be due to a life occurrence that would cause similar symptoms in a younger individual (U.S. National Library of Medicine, 2016).

Myth #6: *Most Older Adults End up in Nursing Homes.*
Reality: Latest figures indicate there are about 44.7 million people age 65 and older in the United States, and the number is steadily growing. This age group accounts for 14.1% of the total population (Administration for Community Living, 2015, December 31; U.S. Census Bureau, 2015, May 8). At any given time, about 4% of the people age 65 and older in this country are in a nursing home.

Research does indicate, however, that 43% of Americans over age 65 will enter a nursing home at some time in their lives. Most of these nursing home stays are for relatively short periods of time, as patients recuperate from surgery or illness. The average nursing home stay is between 2 and 3 years (Public Broadcasting Service, 2012).

The likelihood of being in a nursing home increases with age: 1.4% of those aged 65 to 74 are in a nursing home; 6% of those aged 75 to 84; and 24% of those 85 and older. However, four out of five elderly with long-term care needs live in the community. Only one in five persons with such needs lives in a nursing home. Few families abandon their loved ones in their later years, and few families wantonly "warehouse" older members to a nursing home (American Association of Homes and Services for the Aging, 2012).

Older people are placed in a nursing home for a number of reasons: advancing age; a greater level of chronic disability; deteriorating mental and physical capacities; living alone, or lack of family members to provide help; female gender (women tend to outlive their husbands and end up alone); White race (Whites are twice as likely to enter nursing homes as Blacks); and time spent in a hospital or other health facility. About three out of four nursing home residents are aged 75 or older, and 7 out of 10 are women. The nursing home industry argues that the vast majority of nursing homes have dedicated staffs and try very hard to meet the needs of infirm older people (American Association of Homes and Services for the Aging, 2012).

Myth #7: *Myth: Most Older Adults Are Lonely.*
Reality: The conventional wisdom brings to mind a picture of a frail old man sadly looking off into space, housed in a nursing home with no loved ones or friends visiting him until the day he quietly dies. There are certainly cases like this, but older adults as a group are not necessarily lonely. Some researchers studying loneliness have found that it increases with age, being the strongest among the oldest age groups. Some researchers have found that loneliness decreases with advancing age. And some researchers have found no statistical relationship between age and loneliness (Hall & Havens, 2004).

Loneliness is likely to increase in old age as family and friendship networks become smaller. Social contacts tend to decrease after retirement and may continue to decline with the death of family members, and friends, change in residence after losing one's spouse, mobility difficulties, and poor health. To prevent feelings of isolation and loneliness, it is recommended that individuals keep in regular contact with older family members, friends, and neighbors and help them feel needed and valued. Local communities and groups are advised to increase the availability of programs and services for older people, enhance transportation programs for the elderly, develop low-cost leisure and educational activities, and involve older people in all levels of planning these services (Hall & Havens, 2004).

A study by AARP surveyed 3,012 people ages 45 and above. Using the UCLA Loneliness Scale the researchers found that 35% were chronically lonely, compared to 20% a decade earlier. Loneliness was equally prevalent regardless of race, gender, or level of education. Age, however, did make a difference: those who said they were suffering the most from loneliness were not the oldest but rather adults in their 40s and 50s (Edmondson, 2010).

Myth #8: *Older Adults Are Isolated from Younger Family Members.*
Reality: A national study (Troll, 1997) found that more than half of all people over age 65 who have children live either in the same household with an adult child or in the same neighborhood as a child. Contact with other family members, especially adult children, is rather frequent.

Most older adults enjoy their privacy, preferring not to live in the same house as their adult children and their grandchildren. Of older people who have adult children but live alone, however, half live within 10 minutes from a child. On the day they were interviewed for this study, half of the older people with children reported that they had seen one of their adult children the day they were interviewed, and about three-quarters reported having seen at least one of their adult children during the week preceding the interview. This study also revealed that even in those cases where the geographic distance between them is considerable, older and younger family members tend to stay in contact.

What about the quality of these contacts—a much more difficult characteristic to measure? One way to measure quality is to assess the amount of help family members give each other. In a national study, 7 out of every 10 older adults with children said they helped their children, and 7 out of every 10 older adults said they helped their grandchildren. Five out of every 10 said they even helped their great-grandchildren. Seven out of 10 older people also said they received help from their children. This help included home repairs and housework, care during an illness, and different kinds of gifts. In addition, older people reported that they helped their adult children by caring for grandchildren. In short, it appears that older people are not isolated from younger family members and that these contacts are generally happy ones (Allen, Blieszner, & Roberto, 2000).

Retirement

The stereotypical view of retirement is a dreary, downhill period of life in which people lose their self-esteem and immerse themselves in memories of better days; they stop being productive working citizens and slowly waste away. To the contrary, research shows that retired people are no more likely to be sick or depressed than people of the same age who are still on the job. In fact, most people adapt satisfactorily to retirement, with few long-term changes in their health, psychological well-being, or family relationships.

There are, of course, examples of people who find retirement difficult and depressing. One woman said of her recently retired husband, "He used to be a powerful executive with 200 employees under him. He would work long, hard hours and then come home to relax and enjoy his hobbies. He retired 5 years ago, and ever since he's been terribly depressed."

Most older people adjust well to voluntary retirement, especially those who get involved in new activities.
©Stockbyte/Getty Images

BOX 13.3 At Issue
Alzheimer's

What Is Alzheimer's?

Alzheimer's is the most common form of dementia and results when plaques and tangles develop in the brain and interfere with brain functioning (Alzheimer's Foundation of America, 2016). It is not clear what causes Alzheimer's, and there is no cure. It is progressive, and there is no hope for recovery. The onset of Alzheimer's usually occurs after age 60, with symptoms that include memory loss, decreased thinking and language skills, and behavioral changes. Approximately 10% of all people over the age of 65, and 50% of people over age 85, have Alzheimer's (WebMD, 2016). It has been estimated that the number of people age 65 and older will double by the year 2030 (Alzheimer's Foundation of America, 2016). Because people are living longer, we are seeing an increase in the number of people being diagnosed, resulting in an increase in family issues of caregiving and health care costs. For all involved in the lives of those living with Alzheimer's, it is emotionally, socially, and financially difficult.

Those Who Provide Care

Approximately 70% of people with Alzheimer's live at home (Kantrowitz & Springen, 2007, June 18). It is estimated that one to four family members care for each person who has the disease (Alzheimer's Foundation of America, 2016). Baby Boomers, those born between 1946 and 1964, are typically the caregivers, because it is their parents who are now in the age group most affected. These caregivers are often referred to as "the sandwich generation" because they are caught between caring for their own children, work, and caring for their parents.

People who care for those with Alzheimer's have a heavy burden. One woman talked about how her father could never be left alone, or he would walk out of the house and not know how to get back. Both she and her husband worked, and therefore he had to be in a day care facility during the day. At night they had to lock his bedroom door to prevent him from wandering off. Any change in schedule would mean her children and husband would need to fill in to help with his care. The responsibility was taking a toll on their marriage and family life. An additional component of this story is that he had been an abusive father and husband, which meant caring for him was an unwelcome burden. Her siblings, who lived far away, had no idea how difficult things were, and provided no help, which contributed to resentment toward her brothers and sisters.

Other caregivers include spouses of those with Alzheimer's. These caregivers often still feel love for their spouses, even though the person with Alzheimer's no longer recognizes the person they have been married to for many years. The person with Alzheimer's may become aggressive or even violent, and the weight of what to do next is heavy. One man's wife was relatively easy to care for because, even though she could not carry on a conversation and often did not recognize him, she would accompany him to social events. Even though she did not know what was being said, she would sit quietly and nodded knowingly when engaged in conversation.

Because of the increase in remarriages, there is an increasing number of late-life remarried spouses caring for Alzheimer patients (Sherman & Bauer, 2008). These caregivers sometimes inherit unresolved family issues. The caregiving spouse can end up being on the front lines dealing with family relationships, inheritance issues, and unresolved resentments.

All caregivers can easily become isolated and neglect their own needs. Caregivers often do not feel they have time or resources to have a social life, take time for their own interests, or spend time with family.

Even limited home care is expensive and is usually not covered by Medicare. Ultimately, nursing home care is likely to be necessary, and the cost can run as high as $65,000 to $75,000 per year, or even more. Not all nursing homes are equipped to care for elderly Alzheimer's patients, and therefore some patients may need to live in a facility some distance from family, which can add to the cost of care.

How to Prepare

It is important to talk with aging relatives, including parents, before health issues impact their lives. It is a difficult topic to broach. Who wants to talk about health issues, the loss of control, and finances with one's own parents, even though it is likely these issues will need to be faced at some point? It is also likely that aging relatives will not want to talk about these issues. The conversation might begin by asking parents about their wishes if the time should come when they cannot care for themselves. What would they like to have happen, and what resources are available to make that a reality? In the case of a late-life remarriage, it is especially important to have family discussions about these topics.

One of the issues receiving a great deal of attention is long-term care insurance. It typically covers some of the cost of nursing home or home care. The insurance premiums each month are lower when people begin paying for it early in life before health problems become evident.

Much controversy surrounds long-term care insurance today, with heated arguments coming from those who are for this type of insurance, and from those who are against it. Those who are thinking about this option should do their homework. This would include searching the internet and talking with many people—including family service professionals and other health specialists, insurance agents, and, especially, families who have dealt with Alzheimer's personally. The wrong decision could prove to be a very expensive mistake.

Fortunately, positive retirement stories are the general rule. Most men and women report they adjust quite well to voluntary retirement, and studies consistently find that satisfaction with life remains fairly high for the majority of retired people. Factors predicting a positive adjustment to retirement include good health (many older people leave the workforce because of poor health), economic security, and a supportive social network (Asebedo & Seay, 2014; Darkwa, 2004; Elderly Health Services, 2004).

As with any major life transition, retirement takes some adjustment. Retired people report a number of problems associated with this transition, including sleeplessness, aimlessness, and sadness over not seeing work friends and colleagues regularly. But other retirees are quick to point out that they have gotten involved in so many new activities that they have less free time than they did when they were working and would like to slow down a bit.

Retirement affects marriage in different ways. For couples who place a high value on intimacy and family relationships, retirement can bring more freedom to enjoy each other and the family. Some wives—especially those who always assumed traditional roles and traditional divisions of labor—are pessimistic about the husband's impending retirement, perhaps fearing the retiree will intrude on their domestic territory. This perspective is captured on a bumper sticker: *Retirement: Half as much money, twice as much husband.*

Researchers (Price & Nesteruk, 2015) have collected good advice about retirement from retirees:

1. *Develop a plan.* Early in retirement, retirees need to develop a plan for their lives, and identify activities that motivate them in some way. Too much unstructured time and lack of stimulation can be troublesome.

2. *Prepare financially.* The reality of living on a limited income proves to be difficult for many retirees. Of course, financial preparation for retirement has to begin early in life, and people need to save regularly and begin doing this early in their career.

3. *Expect the unexpected.* Changes in one's health status and unplanned caregiving responsibilities for one's parents or one's partner are likely to arise. Also, there is a good possibility that grandchildren will need care and attention. To meet these challenges, retirees need to be resilient and willing to make the best of the situation.

4. *Reexamine your social network.* The loss of the work role causes disequilibrium for some retirees, including a less hectic schedule, more time with a spouse, lost contact with former work colleagues, and more time alone. This means that the individual will need to reach out to others to reconfigure their social networks and establish new friendships.

As in every other time in life, retirement demands creative and thoughtful responses.

Retirement satisfaction in terms of financial resources can be affected by one's marital history. For example, divorce can affect one's wealth accumulation, which has an impact on how much money one has available in retirement. In a national study with a large sample, it was found that divorce affected wealth in retirement (Ulker, 2009). For those who divorced early in life and remarried, there was little effect on their financial resources in later stages of life because they had time to recover. However, for those who remained single, there was less wealth than for those who remained married, and this was especially true for women.

Long-Term Marriages

Stereotypes about older couples abound in our society. One common belief is that if you have survived many years together, you must be getting along extremely well. Counter to this opinion is the anonymous thought that, "Marriage is forever. And forever is a damned long time."

A number of family researchers have studied long-term marriages, trying to get closer to the truth. From their findings, George Rowe and Marcia Lasswell were able to divide **longevous marriages**—marriages that last 50 years or more—into three categories: (1) couples who are very happy and blissfully in love, (2) couples who are very unhappy but who continue the marriage out of habit or fear, and (3) couples in between, who are neither very happy nor very unhappy and accept the situation (cited in Sweeney, 1982). Lasswell estimated the "very happy" number at roughly 20% of the total and the "very unhappy" number at 20%. Both researchers also found a negative relationship between the number of children couples had and marital happiness: Couples with larger families tended to have less happy marriages. "We can't explain that, except the study indicated that a dip in marital happiness is almost always concurrent with the time the children are a heavy responsibility for parents," Rowe said (p. 23). He theorized that the more children a couple has, the longer this period of responsibility lasts and the more the relationship is drained by parenting responsibilities.

In a similar vein, Timothy Brubaker (1985) reviewed 25 studies of older couples' relationships and identified three common patterns in the studies:

1. Some couples experience a decline in marital quality during the middle years of marriage, and then the marriage improves in the later years.
2. For some couples, the marriage declines gradually in quality as the years go by, with the trend line from the newlywed days to later life moving steadily downward.
3. For some couples, the trend line remains stable in the middle years and into the later years. Those who were happy when the children were at home will remain happy when the children leave home and when they retire. Those who were unhappy as a couple when the kids were at home will continue to be unhappy when the nest empties and they retire.

In general, the quality of the marital relationship shows continuity over the years. Couples who did not get along well in their early years together are likely not to get along well in the later years of their marriage. "In the later years, those who have vital, rewarding relationships will most generally experience continued positive interactions within the marriage, while those who have difficult, unsatisfying relationships will most likely experience continued negative marital interactions" (Brubaker, 1991, p. 229).

What can we conclude? Researchers have found that simply because people remain married for a long time is no guarantee that they are happy with the marriage. Some long-term married couples have very happy marriages, while some have very unhappy marriages. Some may have stayed married for so many years simply out of habit. Some may have stayed married for so many years to honor religious and cultural traditions. Some may have stayed married for so many years because they saw no better options in life. And some may have stayed married for so many years because they genuinely loved and cared for each other and enjoyed each other's company.

We could not find more recent research on long-term marriages, which is unfortunate. But we would hazard this guess: Because divorce is common in our society and because divorce is much more acceptable today than it was in the past, we would predict that fewer and fewer couples will stay together for a long time if they are unhappy. And because of this, in the long run, marriages will steadily improve in quality. In a word, because of the option to divorce, there will be fewer and fewer long-term unhappy marriages. And this will mean that a higher percentage of marriages will be happy ones.

Time, of course, will tell.

Losing a Spouse

After the loss of my husband
The years go fast
But the days and nights are long.

—A BEREAVED 90-YEAR-OLD WIDOW

The death of a spouse is a difficult life transition for most, and for some it is a devastating personal crisis. Brubaker (1990) outlined three characteristic stages of the grieving process:

1. **Crisis-loss stage of grief.** In the first few days and weeks after the loss, the survivor is in a chaotic stage of shock. Common reactions are "I can't believe this is happening to me," "I'll do anything to bring her back," "What am I going to do now?"

2. **Transition stage of grief.** In the transition period, the survivor begins trying to create a new life. Grief lessens in its intensity, and the bereaved person sees the possibility of a life ahead.

3. **New-life stage of grief.** The survivor changes her or his lifestyle and proves to the world and to herself or himself that it is possible to live satisfactorily as a single person. The widow or widower develops an identity without the partner.

Grief lasts longer than was long believed to be the case—up to 2 years, according to research on widows. A widow's grief can include a range of feelings, from sadness and anger to fear and anxiety. The prevalence of anxiety in the first 3 years after a husband's death led one researcher to see its role in mourning as crucial. Other researchers see depression as a significant risk among bereaved spouses (Bruce, 2002).

But other studies question whether depression is universal among the bereaved. These studies also indicate that sudden deaths are not necessarily more distressing than expected ones, and have found that bereaved people who had strained marriages actually feel less grief than those who had close and loving ones. Some widows and widowers experience profound depression in the months and even years following their loss. Many are comforted by "confronting and working through their loss." Yet the majority of older bereaved spouses see death as simply a part of life—albeit a sad part—and for them recovery and resilience is the rule and not the exception (Carr, 2006).

In old age, loved ones with whom one had intimate relationships may no longer be alive, but this does not mean that people no longer feel intimate connections (Troll, 2001). Many older people feel connected to their deceased intimate partners through prayer, photos, visits to the cemetery, and other ways they honor the dead. Commitment and caring are maintained after the death. Cognitive intimacy is maintained by thinking of the departed partner. Though physical encounters cannot continue, some individuals substitute heirlooms or pictures to preserve the physical presence of the loved one. And interdependent intimacy is maintained by hearing the voice of the dead speaking through one's own thoughts.

"Do you talk with Joan?" we asked one elderly husband who had lost his wife to cancer 7 years earlier. "Oh, yes," Bill replied. "She's right here in the kitchen with me now, helping get the tea and cookies together." Bill maintained his intimate emotional connections with his wife after death, and found strength in her presence. As the old adage goes, "To live in the hearts we leave behind is to live forever."

In the United States, 11 out of every 12 people who have lost a spouse are women. This is because women live longer than men and because they tend to marry men older than themselves. Three out of four wives can expect to become widows (Daggett, 2002). While past generations of older people often stayed in difficult marriages because of religious or cultural prohibitions against divorce, Baby Boomers today have more freedom to divorce if their marriage proves unsatisfactory. If the baby boom generation dissolves troubled marriages, the remaining boomers late in life may be more likely to have warm and close relationships, and may be the most grief-stricken upon their loss. It has also been argued that marriage has been idealized in recent decades and we now seek a *soul mate*, who shares our interests and passions, rather than a *helpmate* who just pays the bills or washes the dishes. If our partner is an irreplaceable *soul mate*, the loss can be much more devastating (Carr, 2006). Three years after her husband, President Ronald Reagan, had died, Nancy Reagan said, "I keep thinking of all those people who said time . . . it'll be much better in time." Mrs. Reagan disagreed: "Well, not for me. If anything, it's gotten worse. I miss him more. I'm remembering more little things that we did together. It's harder" (ABC News, 2011).

As one bereaved widow told us, "Society says, 'Get over it. The funeral's over, get off the floor and quit grieving.' But Larry was my best friend for 54 years. You never get over losing your best friend. To hell with society." For one woman's story, see Box 13.4.

Couple Relationships in the Later Years

Because people are living longer, there are more opportunities to develop new couple relationships after a late-life divorce or widowhood. Many in their 60s, 70s, 80s, and even 90s begin new relationships that end up in marriage or cohabiting. Others choose an increasingly popular option of maintaining separate homes while in a committed intimate relationship (Levaro, 2011).

Women's life expectancy is greater than men's, so there are more women available than men. In fact, by the time people reach their late 70s, there three times as many women as men, and most of these women are widowed (Levaro, 2009). Some women may believe that their chances of meeting a man are slim and therefore do not see an intimate relationship as feasible, while men report greater loneliness than women and often marry. Marriage is often viewed as the desirable option for couples because it often meets both social and religious expectations.

There are many reasons, however, why older individuals might not want to marry (Levaro, 2011). For example, there may be financial considerations, where their respective children's inheritance may be affected. There also may be a loss of pension benefits with remarriage, especially for women. Another concern may be potential medical costs or medical care issues, which are often felt by women more than men because women are likely to live longer.

Cohabitation has become an increasingly acceptable choice for aging adults, just as it has for younger generations. Cohabitation allows couples to have an intimate relationship without the legal ramifications of marriage. This arrangement, however, creates new issues for children and grandchildren, who may not know how to respond to this new arrangement (Levaro, 2011). For example, how are family heirlooms to be handled with a new person living in the home? What are the children's and grandchildren's obligations to this new partner? Many children and grandchildren are delighted that their parent or grandparent has found happiness in later life, and others are concerned about how to respond to the new partner.

Levaro (2011) describes a third option that some elderly couples have chosen—**living apart together.** This term describes the living arrangement for couples who are in a committed intimate relationship but choose to maintain separate homes. Women are typically the driving force behind this arrangement, because they often have the most to lose in marriage or cohabiting. This choice allows couples to have a relationship without the issues around inheritance, and it offers freedom from the potential obligation of medical caregiving.

BOX 13.4   At Issue

I Am Aware That I Am No Longer Anyone's "Most Important Person": The Desolation of Grief

As I write, it is 5 months to the day since my darling died. He died in our home, where I had nursed him for the preceding 7 months, with the loving assistance of family and friends, as well as paid carers. For most of that time, Thomas, as I shall call him, was bedridden and incontinent, and was becoming increasingly demented yet subdued by the morphine which gave him effective relief from pain but did not relieve his anxiety state.

In the months before he came home from hospital to live and then to die, Thomas suffered what in hindsight I believe were multiple TIAs (transitory ischemic attacks—silent, indiscernible little strokes), which gradually took from him his ability to initiate thought, to plan, to process or perform complex thoughts and tasks and which caused confusion, loss of balance and co-ordination and falls. One fall, whilst in the acute specialist hospital in which he was receiving tests, resulted in a fractured femur in an artificial hip joint. Despite the fracture being mended with surgery, he never bore his own weight again. Underlying all these misadventures were his cardiac disease treated by stenting, coronary arterial by-pass surgery and a pacemaker and prostate cancer which had progressed to secondaries in his bones. The compounding effects of all of these factors meant I had to take up the Power of Attorney and Enduring Guardianship which Thomas had earlier entrusted to me, as he was no longer competent to manage his affairs.

It was an honor and a privilege to be able to care for him in our home during his final weeks and months. We both knew death was coming and every moment was therefore intense and precious.

Now, today, there is the void. My emotions are many and varied, but predominately that of desolation, despite being surrounded by dear and caring friends and two willing and helpful brothers, and being kept busy with the many tasks that must occupy one in the immediate days and weeks after the death of a next of kin:

- whom to inform, personal, professional and statutory bodies;
- funeral to arrange;
- clothes and personal items to be distributed among his children and other relatives, many of whom are at a distance, with relationships with me and their father strained;
- papers to be prepared for solicitors (probate) and the tax office (inland revenue);
- bank accounts closed;
- and soon, financial assets to be distributed, equitably, if not amicably! ("Where there is a will, there is a relative" has been quoted to me on more than one occasion since his death!)

My emotions: a deep sadness, sense of bewilderment, loss of purpose and focus, and the death of my sense of fun and capacity to enjoy much of anything; anger toward his relatives who stayed away when he so wanted them to visit near to the end. Each morning when I wake, the empty space beside me brings the reality of my loss right back to my consciousness, again and again. I continue to live in the home we have shared for 27 years, and tend the garden in which we were married. Its emptiness makes it a lonely place and yet it is the place richest in our memories. I have surrounded myself with photos of my man, mostly ones of him smiling, at least one in every room, including even at the kitchen sink, so that I can see and talk to him in all those domestic spaces, and as I prepare and eat my meals from which I currently gain little pleasure. I talk to him out loud, voicing my displeasure at his absence, and telling him it is time to come home. I remind him of happy events from our past, and of the debate we used to have about which one of us would die first, so as not to have to empty the attic! (We are both hoarders!) I tell him that it is unfair that he did not let me win that one!

I know that pleasure in eating and in socializing will return in time, but for now, it takes a lot of effort to just do the routine tasks each day. I feel I must keep my "face on," so as to not to pass my sadness on to others and so dampen their spirits. So, sometimes I choose to be alone. Mostly I cry on my own, too. I am aware that I am no longer anyone's "most important person." I am also mindful though, that I have had more happiness from a relationship, for almost half of my life than some people ever have. I am also aware that the effects of chronic stress and fatigue from the caring role I willingly took on will pass and that I will mend.

A Postscript

Four years and four weeks later . . . the pain is still there, but not intense, and certainly not constant. I have again found joy in living, can laugh and sing again. Time and friendships can take the credit! I retain a feeling of disbelief, thinking he will soon walk into our home and explain his lateness! Mail still arrives for him, and that still stings. But now the pain is different: periodic feeling of loneliness, but *always* the sense that I am alone in the world, despite longstanding friends, and some new, fun ones, too. A comfortable home, financial security, creative interests and hobbies, meaningful part-time employment, and still I feel my life lacks direction and purpose. Relationship and intimacy are what I cherish most, and these I still lack. Now, though, I feel ready to love again, and to commit, though I suspect to a partnership that would, inevitably, be different to that of cohabitation and marriage. Not just because, to date, the men I know pale in comparison to the good character, intellect, and capacity for humour of my husband. I am still nobody's most important person . . . .

Source: This story was written by a friend of ours in Australia, a counselor with many years of experience working with grieving families, who wishes to remain anonymous. Printed by permission.

Another benefit is that after so many years, individuals have developed their own habits and preferences about living arrangements. Living apart allows individuals to retain the privacy of their own home and maintain their individual lifestyles.

If we look to aging couples around us, we are likely to see all of these examples of couple relationships. One couple lived together for 15 years, got engaged when both were 61, and at age 62 decided to marry. The bride's maid of honor at the wedding was her granddaughter, age 10, and the best man was the bride's father, who was 90 years old. The priest who married them said he had never conducted a wedding where there was an 80-year age difference between the best man and the maid of honor. Another couple who were both widowed started *dating* when she was 73 and he was 75. They maintained their separate homes but went to dinner and social events together and occasionally took trips together. There are a variety of ways couples develop and maintain relationships in later years of life, and these couples are making choices that fit their life circumstances and preferences.

Changes in Family Dynamics in the Later Years

Sibling relationships in middle and older adulthood have recently become a new area of research. Most sibling relationships remain strong and positive throughout the years and are important for the older adult's well-being. Research indicates in the later years that sisters are the closest, followed by cross-sex siblings, and then brothers (Van Volkom, 2006). Sometimes events in life trigger the opportunity to reconnect in later years, even when siblings had not been particularly close before. A spouse may have died, and relationships with siblings may become closer to fill the void. Here is how two sisters in their 80s developed a closer relationship:

> *Two sisters, one age 80 and the other age 86, have always kept in touch but have not been especially close. They live 1,000 miles apart and have led very different lives. One was married to a chemist, and the other was married to a farmer. Over the years they would see each other once every year or two and would talk on the phone occasionally. In recent years, as they entered old age, they began calling each other regularly—usually every day—to talk about the mundane, but personal and real, events of daily life.*
>
> *One was widowed 4 years ago after 56 years of marriage and did quite well in her grief with the help of family and friends in a very close-knit farming community. Recently her sister's husband died suddenly. Because the sister had no family nearby and lived in a large city, she had less family and community support. She began calling her sister in the farming community even more often—sometimes several times a day. They talked about losing husbands, with the one who has been widowed longer providing sage advice for the sister who just recently experienced her husband's death. They developed a very intimate emotional relationship with these frequent telephone conversations, even though they have not seen each other for 2 years.*

Summary

- Middle age roughly spans ages 35 to 65, a period during which many couples are (1) still raising teenagers, (2) launching young adults and then coping with their absence from or return to the home, and (3) entering retirement.

- For many, the challenges of middle age include coping with routinization in the job, developing a new or second career outside the home (especially for women), coping with the transition of menopause and "male menopause," maintaining the

- emotional and sexual health of the marriage, dealing with the empty or the cluttered nest, and managing the demands of aging parents.
- Marriages fail in the middle years for five main reasons: verbal, physical, or emotional abuse; alcohol or drug abuse; cheating; "falling out of love"; or different values or lifestyles.
- Recommendations for strengthening a marriage in the middle years include making each other the number one priority; being alert to signs of marital trouble; establishing an equal partnership; helping build each other's self-esteem; balancing togetherness and personal growth; finding creative ways to keep the sexual relationship exciting; networking with other committed couples; evaluating the marriage and attending marriage enrichment workshops; changing frustrating job situations; and changing one's lifestyle rather than one's partner to revitalize the marriage. Happiness is key to a content spouse and is the best way to prevent infidelity from occurring.
- People in their middle years are often *sandwiched* between two or more competing responsibilities: caring for adolescents, dealing with boomerang kids (adult children returning to the parental nest), and caring for their own aging parents. The results can be both positive (a closer relationship between the caregiver and the aging parent) and negative (too much stress).
- Grandparenting reinforces continuity of the generations and brings pleasure to most grandparents. Of those 65 or older, 83% have living grandchildren.
- Today, more grandparents are living with a grandchild. Most recent statistics indicate that about 7 million grandparents are living with a grandchild, compared to 5.8 million grandparents doing so in 2000. Among all these grandparents living with grandchildren, 37% were serving as the grandkids' primary caregiver.
- For most American grandparents, however, child care is only an occasional responsibility. One survey found that among grandparents who had helped with child care in the past 12 months, nearly three out of four (72%) said they did so only occasionally. About one in five (22%) said they provided child care regularly.
- U.S. society is undergoing a *demographic revolution* due to the increasing life span of its population. Our average life expectancy is 78.8 years.
- Conventional wisdom about old age includes the following inaccurate beliefs: at 65, *you're over the hill;* most older adults are poor; older adults are not interested in sex; older adults are usually sick; older adults become senile; most older adults end up in nursing homes; most older adults are lonely; and older adults are isolated from younger family members.
- Contrary to stereotypes, retirement is not a negative period of life. Most people who retire voluntarily adapt satisfactorily to retirement, with few long-term effects on their health, psychological well-being, or family relationships.
- Many people might assume that couples who have been married for many years must be very happy with each other. However, research has found that long-term marriages—those that last 50 years or more—can be divided into three categories: (1) couples who are very happy and blissfully in love (perhaps 20% of all long-term marriages); (2) couples who are very unhappy but who continue the marriage out of habit or fear; and (3) couples in between, who are neither very happy nor very unhappy and accept the situation.
- Since divorce is more accepted in our society today, long-term unhappy marriages are less likely in the future. As religious, cultural, and economic constraints diminish, unhappy marriages are more likely to dissolve, rather than drag on year after year after year. Alzheimer's is a disease that affects many people, usually beginning after age 60, with increasing likelihood as one gets older. Caring for someone with this disease can be overwhelming physically, emotionally, and financially, and often this care is provided by family members.
- The death of a spouse is a difficult life transition for most, and for some it is a devastating personal crisis. If our partner is an irreplaceable *soul mate,* the loss can be especially troubling.
- Because people are living longer, there are many opportunities to develop new couple relationships after a late-life divorce or widowhood. Many in their 60s, 70s, 80s, and even 90s begin new relationships that end up in marriage or cohabitation. Others choose an increasingly popular option of maintaining separate homes while in a committed intimate relationship. This arrangement has been called *living apart together.*
- Most sibling relationships remain strong and positive throughout the years and are important for the older adult's well-being. Research indicates that in the later years sisters tend to be the closest, followed by cross-sex siblings, and then brothers.

Key Terms

middle age	boomerang kids
Baby Boomer	cluttered nest
midlife crisis	sandwich generation
menopause	old age
androgen	ageism
male menopause	Alzheimer's disease
empty-nest syndrome	longevous marriage
spacious nest	living apart together

Activities

1. Discuss career issues with a middle-aged man or woman. Ask the individual to trace her or his career development. What conclusions can you come to?
2. Interview your parents (if they are middle-aged) or other middle-aged individuals about the stresses of midlife and their means of coping with them.

3. Interview a middle-aged person who is "sandwiched" between trying to support adolescent or young-adult children and caring for an elderly family member. Prepare 10 or 15 questions for the interview and record 5 or 6 general conclusions.
4. After reading the section on grandparenthood, prepare some questions and interview a grandparent. This can be an easy and rewarding exercise because grandparents and young adults often have an automatic bond.
5. What was your relationship with your grandparents like? What kind of a grandparent do you want to be? Share your thoughts with other members of a small group.
6. Write a short 2- to 3-page story about one of your grandparents.
7. How do you define "old"? When you, personally, are old, what precisely will that mean? Write down your thoughts and then discuss them in a small group.
8. When you are old and, presumably, married, how would you like your marriage to look? Describe the strengths of your marriage on paper and share with a small group.
9. Interview an older couple. Ask them to tell you the story of their family, including information about their parents and grandparents. Focus part of the interview on intergenerational relationships.
10. Write down your feelings about death and share them in a small-group discussion. Record the similarities and differences in the group's observations.

Suggested Readings

AARP. (2016a). Web site: http://www.aarp.org. AARP is a large, well-known, and politically powerful organization providing information and advocacy for people age 50 and older.

AARP. (2016b). Online community. Web site: https://community.aarp.org/t5/Late-Life-Divorce/bd-p/bg41. A very useful resource for older people. Online anonymous discussions on relationships, love, marriage, sex, and myriad other topics of importance to older people. The ongoing dialogue on divorce in later life is especially interesting.

Aiken, L. R. (2004). *Dying, death, and bereavement* (4th ed.). Mahwah, NJ: Erlbaum. A brief but comprehensive survey of research, writings, and professional practices on death and dying.

Aldwin, C. M., Park, C. L., Spiro, A. III, & Abeles, R. P. (2007). *Handbook of health psychology and aging*. New York, NY: The Guilford Press. How biological, psychological, and social factors over the life course affect aging.

Alzheimer's Foundation of America. (2016). Helping more people today than we did yesterday. Web site: http://www.alzfdn.org/.

Booth, S. (2010, February). They're golden. *Real Simple*, pp. 127–135. "There's nothing so nice as a new marriage," the screenwriter Ben Hecht once wrote. But the six couples featured in this magazine story beg to differ. More than 50 years into their marriages, they share their unforgettable moments and secrets of staying together, happily.

Boss, P. (2011). *Loving someone who has dementia: How to find hope while coping with stress and grief*. San Francisco, CA: Jossey-Bass.

Boss, P. (2013). Closure: Why it's a myth. *National Council on Family Relations. Family Focus*, FF58, pp. 1–3. Pauline Boss argues that we need to become more comfortable with the idea of living with grief, rather than closure. Grief comes and goes, with wider intervals between feelings of sadness as time goes on.

Boston Women's Health Book Collective. (2006). *Our bodies, ourselves: Menopause*. New York, NY: Touchstone/Simon & Schuster.

Brubaker, T. H. (1985). *Later life families*. Beverly Hills, CA: Sage.

Brubaker, T. H. (1991). Families in later life: A burgeoning research area. In A. Booth (Ed.), *Contemporary families: Looking forward, looking back* (pp. 226–248). Minneapolis, MN: National Council on Family Relations.

Bruce, M. L. (2002). Psychosocial risk factors for depressive disorders in late life. *Biological Psychiatry, 52*(3), 175–184.

Cacciatore, J., & DeFrain, J. (2015). The world of bereavement: Cultural perspectives on death in families. Cham, Switzerland: Springer International. From a global perspective, the book explores the sensitive balance between personal and private aspects of grief, the social and cultural variables that unite communities in bereavement, and the universal experience of loss.

Daggett, L. M. (2002). Living with loss: Middle-aged men face spousal bereavement. *Qualitative Health Research, 12*(5), 625–639.

Edmondson, B. (2010). All the lonely people. *AARP Magazine*. Researchers find a rise in loneliness in recent years. Web site: http://www.aarp.org/personal-growth/transitions/info-09-2010/all_the_lonely_people.html.

Fry, R., Cohn, D'V., Livingston, G., & Taylor, P. (2011). The rising age gap in economic well-being: The old prosper relative to the young. *Pew Social & Demographic Trends*. Web site: http://www.pewsocialtrends.org/2011/11/07/the-rising-age-gap-in-economic-well-being/. Researchers find that households headed by older adults have made dramatic gains over younger adults the past quarter century in terms of economic well-being.

Kornhaber, A. (2004). *The grandparent solution: How parents can build a family team for practical, emotional, and financial success*. San Francisco, CA: Jossey-Bass.

Kuba, C. A. (2006). *Navigating the journey of aging parents: What care receivers want*. New York, NY: Taylor & Francis.

National Center on Elder Abuse. (2016). NCEA, National Center on Elder Abuse, Administration on Aging. Web site: http://www.ncea.aoa.gov/ Excellent resources for understanding and dealing with elder abuse.

National Institute on Aging. (2016, January 21). Mourning the death of a spouse. Web site: https://www.nia.nih.gov/health/publication/mourning-death-spouse. A very useful discussion of bereavement and grief, and ideas on how to endure the loss.

Niemeyer, R. A. (2011). *Grief and bereavement in contemporary society: Bridging research and practice*. New York, NY: Routledge.

Qualls, S. H. (2013). "Caregiving is just what families do": Challenges of aging families and health. National Council on Family Relations. *Family Focus on Aging*, FF59, pp. F2–F20. Practical information for professionals and families.

Rank, M. R., & Williams, J. H. (2010). A life course approach to understanding poverty among older American adults. *Families in Society: The Journal of Contemporary Social Services, 91*, 337–341. Nearly half of all elderly Americans will encounter at least 1 year of poverty or near poverty between the ages of 60 and 90.

Rowe, D. (2008). *What should I believe? Why our beliefs about the nature of death and the purpose of life dominate our lives*. London and New York: Routledge. If we use our beliefs as a defense against our feelings of worthlessness, we feel compelled to force our beliefs on other people by coercion or aggression. But if we can create a set of beliefs expressed in religious or philosophical metaphors that are meaningful to us, we can live in peace with ourselves and others.

Silverstein, M., & Giarrusso, R. (2010). Aging and family life: A decade review. *Journal of Marriage and Family, 72* (October), 1039–1058. An excellent overview of recent trends in research.

Skogrand, L., Henderson, K., & Higginbotham, B. (2006). Sandwich generation (fact sheet). Utah State University Cooperative Extension. Web site: http://extension.usu.edu/cooperative.

Troll, L. E. (2001). When the world narrows: Intimacy with the dead? *Generations, 25*(2), 55–58.

Ulker, A. (2008). Wealth holdings and portfolio allocation of the elderly: The role of marital history. *Journal of Family Economic Issues, 30*, 90–108. Death and divorce earlier in life can significantly affect the accumulation of wealth among the elderly.

Van Volkom, M. (2006). Sibling relationships in middle and older adulthood: A review of the literature. *Marriage and Family Review, 40*, 151–170.

Visit the text-specific Online Learning Center at **www.mhhe.com/olson9e** for practice tests, chapter summaries, and PowerPoint slides.

Design Element: © Alicia Grünkind/EyeEm/Getty Images

PART FOUR
Challenges and Opportunities

14 Stress, Abuse, and Family Problems

©Pixdeluxe/iStock/Getty Images

- Intimacy, Strengths, and Diversity
- Cross-Cultural Perspectives on Couple and Family Stress
- What We Know About Stress
- War and Its Effect on Families
- Family Coping Strategies
- Domestic Violence
- Child Abuse and Neglect
- Sibling and Child-to-Parent Abuse
- Alcohol Problems in Families
- Summary
- Key Terms
- Activities
- Suggested Readings

Intimacy, Strengths, and Diversity

Individuals, couples, and families have extraordinary abilities when it comes to facing the many problems in the world today. Couple and family intimacy is one of the most important components in successfully dealing with life's problems. We know that pulling together as a family—using close couple and family bonds—helps us get through difficult times. Developing and maintaining close and intimate relationships with friends and extended family, and relying on those relationships, is important in dealing with difficulties. Intimacy involves sharing feelings, sorrows, and joys, which helps people when there is stress in life.

> *One individual had grown up learning to be very independent in life. She had learned that she could handle most crises in life, with little help from friends or family. At age 45 she is going through a divorce and a diagnosis of cancer. Even though she had handled most crises successfully, without relying on others for emotional support, she knew this was different—it was going to be more stressful than anything she had experienced thus far in her life.*
>
> *She approached two close friends and her sister and asked if she could rely on them as she went through the loss of her marriage and her diagnosis with cancer. She already had a close, intimate relationship with each of these people and now she needed to rely on them for support. Each of the people she approached had the same response of surprise. She had never asked for this kind of emotional support before and, of course, they would be there for as long as she needed.*
>
> *She called or got together with these close friends and family member when she needed to cry, needed to make decisions, or when she just needed the comfortable presence of someone who cared about her. Along the way she wished she had learned to rely on intimate relationships in getting through difficult times earlier in her life. Why did she wait until she was middle aged before she learned this important lesson?*

Contrary to the notion that strength means facing a problem without any help, research indicates that the strength to cope with difficulties comes from the close and intimate relationships with loved ones, friends, and relatives.

Every couple and family will experience challenges. Strong marriages and strong families will be able to weather difficult times more successfully than people in marriages and families that are not strong. In this chapter we will describe a study of people who experienced a traumatic childhood and relied on their inner strengths along with using other strategies to become relatively happy and healthy adults. It is common for individuals to tell you that going through difficult times often makes you a better, more caring person. Facing difficulties and coming through the crisis successfully can also result in stronger marriages and families.

There is variability and diversity in how people define problems and difficulties. One of the models of family stress described in this chapter includes the definition the family or individual gives to the event. For example, some cultures have extended-family networks that provide care for children beyond the nuclear family. In such a culture, an adolescent leaving home to live with a relative may not be defined as a crisis. This may be true, for example, in American Indian families. In a culture where children are expected to live with their parents until they are grown, however, this event might be defined as a real crisis, and seen as a child running away from home.

Intimacy, strengths, and diversity all play a part in how people deal with family problems. Close relationships provide resiliency and strength that are not available when one tries to deal with crises alone, and this is true in all cultures.

Cross-Cultural Perspectives on Couple and Family Stress

The following are some of the aspects of family stress that are common across cultural groups. These are generalized principles that emerged from studying family strengths and stressors in different countries and cultures around the world (DeFrain & Asay, 2007).

1. *All stressors either begin or end up in the family.* No matter what the origin of a stressor, it eventually affects the couple and family system and all its members.
2. *Families from all cultural groups experience couple and family stress.* Although the causes of couple and family stress and the types of issues that are most stressful may vary by cultural group, all couples and families experience and understand the concept of stress.
3. *To manage their stress, couples and families tend to first use internal resources (those inside the family system) before seeking external resources (those outside the family system).* Across many cultural groups, most families rely on their internal resources first, seeking external help only after internal resources have proven to be inadequate.
4. *In many cultures, the extended family system is considered "the family" rather than the nuclear family system. In families with strong extended-family structures, the major resources come from inside the extended family, while fewer resources come from the nuclear family.* For this reason, many researchers and practitioners believe the extended family system, when functioning well, can be much stronger and more resilient than a nuclear family system, which may be weak and isolated from sources of support.
5. *All couples and families have some internal strengths for managing stress in their systems.* However, cross-cultural studies of families have seldom sought to identify family strengths within a cultural group. Instead, they have focused on the problems in families from different cultures. By building on a strengths model, we will be able to more clearly identify useful coping strategies across cultures. And when researchers do this, they are likely to find that approaches to stress and coping from one culture to the next can be remarkably similar.

What We Know About Stress

People lead complicated lives, and the term **stress** is used often in today's society to refer to the daily pressure we all encounter (Monat, Lazarus, & Reevy, 2007). Here we will talk about stress and coping as individuals. Later in the chapter we will describe how families experience and manage stress.

There are three levels of stress. First, there is physiological stress, which is the body's harmful reaction to whatever happens. There is a fast-growing body of evidence that stress causes physical reactions in our bodies, such as increased blood pressure or decreased immune response. Second, there is psychological stress, which involves appraising the threat, resulting in an emotional reaction. Finally, there is sociocultural stress, which is the disturbance of social systems. Examples of sociocultural stress might be war, neighborhood violence, unemployment, or poverty. The effect of the stress of war on individuals and families is discussed elsewhere in this chapter. Stress and emotion are interdependent—where there is stress, there is emotion, and sometimes the reverse is true (Lazarus, 2007).

Coping with Stress

We are coping when we say things like "We're hangin' in there" or, as people sometimes say in the Midwest, "It could be worse." Each of us has different ways of coping, and how we cope affects those around us. **Coping** is what we do when we identify something as potentially harmful or stressful (Kleinke, 2007). Coping involves a certain amount of effort or planning, the outcome will not always be positive, and the process takes place over time. Coping can be either problem-focused or emotion-focused. When we do problem-focused coping, we either try to change the situation or behaviors of others or change our attitudes. Emotion-focused coping is managing our own emotional distress and doing such things as exercising or seeking support.

People can respond to stress in a variety of ways, such as confronting the stressful situation, ignoring the stressful situation, or problem solving to change the situation (Kleinke, 2007). Successful coping usually involves being flexible, making accurate appraisals of the situation, and anticipating long-term effects of a coping response. For example, a couple in love is talking about getting married. The stressful situation is that one partner has found a "dream job" several thousand miles away, while the other partner is quite happy in the job she already has in the town where they live. Successful coping for the couple will involve flexible thinking upon the part of both individuals; carefully thinking through the long-term effects of the decision they make; and accurately appraising their relationship as it now stands. How can they come to a solution that meets each other's needs? How much compromise will each have to make? How will they judge if they are doing the right thing? And, if they go ahead with their decision, how will they judge down the road if it was the right decision? If things do not work out, will they be able to avoid blaming each other?

Successful coping means you take on life's challenges with personal control and hope (Kleinke, 2007). It means you try to find solutions to problems by developing a plan to address the situation, get advice and support from others, and use the stressful situation as an opportunity to grow. It usually involves a sense of humor and patience. People all have their own personalities that determine how they respond to stress. What we do know is that how we respond can affect our health and can also affect our future opportunities and choices. See Box 14.1 to learn about "ambiguous loss" and how families cope when there is a lack of closure or uncertainty after the loss of a loved one.

Stress and Life Events

The classic work of Thomas H. Holmes, Richard H. Rahe, and their colleagues (Holmes & Ella, 1989; Holmes & Rahe, 1967) has greatly influenced much of the current research on the relationship between life changes and signs of emotional and physiological stress in individuals (Cooper & Dewe, 2007). These pioneering researchers developed a scale of 43 *life events* that require some type of change of behavior, or readjustment. The scale is called the Holmes and Rahe Social Readjustment Rating Scale, but it is often referred to as the Holmes and Rahe Stress Test. These life events include personal, family, financial, and occupational stressors. Table 14.1 lists the top 14 stressors identified by Holmes and Rahe. It is noteworthy that 11 of the top 14 stressors are clearly marriage and family issues, while all 14 top stressors affect couples and families in some way. In fact, the scale could legitimately be called a Marriage and Family Stress Test.

Holmes and Rahe found a relationship between life changes and health. Of those people who scored between 0 and 150 points on the scale, more than 30% experienced a serious negative health change in the 2 years that followed. (A serious negative health change might be the development of rheumatoid arthritis, clinical depression, cancer, the onset of alcoholism, or a heart attack.) Of those who scored between 151 and 300 points, about 50%

TABLE 14.1 Stress Test by Holmes and Rahe

Event	Points
* 1. Death of spouse	100
* 2. Divorce	73
* 3. Marital separation	65
4. Jail term	63
* 5. Death of close family member	63
6. Personal injury or loss	53
* 7. Marriage	50
8. Fired at work/lost job	47
* 9. Marital reconciliation	45
*10. Retirement	45
*11. Change in health of family member	44
*12. Pregnancy	40
*13. Sex difficulties	39
*14. Gain of new family member	39

*Stressors which are clearly marriage and family issues.

Note: Impact points indicate the severity of the impact of the stressor on individuals, couples, or families.

Source: "The Social Readjustment Rating Scale" by T. H. Holmes and R. H. Rahe, *Journal of Psychosomatic Research, 11,* p. 213.

experienced a serious negative health change in the 2 years that followed. And of those who scored more than 300 points, almost 90% experienced a serious negative health change in the 2 years following the rating.

Holmes and Rahe found that physical and emotional problems are likely to occur when individuals experience a cluster of major and minor changes in life. As an example, a middle-aged woman scored above 700 on the Holmes and Rahe Stress Test. She received her divorce in January and remarried in August; her new husband moved out 3 months later; and by late November she had a new live-in companion. Her mother died during the year, and the woman started and lost two jobs. She had a sprinkling of other life changes during the year, including two car accidents and many bills. As might be predicted, she became very depressed and considered suicide. The relationship between stressful events and major health problems in this woman's life is quite clear. (To take the Holmes-Rahe Stress Inventory yourself, visit the American Stress Institute web site: http://www.stress.org/holmes-rahe-stress-inventory/).

This pioneering work laid the groundwork for what we know today about the link between stress and physical illness (Cooper & Dewe, 2007). There is significant research that connects stress with breast cancer, cardiovascular disease, and the common cold (Jones & Bright, 2007). Some research suggests that all kinds of cancers might be related to stressful life events.

Breast Cancer and Negative Life Events. Research that supports the idea that cancer and stress are related dates back to 1900 (Jones & Bright, 2007). These studies suggested that the loss of a close relative was often the incident that resulted in cancer. More recent work in the 1990s focused on breast cancer and its relation to negative life events. The results of these studies are mixed. Although some studies show a relationship, other studies show

BOX 14.1 At Issue

Ambiguous Loss: When We Are Uncertain If a Person Is In or Out of Our Family

In the 1970s, I was interested in family stress and especially why some families could cope with high stress while others could not. I focused on what I proposed was an immense stressor—**ambiguous loss,** a term I coined, meaning a loss that remained unclear. That is, the loss could not be verified as definite—like a death. Ambiguous loss is a loss without closure, often for years, even for a lifetime. **Boundary ambiguity** is the outcome of ambiguous loss. It means that people are confused about who is in or out of their family system. For example, is a parent who has dementia and no longer knows who you are still perceived as part of your family? Yes, but no longer in the same way. The change is stressful but does not have to mean closing out the ill person. He or she is still present physically and should be visited, talked to, touched, and cared for, even though the relationship is no longer reciprocal. Actually, such a one-sided relationship requires a deeper level of humanity and maturity on our part. We grow deeper and stronger when we are able to stick with such difficult human relationships.

There are two types of ambiguous loss. Type 1 occurs when a loved one is physically absent but kept psychologically present because there is no assurance of death. Examples are loved ones who are missing in action, kidnapped, lost at sea, swept away by floods or a tsunami, vanished without a trace, and so on. More common examples are breakups, divorce, adoption, and uprooting through immigration and migration.

Type 2 ambiguous loss occurs when someone you care about is present but absent psychologically. That is, the person is physically with you but cognitively and emotionally gone. Examples are Alzheimer's disease or other dementias, traumatic brain injury, addiction, depression and other chronic mental illnesses, unresolved grief, autism, and so on. More common examples are homesickness, preoccupation with loss, and obsessions with the internet, computer games, or work. This type of ambiguous loss is the topic of my book, *Loving Someone Who Has Dementia* (Boss, 2011).

Indeed, the ambiguous loss of dementia leads to boundary ambiguity in families. It takes a while to know who is in and who is out in such unclear situations of absence and presence. Hopefully, we can tolerate the ambiguity and continue to care for someone even though they are no longer fully present.

I wrote this book especially for families because I believe that theory can be useful for ordinary people, not just academics or professionals. With the theory of ambiguous loss to guide their thinking and actions, family members who love someone

Pauline Boss
Courtesy of Stephen F. Kistler

---

no relationship. Many of the studies that show a relationship get national attention, and therefore the public is likely to believe that a relationship exists. Jones and Bright (2007) conclude that, although we simply do not know for sure, it seems likely that the relationship between negative life events and breast cancer is negligibly small compared to the role of biological factors.

Chronic Work Stressors and Cardiovascular Disease. The relationship between work stress and heart disease was a focus of research in the 1980s and 1990s. This relationship was generally supported by research findings and often focused on increased blood pressure, which is a component of heart disease (Jones & Bright, 2007). Findings indicate that the most stress in employment comes from jobs with low control and high demand. For example, people in food service or those in the medical field might fit into this category. Other studies suggest that low control, high demand,

who has dementia can find enough resilience for their long journey with ambiguous loss before death brings some measure of finality and clarity.

What I tell family members is this: The lack of clear information about their loved one's absence and presence is immensely stressful and even traumatizing, but the main thing to remember is that the situation is abnormal, not the people experiencing it. The task—when the problem (in this case, dementia) has no solution—is not to seek a solution, but rather, to help people find the strength and resilience to live with the ambiguity. This is not easy in a *can-do* culture that hungers for certainty, but it is possible. I have seen many people find the resiliency to tolerate, even embrace, their ambiguous loss. They learn to think in both-and terms: With dementia, "My loved one is here but also gone," or in the case of a physically missing relative or friend, "My loved one is probably dead, but maybe not."

Paradoxically, with dialectical (*both-and*) thinking, we find the resilience to live with the imperfections of absence and presence and losses that have no closure. Our loved ones are "gone but still here" or "here but also gone."

As a family therapist, and from the narrative perspective, I see a family's ambiguous loss as a story without an ending. Their family tale has a beginning and middle but no end. So people must socially construct their own ending. With ambiguous loss and the inherent lack of information and facts, that ending most often remains in flux. One day, you see the person as fully gone; the next day, you see the person as here again. Back and forth. Ups and downs. To further complicate the situation, family members often see the situation differently, and they fight about what it all means.

I tell them it is okay to see the situation differently at this time. They need to tolerate each other's interpretations of ambiguous loss, as there is no certainty here. Hopefully, they find ways to live without a clear answer. This involves *both-and* thinking. When answers are not forthcoming, or when a problem has no solution, the goal is to find the resilience to withstand the ongoing stress.

Ambiguous loss and its subsequent boundary ambiguity create the most stressful kind of loss because there is no possibility of closure or resolution. The stressor (ambiguous loss) goes on and on, often without finality. It immobilizes individuals and couples by confusing the necessary family processes of decision making, boundary maintenance, role assignments, coping, adaptation, and resiliency. Relationships are ruptured by the ambiguity, roles remain unclear, family boundaries remain blurred, and family celebrations and rituals, the guts of family life, are often canceled. Our task is to make sure family processes continue, although with adaptations, despite ambiguous loss.

Dr. Pauline Boss is professor emeritus of family social science at the University of Minnesota-St. Paul. She is a former president of the National Council on Family Relations and author of *Ambiguous Loss: Learning to Live with Unresolved Grief* (Harvard University Press, 1999); *Loss, Trauma, and Resilience: Therapeutic Work with Ambiguous Loss* (W. W. Norton, 2006); *Loving Someone Who has Dementia: How to Find Hope While Coping with Stress and Grief* (Jossey-Bass, 2011); and coauthor of *Family Stress Management: A Contextual Approach* (Boss, Bryant, & Mancini, Sage, 2017).

Source: Pauline Boss, Ph.D., www.ambiguousloss.com. Reprinted with permission.

---

and low support are the key factors that affect heart disease. Jones and Bright conclude that, at the very least, a situation of high demand and low control leads to increased risk for heart disease.

Stress and the Common Cold and Influenza. There is evidence that stressful life events contribute to the common cold, even when we do not think we are stressed (Jones & Bright, 2007). Interpersonal conflicts and work-related stress as well as minor hassles are often related to getting a cold. Emotional stress is also related to a greater risk of getting an infection and flu.

Other research has delved into whether stressors are linked to negative health behaviors, which then become the real cause of health problems (Jones & Bright, 2007). For example, stress may cause a person to drink more, smoke more, exercise less, or engage in marital conflict, all of which affect one's health. Stress, therefore, may be indirectly related to health issues. The studies are inconclusive, so it is likely that further research will be needed to sort out this complex issue.

Because stress can affect the immune system, it is important to do things to support your body's natural defenses (Somer, 2007). One important thing you can do is to eat well, which means eating breakfast and including low-fat foods in your diet. It is also important to avoid tobacco and limit your consumption of alcohol and caffeine. It is useful to exercise daily and sleep at least 7 hours per day. Emotionally, it is important to think positively, laugh, and use relaxation techniques that you find useful.

Top Five Stressors for Couples

In a study of 20,000 couples, the purpose was to determine what are the top five most stressful issues that couples experienced (Larson & Olson, 2012). The data were collected from dating, engaged, and married couples using the PREPARE-ENRICH Couple Program (Olson, Larson, Olson-Sigg, 2009) that contains a Personal Stress Profile. The Profile contained 25 of the most frequent stressors that were found in previous research by Olson and colleagues (see Table 14.2).

For dating couples, their jobs were the biggest stressor for both males and females and job security and income were also problematic. While women felt that being emotionally upset was their top issue, it was also in the top five stressors for men. Women also were concerned about feeling overweight. This was not an issue for men.

For engaged couples, much of their stress related to the wedding, including the cost of the wedding and how planning reduced their level of exercise and sleep. How the couple handles the wedding is often predictive of how they will handle other major stressors in their life. It is important for them to learn from that experience so they don't repeat the problems from the past.

Interestingly enough, for married couples, both spouses agreed that their most frequent stressor was, in fact, their partner. Blaming one's partner is a very common approach when people feel stressed in a relationship. However, this often indicates that they are not able to work together to resolve issues or support each other during difficult times. The next most stressful issues were their jobs, feeling emotionally upset, and inadequate income. Again, only women were stressed out by their weight, while men were more stressed by job security.

Five Tips for Dealing with Stress in Your Relationship

1. *Share what is most stressing each of you.* What is amazing is that most couples do not know how stressed their partner is feeling and what are the top stressful issues for

TABLE 14.2 Top Five Stressors for Couples

Dating Couples	Engaged Couples	Married Couples
1. My job	My job	My Spouse
2. Feeling emotionally upset	Financial concerns	My Job
3. Inadequate income	Cost of wedding	Feeling emotionally upset
4. Your partner	Lack of exercise	Inadequate income
5. Job security	Lack of sleep	House projects undone

Source: Larson, P. J., & Olson, D. H., Top Five Stressors for Couples, 2012. Web site: http://www.prepare-enrich.com/research.

them. In counseling couples using the Personal Stress Profile from PREPARE-ENRICH, David Olson has found that couples are surprised how little they know about their partner's level of stress. So simply talking about stress is a good beginning since it will provide insight and greater mutual understanding.

2. *Prioritize what stressor to tackle first.* It is not realistic to handle more than one or two major stress issues at one time. So talk about what are the specific stressful issues that you want to work on in the next few weeks.

3. *Develop a plan with specific goals to manage the stress together.* First, set one or two specific goals for each of you. Then brainstorm together some ideas about how to achieve these goals. Working together makes it more of a team effort and will increase the chances that you both will succeed.

4. *Use your communication and relationship skills.* This is the time for you to each practice and use the best communication skills that you have to make this process successful.

5. *Support and praise each other for progress.* Set up a time (say Thursday after dinner) to review the progress each of you has made and to praise each other for good efforts. Try not to blame each other, but find ways to support each other in reaching your goals.

In summary, use these five steps for handling one or two stressful issues for you and your partner over a period of 4 to 5 weeks, with weekly reviews. You will be amazed at the progress if you both work together and support each other. After some success with one issue, you can then move on to tackle together another issue. The good news is that being successful in resolving an issue will not only reduce your stress level, it will also bring you closer together.

The ABC-X Family Crisis Model

The late Reuben Hill (1958, 2016) was a pioneer in the field of family studies at the University of Minnesota. Hill explained why some families do better than others in hard times with what he called the ABC-X Model. The model argues that:

A = the stressor event
B = the family's crisis-meeting resources
C = the definition the family gives to the event
X = the crisis

Hill defined a *stressor* as "a situation for which the family has had little or no prior preparation," and a *crisis* as "any sharp or decisive change for which old patterns are inadequate." The dictionary defines crisis as simply "a turning point in life," and that works fine, also.

To better understand what Hill is saying here, think about a family in which the mother is driving to her job one morning when a speeding driver runs a red light and broadsides the woman's car, injuring her in the crash. The *stressor event,* A, is the accident that causes multiple injuries to this young mother. But simply knowing that the car crash occurred and resulted in serious injuries does not give you a clue about how the crisis will unfold.

If the family possesses important *crisis-meeting resources,* B, the likelihood that the family will survive the crisis and somehow manage to rise above the tragedy increases dramatically. *If* the family's crisis-meeting resources include invaluable relationship strengths among the family members, *if* the family has adequate financial resources, *if* the family has health insurance and access to high-quality medical care, *if* the family is connected to supportive people at work, in the community, in the neighborhood, and in their own extended family. . . . There are literally countless *ifs* to consider, but the more crisis-meeting resources the family can tap into, the better the outcome of the crisis will be for the family.

C, *the definition the family gives to this event,* also plays an important role in how the crisis unfolds. When family members can find some good to hold on to through the tragedy, when they can find good things mixed in among the wreckage of the crash, they can find a way to look to the future and grow together. If they can reframe the situation in a positive light in some way, the likelihood of a more positive resolution to X, *the crisis,* is likely.

So, back to the basic question: "Why do some families fail in a crisis and some families succeed?" The ABC-X Model helps us understand that it is not just the stressor event but the interaction of the event with the family's strengths, the resources they can tap, and how they think about the situation that all combine to determine how severe the crisis will become in their lives. Hill's model is very useful in helping us see how some families rise above the traumatic events they face in life, while other families sink.

Life as a Roller Coaster

Reuben Hill also observed that the path families follow as they deal with a crisis in life looks in many ways like a roller coaster ride, full of ups and downs. Think back to the young mother severely injured in the car crash. Here's just one example from countless possibilities of how the crisis could unfold: Right before the crash as she is driving to work she is thinking about how wonderful her life is and how much she loves her job, her husband, and her children. Seconds later she is broadsided by the speeding driver running the red light and the young mother's life is torn apart. She almost dies on two occasions, on the way to the hospital and during surgery. Her family is thrown into despair—dad, sister, brother, grandparents—everyone believes the young mother will die, and even as she begins to recover, the family becomes disorganized, not knowing how to function effectively or adjust to all the changes necessitated by the mother's incapacity. She endures two surgeries in the first week, and in the following weeks and months she slowly starts to recover from the devastation caused to her body. Complications arise and 3 months after the accident she is back in surgery for reconstructive work to her face. Finally, she leaves the hospital and intensive rehabilitation services begin. Most important of all, she has returned to the shelter of her loving family, who strive to care for her as best they can.

Now, imagine this possibility: Four years after the crash she has made an amazing recovery. However, the family is *not back to normal,* because no family returns to normal after a profound crisis in life. The family has found *a new normal* in life. Mom, partially disabled, has found a new job, a job that is less physically strenuous than her old job. And everyone in the family loves and values each other more than before the catastrophe. They are all much less likely to take each other for granted, as they often did before the crisis. They have learned that life is, indeed, a slender thread, and we all need to cherish each moment because moments simply do not last forever.

Think back to Reuben Hill's idea about how a family crisis can be likened to a roller coaster ride. In Figure 14.1 we have sketched out a very simplified version of how the young mother and other family members might draw the roller coaster ride they were on for 4 years after the accident. Before the crash life was looking up for everyone in the family. When the crash occurred it was as if the whole family fell off the edge of a cliff. Their very

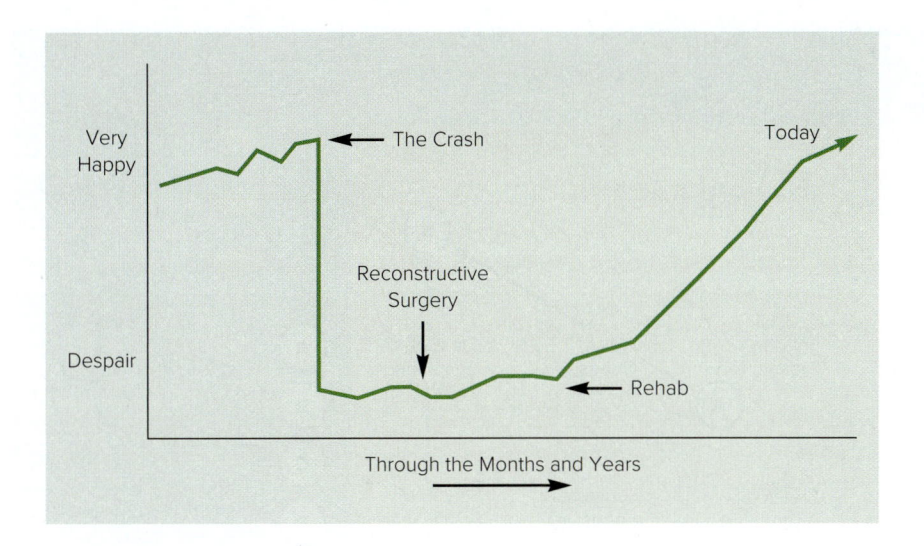

FIGURE 14.1

A Family Endures the Aftermath of a Serious Motor Vehicle Accident

Source: From John DeFrain and the University of Nebraska-Lincoln Extension Family Action Research and Writing Team, Getting Connected, Staying Connected: Loving Each Other Day by Day. 2012, p. 184.

happy life together was plunged into an abyss of fear and despair, wondering whether the mother would live and how they would go on in life. But as life unfolded they gained strength from the shelter of each other's arms and moved on through the ups and downs of the mother's recovery and countless other challenges the family faced. Four years from the time of the crash the family is almost as happy as it was before the crash, and the trend continues to be in a positive direction.

A Roller Coaster Course of Adjustment

The roller coaster model is very relevant for understanding the attacks on America that happened on September 11, 2001, when the World Trade Center in New York and a section of the Pentagon in Washington, D.C., were destroyed.

In considering the attack this country was caught totally by surprise, which created a period of disorganization, both for the country and for the families who had family members in the area. Soon after the attack, the cities of New York and Washington, D.C., the country, and the families started to begin the process of recovery by mobilizing a large variety of resources. This process of recovery took months and years, and eventually the families, the cities, and the country became reorganized. In the process, the reorganized cities and families were changed and in some cases were better than they had been before the crisis. So a crisis can be problematic in the short run and in the long run can strengthen the various components that were initially attacked.

Family Systems Changes Before and After the 9/11 Attacks

An important aspect of family systems is that the family changes to deal with any crises. Let us consider the Greenberg family before and after the destruction of the Twin Towers (Figure 14.2). The father, Henry, worked on the 72nd floor, and it was initially unclear whether he had been able to escape. He had been married for 26 years and had three children ages 22, 20, and 17.

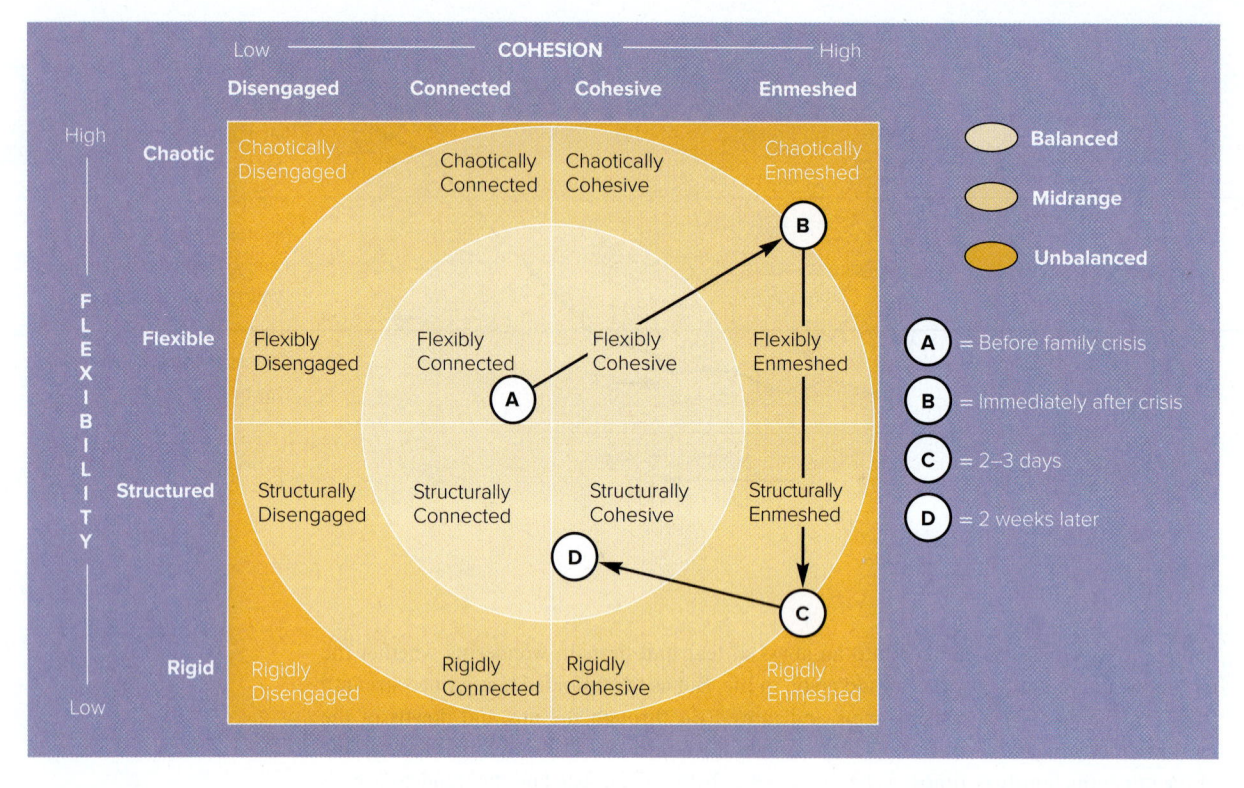

FIGURE 14.2
Family Changes in Response to the 9/11 Attacks.

Before 9/11 (point A), the family was *flexibly connected*, which is appropriate for their stage of the life cycle. Hours after the attack (point B), the family system became *chaotically enmeshed* because the family did not know if the father had escaped from his office. The family, along with close relatives and friends, gathered at their home and huddled together in a mutually supportive way. This high level of closeness and bonding created "enmeshment," and the fact that they did not know if he had survived created a great deal of chaos in their family.

During the next day or two after the attack, the family continued to stay together and were emotionally enmeshed, but they developed a highly organized style of operating, creating a *rigidly enmeshed* system (point C). They got very organized as a group in an attempt to find out what had happened to Henry. This rigidity was an attempt to bring some stability to the chaos by reorganizing some of their family. They decided that their home would be the headquarters and that everyone needed to be in touch by phone. They divided up into teams so they could better search to find out what had happened to Henry. Some family members went to the site of the attack, others went to check out the hospitals, and others stayed at home. They checked in with the home every few hours.

On the third day, a miracle happened from their point of view. They found that Henry was in a downtown hospital but was severely injured in one leg and arm and had some memory loss. He could not remember his phone number but did know his name. That enabled the hospital on the second day to post his name.

Two weeks later, he was home, and the family then changed again, becoming a *structurally cohesive* system (point D). Some of the rigidity was no longer there, but they were still rather organized in order to care for him and to start to get back to their normal routines. Some of the closeness decreased and the family moved from being enmeshed to being cohesive.

Part IV | Challenges and Opportunities

The death of a family member results in a difficult time for that family. The family is likely to experience disorganization for some period following the death.
©Martin Novak/Shutterstock.com

But the family was closer and more organized than before the attack, which was a useful style during the family's recovery from the stress that they had all experienced.

This example illustrates one family's ability to adapt to a crisis. The family changed system types several times over the 6-week period following the attack, and these changes were beneficial in helping the family more effectively deal with this major stressor.

After studying the impact of stress on several hundred couples and families by plotting the changes on the Couple and Family Map, the following general principles of change related to stress were developed. *First*, under stress couples and families often move in the direction of becoming more extreme on both flexibility (a move toward a more chaotic system) and cohesion (a move toward a more enmeshed system). *Second*, communication almost always increases during a stressful event. *Third*, once the stress has abated, couples and families usually return to a similar—but rarely to the same—type of system they had before the stress. *Fourth*, couples and families often require a minimum of 6 months to a year to adjust to a major stress. *Fifth*, balanced couple and family systems tend to become unbalanced during the stress and then return to another balanced system about a year later.

War and Its Effect on Families

The wars that have resulted from the events of 9/11 have affected many aspects of family and community life. One of the issues couples and families face in the military is **deployment**, which is determined by the government and is out of the control of couples. Deployment refers to the time when a military person leaves his or her family and engages in training or combat. Because the couple and family have no control over where or when the family member will be deployed it creates uncertainty. "The only certainty about the deployment of a service member during an era of terrorism, is uncertainty from beginning to end" (Huebner, Mancini, Wilcox, Grass, & Grass, 2007, p. 113).

Chapter 14 | Stress, Abuse, and Family Problems

Those who are deployed may experience the lasting effects of trauma. The family members remaining at home experience effects of separation, reunion, and other difficulties. Finally, communities are faced with the question of how to support these families. There have been many studies about the short-term and long-term effects on military families since the beginning of the wars in Iraq and Afghanistan. It is likely that military deployment and the effects on families will continue for years, and therefore it is likely that research about and services to these families will continue.

Because 55% of military members are married and 43% have children, with nearly half of the children under 5 years of age, family relationships are a major concern for today's military families (Huebner, Mancini, Bowen, & Orthner, 2009). Research regarding the relationship between military deployment and couple and family relationships has been conducted as a result of the current wars in Iraq and Afghanistan.

Couples

Because more than half of military members are married, the marriage relationship for military personnel is a focus of concern. Here is how things worked for one couple anticipating marriage as they dealt with deployment:

> *Jenny and Allen were planning to get married in 4 months. Allen was in the National Guard and knew he could be deployed to Iraq. One day he received his deployment orders—he was expected to leave in 1 month for training before going to Iraq. Jenny and Allen were devastated. They'd known that this could happen, but the reality of living apart under these circumstances was overwhelmingly difficult. They were both 24 years old and were totally unprepared to deal with Allen going to war. Their extended families were wonderfully supportive, but even they had little experience with military life and did not know what to expect.*
>
> *The couple decided to get married before Allen left, and everyone pitched in to put together a lovely wedding in less than a month. This was a bittersweet event, because everyone involved knew that immediately following the wedding Allen would be leaving, and the uncertainty about the couple's future together was difficult for everyone. Jenny was often seen crying as she tried on wedding dresses, selected flowers, and met with the photographer.*
>
> *The wedding was a very difficult experience and not the happy occasion of most weddings. Even the guests felt the sadness that pervaded the ceremony. "'Til death do us part" took on new meaning and brought tears to everyone's eyes.*
>
> *Allen left 2 days after the wedding in a very tearful good-bye with Jenny and all extended family members. Jenny moved in with her parents because she did not want to live alone. Allen is currently in Iraq and hopes to be home soon.*

Jenny and other spouses deal with many stresses as their spouses are engaged in military operations. Spouses, who may be either men or women, fear for their partner, face challenges of maintaining a household, face coping with being the only parent available for children, and experience the marital strain due to separation with an uncertain return (Mansfield et al., 2010).

The stress that couples feel when one partner is deployed can create mental health issues that interfere with marital well-being. According to Mansfield et al. (2010), wives whose husbands had deployed were more likely to have mental health issues than those whose military husbands had not deployed. The kinds of mental health issues included depression, anxiety, and sleep disorders. These researchers also found that these mental health issues increased with length of deployment—the longer the spouse was deployed, the more symptoms occurred and the more likely it was that the at-home spouse would seek mental health services. See Box 14.2 for more information about the impact of war on the families left behind.

Those who have been deployed and have experienced combat can develop multiple mental and physical health issues that can affect marital or couple relationships. Often-cited problems include posttraumatic stress disorder, described below, and **traumatic brain injury** (Thompson, 2008, February 25), which is usually the result of a sudden, violent blow to the head that causes the brain to collide with the inside of the skull. This collision can bruise the brain, tear nerve fibers, and cause bleeding. The resulting symptoms can include severe headaches, problems with memory, confusion, an inability to follow directions, depression, and difficulties concentrating. These issues, along with physical injuries that affect one's ability to continue to earn a living or result in a drastic change in the quality of one's life, can dramatically impact marital quality and happiness. Many of these issues require counseling and therapy, rehabilitation, and the support of family, friends, and community.

It is believed that the divorce rate for military personnel is higher than for civilians. Research on women in the military supports this belief, while studies on men are less clear. The number of women in the military who are divorcing is three times that of men. There is speculation that men who remain at home are at a greater risk for isolation and experience less support than women who stay behind, which may be the reason for this higher percentage of women in the military divorcing (Hull, 2016).

Those who believe divorce is more common among military families cite the increased number of stressors and challenges related to deployment, as well as incentives for early marriage:

1. *Stress:* Repeated and extended family separations; dealing with the soldier's psychological and physical injuries; and difficulty communicating during deployments.
2. *Selection:* The military attracts and selects men and women with preexisting factors for divorce, including a younger age, lower levels of education, having been victims of abuse, or having divorced parents. Other risk factors include substance abuse, lack of emotional response by the military member, depression, domestic violence, and posttraumatic stress disorder (PTSD) (Hull, 2016).

Children

Researchers have focused on the effects of parents' deployment on children. These children experience depression, acting out, poor academic performance, and discipline problems at home (Huebner et al., 2007; National Center for PTSD, 2016; Sahlstein Parcell & Maguire, 2014, March 10). Adolescents experience challenges with their parents' deployment because their ability to cope with such stresses is not fully developed and these stressors add to the existing demands of adolescent development. In fact, children younger than age 8 are unlikely even to understand the concept of war and therefore might know that a parent is gone but have no real understanding about where they are (National Center for PTSD, 2016; O'Malley, Blankemeyer, Walker, & Dellmann-Jenkins, 2007). For children and adolescents whose parent or parents are deployed, there may be issues of relocation, changes in family roles and routines, and loss of a parental figure for extended and unknown periods of time.

In one study of 107 youths 12 to 18 years of age with a deployed parent, researchers found that the youths experienced several effects directly related to the deployment (Huebner et al., 2007; National Center for PTSD, 2016). These youths felt an overall sense of loss and uncertainty. They used words such as *lonely, mad, confused, worried,* and *afraid* to describe these feelings. They also experienced changes in roles and responsibilities because they had to help cover the role filled by their deployed parent. They experienced mental health issues such as depression, changes in sleeping patterns, sadness, crying, and anxiety. Finally, they described conflicts in their relationships at home that often resulted in emotional outbursts. These conflicts were typically focused on the relationships with their mothers, and they talked about how stressed she was. They also talked about how difficult reunions were and how difficult it was to integrate the deployed parent into the family again.

BOX 14.2 At Issue
The Impact of War on Families Left Behind

When you think about one country going to war against another, your immediate concern is for the soldiers who will be fighting on the front lines and the civilians caught in the crossfire. It's easy to imagine—and often to see—the sacrifices they have made as part of their job and their duty. It is not so easy to see the sacrifices made by the families soldiers leave behind.

The U.S. war in Afghanistan began in 2001. The U.S. war in Iraq began in 2003. More than 2.5 million members of the Army, Navy, Marines, Air Force, Coast Guard, and related Reserve and National Guard units have been deployed in these wars, according to Department of Defense data. More than a third of those serving have been deployed more than once: 37,000 Americans had been deployed more than five times, including 10,000 members of Guard or Reserve units. And 400,000 service members had been deployed three or more times (Adams, 2013).

How do these long wars affect the lives of U.S. service members and their families? A study conducted by the RAND Corporation of reservists who had been deployed found that 63% of the service members said their families coped *well or very well* with the deployment; 16% coped *moderately well*; 8% *poorly*; and 13% of the service members did not know or gave no answer. In the same study, spouses of the service members said that 62% of the families coped *well or very well*; 20% coped *moderately well*; 7% coped *poorly*; and 10% did not know or gave no answer (Hosek, 2011).

Problems Related to the Deployment

In the RAND study (p. 36) service members and their spouses reported many different problems related to the deployment:

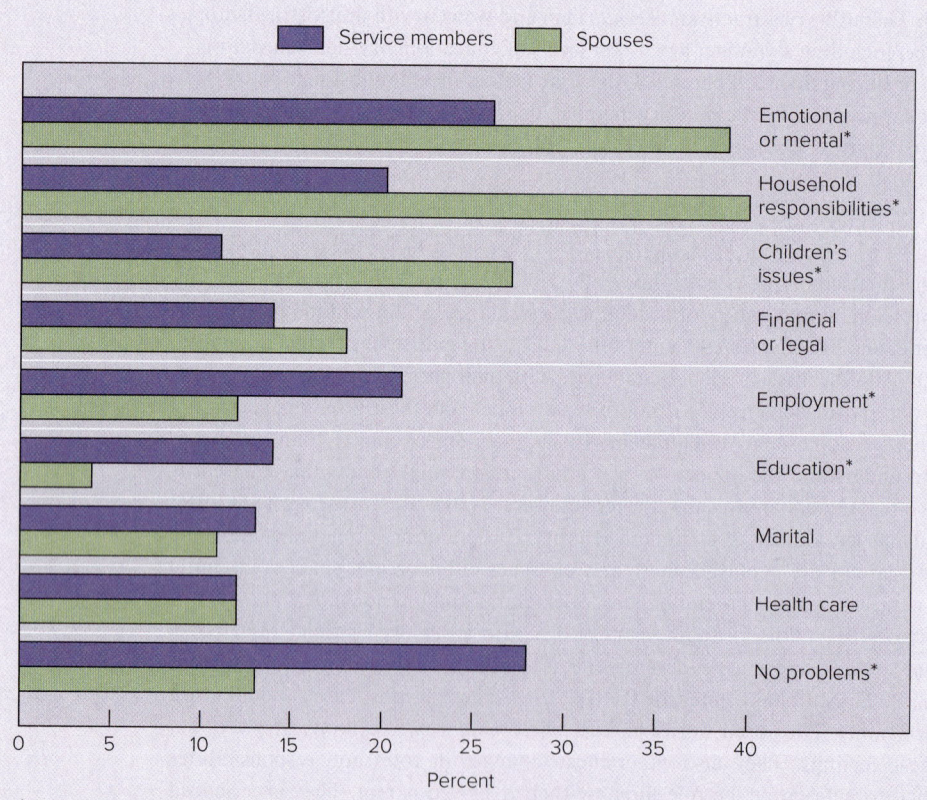

*Statistically significant at p < 0.10.

Positive Aspects of the Deployment

The RAND study (p. 37) also found positive things that were reported by the service members and their spouses in regard to the deployment:

Service members ■ **Spouses** ■

- Family closeness*
- Financial gain*
- Patriotism, pride, civic responsibility*
- Independence, confidence, resilience*
- Employment and education*
- No positives*

Percent (0–30)

*Statistically significant at $p < 0.10$.

Do the Service Members Plan to Stay in the Military Until Retirement?

Just over half of the service members and their spouses indicated in the RAND study (p. 38) that the families intended to stay in the reserve component until they were eligible for retirement. As the figure below indicates, more than that plan to leave before they are eligible for retirement.

Service members ($n = 296$) **Spouses** ($n = 357$)

- Stay until retirement eligible
- Leave before retirement eligible

Percent (0–60)

Chapter 14 | Stress, Abuse, and Family Problems 397

BOX 14.2 (Contd.)

A later study by the RAND Corporation found that the wars in Iraq and Afghanistan have been hard on military marriages. The researchers reported the risk of divorce rose directly in relation to the length of time enlisted service members had been deployed to combat zones (Hosek, 2013).

Some earlier studies had found little or no effects of deployment on divorce rates, or that deployment even somehow helped to decrease the divorce rates. The researchers argued, however, that this new study covered a wider time frame, followed couples for a longer period of time after their marriage, and differentiated between divorce risk before and after the 9/11 attacks. The study also used individual-level information from 462,444 enlisted service members who married while serving in the military from March 1999 to June 2008.

The negative effects of deployment were largest among female military members. Women faced a greater chance of divorce than men under all scenarios studied by the research team. Any type of deployment increases the risk of divorce for members of the military, but the negative consequences were higher for those deployed to the war zones in Afghanistan and Iraq.

Among couples married before the 9/11 attacks, those that experienced deployment of 12 months to war zones were 28% more likely to divorce within 3 years of marriage, when compared with peers who experienced a similar deployment before the wars began. The risk of divorce was higher for hostile deployments than for nonhostile deployments, and women were always more likely to divorce than male service members as a result of time in deployment. Ninety-seven percent of divorces occurred after the service member returned from deployment. The risk of divorce was lower for military families who had children.

The death toll for American military service members continues to mount in Iraq and Afghanistan, and reached almost 6,900 by 2016 (iCasualties.org, 2016). Estimates of the number of Iraqi and Afghani people who have died as a consequence of the conflicts run into the hundreds of thousands. No one knows for sure, and there is a great deal of controversy surrounding the numbers (Casualties of the Iraq War, 2016; Civilian casualties in the war in Afghanistan (2001–present), 2016).

Early in the Iraq war, one team of journalists tried to put a human face on the conflict by looking closer at the American losses. The reporters found that by the end of 2004, almost 1,400 American troops had been killed and approximately 9,000 wounded, along with thousands upon thousands of Iraqis. Among the Americans killed were 27 women, 6 of whom were mothers. Their 10 children were a fraction of the more than 900 who had lost a parent in Iraq by that time (Hoffman & Rainville, 2004).

The reporters found that more than 40% of the American war dead through November 2004 were married, and 429 had children, many of whom were under the age of 10. There are more "married with children" soldiers in this war than in past wars, partly because of the large numbers of reserve forces in Iraq, who tend to be older and more settled than active-duty soldiers (Hoffman & Rainville, 2004).

According to Charles Moskos, a leading military sociologist and Northwestern University professor, we now need to be concerned about orphans as we provide programs for families (Hoffman & Rainville, 2004).

Military families have always had to face different challenges than those faced by civilian families. Often, military families move from city to city, or even country to country, as they follow military orders. Children and spouses have to learn to adapt quickly to new environments and to make new friends they may be with for only a few short months. Spouses must learn to be single parents while their husbands or wives are away for long periods. And these are challenges that occur during peacetime.

During wartime, the challenges are even greater as families cope with uncertainty and loss. An article in *Newsday* (Perez, 2004) described three families' struggles to deal with the holiday season. For one family, Christmas would never be the same, as Army Specialist Victor Martinez, 21, was buried on December 24th.

It is generally found that children's ability to cope with the deployment of a parent is dependent upon the adjustment of the at-home parent (Huebner et al., 2009; National Center for PTSD, 2016; Sahlstein Parcell & Maguire, 2014, March 10). For example, if the at-home mother is depressed, it is more likely that children will experience problems. It is likely that if the at-home parent is not coping well, the children will experience, to some degree, the loss of both parents.

The Role of the Community in Supporting Military Families

Several recently developed social programs help military families deal with stress (Huebner et al., 2009; National Center for PTSD, 2016). Army Child and Youth Services has

He had joined the army to help pay for college and to get a head start on his dream of becoming a police officer. In contrast, the family of Navy Hospital Corpsman Thomas Smith Jr., 23, was celebrating Smith, wounded, who returned home a hero and became a father just five days before Christmas. A third family waited and worried as their only child, Sergeant Francisco Soriano, stationed in Kuwait, waited for his orders to go to Iraq. His mother, who would not put up a tree until her son came home, said, "I don't sleep well. . . . I don't eat well. I can't watch the news. My only desire is to open the door and see his face again."

When soldiers are sent off to war, families undergo emotional cycles. The *Iraq War Clinician Guide,* published by the Department of Veterans Affairs' National Center for Post-Traumatic Stress Disorder (Waldrep, Cozza, & Chen, 2004), describes the emotional cycle's five stages:

1. *Predeployment.* Between the time the family is notified and the time the soldier leaves, families often go through denial and then intense preparation for and anticipation of the departure.

2. *Deployment.* During the first few a months of the soldier's absence, there can be significant emotional turmoil, including depression and feelings of abandonment. Families must find a new balance as they take on the responsibilities of the absent loved one.

3. *Sustainment.* While the soldier is away, families settle into a new routine. Some families, especially those with little outside support, have a more difficult time with this than others, and children may begin to act out in inappropriate ways.

4. *Redeployment.* Just before the soldier is due to return home, families often experience great excitement and anticipation along with great anxiety.

5. *Postdeployment.* While most homecomings are joyous occasions, they can also be accompanied by unrealistic fantasies about the reunion. Soldiers may find it hard to integrate into the family structure that has formed while they were away, and families may have a difficult time giving up new patterns they have created. It may also take time for couples to reestablish physical and emotional intimacy.

The five stages outline some of the emotional impacts on soldiers' families. But there are economic impacts as well. One team of reporters focused on members of the 1161st transportation Company, which had been on the longest deployment of any National Guard unit since World War II (Caplin & McGirt, 2004).

In rural areas like Ephrata, Washington, people often join the National Guard for a second income or as a way to pay for college. However, when a unit ships out, that economic advantage often disappears, Despite popular belief, the U.S. army does not supply all of a soldier's needs, and it's up to the families to make up the difference. One soldier's wife said she had spent about $3,000 on hardware and supplies for her husband, and another $2,200 to ship it all to Iraq. Soldiers and their families also pay for phone calls home. Although they get a discount rate, it often costs more than $1,000 a month to keep in touch (Caplin & McGirt, 2004).

And while federal law requires employers to hold jobs for National Guard troops on active duty, it does not require that their companies pay their salaries or continue to pay health benefits. The U.S. General Accounting Office issued a report in March 2003 stating that 41% of reservists reported that they earned less on active duty than in their civilian jobs. Spouses left at home often have to seek employment or second jobs in order to support their families (Caplin & McGirt, 2004).

The families in Ephrata, Washington, were planning a huge celebration when their loved ones returned home from the war. As one soldier's wife put it, "We deserve a party, too. I truly believe anyone who was left behind serves their country, too" (Caplin & McGirt, 2004).

partnered with National 4-H, which is part of the Extension Service, to provide youth development programs to support military youth and families on U.S. Army installations worldwide. Operation: Military Kids supports military children wherever they live, on or off military bases. The many activities for youth and families focus on recreational, social, and educational programming. The goal is to form friendships and support networks for families. A third program, Essential Life Skills for Military Families, focuses on the relational and practical skills that military reserve families need to help them cope with the uncertainties and challenges of deployment.

Many local communities are creating their own formal and informal support systems for military families. Some help the at-home families of the deployed with house repairs, child care, household bills, or other needs. The overall goal of community programs is to provide military families with support systems to deal with the stress of military life and deployment. These programs help connect potentially isolated family members with services in the community and also provide opportunities for those not in military services to support those who are.

Posttraumatic Stress Disorder and War

With troops deployed in Iraq, Afghanistan, and other places where they are experiencing combat, we have many individuals affected by **posttraumatic stress disorder (PTSD)** and the resulting symptoms. These symptoms are causing stress and disruption in marriage and family relationships (Carey, 2007; Greer, 2005; National Center for PTSD, 2015). According to Sammons (2005), "PTSD can be a chronic and debilitating disorder—one closely associated with related problems such as substance abuse, depression, and domestic and occupational dysfunction" (p. 902). It can result from combat or other traumatic events.

Soldiers are exposed to urban fighting, suicide bombers, and guerilla tactics. When these traumatic events are experienced consistently and over long periods of time, it is a predictor of later mental health problems (Carey, 2007; Greer, 2005; National Center for PTSD, 2015). It makes sense, then, that mental health problems are the second most common reason for medical military discharge, second only to orthopedic injuries (Sammons, 2005). Some reports indicate that as many as 10% of those serving in combat may have a diagnosis of PTSD, which indicates that problems for family life are also substantial for these troops (Fals-Stewart & Kelley, 2005; Sammons, 2005).

A common symptom of PTSD is domestic violence, with one study indicating that the rate of violence for those diagnosed with PTSD was 5.4 times that of veterans who were not diagnosed with the disorder (Sherman, Sautter, Jackson, Lyons, & Han, 2006). Those

Increased family separation has resulted from recent military deployment. Many families are having a difficult time responding to family members repeatedly being deployed to face difficult wartime combat.
©Ariel Skelley/Getty Images

veterans experiencing depression were also more likely to be violent than those veterans who did not experience depression.

Military sexual trauma (MST) is another source of stress for those serving in Iraq and Afghanistan. MST is defined as sexual assault or repeated, threatening sexual harassment that occurs in the military. MST can occur during peacetime, training, or war, and happens to both men and women (National Center for PTSD, 2015). Other mental health symptoms related to PTSD, such as substance abuse and occupational dysfunction, are not as well documented. These issues are also likely to be very disruptive to family life and personal well-being. Treatment for PTSD is usually a combination of drugs and therapy (McGirk, 2009, November 30). Studies also show that veterans with PTSD recover faster if they have a supportive social network of family and friends to help them recover.

Family Coping Strategies

The Chinese pictograph or symbol for the word *crisis* is a composite of two other pictographs: the symbols for *danger* and *opportunity* (Figure 14.3). For thousands of years, the Chinese have understood that a crisis can be a dangerous time but also a time to look for new opportunities. Strong families tend to agree with this idea. Professionals working with those under stress have commonly found that in the midst of the hurt and despair of a serious crisis, there are also some positive outcomes as people draw on their strengths.

What good could possibly come out of a disaster? Many families say that after they have weathered a crisis together, their relationships with each other are stronger, more positive, and more loving. People who have gone through a crisis often relate how they became stronger as individuals as well as closer to their partners and families. They grow to appreciate their families more and become more willing to share with them.

Theoretical Perspectives

Pauline Boss and her colleagues (2002; Boss, Bryant, & Mancini, 2017) clarified the difference between coping as a family resource and coping as a process. Boss explains why the concept of **managing stress** is a more accurate description of how families handle stressors than is *coping with stress:* A family's coping resources are considered strengths, but simply having these strengths available is no guarantee the family will use them to *manage* the stress. Boss also noted that resources are derived from all aspects of life: psychological, economic, and physical.

S. E. Hobfoll and C. D. Spielberger (1992; Hobfoll, 2001) completed an excellent overview of family stress models and research, observing the commonalties and differences

FIGURE 14.3
The Chinese Pictograph for Crisis

TABLE 14.3 — Major Family Coping Strategies

General	Specific
Cognitive	Gain knowledge
	Reframe situation
Emotional	Express feelings
	Resolve negative feelings
	Be sensitive to others' emotional needs
Relationships	Increase cohesion
	Increase adaptability
	Increase trust and cooperation
Community	Seek help and support
Spiritual	Be involved in religious activities
	Maintain faith
Individual development	Develop autonomy, independence

Source: Burr, W. R., & Klein, S. R., *Reexamining Family Stress: New Theory and Research.* Thousand Oaks, CA: Sage, 1994.

among family stress theories and identifying the important family resources across a variety of models. The major resources and strengths were cohesion rather than separateness, flexibility/adaptability rather than rigidity, communication rather than privacy, boundary clarity rather than boundary ambiguity, and order and mastery rather than chaos and helplessness.

Burr and Klein (1994) also provided an excellent summary evaluation of past studies of the most useful coping strategies for families. They identified six general coping strategies that encompass numerous specific strategies. The six general **family coping** strategies are cognitive, emotional, relationships, community, spiritual, and individual development (Table 14.3).

Coping with 9/11

In the September 11, 2001, attack by terrorists, many innocent people were killed. People used a variety of coping resources to deal with this major stress, and we will use this example to illustrate how coping resources are used by families.

In terms of cognitive coping resources, Burr and Klein (1994) described gaining knowledge and reframing the situation. Immediately after people learned of the attacks on the World Trade Center and the Pentagon, they wanted more and more information. Fortunately, the media dropped all other coverage and exclusively reported on the events related to this attack. This media coverage continued nonstop for several days.

Reframing is another cognitive resource, and it involves defining the situation as a challenge that can be conquered rather than denying it is a problem. This attack was so dramatic that it immediately put people into a proactive mode that made them want to overcome the challenge.

Contrary to the notion that strength means facing a problem without any help, research indicates that the strength to cope with problems comes from close connections with loved ones, friends, neighbors, and relatives. Human beings are, indeed, social beings. Good neighbors provide support in countless ways during both good times and troubled times.
©Photodisc/Getty Images

In terms of emotional coping strategies, expressing feelings and being sensitive to others' emotional needs are important resources that help people cope. In the attack on America, we saw endless examples of New Yorkers and others around the country and world expressing their intense feelings about the events and being more open than normal to how others were feeling. With the attack came a dramatic shift in the level and intensity of feelings that were expressed and an interest in sharing with others.

Relationship coping resources include increasing cohesiveness or closeness, increasing flexibility or adaptability, and increasing trust and cooperation. Probably no recent event in our history has brought Americans together more dramatically than this attack. People sought out members of their family and often got reconnected with each other. During crises, people are also willing to forget their normal routine and do whatever it takes to deal with the situation. Their trust and cooperation with each other increase as they bond together to deal with the major problem.

The value of the community as a source of support was clearly demonstrated after the attack. New Yorkers pulled together into a caring community, with strangers helping strangers. The city that had a reputation for being arrogant, distant, and noncaring was transformed into a caring network that rushed to help everyone in need.

The importance of spiritual beliefs was clearly evident from the time of the attack. People were comforted by clergy of all denominations, and prayers were offered by people around the country for those lost and their families. Religious services were packed with people who were there both to comfort and be comforted.

In summary, the terrorist attacks were so dramatic and powerful that they required people to use all the resources described above to begin to better manage the major stress created for all Americans. Because America and Americans are resilient and resourceful, they overcome crises and move on to become stronger people and a stronger country. Box 14.3 provides a summary of the most common strategies for managing stress.

BOX 14.3 Putting It Together
Strategies for Managing Stress

The following is a summary of some of the major strategies for managing stress that were found across a variety of studies of couples and families.

- Look for something positive in every situation.
- Pull together rather than apart.
- Try to be open to sharing our feelings.
- Try to be flexible in handling roles and tasks.
- Try to focus on not worrying about what we cannot change.
- Meet the challenges head on.
- Learn how to go with the flow.
- Be able to cry but also look for humor.
- Take on issues one at a time.
- Do not blame each other.
- Think about the meaning and purpose of life.
- Rely on our spiritual beliefs.
- Show our love for each other.

Domestic Violence

> *Violence is the language of the inarticulate. When people don't know how to talk and communicate with each other.*
>
> —Dr. Charles Steele, president of the Southern Christian Leadership Conference (SCLC)

Domestic violence has been defined as a pattern of abusive behavior in any relationship that is used by one partner to gain or maintain power and control over another intimate partner (National Domestic Violence Hotline, 2016; National Network to End Domestic Violence, 2016; U.S. Department of Justice, 2016). Forms of abuse include physical, sexual, emotional, economic, or psychological actions or threats of actions that influence another person. Abusive behaviors are those that intimidate, manipulate, humiliate, isolate, frighten, terrorize, coerce, threaten, blame, hurt, injure, or wound someone.

Physical abuse: Hitting, slapping, shoving, grabbing, pinching, biting, hair pulling, and so forth are types of physical abuse. This type of abuse also includes denying a partner medical care or forcing alcohol and/or drug use upon her or him.

Sexual abuse: Coercing or attempting to coerce any sexual contact or behavior without consent. Sexual abuse includes, but is certainly not limited to, marital rape, attacks on sexual parts of the body, forcing sex after physical violence has occurred, or treating one in a sexually demeaning manner.

Emotional abuse: Undermining an individual's sense of self-worth and/or self-esteem is abusive. This may include, but is not limited to, constant criticism, diminishing one's abilities, name-calling, or damaging one's relationship with her or his children.

Economic abuse: Is defined as making or attempting to make an individual financially dependent by maintaining total control over financial resources, withholding one's access to money, or forbidding one's attendance at school or employment.

Psychological abuse: Elements of psychological abuse include but are not limited to causing fear by intimidation; threatening physical harm to self, partner, children, or partner's family or friends; destruction of pets and property; and forcing isolation from family, friends, or school and/or work.

Domestic violence is widespread, and can happen to anyone regardless of race, age, sexual orientation, religion, or gender. It affects people in all socioeconomic backgrounds and educational levels. It happens in heterosexual and same-sex relationships, and can happen to intimate partners who are married, living together, or dating (National Domestic Violence Hotline, 2016; National Network to End Domestic Violence, 2016; U.S. Department of Justice, 2016).

The effects of domestic violence are also widespread. Besides affecting those who are abused, domestic violence has a substantial effect on family members, friends, coworkers, other witnesses, and the larger community. Children who grow up witnessing domestic violence are among those who are seriously affected. Frequent exposure to domestic violence predisposes children to numerous social and physical problems and teaches them that violence is normal in life. This increases the child's risk of becoming society's next generation of victims and abusers.

When we hear the term *domestic violence* we often think about a man physically causing harm to his spouse or girlfriend. Many people think of men being the aggressors and women being the victims, with extensive physical harm being done. According to Michael P. Johnson (2008, 2011, 2012) domestic violence takes several forms and the aggressor is not always a male.

Johnson (2008, 2011) identifies three different types of domestic violence between couples. *Intimate terrorism* is violence enacted when taking control over one's partner. This will likely involve physical harm. This type of domestic violence is most often gender specific, with men being the aggressors. This type of violence is often frequent and brutal. Individuals often end up in shelters or hospitals; occasionally, murder is the result (Fergusson, Horwood, & Ridder, 2005; Holtzworth-Munroe, 2005).

The second type of domestic violence involves *violence resistance* and may be in response to a partner's abuse. An example might be when a person inflicts harm on her or his partner in resisting assaults.

The third type of domestic violence identified by Johnson (2008, 2011) is *situational couple violence,* which results when there is a contentious situation or problem in the couple relationship. Situational couple violence is much more common than intimate terrorism. In this type of domestic violence, the aggressor is equally likely to be male or female (Holtzworth-Munroe, 2005). Most studies do not distinguish among the different types of domestic violence, and these distinctions are more likely to be made in future research.

Incidence of Domestic Violence

A wealth of national statistics compiled by the National Coalition Against Domestic Violence (NCADV, 2016) gives a grim picture of domestic violence in the United States. On average, nearly 20 people per minute are physically abused by an intimate partner in the United States. During one year, this comes to more than 10 million women and men. One in three women and one in four men have been victims of some form of physical violence by an intimate partner within their lifetime. One in five women and one in seven men have been victims of severe physical violence by an intimate partner in their lifetime. One in 7 women and 1 in 18 men have been stalked by an intimate partner during their lifetime to the point that they felt very fearful or believed they, or someone close to them, would be harmed or killed. On a typical day there are more than 20,000 phone calls to domestic violence hotlines nationally. Nineteen percent of domestic violence incidents involve a weapon of some kind. The presence of a gun in a domestic violence situation increases the likelihood of homicide by 500%.

Women 18 to 24 years of age have the highest risk of abuse by an intimate partner. Only 34% of those injured by intimate partners receive medical care for their injuries.

One in 5 women and 1 in 71 men in the United States have been raped in their lifetime. Almost half of female victims of rape (46.7%) and male victims of rape (44.9%) were raped by an acquaintance. Of these, 45.4% of female rape victims and 29% of male rape victims were raped by an intimate partner. In the United States, 19.3 million women and 5.1 million men have been stalked sometime during their life. Of these stalking victims, 60.8% of females and 43.5% of males reported being stalked by a current or former intimate partner. A study of intimate partner homicides found that 20% of the victims were not the intimate partners themselves, but family members, friends, neighbors, and persons who intervened, including law enforcement responders and bystanders. Seventy-two percent of all murder-suicides involve an intimate partner, and 94% of the victims of murder-suicides are females. One in 15 American children are exposed to intimate partner violence each year, and 90% of these children are eyewitnesses to the violence (NCADV, 2016).

The economic impact of domestic violence in this country is considerable. Victims of intimate partner violence lose a total of 8.0 million days of paid work each year. The cost of this violence exceeds $8.3 billion per year. Somewhere between 21% and 60% of victims of domestic violence lose their jobs due to reasons stemming from the abuse (NCADV, 2016).

The physical and mental impact of intimate partner violence is also considerable. Women abused by their partners are more vulnerable to contracting HIV and other STIs because of forced intercourse or prolonged exposure to stress. Domestic victimization is correlated with a higher rate of depression and suicidal behavior. Physical, mental, and sexual reproductive health effects have been linked to domestic violence, including adolescent pregnancy, unintended pregnancy in general, miscarriage, stillbirth, intrauterine disorders, chronic pain, disability, anxiety, and posttraumatic stress disorder (PTSD). Add to these effects, noncommunicable diseases such as hypertension, cancer, and cardiovascular diseases. Victims of intimate partner violence are also at increased risk for developing addictions to alcohol, tobacco, and other drugs (NCADV, 2016).

The NCADV (2016) also reports that witnessing violence between one's parents is the strongest risk factor for transmitting violent behavior from one generation to the next. Boys who witness domestic violence are twice as likely to abuse their own partners and children when they become adults, compared to boys who do not witness abuse. And 30% to 60% of those who abuse their partners are also likely to abuse children in the household.

Dating violence is also widespread in our country, with serious long-term and short-term effects. Researchers have found that the dating relationship is apparently more likely to be violent than a marital relationship. Many teenagers do not report the violence because they are afraid to tell friends and family. A nationwide survey by the Centers for Disease Control and Prevention (CDC) found that 23% of females and 14% of males who ever experienced rape, physical violence, or stalking by an intimate partner, first experienced some form of partner violence when they were between 11 and 17 years of age. A subsequent study by the CDC found that approximately 10% of high school students reported physical victimization, and 10% reported victimization from a dating partner in the 12 months before they were surveyed (CDC, 2016, February 1).

Consequences of dating violence include symptoms of depression and anxiety; engagement in unhealthy behaviors, such as tobacco, drug, and alcohol use; involvement in antisocial behaviors; and thoughts of suicide. Furthermore, youths who are victims of dating violence in high school are at higher risk for victimization in college (CDC, 2016, February 1). Young people who are being abused in a dating relationship are encouraged to talk about their situation with their parents and other loved ones, friends, and other trusted people in their lives, including school counselors and religious professionals.

Diversity and Domestic Violence

We know that cultures where men are considered dominant are likely to have higher rates of domestic violence than cultures where men and women are considered equals. We also know that social class, migration, and female dependence on males affect the rates of domestic violence. These factors are very complex, but there are research findings that are beginning to make these relationships more clear (Child Welfare Information Gateway, 2016b).

Some studies show that domestic violence is more prevalent in Latino and African American cultures (Bornstein, 2006). Frias and Angel (2005) found that among poor women, women of Mexican origin reported similar rates of domestic violence to African American women. They found that Latina women from other countries such as Puerto Rico had significantly lower rates of violence. These authors concluded that there are differing cultural views that affect domestic violence for Latinos depending on the country of origin.

We also know that domestic violence is more common among low-income couples (Dingfelder, 2006; Frias & Angel, 2005). Low-income couples are likely to be experiencing considerable stress regarding meeting basic needs, which may affect one's ability to handle issues without violence. It is important to note, however, that domestic violence occurs at all income levels, and the degree to which domestic violence is reported may vary depending on income levels.

There are many factors that affect the willingness to report domestic violence. If a cultural group does not view domestic violence as negative, individuals are less likely to report violence to the police or even self-report violence in research studies. In fact, actions that may be viewed as domestic violence in one culture may not be viewed as domestic violence in another culture. Low-income couples may live in more crowded housing where domestic violence is reported to police by neighbors. Middle- or upper-income couples may live in homes where domestic violence is less likely to be noticed by neighbors and less likely to be reported. Therefore, we must be careful in assuming that reported incidences are an accurate assessment of what is really happening.

National Survey of Domestic Violence

One of the largest national surveys of marriage that also focused on spouse abuse was done by Shuji Asai and David Olson (2004) and is summarized in Table 14.4. This survey of 20,951 married couples from all 50 states had couples complete the ENRICH couple inventory. The average age was 35 for males and 32 for females, and they had been married from 2 to 30 years. Couples were classified into one of four groups based on their level of abuse: nonabusive (61%), only wife abusive (8%), only husband abusive (17%), and volatile—both abusive (13%).

Comparing nonabusive marriages with the other three abusive groups, couples in nonabusive marriages had lower levels of alcohol use and abuse, had less abuse from their parents, and saw less abuse between their parents. In terms of personality styles, couples in nonabusive marriages were more assertive, had higher levels of confidence, less often avoided issues, and less often dominated their partners. Nonabusive marriages had higher levels of couple closeness and flexibility, better communication and conflict resolution, and a more supportive family and friendship network.

In summary, in most ways nonabusive married couples had a much stronger marriage relationship in almost all the major dimensions compared to abusive marriages. This demonstrates that having a strong marriage protects the couple from using more abusive approaches with the partner.

TABLE 14.4	National Survey of Spouse Abuse

- National sample of 20,951 married couples from all 50 states.
- Average age of 35 years for husbands and 32 years for wives who were married 2 to 30 years.
- Classified into nonabusive (61%), only wife abusive (8%), only husband abusive (17%), and volatile—both abusive (13%).
- Greater levels of alcohol use meant a higher level of partner abuse.
- Volatile couples saw more abuse between their parents, more abuse by their parents, and more abuse by others.
- Abused spouses had lower levels of assertiveness and self-confidence and higher levels of avoidance and partner dominance.
- Nonabusive marriages had significantly higher levels of couple closeness, communication, family and friends, personality strengths, couple flexibility, and effective conflict resolution.
- There are five couple types based on the ENRICH inventory: vitalized, harmonious, traditional, conflicted, and devitalized (with ranges from high couple satisfaction to low satisfaction).
- Levels of abuse were highly related to the five couple types: vitalized (5%), harmonious (11%), traditional (20%), conflicted (48%), and devitalized (73%).

Source: Asai, S., & Olson, D. H., National Survey of Spouse Abuse. PREPARE/ENRICH, 2003

Relationship of Physical Abuse and Psychological Abuse

Psychological abuse has been defined as the systematic perpetration of malicious and explicit nonphysical acts against an intimate partner, child, or dependent adult. This can include threatening the physical health of the victim and the victim's loved ones, controlling the victim's freedom, and effectively acting to destabilize or isolate the victim. Psychological abuse frequently occurs before or concurrently with physical or sexual abuse. A number of studies have shown that while psychological abuse increases the trauma of physical and sexual abuse, psychological abuse independently causes long-term damage to its victim's mental health (National Coalition Against Domestic Violence, 2015).

Researchers have found that 95% of men who physically abuse their intimate partners also psychologically abuse them. Psychologically abusive men are also more likely to use a weapon against their partners, have prior criminal arrests, abuse substances, and have employment problems. A woman who is employed and has an unemployed partner is more than twice as likely to be psychologically abused. A woman who has a physical disability is 83% more likely to be psychologically abused. And women who earn 65% or more of their household's income are more likely to be psychologically abused (NCADV, 2015).

Victims of psychological abuse are more likely to experience poor physical health; difficulty concentrating; emotional and/or mental impairment; poor work or school performance; higher likelihood of illegal drugs and alcohol use; and suicidal thoughts and/or suicide attempts (NCADV, 2015).

Physical abuse is almost always accompanied by psychological abuse, but psychological abuse is often present in relationships in which there is no physical violence (Arias & Pape, 1999; Street & Arias, 2001). However, abuse has been conceptualized as a developmental process in which psychological abuse occurs first and eventually may progress into physical aggression. Norina, a college co-ed, describes the escalation of abuse in her relationship with her boyfriend Jerry:

> "In the beginning I thought Jerry was abusive because he was drunk, but then it happened when he wasn't drunk, too. I ignored it at first. I guess I thought he would quit. I also loved him so much I tried to cover it up.
>
> "He became very demeaning toward me, and there was a lot of mental abuse. I wanted to quit seeing him, but he wouldn't accept it. I needed to get away, but he followed me wherever I went and watched every move I made. I didn't realize how bad the situation had become until one night at a party. He had followed me there but didn't speak to me most of the night. He left—or so I thought. Because I was upset, I started to talk with a male friend of mine. Out of the blue my boyfriend returned, picked me up, and carried me outside behind a building. I was scared and started crying. I was so upset I couldn't listen to him. He kept slapping me and telling me to shut up and listen. A few of my friends were watching. They confronted my boyfriend, and he started fighting with them too."

Although a woman who is psychologically abused will not have bruises or visible signs of injury, she will experience damage to her physical and psychological health. Psychologically abused women have an increased chance of serious or chronic illness, lower levels of relationship satisfaction, and lower levels of perceived power and control. These women experience psychological distress, including fear, low self-esteem, depression, an inability to trust others, nightmares, guilt, feelings of inferiority, pessimism, low ego strength, introversion, and helplessness. They also may experience psychophysiological symptoms such as fatigue, backache, headache, general restlessness, and insomnia. Psychological abuse also compromises mothering skills and thus puts children at risk. Psychological abuse has been found to be a major predictor not only of a mother's depression but also of her children's depression and low self-esteem (Arias & Pape, 1999; Street & Arias, 2001). In fact, data suggest that the psychological and behavioral dysfunction of children exposed to interparental psychological abuse is similar to that found in children exposed to interparental physical abuse.

Many symptoms experienced and reported by battered women mirror symptoms of PTSD (posttraumatic stress disorder). An investigation by Arias and Pape (1999) found psychological abuse to be a significant predictor of women's PTSD symptomatology and intentions to end an abusive relationship. Psychologically abused women with low-PTSD symptomatology were highly associated with intentions to terminate the abusive relationship, but there was no significant association for women in the high-PTSD symptomatology group. Arias and Pape suggest that because psychological abuse targets cognitions and is incorporated into self-concept, higher levels of abuse-related distress may decrease a woman's ability to leave the abusive relationship. Based on these findings, Arias and Pape argue that domestic violence shelters need to increase the duration of stay for women to ensure affective and cognitive improvements and to increase the probability that these women will find the support and strength to leave the perpetrator.

Factors Contributing to Domestic Violence

Researchers and clinicians have hypothesized that a number of factors contribute to the likelihood of spouse abuse in a family (American Psychological Association, 2016; Center for Problem-Oriented Policing, 2016; Gelles, 2017; National Council on Family Relations, 2014). These factors are rather similar to those found in the national survey of spouse abuse previously described in Table 14.4 by Asai and Olson (2003).

Violence in the Family of Origin. The family systems theory attributes a tendency toward domestic violence as an adult to growing up in a violent home, where the child learns to be a victim as well as a potential **victimizer**. Abused male children typically learn to be victimizers. They often develop a sort of "pecking order" attitude toward violence: You get beaten up when you're small; then when you're big, you repeat what you learned. Female children typically learn to be victims in their family of origin and are likely to become victims again in their marriage (Frias & Angel, 2005; Gelles, 2000a, 2017). As with child abuse, however, growing up in a home where spouse abuse occurs does not guarantee that one will become a victim or a victimizer as an adult (Gelles, 2000a, 2017). People can and do make positive, life-affirming choices.

Theorists with a psychodynamically oriented approach might see some abusers as having a personality disorder that is facilitated by a "willing" victim. The abuser's sadism is reinforced by the victim's masochism. Another way to think of this is that the abuser is a dominating partner whose dominance is maximized because the abused person is passive rather than assertive.

In a similar vein, **learned helplessness theory** postulates that battered women often learned from childhood that they cannot afford to appear competent around competitive men who like to win. These women give power away to men, and this ingrained passivity leads to a lack of options in life. When abused, they feel they have no way out: nowhere to go, no job skills or career opportunities, no choice except to continue to take their punishment (Nolen, 2016).

Low Self-Esteem. Low self-esteem is a factor in domestic violence. The abusive spouse may feel inadequate and may use violence to gain control. The abused spouse may passively accept the violence, feeling that she or he deserves nothing better (Domesticviolence.org., 2016).

Youth. Age and spouse abuse are statistically related. Marital violence is twice as likely among couples who are under age 30 than among those over age 30 (Center for Problem-Oriented Policing, 2016).

Economic Stress. Although spouse abuse occurs in families at all income levels, economic stress increases the likelihood of wife battering. Spouse abuse is more likely in low-income families, and unemployed men are twice as likely to batter their wives as employed men are (Center for Problem-Oriented Policing, 2016).

Financial Dependency. Financial dependency refers to the degree to which one person relies on another for financial support and in which one member of the couple has considerable control over financial resources (Bornstein, 2006). Financial dependency is positively related to the likelihood of domestic violence. Financial dependency creates an unequal balance of power, which makes it difficult for individuals to move out of the relationship and away from the violence because they have limited or no resources to do so (Bornstein, 2006; Conner, 2014).

Isolation. Social isolation is also a factor in abuse. Abusers often feel isolated and alone. They have fewer contacts with friends, neighbors, and relatives and engage in fewer social activities than nonabusers do. In stressful times, the abusers have no social support network upon which to call (Gelles, 2000a, 2017).

Alcohol. Alcohol is implicated in a high percentage of domestic violence incidents. Many men who assault their wives are found to have been drinking (Asay, DeFrain, Metzger, & Moyer, 2014; Gelles, 2000a, 2017; Substance Abuse and Mental Health Services Administration, n.d.; World Health Organization, 2016). Does drinking cause violence? Some observers argue that alcohol facilitates violence by helping break down the abuser's inhibitions. But alcohol is never the sole cause of a violent episode. Drinking is no more an

Most women who are physically abused by their husbands or partners are reluctant to report the abuse and even more reluctant to end the relationship. One theory for this masochistic behavior is that these women were abused as children and know only the role of victim. Another theory is that throughout their lives they have been conditioned to act passively and as a consequence have few skills and little self-esteem and see no alternative to a brutal relationship.
©Ingram Publishing

excuse for assaulting another human being than it is for killing someone in a car accident. Our system of social justice would break down if people were not held responsible for their behavior.

Male Dominance. Professionals and clinicians studying abuse from a feminist perspective have identified clues as to why men batter women. They note that many in our culture believe that males have the right to control or try to control their partners. Men have also been socialized to believe that aggression is an acceptable, normal response to stress and anger. A patriarchal family system influences males to assume the head-of-the-household role and women to accept subordinate status. Egalitarian decision making is associated with nonviolence in families. Research shows that levels of wife beating and husband beating are higher among husband-dominant couples than among democratic couples (Asay et al., 2014; Gelles, 2000a, 2017; Straus, 2008, March).

Other Cultural Factors. In our culture the depersonalization and objectification of women are reinforced by pornography and by advertising that uses sexy women to sell products. Victim blaming is common, as rape trials often reveal. We live in a society with a high tolerance for overt coercion and the use of physical force to gain control over others (National Council of Juvenile and Family Court Judges, 2012, January 30; Pence & McDonnell, 2000). All of these social factors are viewed as contributing to the epidemic of domestic violence in this country.

Linkage of Animal Abuse and Domestic Violence. There is considerable evidence that mistreatment of animals is a powerful indicator that other forms of violence

Chapter 14 | Stress, Abuse, and Family Problems

may be occurring in the home. Seventy-one percent of pet-owning women entering women's shelters reported that their batterer had injured, maimed, killed, or threatened family pets for revenge or to psychologically control victims; 32% reported their children had hurt or killed animals (American Humane, 2016, August 25; PETA, 2016). Many abused women have companion animals, and many of these companion animals are abused by the perpetrators as a way to hurt and control the women or their children. Some women may choose not to leave the partner or stay separated for long because of their concern for the safety of their companion animals (Fawcett, Gullone, & Johnson, 2002). Other researchers have found that children who abuse animals are often cruel toward people, and they argue that we can intervene in the cycle of abuse by decreasing a child's potential to be abusive toward animals, and, consequently, promote prosocial behavior toward humans (Mickish & Schoen, 2004; Thompson & Gullone, 2003). One study found that half of all the youths surveyed had abused animals at some time in their lives, with boys being more involved in abuse than girls (Baldry, 2003).

Patterns of Domestic Violence

Clinicians commonly see a three-phase, cyclical pattern to wife battering: (1) a tension-building phase; (2) an explosion phase, in which the actual beating occurs; and (3) a loving or honeymoon phase, in which the battered woman is rewarded for staying in the relationship (Walker, 2009, 2016). The third phase can be very pleasant. Many women stay with their spouses or boyfriends because of the promises and gifts that often follow a violent incident.

A common belief in our culture is that venting anger verbally can prevent physical violence. This theory of **catharsis conflict**, as it has been called, is simply not true. Verbal aggression is not a substitute for physical aggression but actually goes hand in hand with physical aggression. The more verbally aggressive a couple is, the more likely they are to be physically aggressive with each other (Gelles, 2000a, 2017; Loseke, Gelles, & Cavanaugh, 2005; Straus, Gelles, & Steinmetz, 2006).

Treatment and Prevention of Domestic Violence

Many clinicians and professionals who work in women's shelters are skeptical that batterers can alter their behavior without professional help and without the genuine desire to change. Some argue that battering men "have a good thing going," with a terrified wife and children who jump every time the batterer says jump.

Counselors commonly advise battered women to leave their husbands and go to a relative's or a friend's home or to a shelter for battered women. But this is easier said than done. Some men panic when women leave because they feel they are losing control. Panic can lead to even more violent behavior. "It's extremely rare that you read about a man who has beaten a woman to death while she's living with him," according to Ellen Pence, a pioneer in the treatment and prevention of domestic violence. "It's when she leaves him that he kills" (National Council of Juvenile and Family Court Judges, 2012, January 30; Pence & McDonnell, 2000).

Responding to pressure from the women's movement, police departments are now more likely to make arrests in cases of domestic violence. Assault against a spouse is seen as a serious offense. After studying research findings indicating that men who had spent time behind bars were less likely to assault their partners again, the Duluth, Minnesota, police department was the first in the United States to make arrest mandatory for suspected

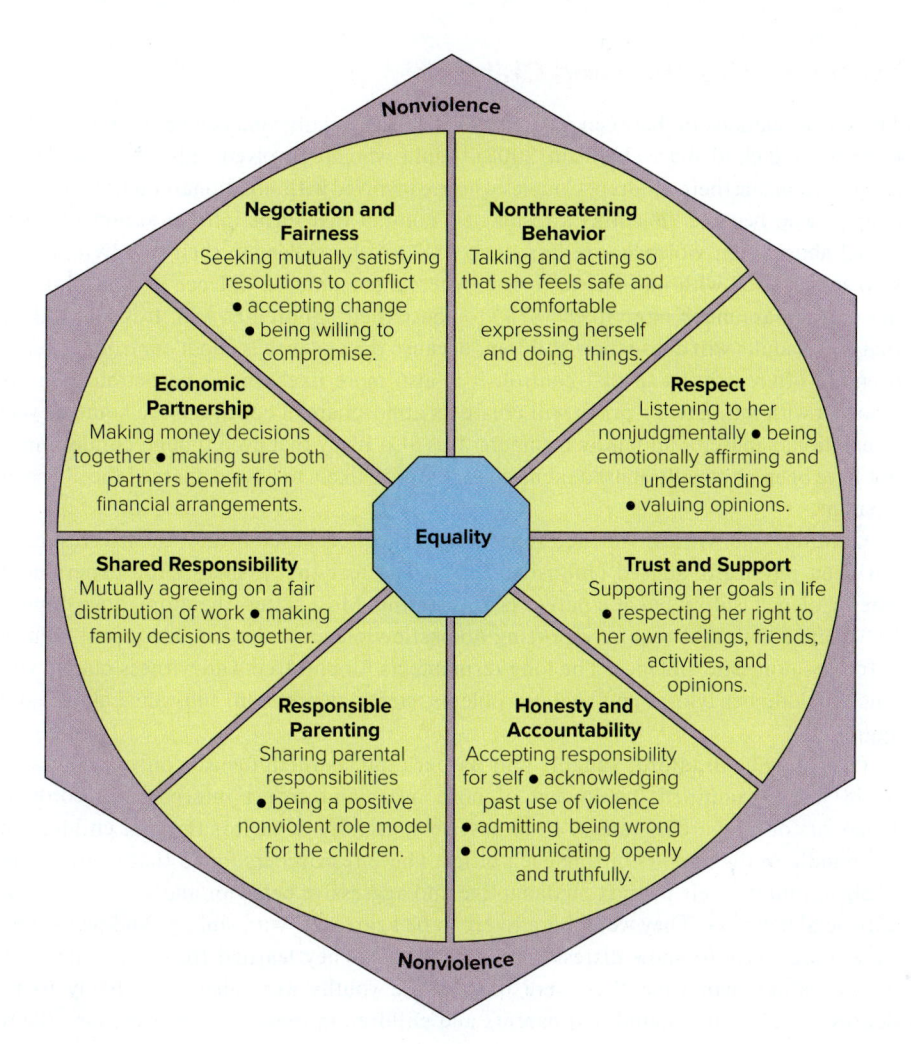

FIGURE 14.4
Equality Wheel
Source: From Domestic Abuse Intervention Programs, https://www.theduluthmodel.org/?s=equality+wheel.

Equality Wheel

Nonviolence

- **Negotiation and Fairness**: Seeking mutually satisfying resolutions to conflict • accepting change • being willing to compromise.
- **Nonthreatening Behavior**: Talking and acting so that she feels safe and comfortable expressing herself and doing things.
- **Economic Partnership**: Making money decisions together • making sure both partners benefit from financial arrangements.
- **Respect**: Listening to her nonjudgmentally • being emotionally affirming and understanding • valuing opinions.
- **Shared Responsibility**: Mutually agreeing on a fair distribution of work • making family decisions together.
- **Trust and Support**: Supporting her goals in life • respecting her right to her own feelings, friends, activities, and opinions.
- **Responsible Parenting**: Sharing parental responsibilities • being a positive nonviolent role model for the children.
- **Honesty and Accountability**: Accepting responsibility for self • acknowledging past use of violence • admitting being wrong • communicating openly and truthfully.

Center: Equality

Nonviolence

---

batterers. The Duluth program requires batterers to attend at least 6 months of counseling and classes. If a man misses two meetings, he risks serving up to 10 days in jail. Studies done 2 years after the program was initiated found that 80% of the women whose partners had completed the program were no longer being battered.

Domestic Abuse Intervention Programs (2016) in Duluth, Minnesota, has developed models for positive treatment of women who have been involved in domestic violence. The Equality Wheel (Figure 14.4) was created by women who have been abused by their male partners. This model also has implications for treatment of all family members and would be a positive way to view all the people who live together in a home.

To help prevent the next generation from falling into the sexism/violence trap, Myriam Miedzian suggests encouraging schools to teach positive approaches to conflict resolution in the classroom and on the playground, and to show children there are alternatives to violent behavior. Television should be prosocial and nonviolent rather than sexist and violent. We need to restrict violent pornography, which both demeans women and glorifies killing. Also boys should be encouraged from a young age to be empathetic rather than aggressive (Miedzian, 2002, 2015).

Domestic Violence and Children

There is a relationship between partner violence, essentially violence between two adult partners, and child abuse (Johnson, 2008). Adults who are involved with partner violence are often abusing their children. Couples who are involved with situational couple violence—couples who become violent as a result of a conflict that turns into an argument, then verbal abuse, then violence—are less likely (31%) to be violent to their children. Those who are involved with intimate terrorism, where a person uses violence to control his or her partner, are much more likely (67%) to abuse their children as well. It is more likely that these adults will abuse their children, because the violence is about control, and children are often a threat to that control. It is also more likely that a perpetrator who is involved with intimate terrorism will create an atmosphere of control in the home by way of emotional abuse of all family members. It is also likely that even though children may not have been physically abused themselves, they are likely to have witnessed the abuse of a parent.

Children who witness violence suffer long-term effects even if they, themselves, have not been physically abused (Johnson, 2008). The fear that a small child experiences when violence is directed at a parent is devastating. Most states, therefore, have domestic violence laws that require reporting domestic violence to human services if a child witnesses domestic violence. The long-term effects for children who witness couple violence include behavioral and social problems, stress, depression, substance abuse, and aggression.

One study by Bradford, Vaughn, and Barber (2008), which focused on youth ages 12 to 18 years, examined the impact of both overt and covert interparental conflict. Behaviors of the parents ranged from passive-aggressive behaviors that put children in the middle to the parents hitting each other. These researchers found that youths were likely to imitate their parents' maladaptive and aggressive behavior and were at risk for antisocial behavior. They were more likely to be aggressive with siblings and peers, and were more likely to show disrespect, yell, and hit. They learned from what they witnessed rather than what they were told. These youths were also more likely to be depressed. The study found that parents and children in these families were also likely to experience conflict.

It is important to realize that, according to the study by Bradford et al. (2008), the effects of conflict, not only violence, can greatly affect children and youth. Parents' treatment of each other can have long-lasting effects on children's social and emotion development.

Child Abuse and Neglect

Child abuse "is any recent act or failure to act on the part of a parent or caretaker, which results in death, serious physical or emotional harm, sexual abuse, or exploitation, or an act or failure to act which presents an imminent risk of serious harm" (Child Welfare Information Gateway, 2016a). Although all states include sexual and physical abuse in their definition of child abuse, not all states include neglect or emotional abuse in their definition.

Child abuse can occur in all kinds of families. We do know, however, that child abuse is reported in low-income families more often than in middle-income families. Reporting could be higher in low-income families because they have fewer resources to cover up the abuse. It is also very likely that the stress related to limited income could contribute to increased abuse in low-income families (Child Welfare Information Gateway, 2016b).

Incidence of Child Abuse and Neglect

In 1974, in response to the Child Abuse Prevention and Treatment Act, the federal government began studies on the incidence of child abuse and neglect nationwide. The findings of the latest research, the *Fourth National Incidence Study of Child Abuse and Neglect* (Sedlak et al., 2010; National Incidence Study of Child Abuse and Neglect, 2016), show that reported maltreatment has decreased by 19% since the last comparable study, which was conducted in 1993. All statistics about child abuse from this report were dependent on actual cases being reported, not estimates of the number of children abused and neglected. Based upon this report, 1 in 58 children experienced abuse or neglect during the year 2005–2006. Forty-four percent of these children were abused, while 61% were neglected. Of those identified as having been abused, 24% were sexually abused.

Some children are more likely to be abused and neglected than others (Sedlak et al., 2010). For example, girls were more likely to be sexually abused than boys. Children under 2 years of age were less likely to be abused than older children. The report suggests that these findings may be a result of underreporting, because younger children are not in school and may not be identified by educational personnel as being abused. Black children were more likely to be abused than White or Hispanic children. Children who were not enrolled in school were sexually abused more often than enrolled children.

There were also differences in the rate of abuse and neglect based upon family characteristics (Sedlak et al., 2010). Not surprisingly, children living with parents who were employed experienced a lower rate of abuse than those whose parents were not employed. Additionally, children living in low-income households, below $15,000 a year, had the highest rate of maltreatment—five times the rate of other children.

Family structure was also related to child maltreatment (Sedlak et al., 2010). Children living with both biological parents had the lowest rate of child maltreatment, and those living with a single parent who was cohabiting had the highest rate, which was eight times higher. Family size was also a factor: families with more than four children and only-child families had the highest rates of abuse. The lowest rates were in families with two children. Finally, rural children were more likely to be abused than urban children.

Some of the factors associated with an increase in child abuse and neglect are related to increased stress and decreased resources, such as not being employed and low income. These findings are not surprising. Other factors, such as living in rural communities versus urban communities, may be less clear. One might speculate that rural communities are more isolating and have limited resources to help parents with parenting issues.

The majority of the abused or neglected children were maltreated by a biological parent (Sedlak et al., 2010). The explanation for this finding might be that children are most often in the care of their biological parents. Consistent with the mother being the primary caregiver is the finding that most children suffer maltreatment by their biological mothers. Sexual abuse, however, was more often committed by males.

Psychological Aggression and Spanking

Psychological aggression by American parents is also quite common. Psychological aggression is yelling, shouting, or threatening a child, but not physically hurting the child. In a nationally representative sample of 991 parents, Straus and Field (2003) found that by the time the child reached age 2, 90% of the parents said they had used one or more forms of psychological aggression during the previous 12 months, and by age 5, 98% of the parents had done so. From ages 6 to 17 the rates of psychological aggression continued in the 90% range. Rates of what the researchers termed severe psychological aggression were

Child maltreatment includes child neglect, physical abuse, sexual abuse, and emotional abuse.

Source: U.S. Department of Health and Human Services, Children's Bureau

Everyone Can Help Prevent Child Abuse

Raise the issue.
Call or write your elected officials to educate them about issues in your community and the need for child abuse prevention, intervention, and treatment programs.

Reach out to kids and parents in your community.
Anything you do to support kids and parents in your family and extended community helps to reduce the likelihood of child abuse and neglect.

Remember the risk factors.
Child abuse and neglect occur in all segments of our society, but the risk factors are greater in isolated families and also when parents or caregivers have other social or emotional problems.

Recognize the warning signs.
The behavior of children may signal abuse or neglect long before any change in physical appearance.

Report suspected abuse or neglect.
If you suspect abuse or neglect is occurring, report it—and keep reporting it—until something is done. Contact child protective services (in your local phone book) or your local police department.

For more information go to
http://nccanch.acf.hhs.gov/topics/prevention

gateways to prevention

Prevent Child Abuse America
200 South Michigan Avenue, 17th Floor
Chicago, Illinois 60604-2404
312.663.3520 tel
www.preventchildabuse.org

U.S. Department of Health and Human Services
Administration for Children and Families
Administration on Children, Youth and Families
Children's Bureau
Office on Child Abuse and Neglect
National Clearinghouse on Child Abuse and Neglect Information
800.394.3366 tel
http://nccanch.acf.hhs.gov

lower: 10% to 20% for toddlers and about 50% for teenagers. Straus and Field found that psychological aggression cut across all social classes and ethnic and cultural groups, indicating that it is a near universal disciplinary tactic of American parents.

Some researchers view spanking as undesirable and see it as the first step in parents' getting out of control and physically abusing their children (Straus, 2008). According to Straus, only a tiny percentage of parents who spank lose control and become physically abusive. However, most of those who become physically abusive began by using spanking as a form of discipline and it got out of control. Therefore, it is argued that preventing spanking will reduce physical abuse.

Currently, 94% of parents with preschoolers spank their children. Some of these parents spank only occasionally; others do it every day. On average, parents spank several times per week (Straus, 2008, 2013). Straus found that children experience trauma when spanked often, even if their parents are loving and caring in every other way. Many parents believe that children under 2 years of age sometimes do not respond to anything but spanking. Straus suggests that children this age do not change their behavior easily, no matter what the consequence. Repetition is the only thing that seems to help young children. Parents, however, sometimes think that if spanking did not work, it was because the spanking needed to happen more often or harder—thus, the potential for it to get out of control.

It has been suggested that putting an end to spanking can decrease physical abuse (Straus, 2008, 2013). In addition, Straus suggests that spanking has harmful side effects for children. Children who have been spanked may hit other children, and when older may hit other adults, such as a dating or marital partner, or their own children. Straus strongly supports the *never hit a child* approach to enhance the well-being of the child and of all those the child will encounter in life.

Alternatives to Spanking

Perhaps the best argument against spanking is that there are many nonviolent approaches to teaching children how to behave in an acceptable manner. Child development specialists have known these approaches for many years and use them successfully in early childhood programs across the country and around the world.

Four commonly used and effective approaches are:

1. *Accentuate the positive.* Focus on what the child is doing right, instead of focusing always on what the child is doing wrong. Focus on rewarding the positive behavior of children by giving them verbal praise, hugs, and occasional material rewards such as food or small gifts when they do the right thing. This makes it important, then, for parents to be watching their children closely to see when they behave correctly. By spending more time on rewarding good behavior and less time on punishing bad behavior, it sets up a loving and friendly family environment in which children are happier, as well as parents.

2. *Call a time-out.* When the kids get out of hand, have them sit down, calm down, and come back with everyone else when they are under control. Time-outs work best when they are short and don't involve angry lectures. Simply state what the child did wrong and have the child sit down until ready to behave properly. This should last only 2 or 3 minutes, if it is done effectively. Long time-outs generally don't work. While the child is calming down in time-out, the parent is also calming down. If everyone is emotionally upset, everyone ends up suffering, so a time-out is as much for the parent as for the child.

3. *Be consistent in how you discipline children.* Make reasonable rules with reasonable consequences, and stick to them.

4. *Teach your children. Don't hit them.* Parents are much more effective when they act as educators, rather than disciplinarians.

The Long-Term Consequences of Child Abuse and Neglect

The price we pay in our society for child abuse and neglect is staggering. It can be seen as we list some of the most common physical, psychological, behavioral, and societal consequences determined by researchers (Child Welfare Information Gateway, 2016b):

Physical Health Consequences. The immediate physical effects of abuse or neglect can be relatively minor (bruises or cuts) or severe (broken bones, hemorrhage, or even death). Though physical effects in some cases are temporary, the suffering caused to the child cannot be discounted. Long-term physical health consequences include: shaken baby syndrome (bleeding in the eye or brain, damage to the spinal cord and neck, and rib or bone fractures); impaired brain development (important regions of the brain fail to form or grow properly); and poor physical health (allergies, arthritis, asthma, bronchitis, high blood pressure, and ulcers).

Psychological Consequences. The immediate emotional effects of abuse and neglect include feelings of isolation, fear, and an inability to trust. Lifelong consequences include low self-esteem, depression, and relationship difficulties. Depression and withdrawal symptoms are common among children as young as 3 who experience emotional, physical, or environmental neglect. In one study as many as 80% of young adults who had been abused met the diagnostic criteria for at least one psychiatric disorder at age 21: depression, anxiety, eating disorders, and suicide attempts. Other researcher teams found psychological and emotional conditions associated with abuse and neglect include panic disorder, dissociative disorders, attention-deficit/hyperactivity disorder, depression, anger, posttraumatic stress disorder, and reactive attachment disorder. Cognitive difficulties associated with abuse and neglect include lower cognitive capacity, language development, academic achievement, and classroom functioning. Social difficulties include antisocial traits, borderline personality disorders, and violent behavior.

Behavioral Consequences. Not all victims of child abuse and neglect experience behavioral consequences; however, problems are more likely among this group, even at a young age. Clinical or borderline levels of behavioral problems among children ages 3 to 5 are displayed at a rate more than twice that of the general population of children. Later in life, child abuse and neglect appear to make difficulties more likely: juvenile delinquency and adult criminality; alcohol and other drug abuse; and abusive behavior toward their own children.

Societal Consequences. The impact of child abuse and neglect does not end within the family, but spills out into the broader society. Child abuse and neglect affect over 1 million children every year. Each incident of child abuse and neglect costs the United States $220 million every day. That is an extraordinary amount of money. How is it calculated? The initial costs include the investigations, foster care, medical treatments, and health care. Later on in the child's life, there are additional costs for special education, juvenile and adult crime, chronic health problems, and other problems that develop across the life span. This all adds up to $80 billion per year to address the costs of child abuse and neglect in this country. Thus, child abuse and neglect affect us all.

Transcending Abuse

Many abusive parents were themselves abused as children, but being abused as a child does not necessarily doom a person to pass the misery along to the next generation. Some abused children grow up to be happy and healthy adults, although transcending the pain of a violent childhood is very difficult. Since the early 1980s, researchers and clinicians have begun to focus on these resilient individuals. What they have found is that a nurturing relative, adult friend, or teacher often helped the troubled individual find a more positive approach to living.

Edward Zigler and his colleagues estimated that the rate of "cross-generational transmission" of child abuse is about 25% to 35%. This means that about one-quarter to one-third of those who are physically or sexually abused or neglected as children will subject their own children to similar abuse. However, the majority (65% to 75%) of people abused as children "will care for their offspring as well as the general population." According to the researchers, "many adults abused as children remember the agony they once suffered and have sworn to give their own children a better start." The research team did make it clear, however, that individuals with a history of abuse are still about six times more likely to abuse their own children than is the average person, who has about a 5% likelihood of doing so (Zigler, 2004). Clearly, the experience of childhood abuse does not predetermine that an abused child will grow up to abuse others later in life (Skogrand, DeFrain, DeFrain, & Jones, 2007).

Families at Risk

Several of these factors have been identified (American Psychological Association, 2016; Centers for Disease Control and Prevention, 2017, April 18; Mayo Clinic, 2015, October 7; National Incidence Study of Child Abuse and Neglect, 2016; Sedlak et al., 2010):

- *Economic distress*. Unemployment, low income, illness in the family, and inability to pay for adequate medical care are stressors in the lives of many abusive parents.
- *Inadequate parenting skills*. Abusive parents often have unrealistic expectations of their children, have little knowledge of child development, and demonstrate an inability to bond with infants.
- *Parental personality problems*. Abusive parents often have low self-esteem and are likely to be more immature, less empathetic, and more self-centered than nonabusive parents. They also tend to be rigid, domineering, self-righteous, moralistic, and prone to anger.
- *Chemical abuse as a means of coping with stress*. Abusive parents often have high stress in their lives but have a difficult time dealing with that stress in a proactive, rational manner. Many turn to alcohol and other drugs to forget their troubles.

Children are more likely to suffer abuse when their parents are under stress because of unemployment, low income, or illness, especially if the parents are immature and know little about the development of children. During stressful times, parents need friends and other sources of support to help them cope with frustrations, and they need to relate to their children in a positive way.
©Doble-d/ iStock/Getty Images

- *Social isolation.* Abusive families tend to be isolated from their community, with few friends or sources of outside support.
- *A special child.* Children with a chronic illness, an emotional disturbance, hyperactivity, mental retardation, or a physical handicap are at higher risk for abuse. Children who were unplanned and are unwanted are also more likely to be abused, as are children whose birth was difficult.
- *Domestic violence in the family of origin.* Many abusive parents witnessed domestic violence between their own parents and were likely to have been physically punished themselves as children.
- *A violent subculture.* Some cultures and subcultures appear to be more tolerant of violent behavior toward children. For example, children who live in an unsafe neighborhood characterized by high levels of violence are at greater risk of being abused than are children growing up in a more peaceful neighborhood.
- *A violent marriage.* Parents who abuse their spouse are more likely to abuse their children than are parents whose marriage is peaceful.
- *Single parent.* Children who live with a single parent are more likely to suffer abuse than are those who live with two parents, perhaps because of the stresses often associated with single parenthood.
- *Stepparent.* A child living with a stepparent is more likely to be abused than is a child living with both natural parents, perhaps because the stepparent's lack of a biological tie with the child can foster intolerance. One study (Daly & Wilson, 1996) of preschoolers found the likelihood for abuse to be 40 times greater for stepchildren.

Treatment and Prevention of Child Abuse

A growing body of professional literature demonstrates that Americans can do something about child abuse (Centers for Disease Control and Prevention, 2017, April 18; Childhelp, 2016; Gelles, 2017; National Child Abuse and Neglect Training and Publications Project, 2014). Parents can learn how to deal more positively and effectively with their children. Education is the key to preventing abuse; education and therapy are needed to help abusive families.

Professionals see child abuse as a family and societal problem. Treating the problem involves three interrelated strategies: (1) increasing the parent's self-esteem, (2) increasing the parent's knowledge of children and positive childrearing techniques, and (3) devising community support networks for families under stress.

Parents who mistreat children are commonly viewed as people who need more positive ways of coping with their many problems. Counselors working with abusive parents are often quite successful in facilitating positive behavioral changes. By focusing on these parents' strengths, a therapist can enhance the development of the parents' self-esteem and parenting skills. A counselor can also provide referrals to other community services: financial aid for families in economic distress, food stamps, aid in finding better housing, family planning and adoption services, and child care services.

Many programs for troubled parents include a parent discussion and support group among the treatment offerings. A group of parents, often facilitated by a professional, gets together to share stories about life's ups and downs and to offer advice and support to each other. Child abuse hotlines are also available to parents around the clock for help in dealing with difficult childrearing situations. And the internet, for those who can afford a computer or have access to one, has a wealth of good information for struggling parents.

There are a number of things we as a society can do to prevent the abuse of children (Centers for Disease Control and Prevention, 2017, April 18; Childhelp, 2016; Gelles, 2017;

National Child Abuse and Neglect Training and Publications Project, 2014). They include working to reduce sources of social stress, such as poverty, racism, inequality, unemployment, and inadequate health care; eliminating sexism in the workplace and the home; providing adequate child care; promoting educational and employment opportunities for both men and women; supporting sex education and family planning programs in an effort to reduce unplanned and unwanted pregnancies; and working to end the social isolation of families in our culture. Child abuse affects all of us, and we all need to work together to help prevent it.

Sibling and Child-to-Parent Abuse

Domestic violence is not initiated only by adults, and it is not directed only at children and partners. Siblings also engage in violence, and children sometimes attack their parents.

Sibling Abuse

The most violent members of American families may be children. Parents often do not recognize sibling abuse for what it is. Parents and society in general tend to expect fights and aggression among brothers and sisters, and because of this parents often don't see sibling abuse as a problem until serious harm has occurred (American Association for Marriage and Family Therapy, 2015; TheSingleMother.com, 2016; University of Michigan Health System, 2012).

Sibling abuse has been defined as the physical, emotional, or sexual abuse of one sibling by another. Physical abuse among siblings can range from mild forms of aggression, such as pushing and shoving, to very violent behavior such as using weapons. Similar to child abuse in general, sibling abuse has both immediate effects and long-term consequences that can last into adulthood.

Researchers have found that sibling abuse is quite common, probably even more common than child abuse by parents or spouse abuse. It has been estimated that 3 children in 100 are dangerously violent toward a brother or sister, and the number of assaults each year to children by a sibling is about 35 per 100 kids. The rates of sibling abuse are similar across income levels and racial and ethnic groups. Sibling incest is believed to be much more common than parent-child incest (University of Michigan Health System, 2012).

All siblings squabble at times and call each other mean names, and some young siblings may "play doctor" with each other. But there is a difference between typical sibling behavior and abuse: If one child is always the victim and the other always the aggressor, it is an abusive situation. Other signs of abuse include: one child always avoids the other sibling; a child exhibits changes in behavior, sleep patterns, eating habits, or has nightmares; a child acts out abuse in play; a child acts out in sexually inappropriate ways; the children's roles are rigid, with one always being the aggressor and the other the victim; and roughness or violence between siblings is increasing over time (American Association for Marriage and Family Therapy, 2015; TheSingleMother.com, 2016; University of Michigan Health System, 2012).

Sibling abuse can be prevented by reducing the rivalries between the children; setting ground rules to prevent emotional abuse and sticking to these ground rules; not giving older children too much responsibility for younger children; setting aside time to regularly talk with the children, one-on-one; knowing when to intervene in the children's conflicts, to prevent an escalation of abuse; learning how to mediate conflicts; modeling good conflict-solving skills for the children; modeling nonviolence; teaching the children to

Child-to-parent abuse is devastating to a family. Children who abuse their parents are likely to be in their teen years or older.
©John Powell Photographer/Alamy Stock Photo

own their own bodies; teaching them to say *no* to unwanted physical contact; creating a family atmosphere where everyone is comfortable talking about sexual issues and problems; keeping an eye on the children's media choices; and, in sum, keeping actively involved in the children's lives and knowing what they are doing (American Association for Marriage and Family Therapy, 2015; TheSingleMother.com, 2016; University of Michigan Health System, 2012).

Child-to-Parent Abuse

Because parents are usually physically and socially more powerful than their children, we assume that parents are immune to abuse by their children. But **child-to-parent abuse** occurs in many families (Envision Counselling & Support Centre, 2016; Women's and Children's Health Network, 2016).

In comparison to child abuse and spouse abuse, parent abuse by their adolescent children has received very little attention by mental health professionals, even though its prevalence is comparable. Studies dating back to the 1950s were showing that the physical abuse of parents was a concern. Recent research found that of all the cases of parent abuse reported to the researchers, 57% were categorized as physical abuse; followed by verbal abuse at 22%; the use of a weapon, usually a knife or gun, at 17%; throwing items at 5%. Regardless of gender, 11% of children under age 10 physically abuse their parents, and this percentage stays steady for boys over age 10. For girls it drops to 7%. Mothers are five times more likely than fathers to experience severe physical abuse from their children, and the highest rate of abuse occurs in families with a single mother (Robinson, Davidson, & Drebot, 2004). Mothers are abused more often than fathers, probably because women usually are not as physically strong as men and because women are commonly viewed as acceptable targets for aggression. Mothers who have been abused by their husbands are more likely to be abused by their children. Teenagers who were once victims of parental violence often grow up to fight back (Gelles, 2000a).

Finally, family caseworkers report many situations in which an adult child physically or emotionally abuses her or his elderly parents. The stress of caring for an aging parent can be great, and abusive adult children sometimes argue that they are paying their parents back for the abuse they suffered as children: "He did it to me. Now I have my chance to get even." Other adult children report they are responding in kind to the abuse their difficult elderly parents have showered on them. Fortunately, many treatment programs are available to help people find positive and satisfying ways to relate to one another across the generations (BBC News, 2012; Buzzetti & Associates, 2010; Envision Counselling and Support Centre, 2016; Purplefairy, 2012; Women's and Children's Health Network, 2016).

Alcohol Problems in Families

More than one in three Americans (36%) say drinking alcohol has been a cause of problems in their family at some point, one of the highest figures Gallup has measured since the 1940s. Reports of alcohol-related family troubles have been much more common in recent decades than they were prior to 1990.

—GALLUP (2014, JULY 29)

A family with a drinking problem is always a family in trouble.
—MARCIA LASSWELL AND THOMAS LASSWELL (1991)

Alcohol is a drug that acts as a depressant to the central nervous system. It is the mood-altering ingredient in wine, beer, and liquor. Alcohol is absorbed into the bloodstream and travels to virtually every part of the body. When ingested in large amounts or over a long period of time, alcohol can kill. It can damage the liver, heart, and pancreas; other consequences include malnutrition, stomach irritation, lowered resistance to disease, irreversible brain or nervous system damage and can cause cancer of the mouth, throat, voice box, esophagus, breast, liver, colon, and rectum (American Cancer Society, 2016; National Institute on Alcohol Abuse and Alcoholism, 2016a).

Alcohol abuse is a generic term that encompasses both **alcoholism**, which is the addiction to alcohol characterized by compulsive drinking, and **problem drinking**, which is alcohol consumption that results in a functional disability. More than one-half of American adults have a close family member who has or has had alcoholism or was a problem drinker. That is to say, about half of all adults in this country grew up with an alcoholic or problem drinker or had a blood relative who was an alcoholic or problem drinker (Centers for Disease Control and Prevention, 2016, February 10; National Institute on Alcohol Abuse and Alcoholism, 2016b).

America's communities are besieged by a highly dangerous, addictive drug. Its users can become agitated and violent, harming themselves and family members. It's incredibly toxic and even lethal at high doses. Many people who start abusing it are unable to quit. It's responsible for nearly 90,000 deaths each year. And in a new survey, more than three-quarters of Americans identified it as a serious problem in their community.
  It's called alcohol.

—CHRISTOPHER INGRAHAM,
THE WASHINGTON POST (2016)

Alcohol is the most widely used psychoactive drug in the United States. It contributes to the death of 88,000 people every year. Approximately 62,000 men and 26,000 women die, making it the third leading cause of preventable death in this country after tobacco and diet/activity patterns. Based on victim reports, 37% of the rapes and sexual assaults in America involved alcohol use by the offender. Fetal alcohol syndrome (FAS), which can occur when women drink during pregnancy, is the leading known environmental cause of mental retardation in Western countries. And, it is estimated that more than 10% of U.S. children live with a parent who has alcohol problems (Center for Behavioral Health Statistics and Quality, 2015; Centers for Disease Control and Prevention, 2016, February 10; National Institute on Alcohol Abuse and Alcoholism, 2016c, 2016d).

Alcohol and Family Violence

Alcohol is commonly associated with marital disruption, domestic violence, and many other family problems (American Association for Marriage and Family Therapy, 2016a; National Council on Alcoholism and Drug Dependence, 2015, June 27; National Institute on Alcohol Abuse and Alcoholism, 2016e). Alcohol abuse is far more common among men than among women, although alcohol abuse by women is growing. Most literature has focused on the husband as the alcohol abuser and the wife and children as victims, but statistics show that alcohol dependence problems among wives are on the rise.

Alcohol abuse and family violence are statistically related. A national sample of more than 2,000 couples found, in general, that the more often a spouse was drunk, the greater likelihood there was of physical violence in the marital relationship. The exception to this finding was when the alcohol abuse was extreme. In this case, when the spouse was "almost always" drunk, the level of physical violence dropped to a lower level.

Even if there is no violence in the family of an alcoholic, there is likely to be a high degree of marital dissatisfaction and a large number of disagreements. Tension and verbal conflict are likely to be frequent. Researchers have estimated that half the divorces and half the juvenile arrests for delinquency in the United States occur in families with at least one alcohol-abusing member.

Spouses and children of alcohol abusers are at risk for developing serious physical and emotional problems. Although the majority of children reared in alcoholic homes are no more prone to suffer some kind of pathology, they are more likely to exhibit a variety of behavioral and emotional problems than are children from families without an alcoholic member. These problems include conduct disorders or delinquency, alcohol abuse, hyperactivity, difficulties with school work, anxiety, depression, or other health problems.

The Family's Reaction to Alcohol Abuse

People don't drink because they're in bad marriages, but . . . drink makes marriages bad.
—GEORGE VAILLANT

In her classic article entitled "The Adjustment of the Family to the Crisis of Alcoholism," Joan K. Jackson (1954) began to develop our modern-day understanding of the effects of alcoholism and other addictions on the family. In a subsequent article Jackson (1964) focused on the developmental problems experienced by children of alcoholics.

Since Jackson began focusing on the family and alcohol, countless family studies have been conducted over the years and these investigations evolved through several stages of primary focus: the alcoholic wife, the alcoholic marriage, the nature of the alcoholic family as a dynamic system, the effects of alcoholism on children and adult children of alcoholics, and family therapy approaches to the treatment of a broad spectrum of substance use disorders (White, 2005).

Jackson (1954) was the first to describe the common dynamics of how families attempt to live with an alcohol-abusing father. It is widely recognized today that there are also many families with alcohol-abusing mothers, of course, and children in a family frequently have

TABLE 14.5   Warning Signs for Alcohol Abuse

The following are some common warning signs of alcohol abuse. The more warning signs that apply, the greater the severity of the problem with alcohol use.

1. Drinking alone or secretively.
2. Using alcohol deliberately and repeatedly to perform or to get through difficult situations.
3. Feeling uncomfortable on occasions when alcohol is not available.
4. Escalating alcohol consumption beyond an already established drinking pattern.
5. Consuming alcohol heavily in risky situations (e.g., before driving).
6. Getting drunk regularly or more frequently than in the past.
7. Drinking in the morning or at other unusual times.

From P.M. Insel and W.T. Roth, *Core Concepts in Health,* Ninth Edition (New York: McGraw_Hill, 2004), p. 268. Copyright © 2004 by McGraw-Hill Education, LLC, reprinted with permission.

drinking problems because young people commonly start drinking at an early age. Jackson's insights, however, remain useful for understanding many different families. She studied a sample of families of Alcoholics Anonymous members and outlined these common processes as families tried to cope. Still, it needs to be further emphasized that every family is unique, and the processes surrounding how families cope with alcohol abuse are widely varied; each story unfolds in a different way. Be that as it may, there are common themes:

- *The family tries to deny the problem.* The problem drinker, when confronted by the sober adult about the drinking behavior, denies there is a problem. The family accepts this statement and tolerates or rationalizes the abuser's drinking episodes.
- *The family tries to eliminate the problem.* When the drinking can no longer be ignored, the sober spouse tries to control the problem drinker with threats, bribes, and/or by hiding the alcohol. Marital conflict increases, and family members isolate themselves from friends and neighbors in a futile effort to conceal the drinker's problem.
- *The family becomes disorganized.* The sober spouse realizes that the problem cannot be rationalized away or concealed from the children or the drinker's employer and co-workers. The sober spouse also recognizes that it is futile to try to curtail the drinker's alcohol consumption. Conflict increases, with the children often caught between arguing parents.
- *The family tries to reorganize.* The sober spouse recognizes that the drinker cannot function adequately in the family—a recognition often precipitated by the drinker's mismanagement of family funds or by the drinker's violence toward the sober spouse or the children—and takes action. The sober spouse may assume the alcohol abuser's role in the family or may decide to leave the alcohol abuser. The sober spouse may seek assistance from various public agencies, counselors, treatment programs, and self-help groups such as Al-Anon. This network of support helps the sober partner gradually regain self-esteem and find the strength to go on. During this process, the problem drinker is likely to bargain with the family, hoping to regain the lost family role and stature. If the family accepts the drinker's bargain but the drinker continues or resumes drinking, the destructive cycle begins again.
- *The family tries to escape the problem.* The sober spouse seeks a legal separation or divorce. The alcohol abuser often gives up drinking for a while, but the sober spouse may have already shifted from inaction to action.
- *The family tries to reorganize a second time.* After legal separation or divorce, the sober spouse assumes the roles formerly held by the problem drinker, and family life

without the problem drinker is generally much better for all family members. The sober spouse may feel guilty for having left the troubled partner. The problem drinker may attempt to reenter the family or may try to get even with the family.
- *The family reorganizes, with the substance abuser seeking help.* If the alcohol-abusing member seeks help and learns to control the drinking, the family may be able to reunite successfully. The process can be difficult, family roles will have to be reassigned once again, and family members will need to reassess their feelings toward the alcohol abuser.

Later therapists built on Jackson's work and outlined a number of coping strategies women commonly use when dealing with alcohol-abusing husbands. These include emotional withdrawal from the marriage; infantilizing the husband; threatening separation or divorce or locking the spouse out of the house; trying to avoid family conflict; assuming control over family finances; and acting out themselves by drinking, threatening suicide, or becoming involved with other men (see Discovery Place, 2015; National Council on Alcoholism and Drug Dependence, 2015, July 26; 2016, February 24; 2017, July 15).

Treatment and Prevention of Alcoholism

Some family therapists have been critical of programs that treat the alcoholic outside the context of the family, whereas some alcoholism treatment therapists have criticized family therapists for assuming that alcoholism can be cured simply by eliminating dysfunctional family patterns. It is probably safe to say that problems in families can contribute to alcohol abuse in individual members, and that the alcohol abuse then contributes to problems for that family. Those who work with alcohol abusers are becoming increasingly aware that family therapy is an important tool in the treatment of alcoholics and their family system (American Association for Marriage and Family Therapy, 2016b; O'Farrell & Fals-Stewart, 2001, 2007; Rowe, 2003).

Self-help groups such as **Alcoholics Anonymous (AA)** (for alcoholics) and **Al-Anon** (for families of alcoholics) have chapters in most U.S. cities and towns. In some metropolitan areas, many different AA meetings are held at a variety of locations each week. These groups offer advice and support for troubled individuals and families. **Alateen,** founded on the AA model, is a support group for young people with alcoholic parents. In weekly meetings, members discuss their problems and learn from others how to move ahead in life from the experiences of others in similar situations.

To get an idea of the size of this volunteer-run movement, and the magnitude of the tragedy of alcoholism in the United States and worldwide, here are some numbers:

- There are 4,689 Alcoholics Anonymous groups in Los Angeles County, California, with 1,388 of them Spanish-speaking, as well as other meetings spoken in Armenian, Farsi, Finnish, French, Japanese, Korean, and Russian. If all these meetings were listed separately by town, they would cover 160 web pages (Alcoholics Anonymous Meetings in Los Angeles County, California, 2012).
- There are 60,698 AA groups in the United States and 5,043 AA groups in Canada. Total members in North America number 1,348,072 (Alcoholics Anonymous, 2017, June).
- Worldwide, there are 117,748 AA groups in 170 countries. Total members in the world number 2,089,698 (Alcoholics Anonymous, 2015).
- Though we could not find numbers for Al-Anon and Alateen groups in the United States and Canada, worldwide numbers are considerable: there are 25,400 autonomous Al-Anon/Alateen groups in more than 130 countries (Al-Anon Family Groups, 2016a).

Alcoholics need to be confronted about their condition by people they trust and in a form they can receive. Even in the most advanced phases, alcoholics can recognize and accept some reality.
©Comstock/Stockbyte/Getty Images

Besides thousands upon thousands of face-to-face support groups meeting each week, AA, Al-Anon, and Alateen have well-developed online programs, including email groups, real-time chat meetings, and internet telephony meetings that help members meet via free conference calls online (Alcoholics Anonymous, 2016b; Al-Anon Family Groups, 2016b, 2016c).

Though no one would say the process is easy, many people have been successful in the process of recovery from the disease of alcoholism and other drugs. Perhaps for the first time, there may be an accurate estimate of how many people in the United States are currently in recovery for an alcohol or other drug problem. A national survey conducted by the Partnership at DrugFree.org and the New York State Office of Alcoholism and Substance Abuse Services (OASAS) indicates that 10% of all adults over age 18 in the United States consider themselves to be in recovery. This means that an estimated 23.5 million Americans have found sustained recovery from involvement with drugs and alcohol that they once considered problematic. The researchers also found that 12% of males are in recovery, and 7% of females (Partnership for Drug-Free Kids, 2012).

The National Council on Alcoholism and Drug Dependence (NCADD) (2016) argues that helping a loved one struggling with alcoholism or drug dependence can be heartbreakingly painful, but with help it also can be remarkably rewarding. At times it can seem so overwhelming that it would be easier to ignore the problem, pretend that nothing is wrong, and just hope it all goes away. But denying or minimizing the problem does not work in the long run and will cause more damage to family and friends and the person who is caught in the trap of addiction.

NCADD (2016) urges family and friends, "Don't wait. Now is the time." To get started, they offer these suggestions:

1. *Learn all you can about alcoholism and drug dependence.* Learn about alcohol, learn about drugs, and learn about family education opportunities.
2. *Speak up and offer your support.* Don't wait for your loved ones to hit bottom. You may be met with excuses, denial, and anger, but be prepared to respond with specific examples of behavior that has you worried.

3. *Don't expect the person to stop without help.* Promises to cut down or stop abusing don't work. Treatment, support, and new coping skills are needed to overcome the addiction to alcohol and drugs, and this journey cannot be made alone.

4. *Support recovery as an ongoing process.* Once your friend or family member is receiving treatment or going to meetings, remain involved. Maintain your commitment to helping them find resources; continue to support their participation in continuing care, meetings, and recovery groups. Continue to show that you are concerned about their successful long-term recovery.

NCADD also lists things you don't want to do:

1. *Don't preach.* Don't lecture, threaten, bribe, or moralize.

2. *Don't be a martyr.* Avoid emotional appeals that may only increase feelings of guilt and the compulsion to drink or use other drugs.

3. *Don't cover up.* Don't lie or make excuses for their behavior.

4. *Don't assume their responsibilities.* Taking over their responsibilities protects them from the consequences of their behavior.

5. *Don't argue when using.* Arguing with the person when they are using alcohol or drugs does not work. They are incapable of having a rational conversation.

6. *Don't feel guilty or responsible for their behavior.* It's not your fault.

7. *Don't join them.* Don't try to keep up with them by drinking or using.

Acknowledging the Dangers of Legal Drugs

Our national fervor to stamp out use of and addiction to illegal drugs has in some ways overshadowed the serious harm legal drugs cause in our society. Alcohol and tobacco cause many times the number of deaths attributable to illegal drugs—and the associated costs, in terms of lost time from work and medical bills, are much greater.

About 570,000 people die every year due to drug use. Breaking this down, 440,000 die from disease related to tobacco, 88,000 due to alcohol, 20,000 due to illicit (illegal drugs), and 20,000 due to prescription drugs (National Institute on Alcohol Abuse and Alcoholism, 2016c; National Institute on Drug Abuse for Teens, 2016). Looking at those numbers from another angle, they tell us that only 3.5% of drug-related deaths in our country each year are related to the use of illegal drugs, leaving 96.5% of the deaths caused by legal drugs. Why in our society do we focus so much attention on illegal drugs, when legal drugs kill so many more people? What do you think is going on?

Medically speaking, alcohol and cigarette addictions can be very difficult habits to break. According to the Centers for Disease Control and Prevention (2016, April 14), tobacco use is started and established primarily during adolescence. Nearly 9 out of 10 cigarette smokers first tried smoking by age 18, and 99% first tried smoking by age 26. It is also known that family functioning is related to adolescent cigarette smoking. For example, William J. Doherty and William Allen (1994) found that families who were low in cohesion (togetherness) and had a parent who smoked were the most likely to have a young adolescent who smoked. Similarly, Janet N. Melby and her colleagues found that harsh and inconsistent parenting was related to adolescent tobacco use and that nurturant and involved parenting was not (Melby, Conger, Conger, & Lorenz, 1993). And Jie Wu Weiss and James A. Garbanati (2004) found that Asian American adolescents who smoked regularly had a lower level of acculturation in this country, compared to nonsmoking Asian American adolescents. This indicates that the smokers had not acquired the culture of this country as well as the nonsmokers. The smokers were also from families demonstrating poorer family functioning, and were more likely to have a father who smokes (Wu Weiss & Garbanati, 2004).

In addition to not smoking themselves, there are a number of other important ways parents can influence their children in the decision to not smoke: by setting rules about movie viewing so that kids don't see a lot of smoking and drinking by the stars (and often subsidized by the tobacco and alcohol companies); communicating positively and regularly with one's children, rather than isolating them and giving them too much alone time or unsupervised time with peers; and being aware of how your behavior as a parent influences your children from an early age. These are all ways that parents can help to reduce their children's chances of smoking (Hood Center for Children and Families, Dartmouth Medical School, 2012).

The family is clearly a major influence in our lives, either as a foundation for health and happiness or as an unhappy battleground. Emotional, physical, and sexual abuse do occur in families, and many families are plagued by alcoholism and addiction to other legal and illegal drugs. But these problems can be treated effectively. Fortunately, most families find ways to create relatively supportive and satisfying relationships among their members, which helps prevent many problems of all sorts.

Summary

- Some of the aspects of family stress are common across cultural groups. These are generalized principles that emerged from studying family strengths and stressors in different countries and cultures around the world: (1) all stressors either begin or end up in the family; (2) families from all cultural groups experience couple and family stress; (3) to manage their stress, couples and families tend to first use internal resources (those inside the family system) before seeking external resources (those outside the family system); (4) in many cultures, the extended family system is considered "the family" rather than the nuclear family system; the major resources come from inside the extended family, while fewer resources come from the nuclear family; and (5) all couples and families have some internal strengths for managing stress in their systems, and approaches to stress and coping from one culture to the next can be remarkably similar.
- The three levels of stress are physiological, psychological, and sociocultural. Physiological stress is what happens to our bodies; psychological stress is what happens to our emotions; and sociocultural stress refers to things around us that cause stress, such as war or poverty.
- Coping is how we respond to something that is potentially harmful. Coping with stress can either be problem-focused or emotion-focused. If we focus on the problem, we try to change the situation, the behavior of others, or our attitudes. If we focus on our emotions, we try to reduce or manage our own stress.
- There is a relationship between stress and health. The strongest association is between work stress and cardiovascular disease.

- The roller coaster course of adjustment to stressors, described by Reuben Hill, involves a period of disorganization, an angle of recovery, and a new level of organization.
- Families draw on a variety of resources and related coping strategies to deal with stressful issues: cognitive resources (reframing the situation), emotional resources (expressing feelings), relationship resources (increasing cohesion), community resources (seeking help and support from outside the family), spiritual resources (praying; seeking help from a spiritual guide), and individual resources (developing autonomy).
- According to family systems theory, family members' behaviors are all interrelated; each member's actions affect the other members and their actions. As such, the family systems approach focuses on helping families resolve relationships by focusing on *where we go next*, instead of *who should we blame*.
- War and deployment of soldiers to training facilities or a war zone affect couple and family relationships. Some of the effects for at-home spouses include mental health issues such as depression, anxiety, and sleep disorders. Those deployed often experience multiple mental and physical health issues.
- Divorce rates have increased for military personnel, with military women divorcing more often than military men.
- Children of parents who are deployed experience an overall sense of loss and uncertainty, often resulting in behavior changes and conflict with the at-home parent.
- Community organizations have been formed to help families with a deployed parent. The support of communities is viewed as important in helping families feel less isolated and alone.

- Family violence is a core social issue in every country around the world. The historical and political bias that events occurring outside the home are more significant than events occurring within the home and that what happens inside the home is private and not public, have helped mask the impact of family violence. Yet, the world is slowly awakening and admitting the fact that family violence is a major problem, and it is hard to conceive how to construct strong nations without creating healthy violence-free families.
- Based on a national survey of spouse abuse with 20,951 married couples, nonabusive marriages were compared with abusive marriages. Couples in nonabusive marriages had used less alcohol, had higher levels of couple closeness and flexibility, had better communication and conflict resolution skills, and had a stronger network of family and friends. In terms of personality, nonabusive marriages had partners who were more assertive, had higher levels of self-confidence, and less often tried to dominate their partners.
- Many of the risk factors for spouse abuse in a family are similar to those for child abuse: victimization as a child, low self-esteem, youth, economic stress, social isolation, alcohol abuse, and a male-dominated relationship. Cultural factors that implicitly support the objectification and denigration of women may also play a part.
- Counselors generally advise battered women to leave their husbands. Shelters for abused women and their children offer emotional support and counseling as well as practical help. Police arrest of perpetrators of domestic violence is more common today, and research indicates that men who spend time behind bars are less likely to assault their partners again.
- Child abuse is physical or emotional harm to children or failure to act that results in harm to a child. Abuse includes physical and sexual abuse as well as neglect.
- The number of reports of child maltreatment has decreased since 1993.
- Some researchers have found that spanking is detrimental to the short-term and long-term development of children. It is suggested that hitting children teaches them to hit others—as children and later as adults.
- Parental and family risk factors for child abuse include economic distress, inadequate parenting skills, parental personality problems, chemical abuse, social isolation, a special child, domestic violence in the abuser's family of origin, a violent subculture or marriage, and single parenthood or stepparenthood.
- Sibling abuse and child-to-parent abuse are more common than might be expected. An estimated 75% of siblings are involved in a violent episode each year, and 10% of parents are victims of their children's violent behavior.
- An estimated 88,000 Americans die each year from alcohol abuse, and about 440,000 Americans die from diseases linked to smoking.

Key Terms

stress
coping
ambiguous loss
boundary ambiguity
deployment
traumatic brain injury
posttraumatic stress
    disorder (PTSD)
managing stress
family coping
victimizer
learned helplessness theory

catharsis conflict
child abuse
sibling abuse
child-to-parent abuse
alcohol abuse
alcoholism
problem drinking
Alcoholics
    Anonymous (AA)
Al-Anon
Alateen

Activities

1. Take the Holmes-Rahe Stress Inventory and see how stressful your life has been in the past year, and the likelihood that you will have serious negative health consequences in the coming two years. To do this, visit the American Stress Institute web site: http://www.stress.org/holmes-rahe-stress-inventory/).
2. Think about how members of your family respond to stress. Ask your parents, siblings, or spouse to describe how your family responds to stress. Are there cultural components to your family's responses? Compare what you have learned from this chapter to what your family does.
3. Identify a family in your community who has a member deployed. Talk to them about what they are experiencing. If it is appropriate and if the parents approve, also talk with the children. Identify ways you can help, and do so.
4. Identify and visit a domestic violence facility in your community. Learn what they do and how they help those who have experienced domestic violence. Or interview a police officer and find out how he or she handles domestic violence calls.
5. In small groups, discuss the extent of alcohol and other drug abuse on campus. Also discuss any violent incidents, such as date rape, related to chemical abuse.
6. About 570,000 people die every year due to drug use. Breaking this down, 440,000 die from disease related to tobacco, 88,000 due to alcohol, 20,000 due to illicit (illegal) drugs, and 20,000 due to prescription drugs. Looking at those numbers from another angle, they tell us that only 3.5% of drug-related deaths in our country are related to the use of illegal drugs, leaving 96.5% of the deaths caused by legal drugs. Why in our society do we focus so much attention on illegal drugs, when legal drugs kill so many more people? In a small group, discuss what you think is going on.

Suggested Readings

Al-Anon Family Groups. (2016b). How does Al-Anon work? Web site: http://al-anon.org/?gclid=CJDyq8vFncwCFQqKaQodmdILJQ. The volunteers with Al-Anon provide education and support for families of alcoholics. Alateen volunteers work with young people who have drinking-related problems.

Al-Anon Family Groups (2016c). Online Al-Anon outreach. Web site: http://www.ola-is.org/. Online education and support for families of alcoholics, and for young people.

Alcoholics Anonymous. (2016a). Welcome to Alcoholics Anonymous. Web site: http://www.aa.org/. Education and support for alcoholics from other alcoholics.

Alcoholics Anonymous. (2016b). Welcome to AAOnline! Web site: http://www.aaonline.org/.

American Humane. (2016, August 25). Understanding the link between animal abuse and family violence. Web site: https://www.americanhumane.org/fact-sheet/understanding-the-link-between-animal-abuse-and-family-violence/.

American Stress Institute. (2016). Holmes-Rahe Stress Inventory. Web site: http://www.stress.org/holmes-rahe-stress-inventory/). This is the class tool for measuring stress in your life, and seeing how likely you are to develop serious negative health changes in the next two years.

Asay, S. M., DeFrain, J., Metzger, M., & Moyer, R. (2014). *Family violence from a global perspective: Strengths-based research and case studies.* Thousand Oaks, CA: Sage. A look at domestic violence from an international perspective, including 17 countries in all the world's major geocultural areas.

Center for Problem-Oriented Policing. (2016). Factors contributing to domestic violence. Web site: http://www.popcenter.org/problems/domestic_violence/2.

Centers for Disease Control and Prevention. (2016, February 10). Alcohol and public health. Web site: http://www.cdc.gov/alcohol/.

Centers for Disease Control and Prevention. (2016, April 14). Youth and tobacco use. Web site: http://www.cdc.gov/tobacco/data_statistics/fact_sheets/youth_data/tobacco_use/.

Centers for Disease Control and Prevention. (2017, April 17). Child abuse and neglect prevention. Web site: http://www.cdc.gov/violenceprevention/childmaltreatment/.

Centers for Disease Control and Prevention. (2017, April 18). Child abuse and neglect: Risk and protective factors. Web site: http://www.cdc.gov/violenceprevention/childmaltreatment/riskprotectivefactors.html.

Cullington, D. (2008). *Breaking up blues.* New York, NY: Routledge.

Faces and Voices of Recovery. (2016). Organizing the recovery community. Web site: http://www.facesandvoicesofrecovery.org/about.

Glaser, G. (2015, April). The irrationality of Alcoholics Anonymous. *The Atlantic.* Web site: http://www.theatlantic.com/magazine/archive/2015/04/the-irrationality-of-alcoholics-anonymous/386255/. The writer argues that the faith-based 12-step program of AA dominates treatment in the United States, but researchers have debunked central tenets of AA doctrine and have found dozens of other treatments more effective.

International Center for Journalists. (2016). Award-winning photojournalist helps put a human face on war. [Video file]. Web site: https://www.youtube.com/watch?v=0xzRkNWeFhQ:. A female war photographer talks about her work showing the realities of war to the world, especially what happens to women and children.

Järvinen, M. (2015). Understanding addiction: Adult children of alcoholics describing their parents' drinking problems. *Journal of Family Issues, 36*(6), 805–825.

Johnson, M. P. (2008). *A typology of domestic violence: Intimate terrorism, violent resistance, and situational couple violence.* Boston, MA: Northeastern University Press.

Johnson, M. P. (2011). Michael P. Johnson on intimate partner violence. [Video file]. Web site: https://www.youtube.com/watch?v=kRmiRvNhVXA.

Kaminer, Y., & Bukstein, O. G. (2008). *Adolescent substance abuse.* New York, NY: Routledge.

Mauritzen, E. (2011). The effect of war-deployment on at-home spouses and partners: A support group manual for group facilitators. University of St. Thomas, Minnesota: Department of Psychology. Web site: http://ir.stthomas.edu/caps_gradpsych_docproj/6/.

McGovern. G. (1997). *Terry: My daughter's life-and-death struggle with alcoholism.* New York, NY: Villard Books/Random House. A prominent statesman searches for an answer to the question why his daughter died as a result of her drinking, and how he could have helped her.

Mickish, J., & Schoen, K. (2004). Colorado Alliance for Cruelty Prevention: Safe pets, safe families, safe communities. *The Colorado Lawyer, 33*(1), 37–40.

National Coalition Against Domestic Violence. (2016). Domestic violence facts. Web site: http://www.ncadv.org/.

National Coalition Against Domestic Violence. (2016). Empowering victims and survivors. Web site: http://www.ncadv.org/. An excellent compilation of statistics.

National Council on Alcoholism and Drug Dependence. (2016). Welcome to NCADD. Web site: http://ncadd.org.

National Domestic Violence Hotline. (2016). Get help. Get involved. Stay safe. Web site: http://www.thehotline.org/about-us/.

National Institute on Alcohol Abuse and Alcoholism. (2016b). Alcohol and your health. Web site: http://www.niaaa.nih.gov/alcohol-health.

National Institute on Alcohol Abuse and Alcoholism. (2016). A guide for marriage and family therapists. Web site: http://pubs.niaaa.nih.gov/publications/niaaa-guide/.

National Institute on Drug Abuse. (2016). Frequently asked questions. Web site: https://www.drugabuse.gov/publications/principles-drug-addiction-treatment/frequently-asked-questions.

National Network to End Domestic Violence. (2016). Because knowledge is power. Womenslaw.org. Web site:

http://www.womenslaw.org/ Provides legal information and support to victims of domestic violence and sexual assault.

Partnership for Drug-Free Kids. (2016). Support and resources for parents dealing with teen drug and alcohol abuse. Web site: http://www.drugfree.org/.

Prevent Child Abuse America. (2016). All children deserve #greatchildhoods. Web site: http://preventchildabuse.org/.

Sahlstein Parcell, E., & Maguire, K. C. (2014, March 10). Turning points and trajectories in military deployment. *Journal of Family Communication*, *14*(2), 129–148. Web site: http://www.tandfonline.com/doi/abs/10.1080/15267431.2013.864293. Researchers found that most military wives in a sample of 50 reflected turbulence in family life during the predeployment and deployment phases, and declining or dipped satisfaction during the postdeployment period.

Scott, M. J. (2007). *Moving on after trauma*. New York, NY: Routledge.

Skogrand, L., DeFrain, N., DeFrain, J., & Jones, J. E. (2007). *Surviving and transcending a traumatic childhood: The dark thread*. New York, NY: Routledge.

Stith, S. M. (2013, Fall). Intimate partner violence in the military. *National Council on Family Relations*. Web site: https://www.ncfr.org/search?keyword=intimate+partner+violence+in+the+military.

U. S. Department of Justice. (2016). Domestic violence. Web site: https://www.justice.gov/ovw/domestic-violence

Walker, L. E. (2009). *The battered woman syndrome: With research associates*. New York, NY: Springer.

Weber, J. G. (2011). *Individual and Family Stress and Crises*. Los Angeles, CA: Sage Publications. An excellent introductory text.

Willows, J. (2008). *Moving on after childhood sexual abuse*. New York, NY: Routledge.

Visit the text-specific Online Learning Center at **www.mhhe.com/olson9e** for practice tests, chapter summaries, and PowerPoint slides.

Design Element: © Alicia Grünkind/EyeEm/Getty Images

15 Divorce, Single-Parent Families, and Stepfamilies

©Mint Images/Getty Images

Intimacy, Strengths, and Diversity

Divorce in Today's Society

Understanding Divorce

Single-Parent Families

Stepfamilies

Summary

Key Terms

Activities

Suggested Readings

Intimacy, Strengths, and Diversity

This chapter is about intimacy and the roller coaster ride of loss of intimacy in divorce, the challenges and strengths of single-parenthood, and newfound intimacy in remarriage resulting in stepfamilies. Intimacy becomes complicated in divorce, when what was once a close relationship turns to the deterioration of the marriage. There was a history of intimacy, and children may have resulted from a close, intimate emotional and sexual relationship. Even though that may be gone in divorce, it is never forgotten. Stepfamily relationships require new and usually more complicated intimate relationships with the addition of stepchildren and new extended-family relationships.

People seek inner strength as they go through a divorce and also as single parents. All types of families can be strong. In fact, single mothers and single fathers can create wonderfully strong family relationships. There is no doubt that life is often more complicated and stressful for single parents and stepfamilies, but many families do well in meeting the challenges.

This chapter is also about the diversity of family forms. This growing family complexity creates challenges for family members, extended-family members, therapists, and policymakers as we try to navigate new territory.

Divorce in Today's Society

Historical Trends

Before we consider the trends in divorce rates, we must look at what has happened with marriage rates. They have declined since the 1960s and continue to decline from 8.2 per 1,000 in the population in 2000 to 6.9 per 1,000 in 2014 (Centers for Disease Control and Prevention, 2015, November 23). This decline is affected by the increase in the number of adults who decide to delay marriage, and the increase in the number of couples who decide to cohabit rather than marry (National Healthy Marriage Resource Center, 2007, January). The proportion of adults who have never married has increased in recent years

Stepfamilies are becoming increasingly common as the number of single parents and divorced parents marry.
©Inti St Clair/Blend Images/Getty Images

(Lewis & Kreider, 2015, March). Those from 20 to 29 years of age are most likely to be in this category. The median age of first marriage has increased. This decline in the numbers of couples who marry and the increased age of marriage affects the corresponding recent decline in divorce rates.

Before the mid-1800s, people married for physical and economic survival. Divorce for most people was not an option. Many marriages were arranged, or women married the farmer down the road with only two or three potential marriage partners available. Very few marriages ended in divorce during this time. By the late 1800s and early 1900s, young people moved from viewing marriage as a way to stay alive to marrying for love.

Divorce rates can change as a result of societal events. Some researchers, although not all, believe that part of the increase in divorce in the 1970s was also related to a change in divorce laws, which made it easier to get divorced. During this time, many states went from fault-based divorce to no-fault divorce, which meant that divorces could be granted without either partner finding fault with their spouse. The highest divorce rates in history occurred in 1979 and 1981, with the rates beginning to decline in 2002 (Centers for Disease Control and Prevention, 2015, November 23). The divorce rate per 1,000 people in the population went from 4.0 in 2000 to 3.2 in 2014. Today the lifetime probability of a marriage ending in divorce is approximately 50%, while those marrying more recently have a probability of divorce which is likely to be lower than that (Greene, Anderson, Forgatch, DeGarmo, & Hetherington, 2012). The explanation for this decrease might be that people today are marrying later, which lowers the probability of divorce.

There are multiple factors that contributed to the peak in divorce rates from 1979 to 1981, since several things were happening in society during that time. Women were entering the workforce in increasing numbers, which meant that they became more independent and could support themselves. Contraception was also more available for women during that time, which allowed women to control childbearing.

Recessions and economic downturns also affect the divorce rate. According to Wilcox (2009), couples are more likely to weather the economic storm by staying together rather than divorcing. Although there are times when it is most important to have a spouse who meets one's emotional needs, during a downturn individuals may choose to stay with someone who can help contribute to house payments. During financially challenging times, marriage becomes an economic partnership and a safety net.

The number of people who cohabit also affects the divorce rate (Daugherty & Copen, 2016, March 17). We do not have any documentation about the number of people who cohabit and then break up, but historically those who break up would have been represented in divorce statistics. This is true to an even greater extent in European countries. For example, the cohabitation rates in Sweden and Denmark have increased to more than 90%, which also results in a decrease in the divorce rates. In some of these countries there is no distinction between marriage and cohabitation, and no one asks if a couple is married or not.

The extent to which people are religious also affects the divorce rate (Popenoe, 2008). Countries where religion is widely practiced are more likely to have higher marriage, lower cohabitation, and lower divorce rates. Spain and Italy are examples where the marriage rate is high, the cohabitation rate is about 3% to 4%, and the divorce rate is also low. These countries are more likely to have more traditional family structures, and religious values affect how couples view marriage. Other information about divorce around the world is provided in Box 15.1.

There are, on the other hand, many who choose not to be in marriages. For example, there is an organization called the Unmarried Equality (www.unmarried.org), which says that they are not opposed to marriage but do not feel marriage is for everyone. The organization

BOX 15.1 Diversity in Families
The Globalization of Divorce

Although America ranks high in the rate of divorce, the rest of the world is catching up. Across Europe, for instance, marriage rates are declining and divorce rates are climbing steadily, with Belgium reporting in 2002 that it had the fewest number of marriages in the European Union (3.9 per 1,000 people) and the highest number of divorces (3.0 per 1,000 people) (UK National Statistics, 2004).

Cultural changes taking place around the world are influencing divorce rates in almost every country. One of the countries changing most rapidly is the Republic of Korea, which in the past 10 to 15 years has become an increasingly open, westernized society.

Prior to 1990, divorce was a cultural and legal taboo in the Republic of Korea (known as South Korea by Westerners), and Korea's divorce rate was one of the lowest in the world (1.1 per 1,000 people). A divorced woman would be ostracized and had a very slim chance of marrying again. She usually lost custody of her children and had a difficult, if not impossible, time finding employment. A divorced man would also have had a hard time finding a job, or if he already had one, would not get promoted. His career path was definitely cut short. His chances at remarriage were not good either, as few women wanted to marry a man who had already shown he could not keep a stable relationship or take care of his family (Lankov, 2004).

The situation began to change in the early 1990s. Within 12 years, Korea's divorce rate rose from 11% in 1990 to 47% in 2002, ranking the country among the top 10 in the world. Some of the reasons for this swift-spreading change include "the collapse of traditional patriarchic values, the rise of a new generation of college-educated women, the growth of employment opportunities for female workers and their ensuing economic independence, and the powerful influence of Western individualism and feminism" (Lankov, 2004).

As a symbol of just how much Korean attitudes toward divorce have changed, in 2004 nearly a quarter of the country's television viewers tuned in once a week to watch a show called *Love and War*, where actors dramatized actual divorce cases and marital conflicts. Viewers could then vote online on whether they thought the couple should stay together or get divorced.

The Republic of Korea isn't the only Asian country to experience a dramatic rise in divorce rates. Below are some divorce statistics and their cultural significance in several other Asian countries:

- *India*. Not so long ago, a woman was so tied to her husband's fate that if he died before she did, she was thrown onto his funeral pyre. Today, that practice is no longer legal, and women in unhappy marriages are now seeking divorce. In 2004, the divorce rate was estimated at 11 per 1,000 people (versus 7.41 in 1991). However, divorce is still not socially accepted by everyone. One divorced woman related to *Time Asia* that divorced women in India always feel a sense of isolation and that "women like her are widely viewed as inferior to those with husbands" (Fitzpatrick, 2004).
- *Japan*. Statistics showed that in 2004 a couple married every 42 seconds in Japan—and that every 2 minutes another couple got divorced. The divorce rate rose from 22% in 1990 to 38% in 2002. The biggest change in Japan, where 70% of

supports the notion that people should have choices about marrying and not feel pressured to marry. Individuals must draw their own conclusions about this issue. Those conclusions are likely to be influenced by the individual's religious beliefs, expectations about the role of happiness in marriage, and personal life experiences.

Remarriage rates are also part of the divorce picture in that remarried adults have a higher likelihood of divorce than those in a first marriage (Lewis & Kreider, 2015, March). Here are some facts about remarriage:

- About half of men and women over age 15 have married only once.
- The proportion of adults who have married only once has decreased since 1996.
- The number of those who have married two times or more has increased between 2008 and 2012 for women aged 50 and men aged 60 and older.
- Those who have married three or more times are more likely to be White, followed by Blacks, Asians, and Hispanics, in that order. This is because Whites are more likely to marry and, thus, remarry more than other ethnic groups.

We are not sure if these recent trends will continue or change, and they may be impacted by a variety of other social factors.

all divorces are initiated by women, was the increase in the number of couples getting divorced after 20 years or more of marriage. In 1975, there were 6,810 such divorces; in 2002, there were 45,536 (Fitzpatrick, 2004).

- *China.* In the past 20 years, the divorce rate in mainland China has doubled—and has tripled in Taiwan. As in Japan, many of these divorced couples are in their 40s and 50s and have been married for many years. People over the age of 50 seeking divorce made up 9% of all divorces in 1980, as compared to 14.7% in 2003. The Association for Asian Research suggested four reasons for increased divorce rates among middle-aged Chinese: (1) the concept of marriage is changing and individual pursuit of happiness is seen as more important than stability; (2) the demands of professional success coupled with the demands of raising a family cause strain on relationships; (3) social acceptance of divorce has increased, and more opportunities exist to meet new partners; and (4) familial support systems—where extended families all lived together and shared responsibilities—are weaker than ever before ("Divorce Rate Climbs," 2004).

In Shanghai, where divorce rates increased by 30% in the 1-year period from 2003 to 2004, the government sent out notices to couples seeking divorce asking them to reconsider the correctness of their decision. One reason for the sharp increase was that procedures for divorce were greatly simplified in 2004, and couples who previously had to wait a month for their divorce agreement now had to wait about 10 minutes ("Divorce Rate on the Increase in Shanghai," 2004).

Elsewhere around the world divorce rates and attitudes toward divorce vary markedly. Africa, for instance, exhibits great disparities. In Morocco, a law was passed in February 2004, stating that women were no longer legally required to obey their husbands. Divorce, however, still brings a woman great shame. In contrast, when a woman in the western Sahara gets a divorce, she throws a party, and men who seek the hand of the newly available woman bring presents like camels, perfume, or money (Harter, 2004).

In another part of the continent, Egypt is struggling to find a more equitable system of granting divorce by changing some of its centuries-old laws and traditions. However, as reported by Human Rights Watch (2004), even the new laws are still biased toward the male population. Egyptian men have an unconditional right to divorce without ever having to go to court; they simply have to make an oral renunciation that can later be ratified by a member of the clergy. Women, on the other hand, must go through complicated legal procedures. If they wish to keep full financial rights, they must show evidence that their husbands inflicted physical harm, a claim they are usually required to support with eyewitness testimony. A woman can file for "no-fault" divorce—if she agrees to forfeit all her financial rights and repay the dowry given to her by her husband when they were wed (Human Rights Watch, 2004).

As the westernization of the world continues, as economic growth in poor countries increases, and as women's rights take on greater dimensions, we can expect the rising global divorce rate to continue to be an unintentional by-product.

Divorce Laws and Views on Divorce

In the early to mid-1900s the granting of a divorce by the legal system was based upon the ability of one of the spouses to successfully place blame on the other. Divorce was a result of a family breakdown, and there was an effort to control the number of divorces by limiting the available grounds for divorce. Because a divorce could not be granted unless one of the partners had done something to break the union, divorces were by definition adversarial. There were times, however, when everyone involved, including lawyers, fulfilled the legal requirement of placing blame, even when both partners agreed that a divorce was in the best interest of the couple.

No-fault divorce statutes eliminated the need to place blame on one partner or the other (Horner, 2014). Incompatibility and irreconcilable differences were added to the grounds for divorce. The first state to enact the no-fault statutes was California in 1969–1970. By 1985 all states had some provisions for no-fault divorce. No-fault divorce resulted in the following changes in how divorces were obtained:

- *Redefinition of the traditional duties of husbands and wives and establishment of equality between the genders as a norm.* Under no-fault laws, the husband is no longer

Because divorce can be a traumatic experience for adults and children, lawyers should not act as adversaries doing battle for their clients but should try to facilitate responsible communication. The lawyer's most important task is to help divorcing parents restructure the family and minimize the emotional damage to both themselves and their children.
©Tanya Constantine/Blend Images/Getty Images

considered by law to be the head of the family. Both spouses are presumed to be equal partners, with equal obligations for financial support and care of their children. Spouses are treated equally with respect to child custody, as well as finances and property. The so-called **tender years doctrine**, which presumed that young children would do better with their mother than with their father, has been replaced by the notion of joint custody as being in the "best interests of the child." Fathers are at least theoretically equal to mothers in questions of custody. In a small number of cases, fathers are winning not only custody but also child support.

- *Elimination of fault-based grounds for divorce.* Under no-fault laws, one spouse does not have to prove the other's adultery, cruelty, or desertion. The concept of *irreconcilable differences* recognizes the irrelevancy of discussing the reasons for the marital dissolution in court.
- *Elimination of the adversarial process.* Proponents of divorce reform argued that the adversarial nature of traditional divorce proceedings was harmful to all parties involved, especially to the children. Under no-fault, by facilitating accurate and responsible communication rather than doing battle, lawyers can help divorcing parents restructure the family and prepare to fulfill their postdivorce parenting responsibilities. Many spouses neither love nor hate each other at the end of a marriage; they are capable of an *amicable divorce* and are good candidates for joint custody of their children.
- *Basing of financial decisions on equity, equality, and economic need rather than on fault or gender-based role assignments.* In a no-fault system, each spouse's economic circumstances are assessed under the principle of equality between the sexes. No-fault

laws adhere to the notion that divorced women should be self-supporting *and when it* is not possible, they should receive fair compensation. Under the newer no-fault divorce laws, older homemakers are more likely to receive alimony than are younger homemakers. In some cases, a woman might receive support while she goes back to school for retraining. Attorneys have been forcefully arguing that women who previously put their husbands through professional school are entitled to a share of their earnings for a period of time after the divorce.

Although no-fault divorce was generally viewed as creating more equality between spouses, inequities still remained. Women typically could not earn as much as men, and women typically were awarded custody of the children (Mercadante et al., 2014). In the 1970s, fathers began to advocate for more involvement in their children's lives and we began to see research focusing on the benefits of fathers being involved in the lives of their children. Fathers began to gain custody of their children in divorce, or at least began to have shared custody of their children.

In the 1990s we began to see research that supported the view that children need both parents in their lives and that with divorce the children become the victims. The result is that states have begun to instigate longer waiting periods and parental counseling to ease the transitions of divorce for children.

Some efforts have been made to put in place safeguards before marriage to reduce the divorce rate. Some states charge less for a marriage license for couples who have participated in premarital education. Other states, such as Louisiana, Arizona, and Arkansas, have implemented the option of covenant marriages. They typically focus on the premise that marriage is more than a contract, it is a covenant with God. In a covenant marriage, the couple agrees to premarital counseling and, if a divorce becomes necessary, fault-based divorce provisions and an extended waiting period before finalizing a divorce. Covenant marriages are typically accepted by couples who are conservative Christians, and may be embraced by clergy and promoted in their congregations.

Understanding Divorce

No emptiness on earth can compare with the loss of love.
—PAUL THEROUX (1996, P. 425)

Both partners in a divorce often spend considerable time trying to unravel the reasons why their marriage ended. Although the task is difficult, it is essential to the postdivorce recovery process. The search for the "causes" of a divorce must take into consideration a number of factors and many points of view. In this section we will look at several important issues to understand why people divorce.

The Culture of Divorce

Divorce culture is the notion that divorce has now become so accepted that it is almost the expected outcome of marriage. Before the 1950s, divorce was rare, and there was considerable social pressure to stay married, even if it was a bad and abusive marriage. But now divorce is linked with the pursuit of individual satisfaction, and there is less social pressure to stay married. Even the presence of children is not a deterrent to getting divorced as it was in the past. The challenges of divorce are even fodder for comedy, as in the movie *Mrs. Doubtfire,* in which a mother unknowingly hires the separated father (dressed up as a woman) as a nanny to care for their children.

Usdansky (2009) recently concluded that as a society we are less critical of single-parent families when they have resulted from divorce than when they have resulted from nonmarital births. She indicates we currently have an *ambivalent acceptance of divorce*. Other researchers have also contributed to this discussion in that divorce is about individual rights and that in many cases divorce is necessary because of the right to be free of violence or other unfortunate circumstances (Cherlin, 2009). The views about nonmarital births, however, according to Cherlin, are tied to views about morality, and nonmarital births thus are viewed as less acceptable. Not surprisingly, nonmarital births are more accepted in low-income communities than in middle-income neighborhoods. It is expected by some that, in the future, views will change and the ambivalent acceptance of divorce will likely extend to women having children outside of marriage.

The Impact of Divorce on Adults

There are potentially multiple issues that divorced adults deal with as they move on after a failed marriage. The legal divorce is usually not the end of stress and unhappiness. Some of these issues include having major responsibility for children as the custodial parent, decreased contact with children for the noncustodial parent, difficulty dealing with reduced income, decreased social support, and potentially continued conflict with the ex-spouse over child support or custody issues (Greene et al., 2012). People differ in their ability to

Happy couples share fun and laughter together. This is because they have good relationship skills and are able to resolve any problematic issues.
©Kali9/E+/Getty Images

BOX 15.2 At Issue
Fathers' Experiences with Marital Separation

A qualitative research study of eight husbands and fathers in Australia describes their experiences during marital separation (Mercadante, Taylor, & Pooley, 2014). Although this study was conducted with Australian participants, it seems that these experiences might resonate with husbands and fathers in the United States or in other developed countries.

These authors (Mercadante et al., 2014) conclude that when couples decide to separate, generally one person is eager to get out of the relationship and the other is taken by surprise or is not ready to end the relationship. This leads to more trauma on the part of one of the individuals. Because women often are the initiators of separation and see it as a relief, while men typically describe it as difficult, the findings of this study are important in understanding what husbands and fathers sometimes experience.

According to Mercadante and colleagues (2014), the abruptness of the separation was a very difficult adjustment. Half of the fathers and husbands had no idea there was a problem in their marriages. They felt completely blindsided. The other four participants knew their relationships were unstable, but were surprised by what they viewed as abruptness of the termination. One man who was unaware of problems in his marriage came home to an empty house. His wife had taken everything. He could not believe he had been so unaware of the problems in their relationship. The fathers not only lost the connection with their spouse; most lost what they thought would be a 50/50 shared arrangement with their children. These fathers were, to some degree, at the mercy of their wives' determination of how much time they would have with their children.

The men in this study (Mercadante et al., 2014) also talked about the turmoil they felt when the separation was announced by their spouse. Because it was often abrupt, they usually had to find a place to live quickly. Even if they ended up staying in the home, with their wife and children moving out, the relationships ended quickly. They felt emptiness and anguish, especially in the relationships with their children. There was no preparation for this; they had lost all sense of control. Because the wives had typically initiated the separation, they had already spent time grieving and adjusting to the situation. This was not true for the men, however. These men not only had to try to adapt to their new physical situation, but they had to deal with the pain and grief of losing a marriage and changes in their relationships with their children. The husbands and fathers all felt it was an experience they would not wish on anyone else. One father said, "... I wouldn't wish it on my worst enemy" (Mercadante et al., 2014, p. 335).

It is clear from this study that the biggest change for these men was in their parenting role. In Australia only 17% of fathers receive equal or shared care arrangement for their children (Mercadante et al., 2014), and in the United States this percentage is just slightly higher. It, therefore, can be assumed many fathers and husbands in the United States have similar experiences with marital separation. It is truly a painful experience. These findings might be useful for divorce lawyers and judges in considering postdivorce arrangements. They also might be helpful for clinicians in understanding how to help families, especially fathers, in the separation process.

---

address these issues. For example, the ability to develop social support is dependent upon one's social skills and one's ability to construct new social networks. Individuals' ability to define their new status as a single person will also affect their ability to move on. Those who see their singlehood as an opportunity for personal growth, rather than a tragedy, will adjust more readily and successfully to life after divorce.

Often the road to adjustment and happiness is bumpy and difficult (Greene et al., 2012). Many adults who have experienced a divorce have a variety of problems as they adjust to a new life. There can be increased drug and alcohol use, suicide or attempted suicide, increase in motor vehicle accidents, and even death. As we see from Box 15.2, divorce is a painful process, and this process takes its toll on one's physical and emotional health.

More recent research indicates that the extent of these behaviors can be affected by gender, economic resources, the presence of preschool children, and the quality of the marriage (Greene et al., 2012). For example, low economic resources and the presence of preschool children increases the likelihood of problems with mental and physical health because they add stress to one's life. Women are more likely to experience difficulties when they are caring for preschool children because of parental stress. On the other hand, if one came out of an unsatisfying marriage, it can be a relief to separate or divorce and may actually improve a person's mental and physical health.

The Impact of Divorce on Children

The increase in divorce and the resulting impact on the well-being of children have been a major focus of research for many years. It is estimated that 50% of all children will experience divorce before reaching adulthood (Amato, 2010). Most studies show that children with divorced parents have higher rates of emotional and social problems than children from intact families.

Some of the most vocal professionals describing the negative impact of divorce on children include Judith Wallerstein and her colleagues (Wallerstein & Lewis, 2004). They conducted a longitudinal study of children of divorce using a small sample of families and concluded that divorce has a long-term impact on children. Even 5 years after a divorce, they found more than one-third of the children showed signs of moderate-to-severe depression. After 10 years, some of the adult children were underachieving and having emotional problems, and after 15 years, some adult children were having problems in their love relationships. This study had a small and biased sample of 60 families and no control group, although it did follow the same people over time, and provided a negative perspective on divorce.

A recent longitudinal study looked at how parental separation affected children's behavioral and emotional problems (Stadelmann, Perren, Groeben, & von Klitzing, 2010). In this large study of almost 200 5- and 6-year-old children, researchers investigated parental separation, family conflict, and children's views of their parents' relationships as these variables related to behavioral problems. The researchers found that parental separation and family conflict predicted and increased the level of behavior problems. They also found that if parents got along well, the behavioral problems were diminished.

Constance Ahrons, a long-time researcher of divorce, concludes that the effect of divorce on children varies depending on a multitude of interactive factors (Ahrons, 2007). These factors take into account the child, the parents, the pre- and postdivorce family, and the environmental and social factors. She concludes that most children of divorced parents grow up to be healthy and well adjusted, while another smaller group does less well.

The personalities of children affect how they react and respond to divorce (Ahrons, 2007). For example, the child's temperament and ways of coping have an impact on his or her ability to deal with this major family change. Is the child easy going, or does he or she respond dramatically to family transitions? Has the child developed ways of coping with difficulties? A child's emotional health before the divorce also affects his or her ability to deal with divorce. In addition, the relationship the child had with each parent before the divorce has an impact on the child's divorce experience.

A major factor in children's adjustment to divorce is also how well the parents deal with the divorce. The parents may lack the emotional health to handle the divorce in a mature way, and children get caught in the middle of parents who may not realize the impact of their behavior on the children. In addition, parents experience anger and grief and many other emotions and may not be able to help their children with those same feelings. As a result, the children can be left to fend for themselves.

Ahrons (2007) reported on a longitudinal interview study following 173 children of divorce over 20 years. Because longitudinal studies are rare, and the sample is relatively large, this study is very telling of what we know about the effects of divorce on children over time. This study focused on the long-term effects of divorce and the impact of a new partner in their parents' lives.

A focus of the Ahrons (2007) study was how well their divorced parents got along. Sixty percent of the adult children said their parents were cooperative, whereas when the divorce occurred only 40% were cooperative. Children whose parents did not get along describe the effort they had to make to maneuver relationships between both parents.

They talked retrospectively about not being able to talk about one parent when they were in the presence of the other. They also talked about dreading the transition times when moving between households. As adults they had to deal with weddings, funerals, and other family celebrations, often wondering how their divorced parents would behave toward each other. The major factor related to their personal well-being was how well their divorced parents got along. If the parents did not get along, the children did not do well. This finding supports other short-term findings, but according to this study, it was also true 20 years later. Not surprisingly, the relationships they had with their extended family also depended on how well their parents got along. This is consistent with the knowledge that family can be an important support system in getting through difficult times in life.

It does need to be noted that this study was conducted with adults whose parents divorced in the 1970s and 1980s. Times have changed, when it comes to parent custody issues and views about divorce and remarriage. Children whose parents divorce today may have a slightly different experience.

A more recent study by Amato, Kane, and James (2011) compared three groups of parents following divorce. The three groups were cooperative parenting, parallel parenting, and single parenting to see how children did in terms of behavior problems following a divorce. Cooperative parenting meant that parents worked together after the divorce and was coined by these authors as the *good divorce.* Youth who had parents who worked together in a positive way had fewer behavior problems and had better relationships with their fathers than the other two groups. However, these youth were no better off than the other two groups in terms of self-esteem, substance abuse, or early sexual activity. In conclusion, these authors question whether there really is such a thing as a good divorce.

Because same-sex relationships are becoming more prevalent, studies are now appearing that focus on the breakup of same-sex couples. A recent study of lesbian couple breakups, most of whom did not have a legal marriage relationship, indicated that if the children had been adopted by the nonbiological parent there was a closer relationship with both mothers after the separation (Gartrell, Bos, Preyser, Deck, & Rodas, 2011).

To put this discussion in perspective, Greene et al. (2012) conclude that although children experiencing divorce have a higher risk of problems than those who do not experience divorce, 80% of these children do not experience problems. Many children do extremely well navigating the challenges of their parents separating.

Binuclear Families Compared to Single-Parent Families. Terminology often can help in understanding how families are reorganized after divorce. Researchers sometimes prefer the term *binuclear family* to *single-parent family* because it acknowledges the positive outcome that results from divorce or separation of biological parents. Divorce or separation is a process that results in family reorganization rather than disintegration of the family system. This reorganization of the nuclear family frequently results in the establishment of two households, the mother's and the father's. If one ex-partner does not drop out of the family after the separation and the two households continue to interrelate, then a **binuclear family** has been established.

In some binuclear families, children have a primary and a secondary home: One parent has **sole custody**, and the children live with that parent in the primary home; the other parent in the secondary home has rights of visitation with the children. In a smaller proportion of families, the homes of both parents have equal importance—"one child, two homes." This arrangement has been termed **joint custody**. In an even smaller proportion of families, one parent has sole custody of one or more of the children, and the other parent has sole custody of the other child or children—an arrangement called **split custody**.

In binuclear families, relationships between the two households can vary greatly. Some ex-partners continue the preseparation wars into the postseparation years, whereas others get along wonderfully. A few binuclear families even share some holidays. The majority, however, rarely get together as a group.

Joint Custody. Joint custody is defined as either physical custody, where the child spends about equal time with both parents, or shared legal custody, where the child spends more time with one parent but both parents are involved in the child's life. In general, joint custody can be successful only if both parents are willing and able to work together in the best interests of the child or children.

While no particular custody arrangement is best for all families, joint custody can work if parents can work together. What is best for the children has to be decided on the basis of answers to numerous questions, including these: (1) Do the children and both parents feel it best that both parents continue to have contact with the children after the divorce? (2) Are both parents capable of maintaining an adequate home for the children? (3) Can the parents get along with each other well enough to manage a joint-custody arrangement after the divorce? If all members of the family can honestly answer yes to all three questions, then joint custody can potentially be successful.

Joint-custody parents report less stress than sole-custody parents. Joint-custody parents also have more time to pursue their own interests, because the ex-spouse assumes a share of the child care responsibilities. Joint-custody parents are more likely to come from a devitalized or burned-out marriage; they are likely to neither love nor hate each other but are able to deal rationally with each other.

Coping Successfully on Becoming a Single Parent. Becoming a single parent after a divorce is difficult. It is a process of finding one's way in a new world. Single parents have developed a number of successful strategies for coping with their unique station in life and offer the following suggestions for other single parents:

- Don't rush into a new couple relationship, particularly in an attempt to transfer your dependence onto another person. Let go of the past and move on.
- Realistically face what has happened. Learn from it; don't repeat it.
- Don't succumb to feelings of failure and worthlessness. Make the best of the situation and don't blame yourself completely.
- Keep busy with constructive activities. Take up new (or old) activities you always wanted to find time to enjoy.
- Listen to others but make your own decisions.
- Take one day at a time, setting small goals at first.
- Consider going back to school.
- Be flexible, adaptable, and independent.

Single-Parent Families

The number of children who at some point live in single-parent families increased from 1960 through 2000, and then began to level off (see Figure 15.1). Figure 15.1 indicates that there are differences in different cultural groups, with a higher rate of single parenthood for Blacks than Whites. In 1960, 9% of all children lived with one parent, and in 2008 it was 26% (Wilcox, 2009), with the majority of these families being headed by mothers. The percentage of single-parent families headed by fathers has increased substantially in recent years, with the number currently at 18%. It needs to be noted, however, that in 20% of separations and divorces, parents have joint legal custody of children and children share equal time with both parents.

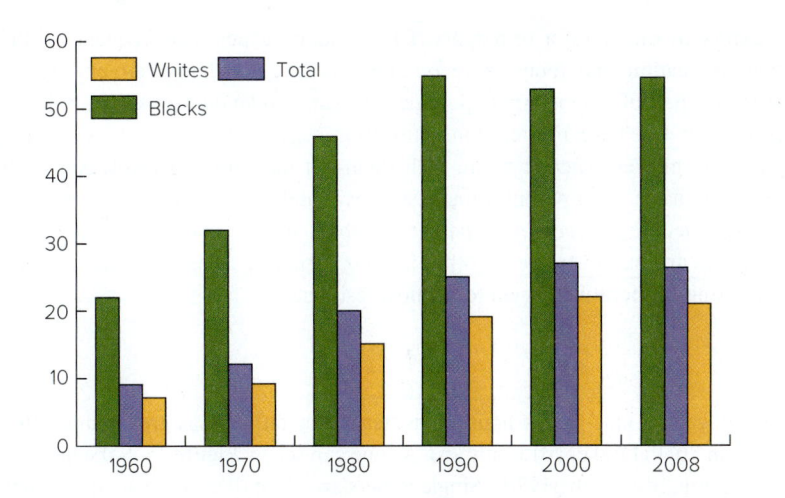

FIGURE 15.1

Percentage of children under age 18 living with a single parent, by year, United States

Source: U.S. Dept. of Agriculture, Center for Nutrition Policy and Promotion.

The increase in single-parent families has resulted from divorce, cohabitation, and births outside of marriage. Children born to cohabiting couples account for the largest increase in single-parent families. Multiple studies point to the varying ways single-parent families manage time with children and the varying factors that impact nonresidential parents' involvement in the lives of their children.

The literature is clear that unless there is abuse or neglect on the part of the noncustodial parent, most children want to have a relationship with both parents. Because most of the noncustodial parents are fathers, studies have typically focused on the time children are allowed to spend with their fathers. Generally, the quality of the parent–child relationship, the amount of contact, the amount of active involvement, and the type of parenting provided are related to more positive outcomes for children. This involvement usually results in fewer behavioral problems, better communication skills, and better academic performance.

Based upon existing literature, Kelly (2007) describes three types of coparenting relationships following separation or divorce. First, there is *conflicted coparenting,* which makes

Coparenting has become increasingly popular and has resulted in more fathers having quality time with their children.

©Digital Vision/Getty Images

Chapter 15 | Divorce, Single-Parent Families, and Stepfamilies up approximately one-quarter of parents. These couples experience frequent conflicts and poor communication and focus more on their own needs than their children's needs. Approximately half of parents are in *parallel coparenting relationships* and have low conflict with each other but have limited communication regarding parenting issues. They ultimately parent children when they are with them but have limited involvement when the children are with the other parent. Finally, approximately one-fourth of parents may be categorized as practicing *cooperative coparenting,* which involves planning together for their children's lives and supporting each other in their parenting roles. Children whose parents are coparenting cooperatively seem to be most resilient.

Fathers

The percentage of single-parent households headed by fathers has grown since 1960 from 14% to 24% in 2011 (Drake, 2013, July 15). As one can see by Figure 15.2, the number began to rise substantially after the 1990s. Single fathers are more likely than single mothers to be living with a partner (41% versus 16%). Typically, single fathers have higher incomes than single mothers and are less likely to be living in poverty.

Because the majority of children still end up residing with their mothers, the fathers often have less time with their children and typically are the noncustodial parent. This often creates a disparity between biological mothers and fathers in terms of the time spent with children. Because the amount of time fathers spend with children has important implications for their development, much research has focused on father–child relationships. From 1976 to 2002 the amount of time spent with 6- to 12-year-olds increased. Some noncustodial fathers spend little time with their children because it is too painful to have a minimal visiting role in the lives of their children. Mothers are often referred to as *gatekeepers* of children, and control how much time fathers spend with their children. This may be

FIGURE 15.2

Types of Living Arrangements in Households with Children Under 18, 1960–2011

Source: Pew Research Center, "The Rise of Single Fathers," July 2, 2013. Website: http://www.pewsocialtrends.org/2013/07/02/the-rise-of-single-fathers/

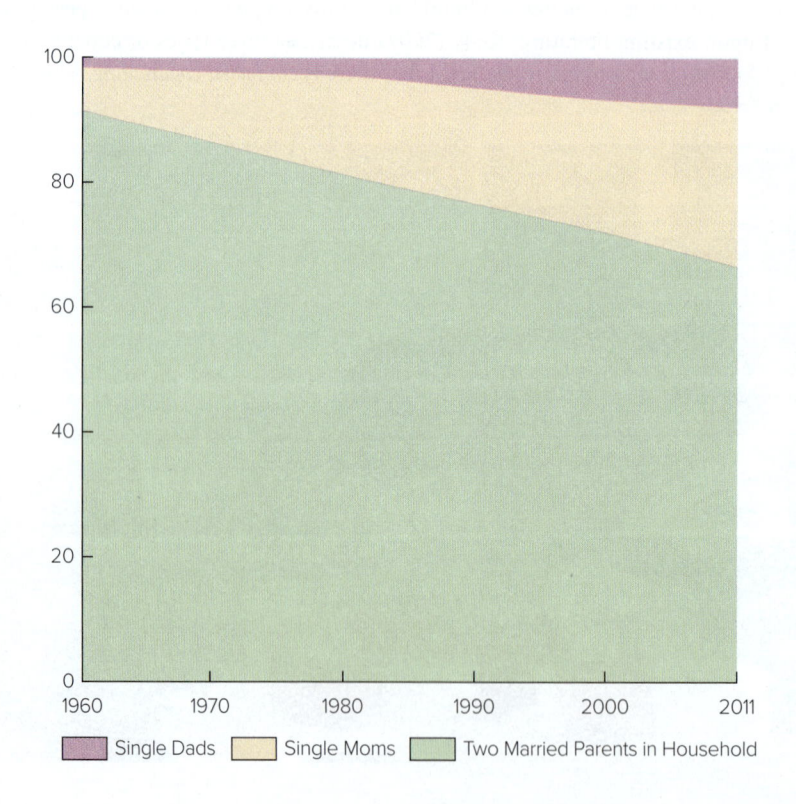

Many people who remarry have children from a previous marriage, and the resulting combination can be a large stepfamily with complex dynamics. The children must establish relationships with their stepparent and their stepsiblings, and the adults must learn new roles as stepparents.
©Purestock/Getty Images

due to beliefs, held by both mothers and fathers, that caring for children is the mother's responsibility and that fathers are less competent in this regard.

Fathers' involvement with their biological children is influenced by many factors, one of which is the degree to which they are paying child support. If fathers are paying child support, they are more likely to be spending time with their children. Fathers who were once married to their children's mother are also more likely to be involved in their children's lives. Hostility over a separation or divorce is also directly related to involvement with their children—with less contact if there was hostility during the breakup. For couples who were not married, better relationships between parents and the parents' relationships with each other's extended family are positively related to increased involvement with their children (Ryan, Kalil, & Ziol-Guest, 2008).

Several other factors can affect the involvement of the noncustodial parent in the lives of the children. Moving away, especially more than 75 miles, can affect time with children. This may be a substantial barrier for parents with limited economic resources or whose work does not allow for flexibility in spending time with children. If the parents are hostile toward each other or have coparenting conflict, it can lead to breakdown in communication and complicates the planning and execution of time with children. Finally, remarriage or having a new romantic relationship can also affect time together. Typically, when such problems or barriers interfere with spending time with children, time together decreases and closeness between the noncustodial parent and children diminishes.

Here are several research findings that help us understand the role of fathers in the lives of their noncustodial children:

Fathers rely on others for support. Noncustodial divorced fathers relied more on relatives and former spouses regarding parenting than did custodial parents. Custodial parents relied more on romantic partners for parenting support. This support, no matter where it came from, helped fathers buffer the daily stresses of role overload (DeGarmo, Patras, & Eap, 2008).

Shared physical placement supports the father-child relationship long term. A study of over 1,500 mothers and fathers found that fathers who have shared placement, meaning their children live with them part of the time, are likely to continue to maintain the initial shared physical placement 3 years later (Berger, Brown, Joung, Melli, & Wimer, 2008). It appears that the court-ordered shared physical placement supports fathers in continuing to have quality time with their children.

Close relationships with mother are related to close relationships with the noncustodial father. In one study of almost 500 adolescents, it was found that children were more likely to have a close relationship with their noncustodial father if they had a close relationship with their mother (Scott, Booth, King, & Johnson, 2007). These relationships were maintained long term.

Relationships with children have positive effects on the father's well-being. In a study of economically disadvantaged new fathers, it was found that increased commitment to fathering led to fathers having more religious participation, improved well-being, and increased work hours. In other words, fathers' contact with their children improved the fathers' lives—a relationship between parent and child is beneficial to both parent and child (Knoester, Petts, & Eggebeen, 2007).

The parent–child relationships after divorce or separation will continue to evolve. Currently fathers are viewed as essential in a child's development, and custody laws have changed to reflect fathers' important role in children's lives.

Strengths of Single-Parent Families

In the past most research focused on single-parent families that were the result of a divorce. Even today, much research also has that focus. Current estimates reveal the divorce rate in the United States to be somewhere between 40% and 50%, resulting in many single-parent families. However, in recent years the number of single-parent families has increased dramatically because of the number of children born to unmarried parents and children born in cohabiting relationships (Wilcox, 2009).

The largest increase in single-parent families is currently coming from cohabiting couples who have children, and who are legally defined as single-parent families. It is estimated that 60% of all adults cohabit at some time during their lifetime, and 40% of those who cohabit have children (Wilcox, 2010). It is also estimated that half of nonmarital births are to mothers in cohabiting relationships. Many of these couples, even though they are not married, see themselves as being in a stable couple relationship with children they parent together. Therefore, for many of the cohabiting couples, both parents may be very involved in the life of the child/children and in all aspects of family life and family responsibilities.

Currently, over 41% of all children are born to single mothers (Wang, Parker, & Taylor, 2013, May 29), with that percentage having increased dramatically in recent years. At the current time, approximately 28% of children live in single-parent households (Amato, 2010). But keep in mind what we have just stated, half of the children born to single mothers are in cohabiting households. Therefore, we are left with 20% of children born to mothers who we might assume have limited or no support from a significant other.

We also are aware that some single-parent families live in extended family households, which means there may be multiple sources of support in terms of raising children and/or financial support. For example, there has been an increase in multi-generational family households in recent years. The percentage of the U.S. population living in households that include at least two adult generations has increased from 12% several years ago to 16%, according to recent figures (Pew Research Center, 2010). Although some of this increase may be because of adult children returning home or never leaving home, some is attributed to the increase in single-parent families who seek help and support from their parents.

Single-parent families from diverse cultures are likely to look different from those from White middle-class single-parent families. Do Latino, African American, and Asian American single-parent families have differing living arrangements than the members of the European American culture? We expect that to be true. Compared to other ethnic groups, African Americans have the highest percentage of mothers being in single-parent families, followed by Hispanics (Wang et al., 2013, May 29). For example, 40% of never-married mothers were Black and 24% were Hispanic. We also know, however, that the institution of the family is highly valued in African American culture. Family is also highly valued in other cultural groups as well. Family, for African Americans, means nuclear family, extended family, and friends who may be viewed as family members (Skogrand, Barrios-Bell, & Higginbotham, 2009). Therefore, single-parent families are often living with extended family members who support them in parenting and provide other resources. Moreover, in Black communities there is a strong religious orientation among many families (Taylor, Lincoln, & Chatters, 2005). It has been found that many members of the Black community view their church as an important means of support, and churches actually function as families and supplement the efforts of the family network. Churches in the African American culture help and support single-parent families. Other ethnic groups in the United States have similar family and informal community support systems in place and are a strength and resource for members of single-parent families.

One more component of single-parent families is the nonresidential fathers' involvement in the lives of the children. Approximately 35% of divorced parents have joint custody of children. It is estimated that 30% or more of children have at least weekly contact with their fathers, and this percentage has increased in recent years.

In a recent summary of 52 studies of nonresidential involvement of fathers, Adamsons and Johnson (2013) found that their involvement can have positive effects on children. The quality of involvement, however, matters more than the quantity of time. According to these researchers, father involvement positively affected children's social, behavioral, emotional, and academic outcomes. Historically, we have had a stereotypical view of the "deadbeat dad," but in the United States there is evidence this is changing. There have been policy changes that support father involvement with their children because we know more about the important role fathers play in their lives—because dads want to spend time with their kids.

We also have a significant number of gay and lesbian families that include a second, same-sex parent, who in many states in the United States is not recognized as a legal parent. However, a recent ruling by the United States Supreme Court recognizes same-sex marriages at the federal level. An estimated 25% of gay and lesbian couples have children living with them, and another 45% of these couples want to have children. In many cases, these children are legally living in single-parent families, even though there may be a very involved and active second parent living in the home (Gates, 2008).

There is much lamenting about the increase of single-parent families. We should be concerned about this change in family structure. However, single-parent families do not only result from divorce. They may involve a second parent who lives in the home, but where the couple is not married, as in the case of cohabiting couples. They are choosing to create a family without marriage—or as in the case of gay and lesbian couples, are not allowed to marry in many states. Nonresidential parents, usually fathers, are often very involved in the life of children even if he or she does not live in the home. There may be other caring adults who are considered *family* who provide love, resources, and support in single-parent families. We may conclude, therefore, that it is not about family structure, but it is about family function. We need to look at how single-parent families function and who is part of what is considered *family*. We need to see what strengths and resources are available to family members.

Challenges of Being in Single-Parent Families

Challenges in single-parent families may be more evident for those who truly feel like they are *going it alone,* with little or no support from others. Even those who are not going it alone may be able to relate to the challenges identified in the literature. It is important to note that research is still mostly about how poorly single-parent families are doing, and how the outcomes for children in single-parent families are not very promising. The research talks about outcomes, not the multiple challenges families encounter and the strength it takes to meet those challenges. The challenges identified below have been identified in the literature:

Financially, many single-parent families struggle. Most children in single-parent homes live primarily with their mothers (approximately 75%). Most women in the workforce make less money than men. In addition, there is only one income rather than two incomes in single-parent families versus two-parent families. Therefore, children in single-parent homes are more likely to have limited income than children in two-parent families (Poverty Solutions, n.d.; National Marriage Project, 2007, July). In addition, adequate financial resources seem to make the most significant difference in how well a family does. If a parent has an education that allows for working only one job, if that parent can spend time with his or her children, and can generally feel good about his or her role as a parent, things will more easily fall into place. If, however, a parent has limited education and has to support himself or herself and children by working multiple—sometimes dead-end jobs—the parent is likely to feel tired and depressed. Children may not get enough time or supervision from an adult, and basic needs such as health care, food, shelter, and clothing may not be optimal. This can also mean that single-parent families live in communities that are unsafe (and environment does count), less likely to go to the best schools, and are less likely to be involved in high-quality and supervised activities. Financial issues also tend to have a domino effect. Here is an example: A single-mother is working two jobs, driving an old car that often breaks down, has health insurance with one of her jobs, but generally has no money left over after paying bills. The car breaks down, with no money to repair the car. Jobs are lost, health insurance is lost, and soon housing will be lost. There is no safety net when finances are really tight.

Lack of financial resources can affect all areas of well-being. Parents become depressed, exhausted, burned out. Self-esteem diminishes. A person who has low self-esteem and is depressed is not a good parent and, therefore, there is stress on all family members. Lack of financial security may be the single most important issue for single-parent families, because it has such far-reaching effects.

Experiencing the stigma of being in a single-parent family. Much is written about the problems of both adults and children in single-parent families. Adults and children often feel a sense of failure for not being successful in marriage, not providing a second parent for their child, for not living up to society's family standards. Even at a young age, children experience the stigma. Recently, a single mom talked about how she gave her little boy so many things he did not need to compensate for being in a single-parent family. The single mom added, "I could never do enough to compensate for him not having a dad in his life."

Single parents also sometimes talk about how hard it is to attend family events, because most people there are in two-parent families. Or how hard it is to go to any kind of event where nuclear families—two parents and children—are present, because they are faced with the fact they are alone and their children do not have two married parents. Even though the number of people marrying in the United States has decreased in recent years, due to delaying marriage and cohabitation, still the majority of people, over 90%, want to be married—they still see marriage as *the prize* (Waite, Luo, & Lewin, 2009) and 90% of adults will eventually marry. To not be in a two-parent family is a stigma felt by many single-parent families.

Having to juggle everything alone and making decisions alone. If there is a supportive other parent or a significant *other* in their lives, it may not be as difficult. However, many single parents talk about juggling many activities and obligations alone. They talk about always feeling they are in a survival mode, always feeling unsettled. There often is no time to nurture oneself, or even have time or energy to go on a date. This can result in feeling vulnerable. *What if I make a poor financial decision? What if I choose the wrong school for my child? What if I make the wrong decision regarding a child's well-being?* There is often the feeling of not having someone to bounce ideas off, and the feeling of not having anyone to help out when schedules get out of hand. This can affect emotional well-being and can contribute to feelings of being inadequate.

Benefits of Being in Single-Parent Families

There are several benefits of being in a single-parent family that are identified in the literature and they include the following:

There is closeness between the parent and child/children. Members of single-parent families often have a strong family bond. Because they need to work together to make things happen, they understand and empathize with each other and they become close. The parent and child or children also need to do most things together, since children cannot be left with the other parent. They often rely on each other exclusively when they need comfort and experience joys. They have a bond because they are aware of struggles and challenges that no one else knows about.

The parent and child/children "get to do hard things." Being a child in a single-parent family should not necessarily mean you have to do adult things such as taking on added household responsibility, moving to a new neighborhood, or taking care of one's own needs. There are, however, times when children in single-parent families have to experience these *hard things* to a greater degree than children in two-parent families. These hard things may include mowing the lawn earlier than other children, having to learn to walk to school rather than getting a ride, or having to earn their own money to buy clothes. These things may seem like negative experiences; however, these children may experience the positive result of accelerated growth and development that can help them in life. This may mean children develop social skills and learn to empathize with people at an earlier age. For example, one single mom said her child learned what it meant to be poor as a result of being in a single-parent family, and developed an increased capacity to empathize with people who had little money. As this child became an adult, he expressed his appreciation for this experience.

Parents, of course, also do hard things. They may *go without* because money does not stretch. They may not be able to spend as much time with adult friends because they need to focus on children's needs. They may need to sacrifice their own needs for the benefit of the family, because there just are not enough resources to go around. Both children and adults may learn coping skills that prepare them for all kinds of challenges.

Everyone, adults and children, may be forced into situations that are ultimately beneficial. Sometimes parents are pushed to use skills and abilities they did not know they had or are forced, in all kinds of ways, to move out of their comfort zone. A single-parent may decide to get an advanced degree to better provide for the family. As a result, this person meets new and interesting people, and the person experiences a whole new world—and children get the experience of seeing their parent do this. What a single-parent was at one point forced into learning or doing may, at a later time, be viewed as a strength. As one single parent said, "All the hard things I have had to do as a single parent have served me well."

Parenting and decision making do not need to be negotiated with another adult. The other side of having to do everything alone is that a parent gets *to do everything alone*. Parents often talk about not having to work out differences in parenting styles, or come to compromises on household decisions. They do not have to talk about these decisions—they just make them. This can create less conflict in the family.

What Resources Do Single-Parent Families Rely On?

Research in this area is very limited, almost nonexistent. Some resources, however, can be gleaned from the literature. It needs to be noted, however, that some resources may be useful to one single-parent family and this same resource may not be useful to another:

Family and friends. Family members, especially parents of the single parent, often help out with finances and emotional support. In some cases the single-parent resides with parents in the early years as a single-parent. Friends may also become like family and help each other with any needs that arise. Single parents often have a network of friends that all help each other with child care, finances, getting children to important events, moving, and any other issue or challenge that arises. What is assumed with this group of friends is that "I will help you, because you have been there for me when I needed help." Having a social network is critical for maintaining a successful single-parent family.

Spiritual and/or religious resources. Strong families of all kinds rely on spiritual and religious resources for strength and guidance. Although this can be a religion, it can also be a common set of values that help the family work together toward a common goal. For example, a family may be dedicated to caring for the environment, and even though this is not religion it is a shared value. Family members work together toward a common goal. In terms of religion, however, a single parent may view a higher being as someone to go to, to ask for guidance, support, or comfort. As one single parent said, "Without God in my life, I would never make it." This parent feels less alone in making important decisions because she relies on answers to prayer to help her with these decisions.

A positive attitude. There is little in the literature about the importance of members of single-parent families having a positive attitude. Family stress theory, however, indicates that how one perceives a crisis is an important component determining the outcome for the family. How a single parent views the challenges they face and their family situation is an important determinant of well-being and hope for the entire family. Some single parents see themselves and their families as victims of some injustice on the part of the ex-partner, or someone else who got them into this *less than optimal* family situation. Lots of energy goes into those feelings, with less remaining for positive family interactions. It can lead to depression and low self-esteem. Many single parents indicate the importance of seeing things in a positive light, and sometimes it is for the sake of their children—so that they, too, feel positive. A positive attitude leads to positive communication, positive interaction, and hope for the future.

Members of single-parent families generally have reason to be positive. They are accomplishing amazing things. They are addressing challenges, they are doing well. We know that approximately 25% of single mothers live in poverty compared with 15% of the general population (Poverty Solutions, n.d.). Therefore, 75% of single mothers do not live in poverty. That is something to feel positive about. These families, given all the challenges, are generally doing well.

A sense of humor. Although single-parent families may experience more stress than two-parent families, having a sense of humor helps. A sense of humor goes with a positive attitude. If you view something in a positive light, you are more likely to laugh about it. We know that laughter helps us physically and chemically—it releases health-enhancing hormones into our system and reduces stress hormones. So it is healthy to laugh. It is often said, "If I didn't laugh, I would cry." That comment can be made by anyone, not just single parents. It seems that members of single-parent families who have a sense of humor as a response to some of the challenges they face do better.

We need more research to better understand the dynamics and strengths of single-parent families—especially cohabiting families, nonresidential parent-supported families, and other families that have other adults and support systems in place. We need research to learn more about how children and adults use the strengths they develop to meet future challenges—how these strengths benefit them in the long run.

Stepfamilies

A **stepfamily** is a family in which one or both partners in a relationship have a child or children from a previous relationship. Although some stepfamilies result when there is a divorce involving a child and one of the partners remarries, more recently the term includes children who came from or become part of a cohabiting relationship. For example, a child may have been born to a single mother. The mother then cohabits with a man and brings the child into that new relationship. This new relationship is a stepfamily relationship because one partner (she) had a child from a previous relationship. The increase in the number of single-parent and cohabiting families has contributed to this evolution of the definition of stepfamilies.

Approximately 9% of married couples have a stepchild in their family, and approximately 12% of cohabiting households have a stepchild (Pasley & Garneau, 2012). These data are cross-sectional and reflect the number of stepfamilies at any given point in time. It is estimated that 40% of all mothers and 30% of all children will at some point be in a stepfamily, if we look at individuals' lifetime experiences.

The joining together of two families in a second or subsequent relationship adds considerable complexity to a family system. A child of divorced parents who both remarry will have two stepparents; a range of possible combinations of biological siblings, stepsiblings, and half-siblings; up to eight grandparents; and numerous extended relatives (aunts, uncles, cousins, etc.).

Stepfamilies are also formed in gay and lesbian relationships. A common same-sex stepfamily results from a child who was born in a heterosexual relationship and is now part of a same-sex stepfamily. It is estimated that just over 25% of female same-sex couples have children in their couple relationships, and 8% of male same-sex couples have children (Sweeney, 2010). In addition, however, children are currently becoming part of gay and lesbian families by adoption or the use of reproductive technologies. These numbers are unknown because they are not tracked.

As important new people are added to a family system, the number of potentially positive and negative human relationships increases geometrically. Take, for example, a man from a relatively small family who married a woman with a huge extended family. The fellow's mother-in-law has nine brothers and sisters and countless nieces and nephews. His father-in-law has four brothers and sisters, and these folks also have a considerable number of progeny. "I have to have a program in hand when I go to a family picnic," the fellow chuckles. "Sometimes there will be more than 200 people at these gatherings."

Differences Between Nuclear Families and Stepfamilies

Many stepfamilies assume that they are like nuclear families, but there are differences between nuclear families and stepfamilies. Because there are usually two biological parents in a nuclear family, the children are clearer about their biological heritage. In a stepfamily, one parent is not a biological parent, which can increase children's feelings of attachment to their biological parent. In a nuclear family the parents' marriage or relationship is ongoing and may have lasted many years, but in a stepfamily, one partner may have changed. The new couple have to balance their investment in the new relationship with the handling of parenting and stepparenting issues.

Children from previous relationships put stepfamily couples at higher risk for divorce or separation (Pasley & Garneau, 2012). Unlike nuclear families, the relationship with stepchildren can create challenges that make it more difficult for couples to maintain a healthy relationship. Issues of expectations of how the stepfamily should function, consensus about child rearing, biological parent–child relationships, and stepparent–stepchildren relationships all create additional stress for couples in stepfamilies, compared to nuclear families (Pasley & Garneau, 2012).

The bonds that children feel with their parents and vice versa are often stronger in nuclear families than in stepfamilies. There are often loyalty issues in stepfamilies, with

Healthy single-parent families share the same strengths that contribute to the well-being of strong two-parent families. This father genuinely enjoys spending leisure time with his children.
©Polka Dot Images/Getty Images

Although fewer men than women have sole custody of the children after a divorce, research shows that single fathers do just as good a job of childrearing as single mothers do and that they experience the same stresses of loneliness and limited time and money.
©Siri Stafford/DigitalVision/Getty Images

children, particularly adolescents, feeling greater loyalty to their biological parents than to the stepparent. Many stepfamilies struggle with complex and sometimes conflictual dynamics. Issues regarding grandparents and stepgrandparents add to the complexity. There can also be struggles between stepsiblings when both spouses bring children to the new family. Financial issues can also be complex. When both parents in a stepfamily have children, the financial resources available for child support payments and for meeting the financial demands of all the children can be limited.

Though they may be fearful of entering into a new relationship most single parents want to find a new mate. Even more difficult than finding a new partner is finding one who cares about the children, and one whom the children like also. Single parents who marry again then face the challenge of developing a stepfamily system that works.

Children in Stepfamilies

It has been well documented that children in stepfamilies are more likely to experience emotional, behavioral, and academic achievement problems than children in nuclear families. This is comparable to children in single-parent families (Pasley & Garneau, 2012; Sweeney, 2010). From the perspective of a child living in a stepfamily, life can be extremely challenging (Pasley & Garneau, 2012; Sweeney, 2010). Children often need to share space and attention with new stepsiblings, develop relationships with new sets of extended family members, develop a new relationship with a stepparent, adjust to new ways of parenting, and adjust to multiple losses. The new couple relationship may be romantic and exciting and leave little time to focus on the needs of children.

Jensen and Howard (2015) reviewed 23 studies to assess the most pervasive conclusions regarding what made stepchildren and stepparents' relationships strong from the perspectives of stepchildren. These authors found that the relationship between the biological parent and their child was most important in determining the quality of the stepparent–stepchild relationship. These researchers conclude that focusing on the couple relationship alone will not help the stepchildren adjust to the new family structure.

Stepparent–stepchild relationships were also better when the stepparent did not speak disparagingly about the biological parent, and when the child was involved in the development of the stepfamily. In another study, Speer and Giles (2013) found that stepparents who accommodated their communication behavior to that of their stepchildren had better relationships with their stepchildren. This accommodation meant that stepparents communicated in a way that was emotionally warm and respectful, which enhanced the child's sense of self.

Given all of the adjustments children in stepfamilies encounter, Nicholson et al. (2008) provide a list of potential issues children in stepfamilies might be experiencing (see Table 15.1). It would be helpful for parents to be understanding of these multiple stresses, because if the children's needs are being met, it is more likely the couple relationship can prosper.

Many children in stepfamilies become adopted by a nonbiological parent. In fact, 25% of all adoptions include children who are adopted by a stepparent (Stewart, 2010). Stewart learned from her study that children adopted by a stepparent at an early age had about the same number of emotional problems as children in two-parent biological families. However, children who were older when they were adopted were similar in terms of well-being as children who lived in stepfamilies but were not adopted—both having more behavioral problems than children in families with both biological parents. Therefore, when children are older there does not seem to be an advantage to going through the adoption process.

It has been suggested that children be included in stepfamily education so they can be part of learning about the many adjustments all family members are experiencing (Higginbotham, Skogrand, & Torres, 2010). According to these researchers, children participating in a research-based stepfamily education program were able to learn to better express their feelings, develop relationship skills, and feel support from peers and facilitators. They felt *normal* after realizing other children in stepfamilies had similar experiences. Parents also benefited in stepfamily education that included their children. They were more able to empathize with the issues children were experiencing, they became more engaged in family activities, and they were able to improved parent–child relationship skills. Because the challenge of meeting the needs of children in stepfamilies is so great, it is important for educational programming to include children, because a more unified family is likely to be a result.

Couples in Stepfamilies

Couple relationships are more difficult to maintain in stepfamilies than in nuclear families. The multiple challenges of children and ex-partners create stress for the couple's relationship. In a national sample of more than 50,000 couples in stepcouple relationships, *remarriage stumbling blocks* were identified (Deal & Olson, 2010). These anticipated problems of stepcouples are listed in rank order below:

- They expect difficulty dealing with complex stepfamily issues. (88%)
- They believe having children from previous relationships will put an additional strain on their marriage. (66%)
- Creating a stepfamily puts more strain on their relationship. (85%)
- Having different patterns of childrearing in their birth family can be problematic. (82%)
- They expect stepfamily adjustment to be difficult. (78%)
- They don't have a specific plan for money management. (73%)
- They have concerns over unpaid bills, debts, or settlements. (66%)
- They feel their partner is too stubborn. (65%)
- One or both of the partners goes out of their way to avoid conflict with the other. (63%)
- They have a fear of another marital failure. (63%)

The above problems identified by couples are real, and many couples in stepfamilies encounter challenges related to these issues.

TABLE 15.1 Factors Influencing the Adjustment of Children in Stepfamilies*

Fears of Being Replaced or Unloved
Being hurt by Mom wanting to spend time alone with stepdad
Feeling sad when stepdad appears more loving toward his own children
Feeling jealous of Mom spending time with stepchildren

Grief over Losing Original Family
Feeling sad about Mom and Dad not getting back together
Resentment at stepdad for causing the divorce

Loyalty Conflicts
Feeling compelled to stick up for Mom when Dad is criticizing her
Feeling upset that stepdad is trying to replace Dad
Being afraid that liking stepdad will make Dad angry
Being anxious about saying the wrong things when asked about the other household

Uncertainty over Family Relationships
Being afraid of being expected to love stepdad and his kids
Being unsure what stepdad can and can't do
Being confused when stepdad is sometimes nice and at other times is cross

Uncertainty About the Future
Hearing Mom and stepdad fight and being afraid the new family will break up
Feeling it is pointless getting to know the stepdad because he will leave, just like Dad did
Worrying about being responsible for family fights

Exposure to Conflict
Feeling upset by Mom and Dad saying bad things about each other
Feeling caught in the middle passing messages between parents

Changes in Roles and Status
Losing that special feeling of not being the youngest or oldest anymore
Resentment of the stepdad taking over
Feeling rejected when Mom confides in stepdad and not me

Feeling Invaded
Feeling resentful over having to share room or possessions with stepsiblings

Changes in Rules and Expectations
Resentment about changes in what is expected and what is okay
Being uncertain about whether I will get yelled at
Being confused when Mom overrides what stepdad says

* Examples written for biological mother/stepfather family.
Source: Pryor, J. (Ed.), *The International Handbook of Stepfamilies: Policy and Practice in Legal, Research, and Clinical Environments.* Hoboken, NJ: John Wiley & Sons, 2008

Deal and Olson (2010) also identified the top five strengths that distinguish great relationships from unhappy relationships. They are provided in Figure 15.3. The personality of each partner is the factor most often identified as distinguishing happy from unhappy stepcouples. Personality refers to such things as stubbornness or being withdrawn, jealous, critical, or controlling. These characteristics make relationships difficult and are likely to contribute to unhappiness. The other factors that make a difference for couples in stepfami-

FIGURE 15.3

Keys to Marital Happiness

Source: Deal, R. L., & Olson, D., *The Remarriage Checkup.* Minneapolis, MN: Bethany House, 2010.

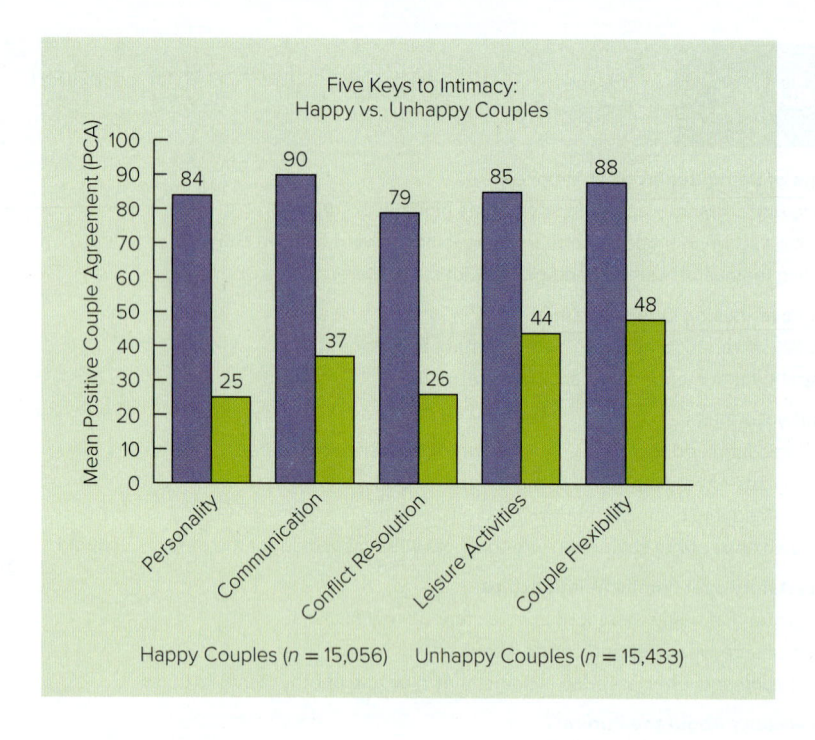

Five Keys to Intimacy: Happy vs. Unhappy Couples

Key	Happy Couples	Unhappy Couples
Personality	84	25
Communication	90	37
Conflict Resolution	79	26
Leisure Activities	85	44
Couple Flexibility	88	48

Happy Couples (n = 15,056)   Unhappy Couples (n = 15,433)

Mean Positive Couple Agreement (PCA)

lies include healthy communication, ability to resolve conflict and solve problems, spending leisure time together, and the ability to be flexible.

In a study of the reasons why couples attended stepfamily courses, it was found that most couples attend because they are seeking information about children, stepchildren, and parenting issues (Skogrand, Reck, Higginbotham, Adler-Baeder, & Dansie, 2010). As mentioned previously, the parent-child and stepparent-stepchild relationships are often the most troublesome, and these relationships will impact the couple relationships.

A study by Skogrand, Mendez, and Higginbotham (2013) explored the benefits of two lesbian couples in stepfamilies attending a stepfamily course with other members of the course being heterosexual couples. These two lesbian couples found the course very helpful in that stepparent-stepchildren relationships were the most problematic before attending the course. These couples benefited by learning how to address these challenges resulting in improved parent-child relationships and, thus, resulting in improved family relationships. These researchers concluded that the shared experience of being in a stepfamily created a bond with heterosexual couples that was more important than the nonshared experience of being lesbian couples in stepfamilies.

Stepfamilies in Diverse Populations

It is difficult to know the ethnic makeup of stepfamilies in this country. In some cultures, such as the African American and Latino populations, cohabitation is more common than in the European American population, which would result in more unidentified stepfamilies in these populations (Coltrane, Gutierrez, & Parke, 2008).

Although limited research exists about stepfamilies in various cultures, Coltrane et al. (2008) studied Mexican stepfamilies and identified specific issues that were unique to this population. One of the issues they identified was that children often had little or no contact with their noncustodial birth father, which is different from children in European American stepfamilies. According to Skogrand et al. (2009), this may be due to the strong influence of religion and familism in Latino culture. It is suggested by these authors that beliefs about the sanctity of marriage can negatively affect feelings about divorce and remarriage and, as a result, that Latino stepfamilies mimic the nuclear family structure. Stepfamilies may come together with little acknowledgment of past marriage or couple relationships. This would also mean that relationships with nonresidential parents may be discouraged. The Mexican stepfathers in the Coltrane study took on more of a father role than was typical of European American stepfathers. Other unique qualities of Mexican stepfamilies included recent immigration issues and dealing with language barriers.

Little is known about how stepfamilies function in other ethnic cultures. We might speculate, however, that values about family and religion will differ and, thus, impact stepfamily relationships. More research needs to be conducted to learn more about stepfamilies in diverse populations.

Boundary Ambiguity in Stepfamilies

Family boundary ambiguity refers to a lack of clarity regarding who is included and who is not included in the family, and this lack of clarity regarding family composition is associated with stress for family members (Sweeney, 2010; Suanet, van der Pas, & van Tilburg, 2013). Because of the multiple and complex family compositions that can result in stepfamilies, boundary ambiguity is likely to result.

Ambiguity is also increased because laws vary from state to state about custody and visitation. There is also ambiguity about the stepparent–stepchild relationship. Stepfamilies seem to have a variety of ways to handle these relationships with no best way. It seems that people have a tendency to define family as those who live with you, and those who are out of sight are also out of mind. In addition, when the stepfamily is structurally more complex, there is likely to be more boundary ambiguity, such as when parents have multiple sets of children.

Stepfamilies in Later Life

Stepfamilies are increasing as a family structure in later life, which adds complexity to relationships with adult stepchildren, care of elderly stepparents, and inheritance issues. Couples are experiencing the opportunity for a second chance as they find love and remarriage in later years, but they are also faced with unique and complex challenges in the new multifamily relationships. There are no clear rules for these relationships because it is a relatively new phenomenon (de Jong Gierveld & Merz, 2013). Family members may not know who they are to each other. For example, if the remarriage occurs after all the children are adults, are they still stepbrothers and -sisters to their stepparent's children? They are faced with new responsibilities. Who cares for an aging stepmother? They are also faced with issues around finances and inheritance. Who inherits the family business? These relationships require increased patience, communication, and commitment to navigate this new territory.

Just because a first marriage ended in divorce does not mean a new marriage will also fail. In fact, the painful process of divorce can be a tremendous learning experience and can help provide the foundation for a successful new marriage and a strong stepfamily.

Building Stepfamily Strengths

Developing stepfamily relationships after divorce and remarriage is difficult. Stepparents face many challenges in dealing with the offspring of their new spouse (Ahrons, 2004). Stepparents must remember that they are taking on someone else's child and many of the childrearing responsibilities formerly held by a biological parent. Stepparents often find themselves either overidealized by their stepchildren early in the relationship or the victim of displaced hostility.

Not all members of a stepfamily are biologically related. This is an obvious enough fact and one that should, in theory, be relatively simple to deal with. But our culture considers biological family ties special. "Blood is thicker than water," the old saying goes. Biological family bonds are difficult to break. Many children of divorce keep hoping that Mom and Dad will reunite, and the new marriage of one of the parents dashes those hopes. When a stepparent enters the family, children truly know that their mother and father will never get back together. This can cause despair and bitterness toward the stepparent. The stepparent can become the personification of evil in the child's mind: "If only *she* weren't around, Mom and Dad would get back together."

Even though the relationships between biological parent and child are well established, the couple in a stepfamily are newlyweds. It can be very difficult for the couple to balance marital needs and the children's needs. Family members' loyalties are divided in new and complex ways when a new family member comes on the scene. If a stepparent does not recognize the stepchildren's long-standing bonds with the biological parent and move carefully, the stepparent can end up in a very difficult love triangle.

A common example is a single mother who lives alone with her children for a number of years before marrying again. The mother may have developed strong ties and a comfortable pattern of parenting with her children. If she has an adolescent son or daughter, the mother's relationship with the child may be more like that of a big sister than that of a parent. The adolescent may become very jealous of the new spouse. "She always used to want to talk to me after school. Now she spends all her time with him!"

In the case of single-parent families headed by a male, girls may develop an almost "wifelike" relationship with their father during the single-parent period. Daughters often serve as confidante and household manager for their father, and many enjoy their new status. When the father marries again, the daughter may see the stepmother as a competitor for Dad's time and affection and an intruder on her wifelike roles.

Stepparents must avoid the tendency to try too hard; bonding takes a good deal of time. Newlyweds generally go out of their way to please each other, but the same approach taken with the stepchildren can create problems for the new stepparent. The stepparent knows that his or her new spouse's children are a major hurdle in establishing a successful marriage and feels that if she or he can only get along with the children, the chances for success in this new marriage are vastly improved. But children do not easily forsake the love of their birth parent for a stepparent. Adolescents, in particular, are often not very open to including an "outsider" in their family.

The stepparent needs to avoid the trap of trying to replace the former parent. In reality, the stepparent is not so much a new parent in the family as a new adult in the family. The parent role has to develop slowly. The urge to build a solid new marriage can spur stepparents to play the "superstepmother" or "superstepfather" role, which is neither realistic nor beneficial.

Stepparents must also avoid favoritism in dealing simultaneously with their "real" children and their stepchildren. Children are not always pleasant to be around; they can at times be selfish, whiney, disobedient, and intrusive. Just as many parents have difficulty loving their own children when they are not acting lovable, so it is difficult for stepparents to love someone else's children at times. It is also important that stepparents not overcompensate for their tendency to favor their biological children by being more lenient with their stepchildren.

Stepparents also need to develop skills in dealing with complex financial realities in their new families (Sweeney, 2010). Although people who are marrying again are usually painfully aware of how challenging family money problems can be, few feel comfortable discussing money matters and financial planning before remarriage. Some even prefer to avoid talking about minor financial issues until they become more serious problems. Money problems are common in stepfamilies. For example, a father who remarries is sometimes in the difficult position of sending child support payments to his biological children, supporting his new family, and hoping that his new spouse's former husband will continue to provide financial support for the stepchildren.

Summary

- The number of marriages has declined from 2000 to 2014. This was followed by a decrease in divorce rates over the same period of time.
- The number of people cohabiting has increased in recent years, which may have implications for the declining divorce rate. If fewer people marry, fewer people will divorce. Couples who cohabit and then separate are not identified and may historically been reflected in divorce statistics.
- No-fault divorce laws eliminated (1) fault as grounds for divorce, (2) gender-based division of responsibilities, (3) the adversarial nature of divorce, and (4) linkage of the financial settlement to the determination of fault. Some argue, however, that no-fault's principle of equity between the sexes penalizes divorced women financially.
- Individuals differ greatly in their ability to address the issues of divorce. However, most go on to do as well as or better than before the divorce.
- Children, however, do not always do as well as adults in the aftermath of divorce. A key factor in how well children do after a divorce is related to how well their parents get along.
- In one 20-year study, Ahrons (2007) found that, looking back, children felt caught between their parents when they did not get along postdivorce. They felt they could not talk to one parent about the other. Even into adulthood they felt they had to manage family events so their parents did not cause problems. Clearly, when parents got along after a divorce, children's well-being improved, even into adulthood.
- The duration and experience of the entire process of divorce vary with each individual. It appears, however, that when people can talk openly about divorce and accept it as an important part of their lives, they can move on as happy single individuals.
- It is estimated, that 50% of all children will live in a single-parent household at some point in their lives.
- Generally, children want to have contact with both of their biological parents.
- Of the children whose biological parents do not live together, the majority end up living with their mothers. Fathers, however, are increasingly taking a more active role in the lives of their noncustodial children.
- It has been found that when noncustodial fathers have contact with their children, it helps the children but also is beneficial to the fathers in that they are more likely to increase their work hours and have more religious participation.
- Single-parent families also have many strengths, challenges, and even benefits of being in a single-parent family. There are also resources single parents rely upon.
- Stepfamilies are created when one or both partners in a relationship have a child or children from a previous relationship.
- Stepfamilies are not only created when there is a divorce and remarriage. The number of stepfamilies has increased because many children are part of or become part of cohabiting relationships.
- Children brought into a stepfamily increase the risk for divorce or separation. Issues around parenting and parent–child relationships contribute to this stress.
- Children in stepfamilies experience multiple stresses and challenges. It is important for parents and stepparents to understand what children are experiencing.

Key Terms

no-fault divorce
tender years doctrine
divorce culture
binuclear family

sole custody
joint custody
split custody
stepfamily

Activities

1. Interview someone who has been divorced. Ask her or him to recount experiences encountered throughout the entire divorce process. Determine whether that person's experience was similar to or different from the literature in this chapter.
2. Interview a member of a single-parent family. Ask not only about the stresses the family faces but also about the strengths in the family. How is the family different from a two-parent family? How is it similar? Discuss your findings with other students.
3. Interview a member of a stepfamily, focusing on both the strengths and the stresses in the family. Compare and contrast the family with a nuclear family. Share your findings with other students.

4. Talk to an adult who grew up in a stepfamily—maybe another student. Ask the person to look at the list of possible issues stepchildren often go through on Table 15.1 and talk about his or her experiences with each of those issues.

Suggested Readings

Ahrons, C. (2007). Family ties after divorce: Long-term implications for children. *Family Process, 46*, 53–65.

Centers for Disease Control and Prevention (2015, November 23). *National marriage and divorce rate trends.* National Vital Statistics System. Web site: https://www.cdc.gov/nchs/nvss/marriage_divorce_tables.htm

Deal, R. L., & Olson, D. (2010). *The remarriage checkup.* Minneapolis, MN: Bethany House.

Emery, R. E. (2012). *Renegotiating family relationships: Divorce, child custody, and mediation* (2nd ed.). New York, NY: Guilford Press.

Greene, S. M., Anderson, E. R., Forgatch, M. S., DeGarmo, D. S., & Hetherington, E. M. (2012). Risk and resilience after divorce. In F. Walsh (Ed.), *Normal family processes* (pp. 102–127). New York, NY: Guilford Press.

Pasley, K., & Garneau, C. (2012). Remarriage and stepfamily life. In F. Walsh (Ed.), *Normal family processes* (pp. 102–127). New York, NY: Guilford Press.

Skogrand, L., Mendez, E., & Higginbotham, B. (2013). Stepfamily education: A case study of two lesbian couples. *Marriage & Family Review, 49*, 504–519.

Wallerstein J. S., & Kelly, J. B. (2008). *Surviving the breakup.* New York, NY: Basic Books.

Wang, W., Parker, K., & Taylor, P. (2013, May 29). *Single mothers.* Pew Research Center. Web site: http://www.pewsocialtrends.org/2013/05/29/chapter-4-single-mothers/.

Wilcox, B. (2009). *The state of our unions: Marriage in America 2009.* Retrieved from the National Marriage Project Web site: http://stateofourunions.org/2009/index.php.

Visit the text-specific Online Learning Center at **www.mhhe.com/olson9e** for practice tests, chapter summaries, and PowerPoint slides.

Design Element: © Alicia Grünkind/EyeEm/Getty Images

16 Strengthening Marriages and Families Worldwide

©Purestock/Getty Images

Global Perspectives on Family, Community, and Cultural Strengths

Premarital and Marriage Programs

Marital and Family Therapy

Strengthening Your Marriage and Family Relationships

The Future of Your Family

Summary

Activities

Suggested Readings

As the world shrinks, the need for international cooperation expands. The family, in all its magnificent diversity, is the basic foundation for all known world cultures throughout history. Worldwide research on family strengths, community strengths, and cultural strengths, which began more than 35 years ago, is making it quite clear that what makes families work well is much more similar than different from culture to culture, giving human beings solid common ground upon which to build a better world together. And, as David H. Olson has noted, "All the problems in the world either begin in the family or end up in the family" (Olson, Olson-Sigg, & Larson, 2008).

Therefore, the need for strengthening couple and family relationships is a global concern that unites all of us on planet Earth, and the work we can do together needs to be done on multiple levels simultaneously: work strengthening our personal relationships as couples and families; work building communities that are more supportive of couple and family relationships; and work to grow our national and international networks to be more cognizant of the critical importance of positive human relationships that begin in families of one kind or another.

In this final chapter of *Marriages and Families: Intimacy, Diversity, and Strengths,* we will begin by taking a broad look at the strengths and challenges couples and families face, from the *micro level* to the *macro level.* New global-level research has discovered that family strengths, community strengths, and the broader cultural strengths from country to country around the world are remarkably similar. After this discussion from a world perspective, we will return once again to the micro level and look at premarital and marriage programs that serve individual couples. These programs aim to build a strong foundation for couples in the early years of their relationship, and to strengthen the connections of those couples who are not in the midst of a marital crisis but would like to prevent difficulties and enhance their love for each other in a group educational setting. This section on educational prevention programs will be followed by a section on therapeutic intervention: a discussion of marital and family therapy for those who have significant challenges. Research has shown that the vast majority of couples who have experienced marital therapy find the process useful in helping them to overcome difficulties they are facing and improving their communication and conflict resolution skills. We then present a summary of the best advice experts around the world have for strengthening marriage and family relationships. The chapter ends with some very personal stories about different people's views of the future of their couple and family relationships.

Global Perspectives on Family, Community, and Cultural Strengths

Research on couple and family strengths and challenges around the world confirms what investigators have long suspected: that family strengths from culture to culture are remarkably similar—much more similar than different. The research team working on this two-phase project included 56 investigators in 20 countries, including countries and cultures in each of the world's seven major geocultural areas: Africa (Botswana, Kenya, Somalia, South Africa); Asia (China, India, Korea); Europe (Greece, Moldova, Romania, Russia); the Middle East (Israel, Oman, Palestine); Latin America (Brazil, Mexico); North America (Canada, USA); and Oceania (Australia, New Zealand). This two-phase research also shows that community strengths and cultural strengths worldwide look much the same from a global perspective (DeFrain & Asay, 2007; Asay, DeFrain, Metzger, & Moyer, 2014).

Family Strengths

The reader is well aware by now of the International Family Strengths Model, which includes six major qualities or strengths. When people around the world describe the qualities that make their family strong, they commonly talk about:

1. Appreciation and affection
2. Positive communication
3. Commitment to the family
4. Enjoyable time together
5. A sense of spiritual well-being and shared values
6. The ability to manage stress and crisis effectively

Family members in each country tend to talk about strengths in unique and different ways; and strengths are manifested somewhat differently from culture to culture in the ways people in families behave toward each other. But broadly speaking, it is difficult to deny the basic premise that the strengths concepts family members talk about around the world share a great deal in common with each other no matter where they are on earth. In terms of family strengths, human beings speak a common language.

Community Strengths

This research also found that when talking about the strengths of the community in which they live, people around the world also share a common language. A qualitative analysis of community strengths in the 20 countries in the world's seven major geocultural areas indicates that what makes a community work well in a particular culture is quite similar to what makes a community effective globally. Five basic community strengths emerged from the research:

1. A supportive environment that genuinely values families, and a general willingness and natural generosity infused in the culture to help when families are in need
2. An effective educational delivery system
3. Religious communities for families seeking this kind of support
4. Family service programs developed by government and nongovernmental organizations for families who cannot find the help they need from their own extended family, friends, and neighbors
5. A safe, secure, and healthful environment

Cultural Strengths

Finally, the global research team found that cultural strengths also were remarkably similar from country to country and culture to culture. The study discovered five worldwide cultural strengths:

1. A rich cultural history
2. Shared cultural meanings
3. A stable political process
4. A viable economy
5. An understanding of the global society

FIGURE 16.1

The Relationship of Family, Community, and Cultural Strengths: Concentric Circles

Source: DeFrain, J. & Asay, S. M., *Strong Families Around the World: Strengths-Based Research and Perspectives.* The Haworth Press, Taylor & Francis, 2007.

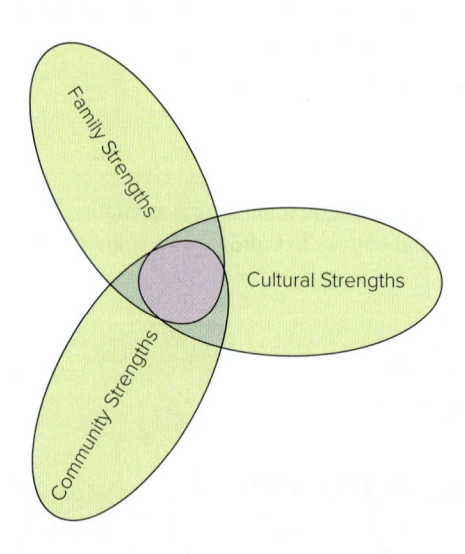

Two Visual Models Integrating Family, Community, and Cultural Strengths

How do family strengths, community strengths, and cultural strengths fit together? How do these strengths interact with and influence each other? We believe that strong families help build strong communities and that strong communities contribute significantly to the health of nations. Figure 16.1 simplifies the very complex processes involved in the interactions among family strengths, community strengths, and cultural strengths. In this model the three areas of strengths move out and away from the single-family unit to the broader cultural contexts in a concentric fashion. The health of each level of society from the micro level of the family to the community that surrounds the family and on to the macro level of the national-level social culture is affected by what is happening in each other level. The three concentric circles not only interact with each other but have depth, indicating complex interactions on various levels. (See Figure 16.1.)

Figure 16.2 shows the relationships among family strengths, community strengths, and cultural strengths in another way, a Venn diagram with intersecting strengths. The intersection of the three areas of strengths represents the strong family (the darkest blue area). Although families can have many strengths even when they live in a community or a culture without significant strengths, the most fortunate families are those where significant family strengths, community strengths, and cultural strengths intersect. In this way of thinking about families, a family caught up by the terrible forces of war or economic depression can still be strong, in spite of the difficult environment in which they live. Conversely, in a

FIGURE 16.2

The Relationship of Family, Community, and Cultural Strengths: A Venn Diagram

Source: DeFrain, J. & Asay, S. M., *Strong Families Around the World: Strengths-Based Research and Perspectives.* The Haworth Press, Taylor & Francis, 2007.

466   Part IV | Challenges and Opportunities

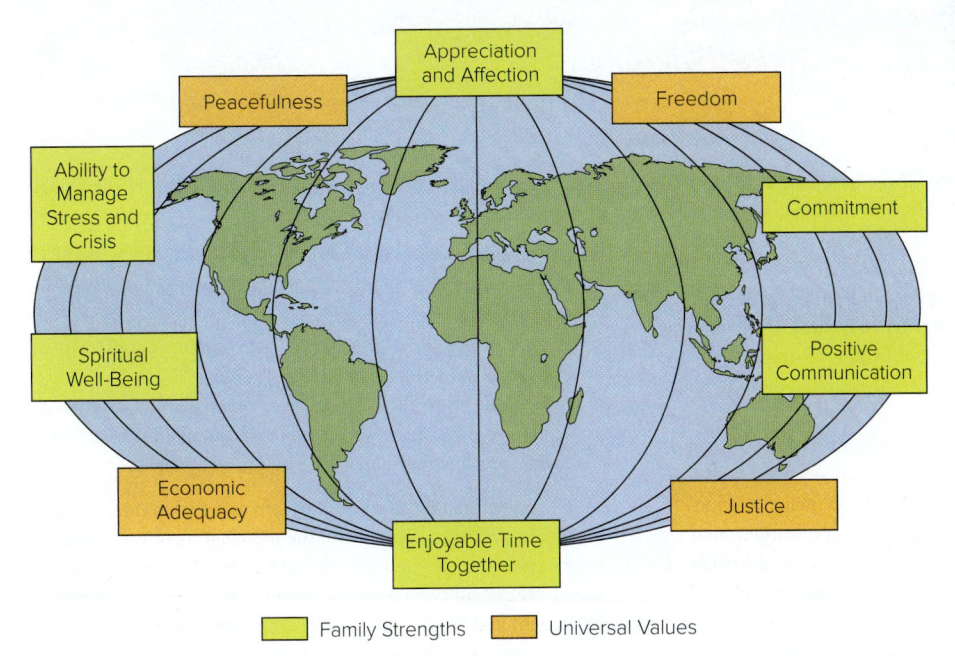

FIGURE 16.3

Family Strengths and Universal Values Around the World: A Proposed Model

Source: Illustration by Arnie DeFrain.

healthy community and healthy national cultural environment there will be troubled families without many significant family strengths. (See Figure 16.2.)

Another global perspective that fits well here is the work of Kenneth Boulding (1985), an economist and philosopher who believes that human betterment is the end toward which we individually and collectively should strive. Human betterment is an increase in the *ultimate good,* that which is good in itself. Four great virtues make up this ultimate good:

- *Economic adequacy.* "Riches," in contrast to poverty; nourishment, in contrast to starvation; adequate housing, clothing, health care, and other essentials of life
- *Justice,* in contrast to injustice; equality, rather than inequality, in access to work, education, and health
- *Freedom,* in contrast to coercion and confinement
- *Peacefulness,* in contrast to war and strife

The four great virtues from Boulding and the International Family Strengths Model of DeFrain and Stinnett are illustrated in Figure 16.3. And for another discussion of universal values, see The Perennial Philosophy in Box 16.1.

We give strength to each other as individuals, family members, and citizens of our communities. Novelist James A. Michener, a self-described citizen of the world, dedicated a lifetime to understanding people around the world. Michener and his wife Mari Yoriko Sabusawa would live in an area for many months and write about what they saw and learned. Some of his internationally acclaimed novels and stories include: *Tales of the South Pacific, Caravans, The Source, Caribbean, Mexico, Centennial, Poland, Texas, Alaska,* and *Hawaii.* Late in his long life Michener concluded:

We are all brothers [and sisters]. We all face the same problems and find the same satisfactions. We are united in one great band. I am one with all of them, in all lands, in all climates, in all conditions. Since we brothers [and sisters] occupy the entire earth, the world is our home. (Michener, 1991, p. 249)

BOX 16.1 Diversity in Families
The Perennial Philosophy

Because the focus of this section of the book is on global perspectives of families, communities, and cultures, we would like to include here a discussion of matters of the spirit. Though religions around the world are remarkably diverse and fascinating to learn about, many theologians and philosophers have argued since at least the 16th century that there is a perennial philosophy—an eternal philosophy, if you will—that all great world religions share and that unites them in a common view of what is sacred in life.

In 1540, Augustinus Steuchis, the librarian of the Vatican in Rome, wrote of a *philosophia perennis*—a way of thinking about the world and our lives that is "universal and inclusive, internally coherent, fruitful of new insights and applications, and reasoned so conclusively that attacks cannot refute, and written or presented so convincingly that reasonable minds cannot resist it" (Cline Horowitz, 2005).

Gottfried Leibniz (1646–1716), a German philosopher and mathematician, expanded upon Steuchis's thinking about a perennial philosophy, one with qualities that would ensure its survival through time and change and become, by generalization, a permanently significant philosophy. Analysis of all religions and philosophies both ancient and modern would "draw the gold from the dross, the diamond from its mine, the light from the shadows; and this would be in effect a kind of perennial philosophy."

Aldous Huxley (1894–1963), an English writer, was the most prominent person in the 20th century to look for the gold, the diamond, the light. He studied world religions at length and in 1945 wrote of the enduring intellectual and personal insights that, he argued, are repeated in all variations of thought and conviction and that can serve as an ideal for living. He described this perennial philosophy as

- the *metaphysic* or way of defining and understanding reality that recognizes "a divine Reality substantial to the world of things and lives and minds,"
- the *psychology* that "finds in the soul something similar to, or even identical with, divine Reality," and
- the *ethic* or principle of moral living that places human beings' final purpose in life as seeking knowledge of "the immanent and transcendent Ground of all being." (Huxley, 1945, p. vii)

Huxley wrote that this belief system came from time immemorial, beginning so far back in the past that its origins could not be traced. He argued that this perennial philosophy is universal. Rudiments of it could be found in the traditional lore of all ancient and modern peoples in every region of the world. In its fully developed forms it could be found in the texts of every one of the great religions of the world. Each belief system might express these ideas using different terminology and examples reflecting different cultural contexts, but Huxley was convinced that the core concepts were similar.

What relevance does this so-called perennial philosophy, with roots going back literally thousands of years, have for us today? The theologians and philosophers arguing from this perspective believe that the core beliefs of all the world's religions are much more alike than different, and that if we recognize this common spiritual ground, we can use this knowledge to find ways of living peacefully with each other in our families, in our communities, and among nations. Our personal religious beliefs can bring us together.

Premarital and Marriage Programs

Today's families live in a global society that is complex, interconnected, and continuously evolving because of the rapid pace of change in the world economy, technology, and migration. Change worldwide affects couples and families everywhere. Therefore international efforts, aided by technology, are growing as researchers and family educators work together around the globe to develop programs to help strengthen couple and family relationships. One study of global family concerns and the role of family life education represented six continents and 50 countries. The researchers found that family education and related coursework were available in all the continents of the world, and there was worldwide public interest in the need for family life education programs (Darling & Turkii, 2009).

In the rest of this chapter we will shift our focus from the macro level, the global perspective on couples and families, back to the micro level. We will see how couples can find effective premarital and marriage education programs to enhance their relationships. Then we will look at marital and family therapy and how it can be helpful for those facing more difficult challenges. Finally, we will be summing up the best advice that can be found today

TABLE 16.1 Programs for Couples and Families

	Service	Goal	Provider
Education courses for students	Functional marriage and family courses	Awareness and knowledge	High school and college teachers
Couple education programs	Premarital and marital programs	Insight and skills in communication and conflict resolution	Clergy, counselors, and marital therapists
Couple and family therapy	Marital and family therapy	Insight and change in relationship dynamics	Marital and family therapists, psychologists

for strengthening couple and family relationships, and think a bit about the future—what the future will bring for each of us in our own personal quest to create strong, loving, and caring couple and family relationships.

Programs and services for couples and families range from informal networks to couple and family therapy. Table 16.1 lists program types in order of their therapeutic impact, from least to most intensive. As couple and family issues become more serious and chronic, a higher intensity of treatment is recommended. For example, it would be more appropriate for a couple who has been having marital problems for several years and has seriously considered divorce to see a couple therapist rather than to attend a self-help group.

Couple education programs can be very useful resources for couples without serious problems. These programs can help couples meet and learn from other couples. They can also learn from skill-building programs that focus on communication and conflict-resolution skills. These are relationship skills that couples can use to improve their relationships and resolve the differences that inevitably arise in any close relationship.

Couple therapy and family therapy are recommended when relationship problems between partners or among family members are chronic and intense. When problems involve the children, family therapy is called for. In families headed by two parents, the parents may also benefit from couple therapy, because parenting can put a great deal of stress on the couple relationship. Couple therapy and family therapy are most effective when begun before problems become severe and chronic.

Premarital Programs for Marriage

Failing to prepare is like preparing to fail.

This quote emphasizes the importance of being prepared for marriage, which is one of the most challenging tasks that you will experience in your life. Because the risk of divorce is still very high and because of the considerable value couples place on a happy marriage, more couples are seeking premarital counseling from the clergy performing their marriage ceremony or from a professional counselor.

There is increasing evidence that skill-based premarital and couples education programs can increase satisfaction and enhance the maintenance of healthy, committed relationships (Bakhurst, Loew, McGuire, Halford, & Markman, 2016; Murray, 2006). Marriage education evaluation studies indicate that participants from a wide variety of ethnic/cultural groups, levels of household income, and family structure types can benefit from involvement in these types of programs. These benefits include an increased knowledge of relationships, including the ability to identify unhealthy relationship patterns. Participants also can develop more realistic beliefs about relationships/marriages and decrease their level of verbal aggression (Adler-Baeder, Kerpelman, Schramm, Higginbotham, & Paulk, 2007).

As discussed in Chapter 11, an effective premarital program has at least three essential components: (1) a premarital inventory with individual feedback for each couple, (2) a skill-building component that focuses on communication and problem solving, and (3) small-group discussions in which couples can air their mutual issues. The program should last 6 to 8 weeks and should be started a year before the marriage so that the partners have time to develop their relationship skills and deal with any important issues.

Concerned by continuing high divorce rates, the federal government and many states began working in the early 2000s to develop premarital counseling and marriage education programs. One survey of premarital counseling providers, primarily members of the clergy and mental health professionals, held favorable opinions of the government efforts to help strengthen marriages (Murray, 2006). Good candidates for marriage preparation programs include couples who value marriage, are kind and considerate to each other, and are both mature in their judgments and views of the world (Duncan, Holman, & Yang, 2007).

One of the most popular premarital programs in the United States is the *PREPARE Program,* which is offered by over 75,000 counselors and clergy. As mentioned in Chapter 11, more than 3 million couples have participated in this program since 1980. The program is also available in 13 other countries around the world. The six goals of the program are to (1) help the couple explore their relationship strengths and growth areas; (2) teach the couple the communication skills of assertiveness and active listening; (3) help the couple learn to resolve conflict effectively using a 10-step conflict resolution model; (4) help the couple discuss their families of origin; (5) develop a workable budget and financial plan; and (6) develop personal, couple, and family goals. The PREPARE Program focuses on 20 important relationship areas, including communication, conflict resolution, financial management, and egalitarian roles. For more information on the PREPARE Program and the location of a professional in your community, and to take a sample *Couple Quiz,* visit the web site at www.prepare-enrich.com.

Educational programs for couples are increasingly popular, both as a means for helping couples learn new relationship skills and as a way to strengthen an already effective relationship. Either way, there is always room for improvement.
©John Moore/Getty Images

Couple Education Programs

Interest in couple programs is on the rise. There are two types of couple programs. One type, referred to simply as a couple enrichment program, usually lasts 1 or 2 days and often takes place on a weekend. The focus is on motivating the couple to increase the amount of personal information they share with each other. These relatively brief programs are helpful to some couples who already have a good marriage and want to improve it. However, for couples with more serious relationship issues, such programs can create problems by raising expectations for a better relationship, but not providing the relationship skills to achieve it. For example, couples struggling with especially challenging family problems, including alcohol and other drug-related problems, family violence, or sexual abuse in the family, are not likely to benefit a great deal from relatively brief couple enrichment programs.

The second type of program, couple education, focuses on teaching communication and conflict resolution skills. These programs are more effective than the 1- or 2-day couple enrichment programs. They usually last about 6 weeks and meet each week for about 2 hours. Skill-building programs have demonstrated their effectiveness and value to couples.

The following four marriage education programs are high quality and have developed and been refined over the last 25 years (American Psychological Association, 2016):

- *Couple Communication Program*—Sherod Miller and Phyllis Miller (2016)
- *PAIRS Program*—Lori Gordon (2016)
- *PREP Program*—Howard Markman and Scott Stanley (2016)
- *PREPARE/ENRICH Program*—David H. Olson (2016)

To learn more about these programs and other couple education programs, go to the Smart Marriages web site at www.smartmarriages.com.

Marital and Family Therapy

If you did nothing more when you have a family together than to make it possible for them to really look at each other, really touch each other, you would have already swung the pendulum in the direction of a new start.

—Virginia Satir (1988)

Couples with persistent relationship problems should seek marital therapy as early as possible. Couples and families who receive help with problems before they become too severe have a much better chance of overcoming the difficulties and building a stronger relationship than do those who wait. An analogy can be made to treating cancer and a problematic marriage: the sooner you seek treatment, the more effective the treatment and the better the outcome.

Common Problems in Couple Relationships

The national survey of 21,501 married couples identified 10 of the most common marital problems for married couples from newlyweds to retired couples (Olson & Olson, 2001). The top 10 issues or stumbling blocks were obtained across both happy and unhappy couples and they are summarized in Table 16.2.

In reviewing the common stumbling blocks for married couples, it is striking that a high percentage of both happy and unhappy couples (ranging from 78% to 93%) have these problems. The most problematic issue for couples is sharing leadership equally, with 93% agreeing that this is a problem. Over 80% of the couples agreed that their partner was too

TABLE 16.2 — Top 10 Stumbling Blocks for Couples

A nationwide survey of 21,501 married couples from newlyweds to retirees uncovered the 10 most common difficulties they face:

Issue/Problem	Percentage of Couples
1. We have problems sharing leadership equally.	93%
2. My partner is sometimes too stubborn.	87
3. Having children reduces our marital satisfaction.	84
4. My partner is too negative or critical.	83
5. I wish my partner had more time and energy for recreation with me.	82
6. I wish my partner were more willing to share feelings.	82
7. I always end up feeling responsible for the problem.	81
8. I go out of my way to avoid conflict with my partner.	79
9. We have difficulty completing tasks or projects.	79
10. Our differences never seem to get resolved.	78

stubborn, that children reduced their marital satisfaction, that their partner was too negative or critical, that they wish they had more time to be together, that they wish their partner would share more feelings, and that they often ended up feeling responsible for problems. Three other very common issues were avoiding conflict with their partner, having difficulty completing tasks, and that differences never seemed to get resolved.

When clustering these 10 items into topic areas, the most common areas were regarding conflict resolution (3 items); couple flexibility (2 items); personality issues (2 items); and 1 item in communication, leisure activities, and parenting. These are issues that marital and family therapists often observe when working with couples having marital problems.

Problems Related to Closeness and Flexibility

Marital and family therapists working with couples and families with problems often use the Couple and Family Map. Because it focuses on the key dimensions of cohesion, flexibility, and communication, the Couple and Family Map provides a useful framework for diagnosing and treating several common problems in marital and family systems.

One frequent problem couples seeking counseling describe is the feeling that they are at opposite extremes on the same dimension of the model. On the cohesion dimension, for example, one partner may want more togetherness, whereas the other partner may want more autonomy. Similarly, on the flexibility dimension, one partner may desire more flexibility in the family, whereas the other partner may want more rules (that is, rigidity). When couples disagree on the balance of separateness (autonomy) and togetherness in their relationship, they can negotiate by jointly planning their schedules. When couples disagree on flexibility issues (rules or roles), they might try reversing roles at home for a week.

Another common problem for couples occurs when both partners are at the same extreme on one or both model dimensions. Both may be disengaged from the relationship because they are so heavily involved in career or outside interests that they have little time or energy for the marriage. Or both may be enmeshed, so invested in the partner that they have little room to develop personal interests and skills. When couples are disengaged, it is important for them to assess their commitment to the relationship. When couples are too enmeshed, one solution is for each of them to develop more separate interests and spend more time apart.

Family gatherings can be a great way for different generations to connect and build a stronger family network.
©Hero Images/Getty Images

This all may sound quite simple, but difficulties arise because people see their relationships differently and have conflicting expectations about them. For example, the wife and the husband often offer different couple and family descriptions and goals. Add a teenage child, and the child's description will tend to be different from that of the parents. In fact, adolescents will describe their family as more extreme on the dimensions of cohesion and flexibility (to unbalanced levels), whereas their parents will tend to see their family as more healthy and balanced on the Couple and Family Map (Figure 16.4).

There is no avoiding this dilemma of differing family perceptions. By interviewing only one person in the family, the husband or wife or adolescent, a counselor would get only a snapshot rather than a panoramic view of the entire family and its complexity. The solution lies in getting everyone together, asking many questions, and dealing with the conflicting perspectives of all the family members. This approach produces a more valid—and also a more complex—picture of the family's dynamics.

Common Questions About Marital and Family Therapy

The American Association for Marriage and Family Therapy (AAMFT), which is the professional organization representing the interests of approximately 26,000 marriage and family therapists nationally, argues that research studies have repeatedly demonstrated the effectiveness of marriage and family therapy for treating a wide range of mental and emotional disorders and health problems. Marriage and family therapists treat not only marital distress and conflict, but also adolescent drug abuse, depression, alcoholism, obesity, and dementia in the elderly, because these issues all have a family component (AAMFT, 2016).

People have many questions about marriage and family therapy; therefore, we will pose several of these here and offer the best answers we found (DeFrain & the University of Nebraska Family Action Research and Writing Team, 2012).

What happens in marital counseling? The counselor sometimes plays the role of referee, helping partners calm down and really listen to each other. In other cases where the couple has closed down communication, the approach is to help them open up and learn what is happening in their relationship. Basically, the purpose is to help couples learn to communicate effectively with each other and resolve conflicts effectively. A good counselor knows how to smooth the waters, help couples talk clearly and honestly with each other, and look for solutions to problems that they alone cannot seem to resolve.

Is something wrong with people who go to a professional counselor? One useful way of answering this question is to ask another question: Is there something wrong with a man who takes his car to a good mechanic when it is running poorly? Or another question: Is there something wrong with a woman who calls a doctor when she thinks she is having a heart attack? The fact of the matter is that none of us are experts in everything. We can't fix everything in our life, and this long list sometimes includes our marriage and family relationships. So, we do the wise thing and seek help from someone who is trained and highly experienced in dealing effectively with such difficulties.

What if one partner is willing to go to a therapist, but the other partner is not willing? Wives are often the ones who want the couple to seek counseling, and husbands sometimes are resistant (Eubanks Fleming & Córdova, 2012). The prognosis for healing a relationship is much better if both partners are intensely involved in the process. However, one partner may be totally resistant to seeking help, but in this case it is still useful for the other partner to spend some time with a professional to get some ideas of how to proceed in her or his situation.

What about marital therapy for situations in which violence is possible? In some volatile situations it is not wise to involve both partners in therapy. There may be genuine danger, usually for an abused wife. One therapist we know told the story of a couple who sought therapy with her. During the session it became very clear that the husband was abusive and that the wife needed help in telling her husband she was leaving him and wanted a divorce. Upon learning this, the husband stormed out of the counselor's office in a rage. Two days later he walked into a restaurant where his wife was having lunch and shot her.

She survived, but the marriage did not.

Marriage and family therapists have done a great deal of good for many couples. However, in the case of domestic violence the endangered spouse is encouraged to seek counsel from programs and professionals who specialize in dealing with family violence, because safety is a critical concern. The situation may be so dangerous for the woman that she and her children need to remain hidden in a secret family shelter provided by the community until the man is jailed by the police or calms down and is deemed nonviolent. And, as we saw earlier in this book, alcohol and other drug abuse problems often go hand-in-hand with domestic violence. When seeking help with these kinds of situations, it is important to approach programs and specialists who focus on substance abuse issues.

Not all marriages can be saved, even with professional help. And not all marriages should be saved.

What kinds of qualifications should the therapist have? Licensed marital and family therapists who are certified by the American Association for Marriage and Family Therapy (AAMFT) are specially trained to deal with relationship problems and work directly with couples and families. Some psychologists, psychiatrists, social workers, and other counselors have some additional training for work with couples and families, but these tend to be the minority in their professions. For more information about the AAMFT, visit their web site at http://www.aamft.org.

How can a person find a marital or relationship therapist? A good place to start is the AAMFT web site. There is a very handy *Therapist Locator* tool. Type in your zip code and check how far you would be willing to drive (5 miles, 10 miles, 25 miles, 50 miles, and so forth). The search can be done in several other ways, also: by city or state, or by the last name of the therapist. The *Therapist Locator* then lists professionals in your area and the qualifications of each therapist. If a computer is not available, in many cities and towns marital and family therapists are listed under "Marital and Family Counseling" in the yellow pages. A person could also consult a family service organization or the United Way for a list of names. And finally, a good way is to ask friends and loved ones. Someone you know and trust often will have experience with professional marriage and family therapists, and can give good advice.

Here are some useful, specific questions to ask the potential marital and family therapist:

- What is your professional training and degree?
- How much specialized training and experience have you had in marital and family therapy?
- Do you usually see couples and families together or as individuals?
- What procedure will you use to evaluate our relationship?
- How much will you charge for that assessment?
- How frequently will we have sessions, and how long will they last?
- What will each session cost?

The more comfortable you feel about the therapist's answers to these questions, the more confidence you can have in the therapist's ability to help you as a couple or family.

What if my partner or I don't like the counselor? Regarding a marriage partner, you have probably been advised by someone at some time in your life to shop around and not marry the first person you run into. Likewise, couples seeking counseling together need to talk with a few professionals before they settle on one who both of them feel comfortable with and believe is competent to deal with their problems. If it doesn't go well with this first choice, we encourage the couple not to give up on therapy, but simply find another therapist.

Can I afford this? What is it going to cost? And how long will it take? The hourly cost of marriage and family therapy in the United States can vary widely, from perhaps $75 to $500 per hour, with an average cost of $100 up to $200 per hour. The cost can sound steep to a couple living on a tight budget, but they need to remember that if you get the oil changed in your car it might be costing you $65 an hour or more. Fortunately, some therapists and family service agencies offer sliding fee scales and the cost of therapy can be quite reasonable for a couple on a limited budget. Also, health insurance policies cover marriage and family therapy with a small copay. A couple visiting with a counselor an hour a week for 3 months might expect to pay $1,200 to $2,400 at $100 to $200 per hour. Be sure you are very clear on the cost *before* therapy begins.

Is marriage and family therapy effective? The short answer to this question is, *Not always, but quite often*. A research team in the mid-1990s led by Bill Doherty at the University of Minnesota concluded that marital and family therapy is a rather cost-effective and efficient approach to dealing with a range of emotional and relationship problems in individuals, couples, and families (Doherty & Simmons, 1996). Similarly, a more recent study by Andrew Christensen (Christensen, Atkins, Baucom, & Yi, 2010; Christensen, 2016) at UCLA and other colleagues around the United States looked at traditional and nontraditional approaches to marriage and family therapy for troubled couples. The researchers found substantial positive effects as a result of the therapy. These positive effects proved true even for seriously and chronically distressed couples.

However, the research team also concluded that going to a therapist is no guarantee that a marriage will be saved. Within 2 years of therapy, more than 25% of the couples in the study ended up separated or divorced.

We certainly do not want to sound repetitious, but it is important to stress that couples should be proactive in regard to marriage problems: When things aren't going well, don't be afraid to talk about the situation with your partner and work together toward a solution. Don't wait until it's too late. These problems, like your broken-down car, just don't fix themselves. It is important to remember that if we can talk about a troubling issue, we can find a way to make it better—not perfect, but better. Anything mentionable is manageable.

Family Therapy Case Study

The Davis family has five members: Mary and Don, the parents; 18-year-old Ann; 16-year-old Julie; and 9-year-old Peter. Mary drank to relieve feelings of inadequacy in a family dominated by high achievers: Don and the oldest daughter, Ann. The middle daughter, Julie, also felt inadequate but tried to console her mother and was responsible enough to be a surrogate mother to Peter, the youngest child. The family came in for therapy shortly after Mary began treatment for her dependence on alcohol. Ann subsequently left home, angry at Mary for all the problems she had caused. Julie felt lost because her mother was being "taken care of" by other people and Julie's role as chief counselor had been usurped.

In terms of the Couple and Family Map, the Davis family would be classified as a *rigidly enmeshed* family, which is an unbalanced family type because they are at the extreme levels of both cohesion and flexibility. The goal for therapy in terms of their family system is to move them one level toward the balanced part of the model, which would move them to the *structurally cohesive* family type (see Figure 16.4).

FIGURE 16.4
Couple and Family Map: Before and After Therapy

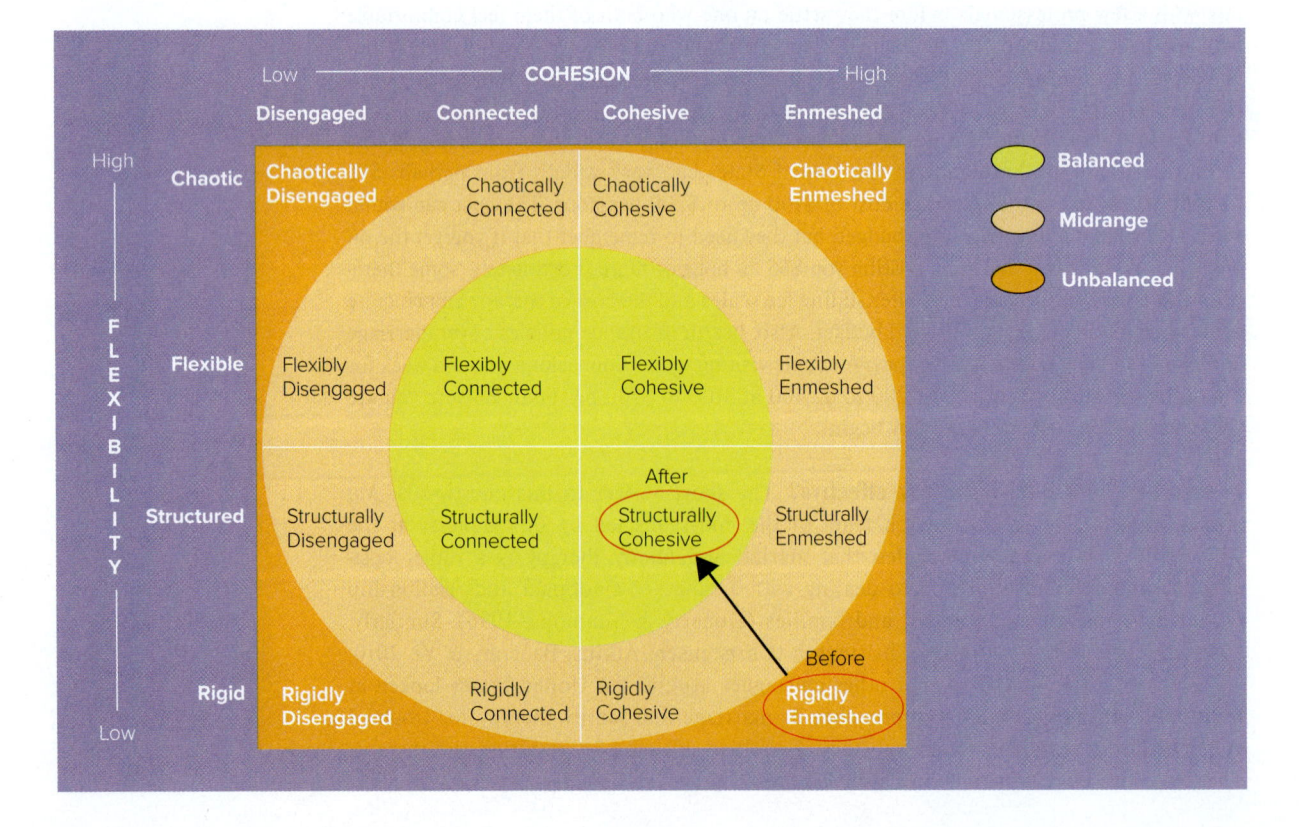

Diagnosis. In terms of cohesion, the Davis family was *enmeshed*. They evidenced high emotional bonding as well as high mutual dependency. The mother and the two daughters competed intensely for approval from each other and from Dad. The family's external boundaries were closed. No one felt free to interact with people outside the family, partly because they were afraid Mary would be drunk and embarrass everyone. Friends and relatives were kept at a distance. The only time husband and wife made contact was when one of the children misbehaved. Then the two would team up as parents and support each other; otherwise, they did not interact much. The father–daughter coalitions, especially that between Don and Ann, were strong. In many ways, Don and Ann played the role of parents in the family, because Mary's drinking often made her incapable of parenting.

Individual activities were permitted but only within family-approved guidelines. Don and Ann spent a lot of time playing tennis together, but Julie's desire to spend the same amount of time away from the family *partying* with friends was not approved. Close friends, especially males, were not allowed. The family tried desperately to have fun at their cabin on the weekends. Everyone was required to go, and the implicit message was, "You *will* have fun!" The result was that nobody enjoyed the weekends at the cabin. Tending to Peter's needs kept Julie connected to the family after she became adrift when her mother entered the alcohol treatment program.

Much of the conflict in the family seemed to stem from its *rigidity*. The family system and each of its members could seldom think of new ways to solve problems. Also, no one in the family knew how to be appropriately assertive. Rather than making their point firmly but without malice or yelling, family members resorted to aggressive behaviors: screaming, throwing things, and occasionally striking each other.

Family roles were stereotypic and rigid. Mary saw herself as being in charge of the house, and she saw Don as the boss of the children, the rule enforcer. Mary made many threats but rarely carried them out. When things got out of hand, Don delivered punishment in a heavy-handed manner. When Mary felt upset about life, she tended to clean house

Although the challenges can be formidable, families are capable of dramatic and positive change. Marital and family therapists can be helpful guides on the journey towards healing.
©FatCamera/iStock/Getty Images

or drink. She made life difficult for everyone by insisting that each be as compulsive about housekeeping standards as she was.

All in all, family leadership, rules, and roles were very rigid. As new situations developed in the family, the members did not have the flexibility to negotiate and create solutions that were reasonable. Ann and Julie could not discuss possible changes in a rational fashion with their parents. The Davises were locked in a dysfunctional family system that was *rigidly enmeshed*.

Treatment. The family therapist sought to focus on those issues in the family in which some positive movement was already under way. On the dimension of cohesion, the goal was to increase the level of individual autonomy in the family—in short, to give each member more space. A related goal was to strengthen the marriage.

In terms of flexibility, the family therapist taught family members how to negotiate and compromise with each other, rather than alternating between quiet passivity and conflict. Members were taught to see family rules as general guidelines to be discussed and interpreted as new situations arose in day-to-day living. This gave the children a chance to argue their points and even to change their parents' minds occasionally. When the family as a whole had improved on these dimensions, the focus shifted to the marriage.

Don and Mary continued in marital therapy as a couple. The therapist focused on ways the couple could learn to enjoy each other's company again. They were encouraged to go out on dates without the children and to do things they felt they hadn't had time to do together for many years. As the marriage improved, the number of disagreements with the children diminished. Why was this? As the marital coalition strengthened and Mary took back her rightful place on the parental team, it was less necessary for Julie and Ann to struggle for a position in coalition with Dad, and Julie no longer felt it necessary to try to fill the vacuum.

The family therapist got a good deal of help from Mary's alcohol counselors and from Alcoholics Anonymous. The chemical dependence specialists were adept at helping Mary

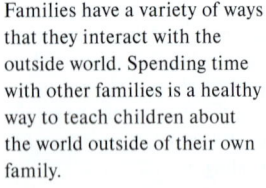

Families have a variety of ways that they interact with the outside world. Spending time with other families is a healthy way to teach children about the world outside of their own family.
©Ariel Skelley/Blend Images/Getty Images

maintain sobriety once she had attained it. Al-Anon, which focuses on the family of the alcoholic, gave Don and the children support and ideas in their struggle to live with an alcoholic. As Mary became more secure in her marriage with Don, she was able to be more supportive of Julie in her growth as an individual. The family became more adept at both separating from and connecting with each other.

As a result of couple therapy to strengthen the marriage, and family therapy to improve the family functioning, after about 10 sessions the family was now functioning as a *structurally cohesive* family (see the Couple and Family Map, Figure 16.4). In terms of cohesion, they had moved from being *enmeshed* to being less connected as a *cohesive* family. Don and Mary became more emotionally connected to each other, and this helped to reduce the dysfunctional parent–adolescent coalition of Don and daughter Ann. In terms of flexibility, the family moved from being *rigid* to being *structured*. The parents started to work more as a cooperating team and gave their adolescents a little more freedom and autonomy. All family members were happy with how the family had changed, and they were more clear about how they could continue to improve their family over time.

Strengthening Your Marriage and Family Relationships

What is the best advice we can give about building stronger marriage and family relationships?

1. *Carefully choose a good partner, prepare for your marriage, and once you are married, continue to find ways to build a stronger marriage.* Read together, talk with other more experienced couples about marriage, attend educational programs for couples, and engage in premarital counseling with a skillful professional.

2. *Do things every day that continually build a stronger couple and marital relationship.* Praise your partner at least once or twice a day. This is just as important as going to school, going to work, eating, sleeping, and breathing.

3. *Work on building your family strengths, which ultimately impact the quality of your individual, couple, and parent–child relationships.* You don't marry an individual, you marry a whole family and the culture that surrounds that family. You can't afford to try to ignore or escape this fact, so find ways to get along well with your partner's family and your own family. Don't try to isolate yourselves as a couple from the rest of your families.

Building a Stronger Marriage

The couple relationship is the foundation of a strong family, so it is important that the couple develop a strong and healthy relationship. As we have seen earlier in this textbook, a strong marriage has a positive impact on the emotional and physical health of the individuals.

There are a variety of very specific things that couples can do to build a stronger relationship. Box 16.2 lists 10 suggestions that have been found to be important across numerous studies. These suggestions include giving compliments, finding time to dialogue, having a weekly date, being assertive, listening with care, resolving issues before they become serious, and seeking help if you have problems that you are unable to resolve.

BOX 16.2 Putting It Together

Building a Stronger Marriage

Relationships, like children, need to be nurtured and protected in order to grow and remain healthy. One of the natural consequences of long-term relationships is that couples become complacent about each other and about the strengths upon which their relationship was built. The 10 suggestions listed here can help couples keep relationships vital and healthy.

1. Give one or two compliments or more to your partner each day.
2. Find time to dialogue for 5 minutes each day about your relationship.
3. Have a weekly meeting for about 15 minutes with your partner and discuss one or two issues and one or two strengths of your relationship.
4. One night a week, have a date with each other, just as you did before marriage.
5. Be assertive—ask for what you want—so your partner does not have to guess.
6. Share feelings with each other and remember to listen, listen, and listen.
7. Resolve issues as soon as possible.
8. If a problem persists for 2 to 3 months, try the 16 suggestions for resolving disagreements between individuals in a couple relationship (see Chapter 5 on conflict resolution).
9. If you are unable to resolve your conflict, seek professional counseling from a marital therapist.
10. At least once a year, try to attend a workshop to enrich your marriage.

Because marriages change over time, it is important to keep working on improving the relationship. One way is to look for opportunities to attend couple enrichment programs with other couples.

Building a Stronger Family

In numerous studies, we have found that strong families successfully manage life's difficulties in a variety of creative ways. These are some of their strategies:

- *Look for something positive in difficult situations.* No matter how difficult, most problems teach us something about ourselves and others that we can draw on in future situations.
- *Pull together.* Think of the problem not as one family member's difficulty, but as a challenge for the family as a whole.
- *Create open channels of communication.* Challenges cannot be met when communication shuts down.
- *Keep things in perspective.* "These things, too, shall pass."
- *Adopt new roles in a flexible manner.* Crises often demand that individuals learn new approaches to life and take on different responsibilities.
- *Focus to minimize fragmentation.* Look at the big picture. Focusing on the details rather than the essentials can make people edgy and anxious.
- *Create a life full of meaning and purpose.* We all face severe crises in life. These challenges are simply unavoidable. Our aim should be to live a useful life of service to our community. Giving of ourselves brings a richness and dignity to our lives, in spite of the troubles we endure.
- *Actively meet challenges head on.* Life's disasters do not go away when we try to hide our head in the sand.

Although the foundation of a strong two-parent family is a strong marriage or couple relationship, more families today are composed of single parents and also are stepfamilies, where children and parenting came before the marriage. Please take a look at Box 16.3 for 10 suggestions that single-parent families, stepfamilies, and two-parent families can use to strengthen their relationships (DeFrain et al., 2007).

BOX 16.3 Putting It Together

Building a Stronger Family

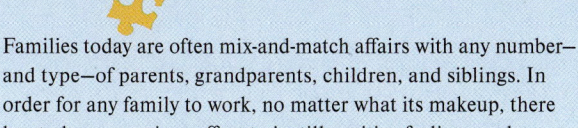

Families today are often mix-and-match affairs with any number—and type—of parents, grandparents, children, and siblings. In order for any family to work, no matter what its makeup, there has to be a conscious effort to instill positive feelings and a sense that every family member is equally important. Here are 10 suggestions for keeping families strong.

1. Give at least one compliment to each family member each day.
2. Do a daily dialogue for 5 to 10 minutes each day about what is happening with each family member.
3. Try to have your family meal together with everyone present.
4. Have a weekly family meeting for about 30 to 45 minutes with all family members attending. Each member should say one thing they like about the family and one issue they have with their family that everyone will work on during the following week.
5. Give top priority to your marriage.
6. Be as assertive as your children are with you. (Not aggressive but assertive.)
7. Remember to listen, listen, and listen.
8. Spend 1 hour of quality time each week with each child (one on one).
9. If a problem persists, bring it to the family meeting and try using the 16 suggestions for resolving conflicts (see Chapter 5).
10. If a parenting problem lasts for 2 to 3 months, seek professional help from a family therapist.

The Future of Your Family

The future of couples and families around the world begins with each of us as we create the future in our own family. We have asked many people, "What is the future of your family?" Here is what some of them said:

> "That's a really hard question, Grandpa!" exclaimed Cole, age 6. But he quickly turned to his Mommie and Daddy and smiled: "I want you guys to be alive with me forever because you always snuggle."
>
> * * * * *
>
> "The future for my family?" 19-year-old Rachel replied. "I'm not sure. My parents have been divorced for almost 15 years, and they're both remarried. My mom's happily remarried. My dad is not so happy. He always talks about my mom and what she's doing and what they'd be like if they were still together. My mom has done a really good job of showing us things are okay, even with stressful events. She has raised us very well, I believe. My father, he had a girlfriend . . . he screwed up, and he's realizing it now. And I just don't know what to say to him. Yeah, Dad, you blew it. And I think he's going to get divorced again. For myself, I have the biggest hopes. I know everyone does."
>
> * * * * *
>
> "As far as where we're going," 21-year-old Tanya noted, "I think we'll be okay because my partner, Darren, has a strong family. But I don't want my dysfunctional family to overshadow our life because that's something I want to overcome. I want to overcome the statistics and have a strong marriage."
>
> * * * * *
>
> "For the future," said 26-year-old Allan, "I want to raise my family like my family raised me. We were a close family and had good communication. We had fun together and got much love from one another, because our family cared for each other."
>
> * * * * *
>
> "I think we're a happier family than we were in the past because we laugh a lot," answered Marta, a 40-year-old divorced mother of three. "The children think I have done really well as a single mom

taking care of them and developing my career. That's pretty exciting. Young people need to hang in there with their parents and try to understand them, because they love you and they just want the very best for you."

* * * * *

"Well, gosh, I haven't really thought much about the future," 62-year-old Richard said. "But that's a great question, so here goes: I think I'll keep chugging along in a lot of ways pretty much as I have been for many, many years. I'll probably retire, as they say, in a couple years and that will give me much more time to enjoy with Lynn, and with our grown-up kids and grandkids. She's had some health problems the past few years and I learned never to take your loved ones for granted. So, we'll travel a bit more and I'll probably get involved in some volunteer activities I like that will help the community a bit. Mostly I'll enjoy being with Lynn. You know, we've been best friends, really, for just about forever."

* * * * *

"The future?" 92-year-old Helen pondered. "When you're my age it's pretty certain you have learned to live in the moment because anything can happen to older people any second. But, your question is a serious question, so I'll give you a serious answer: I'm not so concerned about my future. My life has been a long life, a good life. I miss Jim, just as lots of widows miss their husbands. I miss him terribly. But my life still has meaning because I am connected to my children and grandchildren and the few old friends that have lived as long as I have. I may go in a few years or I may go this afternoon. That's really not important. The important thing to me is that my family will survive after I'm gone. Their lives will go on and on. And I hope they will remember me and think kindly of me and remember how much I cared for them. That sums up a pretty good life."

It has been said that when our life comes to an end, all we really have left is our story. We won't be taking our money or possessions or résumé with us when we make the transition from this world to whatever will come next for us. All we have at the end of a hopefully long and meaningful life will be the story of our journey. Will our story, as it comes to an end, be a happy one or a sad one? Will it include touching elements of warm and affectionate relationships, or will it be a story of loneliness and despair?

We hope you have seen as you were reading this book that happiness, in many ways, is a choice human beings make in life. And we also hope that it has become clear to you that loving couple and family relationships are created every day by people who have educated themselves to meet the challenges of intimate living. These fortunate souls have joined together with the special people in their world to write a family story full of life: meaningful work, significant opportunities to learn and grow, chances that were taken for adventure and reaching out, and much love given and received from people for whom they deeply care.

Summary

- As the world shrinks, the need for international cooperation expands. The family, in all its magnificent diversity, is the basic foundation for all known world cultures throughout history.
- Worldwide research on family strengths, community strengths, and cultural strengths is making it quite clear that what makes families work well is much more similar than different from culture to culture, giving human beings solid common ground upon which to build a better world together.
- Family strengths worldwide include appreciation and affection; positive communication; commitment to the family; enjoyable times together; a sense of spiritual well-being and shared values; and the ability to manage stress and crisis effectively.
- Community strengths from a global perspective include a supportive environment that genuinely values families, and a general willingness and natural generosity infused in the culture to help when families are in need; an effective educational delivery system; religious communities for families seeking this kind of support; family service programs developed by government and nongovernmental organizations for families who cannot find the help they need from their own

- extended families, friends, and neighbors; and a safe, secure, and healthful environment.
- Cultural strengths around the world include a rich cultural history; shared cultural meanings; a stable political process; a viable economy; and an understanding of the global society.
- Strong families help build strong communities, and strong communities contribute significantly to the health of nations. The health of each level of society, from the micro level of the family to the community that surrounds the family and on to the macro level of the national-level social culture, is affected by what is happening in every other level.
- Although families can have many strengths even when they live in a community or a culture without significant strengths, the most fortunate families are those where significant family strengths, community strengths, and cultural strengths intersect. In this way of thinking about families, a family caught up by the terrible forces of war or economic depression can still be strong, in spite of the difficult environment in which they live. Conversely, in a healthy community and healthy national cultural environment there will be troubled families without many significant family strengths.
- Economist Kenneth Boulding believes that there are four great virtues that make up the *ultimate good* and we should individually and collectively strive to achieve these: *economic adequacy, justice, freedom,* and *peacefulness.*
- Within the world, focusing on our similarities as human beings can help unite us and understand one another. Within families, focusing on family strengths emphasizes these strengths and helps us build successful ways of relating to one another.
- There are many ways individuals, couples, and families seek support, advice, and education, ranging from *informal networks* to *professional therapy.* The intensity level of the program should correspond to the level of need.
- A good premarital program can reduce a couple's chances of divorce and improve their overall relationship. One important way we can strengthen marriages is to offer good premarital programs that give couples the skills to help them through their lives together.
- There are two types of couple programs: *couple enrichment programs* and *couple education programs.* Couple enrichment programs typically last 1 or 2 days and improve the couple relationship by increasing the sharing between the couple. Couple education programs are skill based, more comprehensive, and more effective in helping couples build stronger relationships.
- The top five stumbling blocks identified by couples in a national survey were the following: They have problems sharing leadership equally, they feel their partner is sometimes too stubborn, they are less satisfied with their marriage since having children, they feel their partner is too negative or critical, and they wish their partner had more time and energy for recreation.
- Family members often have different perceptions of the issues, events, and dynamics in their family. This is one reason the Couple and Family Map is helpful in assessing each family member's perceptions and providing a reference point for therapy.

- The American Association for Marriage and Family Therapy (AAMFT), which is the professional organization representing the interests of approximately 26,000 marriage and family therapists nationally, argues that research studies have repeatedly demonstrated the effectiveness of marriage and family therapy for treating a wide range of mental and emotional disorders and health problems. Marriage and family therapists treat not only marital distress and conflict, but also adolescent drug abuse, depression, alcoholism, obesity, and dementia in the elderly, because these issues all have a family component.
- Building strong marriages begins with your being proactive about your relationship skills and developing good relationships with others. Choosing a good partner and premarital education are the first steps you can take to develop a strong marriage. Then, as a couple, seek out couple education programs. When you have a family, remember to build on your strengths as individuals, as a couple, and as a family.
- Ways to build a strong family are to compliment each family member regularly; have a 5- to 10-minute daily dialogue about what is happening with each family member; try to have the family meal with everyone present; have a 30- to 45-minute weekly family meeting with all family members attending; give top priority to your marriage; be assertive like your children are with you; listen, listen, listen; spend 1 hour of quality time each week with each child one on one; if problems persist, use the 16 suggestions listed in Chapter 5 for resolving the conflict; and seek professional help if a parenting problem lasts 2 or 3 months.

Activities

1. Draw a model outlining the strengths of your family, community, and culture. Pick either the concentric circles model or the Venn diagram model. Share your model with a small group of other people and discuss what you are seeing together.
2. Write down the strengths in your family of origin that you want to bring into your marriage.
3. Write down the problematic issues in your family of origin, and think about ways you can avoid bringing them into your marriage.
4. What are the pros and cons of premarital counseling?
5. Will cohabitation help you personally prepare for marriage?
6. Would you attend a couple program or go to marital therapy? Why? Why not?

Suggested Readings

American Association for Marriage and Family Therapy (AAMFT). (2016). Founded in 1942, AAMFT is the professional association for the field of marriage and family therapy, representing the professional interests of more than 26,000 marriage and family therapists in the United States, Canada, and abroad. AAMFT publishes the *Journal of Marital and Family Therapy* and *Family Therapy Magazine.* Web site: www.aamft.org.

American Family Strengths Inventory (AFSI). (2016). An at-home, free assessment of couple and family strengths. Take the inventory with your partner and other family members and plan how to enhance your strengths and improve areas of potential growth in your relationships. Web site: http://extensionpublications.unl.edu/assets/pdf/g1881.pdf.

American Psychological Association. (2016). Marital education programs help keep couples together. Web site: http://www.apa.org/research/action/marital.aspx.

Asay, S. M., DeFrain, J., Metzger, M., & Moyer, B. (2014). *Family violence from a global perspective: A strengths-based approach.* Thousand Oaks, CA: Sage. Further developments in international research on individual strengths, family strengths, community strengths, and cultural strengths.

Atwood, J., & Genovese, F. (2006). *Therapy with single parents: A social constructivist approach.* New York, NY: Haworth Press.

Bigner, J., & Gottlieb, A. (2007). (Eds.). *Interventions with families of gay, lesbian, bisexual, and transgender people: From the inside out.* Binghamton, NY: Haworth Press.

CoupleCARE. (2016). Couple commitment and relationship enhancement. Queensland, Australia: Australian Academic Press. Web site: http://www.couplecare.info/. Complete educator kit.

DeFrain, J., & the University of Nebraska-Lincoln Extension Family Action Research and Writing Team. (2007). *Family treasures: Creating strong families.* University of Nebraska-Lincoln Extension. Bloomington, IN: iUniverse. Sixty-three couple and family activities keyed to each of the six major strengths.

DeFrain, J., & the University of Nebraska–Lincoln Extension Family Action Research and Writing Team. (2012). *Getting connected, staying connected: Loving each other day by day.* Bloomington, IN: iUniverse. Very clear and specific activities to strengthen couple and family relationships.

DeFrain, J., & Asay, S. M. (2007). *Strong families around the world: Strengths-based research and perspectives.* London: Routledge/Taylor & Francis Group. The best source for understanding the research on international family strengths, community strengths, and cultural strengths.

Eubanks Fleming, C. J., & Córdova, J. V. (2012). Predicting relationship help seeking prior to a marriage checkup. *Family Relations, 61*(February), 90–100.

Ferrer, M. (2015). Stepping stones for stepfamilies. A six-lesson curriculum for enhancing stepfamily relationships developed by the University of Florida Extension. Web site: http://edis.ifas.ufl.edu/topic_program_stepping_stones_for_stepfamilies.

Gil, E. (2006). *Helping abused and traumatized children: Integrating directive and nondirective approaches.* New York, NY: Guilford Press.

Gurman, A. S., Lebow, J. L., & Snyder, D. K. (Eds.). (2015). *Clinical handbook of couple therapy.* New York, NY: Guilford Press.

Hennon, C. B., & Wilson, S. M. (Eds.). (2008). *Families in a global context.* London: Routledge/Taylor & Francis Group. How are families the same or different around the world? An in-depth analysis of family life in 17 countries.

Huxley, A. (1945). *The perennial philosophy.* New York, NY: Harper & Brothers.

Imber-Black, E. (Ed.). (2010) Couple and family therapy theory and practice: Innovations in 2010. *Family Process, 49* (3), 265–267. A special issue of the respected journal.

Journal of GLBT Family Studies. (2016). Taylor & Francis Online. Web site: http://www.tandfonline.com/doi/abs/10.1080/1550428X.2015.1072389?journalCode=wgfs20.

Markman, H. J., & Stanley, S. M. (2016). PREP Program: Successful relationships, successful lives. Web site: https://www.prepinc.com/content/about-us/what-is-prep.htm.

Miller, S., & Miller, P. (2016). Couple Communication. Web site: http://www.smartmarriages.com/directory/17.

Minuchin, P., Colapinto, J., & Minuchin, S. (2007). *Working with families of the poor* (2nd ed.). New York, NY: Guilford Press.

Moore, B. A. (2011). *Handbook of counseling military couples.* New York and London: Routledge/Taylor & Francis Group.

National Council on Family Relations. (2016). NCFR, founded in 1938, is the oldest multidisciplinary and nonpartisan professional organization focused solely on family research, practice, and education. NCFR publishes three scholarly journals: *Journal of Marriage and Family, Family Relations: Interdisciplinary Journal of Applied Family Studies,* and *Journal of Family Theory & Review.* Web site: www.ncfr.org.

Olson, D. H., Olson-Sigg, A., & Larson, P. J. (2008). *The couple checkup: Finding your relationship strengths.* Nashville, TN: Thomas Nelson.

Onedera, J. D. (2007). *The role of religion in marriage and family counseling.* London: Routledge/Taylor & Francis Group. Focuses on how each of the major world religions can influence family dynamics.

Paragament, K. I. (2007). *Spiritually integrated psychotherapy: Understanding and addressing the sacred.* New York, NY: Guilford Press.

PREPARE-ENRICH. (2016). Building strong marriages. Web site: https://www.prepare-enrich.com/.

Rivett, M. (2009). *Family therapy: 100 key points and techniques.* London: Routledge/Taylor & Francis Group. Family therapy theory and practice; concise and jargon-free.

University of Nebraska–Lincoln Extension. (2016). Educational materials for strengthening couple and family relationships. Web site: http://extensionpubs.unl.edu/.

Wetchler, J. L., & Hecker, L. (Eds.). (2015). *An introduction to marriage and family therapy.* New York, NY: Routledge/Taylor & Francis Group.

Visit the text-specific Online Learning Center at **www.mhhe.com/olson9e** for practice tests, chapter summaries, and PowerPoint slides.

Design Element: © Alicia Grünkind/EyeEm/Getty Images

Couple and Family Scales

Couple and Family Map

Appendix A

Couple and Family Map

The Couple and Family Map can be used to define the way in which a couple or a family interacts—that is, to describe the family system. The Couple and Family Scales are the tools an interviewer uses to place the couple or family in the Couple and Family Map. In this resource section we will outline the instructions for using these scales. The process consists of six steps:

1. Understanding the dimensions and concepts of the Couple and Family Map
2. Interviewing the couple or family
3. Completing the Coalition Rating Scale
4. Assigning a scale value for each concept
5. Assigning a global rating for each dimension
6. Plotting the global ratings on the Couple and Family Map

Step 1: Dimensions and Concepts

There are three primary dimensions in the Couple and Family Map: family cohesion, family flexibility, and family communication. Each dimension has several concepts that help define and describe it. Before doing an assessment of a couple or a family, the interviewer reviews all the concepts and their descriptions for each of the three dimensions.

Step 2: Interview Questions

To assess a couple or a family, the interviewer, usually through a semistructured interview, evaluates the couple's or family's interactions in terms of each of the concepts for each dimension. Those experienced in using the Family and Couple Scales find it helpful to encourage the couple or family to discuss with each other the interview questions in Table A.1. The questions focus on the two dimensions of cohesion and flexibility but not on communication. To assess communication, the interviewer simply observes how the couple or family communicates while they are discussing the interview questions. The interviewer should encourage the couple or the family to talk directly to each other—*not* to the interviewer—so that the interviewer can observe how they interact with each other.

Step 3: The Coalition Rating Scale

After the interview, the interviewer first completes the Coalition Rating Scale (shown in Table A.2), if it applies. It is necessary to use this scale if one or more family members function differently from the rest of the family. For example, it is possible to have a *rigidly enmeshed* family with a *chaotically disengaged* husband. If there is a disengaged member or a coalition (see definitions given in Table A.2), these family members are rated separately from the rest of the family system. The interviewer completes the Coalition Rating Scale *first*, before completing the other scales.

TABLE A.1   Interview Questions for Assessing Family Cohesion and Flexibility

Questions for Assessing Family Cohesion
1. *Separateness/togetherness*: How much do family members go their own way versus spending time with the family?
2. *I–we balance*: Do family members have a good balance of time apart and together?
3. *Closeness*: Do people feel close to each other?
4. *Loyalty*: Is the family a top priority compared with work or friends?
5. *Activities*: Do people spend much time having fun together?
6. *Dependence/independence*: Do family members stay in close contact?

Other Useful Questions to Assess Family Cohesion
1. How does your family celebrate birthdays and holidays?
2. Describe your typical dinnertime meal in terms of who is present, who prepares the meal, who cleans up, and the type of family interaction that occurs.
3. What is a typical weekend like in your family?
4. Do you have special times when you get together as a family?

Questions for Assessing Family Flexibility
1. *Leadership*: Is leadership shared between parents?
2. *Discipline*: Is (was) discipline strict?
3. *Negotiation*: How do you negotiate differences in your family?
4. *Roles*: Does each spouse do only certain tasks?
5. *Rules*: Do rules change in your family?
6. *Change*: Is change upsetting to your family?

Other Useful Questions to Assess Family Adaptability
1. How open is your family to change?
2. Is your family good at problem solving?
3. Does your family seem disorganized?
4. Who is in charge—the parent(s) or the child(ren)?

TABLE A.2 The Coalition Rating Scale

Instructions

The functioning of most families can be adequately described on the basis of their assessment as a unit or group. However, some families include individuals or dyadic units (coalitions) whose functioning may be markedly different from that of the rest of the family as a group.

This Coalition Rating Scale provides a way of noting coalitions' or disengaged individuals' patterns in family systems. After observing the family's interactions, any coalitions or disengaged individuals should be identified by checking the relevant categories below.

Definitions

Coalition. A coalition is two or more people with a high degree of emotional closeness to one another. During family interaction, the members of a coalition are very connected to one another and may at times exclude other family members.

Disengaged individual(s). A disengaged individual is emotionally separated from the rest of the family. Disengaged individuals often exhibit a low degree of involvement and interaction with other family members.

Coalitions

____ Mother–son
____ Mother–daughter
____ Father–son
____ Father–daughter
____ Son–daughter
____ Same-sex siblings
____ Other

Disengaged Individuals

____ Disengaged mother
____ Disengaged father
____ Disengaged child(ren)
____ Other

(A husband–wife coalition is considered a positive dyad and is therefore not listed.)

Step 4: Assigning Scale Values

After interviewing the couple or family, the interviewer rates them on each of the concepts that make up the three dimensions, using the scales in Table A.3. Before selecting a value, the interviewer carefully reads the descriptions for each concept and then selects a value from 1 to 8 that most closely represents the couple or family as a unit.

Step 5: Assigning Global Ratings

After assigning a rating for each concept in each of the three dimensions and recording those ratings on Table A.4, the interviewer makes a global rating for each of the three dimensions (cohesion, flexibility, and communication) and records the global ratings on Table A.4. The global rating for each dimension should be based on an overall evaluation rather than on a sum of the subscale (concept) ratings.

Step 6: Plotting a Family System Type on the Couple and Family Map

Finally, the interviewer plots the couple's or the family's global ratings on cohesion and flexibility on the Couple and Family Map (Figure A.1). This determines the marital or family system type. If, for example, the interviewer assigns a family a global rating of 5 on the cohesion dimension and 4 on the flexibility dimension, the model will identify the family as *structurally cohesive*, one of the four balanced family types on the Couple and Family Map. If the family contains a coalition or a disengaged member, the interviewer also plots the coalition or member on the map.

TABLE A.3 Couple and Family Scales

Levels of Family Cohesion

COHESION

	Disengaged (Unbalanced)		Connected (Balanced)		Cohesive (Balanced)		Enmeshed (Unbalanced)	
Score	1	2	3	4	5	6	7	8
Separateness/togetherness	High separateness		More separateness than togetherness		More togetherness than separateness		Very high togetherness	
I–we balance	Primarily "I"		More "I" than "we"				More "we" than "I"	
	Primarily "we"							
Closeness	Little closeness		Low-to-moderate closeness		Moderate-to-high closeness		Very high closeness	
Loyalty	Lack of loyalty		Some loyalty		Considerable loyalty		High loyalty	
Activities	Mainly separate		More separate than shared		More shared than separate		Mainly shared	
Dependence/independence	High independence		More independence than dependence		More dependence than independence		High dependence	
	High dependence							

Levels of Family Flexibility

FLEXIBILITY

	Rigid (Unbalanced)		Structured (Balanced)		Flexible (Balanced)		Chaotic (Unbalanced)	
Score	1	2	3	4	5	6	7	8
Leadership	Authoritarian		Sometimes shared		Often shared		Lack of leadership	
Discipline	Strict discipline		Somewhat democratic		Democratic		Erratic/inconsistent	
Negotiation	Limited discussion		Organized discussion		Open discussion		Endless discussion	
Roles	Roles very stable		Roles stable		Role sharing		Dramatic role shifts	
Rules	Unchanging rules		Few rule changes		Some rule changes		Frequent rule changes	
Change	Very little change		Moderate change		Some change		Considerable change	

Levels of Family Communication

COMMUNICATION

	Poor		Good		Very Good	
Score	1	2	3	4	5	6
Listening skills	Poor listening skills		Appears to listen, but feedback is limited		Gives feedback, indicating good listening skills	
Speaking skills	Often speaks for others		Speaks for oneself more than for others		Speaks mainly for oneself rather than for others	
Self-disclosure	Low sharing of feelings		High sharing of feelings		Moderate sharing of feelings	
Clarity	Inconsistent messages		Clear messages		Very clear messages	
Staying on topic	Seldom stays on topic		Often stays on topic		Mainly stays on topic	
Respect and regard	Low to moderate		Moderate to high		High	

TABLE A.4 Couple and Family Rating Form

COHESION

	Disengaged		Connected		Cohesive		Enmeshed	
Score	1	2	3	4	5	6	7	8
Separateness/togetherness	☐	☐	☐	☐	☐	☐	☐	☐
I–we balance	☐	☐	☐	☐	☐	☐	☐	☐
Closeness	☐	☐	☐	☐	☐	☐	☐	☐
Loyalty	☐	☐	☐	☐	☐	☐	☐	☐
Activities	☐	☐	☐	☐	☐	☐	☐	☐
Dependence/independence	☐	☐	☐	☐	☐	☐	☐	☐
Global rating	☐	☐	☐	☐	☐	☐	☐	☐

FLEXIBILITY

	Rigid		Structured		Flexible		Chaotic	
Score	1	2	3	4	5	6	7	8
Leadership	☐	☐	☐	☐	☐	☐	☐	☐
Discipline	☐	☐	☐	☐	☐	☐	☐	☐
Negotiation	☐	☐	☐	☐	☐	☐	☐	☐
Roles	☐	☐	☐	☐	☐	☐	☐	☐
Rules	☐	☐	☐	☐	☐	☐	☐	☐
Change	☐	☐	☐	☐	☐	☐	☐	☐
Global rating	☐	☐	☐	☐	☐	☐	☐	☐

COMMUNICATION

	Poor			Good		Very Good
Score	1	2	3	4	5	6
Listening skills	☐	☐	☐	☐	☐	☐
Speaking skills	☐	☐	☐	☐	☐	☐
Self-disclosure	☐	☐	☐	☐	☐	☐
Clarity	☐	☐	☐	☐	☐	☐
Staying on topic	☐	☐	☐	☐	☐	☐
Respect and regard	☐	☐	☐	☐	☐	☐
Global rating	☐	☐	☐	☐	☐	☐

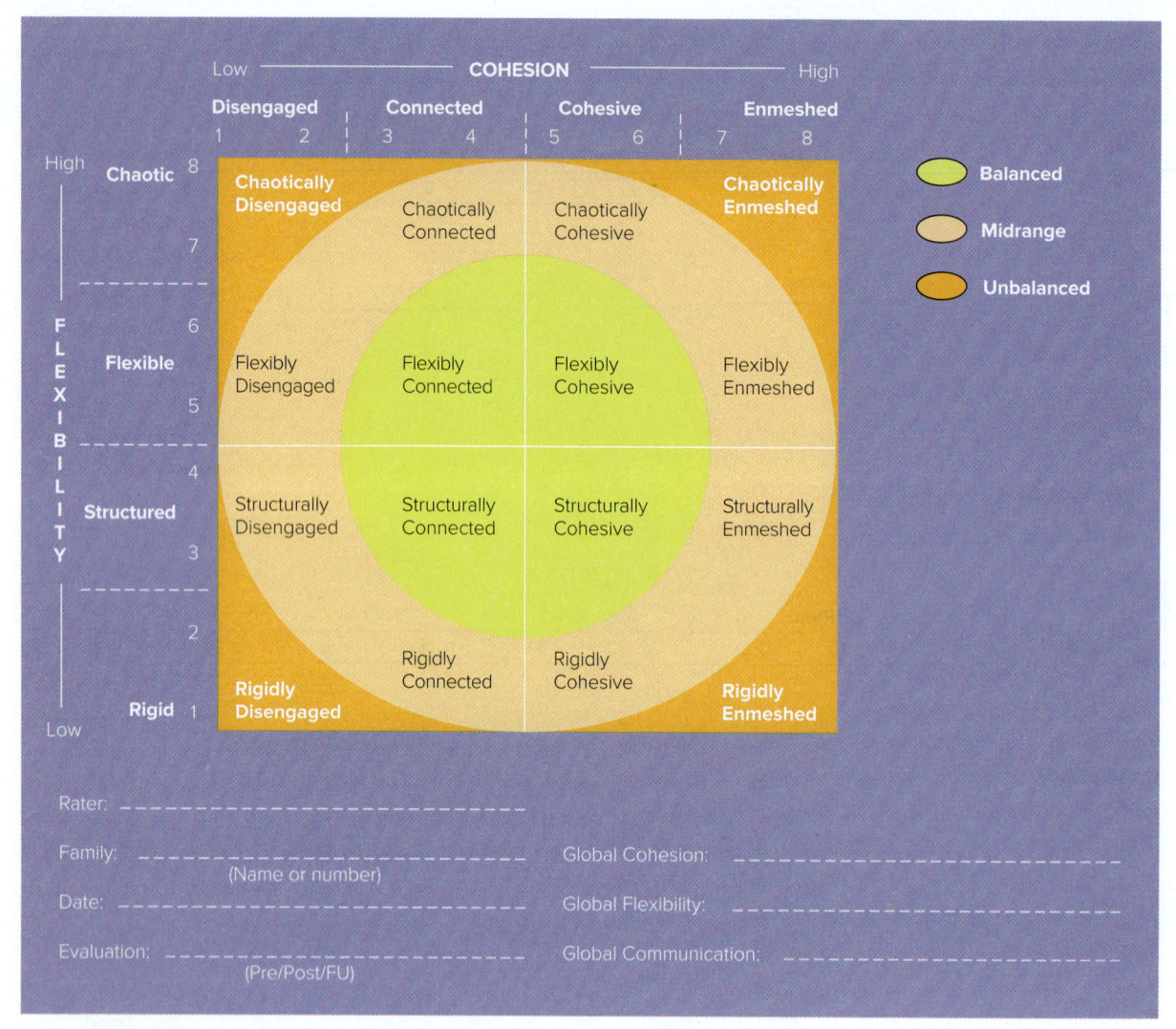

FIGURE A.1
Couple and Family Map

Source: Carlson, K.J., Eisenstat, S. A., and Ziporyn T., *The Harvard Guide to Women's Health.* Cambridge, MA: Harvard University Press, 1996.

Family Science and Family Research Methods

Appendix B

A Knowledge Explosion
Family Research Methods
Research Designs
A Final Word About Research

Family science, also called family studies, is growing rapidly, as a profession and as a social and behavioral science. In recent years, research on the family has improved in both quality and quantity. Family researchers use many of the same methods as other social scientists, but they tailor these methods to their own interests and purposes as they focus on couple and family issues. This section describes several research methods, including questionnaires, interviews, case studies, and observational approaches.

A Knowledge Explosion

Family science is a multidisciplinary field, which has an impact on many disciplines. These disciplines in turn contribute to the understanding of families (Table B.1). Over the past 40 years, this science has emerged as a genuine discipline unto itself. Its primary goal is to achieve a better understanding of families in order to enhance the quality of family life. Professionals whose main interests are research, theory, and the development of programs for families tend to call themselves *family scientists*. Those who develop educational programs for couples and families call themselves *family life educators*. Those who work clinically with troubled families are called *marital and family therapists*.

Family scientists have backgrounds in a wide variety of disciplines: human development, family science, human sciences, social work, nursing, educational psychology, psychology, sociology, psychiatry, and anthropology. Family scientists may be researchers, professors, teachers, family life educators, family therapists, ministers, nurses, social workers, or attorneys.

This multidisciplinary contribution to the field of family science has resulted in increased collaboration among researchers, with more articles being coauthored in recent years (Moody, 2004). Nearly half of all social science articles in family science are coauthored. This trend might be the result of funding requirements of projects in the field or the need for differing skills on any given article. Family science is also more likely to have coauthors than many of the other social science areas because it is already a multidisciplinary field of study.

Family Research Methods

The whole of science is nothing more than a refinement of everyday thinking.

—Albert Einstein

It is primarily through research that new ideas and facts are discovered. The word *research* is derived from the Middle French word *recherché*, meaning "to investigate thoroughly." Science, in the final analysis, is an examination of events or information in an attempt to make new discoveries.

TABLE B.1 Disciplines Contributing to Family Science

Discipline	Topics in Family Science
Anthropology	Cross-cultural studies; kinship; diversity in families
Biology	Conception and reproduction; growth, development, and aging
Child development	Development of infant and child; interpersonal skills
Communication studies	Couple and family communication
Economics	Family finances; consumer behavior
Education	Family life education; marriage preparation
History	Historical perspectives on the family throughout time
Human sciences	Ecosystem perspectives on family, nutrition, housing, clothing
Law	Marriage and divorce laws; child custody laws
Literature	Marriages and families in fiction, present and past
Marital and family therapy	Treating couple and family relationships
Medicine and nursing	Families and health
Psychiatry	Treating mental health problems
Psychology	Family psychology; assessment of couples and families
Social work	Treating family problems; family policy
Sociology	Marriage and divorce statistics; sociological theories about families

It has been argued that the family is the most difficult institution in human society to study. The reason for this is that families tend to be closed to outsiders; they show their best side, their best behavior to the world, and the darker side of family life is hidden behind closed doors. To study important issues and to solve family problems, researchers and practitioners have to get below the surface and deal with both the positive and the negative aspects of family life.

Family researchers have a creative mix of tools and techniques for learning more about family realities, using both "insider" and "outsider" perspectives. An **insider perspective** is provided by family members when they describe how they see their relationships. An **outsider perspective** is provided by researchers or therapists observing and describing the activity from their point of view. Methods that tap the insider perspective are questionnaires, interviews, and case studies. Outsider perspectives are obtained through observational approaches. Family researchers often use only one method in a particular study, but there are advantages to a multimethod approach that uses both insider and outsider perspectives.

Family researchers study couple and family issues from both quantitative and qualitative perspectives. **Quantitative research** typically uses structured questionnaires and scales to assess family members' perceptions of their relationships, their attitudes, and behaviors. Their responses are typically converted to numbers that can be summed and analyzed using statistical methods. Most family science researchers believe that in the past 20 years qualitative research has become more accepted as a legitimate and systematic mode of inquiry (Creswell, 2013). **Qualitative research** tends to be based on more or less open-ended interviews of people talking about how they see their relationships. Their verbal responses are analyzed looking for themes in their comments. Ultimately, quantitative studies produce numbers that can be analyzed, whereas qualitative studies are more often looking for themes in stories from persons about a given topic.

Because quantitative studies rely on questionnaires and scales rather than personal interviews, quantitative studies usually have a larger sample of participants than qualitative studies. In qualitative research, data collection is often more involved and time consuming, because the interviews or written testimony can be much longer and in depth. This usually requires a great deal more time to transcribe into written testimony from the participants. This is why it has been said that, "Quantitative research learns a little about a lot of people, and qualitative research learns a lot about a few." This statement is an oversimplification of the difference between these two different research traditions, but it does highlight their differences.

Neither approach is "better" than the other. They are simply two different ways to study families. There is a growing movement today to use so-called **mixed-methods research** approaches, which rely on both qualitative and quantitative methods in the same study. For example, a research team focusing on marital quality might want to begin with 10 in-depth, face-to-face interviews, in which time is spent talking with couples about their marriages in a relatively unstructured and open-ended fashion. The researcher might ask a few broad, leading questions and then listen as the couple talk about how they view the particular issues, all of which is tape recorded or videotaped.

After completing a series of these in-depth interviews and transcribing the data—that is to say, the couples' thoughts about the issues—the researchers can then design the quantitative phase of the study. The open-ended interview questions can then be transformed into a more structured questionnaire with closed-end questions, that is, questions that have a series of fixed responses. The questionnaire can then be mailed to hundreds of couples in a wide geographic area. By using a qualitative approach, the researchers develop an in-depth understanding of the dynamics of marital quality based on a small sample of couples. Expanding the sample size and the breadth of the study to many more couples using the quantitative approach then increases the sample size and the ability to use statistical analysis with the data. The mixed-methods approach gives the investigator, in sum, "the best of both worlds."

Research methods need to be suitable for the population being studied. Written questions, for example, are inappropriate for people whose culture is predominantly an oral culture.

Questionnaires

Perhaps the most common method of studying families is the questionnaire. The researcher carefully prepares a series of questions based on a review of previous research on the topic. *Fixed-response questions* require an individual to pick his or her response from a selection of possible responses; *open-ended questions* allow the individual to respond in her or his own words. A questionnaire might contain either or both types of questions.

Developing a questionnaire is a challenge. What questions one asks and the manner in which the questions are phrased can greatly influence the results of a study. Researchers are wise to do a trial run with a small sample of families to see whether the questions are clear and precise. Next, the process of **validation** of a survey instrument—ensuring that the instrument measures what it is intended to measure—often takes researchers several months or even a number of years, depending on the complexity of the problem they are studying.

After the questionnaire is deemed satisfactory by the research team, it is distributed to a sufficiently large sample of family members. A number of factors determine the size of the sample, including how much money the research team has to spend on the project, how important the topic is to the researchers, and how difficult it is to find a group of families who are willing to participate in the study.

In the past, it was quite common for family researchers to limit their studies to what mothers thought was going on in their families. Fathers and children were often ignored. Researchers assumed that one individual could speak for the family as a whole. Furthermore, researchers favored this approach to studies of multiple family members because the latter were much more time consuming, expensive, and difficult to analyze. Today, most researchers recognize that fathers, mothers, and children often differ in their perceptions of family life and that a good study demands information and perceptions gathered from multiple family members.

Interviews

The interview—whether face to face or by telephone or online—is another family research method. Some investigators believe that interview data are more valid than data from questionnaires because the researcher can ask follow-up questions and get more information. On the other hand, some research has found that people are more honest on questionnaires. Furthermore, interviews tend to take more time, cost more money, and thus reach fewer people than is possible with questionnaires. Variation from one interviewer to another may also taint the results; questionnaires, of course, are standardized. Perhaps the best approach is to use both questionnaires and interviews. The results can then be compared with each other to provide **cross-validation**.

Case Studies

Some of the most emotionally gripping research findings have come from family therapists and researchers using the case study method. A **case study** is a detailed description of a person or family whose interactions illustrate some specific idea, concept, or principle of family science. Using this method, researchers record in narrative form and analyze the complexities of family dynamics. Great care is taken to protect the privacy and anonymity of the family members, in part by concealing their names and disguising any identifying family characteristics.

The major problem with case studies is that the families described are probably not representative of all American families. For example, if a researcher were to analyze the case of a stepfamily in treatment at a counseling agency, the researcher might conclude that stepfamilies have numerous problems. This conclusion would be biased, however, because it was based on a family who had come for help. If the researcher were to question stepfamilies by randomly telephoning people in the community, the result would be a more **representative sample**—that is, a random selection—of stepfamilies and probably a more positive description of interactions in this type of family.

Observational Approaches

Researchers who study families and family therapists who treat families with problems tend to work by observing family interactions in natural settings, such as the home. Observational approaches, which tap the outsider perspective, have both strengths and limitations. One strength is that the researcher does not have to rely on family members' self-reports of their own behavior. One major limitation is that the presence of a stranger (the therapist or researcher) influences family members' behavior, making it less natural. Researchers also need to consider whether families who volunteer for such studies differ in some ways from families who do not volunteer. These are important issues in any research study, but they are more problematic in observational studies.

Sometimes a family is brought into a research laboratory for a study. Often the laboratory is set up like a living room or a dining room, and the family is asked to perform a particular task together, such as playing a game. The researchers videotape the interaction and later study the video to analyze and evaluate the family members' communication styles. Many families are not willing to participate in such studies, of course, and those who do may act differently than they do when in the privacy of their own home. Despite the difficulties associated with observational research, however, many creative observational family studies have contributed significantly to the field of family science.

Historical Studies

Studies of families from earlier generations are often useful and interesting to us today. As historians point out, we cannot know where we are going in the future unless we know where we have been. Historical research, which often relies on diaries and historical statistics about families, can help us understand families in the past.

Feminists argue that much of what has been presented as family history in the past has focused on the lives of men (*his*-story) and has neglected the lives of women (*her*-story). The history of the family, which in many cultures is traditionally the domain of women, has received little attention from historians (who have for the most part been men). But in recent decades, a resurgent feminist history movement has begun to look at the past from women's perspectives.

Multicultural Studies

Multicultural studies of families can contribute rich insights into family life and family interactions. The United States has innumerable family cultures: African American, Caucasian, Latino, Italian American, Chicago suburban, inner-city Boston, gay-male, lesbian, middle class, upper class, rural, urban, and so forth. Family life is different in each of these cultures. A family in the commuter culture of Los Angeles, for example, lives a life quite different from that of a family in rural Iowa. Diversity in families is discussed in greater detail in Chapter 2.

Conducting research with economically disadvantaged and diverse populations has been an area of focus in the social sciences in recent years (Knight, Roosa, & Umaña-Taylor, 2009; Trimble & Fisher, 2006). This increased interest is primarily because minority populations in this country are increasing.

Research on economically disadvantaged and diverse populations has often been conducted inappropriately. Instruments and measurements have typically been developed with samples of European Americans, and it cannot be assumed that these research tools are appropriate for all cultures. In addition, researchers have not always treated diverse populations with respect and consideration. For example, findings often are not reported within the context of cultural beliefs but instead are interpreted in terms of the dominant culture. Also, the people studied may not have received any reports of findings or received any benefit from the studies and feel "used" in the process. Therefore, there are new resources about how to ethically and appropriately conduct research with these populations. This usually means research needs to be conducted with an understanding about how a behavior might fit into the context of cultural values and beliefs, subjects must be compensated for their time, they must be adequately informed about the research process, and members of the community studied need to be part of or inform the research team (Trimble & Fisher, 2006).

Research Designs

Researchers are often interested in how particular families grow and change over time. Three types of research designs that take the passage of time into consideration are longitudinal studies, cross-sectional studies, and cross-sectional cohort studies.

Longitudinal Studies

In a **longitudinal study**, the researcher interviews or observes a family several times over a period of months or years. This approach obviously takes a considerable amount of time, effort, and money. For these reasons, only a small proportion of family research is longitudinal. The results of such projects, however, are often well worth the effort because they provide valuable information about long-term processes, such as the effect of the birth of a child on a marriage.

An example of a longitudinal study would be an investigation of the process of marital adaptation. A sample of couples would be interviewed over several years, from the dating period before they were married, to living together and/or early marriage, to the advent of parenthood, and so on. The study could continue for a very long time, dependent on the energy and dedication of the researchers; the interest of the couples in continuing to be involved in the study; and the funding stream.

Cross-Sectional Studies

In a **cross-sectional study**, a researcher selects couples or families at various stages of the family life cycle and compares the differences between the various stages. For example, a researcher could compare four stages of the life cycle by selecting some newlywed couples, some couples with young children, some couples with adolescents, and some older couples whose children had left home. The aim of this approach is to describe the similarities and differences between couples and families at these four stages.

The advantage of the cross-sectional design is efficiency: Data can be collected from all four groups at about the same time and then immediately compared. A disadvantage of this type of study is that it is not possible to know if identified similarities and differences are due only to the stage of the life cycle or to the characteristics of these specific families—a question that could only be answered by a longitudinal study that followed the same families over time. Furthermore, cross-sectional studies cannot reveal whether the historical context for each group (past experiences, crises, etc.) influenced the findings.

Family Science and Family Research Methods   A-11

Cross-Sectional Cohort Studies

Because of the problems with both longitudinal and cross-sectional studies, researchers have designed a shortcut known as the **cross-sectional cohort study**. Using this approach, researchers do not follow a group of families for many years; instead, they study various families at different stages of the family life cycle for shorter periods. They might, for example, study a group of families with a 10-year-old, another group with a 12-year-old, a third group with a 14-year-old, and a fourth group with a 16-year-old. If they follow these families for 5 years, they could analyze changes from age 10 to 15, 12 to 17, 14 to 19, and 16 to 21. The result would be an overview of an 11-year period (age 10 to age 21) achieved in only 5 years of research.

A Final Word About Research

No single study can provide definitive answers to important questions in family science. In fact, each study almost invariably raises new questions that are complex and difficult to answer. The advancement of scientific knowledge is a slow and painstaking process. People researching a particular topic in family science have to examine data from many related studies on the topic.

Sometimes studies produce findings that conflict with the results of other studies. These discrepancies may be due to variations in the type of questions asked, the method of research used, or the specific sample studied. For example, a sample of families drawn from the Midwest may look at gender-role issues in families somewhat differently from a sample of families drawn from Latino families living in California. Likewise, two-parent traditional American families may have a different way of looking at certain issues than do single-parent families.

Although studies on similar topics may have differing results, good studies tend to complement each other. When dozens of researchers from various parts of the United States or around the world look at a problem from many different theoretical approaches, using different research methods and different statistical analyses, a fairly comprehensive picture emerges. When the findings are similar in spite of all the differences in the sample, method, and analysis, the results are more conclusive and help build more valid findings and theories about couples and families.

Key Terms

family science
insider perspective
outsider perspective
quantitative research
qualitative research
mixed-methods research
validation
cross-validation
case study
representative sample
longitudinal study
cross-sectional study
cross-sectional cohort study

Glossary

A

ability to manage stress and crisis effectively One of the six major qualities (commonly found in emotionally healthy families) identified by researchers working within the family strengths framework.

abortion Expulsion of a fetus from the uterus before it is sufficiently developed to survive on its own; commonly used to describe only artificially induced terminations of pregnancy.

abortion pill (RU-486) A medication abortion method. The drug mifepristone combined with misoprostol has been widely used in Europe for early abortions and now is used routinely in the United States. *See also* medication abortion.

acculturation The intermeshing of cultural traits and values with those of the dominant culture.

afterbirth The placenta and fetal membranes, which are expelled from the uterus during the third stage of labor.

ageism A form of prejudice or discrimination in which one judges an older person negatively solely on the basis of age.

aggressive communication A style of interpersonal communication that attempts to hurt or put down the receiver while protecting the aggressor's self-esteem.

Al-Anon A self-help group for families of alcoholics.

Alateen A support group for young people with alcoholic parents, based on the Alcoholics Anonymous model.

alcohol abuse A generic term that encompasses both alcoholism (addiction to alcohol characterized by compulsive drinking) and problem drinking (alcohol consumption that results in functional disability).

Alcoholics Anonymous (AA) A self-help group for alcoholics.

alcoholism Addiction to alcohol characterized by compulsive drinking.

Alexander Technique An educational process approach to childbirth designed to improve the mother's ease and freedom of movement, balance, flexibility, and coordination. Ideally, mothers take weekly practice sessions while pregnant. Goals include improving comfort during pregnancy; increasing pushing effectiveness during delivery; aiding in recovery from childbirth; and easing the discomfort of nursing.

alimony Court-ordered financial support to a spouse or former spouse following separation or divorce.

Alzheimer's disease A progressive neurologic disease of the brain that leads to the irreversible loss of neurons and dementia. Clinical hallmarks of the disease include impairment in memory, judgment, decision making, orientation to physical surroundings, and language.

ambiguous loss When a family member is physically absent but psychologically present, the family experiences highly stressful feelings. People need to find ways to accept a loss before they can move on through the grieving process, but this is difficult when there is significant ambiguity in the situation. *See also* boundary ambiguity.

amniotic sac The membrane that encloses the fetus and holds the amniotic fluid, which insulates the fetus.

androgen Any of the hormones that develop and maintain male secondary sex characteristics.

anorgasmia A sexual dysfunction that prevents a woman from having an orgasm; failure to achieve orgasm (climax) during sexual intercourse.

appreciation and affection One of the six major qualities (commonly found in emotionally healthy families) identified by researchers working within the family strengths framework.

arranged marriage *See* parent-arranged marriage.

assertive communication A style of interpersonal communication that involves expressing one's self-interests and wishes without degrading or putting down the other person.

assertiveness A person's ability to express her or his feelings and desires.

assimilation Adopting the cultural traits and values of the dominant culture.

attachment theory This theory focuses on the ways that children develop attachment to their caregivers, usually their parents, during infancy. The most important tenet of attachment theory is that a young child needs to develop a relationship with at least one primary caregiver for social and emotional development to occur normally. This theory has recently been applied to adults in romantic relationships.

attentive listening A style of listening focused on fully understanding the speaker's point of view; characterized by encouragement rather than trying to direct or control the speaker.

authoritarian parenting A parenting style characterized by the demand for absolute obedience to rigid rules and the use of punitive, forceful disciplinary measures.

avoidance A person's tendency to minimize issues and a reluctance to deal with issues directly.

B

Baby Boomer A person who was born during the demographic post–World War II baby boom, between 1946 and 1964. The term is sometimes used in a cultural context and sometimes used in a demographic context.

balanced families Families who fit into the four central categories of the Couple and Family Map: families who are flexibly connected, flexibly cohesive, structurally connected, or structurally cohesive. *See also* midrange families; unbalanced families.

bankruptcy The state of being financially insolvent or unable to pay one's bills.

barrier methods of contraception Devices that prevent pregnancy by physically blocking the sperm from entering the uterus, including condoms, diaphragms, and cervical caps.

behaviorist A clinician who, based on learning theories, has developed practical, positive ways of dealing with children's behavior; rather than focusing on punishment, behaviorists encourage "accentuating the positive." *See also* reinforcement.

belief system One of the four major components of the sociocultural context in which families live, centering on religious/spiritual/ethical beliefs and other ideas about how to live successfully and happily in the world. *See also* extended-family system; family system; social system.

bidirectional effects Both the influence of the child on the parent and the influence of the parent on the child; child development specialists and family scientists concur that studying these effects is important to an understanding of parent–child dynamics.

bilateral descent A method of tracing the lineage of children equally through ancestors of both mother and father.

binuclear family A postdivorce family in which both parents participate in the raising of their children despite living in separate households; the children generally reside with one of the parents.

bisexual Sexual orientation toward members of both sexes.

blamer A person whose style of anger management is characterized by a short temper, emotionally intense responses to stress, and the belief that others are responsible for her or his feelings and problems.

blastocyst An early stage of the fertilized egg, containing about 100 cells; implants itself in the uterine lining (endometrium).

blended family A term used to describe a stepfamily. Some researchers object to the term because it creates unrealistic expectations that the new family will quickly and easily "blend" together harmoniously and because it assumes a homogeneous unit, one without a previous history or background. *See also* stepfamily.

boomerang kids Adult children who come back to their parents' home to live as a result of divorce, job loss, or an inability to make it in the "real world."

boundaries The lines that both separate systems from and connect systems to each other. The notion of a boundary implies a hierarchy of interconnected systems, each larger than the one before it.

boundary ambiguity Lack of clarity about whether a person is either in or out of the family system; related to family stress levels. The concept includes two variables: physical and psychological presence or absence. High ambiguity (conflicting variables) produces high levels of stress.

Bradley Method This approach to childbirth, also called husband-coached birth, prepares the mother with relaxation techniques to deliver without pain medications and helps the father learn how to be mom's birth coach. The aim is to give birth without medications, but the Bradley Method also prepares parents for the possibility of unexpected situations, such as an emergency cesarean section. This 12-session course also covers the importance of nutrition and exercise; labor rehearsals; postpartum care; and breastfeeding.

breastfeeding Feeding a baby from the mother's breast rather than from a bottle; usually better than bottle-feeding for the physical well-being of the baby.

budgeting The regular, systematic balancing of income and expenses.

C

cascading circumstances When one crisis has an impact on other issues in one's life. An example would be when a person loses a job, and the job loss results in losing one's apartment, and the loss of an apartment results in having one's children removed from the home.

case study A detailed description of a person or a family that illustrates a specific idea, concept, or principle of family science.

catharsis conflict The false belief that venting anger verbally prevents physical violence. Researchers who study family violence have found that verbal and physical violence are related.

centrifugal interaction Behavior that pushes system components away from one another, decreasing the system's connectedness.

centripetal interaction Behavior that pulls system components toward one another, resulting in the system's increasing connectedness.

cervical cap A thimble-shaped contraceptive device that fits snugly over the cervix; must be fitted by a physician and used with a spermicide.

cesarean section (C-section) Surgical delivery of the fetus by incising the mother's abdominal and uterine walls.

child abuse Any recent act, or failure to act, by a parent or caretaker, that results in a child's death, serious physical or emotional harm, sexual abuse, or exploitation, or an act or failure to act that presents an imminent risk of serious harm to a child.

child-free alternative The decision by married or cohabiting adults not to have children.

child-to-parent abuse Violence directed at a parent by a child.

circular causality model An interpersonal communication model that describes an interaction pattern in which both parties view their behavior as a reaction to the other's behavior rather than as something for which they are each responsible. The first person sends out a message that causes a change in and a response from the second person. That response causes a new response in the first person, whose response initiates another response from the second person, and so on. This type of communication cycle can escalate into conflict.

closed system A family system that has the capacity to maintain the status quo and avoids change; also called a *morphostatic system*.

cluttered nest The period during which young adults return to their parental home until they are established professionally and financially and can move into an apartment or home of their own.

coculture A distinct cultural or social group living within a dominant culture but also having membership in another culture, such as gay men and lesbians.

cognitive development theory A model of child development that views growth as the mastery of specific ways of perceiving, thinking, and doing; growth occurs at discrete stages.

cohabiting The sharing of living quarters by unrelated and unmarried heterosexual or same-sex adults who have an emotional and sexual relationship.

cohabiting The sharing of living quarters by unrelated and unmarried heterosexual or same-sex adults who have an emotional and sexual relationship.

cohesion *See* family cohesion.

collective worldview The group is viewed as more important than the individual.

commitment Attachment to another. One of the six major qualities (commonly found in emotionally healthy families) identified by researchers working within the family strengths framework; also, the cognitive component of Sternberg's three dimensions of love.

communication The way humans create and share meaning, both verbally and nonverbally; the foundation for developing and maintaining human relationships, especially intimate relationships. *See also* family communication; positive communication.

companionate love A type of love relationship characterized by commitment and intimacy but lacking intense passion; common between partners who have been together for many years.

complex stepfamily A stepfamily that includes children from both parents. *See also* simple stepfamily.

conception The union of a sperm cell and the nucleus of an ovum (egg), which begins the development of the fetus; also called *fertilization*.

conceptual framework A set of interconnected ideas, concepts, and assumptions that helps organize thinking from a particular perspective. The field of family science includes a variety of major conceptual frameworks: family systems theory (or the family systems framework), the family strengths framework, the family development framework, the symbolic interaction framework, the social construction framework, and the feminist framework.

condom A rubber sheath placed over the penis before intercourse to prevent pregnancy and protect against sexually transmitted diseases.

conflict When one person opposes another person's position. It can occur between adults, between adults and children, and between children.

conflicted couple A type of premarital and married couple characterized by few relationship strengths, low levels of relationship satisfaction, and a high risk of divorce.

conjugal family system A family consisting of a husband, a wife, and children; also called a *nuclear family*.

consanguineal family system A family system that emphasizes blood ties more than marital ties.

constructive intimacy game A game, or exercise, designed to increase intimacy in a relationship; people participate voluntarily, and they know the rules and goals of the game. *See also* destructive intimacy game.

consummate love A type of love relationship characterized by commitment, intimacy, and passion.

continuous partial attention To keep up with the relentless flow of information, ideas, and exchanges, we often find ourselves in a state of continuous partial attention. As we attend to our email, cell phone, computer, television, laptop, iPod, and so forth, we also are often trying to hold a genuine conversation with a friend. This form of multitasking, when it comes to developing and maintaining intimate relationships, simply does not work.

contraception A deliberate action (use of a device, drug, or technique) taken to prevent conception (pregnancy).

contractions Tightenings of the muscles, especially those of the uterus, during labor.

conventional couple A type of couple that usually has disagreements in several areas in the marriage. They often struggle with communication and resolving conflict. They are fairly satisfied with their marriage and have strengths in spiritual beliefs, traditional roles, and have a network of friends and family.

coparenting A style of parenting in which both parents take on tasks and roles traditionally associated with only the mother or the father.

coping What we do when we identify something as potentially harmful or stressful.

Couple and Family Map A graphic representation of dynamic relationships within families, comprising three central dimensions: cohesion (togetherness), flexibility (ability to change), and communication (a facilitating dimension that helps families move between the extremes on the cohesion and flexibility dimensions). Identifies 16 types of family relationship.

couple-arranged marriage Freedom of choice in marriage. This approach is sometimes referred to as the *love match*, though love is not always the goal of marriage in Western industrialized societies. *See also* parent-arranged marriage.

crisis-loss stage of grief A period of chaotic shock; the first of Brubaker's three stages of the grieving process. *See also* new-life stage of grief; transition stage of grief.

cross-cultural family study A research study focused on how cultural context influences family issues, among them, values and behaviors, courtship and marriage patterns, communication, roles, work and the family, childrearing patterns, and sexuality.

cross-sectional cohort study Using this approach, researchers do not follow a group of families for many years; instead, they study various families at different stages of the family life cycle for shorter periods.

cross-sectional study A type of observational study that analyzes data collected from a population, or a representative subset, at a specific point in time.

cross-validation A comparison of the results from one research method with those of another research method to see if the findings are similar or identical.

cultural competence The ability to be effective in working with a variety of cultural groups. This ability involves awareness, knowledge, and skills.

cultural group A set of people who embrace core beliefs, behaviors, values, and norms and transmit them from generation to generation.

cultural identity A feeling of belonging that evolves from the shared beliefs, values, and attitudes of a group of people; the structure of the group's marital, sexual, and kinship relationships.

curvilinear relationship Researchers have found that the relationship between stress and effective outcomes for people is curvilinear—both too much and too little stress are problematic for individual and family functioning, but moderate levels of stress are usually positive.

D

dance of anger Lerner's metaphor to describe styles of managing anger and ways in which these styles interact.

dating A form of courtship involving a series of appointed meetings for social interaction and activities during which an exclusive relationship may evolve between two people. Also called *individual-choice courtship*.

definition of the situation The concept that a situation is based on a person's subjective interpretation; hence, people can have different views of the same situation.

delivery The second stage of labor, lasting from the time the cervix is completely dilated until the fetus is expelled or removed by cesarean section.

democratic parenting A parenting style that establishes the parents' legitimate power to set rules while also recognizing the child's feelings, individuality, and need to develop autonomy; uses positive reinforcement, seldom punishment, to enforce standards. Also called *authoritative parenting*.

deployment When a person in the military engages in military training or combat.

Depo-Provera (DMPA) A progestin that is administered by injection.

destructive intimacy game A game that reduces intimacy because people are often unaware of the game, do not voluntarily participate, and are often manipulated to behave in certain ways. *See also* constructive intimacy game.

devitalized couple The unhappiest type of married couple; characterized by few couple strengths and the highest risk for divorce.

diaphragm A cup-shaped rubber contraceptive device that is inserted in the vagina before intercourse to cover the cervical opening and block sperm from entering the uterus; must be fitted by a physician and used with a spermicide.

dilation and curettage (D & C) An abortion technique used in the second trimester of pregnancy; performed in a hospital under general anesthetic. After the cervix is dilated (opened), the embryo is removed from the uterus with a sharp instrument (curette).

dilation and evacuation (D & E) An abortion technique used in the second trimester of pregnancy. Suction and forceps are used to remove the embryo or fetus.

DINS dilemma Inhibited or hypoactive sexual desire in couples with many demands on their time. DINS stands for *double income, no sex.*

directive listening A style of listening in which the listener attempts to control the direction of the conversation through the use of questions.

distancer An individual who (1) wants emotional space when stress is high, (2) is self-reliant rather than a help-seeker, and (3) values privacy.

distress Feelings of discomfort caused by high levels of stress.

divorce culture The notion that divorce has become so accepted in the United States that it is almost expected as the outcome of marriage.

double bind A situation in which the message relayed by the speaker calls into question the type of relationship the receiver has with the speaker.

E

ecofeminism Politics that focuses on human beings' domination of nature.

ecology The study of how all the organisms in a system relate to one another.

egalitarian group In these types of groups, the ideals of democracy prevail and the rights and perspectives of both genders and all generations are respected.

egalitarian roles Social equality between the sexes; equal sharing of practical responsibilities and decision making by men and women. Also called *equalitarian roles*.

emerging adulthood A new stage of development between childhood and adulthood that is the age from 18 to 25. This is a prolonged period of role exploration focusing on identity exploration.

emic perspective The analysis of a society from the inside. *See also* etic perspective.

empty love A type of love relationship involving commitment but no passion or intimacy.

empty-nest syndrome Feelings of malaise, emptiness, and lack of purpose that some parents experience when their last child leaves home. *See also* spacious nest.

endogamy The practice of choosing a mate from within one's own ethnic, religious, socioeconomic, or general age group.

enjoyable time together One of the six major qualities (commonly found in emotionally healthy families) identified by researchers working within the family strengths framework.

ENRICH A comprehensive marital inventory containing 125 questions in categories that are relevant to married couples and their satisfaction with their relationship. ENRICH is an acronym for **EN**riching **R**elationship **I**ssues, **C**ommunication, and **H**appiness.

episiotomy A surgical incision from the vagina toward the anus, performed to prevent tearing of the perineum during childbirth.

erectile dysfunction A sexual dysfunction in which a man has difficulty achieving or maintaining penile erection that is firm enough for intercourse.

estrogen Although often called the *female hormone*, any of a group of hormones, produced primarily by the ovaries, that are significant in controlling female physiological functions and directing the development of female secondary sex characteristics at puberty.

ethnic group A set of people who are embedded within a larger cultural group or society and who share beliefs, behaviors, values, and norms that are transmitted from generation to generation.

ethnic identity The geographic origin of a minority group within a country or culture; cultural identity transcends ethnic identity.

ethnocentrism The assumption that one's own culture is the standard by which to judge other cultures.

etic perspective The analysis of a society from the outside. *See also* emic perspective.

eugenics Breeding to improve inherited characteristics.

eustress A moderate-to-high level or a low-to-moderate level of stress that is energizing, motivating, positive, and healthy.

exogamy The practice of choosing a mate from outside one's own group.

expressive role According to the Parsons and Bales model of the modern family, the wife-mother's role is to be expressive—caring for the emotional well-being of the family, providing nurturing and comfort. *See also* instrumental role.

extended family A nuclear family and those related to its members by blood, such as aunts, uncles, cousins, and grandparents.

extended-family system One of the four major components of the sociocultural context in which families live; focuses on the degree of importance relatives outside the nuclear family have on the family's life. *See also* belief system; family system; social system.

F

family Two or more people who are committed to each other and who share intimacy, resources, decision-making responsibilities, and values; people who love and care for each other.

family cohesion The togetherness or closeness of a family; one of the three dimensions of the Couple and Family Map.

family communication Interaction; sharing of thoughts and feelings; the facilitating dimension of the Couple and Family Map.

family coping A family's ability to manage stressful events or situations as a unit with minimal or no detrimental effects on any individual members.

family coping resources Resources of a healthy family system on which the family can draw in times of stress, including cohesion, adaptability, and a willingness to adopt nontraditional family roles in the face of changing economic circumstances. *See also* personal coping resources.

family development framework A conceptual framework that focuses on how family members deal with roles and developmental tasks within the family unit as they move through the stages of the life cycle.

family flexibility A family's ability to change and adapt in the face of stress or crisis; one of the three dimensions of the Couple and Family Map.

family of origin The family in which a person is raised during childhood.

family power The ability of one family member to change the behavior of the other family members.

family science An interdisciplinary field whose primary focus is to better understand families in order to enhance the quality of family life. Professionals whose main focus of applied or action research is the family tend to call themselves *family scientists*; those who develop educational programs for families sometimes call themselves *family life educators* or *family educators*; those who work clinically with troubled families are called *marriage* (or *marital*) *and family therapists*.

family strengths framework A conceptual framework proposing that if researchers study only family problems, they will find only problems in families, but that if they are interested in family strengths, they must study strong families; identifies six qualities that strong families commonly demonstrate: commitment, appreciation and affection, positive communication, enjoyable time together, spiritual well-being, and the ability to manage stress and crisis effectively.

family system One of the four major components of the sociocultural context in which families live; focuses on the interconnectedness of family members. *See also* belief system; extended-family system; social system.

family systems theory (or family systems framework) A conceptual framework that views everything that happens to any family member as having an impact on everyone else in the family, because family members are interconnected and operate as a group, or family system.

family therapy An approach to helping families; based on the belief that the roots of an individual's problems may be traced to troubled family dynamics, and solutions can come by working with the whole family.

fatuous love A type of love relationship in which commitment is based on passion but in which there has not yet been time to develop true intimacy.

femininity A gender-linked constellation of personality traits and behavioral patterns traditionally associated with females in a society.

feminist framework A conceptual framework that emphasizes the value of women's perspectives on society and the family, that recognizes women's subordination, and that promotes change in that status.

fertility awareness A variety of contraceptive methods based on predicting a woman's fertile period and avoiding intercourse during that interval (or using an additional method of contraception during that time).

fertilization The union of a sperm cell and the nucleus of an ovum (egg); also known as *conception*.

fetal alcohol syndrome (FAS) Serious malformations (particularly of the facial features and the eyes) seen in children whose mothers drank excessively during their pregnancy.

flexibility *See* family flexibility.

foreign born A person whose birth place is somewhere other than the United States.

G

gay and lesbian family A same-sex couple, such as two men or two women, develops an intimate, caring, loving relationship and includes children in that relationship.

gender The learned characteristics and behaviors associated with biological sex in a particular culture. *See also* sex.

gender identity A person's internal sense of being female or male, which is expressed in personality and behavior.

gender role The traits and behaviors assigned to males and females in a culture.

gender-role stereotype A rigid, simplistic belief about the distinctive psychological characteristics and behavioral patterns attributable to a man or woman based exclusively on sex.

general systems theory A set of principles and concepts that can be applied to all types of systems, living and nonliving.

GLBT An acronym that stands for gay, lesbian, bisexual, and transgender.

goals Specific, achievable objectives or purposes.

H

harmonious couple A type of premarital and married couple characterized by many couple strengths, relationship satisfaction, and a low risk of divorce.

heterosexual Sexual orientation toward members of the other sex.

historical trauma The loss, of things such as land, language, or culture, that results in loss of identity and social problems for individuals and families.

HIV *See* human immunodeficiency virus.

homogamy The tendency to marry someone of the same ethnic group, educational level, socioeconomic status, religion, and values.

homosexual Sexual orientation toward members of the same sex.

hooking up Having a sexual encounter with someone who is an acquaintance or someone who is a stranger. The sexual encounter may or may not include intercourse.

hormonal methods of contraception These include oral contraceptives, the birth control shot, and the birth control patch. The *pill*, a combination oral contraceptive, contains the hormones estrogen and progestin. In addition to preventing pregnancy, the pill makes the menstrual cycle more regular, tends to reduce menstrual cramping, and is associated with lower incidences of breast and ovarian cysts and pelvic inflammatory disease (PID).

human ecosystem A model showing how various human subsystems interrelate among each other. To really understand a specific family system, one also needs to consider the various system levels it influences and that influence it.

human immunodeficiency virus (HIV) The virus that causes AIDS.

HypnoBirthing This method of childbirth, also called the Mongan method, is a relaxed natural childbirth education approach enhanced with self-hypnosis techniques. Teachers emphasize pregnancy and childbirth, as well as prebirth parenting and the consciousness of the preborn child.

hypothesis An assertion subject to verification or proof; a presumed relationship between variables.

I

idiographic approach A theoretical approach that focuses on the study of individuals and individual differences. *See also* nomothetic approach.

immigrant A person who comes to the United States for a better life.

incest taboo The nearly universal societal prohibition of intercourse between parents and children and between siblings.

individualistic worldview The individual is viewed as more important than the group.

induced labor A method of abortion performed in the late second trimester, generally in a hospital, in which a saline solution or prostaglandins are injected into the amniotic sac to cause the woman's body to expel the fetus.

infant mortality The death of a baby in its first year of life. An important indicator of the health of a nation, it is associated with a variety of factors such as maternal health, quality and access to medical care, socioeconomic conditions, and public health practices.

infatuation A type of love relationship characterized by passion and lacking both intimacy and commitment.

insider perspective How people inside the family describe their relationships. *See also* outsider perspective.

instrumental role According to the Parsons and Bales model of the modern family, the husband-father's role—being the breadwinner, the manager, and the leader of the family. *See also* expressive role.

interdependence of parts A characteristic of systems; the parts or elements of a system are interconnected in such a way that if one part is changed, other parts are automatically affected.

international family strengths framework A conceptual framework proposing that if researchers study only family problems, they will find only problems in families, but that if they are interested in family strengths, they must study strong families. The international family strengths framework identifies six qualities that strong families commonly demonstrate around the world: commitment, appreciation and affection, positive communication, enjoyable time together, spiritual well-being and shared values, and the ability to manage stress and crisis effectively.

intimacy Sharing intellectually, physically, and/or emotionally with another person; the emotional component of Sternberg's three dimensions of love.

intimate experience An experience in which one feels close to another or shares oneself in one area of life, such as intellectually, socially, emotionally, or sexually.

intimate partner violence Verbal, emotional, physical, or sexual abuse directed at a romantic partner.

intimate relationship A partnership involving an emotional bond between two people, with proven mutual commitment and trust, that provides personal and relationship security and rewards; a relationship in which one shares intimate experiences in several areas of life over time, with expectations that this sharing will continue.

intrauterine contraceptive (IUC) or intrauterine device (IUD) A small, flexible plastic contraceptive device that is inserted by a physician into the uterus. An IUC can be left in place for 3, 5, or 10 years, depending on the type, or until the woman wants the device removed. IUCs prevent pregnancy by killing or immobilizing sperm; preventing sperm from fertilizing the egg; and creating an inflammatory reaction inside the uterus.

J

jealousy The condition of being resentful and suspicious of a rival.

joint custody A legal child custody arrangement following a divorce in which children divide their time between the homes of both parents, with both homes having equal importance: "one child, two homes."

K

kinship The relatedness of certain individuals within a group. Cultures have norms and expectations that structure and govern kin behavior.

L

labor The stages of delivering a baby, consisting of contractions of the uterine muscles and dilation of the cervix, the birth itself, and the expulsion of the placenta.

Lamaze Method A "prepared childbirth" approach introduced by French obstetrician Fernand Lamaze in the 1950s and the most widely used method today. The baby's father or a friend or relative serves as a coach for the mother; and prenatal classes emphasize relaxation and breathing techniques for dealing with the intensity of labor, allowing the woman to remain active and alert during the birth of her baby.

learned helplessness theory A theory that a learned passivity develops from giving power over oneself to another; that passivity increases helplessness, reduces problem-solving abilities, and limits options.

learning theories Approaches to understanding human development that focus on how people learn to behave the way they do.

Leboyer's "Gentle Birthing" A childbirth method introduced by French physician Frederick Leboyer in 1995. The approach advocates methods for reducing the shock of birth to the baby. The delivery area is a quiet, dimly lit, warm setting. The baby lies on the mother's abdomen for a while before the umbilical cord is cut and then receives a gentle, warm bath.

life course (as compared to life cycle or life stage) A term to describe the transitions that one makes through life. It is fluid to reflect the unpredictable changes such as divorce, remarriage, or early retirement that are not tied to traditional age stages.

liking A type of love relationship characterized by intimacy but lacking passion and commitment.

lineage Line of descent, influenced by cultural norms. Lineage determines membership in a kinship group, patterns of inheritance, and kinship obligations or responsibilities. *See also* matrilineal society; patrilineal society.

linear causality model An interpersonal communication model that assumes a direct, or linear, relationship between cause and effect.

living apart together A living arrangement for couples who are in a committed intimate relationship but choose to maintain separate homes. Women are typically the driving force behind this arrangement, because they often have the most to lose in marriage or cohabiting.

longevous marriage A long-term marriage that lasts 50 years or more.

longitudinal study An observational research method in which data is gathered for the same subjects repeatedly over a period of time.

looking-glass self The idea that you learn about yourself based on the feedback you receive from others.

low sexual desire The woman's desire to have sex is low or absent.

M

male menopause Physical changes in men related to age, similar to those that occur in women during menopause.

managing stress Pauline Boss's alternative to the phrase *coping with stress;* individual family members' use of their own resources to help their family deal with a stressor or work through a crisis.

marriage An emotional and legal commitment between two people to share emotional and physical intimacy, various tasks, and economic resources.

masculinity A gender-linked constellation of personality traits and behavioral patterns traditionally associated with males in a society.

masturbation Self-stimulation of the genitals; also called *autoeroticism*.

maternal gatekeeping When mothers are ambivalent about giving up their role as the parent who knows the most about caring for children.

mating gradient The tendency of women to marry men who are better educated or more successful than they are.

matriarchal group A group in which the mother or eldest female is recognized as the head of the family, kinship group, or tribe. Descent is traced through this woman.

matrilineal society A society in which descent, or lineage, is traced through females.

matrilocal society A society that encourages newly married couples to live with or near the wife's kin, especially her mother's kinship group.

medication abortion A method of abortion, also called the *abortion pill*. The drug mifepristone combined with misoprostol has been widely used in Europe for early abortions and now is used routinely in the United States. *See* abortion pill; RU-486.

menopause The cessation of ovulation, menstruation, and fertility in women as a result of aging.

menses The menstrual flow in which the endometrial tissue is discharged.

menstruation The discharge from the uterus through the vagina of blood and the unfertilized ova; occurs about every 28 days in nonpregnant women between puberty and menopause.

metacommunication Communicating about communi-cating.

middle age Generally speaking, the years between the ages of 35 and 65; from the standpoint of the family development conceptual framework, the middle years of the family life cycle are the launching period for young-adult children and the period before the parents' retirement.

midlife crisis A period of questioning one's worth, values, and contributions in life, usually beginning in a person's 40s or early 50s.

midrange families Families who are extreme on one dimension of the Couple and Family Map but balanced on the other dimension. There are eight midrange family types. For example, a family might be structurally enmeshed: extreme on cohesion (enmeshed) but balanced on flexibility (structured). *See also* balanced families; unbalanced families.

midwife A nonphysician who attends and facilitates a birth.

minority group A social group that differs from the rest of the population in some ways and that often experiences discrimination and prejudice.

miscarriage The termination of a pregnancy from natural causes before the fetus is viable outside of the mother (during the first or second trimester of pregnancy).

mixed message A message in which there is a discrepancy between the verbal and the nonverbal components: The receiver hears one thing but simultaneously feels something else.

mixed-methods research This is a type of study in which family researchers use both qualitative and quantitative research techniques, thus benefiting from the strengths of both approaches to research.

monogamy A relationship in which a man or a woman has only one mate.

morning sickness Nausea experienced by many women during the first trimester of pregnancy, often but not exclusively in the morning.

morphogenic system A system that is open to growth and change; also called an *open system*.

morphostatic system A system that has the capacity to maintain the status quo, thus avoiding change; also called a *closed system*.

multicultural marriage Marriage between two people from two different cultural or ethnic groups.

multiple system levels General systems theory holds that systems are embedded within other systems, layer upon layer.

multiracial marriage Marriage between people from two different cultural or ethnic groups.

N

negative feedback Information or communication that is intended to minimize change in a system.

neolocal society In this type of group, norms encourage newly married couples to establish a separate, autonomous residence, autonomous of either partner's kinship group.

new-life stage of grief The period during which the bereaved establishes a new lifestyle and exhibits to society and himself or herself that he or she can live satisfactorily as a single person; the last of Brubaker's three stages of the grieving process. *See also* crisis-loss stage of grief; transition stage of grief.

no-fault divorce Divorce laws that do not place blame (fault) for the divorce on either spouse. One party's assertion that irreconcilable differences exist is sufficient grounds for dissolving the marriage.

nomothetic approach A theoretical approach that focuses on developing a theory that works for a great number of cases. Researchers using this approach believe it is possible to develop a general family theory. *See also* idiographic approach.

non-love A type of love relationship characterized by the absence of commitment, intimacy, and passion.

nonverbal communication The communication of emotions by means other than words, such as touch, body movement, facial expression, and eye contact.

Norplant The trade name of a contraceptive implant placed under the skin on the inside of a woman's upper arm; releases the hormone progestin.

nuclear family A kinship group in which a husband, a wife, and their children live together in one household; also called a *conjugal family system*.

O

old age Arbitrarily defined as beginning at age 65, which coincides for most people with retirement.

open system A family system that is open to growth and change; also called a *morphogenic system*.

oral contraceptives Birth control pills taken by mouth that contain hormones that suspend ovulation and thus prevent conception.

organic sexual dysfunction Organic factors cause 10% to 20% of all cases of sexual dysfunction, and contribute to the dysfunction in another 15% of all cases, according to one source. For example, a man may have difficulty achieving or maintaining an erection as a result of numerous medical conditions, including diabetes and alcoholism.

organismic theory Developed by Jean Piaget and expanded by later theorists, a theory of child development emphasizing that children's minds develop through various stages and that children think very differently from adults; sees child-thought as primitive and mystical, with logical reasoning developing slowly into adulthood.

orgasmic disorder The woman cannot experience an orgasm.

orgasmic dysfunction Impairment of the ordinary physical responses of sexual excitement or orgasm as the result of physical or medical factors, such as illness, injury, or drugs.

outsider perspective How researchers or therapists perceive a family, in contrast with how family members perceive the family. *See also* insider perspective.

overfunctioner An individual who knows what is best not only for herself or himself but for everybody else as well; overfunctioners cannot let others solve their problems themselves.

oviduct In the female reproductive system, one of a pair of tubes through which ova (eggs) travel from an ovary to the uterus. Also called *fallopian tube*.

ovulation The regular monthly release in the female of one or more eggs from an ovary.

P

painful intercourse A sexual dysfunction characterized by intense discomfort during sex; experienced by both women and men and often related to physical problems with the sex organs.

parent education A lecture-and-discussion format for small or large groups of parents that is aimed at helping them learn how to raise children successfully.

parental control The degree of flexibility exhibited by a parent in terms of enforcing rules and disciplining her or his child(ren).

parental support The amount of caring, closeness, and affection a parent exhibits or gives to her or his child(ren).

parent-arranged marriage A practice, common in nonindustrialized societies, in which the parents of the bride and groom select the future spouse and arrange the marriage ceremony. Based on the principle that the elders in a community have the wisdom to select an appropriate spouse, this type of marriage generally extends existing family units rather than creating new units. *See also* couple-arranged marriage.

partner dominance The degree to which a person feels her or his partner tries to be controlling and dominant in their relationship.

passion Intense physiological arousal; the motivational component of Sternberg's three dimensions of love.

passive communication A style of interpersonal communication characterized by an unwillingness to say what one thinks, feels, or wants.

patriarchal group A group in which the father or eldest male is recognized as the head of the family, kinship group, or tribe. Descent is traced through this man.

patrilineal society A society in which descent, or lineage, is traced through males.

patrilocal society A society that encourages newly married couples to live with or near the husband's kin, especially his father's kinship group.

perennial philosophy Though religions around the world are remarkably diverse and fascinating to learn about, many theologians and philosophers have argued since at least the 16 century that there is a perennial philosophy—an eternal philosophy, if you will—that all great world religions share and that unites them in a common view of that which is sacred in life.

permissive parenting A style of parenting in which the parents (1) permit the child's preferences to take over their ideals and (2) rarely force the child to conform to their standards.

personal coping resources Qualities that help people deal with stressors across the life cycle, such as an individual's self-esteem and mastery (confidence in personal abilities). *See also* family coping resources.

personification The belief that everything one's partner does is a reflection on oneself; leads to attempts to control the partner's behavior.

persuasive listening A style of listening in which the "listener" is looking only for an opportunity to take over and control the direction of the conversation.

placenta A vascular organ that joins the fetus with the mother's uterus and through which the fetus receives nutrients and discharges wastes; expelled in the final stage of labor, following the birth of the baby.

plural marriage A marriage in which a man has more than one wife (polygyny) or a woman has more than one husband (polyandry).

polyandry A plural marriage in which a woman has more than one husband.

polygamy A marriage in which a man or a woman has more than one mate; a plural marriage.

polygyny A plural marriage in which a man has more than one wife.

positive communication One of the six major qualities (commonly found in emotionally healthy families) identified by researchers working from a family strengths perspective.

positive feedback Information or communication that is intended to create change in a system.

postmodernism A belief system that emphasizes multiple perspectives or "truths." Postmodernists are extremely skeptical in regard to questions of truth, meaning, and historical interpretation. No objective, universal truth can be seen, once and for all, and readily agreed upon. Instead, there is only a collection of subjective truths shaped by the particular subcultures in which we live. These multiple subjective truths are constantly competing for our attention and allegiance.

postpartum depression A feeling of depression after giving birth, characterized by irritability, crying, loss of appetite, and difficulty sleeping; thought to be a result of the many physiological changes that occur after delivery.

posttraumatic stress disorder (PTSD) A severe stress reaction characterized by the reexperiencing of past traumatic events.

power The ability of an individual in a social system to change the behavior of other members of the system through will, influence, or control.

prejudice Negative judgment or opinion having no or limited basis in fact; hostility to a person or a group based on physical characteristics.

premature ejaculation A sexual dysfunction in which a man is unable to control his ejaculation reflex voluntarily and reaches orgasm sooner than he or his partner wishes.

PREPARE A comprehensive premarital inventory that assesses a couple's relationship and determines how idealistic or realistic each person is in regard to marriage, how well the couple communicates, and how well the couple resolves conflicts and financial issues; acronym for **PRE**-marital **P**ersonal **A**nd **R**elationship **E**valuation.

problem drinking Alcohol consumption that results in functional disability.

progestin A hormone connected with pregnancy and contained in oral contraceptives.

prosocial spending Spending one's personal money to help others. It provides a positive feeling and a sense of well-being.

pseudo-kin group A type of kinship group in which relationships resembling kinship ties develop among "unrelated" individuals.

psychodynamic theory Developed by Freud and his followers, a theory of human development that emphasizes the importance of providing a positive emotional environment during early childhood, when the foundation for later life is laid down.

psychosocial sexual dysfunction Impairment of the ordinary physical responses of sexual excitement or orgasm as a result of psychological, developmental, interpersonal, environmental, or cultural factors; these causes of sexual problems include untreated anxiety or depression and long-term stress.

pursuer An individual who wants a very high degree of togetherness and expression of feelings in a relationship.

Q

qualitative research Qualitative research in the field of family science tends to focus on family members' perceptions of their world and how they live in it. Data are recorded in the form of words and stories that the family members tell. These verbal or written perceptions are analyzed by researchers looking for common themes that explain the processes of life in families.

quantitative research Quantitative research in the field of family science reduces family members' attitudes and behaviors to numbers that can be analyzed using statistical methods. Rather than work with the words and stories collected in qualitative investigations, quantitative researchers work with data that are numerical.

R

race A group of people with similar and distinctive physical characteristics.

racism A belief that all individuals who represent a particular race have the same qualities and abilities.

refugee A person who comes to the United States to avoid persecution, because her or his native country is unsafe.

reinforcement Rewarding desired behavior to increase the likelihood that it will be repeated.

rejecting parenting A style of parenting in which parents pay little attention to their children's needs and set few or no expectations for their children's behavior.

remarriage A marriage in which one or both partners marry following divorce or the death of a spouse; in this book, remarriage refers to couples who have never been married to each other before.

representative sample A random selection of individuals who accurately reflect the characteristics of a particular group.

research study Careful, systematic, and patient investigation in a field of knowledge to establish facts or principles, test hypotheses, or better understand processes.

role The expected behavior of a person or group in a given social category, such as husband, wife, supervisor, or teacher.

role making The process of creating new roles or revising existing roles.

role taking The process whereby people learn how to play roles correctly by practicing and getting feedback from others.

romantic love A type of love relationship characterized by intimacy and passion but lacking commitment.

routinization A situation, often encountered in middle age, in which one's job lacks the challenge it once offered and becomes boring.

RU-486 A method of *medication abortion*, also called the *abortion pill*. The drug mifepristone combined with misoprostol has been widely used in Europe for early abortions and now is used routinely in the United States. See abortion pill; medication abortion.

S

sandwich generation Parents, usually in their 50s and older, who are simultaneously responsible for child rearing and for caring for their own aging parents; individuals who are "caught in the middle" between two generations.

segregation Isolation of an ethnic group within the dominant culture.

self-confidence A measure of how a person feels about herself or himself and the ability to control things in her or his life.

self-disclosure Revealing to another person personal information or feelings that that individual could not otherwise learn.

sex Being biologically male or female; also, sexual activity or behavior. *See also* gender.

sex educator A trained teacher who provides information and principles about sex and sexuality, generally in a group setting.

sex ratio The relationship between the number of men and the number of women of a given age.

sex therapist A trained individual who teaches and counsels clients individually, in pairs, or in small groups about sex and sexuality.

sex therapy A process of education and counseling designed to help people overcome sexual problems.

sexual arousal disorder The woman cannot maintain arousal during sexual activity, or cannot become aroused even when she wishes to have sex.

sexual dysfunction A state in which one's sexual behavior or lack of it is a source of distress; any malfunction of the human sexual response that inhibits the achievement of orgasm, either alone or with a partner.

sexual orientation A person's self-identification as a heterosexual, homosexual, bisexual, or transgender.

sexual pain disorder The woman experiences pain during sexual contact.

sexuality The set of beliefs, values, and behaviors by which one defines oneself as a sexual being.

sibling abuse Physical violence between siblings; probably the most common form of abuse of children.

SIDS *See* sudden infant death syndrome.

simple stepfamily A stepfamily that includes children from only one parent. *See also* complex stepfamily.

singlehood The state of being unmarried, divorced, or unattached to another person.

social construction framework A conceptual framework that proposes that human beings are profoundly immersed in the social world and that our understanding of this world and beliefs about this world are social products.

social environment All the factors, both positive and negative, in society that impact individuals and their relationships, such as mass media, the internet, changing gender roles, and growing urban crowding.

social learning theory A psychological theory of development that focuses on learning through observation, imitation, and reinforcement.

social system One of the four major components of the sociocultural context in which families live; encompasses the influence of the community, laws, economic resources, educational opportunities, and other external factors on the family. *See also* belief system; extended-family system; family system.

sole custody A child custody arrangement following a divorce in which only one parent has legal and physical custody of the child or children; the other parent generally has visitation rights.

spacious nest A positive descriptive term for the time in a marriage when the children have left home. *See also* empty-nest syndrome.

sperm The male reproductive cells produced by the testes.

spermicide A contraceptive substance (gel, cream, foam, or vaginal insert) that is toxic to sperm; usually used with a barrier device; may protect against certain sexually transmitted diseases.

spiritual well-being One of the six major qualities (commonly found in emotionally healthy families) identified by researchers working within the family strengths framework.

split custody A legal child custody arrangement following a divorce in which each parent has sole custody of one or more of the children.

STD *See* sexually transmitted disease.

stepfamily The family created when one or both partners in a marriage have a child or children from a previous marriage. *See also* blended family.

stepparent An adult who is married to one's biological parent but who is not one's birth parent.

Stepping Ahead Program An eight-step program designed to build strengths in stepfamilies.

stereotype A standardized, oversimplified, often foolish and mean-spirited view of someone or something.

sterilization Any procedure, but usually a surgical one, by which an individual is made incapable of reproduction.

stillbirth The term health care providers use when describing the loss of a pregnancy after the 20th week of pregnancy, due to natural causes. Unlike miscarriages, stillborn babies could have lived successfully outside the womb, but for many different reasons have died inside the mother.

stress The nonspecific response of the body to any demand made upon it.

stress pileup The occurrence and after-effects of several stresses within a short period of time, which can strain an individual's or a family's coping abilities.

stressor An external event that causes an emotional and/or a physical response and that can precipitate a crisis.

strong family Two or more people who share significant relationship strengths, which are likely to include appreciation and affection for each other; commitment to the family; positive communication with each other; enjoyable time together; a sense of spiritual well-being; and the ability to manage stress and crisis effectively. Also can be defined as people who love and care for each other.

subsystem In the general systems theory, a small system that is part of a larger suprasystem.

sudden infant death syndrome (SIDS) The sudden, unexpected death of an infant, which cannot be explained by postmortem examination or tests.

suprasystem In the general systems theory, a large system that incorporates smaller subsystems.

symbolic interaction framework A conceptual framework that focuses on the internal perceptions of family members and examines how they learn roles and rules in society through interaction and shared meaning.

system A set of interconnected components that form a whole; what happens to one component affects all the other components.

T

tender years doctrine The legal presumption under traditional divorce laws that young children would do better with their mother than with their father after a divorce.

theory Systematically organized knowledge applicable in a wide variety of circumstances; especially, a system of assumptions, accepted principles, and rules of procedure devised to analyze, predict, or otherwise explain the nature or behavior of a specified set of phenomena.

traditional couple A type of premarital and married couple characterized by some external strengths (such as religion and friends) but fewer internal strengths (such as communication and conflict resolution skills).

transgender An individual who believes that he or she is a victim of a biologic accident that occurred before birth and has been living within a body incompatible with his or her real gender identity. A majority of transgender persons are biologic males who identify themselves as females, usually early in childhood.

transition stage of grief The period during which the bereaved's grief lessens and he or she begins to recognize that a new life is possible; the second of Brubaker's three stages of the grieving process. *See also* crisis-loss stage of grief; new-life stage of grief.

traumatic brain injury Damage to the brain, usually the result of a sudden, violent blow to the head that launches the brain on a collision course with the inside of the skull. This collision can bruise the brain, tear nerve fibers, and cause bleeding. The resulting symptoms can include severe headaches, problems with memory, confusion, an inability to follow directions, depression, and difficulty concentrating.

trimester One of three periods of about 3 months each into which pregnancy is divided.

tubal ligation A female sterilization procedure in which the oviducts (fallopian tubes) are cut or tied and sealed.

U

umbilical cord A flexible structure that connects the fetus to the placenta and through which nutrients pass to the fetus and waste products are discharged.

unbalanced families Families who fall at the extremes on both the flexibility and the cohesion dimensions of the Couple and Family Map: chaotically enmeshed, chaotically disengaged, rigidly enmeshed, or rigidly disengaged, families. *See also* balanced families; midrange families.

uncontested divorce Under traditional divorce law, a divorce in which one party would charge the other party with an infraction that was considered by the court as grounds for granting a divorce and the accused party would agree not to challenge the accuser in court. In many cases, parties were forced to collude and to perjure themselves in order to divorce.

underfunctioner An individual who is too highly flexible and disorganized and becomes less competent under stress.

uninvolved parenting A style of parenting in which parents ignore their children and let them do what they wish unless it interferes with the parents' activities.

V

vacuum aspiration An abortion method, used during the first trimester of pregnancy, in which the uterine contents are removed by suction.

vaginismus A sexual dysfunction in which a woman's vaginal muscles involuntarily constrict, preventing intercourse; a muscular contraction that causes the vagina to close. Vaginismus is usually an anxiety reaction before coitus or a pelvic examination.

validation The process of ensuring that a research instrument measures what it is intended to measure.

vasectomy A male sterilization procedure in which the vasa deferentia are severed and tied.

victimizer One who victimizes others. Children who grow up with violence often learn the potential for victimizing others as adults.

vitalized couple A type of premarital and married couple characterized by many couple strengths, high marital satisfaction, and a low risk of divorce.

vulva The external female genital organs.

W

water birth Using this approach to childbirth means that for at least part of a mother's labor, delivery, or both, the woman is in a birth pool filled with warm water. Using a birthing pool in the first stage of labor might help ease pain; keep a mother from needing anesthesia; and speed up the process of labor, but the American College of Obstetricians and Gynecologists (ACOG) argues that water birth should be considered an experimental procedure with risks.

wholeness A characteristic of systems; general systems theorists believe that the whole is more than the sum of its parts.

Z

zero-sum game A game in which one side's margin of victory equals the other side's margin of defeat, producing a final sum of zero; what one person wins, the other loses.

zygote The fertilized ovum (egg).

References

AARP. (2016a). Official site. Web site: http://www.aarp.org.

AARP. (2016b) Online community. Web site: https://community.aarp.org/t5/Late-Life-Divorce/bd-p/bg41.

ABC News. (2011). Exclusive: Nancy Reagan misses husband now more than ever. Web site: http://abcnews.go.com/GMA/story?id=3193730.

ABC News. (2012). U.S. gun homicide rate higher than other developed countries. Web site: http://abcnews.go/com/blogs/headlines/2012/12/us-gun-ownership-homicide-rate-higher-than-other-develo...

ABC News–Washington Post. (2001, January 11–15). Poll: Views about abortion. Cited in T. Raum. Associated Press (2001, January 23). Bush's early gamble: The new president will find it hard to finesse the thorny issue of abortion. Lincoln [NE] *Journal Star,* p. 5A.

Abma, J. C., et al. (2004). Teenagers in the United States: Sexual activity, contraceptive use, and childbearing, 2002. *Vital and Health Statistics, 23*(24). Web site: http://www.cdc.gov/nchs/data/series/sr_23/sr23_024.pdf.

Abma, J. C., Martinez, G. M., & Copen, C. E. (2010). Teenagers in the United States: Sexual activity, contraceptive use, and childbearing, National Survey of Family Growth 2006–2008. National Center for Health Statistics. *Vital Health Statistics, 23*(30). Web site: http://www.cdc.gov/nchs/data/series/sr_23/sr23_030.pdf.

Abma, J. C., Martinez, G. M., Mosher, W. D., & Dawson, B. S. (2004, December). Teenagers in the United States: Sexual activity, contraceptive use, and childbearing, Series 23, Number 24. Washington, DC: Centers for Disease Control and Prevention.

Abortion foes vow to fight: Maryland's governor OKs abortion-rights law. (1991, February 19). Lincoln [NE] *Journal Star,* p. 2.

Abrahms, S. (2012, June). *Aarp.org/bulletin.* Washington, DC: American Association of Retired Persons.

Abrahms, S. (2012, June 26). Life after divorce: More boomers are calling it quits after years of marriage. *AARP Bulletin.* Web site: http://www.aarp.org/home-family/friends-family/info-05-2012/life-after-divorce.html.

Adams, C. (2013). Millions went to war in Iraq, Afghanistan, leaving many with lifelong scars. *McClatchy DC Bureau.* Web site: http://www.mcclatchydc.com/news/nation-world/national/article24746680.html.

Adamsons, K., & Johnson, S. K. (2013). An updated and expanded meta-analysis of nonresident fathering and child well-being. *Journal of Family Psychology, 27,* 589–599.

Addis, M. E., & Mahalik, J. R. (2003). Men, masculinity, and the context of help seeking. *American Psychologist, 58*(1), 5–14.

Adler-Baeder, F., Kerpelman, J. L., Schramm, D. G., Higginbotham, B., & Paulk, A. (2007). The impact of relationship education on adolescents of diverse backgrounds. *Family Relations, 56* (July), 291–303.

Adler, N. E., David, H. P., Major, B. N., Roth, S. H., Russo, N. F., & Wyatt, G. E. (1992). Psychological factors in abortion: A review. *American Psychologist, 47,* 1194–1204.

Adler, N. E., Ozer, E. J., & Tschann, J. (2003, March). Abortion among adolescents. *American Psychologist,* 211–217.

Administration for Children and Families. (2003). Child maltreatment 2001. U.S. Department of Health and Human Services. Washington, DC: http://www.acf.hhs.gov/programs/cb/publications/cm01/index.htm.

Administration for Children and Families. (2004). Child maltreatment 2002. U.S. Department of Health and Human Services. Washington, DC: http://www.acf.hhs.gov.programs/cb/publications/cm02/chapterthree.htm.

Administration for Children and Families. (2007). The Healthy Marriage Initiative. Web site: http://www.acf.hhs.gov/healthymarriage/about/mission.html#ms.

Administration for Children and Families. (2016). What is the Administration for Children and Families? Web site: https://www.acf.hhs.gov/.

Administration for Children and Families. (n.d.). 2015–2016 *ACF Strategic Plan.* Web site: https://www.acf.hhs.gov/sites/default/files/assets/acf_2015_2016_strategic_plan.pdf.

Administration for Community Living. (2016, March 17). Aging statistics. Web site: https://www.acl.gov/about-acl/public-input.

Administration for Community Living. (2015, December 31). Projected future growth of older population. Web site: https://www.acl.gov/aging-and-disability-in-america/data-and-research/projected-future-growth-older-population.

Administration on Aging. (2011). Aging statistics. Web site: http://www.aoa.gov/aoaroot/aging_statistics/index.aspx.

Advocates for Youth. (2016). Rights. Respect. Responsibility. "Established in 1980 as the Center for Population Options, Advocates for Youth champions efforts that help young people make informed and responsible decisions about their reproductive and sexual health. Advocates believes it can best serve the field by boldly advocating for a more positive and realistic approach to adolescent sexual health." The work focuses on 14- to 25-year-olds in the United States and internationally. Web site: http://www.advocatesforyouth.org.

Advocates for Youth. (2016a). Are parents and teens talking about sex? Web site: http://www.advocatesforyouth.org/parents/136?task=view.

Advocates for Youth. (2010b). Comprehensive sex education: Research and results. Web site: http://www.advocatesforyouth.org.

AFL-CIO and the Institute for Women's Policy Research. (1999). Equal pay for working families: National and state data. http://www.aflcio.org/issuepolitics/women/equalpay/EqualPayForWorkingFamilies.cfm.

Agrillo, C., & Nelini, C. (2008). Childlfree by choice: A review. *Journal of Cultural Geography, 25,* 347–363.

Ahlburg, D. A., Jensen, E. R., & Perez, A. E. (1997). Determinants of extramarital sex in the Philippines. *Health Transition Review,* Suppl. to Vol. *7,* pp. 467–479.

Ahrons, C. (2007). Family ties after divorce: Long-term implications for children. *Family Process, 46,* 53–65.

Ahrons, C. R. (2004). *We're still family: What grown children have to say about their parents' divorce.* New York, NY: HarperCollins.

Ahrons, C. R. (2006, May/June). Long-term effects of divorce on children. *Family Therapy Magazine,* pp. 24–27.

Aiken, L. R. (2004). *Dying, death, and bereavement* (4th ed.). Mahwah, NJ: Erlbaum. A brief but comprehensive survey of research, writings, and professional practices on death and dying.

Aknin, L. B., Dunn, E. W., Helliwell, J. F., Biswas-Diener, R., Nyende, P., Barrington-Leigh, C., . . . & Norton, M. I. (2013). Prosocial spending and well-being: Cross-cultural evidence for a psychological universal. *Journal of Personality and Social Psychology, 104,* 635–652.

Alan Guttmacher Institute. (1999). *Teenage pregnancy: Overall trends and state-by-state information* (Table 1). New York, NY: Author.

Alan Guttmacher Institute. (2000). *Induced abortion.* New York, NY: Author (http://www.agi-usa-org/pubs/fb_induced_abortion.html).

Alan Guttmacher Institute. (2002). Teen pregnancy: Trends and lessons learned. *The Guttmacher Report on Public Policy, 5*(1), 2.

Alan Guttmacher Institute. (2008). Facts on induced abortion in the United States. Web site: http://www.guttmacher.org/pubs/fb_induced_abortion.html.

Alan Guttmacher Institute. (2009c). Get "in the know": Questions about pregnancy, contraception and abortion. Web site: http://www.guttmacher.org/in-the-know/incidence.html.

Alan Guttmacher Institute. (2009d). Safety of abortion. Web site: http://www.guttmacher.org/in-the-know/safety.html.

Alan Guttmacher Institute. (2016). Web site: https://www.guttmacher.org/.

Al-Anon Family Groups. (2016). Since 1951, Al-Anon (which includes Alateen for younger members) has been offering strength and hope for friends and families of problem drinkers. It is estimated that each alcoholic affects the lives of at least four other people . . . alcoholism is truly a family disease. No matter what relationship you have with an alcoholic, whether they are still drinking or not, all who have been affected by someone else's drinking can find solutions that lead to serenity in the Al-Anon/Alateen fellowship. Web site: http://www.al-anon.alateen.-org/english.html.

Al-Anon Family Groups. (2016a). Al-Anon history. Web site: https://al-anon.org/newcomers/what-is-al-anon-and-alateen/history/.

Al-Anon Family Groups. (2016b). Who are Al-Anon members? Web site: http://al-anon.org/?gclid=CJDyq8vFncwCFQqKaQodmdILJQ.

Al-Anon Family Groups. (2016c). Online Al-Anon. A gathering. . . Al-Anon family groups on the internet. Web site: http://www.ola-is.org/.

Alberti, R., & Emmons, M. (2008). *Your perfect right: Assertiveness and equality in your life and relationships* (9th ed.). Atascadero, CA: Impact.

Alcoholics Anonymous Meetings in Los Angeles County, California. (2012). Web site: http://www.simeetings.com/LA/LAMtgs.html.

Alcoholics Anonymous. (2015). Estimated worldwide A.A. individual and group membership. Web site: http://www.aa.org/assets/en_US/smf-132_en.pdf.

Alcoholics Anonymous. (2016). In their own words, AA is "a fellowship of men and women who share their experience, strength and hope with each other that they may solve their common problem and help others to recover from alcoholism. The only requirement for membership is a desire to stop drinking." AA charges no dues or fees for membership and is self-supporting through member contributions. It is not allied with any sect, denomination, politics, organization, or institution. AA does not wish to engage in any controversy, and neither endorses nor opposes any causes. "Our primary purpose is to stay sober and help other alcoholics to achieve sobriety." Web site: http://www.aa.org/lang/en/subpage.cfm?page=1.

Alcoholics Anonymous. (2016a). Welcome to Alcoholics Anonymous. Web site: http://www.aa.org/.

Alcoholics Anonymous. (2016b). Welcome to AAOnline! Web site: http://www.aaonline.org/.

Alcoholics Anonymous. (2017, June). Estimates of A.A. groups and members as of January 1, 2017. Web site: http://www.aa.org/assets/en_US/smf-53_en.pdf.

Aldwin, C. M., & Levenson, M. R. (2001). Stress, coping, and health at midlife: A developmental perspective. In M. E. Lachman (Ed.), *Handbook of midlife development* (pp. 188–216). New York, NY: Wiley.

Aldwin, C. M., Park, C. L., Spiro, A. III, & Abeles, R. P. (2007). *Handbook of health psychology and aging.* New York, NY: The Guilford Press. How biological, psychological, and social factors over the life course affect aging.

Allen, E. S., Rhoades, G., Stanley, S. M., Loew, B., & Markman, H. J. (2012). The effects of marriage education for army couples with a history of infidelity. *Journal of Family Psychology, 26,* 26–35.

Allen, K. R., Blieszner, R., & Roberto, K. A. (2000). Families in the middle and later years: A review and critique of research in the 1990s. *Journal of Marriage and the Family, 62*(4), 911–926.

Allen, R. E., Wiles, J. L. (2013). How older people position their late-life childlessness: A qualitative study. *Journal of Marriage and Family, 75,* 206–220.

Allen, S. M., & Hawkins, A. J. (1999). Mothers' beliefs and behaviors that inhibit greater father involvement in family. *Journal of Marriage and the Family, 61,* 199–212.

Allgeier, E. R., & Allgeier, A. R. (2000). *Sexual interactions: Basic understandings* (6th ed.). Boston, MA: Houghton Mifflin.

Alliance for Aging Research. (2016). Shattering the myths of old age. Web site: http://www.agingresearch.org/newsletters/issue/3.

Alliance for Children and Families. (2004). 11700 West Lake Park Drive, Milwaukee, WI 53224-3099: http://www.info@alliance1.org.

Altura, J. (1974). Poem. In J. Gillies, *My needs, your needs.* New York, NY: Doubleday.

Alzheimer's Foundation of America. (2016). Helping more people today than we did yesterday. Web site: http://www.alzfdn.org/.

Amato, P. R. (2000). The consequences of divorce for adults and children. *Journal of Marriage and the Family, 62*(4), 1269–1287.

Amato, P. R. (2010). Interpreting divorce rates, marriage rates, and data on the percentage of children with single parents. National Healthy Marriage Resource Center, Research Brief. Web site: http://www.healthymarriageinfo.org/resource-detail/download.aspx?id=325.

Amato, P. R., Kane, J. B., & James, S. (2011). Reconsidering the "Good Divorce." *Family Relations, 60,* 511–524.

American Academy of Pediatrics. (2005). Policy statement: Breastfeeding and the use of human milk. *Pediatrics, 115*(2), 496–506.

American Academy of Pediatrics (AAP). (2016). Why breastfeed. Web site: https://www.healthychildren.org/English/ages-stages/baby/breastfeeding/Pages/Why-Breastfeed.aspx.

American Academy of Pediatrics. (2016). Working mothers. Web site: https://www.healthychildren.org/English/family-life/work-play/Pages/Working-Mothers.aspx.

American Association for Marriage and Family Therapy. (2015). Sibling violence. Web site: https://www.aamft.org/iMIS15/AAMFT/Content/Consumer_Updates/Sibling_Violence.aspx.

American Association for Marriage and Family Therapy. (2016). Frequently asked questions about AAMFT membership. Web site: https://www.aamft.org/iMIS15/AAMFT/Content/membership/membership_faqs.aspx.

American Association for Marriage and Family Therapy. (2016). Infidelity. Web site: https://www.aamft.org/iMIS15/AAMFT/Content/consumer_updates/infidelity.aspx.

American Association for Marriage and Family Therapy. (2016a). Substance abuse and intimate relationships. Web site: https://www.aamft.org/iMIS15/AAMFT/Content/Consumer_Updates/Substance_Abuse_and_Intimate_Relationships.aspx.

American Association for Marriage and Family Therapy. (2016b). Alcohol problems. Web site: https://www.aamft.org/iMIS15/AAMFT/Content/consumer_Updates/Alcohol_problems.aspx.

American Association of Family and Consumer Sciences. (2015). AAFCS: Connecting professionals, touching lives. Web site: https://www.aafcs.org/AboutUs/FAQ.asp.

American Association of Homes and Services for the Aging. (2012). Web site: http://www.healthfinder.gov/orgs/HR0456.htm.

American Association of Retired Persons. (2016). AARP: Real possibilities. Web site: http://www.aarp.org/. An excellent resource for older persons and those interested in the process of aging.

American Association of Sexuality Educators, Counselors and Therapists (AASECT). (2016). A not-for-profit, interdisciplinary professional organization promoting the understanding of human sexuality and healthy sexual behavior. "AASECT members include sexuality educators, sexuality counselors and sex therapists, physicians, nurses, social workers, psychologists, allied health professionals, clergy members, lawyers, sociologists, marriage and family counselors and therapists, family planning specialists and researchers, as well as students in relevant professional disciplines." Web site: http://www.aasect.org/.

American Cancer Society. (2012). Alcohol and cancer. Web site: http://www.cancer.org.

American Cancer Society. (2016). Alcohol use and cancer. Web site: http://www.cancer.org/cancer/cancercauses/dietandphysicalactivity/alcohol-use-and-cancer.

American Family Strengths Inventory (AFSI). (2016). An at-home, free assessment of couple and family strengths. Take the inventory with your partner and other family members and plan how to enhance your strengths and improve areas of potential growth in your relationships. Web site: http://extensionpublications.unl.edu/assets/pdf/g1881.pdf.

American Family Strengths Inventory. (2016). University of Nebraska-Lincoln Extension. Web site: http://extensionpublications.unl.edu/assets/pdf/g1881.pdf.

American Humane. (2016, August 25). Understanding the link between animal abuse and family violence. Web site: https://www.americanhumane.org/fact-sheet/understanding-the-link-between-animal-abuse-and-family-violence/.

American Institute of Stress. (2016). The Holmes-Rahe Stress Inventory. Web site: http://www.stress.org/holmes-rahe-stress-inventory/.

American Planning Association. (2011). *Child care and sustainable community development*. Web site: www.planning.org.

American Psychological Association. (2008, August 13). Report of the APA Task Force on Mental Health and Abortion. Web site: http://www.apa.-org/releases/abortion-report.pdf.

American Psychological Association. (2014, April). Is pornography addictive? APA Monitor, *45*(4). Web site: http://www.apa.org/monitor/2014/04/pornography.aspx.

American Psychological Association. (2016). Marital education programs help keep couples together. Web site: http://www.apa.org/research/action/marital.aspx.

American Psychological Association. (2016). Marriage and divorce. Web site: http://www.apa.org/topics/divorce/.

American Psychological Association. (2016). Mental health and abortion. Web site: http://www.apa.org/about/gr/issues/women/mental-health-and-abortion.aspx.

American Psychological Association. (2016). Sexual orientation and gender identity. Web site: http://www.apa.org/helpcenter/sexual-orientation.aspx.

American Psychological Association. (2016). Understanding and preventing child abuse and neglect. Web site: http://www.apa.org/pi/families/resources/understanding-child-abuse.aspx.

American University. (2016). Barry McCarthy. Web site: http://www.american.edu/cas/faculty/bmccar.cfm.

Anderson, B. L. (2010). *Finances in strong African American marriages* (Unpublished master's thesis). Utah State University, Logan, Utah.

Anderson, J. R., & Doherty, W. J. (2005). Democratic community initiatives: The case of overscheduled children. *Family Relations, 54*, 654–665.

Anderson, L. R. (2016). High school seniors' attitudes on cohabitation as a testing ground for marriage. *Family Profiles*, FB-16-13. Bowling Green, OH: National Center for Family & Marriage Research. Web site: http://www.bgsu.edu/content/dam/BGSU/college-of-arts-and-sciences/NCFMR/documents/FP/anderson-teen-attitudes-cohab-marriage-fp-16-13.pdf.

Anderson, M. (2015, April 9). *A rising share of the U.S. Black population is foreign born*. Pew Research Center. Web site: http://www.pewsocialtrends.org/2015/04/09/a-rising-share-of-the-u-s-black-population-is-foreign-born/.

Antonovics, K., & Town, R. (2004). Are all the good men married? Uncovering the sources of the marital wage premium. *American Economic Review, 68*(1), 137–154.

Apter, T. (2009). *What do you want from me?* New York, NY: Norton.

Arditti, J., Burton, L., & Neeves-Botelho, S. (2010). Maternal distress and parenting in the context of cumulative disadvantage. *Family Process, 49*, 142–164.

Arias, I., & Pape, K. T. (1999). Psychological abuse: Implications for adjustment and commitment to leave violent partners. *Violence and Victims, 14*(1), 55–67.

Arnett, J. J. (2007). Emerging adulthood: What is it, and what is it good for? *Child Development Perspectives, 1*(2), 68–73.

Arnett, J. J. (2015). *Emerging adulthood: The winding road from the late teens through the twenties* (2nd ed.). New York, NY: Oxford University Press.

Arond, M., & Pauker, S. L. (1987). *The first year of marriage*. New York, NY: Warner Books.

Asai, S. G. (2004). Culturally sensitive adaptation of PREPARE with Japanese premarital couples. *Journal of Marital and Family Therapy, 30*(4), 411–426.

Asai, S., & Olson, D. H. (2003). National Survey of Spouse Abuse. PREPARE / ENRICH. Web site: https://www.prepare-enrich.com/pe/pdf/research/abuse.pdf.

Asai, S. G., & Olson, D. H. (2004). *National couple abuse study*. Roseville, MN: Life Innovations. Web site: http://lifeinnovations.com.

Asay, S. M., DeFrain, J., Metzger, M., & Moyer, B. (2014). *Family violence from a global perspective: A strengths-based approach.* Thousand Oaks, CA: Sage.

Asebedo, S. D., & Seay, M. C. (2014). Positive psychological attributes and retirement satisfaction. *Journal of Financial Counseling and Planning, 25*(2), 161–173. Web site: http://afcpe.org/assets/pdf/volume_25_2/09013_pg161-173.pdf.

Atwood, J., & Genovese, F. (2006). *Therapy with single parents: A social constructivist approach.* New York, NY: Haworth Press.

Austin, W., & Walster, E. (1974). Reactions to confirmations and disconfirmations of expectancies and inequity. *Journal of Personality and Social Psychology, 30,* 208–216.

Australian Bureau of Statistics. (2013). What is a family? Web site: http://www.abs.gov.au/ausstats/abs@.nsf/Products/6224.0.55.001~Jun%202012~Chapter~What%20is%20a%20Family%3F.

Australian Government. (2008). *Families in Australia: 2008.* Canberra: Department of Prime Minister and Cabinet, p. 1.

Australian Institute of Family Studies. (2010). Effects of child abuse and neglect for children and adolescents. Web site: http://www.aifs.gov.au/nch/pubs/sheets/rs17/4s17.html.

Axtell, R. E. (2007). *Essential do's and taboos: The complete guide to international business and leisure travel.* Hoboken, NJ: Wiley. A fun and funny book.

Axtell, R. G. (1999). *Do's and taboos of humor around the world: Stories and tips from business and life.* New York, NY: Wiley.

Azar, S. T., & Bober, S. L. (1999). Children of abusive parents. In W. K. Silverman & T. O. Ollendick (Eds.), *Developmental issues in the clinical treatment of children* (pp. 371–392). Needham Heights, MA: Allyn & Bacon.

Azar, S. T., & Gehl, K. S. (1999). Physical abuse and neglect. In R. T. Ammerman et al. (Eds.), *Handbook of prescriptive treatments for children and adolescents* (2nd ed., pp. 329–345). Needham Heights, MA: Allyn & Bacon.

Babycenter. (2011, July). *How much you'll spend on childcare.* Retrieved from http://www.babycenter.com/0_how-much-youll-spend-on-childcare_1199776.bc.

Baca Zinn, M., & Pok, A. Y. H. (2002). Tradition and transition in Mexican-origin families. In R. L. Taylor (Ed.), *Minority families in the United States: A multicultural perspective* (pp. 77–100). Upper Saddle Creek, NJ: Prentice Hall.

Bach, G., & Wyden, P. (1969). *The intimate enemy: How to fight fair in love and marriage.* New York, NY: Morrow.

Bachman, H. J., & Chase-Lansdale, P. L. (2005). Custodial grandmothers' physical, mental, and economic well-being: Comparisons of primary caregivers from low-income neighborhoods. *Family Relations, 54,* 475–487.

Bailey, M. J., & Danziger, S. (2013). *Legacies of the war on poverty.* New York, NY: Russell Sage Foundation.

Bailey, S. J. (2003). Challenges and strengths in nonresidential parenting following divorce. *Marriage and Family Review, 35*(1/2), 59–80.

Bakhurst, M. G., Loew, B., McGuire, A. C. L., Halford, W. K., & Markman, H. J. (2016). Relationship education for military couples: Recommendations for best practice. *Family Process* (March 2). Web site: http://www.ncbi.nlm.nih.gov/pubmed/26932356.

Baldry, A. C. (2003). Animal abuse and exposure to interpersonal violence in Italian youth. *Journal of Interpersonal Violence, 18*(3), 258–281.

Baldwin, S. E., & Baranoski, M. V. (1990). Family interactions and sex education in the home. *Adolescence, 25,* 573–582.

Bámaca, M. Y., Umaña-Taylor, A. J., Shin, N., & Alfaro, E. C. (2005). Latino adolescents' perception of parenting behaviors and self-esteem: Examining the role of neighborhood risk. *Family Relations, 54,* 621–632.

Barry, E. (2007, February). Eagerness and some resignation as Civil Union Law takes effect. *The New York Times.* Web site: http://www.nytimes.com/2007/02/20/nyregion/20civil.html.

Barstad, A. (2014). Equality is bliss? Relationship quality and the gender division of household labor. *Journal of Family Issues, 35,* 972–992.

Barta, P. L. (2001). Blended families: How to make sense of your new stepfamily. *In Touch.* Missoula, MT: APS Healthcare.

Bass, B. L., Butler, A. B., Grzywacz, J. G., & Linney, K. D. (2009). Do job demands undermine parenting? A daily analysis of spillover and crossover effects. *Family Relations, 58,* 201–215.

Bateson, G., Jackson, D. D., Haley, J., & Weakland, J. (1956). Toward a theory of schizophrenia. *Behavioral Science, 1,* 251–264.

Batson, C. D., Qian, Z., & Lichter, D. T. (2006). Interracial and intraracial patterns of mate selection among America's diverse Black population. *Journal of Marriage and the Family, 68,* 658–672.

Bauer, J. W., & Wollen, B. J. (1990). *Financial management extension consultant program: Young singles and young couples.* St. Paul, MN: Minnesota Extension Service.

Baumbusch, J. L. (2004). Unclaimed treasures: Older women's reflections on lifelong singlehood. *Journal of Women and Aging, 16*(1/2), 105–121. Lifelong single women strongly emphasize their independence and "ability to be alone" as significant benefits, while discussing drawbacks, including loneliness and the absence of a social support network, which became more important as they experienced increasing age and frailty.

Baumrind, D. (1991). The influence of parenting style on adolescent competence and substance abuse. *Journal of Early Adolescence, 11*(1), 56–95.

Baumrind, D. (1995). *Child maltreatment and optimal caregiving in social contexts.* New York, NY: Garland.

Baumrind, D. (1996). The discipline controversy revisited. *Family Relations, 45,* 405–414.

BBC News. (2004, November 16). STUC urges gender pay gap action. Web site: http://news.bbc.co.uk/go/pr/fr/-/2/us_news/scotland/4013675.stm.

BBC News. (2012). Abused by their own children. Web site: http://news.bbc.co.uk/2/hi/uk_news/magazine/8366113.stm.

Beach, S. R., Hurt, T., Franklin, K., Fincham, F. D., McNair, L. M., & Stanley, S. M. (2011). Enhancing marital enrichment through spirituality: Efficacy data for prayer focused relationship enhancement. *Psychology of Religion and Spirituality, 3,* 201–216.

Bean, R. A., Barber, B. K., & Crane, D. R. (2006). Parental support, behavioral control, and psychological control among African American youth. *Journal of Family Issues, 27*(10), 1335–1355.

Becvar, D. S., & Becvar, R. J. (2013). *Family therapy: A systemic integration* (8th ed.). Boston, MA: Pearson Education.

Beers, M. H. (Ed.). (2003). *The Merck manual of medical information.* Whitehouse Station, NJ: Merck Research Laboratories.

Bell, R. Q. (1977). *Child effects on adults.* Hillsdale, NJ: Erlbaum.

Bellous, J. E. (2010). *Children, spirituality, loss and recovery.* New York, NY: Routledge.

Belsky, J., & Kelly, J. (1994). *The transition to parenthood: How a first child changes a marriage: Why some couples grow closer and others apart.* New York, NY: Delacorte.

Belsky, J. (2006). Early child care and early child development: Major findings of the NICHD study of early child care. *European Journal of Developmental Psychology, 3,* 95–110.

Bent-Goodley, T. B. (2005). An African-centered approach to domestic violence. *Families in Society, 86,* 197–206.

Berger, L. M., Brown, P. R., Joung, E., Melli, M. S., & Wimer, L. (2008). The stability of child physical placements following divorce: Descriptive evidence from Wisconsin. *Journal of Marriage and the Family, 70,* 273–283.

Berger, R., & Hannah, M. T. (1999). *Preventive approaches in couples therapy.* Philadelphia, PA: Brunner/Mazel.

Berkowitz, D. (2009). Theorizing lesbian and gay parenting: Past, present, and future scholarship. *Journal of Family Theory & Review, 1,* 117–132.

Berkowitz, D., & Marsiglio, W. (2007). Gay men: Negotiating procreative, father, and family identities. *Journal of Marriage and the Family, 69,* 366–381.

Berman, J. (2010, September 15). What makes a family? Children, say many Americans. *ABC World News.* Web site: http://abcnews.go.com/WN/defines-family-children-americans-survey/story?id=11644693.

Berman, M. (2015, July 9). Federal marriage benefits now available to same-sex couples nationwide. *The Washington Post.* Web site: https://www.washingtonpost.com/news/post-nation/wp/2015/07/09/federal-marriage-benefits-now-available-to-same-sex-couples-nationwide/?utm_term=.061c38911189.

Bernard, J. (1970). Women, marriage, and the future. *Futurist, 4,* 41–43.

Bernard, J. (1972). *The future of marriage.* New York, NY: World.

Berscheid, E. (1999). The greening of relationship science. *American Psychologist, 54*(4), 260–266.

Berscheid, E. (2006). Seasons of the heart. In M. Mikulincer & G. S. Goodman (Eds.), *Dynamics of romantic love: Attachment, caregiving, and sex* (pp. 404–422). New York, NY: Guilford.

Berscheid, E. (2010). Love in the fourth dimension. Web site: http://www.annualreviews.org/doi/pdf/10.1146/annurev.psych.093008.100318.

Berzon, B. (2004). *Permanent partners: Building gay and lesbian relationships that last* (rev. ed.). New York, NY: Penguin. Suggestions by a psychotherapist specializing in same-sex relationships for resolving conflicts over power and control, jealousy, differences in sexual desire, money, and family demands.

Berzon, B. (2016). Betty Berzon. *Wikipedia.* Web site: https://en.wikipedia.org/wiki/Betty_Berzon.

Best, J., & Bogle, K. A. (2014). *Kids gone wild.* New York, NY: New York University Press.

Bhopal, K. (1997). South Asian women within households: Dowries, degradation and despair. *Women's Studies International Forum, 20*(4), 489–492.

Bhopal, K. (2008). Arranged and forced marriages: The impact of education. In *Understanding the issues around forced marriage: "16 days of action to end violence against women."* Stirling, Scotland, November 26. Web site: http://eprints.soton.ac.uk/64141/.

Bhugra, D., Popelyuk, D., & McMullen, I. (2010). Paraphilias across cultures: Contexts and controversies. *Journal of Sex Research, 47,* 242–256.

Biblarz, T. J., & Stacey, J. (2010). How does the gender of parents matter? *Journal of Marriage and Family, 72,* 3–22.

Bierstedt, R. (1950). An analysis of social power. *American Sociological Review, 6,* 7–30.

Bigner, J., & Gottlieb, A. (2007). (Eds.). *Interventions with families of gay, lesbian, bisexual, and transgender people: From the inside out.* Binghamton, NY: Haworth Press.

Billingsley, A. (1986). *Black families in White America.* Englewood Cliffs, NJ: Prentice Hall.

Billingsley, A. (1992). *Climbing Jacob's ladder: The ending legacy of African-American families.* New York, NY: Touchstone.

Binik, Y. M., & Hall, S. K. (2014). *Principles and practice of sex therapy* (5th ed.). New York, NY: Guilford Press.

Binner, J. M., & Dnes, A. W. (2001). Marriage, divorce, and legal change: New evidence from England and Wales. *Economic Inquiry, 39*(2), 298–306.

Binson, D., Michaels, S., Stall, R., Coates, T. J., Gagnon, J. H., & Catania, J. A. (1995). Prevalence and social distribution of men who have sex with men: United States and its urban centers. *Journal of Sex Research, 32*(3), 245–254.

Biracial couples find more tolerance. (2001, July 6). Lincoln [NE] *Journal Star,* p. 5A.

Bissell, M. (2000). Socio-economic outcomes of teen pregnancy and parenthood: A review of the literature. *Canadian Journal of Human Sexuality, 9*(3), 191–204.

Bjorklund, G. (1977). Historical perspectives on parent education in America. Paper presented at *Toward the Competent Parent:* An *Interdisciplinary Conference on Parenting,* Atlanta, GA, February 21–22.

Blackman, L., Clayton, O., Glenn, N., Malone-Colon, L., & Roberts, A. (2005). *The consequences of marriage for African Americans: A comprehensive literature review.* New York, NY: Institute for American Values.

Blankenhorn, D. (2004). About David Blankenhorn. American Values.org Web site: http://www.americanvalues.org/htmolabout_david_blankenhorn.html.

Blankenhorn, D. (2007). *The future of marriage.* New York, NY: Encounter Books.

Bloch, E. (2007). The daddy difference. *Parenting, 21*(5), 81–84. The author argues that fathers let kids take risks while mothers are too protective because of their attachment to the child, which developed during pregnancy. And fathers trust themselves more than experts, while mothers are more sensitive to getting it right; they tend to compare notes with other parents more than dads do.

Blow, A. J., & Hartnett, K. (2005). Infidelity in committed relationships II: A substantive review. *Journal of Marital and Family Therapy, 31,* 217–233.

Bogle, K. A. (2007). The shift from dating to hooking up in college: What scholars have missed. *Sociology Compass, 1,* 775–788.

Bogle, K. A. (2008a). *Hooking up: Sex, dating and relationships on campus.* New York, NY: New York University Press.

Bogle, K. A. (2008b). The sociology of "hooking up": An interview with Kathleen Bogle. *Inside Higher Education.* Web site: ttp://www.insidehighered.com/news/2008/01/29/hookups.

Bohannan, P. (1970). The six stations of divorce. In P. Bohannan (Ed.), *Divorce and after* (pp. 29–55). New York, NY: Doubleday.

Bond, B. J., Hefner, V., & Drogos, K. L. (2009). Information-seeking practices during the sexual development of lesbian, gay, and bisexual individuals: The influence and effects of coming out in a mediated environment. *Sexuality & Culture, 13,* 32–50.

Boonstra, H. (2000). Promoting contraceptive use and choice: France's approach to teen pregnancy and abortion. *The Guttmacher Report on Public Policy, 3*(3).

Boonstra, H. D. (2007a). The case for a new approach to sex education mounts: Will policymakers heed the message? *Guttmacher Policy Review, 10*(2), p. 4. Web site: http://www.guttmacher.org/pubs/gpr/10/2/gpr100202.html.

Booth, S. (2010, February). They're golden. *Real Simple,* pp. 127–135. "There's nothing so nice as a new marriage," the screenwriter Ben

Hecht once wrote. But the six couples featured in this magazine story beg to differ. More than 50 years into their marriages, they share their unforgettable moments and secrets of staying together, happily.

Borcherdt, B. (1996). *Head over heart in love: 25 guides to rational passion.* Sarasota, FL: Professional Resource Press.

Borcherdt, B. (2000). *You can control your anger! 21 ways to do it.* Sarasota, FL: Professional Resource Press.

Borcherdt, B. (2000). *You can control your anger! 21 ways to do it.* Sarasota, FL: Professional Resource Press. A practical guide for people who would like to change.

Bornstein, R. F. (2006). The complex relationship between dependency and domestic violence. *American Psychologist, 61,* 595–606.

Boss, P. (1988). *Family stress management.* Newbury Park, CA: Sage.

Boss, P. (1992). Primacy of perception in family stress theory and measurement. *Journal of Family Psychology, 6*(2), 113–119.

Boss, P. (1999). *Ambiguous loss: Learning to live with unresolved grief.* Cambridge, MA: Harvard University Press.

Boss, P. (2002). *Family stress management: A contextual approach.* Thousand Oaks, CA: Sage.

Boss, P. (2006). *Loss, trauma, and resilience: Therapeutic work with ambiguous loss.* Dunmore, PA: Norton.

Boss, P. (2007). Ambiguous loss theory: Challenges for scholars and practitioners. *Family Relations, 56,* 105–111.

Boss, P. (2011). *Loving someone who has dementia: How to find hope while coping with stress and grief.* San Francisco, CA: Jossey-Bass.

Boss, P. (2013). Closure: Why it's a myth. National Council on Family Relations. *Family Focus, FF58,* 1–3.

Boss, P., et al. (2009). *Sourcebook of family theories and methods: A contextual approach.* St. Paul, MN: Springer.

Boss, P., Bryant, C., & Mancini, J. A. (Eds.). (2017). *Family stress management* (3rd ed.). Los Angeles, CA: Sage.

Boston Women's Health Book Collective. (1998). *Our bodies, ourselves for the new century: A book by and for women.* New York, NY: Touchstone/Simon & Schuster.

Boston Women's Health Book Collective. (2005). *Our bodies, ourselves: A new edition for a new era* (35th anniversary edition). New York, NY: Simon & Schuster.

Boston Women's Health Book Collective. (2006). *Our bodies, ourselves: Menopause.* New York, NY: Touchstone/Simon & Schuster.

Boston Women's Health Book Collective. (2008). *Our bodies, ourselves: Pregnancy and birth.* New York, NY: Touchstone.

Boston Women's Health Book Collective. (2011). *Our bodies, ourselves.* New York, NY: Touchstone.

Boulding, K. (1985). *Human betterment.* Beverly Hills, CA: Sage.

Bowen, G. L., Pittman, J. F., Pleck, J. H., Haas, L., & Voydanoff, P. (Eds.). (1995). *The work and family interface: Toward a contextual effects perspective.* Minneapolis, MN: National Council on Family Relations.

Boyd-Franklin, N. (2003). *Black families in therapy: Understanding the African American experience* (2nd ed.). New York, NY: Guilford Press.

Boyd-Franklin, N., Franklin, A. J., & Toussaint, P. A. (2000). *Boys into men: Raising our African American teenage sons.* New York, NY: Dutton.

Bradford, K., Vaughn, L., & Barber, B. (2008). When there is conflict. *Journal of Family Issues, 29,* 780–805.

Braithwaite, D. (2008, December 11). Braithwaite delves into voluntary kin. *Scarlet.* Web site: http://scarlet.unl.edu/p=872.

Braithwaite, D. O., Wackernagel Bach, B., Baxter, L. A., DiVerniero, R., Hammonds, J. R., Hosek, A. M., Willer, E. K., & Wolf, B. M. (2010). Constructing family: A typology of voluntary kin. *Journal of Social and Personal Relationships, 27*(3), 388–407.

Brandeis University Institute for Health Policy. (1993). Substance abuse: The nation's number one health problem. Cited by National Council on Alcoholism and Drug Dependence: http://www.ncadd.org.

Brandeis University Institute for Health Policy. (2001). Substance abuse: The nation's number one health problem. Cited by National Council on Alcoholism and Drug Dependence: http://www.ncadd.org.

"Breasts Shaped by Evolution for Babies, Not Men." (2010). Breastfeeding.com. Web site: http://www.breastfeeding.com/reading_room/breasts_shaped_babies.html.

Brick, P., & Taverner, B. (2001). *Positive images: Teaching abstinence, contraception, and sexual health* (3rd ed.). Morristown, NJ: Planned Parenthood of Greater Northern New Jersey.

Broderick, C. B. (1992). *Marriage and the family* (4th ed.). Englewood Cliffs, NJ: Prentice Hall.

Broderick, C. B. (1993). *Understanding family process: Basics of family systems theory.* Newbury Park, CA: Sage.

Broderick, C. (2016). Carlfred Broderick. *Wikipedia.* Web site: https://en.wikipedia.org/wiki/Carlfred_Broderick.

Brown, E. (1999). *Affairs: A guide to working through the repercussions of infidelity.* San Francisco, CA: Jossey-Bass.

Brown, E. (2000). Working with marital affairs: Learning from the Clinton triangles. In L. Vandecreek & T. L. Jackson (Eds.), *Innovations in clinical practice: A source book* (vol. 18, pp. 471–478). Sarasota, FL: Professional Resource Press/Professional Resource Exchange.

Brown, E. (2016). Affairs—Help with Emily Brown. Web site: http://www.affairs-help.com/about-emily-brown.

Brown, E., Hendrix, S., & Svriuga, S. (2015, June 14). Drinking is central to college culture—and to sexual assault. *The Washington Post.* Web site: https://www.washingtonpost.com/local/education/beer-pong-body-shots-keg-stands-alcohol-central-to-college-and-assault/2015/06/14/7430e13c-04bb-11e5-a428-c984eb077d4e_story.html.

Brown, S., Bulanda, J. R., & Lee, G. R. (2012). Transitions into and out of cohabitation in later life. *Journal of Marriage and Family, 74,* 774–793.

Brown, S. L. (2010). Marriage and child well-being: Research and policy perspectives. *Journal of Marriage and Family, 72,* 1059–1077.

Brown, S. L., & Lin, I-F. (2015). The gray divorce revolution. *Family Focus,* Winter, pp. 4, 6. Web site: https://www.ncfr.org/sites/default/files/winter_2015_focus_0.pdf.

Brown, T. B. (2015, April 28). Did you know in most states it's legal to discriminate against LGBT people? *NPR Net Radio.* Web site: http://www.npr.org/sections/itsallpolitics/2015/04/28/402774189/activists-urge-states-to-protect-the-civil-rights-of-lgbt-people.

Brown University Center for Alcohol and Addiction Studies. (2000). Position paper on drug policy. Physician Leadership on National Drug Policy. Cited by National Council on Alcoholism and Drug Dependence: http://www.ncadd.org.

Browning, R. (1864). Grow old along with me! In I. Jack (Ed.), *Browning: Poetical works, 1833–1864.* Oxford, UK: Oxford University Press. (Original work published in 1864.)

Brown-Rice, K. (2013). Examining the theory of historical trauma among Native Americans. *The Professional Counselor, 3,* 117–130.

Brubaker, T. H. (1985). *Later life families.* Beverly Hills, CA: Sage.

Brubaker, T. H. (Ed.). (1990). *Family relationships in later life* (2nd ed.). Newbury Park, CA: Sage.

Brubaker, T. H. (1991). Families in later life: A burgeoning research area. In A. Booth (Ed.), *Contemporary families: Looking forward, looking back* (pp. 226–248). Minneapolis, MN: National Council on Family Relations.

Bruce, M. L. (2002). Psychosocial risk factors for depressive disorders in late life. *Biological Psychiatry, 52*(3), 175–184.

Bryant, J., & Bryant, J. A. (2001). *Television and the American family.* (2nd ed.). Mahwah, NJ: Erlbaum.

Buchanan, C. M., & Heiges, K. L. (2001). When conflict continues after the marriage ends: Effects of post-divorce conflict on children. In J. H. Grych & F. D. Fincham (Eds.), *Interparental conflict and child development: Theory, research, and applications* (pp. 337–362). New York, NY: Cambridge University Press.

Buchanan, C. M., Maccoby, E. E., & Dornbusch, S. M. (1996). *Adolescents after divorce.* Cambridge, MA: Harvard University Press.

Buckingham, M., & Clifton, D. O. (2005). *Now, discover your strengths.* Lincoln, NE: Gallup Press.

Buehler, C., & O'Brian, M. (2011). Mothers' part-time employment: Associations with mother and family well-being. *Journal of Family Psychology, 25,* 895–906.

Bumpass, L. (1999, March). (Interviewed by Nadya Labi.) A bad start: Living together may be the road to divorce. *Time,* p. 61.

Bumpass, L., & Lu, H. H. (1998). *Trends in cohabitation and implications for children's family contexts.* Unpublished manuscript, University of Wisconsin, Madison, Center for Demography.

Bumpass, L., & Lu, H. H. (2000a). Cohabitation: How the families of U.S. children are changing. *Focus, 21*(1), 5–8.

Buono, A. J., & Weisenbach, S. (Eds.). (2004). *We met online! Stories of married Catholics who met their spouses on the Internet.* Philadelphia, PA: Xlibris.

Burgess, E. W., & Wallin, P. (1943). Homogamy in social characteristics. *American Journal of Sociology, 49*(2), 109–124.

Burr, W. R., Day, R. D., & Bahr, K. S. (1993). *Family science.* Pacific Grove, CA: Brooks/Cole.

Burr, W. R., & Klein, S. R. (1994). *Reexamining family stress.* Thousand Oaks, CA: Sage.

Burton, L. M., Cherlin, A., Winn, D., Estacion, A., & Holder-Taylor, C. (2009). The role of trust in low-income mothers' intimate unions. *Journal of Marriage and the Family, 71,* 1107–1124.

Butler, M. H., Harper, J. M., & Seedall, R. B. (2009). Facilitated disclosure versus clinical accommodation of infidelity secrets: An early pivot point in couple therapy. *Journal of Marital and Family Therapy, 35,* 125–143.

Buzzetti, A. L., & Associates. (2010). Children abusing elderly parents: A growing concern in New Jersey. Web site: http://www.24-7pressrelease.com/press-release/children-abusing-elderly-parents-a-growing-concern-in-. . .

Byrne, D. (1983). Sex without contraception. In D. Byrne & W. A. Fisher (Eds.), *Adolescents, sex, and contraception.* Hillsdale, NJ: Erlbaum.

Byrne, D. (2009). Professional profile. Web site: http://www.byrne.socialpsychology.org/.

Cacciatore, J., & DeFrain, J. (2015). The world of bereavement: Cultural perspectives on death in families. Cham, Switzerland: Springer International.

Cacciatore, J., DeFrain, J., Jones, K., & Jones, H. (2008). The couple and the death of a baby. *Journal of Family Social Work, 11*(4), 351–370.

Cacioppo, J. T., & Patrick, W. (2008). *Loneliness: Human nature and the need for social connection.* New York, NY: W. W. Norton.

Camarota, S. A., & Zeigler, K. (2014, September). *U.S. immigrant population record 41.3 million in 2013.* Washington, DC: Center for Immigration Studies. Web site: http://cis.org/sites/cis.org/files/camarota-record-immigrant-pop.pdf.

Campbell, R. (2016). Rural Sociology, University of Missouri. Web site: http://dass.missouri.edu/ruralsoc/faculty/campbell-r.php.

Canary, H. E., & Canary, D. J. (2013). *Family conflict.* Cambridge, UK: Polity Press.

Cano, A., Christian-Herman, J., O'Leary, K. D., & Avery-Leaf, S. (2002). Antecedents and consequences of negative marital stressors. *Journal of Marital and Family Therapy, 28,* 145–151.

Caplin, J., & McGirt, E. (2004, August 1). Ephrata, Washington pays for the war: A small town's National Guard soldiers trained hard for duty in Iraq. No one trained their families for the financial burden of their absence. *Money.* Web site: www.guardfamily.org/A00_admin/A0017_news%5Chtm%5CNYCU_07_12_2004.htm#Homefront_dealing_with_deployment.

Carey, B. (2007). Stress on troops adds to U.S. hurdles in Iraq. *The New York Times.* Web site: http://topics.nytimes.com/top/reference/timestopics/subjects/v/veterans/posttraumatic_stress_disorder/in. . .

Carr, D. (2006). Good grief: Bouncing back from a spouse's death in later life. *Contexts, 5*(4), 22–27.

Carroll, J. (2007, December 31). Most Americans "very satisfied" with their personal lives. Gallup Poll. Web site: http://www.gallup.com/poll/103483/most-americans-very-satisfied-their-personal-lives.aspx.

Carson, D. K., Dail, P. W., Greeley, S., & Kenote, T. (1990). Stresses and strengths of Native American reservation families in poverty. *Family Perspective, 24*(4), 383–400.

Cassidy, J., & Shaver, P. R. (Eds.). (2008). *Handbook of attachment: Theory, research, and clinical application* (2nd ed.). New York, NY: Guilford Press.

Casualties of the Iraq war. (2016). *Wikipedia.* Web site: https://en.wikipedia.org/wiki/Casualties_of_the_Iraq_War.

Caughlin, J. P., & Basinger, E. D. (2015). Completely open and honest communication: Is that really what we want? *Family Focus, Issue FF64,* pp. F1–F3.

Caughy, M. O., O'Campo, P. J., Nettles, S. M., & Lohrfink, K. F. (2006). Neighborhood matters: Racial socialization of African American children. *Child Development, 77,* 1220–1236.

Cavedo, C., & Guerney, B. G. (1999). Relationship enhancement, enrichment and problem prevention. In R. Berger & M. T. Hannah (Eds.), *Preventive approaches in couple therapy* (pp. 73–105). Philadelphia, PA: Brunner/Mazel.

Center for Behavioral Health Statistics and Quality. (2015). Behavioral health trends in the United States: Results from the 2014 National Survey on Drug Use and Health (HHS Publication No. SMA 15-4927, NSDUH Series H-50). Web site: https://www.samhsa.gov/data/sites/default/files/NSDUH-FRR1-2014/NSDUH-FRR1-2014.htm.

Center for Problem-Oriented Policing. (2016). Factors contributing to domestic violence. Web site: http://www.popcenter.org/problems/domestic_violence/2.

Centers for Disease Control. (2010a). HIV/AIDS in the United States. Department of Health and Human Services. Web site: http://www.cdc.gov/hiv/resources/factsheets/u.s.htm.

Centers for Disease Control and Prevention. (2004a). Actual causes of death in the United States, 2000. National Center for Chronic Disease Prevention and Health Promotion. Web site: http://www.cdc.gov/nccdphp/factsheets/death_causes2000.htm.

Centers for Disease Control and Prevention. (2004c, May 21). Youth risk behavior surveillance—United States, 2003. *Morbidity and Mortality Weekly Report, 53*(SS-2).

Centers for Disease Control and Prevention. (CDC). (2006). Abortion surveillance—United States, 2003. *Morbidity and Mortality Weekly Report, 55,* SS-11, pp. 1–32. Web site: http://www.cdc.gov/mmwr/preview/mmwrhtml/ss5511a1.htm.

Centers for Disease Control and Prevention. (2009b). Suicide. Web site: http://www.cdc.-gov/violenceprevention.

Centers for Disease Control and Prevention. (CDC). (2013, November 29). Abortion surveillance—United States, 2010. *Morbidity and Mortality Weekly Report, 62,* SS-8, pp. 1-44. Web site: http://www.cdc.gov/mmwr/preview/mmwrhtml/ss6208a1.htm.

Centers for Disease Control and Prevention. (2015, March 10). The National Intimate Partner and Sexual Violence Survey. Web site: http://www.cdc.gov/violenceprevention/nisvs/.

Centers for Disease Control and Prevention. (2015, November). CDC Fact Sheet. Reported STDs in the United States, 2014 National Data for Chlamydia, Gonorrhea, and Syphilis. Web site: http://www.cdc.gov/std/stats14/std-trends-508.pdf.

Centers for Disease Control and Prevention. (2015, November 6). Drug-poisoning deaths involving heroin: United States, 2000-2013. Web site: http://www.cdc.gov/nchs/data/databriefs/db190.htm.

Centers for Disease Control and Prevention. (2015, November 23). National marriage and divorce rate trends. Web site: http://www.cdc.gov/nchs/nvss/marriage_divorce_tables.htm.

Centers for Disease Control and Prevention. (2016). National Vital Statistics System. Birth data. Web site: https://www.cdc.gov/nchs/nvss/births.htm.

Centers for Disease Control and Prevention. (2016a). Fetal Alcohol Spectrum Disorders (FASDs). Web site: http://www.cdc.gov/ncbddd/fasd/data.html.

Centers for Disease Control and Prevention. (2016b). Breastfeeding report card: United States / 2014. Web site: http://www.cdc.gov/breastfeeding/pdf/2014breastfeedingreportcard.pdf.

Centers for Disease Control and Prevention. (2016c). Births and natality. Web site: http://www.cdc.gov/nchs/fastats/births.htm.

Centers for Disease Control and Prevention. (2016d). Infant mortality. Web site: http://www.cdc.gov/reproductivehealth/maternalinfanthealth/infantmortality.htm.

Centers for Disease Control and Prevention. (2016e). HIV/AIDS. Web site: http://www.cdc.gov/hiv/.

Centers for Disease Control and Prevention. (2016f). Six tips for college health and safety. Web site: http://www.cdc.gov/features/collegehealth/.

Centers for Disease Control and Prevention. (2016, February 1). Teen dating violence. Web site: http://www.cdc.gov/violenceprevention/intimatepartnerviolence/teen_dating_violence.html.

Centers for Disease Control and Prevention. (2016, February 9). CDC Wonder Online Databases. Web site: http://wonder.cdc.gov/.

Centers for Disease Control and Prevention. (2016, February 10). Alcohol and public health. Web site: http://www.cdc.gov/alcohol/.

Centers for Disease Control and Prevention. (2016, February 25). Life expectancy. Web site: http://www.cdc.gov/nchs/fastats/life-expectancy.htm.

Centers for Disease Control and Prevention. (2016, February 29). Alcohol use and your health. Web site: http://www.cdc.gov/alcohol/fact-sheets/alcohol-use.htm.

Centers for Disease Control and Prevention. (2016, April 14). Youth and tobacco use. Web site: https://www.cdc.gov/tobacco/data_statistics/fact_sheets/youth_data/tobacco_use/.

Centers for Disease Control and Prevention. (2017, April 17). Child abuse and neglect prevention. Web site: http://www.cdc.gov/violenceprevention/childmaltreatment/.

Centers for Disease Control and Prevention. (2017, April 18). Child abuse and neglect: Risk and protective factors. Web site: http://www.cdc.gov/violenceprevention/childmaltreatment/riskprotectivefactors.html.

Chamberlin, J. (2005, April). "A crucial time" for LGB research. *Monitor on Psychology, 36,* 84-85.

Chambers, A. L., & Kravitz, A. (2011). Understanding the disproportionately low marriage rate among African Americans: An amalgam of sociological and psychological constraints. *Family Relations, 60,* 648-660.

Chaney, C. (2014). "No matter what, good or bad, love is still there": Motivations for romantic commitment among Black cohabiting couples. *Marriage & Family Review, 50,* 216-245.

Chaney, C., Shirisia, L., & Skogrand, L. (2016). Whatever God has yoked together, let no man put apart: The effect of religion on Black marriages. *The Western Journal of Black Studies, 40,* 24-41.

Chaney, C., & Skogrand, L. (2009, June). *Strong Black marriages.* Paper presented at the African American Healthy Marriage Initiative Research to Practice Conference, Chapel Hill, NC.

Chapman, M., & Perreira, K. (2005). The well-being of immigrant Latino youth: A framework to inform practice. *Families in Society, 86,* 104-111.

Chase-Lansdale, P. L., Cherlin, A. J., & Kiernan, K. E. (1995). The long-term effects of parental divorce on the mental health of young adults: A developmental perspective. *Child Development, 66,* 1614-1634.

Cherlin, A. J. (2009). *The marriage-go-around: The state of marriage and the family in America today.* New York, NY: Vintage Books.

Cherlin, A. J. (2009b). The origins of the ambivalent acceptance of divorce. *Journal of Marriage and Family, 71,* 226-229.

Cherlin, A. J. (2010). Demographic trends in the United States: A review of research in the 2000s. *Journal of Marriage and Family, 72,* 403-419.

Cherlin, A. (2014). *Love's labor lost: The rise and fall of the working-class family in America.* New York, NY: Russell Sage Foundation.

Chicago Tribune (2013, January 14). *Study shows younger Americans deeper in credit card debt.* Web site: http://www.chicagotribune.com/business/breaking/chi-study-shows-younger-americans-deeper-in-credit-card-debt-20130114,0,7710181.story.

Child Development Institute. (2015). Internet safety for kids and teens: 10 ways to keep your family safe online. Web site: http://childdevelopmentinfo.com/family-living/kids-media-safety/children-teens-web-internet-safety/.

Childhelp. (2012). Prevention and treatment of child abuse. Web site: http://www.childhelp.org.

Childhelp. (2016). Five too many: Close to 5 children die every day as a result of child abuse in the United States. Web site: https://www.childhelp.org/?gclid=COXHkInWmMwCFdgMgQodSoELbg.

Child Trends. (2017, January 4). *Births to unmarried women.* Child Trends Databank Indicator. Web site: https://www.childtrends.org/indicators/births-to-unmarried-women/.

Child Trends Databank. (2013). Family structure. Web site: http://www.childtrendsdatabank.org/?q=node/231.

Child Trends Databank. (2015, December). Family structure. Web site: http://childtrends.org/?indicators=family-structure.

Child Welfare Information Gateway. (2015). Child maltreatment 2013: Summary of key findings. Washington, DC: U.S. Department of Health and Human Services, Children's Bureau.

Child Welfare Information Gateway. (2016a). Child abuse & neglect. Web site: https://www.childwelfare.gov/topics/can/.

Child Welfare Information Gateway. (2016b). Cultural competence in domestic violence services. U.S. Department of Health and Human Services. Web site: https://www.childwelfare.gov/topics/systemwide/cultural/services/domviolence/.

Chilisa, B. (2012). *Indigenous research methodologies*. Los Angeles, CA: Sage.

Chiriboga, D., Zettle, L., Connidis, I., Koropeckyj-Cox, T., Bluck, S., Luecking, G., Rook, K., Dykstra, P., DePaulo, B., Morris, W., & Hertel, J. (2004). The never-marrieds in later life: Potentials, problems, and paradoxes. *The Gerontologist, 44*(1), 145. A cross-national perspective on conceptual models and research findings, including discussions of social supports available to never-married men and women, advantages and disadvantages of never being married, how society views individuals representing this role status, and the variety of types of never-marrieds.

Choi, H., & Marks, N. F. (2013). Marital quality, socioeconomic status, and physical health. *Journal of Marriage and Family, 75*, 903-919.

Chong, A., & Mickelson, K. D. (2016). Perceived fairness and relationship satisfaction during the transition to parenthood: The mediating role of spousal support. *Journal of Family Issues, 37*, 3-28.

Christensen, A. (2016). Andrew Christensen, Ph.D. Web site: http://drandrewchristensen.com/.

Christensen, A., Atkins, D. C., Baucom, B., & Yi, J. (2010). Marital status and satisfaction five years following a randomized clinical trial comparing traditional versus integrative behavioral couple therapy. *Journal of Consulting and Clinical Psychology, 78*(2), 225-235.

Christopher, F. S. (2001). *To dance the dance: A symbolic interactional exploration of premarital sexuality*. Mahwah, NJ: Erlbaum.

Chung, A. Y. (2016). *Saving face: The emotional costs of the Asian immigrant family myth*. Chapel Hill, NC: Rutgers University Press.

Cicirelli, V. G. (2001). Intergenerational decision making by mother and adult child: Effects of adult child gender and age of dyad. *The Gerontologist, 41*(1), 12.

Cicirelli, V. G. (2003). Caregiving decision making by older mother and adult child: Process and expected outcome. *The Gerontologist, 43*(1), 364.

Cinotto, S. (2006). "Everyone would be around the table": American family mealtimes in historical perspective, 1850-1960. In R. W. Larson, A. R. Wiley, & K. R. Branscomb (Eds.), *Family mealtimes as a context of development and socialization* (pp. 17-34). San Francisco, CA: Jossey-Bass.

Civilian casualties in the war in Afghanistan (2001-present). (2016). Wikipedia. Web site: https://en.wikipedia.org/wiki/Civilian_casualties_in_the_war_in_Afghanistan_(2001%E2%80%93present).

Clark, R. A., Richard-Davis, G., Hayes, J., Murphy, M., & Pucheu Theall, K. (2009). *Planning parenthood: Strategies for success in fertility assistance, adoption, and surrogacy*. Baltimore, MD: Johns Hopkins University Press.

Claxton, A., & Perry-Jenkins, M. (2008). No fun anymore: Leisure and marital quality across the transition to parenthood. *Journal of Marriage and the Family, 70*, 28-43.

Claxton-Oldfield, S. (2000). Deconstructing the myth of the wicked stepparent. *Marriage and Family Review, 30*(1-2), 51-58.

Clay, R. A. (2009). The debate over low libidos: Psychologists differ on how to treat a lack of desire among some women. *APA Online Monitor on Psychology, 40*(4), 32. Web site: http://www.apa.org/monitor/2009/04/libidos.html.

Clift, E. (1992, July 13). Abortion angst: How the court's ruling will affect women, doctors and activists on both sides. *Newsweek*, pp. 16-19.

Cline Horowitz, M. (Ed.). (2005). *New dictionary of the history of ideas*. New York, NY: Charles Scribner's Sons.

CNN. (2015, June 27). Supreme Court rules in favor of same-sex marriage nationwide. Web site: http://www.cnn.com/2015/06/26/politics/supreme-court-same-sex-marriage-ruling/.

Cohen, P. (2014). Recession and divorce in the United States, 2008-2011. *Population Research and Policy Review, 33*, 615-628.

Cohn, D'V. (2011, December 14). Barely half of U.S. adults are married—A record low. Pew Research Center. Web site: http://www.pewsocialtrends.org/2011/12/14/barely-half-of-u-s-adults-are-married-a-record-low/.

Colby, S. L., & Ortman, J. M. (2015, March). *Projections of the size and composition of the U.S. population: 2014 to 2060*, Current Population Reports, P25-1143. Washington, DC: U.S. Census Bureau. Web site: https://www.census.gov/content/dam/Census/library/publications/2015/demo/p25-1143.pdf.

Coleman, M., & Ganong, L. H. (2004). *Handbook of contemporary families: Considering the past, contemplating the future*. Thousand Oaks, CA: Sage.

Coleman, M., Ganong, L., & Fine, M. (2000). Reinvestigating remarriage: Another decade of progress. *Journal of Marriage and the Family, 62*(4), 1288-1307.

Coles, R. L. (2003). Black single custodial fathers: Factors influencing the decision to parent. *Families in Society: The Journal of Contemporary Human Services, 84*(2), 247-258.

Coley, R. L., & Chase-Lansdale, P. L. (1998). Adolescent pregnancy and parenthood: Recent evidence and future directions. *American Psychologist, 53*(2), 152-166.

Coles, R. L., & Green, C. (2010). *The myth of the missing Black father*. New York, NY: Columbia University Press.

Coltrane, S., Gutierrez, E., & Parke, R. (2008). Stepfathers in cultural context: Mexican American families in the United States. In J. Pryor (Ed.), *The international handbook of stepfamilies: Policy and practice in legal, research, and clinical environments* (pp. 100-121). Hoboken, NJ: Wiley.

Compassionate Friends. (2016). Supporting family after a child dies. Web site: http://www.compassionatefriends.org/home.aspx.

Conner, D. H. (2014). Financial freedom: Women, money, and domestic abuse. *William & Mary Journal of Women and the Law, 339*. Web site: http://scholarship.law.wm.edu/wmjowl/vol20/iss2/4.

Constantine, N. A., Jerman, P., & Huang, A. X. (2007). California parents' preferences and beliefs regarding school-based sex education policy. *Perspectives on Sexual and Reproductive Health, 39*(3), 167-175.

Consumer Reports. (2005). CR's guide to contraception. *Consumer Reports* (February), 34-38. Sections on condoms for extra protection; birth control, more and safer choices; a comparative guide to contraceptives; and abortion options.

Cook, R., & DeFrain, J. (2005). Using discourse analysis to explore family strengths: A preliminary study. *Marriage and Family Review, 38*(1), 3-12.

Coontz, S. (Ed.). (2008). *American families: A multicultural reader*. New York, NY: Routledge.

Coontz, S. (2011). *A strange stirring*. New York, NY: Basic Books.

Cooper, C. L., & Dewe, P. (2007). Stress: A brief history from the 1950s. In A. Monat, R. S. Lazarus, & R. Reevy (Eds.), *The Praeger handbook on stress and coping* (vol. 1, pp. 7-32). Westport, CT: Praeger.

Coop Gordon, K., Hughes, F. M., Tomcik, N. D., Dixon, L. J., & Litzinger, S. C. (2009). Widening spheres of impact: The role of forgiveness in marital and family functioning. *Journal of Family Psychology, 23*(1), 1-13.

Copeland, L. (2014, October 9). Life expectancy in the USA hits a record high. *USA Today.* Web site: http://www.usatoday.com/story/news/nation/2014/10/08/us-life-expectancy-hits-record-high/16874039/.

Copen, C. E., Daniels, K., Vespa, J., & Mosher, W. D. (2012, March). *First marriages in the United States: Data from the 2006-2010 National Survey of Family Growth.* National Health Statistics Reports, U.S. Department of Vital Statistics, U. S. Department of Health and Human Services. Web site: http://www.cdc.gov/nchs/data/nhsr/nhsr049.pdf.

CoupleCARE. (2016). Couple commitment and relationship enhancement. Web site: http://www.couplecare.info/.

Cowan, P. A., & Cowan, C. P. (2011, summer). After the baby: Keeping the couple relationship alive. *Family Focus, 56.2*(49), 1, 2, 5.

Cowley, G. (1989, March 13). How the mind was designed: Evolutionary theory is yielding rich new insights into everything from cognition to sexual desire. *Newsweek,* pp. 56-58.

Cox, C. B. (2007). Grandparent-headed families: Needs and implications for social work interventions and advocacy. *Families in Society: The Journal of Contemporary Social Services, 88,* 561-566.

Craig, L. (2015). How mothers and fathers allocate time to children: Trends, resources, and policy context. *Family Focus, FF66,* F9-F10.

Creswell, J. W. (2007). *Qualitative inquiry & research design: Choosing among five approaches* (2nd ed.). Thousand Oaks, CA: Sage.

Creswell, J. W. (2013). *Qualitative inquiry and research design: Choosing among five approaches* (3rd ed.). Los Angeles, CA: Sage.

Crittenden, A. (2001). *The price of motherhood: Why the most important job in the world is still the least valued.* New York, NY: Metropolitan Books. "An easy, informative, enjoyable read."

Crockenberg, S. C. (2003). Rescuing the baby from the bathwater: How gender and temperament (may) influence how child care affects child development. *Child Development, 74*(4), 1034-1038.

Csikszentmihalyi, M. (1999). If we are so rich, why aren't we happy? *American Psychologist, 54*(10), 821-827.

Cui, M., Ueno, K., Gordon, M., & Fincham, F. D. (2013). The continuation of intimate partner violence from adolescence to young adulthood. *Journal of Marriage and Family, 75,* 300-313.

Cullington, D. (2008). *Breaking up blues.* New York, NY: Routledge.

Cummins, H. J. (2001). *Advice for those experiencing ambiguous loss.* Minneapolis, MN: Minneapolis Star and Tribune.

CYFERnet. (2010). Financial literacy. Children, Youth and Families Education and Research Network. Web site: http://www.cnpp.usda.gov/ExpendituresonChildrenbyFamilies.htm.

Cynkar, A. (2007). Early-career insights: Seven steps to stomp out debt. *Monitor on Psychology, 38.* Web site: http://www.apa.org/monitor/may07/sevensteps.html.

Daggett, L. M. (2002). Living with loss: Middle-aged men face spousal bereavement. *Qualitative Health Research, 12*(5), 625-639.

Dahl, T. (1980). *Model of stress.* Unpublished manuscript University of Minnesota, Minneapolis.

Dalla, R., DeFrain, J., Johnson, J., & Abbott, D. A. (Eds.). (2009). *Strengths and challenges of new immigrant families: Implications for research, education, policy, and service.* Lanham, MD: Lexington Press.

Dalla, R., DeFrain, J., Johnson, J., & Abbott, D. A. (2009). *Strengths and challenges of new immigrant families: Implications for research, education, policy, and service.* Lanham, MD: Lexington Books/Rowman & Littlefield.

Daly, M., & Wilson, M. I. (1996). *Current Directions in Psychological Science, 5,* 77-81.

Danes, S. M., & Haberman, H. R. (2007). Teen financial knowledge, self-efficacy, and behavior: A gendered view. *Financial Counseling and Planning, 18*(1), 48-60.

Darkwa, O. (2004). *Social welfare services for the aged.* Chicago, IL: University of Illinois. Web site: http://www.uic.edu/classes/socw/socw550/AGING/sld001.htm.

Darling, C. A., & Turkki, K. (2009). Global family concerns and the role of family life education: An ecosystemic analysis. *Family Relations: Interdisciplinary Journal of Applied Family Studies, 58* (February), 4-27.

Daugherty, J., & Copen, C. (2016, March 17). Trends in attitudes about marriage, childbearing, and sexual behavior: United States, 2002, 2006-2010, and 2011-2013 (Report No. 92). National Health Statistics Reports. Web site: https://www.cdc.gov/nchs/data/nhsr/nhsr092.pdf.

David, P., & Stafford, L. (2015). A relational approach to religion and spirituality in marriage: The role of couples' religious communication in marital satisfaction. *Journal of Family Issues, 36,* 232-249.

Davis, D. J., & Chaney, C. (2013). *Black women in leadership: Their historical and contemporary contributions.* New York, NY: Peter Lang Publishing.

Davis, K. E. (2004). *Love's many faces apprehended.* Washington, DC: American Psychological Association.

Davis, K. E. (2014). Two concepts of love. Web site: http://www.psych.sc.edu/faculty/Keith_Davis.

Dawson, D. A., & Grant, B. F. (1998). Family history of alcoholism and gender: Their combined effects on DSM-IV alcohol dependence and major depression. *Journal of Studies on Alcohol, 59*(1), 97-106.

Deal, R. L., & Olson, D. (2010). *The remarriage checkup.* Minneapolis, MN: Bethany House.

Deal, R. L., & Olson, D. H. (2010). *The remarriage checkup: Tools to help your marriage last a lifetime.* Minneapolis, MN: Bethany House. Ways in which remarried couples can build on their strengths and overcome relationship problems.

Dean, L., Joo, S., Gudmunson, C., Fischer, J. L., & Lambert, N. (2013, March). Debt begets debt: Examining negative credit card behaviors and other forms of consumer debt. *Journal of Financial Service Professionals, 67*(2), 72-84.

Dee, T. S. (2001). The effects of minimum legal drinking ages on teen childbearing. *Journal of Human Resources 36*(4), 824-838.

Deen, M. R. (2005, June). Family values reconsidered. *Family Focus,* pp. 5-6.

Deets, H. B. (1996). Aging in America: A women's issue. Workshop on social protection, poverty, and older persons at risk, American Association of Retired Persons and UN/ECE. Web site: http://www.unece.org/spot/deets.htm.

DeFrain, J., & the University of Nebraska-Lincoln Extension Family Action Research and Writing Team. (2007). *Family treasures: Creating strong families.* University of Nebraska-Lincoln Extension. Bloomington, IN: iUniverse.

DeFrain, J., & the University of Nebraska-Lincoln Extension Family Action Research and Writing Team. (2007). *Family treasures: Creating strong families.* University of Nebraska-Lincoln Extension. Bloomington, IN: iUniverse. Sixty-three couple and family activities keyed to each of the six major strengths.

DeFrain, J., & the University of Nebraska-Lincoln Extension Family Action Research and Writing Team. (2012). *Getting connected, staying connected: Loving each other day by day.* Bloomington, IN: iUniverse.

DeFrain, J., & the University of Nebraska–Lincoln Extension Family Action Research and Writing Team. (2012). *Getting connected, staying connected: Loving each other day by day*. Bloomington, IN: iUniverse. Very clear and specific activities to strengthen couple and family relationships.

DeFrain, J., & Asay, S. (Eds.). (2007). *Strong families around the world: The family strengths perspective*. New York, NY: Haworth.

DeFrain, J., & Asay, S. M. (Eds.). (2007). *Strong families around the world: Strengths-based research and perspectives*. London and New York: Haworth Press/Taylor & Francis.

DeFrain, J., & Asay, S. M. (2007). *Strong families around the world: Strengths-based research and perspectives*. London: Routledge/Taylor & Francis Group.

DeFrain, J., & Asay, S. M. (2008). *Strong families around the world: Strengths-based research and perspectives*. London: Routledge/Taylor & Francis Group. Web site: https://www.routledge.com/products/9780789036032.

DeFrain, J., Cook, R., & Gonzalez-Kruger, G. (2005). Family health and dysfunction. In R. J. Coombs (Ed.), *Family Therapy Review* (pp. 3–20). Mahwah, NJ: Lawrence Erlbaum Associates

DeFrain, J., Fricke, J., & Elmen, J. (1987). *On our own: A single parent's survival guide*. Lexington, MA: Lexington Books/Heath.

DeGarmo, D. S., Patras, J., & Eap, S. (2008). Social support for divorced fathers' parenting: Testing a stress-buffering model. *Family Relations, 57*, 35–48.

de Jong Gierveld, J., & Merz, E.-M. (2013). Parents' partnership decision making after divorce or widowhood: The role of (step) children. *Journal of Marriage and Family, 75*, 1098–1113.

DePaulo, B. M. (2006). *Singled out: How singles are stereotyped, stigmatized, and ignored and still live happily ever after*. New York, NY: St. Martin's.

Desmond, M. (2016). *Evicted*. New York, NY: Crown Publishers.

de Vries, J. M., Swenson, L., & Walsh, R. P. (2007). Hot picture or self-description: Predicting mediated dating success with Parental Investment Theory. *Marriage and Family Review, 42*, 7–33.

Dew, J. (2007). Two sides of the same coin? The differing roles of assets and consumer debt in marriage. *Journal of Family and Economic Issues, 28*, 89–104.

Dew, J. (2008a). Debt change and marital satisfaction change in recently married couples. *Family Relations, 57*, 60–71.

Dew, J. (2008b). Themes and trends of *Journal of Family and Economic Issues*: A review of twenty years (1988–2007). *Journal of Family and Economic Issues, 29*, 496–540.

Dew, J. (2009). The gendered meanings of assets for divorce. *Journal of Family and Economic Issues, 30*, 20–31.

Dew, J. (2011). Financial issues and relationship outcomes among cohabiting individuals. *Family Relations, 60*, 178–190.

Dew, J. (2015). The many interfaces between money and marriage. *Family Focus, 13* (Spring), F11–F12.

Dew, J., Anderson, B., Skogrand, L., & Chaney, C. (2016). *Financial issues in strong African American marriages: A strengths-based qualitative approach*. Manuscript submitted for publication. Logan, UT: Department of Family, Consumer, and Human Development, Utah State University.

Dew, J., Britt, S., & Huston, S. (2012). Examining the relationship between financial issues and divorce. *Family Relations, 61*, 615–628.

Diamond, M. (2007). *My father before me: How fathers and sons influence each other throughout their lives*. New York, NY: W. W. Norton.

DiCenso, A., Guyatt, G., Willan, A., & Griffith, L. (2002). Interventions to reduce unintended pregnancies among adolescents: Systematic review of randomized controlled trials. *British Medical Journal, 324*(7351), 1426–1430.

Dickler, J. (2012, May 15). Boomerang kids: 85% of college grads move home. *CNNMoney*. Web site: http://money.cnn.com/2010/10/14/pf/boomerang_kids_move_home/index.htm.

Dick-Read, G. (1984). *Childbirth without fear: The original approach to natural childbirth*. New York, NY: Harper & Row. (Original work published 1932.)

Dindia, K. (2000). Self-disclosure, identity, and relationship development: A dialectic perspective. In K. Dindia & S. Duck (Eds.), *Communication and personal relationships* (pp. 147–162). New York, NY: Wiley.

Dingfelder, S. (2006). Violence in the home takes many forms. *Monitor in Psychology, 37,* 18.

Dirie, W. (1998). *Desert flower*. New York, NY: Morrow.

Discovery Place. (2015). The secrets to helping an alcoholic family member or friend. Web site: https://www.discoveryplace.info/secrets-helping-alcoholic-family-member-or-friend.

Divorce rate climbs among middle-aged Chinese. (2004, February 1). *The Epoch Times*. Web site: http//www.asianresearch.org/articles/1846.htm.

Divorce rate on the increase in Shanghai. (2004, December 16). *Shanghai Daily*. Web site: http://www.china.org.cn/english/Life/115127.htm.

Dobson, J. C. (1999). *Love must be tough: New hope for families in crisis*. Nashville, TN: Word.

Doherty, W. H. (2016). About the Families and Democracy Project. The Doherty Relationship Institute. Web site: http://dohertyrelationshipinstitute.com/about/citizen-democracy/.

Doherty, W. J. (2000). *Take back your kids*. Notre Dame, IN: Sorin Books.

Doherty, W. J. (2001). *Take back your marriage: Sticking together in a world that pulls us apart*. New York, NY: Guilford.

Doherty, W. J., & Allen, W. (1994). Family functioning and parental smoking as predictors of adolescent cigarette use: A six-year prospective study. *Journal of Family Psychology, 8*(3), 347–353.

Doherty, W. J., & Anderson, J. R. (2004). Community marriage initiatives. *Family Relations, 53,* 425–432.

Doherty, W. J., Erickson, M. F., & LaRossa, R. (2006). An intervention to increase father involvement and skills with infants during the transition to parenthood. *Journal of Family Psychology, 20*(3), 438–447.

Doherty, W. J., Jacob, J., & Cutting, B. (2009). Community engaged parent education: Strengthening civic engagement among parents and parent educators. *Family Relations, 58*, 303–315.

Doherty, W. J., & Simmons, D. S. (1996). Clinical practice patterns of marriage and family therapists: A national survey of therapists and their clients. *Journal of Marital and Family Therapy, 22*, 9–25.

Dolbin-MacNab, M., & Keiley, M. K. (2009). Navigating interdependence: How adolescents raised solely by grandparents experience their family relationships. *Family Relations, 58*, 172–175.

Dolbin-MacNab, M. L. (2006). Just like raising your own? Grandmothers' perceptions of parenting a second time around. *Family Relations, 55*, 564–575.

Dolbin-MacNab, M. L. (2016). An exploration of the health of adolescents raised by grandparents. In M. Harrington Meyer & Y. Abdul-Malak (Eds.), *Grandparenting in the US*. Amityville, NY: Baywood.

Domestic Abuse Intervention Programs. (2016). Wheels. Web site: http://www.theduluthmodel.org/training/wheels.html.

Domesticviolence.org. (2016). Who are the abusers? Web site: http://www.domesticviolence.org/who-are-the-abusers/.

Dorey-Stein, C. (2015). A brief history: The three waves of feminism. *Progressive Women's Leadership*. Web site: https://www.progressivewomensleadership.com/a-brief-history-the-three-waves-of-feminism/.

Douglas, S. J., & Michaels, M. W. (2004). *The mommy myth: The idealization of motherhood and how it has undermined women*. New York, NY: Free Press.

Drago, R. W. (2007). *Work, family, life*. Boston, MA: Dollars & Sense Publishers.

Drake, B. (2013, July 15). The number of American single fathers has grown substantially. Pew Research Center. Web site: http://www.pewresearch.org/fact-tank/2013/07/15/the-number-of-american-single-fathers-has-grown-substantially/.

Dreby, J. (2010). *Divided by borders: Mexican migrants and their children*. Berkeley, CA: University of California Press.

Driver, J., Tabares, A., Shapiro, A. F., & Gottman, J. M. (2012). Couple interaction in happy and unhappy marriages. In F. Walsh (Ed.), *Normal family processes* (4th ed., pp. 57–77). New York, NY: Guilford Press.

Dugas, C. (2012, October 24). Gender pay gap persists. *USA Today*. Web site: http://www.usatoday.com/story/money/personalfinance/2012/10/24/gender-pay-gap/1652511/.

Duncan, S. F., Holman, T. B., & Yang, C. (2007). Factors associated with involvements in marriage preparation programs. *Family Relations: Interdisciplinary Journal of Applied Family Studies, 56* (July), 270–278.

Dunn, E. W., Aknin, L. B., & Norton, M. I. (2014). Prosocial spending and happiness. *Current Directions in Psychological Science, 23*(1), 41–47. Web site: http://journals.sagepub.com/doi/full/10.1177/0963721413512503.

Durham, W., & Braithwaite, D. O. (2009). Communication privacy management with the family planning trajectories of voluntarily child-free couples. *Journal of Family Communication, 9*, 43–65.

Duvall, E. M. (2001). Evelyn Duvall's life. *Marriage and Family Review, 32*(1/2), 7–23.

Duvander, A.-Z. E. (1999). The transition from cohabitation to marriage: A longitudinal study of the propensity to marry in Sweden in the early 1990s. *Journal of Family Issues, 20*(5), 698–717.

Dye, J. L. (2008). Fertility of American women: 2006. *Current Population Reports*, P20-558. U.S. Census Bureau. Web site: https://www.census.gov/prod/2008pubs/p20-558.pdf.

Dykstra, P. A., & Hagestad, G. O. (2007). Roads less taken: Developing a nuanced view of older adults without children. *Journal of Family Issues, 28*, 1275–1310.

Economics and Statistics Administration. (2011). Exploring the digital nation—Computer and Internet use at home. Web site: http://www.esa.doc.gov/Reports/exploring-digital-nation-computer-and-internet-use-home.

Edmondson, B. (2010). All the lonely people. American Association of Retired Persons. Web site: http://www.aarp.org/personal-growth/transitions/info-09-2010/all_the_lonely_people.html.

Edmondson, B. (2010). All the lonely people. *AARP Magazine*. Researchers find a rise in loneliness in recent years. Web site: http://www.aarp.org/personal-growth/transitions/info-09-2010/all_the_lonely_people.html.

Edwards, B. G. (2014). 10 essential elements of Carl Whitaker's theory and therapy. GoodTherapy.org Web site: http://www.goodtherapy.org/blog/10-essential-elements-of-carl-whitakers-theory-and-therapy-1212144.

Elderly Health Services. (2004). Self-help tips for the elderly. Hong Kong, People's Republic of China: Elderly Health Services Head Office. Web site: http://www.info.gov.hk/elderly/english/healthinfo/selfhelptips/adjustmenttoretirement-e.htm.

El Issa, E. (2016). *2016 American household credit card debt study*. Nerdwallet, Inc. Web site: https://www.nerdwallet.com/blog/average-credit-card-debt-household/.

Elliott, D. B., & Simmons, T. (2011, August). *Marital events of Americans: 2009, ACS 13*. U.S. Census Bureau. Web site: https://www.census.gov/prod/2011pubs/acs-13.pdf.

Ellison, C. G., & Bradshaw, M. (2009). Religious beliefs, sociopolitical ideology, and attitudes toward corporal punishment. *Journal of Family Issues, 30*, 320–340.

Emery, R. E. (2012). *Renegotiating family relationships: Divorce, child custody, and mediation* (2nd ed.). New York, NY: Guilford Press.

Emmers-Sommer, T. M., Rhea, D., Triplett, L., & O'Neil, B. (2003). Accounts of single fatherhood: A qualitative study. *Marriage and Family Review, 35*(1/2), 99–115.

Encyclopedia Britannica. (2004). Biography: Dirie, Waris. Web site: http://www.britannica.com/eb/article?eu=368479.

Encyclopedia Britannica. (2015). Mass extinction. Web site: http://www.britannica.com/science/extinction-biology.

Encyclopedia Britannica. (2015). Masters and Johnson: American research team. Web site: http://www.britannica.com/biography/Masters-and-Johnson.

Encyclopedia Britannica. (2015). Natural childbirth. Web site: https://www.britannica.com/science/natural-childbirth-biology.

Ennis, S. R., Rios-Vargas, M., & Albert, N. G. (2011, May). *The Hispanic population: 2010*. (U. S. Census Bureau Report C2010BR-04). Web site: http://www.census.gov/prod/cen2010/briefs/c2010br-04.pdf.

Enright, E. (2004, July and August). A house divided. *American Association of Retired Persons Magazine*, pp. 60, 64–66, 68, 81.

Envision Counselling & Support Centre. (2016). Parent abuse. Web site: http://envisioncounsellingcentre.com/innerpage/resources/parent-abuse/.

Erasing 76 Crimes. (2016, April 21). The human toll of 76 countries' anti-gay laws. The struggle to repeal them. Web site: https://76crimes.com/76-countries-where-homosexuality-is-illegal/.

Erickson, R. (2005). Why emotion work matters: Sex, gender, and the division of household labor. *Journal of Marriage and the Family, 67*, 337–351.

Erikson, E. H. (1950). *Childhood and society*. New York, NY: Norton.

Erikson, E. H. (1963). *Childhood and society* (2nd ed.). New York, NY: Norton.

Esteinou, R. (2009). *Construyendo relaciones y fortalezas familiares: Un panorama internacional*. Mexico, D.F.: Centro de Investigaciones y Estudios Superiores en Anthropologia Social. This book, published in Spanish in Mexico City, is the first book in Latin America to focus on family strengths. The book is the result of the Mexican Family Strengths Conference held in Cuernavaca, and includes articles from Mexico, Australia, Botswana, China, Italy, Korea, and the United States.

Eubanks Fleming, C. J., & Córdova, J. V. (2012). Predicting relationship help seeking prior to a marriage checkup. *Family Relations, 61* (February), 90–100.

Eunice Kennedy Shriver National Institute of Child Health and Human Development, NIH, DHHS. (2006). *The NICHD study of early child care and youth development (SECCYD): Findings for children up to age 4½ years (05-4318)*. Washington, DC: U.S. Government Printing Office. Web site: http://www.nichd.nih.gov/publications/.

Evans-Campbell, T. (2008). Historical trauma in American Indian/Native Alaska communities. *Journal of Interpersonal Violence, 23*, 316-338.

Everythingconnects.org. (2013). Effects of human overpopulation. Web site: http://everythingconnects.org/overpopulation-effects.html.

Faces and Voices of Recovery. (2016). Organizing the recovery community. Web site: http://www.facesandvoicesofrecovery.org/about.

Fadiman, G., & Bernard, A. (2000). *Bartett's book of anecdotes*. Boston, MA: Little, Brown.

Faiola, A. (2004, August 31). Japanese women live, and like it, on their own. *The Washington Post*, p. A01.

Falicov, C. J. (1998). *Latino families in therapy: A guide to multicultural practice*. New York, NY: Guilford Press.

Falicov, C. J. (2010). Changing construction of machismo for Latino men in therapy: "The devil never sleeps." *Family Process, 49*, 309-329.

Fals-Stewart, W., & Kelley, M. (2005). When family members go to war—A systemic perspective on harm and healing. *Journal of Family Psychology, 19*, 233-236.

Family Action Centre, University of Newcastle, Australia. (2010). Useful information and resources on parenthood. Web site: www.newcastle.edu.au/centre/fac.

Family Focus. (2005, June). American families: By the numbers. *Family Focus*, pp. 6, 14.

Family Service Association. (2012). How do you define your family? Web site: http://www.fsabc.org/mission/family/.

Family violence tops health issue. (1991, October 17). Lincoln [NE] *Journal Star*, p. 3.

Faris, E. (1940, summer). Seven pillars of family strength. *Living*, 69-76.

Fawcett, N. R., Gullone, E., & Johnson, J. (2002, March). The relationship between animal abuse and domestic violence: Implications for animal welfare agencies and domestic violence. *Australian Domestic and Family Violence Clearinghouse Newsletter*, *10*, 4-7.

Fay, R., Turner, C., Klassen, A., & Gagnon, J. (1989). Prevalence and patterns of same-gender sexual contact among men. *Science, 246*, 338-348.

Federal Bureau of Investigation. (2011). Child predators: The online threat continues to grow. Web site: https://www.fbi.gov/news/stories/child-predators.

Federal Bureau of Investigation. (2015). Property crime. Web site: https://www.fbi.gov/about-us/cjis/ucr/crime-in-the-u.s/2010/crime-in-the-u.s.-2010/property-crime.

Federal Interagency Forum on Aging-Related Statistics. (2016, August). *Older Americans 2016: Key indicators of well-being*. Washington, DC: U.S. Government Printing Office. Web site: https://agingstats.gov/docs/LatestReport/Older-Americans-2016-Key-Indicators-of-WellBeing.pdf.

Fehr, B. (2004). A prototype model of intimacy interactions in same-sex friendships. In D. J. Mashek & A. Aron (Eds.), *Handbook of closeness and intimacy* (pp. 9-26). Mahwah, NJ: Erlbaum.

Feldman, R. (2015). *Discovering the life span*. Boston, MA: Pearson.

Fenell, D. L., & Weinhold, B. K. (1997). *Counseling families: An introduction to marriage and family therapy* (2nd ed.). Denver, CO: Love.

Ferguson, S. J. (2000). Challenging traditional marriage: Never married Chinese American and Japanese American women. *Gender and Society, 14*(1), 136-159. Why do some heterosexual Chinese American and Japanese American women never marry? The four most significant reasons are the effect of their parents' marriages, their status as eldest daughter, their pursuit of education, and the lack of eligible suitors. Parents' traditional marriages and duties as eldest daughter caused many to have negative views of marriage and childbearing. The number of suitors was limited for 46 of 62 respondents because their parents placed strict restrictions on them concerning the types of men they are allowed to marry.

Fergusson, D. M., Horwood, L. J., & Ridder, E. M. (2005). Rejoinder. *Journal of Marriage and the Family, 67*, 1131-1136.

Ferrer, M. (2015). Stepping stones for stepfamilies. A six-lesson curriculum for enhancing stepfamily relationships developed by the University of Florida Extension. Web site: http://edis.ifas.ufl.edu/topic_program_stepping_stones_for_stepfamilies.

Field, T. (2011). Romantic breakup, heartbreak and bereavement. *Psychology, 2*, 382-387.

Fincham, F. D. (2013). Religion, spirituality, and families. *Family Focus*, pp. F5-F7.

Fincham, F. D., & Beach, S. R. H. (2002). Forgiveness in marriage: Implications for psychological aggression and constructive communication. *Personal Relationships, 9*, 239-251.

Fincham, F. D., & Beach, S. R. (2013). I say a little prayer for you: Praying for partner increases commitment in romantic relationships. *Journal of Family Psychology, 28*, 587-593.

Fincham, F. D., Hall, J., & Beach, S. R. (2006). Forgiveness in marriage: Current status and future directions. *Family Relations, 55*, 415-427.

Finer, L. (2007). Trends in premarital sex in the United States, 1954-2003. *Public Health Reports, 122*, 73-78.

Finer, L. B., & Zolna, M. R. (2011). Unintended pregnancy in the United States: Incidence and disparities, 2006. *Contraception, 84*(5), 478-485.

Finer, L. B., et al. (2006). Timing of steps and reasons for delays in obtaining abortions in the United States. *Contraception, 74*(4), 334-344.

Fingerman, K., Sechrist, J., & Birditt, K. (2012). Intergenerational ties in a changing world. *Gerontology, 59*, 64-70.

Finkelhor, D. (2009). The prevention of childhood sexual abuse. The future of children. Web site: http://www.unh.edu/ccrc/pdf/CV192.pdf.

Fisher, H. E. (2010). *Why him? Why her: How to find and keep lasting love*. New York, NY: Henry Holt.

Fisher, H. E. (2016). *Anatomy of love: A natural history of mating, marriage, and why we stray*. New York, NY: W. W. Norton.

Fisher, H. E., Aron, A., & Brown, L. (2006). Romantic love: A mammalian brain system for mate choice. *Philosophical Transactions of the Royal Society B, 361*, 2173-2186.

Fisher, H. E., Brown, L. L., Aron, A., Strong, G., & Mashek, D. (2010). Reward, addiction, and emotion regulation systems associated with rejection in life. *Journal of Neurophysiology, 104*, 51-60. Web site: http://www.helenfisher.com/downloads/articles/Fisher-et-al-Rejection.pdf.

Fisher, L. L., et al. (2010). Sex, romance, and relationships: AARP survey of midlife and older adults. American Association for Retired Persons. Web site: http://assets.aarp.org/rgcenter/general/srr_09.pdf.

Fisher, W. A., Fisher, J. D., Singh, R., & Baron, R. A. (2015). Donn Byrne (1931-2014). *American Psychologist, 70*, 477.

Fitzpatrick, L. (2004, March 29). Getting out. *Time Asia.* Web site: http://www.time.com/time/asia/magazine/printout/0,13675,501040405-605534,00.html.

Fletcher, W. L., & Hansson, R. O. (1991, March). Assessing the social components of retirement anxiety. *Psychology and Aging, 6,* 76–85.

Foote, J., Wilkens, C., & Kosanke, N. (2014). *Beyond addiction.* New York, NY: Scribner.

Fowers, B., & Davidov, B. (2006). The virtue of multiculturalism: Person transformation, character, and openness to the other. *American Psychologist, 61,* 581–594.

Fowers, B. J., & Olson, D. H. (1986). Predicting marital success with PREPARE: A predictive validity study. *Journal of Marital and Family Therapy, 12*(4), 403–413.

Fox, G. L., & Murry, V. M. (2000). Gender and families: Feminist perspectives and family research. *Journal of Marriage and the Family, 62*(4), 1160–1172.

Francoeur, R. T. (1982). *Becoming a sexual person.* New York, NY: Wiley.

Francoeur, R. T. (Ed.). (1997). *International encyclopedia of sexuality.* New York, NY: Continuum.

Franklin, A. J. (2006). A dialogue about gender, race, and invisibility in psychotherapy with African American men. In J. C. Muran (Ed.). *Dialogues on difference: Diversity studies of the therapeutic relationship* (pp. 117–131). Washington, DC: American Psychological Association Books.

Fravel, D. L. (1995). *Boundary ambiguity perceptions of adoptive parents experiencing various levels of openness in adoption.* Unpublished doctoral dissertation, University of Minnesota, St. Paul.

Freedom to Marry. (2016). Winning the freedom to marry nationwide. Web site: http://www.freedomtomarry.org/.

French, M. (2014, February 15). How supermodel Waris Dirie saved girl from female genital mutilation. *The Observer.* Web site: http://www.theguardian.com/society/2014/feb/16/supermodel-waris-dirie-female-genital-mutilation-fgmhttp://www.theguardian.com/society/2014/feb/16/supermodel-waris-dirie-female-genital-mutilation-fgm.

Frey, W. H. (2014, November 28). *The major demographic shift that's upending: How we think about race.* New Republic. Web site: https://newrepublic.com/article/120387/people-identifying-white-and-black-are-future-america.

Frias, S. M., & Angel, R. J. (2005). The risk of partner violence among low-income Hispanic subgroups. *Journal of Marriage and the Family, 67,* 552–564.

Friedan, B. (1963). *The feminine mystique.* New York, NY: Norton.

Friedan, B. (1997). *Beyond gender: The new politics of work and family.* Washington, DC: The Woodrow Wilson Center Press, book jacket.

Frieden, T. (2012). U.S. violent crime down for fifth straight year. *CNN Justice.* Web site: http://www.cnn.com/2012/10/29/justice/us-violent-crime/index.html.

Fromm, E. (2000). *The art of loving.* New York, NY: Continuum.

Frost, D. M. (2011). Stigma and intimacy in same-sex relationships: A narrative approach. *Journal of Family Psychology, 25,* 1–10.

Fry, R., Cohn, D'V., Livingston, G., & Taylor, P. (2011). The rising age gap in economic well-being: The old prosper relative to the young. *Pew Social & Demographic Trends.* Web site: http://www.pewsocialtrends.org/2011/11/07/the-rising-age-gap-in-economic-well-being/.

Fu, V. K. (2008). Interracial-interethnic unions and fertility in the United States. *Journal of Marriage and the Family, 70* (August), 783–795.

Gagnon, J. (2010). John Gagnon, personal profile. Web site: http://www.stonybrook.edu/sociology/?faculty/Gagnon/gagnon.

Gagnon, J. (2016). John Gagnon. *Wikipedia.* Web site: https://en.wikipedia.org/wiki/John_Gagnon.

Gagnon, J. H. (2004). *An interpretation of desire: Essays in the study of sexuality.* Chicago, IL: University of Chicago Press.

Gallup. (2014, July 29). Reports of alcohol-related family trouble remain up in U.S. Web site: http://www.gallup.com/poll/174200/reports-alcohol-related-family-trouble-remain.aspx.

Gallup. (2015, October 22). More Americans say crime is rising in U.S. Web site: http://www.gallup.com/poll/186308/americans-say-crime-rising.aspx.

Gallup, Inc. (1989). *Love and marriage.* Princeton, NJ: The Gallup Organization.

Gallup, Inc. (2004, June 22). The cultural landscape: What's morally acceptable? Web site: http://www.gallup.com/content/login.aspx?ci=12061.

Gallup poll. (1996). *Gender and society: Status and stereotypes.* Princeton, NJ: The Gallup Organization.

Galvin, K. M., & Brommel, B. J. (1986). *Family communication: Cohesion and change* (2nd ed.). Glenview, IL: Scott, Foresman.

Galvin, K. M., & Brommel, B. J. (2000). *Family communication: Cohesion and change* (5th ed.). New York, NY: Longman.

Gamache, S. (2001). Stepfamily life . . . and then some. British Columbia Council for Families, Vancouver, BC. Web site: http://www.bccf.bc.ca/learn/fl_stepfam.html.

Ganong, L. H., & Coleman, M. (1994). *Remarried family relationships.* Thousand Oaks, CA: Sage.

Ganong, L. H., & Coleman, M. (1999). *Changing families, changing responsibilities: Family obligations following divorce and remarriage.* Mahwah, NJ: Erlbaum.

Ganong, L. H., & Coleman, M. (2000). Remarried families. In C. Hendrick & S. S. Hendrick (Eds.), *Close relationships: A sourcebook* (pp. 155–168). Thousand Oaks, CA: Sage.

Garbarino, J. (2000). The soul of fatherhood. *Marriage and Family Review, 29*(2/3), 11–21.

Garman, E. T., & Forgue, R. E. (1997). *Personal finance* (5th ed.). Boston, MA: Houghton Mifflin.

Garman, E. T., & Forgue, R. E. (2002). *Personal finance* (7th ed.). Boston, MA: Houghton Mifflin.

Gartrell, N., & Bos, H. (2010). U.S. National Longitudinal Lesbian Family Study: Psychological adjustment of 17-year-old adolescents. *Pediatrics, 126,* 1–9. Web site: http://escholarship.org/uc/item/7f06z3sv.

Gartrell, N., Bos, H., Peyser, H., Deck, A., & Rodas, C. (2011). Family characteristics, custody arrangements, and adolescent psychological well-being after lesbian mothers break up. *Family Relations, 60,* 572–585.

Gary, L. E., Beatty, L. A., & Berry, G. L. (1986). Strong Black families: Models of program development for Black families. In S. Van Zandt, H. Lingren, G. Rowe, P. Zeece, L. Kimmons, P. Lee, D. Shell, & N. Stinnett (Eds.), *Family strengths 7: Vital connections* (pp. 453–468). Lincoln, NE: University of Nebraska Press.

Gates, G. (2008). Diversity among same-sex couples and their children. In S. Coontz, M. Parson, & G. Raley (Eds.), *American families* (pp. 394–399). New York, NY: Routledge.

Gates, G. J. (2011, April). How many people are lesbian, gay, bisexual and transgender? The Williams Institute, University of California at Los Angeles School of Law. Web site: http://williamsinstitute.law.ucla.edu/research/census-lgbt-demographics-studies/how-many-people-are-lesbian-gay-bisexual-and-transgender/.

Gaunt, R. (2009). Maternal gatekeeping: Antecedents and consequences. *Journal of Family Issues, 29*(3), 373–395.

Gay and Lesbian Times. (2003, October 9). Sex clampdown proposed in Indonesia. Web site: http://www.gaylesbiantimes.com/?id=1167&issue=824.

Gelles, R. J. (2000a). Family violence. In M. H. Tonry (Ed.), *The handbook of crime and punishment* (pp. 178–206). New York, NY: Oxford University Press.

Gelles, R. J. (2000b). Treatment resistant families. In R. M. Reece (Ed.), *Treatment of child abuse: Common ground for mental health, medical, and legal practitioners* (pp. 304–312). Baltimore, MD: Johns Hopkins University Press.

Gelles, R. J. (2017). *Intimate violence in families* (4th ed.). New York, NY: Oxford University Press.

General Social Survey. (2016). NORC at University of Chicago. Web site: http://www.norc.org/Research/Projects/Pages/general-social-survey.aspx.

Gershoff, E. T., & Bitenskty, S. H. (2007). The case against corporal punishment of children. *Psychology, Public Policy, and Law, 13*, 231–272.

Gershoff, E. T., Lansford, J. E., Zelli, A., Grogan-Kaylor, A., Chang, L., Deater-Deckard, K., & Dodge, K. A. (2010). Parent discipline practices in an international sample: Associations with child behaviors and moderation by perceived normativeness. *Child Development, 81*, 487–502.

Gerson, K. (2010). *The unfinished revolution: How a new generation is reshaping family, work, and gender in American.* New York, NY: Oxford University Press.

Gibbs, N. (2001, July 30). Who's in charge here? *Time,* pp. 40–49.

Gibran, K. (1976). *The prophet.* New York, NY: Knopf. (Original work published 1923.)

Gibson, P. A. (2002). Caregiving role affects family relationships of African-American grandmothers as new mothers again: A phenomenological perspective. *Journal of Marital and Family Therapy, 28*(3), 341–353.

Gibson, P. A. (2005). Intergenerational parenting from the perspective of African American grandmothers. *Family Relations, 54*, 280–297.

Gil, E. (2006). *Helping abused and traumatized children: Integrating directive and nondirective approaches.* New York, NY: Guilford Press.

Gilbert, N. (2008). *A mother's work: How feminism, the market, and policy shape family life.* New Haven, CT: Yale University Press.

Giles, J. (2008). *The nature of sexual desire.* Landham, MD: University Press of America.

Giles, J. (2016). James Giles (philosopher). *Wikipedia.* Web site: https://en.wikipedia.org/wiki/James_Giles_(philosopher).

Giving USA. (2015, June 29). *Giving USA: Americans donated an estimated $358.38 billion to charity in 2014: Highest total in report's 60-year history.* Web site: https://givingusa.org/giving-usa-2015-press-release-giving-usa-americans-donated-an-estimated-358-38-billion-to-charity-in-2014-highest-total-in-reports-60-year-history/.

GLAAD. (2016). GLAAD media reference guide: Terms to avoid. Web site: http://www.glaad.org/reference/offensive.

Glaser, G. (2015, April). The irrationality of Alcoholics Anonymous. *The Atlantic.* Web site: http://www.theatlantic.com/magazine/archive/2015/04/the-irrationality-of-alcoholics-anonymous/386255/.

Globalist. (2016, February 10). U.S. vs the world? Women as top political leaders. Web site: http://www.theglobalist.com/women-on-top-of-the-political-world/.

Goldberg, A. E. (2007). Talking about family: Disclosure practices of adults raised by lesbian, gay, and bisexual parents. *Journal of Family Issues, 28*, 100–131.

Goldberg, A. E., Downing, J. B., & Sauck, C. (2008). Perceptions of children's parental preferences in Lesbian twomother households. *Journal of Marriage and the Family, 70*(May), 419–434.

Goldberg, A. E., & Smith, J. (2014). Predictors of parenting stress in lesbian, gay, and heterosexual adoptive parents during early parenthood. *Journal of Family Psychology, 28*, 128–137.

Goldenberg & Goldenberg Eunice Kennedy Shriver National Institute of Child Health and Human Development, NIH, DHHS. (2006). The NICHD study of early child care and youth development (SECCYD): Findings for children up to age 4½ years (05-4318). Washington, DC: U.S. Government Printing Office.

Goldenberg, I., Stanton, M., & Goldenberg, H. (2016). *Family therapy: An overview* (9th ed.). San Francisco, CA: Cengage Learning.

Goldstein, S. (1940, winter). The family as a dynamic factor in American society. *Living,* 8–19.

Gomel, J. N., Tinsley, B. J., Parke, R. D., & Clark, K. M. (1998). The effects of economic hardship on family relationships among African American, Latino, and Euro-American families. *Journal of Family Issues, 19*(4), 436–476.

Gomez, A. (2016, September 9–11). Hispanic growth rate at record low. *USA Today.* 1A–2A.

Gone, J. P. (2009). A community-based treatment for Native American historical trauma: Prospects for evidence-based practice. *Journal of Consulting and Clinical Psychology, 1*, 78–94.

Gonzalez, J., & Holmes, T. (n.d.). *Credit card debt statistics.* CreditCards.com. Web site: http://www.creditcards.com/credit-card-news/credit-card-debt-statistics-1276.php.

Goodman, C. C., & Silverstein, M. (2006). Grand-mothers raising grandchildren. *Journal of Family Issues, 27,* 1605–1626.

Goodman, E. (2001, February 26). Clear up contraceptive issue before it's 2-LATE. Lincoln [NE] *Journal Star,* p. 4B.

Goodwin, R. (2009). *Changing relations.* New York, NY: Cambridge University Press.

Goodwin, R. (2016). Robin Goodwin, Professor, University of Warwick. Web site: http://www2.warwick.ac.uk/fac/sci/psych/people/rgoodwin/.

Gordon, K., Baucom, D. H., & Snyder, D. K. (2005). Forgiveness in couples: Divorce, infidelity, and couples therapy. In E. L. Worthington (Ed.), *Handbook of forgiveness* (pp. 407–422). New York, NY: Routledge.

Gordon, K. C., & Baucom, D. H. (2003). Forgiveness and marriage: Preliminary support for a synthesized model of recovery from a marital betrayal. *American Journal of Family Therapy, 31*, 179–199.

Gordon, L. (2016). PAIRS Program: Practical skills for love, for life. Web site: http://participant.pairs.com/about.

Gordon, P. A. (2003). The decision to remain single: Implications for women across cultures. *Journal of Mental Health Counseling, 25*(1), 33–45.

Gordon, S., & Gordon, J. (2000). *Raising a child responsibly in a sexually permissive world* (2nd ed.). Cincinnati, OH: Adams Media.

Gotta, G., Green, R., Rothblum, E., Solomon, S., Balsam, K., & Swartz, P. (2011). Heterosexual, lesbian, and gay male relationships: A comparison of couples in 1975 and 2000. *Family Process, 50,* 353–376.

Gottman, J., & Gottman, J. S. (2016). Same-sex couples. Web site: https://www.gottman.com/about/research/same-sex-couples/.

Gottman, J. M. (2007). *And baby makes three: The six-step plan for preserving marital intimacy and rekindling romance after baby arrives.* New York, NY: Crown.

Gottman, J. M. (2011). *The science of trust: Emotional attunement for couples.* New York, NY: W. W. Norton.

Gottman, J. M. (2011). *The science of trust: Emotional attunement for couples.* New York, NY: W. W. Norton. *Journal of Family Communication.* Philadelphia, PA: Routledge. Web site: http://www.tandf.co.uk/journals/hjfc.

Gottman, J. M., & DeClaire, J. (2001). *The relationship cure: A five-step guide for building better connections with family, friends, and lovers.* New York, NY: Crown.

Gottman, J. M., & Notarius, C. I. (2000). Decade review: Observing marital interaction. *Journal of Marriage and the Family, 62,* 927–947.

Gottman, J. M., Schwartz Gottman, J., & DeClaire, J. (2006). *Ten lessons to transform your marriage: America's love lab experts share their strategies for strengthening your relationship.* New York, NY: Crown.

Gottman, J. M., & Silver, N. (1994). *Why marriages succeed or fail.* New York, NY: Simon & Schuster.

Gouin, J.-P., Kiecolt-Glaser, J. K., Malarkey, W. B., & Glaser, R. (2008). The influence of anger expression on wound healing. *Brain, Behavior, and Immunity, 22,* 699–708.

Graber, E. C., Laurenceau, J., Miga, E, Chango, J., & Coan, J. (2011). Conflict and love: Predicting newlywed marital outcomes from two interaction contexts. *Journal of Family Psychology, 25,* 541–550.

Graham, J. L., Keneski, E., & Loving, T. J. (2014). Mental and physical health correlates of nonmarital relationship dissolution. *Family Focus, FF62,* F7–F9.

Graham, L. (1998, December 13). Where have all the small towns gone? *Parade,* pp. 6–9.

Graves, J. L., Jr. (2004). *The race myth: Why we pretend race exists in America.* New York, NY: Dutton. Dr. Graves, an evolutionary biologist at Fairleigh Dickinson University in New Jersey, argues, *We have paid dearly for the policies of racism, and are continuing to pay in a currency of despair, unfulfilled dreams, and blood. . . . Every time we pay, we slide closer toward hell on a road paved with our racial misconceptions. We will continue to pay until we reject the notion that there are biological races in the human species, and that race determines an individual's worth.*

Gray, E. (2015, April 9). A record percentage of women don't have kids. Here's why that makes sense. *The Huffington Post.* Web site: http://www.huffingtonpost.com/2015/04/09/childless-more-women-are-not-having-kids-says-census_n_7032258.html.

Gray, P. (1998, January 18). Paradise found. *Time,* p. 67.

Green, R. (2012). Gay and lesbian family life. In F. Walsh (Ed.), *Normal family process* (4th ed., pp. 172–195). New York, NY: Guilford Press.

Greene, S. M., Anderson, E. R., Forgatch, M. S., DeGarmo, D. S., & Hetherington, E. M. (2012). Risk and resilience after divorce. In F. Walsh (Ed.), *Normal family processes* (pp. 102–127). New York, NY: Guilford Press.

Greenspan, S. I. (2003). Child care research: A clinical perspective. *Child Development, 74*(4), 1064–1068.

Greer, M. (2005). A new kind of war. *Monitor on Psychology, 36,* 38.

Grieco, E. M., Acosta, Y. E., de la Cruz, C. P., Gumbino, C., Gryn, T., Laron, L. J. . . . & Walters, N. P. (2012, May). The foreign-born population in the United States: 2010. U.S. Census Bureau. Web site: http://www.census.gov/prod/2012pubs/acs-19.pdf.

Gudmunson, C. G., Beutler, I. F., Israelsen, C. L., McCoy, J. K., & Hill, E. J. (2007). Linking financial strain to marital instability: Examining the roles of emotional distress and marital interaction. *Journal of Family and Economic Issues, 28,* 357–376.

Gurman, A. S., Lebow, J. L., & Snyder, D. K. (Eds.). (2015). *Clinical handbook of couple therapy.* New York, NY: Guilford Press.

Gustafson, R. (2005). Is pornography addictive? Web site: http://www.parentstov.org.

Guttmacher Institute. (2014). Fact sheet: Induced abortion in the United States. Web site: https://www.guttmacher.org/fact-sheet/induced-abortion-united-states.

Guttmacher Institute. (2014, May). American teens' sexual and reproductive health. Web site: http://www.guttmacher.org/pubs/FB-ATSRH.html.

Guttmacher Institute. (2014, May 5). U.S. teen pregnancy, birth and abortion rates reach historic lows. Web site: https://www.guttmacher.org/media/nr/2014/05/05/.

Guttmacher Institute. (2015). Fact sheet: Contraceptive use in the United States. Web site: http://www.guttmacher.org/pubs/fb_contr_use.html.

Guttmacher Institute. (2015, January 23). Teen pregnancy rates declined in many countries between the mid-1990s and 2011. Web site: https://www.guttmacher.org/media/nr/2015/01/23/.

Guttmacher Institute. (2016). "Now in its fifth decade, the Guttmacher Institute continues to advance sexual and reproductive health and rights through an interrelated program of research, policy analysis and public education designed to generate new ideas, encourage enlightened public debate and promote sound policy and program development. The Institute's overarching goal is to ensure the highest standard of sexual and reproductive health for all people worldwide." Web site: https://www.guttmacher.org.

Guttmacher Institute. (2016a). Fact sheet: Abortion. Web site: https://www.guttmacher.org/sections/abortion.php.

Guttmacher Institute. (2016b). State policies in brief: An overview of abortion laws. As of August 1, 2017. Web site: http://www.guttmacher.org/statecenter/spibs/spib_OAL.pdf.

Hagestad, G. O., & Call, V. (2007). Pathways to childlessness: A life perspective. *Journal of Family Issues, 28,* 1338–1361.

Haley, J. (1959). The family of the schizophrenic: A model system. *Journal of Nervous and Mental Disease, 129,* 357–374.

Haley, J. (2016). What is strategic therapy? *Jay Haley on Therapy.* Web site: http://www.jay-haley-on-therapy.com/html/strategic_therapy.html.

Halgunseth, L. C., Ispa, J. M., & Rudy, D. (2006). Parental control in Latino families: An integrated review of the literature. *Child Development, 77,* 1282–1297.

Hall, M., & Havens, B. (2004). Social isolation and social loneliness. Division of Aging and Seniors, Health Canada. Web site: http://www.hc-sc.gc.ca/seniors-aines/naca/writings_gerontology/writ18/writ18_3_e.htm.

Halpern, D. F. (2005). Psychology at the intersection of work and family: Recommendations for employers, working families, and policy makers. *American Psychologist, 60,* 367–409.

Halpern, D. F., & Cheung, F. M. (2008). *Women at the top: Powerful leaders tell us how to combine work and family.* West Sussex, UK: Wiley-Blackwell.

Hamilton, B., Martin, J. A., Osterman, M., Curtin, S., & Mathews, T. J. (2015, December 23). *Births: Final data for 2014.* National Vital Statistics Reports, 64. Web site: https://www.cdc.gov/nchs/data/nvsr/nvsr64/nvsr64_12.pdf.

Hamon, R. R., & Ingoldsby, B. B. (Eds.). (2003). *Mate selection across cultures.* Thousand Oaks, CA: Sage. The meaningful processes, traditions, and practices related to couple formation around the world, including chapters from North America, the Caribbean and South America, Africa, the Middle East, Europe, and Asia.

Hancock, A. M., Jorgensen, B. L., & Swanson, M. S. (2013). College students and credit card use: The role of parents, work experience, financial knowledge, and credit card attitudes. *Journal of Family and Economic Issues, 34*, 369–381.

Hanna, S. L., Suggett, R., & Radtke, D. (2008). *Person to person: Positive relationships don't just happen* (5th ed.). Upper Saddle River, NJ: Pearson/Prentice Hall.

Hare, J., & Skinner, D. (2008). "Whose child is this?" Determining legal status for lesbian parents who used assisted reproductive technologies. *Family Relations, 57*, 365–375.

Harmon, A. (1998, August 30). Researchers say cyberspace sad, lonely: People who spend time online are more depressed. Lincoln [NE] *Journal Star*, p. 5A.

Harris, A. H., & Thoresen, C. E. (2005). Forgiveness, unforgiveness, health and disease. In E. L. Worthington (Ed.), *Handbook of forgiveness* (pp. 321–334). New York, NY: Routledge.

Harris, G. (2004, May 1). FDA restricts pill's availability. *The New York Times* report in the Minneapolis *Star Tribune*, p. A2.

Harris, J. R. (2009). *The nurture assumption* (2nd ed.). New York, NY: Free Press/Simon & Schuster.

Hart, A. D., Weber, C. H., & Taylor, D. (1998). *Secrets of Eve: Understand the mystery of female sexuality.* Nashville, TN: Word.

Harter, P. (2004, August 4). Divorce divides Morocco and W Sahara. *BBC News.* Web site: http://news.bbc.co.uk/go/pr/fr/-/1/hi/world/africa/3532612.stm.

Hartshorne, J. K., Salem-Hartshorne, N., & Hartshorne, T. (2009). Birth order effects in the formation of long-term relationships. *Journal of Individual Psychology, 65*, 156–176.

Harvey, J. H. (Ed.). (2004). *The handbook of sexuality in close relationships.* Mahwah, NJ: Erlbaum. Enhances the dialogue about the centrality of sexual issues in close relationships.

Hatcher, R. A., Trussell, J., Nelson, A. L., Cates, Jr., W., Kowal, D., & Policar, M. S. (2011). *Contraceptive technology* (20th rev. ed.). New York, NY: Ardent Media.

Hawkins, A. J., Amato, P. R., & Kinghorn, A. (2013). Are government-supported healthy marriage initiatives affecting family demographics? A state-level analysis. *Family Relations, 62*, 501–513.

Hawkins, A. J., Blanchard, V. L., Baldwin, S. A., & Fawcett, E. B. (2008). Does marriage and relationship education work? A meta-analytic study. *Journal of Consulting and Clinical Psychology, 76*(5), 723.

Hawkins, A. J., Stanley, S., Cowan, P. A., Fincham, F. D., Beach, S. R. H., Cowan, C. P., . . . & Daire, A. P. (2013, February–March). A more optimistic perspective on government-supported marriage and relationship education programs for lower income couples. *American Psychologist, 68*, 110–112.

Hawley, D. R., & Olson, D. H. (1995). Enriching newlyweds: An evaluation of three enrichment programs. *American Journal of Family Therapy, 23,* 129–147.

Hawthorne, B. (2000). Split custody as a viable post-divorce option. *Journal of Divorce and Remarriage, 33*(4), 1–19.

Hayes, A., & Higgins, D. (Eds.). (2014). *Families, policy and the law: Selected essays on contemporary issues for Australia.* Melbourne: Australian Institute of Family Studies. Web site: https://aifs.gov.au/publications/families-policy-and-law.

Haynes, C., Merolla, J., & Ramakrishnan, S. K. (2016). *Framing immigrants.* New York, NY: Russell Sage Foundation.

He, W., Sengupta, M., Velkoff, V. A., & DeBarros, K. A. (2005). 65+ in the United States: 2005. *Current population reports.* Washington, DC: Government Printing Office.

Healey, J. F., & O'Brien, E. (2015). *Race, ethnicity, gender, and class.* (7th ed.). Thousand Oaks, CA: Sage Publications.

Heart, M., Chase, J., Elkins, J., & Altschul, D. B. (2011). Historical trauma among indigenous peoples of the Americas: Concepts, research, and clinical considerations. *Journal of Psychoactive Drugs, 43*, 282–290.

Helliwell, J. F., & Grover, S. (2014). National Bureau of Economic Research. Working Paper No. 20794. Web site: http://www.nber.org/papers/w20794.

Hellmich, N. (1990, April 4). Marriage is no. 1 with men. *USA Today,* p. 1D.

Hennigan, R., & Ladd, L. (2015). Conflict resolution methods in heterosexual and same-sex relationships. *Family Focus, FF64,* F7–F9.

Hennon, C. B., & Wilson, S. M. (Eds.). (2008). *Families in a global context.* London: Routledge/Taylor & Francis Group. How are families the same or different around the world? An in-depth analysis of family life in 17 countries.

Henshaw, S. K. (1999). *U.S. teenage pregnancy statistics with comparative statistics for women aged 20–24* (p. 5). New York, NY: Alan Guttmacher Institute.

Herbenick, D., Reece, M., Schick, V., Sanders, S. A., Dodge, B., & Fortenberry, J. D. (2010). Sexual behavior in the United States: Results from a national probability sample of men and women ages 14–94. *Journal of Sexual Medicine, 7*, 255–265.

Herbenick, D., Reece, M., Schick, V., Sanders, S. A., Dodge, B., & Fortenberry, J. D. (2010). Sexual behavior in the United States: Results from a national probability sample of men and women ages 14–94. Center for Sexual Health Promotion, Indiana University. *Journal of Sexual Medicine, 7,* Supplement 5. Web site: http://onlinelibrary.wiley.com/doi/10.1111/j.1743-6109.2010.02012.x/abstract.

Herbert, W. (1999, February 22). Not tonight, dear: Americans say their sex lives leave a lot to be desired. *U.S. News and World Report,* pp. 57–59.

Herek, G. M. (2006). Legal recognition of same-sex relationships in the United States. *American Psychologist, 61*(6), 607–621.

Hernandez, D. J. (1997). Child development and the social demography of childhood. *Child Development, 68*(1), 149–169.

Higginbotham, B., Skogrand, L., & Torres, E. (2010). Stepfamily education: Perceived benefits for children. *Journal of Divorce & Remarriage, 51,* 36–49.

Higginson, J. G. (1998). Competitive parenting: The culture of teen mothers. *Journal of Marriage and the Family, 60,* 135–149.

Hill, M. S., Freedmen, S. R., & Enright, R. D. (2007). Towards a feminist empowerment model of forgiveness psychotherapy. *Psychotherapy: Theory, Research, Practice, Training, 44,* 14–29.

Hill, R. (1949). *Families under stress: Adjustment to the crises of war separation and reunion.* New York, NY: Harper.

Hill, R. (1958). Generic features of families under stress. *Social Casework, 49,* 139–150.

Hill, R. (1971). *The strengths of Black families.* New York, NY: Emerson Hall.

Hill, R. (2016). ISA past presidents: Reuben Hill. International Sociological Association. Web site: http://www.isa-sociology.org/en/about-isa/history-of-isa/isa-past-presidents/list-of-presidents/reuben-hill/.

Hine, D. C. (2007). Family first, then the world. In H. McAdoo (Ed.), *Black families* (4th ed., pp. 238–247). Thousand Oaks, CA: Sage.

Hines, P. M., & Boyd-Franklin, N. (1996). African American families. In M. McGoldrick, J. Giordano, & J. K. Pearce (Eds.), *Ethnicity and family therapy* (pp. 66–84). New York, NY: Guilford.

Hingson, R. W., & Howland, J. (2002). Comprehensive community interventions to promote health: Implications for college-age drinking problems. *Journal of Studies on Alcohol,* Suppl. No. 14, 226–240.

Hobfoll, S. (2001). The influence of culture, community, and the nested-self in the stress process: Advancing conservation of resources theory. *Applied Psychology: An International Review, 50,* 337–421.

Hobfoll, S. E., & Spielberger, C. D. (1992). Family stress: Integrating theory and measurement. *Journal of Family Psychology, 6*(2), 99–112.

Hochschild, A. (2009, October 16). The state of families, class and culture. *The New York Times.* Web site: http://www.nytimes.com/2009/10/18/books/review/Hochschild-t.hml/_r=2.

Hochschild, A. (2010). Berkeley sociology faculty profile. Web site: http://sociology.berkeley.-edu/profiles/hochschild/.

Hochschild, A. R. (1997). *The time bind: When work becomes home and home becomes work.* New York, NY: Metropolitan Books.

Hoffman, L., & Rainville, A. (2004, December 15). Children of the fallen. Scripps Howard News Service. Web site: www.shns.com/shns/warkids.

Holley, S. R., Haase, C. M., & Levenson, C. M. (2013). Age-related changes in demand-withdraw communication behaviors. *Journal of Marriage and Family, 75,* 822–836.

Holmes, P., & Fairfield, S. (2014). *The Routledge handbook of attachment: Theory.* New York, NY: Routledge/Taylor & Francis.

Holmes, T. H., & Ella, D. M. (Eds.). (1989). *Life change, life events, and illness: Selected papers.* New York, NY: Praeger.

Holmes, T. H., & Rahe, R. H. (1967). The social readjustment rating scale. *Journal of Psychosomatic Research, 11,* 213–218.

Holstein, J. A., & Gubrium, J. F. (Eds.). (2008). *Handbook of constructionist research.* New York, NY: Guilford Press.

Holtzman, M. (2011). Nonmarital unions, family decisions, and custody decision making. *Family Relations, 60*(5), 617–632.

Holtzworth-Munroe, A. (2005). Male versus female intimate partner violence: Putting controversial findings into context. *Journal of Marriage and the Family, 67,* 1120–1125.

Homer, M. M., Freeman, P. A., Zabriskie, R. B., & Eggett, D. L. (2007). Rituals and relationships: Examining the relationship between family of origin rituals and young adult attachment. *Marriage and Family Review, 42,* 5–27.

Hood Center for Children and Families, Dartmouth Medical College. (2012). Smoking. Web site: http://hoodcenter.dartmouth.edu/research-programs/smoking/parent-family_influences.html.

Horn, W. (2010). "Wade Horn." Wikipedia. Web site: http://en.wikipedia.org/wiki/-Wade_Horn.

Horn, W. F. (1995). *Father facts.* Lancaster, PA: The National Fatherhood Initiative.

Horner, E. M. (2014). Continued pursuit of happily ever after: Low barriers to divorce and happiness. *Journal of Family and Economic Issues, 35,* 228–240.

Hornik, D. (2001). Can the church get in step with stepfamilies? *US Catholic, 66*(7), 30–31.

Hosek, J. (Ed.). (2011). How is deployment to Iraq and Afghanistan affecting U.S. service members and their families? An overview of early RAND research on the topic. RAND National Defense Research Institute. Web site: rand.org/content/dam/rand/occasional_papers/2011/RAND_OP316.pdf.

Hosek, J. (2013). Lengthy military deployments increase divorce risk for U.S. enlisted service members. Rand Corporation. Web site: http://www.rand.org/news/press/2013/09/03.html.

Hoskins, M. (2005, winter). Merger of minds: Buffet/Gates. *Nebraska Magazine,* 30–35. Web site: http://ncsu.edu/ffci/publications/2009/v14-n1-2009-spring/olsen-skogrand.php.

Houseknecht, S. K., & Lewis, S. K. (2005). Explaining teen childbearing and cohabitation: Community embeddedness and primary ties. *Family Relations, 54,* 607–620.

Houseknecht, S. K., & Sastry, J. (1996). Family decline and child well-being: A comparative analysis. *Journal of Marriage and the Family, 58,* 726–739.

Howard, J. (2002). In A. Gore and T. Gore, *The spirit of family.* New York, NY: Henry Holt (back cover).

Howden, L. M., & Meyer, J. A. (2011, May). *Age and sex composition: 2010.* U.S. Census Bureau, U. S. Census Briefs. Web site: http://www.census.gov/prod/cen2010/briefs/c2010br-03.pdf.

Hoyt, C. (2012). The pedagogy of the meaning of racism: Reconciling a discordant discourse. *Social Work, 57,* 225–234.

Huebner, A. J., Mancini, J. A., Bowen, G. L., & Orthner, D. K. (2009). Shadowed by war: Building community capacity to support military families. *Family Relations, 58,* 216–228.

Huebner, A. J., Mancini, J. A., Wilcox, R. M., Grass, S. R., & Grass, G. A. (2007). Parental deployment and youth in military families: Exploring uncertainty and ambiguous loss. *Family Relations, 56,* 112–122.

Huffington Post. (2016). Here's how many people fatally overdosed on marijuana last year. Web site: http://www.huffingtonpost.com/entry/marijuana-deaths-2014_us_56816417e4b06fa68880a217.

Hull, E. (2011). Military service and marriage: A review of research. National Healthy Marriage Resource Center. Web site: http://www.healthymarriageinfo.org.

Hull, E. (2016). Military service and marriage: A review of research. National Healthy Marriage Resource Center. Web site: http://www.healthymarriageinfo.org/resource-detail/download.aspx?id=1129.

Human Rights Watch. (2004, November 29). Divorced from justice: Women's unequal access to divorce in Egypt. Web site: http://hrw.org/reports/2004/egypt1204/1.htm.

Humes, K. R., Jones, N. A., & Ramirez, R. R. (2011, March). *Overview of race and Hispanic origin: 2010* (U.S. Census Bureau Report C2010BR-02). Web site: http://www.census.gov/prod/cen2010/briefs/c2010br-02.pdf.

Hunt, R. A., Hof, L., & DeMaria, R. (Eds.). (1998). *Marriage enrichment: Preparation, mentoring and outreach.* Philadelphia, PA: Brunner/Mazel.

Hunt, S. (2005). *The life course: A sociological introduction.* New York, NY: Palgrave MacMillan.

Hunter, A. G. (1997). Counting on grandmothers: Black mothers' and fathers' reliance on grandmothers for parenting support. *Journal of Family Issues, 18*(3), 251–269.

Hutson, M. (2015, January/February). You're just like me. *The Atlantic,* 25.

Huxley, A. (1945). *The perennial philosophy.* New York, NY: Harper & Brothers.

Hyde, J. S., & DeLamater, J. D. (2014). *Understanding human sexuality* (12th ed.). New York, NY: McGraw-Hill.

Iasenza, S. (2010). What is queer about sex?: Expanding sexual frames in theory and practice. *Family Process, 49,* 291–308.

Iasenza, S. (2014). Expanding sexual frames in couples therapy. The Ackerman Institute, New York. Web site: https://www.youtube.com/watch?v=6TmfKf0G95k.

iCasualties.org. (2016). Operation Iraqi Freedom and Operation Enduring Freedom/Afghanistan. Web site: http://icasualties.org/.

Ihinger-Tallman, M., & Pasley, K. (1987). *Remarriage.* Newbury Park, CA: Sage.

Ihinger-Tallman, M., & Pasley, K. (1997). Stepfamilies in 1984 and today: A scholarly perspective. *Marriage and Family Review, 27*(1-2), 19-40.

Ikkink, K. K., van Tilburg, T., & Knipscheer, K. C. P. M. (1999). Perceived instrumental support exchanges in relationships between elderly parents and their adult children: Normative and structural explanations. *Journal of Marriage and the Family, 61,* 831-844.

Imber-Black, E. (Ed.). (2010). Couple and family therapy theory and practice: Innovations in 2010. *Family Process, 49*(3), 265-267.

Indiana University Bloomington. (2016). Center for Sexual Health Promotion. Web site: http://www.sexualhealth.indiana.edu/.

Ingraham, C. (2016, March 28). America's biggest drug threat is 100% legal. *The Washington Post.* Web site: https://www.washingtonpost.com/news/wonk/wp/2016/03/28/americas-biggest-drug-threat-is-100-legal/?utm_term=.5f90f07259ed.

Inman, A. G., Altman, A., Kaduvettoor-Davidson, A., Carr, A., & Walker, J. (2011). Cultural intersections: A qualitative inquiry into the experience of Asian Indian-White interracial couples. *Family Process, 50,* 248-266.

Insel, P. M., & Roth, W. T. (2013). *Core concepts in health* (13th ed.). New York, NY: McGraw-Hill.

Inskeep, S., & Ludden, J. (2014, December 15). When grandma's house is home: The rise of grandfamilies. National Public Radio. Web site: http://www.npr.org/2014/12/15/369366596/when-grandmas-house-is-home-the-rise-of-grandfamilies.

International Center for Journalists. (2016). Award-winning photojournalist helps put a human face on war. Web site: https://www.youtube.com/watch?v=0xzRkNWeFhQ:.

International Lesbian, Gay, Bisexual, Trans and Intersex Association. (2016). ILGA. Web site: http://ilga.org/.

Jackson, J. K. (1954). The adjustments of the family to the crisis of alcoholism. *Quarterly Journal of Studies on Alcohol, 15,* 562-586.

Jackson, J. K. (1964). Drinking, drunkenness, and the family. In R. McCarthy (Ed.), *Alcohol education for classroom and community* (pp. 155-166). New York, NY: McGraw Hill.

James, S. (2014). Longitudinal patterns of women's marital quality: The case of divorce, cohabitation, and race-ethnicity. *Marriage & Family Review, 50,* 738-763.

Janus, S. S., & Janus, C. L. (1993). *The Janus report on sexual behavior.* New York, NY: Wiley.

Järvinen, M. (2015). Understanding addiction: Adult children of alcoholics describing their parents' drinking problems. *Journal of Family Issues, 36*(6), 805-825.

Jayson, S. (2010). Free as a bird and loving it. In K. Gilbert (Ed.), *Annual edition: The family 10/11* (pp. 47-48). Boston, MA: McGraw-Hill.

Jensen, T. M., & Howard, M. O. (2015). Perceived stepparent-child relationship quality: A systematic review of stepchildren's perspectives. *Marriage & Family Review, 51,* 99-153.

Johansen, A. S., Leibowitz, A., & Waite, L. J. (1996). The importance of child-care characteristics to choice of care. *Journal of Marriage and the Family, 58,* 759-772.

Johnson, B. (2004). Older women talk about sex. *Selfhelp.* Web site: http://www.selfhelpmagazine.com/articles/aging/eldersex.html.

Johnson, M. (2008, December). Domestic violence and child abuse: What is the connection—Do we know? *Family Focus, 40,* F17-F19.

Johnson, M. P. (2008). A typology of domestic violence: Intimate terrorism, violent resistance, and situational couple violence. Boston, MA: Northeastern University Press.

Johnson, M. P. (2011). Michael P. Johnson on intimate partner violence. [Video file]. Web site: https://www.youtube.com/watch?v=kRmiRvNhVXA.

Johnson, M. P. (2012). Professional. Web site: http://www.personal.psu.edu/MPJ/Welcome.html.

Joint United Nations Programme on HIV/AIDS and World Health Organization. (2009, November). 09 AIDS epidemic update. Web site: unaids.org.

Jones, E. F., & Stahmann, R. F. (1994). Clergy beliefs, preparation, and practice in premarital counseling. *Journal of Pastoral Care, 48,* 181-186.

Jones, F., & Bright, J. (2007). Stress: Health and illness. In A. Monat, R. S. Lazarus, & R. Reevy (Eds.), *The Praeger handbook on stress and coping* (vol. 1, pp. 141-168). Westport, CT: Praeger.

Jones, R. K., & Henshaw, S. K. (2002). Mifepristone for early medical abortion: Experiences in France, Great Britain and Sweden. *Perspectives on Sexual and Reproductive Health, 34,* 154-161.

Jones-Sanpei, H., Holmes, E. K., & Day, R. D. (2009). Family process environmental measures. In the NLSY97: Variation by race and socioeconomic conditions. *Marriage & Family Review, 45,* 168-188.

Joseph, A. L., & Afifi, T. D. (2010). Military wives' stressful disclosures to their deployed husbands: The role of protective buffering. *Journal of Applied Communication Research, 38,* 412-434.

Jouriles, E. N., Norwood, W. D., McDonald, R., & Peters, B. (2001). Domestic violence and child adjustment. In J. H. Grych & F. D. Fincham (Eds.), *Interparental conflict and child development: Theory, research, and applications* (pp. 315-336). New York, NY: Cambridge University Press.

Julien, D., Chartrand, E., Simard, M., Bouthillier, D., & Begin, J. (2003). Conflict, social support, and relationship quality: An observational study of heterosexual, gay male and lesbian couples' communication. *Journal of Family Psychology, 17*(3), 419-428.

Journal of Family Communication. Philadelphia, PA: Routledge. *JFC* publishes original empirical and theoretical papers that advance the understanding of the communication processes within or about families. *JFC* is also committed to publishing manuscripts that address issues related to the intersection between families, communication, and social systems, such as mass media, education, health care, and law and policy. Web site: http://www.tandf.co.uk/journals/hjfc.

Journal of GLBT Family Studies. (2016). Taylor & Francis Online. Web site: http://www.tandfonline.com/doi/abs/10.1080/1550428X.2015.1072389?journalCode=wgfs20.

Kagan, J. (1964). *The nature of the child.* New York, NY: Basic Books.

Kahn, J., García-Manglano, J., & Bianchi, S. (2014). The motherhood penalty at midlife: Long-term effects of children on women's careers. *Journal of Marriage and Family, 76,* 56-72.

Kaminer, Y., & Bukstein, O. G. (2008). *Adolescent substance abuse.* New York, NY: Routledge.

Kantrowitz, B., & Springen, K. (2007, June 18). Confronting Alzheimer's. *Newsweek,* pp. 55-61.

Kapungu, C. T., Baptiste, D., Holmbeck, G., McBride, C., Robinson-Brown, M., Sturdivant, A., Crown, L., & Paikoff, R. (2010). Beyond the "birds and the bees": Gender differences in sex-related communication among urban African-American adolescents. *Family Process, 49,* 251-264.

Karis, T. A., & Killian, K. D. (2008). *Intercultural couples.* London: Routledge/Taylor & Francis Group.

Kartemquin Films. (2008). *The new Americans*. Web site: kartemquin.com. Follows 4 years in the lives of a diverse group of contemporary immigrants and refugees as they start new lives in America. An Indian couple is viewed through the dot-com boom and bust in Silicon Valley. A Mexican meatpacker struggles to reunite his family in rural Kansas. Two families of Nigerian refugees escape government persecution. Two Los Angeles Dodgers prospects follow their big dreams of escaping the barrios of the Dominican Republic. And a Palestinian woman marries into a new life in Chicago, only to discover that in the wake of 9/11, she cannot leave behind the pain of the conflict in her homeland.

Kaufman, A. (2011). *Personality, partner similarity and couple satisfaction: Do opposites attract or birds of a feather flock together*. Prepare Enrich. Web site: https://www.prepare-enrich.com/pe/pdf/research/2011/personality_and_couple_satisfaction_kaufmann_2011.pdf.

Kaufman, M. (2000, September 30). RU-486 user: It's easier, but not easy. *Washington Post* article published in the Lincoln [NE] *Journal Star*, p. 6A.

Kaufman, M. (2011). Sex education for children: Why parents should talk to their kids about sex. About Kids Health. Web site: http://www.aboutkidshealth.ca/En/HealthAZ/FamilyandPeerRelations/Sexuality/Pages/Sex-Education-for-Children-Why-Parents-Should-Talk-to-their-Kids-About-Sex.aspx.

Keillor, G. (1994, October 17). It's good old monogamy that's really sexy. *Time*, p. 71.

Keillor, G. (2005). *Lake Wobegon days*. New York, NY: Viking Penguin.

Keillor, G. (2009). *A Prairie Home Companion* with Garrison Keillor. Web site: http://prairiehome.publicradio.org/.

Kelly, G. F. (2011). *Sexuality today* (10th ed.). New York, NY: McGraw-Hill.

Kelly, J. B. (2007). Children's living arrangements: Following separation and divorce: Insights from empirical and clinical research. *Family Process, 46*, 35–52.

Kendig, H., Dykstra, P. A., Gaalen, P. A., & Melkas, T. (2007). Health of aging parents and childless individuals. *Journal of Family Issues, 28*, 1457–1486.

Kennedy, J. F. (1990). Inaugural address. In D. B. Baker (Ed.), *Political quotations*. Detroit, MI: Gale Research. (Original work published 1961.)

Kennedy, S., & Bumpass, L. L. (2008). Cohabitation and children's living arrangements: New estimates from the United States. *Demographic Research, 19*, 1663–1692.

Kennedy, S., & Fitch, C. (2012). Measuring cohabitation and family structure in the United States: Assessing the impact of new data from the Current Population Survey. *Demography, 49*(4), 1479–1498. Web site: http://www.ncbi.nlm.nih.gov/pmc/articles/PMC3496021/.

Kensinger-Rose, K., & Elicker, J. (2008). Parental decision making about child care. *Journal of Family Issues, 29*(9), 1161–1184.

Kersting, K. (2005, March). Happiness in men usually drops after age 65, study finds. *American Psychological Association Monitor*. Web site: apa.org/monitor/march05/happiness.aspx.

Kiang, L., Gonzales-Backen, M., Yip, T., Witkow, M., & Fuligni, A. (2006). Ethnic identity and the daily psy-chological well-being of adolescents from Mexican and Chinese backgrounds. *Child Development, 77*, 1338–1350.

Kindlon, D. (2001). *Too much of a good thing: Raising children of character in an indulgent age*. New York, NY: Talk Miramax.

King, V., & Scott, M. E. (2005). A comparison of cohabiting relationships among older and younger adults. *Journal of Marriage and the Family, 67*(May), 271–285.

Kinsey Institute for Research in Sex, Gender, and Reproduction (2016). The Kinsey Institute at Indiana University promotes interdisciplinary research and scholarship in the fields of human sexuality, gender, and reproduction. Web site: http://www.kinseyinstitute.org/.

Kinsey Institute. (2016). Kinsey's heterosexual-homosexual rating scale. Web site: http://www.kinseyinstitute.org/research/ak-hhscale.html.

Klein, D. M., & White, J. M. (1996). *Family theories*. Thousand Oaks, CA: Sage.

Klein, M., & Gordon, S. (1992). Sex education. In C. E. Walker & M. C. Roberts (Eds.), *Handbook of clinical child psychology* (2nd ed., pp. 933–949). New York, NY: Wiley.

Kleinke, C. L. (2007). What does it mean to cope? In A. Monat, R. S. Lazarus, & R. Reevy (Eds.), *The Praeger handbook on stress and coping* (vol. 2, pp. 289–308). Westport, CT: Praeger.

Knapp, M. L., Hall, J. A., & Horgan, T. G. (2014). *Nonverbal communication in human interaction* (8th ed.). Boston, MA: Wadsworth.

Knapp, M. L., & Vangelisti, A. L. (2009). *Interpersonal communication and human relationships* (6th ed.). Boston, MA: Pearson/Allyn & Bacon.

Knight, G. P., Roosa, M. W., & Umaña-Taylor, A. J. (2009). *Studying ethnic minority and economically disadvantaged populations: Methodological challenges and best practices*. Washington, DC: American Psychological Association.

Knoester, C., Petts, R. J., & Eggebeen, D. J. (2007). Commitments to fathering and the well-being and social participation of new, disadvantaged fathers. *Journal of Marriage and the Family, 69*, 991–1004.

Knudson-Martin, C. (2012). Changing gender norms in families and society. In F. Walsh (Ed.), *Normal family process* (4th ed., pp. 297–323). New York, NY: Guilford Press.

Knudson-Martin, C. (2012). Why power matters: Creating a foundation of mutual support in couple relationships. *Family Process, 52*, 5–18.

Knutson, L., & Olson, D. H. (2003). Effectiveness of PREPARE Program with premarital couples in a community setting. *Marriage and Family, 6*(4), 529–546.

Kohlberg, L. (1966). Cognitive stages and preschool education. *Human Development, 9*, 5–17.

Kolak, A. M., & Volling, B. L. (2007). Parental expressiveness as a moderator of coparenting and marital relationship quality. *Family Relations, 56* (December), 467–478.

Kolbert, E. (2014). *The sixth mass extinction: An unnatural history*. New York: Henry Holt.

Korman, J. (2016, December 9). How to choose the right device for better work/life balance. *USA Today*. Web site: http://www.usatoday.com/story/sponsor-story/alcatel/2016/11/30/all-work-all-play-future-flexible-productivity/94634892/.

Kornhaber, A. (2004). *The grandparent solution: How parents can build a family team for practical, emotional, and financial success*. San Francisco, CA: Jossey-Bass.

Koropeckyj-Cox, T., & Call, V. (2007). Characteristics of older childless persons and parents: Cross-national comparisons. *Journal of Family Issues, 28*, 1362–1414.

Koropeckyj-Cox, T., & Pendell, G. (2007). The gender gap in attitudes about childlessness in the United States. *Journal of Marriage and the Family, 69* (November), 899–915.

Koropeckyj-Cox, T., & Pendell, G. (2009). Attitudes about childlessness in the United States. *Journal of Family Issues, 28*(8), 1054–1082.

Kostelnik, M. (2005). *What is a high quality early childhood program?* Lincoln, NE: University of Nebraska, College of Education and Human Sciences.

Kottak, C. P. (2004). *Anthropology: The exploration of human diversity* (10th ed.). Boston, MA: McGraw-Hill.

Kraut, R., Patterson, M., Lundmark, V., Kiesler, S., Mukopadhyay, T., & Scherlis, W. (1998). Internet paradox: A social technology that reduces social involvement and psychological well-being? *American Psychologist, 53*(9), 1017–1031.

Kreider, R. M. (2010). Increase in opposite-sex cohabiting couples from 2009 to 2010 in the Annual Social and Economic Supplement (ASEC) to the Current Population Survey (CPS). Washington, DC: U.S. Census Bureau, Housing and Household Economic Statistics Division. Web site: http://www.census.gov/population/www/socdemo/Inc-Opp-sex-2009-to-2010.pdf.

Kuba, C. A. (2006). *Navigating the journey of aging parents: What care receivers want*. New York, NY: Taylor & Francis.

Kulthau, K., & Mason, K. O. (1996). Market child care versus care by relatives: Choices made by employed and nonemployed mothers. *Journal of Family Issues, 17*(4), 561–578.

Kurdek, L. A. (2000). Attractions and constraints as determinants of relationship commitment: Longitudinal evidence from gay, lesbian, and heterosexual couples. *Personal Relationships, 7*(3), 245–262.

Kurdek, L. A. (2003). On being insecure about the assessment of attachment styles. *Journal of Social and Personal Relationships, 19*(6), 811–834.

Kurdek, L. A. (2004). Are gay and lesbian cohabiting couples *really* different from heterosexual married couples? *Journal of Marriage and the Family, 66*, 880–900.

Kurdek, L. A. (2006). Differences between partners from heterosexual, gay, and lesbian cohabiting couples. *Journal of Marriage and the Family, 68*, 509–528.

Kurdek, L. A. (2008). Change in relationship quality for partners from lesbian, gay male, and heterosexual couples. *Journal of Family Psychology, 22*(5), 701–711.

Lacayo, R. (1997, April 14). The kids are all right: Day care—A new study says it's mostly harmless, sometimes helpful and less important than home. *Time*, p. 76.

Lachman, M. E. (2004). Development in midlife. *Annual Review of Psychology, 55*, 305–331.

LaMastro, V. (2001). Childless by choice? Attributions and attitudes concerning family size. *Social Behavior and Personality, 29*(3), 231–243.

Landers, A. (1997, June 30). How to tell if a date or mate is a potential batterer. Minneapolis [MN] *Star Tribune*, p. 16.

Landers, S. (1989, March). Koop will not release abortion effects report. *American Psychological Association Monitor*, p. 1.

Langer, G., Arnedt, C., & Sussman, D. (2004). ABC News: Primetime Live poll: American sex survey. Web site: http://abcnews.go.com/Primetime/News/story?id=156921@page=1.

Lankov, A. (2004, August 9). The dawn of modern Korea: Changes for better or worse. *The Korea Times*. Web site: http://times.hankooki.com/cgi-bin/hkiprn.cgi?pa=/1page/opinion/200408/kt2004080916572054130.htm&ur=times.hankooki.com&fo=print_kt.htm.

Lannutti, P. (2013). Same-sex marriage and privacy management: Examining couples' communication with family members. *Journal of Family Communication, 13*, 60–75.

Larsen, A. S., & Olson, D. H. (1989). Predicting marital satisfaction using PREPARE: A replication study. *Journal of Marital and Family Therapy, 15*, 311–322.

Larson, P. J., & Olson, D. H. (2004). Spiritual beliefs and marriage: A national survey based on ENRICH. *The Family Psychologist, 20*(2), 4–8.

Larson, P. J., & Olson, D. H. (2012). Top five stressors for couples. Web site: http://www.prepare-enrich.com/research.

Larson, R. W., Branscomb, K. R., & Wiley, A. R. (2006). Forms and function of family mealtimes: Multidisciplinary perspectives. In R. W. Larson, A. R. Wiley, & K. R. Branscomb (Eds.), *Family mealtimes as a context of development and socialization* (pp. 1–15). San Francisco, CA: Jossey-Bass.

Lasswell, M., & Lasswell, T. (1991). A family with a drinking problem is always a family in trouble. *Marriage and the family* (3rd ed., p. 256). Belmont, CA: Wadsworth.

Laughlin, L. (2013, April). *Who's minding the kids? Child Care Arrangements: Spring 2011*. U.S. Census Bureau, Household Income Studies, P70-135. Web site: https://www.census.gov/prod/2013pubs/p70-135.pdf.

Laughlin, L. (2010). Who's minding the kids? Child care arrangements: Spring 2005/Summer 2006. Household Economic Studies, U.S. Census Bureau. Web site: http://www.census.gov/hhes/childcare/.

Laumann, E. O. (2010). Edward O. Laumann, Department of Sociology, University of Chicago. Web site: http://sociology.uchicago.edu/people/faculty/laumann.shtml.

Laumann, E. O. (2016). Edward O. Laumann. Web site: http://sociology.uchicago.edu/people/faculty/laumann.shtml.

Laumann, E. O., et al. (Eds.). (2004). *The sexual organization of the city*. Chicago, IL: University of Chicago Press.

Laumann, E. O., Gagnon, J. H., Michael, R. T., & Michaels, S. (1994). *The social organization of sexuality: Sexual practices in the United States*. Chicago, IL: University of Chicago Press.

Laumann, E. O., Gagnon, J. H., Michael, R. T., Michaels, S., & Kolata, G. (1995). *Sex in America: A definitive survey*. Boston, MA: Little, Brown.

Laumann, E. O., & Michael, R. T. (2000). *Sex, love, and health in America: Private choices and public policies*. Chicago, IL: University of Chicago Press.

Laumann, E. O., Paik, A., & Rosen, R. C. (1999). Sexual dysfunction in the United States: Prevalence and predictors. *Journal of the American Medical Association, 28*(6), 537–544.

Lawrence, E., Rothman, A. D., Cobb, R. J., Rothman, M. T., & Bradbury, T. N. (2008). Marital satisfaction across the transition in parenthood. *Journal of Family Psychology, 22*(1), 41–50.

Lazarus, R. S. (2007). Stress and emotion: A new synthesis. In A. Monat, R. S. Lazarus, & R. Reevy (Eds.), *The Praeger handbook on stress and coping* (vol. 1, pp. 33–52). Westport, CT: Praeger.

Leboyer, F. (1995). *Birth without violence: The book that revolutionized the way we bring our children into the world*. Rochester, VT: Healing Arts Press.

Lee, C. Y. S., & Doherty, W. J. (2007). Marital satisfaction and father involvement during the transition to parenthood. *Fathering, 5*, 75–98.

Lee, G. R., Peek, C. W., & Coward, R. T. (1998). Race differences in filial responsibility expectations among older parents. *Journal of Marriage and the Family, 60*, 404–412.

Lee, V. (1996). Asian American families: An overview. In M. McGoldrick, J. Giordano, & J. K. Pearce (Eds.), *Ethnicity and family therapy* (pp. 227–248). New York, NY: Guilford.

Lee, Y., & Waite, L. (2005). Husbands' and wives' time spent on housework: A comparison of measures. *Journal of Marriage and the Family, 67*, 328–336.

Leiblum, S., & Rosen, R. (2000). *Principles and practices of sex therapy*. New York, NY: Guilford.

Leininger, L. J., & Kalil, A. (2014). Economic strain and children's behavior in the aftermath of the Great Recession. *Journal of Marriage and Family, 76*, 998–1010.

LeMasters, E. E. (1957). Parenthood as crisis. *Marriage and Family Living, 19,* 325-355.

Leon, K., & Jacobvitz, D. B. (2003). Relationships between adult attachment representations and family ritual quality: A prospective, longitudinal study. *Family Process, 42*(3), 419-432.

Lerner, H. G. (2012). *Marriage rules: A manual for the married and the coupled up.* New York, NY: Gotham Books.

Lerner, H. G. (2012). *Marriage rules: A manual for the married and the coupled up.* New York, NY: Gotham Books. Good advice from the much-admired couple and family therapist.

Lerner, H. G. (2014). *The dance of anger.* New York, NY: HarperCollins.

Letiecq, B. L., Bailey, S. J., & Kurtz, M. A. (2008). Depression among rural Native American and European American grandparents rearing their grandchildren. *Journal of Family Issues, 29,* 334-356.

Levaro, E. B. (2011). Theorizing age and gender in the pursuit of love in later life. Doctoral dissertation. Corvallis, OR: Oregon State University. Web site: http://www.ir.library.oregonstate.edu/xmlui/bitstream/handle/1957/22664/L.

Levaro, L. B. (2009, summer). Living together or living apart together: New choices for old lovers. *Family Focus,* pp. 9-10.

Levin, D. E., & Kilbourne, J. (2008). *So sexy so soon: The new sexualized childhood and what parents can do to protect their kids.* New York, NY: Ballantine Books. Sex is everywhere in American commercial culture. How to help children live in such an environment.

Levine, J. R., & Markman, H. J. (Eds.). (2001). *Why do fools fall in love? Experiencing the magic, mystery, and meaning of successful relationships.* San Francisco, CA: Jossey-Bass.

Levy, K., Kelly, K. M., & Jack, E. L. (2006). Sex differences in *Jealousy:* A matter of evolution or attachment theory? In M. Mikulincer & G. S. Goodman (Eds.), *Dynamics of romantic love: Attachment, caregiving, and sex* (pp. 128-145). New York, NY: Guilford.

Lewis, J. M., & Kreider, R. M. (2015, March). *Remarriage in the United States.* U.S. Census Bureau. Web site: https://www.census.gov/content/dam/Census/library/publications/2015/acs/acs-30.pdf.

Lewis, M. A., Granato, H., Blayney, J. A., Lostutter, T. W., & Kilmer, J. R. (2012). Predictors of hooking up sexual behaviors and emotional reactions among U.S. college students. *Archives of Sexual Behavior, 41,* 1219-1229.

LGBT rights in the United States. (2016). *Wikipedia.* Web site: https://en.wikipedia.org/wiki/LGBT_rights_in_the_United_States.

Limb, G. E., & Hodge, D. R. (2008). Developing spiritual competency with Native Americans: Promoting wellness through balance and harmony. *Journal of Contemporary Social Sciences, 89,* 615-622.

Lindau, S. T., Schumm, L. P., Laumann, E. O., Levinson, W., O'Muircheartaigh, C. A., & Waite, L. J. (2007). A study of sexuality and health among older adults in the United States. *New England Journal of Medicine, 357,* 762-774.

Lindstrom, R., Monk, J. K., & Vennum, A. (2014). Together again: The emerging trend of on-again/off-again relationships. *Family Focus, FF62,* F5-F6.

Lino, M. (2004). *Expenditures on children by families, 2003.* U.S. Department of Agriculture, Center for Nutrition Policy and Promotion. Miscellaneous Publication No. 1528-2003. Washington, DC. Web site: http://www.cnpp.usda.gov.

Lino, M., Kuczynski, K., Rodriguez, N., & Schap, T. (2017, January). *Expenditures on children by families, 2015.* (Miscellaneous Report No. 1528-2015). USDA Center for Nutrition Policy and Promotion. Web site: https://www.cnpp.usda.gov/sites/default/files/expenditures_on_children_by_families/crc2015.pdf.

Lisle, J. (2004, November 24). Single women become a force in home buying. Web site: http://www.realestatejournal.com/buysell/salestrends/20041124-lisle.html.

Liu, H., & Reczek, C. (2012). Cohabitation and U.S. adult mortality: An examination by gender and race. *Journal of Marriage and Family, 74,* 794-811.

Livingston, G., & Parker, K. (2010, September 9). Since the start of the Great Recession, more children raised by grandparents. Pew Research Center. Web site: http://www.pewsocialtrends.org.

Loseke, D. R., Gelles, R. J., & Cavanaugh, M. M. (Eds.). (2005). *Current controversies on family violence.* Thousand Oaks, CA: Sage.

Lunneborg, P. (1999). *The chosen lives of childfree men.* Westport, CT: Bergin & Garvey/Greenwood.

Lykken, D. (1999). *Happiness.* New York, NY: Golden Books.

Maccoby, E. E., & Lewis, C. C. (2003). Less day care or different day care? *Child Development, 74*(4), 1069-1075.

MacDonald, W. L., & DeMaris, A. (1995). Remarriage, stepchildren, and marital conflict: Challenges to the incomplete institutionalization hypothesis. *Journal of Marriage and the Family, 57,* 387-398.

MacDorman, M. F., Mathews, T. J., Mohangoo, A. D., & Zeitlin, J. (2014, September 24). International comparisons of infant mortality and related factors: United States and Europe, 2010. *National Vital Statistics Reports, 63*(5). Web site: http://www.cdc.gov/nchs/data/nvsr/nvsr63/nvsr63_05.pdf.

Mace, D., & Mace, V. (1980). Enriching marriages: The foundation stone of family strength. In N. Stinnett, B. Chesser, J. DeFrain, & P. Knaub (Eds.), *Family strengths: Positive models for family life.* Lincoln, NE: University of Nebraska Press.

Maciel, J. A., Van Putten, Z., & Knudson-Martin. (2009). Gendered power in cultural contexts: Part I. Immigrant couples. *Family Process, 48,* 9-23.

Mahoney, A. (2010). Religion in families, 1999-2009: A relational spirituality framework. *Journal of Marriage and Family, 72* (August), 805-827.

Maier, T. (2009). *Masters of sex: The life and times of William Masters and Virginia Johnson, the couple who taught America how to love* (p. 262). New York, NY: Basic Books.

Malinowski, B. (1929). *The sexual life of savages.* New York, NY: Harcourt.

Manning, W., & Brown, S. (2006). Children's economic well-being in married and cohabiting parent families. *Journal of Marriage and the Family, 68,* 345-362.

Manning, W., & Smock, P. (2005). Measuring and modeling cohabitation: New perspectives from qualitative data. *Journal of Marriage and the Family, 67,* 989-1002.

Manning, W. D., Giordano, P. C., & Longmore, M. A. (2006). Hooking up: The relationship contexts of "nonrelationship" sex. *Journal of Adolescent Research, 21,* 459-483.

Manning, W. D., Longmore, M. A., & Giordano, P. C. (2007). The changing institution of marriage: Adolescents' expectations to cohabit and to marry. *Journal of Marriage and the Family, 69* (August), 559-575.

Manning, W. D., Stewart, S. D., & Smock, P. J. (2003). The complexity of fathers' parenting responsibilities and involvement with nonresident children. *Journal of Family Issues, 24*(5), 645-667.

Mansfield, A. J., Kaufman, J. S., Marshall, S. W., Gaynes, B. N., Morrissey, J. P., & Engle, C. C. (2010). Deployment and the use of mental health services among U. S. Army wives. *New England Journal of Medicine, 362,* 101-109.

Manzi, C., Vignoles, V. L., Regalia, C., & Scabini, E. (2006). Cohesion and enmeshment revisited: Differentiation, identity, and well-being in two European cultures. *Journal of Marriage and the Family, 68,* 673-689.

March of Dimes. (2016). Stillbirth. Web site: http://www.marchofdimes.org/complications/stillbirth.aspx#.

Marelich, W. D., Gaines, S. O., & Banzet, M. R. (2003). Commitment, insecurity and arousability: Testing a transactional model of jealousy. *Representative Research in Social Psychology, 27,* 23–31.

Markman, H. J., Rhodes, G. K., Stanley, S. M., & Ragan, E. P. (2010). The premarital communication roots of marital distress and divorce: The first five years of marriage. *Journal of Family Psychology, 24,* 289–298.

Markman, H. J., & Stanley, S. M. (2016). PREP Program: Successful relationships, successful lives. Web site: https://www.prepinc.com/content/about-us/what-is-prep.htm.

Marks, L., Hopkins, K., Chaney, C., Monroe, P., Nesteruk, O., & Sasser, D. D. (2008). "Together, we are strong": A qualitative study of happy, enduring African American marriages. *Family Relations, 57,* 172–185.

Marks, L. D., Nesteruk, O., Hopkins-Williams, K., Swanson, M., & Davis, T. (2006). Stressors in African American marriages and families: A qualitative study. *Stress, Trauma, and Crisis: An International Journal, 9,* 203–225.

Marmot, M. (2004). *Status syndrome: How your social standing directly affects your health and life expectancy.* New York, NY: Times Books.

Marquardt, E., Blankenhorn, D., Lerman, R., Malone-Colon, L., & Wilcox, B. (2012). *The state of our unions 2012: The president's marriage agenda for the forgotten sixty percent.* University of Virginia, The National Marriage Project. Web site: http://www.stateofourunions.org/.

Marsh, J. C. (2003). Arguments for family strengths research. *Social Work, 48*(2), 147–149.

Martin, J. A., Hamilton, B. E., Sutton, P. D., Ventura, S. J., et al. (2009). Births: Final data for 2006. National Vital Statistics Reports, 57(7). Hyattsville, MD: National Center for Health Statistics.

Martinez-Brawley, E. E., & Zorita, P. (2011). Immigration and human services: The perils of professionalization. *The Journal of Contemporary Social Services, 92,* 133–137.

Mashek, D. J., & Aron, A. (Eds.). (2004). *Handbook of closeness and intimacy.* Mahwah, NJ: Erlbaum. Written by scholars in the field, this book provides the most comprehensive summary of a wealth of ideas about closeness and intimacy.

Masters, W. H., Johnson, V. E., & Kolodny, R. C. (1998). *Heterosexuality.* New York, NY: Gramercy Books.

Mauritzen, E. (2011). The effect of war-deployment on at-home spouses and partners: A support group manual for group facilitators. University of St. Thomas, Minnesota: Department of Psychology. Web site: http://ir.stthomas.edu/caps_gradpsych_docproj/6/.

May, R. (1969). *Love and will.* New York, NY: Norton.

Mayo Clinic. (2009a). Coping with pregnancy loss. Web site: http://www.mayoclinic.com-/health/pregnancy-loss/PR00098.

Mayo Clinic. (2009b). Miscarriage. Web site: http://www.mayoclinic.com-/health/miscarriage/DS01105.

Mayo Clinic. (2010a). Female sexual dysfunction. Web site: http://www.mayoclinic.com/health/female-sexual-dysfunction/DS0070.

Mayo Clinic. (2010b). Female orgasm: Why can't I climax during sexual intercourse? Web site: http://www.mayoclinic.com/health/female-orgasm/AN0172/METHO.

Mayo Clinic. (2010c). Viagra for women: Why doesn't it exist? Web site: http://www.mayoclinic.com/health/viagra-for-women/AN01987?ME.

Mayo Clinic. (2014, August 7). Male menopause. Web site: http://www.webmd.com/men/guide/male-menopause.

Mayo Clinic. (2015, January 7). Menopause. Web site: http://www.mayoclinic.org/diseases-conditions/menopause/basics/definition/con-20019726.

Mayo Clinic. (2015, April 14). Hormone therapy: Is it right for you? Web site: http://www.mayoclinic.org/diseases-conditions/menopause/in-depth/hormone-therapy/art-20046372.

Mayo Clinic. (2015, October 7). Child abuse: Risk factors. Web site: http://www.mayoclinic.org/diseases-conditions/child-abuse/basics/risk-factors/con-20033789.

Mayo Clinic. (2016a). Men's sexual health. Web site: http://www.mayoclinic.org/healthy-lifestyle/sexual-health/basics/mens-sexual-health/hlv-20049432.

Mayo Clinic. (2016b). Female sexual dysfunction. Web site: http://www.mayoclinic.org/diseases-conditions/female-sexual-dysfunction/basics/definition/con-20027721.

Mayo Clinic. (2016c). Miscarriage. Web site: http://www.mayoclinic.org/diseases-conditions/pregnancy-loss-miscarriage/basics/definition/con-20033827.

Mayo Clinic. (2016d). Sudden infant death syndrome (SIDS). Web site: http://www.mayoclinic.org/diseases-conditions/sudden-infant-death-syndrome/basics/definition/con-20020269.

Mayo Clinic. (n.d.). Mayo Clinic Health Information. Web site: http://www.mayoclinic.com/health-information/.

McCarthy, B. (2001). Male sexuality after fifty. *Journal of Family Psychotherapy, 12*(1), 29–37.

McCarthy, B. (2003). Marital sex as it ought to be. *Journal of Family Psychotherapy, 14*(2), 1–12.

McCarthy, B., & McCarthy, E. (2014). *Rekindling desire* (2nd ed.). London: Routledge/Taylor & Francis Group. Web site: https://www.routledge.com/products/9780415823524?utm_source=web&utm_medium=cms&utm_campaign=SBU2_JKG_2PR_8cm_4PSY_00000_Self%20Improvement%20Month.

McCarthy, B. W. (2007). *Men's sexual health: Fitness for satisfying sex.* London: Routledge Mental Health/Taylor & Francis Group.

McCarthy, B. W. (2009). *Discovering your couple sexual style: Sharing desire, pleasure, and satisfaction.* New York, NY: Routledge.

McConaghy, N., Hadzi-Pavlovic, D., Stevens, C., & Manicavasagar, V. (2006). Fraternal birth order and ratio of heterosexual/homosexual feelings in women and men. *Journal of Homosexuality, 4*(51), 161–174.

McCullough, M. (2000, September 29). RU-486 wins FDA approval: Abortion pill available in a month. Knight Ridder Newspapers article published in the Lincoln [NE] *Journal Star,* p. 1A.

McGinley, E., & Sabbadini, A. (2006). *Play Misty for Me* (1971): The perversion of love. *International Journal of Psychoanalysis, 87*(2), 589–597.

McGirk, T. (2009, November 30). The hell of PTSD. *Time,* pp. 41–43.

McGoldrick, M., & Ashton, D. (2012). A challenge to concepts of normality. In F. Walsh (Ed.). *Normal family processes* (4th ed., pp. 249–273). New York, NY: Guilford Press.

McGoldrick, M., Giordano, J., & Preto, N. G. (2008). *Ethnicity and family therapy.* New York, NY: Guilford.

McGoldrick, M., & Hardy, K. V. (Eds.). (2008). *Re-visioning family therapy: Race, culture, and gender in clinical practice.* New York, NY: Guilford Press.

McGovern. G. (1997). *Terry: My daughter's life-and-death struggle with alcoholism.* New York, NY: Villard Books/Random House.

McGraw, L.A., & Walker, A. J. (2004). Negotiating care: Ties between aging mothers and their caregiving daughters. *Journals of Gerontology, Series B, Psychological Sciences and Social Sciences, 59*(6), S324–32. Web site: http://www.ncbi.nlm.nih.gov/pubmed/15576863.

McKee, M. (2016). Talking with kids openly about sexuality. Advocates for Youth. Web site: http://www.advocatesforyouth.org/parents/175?task=view.

McLeod, B. (1986, July). The oriental express. *Psychology Today*, pp. 48–52.

McNulty, J. K. (2008). Forgiveness in marriage: Putting the benefits into context. *Journal of Family Psychology, 22*, 171–175.

Mead, M. (1935). *Sex and temperament in three primitive societies*. New York, NY: Morrow/Quill.

Mead, M. (1995). *Blackberry winter*. New York, NY: Kodansha International.

Mehta, V. (2013, August 5). What women want in men: A recent study reveals the qualities women look for in a partner. *Psychology Today*. Web site: https://www.psychologytoday.com/blog/head-games/201308/what-women-want-in-men.

Meier, J. A., McNaughton-Cassill, M., & Lynch, M. (2006). The management of household and childcare tasks and relationship satisfaction in parenting couples. *Marriage and Family Review, 40*, 61–88.

Melby, J. N., Conger, R. D., Conger, K. J., & Lorenz, F. O. (1993). Effects of parental behavior on tobacco use by young male adolescents. *Journal of Marriage and the Family, 55*, 439–454.

Mendenhall, T. J., Grotevant, H. D., & McRoy, R. G. (1996). Adoptive couples: Communication and changes made in openness levels. *Family Relations, 45*, 223–229.

Mercadante, C., Taylor, M. F., & Pooley, J. A. (2014). "I wouldn't wish it on my worst enemy": Western Australian fathers' perspectives on their marital separation experiences. *Marriage & Family Review, 50*, 318–341.

Merck & Co. (2016). Merck manual, consumer version. Web site: http://www.merckmanuals.com/home. An excellent online medical library.

Merck Manual, Consumer Version. (2016a). Intrauterine devices. Web site: http://www.merckmanuals.com/home/women's-health-issues/family-planning/intrauterine-devices.

Merck Manual, Consumer Version. (2016b). Fertility awareness-based methods of contraception. Web site: http://www.merckmanuals.com/professional/gynecology-and-obstetrics/family-planning/fertility-awareness%E2%80%92based-methods-of-contraception.

Merck Manual, Consumer Version. (2016c). Abortion. Web site: http://www.merckmanuals.com/home/women's-health-issues/family-planning/abortion.

Merck Manual, Consumer Version. (2016d). Introduction to symptoms during pregnancy. Web site: http://www.merckmanuals.com/home/women's-health-issues/symptoms-during-pregnancy/introduction-to-symptoms-during-pregnancy.

Merck Manual, Consumer Version. (2016e). Stages of development of the fetus. Web site: http://www.merckmanuals.com/home/women's-health-issues/normal-pregnancy/stages-of-development-of-the-fetus.

Merck Manual, Consumer Version. (2016f). Overview of labor and delivery. Web site: https://www.merckmanuals.com/home/women's-health-issues/normal-labor-and-delivery/overview-of-labor-and-delivery.

Merck Manual, Consumer Version. (2016g). Self-care during pregnancy. Web site: https://www.merckmanuals.com/home/women's-health-issues/normal-pregnancy/self-care-during-pregnancy.

Merck Manual, Consumer Version. (2016h). Drug use during pregnancy. Web site: http://www.merckmanuals.com/home/women's-health-issues/drug-use-during-pregnancy/drug-use-during-pregnancy.

Merck Manual, Consumer Version. (2016i). Cesarean delivery (C-section). Web site: http://www.merckmanuals.com/home/women's-health-issues/complications-of-labor-and-delivery/cesarean-delivery.

Merck Manual, Consumer Version. (2016j). Miscarriage. Web site: http://www.merckmanuals.com/home/women-s-health-issues/complications-of-pregnancy/miscarriage.

Merck Manual, Professional Version. (2016a). Conception and prenatal development. Web site: http://www.merckmanuals.com/professional/gynecology-and-obstetrics/approach-to-the-pregnant-woman-and-prenatal-care/conception-and-prenatal-development.

Merck Manual, Professional Version. (2016b). Overview of infertility. Web site: http://www.merckmanuals.com/professional/gynecology-and-obstetrics/infertility/overview-of-infertility.

Merck Manual, Professional Version. (2016c). Postpartum depression. Web site: http://www.merckmanuals.com/professional/gynecology-and-obstetrics/postpartum-care-and-associated-disorders/postpartum-depression.

Merriam-Webster Dictionary. (2016). Family. Web site: https://www.merriam-webster.com/dictionary/family.

Mertensmeyer, C., & Fine, M. (2000). ParentLink: A model of integration and support for parents. *Family Relations, 49*, 257–265.

Metro.co.uk. (2015). Earth Day 2015: 10 simple things you can do to help the environment—and save money. Web site: http://metro.co.uk/2015/04/22/earth-day-2015-10-simple-things-you-can-do-to-help-the-environment-and-save-money-5159726/.

Michener, J. A. (1991). *The world is my home*. New York, NY: Random House.

Mickish, J., & Schoen, K. (2004). Colorado Alliance for Cruelty Prevention: Safe pets, safe families, safe communities. *The Colorado Lawyer, 33*(1), 37–40.

Miedzian, M. (2002). *Boys will be boys: Breaking the link between masculinity and violence*. New York, NY: Lantern Books.

Miedzian, M. (2015). Myriam Miedzian on roots of terrorism and war. International Psychohistorical Association. Web site: https://www.youtube.com/watch?v=MVoRC9WDnp8.

Mikulincer, M., & Shaver, P. R. (2007). *Attachment in adulthood*. New York, NY: Guilford Press.

Miller, B. C. (2002). Family influences on adolescent sexual and contraceptive behavior. *Journal of Sex Research, 39*(1), 22–26.

Miller, B. C., Benson, B., & Galbraith, K. A. (2001). Family relationships and adolescent pregnancy risk: A research synthesis. *Developmental Review, 21*(1), 1–38.

Miller, B. C., Sage, R., & Winward, B. W. (2006). Teen childbearing and public policy. In L. Kowaleski-Jones & N. H. Wolfinger (Eds.), *Fragile families and the marriage agenda* (pp. 47–72). New York, NY: Springer.

Miller, S., & Miller, P. A. (1997). *Core communication: Skills and processes*. Littleton, CO: Interpersonal Communication Programs.

Miller, S., & Miller, P. (2016). Couple communication. Web site: http://www.smartmarriages.com/directory/17.

Mindel, C. H., Habenstein, R. W., & Wright, R., Jr. (Eds.). (1988). *Ethnic families in America: Patterns and variations* (3rd ed.). New York, NY: Elsevier.

Minuchin, P., Colapinto, J., & Minuchin, S. (2007). *Working with families of the poor* (2nd ed.). New York, NY: Guilford Press.

MISS Foundation. (2016). When a child dies: Twenty years of compassion. Web site: https://www.facebook.com/missfoundation.

M.I.S.S. Foundation. (2016). The MISS Foundation is a 501 (c) 3, volunteer-based organization committed to providing crisis support and long-term aid to families after the death of a child from any cause. Web site: http://www.missfoundation.org/.

Moglia, R. F., & Knowles, J. (Eds.). (1997). *All about sex: A family resource on sex and sexuality*. New York, NY: Three Rivers Press.

Mohatt, G., & Thomas, L. (2006). "I wonder, why would you do it that way?" In J. E. Trimble & C. B. Fisher (Eds.), *The handbook of ethical research with ethnocultural populations and communities*. Thousand Oaks, CA: Sage.

Monaghan, L., Goodman, J. E., & Robinson, J. M. (Eds.). (2012). *A cultural approach to interpersonal communication: Essential readings*. Malden, MA: Wiley-Blackwell.

Monat, A. Lazarus, R. S., & Reevy, G. (Eds.). (2007). *The Praeger handbook on stress and coping* (vol. 1). Westport, CT: Praeger.

Monserud, M. A. (2008). Intergenerational relationships and affectual solidarity between grandparents and young adults. *Journal of Marriage and the Family, 70*, 182–195.

Montagu, A. (1964). *Man's most dangerous myth: The fallacy of race*. Cleveland, OH: World.

Montenegro, X. P. (2004). *The divorce experience: A study of divorce at midlife and beyond*. Washington, DC: American Association of Retired Persons. Web site: http://www.assets.arp.org.rgcenter/general/divorce.pdf.

Moody, J. (2004). The structure of social science collaboration network: Disciplinary cohesion from 1963 to 1999. *American Sociological Review, 69*, 213–238.

Moore, B. A. (2011). *Handbook of counseling military couples*. New York and London: Routledge/Taylor & Francis Group.

Moore, F. (2009). *The effects of female control of resources on sex-differentiated mate preferences*. Evolution and Human Behavior (May).

Moore, K. A. (2010). *Kristin A. Moore, senior scholar and program area director*. Child Trends. Web site: http://www.childtrends.org/_staffmemdisp_page.cfm?LID=05A6959E-2D9F-470F-804052FAE261DD83.

Moore, T. (2015). Rethinking homeownership. *Family Focus*, Spring, pp. F5–F6.

Morbidity and Mortality Weekly Report. (2006, June). Epidemiology of HIV/AIDS–United States, 1981–2005. *Morbidity and Mortality Weekly Report, 55*, 589–592.

Morgan, S. P., & Chen, R. (1992). Predicting childlessness for recent cohorts of American women. *International Journal of Forecasting, 8*, 477–493.

Morrill, P. (2006). *Couples in great marriages with a traditional structure and egalitarian relationship*. Unpublished master's thesis, Utah State University, Logan.

Morrill, P., Bradford, K., Higginbotham, B., & Skogrand, L. (2013). Evaluations of "How to Avoid Falling for a Jerk (ette)." Unpublished raw data.

Mroczek, D., & Spiro, A. (2005). Change in life satisfaction over 20 years during adulthood: Findings from the VA Normative Aging Study. *Journal of Personality and Social Psychology, 86*(1), 189–202.

Mroczek, D. K., & Spiro, A., III. (2003). Modeling intra-individual change in personality traits: Findings from the Normative Aging Study. *Journals of Gerontology: Series B: Psychological Sciences and Social Sciences, 58B*(3), 153–165.

Muller, D. (2002). Fault or no fault? *Christian Century, 119*(12), 28–31.

Mulvihill, G. (2007, February). N.J. civil union law goes into effect with gay couples vowing to push for marriage. *StarTribune*. Web site: http://www.startribune.com/484/v-print/story/1013013.html.

Munk-Olsen, T., Munk Laursen, T., Pedersen C. B., Lidegaard, O., & Mortensen, P. B. (2011). Induced first-trimester abortion and risk of mental disorder. *New England Journal of Medicine, 364*, 332–339.

Murray, C. E. (2006). Professional responses to government-endorsed premarital counseling. *Marriage & Family Review, 40*(1), 53–67.

Murry, V. M., Smith, E. P., & Hill, N. E. (2001). Race, ethnicity, and culture in studies of families in context. *Journal of Marriage and Family, 63*, 911–914.

Murstein, B. I. (1980). Mate selection in the 1970s. *Journal of Marriage and the Family, 42*, 52–54.

Mussen, P. H. (1969). Early sex-role development. In D. A. Goslin (Ed.), *Handbook of socialization theory and research*. Chicago, IL: Rand McNally.

Mydans, S. (2004, November 20). There she is, "Miss Spinster of Thailand" and proud of it. *The New York Times*.

Myers, J. E., Madathil, J., & Tingle, L. R. (2005). Marriage satisfaction and wellness in India and the United States: A preliminary comparison of arranged marriages and marriages of choice. *Journal of Counseling & Development, 83*, 183–190.

Myerson, B. (1987). *Miss America, 1945: Bess Myerson's own story*. New York, NY: Newmarket Press.

Najman, J. M., Dunne, M. P., Purdie, D. M., Boyle, F. M., & Coxeter, P. D. (2006). Sexual partner preferences: Evolutionary imperative, emotional attachment or hedonism? *Marriage & Family Review, 40*, 5–23.

Nakonezny, P. A., Shull, R. D., & Rodgers, J. L. (1995). The effect of no-fault divorce law on the divorce rate across the 50 states and its relation to income, education, and religiosity. *Journal of Marriage and the Family, 57*(2), 477–488.

Nance-Nash, S. (2012). Five survival tips for parents with "boomerang" kids. Forbes. Web site: http://www.forbes.com.

Nasdaq. (2016). Credit card debt statistics. Web site: http://www.nasdaq.com/article/credit-card-debt-statistics-cm393820.

National Campaign to Prevent Teen and Unplanned Pregnancy. (2012). DCR report. Web site: https://thenationalcampaign.org/resource/dcr-report%E2%80%94full-report.

National Center for Children in Poverty. (2016). Child poverty. Web site: http://www.nccp.org/topics/childpoverty.html.

National Center for Family & Marriage Research. (n.d). Bowling Green State University. Web site: http://www.bgsu.edu/ncfmr.html.

National Center for Health Statistics. (n.d.). Centers for Disease Control and Prevention. Web site: https://www.cdc.gov/nchs/.

National Center for Injury Prevention and Control. (2005). Violence. Web site: http://www.cdc.gov/ncipc/default.htm.

National Center for PTSD. (2015, August 13). Mental health effects of serving in Afghanistan and Iraq. U.S. Department of Veterans Affairs. Web site: http://www.ptsd.va.gov/public/PTSD-overview/reintegration/overview-mental-health-effects.asp.

National Center for PTSD. (2016, February 23). How deployment stress affects children and families: Research findings. U.S. Department of Veterans Affairs. Web site: http://www.ptsd.va.gov/professional/treatment/family/pro_deployment_stress_children.asp.

National Center on Caregiving. (2015). Selected long-term care statistics. Family Caregiver Alliance. Web site: https://www.caregiver.org/selected-long-term-care-statistics.

National Center on Elder Abuse. (2016). NCEA, National Center on Elder Abuse, Administration on Aging. Web site: https://ncea.acl.gov/.

National Child Abuse and Neglect Training and Publications Project. (2014). *The Child Abuse Prevention and Treatment Act: 40 years of safeguarding America's children*. Washington, DC: U.S. Department of Health and Human Services, Children's Bureau.

National Child Care Information and Technical Assistance Center. (2008, June). National Task force on Early Childhood Education for Hispanics in the United States. Web site: http://nccic.acf.hhs.gov/library/index.cfm/do=oll.viewitem&itemid=41292http://nccic.acf.hhs.gov/library/index.cfm?do=oll.viewitem&itemid=41292.

National Child Care Information Center. (2004a, September). Hispanics and child care: The changing landscape. U.S. Department of Health and Human Services, Washington, DC.

National Child Care Information Center. (2004b). National Leadership Forum on Child Care Issued of the Hispanic Community. Child Care Bulleting Issue 24. U.S. Department of Health and Human Services, Washington, DC.

National Coalition Against Domestic Violence. (2012). Domestic violence facts. Web site: http://www.ncadv.org/.

National Coalition Against Domestic Violence. (2015). Facts about domestic violence and psychological abuse. Web site: http://ncadv.org/files/Domestic%20Violence%20and%20Psychological%20Abuse%20NCADV.pdf.

National Coalition Against Domestic Violence. (2016). Empowering victims and survivors. Web site: http://www.ncadv.org/.

National Coalition for the Homeless. (2004, September). How many people experience homelessness? NCH Fact Sheet #2. Washington, DC. Web site: http://www.nationalhomeless.org/numbers.html.

National Coalition for the Homeless. (2009, July). Web site: http://www.nationalhomeless.org/-factsheets/.

National Council of Juvenile and Family Court Judges. (2012, January 30). Remembering Ellen Pence. Web site: http://www.ncjfcj.org/remembering-ellen-pence.

National Council on Alcoholism and Drug Dependence. (2015, June 27). Alcohol, drugs, and crime. Web site: https://ncadd.org/about-addiction/alcohol-drugs-and-crime.

National Council on Alcoholism and Drug Dependence. (2015, July 26). Alcohol and drug abuse affects everyone in the family. Web site: https://ncadd.org/family-friends/alcohol-and-drug-abuse-affects-everyone-in-the-family.

National Council on Alcoholism and Drug Dependence. (2016). Addiction is a disease. Treatment is available. Recovery brings joy. Web site: https://www.ncadd.org/.

National Council on Alcoholism and Drug Dependence. (2016, February 24). Family disease. Web site: https://ncadd.org/family-friends/there-is-help/family-disease.

National Council on Alcoholism and Drug Dependence. (2017, July 15). National prevention week 2018. Web site: https://www.ncadd.org/blogs/in-the-news/national-prevention-week-2918-may-13-to-19-2018.

National Council on Family Relations. (2010). Certified Family Life Educator certification. Web site: http://www.ncfr.org/cert/index.asp.

National Council on Family Relations. (2014, Fall). Family Focus on Intimate Partner Violence. Web site: https://www.ncfr.org/ncfr-report/focus/family-focus-international-intimate-partner-violence.

National Council on Family Relations. (2016). NCFR, founded in 1938, is the oldest multidisciplinary and nonpartisan professional organization focused solely on family research, practice, and education. NCFR publishes three scholarly journals: *Journal of Marriage and Family, Family Relations: Interdisciplinary Journal of Applied Family Studies,* and *Journal of Family Theory & Review.* Web site: www.ncfr.org.

National Crime Victimization Survey. (2002). *Crime and victims statistics.* Washington, DC: U.S. Department of Justice, Office of Justice Programs. Web site: http://www.ojp.usdoj.gov/bjs/cvict.htm.

National Domestic Violence Hotline. (2016). Statistics. Web site: http://www.thehotline.org/resources/statistics/.

National Healthy Marriage Resource Center (2007, January). Trends in marriage rates. Web site: http://www.healthymarriageinfo.org/resource-detail/index.aspx?rid=2258.

National Healthy Marriage Resource Center. (2012). Web site: http://www.healthymarriageinfo.org.

National Healthy Marriage Resource Center. (2013). Remarriage trends in the United States. Web site: http://www.healthymarriageinfo.org.

National Healthy Marriage Resource Center (n.d.). Web site: http://www.healthymarriageinfo.org/curricula/index.cfm.

National Incidence Study of Child Abuse and Neglect (NIS-4), 2004–2009. (2016). Office of Planning, Research & Evaluation, Office of the Administration for Children & Families. Web site: http://www.acf.hhs.gov/programs/opre/research/project/national-incidence-study-of-child-abuse-and-neglect-nis-4-2004-2009.

National Institute of Child Health Research Network. (2003). *Child Development, 74*(4), 976–1005.

National Institutes of Health. (2016a). Miscarriage. Web site: https://medlineplus.gov/miscarriage.html.

National Institutes of Health. (2016b). Stillbirth. Web site: https://medlineplus.gov/stillbirth.html.

National Institute of Mental Health. (2015, April). Suicide prevention. Web site: https://www.nimh.nih.gov/health/topics/suicide-prevention/index.shtml.

National Institute on Aging. (2016, January 21). Mourning the death of a spouse. Web site: https://www.nia.nih.gov/health/publication/mourning-death-spouse.

National Institute on Alcohol Abuse and Alcoholism. (2016a). Alcohol consumption and the risk of cancer: A meta-analysis. Web site: http://pubs.niaaa.nih.gov/publications/arh25-4/263-270.htm.

National Institute on Alcohol Abuse and Alcoholism. (2016b). Alcohol & your health. Web site: http://www.niaaa.nih.gov/alcohol-health.

National Institute on Alcohol Abuse and Alcoholism. (2016c). Alcohol facts and statistics. Web site: http://www.niaaa.nih.gov/alcohol-health/overview-alcohol-consumption/alcohol-facts-and-statistics.

National Institute on Alcohol Abuse and Alcoholism. (2016d). Alcohol and sexual assault. Web site: http://pubs.niaaa.nih.gov/publications/arh25-1/43-51.htm.

National Institute on Alcohol Abuse and Alcoholism. (2016e). Module 8: Alcohol and intimate partner violence. Web site: http://pubs.niaaa.nih.gov/publications/Social/Module8IntimatePartnerViolence/Module8.html.

National Institute on Drug Abuse. (2016). Frequently asked questions. Web site: https://www.drugabuse.gov/publications/principles-drug-addiction-treatment/frequently-asked-questions.

National Institute on Drug Abuse for Teens. (2016). How many people die each year from drug usage? Web site: http://teens.drugabuse.gov/national-drug-facts-week/how-many-people-die-each-year-drug-usage.

National Marriage Project. (2007, July). *The state of our unions 2007: The social health of marriage in America*. Piscataway, NJ: Rutgers, The State University of New Jersey. Web site: http://stateofourunions.org/pdfs/SOOU2007.pdf.

National Marriage Project. (2012). *The state of our unions: Marriage in America 2012*. Web site: http://www.stateofourunions.org/.

National Marriage Project. (2012). *The state of our unions: Marriage in America 2012*. Web site: http://www.nationalmarriageproject.org.

National Marriage Project. (2016). Mission. Web site: http://nationalmarriageproject.org/about/.

National Marriage Project. (n.d.). Research and analysis on the health of marriage and family in America. Web site: http://nationalmarriageproject.org/about/.

National Network to End Domestic Violence. (2016). Because knowledge is power. Web site: http://www.womenslaw.org/.

National Opinion Research Center. (1996). *General social survey.* Chicago, IL: University of Chicago.

National Organization on Fetal Alcohol Syndrome. (2016). Play it smart. Alcohol and pregnancy don't mix. Web site: http://www.nofas.org/.

National Public Radio (NPR). (2012). What spermicide users should know, but often don't. Web site: http://www.npr.org/sections/health-shots/2012/02/06/146343080/what-spermicide-users-should-know-but-often-dont.

National Right to Life. (2016). Protecting life in America since 1968. Web site: http://www.nrlc.org/.

National Stepfamilies Resource Center. (2016). Web site: http://stepfamilies.info.

Northern Territory Government. (2008). *Strong families: Sharing cultural parenting knowledge.* Darwin, N.T., Australia: Department of Health and Community Services.

National Women's Hall of Fame. (2016). Showcasing great women... Inspiring all! Web site: https://www.womenofthehall.org/.

National Youth Violence Prevention Resource Center. (2009). Dating violence warning signs. Web site: http://www.safeyouth.org/scripts/faq/datingwarning.asp.

Nation's legal drugs may be its worst drugs. (1986, November 23). Lincoln [NE] *Journal Star,* pp. 1D, 3D.

Nelson, L. J., & Barry, C. M. (2005). Distinguishing features of emerging adulthood: The role of self-classification as an adult. *Journal of Adolescent Research, 20,* 242–262. New York, NY: Touchstone.

Neugarten, B. (1968). The awareness of middle age. In B. Neugarten (Ed.), *Middle age and aging.* Chicago, IL: University of Chicago Press.

Newport, F. (2013, January 3). Americans optimistic about life in 2013. Gallup Poll. Web site: http://www.gallup.com/poll/159698/americans-optimistic-life-2013.aspx.

New York Life. (2012). Adult children moving back home: Don't let "boomerang kids" derail your goals. Web site: http://www.newyorklife.com/.

New York State Administrative Regulations. (1995). 9 N.Y.C.R.R. 2104.6(d)(3).

Nicholson, J. M., Sanders, M. R., Halford, W. K., Phillips, M., & Whitton, S. W. (2008). The prevention and treatment of children's adjustment problems in stepfamilies. In J. Pryor (Ed.), *The international handbook of stepfamilies: Policy and practice in legal, research, and clinical environments* (pp. 485–521). Hoboken, NJ: Wiley.

Nicholson, T. (2001). 50+ world—Bright scene with shadows. *AARP Bulletin,* p. 25.

Niebuhr, R. (1988). Serenity prayer. In G. Carruth & E. Ehrlich (Eds.), *Harper book of American quotations.* New York, NY: Harper & Row. (Original work published 1951.)

Niemeyer, R. A. (2011). *Grief and bereavement in contemporary society: Bridging research and practice.* New York, NY: Routledge.

Noar, S. M., Carlyle, K., & Cole, C. (2006). Why communication is crucial: Meta-analysis of the relationship between safer sexual communication and condom use. *Journal of Health Communication, 11,* 365–390.

Noel, R. (2014, November). *Income and spending patterns among Black households.* United States Department of Labor, Bureau of Labor Statistics (vol. 3). Web site: https://www.bls.gov/opub/btn/volume-3/income-and-spending-patterns-among-black-households.htm.

Nolen, J. L. (2016). Learned helplessness. *Encyclopedia Britannica.* Web site: http://www.britannica.com/topic/learned-helplessness.

Norris, C. (1990). *What's wrong with postmodernism: Critical theory and the ends of philosophy.* Baltimore, MD: Johns Hopkins University Press.

Norris, T., Vines, P. L., & Hoeffel, E. M. (2012, January). *The American Indian and Alaska Native population: 2010.* (U.S. Census Bureau Report C2010BR-10). Web site: http://www.census.gov/prod/cen2010/briefs/c2010br-10.pdf.

Norwood, E. (1998). Poor folks have dreams. In C. L. Nelson & K. A. Wilson (Eds.), *Seeding the process of multicultural education* (pp. 73–78). Plymouth, MN: Minnesota Inclusiveness Program.

Notter, M. L., MacTavish, K. A., & Shamah, D. (2008). Pathways toward resilience among women in rural trailer parks. *Family Relations, 57,* 613–624.

NPR. (2004). Sex education in America: An NPR/Kaiser/Kennedy School poll. Web site: http://www.npr.org/templates/story/story.php?storyID=1622610.

Ochs, E., & Shohet, M. (2006). The cultural structuring of mealtime socialization. In R. W. Larson, A. R. Wiley, & K. R. Branscomb (Eds.), *Family mealtimes as a context of development and socialization* (pp. 35–49). San Francisco, CA: Jossey-Bass.

O'Farrell, T. J., & Fals-Stewart, W. (2001). Family-involved alcoholism treatment: An update. *Recent Developments in Alcoholism, 15,* 329–356.

O'Farrell, T. J., & Fals-Stewart, W. (2007). Alcohol abuse. *Journal of Marital and Family Therapy, 29*(1), 121–146.

Office of Population Research at Princeton University & the Association of Reproductive Health Professionals. (2016). Types of emergency contraception. Web site: http://ec.princeton.edu/questions/dose.html.

Olds, S. B., London, M. L., & Ladewig, P. (2004). *Maternal–newborn nursing and women's healthcare* (7th ed.). Upper Saddle River, NJ: Pearson/Prentice Hall.

Olsen, C., & Skogrand, L. (2009). Cultural implications and guidelines for Extension and familylife programming with Latino/Hispanic audiences. *The Forum for Family and Consumer Issues, 14.* Online journal: http://ncsu.edu/ffci/publications/2009/v14n1-2009-spring/olsen-skogrand.php.

Olsen, C. S. (2004). PeopleTALK: Enhancing Your Relationships. Kansas State University Agricultural Experiment Station and Cooperative Extension Service. Web site: http://www.bookstore.ksre.ksu.edu/pubs/MF2651.pdf.

Olson, A., & Olson, D. H. (2001). Ten traits of love. In J. R. Levine & H. J. Markman (Eds.), *Why do fools fall in love? Experiencing the magic, mystery, and meaning of successful relationships.* San Francisco, CA: Jossey-Bass.

Olson, D., Olson-Sigg, A., & Larson, P. (2008). *The couple checkup.* Nashville, TN: Thomas Nelson.

Olson, D. H. (1997). Family stress and coping: A multisystem perspective. In S. Dreman (Ed.), *The family on the threshold of the 21st century: Trends and implications* (pp. 259–280). Mahwah, NJ: Erlbaum.

Olson, D. H. (2011). FACES IV and the Circumplex Model: Validation study. *Journal of Marital & Family Therapy, 3,* 64–80.

Olson, D. H. (2016). Brief vitae on David H. Olson. PREPARE/ENRICH. Web site: https://www.prepare-enrich.com/webapp/pe/about_us/template/DisplaySecureContent.vm?id=pe*about_us*david_vitae.html.

Olson, D. H., Fournier, D. G., & Druckman, J. M. (2001). *PREPARE, PREPARE-MC and ENRICH inventories* (4th ed.). Minneapolis, MN: PREPARE/ENRICH.

Olson, D. H., Fye, S., & Olson, A. (1999). *National survey of happy and unhappy married couples.* Minneapolis, MN: Life Innovations.

Olson, D. H., & Gorall, D. M. (2003). Circumplex model of marital and family patterns. In F. Walsh (Ed.), *Normal family processes* (3rd ed., pp. 514-548). New York, NY: Guilford Press.

Olson, D. H., Larson, P. J., & Olson-Sigg, A. (2009). *PREPARE-ENRICH Program: Customized Version.* Minneapolis, MN: Life Innovations, Inc. Web site: http:// www.prepare-enrich.com.

Olson, D. H., Olson-Sigg, A., & Larson, P. J. (2008). *The couple checkup: Finding your relationship strengths.* Nashville, TN: Thomas Nelson.

Olson, D. H., Olson-Sigg, A., & Larson, P. J. (2008). *The couple checkup.* Nashville, TN: Thomas Nelson. Based on a survey of 50,000 couples, the book is an effort to help couples find the strengths in their relationship and build on these strengths.

Olson, D. H., Olson-Sigg, A., & Larson, P. J. (2009). National survey of marriage: Based on over 50,000 couples who took ENRICH. Unpublished manuscript. Minneapolis, MN: Live Innovations.

Olson, D. H., & Stewart, K. L. (1991). Family systems and health behaviors. In H. E. Schroeder (Ed.), *New directions in health psychology assessment. Series in applied psychology: Social issues and questions* (pp. 27-64). Washington, DC: Hemisphere.

O'Malley, C. J., Blankemeyer, M., Walker, K. K., & Dellmann-Jenkins, M. (2007). Children's reported communication with their parents about war. *Journal of Family Issues, 28,* 1639-1662.

Onedera, J. D. (2007). *The role of religion in marriage and family counseling.* London: Routledge/Taylor & Francis Group. Focuses on how each of the major world religions can influence family dynamics.

Ooms, T. (1998). *Toward more perfect unions: Putting marriage on the public agenda.* Washington, DC: Family Impact Seminar.

Oord, T. J. (2008) (Ed.). *The altruism reader: Selections from writings on love, religion, and science.* West Conshohocken, PA: Templeton Foundation Press.

Orwell, G. (1951). *Animal farm.* New York, NY: Penguin.

Osborn, F. (1939, Spring and Summer). The comprehensive program of eugenics and its social implications. *Living, 33*-38.

Otters, R. V., & Hollander, J. F. (2015). Leaving home and boomerang decisions: A family simulation protocol. *Marriage & Family Review, 51,* 39-58.

Ouytsel, J. V., Ponnet, K., & Walrave, M. (2017). The association of adolescents' dating violence victimization, well-being and engagement in risk behaviors. *Journal of Adolescence, 55,* 66-71.

Owen, J., & Fincham, F. D. (2011). Young adults' emotional reactions after hooking up encounters. *Archives of Sexual Behavior, 40,* 321-330.

Owen, J., Manthos, M., & Quirk, K. (2013). Dismantling study of Prevention and Relationship Education program: The effects of a structured communication intervention. *Journal of Family Psychology, 27,* 336-341.

Owens, T. J., & Suitor, J. J. (Eds.). (2007). *Advances in life course research: Vol. 12. Interpersonal relations across the life course.* Amsterdam: Elsevier.

Owings, A. (2011). *Indian voices: Listening to Native Americans.* New Brunswick, NJ: Rutgers University Press.

Padgett, D. (1997). The contribution of support networks to household labor in African American families. *Journal of Family Issues, 18*(3), 227-250.

Pan, P. A. (2000, December 26). Thoroughly modern women disconcert many in China. *The Washington Post,* p. A20.

Pan, Y. (2002). *On the freedom of mate selection.* Paper presented at the Building Family Strengths Conference, Shanghai Academy of Social Sciences, Shanghai, China.

Paragament, K. I. (2007). *Spiritually integrated psychotherapy: Understanding and addressing the sacred.* New York, NY: Guilford Press.

Parents Without Partners. (2010). Home page. Web site: http://www.parentswithoutpartners.org/.

Parkman, A. M. (1995). The deterioration of the family: A law and economics perspective. In G. B. Melton (Ed.), *The individual, the family, and social good: Personal fulfillment in times of change* (pp. 21-52). Lincoln, NE: University of Nebraska Press.

Parkman, A. M. (2000). *Good intentions gone awry: No-fault divorce and the American family.* Lanham, MD: Rowman & Littlefield.

Parsons, T. (1955). The American family: Its relations to personality and the social structure. In T. Parsons & R. F. Bales (Eds.), *Family socialization and interaction process* (pp. 3-21). Glencoe, IL: Free Press.

Parsons, T. (1965). The normal American family. In S. M. Farber, P. Mustacchi, & R. H. L. Wilson (Eds.), *Man and civilization: The family's search for survival* (pp. 31-50). New York, NY: McGraw-Hill.

Parsons, T., & Bales, R. F. (1955). *Family socialization and interaction process.* Glencoe, IL: Free Press.

Partnership for Drug-Free Kids. (2012, March 6). Survey: Ten percent of American adults report being in recovery from substance abuse or addiction. Web site: http://www.drugfree.org/newsroom/survey-ten-percent-of-american-adults-report-being-in-recovery-from-substance-abuse-or-addiction/.

Partnership for Drug-Free Kids. (2016). Support and resources for parents dealing with teen drug and alcohol abuse. Web site: http://www.drugfree.org/.

Pasley, K., & Garneau, C. (2012). Remarriage and stepfamily life. In F. Walsh (Ed.), *Normal family processes* (pp. 102-127). New York, NY: Guilford Press.

Passel, J. S., Wang, W., & Taylor, P. (2010, June 4). *One-in-seven new U.S. marriages is interracial or interethnic.* Pew Research Center. Web site: http://www.pewsocialtrends.org/2010/06/04/marrying-out/.

Patterson, C. (2009). Children of lesbian and gay parents: Psychology, law, and policy. *American Psychologist, 64,* 727-736.

Pawelski, J., Perrin, E. C., Fly, J. M., Allen, C. E., Crawford, J. E., Del Monte, M., et al. (2006). *Pediatrics, 118,* 349-363.

Peele, S., with Brodsky, A. (1991). *Love and addiction.* New York, NY: Taplinger.

Pelucchi, S., Paleari, F. G., Regalia, C., & Fincham, F. D. (2013). Self-forgiveness in romantic relationships: It matters to both of us. *Journal of Family Psychology, 27,* 541-549.

Peluso, P. (Ed.) (2007). *Infidelity: A practitioner's guide to working with couples in crisis.* London: Routledge Mental Health/Taylor & Francis Group. When one partner in a relationship is unfaithful to the other, salvaging the relationship takes a lot of work by both parties.

Pence, E. L., & McDonnell, C. (2000). Developing policies and protocols in Duluth, Minnesota. In J. Hanmer & C. Itzin (Eds.), *Home truths about domestic violence: Feminist influences on policy and practice* (pp. 249-268). London: RoutledgeFalmer.

Pensanti, H. (2001). *Better sex for you: A natural approach to finding new levels of sexual satisfaction.* Lake Maru, FL: Siloam Press.

Peplau, L. A., & Fingerhut, A. W. (2007). The close relationships of lesbians and gay men. *Annual Review of Psychology, 58,* 405-424. Web site: http://www.ppcok.org/brochure.php?id=2.

Peplau, L. A., Veniegas, R. C., & Campbell, S. M. (1996). Gay and lesbian relationships. In R. C. Savin-Williams & K. M. Cohen (Eds.), *The lives of lesbians, gays, and bisexuals: Children to adults* (pp. 250–273). Ft. Worth, TX: Harcourt.

Perez, L. (2004, December 26). In three city homes, grief for the ultimate loss, fear for a son sent to Iraq, and relief for one who is back. *Newsday*. Web site: www.newsday.com/news/printedition/newyork/nyc-nyiraq264096646dec26,0,7962315.print.story?coll=nyc-nynews-print.

Perreira, K., Chapman, M., & Stein, G. (2006). Becoming an American parent: Overcoming challenges and finding strength in a new immigrant Latino community. *Journal of Family Issues, 27*, 1383–1414.

Perrin, E. C., & Siegel, B. S. (2013). *Promoting the well-being of children whose parents are gay or lesbian*. Technical Report from American Academy of Pediatrics. Web site: http://pediatrics.aappublications.org/content/pediatrics/early/2013/03/18/peds.2013-0376.full.pdf.

PETA. (2016). Cruelty to animals and family violence. Web site: http://www.peta.org/issues/companion-animal-issues/cruel-practices/human-animal-abuse/animal-family-violence/.

Peters, M. F. (1981). Strengths of Black families. In N. Stinnett, J. DeFrain, K. King, P. Knaub, & G. Rowe (Eds.), *Family strengths 3: Roots of well-being* (pp. 73–91). Lincoln, NE: University of Nebraska Press.

Peterson, K. S. (1992a, March 12). Adults should know status of parents. *USA Today*, p. 1D.

Peterson, K. S. (1992b, March 12). Parents hand down financial attitudes. *USA Today*, p. 4D.

Pew Research Center. (2006, February 13). Are we happy yet? Web site: http://pewsocialtrends.org/assets/pdf/AreWeHappyYet.pdf.

Pew Research Center. (2007, September 14). 78% favor sex education in public schools. Web site: http://www.pewresearch.org/daily-number/favor-sex-education-in-public-schools/.

Pew Research Center. (2008, February 11). U.S. population projections: 2005–2050. Web site: http://www.pewsocialtrends.org/2008/02/11/us-population-projections-2005-2050/.

Pew Research Center (2010). *The return of multi-generational family household*. Web site: http://pewsocialtrends.org.

Pew Research Center. (2013, January 30). The sandwich generation: Rising financial burdens for middle-aged Americans. Web site: http://www.pewsocialtrends.org/2013/01/30/the-sandwich-generation/.

Pew Research Center (2013, April 4). The rise of Asian Americans. Web site: http://www.pewsocialtrends.org/2012/06/19/the-rise-of-asian-americans/.

Pew Research Center. (2014, January 14). French more accepting of infidelity than people in other countries. Web site: http://www.pewresearch.org/fact-tank/2014/01/14/french-more-accepting-of-infidelity-than-people-in-other-countries/.

Pew Research Center. (2014, April 8). After decades of decline, a rise in stay-at-home mothers. Web site: http://www.pewsocialtrends.org/2014/04/08/after-decades-of-decline-a-rise-in-stay-at-home-mothers/.

Pew Research Center. (2014, April 15). What's morally acceptable? It depends on where in the world you live. Web site: http://www.pewresearch.org/fact-tank/2014/04/15/whats-morally-acceptable-it-depends-on-where-in-the-world-you-live/.

Pew Research Center. (2014, September 24). Record share of Americans have never married as values, economics and gender patterns change. Pew Research Center. Web site: http://www.pewsocialtrends.org/2014/09/24/record-share-of-americans-have-never-married/.

Pew Research Center. (2014, December 22). Fewer than half of U.S. kids today live in a 'traditional' family. Web site: http://www.pewresearch.org/fact-tank/2014/12/22/less-than-half-of-u-s-kids-today-live-in-a-traditional-family/.

Pew Research Center. (2015, January 16). Pew: Only 46 percent of US families are 'traditional'. Web site: http://www.newsmax.com/US/Family-single-parent-children-Pew-Research/2015/01/16/id/619047/.

Pew Research Center. (2015, June 26). Americans' internet access: 2000–2015. Web site: http://www.pewinternet.org/2015/06/26/americans-internet-access-2000-2015/.

Pew Research Center. (2015, June 29). Most Americans now say learning their child is gay wouldn't upset them. Web site: http://www.pewresearch.org/fact-tank/2015/06/29/most-americans-now-say-learning-their-child-is-gay-wouldnt-upset-them/.

Pew Research Center. (2015, September 13). 5 facts about American grandparents. Web site: http://www.pewresearch.org/fact-tank/2015/09/13/5-facts-about-american-grandparents/.

Pew Research Center. (2016, February 29). 5 facts about online dating. Web site: http://www.pewresearch.org/fact-tank/2016/02/29/5-facts-about-online-dating/.

Pew Research Center (2016, March 31). Campaign exposes fissures over issues, values and how life has changed in the U.S. Web site: http://www.people-press.org/2016/03/31/campaign-exposes-fissures-over-issues-values-and-how-life-has-changed-in-the-u-s/.

Pew Research Center. (2016). Marriage and family. Web site: http://www.pewsocialtrends.org/series/the-decline-of-marriage/.

Pew Research Center. (2017, January 26). 5 facts about abortion. Web site: http://www.pewresearch.org/fact-tank/2017/01/26/5-facts-about-abortion/.

Pew Research Center for the People and the Press. (2005, August 3). Abortion and rights of terror suspects top court issues. Web site: http://people-press.org/reports/display.php3?ReportID=253.

Physician Leadership on National Drug Policy. (2000). Position paper on drug policy. Providence, RI: Brown University Center for Alcohol and Addiction Studies.

Pick Program (n.d.). Love Thinks. Web site: http://www.lovethinks.com/PICK/PICK_Program.

Pieve, L. (2001). An ethnographic study of the perceptions of Puerto Rican pregnant teenagers. *Dissertation Abstracts International-A, 62*(03), 1226.

Pines, A. M. (2005). *Falling in love: Why we choose the lovers we choose* (2nd ed.). New York, NY: Routledge/Taylor & Francis Group.

Planned Parenthood. (2006). 5 ways to prevent abortion (and one way that won't work). Web site: http://www.jhu.edu/choice/files/5waystopreventabortion.pdf.

Planned Parenthood. (2009). Pregnancy test. Web site: http://www.plannedparenthood.org/health-topics/pregnancy/pregnancy-test-21227.htm.

Planned Parenthood. (2014). By the numbers. Web site: https://www.plannedparenthood.org/files/9313/9611/7194/Planned_Parenthood_By_The_Numbers.pdf.

Planned Parenthood. (2016a). Birth control patch. Web site: https://www.plannedparenthood.org/learn/birth-control/birth-control-patch.

Planned Parenthood. (2016b). Abortion. Web site: https://www.plannedparenthood.org/learn/abortion.

Planned Parenthood. (2016c). Worried? Chat now. Web site: https://www.plannedparenthood.org/online-tools/chat.

Planned Parenthood. (2016d). Care. No matter what. Web site: https://www.plannedparenthood.org/.

Planned Parenthood. (2016e). Infertility. Web site: https://www.plannedparenthood.org/learn/pregnancy/infertility.

Planned Parenthood. (2016f). Am I pregnant? Web site: https://www.plannedparenthood.org/online-tools/am-i-pregnant.

Planned Parenthood Affiliates of New Jersey. (2006). Five ways to prevent abortion. Web site: http://www.plannedparenthoodnj.org/library/topic/planned_parenthood/five_ways_prevent-abortion.

Planned Parenthood Federation of America. (1985, Spring). Five ways to prevent abortion (and one way that won't). In *Family matters* (p. 2). Lincoln, NE: Planned Parenthood of Lincoln.

Planned Parenthood of Central Oklahoma. (2010). Ten ridiculous ideas that will make a father out of you. Web site: http://www.ppcok.org/brochure.php?id=2.

Planned Parenthood of the Gulf Coast. (2016). Family planning—A special and urgent concern. Web site: https://www.plannedparenthood.org/planned-parenthood-gulf-coast/mlk-acceptance-speech.

Pool, J. N., & Olson-Sigg, A. (2010). *PREPARE-ENRICH-INSPIRE for Teens: Preparing Youth, Enriching Relationships and Inspiring Futures*. Berkeley, CA: The Dibble Institute.

Poortman, A., & van der Lippe, T. (2009). Attitudes toward housework and child care and the gendered division of labor. *Journal of Marriage and Family, 71*, 526–541.

Popenoe, D. (2008). *Cohabitation, marriage, and child wellbeing: A cross-national perspective*. Retrieved from the National Marriage Project Web site: http://www.virginia.edu/marriageproject/pdfs/NMP2008 CohabitationReport.pdf.

Popenoe, D., & Whitehead, B. D. (1999a). *Should we live together? What young adults need to know about cohabitation before marriage*. New Brunswick, NJ: Rutgers University, National Marriage Project.

Popenoe, D., & Whitehead, B. D. (1999b). *The state of our unions*. 1996 New Brunswick, NJ: Rutgers University, National Marriage Project.

Popenoe, D., & Whitehead, B. D. (2004). *The state of our unions 2004*. New Brunswick, NJ: Rutgers University, National Marriage Project.

Popenoe, D., & Whitehead, R. D. (2010). *The state of our unions 2010*. Piscataway, NJ: National Marriage Project, Rutgers University.

Population Reference Bureau. (2012). Fact sheet: The decline in U.S. fertility. Web site: http://www.prb.org/publications/datasheets/2012/world-population-data-sheet/fact-sheet-us-population.aspx.

Porche, M. V., & Purvin, D. M. (2008). "Never in our lifetime": Legal marriage for same-sex couples in long-term relationships. *Family Relations, 57*, 144–159.

Porter, J. (1999, January 10). It's time to start thinking about electing a female president. Lincoln [NE] *Journal Star*, p. 6D.

Poverty Solutions. (n.d.). Poverty facts. University of Michigan. Web site: http://www.npc.umich.edu/poverty/.

Powell, B., Bolzendahl, C., Geist, C., & Carr Steelman, L. (2010). *Counted out: Same-sex relations and Americans' definitions of family*. New York, NY: Russell Sage Foundation.

PREPARE-ENRICH. (2016). Building strong marriages. Web site: https://www.prepare-enrich.com/webapp/pe/faq/template/DisplaySecureContent.vm?id=pe*faq*overview.html.

Prevent Child Abuse America. (2016). All children deserve #greatchildhoods. Web site: http://preventchildabuse.org/.

Price, C. A., & Nesteruk, O. (2015). What to expect when you retire: By women for women. *Marriage & Family Review, 51*, 418–440.

ProCon.org. (2016). Gay marriage timeline: History of the same-sex marriage debate. Web site: http://gaymarriage.procon.org/view.timeline.php?timelineID=000030.

Proctor, B. D., & Dalaker, J. (2003). *Poverty in the United States: 2002*. Current Population Reports, Consumer Income. Washington, DC: U.S. Census Bureau.

Proctor, B. D., Semega, J. L., & Kollar, M. (2016, September). *Income and poverty in the United States: 2015*. U.S. Census Bureau, Current Population Reports. Web site: https://www.census.gov/content/dam/Census/library/publications/2016/demo/p60-256.pdf.

Pryor, J. (2008). (Ed.). *The international handbook of stepfamilies: Policy and practice in legal, research, and clinical environments*. Hoboken, NJ: Wiley.

Public Broadcasting Service. (2012). Senior living. *Independent Lens*. Web site: http://www.pbs.org/independentlens/almosthome/senior.html.

Puente, S., & Cohen, D. (2003). Jealousy and the meaning (or non-meaning) of violence. *Personality and Social Psychology Bulletin, 29*(4), 449–460.

Purplefairy, L. (2012). The silent suffering of parent abuse: When children abuse parents. Web site: http://222.loupurplefairy.hubpages.com/hub/The-Silent-Suffering-of-Parent-Abuse-When-Children-Abuse-P...

Putman, R. D. (2015). *Our kids*. New York, NY: Simon & Schuster.

Qian, Z., & Lichter, D. T. (2007). Social boundaries and marital assimilation: Interpreting trends in racial and ethnic intermarriage. *American Sociological Review, 72*, 68–94.

Qian, Z., & Lichter, D. T. (2011). Changing patterns of interracial marriage in a multiracial society. *Journal of Marriage and Family, 73*, 1065–1083.

Qualls, S. H. (2013). "Caregiving is just what families do": Challenges of aging families and health. National Council on Family Relations. *Family Focus on Aging*, FF59, pp. F2–F20.

Raetz, K. (2011). *Birth order and couple satisfaction*. Prepare Enrich. Web site: https://www.prepare-enrich.com/pe/pdf/research/2011/birth_order_and_couple_satisfaction_Raetz_2011.pdf.

Raley, S. B., Mattingly, M. J., & Bianchi, S. (2006). How dual are dual-income couples? Documenting change from 1970–2001. *Journal of Marriage and the Family, 68*, 11–28.

Rank, M. R., & Hirschl, T. A. (1999). The economic risk of childhood in America: Estimating the probability of poverty across the formative years. *Journal of Marriage and the Family, 61*, 1058–1067.

Rank, M. R., & Hirschl, T. A. (2015). The likelihood of experiencing relative poverty over the life course. *PLoS One, 10*(7). Web site: http://www.ncbi.nlm.nih.gov/pmc/articles/PMC4511740/.

Rank, M. R., & Williams, J. H. (2010). A life course approach to understanding poverty among older American adults. *Families in Society: The Journal of Contemporary Social Services, 91*(4), 337–441.

Rappleyea, D. L., Taylor, A. C., & Fang, X. (2014). Gender differences and communication technology use among emerging adults in the initiation of dating relationships. *Marriage & Family Review, 50*, 269–284.

Raymond, E. G., & Grimes, D. A. (2012, February). The comparative safety of legal induced abortion and childbirth in the United States. *Obstetrics and Gynecology, 119*, 215–219. Web site: http://www.ncbi.nlm.nih.gov/pubmed/22270271.

Real Simple. (2012, June). *The simple list*, p. 8.

Recker, N. K. (2001). The wicked stepmother myth. Family Life Month Packet. Columbus, OH: Ohio State University Extension Web site: http://ohioline.osu.edu/flm01/FS04.html.

Reed, J., England, P., Littlejohn, K., Conroy Bass, B., & Caudillo, M. L. (2014). Consistent and inconsistent contraception among young women: Insights from qualitative interviews. *Family Relations, 63*(April), 244–258.

Regnerus, M. (2012). How different are the adult children of parents who have same-sex relationships? Findings from the New Family Structures Study. *Social Science Research, 41,* 752-770.

Reid, G. (2015, May 15). Outlawed: Legal discrimination against gays and lesbians. Human Rights Watch. Web site: https://www.hrw.org/news/2015/05/15/outlawed-legal-discrimination-against-gays-and-lesbians.

Reinisch, J., & Beasley, R. (1994). *The Kinsey Institute new report on sex* (p. 45). New York, NY: St. Martin's.

Remez, L. (1998). In Turkey, women's fertility is linked to education, employment and freedom to choose a husband. *International Family Planning Perspectives, 24*(2), 97-98.

Rennison, C. M. (2003, February). Intimate partner violence, 1993-2001. U.S. Department of Justice, Office of Justice Programs. Web site: http://www.ojp.usdoj.gov/bjs.

Rettig, K. D., Christensen, D. H., & Dahl, C. M. (1991). Impact of child support guidelines on the economic well-being of children. *Family Relations, 40,* 167-175.

Rettig, K. D., Leichtentritt, R. D., & Stanton, L. M. (1999). Understanding noncustodial fathers' family and life satisfaction from resource theory perspective. *Journal of Family Issues, 20*(4), 507-538.

Rich, J. (2003). *The couple's guide to love and money.* Oakland, CA: New Harbinger.

Ridley, C. A., Peterman, D. J., & Avery, A. W. (1978, April). Cohabitation: Does it make for a better marriage? *Family Coordinator,* pp. 129-136.

Rilke, R. M. (1904). *Letters to a young poet.* Letter 7, March 14. New York, NY: W. W. Norton.

Rilke, R. M. (1993). *Letters to a young poet.* Boston, MA: Shambhala.

Rivett, M. (2009). *Family therapy: 100 key points and techniques.* London: Routledge/Taylor & Francis Group. Family therapy theory and practice; concise and jargon-free.

Rix, S. E. (2014, September). America's aging labor force. AARP Public Policy Institute. Web site: http://www.aarp.org/content/dam/aarp/ppi/2014-10/aging-labor-force-fact-sheet-aarp.pdf.

Robbins, R., Scherman, A., Holman, H., & Wilson, J. (2005). Roles of American Indian grandparents in times of cultural crises. *Journal of Cultural Diversity, 12,* 62-68.

Roberts, L. (2005). Alcohol and the marital relationship. *Family Focus,* pp. 12-13.

Roberts, S. (2006, October 15). To be married means to be outnumbered in America. *The New York Times,* p. A22.

Robinson, J. (2012). *Communication miracles for couples. Easy and effective tools to create more love and less conflict.* San Francisco, CA: Red Wheel.

Robinson, P. W., Davidson, L. J., & Drebot, M. E. (2004). Parent abuse on the rise: A historical review. *American Association of Behavioral Social Science Online Journal.* Web site: http://www.aabss.org.

Rodgers, J. L., Nakonezny, P. A., & Shull, R. D. (1997). The effect of no-fault divorce legislation on divorce rates: A response to a reconsideration. *Journal of Marriage and the Family, 59*(4), 1026-1030.

Rogers, F. (2009). *Good reads.* Web site: http://www.goodreads.com/quotes/show/157666.

Rokach, A. (2005). Coping with loneliness during pregnancy and motherhood. *Psychology and Education, 42*(1), 1-12.

Rokach, A. (2006). Loneliness in domestically abused women. *Psychological Reports, 98*(2), 367-373.

Roosa, M. W., Tein, J.-Y., Groppenbacher, N., Michaels, M., & Dumka, L. (1993). Mothers' parenting behavior and child mental health in families with a problem drinking parent. *Journal of Marriage and the Family, 55,* 107-118.

Rosato, D. (2012). The best reason to rethink retirement, says psychologist Laura Carstensen, is the fact that we'll be spending so many more years in it. *CNNMoney.com,* pp. 99-102.

Rosenblum, K., & Travis, T. (2016). *The meaning of difference* (7th ed.). New York, NY: McGraw-Hill.

Rosenfeld, M. J., & Thomas, R. J. (2012). Searching for a mate: The rise of the Internet as a social intermediary. *American Sociological Review, 77,* 523-547.

Ross, M. E., & Aday, L. A. (2006). Stress and coping in African American grandparents who are raising their grandchildren. *Journal of Family Issues, 27,* 912-932.

Rowe, C. L. (2003). Family-based interventions for substance abuse: A profile of two models. *The Family Psychologist, 19*(4), 4-9.

Rowe, D. (2008). *What should I believe? Why our beliefs about the nature of death and the purpose of life dominate our lives.* London and New York: Routledge. If we use our beliefs as a defense against our feelings of worthlessness, we feel compelled to force our beliefs on other people by coercion or aggression. But if we can create a set of beliefs expressed in religious or philosophical metaphors that are meaningful to us, we can live in peace with ourselves and others.

Rudy, D., & Grusec, J. E. (2006). Authoritarian parenting in individualist and collectivist groups: Associations with maternal emotion and cognition and children's self-esteem. *Journal of Family Psychology, 20*(1), 68-78.

Russell, B. (1938). *Power: A new social analysis.* New York, NY: Norton.

Russell, S. T., & Horn, S. S. (2016). *Sexual orientation, gender identity, and schooling.* New York, NY: Oxford University Press.

Russo, N. F., & Dabul, A. J. (1997). The relationship of abortion to well-being: Do race and religion make a difference? *Professional Psychology: Research and Practice, 28*(1), 23-31.

Ryan, R. M., Kalil, A., & Ziol-Guest, K. M. (2008). Longitudinal patterns of nonresident fathers' involvement: The role of resources and relations. *Journal of Marriage and the Family, 70,* 962-977.

Rye, B. J., & Meaney, G. L. (2010). Self-defense, sexism, and etiological beliefs: Predictors of attitudes toward gay and lesbian adoption. *Journal of GLBT Family Studies, 6,* 1-24.

Sager, C. J., Brown, H. S., Crohn, H., Engel, T., Rodstein, E., & Walker, L. (1983). *Treating the remarried family.* New York, NY: Brunner/Mazel.

Sahlstein Parcell, E. M., & Maguire, K. C. (2014, March 10). Turning points and trajectories in military deployment. *Journal of Family Communication, 14*(2), 129-148. Web site: http://www.tandfonline.com/doi/abs/10.1080/15267431.2013.864293. Researchers found that most military wives in a sample of 50 reflected turbulence in family life during the predeployment and deployment phases, and declining or dipped satisfaction during the postdeployment period.

Saluter, A. (1996). *Marital status and living arrangements.* Washington, DC: United States Bureau of the Census.

Same-Sex Marriage. (2016). *Wikipedia.* Web site: https://en.wikipedia.org/wiki/Same-sex_marriage.

Sammons, M. T. (2005). Psychology in the public sector: Addressing the psychological effects of combat in the U.S. Navy. *American Psychologist, 162,* 123-129.

Sandler, L. (2010, July 19). One and done. *Time, 176*(3), 34-41.

Sarkisian, N. (March, 2007). Race, class, and extended family involvement. *Family Focus,* pp. 14-15.

Sarkisian, N., Gerena, M., & Gerstel, N. (2006). Extended family ties among Mexicans, Puerto Ricans, and Whites: Superintegration or disintegration? *Family Relations, 55,* 331-344.

Sassler, S. (2010). Partnering across the life course: Sex, relationships, and mate selection. *Journal of Marriage and Family, 72*, 557–574.

Sassler, S., & Miller, A. (2011). Class differences in cohabitation processes. *Family Relations, 60*, 163–177.

Satir, V. (1988). *The new peoplemaking.* Palo Alto, CA: Science and Behavior Books.

Saving 2 Invest (n.d.). *A look at the average American income, earnings and poverty by household, gender and race.* Web site: http://www.savingtoinvest.com/2010/10/income-earnings-and-poverty-by-household-gender-and-race.html.

Schachner, D. A., Shaver, P. R., & Gillath, O. (2008). Attachment style and long-term singlehood. *Personal Relationships, 15*, 479–491. Web site: http://onlinelibrary.wiley.com/doi/10.1111/j.1475-6811.2008.00211.x/abstract.

Scheinkman, M. (2005). Beyond the trauma of betrayal: Reconsidering affairs in couples therapy. *Family Process, 44*, 227–244.

Schneider, D. (2015). The Great Recession, fertility, and uncertainty: Evidence from the United States. *Journal of Marriage and Family, 77*, 1144–1156.

Schneider, D., Harknett, K., & McLanahan, S. (2016). Intimate partner violence in the Great Recession. *Demography, 53*, 471–505.

Schooler, J. E., & Atwood, T. C. (2008). *The whole life adoption book: Realistic advice for building a healthy adoptive family.* Colorado Springs, CO: NavPress.

Schoppe-Sullivan, S. (2010, Summer). Maternal gatekeeping: Listening for the "creeaak." *NCFR Report, 55.2*, F6–F8.

Schoppe-Sullivan, S. (2010, Winter). Maternal gatekeeping: Listening for the "creeaak." *Family Focus, Issue 55.3*(47), 24, 26.

Schramm, D. G. (2006). Individual and social costs of divorce in Utah. *Journal of Family and Economic Issues, 27*, 133–151.

Schramm, D. G., Marshall, J. P., Harris, V. W., & Lee, T. R. (2005). After "I do": The newlywed transition. *Marriage and Family Review, 38*, 45–67.

Schultz, N. C., Schultz, C. L., & Olson, D. H. (1991). Couple strengths and stressors in complex and simple stepfamilies in Australia. *Journal of Marriage and the Family, 53*, 555–564.

Schwartz, J., Raine, G., & Robins, K. (1987, May 11). A "superminority" tops out. *Newsweek*, pp. 48–49.

Schwartz, P. (2015). *Better sex: AARP's guide to sex after 50.* AARP. Web site: http://www.aarp.org/entertainment/books/bookstore/home-family-caregiving/info-2016/better-sex-after-50.html.

Scientific American. (2013). Is divorce bad for children? Web site: http://www.scientificamerican.com/article/is-divorce-bad-for-children/.

Scott, M., Booth, A., King, V., & Johnson, D. (2007). Postdivorce father-adolescent closeness. *Journal of Marriage and the Family, 69*, 1194–1209.

Scott, M. J. (2007). *Moving on after trauma.* New York, NY: Routledge.

Search Institute. (2006). *Introduction to assets.* Minneapolis, MN: Author. Web site: http://www.search-institute.org/assets.

Search Institute. (2013). Discovering what kids need to succeed. Web site: http://www.search-institute.org/.

Sedlak, A. J., Mettenburg, J., Basena, M., Petta, I., McPherson, K., Greene, A., & Li, S. (2010). *Fourth national incidence study of child abuse and neglect (NIS-4): Report to Congress.* Washington, DC: U. S. Department of Health and Human Services, Administration for Children and Families. Web site: http://www.acf.hhs.gov/programs/opre/abuse_neglect/natl_incid/nis4_report_congress_full_pdf_jan2010.pdf.

Seidman, G. (2014, October 28). What's really behind jealousy, and what to do about it. *Psychology Today.* Web site: https://www.psychologytoday.com/blog/close-encounters/201410/whats-really-behind-jealousy-and-what-do-about-it.

Seiler, W. J., & Beall, M. L. (2011). *Communication: Making connections* (8th ed.). Boston, MA: Pearson/Allyn and Bacon.

Seligman, M. E. (2002). *Authentic happiness.* New York, NY: Free Press.

Selle, R. (1998, May). People in the news: Feminism's matriarch. *The World and I*, p. 51.

Selye, H. (1974). *The stress of life* (2nd ed.). New York, NY: McGraw-Hill.

Sen, A. (2001, October 27–November 9). Many faces of gender inequality. *Frontline.* Web site: http://www.flonnet.com/fl18220040.htm.

Sex Education in the United States. (2016). *Wikipedia.* Web site: https://en.wikipedia.org/wiki/Sex_education_in_the_United_States.

Sex Information and Education Council of the U.S. (2001). Community action kit. Web site: http://www.siecus.org/advocacy/kits0005.html.

Sex Information and Education Council of the U.S. (2004). Adolescence and abstinence fact sheet. Web site: http://www.siecus.org/pubs/fact/fact0001.html.

Sexuality Information and Education Council of the United States (SIECUS). (2016). Founded by Dr. Mary S. Calderone in 1964, who was concerned about the lack of information about sexuality for both young people and adults. So, at the age of 60, "with determination to live in a world in which sexuality was viewed as a natural and healthy part of life," she founded SIECUS, which publishes books, journals, and resources for professionals, parents, and the public. Web site: http://www.siecus.org/.

Sharp, E. A., & Ganong, L. (2011). "I'm a loser, I'm not married, let's just all look at me": Ever-single women's perceptions of their social environment. *Journal of Family Issues, 32*, 956–980.

Sheldon, A. (2009). *Big brother now: A story about me and our new baby* and *Big sister now: A story about me and our new baby.* Magination Press. Web site: http://www.magination-press.com.

Sherman, C. W. (2006, December). Remarriage and stepfamily in later life. *Family Focus*, pp. 8–9.

Sherman, C. W., & Bauer, J. W. (2008). Financial conflicts facing late-life remarried Alzheimer's disease caregivers. *Family Relations, 57*, 492–503.

Shoemake, E. (2007). Human mate selection theory: An integrated evolutionary and social approach. *Journal of Scientific Psychology, Fall*, 35–41.

Shorris, E. (1992). *Latinos: A biography of the people.* New York, NY: Norton.

Shostak, A. (1987). Singlehood. In M. Sussman & S. Steinmetz (Eds.), *Handbook of marriage and the family.* New York, NY: Plenum.

Shpancer, N. (2014, December 2). Laws of attractiveness: How do we select a life partner? *Psychology Today.* Web site: https://www.psychologytoday.com/blog/insight-therapy/201412/laws-attraction-how-do-we-select-life-partner.

Silva, M. (2002). The effectiveness of school-based sex education programs in the promotion of abstinent behavior: A meta-analysis. *Health Education Research, 17*(4), 471–481.

Silverstein, L. B. (2010). Louise Bordeaux Silverstein, Yeshiva University. Web site: http://www.yu.edu/Ferkauf/people/Silverstein.asp.

Silverstein, M., & Giarrusso, R. (2010). Aging and family life: A decade review. *Journal of Marriage and Family, 72* (October), 1039–1058. An excellent overview of recent trends in research.

Simons, J., & Carey, M. P. (2008). Prevalence of sexual dysfunction. Published at PubMed Central (PMC), and archive of the National

Institutes of Health's National Library of Medicine. Web site: http://www.ncbi.nlh.gov/pmc/articles/PMC2426773/.

Singletary, M. (2004, October 20). College students should steer clear of credit cards. *The Washington Post.* Web site: http://washingtonpost.com/wp-dyn/articles/A50054-2004(ct20.html).

Skogrand, L. (2004). A process for learning about and creating programming for culturally diverse audiences. *Forum of Family and Consumer Issues, 9*. Online journal: http://www.ces.ncsu.edu/depts/fcs/pub/forum.html.

Skogrand, L., Barrios-Bell, A., & Higginbotham, B. (2009). Stepfamily education for Latino families: Implications for practice. *Journal of Couple and Relationship Therapy: Innovations in Clinical and Educational Interventions, 8*, 113-128.

Skogrand, L., & Chaney, C. (2010). Strong marriages in African American culture. Unpublished raw data.

Skogrand, L., DeFrain, N., DeFrain, J., & Jones, J. (2007). *Surviving and transcending a traumatic childhood: The dark thread.* New York, NY: Haworth.

Skogrand, L., DeFrain, N., DeFrain, J., & Jones, J. E. (2007). *Surviving and transcending a traumatic childhood: The dark thread.* New York, NY: Routledge.

Skogrand, L., Hatch, D., & Singh, A. (2009). Strong marriages in Latino culture. In R. Dalla, J. DeFrain, J. Johnson, & D. Abbott (Eds.), *Strengths and challenges of new immigrant families: Implications for research, policy, education, and service* (pp. 117-134). Lexington, MA: Lexington Press.

Skogrand, L., Henderson, K., & Higginbotham, B. (2006). Sandwich generation (fact sheet). Utah State University Cooperative Extension. Web site: http://extension.usu.edu/cooperative.

Skogrand, L., Johnson, A. C., Horrocks, A., & DeFrain, J. (2011). Financial management practices of couples with great marriages. *Journal of Family and Economic Issues, 32*, 27-35.

Skogrand, L., Mendez, E., & Higginbotham, B. (2013). Stepfamily education: A case study of two lesbian couples. *Marriage & Family Review, 49*, 504-519.

Skogrand, L., Mendez, E., & Higginbotham, B. (2014). Latina women's experiences in a stepfamily education course. *The Family Journal, 22*, 49-55.

Skogrand, L., Mueller, L., Crook, R., Spotted Elk, D., Dayzie, I., LeBlanc, H., & Rosenband, R. (2007). *Strong marriages for Navajo couples: Couple activity book*. Web site http://extension.usu.edu/files/publications/publication/pub__8139744.pdf.

Skogrand, L., Mueller, M. L., Arrington, R., LeBlanc, H., Spotted Elk, D., Dayzie, I., & Rosenband, R. (2008). Strong Navajo marriages. *American Indian and Alaska Native Mental Health Research: The Journal of the National Center, 15*, 25-41. Online journal: http://aianp.uchsc.edu/ncaianmhr/journal_online.htm.

Skogrand, L., Mueller, M. L., Arrington, R., LeBlanc, H., Spotted Elk, D., Dayzie, I., & Rosenband, R. (2008). Strong Navajo marriages. *American Indian and Alaska Native Mental Health Research: The Journal of the National Center, 15*, 25-41. Web site: http://www.ucdenver.edu/academics/colleges/PublicHealth/research/centers/CAIANH/journal/Documents/Volume%2015/15(2)_Skogrand_Strong_Navajo_Marriages_25-41.pdf.

Skogrand, L., Reck, K., Higginbotham, B., Adler-Baeder, F., & Dansie, L. (2010). Recruitment and retention for stepfamily education. *Journal of Couple & Relationship Therapy, 9*, 448-465.

Skogrand, L., Schramm, D. G., Marshall, J. P., & Lee, T. (2005). The effects of debt on newlyweds and implications for education. *Journal of Extension, 43.* Web site: http://www.joe.org/joe/2005june/rb7.shtml.

Skolnick, A. S., & Skolnick, J. H. (1977). *Family in transition.* Boston, MA: Little, Brown.

Slater, L. (2006, February). This thing called love. *National Geographic*, 32-49.

Smart Marriages®. (2016). The coalition for marriage, family, and couples education. Web site: http://www.smartmarriages.com/index.html.

Smiler, A. P. (2008). "I wanted to get to know her better": Adolescent boys' dating motives, masculinity ideology, and sexual behavior. *Journal of Adolescence, 31*, 17-32.

Smith, A. (2016, February 11). *15% of American adults have used online dating sites or mobile dating apps*. Pew Research Center. Web site: http://www.pewinternet.org/2016/02/11/15-percent-of-american-adults-have-used-online-dating-sites-or-mobile-dating-apps/.

Smith, A. (2016, February 29). *5 facts about online dating*. Pew Research Center. Web site: http://www.pewresearch.org/fact-tank/2016/02/29/5-facts-about-online-dating/.

Smith, J. A. (2009). *The daddy shift: How stay-at-home dads, breadwinning moms, and shared parenting are transforming the American family*. Boston, MA: Beacon Press.

Smith, K. (2002). *Who's minding the kids? Child care arrangements: Spring 1997* (pp. 70-86). Washington, DC: U.S. Census Bureau.

Smith, S. R., & Hamon, R. R. (2012). *Exploring family theories* (3rd ed.). New York, NY: Oxford University Press.

Smith, T. W. (2006). American sexual behavior: Trends, socio-demographic differences, and risk behavior. National Opinion Research Center, University of Chicago. *General Social Survey Topical Report No. 25*. Web site: http://www.norc.org/PDFs/Publications/AmericanSexualBehavior2006.pdf.

Solheim, C. (2008, June). Family resource management through multicultural lenses. *Family Focus, FF38*, 1-2, 4.

Solot, D., & Miller, M. (2000). Ten ways to improve your chances for a good marriage after cohabitation. Alternatives to marriage. Web site: http://www.unmarried.org/ten-ways-to-improve-your-chances-for-a-good-marriage.

Solot, D., & Miller, M. (2009). Sex discussed here! Sex education unlike any you've had before. Web site: http://www.sexualityeducation.com/.

Somer, E. (2007). Stress and diet. In A. Monat, R. S. Lazarus, & R. Reevy (Eds.), *The Praeger handbook on stress and coping* (vol. 2, pp. 509-528). Westport, CT: Praeger.

Sorkhabi, N., & Mandara, J. (2013). Are the effects of Baumrind's parenting styles culturally specific or culturally equivalent? In R. E. Larzelere, A. S. Morris, & A. W. Harrist (Eds.), *Authoritative parenting: Synthesizing nurturance and discipline for optimal child development* (pp. 113-135). Washington, DC: American Psychological Association.

Specter, M. (2015, August 20). Planned Parenthood means fewer abortions. *The New Yorker*. Web site: http://www.newyorker.com/news/daily-comment/planned-parenthood-means-fewer-abortions.

Speer, R. B., & Giles, H. (2013). Investigating stepparent-stepchild interactions: The role of communication accommodation. *Journal of Family Communication, 13*, 218-241.

Spencer, M. (2006). Revisiting the 1990 *Special Issue on Minority Children:* An editorial perspective 15 years later. *Child Development, 77*, 1149-1154.

Sprecher, S. (2001). Equity and social exchange in dating couples: Associations with satisfaction, commitment, and stability. *Journal of Marriage and Family, 63*, 599-613.

Sprey, J. (1990). Theoretical practice in family studies. In J. Sprey (Ed.), *Fashioning family theory: New approaches* (pp. 9-33). Newbury Park, CA: Sage.

Stacey, J., & Biblarz, T. (2001). (How) does the sexual orientation of parents matter? *American Sociological Review, 66*, 159-183.

Stadelmann, S., Perren, S., Groeben, M., & von Klitzing, K. (2010). Parental separation and children's behavioral/emotional problems: The impact of parental representations and family conflict. *Family Process, 49*, 92-108.

Stanley, S. M., Whitton, S. W., Sadberry, S. L., Clements, M. L., & Markman, H. J. (2006). Sacrifice as a predictor of marital outcomes. *Family Process, 45*, 289-303.

Stauss, J. H. (1986). The study of American families: Implications for applied research. *Family Perspective, 20*(4), 337-350.

Stepler, R., & Brown, A. (2016, April 19). *Statistical portrait of Hispanics in the United States.* Pew Research Center: Hispanic Trends. Web site: http://www.pewhispanic.org/2016/04/19/statistical-portrait-of-hispanics-in-the-united-states/.

Sternberg, R. J. (2006). A duplex theory of love. In R. J. Sternberg & K. Weis (Eds.), *The new psychology of love* (pp. 184-199). New Haven, CT: Yale University Press. See also, web site: http://www.robertjsternberg.com/love/.

Sternberg, R. J. (2007a). Triangular theory of love. Web site: http://en.wikipedia.org/wiki/Triangular_theory_of_love.

Sternberg, R. J. (2007b). Robert J. Sternberg homepage. Web site: http://yale.edu/rjsternberg.

Sternberg, R. J. (2008). Triangulating love. In T. J. Oord (Ed.), *The altruism reader: Selections from writings on love, religion, and science* (pp. 331-347). West Conshohocken, PA: Templeton Foundation Press.

Sternberg, R. J. (2013a). Measuring love. *The Psychologist, 26*(2), 101.

Sternberg, R. J. (2013b). Searching for love. *The Psychologist, 26*(2), 98-101.

Sternberg, R. J., & Barnes, M. (Eds.). (1988). *The psychology of love.* New Haven, CT: Yale University Press.

Sternberg, R., & Weis, K. (Eds.). (2008). *The new psychology of love.* New Haven, CT: Yale University Press.

Stewart, J. (Ed.). (2009). *Bridges not walls* (10th ed.). Boston, MA: McGraw-Hill.

Stewart, K. L. (1989). Stress and adaptation: A multisystem model of individual, couple, family, and work systems. *Dissertation Abstracts International-A, 49*(08).

Stewart, S. (2010). The characteristics and well-being of adopted stepchildren. *Family Relations, 59*, 558-571.

Stinnett, N., & DeFrain, J. (1985). *Secrets of strong families.* Boston, MA: Little, Brown.

Stinnett, N., & Sauer, K. H. (1977). Relationship characteristics of strong families. *Family Perspective, 11*, 3-11.

Stinnett, N., Sanders, G., & DeFrain, J. (1981). Strong families: A national study. In N. Stinnett, J. DeFrain, K. King, P. Knaub, & G. Rowe (Eds.), *Family strengths 3: Roots of well-being* (pp. 33-42). Lincoln, NE: University of Nebraska Press.

Stith, S. M. (2013, Fall). Intimate partner violence in the military. *National Council on Family Relations.* Web site: https://www.ncfr.org/search?keyword=intimate+partner+violence+in+the+military.

Stokes, B. (2007, July 24). Happiness is increasing in many countries—But why? Pew Research Center. Web site: http://pewglobal.org/commentary/display.php?AnalysisID=1020.

Stolzer, J. (2005). Breastfeeding in the 21st century: A theoretical perspective. *International Journal of Sociology and the Family, 31*(1), 39-55.

Stolzer, J. (2006). Breastfeeding: An interdisciplinary review of the literature. *International Review of Modern Sociology, 32*(1), 103-128.

Stolzer, J. M. (2011). Breastfeeding and obesity: A meta-analysis. *Open Journal of Preventive Medicine, 1*(3), 88-93.

Stolzer, J. M., & Hossain, S. A. (2014). Breastfeeding education: A physician and patient assessment. *Child Development Research.* Web site: http://dx.doi.org/10.1155/2014/413053.

Stone, A. A., Schwartz, J. E., Broderick, J. E., & Deaton, A. (2010). A snapshot of the age distribution of psychological well-being in the United States. *Proceedings of the National Academy of Sciences.* Web site: http://www.pnas.org/content/early/2010/05/04/1003744107.abstract.

Straus, J. (2006). *Unhooked generation: The truth about why we're still single.* New York, NY: Hyperion.

Straus, M. (2008, December). Ending spanking can make a major contribution to preventing physical abuse. *Family Focus, 40*, F14-F16.

Straus, M. A. (2005). Children should never, ever, be spanked no matter what the circumstances. In D. R. Loseke, R. J. Gelles, & M. M. Cavanaugh (Eds.), *Current controversies about family violence* (2nd ed., pp. 137-157). Thousand Oak, CA: Sage.

Straus, M. A. (2008, March). Dominance and symmetry in partner violence by male and female university students in 32 nations. *Children and Youth Services Review, 30*, 252-275. Web site: https://www.researchgate.net/publication/4750591_Dominance_and_symmetry_in_partner_violence_by_male_and_female_university_students_in_32_nations.

Straus, M. A. (2013, December 19). The case against spanking. *UNH Today.* Web site: http://www.unh.edu/unhtoday/2013/12/case-against-spanking.

Straus, M. A., & Field, C. (2003). Psychological aggression by American parents: National data on prevalence, chronicity, and severity. *Journal of Marriage and Family, 65*, 795-808.

Straus, M. A., Gelles, R. J., & Steinmetz, S. K. (2006). *Behind closed doors: Violence in the American family.* New Brunswick, NJ: Translation Publishers.

Street, A. E., & Arias, I. (2001). Psychological abuse and posttraumatic stress disorder in battered women: Examining the roles of shame and guilt. *Violence and Victims, 16*(1), 65-78.

Struthers, C. B., & Bokemeier, J. L. (2000). Myths and realities of raising children and creating family life in a rural county. *Journal of Family Issues, 21*(1), 17-46.

Suanet, B., van der Pas, S., & van Tilburg, T. G. (2013). Who is in the stepfamily? Change in stepparents' family boundaries between 1992 and 2007. *Journal of Marriage and Family, 75*, 1070-1083.

Sue, D. W., & Sue, D. (2016). *Counseling the culturally diverse* (7th ed.). Hoboken, NJ: Wiley

Suitor, J. J., Sechrist, J., Gilligan, M., & Pillemer, K. Intergenerational relations in later-life families. In R. Settersten & J. Angel (Eds.), *Handbook of sociology of aging.* New York, NY: Springer Publishing, pp. 161-178.

Supreme Court of the United States. (2015, June 26). *Obergefell et al. v. Hodges,* Director, Ohio Department of Health, et al. Web site: http://www.supremecourt.gov/opinions/14pdf/14-556_3204.pdf.

Suter, E. A., Daas, K. L., & Bergen, K. M. (2008). Negotiating lesbian family identify via symbols and rituals. *Journal of Family Issues, 29*, 26-47.

Sutton, C. E. T., & Broken Nose, M. A. (1996). American Indian families: An overview. In M. McGoldrick & J. Giordano (Eds.), *Ethnicity and family therapy* (2nd ed., pp. 31-44). New York, NY: Guilford.

Sutton, C. T., & Broken Nose, M. A. (2005). American Indian families: An overview. In M. McGoldrick, J. Giordano, & N. Garcia-Preto (Eds.), *Ethnicity and family therapy* (3rd ed.). New York, NY: Guilford Press.

Sweeney, J. (1982, June 21). Taking the long view of marriage: Why do some endure? *Los Angeles Times*, pp. 1, 21-23.

Sweeney, M. M. (2010). Remarriage and stepfamilies: Strategic sites for family scholarship in the 21st century. *Journal of Marriage and Family, 72*, 667-684.

Switala, K. (2016). *The feminist theory website*. Web site: http://www.cddc.vt.edu/feminism/enin.html.

Taffel, S. M., Placek, P. J., Moien, M., & Kosary, C. L. (1991). 1989 U.S. cesarean section rate steadies—VBAC rate rises to nearly one in five. *Birth, 18*, 73-77.

Tamis-Lemonda, C. S., & Cabrera, N. (2003). *Handbook of father involvement: Multidisciplinary perspectives.* Mahwah, NJ: Erlbaum. Experts from diverse scientific disciplines share their interests in the topic of father involvement in the lives of children.

Tasker, F., & Patterson, C. J. (2007). Research on gay and lesbian parenting. *Journal of GLBT Family Studies, 3*, 9-34.

Tatara, T. (Ed.). (1998). *Understanding elder abuse in minority populations*. Philadelphia, PA: Brunner/Mazel.

Tatkin, S. (2016). *Wired for dating*. Oakland, CA: New Harbinger Publications.

Tavernise, S. (2011, May 26). Married couples are no longer a majority, census finds. *The New York Times*. Web site: http://www.nytimes.com/2011/05/26/us/26marry.html?_r=0.

Taylor, J. L. (2009). Midlife impacts of adolescent parenthood. *Journal of Family Issues, 30*, 484-510.

Taylor, R. J., Jackson, J. S., and Chatters, L. M. (Eds.). (1997). *Family life in Black America*. Thousand Oaks, CA: Sage.

Taylor, R. J., Lincoln, K. D., & Chatters, L. M. (2005). Supportive relationships with church members among African Americans. *Family Relations, 54*, 501-511.

The Dictionary of the History of Ideas. (2003). Electronic Text Center. Charlottesville, VA: University of Virginia Library and the Gale Group. Web site: http://etext.virginia.edu/cgi-local/DHI/dhi.cgi?id=dv3-56.

The Economist (2007, July 14). Where money seems to talk. *The Economist, 384*, pp. 63-64.

Theroux, P. (1996). *My other life: A novel.* Boston, MA: Houghton Mifflin.

TheSingleMother.com. (2016). Sibling abuse help guide. Web site: http://thesinglemother.com/sibling-abuse-help-guide/.

Thiele, D. M., & Whelan, T. A. (2006). The nature and dimension of the grandparent role. *Marriage and Family Review, 40*, 93-108.

Thiele, D. M., & Whelan, T. A. (2008). The relationship between grandparent satisfaction, meaning, and generativity. *International Journal of Aging and Human Development, 66*(1), 21-48.

Thomas, V., & Olson, D. H. (1993). Problem families and the Circumplex Model: Observational assessment using the clinical rating scale. *Journal of Marital and Family Therapy, 19*(2), 159-175.

Thompson, K. L., & Gullone, E. (2003). Promotion of empathy and prosocial behaviour in children through humane education. *Australian Psychologist, 38*(3), 175-182.

Thompson, M. (2008, February 25). Death at the Army's hands. *Time*, pp. 40-42.

Thompson, S. H., & Lougheed, E. (2012, March). Frazzled by Facebook? An exploratory study of gender differences in social network communication among undergraduate men and women. *College Student Journal, 46*, 88-98.

Thorne, D. (2010). Extreme financial strain: Emergent chores, gender inequality and emotional distress. *Journal of Family and Economic Issues, 31*, 185-197.

Thrift nation. (2009, April 27). *Time*, pp. 20-23.

Tichenor, V. J. (1999). Status and income as gendered resources: The case for marital power. *Journal of Marriage and the Family, 61*, 638-650.

Todd, M. (2011). *The process of becoming a strong GLBT family*. (Doctoral dissertation). Digital Commons. Web site: http://digitalcommons.unl.edu/cgi/viewcontent.cgi?article=1096&context=cehsdiss.

Tolstoy, L. (1869). *War and Peace*, Book IV, Ch. 11. 1999 version. Köln, Germany: Könemann.

Tong, R. (2014). *Feminist thought: A more comprehensive introduction* (4th ed.). Boulder, CO: Westview Press.

Treas, J. (2015). Going global: A cross-national view of couples and housework. *Family Focus, FF66*, F10-F12.

Treas, J., & Drobnic, S. (Eds.). (2010). *Dividing the domestic: Men, women, and household work in cross-national perspective.* Stanford, CA: Stanford University Press.

Trimble, J., & Fisher, C. (2006). Our shared journey: Lessons from the past to protect the future. In J. Trimble & C. Fisher (Eds.), *The handbook of ethical research with ethnocultural populations and communities* (pp. xv-xxix). Thousand Oaks, CA: Sage.

Trimble, J., & Fisher, C. (2006). *The handbook of ethical research with ethnocultural populations & communities.* Thousand Oaks, CA: Sage.

Trimble, J. E., & Gonzalez, J. (2008). Cultural considerations and perspectives for providing psychological counseling for Native American Indians. In P. Pedersen, J. Draguns, W. Lonner, & J. Trimble (Eds.), *Counseling across cultures* (4th ed., pp. 93-112). Los Angeles, CA: Sage.

Troll, L. E. (1997). Growing old in families. In I. Deitch & C. Ward Howell (Eds.), *Counseling the aging and their families* (pp. 3-16). Alexandria, VA: American Counseling Association.

Troll, L. E. (2001). When the world narrows: Intimacy with the dead? *Generations, 25*(2), 55-58.

Trussell, D. E., & Shaw, S. M. (2009). Changing family life in the rural context: Women's perspectives of family leisure on the farm. *Leisure Sciences, 31*(5), 434-449. Web site: http://www.tandfonline.com/doi/pdf/10.1080/01490400903199468.

Tubbs, C. Y. (2016). St. Mary's University. Web site: https://www.stmarytx.edu/academics/humanities/faculty/carolyn-y-tubbs-ph-d/.

Tubbs, C. Y., Roy, K. M., & Burton, L. M. (2005). Family ties: Constructing family time in low-income families. *Family Process, 44*, 77-91.

Tudge, J. (2008). *The everyday lives of young children: Culture, class, and child rearing in diverse societies.* New York, NY: Cambridge University Press.

UK National Statistics. (2004, January 24). Marriage and divorce rates: EU comparison, 2002. Web site: http://www.statistics.gove.uk/STATBASE/ssdataset.asp?vlnk117625&More=Y.

Ulker, A. (2008). Wealth holdings and portfolio allocation of the elderly: The role of marital history. *Journal of Family Economic Issues, 30*, 90-108. Death and divorce earlier in life can significantly affect the accumulation of wealth among the elderly.

Ulker, A. (2009). Wealth holdings and portfolio allocations of the elderly: The role of marital history. *Journal of Family and Economic Issues, 30*, 90-108.

Umberson, D., Pudrovska, T., & Reczek, C. (2010). Parenthood, childlessness, and well-being: A life course perspective. *Journal of Marriage and Family, 72*, 612-629.

United Nations. (2015). World population projected to reach 9.7 billion by 2050. Department of Economic and Social Affairs. Web site: http://www.un.org/en/development/desa/news/population/2015-report.html.

United Nations AIDS. (2004). A global overview of the AIDS epidemic. Web site: http://www.unaids.org/EN/resources/epidemiology.asp.

United Nations International Labour Office. (2004a). *Breaking through the glass ceiling: Women in management—update 2004.* Geneva: Author.

United Nations International Labour Office. (2004b). *Global employment trends for women 2004.* Geneva: Author.

United States Courts (n.d.). *2011 BAPCPA report highlights.* Web site: http://www.uscourts.gov/Statistics/BankruptcyStatistics/bapcpa-report-highlights.aspx.

University of Arkansas News. (2013, July 2). Research: Genders communicate consent to sex differently. Web site: http://news.uark.edu/articles/21460/research-genders-communicate-consent-to-sex-differently.

University of Michigan. (2003). Monitoring the future: National results on adolescent drug use: Overview of key findings, 2002. Cited by the U.S. Department of Justice, Office of Justice Programs, Bureau of Justice Statistics. Web site: http://www.ojp.us.doj.gov/bjs/dcf/du.htm.

University of Michigan Health System. (2012). Sibling abuse. Web site: http://www.med.umich.edu/yourchild/topics/sibabuse.htm.

University of Missouri at Columbia Extension. (2010). Information on parenthood and families. Web site: www.extension.missouri.edu-/main/family/.

University of Nebraska–Lincoln Extension. (2010). Parenting and family issues from a strengths-based perspective. Web site: www.ianrpubs.unl.edu/-epublic/pages/index.jsp.

University of Nebraska–Lincoln Extension. (2016). Educational materials for strengthening couple and family relationships. Web site: http://extensionpubs.unl.edu/.

Urban Institute. (2000, February 1). A new look at homelessness in America. Web site: http://www.urban.org.

U.S. Administration on Aging. (2009). A profile of older Americans: 2008. Web site: http://www.aoa.gov/AoARoot/Aging_Statistics/Profile/2008/3.aspx.

U.S. Advisory Board on Child Abuse and Neglect. (1990). *Child abuse and neglect: Critical first steps in response to a national emergency.* Washington, DC: U.S. Government Printing Office.

USC Annenberg. (2016). Center for the Digital Future, University of Southern California. Web site: http://www.digitalcenter.org/.

U.S. Census Bureau. (n.d.). *Annual estimates of the resident population by sex, age, race, and Hispanic origin for the United States and States: April 1, 2010 to July 1, 2015.* American Fact Finder. Web site: http://factfinder.census.gov/faces/tableservices/jsf/pages/productview.xhtml?src=bkmk.

U.S. Census Bureau. (2005). Hispanic heritage month 2005: September 15–October 15. Web site: http://www.census.gov/Press-Release/www/releases/archives/.

U.S. Census Bureau. (2006a). Hispanic heritage month. *Facts for features.* Web site: http://www.census .gov/Press-Release.

U.S. Census Bureau. (2008, May 1). U.S. Hispanic population surpasses 45 million: Now 15 percent of total. Web site: http://www.census.gov/Press-Release/www/releases/archives/.

U.S. Census Bureau. (2008, July 1). Median age of the population by race and Hispanic origin for the United States and states. Web site: http://data.iowadatacenter.org/datatables/UnitedStates/-usstmedianagebyrace 2008.pdf.

U.S. Census Bureau. (2009, September 21). Current population trends in the Hispanic population. Web site: http://www.census.gov/population/www/socdemo/hispanic/files/-Internet_Hispanic_in_US_2006.pdf.

U.S. Census Bureau. (2009a). Older Americans month: May 2009. Web site: http://www.census.gov/Press-Release/www/releases/archives/-facts_for_features_special_editions/013384.html.

U.S. Census Bureau (2010a). American Community Survey 1-year estimates. Grandchildren under 18 years living with a grandparent householder by grandparent responsibility and presence of parent. Web site: http://www.census.gov/acs/www.

U.S. Census Bureau. (2012). *About poverty.* Web site: http://www.census.gov/hhes/www/poverty/about/overview/measure.html.

U.S. Census Bureau. (2012). *Average earnings of year-round, full-time workers by educational attainment: 2009* (Table 703). Statistical Abstract of the United States. Web site: http://www.census.gov/compendia/statab/2012/tables/12s0703.pdf.

U.S. Census Bureau. (2012). Educational attainment by race and Hispanic origin: 1970–2010, Table 229. *Statistical Abstract of the United States 2012.* Web site: http://www.census.gov/compendia/statab/2012/tables/12s0695.pdf.

U.S. Census Bureau. (2012). Families below poverty level and below 125 percent of poverty By race and Hispanic origin: 1980 to 2009, Table 715. Statistical Abstract of the United States: 2012. Web site: http://www.census.gov/compendia/statab/cats/population/households_families_group_quarters.html.

U.S. Census Bureau. (2012). *Statistical abstract of the United States: 2012.* Table 133. Marriages and divorces: Number and rate by state: 1990 to 2009, p. 98. Web site: http://www.census.gov/compendia/statab/2012/tables/12s0133.pdf.

U.S. Census Bureau. (2012). Table 67. Family groups with children under 18 years old by race and Hispanic origin: 1990 to 2010. Web site: http://www.census.gov/compendia/statab/2012/tables/12s0067.pdf.

U.S. Census Bureau. (2013, April). Who's minding the kids? Child care arrangements: Spring 2011. Household Economic Studies. Web site: https://www.census.gov/library/publications/2013/demo/p70-135.html.

U.S. Census Bureau. (2013, June 13). Asians fastest-growing race or ethnic group in 2012, Census Bureau reports. News Release Number CB13-112. Web site: http://www.census.gov/newsroom/press-releases/2013/cb13-112.html.

U.S. Census Bureau. (2014, October 22). 10 percent of grandparents live with a grandchild, Census Bureau reports. Web site: http://www.census.gov/newsroom/press-releases/2014/cb14-194.html.

U.S. Census Bureau. (2015). Median age at first marriage: 1890 to the present. Decennial Censuses, 1890 to 1940, and Current Population Survey, Annual Social and Economic Supplements, 1947 to 2015. Web site: https://www.census.gov/content/dam/Census/library/visualizations/time-series/demo/families-and-households/ms-2.pdf.

U.S. Census Bureau. (2015, May 8). Older Americans month: May 2015. Web site: https://www.census.gov/newsroom/facts-for-features/2015/cb15-ff09.html.

U.S. Census Bureau. (2015, September 15). Unmarried and Single Americans Week. Web site: https://www.census.gov/newsroom/facts-for-features/2015/cb15-ff19.html.

U.S. Census Bureau. (2016). Income. FAQs. Web site: https://www.census.gov/topics/income-poverty/income/about/faqs.html.

U.S. Census Bureau. (2016, May 7). U.S. and world population clock. Web site: http://www.census.gov/popclock/.

U.S. Census Bureau, Housing and Household Economic Statistics Division. (2008). Current population survey—Definitions and explanations. Web site: http://www.census.gov/-/population/www/cps/cpsdef.html.

U.S. Census Bureau. (2017, April 10). Facts for Features: Older Americans Month: May 2017. Web site: https://www.prnewswire.com/news-releases/us-census-bureau-facts-for-features-older-americans-month-may-2017-300437489.html

U.S. Census Bureau News. (2004, June 14). Hispanic and Asian American increasing faster than overall population.

U.S. Census Bureau Quick Facts. (n.d.). *Quick Facts, United States.* Web site: http://www.census.gov/quickfacts/table/PST045215/00.

Usdansky, M. L. (2009). A weak embrace: Popular and scholarly depictions of single-parent families. *Journal of Marriage and Family, 71,* 209–225.

U.S. Department of Agriculture. (2015, September 15). Household food security in the United States, 2014. Web site: https://www.ers.usda.gov/publications/pub-details/?pubid=79760.

U.S. Department of Commerce. (2011). *Women in America.* Washington, DC: White House Council on Women and Girls. Web site: http://www.esa.doc.gov/sites/default/files/womeninamerica.pdf.

U.S. Department of Health and Human Services. (2016). Female genital cutting. *Women's Health.gov.* Web site: http://womenshealth.gov/publications/our-publications/fact-sheet/female-genital-cutting.html.

U.S. Department of the Interior. (2014, January 16). 2013 American Indian population and labor force report. Office of the Secretary Office of the Assistant Secretary—Indian Affairs. Web site: http://www.bia.gov/cs/groups/public/documents/text/idc1-024782.pdf.

U.S. Department of Justice. (2005a). Victims of crime. Web site: http://www.usdoj.gov.

U.S. Department of Justice. (2005a, b). Bureau of Justice Statistics. Intimate homicide victims by gender. Web site: http://bjs.ojp.usdoj.gov/content/homicide/intimates.cfm.

U.S. Department of Justice. (2016). Domestic violence. Web site: https://www.justice.gov/ovw/domestic-violence.

U.S. Department of Labor (n.d.). *Women in the labor force.* Web site: https://www.dol.gov/wb/stats/stats_data.htm#mothers.

U.S. Department of Labor. (2010, February 5). The unemployment situation—January 2010. Web site: http://www.bls.gov/news.release/pdf/empsit.pdf.

U.S. General Accounting Office. (2003). *Women's earnings: Work patterns partially explain difference between men's and women's earnings.* Report to Congressional requesters. Washington, DC: Author.

U.S. National Center for Health Statistics. (2017, January 6). *Reproductive health: Teen pregnancy.* Web site: https://www.cdc.gov/teenpregnancy/index.htm.

U.S. National Library of Medicine. (2016). Dementia. Web site: https://www.nlm.nih.gov/medlineplus/dementia.html.

Vaillant, G. (2012). *Triumphs of experience: The men of the Harvard Grant Study.* Cambridge, MA: The Belknap Press of Harvard University Press.

Vandell, D. L., Burchinal, M., Vandergrift, N., Belsky, J., Steinberg, L., & NICHD Early Child Care Research Network. (2010). Do effects of early child care extend to age 15 years? Results from the NICHD study of early child care and youth development. *Child Development, 81,* 737–756.

Van Dorn, R. A., Bowen, G. L., & Blau, J. R. (2006). The impact of community diversity and consolidated inequality on dropping out of high school. *Family Relations, 55,* 105–118.

van Dulmen, M., Miller, B. C., Grotevant, H. D., Fan, X., & Christensen, M. (2000). Comparisons of adopted and nonadopted adolescents in a large, nationally representative sample. *Child Development, 71*(5), 1458–1473.

Van Epp, J. (2008). *How to avoid falling in love with a jerk.* New York, NY: McGraw-Hill.

Vannier, S. A., & O'Sullivan, L. F. (2011). Communicating interest in sex: Verbal and nonverbal initiation of sexual activity in young adults' romantic dating relationships. *Archives of Sexual Behavior, 40,* 961–969.

Van Volkom, M. (2006). Sibling relationships in middle and older adulthood: A review of the literature. *Marriage and Family Review, 40,* 151–170.

Vaterlaus, J. M., Skogrand, L., Chaney, C., & Gahagan, K. (2016). Marital expectations in strong African American marriages. *Family Process.* Online: doi10.1111/famp.12263.

Veniegas, R. C., & Peplau, L. A. (1997). Power and the quality of same-sex friendships. *Psychology of Women Quarterly, 21*(3), 279–297.

Vespa, J. (2014). Historical trends in the marital intentions of onetime and serial cohabitors. *Journal of Marriage and Family, 76,* 207–217.

Vincent, J. P., & Jouriles, E. N. (2000). *Domestic violence: Guidelines for research-informed practice.* London: Jessica Kingsley.

Visher, E. B. (1989). The Stepping Ahead Program. In M. Burt (Ed.), *Stepfamilies stepping ahead* (3rd ed., pp. 57–89). Lincoln, NE: Stepfamilies Press.

Visher, E. B., & Visher, J. S. (1992). *How to win as a stepfamily* (2nd ed.). New York, NY: Brunner/Mazel.

Visher, E. B., Visher, J. S., & Pasley, K. (1997). Stepfamily therapy from the client's perspective. *Marriage and Family Review, 27*(1–2), 191–213.

von Bertalanffy, L. (1968). *General system theory: Foundation, development, applications.* New York, NY: Braziller.

Voydanoff, P. (2008). A conceptual model of the work-family interface. In K. Korabik, D. S. Lero, & D. L. Whitehead (Eds.), *Handbook of work-family integration,* chap. 2. St. Louis, MO: Elsevier.

Wagner, J., Wrzus, C., Neyer, F. J., & Lang, F. (2015). Social network characteristics of early midlife voluntary and involuntarily childless couples. *Journal of Family Issues, 36,* 87–110.

Waite, L. J. (1998). Why marriage matters. In T. Ooms (Ed.), *Strategies to strengthen marriage* (pp. 1–22). Washington, DC: Family Impact Seminar.

Waite, L. J. (2001, April). 5 marriage myths, 6 marriage benefits. *Marriage and Families,* pp. 19–25.

Waite, L. J. (2003, April). Uncommitted cohabitation versus marriage. *Terskel, 76,* 17–20.

Waite, L. J., & Gallagher, M. (2000). *The case for marriage: Why married people are happier, healthier, and better off financially.* New York, NY: Doubleday.

Waite, L. J., & Lehrer, L. (2003). The benefits from marriage and religion in the United States: A comparative analysis. *Population and Developmental Review, 29*(2), 255–275.

Waite, L. (2016). National Opinion Research Center at the University of Chicago. Web site: http://www.norc.org/Experts/Pages/linda-waite.aspx.

Waite, L., Luo, Y., & Lewin, A. (2009). Marital happiness and marital stability: Consequences for psychological well-being. *Social Science Research, 38,* 201–212.

Waldegrave, C. (2009). Culture, gender, and socioeconomic context in therapeutic and social policy work. *Family Process, 48,* 85–101.

Waldrep, D. A., Cozza, S. J., & Chen, R. S. (2004, June). The impact of deployment on the military family. In *Iraq War Clinician Guide* (2nd ed., pp. 83–86). Washington, DC: Department of Veterans Affairs, National Center for PTSD.

Walker, A. J., & McGraw, L. A. (1999). Interdependence between mothers and daughters in middle and later life: Patterns of connection and autonomy. Poster presented at the 61st Annual Conference of the National Council on Family Relations, Irvine, CA, November 12–15.

Walker, L. E. (2000). *The battered woman syndrome* (2nd ed.). New York, NY: Springer.

Walker, L. E. (2009). *The battered woman syndrome: With research associates*. New York, NY: Springer.

Walker, L. E. (2016). Lenore E. Walker. *Wikipedia*. Web site: https://en.wikipedia.org/wiki/Lenore_E._Walker.

Walkner, A. J., & Rueter, M. A. (2014). Adoption status and family relationships during the transition to young adulthood. *Journal of Family Psychology, 28*, 877–886. Web site: https://www.ncbi.nlm.nih.gov/pmc/articles/PMC4307793/.

Waller, M. R., & Peters, H. E. (2008). The risk of divorce as a barrier to marriage among parents of young children. *Social Science Research, 37*, 1188–1199.

Waller, W. (1951). *The family* [revised by R. Hill]. New York, NY: Dryden.

Wallerstein J. S., & Kelly, J. B. (2008). *Surviving the breakup*. New York, NY: Basic Books.

Wallerstein, J. S. & Lewis, J. M. (2004). The unexpected legacy of divorce: Report of a 25-year study. *Psychoanalytic Psychology, 21*, 353–370.

Walsh, F. (1998). *Strengthening family resilience*. New York, NY: Guilford.

Walsh, F. (2006). *Strengthening family resilience* (2nd ed.). New York, NY: Guilford.

Walsh, F. (Ed.). (2015). *Normal family processes: Growing diversity and complexity* (4th ed.). New York, NY: Guilford.

Walster, E. G., Walster, W., & Bersheid, E. (1978). *Equity: Theory and research*. Boston, MA: Allyn & Bacon.

Wang, B., Hertog, S., Meier, A., Lou, C., & Gao, E., & Wang, B. B. (2005, June). The potential of comprehensive sex education in China: Findings from suburban Shanghai. *International Family Planning Perspectives, 31*(2), 63–72.

Wang, R., Bianchi, S., & Raley, S. (2005). Teenagers' Internet use and family rules: A research note. *Journal of Marriage and the Family, 67*, 1249–1258.

Wang, W. (2012, February 16). *The rise of intermarriage*. Pew Research Center. Web site: http://www.pewsocialtrends.org/2012/02/16/the-rise-of-intermarriage/.

Wang, W., & Morin, R. (2009, November 24). Home for the holidays . . . and every other day: Recession brings many young adults back to the nest. Pew Research Center Publications. Web site: http://pewresearch.org/pubs/1423/home-for-the-holidays-boomeranged-parents.

Wang, W., Parker, K., & Taylor, P. (2013, May 29). Single mothers. Pew Research Center. http://www.pewsocialtrends.org/2013/05/29/chapter-4-single-mothers/.

Washington Post. (2012). Faces of the fallen. Web site: http://apps.washingtonpost.com/national/fallen/.

Washington Post. (2014, February 24). Here are the 10 countries where homosexuality may be punished by death. Web site: https://www.washingtonpost.com/news/worldviews/wp/2014/02/24/here-are-the-10-countries-where-homosexuality-may-be-punished-by-death/.

Washington Post. (2014, August 6). 'The Second Shift' at 25: Q & A with Arlie Hochschild. Web site: https://www.washingtonpost.com/blogs/she-the-people/wp/2014/08/06/the-second-shift-at-25-q-a-with-arlie-hochschild/.

Washington Post. (2015, April 28). There are 390,000 gay marriages in the U.S. The Supreme Court could quickly make it half a million. Web site: https://www.washingtonpost.com/news/the-fix/wp/2015/04/28/heres-how-many-gay-marriages-the-supreme-court-could-make-way-for/.

Watamura, S. E., Sebanc, A. M., & Gunnar, M. R. (2002). Rising cortisol at childcare: Relations with nap, rest, and temperament. *Developmental Psychobiology, 40*(1), 33–42.

WebMD. (2010, April 16). Statins may lower testosterone, libido. Web site: http://www.webmd.com/erectile-dysfunction/news/20100416/statins_may_lower_testosterone_libido.

WebMD. (2014, August 17). Male menopause. Web site: http://www.webmd.com/men/guide/male-menopause.

WebMD. (2016). Alzheimer's disease health center. Web site: http://www.webmd.com/alzheimers/.

WebMD. (2016). Menopause health center. Web site: http://www.webmd.com/menopause/guide/menopause-symptoms-types.

WebMD. (2016a). Barrier methods of birth control. Web site: http://www.webmd.com/sex/birth-control/barrier-methods-of-birth-control-19059.

WebMD. (2016b). Birth control health center. Web site: http://www.webmd.com/sex/birth-control/.

WebMD. (2016c). Spermicide for birth control—Topic overview. Web site: http://www.webmd.com/sex/birth-control/tc/spermicide-for-birth-control-topic-overview.

WebMD. (2016d). Many young women use "withdrawal" for birth control, but new study confirms that it's not good for preventing pregnancy. Web site: http://www.webmd.com/sex/birth-control/news/20130806/1-in-3-young-us-women-uses-withdrawal–for-birth-control.

WebMD. (2016e). Birth control myths. Web site: http://www.webmd.com/sex/birth-control/birth-control-contraceptive-myths.

WebMD. (2016f). Vaginal douching: Helpful or harmful? Web site: http://www.webmd.com/women/guide/vaginal-douching-helpful-or-harmful.

WebMD. (2016g). Fertility awareness. Web site: http://www.webmd.com/infertility-and-reproduction/fertility-awareness.

WebMD. (2016h). What's the best birth control? Web site: http://www.webmd.com/sex/birth-control/best-effective-birth-control.

WebMD. (2016i). Abortion—Topic overview. Web site: http://www.webmd.com/women/tc/abortion-topic-overview.

WebMD. (2016j). Pregnancy and conception. Web site: http://www.webmd.com/baby/guide/understanding-conception.

WebMD. (2016j). Xulane patch, transdermal weekly. Web site: https://www.webmd.com/drugs/2/drug-166145/xulane-transdermal/details

WebMD. (2016k). Infertility & reproduction health center. Web site: http://www.webmd.com/infertility-and-reproduction/.

WebMD. (2016l). Normal labor and delivery process. Web site: http://www.webmd.com/baby/guide/normal-labor-and-delivery-process.

WebMD. (2016m). 8 early signs of pregnancy. Web site: http://www.webmd.com/baby/features/8-early-signs-of-pregnancy.

WebMD. (2016n). Types of childbirth classes. Web site: http://www.webmd.com/baby/guide/childbirth-class-options.

WebMD. (2016o). Self-care during pregnancy. Web site: http://www.webmd.com/baby/pregnancy-self-care.

WebMD. (2016p). Drug use and pregnancy. Web site: http://www.webmd.com/baby/drug-use-and-pregnancy.

WebMD. (2016q). Pregnant? Keep sex on your agenda. Web site: http://www.webmd.com/baby/pregnancy-sex.

WebMD. (2016r). Labor and delivery—Topic overview. Web site: http://www.webmd.com/baby/tc/labor-delivery-and-postpartum-period-topic-overview.

WebMD. (2016s). Cesarean section—Topic overview. Web site: http://www.webmd.com/baby/guide/cesarean-section-topic-overview.

WebMD. (2016t). Types of childbirth classes. Web site: http://www.webmd.com/baby/guide/childbirth-class-options.

WebMD. (2016u). Home birth: Is it safe for you? Web site: http://www.webmd.com/baby/home-birth-is-it-safe-for-you.

WebMD. (2016v). The basics of water birth. Web site: http://www.webmd.com/baby/guide/water-birth.

WebMD. (2016w). Postpartum depression. Web site: http://www.webmd.com/depression/guide/postpartum-depression.

WebMD. (2016x). Bonding with baby before birth. Web site: http://www.webmd.com/baby/features/bonding-with-baby-before-birth.

WebMD. (2016y). Stillbirth: Topic overview. Web site: http://www.webmd.com/baby/tc/stillbirth-topic-overview#1.

Weinberg, D. (2008). The philosophical foundations of constructionist research. In J. A. Holstein & J. F. Gubrium (Eds.), *Handbook of constructionist research* (pp. 13–40). New York, NY: Guilford Press.

Weiser, D. A., & Niehuis, S. (2014). Relationship initiation and early dating. *Family Focus, FF62,* F3–F4.

Weitz, T. A., et al. (2013). Safety of aspiration abortion performed by nurse practitioners, certified nurse midwives, and physician assistants under a California legal waiver. *American Journal of Public Health, 103*(3), 454–461.

Weitzman, L. J., & Dixon, R. B. (1992). The transformation of legal marriage through no-fault divorce. In A. S. Skolnick & J. H. Skolnick (Eds.), *Family in transition: Rethinking marriage, sexuality, child rearing, and family organization* (7th ed., pp. 217–289). New York, NY: HarperCollins.

Wenger, G. C., Dykstra, P. A., Melkas, T., & Knipscheer, K. (2007). Social embeddedness and late-life parenthood: Community activities, close ties, and support networks. *Journal of Family Issues, 28,* 1419–1456.

Westman, J. C. (1998). Grandparenthood. Parenthood in America, General Library System, University of Wisconsin–Madison. Web site: http://parenthood.library.wisc.edu/Westman/Westman-Grandparenthood.html.

Wetchler, J. L., & Hecker, L. (Eds.). (2015). *An introduction to marriage and family therapy.* New York, NY: Routledge/Taylor & Francis Group.

Where money seems to talk. (2009, July 14). *The Economist.* 63–64.

Whisman, M. A., Coop Gordman, K., & Chatav, Y. (2007). Predicting sexual infidelity in a population-based sample of married individuals. *Journal of Family Psychology, 21*(2), 320–324.

Whitaker, C. (2016). *Wikipedia.* Web site: https://en.wikipedia.org/wiki/Carl_Whitaker.

White, J. M., Klein, D. M., & Martin, T. F. (2015). *Family theories: An introduction* (4th ed.). Los Angeles, CA: Sage.

White, M. (2016). Michael White archive. Dulwich Centre. Web site: http://dulwichcentre.com.au/michael-white-archive/.

White, M., & Epston, D. (1990). *Narrative means to therapeutic ends.* New York, NY: Norton.

White, M., & Morgan, A. (2006). *Narrative therapy with children and their families.* Adelaide, Australia: Dulwich Centre Publishers.

White, W. L. (2005). Fire in the family: Historical perspectives on the intergenerational effects of addiction. *Counselor, 6*(1), 20–25.

Whitehead, B. D. (1997). *The divorce culture.* New York, NY: Knopf.

Whitehead, B. D. (2003). *Why there are no good men left.* New York, NY: Broadway Books.

Whitehead, B. D., & Popenoe, D. (2001). *The states of our unions.* Rutgers University, National Marriage Project.

Whitehead, D., & Doherty, W. J. (1989). Systems dynamics in cigarette smoking: An exploratory study. *Family Systems Medicine, 7*(3), 264–273.

White House. (2004). Summary fact sheet on HIV/AIDS. Web site: http://www.whitehouse.gov/onap/facts.html.

White House. (2014). Consequences of illicit drug use in America. Web site: https://obamawhitehouse.archives.gov/sites/default/files/ondcp/Fact_Sheets/consequences_of_illicit_drug_use_-_fact_sheet_april_2014.pdf.

Whitman, C. T. (1995, May 31). Wheaton College commencement address. *Good Morning America.* New York, NY: ABC Television.

Whitton, S., & Buzzella, B. A. (2011). Relationship education with same-sex couples. *Family Focus, 56.4,* F13–F115.

Widman, L., Choukas-Bradley, S., Helms, S. W., Golin, C. E., & Prinstein, M. J. (2014). Sexual communication between early adolescents and their dating partners, parents, and best friends. *The Journal of Sexual Research, 51,* 731–741.

Wiener, N. (1956). *I am a mathematician.* New York, NY: Doubleday.

Wight, V. R., Bianchi, S. M., & Hunt B. R. (2012). Explaining racial/ethnic variation in partnered women's and men's housework: Does one size fit all? *Journal of Family Issues, 34,* 394–427.

Wilcox, B. (2009). *The state of our unions: Marriage in America 2009.* Retrieved from the National Marriage Project Web site: http://stateofourunions.org/2009/index.php.

Wilcox, B. (2010). *The state of our unions: When marriage disappears.* Charlottesville, VA: The National Marriage Project, University of Virginia. Web site: http://nationalmarriageproject.org/wp-content/uploads/2012/06/Union_11_12_10.pdf.

Wilcox, B. (2010). *The state of our unions: When marriage disappears.* Retrieved from the National Marriage Project Web site: http://www.stateofourunions.org/2010/index.php.

Wilcox, B. (2011). *The state of our unions: When baby makes three.* Web site: http://www.stateofourunions.org/2011/SOOU2011.pdf.

Wilcox, W. B. (2009). The great recession's silver lining. In W. B. Wilcox (Ed.), *The state of our unions* (pp. 15–22). Charlottesville, VA: National Marriage Project. Web site: http://stateofourunions.org/2009/great_recession.php.

Wilcox, W. B., & Marquardt, E. (Eds.). (2011). The state of our unions 2011. National Marriage Project at the University of Virginia and the Center for Marriage and Families at the Institute for American Values. Web site: http://www.stateofourunions.org/.

Williams, K. (2011). A socio-emotional relational framework for infidelity: The relational justice approach. *Family Process, 50,* 516–528.

Willoughby, B. J., & Belt, D. (2012). Marital orientation and relationship well-being among cohabiting couples. *Journal of Family Psychology, 3,* 181–192.

Willoughby, B. J., & Carroll, J. S. (2010). Sexual experience and couple formation attitudes among emerging adults. *Journal of Adult Development, 17*(1), 1–11.

Willoughby, B. J., & Dworkin, J. (2009). The relationship between emerging adults' expressed desire to marry and frequency of participation in risk-taking behaviors. *Youth & Society, 40,* 426–450.

Willoughby, B. J., Madsen, B., Carroll, J. S., & Busby, D. M. (2015). "Want to stay over?" Demographic, intrapersonal, and relational differences among those who date, stay over and cohabit. *Marriage & Family Review, 51,* 587–609.

Willows, J. (2008). *Moving on after childhood sexual abuse.* New York, NY: Routledge.

Wincze, J. P. (2009). *Enhancing sexuality: A problem-solving approach to treating dysfunction: Therapist guide* (2nd ed.). New York, NY: Oxford University Press. An excellent overview of sex therapy today.

Wolak, J., Mitchell, K., & Finkelhor, D. (2006). Online victimization of youth: Five years later. Web site: http://www.missingkids.com.

Wolfe, A. (1999, September). The mystique of Betty Friedan. *The Atlantic Online*: http://www.theatlantic.com/issues/99sep/9909friedan.htm.

Women in Leadership. (2010). Web site: http://www.guide2womenleaders.com/.

Women's and Children's Health Network. (2016). Parenting and Child Health. Violence towards parents by young people. Web site: http://www.cyh.com/HealthTopics/HealthTopicDetails.aspx?p=114&np=99&id=1729.

Wood, J. T. (2009). Gendered standpoints on personal relationships. In J. Stewart (Ed.), *Bridges not walls* (pp. 358–364). Boston, MA: McGraw-Hill.

Wood, S., & Liossis, P. (2007). Potentially stressful life events and emotional closeness between grandparents and adult grandchildren. *Journal of Family Issues, 28*, 380–398.

World Health Organization. (2016, February). Female genital mutilation. Web site: http://www.who.int/mediacentre/factsheets/fs241/en/.

World Health Organization. (2016). *World Health Organization intimate partner violence and alcohol fact sheet*. Web site: http://www.who.int/violence_injury_prevention/violence/world_report/factsheets/ft_intimate.pdf.

Worthington, E. L. (Ed.). (2005). *Handbook of forgiveness*. New York, NY: Routledge.

Wright, P. J. (2009). Father-child sexual communication in the United States: A review and synthesis. *Journal of Family Communication, 9*, 233–250.

Wrobel, G. M., Ayers-Lopez, S., Grotevant, H. D., & McRoy, R. G. (1996). Openness in adoption and the level of child participation. *Child Development, 67*(5), 2358–2374.

Wuerffel, J., DeFrain, J., & Stinnett, N. (1990, Fall). How strong families use humor. *Family Perspective*, pp. 129–142.

Wu Weiss, J., and Garbanati, J. A. (2004). Relationship of acculturation and family functioning to smoking attitudes and behaviors among Asian-American adolescents. *Journal of Child and Family Studies, 13*(2), 193–204.

Wynne, L. (1958). Pseudo-mutuality in the family relations of schizophrenics. *Psychiatry, 21*, 205–222.

Wynne, L. (2016). About Lyman Wynne. University of Rochester Medical Center. Web site: https://www.urmc.rochester.edu/psychiatry/institute-for-the-family/wynne-center/about-lyman-wynne.aspx.

Xiao, J. J. (Ed.). (2008). *Handbook of consumer finance research*. New York, NY: Springer.

Xu, A., DeFrain, J., & Liu, W. (2017). *The Chinese family today*. London: Routledge/Taylor & Francis Group.

Xu, A., Xie, X., Liu, W., Xia, Y., & Liu, D. (2007). Chinese family strengths and resiliency. In DeFrain, J. & Asay, S. M. (Eds.), *Strong families around the world: Strengths-based research and perspectives*. London: Routledge/Taylor & Francis Group.

Yalom, M. (1997). *A history of the breast*. New York, NY: Alfred A. Knopf.

Yalom, M. (2001). *A history of the wife*. New York, NY: HarperCollins.

Yalom, M. (2016). Marilyn Yalom: Biographical sketch. Web site: http://www.myalom.com/biography.html.

Yarber, W. L., & Sayad, B. W. (2013). *Human sexuality: Diversity in contemporary America* (8th ed.). New York, NY: McGraw-Hill.

Yarrow, P. (1972). River of Jordan. *PP&M Lifelines*. Mary Beth Music, ASCAP. Burbank, CA: Warner Bros. Records.

Zambrana, R. E. (Ed.). (1995). *Understanding Latino families*. Thousand Oaks, CA: Sage.

Zambrana, R. E., & Capello, D. (2003). Promoting Latino child and family welfare: Strategies for strengthening the child welfare system. *Children and Youth Services Review, 25*(10), 755–780.

Zaslow, M., & Eldred, C. (1998). Parenting behavior in a sample of young mothers in poverty. *APA Monitor*. Washington, DC: American Psychological Association.

Zhang, N., Parish, W. L., Huang, Y., & Pan, S. (2012, August). Sexual infidelity in China: Prevalence and gender-specific correlates. *Archives of Sexual Behavior, 41*(4), 861–873. Web site: http://www.ncbi.nlm.nih.gov/pubmed/22544304.

Zhang, Y. (2010). A mixed-methods analysis of extramarital sex in contemporary China. *Marriage & Family Review, 46*, 170–190.

Zhou, M., & Lee, J. (2008). Asian American youth: Culture, identity, and ethnicity. In S. Coontz (Ed.), *American families: A multicultural reader* (pp. 294–300). New York, NY: Routledge/Taylor & Francis Group.

Zigler, E. F. (2004). Research interests. Yale University, Department of Psychology, New Haven, CT. Web site: http://www.yale.edu/psychology/FacInfo/Zigler.html.

Zvonkovic, A. M., Lee, K., Brooks-Hurst, E., & Lee, N. (2014). Recession jitters among professional class families: Perceptions of economic strain and family adjustments. *Journal of Family Issues, 35*, 755–775.

Name Index

Abbott, D. A., 36, 69
Abeles, R. P., 379, 349
Abma, J. C., 165
Abrahms, S., 358
Adams, M., 396
Aday, L. A., 363
Adler-Baeder, F., 296, 458, 470
Afifi, T. D., 121
Agrillo, C., 322, 323
Ahrons, C., 442, 459, 461, 462
Aiken, L. R., 379, 402
Aknin, L. B., 213
Albert, N. G., 41
Alberti, R., 148, 158
Aldwin, C. M., 354, 379
Alfaro, E. C., 18
Allen, E. S., 176
Allen, K., 370
Allen, S. M., 192
Allen, W., 173, 323, 428
Altman, A., 277
Altschul, D. B., 62
Amato, P., 12, 310, 442, 443, 448
Anderson, E. R., 435, 440, 441, 443, 462
Anderson, J. R., 217, 283, 296
Anderson, N. B., 39, 42, 43, 64
Angel, R. J., 407, 410
Antonovics, K., 12
Apter, T., 311
Arditti, J., 332
Arias, I., 408, 409
Arias, L., 408, 409
Arnedt, C., 160
Arnett, J. J., 87, 103
Aron, A., 241, 263
Arrington, R., 38, 50, 59, 69, 92
Asai, S., 200, 407, 408, 409
Asay, S. M., 2, 15, 18, 35, 36, 53, 55, 81, 112, 383, 410, 411, 431, 464, 466, 480, 484
Asebedo, S. D., 372
Ashton, D., 41
Atkins, D. C., 475
Atwood, J., 484

Atwood, T. C., 321, 349
Avery-Leaf, S., 144
Axtell, R. E., 110, 127

Bachman, H. J., 363
Bailey, M. J., 233
Bailey, S. J., 363
Bakhurst, M. G., 469
Baldry, A. C., 412
Baldwin, S. E., 296, 310
Bales, R. F., 90
Bámaca, M. Y., 18
Banzet, M. R., 242
Barber, B., 325, 414
Barrios-Bell, A., 58, 198, 297, 449, 459
Barry, C. M., 87
Barstad, A., 197
Basinger, E. D., 121
Bass, B. L., 209
Bateson, G., 116
Batson, C. D., 66
Baucom, D. H., 144, 307, 475
Bauer, J. W., 371
Baumbusch, J. L., 263
Baumrind, D., 326, 327, 328
Beach, S. R. H., 144, 307, 308, 309
Beall, M. L., 128
Bean, R. A., 325, 326
Becvar, D. S., 80
Becvar, R. J., 80
Begin, J., 140
Bell, R., 329
Bellous, J. E., 348
Belsky, J., 348
Belt, D., 283
Benson, B., 169
Bent-Goodley, T. B., 39
Bergen, K. M., 49
Berger, L. M., 447
Berkowitz, D., 46, 49
Berman, J., 6, 45
Bernard, A., 189
Bernard, J., 7, 16, 17, 88, 205

Berscheid, E., 74
Berzon, B., 183
Best, J., 287
Bhopal, K., 265, 266
Bhugra, D., 157
Bianchi, S. M., 29, 194, 198, 209
Bianchi, S., 209
Biblarz, T., 46, 47
Bigner, J., 484
Billingsley, A., 57
Binik, Y. M., 179
Bitensky, S. H., 332, 333
Bjorklund, G., 343
Blackman, L., 292
Blanchard, V. L., 296, 310
Blankemeyer, M., 395
Blankenhorn, D., 259, 288, 340
Blau, J. R., 18
Blayney, J. A., 269
Blieszner, R., 370
Bloch, E., 348
Blow, A. J., 150, 175, 183
Bluck, S., 263
Blumberg, S. L., 113, 126, 127
Bogle, K. A., 268, 269, 287
Bolzendahl, C., 6
Bond, B. J., 111
Boonstra, H. D., 165
Booth, S., 379, 448
Borcherdt, B., 134, 135, 148
Bornstein, R., 407, 410
Bos, H., 46, 443
Boss, P., 103, 379, 386, 387, 401
Boulding, K., 467
Bouthillier, D., 140
Bowen, G. L., 18, 394
Bowlby, J., 254
Boyd-Franklin, N., 199
Boyle, F. M., 244
Bradford, K., 279, 414
Bradshaw, M., 332
Braithwaite, D. O., 5, 324
Branscomb, K. R., 112
Bright, J., 385, 386, 387, 388

Britt, S., 215, 233
Broderick, C., 3, 365
Broderick, J. E., 365
Broken Nose, M. A., 199
Brommel, B. J., 205
Brooks-Hurst, E., 211
Brown, E., 41, 42, 172, 175
Brown, K. G., 283, 310, 358
Brown, L., 241
Brown, P. R., 447
Brown, S., 17
Brown, T. B., 155
Browning, R., 366
Brown-Rice, K., 62
Brubaker, T. H., 379
Brubaker, T., 373, 374
Bruce, M. L., 374, 379
Bryant, J. A., 36
Bryant, J., 36
Bryant, M., 387, 401
Buechner, F., 340
Buehler, C., 194
Buffett, W., 212
Bukstein, O. G., 431
Bulanda, J. R., 283
Bumpass, L., 9
Buono, A. J., 263
Burgess, E., 7, 88
Burr, W. R., 402
Burton, L., 20, 93, 332
Busby, D. M., 284
Buss, D. M., 196, 197
Butler, A. B., 209
Butler, M. H., 176
Buzzela, B. A., 45

Cacciatore, J., 379
Cacioppo, J. T., 260, 263
Call, V., 355
Camarota, S. A., 43
Campbell, R., 30
Canary, D. J., 130, 146, 147, 148
Canary, H. E., 130, 146, 147, 148
Cano, A., 144
Caplin, J., 399
Carey, B., 400
Carey, M. P., 179, 180
Carlson, K. J., A-6
Carlson, S. A., A-6
Carlyle, K., 110
Carr, D., 277, 374, 375
Carroll, J. S., 87, 284
Cassidy, J., 280
Caughlin, J. P., 121
Caughy, M. O., 18

Cavanaugh, M. M., 412
Chamberlin, J., 155
Chambers, A. L., 292
Chaney, C., 38, 57, 209, 217, 285, 292
Chango, J., 303
Chapman, M., 39, 50
Chartrand, E., 140
Chase, J., 62
Chase-Lansdale, P. L., 363
Chatav, Y., 177
Chatters, L. M., 449
Chen, R., 322, 399
Cherlin, A. J., 268, 287, 311, 440
Cherlin, A., 36, 43, 93, 358, 440
Cheung, F. M., 194, 209
Chilisa, B., 39
Chiriboga, D., 263
Choi, H., 310
Chong, A., 319, 348
Choukas-Bradley, S., 110
Christensen, A., 475
Christian-Herman, J., 144
Chse-Lansdale, P. L., 363
Chung, A. Y., 68
Cicirelli, V. G., 360
Cinotto, S., 112
Clark, R. A., 348
Claxton, A., 92
Clay, R. A., 180, 183
Clayton, O., 292
Clements, M. L., 309, 311
Clinic, M., 179, 180
Clooney, G., 260
Coan, J., 303
Cohen, D., 221, 240, 263
Cohn, D'V., 294, 367, 379
Colapinto, J., 484
Colby, S. L., 44
Cole, C. L., 110
Coles, R. L., 68
Coltrane, S., 458, 459
Conger, K. J., 428
Conger, R. D., 428
Conner, D. H., 410
Connidis, I., 263
Constantine, N. A., 168
Cook, R., 81, 89
Cooley, C., 88
Coontz, S., 69, 209
Coop Gordman, K., 177
Coop Gordon, K., 144, 148
Cooper, C. L., 384, 385
Copen, C. E., 165, 275, 283, 284, 435

Córdova, J. V., 474, 484
Cowan, C. P., 319
Cowan, P. A., 319
Cox, C. B., 363
Coxeter, P. D., 244
Cozza, S. J., 399
Craig, L., 191
Crane, D. R., 325
Creswell, J. W., A-9
Crook, R., 92
Cui, M., 280, 281, 287
Cullington, D., 431
Curtin, S., 338
Cutting, B., 348
Cynkar, A., 219

Daas, K. L., 49
Daggett, L. M., 375, 379
Dalla, R., 36, 69, 349
Daly, M., 420
Danes, S., 320
Daniels, K., 275, 283, 284
Dansie, L., 458
Danziger, S., 233
Darkwa, O., 372
Darling, C. A., 468
Darwin, N. T., 36
Daugherty, J., 435
David, P., 311
Davidov, B., 50, 51
Davidson, L. J., 422
Davis, D. J., 209
Davis, K. E., 235
Davis, T., 57
Davis, W., 38
Day, R. D., 212
Dayzie, I., 38, 50, 59, 69
de Jong Gierveld, J., 459
De Staël, M., 236
de Vries, J. M., 244
Deal, R. L., 36, 456, 457, 458, 462
Dean, L., 228, 229
Deaton, A., 365
Deck, A., 443
DeClaire, J., 118, 125, 127, 148
Dee, T. S., 172
DeFrain, A., 480
DeFrain, J., 2, 12, 15, 18, 35, 36, 53, 55, 56, 69, 81, 83, 89, 112, 142, 148, 157, 213, 330, 379, 383, 391, 410, 411, 419, 431, 432, 464, 466, 480, 484
DeFrain, N., 74, 419, 431, 432
DeGarmo, D. S., 435, 440, 441, 443, 447, 462

I-2   Name Index

DeLamater, J. D., 150, 155, 156, 157, 179, 182, 184, 357
Dellmann-Jenkins, M., 395
DePaulo, B., 263
DePaulo, B. M., 263
Desmond, M., 233
Devahastin, S., 259
Dew, J., 211, 215, 216, 217, 233, 285
Dewe, P., 384, 385
Diamond, M., 348
Dickler, J., 359
Dindia, K., 118
Dingfelder, S., 407
Dirie, W., 157
Dixon, L. J., 144, 148
Doherty, B., 331
Doherty, W., 33, 307, 341, 296
Doherty, W. J., 348, 428
Dolbin-MacNab, M., 92, 362, 363
Dole, B., 189
Dole, E., 189
Dorey-Stein, C., 90
Douglas, S. J., 98, 348
Downing, J. B., 93, 340
Drago, R. W., 209
Drake, B., 446
Drebot, M. E., 422
Dreby, J., 69
Driver, J., 300, 311
Drobnic, S., 209
Drogos, K. L., 111
Dugas, C., 204
Duncan, S. F., 470
Dunn, L., 213, 228
Dunne, M. P., 244
Durham, W., 324
Duvall, E., 87
Dworkin, J., 87, 280
Dye, J. L., 338
Dykstra, P., 263, 355

Eap, S., 447
Edmondson, B., 369, 379
Edwards, B. G., 75
Eggebeen, D. J., 448
Eggett, D. L., 255
Einstein, A., A-8
Eisenstat, S. A., A-6
El Issa, E., 227
Elicker, J., 334
Elkins, J., 62
Ella, D. M., 384
Elliott, D. B., 291
Ellison, C. G., 332

Emery, R. E., 148, 462
Emmons, M., 136, 148
Ennis, S. R., 41
Enright, E., 358
Enright, R. D., 93
Epp, John Van, 279
Erickson, M. F., 341
Erickson, R., 191
Erikson, E., 147, 352
Estacion, A., 93
Esteinou, R., 36
Eubanks Fleming, C. J., 474, 484
Evans-Campbell, T., 62

Fadiman, G., 189
Faiola, A., 259
Fairfield, S., 254, 263
Falicov, C. J., 198, 199
Fals-Stewart, W., 400, 426
Fang, X., 271
Faris, E., 73
Fawcett, N. R., 296, 310, 412
Fehr, B., 245
Feldman, R., 352
Ferguson, S. J., 263
Fergusson, D. M., 405
Ferrer, M., 484
Fields, J., 273, 415, 416
Fincham, F. D., 270, 280, 281, 287, 307, 308, 309
Fincham, F., 144
Finer, L., 165, 172
Finkelhor, D., 29
Fischer, J. L., 228
Fisher, C., 49, A-11
Fisher, H. E., 241, 263
Fisher, L. L., 159, 162, 183
Fitch, C., 9
Fitzpatrick, L., 436, 437
Foote, J., 141
Forgatch, M. S., 435, 440, 441, 443, 462
Fowers, B., 50, 51
Fox, G. L., 90
Franklin, A., 199
Freedmen, S. R., 93
Freeman, P. A., 255
Frey, W. H., 66
Frias, S. M., 407, 410
Friedan, B., 34, 90
Fromm, E., 236
Frost, D. M., 47, 48
Fry, R., 367, 379
Fu, V. K., 279
Fuligni, A., 50

Gaalen, P. A., 355
Gagnon, J. H., 176
Gahagan, K., 292
Gaines, S. O., 242
Galbraith, K. A., 169
Gallagher, M., 12, 15, 16, 17, 34, 291
Galvin, K. M., 205
Ganong, L., 260
Garbanati, J. A., 428, 429
Garbarino, J., 340
Garcia-Manglano, J., 209
Garneau, C., 453, 454, 455, 462
Gartrell, N., 46, 443
Gates, B., 212
Gates, G., 46, 153, 449
Gaunt, R., 340
Geist, C., 6
Gelles, R., 36, 409, 410, 411, 412, 420, 422
Genovese, F., 484
Gerena, M., 39
Gershoff, E. T., 332, 333
Gerson, K., 209
Gerstel, N., 39
Giarrusso, R., 380
Gibbs, N., 331
Gibran, K., 94, 346
Gibson, P. A., 363, 364
Gil, E., 484
Gilbert, N., 209
Giles. J., 184, 456
Gillath, O., 254
Giordano, J., 277
Giordano, P. C., 270, 283
Glaser, G., 431
Glaser, R., 135
Glenn, N., 292
Goldberg, A. E., 45, 93, 321, 340
Goldenberg, H., 74, 75, 76, 77, 78, 80, 103
Goldenberg, I., 74, 75, 76, 77, 78, 80, 103
Goldstein, S., 73
Golin, C. E., 110
Gomez, A., 41
Gone, J. P., 62
Gonzales-Backen, M., 50
Gonzalez, J., 60, 62, 227, 233
Gonzalez-Kruger, G., 81
Goodman, C. C., 363
Goodman, J. E., 128
Goodwin, R., 236–237, 238, 263
Gorall, D., 91, 95
Gordman, K., 177
Gordon, K. C., 148

Name Index   I-3

Gordon, K. L., 144
Gordon, L., 471
Gordon, M., 280, 281, 287, 307
Gordon, P. A., 258, 259
Gotta, G., 154, 163, 164
Gottlieb, A., 484
Gottman, J. M., 118, 125, 127, 148, 154, 311, 348
Gottman, J. S., 148, 154
Gottman, J., 127, 300
Gouin, J.-P., 135
Graber, E. C., 303
Graham, L., 30, 273
Granato, H., 269
Grass, G. A., 393
Grass, S. R., 393
Gray, P., 40 323
Green, C., 68
Green, R., 154, 164
Greene, S. M., 435, 440, 441, 443, 462
Greer, M., 400
Grieco, E. M., 43
Groeben, M., 442
Grover, S., 12
Grusec, J. E., 327
Grzywacz, J. G., 209
Gubrium, J. F., 103
Gudmunson, C. G., 214, 228
Gullone, E., 412
Gurman, A. S., 484
Gustafson, R., 29
Gutierrez, D., 458

Haase, C. M., 141
Haberman, H. R., 320
Hadzi-Pavlovic, D., 163
Hagestad, G. O., 355
Haley, J., 97, 116
Halford, W. K., 469
Halgunseth, L. C., 58
Hall, J. A., 114, 127, 179
Hall, J., 307, 308
Hall, M., 369
Halpern, D. F., 194, 195, 209
Halpern, D. F., 209
Ham, J., 152
Hamilton, B. E., 338
Hamon, R. R., 104, 287
Han, X., 400
Hancock, A. M., 228
Hare, J., 48
Harknett, K., 221
Harper, J. M., 176
Harris, A. H., 307
Harris, J. R., 331

Harris, S., 265
Harris, V. W., 303, 304
Harter, P., 437
Hartnett, K., 150, 175, 183
Hartshorne, J. K., 276
Harvey, J. H., 184
Hatch, D., 38, 49, 58, 69, 216, 297, 323, 349
Havens, B., 369
Hawkins, A. J., 192, 296, 310
Hayes, A., 348
Hayes, J., 348
Haynes, C., 69
Hazan, C., 254
Healey, J. F., 233
Heart, M., 62
Hecker, L., 484
Hefner, V., 111
Helliwell, J. F., 12
Hellmich, N., 173
Helms, S. W., 110
Henderson, K., 351, 380
Hendrix, S., 172
Hennigan, 136, 137
Hennon, C. B., 484
Herbenick, D., 12, 150, 159, 160
Herek, G. M., 155
Herlihy, J. L., 236
Hertel, J., 263
Hertog, S., 158
Hertwig, O., 152
Hetherington, E. M., 12, 435, 440, 441, 443, 462
Higginbotham, B., 46, 58, 198, 279, 296, 297, 351, 360, 380, 449, 456, 458, 459, 462, 470
Higgins, D., 348
Hill, N. E., 39
Hill, R., 57, 87, 93, 389, 390, 429
Hill, T. L., 364
Hine, D. C., 57
Hingson, R. W., 172
Hirschl, T. A., 12
Hobfoll, S. E., 401
Hochschild, A., 20
Hodge, D. R., 61
Hoeffel, E. M., 43
Hoffman, L., 398
Holder-Taylor, C., 93
Hollander, J. F., 359
Holley, S. R., 141
Holman, H., 362
Holman, T. B., 470
Holmes, E. K., 212
Holmes, P., 254, 263

Holmes, T., 227, 233
Holmes, T. H., 384, 385
Holstein, J. A., 103
Holtzman, M., 5
Holtzworth-Munroe, A., 405
Holzner, C., 217
Homer, M. M., 255
Hopkins-Williams, K., 57
Horgan, T. G., 114, 127
Horn, S. S., 69
Horn, W., 340
Horner, E. M., 437
Horowitz, C., 468
Horrocks, A., 213
Horwood, L. J., 405
Hosek, J., 396, 398
Hoskins, M., 212
Houseknecht, S. K., 18
Howard, J., 5, 455
Howden, L. M., 275
Howland, J., 172
Huang, A. X., 168, 176
Huebner, A. J., 393, 394, 395, 398
Hughes, F. M., 144, 148
Hull, E., 395
Humes, K. R., 41
Hunt, B. R., 198, 209
Hunt, S., 87, 103
Huston, S., 215, 233, 275
Huxley, A., 468, 484
Hyde, J. S., 150, 155, 179, 182, 184, 357

Iasenza, S., 181
Imber-Black, E., 484
Ingoldsby, B. B., 287
Ingraham, C., 423
Inman, A. G., 277
Insel, P. M., 150, 180, 184, 425
Inskeep, S., 362, 363
Ispa, J. M., 58

Jack, E. L., 51, 242
Jackson, D. D., 116
Jackson, J. K., 424
Jackson, M. H., 400–401
Jacob, J., 348
Jacobvitz, D. B., 85
James, S., 292, 443
Järvinen, M., 431
Jayson, S., 258
Jenkins, N. H., 113, 126, 127
Jensen, L. A., 455
Jerman, P., 168
Johnson, A. C., 213

Johnson, D., 448
Johnson, J., 36, 69, 412
Johnson, M., 405, 414, 431, 449
Johnson, V., 173
Jones, F., 385, 386, 387, 388
Jones, J. E., 419, 432
Jones-Sanpei, H., 212
Joo, S., 228
Jorgensen, B. L., 228
Joseph, A. L., 121
Jossey-Bass, P., 387
Joung, E., 447
Jozkowski, K., 110
Julien, D., 140

Kaduvettoor-Davidson, A., 277
Kagan, J., 201
Kahn, J., 209
Kaiser, H. J., 170, 171, 172, 212, 214
Kalil, A., 211, 447
Kaminer, Y., 431
Kane, J. B., 443
Kantrowitz, B., 371
Kapungu, C. T., 169
Karis, T. A., 287
Kaufman, A., 168, 276
Keaton, D., 173
Keiley, M. K., 92
Keillor, G., 193
Kelley, M., 400
Kelly, G. F., 150, 179, 181, 182, 184, 445
Kelly, J. B., 462
Kelly, J., 12
Kelly, K. M., 242
Kendig, H., 355
Keneski, E., 273
Kennedy, S., 9
Kensinger-Rose, K., 334
Kerpelman, J. L., 296, 470
Kersting, K., 365
Kiang, L., 50
Kiecolt-Glaser, J. K., 135
Kilbourne, J., 184
Killian, K. D., 287
Kilmer, J. R., 269
Kindlon, D., 331
King, M. L., 57
King, V., 448
Kinghorn, A., 310
Kirkpatrick, L. A., 197
Klein, D. M., 88
Klein, S. R., 402
Kleinke, C. L., 384
Knapp, M. L., 114, 127

Knight, G. P., A-11
Knipscheer, K., 355
Knoester, C., 448
Knudson-Martin, 188, 200, 205
Knutson, L., 299, 311
Kohlberg, L., 201
Kolak, A. M., 338
Kolbert, E., 32
Kollar, M., 220, 221, 222, 233
Kolodny, R., 173
Korman, J., 118
Kornhaber, A., 379
Koropeckyj-Cox, T., 263, 322, 355
Kosanke, N., 141
Kravitz, A., 292
Kreider, R. M., 9, 10, 290, 435, 436
Kuba, C. A., 379
Kuczynski, K., 320
Kurdek, L., 45, 154, 155
Kurtz, M. A., 363

Lachman, M. E., 354
Ladd, L., 136, 137
Lambert, N., 228
Landers, A., 172
Lang, F., 323
Langer, G., 160
Lankov, A., 436
Lannutti, P., 111, 112
LaRossa, R., 341
Larsen, R. J., 206
Larson, P. J., 32, 36, 85, 97, 98, 107, 108, 112, 123, 124, 125, 126, 128, 130, 131, 148, 150, 151, 188, 189, 197, 206, 213, 247, 300, 305, 306, 311, 313, 314, 388, 464, 484
Larson, R. W., 112
Lasswell, M., 373, 423
Lasswell, T., 423
Laughlin, L., 333
Laumann, E. O., 176
Laurenceau, J., 303
Lawrence, E., 318
Layden, M. A., 27
Lazarus, R. S., 383
Le Guin, U. K., 236
LeBlanc, H., 38, 50, 59, 69
Lebow, J., 358, 484
Lee, C., 341
Lee, E., 200
Lee, J., 58
Lee, T. R., 303
Lee, T., 211, 215, 233, 283, 303, 304
Lee, Y., 190
Lehrer, L., 15-17

Leibniz, G., 468
Leininger, L. J., 211
LeMasters, E. E., 318
Leon, K., 85
Lerman, R., 259, 288
Lerner, H. G., 138, 140, 148, 311
Letiecq, B. L., 363
Levaro, E. B., 375
Levenson, M. R., 354
Levin, D. E., 184
Levy, K., 242
Lewin, A., 15-17, 450
Lewis, C. S., 269, 290, 435, 436, 442
Lewis, S. K., 18
Lichter, D. T., 66, 280
Limb, G. E., 61
Lin, I-F., 358
Lincoln, A., 246
Lincoln, K. D., 449
Lindau, S. T., 367
Lindstrom, R., 272, 273
Linney, K. D., 209
Lino, M., 320
Liossis, P., 361
Lisle, J., 258
Litzinger, S. C., 144, 148
Liu, W., 12
Liu, D., 12
Liu, H., 157
Livingston, G., 294, 362, 367, 379
Loew, B., 176, 469
Lohrfink, K. F., 18
Longmore, M. A., 270, 283
Lorenz, F. O., 428
Loseke, D. R., 412
Lostutter, T. W., 269
Lougheed, E., 117
Louis, St., 173
Loving, T. J., 273
Ludden, J., 362, 363
Luecking, G., 263
Lund, M., 149
Luo, Y., 15-17, 450
Lynch, M., 190, 191, 209
Lyons, J. A., 400

Mace, D., 7, 296
Mace, V., 7, 296
Maciel, J. A., 200
MacTavish, K. A., 213
Madathil, J., 265
Madsen, B., 284
Maguire, K. C., 395, 398, 432
Mahoney, A., 104

Maier, T., 184
Malarkey, W. B., 135
Malinowski, B., 156
Malone-Colon, L., 259, 288, 292
Mancini, J. A., 387, 393, 394, 401
Mandara, J., 326, 328, 349
Manicavasagar, V., 163
Mankiller, W., 200
Manning, W., 17, 270, 283
Mansfield, A. J., 394
Manthos, M., 113
Manzi, C., 326
Marelich, W. D., 242
Markman, H. J., 113, 126, 127, 176, 309, 311, 469, 471, 484
Marks, L., 57, 310
Marmot, M., 366
Marquardt, E., 259, 288, 293
Marsh, J. C., 81
Marshall, J. P., 215, 233, 303
Marsiglio, W., 49
Martin, J. A., 88, 338
Martinez, V., 162
Martinez-Brawley, E. E., 44
Mashek, D. J., 241, 263
Masters, W., 173
Mathews, T. J., 338
Mattingly, M. J., 194
Mauritzen, E., 431
May, R., 134
McCarthy, B., 173, 174, 184
McCarthy, B. W., 184
McCarthy, E., 174, 184
McConaghy, N., 163
McDonnell, C., 411, 412
McGinley, E., 240
McGirk, T., 401
McGirt, E., 399
McGoldrick, M., 41, 277, 278
McGovern. G., 431
McGraw, L. A., 360
McGuire, A. C. L., 469
McLanahan, S., 221
McLaughlin, M., 121
McMullen, I., 157
McNaughton-Cassill, M., 190, 191, 209
McNulty, J. K., 308
Mead, G., 88
Mead, M., 194, 340, 360
Meaney, G. L., 321
Mehta, V., 244
Meier, J. A., 190, 191, 209
Melby, J. N., 428
Melkas, T., 355

Melli, M. S., 447
Mencken, H. L., 236
Mendez, E., 46, 297, 458, 462
Mercadante, C., 439, 441
Merolla, J., 69
Merz, E.-M., 459
Metzger, M., 18, 35, 410, 411, 431, 464, 484
Meyer, J. A., 275
Michael, R. T., 176
Michaels, M. W., 348
Michaels, S., 176
Michener, J. A., 467
Mickelson, K. D., 319, 348
Mickish, J., 412, 431
Miedzian, M., 413
Miga, E., 303
Mikulincer, M., 254, 255, 263
Miller, A., 258, 284
Miller, B., 169, 170
Miller, M., 286
Miller, P., 122, 471, 484
Miller, S., 122, 471, 484
Minuchin, P., 484
Minuchin, S., 484
Mitchell, K., 29
Mohatt, G., 49, 69
Monaghan, L., 128
Monat, A., 383
Monk, J. K., 272
Monserud, M. A., 361
Montenegro, X. P., 358
Moody, J., A–8
Moore, B. A., 484
Moore, K. A., 342
Moore, T., 228
Morgan, A., 89
Morgan, S. P., 322
Mori, Y., 259
Morin, R., 359
Morrill, P., 279, 309
Morris, W., 263
Morrison, T., 39
Mosher, W. D., 275, 283, 284
Moskos, C., 398
Moyer, B., 18, 35, 464, 484
Moyer, R., 410, 411, 431
Mroczek, D., 365
Mueller, L., 92
Mueller, M. L., 38, 50, 59, 69, 92
Murphy, M., 348
Murray, C. E., 469, 470
Murry, V. M., 39, 90
Murstein, B. I., 268

Mussen, P., 202
Mydans, S., 259
Myers, J. E., 265

Najman, J. M., 244
Nance-Nash, S., 359
Neeves-Botelho, S., 332
Nelini, C., 322, 323
Nelson, L. J., 87
Nesteruk, O., 57, 372
Nettles, S. M., 18
Neugarten, B., 353
Neyer, F. J., 323
Nicholson, J. M., 456
Niehuis, S., 272
Niemeyer, R. A., 379
Noar, 110
Noel, R., 43
Nolen, J. L., 410
Norris, T., 43
Norton, W. W., 127, 213, 263, 311, 348, 387
Notter, M. L., 213

O'Brien, E., 194, 233
O'Campo, P. J., 18
O'Farrell, T. J., 426
O'Leary, K. D., 144
O'Malley, C. J., 395
O'Sullivan, L. F., 110
Obama, B., 278
Ochs, E., 112
Olsen, C., 58, 297
Olson, A., 237
Olson, D. H., 32, 36, 53, 85, 91, 95, 97, 98, 100, 107, 108, 123, 124, 125, 126, 128, 130, 131, 148, 150, 151, 188, 189, 206, 213, 237, 247, 299, 300, 305, 306, 311, 313, 314, 388, 389, 407, 408, 409, 456, 457, 458, 462, 464, 471, 484
Olson-Sigg, A., 32, 36, 97, 98, 107, 108, 123, 124, 125, 126, 128, 130, 131, 148, 150, 151, 188, 189, 206, 213, 247, 300, 305, 306, 311, 313, 314, 388, 464, 484
Onedera, J. D., 484
Ooms, T., 290, 291
Oord, T. J., 236, 263
Orthner, D. K., 394
Ortman, J. M., 44
Orwell, G., 186
Osborn, F., 72
Osterman, M., 338
Otters, R. V., 359

Ouytsel, J. V., 280, 281
Owen, J., 113, 270
Owens, T. J., 104
Owings, A., 69

Palacio, J., 79
Paleari, F. G., 308
Pan, P. A., 259
Pan, S., 176
Pan, Y., 267
Pape, K. T., 408, 409
Paracelsus, 236
Paragament, K. I., 484
Parish, W. L., 176
Park, C. L., 379
Parke, R., 458
Parker, K., 362, 448, 449, 462
Parshall, S., 40
Parsons, T., 90, 193, 208
Pasley, K., 453, 454, 455, 462
Passel, J., 66, 294
Patras, J., 447
Patrick, W., 260, 263
Patterson, C., 46
Patterson, C. J., 339
Paulk, A., 296, 470
Pawelski, J., 155
Pelucchi, S., 308
Peluso, P., 184
Pence, E., 411, 412
Pendell, G., 322
Perez, L., 398
Perreira, K., 39, 50
Perren, S., 442
Perry-Jenkins, M., 92
Peters, H. E., 280
Petts, R. J., 448
Piaget, J., 329
Pines, A. M., 242
Ponnet, K., 280, 281
Pooley, J. A., 441
Poortman, A., 190
Popelyuk, D., 157
Popenoe, D., 8, 12, 257, 258, 284, 293, 435
Porche, M. V., 45
Powell, B., 6
Preto, N. G., 277
Preyser, H., 443
Price, C. A., 372
Prinstein, M. J., 110
Proctor, B. D., 220, 221, 222, 233
Pryor, J., 457
Pucheu Theall, K., 348
Pudrovska, T., 325

Puente, S., 240, 263
Purdie, D. M., 244
Purplefairy, L., 423
Purvin, D. M., 45
Putman, R. D., 69, 112, 191

Qian, Z., 66, 280
Qualls, S. H., 379
Quirk, K., 113

Raetz, K., 276
Ragan, E. P., 113
Rahe, R. H., 384, 385
Rainville, A., 398
Raley, S., 29, 194
Ramakrishnan, S. K., 69
Rank, M. R., 12, 367, 379
Rappleyea, D. L., 271
Reagan, N., 375
Reagan, R., 375
Reck, K., 458
Reczek, C., 12, 325
Reece, M., 12
Reevy, G., 383
Regalia, C., 308, 326
Regnerus, M., 46
Reid, G., 155
Rhoades, G., 113, 176
Richard-Davis, G., 248
Ridder, E. M., 405
Rilke, R. M, 131, 236
Rios-Vargas, M., 41
Rivett, M., 484
Rix, S. E., 354
Robbins, R., 362
Roberto, K. A., 370
Roberts, A., 292
Roberts, S., 8
Robinson, J. M., 128
Robinson, J., 148
Robinson, P. W., 422
Rodas, C., 443
Rodriguez, N., 320
Rokach, A., 247
Rook, K., 263
Roosa, M. W., A-11
Rosato, D., 354
Rosenband, R., 38, 50, 59, 69
Rosenblum, K., 209
Rosenfeld, M. J., 250, 270–271
Ross, M. E., 363
Roth, W. T., 150, 180, 184, 425
Rowe, C. L., 426
Rowe, D., 380
Rowe, G., 373

Roy, K. M., 20
Rudy, D., 58, 327
Rueter, M. A., 320, 321
Russell, B., 204
Russell, C., 98
Russell, S. T., 69
Ryan, R. M., 447
Rye, B. J., 321

Sabbadini, A., 240
Sabusawa, M. Y., 467
Sadberry, S. L., 309, 311
Sage, R., 169, 170, 387
Sahlstein Parcell, E., 395, 398, 432
Saint Augustine, 240
Salem-Hartshorne, N., 276
Saluter, A., 364
Sammons, M. T., 400
Sand, G., 236
Sanders, M. R., 55
Sandler, L., 322
Sarkisian, N., 39, 57
Sassler, S., 273, 274, 280, 284, 285
Satir, V., 471
Sauck, C., 93, 340
Sauer, K. H., 55
Sautter, F., 400
Sayad, B. W., 150, 184
Scabini, E., 326
Schachner, D. A., 254
Schap, T., 320
Scheinkman, M., 150
Scherman, A., 362
Schneider, D., 221
Schoen, K., 412, 431
Schooler, J. E., 321, 349
Schoppe-Sullivan, S., 192, 341
Schramm, D. G., 215, 218, 233, 296, 303, 304, 470
Schwartz Gottman, J., 118, 125, 127, 148
Schwartz, J. E., 365
Schwartz, P., 288
Scott, M. J., 432, 448
Seay, M. C., 372
Sedlak, A. J., 415, 419
Seedall, R. B., 176
Seidman, G., 240, 242
Seiler, W. J., 128
Semega, J. L., 220, 221, 222, 233
Sen, A., 204
Shackelford, T. K., 197
Shamah, D., 213
Shapiro, A. F., 300, 311
Sharp, E. A., 260

Shaver, P. R., 254, 255, 263, 280
Shaw, S. M., 30
Sheldon, A., 349
Sherman, C. W., 371
Sherman, M. D., 400-401
Shin, N., 18
Shirisia, L, 57
Shoemake, E., 280
Shohet, M., 112
Shpancer, N., 275
Siegel, D. H., 339
Signoret, S., 236
Silverstein, L. B., 341
Silverstein, M., 363, 380
Simard, M., 140
Simmons, D. S., 291, 475
Simons, J., 179, 180
Singh, A., 349
Singh, A., 38, 49, 58, 69, 216, 297, 323
Skinner, D., 48
Skogrand, L., 38, 46, 49, 50, 51, 57, 58, 59, 69, 92, 112, 198, 213, 215, 216, 217, 227, 233, 279, 292, 296, 297, 323, 349, 351, 360, 380, 419, 432, 449, 456, 458, 459, 462
Skolnick, A. S., 7
Skolnick, J. H., 7
Slater, L., 241
Smiler, A. P., 280
Smith, A., 271
Smith, E. P., 39
Smith, J., 321
Smith, J. A., 338, 349
Smith, S. R., 104
Smith, T., Jr., 399
Smith, T. W., 159
Snyder, D. K., 307, 484
Solheim, C., 217
Solot, D., 286
Somer, E., 388
Sorkhabi, N., 326, 328, 349
Sorokin, P., 7
Speer, R. B., 456
Spencer, M., 50
Spielberger, C. D., 401
Spiro, A., III, 365, 379
Spotted Elk, D., 38, 50, 59, 69
Sprecher, S., 280
Sprenkle, D., 98
Springen, K., 371
Stacey, J., 46, 47
Stadelmann, S., 442
Stafford, L., 309, 311
Stanley, S. M., 74, 75, 76, 77, 78, 80, 113, 126, 127, 176, 309, 311, 471, 484

Stanton, M., 103
Steele, C., 404
Stein, G., 39
Steinmetz, S., 36, 412
Stepler, R., 41, 42
Sternberg, R. J., 239, 240, 263
Steuchis, A., 468
Stevens, C., 163
Stewart, J., 107, 456
Stewart, S., 456
Stinnett, N., 55, 81, 83, 467
Stith, S. M., 432
Stokes, B., 211
Stone, A. A., 365
Straus, J., 263
Straus, M., 36, 411, 412, 415, 416, 417
Street, A. E., 408, 409
Strong, G., 241
Struthers, C. B., 30
Suanet, B., 459
Sue, D. W., 43, 57, 58, 60, 61, 199, 200, 201
Sue, D., 43, 57, 58, 60, 61, 199, 200, 201
Suitor, J. J., 104
Sullivan, H. S., 236
Sussman, D., 160
Suter, E. A., 49
Sutton, C. T., 199
Sutton, P. D., 338
Svriuga, S., 172
Swanson, M., 57, 228
Sweeney, J., 373, 453, 455, 459, 460
Swenson, L., 244
Switala, K., 89, 104

Tabares, A., 300, 311
Tasker, F., 339
Tatkin, S., 288
Tavernise, S., 2
Taylor, J. L., 166, 271
Taylor, P., 367, 379, 441, 448, 449, 462
Taylor, R. J., 15, 66, 448
Theroux, Paul, 439
Thiele, D. M., 361, 362
Thomas, L., 49, 69
Thomas, R. J., 250, 270, 271
Thomas, V., 99, 100
Thomas, W., 88
Thompson, K. L., 117, 118, 395, 412
Thoresen, C. E., 307
Thorne, D., 231
Tingle, L. R., 265
Todd, M., 46
Tolstoy, L., 236

Tomcik, N. D., 144, 148
Tong, R., 105
Tong, R., 90, 91, 105
Torres, E., 296, 456
Town, R., 12
Travis, T., 209
Treas, J., 197, 209
Trimble, J., 49, 60, 62, A-11
Troll, L. E., 369, 374, 380
Trussell, D. E., 30
Tubbs, C. Y., 20
Tudge, J., 69
Turkki, K., 468
Twain, M., 134

Ueno, K., 280, 281, 287
Ulker, A., 372, 380
Umaña-Taylor, A. J., 18, A-11
Umberson, D., 325
Usdansky, M. L., 440

Vaillant, G., 236, 424
van der Lippe, T., 190
van der Pas, S., 459
Van Dorn, R. A., 18
Van Epp, J., 279, 288
van Leeuwenhoek, A., 152
Van Putten, Z., 200
van Tilburg, T. G., 459
Van Volkom, M., 377, 380
Vandell, D. L., 336
Vannier, S. A., 110
Vaterlaus, J. M., 292
Vaughn, L., 414
Vennum, A., 272
Ventura, S. J., 338
Vespa, J., 275, 283, 284
Vignoles, V. L., 326
Vines, P. L., 43
Volling, B. L., 338
von Bertalanffy, L., 75
von Klitzing, K., 442
Voydanoff, P., 194, 195

Wagner, J., 323
Waite, L., 12, 15, 16, 17, 34, 190, 291, 450
Waldegrave, C., 38
Waldrep, A. J., 399
Walker, A. J., 360
Walker, J., 277
Walker, K. K., 395
Walker, L. E., 412, 432
Walkner, A. J., 320, 321
Waller, M. R., 280

I-8 Name Index

Wallerstein, J. S., 442, 462
Wallin, P., 88
Walrave, M., 280, 281
Walsh, F., 53, 54, 105
Walsh, R. P., 244
Wang, R., 29, 66
Wang, W., 158, 277, 294, 359, 448, 449, 462
Watson, J. B., 7
Weakland, J., 116
Weber, J. G., 432
Weinberg, D., 89
Weis, K., 239, 263
Weisenbach, S., 263
Weiser, D. A., 272
Weiss, J. W., 428, 429
Wenger, G. C., 355
West, R., 89
Wetchler, J. L., 484
Whelan, T. A., 361, 362
Whisman, M. A., 177
Whitaker, C., 75
White, J. M., 88, 89
White, M., 89
White, W. L., 424
Whitehead, B., 8, 12, 257, 258, 276, 284
Whitton, S. W., 309, 311

Whitton, S., 45
Widman, L., 110
Wiener, N., 297
Wiener, N., 297
Wight, V. R., 198, 209
Wilcox, B., 259, 283, 284, 288, 293, 313, 314, 322, 349, 435, 444, 448, 462
Wilcox, R. M., 393
Wilcox, W. B., 293
Wiles, J. L., 323
Wiley, A. R., 112
Wiley, J., 457
Wilkens, C., 141
Williams, J. H., 367, 379
Williams, K., 175
Williams, S., 6
Williams, V., 6
Willoughby, B. J., 87, 280, 283, 284
Willows, J., 432
Wilson, J., 362
Wilson, M. I., 420
Wilson, S. M., 484
Wimer, L., 447
Wincze, J. P., 184
Winn, D., 93
Winward, B. W., 169, 170

Witkow, M., 50
Wolak, J., 29
Wood, S., 108, 109, 361
Worthington, E. L., 307, 311
Worthington, E. L., Jr., 144
Wright, P. J., 169
Wuerffel, J., 83
Wynne, L., 97

Xiao, J. J., 233
Xu, A., 12, 157, 267

Yalom, M., 157
Yang, C., 470
Yarber, W. L., 150, 184
Yip, T., 50

Zabriskie, R. B., 255
Zettle, L., 263
Zhang, Y., 176
Zhou, M., 59
Zigler, E, 419
Zimmerman, C, 7
Ziol-Guest, K. M., 447
Ziporyn, T., A-6
Zolna, M. R., 165
Zorita, P., 44
Zvonkovic, A. M., 211

Subject Index

Page numbers in *italics* denote figures and tables.

A Prairie Home Companion (radio show), 193
AA. *See* Alcoholics Anonymous (AA)
AAMFT. *See* American Association for Marriage and Family Therapy (AAMFT)
AARP. *See* American Association of Retired Persons (AARP)
AASECT. *See* American Association of Sexuality Educators, Counselors, and Therapists (AASECT)
ABC-X family crisis model, 389–390
Ability to manage stress and crisis, 85–86
Abrazo (hug), 111
Absent father, 340
Abstinence-only-until-marriage approach, 167
Abuse, 240
   animal, 411–412
   child-to-parent, 422–423
   economic, 404
   emotional, 404
   physical, 404, 408–409
   psychological, 404, 408–409
   sexual, 404
   sibling, 421–422
   transcending, 418–419
   See also Alcohol abuse; Child abuse; Violence
Abusive behaviors, 22, 404
Accelerated-consensus trajectory, 324
Acceptance, 235
Acculturation, 63–65, 277–278
Administration for Children and Families (ACF), 310
Adolescents/adolescence, 147, 171, 318
   sexual behavior among, 165–176
Adoption, 320–321
   adoptive family, 321

Adults, divorce impact on, 440–441
African Americans, 42
   awareness, 50
   changes in family structure, 12
   characteristics of families, *42*
   child care, 333
   cohabitation, 285, 458
   culture, 38, 199
   domestic violence, 407
   drop out of school, 18
   economic issues of couples, 217
   families strengths, 57
   gay and lesbian families, 46–47
   grandparents raising grandchildren, 362–363
   marital expectations, 292
   marital status of U.S. population, *8*
   multiracial marriages, 66
   population, 42–43
   racial and ethnic differences, 27
   single-parent families, 448
   single mothers, 338
   victims of abuse and neglect, 23
Age(ism), 366
   differences, 27
   and finding mate, 275–276
Aggression/aggressiveness, 123, 124, 134, 411
   aggressive behavior, 123
   aggressive communication, 123–124
Agriculturally oriented family, 67
AI/ANs. *See* American Indians and Alaska Natives (AI/ANs)
Al-Anon Family Groups, 425–427, 479
Alaska Native populations, 43
Alateen groups, 426–427
Alcohol(ism), 269, 410–411, 423
   acknowledging dangers of legal drugs, 428–429
   and family violence, 424
   problems in families, 423
   sexual behavior, 171–172

   treatment and prevention of, 426–428
   treatment and prevention of alcoholism, 426–428
   use, 25–27
Alcohol abuse, 423
   family's reaction to, 424–426
   warning signs for, *425*
   See also Child abuse
Alcoholics, 427
Alcoholics Anonymous (AA), 426
Alzheimer's disease, 368, 371
Ambiguity, 459
Ambiguous loss, 386–387
American Association for Marriage and Family Therapy (AAMFT), 72, 176, 343, 473, 474
American Association of Retired Persons (AARP), 162, 358
American Association of Sexuality Educators, Counselors, and Therapists (AASECT), 181
American Community Survey, 3
American culture, 66
American Indians, 62
   culture, 199–200
   families strengths, 60–62
   population, 41, 43
American Indians and Alaska Natives (AI/ANs), 43, 60
American morality, 177, 178
American sexual health and behavior, 159
   American sex survey by ABC news, 160–161
   gay-male and lesbian sexual behavior, 163–164
   National Survey of Sexual Health and Behavior, 159–160
   sexuality in later years, 162–163
American society. *See* United States
American style dating, 266
Androgen, 354
   decline. *See* Male menopause

I-11

Anger, 131, 174
  in balance, 137
  and conflict taboos, 133-134
  hierarchy of conflict, 131-133
  myths, theories, and facts about, 134-136
Animal abuse, 411-412
Antiretroviral therapy (ART), 158, 159
Anxious attachment, 254
Appreciation and affection, 82-83
Argument, 253
ART. *See* Antiretroviral therapy (ART)
Asian Americans
  changes in family structure, 12
  characteristics of families, *42*
  culture, 200
  families strengths, 59-60
  household income level, 220-221
  marital status of U.S. population, *8*
  multiracial marriages, 66
  population, 43
  single-parent families, 448
Assertiveness, 124
  assertive communication, 123-124
  positive influence of, 125
Assimilation, 63-65
Astrological signs, 265
Attachment, 238
  avoidant, 254
  theory, 254-255, 280
Attentive listening, 122
Attractiveness, 244
Avoidance, 124
  avoidant attachment, 254
  avoidant style, 124
  debt, 231
  negative influence of, 125-126

Baby boomers, 353
Bad memories, 300
Balanced families, 98-99
Balanced relationships, 99-100
Bamboocioni. *See* Big babies
Bankruptcy, 231
Basic institutional inequality, 204
Behavioral consequences, 418
Behaviorists, 330
Behavior problems, 281
Being single, 255
  cohabitation, 257-258
  diversity in families, 258
  historical perspective on, 257
  individuals, 259-260
  loneliness, 260-262

Pew Research Center, 255-256
  statistics, 256-257
Belief system, 53-55
Best-friend couples, 174
Bidirectional effects, 329
Big babies, 359
Bilateral-persuasion trajectory, 324
Bilateral descent, 53
Binge drinking, 25
Binuclear family, 443
Biological parent, 454
Biological reality, 366
Birth order, 276
Bisexuals, 152, 163
Black Americans, 42-43
  drop out of school, 18
  household income level, 220-221
  marriage and, 292
  population, 41
  racial and ethnic differences, 27
Blamers, 139, 140
Blaming one's partner approach, 388
Blood pressure, 386
Boomerang kids, 359
Boundaries, 75
Boundary ambiguity, 386
  in stepfamilies, 459
Breast cancer, 385-386
"Broken heart syndrome", 273
Budgeting, 219, 225-226
Buying home, 230

Cardiovascular disease, 386-387
Careless spending, 231
Cascading circumstances, 332
Case studies, 476-479, A-10
Catharsis conflict, 412
Caucasian Americans
  changes in family structure, 12
  communication, 56
  marital status of U.S. population, *8*
  multicultural studies, A-11
  single mother, 13
CCC. *See* Civilian Conservation Corps (CCC)
CCCS. *See* Consumer Credit Counseling Service (CCCS)
CD4 cells, 158
Centers for Disease Control and Prevention (CDC), 25, 27, 158, 406
Centrifugal interactions, 78
Centripetal interactions, 78
Certified Family Life Educator (CFLE), 343

CFLE. *See* Certified Family Life Educator (CFLE)
Change
  balancing, 77-78, *96*, 96-97
  chaotic, 95-96
  cultural, 157-158
Chaotically cohesive family, 102
Chaotically disengaged husband, A-2
Chaotically disengaged pattern, 327
Chaotically enmeshed family system, 392
Chaotically enmeshed style, 327
Chaotic change, 95-96
Chemical dependency, 275
Chicano/a families. *See* Hispanic Americans
Child abuse, 414
  cost of raising child, *320*
  cross-generational transmission, 419
  incidence, 415
  long-term consequences, 417-418
  treatment and prevention, 420-421
  See also Alcohol abuse
Child Abuse Prevention and Treatment Act, 415
Child care, 333-337
  for growing Hispanic population, 334
  high quality child care program and positive caregiving, 336-337
  increasing use of child care outside family, 21
Child Effects on Adults, 329
Childfree, 355
Childlessness, 322, 355
Childrearing theories, 328-330
Children, 58
  changing reactions to gay child, *164*
  child-free alternative, 322-325
  child-thought, 329
  child-to-parent abuse, 422-423
  conflict between parents and, 146-147
  and couple happiness, 314
  dies, 342-343
  divorce impact on, 442-444
  domestic violence and, 414
  financial issues and, 320
  and individual happiness, 313
  living arrangements, *11*
  maltreatment, 416
  percentage of children living with single parent, *445*
  relationships with parents and, 67
  in stepfamilies, 455-457, *457*
  war and effect on families, 395, 398

I-12   Subject Index

Chronic obstructive pulmonary disease (COPD), 26
Chronic work stressors, 386-387
Circular causality model, 114
Circumplex Model of Marital and Family Systems, 98
Civilian Conservation Corps (CCC), 72
Clarity, 97, 98
Class differences, 27
Closed system, 77
Closeness, problems relating to, 472-473
Cluttered nest, 358-359
Coalition Rating Scale, A-2, A-3
Cognitive development theory, 201-203
Cohabiting/cohabitation, 268, 274, 280, 283, 284, 286, 375
   dramatic increase, 283-283
   parents, 313
   reasons for, 284-286
   reasons for cohabiting, 284-286
   trends in, 8-9
Cohesion, 78-80, 302
   balancing between separateness and togetherness, 92-94
   in couples and families, 91
   extreme togetherness and extreme separateness, 94-95
   levels of couple and family cohesion, 94
Cohesive relationships, 93
Collective worldview, 216
Command of communication, 114
Commitment, 83, 239, 240
Common cold, 387-388
Communication, 80, 107
   all together at family mealtimes, 112
   assertive, 123-124
   component of, 114
   in couples and families, 97-98
   couple strengths and issues in, 107-108
   cultural differences in, 110-111
   cycle, 114, *125*
   to developing intimacy, 113-118
   gender differences in, 108-110
   with GLBT individuals and couples, 111-112
   to increasing intimacy, 124
   intimacy and, 245-246
   to maintaining intimacy, 118-124
   patterns, 126
   positive and negative communication cycles, 124-126
   problems for couples, *108*
   about sex, 110
   skills, 154, 248
   strategies for communicating about difficult issues, 142-145
   strengths of happy couples *vs.* unhappy couples, *108*
Community
   differences, 27
   strengths, 465, 466
Companionate love, 240
Complementary couples, 174
Compulsive spending, 231
Conceptual frameworks
   for describing marriage and family dynamics, 71
   family development framework, 86-88, 92-93
   family systems theory, 74-80, 92
   feminist framework, 89-91, 93
   international family strengths framework, 81-86, 92
   social construction framework, 88-89, 93
   symbolic interaction framework, 88, 93
   theories and research, 92
   for understanding couples and families, 74
Confiding, 236
Conflict, 130
   and anger, 131-136
   conflict-minimizing couples, 174
   conflicted coparenting, 445-446
   conflicted couples, 305
   hierarchy of, 131-133, *132*
   intimacy and conflict, 136
   between parents and children, 146-147
   problems for couples, *131*
   in relationships, 280-283
   resolving conflict, 141-145
   and supportiveness in heterosexual couples, 140-141
   taboos, 133-134
Conflict resolution for couples, 136, 249
   couple strengths and issues, *130*, 130-131
   dance of anger, 138-140
   love and anger in balance, 137
Conjugal family system, 52
Connectedness, balance of, 78-80
Connected relationships, 93
Connected systems hierarchy, 75-77
Conquest mentality, 269

Consanguineal family systems, 52
Constructive intimacy games, 251
Consumer Credit Counseling Service (CCCS), 232
Consummate love, 240
Contemporary families, 11
Contemporary views of gender roles, 193, 195
   work-family interface, 194-195
Contempt, 300
Content messages, 114
Continuous partial attention, 117-118
Conventional couples, 305
Cooperative coparenting, 446
Cooperative endeavor, communication as, 113-114
Coparenting, 337-339, 445-446
COPD. *See* Chronic obstructive pulmonary disease (COPD)
Coping
   with 9/11, 402-403
   abilities, 54
   with stress, 384
Corporal punishment and consequences, 332-333
Cost
   of divorce, 218
   of home loans, 230
   of raising child, *320*
Counseling
   PREPARE program for premarital, 299
   financial, 231-232
   marriage, 137
   See also Marital and family therapy
Couple & family system, 299
Couple and Family Map, 71, 98, *99*, 101, 138, 313, 472, 473, 476, A-2, A-6
   assigning global ratings, A-3
   assigning scale values, A-3
   balanced relationships, 99-100
   balanced *vs.* unbalanced families, 98-99
   change over time, *101*
   coalition rating scale, A-2, A-3
   couple and family rating form, A-5
   couple and family scales, A-4
   dimensions and concepts, A-2
   interview questions, A-2
   parenting styles and, *325*
   plotting family system type, A-3
   value, 100-101
Couple Communication Program, 299, 471

Couple relationship, 479
  common problems in, 471-472
  intimacy development in, 247-249
  power in, 205-206
Couple(s), 382
  closeness, 248
  communication problems for, *108*
  conflict problems for, *131*
  conflict resolution for, 136-141
  couple-arranged marriage, 267
  cross-cultural perspectives on, 383
  devitalized, 306
  education programs, 469, 471
  and family scales, *104*
  flexibility, 248
  happy couples versus unhappy couples viewing roles, *189*
  levels, *94, 96, 97*
  meeting, *271*
  parenting issues in, 314-315, *315*, 330
  programs for, *469*
  relationship education, 113
  relationships in later years, 375-377
  role problems for, *189*
  role relationships in happy couples *vs.* unhappy couples, *206*
  sexual problems for, *151*
  in stepfamilies, 456-458
  social environment elements effects, *19*
  stressors for, 388
  stumbling blocks, *472*
  therapists, 177
  therapy, 469
  war and effect on families, 394-395
Couples and families
  cohesion in, 91-95
  communication in, 97-98
  conceptual frameworks for understanding, 74
  family development framework, 86-88, 92-93
  family systems theory, 74-80, 92
  feminist framework, 89-91, 93
  flexibility in, 95-97
  international family strengths framework, 81-86, 92
  social construction framework, 88-89, 93
  symbolic interaction framework, 88, 93
  theories and research, 92

Couple relationships, developing intimacy in, 247
  communication skills, 248
  conflict resolution, 249
  couple closeness, 248
  couple flexibility, 248
  happily *vs.* unhappily married couples, *247*
  personality compatibility, 248
Couple strengths, 314-315
  and issues in communication, 107-108
  and issues in conflict resolution, 130-131
  and sexual issues, 150-151
Courtship patterns, 265
  breaking up, 273
  dating, 268
  dating with older people, 273-274
  ongoing relationships, 272
  parent-arranged marriages, 265-268
  trends in searching for partner, 270-271
Credit, 227
  avoiding debt and bankruptcy, 231
  clinics, 232
  credit cards, 227
  financial counseling, 231-232
  protection, 219
  purchasing home, 228-230
  spending, 231
Credit cards, 227
  debt, 219
Cretaceous-Paleogene extinction (K-Pg extinction), 32
Cretaceous-Tertiary extinction (K-T extinction), 32
Criminal victimization, 22-25
Crisis, 318, 319, 389, 401
  Chinese pictograph for, *401*
  crisis-loss stage of grief, 374
  crisis-meeting resources, 390
  crisis-resolution phase, 132
  spending, 231
Criticism, 146, 300
Cross-cultural family studies, 63
Cross-cultural phenomenon, 65
"Cross-generational transmission" of child abuse, 419
Cross-sectional cohort studies, A-12
Cross-sectional studies, A-11
Cross-validation, A-10
Cultural competence, 50
  awareness, 50-51
  knowledge, 51
  skills, 51

Cultural/culture, 38-41, 237
  change, 157-158
  conflicts for female Chicana college student, 79
  differences in communication, 110-111
  diversity, 2, 38
  of divorce, 22
  factors, 411
  familiarity, 279
  groups, 2, 39, 40, 41
  identity, 41
  kin relationships across, 51-53
  norms, 52
  recovery, 62
  standards, 156
  strengths, 38, 465, 466
  variations, 267
Cumulative circumstances. *See* Cascading circumstances

Dance of anger, The, 138-140
Dating, 268, 272
  American style, 266
  contemporary *vs.* traditional, *195*
  Internet, 242-243, 271, 280
  with older people, 273-274
  violence, 406
  See also Mate selection
Debt
  avoiding, 231
  effects on newlyweds, 215
  in United States, 228, 229
  See also Credit
Decision making, 131, 132
Decline in marriage, 293
Defensiveness, 300
Definition of situation, 88
Degree of adjustment, 277-279
Demand-withdrawal communication, 141
Democratic parenting, 328
Deployment, 393, 399
Depression, 273, 275
Desolation of grief, 376
Destructive intimacy games, 249-253
Devitalized couples, 306
Devonian extinctions, 32
Digital technology, 242
DINS dilemma. *See* Double income, no sex dilemma (DINS dilemma)
Directive listening, 122
Disagreements, 285
Discipline, 331,. 333

Disengaged relationships, 93
Distancers, 138–139
Diverse populations, stepfamilies in, 458–459
Diverse programs, 343–346
Diversity, 39, 150, 186, 290, 351–352, 382, 434
  and domestic violence, 407
  in families, 38, 40, 64, 258, 468
  and financial style, 216–218
  increasing diversity in America, *44*
  themes of, 2–3
Divorce, 266, 293, 434, 439
  cost of, 218
  culture, 439–440
  globalization, 436–437
  historical trends, 434–436
  impact on adults, 440–441
  impact on children, 442–444
  laws, 437–439
  during middle and later years, 358
  statistics on, *12*
  in today's society, 434
  trends in, 9–11
  views on, 437–439
Domestic Abuse Intervention Programs, 413
Domestic violence, 404
  and children, 414
  diversity and, 407
  effects, 405
  factors contributing to, 409–412
  in family of origin, 409–410
  incidence, 405–406
  linkage of animal abuse and, 411–412
  National Survey of Domestic Violence, 407, 408
  patterns, 412
  physical and psychological abuse relationship, 408–409
  treatment and prevention, 412–413
Dopamine, 241
Double bind communications, 115–116
Double income, no sex dilemma (DINS dilemma), 173
Drinking, 25
Drugs use, 25–27
Duluth program, 413
Duvall's traditional family life cycle stages, 87–88
Dynamics change in relationships over time, 101–102

Eclectic approach, 71
Ecofeminism, 91
Ecology, 76
Economic
  abuse, 404
  adequacy, 467
  hardship, 310
  stress, 410
Education
  as investment, 222
  level, 39
  marriage, 296–300, 304
  median earnings, *223*
  programs and resources for parents, 343–346
  for sexuality, 167–168
Egalitarian(ism), 186
  decision making, 154
  groups, 53
  roles, 193–194, 206–207
Embarrassment, 62
Emerging adulthood, 87
Emic perspective, 63
Emotion(al), 133
  abuse, 404
  bonding, 16
  closeness, 95
  coping strategies, 403
  disengagement, 300
  disorders, 275
  emotional-only infidelity, 175
  expressive couples, 174
  infidelity, 175
  stress, 387
  work in marriage and family, 191
Empty-nest syndrome, 358–359
Empty love, 240
End-Triassic extinction, 32
Endogamy, 276
Enjoyable time together, 20, 54–56, 84–85
Enjoyment, 235
Enmeshed relationships, 93
Enmeshment, 94
ENRICH Inventory, 247
Equalitarian roles, 193–194
Equality Wheel, *413*
"Equal pay for comparable work" approach, 224
Equity theory, 280
Erectile dysfunction, 180
Ethnic diversity, 2, 38
Ethnic families, challenges for, 63
  advantages of being in majority, 65–66
  assimilation, acculturation, and segregation, 63–65
  marriage outside group, 66
  relationships between men and women, 66–67
  relationships between parents and children, 67
Ethnic groups, 38, 41
  characteristics of families from various, *42*
  family strengths and challenges across, 55
  gender roles across, 198–201
  historical trauma and American Indians, 62
  self-assessment, 56
  strengths of African American families, 57
  strengths of American Indian families, 60–62
  strengths of Asian American families, 59–60
  strengths of European American families, 55–56
  strengths of Latino families, 57–59
Ethnic identity, 50, 67
Ethnicity, 39–41
Ethnic variations, 198
Ethnocentrism, 63
Etic perspective, 63
Eugenics, 72
European American
  families strengths, 55–56
  gay and lesbian families, 46–47
Excessive drinking, 25
Exchange theory, 280
Exclusionists, 6
Exclusivity, 16
Exogamy, 276
Explicit rules, 253
Explosion phase, 412
Expressive role, 90
Extended family, 52, 53, 61
  agreement, 279
  system, 54, 55
Extramarital sexual behavior, 172
  infidelity, 174–176, 177–178
  marital styles and, 174
  sex within marriage, 172–174
Extreme change, 97
Extreme separateness, 94–95
Extreme stability, 97
Extreme togetherness, 94–95

Fabric of friendship, 235–237
Facebook (FB), 117–118
Families and Democracy Model, 33

Subject Index   I-15

Familism, 58
Family cohesion, 54, 60, A-2
　couple and family rating form, A-5
　couple and family scales, A-4
　levels, *91*, *93*, *94*
　interview questions, A-2
Family communication, 54, 97, A-2, A-4
　couple and family rating form, A-5
　couple and family scales, A-4
　levels, *97*
　See also Communication
Family coping strategies, 401, *402*
　Chinese pictograph for crisis, *401*
　coping with 9/11, 402–403
　theoretical perspectives, 401–402
Family expenses, 220–225
　annual expenditures for necessities, *225*
　"equal pay for comparable work" approach, 224
　pay to work outside the home, 224–225
Family/families, 3, 4–6, 38, 90
　boundary ambiguity, 459
　changes in response, *392*
　continuity in, 14
　day care, 333
　development framework, 71, 74, 86–88, 92–93
　divorce and remarriage, trends in, 9–11
　diversity in, 258
　emotion work in, 191
　and environment, 31–33
　family structure, trends in, 11–14
　and friends, 452
　households, 448
　income, 220–224
　intimacy, 382
　marital status of U.S. population, *8*
　in marriage, 301–303
　marriage and cohabitation, trends in, 8–9
　motor vehicle accident, *391*
　of origin, *301*
　power, 67, 205
　practice, 74
　prioritization, 216
　programs for, *469*
　relations, 72
　researchers, A-8, A-9
　at risk, 419–420
　scales, *104*
　scientists, A-8
　therapists, 79, 81
　therapy, 343, 469
　trends in, 6
　violence, 424
　work distribution by gender, 190–191
Family flexibility, 54, A-2, A-4
　couple and family rating form, A-5
　couple and family scales, A-4
　interview questions, A-2
　levels, *96*
Family in Transition, 7
Family life, 188–190
　education, 72
　educators, A-8
　immigration and, 43–44
　in later years, 364–377
　in middle years, 352–364
Family research methods, A-8, A-9
　case studies, A-10
　historical studies, A-10, A-11
　interviews, A-10
　multicultural studies, A-11
　observational approaches, A-10
　questionnaires, A-9, A-10
Family science, 71, A-8
　current status, 73–74
　disciplines contributing to, *73*, A-8
　in early years, 72–73
　knowledge explosion, A-8
Family strengths, 465, 466
　of African American families, 57
　of American Indian families, 60–62
　of Asian American families, 59–60
　and challenges across ethnic groups, 55
　focus on, 14–15
　historical trauma and American Indians, 62
　of Latino families, 57–59
　perspective, 2
　self-assessment, 56
　strengths of European American families, 55–56
Family stress, cross-cultural perspectives on, 383
Family structure
　challenges for ethnic families, 63–67
　challenge to researchers and practitioners, 49–50
　cross-cultural family studies, 63
　cultural competence, 50–51
　culture, 38–41
　diversity and strengths in family structure and cultural context, 38
　diversity in families, 40, 64
　ethnicity concept, 39–41
　ethnic or cultural differences, 40
　family strengths and challenges across ethnic groups, 55–62
　family system and sociocultural characteristics, 53
　Gay and Lesbian couples and families, 45–49
　intimacy and diversity, 39
　kin relationships across cultures, 51–53
　race concept, 39–41
　U.S. demographics and future trends, 41–44
Family studies. See Family science
Family system, 53–54, 74–75
　changing before and after 9/11 attacks, 391–393
　and sociocultural characteristics, *54*
　function, 80
Family systems theory, 71, 74, 92, 203
　cohesion, 78–80
　cultural conflicts for female Chicana college student, 79
　feedback within system, 80
　flexibility, 77–78
　hierarchy of connected systems, 75–77
　reorganization of family system after car accident, 78
"Family tree" approach, 53
FAS. See Fetal alcohol syndrome (FAS)
FASDs. See Fetal alcohol spectrum disorders (FASDs)
Father
　absent father, 340
　father-child communication about sex, 169
　as nurturer, 340
　single-parent families, 446–448
Fatherhood, 339–342
Fatuous love, 240
FB. See Facebook (FB)
Fear, 22–25
Federal Healthy Marriage Initiative, 310
Feedback within system, 80
Feelings, 131, 239
　work, 140

I-16　Subject Index

Female/feminism, 90, 91
  circumcision in Africa, 157
  sexual dysfunction, 179
Female genital mutilation (FGM), 157
Femininity, 187–188
Feminist framework, 71, 74, 89–91, 93, 203
  gender inequality as global problem, 204
Feminist theories, 90, 280
Fertility rates, *14*, 221
Fetal alcohol spectrum disorders (FASDs), 26
Fetal alcohol syndrome (FAS), 423–424
FGM. *See* Female genital mutilation (FGM)
Financial/finances
  causing problems, 218–220
  counseling, 231–232
  for couples, 226
  dependency, 410
  financial freedom, steps to, 219
  financial style, diversity and, 216–218
  issues, 30
  issues and children, 320
  problems and global economy, 30–31
  strengths of happy *vs.* unhappy couples regarding, *214*
  stress, 39
Firearms, 24
Firm and assertive statements, 135
Flexibility, 77–78
  balance between stability and change, 96–97
  in couples and families, 95
  extreme stability and extreme change, 97
  flexible level, 95–96
  levels of couple and family flexibility, 96
  problems relating to, 472–473
"Flexibly cohesive" relationship, 101
Flexibly connected family, 392
Flooding, 300
Food security in American households and communities, 30
Foreign born, 43
Forgiveness in marriage, 307–308
Fourth National Incidence Study of Child Abuse and Neglect, 415
Freedom, 467

Friendship, 235, 235–244
  fabric of friendship, 235–237
  self-disclosure in, 119–121

G-8. *See* Group of Eight (G-8)
Gatekeepers of children, 446
Gay-male and lesbian sexual behavior, 163–164
Gay and Lesbian couples and families, 45, 46–47
  challenges, 47–49
  communication for, 111
  gay and lesbian parenting, 339
  same-sex couple relationships and marriages, 45–46
Gay couples, 136, 140–141, 153–155
Gay, lesbian, bisexual, transgender (GLBT), 154
  communication with GLBT individuals and couples, 111–112
Gender, 90, 152
  differences in communication, 108–110
  income differences, 222
  inequality as global problem, 204
  issues for immigrant couples, 200–201
  norms, 188–190
Gender roles, 186
  African American culture, 199
  American Indian culture, 199–200
  Asian American culture, 200
  changing gender roles and balance of power, 29–30
  cognitive development theory, 201–203
  distribution of family work by gender, 190–191
  egalitarian roles, 193–194
  emotion work in marriage and family, 191
  across ethnic groups, 198–201
  facts about women and men in United States, 186
  family systems theory, 203
  feminist framework, 203–204
  gender issues for immigrant couples, 200–201
  gender norms and family life, 188–190
  international perspective, 194, 196–198
  intimacy, strengths, and diversity, 186
  Latino/a culture, 198–199

  maternal gatekeeping, 192
  social learning theory, 201
  spending time with children, 191
  stereotypes, 187
  traditional *vs.* contemporary views, 193–195
General systems theory, 75
GLBT. *See* Gay, lesbian, bisexual, transgender (GLBT)
Global economy, financial problems and, 30–31
Globalization of divorce, 436–437
Global morality, 177
Goal identification, 219
Good listeners, 123
Grandchild/grandparent relationship, 361
Grandfamilies, 364
Grandparenthood, 360–362
Grandparents, 364
  raising grandchildren, 362–363
Gray divorce, 358
Great Depression, 322
Great Recession, 293, 354
Grieving process, 374
Group of Eight (G-8), 24–25
Growing edge, 137
Gun violence, 24

Handbook of Forgiveness, 307
Happiness
  children and, 313–314
  money and, 211–213, *212*
Happy couples, 130, 314
  strengths regarding parenting, 315
Harmonious couples, 305
Harsh disciplinary, 332
Hate, 134
Healthy conversation, 141
Healthy couple relationships, 214
Healthy families, 77, 81, 100
  communication in, 83
  degree of balance, *100*
Healthy Marriage Initiative, 296
Healthy marriages, 296, 310
Helpmate, 375
"Hereditary defectives, borderline cases, and persons with marked ability", 72
Heterosexual, 152, 163
  conflict and supportiveness in, 140–141
  couples, 45
  relationships, 164
Hierarchy of conflict, 131–133, *132*

Hispanic Americans
  changes in family structure, 12
  characteristics of families, *42*
  child care, 333
  cohabitation, 458
  culture, 38, 58, 198–199
  domestic violence, 407
  families strengths, 57–59
  gay and lesbian families, 46–47
  grandparents raising grandchildren, 363–364
  household income level, 220–221, *221*
  marital status of U.S. population, *8*
  marriage study, 59
  multiracial marriages, 66
  population, 41–42
  racial and ethnic differences, 27
  single-parent families, 448
  victims of abuse and neglect, 23
Historical trauma, 62
HIV. *See* Human immunodeficiency virus (HIV)
Holmes and Rahe Social Readjustment Rating Scale, 384
Holmes and Rahe Stress Test, 384, 385, *385*
Home loans, cost of, 230
Homosexuality, 152, 177
Honesty, 246
Hooking Up: Sex, Dating and Relationships on Campus, 269
Hooking up, 268–270, 280
Hormonal conditions, 179
Hormone therapy, 356
Household income by race and Hispanic origin, 220–221, *221*
Household inequality, 204
How to Avoid Falling for a Jerk (ette), 279
Human betterment, 467
Human ecosystem, 76
Human emotions, 134–135
Human immunodeficiency virus (HIV), 158
Human relationships, Internet and, 27–29
Human systems, ecological approach to, 76, *76*
Humor, 83
Hypoactive, 173
Hypotheses, 71

Idiographic approach, 71
"I Don't Care. You Decide", games, 251–252

Immigrants, 43, 237
  immigrant couples, gender issues for, 200–201
Immigration and family life, 43–44
Implicit rules, 253
Impotence, 180
Impulsive spending. *See* Careless spending
Incest taboos, 155
Inclusionists, 6
Individualistic worldview, 216
Individuals, 324
Infatuation, 240
Infidelity, 174–176
  morally acceptable, 177–178
Influenza, 387–388
Insiders, 55
  perspective, A-9
Instability of couple and family relationships, 22
Instrumental role, 90
Intercultural marriages, 265
Interdependence, 134, 137
  of parts, 77
Interfaith marriages, 276–279
Intermarriage, 279
International family strengths framework, 71, 74, 81, 92, 465
  ability to manage stress and crisis effectively, 85–86
  appreciation and affection, 82–83
  commitment, 83
  enjoyable time together, 84–85
  positive communication, 83–84
  qualities of strong families, *81*
  spiritual well-being and shared values, 85
International perspective, 194, 196–198
Internet, 271
  dating, 242–243, *243*, 271, 280
  and human relationships, 27–29
  love on, 242–244
  Internet dating, 242–243, 271, 280
  attitudes toward, *243*
  sites and mobile apps usage, *243*
Interpersonal area in PREPARE/ENRICH program, 299
Interracial couples, 278
Interracial marriages, 276–279
Interviews, A-10
Intimacy, 39, 126, 136, 150, 186, 239, 240, 290, 295, 351–352, 382, 434
  attachment theory and, 254–255

  and communication, 245–246
  using communication to developing, 113–118
  using communication to increasing, 124
  using communication to maintaining, 118–124
  developing in couple relationships, 247–249
  intimate experiences *vs.* intimate relationship, 246
  paradox of marriage and, 246–247
  paths to intimacy differs in males and females, 244–245
  themes of, 2–3
Intimacy games, 249
  constructive intimacy games, 251
  destructive intimacy games, 251–253
  dimensions of, *250*
  limiting destructive games, 253–254
Intimate experiences, 246
Intimate partner violence, 23, 280
Intimate relationships, 2, 246
  advantages of marriage, 15–18
  changing social environment, 33
  family, 3, 4–6
  focus on marital and family strengths, 14–15
  learning to focus on strengths, 15
  marriage, 3–4
  positive responses to social environment, 34
  self-disclosure in, 119–121
  impact of social environment on relationships, 18–33
  themes of intimacy, strengths, and diversity, 2–3
  trends in marriage and family, 6–14
Intimate terrorism, 405
Intrapersonal areas in PREPARE/ENRICH program, 299
Isolation, 410

Jealousy, 240–242
Jim's family of origin, 302
Joint custody, 443, 444
Journal of Marriage and Family, 72
Justice, 467

K-Pg extinction. *See* Cretaceous-Paleogene extinction (K-Pg extinction)
K-T extinction. *See* Cretaceous-Tertiary extinction (K-T extinction)

Key relationship concepts, 91
   cohesion in couples and families, 91–95
   communication in couples and families, 97–98
   flexibility in couples and families, 95–97
Kids in Parents' Pockets Eroding Retirement Savings (KIPPERS), 359
Kin relationships across cultures, 51–53
Kinship, 51
   bonds, 57
   groups, 52
KIPPERS. *See* Kids in Parents' Pockets Eroding Retirement Savings (KIPPERS)
Knowledge-positions, 89
Knowledge explosion, A-8

Later years, family life in, 364
   changes in family dynamics, 377
   conventional wisdom about old age, 366–369
   couple relationships, 375–377
   long-term marriages, 372–373
   losing spouse, 374–375
   median net worth by age of householder, *367*
   old age, 365–366
   retirement, 370–372
   See also Middle years, family life in
Law of enlightened self-interest, 295
Learned helplessness theory, 410
Learning theories, 330
Legal drugs, acknowledging dangers of, 428–429
Lerner, 139
Lesbian couples, 136, 140–141, 153–155
Life
   course, 87
   course theories, 280
   cycle, 87
   experiences, 39
   as roller coaster, 390–391
   stages, 87
Liking, 240
Lineage, 52
Linear causality model, 114
Lines of descent, 52
Listening, 121–123
   skills, 97
Living, 72

Living apart together, 375
Living arrangements, 448
   of children, by race and Hispanic origin, *11*
   types in households with children, *446*
Living in poverty, 220
Living together, 281, 283
   cohabitations dramatic increase, 283–283
   difficult choices, 286
   reasons for cohabiting, 284–286
Loneliness: Human Nature and the Need for Social Connection, 260
Long-term contract, 16
Long-term health risks, 26
Long-term loving relationships, 145
Long-term marriages, 372–373
Longevous marriages, 373
Longitudinal studies, A-11
Looking-glass self, 88
Losing spouse, 374–375
Love, 134, 174, 235, *236*, 300
   in balance, 137
   on Internet, 242–244
   jealousy, 240–242
   LOVE-based mate selection, 267
   match, 267
   relationship, 265
   and science, 241
   tapestry of, 237–238
   traits of, 238
   triangle, 239–240
   See also Intimacy
Love and War (Korea), 436
Lovers, 235–244
Loving
   or honeymoon phase, 412
   relationships, 144, 294
Loving Someone Who Has Dementia (Boss), 386
Low-income couples, 407
Low-income families, 217
Lower-middle-income families, 220
Low self-esteem, 410
Low sexual desire, 179

"Majority-minority" population, 41
Male dominance, 411
Male menopause, 354, 356–357
Male sexual dysfunction, 180
Maltreatment, 24
Mama's boys, 359
Mammoni. *See* Mama's boys

Marital and family therapists, 142, A-8
Marital and family therapy, 471
   case study, 476–479
   common problems in couple relationships, 471–472
   problems relating to closeness and flexibility, 472–473
   questions, 473–476
   stumbling blocks for couples, 472
Marital betrayal, 144
Marital happiness, keys to, 458
Marital realities, *304*
Marital satisfaction, 206–207
Marital separation, fathers' experiences with, 441
Marital sexual behavior, 172–176
Marital strengths, focus on, 14–15
Marital success prediction, 300
Marriage, 3, 6, 246–247, 265, 274
   advantages, 15–18
   benefits, 291–292
   and black Americans, 292
   components of successful marriage, 294–296
   continuity in, 14
   counseling, 137
   decline in, 293
   effects of debt on newlyweds, 215
   emotion work in, 191
   encounter, 296
   factors Americans associate with successful, *322*
   facts about, *294*
   families of origin in, 301–303
   Federal Healthy Marriage Initiative, 310
   forgiveness in, 307–308
   goals for, 302–303
   intimacy, strengths, and diversity, 290
   keeping marriages strong, 305–307
   marital status of U.S. population, *8*
   marriages over time, 292–293
   middle-aged, 357–358
   and money, 213–216
   movement, 296
   newlywed years, 303–304
   outside group, 66
   patterns, *195*
   perspectives on, 290
   prayer in, 308
   relationship, 150
   sacrifice in, 308
   same-sex marriage, 4

Marriage (*continued*)
   statistics on, *12*
   strengths of happy *vs.* unhappy couples regarding finances, 214
   trends in divorce and remarriage, 9–11
   trends in family structure, 11–14
   trends in marriage and cohabitation, 8–9
   types of, *301*, 305–306
Marriage and family dynamics, 71
   conceptual frameworks for understanding couples and families, 74–91
   Couple and Family Map, 98–101
   couple and family scales, 104
   dynamics change in relationships over time, 101–102
   frameworks for, 71
   history of family science, 71–74
   key relationship concepts, 91–98
Marriage and Family Stress Test, 384
Marriage education, 296, 304
   effective premarital program, 298–299
   inventories, 290
   predicting successful marriage, 300
   premarital education, 297
   stepfamilies, 296–297
Married couples, 2, 3, 14, 121
   building stronger marriage, and families, 22
   communication cycle, 124
   conflict resolution problems, 131
   financial wealth, 17
   households, 8
   in matrilocal society, 53
   kinship group, 52
   pooling, 227
   problematic issues for, 107
   same-sex, 45
   sexual health and behavior, 159
   sexual issues, 150
   sexual relationship, 16
   strengths, 130, 150
   stressors, *388*
   types, *306*
Masculinity, 187–188
Masturbation, 157
Matchmaker, 267
Materialism, 19–20
Maternal gatekeeping, 192
Mate selection, 274
   age and finding mate, 275–276
   birth order, 276
   determinants in, 275
   finding good mate, 279
   interracial and interfaith marriages, 276–279
   patterns of, 279–280
   similar personalities or different personalities, 276
   See also Dating
Mating gradient, 275
Matriarchal group, 53
Matrilineal societies, 52–53
Matrilineal society, 53
Matrilocal society, 53
Mature marriage, 137
Medical care issues, 375
Men
   relationships with women and, 66–67
   sexual behaviors, 160
   in United States, 186
Menopause, 354, 356
Mental disorders, 275
Mental health issues, 394
Metacommunication, 116–117
Middle age, 352–353
   sexuality in, 354–357
Middle-aged marriage, 357–358
Middle-aged person, 354
Middle-old, 365
Middlescence, 352
Middle years, family life in, 352
   divorce during middle and later years, 358
   empty nest, spacious nest, or cluttered nest, 358–359
   grandparenthood, 360–362
   grandparents raising grandchildren, 362–363
   middle-aged marriage, 357–358
   middle-aged person and working world, 354
   middle age, 352–353
   midlife crisis, 353–354
   sandwich generation, 359–360
   sexuality in middle age, 354–357
   See also Later years, family life in
Midlife crisis, 353–354
Midrange families, 98
Military families, role of community in supporting, 398–400
Military sexual trauma (MST), 401
Minimizing power issues, suggestions for, 207–208
Minority populations, 44
Mixed-methods research approaches, A-9
Mixed cultural marriages, 265
Mixed messages, 115–116
Moderates, 6
Modern-day friendships, 236
Money
   and happiness, 211–213, *212*
   marriage and, 213–216
Monogamous relationships, 164
Monogamy, 52
Morality of extramarital affairs around world, 177
Morphogenic system, 77
Morphostatic system, 77
Mortality inequality, 204
Motherhood, 339–342
Mother's Book, The, 333
MRI technology, 241
MST. *See* Military sexual trauma (MST)
Multicultural feminism, 91
Multicultural studies, A-11
Multiple system levels, 75
Multiracial marriages, 66
Mutual-negotiation trajectory, 324
Mutual assistance, 236
Mutual disclosure, 120
Myths, 131
   about anger, 134–136

Nakode, 267
Narrative therapy, 89
Natality inequality, 204
National 4-H, 399
National Coalition Against Domestic Violence (NCADV), 405, 406
National Council on Alcoholism and Drug Dependence (NCADD), 427
National Council on Family Relations (NCFR), 72
National Healthy Marriage Resource Center, 10, 298–299
National Institute of Child Health and Human Development Study of Early Child Care and Youth Development (NICHD), 335–336
National Public Radio (NPR), 167
National Survey of Domestic Violence, 407, 408
National Survey of Sexual Health and Behavior, 159–160
National Survey of Spouse Abuse, *408*
NCADD. *See* National Council on Alcoholism and Drug Dependence (NCADD)

NCADV. *See* National Coalition Against Domestic Violence (NCADV)
NCFR. *See* National Council on Family Relations (NCFR)
Negative communication cycles, 124
   negative influence of avoidance, 125-126
Negative feedback, 80
Negative life events, 385-386
Negative stigma, 48
Neglect, 414
   incidence, 415
   long-term consequences, 417-418
Neolocal society, 53
New-life stage of grief, 374
Newlywed years, 303-304
New York Times, 318
NICHD. *See* National Institute of Child Health and Human Development Study of Early Child Care and Youth Development (NICHD)
9/11 attacks
   coping with, 402-403
   family systems changing before and after, 391-393
No-fault divorce, 437, 439
Nomothetic approach, 71
Non-love, 240
Nonabusive marriages, 407
Noncustodial birth father, 459
Nonindulgent families, 331
Nonmarital births, 440
Nonparenthood, 322
Nonverbal communication, 114-115
NPR. *See* National Public Radio (NPR)
Nuclear families, 52, 61
   differences between stepfamilies and, 454-455

OASAS. *See* Office of Alcoholism and Substance Abuse Services (OASAS)
Observational approaches, A-10
Obsessive-compulsive disorder, 241
Office of Alcoholism and Substance Abuse Services (OASAS), 427
Old age, 365-366
   conventional wisdom about, 366-369
Older adults, 24
Older couples, 366
Old-old, 365
"On-again/off-again" relationship, 272-273

Online dating. *See* Internet—dating
Open communication, 246, 248
Open system, 77
Oral sex, 160
Ordovician-Silurian extinction, 32
Organismic theory, 329
Orgasmic disorder, 179
Orgasmic dysfunction, 180
Outsiders, 55
   perspective, A-9
Overcrowding, 30
Overfunctioners, 139, 140
Ownership inequality, 204
Oxytocin, 241

Painful intercourse, 180
PAIRS Program, 299, 471
Paradox of marriage and intimacy, 246-247
Parallel coparenting relationships, 446
Parasite singles, 359
Parent-arranged marriages, 265-268
Parental control, 325
Parental support, 325
Parent–child relationship, 253
Parent/child violence, 281
Parent education, 343
Parenthood, 14
   adoption, 320-321
   challenge, 315-320
   child-free alternative, 322-325
   childrearing theories, 328-330
   children and happiness, 313-314
   couple strengths and issues in parenting, 314-315
   financial issues and children, 320
   issues in parenting, 330-346
   joy and enduring satisfaction of, 346-347
   myths and realities, 316-318
   roots and wings, 313
   society, 315-316
   styles of parenting, 325-328
   transition to parenthood, 318-319
Parenting styles, 325
   authoritarian style, 327
   and children's behavior, *326*
   democratic parenting works best, 328
   democratic style, 326
   permissive style, 327
   rejecting style, 327
   uninvolved style, 327
Parents/parenting, 313, 328
   child care, 333-337
   child dies, 342-343

   conflict between children and, 146-147
   coparenting, 337-338
   corporal punishment and consequences, 332-333
   educational programs and resources, 343-346
   fatherhood and motherhood, 339-342
   gay and lesbian, 339
   issues in, 314-315, *315*, 330
   positive discipline, 331
   relationships with children and, 67
   single mothers, 338
   strengths of happy couples *vs.* unhappy couples, *315*
   styles and Couple and Family Map, *325*
Parsons theory, 193
Partner
   dominance, 124
   violence warning signs, 282
"Partying", 268
Passion, 239, 240
Passive-aggressive behaviors, 414
Passive–aggressive approach, 295
Passive communication, 123-124
Passiveness, 124
Patriarchal group, 53
Patrilineal societies, 52-53
Patrilocal societies, 53
Peacefulness, 467
PEP. *See* Post-exposure prophylaxis (PEP)
Perennial philosophy, 468
Permian extinction, 32
Permissive parenting, 327
Personality, 457
   compatibility, 248
   types, 276
Personification, 94
Perspective, 63
Persuasive listening, 122
Physical abuse, 404, 408-409
Physical conditions, 179
Physical health consequences, 418
Physical intimacy, 290
"Physical, mental and social inadequacy", 72
Physiological stress, 383
Pick Program, 279
Players, 269
Plural marriage, 52
Polyandry, 52
Polygamy, 52

Polygyny, 52
Pooling money, 226–227
Positive attitude, 452
Positive caregiving, 337
Positive communication, 54, 56, 83–84, 107, 113
　cycles, 124
　positive influence of assertiveness, 125
Positive discipline, 331
Positive feedback, 80
Positive parent–child relationships, 154
Post-exposure prophylaxis (PEP), 159
Postdeployment, 399
Postmodernism, 89
Posttraumatic stress disorder (PTSD), 395, 400–401, 406, 409
Poverty, 39
Power in family, 186, 204
　egalitarian roles and marital satisfaction, 206–207
　power in couple relationships, 205–206
　suggestions for minimizing power issues, 207–208
Prayer in marriage, 308
Pre-exposure prophylaxis (PrEP), 159
Predeployment, 399
Prejudice, 39, 65
Premarital and marriage programs, 468, 469
　couple education programs, 471
　for couples and families, 469
　PREPARE Program, 470
Premarital education, 297
Premarital fantasies, *304*
Premarital program, 298–299
Premarital sex in America, 165, *165*
Premature ejaculation, 180
PrEP. *See* Pre-exposure prophylaxis (PrEP)
PREP. *See* Prevention and Relationship Enhancement Program (PREP)
PREPARE-ENRICH Couple Program, 388
PREPARE/ENRICH programs, 299, 471
PREPARE program, 290, 296, 470
　for premarital counseling, 299
Prevention and Relationship Enhancement Program (PREP), 113, 125, 296, 299, 471
Problem drinking, 423
Problem families, 99
　degree of balance, *100*

Problem-solving phase, 132
Professional inequality, 204
Prosocial spending, 213
Proximity, 16
Pseudo-kin group, 52
Psychodynamic theory, 329
Psychological
　abuse, 404, 408–409
　aggression, 415–417
　consequences, 418
　perceptive, 154
　phenomenon, 366
　and social causes, 180
　stress, 383
PTSD. *See* Posttraumatic stress disorder (PTSD)
Purchasing home, 228–230
Pursuers, 138

Qualitative research, A-9
Quantitative research, A-9
Questionnaires, A-9, A-10

Race, 39–41
　household income by, 220–221, *221*
Racial and ethnic differences, 27
Racism, 65
Rape, 156, 406
　See also Domestic violence
Rapid ejaculation. *See* Premature ejaculation
Reading scholarly information, 51
Recession, 221
Redeployment, 399
Reframing, 402
Refugees, 44
Reinforcement, 330
Rejecting parenting style, 327
Relationship Enhancement Program, 299
Relationships, 74, 239
　of communication, 114
　component, 115, 116
　conflict and violence in, 280–283
　coping resources, 403
　dynamics, 299
　dynamics change, 101–102
　messages, 114
　positive and negative comments by, *120*
　skills, 45
　social environment elements effects, *19*
Religion, 58, 278
　religious beliefs, 85

religious groups, 45
Remarriage, 436
　stumbling blocks, 456
　trends in, 9–11
Renting home, 230
Repetition, 417
Report component of communication, 114
Representative sample, A-10
Reproductive rights, 90
Research, A-10
　study, 71
Research designs, A-11
　cross-sectional cohort studies, A-12
　cross-sectional studies, A-11
　longitudinal studies, A-11
Resolving conflict, 141
　healthy conversation, 141
　strategies for communicating about difficult issues, 142–145
Respect, 236
　and regard, 97, 98
Retirement, 370–372
　fund, 219
Rigid change, 95–96
Rigidly disengaged style, 327
Rigidly enmeshed family system, 327, 392, 476, A-2
Role, 88
　flexibility, 57
　making, 88
　taking, 88
Roller coaster
　course of adjustment, 391
　life as, 390–391
Romantic love, 237, 240, 241, 254, 255

Sacrifice in marriage, 308
Same-sex
　couple relationships and marriages, 45–46
　marriage, 4
Sandwich generation, 351, 359–360
Savings, 219
Science, love and, 241
Secure romantic attachment, 254
Segregation, 63–65
Selection, 395
Self-assessment, 56
Self-confidence, 124
Self-disclosure, 97, 98, *120*, 121, 246
　in friendships and intimate relationships, 119–121
　and intimacy, 119

Self-forgiveness, 308
Self-help groups, 426
Semiarranged marriages, 267
Senility, 368
Sensate focus, 182
Sense of humor, 453
Separateness
　balance of, 78-80
　balancing and, *91*, 92-94
Separation. *See* Divorce
Seven Pillars of Family Strength, 73
Sex and Temperament in Three Primitive Societies, 194-195
Sex(ual), 140, 255, 278
　abuse, 404
　activity, 87
　arousal disorder, 179
　attitudes, 150, 157
　desire, 173
　drive, 241
　dysfunction, 150, 153, 179-181
　education effective, 170-171
　educators, 181
　fidelity, 83
　gay and lesbian couples, 153-155
　historical perspectives on, 152-153
　HIV/AIDS, 158-159
　infidelity, 175
　within marriage, 172-174
　orientation, 152, 163
　pain disorder, 179
　problems for couples, *151*
　ratio, 275
　sex-related behavior, 201
　sexuality across cultures, 155-158
　sexuality, sex, and gender, 152
　and society, 152
　therapists, 181
　therapy, 181-182
　violence, 23
　See also Sexual intimacy
Sexual behavior, 150, 156
　alcohol, and college, 171-172
　among adolescents and young adults, 165
　education for sexuality, 167-168
　risky, *172*
　sex education effective, 170-171
　sexuality education and parents, 168-170
　unintended consequences, 165-167
Sexual health, 176
　sex therapy, 181-182
　sexual dysfunction, 179-181
Sexual intimacy

American sexual health and behavior, 159-164
couple strengths and sexual issues, 150-151
intimacy, strengths, and diversity, 150
marital and extramarital sexual behavior, 172-176
sex and society, 152-159
sexual behavior among adolescents and young adults, 165-172
toward sexual health, 176, 179-182
Sexuality, 90, 152
　across cultures, 155-158
　education and parents, 168-170
　in later years, 162-163
　in middle age, 354-357
　strengths of happy couples *vs.* unhappy couples, *151*
Sexually transmitted infections (STIs), 157-158, 165-167
Sexual-only infidelity, 175
Sexy relationship, 173
Shared values, 85
Short-term health risks, 25-26
Sibling abuse, 421-422
Silent passage, 354
Single-parent families, 47, 444
　benefits of being in, 451-452
　challenges of being in, 449-451
　conflicted coparenting, 445-446
　fathers, 446-448
　percentage of children under age 18 living with, 445
　resources, 452-453
　strengths, 448-449
　types of living arrangements in households with children, *446*
Singlehood, 258
Single mothers, 338
Situational couple violence, 405
Skill-building programs, 471
Sluts, 269
Smart money management, 225
　budgeting, 225-226
　pooling money, 226-227
Smartphones, 242
Smoking, 25, 26
Social, Change, Organization, Pleasing, Emotionally stable personality scales (SCOPE personality scales), 299
Social construction framework, 71, 74, 88-89, 93

Social construction theories, 89
Social environment
　changing, 33
　changing gender roles and balance of power, 29-30
　elements, *19*
　family and environment, 31-33
　financial problems and global economy, 30-31
　impact on relationships, 18
　increasing use of child care outside family, 21
　instability of couple and family relationships, 22
　internet and human relationships, 27-29
　lack of time for oneself and significant others, 20-21
　positive responses to, 34
　stress, change, and materialism, 19-20
　urban migration and overcrowding, 30
　use of alcohol, tobacco, and other drugs, 25-27
　violence, criminal victimization, and fear, 22-25
Social isolation, 410
Socializing children, 320
Social learning theory, 201
Social phenomenon, 366
Social stigma, 284
Social system, 53-55
Societal consequences, 418
Sociobiological theory, 280
Sociocultural characteristics, 53, *54*, 54-55
Sociocultural stress, 383
Socioeconomic differences, 278
Sole custody, 443
Somali immigrants, financial issues of, 217
Soul mate, 375
"Soul wounds", 62
Spacious nest, 358-359
Spanking, 415-417
Speaker-Listener technique, 113
Speaking, 118-121
　skills, 97-98
Special opportunity inequality, 204
Spending time with children, 191
Spirituality, 61
　spiritual and/or religious resources, 452
　spiritual beliefs, 85, 403
　spiritual well-being, 85

Subject Index　**I-23**

Split custody, 443
Spontaneity, 236
Spouse abuse. *See* Domestic violence
Squeeze technique, 182
Stability, balancing, 77-78, *96*, 96-97
Stalking, 23
Standards of attractiveness, 156
Staying on topic, 97, 98
Stepfamilies, 296-297, 434, 453
   boundary ambiguity in, 459
   building stepfamily strengths, 459-461
   children in, 455-457, *457*
   couples in, 456-458
   differences between nuclear families and, 454-455
   in diverse populations, 458-459
   education, 46
   keys to marital happiness, 458
   in later life, 459
Stepparents, 460
Stepparent-stepchild relationships, 456
Stereotypes, 65
STIs. *See* Sexually transmitted infections (STIs)
Stonewalling, 124, 300
Stop-and-go technique, 182
Strain-based demands, 194
Strengthening marriages and families, 464, 479
   building stronger family, 480-481
   building stronger marriage, 479-480
   community strengths, 465, 466
   cultural strengths, 465, 466
   family strengths, 465, 466
   family strengths and universal values around World, 467
   future, 481-482
   global perspectives, 464
   marital and family therapy, 471-479
   premarital and marriage programs, 468-471
   Venn diagram, 466
   visual models integrating family, community, and cultural strengths, 466-467
Strengths, 186, 290, 351-352, 382, 434
   in family structure and cultural context, 38
   sexual intimacy, 150
   themes of, 2-3
Stress, 19-20, 383, 387-388, 395
   ABC-X family crisis model, 389-390
   coping with, 384

   family enduring aftermath of motor vehicle accident, 391
   family systems changing before and after 9/11 attacks, 391-393
   life as roller coaster, 390-391
   management, 401, 404
   roller coaster course of adjustment, 391
   stressors for couples, *388*
   tips for dealing with stress in relationship, 389
Stress and life events, 384
   breast cancer, 385-386
   cardiovascular disease, 386-387
   chronic work stressors, 386-387
   common cold, 387-388
   influenza, 387-388
   negative, 385-386
Stressor, 389
   for couples, 388
   event, 389
Strong families qualities, *81*
Strong two-parent family, 480
Structurally cohesive family type, 476, 479
Structurally cohesive system, 392
"Structurally connected" relationship, 102
Structured level, 95-96
Subsystem, 75
Suffocation, 24
Suicide, 24
   suicidal tendencies, 24
Superior heredity capacity, 72
"Superstepfather" role, 460
Superstepmother role, 460
Suprasystem, 75
Sustainment, 399
Symbolic interaction framework, 71, 74, 88, 93
System, 75

T-cells, 158
Taboos, 131
   conflict, 133-134
   incest, 155
Take Back Your Kids, 331
Take Back Your Marriage, 307
Tapestry of love, 237-238
Teenage relationship violence, 281
Teen pregnancies, 165-167
Teens, 283
Temptation, 245
Tender years doctrine, 438
Tension-building phase, 412

Theory, 71
Therapist Locator tool, 474, 475
"The Ties That Bind", games, 253
TIAs. *See* Transitory ischemic attacks (TIAs)
Time-based demands, 194
Time-outs, 417
TLC approach, 331
Tobacco use, 25-27
Togetherness, balancing with separateness and, *91*, 92-94
Too Much of a Good Thing: Raising Children of Character in an Indulgent Age, 331
Traditional date, 268
Traditional gender-role, 203
Traditional views of gender roles, 193, 195
   work-family interface, 194-195
Transcending abuse, 418-419
Transgender, 152
Transition stage of grief, 374
Transitory ischemic attacks (TIAs), 376
Traumatic brain injury, 395
Trouble, 143
Trust, 236

UN. *See* United Nations (UN)
Unbalanced families, 98-99
Underfunctioners, 139, 140
Understanding, 236
Unhappy couples, 130, 314
   strengths regarding parenting, 315
Unilateral-persuasion trajectory, 324
Unintended consequences, 165-167
Uninvolved parenting style, 327
United Nations (UN), 157
United States, 38
   percentage of children living with single parent, *445*
   debt in, 228, 229
   increasing diversity, 44
   premarital sex in, 165, *165*
   U.S. Teen Pregnancy, Birth, and Abortion Rates, *166*
   very happy Americans, *212*
   women and men in, 186
University of Southern California (USC), 28
Unmarried couples, 6
Unmarried equality, 435
Unveiling game strategies, 254
Unwritten rules, 277
Up in the Air, 260
Urban migration, 30

USC. *See* University of Southern California (USC)
U.S. Census Bureau, 3, 21
U.S. demographics and future trends, 41
  African American population, 42-43
  AI/AN, 43
  Asian American population, 43
  characteristics of families from various ethnic groups, *42*
  future, 44
  Hispanic population, 41-42
  immigration and family life, 43-44

Validation, A-9, A-10
Values, 277
Verbal communication, 114
Victimizer, 409
Violence, 22-25
  in relationships, 280-283
  resistance, 405
  See also Domestic violence
Violent date, 282
Violent pornography, 413

Vitalized couples, 305
VOICES, 40
Voluntary childlessness, 322, 325

Walk of shame, 269
War and effect on families, 393
  children, 395, 398
  couples, 394-395
  deployment, 393
  impact, 396-399
  PTSD, 400-401
  role of community in supporting military families, 398-400
White Americans
  characteristics of families, *42*
  drop out of school, 18
  grandparents raising grandchildren, 363-364
  household income level, 220-221
  multiracial marriages, 66
  population, 41, 44
  victims of abuse and neglect, 23
Wholeness, 76
Why There Are No Good Men Left, 276

Women
  drop out of labor force, 223
  fight for equal contract and property rights, 90
  relationships with men and, 66-67
  sexual behaviors, 160
  in United States, 186
Work-family interface, 194-195
Working world, 354
Work orientation, 307
Worldview, 216
Written communication, 114

Young adults, sexual behavior among, 165-176
Young Mother's diary, 347
Young-old, 365, 366
Youth, 410
"You" statements, 125, 143
You've Got Mail (film), 27

Zero-sum game, 249